MOON HA

NEVADA

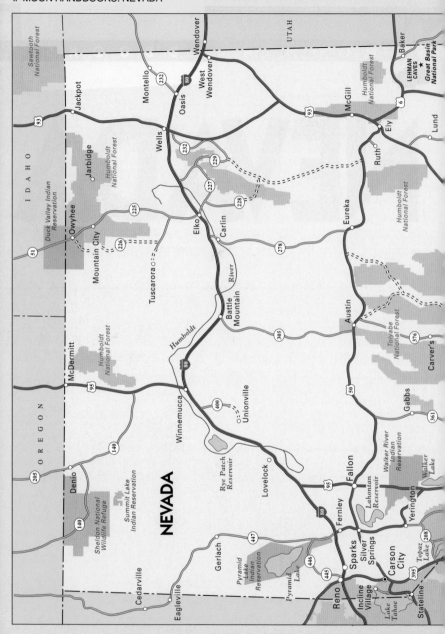

MOON HANDBOOKS

NEVADA

SIXTH EDITION

DEKE CASTLEMAN

AVALON
TRAVEL

MOON HANDBOOKS: NEVADA
SIXTH EDITION

By Deke Castleman
Sixth edition updated by Nancy Keller and Kathleen Dodge

Published by
Avalon Travel Publishing
5855 Beaudry St.
Emeryville, CA 94608, USA

Text © Avalon Travel Publishing Inc., 2001.
All rights reserved.
Cover, illustrations, photos,
and maps © Avalon Travel Publishing Inc., 2001.
All rights reserved.
Some photos and illustrations are used by permission
and are the property of the original copyright owners.

ISBN: 1-56691-276-8
ISSN: 1531-6629

Editor: Erin Van Rheenen
Series Manager: Erin Van Rheenen
Graphics Coordinator: Erika Howsare
Production Coordinator: Darren Alessi
Map Editors: Mike Ferguson, Naomi Dancis
Cartographer: Mike Morgenfeld, Jeremy Shaw, Eurydice Thomas
Index: Deana Shields

Front cover photo: Highway 50 © John Elk III

Distributed in the U.S.A. by Publishers Group West

Printed in the United States by R.R. Donnelley

Please send all comments,
corrections, additions,
amendments, and critiques to:

**MOON HANDBOOKS: NEVADA
AVALON TRAVEL PUBLISHING
5855 BEAUDRY ST.
EMERYVILLE, CA 94608, USA
email: info@travelmatters.com
www.travelmatters.com**

Printing History
First edition—1989
Sixth edition—May 2001
5 4 3 2 1

CONTENTS

SPECIAL TOPICS

MAPS

MAP SYMBOLS

═══	Superhighway	⬭	Interstate	▪	Other Location
═══	Primary Road	⬯	U.S. Highway	⚑	State Park
═══	Secondary Road	◯	State Highway	▲	Mountain
┝━┿━┥	Railroad	◉	State Capital	//	Mountain Pass
─ ─ ─	Trail	○	City/Town	✈	International Airport
·········	Unpaved Road	•	Accommodation	✈	Airport/Airstrip
⟨▱⟩	Dry Lake	▾	Restaurant/Bar	Λ	Campground
		★	Point of Interest		

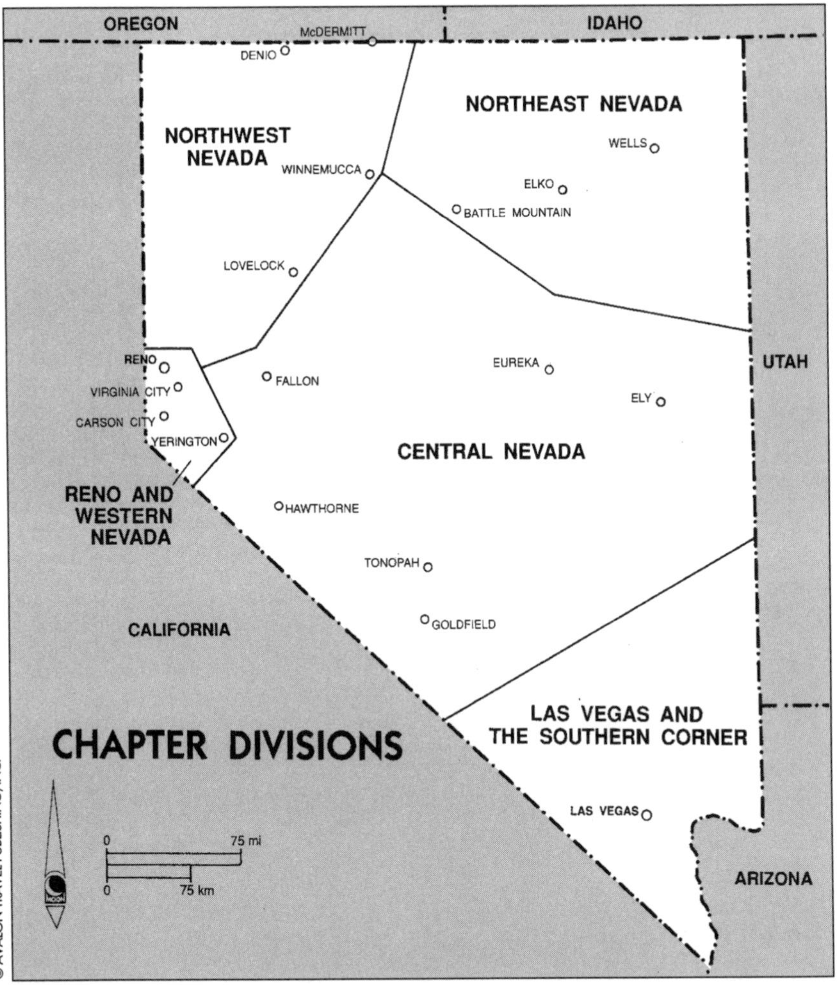

CHAPTER DIVISIONS

OREGON

IDAHO

McDERMITT

DENIO

NORTHEAST NEVADA

WELLS

NORTHWEST NEVADA

WINNEMUCCA

ELKO

BATTLE MOUNTAIN

LOVELOCK

RENO

VIRGINIA CITY

CARSON CITY

YERINGTON

FALLON

EUREKA

ELY

UTAH

CENTRAL NEVADA

RENO AND WESTERN NEVADA

HAWTHORNE

TONOPAH

CALIFORNIA

GOLDFIELD

LAS VEGAS AND THE SOUTHERN CORNER

LAS VEGAS

ARIZONA

0   75 mi

0   75 km

© AVALON TRAVEL PUBLISHING, INC.

ABBREVIATIONS

B&B—bed and breakfast
d—double occupancy
F—Fahrenheit
4WD—four-wheel drive

km—kilometer
mph—miles per hour
Mt.—Mount
s—single occupancy

IS THIS BOOK OUTTA DATE?

Writing a guidebook is a lot like eating ice cream in the Mojave—trying to maintain the consistency and capture the flavor before the sun melts it all into warm mush. You can't turn down the heat (of change), but you also don't want to gulp the scoop so lickety-split that you bypass the taste buds or get a headache from the cold. These guidebooks are completely updated every two years. Although we make herculean efforts to keep up to date, the task is enormous and sometimes overwhelms us.

You can help.

If something in this handbook no longer exists, if you've uncovered anything new, or if certain suggestions are misleading, please write in. If you feel we've overlooked important facts or details, or made mountains out of molehills, let us know. Inaccuracies? Inconsistencies? Bad jokes? Point them out. Women travelers sometimes run into situations that warrant special attention—if you share them with us, we'll share them with others. Letters from Nevadans are particularly appreciated. And if there's anything *good* about the book, we always like to hear *that* too!

When writing, please be as specific and accurate as possible. Notes made on the spot are much better than later recollections. Write your comments into the margins of *Moon Handbooks: Nevada* and send us a summary when you get home. This book speaks for you, the independent traveler; all feedback will be checked out and considered for the reprint or next edition. Address your letters to:

> *Moon Handbooks: Nevada*
> Avalon Travel Publishing
> 5855 Beaudry St.
> Emeryville, CA 94608, USA
> email: info@travelmatters.com

PREFACE

Stare long enough at a large blank map of Nevada, just the outline of the state boundaries, and it starts to look like a cartoon balloon, emanating from the mouth of a caricature of, say, Mark Twain, exclaiming, "And so! Ho for Washoe!" Now paint the balloon with Nevada's colors: the sandy brown of the great western deserts and the silvery green of its sage and creosote carpet. Fill up the outline with carob-colored mountains, which look like a herd of earthworms marching to Mexico. Stipple the lower ranges with forest green and daub icy-white dots on the mountaintops. Imbue the western and southern borders with ovals of deep blue. Now tilt the picture horizontally so that the whole thing is a pitted wedge, high end at the north, with a long slow slope to the south. Draw on a few bold black highways (with a yellow stripe down the middle) and thin gray byways. Finally, spotlight the cities and bordertowns with full-spectrum neon and blinking incandescent bulbs; dot the small towns and remote highway junctions with red lights; and add a soundtrack of coins jangling, crowds jostling, and machines shrieking—and you have Nevada in a nutshell.

Encompassing 110,000 square miles, Nevada is the seventh largest state in the Union. It's home to huge hunks of the Great Basin and Mojave deserts and boasts more than 200 individual mountain ranges, half a dozen rivers to nowhere, and the majority of the wild horses in the country. Only a few thousand years ago, it was covered with vast lakes, thick forests, and advanced native cultures. Its Indians' first contact with explorers from the east and south occurred only 170 years ago, in the last piece of the west to be found, claimed, and conquered.

Since then we have altered, are altering, are planning to alter, or have not prevented from being altered, in a word, everything. We grabbed it, put a political boundary around it, sliced it into jigsaw pieces, dug into it, dumped on it, dammed it up, even detonated all over it. We've grazed it, paved it, run our wires and pipes over and under it, and filled up the airwaves. We've continuously bought, sold, traded, and inherited tiny parcels of it, some of which by now is the most expensive real estate on Earth. This eruption of change over the past century-plus cannot be reversed, stopped, or even slowed.

Yet in spite of all *that*, Nevada has retained the last vast rugged and remote Wild Country in the contiguous United States. You can travel on gravel or hike clear across a mountain range and not see another soul for days. In the middle of the driest land on the continent, you can fish for huge trout, houseboat among hidden coves, and surf whitecaps. You can search for wildlife galore, from pelicans to pronghorns, from falcons to mountain lions. And you can get as wild indoors as out, winning or losing fortunes on the turn of a card or the spin of a wheel.

Most people, however, drive across Nevada east and west on long dull stretches of highway, never noticing its subtle beauty, great variety, or electric excitement. Too many people believe in the stereotypes of the state: that "there's nothing there" except land suitable only for the testing of atomic bombs and smoky casinos filled with degenerate gamblers. But you can pick a page, any page, in this book, and if I've done my job, then those myths should not only be debunked once and for all, but Nevada should also come across as the most unusual, exotic, and inviting state of them all.

BOB RACE

INTRODUCTION
THE LAND

GEOLOGY

Half a billion years ago or so, Nevada rested underwater, the eastern half a narrow shelf that slanted westward into a deep ocean trench. Where Salt Lake City now sits was the shoreline; the equator passed nearby and the region teemed with tropical Precambrian life. Soft-shelled brachiopods, primitive trilobites, tiny spiny starfish, single-celled radiolaria, and algae all populated the tidal flats, reefs, lagoons, estuaries, and wide bays of the shallow sea. For roughly 150 million years, skeletons and sediments accumulated on the ocean floor and were pressurized into limestone. At least twice during the mysterious 300-million-year Paleozoic era, violent and titanic orogenies (episodes of uplift) raised the land, draining the sea and leaving towering mesas and alluvial plains. Gravity pulled the upland rubble into the low-lying basins, which sunk under their own weight, creating new lanes for the seawater to flow back. Then, toward the end of the Paleozoic in the period known as the Permian, supercontinental collision flattened massive ridges in the ocean, forcing the ocean into retreat again and, incidentally, triggering the first of the two near-global extinctions in the history of Earth.

This mass extinction of plants and animals extinguished most of the carbon, creating a superabundance of oxygen (which is usually bound up by carbon). Thus the oxygen resorted to rusting the ubiquitous ferrous iron in the Earth's crust, turning it red. During the Triassic period of the new Mesozoic era, 230 million years ago, the exposed and oxidized sediments eroded. Ferric red sands blew southward and collected in dunes, which petrified into sandstone mountains, to be sculpted in later eons by wind and water.

During the Jurassic, 175 million years ago,

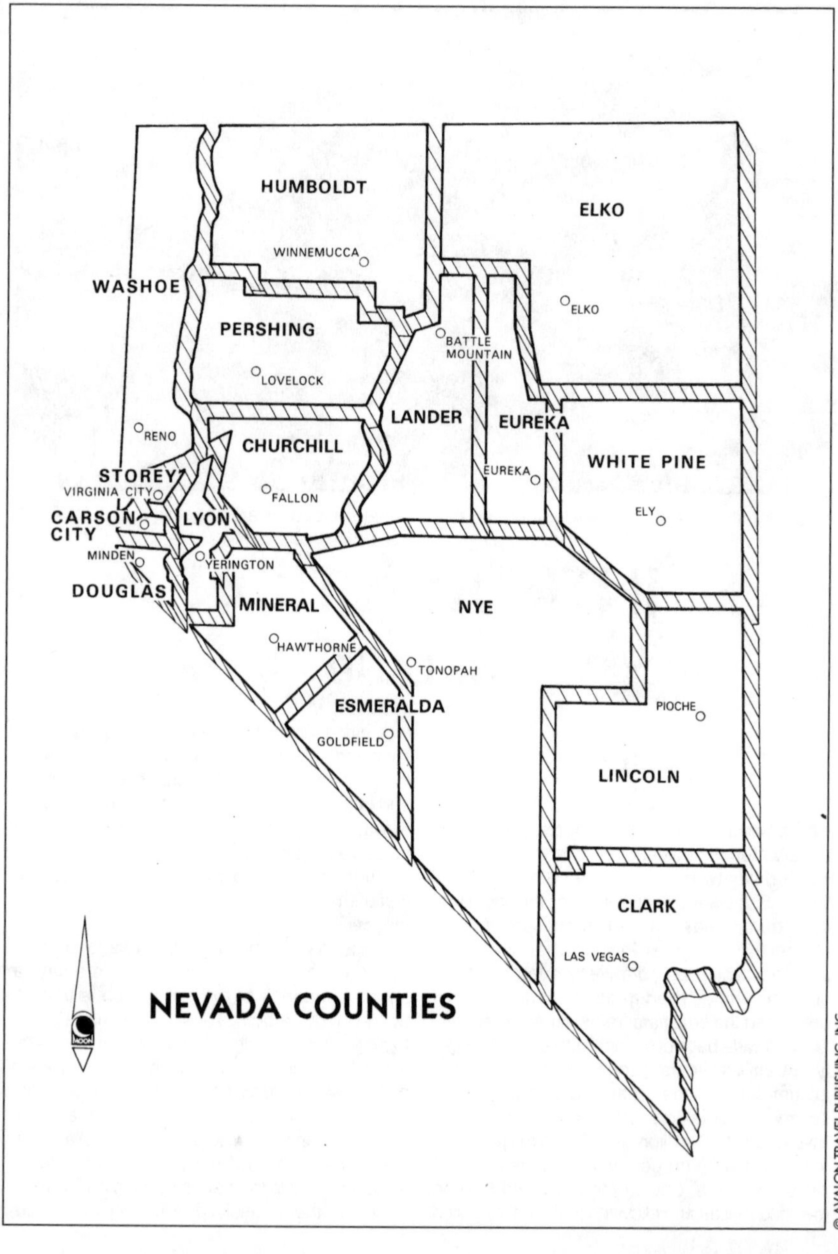

WASHOE

HUMBOLDT

WINNEMUCCA

ELKO

ELKO

PERSHING

LOVELOCK

BATTLE MOUNTAIN

LANDER

EUREKA

WHITE PINE

RENO

CHURCHILL

EUREKA

STOREY

VIRGINIA CITY

CARSON CITY

MINDEN

LYON

FALLON

ELY

YERINGTON

DOUGLAS

MINERAL

NYE

HAWTHORNE

TONOPAH

PIOCHE

ESMERALDA

GOLDFIELD

LINCOLN

CLARK

LAS VEGAS

NEVADA COUNTIES

© AVALON TRAVEL PUBLISHING, INC.

the fused supercontinent tore asunder, a cataclysmic megashear resulting in global-scale tectonics, which again caused the flooding of North America. This triggered what's known as the Nevada Phase of the Cordilleran Orogeny, a violently unstable and confused era. The earth squeezed together, folded, and thrust up from the sea. Huge blocks of sediment faulted, tipped, and rose thousands of feet. Earthquakes shuffled the ranges like a deck of cards. Great crustal fissures cracked open. Molten lava, gaseous plumes, and hot springs spewed out, bearing solutions of gold, silver, copper, silica. Volcanoes blasted hot rock and ash from their bowels. During the greatest period of granite formation in Earth's history, the ancestral Sierra Nevada were raised. Flash floods gouged the mountains—leaching, oxidizing, concentrating the ores. Two families of creatures that had survived the Permian Extinction—marine and flying reptiles and dinosaurs—evolved, over the 165 million years of the Mesozoic, into giants. But then, 65 million years ago, another cosmic cataclysm, the Cretaceous Extinction, again erased almost all life and ended the Mesozoic, framing "an era of burgeoning creation," as John McPhee puts it, "within deadly brackets of time."

The Cordilleran Orogeny ended shortly thereafter, followed by the Laramide Igneous Gap, 25 million years of gradual erosion. Then, during the Oligocene, 40 million years ago, another colossal episode, this time of volcanism, obliterated the Nevadan landscape. Up through fractures, fissures, and vents spewed an unimaginably titanic disgorgement of white-hot steam, ash, and particulates, burying the surface under thousands of feet of ash-flow sheets, turning the topmost sheet into a single continuous and uniform plain.

Finally, 17 million years ago during the Miocene epoch, the continental collision course stretched and lifted the crust, bowing the vast volcanic-ash plain upward like an arch. The crust pulled apart, thinned, then crumpled into blocks that tilted and slid into each other—the high edges became the ridgelines of the ranges, the low edges V-shaped canyons. As they began to fill with eroded sediment, the canyons spread into basins, tilting the blocks further upward. Large cracks ripped open between the rising mountains and sinking valleys; the blocks still

quake the land at the faults today, as the crust continues to adjust. Still spreading, the Basin and Range could very well be cracking open a new sea-lane, by way of the Gulf of California, the Salton Sea, and the Mojave Desert (the latter two already below sea level in places), and basins northward. California becomes an island. Nevada drowns again.

Meanwhile, erosion continues to litter the valleys with mountain material. Some ranges have been whittled down over the past 15 million years to a mere 12,000 feet. Others have been completely buried in their own shavings. Still other ranges are growing, as their blocks tilt more steeply. Some hills are really the peaks of mountains that extend thousands of feet below the surface, iceberg-style, resting on bedrock. Roughly 200 discrete ranges have been named in Nevada, 90% of them oriented northeast-southwest. The other 10% constitute what's known as a discontinuous fault zone—hooked, curved, folded toward all points on the compass. Collectively referred to as the Walker Belt, these

---

IT'S ALIVE!

The lesson is that the whole thing—the whole Basin and Range, or most of it—is alive. The earth is moving. The faults are moving. There are hot springs all over the province. There are young volcanic rocks. Fault scars everywhere. The world is splitting open and coming apart. You see a sudden break in the sage like this and it says to you that a fault is there and a fault block is coming up. This is a gorgeous, fresh, young, active fault scarp. It's growing. The range is lifting up. This Nevada topography is what you see during mountain building. There are no foothills. It is all too young. It is live country. This is the tectonic, active, spreading, mountain-building world. To a nongeologist, it's just ranges, ranges, ranges.

— *BASIN AND RANGE*, JOHN MCPHEE

individually scrambled mountains at the same time occur in a line, northwest-southeast, roughly 400 miles long, along the geologically uneasy California-Nevada state line.

(Appropriately enough, the locale where the structural continuity is most disturbed, where the southwest-trending cavalcade jams up at a southeast-trending dead end, where a cosmic X marks the spot, is right there at the edge of Las Vegas Valley. To geologists, this phenomenon is known, with no apparent irony, as the Las Vegas Zone of Deformation.)

The final uplift of the Sierra Nevada occurred roughly 10 million years ago; the rainshadow it cast transformed the terrain east of the great range of granite mountains into a wide desert. The Pleistocene, beginning a little less than two million years ago, ushered four great ice ages into history. Alternately warm and cool, the humidity remained constant. The soil was moist, rich, and full of minerals from decomposed lava. Forests of giant fir, pine, and sequoia towered over a lush undergrowth of moss, fern, and willow. Great lakes covered much of Nevada, mountain peaks poking out as islands. Lakeshore grasses and woodlands supported great Pleistocene fauna: sabre-toothed cats, ground sloths, tapirs, camels, two-horned teleoceras, three-toed horses, and four-horned antelope in warmer times; musk ox, woolly mammoth, bison, mastodon, and caribou in cooler. The last glacial epoch, the Wisconsin, expired roughly 15,000 years ago, inaugurating a warm dry climate that persists to this day.

TWO STATES IN ONE

Unlike Nevada's next-door-neighbor state to the west, whose demarcation between its northern and southern zones is variable, based as much on a state of mind as a point of geography, northern and southern Nevada can be pinpointed fairly specifically. Simply stated, Nevada's two deserts separate the state into its two distinct parts. Northern Nevada is usually considered to comprise everything within the Great Basin Desert, while southern Nevada occupies the Mojave Desert. The differences in the field probably wouldn't be immediately apparent to the untrained eye, but the two primary related factors are elevation and vegetation.

The base elevation of the Great Basin Desert ranges from around 4,500 to 6,200 feet, where the predominant vegetation is sagebrush. The Mojave's elevation in Nevada starts at 490 feet (the lowest and southernmost point in Nevada at the Colorado River near Laughlin) and ascends, in latitude as well as elevation, to the Great Basin; the predominant vegetation below 4,000 feet is creosote.

It isn't an exact science, but generally speaking, a digitated line can be drawn from around Beatty in the west to around Caliente in the east in terms of elevation, vegetation, and drainage to denote southern Nevada. The WPA's *Nevada* reported that roughly 15 miles south of Tonopah, "A distinct change in the vegetation is noted; northward is the sagebrush zone, southward the creosote bush. The line of demarcation between the zones is so sharp that in this area not a single piece of sagebrush is found within a few hundred feet south of it and not a creosote bush a hundred feet north."

Too, Caliente is surrounded by sage above 4,000 feet, but because its Meadow Valley Wash is drained southward into the Colorado system, it's generally considered not part of the Great Basin, whose drainage is internal, without an outlet to the sea. Of course, all the life zones are found on the mountain ranges of the Mojave, but the Great Basin does not lower itself to the Mojave's own zone.

Though the northern part of the state accounts for the vast majority of land, the southern part accounts for the vast majority of population. Roughly 80% of the real estate is in the north, and 80% of the residents are in the south. As for climate, the farther south you travel in Nevada, the hotter and drier it gets. Las Vegas has some of the least precipitation and the lowest relative humidity of any metropolitan area in the country; Laughlin, at the extreme southern tip of the state, is second only to Laredo, Texas, for the most record-high temperatures in the country.

Who Owns all this Land, Anyway?
Nevada's 110,000 square miles, or 70,264,320 acres, make it the seventh-largest state in the United States. The federal government owns nearly 60 million of those acres, or 85.28% of the total land area in the state. Of the federally claimed acreage, nearly 50 million acres are man-

aged by the Bureau of Land Management, with just over five million acres controlled by the U.S. Forest Service. The military rules over four million acres, which it uses for bases, training grounds, and test sites, and that number is growing.

Tribal reservations, national wildlife refuges, and wilderness areas account for the remainder of the federal total. Twenty-three state parks preserve roughly 50,000 acres. The rest is privately owned.

THE DESERT

Great Basin

The Great Basin Desert is one of the major geographic features in the United States. It stretches 500 miles wide between California's Sierra Nevada and Utah's Wasatch Mountains, up to 750 miles long between Oregon's Columbia Plateau and southern Nevada's Mojave Desert,

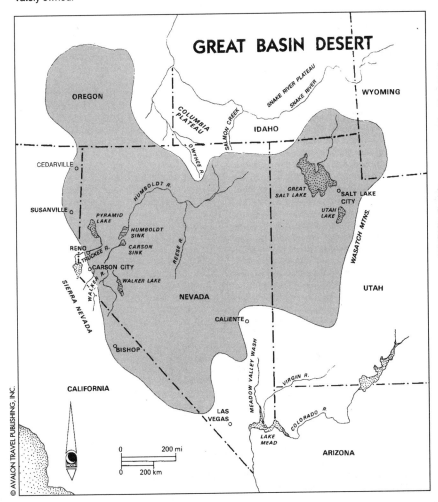

and makes up a large part of the Basin and Range Physiographic Province. John C. Frémont named the Great Basin in 1844 for a curious and unique phenomenon: internal drainage. None of the rivers that flow into this desert ever flow out. Instead, they empty into lakes, disappear into sinks, or just peter out and evaporate.

The Great Basin is not a basin at all. The image of a bowl-shaped depression between the two major mountain ranges couldn't be further from the truth. It's more like a square of corrugated cardboard inside a shallow box. Some of the interior ridges rise higher than the sides of the box. All of the ridges, no matter what their height, have troughs between them. This desert is not even *shaped* anything like its name might imply. Stare at the "Great Basin" map for a hundred years and you won't see a basin. Frémont did get one thing right in the name, though. It *is* great.

Roughly 75% of Nevada is occupied by the Great Basin Desert. At the same time, roughly 75% of the Great Basin Desert is in Nevada. Only a few thousand years ago, a large proportion of this desert was covered by great lakes left over from the wet Pleistocene. The earth is highly mineralized: copper, lead, iron, gypsum, salt, magnesite, brucite, diatomaceous earth, silver, and gold have all been mined in unimaginable quantities. But this desert's most unmistakable characteristic is the basin and range corrugation. There are upwards of 200 separate mountain ranges; most are oriented northeast-southwest, are between 50 and 100 miles long, and are separated by valleys of equal length. The average base elevation (where the basins meet the ranges) is 5,000 feet above sea level, slightly lower in the west, slightly higher in the east. The bottom of the basins here are higher than most mountains east of the Mississippi. The overwhelmingly predominant vegetation is sagebrush, the state flower. Piñon pine and juniper, mountain mahogany and aspen, fir, pine, and spruce inhabit the higher life zones, where many creatures, from field mice and jackrabbits to pronghorn and bobcat, reside.

Mojave Desert

At the southern tip of Nevada, the Mojave Desert borders the northern boundary of the great Sonoran Desert, which encompasses southwestern Arizona, southeastern California, Mexico's north-

desert horned lizard

BOB RACE

western state of Sonora, and nearly the entire Baja California Peninsula. Ironically, the Mojave Desert is a basin, sluicing south, down to and out of the main drain pipe (the Colorado River). Elevations begin to plummet south of Goldfield on the west and Caliente on the east: down to Las Vegas at around 2,000 feet, then down to Laughlin at around 500 feet. The Mojave is not only lower, but also hotter and drier, than its northern Nevada counterpart. Its prevalent vegetation consists of creosote, yucca, and Joshua tree. Snakes, lizards, and bighorn sheep predominate.

Outside of the Deserts

Two tiny nondesert tableaux impinge upon Nevada: the sheer eastern escarpment of the Sierra Nevada from just west of Reno to just south of Lake Tahoe, and the little nipple of northeastern Nevada that separates the Great Basin from the Snake River Plateau in southwestern Idaho. Lake Tahoe sits in a mountain bowl at roughly 6,200–6,300 feet, its east shore (Nevada side) contained by the Sierra's Carson Range. These rugged, heavily forested (second growth) granite mountains drop precipitously into the desert; the Carson Range, right on the California state line, is the only part of northwestern and north-central Nevada that's outside the Sierra rain-shadow. The Sierra are responsible for both the paltry rainfall to the east of them and the Truckee, Carson, and Walker rivers that form from the runoff from the wet peaks. The summit of Mt. Rose in the Carson Range (10,778 feet) attracts more than 30 inches of precipitation in a normal year, while Washoe City, at Mt. Rose's eastern foot, receives less than five inches annually.

The jumbled U-shaped ridgeline of the Jarbidge Wilderness along the Nevada/Idaho border consists of eight peaks higher than 8,000 feet and three over 10,000. The Bruneau, Owyhee, and Salmon rivers flow north from there into the Columbia drainage system. And the vast Snake River Plateau stretches from this part of northeastern Nevada north into infinity. These three anomalies abundantly substantiate that this corner of northeastern Nevada isn't the Great Basin anymore, Dorothy.

THE MOUNTAINS

Depending on who's counting and how, between 150 and 250 mountain ranges have been enumerated and enamerated (named, that is) within Nevada's borders. Most were uplifted and eroded by similar forces; therefore, most share similar geological characteristics. These ranges were created by the tectonic pressure exerted on the western continental crustal surface from the strain of the Pacific plate edging north against the North American plate, right at the San Andreas fault. This colossal jostle has fractured the crust at numerous places; at the cracks, some chunks have sunk down, some have lifted up, and some have listed over. A typical Nevada range is approximately 50 miles long (but can stretch as much as 100–150 miles from one end to the other) and is 10 miles wide. Each is slanted: a long gentle slope on one side, and a sheer scarp on the other. Boundary and Wheeler, the two highest peaks, reach just over 13,000 feet. Mount Moriah, Mt. Jefferson, Mt. Charleston, Arc Dome,

Pyramid Peak, and South Schell Peak hover around 12,000 feet. A score rise higher than 10,000 feet.

In the early mists of time, Nevada was covered by a shallow inland sea, then a vast duney desert. Limestone and sandstone, respectively, remind us of those times, hundreds of millions of years ago. Limestone ranges occur primarily in eastern Nevada. From the Tuscarora Mountains to the Las Vegas Range, several dozen ranges are built from this ancient rock, laid down during the dim Paleozoic era, from 570 to 230 million years ago. The Schell Creeks, Egans, and Snakes around Ely are the best known and most representative of the limestone massifs; the Snakes contain Great Basin National Park, within which Lehman Caves provide a graphic lesson in mountain building and erosion. The sandstone ranges occur in the southern Mojave: the Spring and Muddy mountains, outside of Las Vegas. After the sea retreated, massive sand dunes covered the land. Chemical and thermal reactions petrified the dunes into polychrome sandstone; wind and water erosion sculpted it into the strange and wondrous shapes on view at Red Rock Canyon and Valley of Fire.

The granite ranges mostly cluster in the west-central part of Nevada around the most magnificent granite mountains of them all: the Sierra Nevada. Granite, the major mountain-building rock, is forced up into the crust as molten magma, then cools slowly. The Granite and Se-

polychrome sandstone at Red Rock Canyon

PHIL GUERRERO/B.L.M.

BOB RACE

cougar

lenite ranges around the Black Rock Desert and the Pine Nut and Wassuk ranges around Topaz and Walker lakes are examples.

When magma cools slowly it forms granite; when it cools quickly it forms basalt and rhyolite. The volcanics are the youngest and most active of Nevada's many types of ranges and mark the eastern edge of the famous Pacific Ring of Fire. The Virginia Range is one of the older, more eroded, and most mineralized of the volcanic ranges—having yielded hundreds of millions of dollars in gold and silver. The Monte Cristos west of Tonopah are an anomaly in the Great Basin—crescent-shaped, mazed by badlands, and brightly colored with pinks, purples, yellows, and whites. The Pancake Range is only a few thousand years old, and the Apollo astronauts used its Lunar Cuesta to simulate the craters, lava flows, and calderas of the moon.

The rest of Nevada's many mountain ranges are composites, exhibiting a great variety of granite, sedimentary, volcanic, and metamorphic signs. The Humboldts, Santa Rosas, Stillwaters, and Toiyabes are composite ranges; the Toiyabes have been called "the archetype of Nevada ranges."

THE RIVERS

As trail-guide author John Hart has written, "Only two large areas of North America were unexplored by 1825: the interior of Alaska and the inner areas of the Basin." (For more comparisons between Alaska and Nevada, please see the Special Topic "Alaska-Nevada Comparison.") The first explorers were looking primarily for rivers, seeking their beaver pelts and drinking water. They also had it half in mind to find the mythical San Buenaventura River, believed to flow from the Rocky Mountains through the great unknown expanse of the west all the way to the Pacific Ocean.

Ten rivers of note snake around Nevada. The Truckee, Carson, and Walker flow in, while the Bruneau, Owyhee, and Salmon flow out. The Humboldt and Reese are born and die in the Great Basin. The state's southeast boundary is formed by the Colorado, which meanders for 150 miles along the edge. The Amargosa rises in the Nuclear Test Site, waters Beatty slightly, then flows underground to Death Valley. Seven of the ten are dammed.

Only the Colorado was a large enough river to be served by riverboats. The legendary Reese, however, looked good enough on the early maps to foster one of the great scams in Nevada history: a phony navigation company. The Humboldt was both the scourge (the highly alkali water was as good as undrinkable) and the salvation (both for its stock-feeding grasses and its trail along the riverbank) of thousands of pioneers. The Carson, Truckee, and Walker rivers are life givers and sustainers for most of western Nevada.

In these greatest of American deserts, the stories that have arisen from the banks of these precious rivers are priceless. Not even the stories emanating from the tunnels of gold and silver can touch them. Read on.

The Humboldt

Jedediah Smith came west from Wyoming in 1825, trapping beaver as he explored. He sniffed out a river in the great desert and named it Mary's, after his Indian wife. Apparently, Peter Skene Ogden hadn't heard about that, because when he located it from the north in 1828 he named it Unknown River. Walkin' Joe Walker, in spite of Ogden's name, found it and followed it in 1834. Namin' John Frémont was the last one to label it, in honor of a German scientist so eminent that not only did the name stick like glue, but the river trail, three mountain ranges, a mining district, a sink, and a county were named for him, too.

Originating in northeastern Nevada, it flows southwest, picking up runoff from the East Humboldts, Rubies, and a half-dozen mountain ranges north and south of it between there and

Beowawe. It cuts northwest up to Winnemucca and back southwest into the Rye Patch Reservoir. Beyond the dam, it disappears into its own sour sink. The emigrants cursed its foul water and harvested all the vegetation from its banks, and reclamation projects dammed it to irrigate Pershing County. A railroad, U.S. defense highway, and interstate superhighway have been built next to it. If you remember only one thing from this book, it should be the name of this river: the Humboldt.

The Colorado
Nevada got lucky in 1866 when, only two years after its boundaries were surveyed, the state was allowed to extend its southern borders into Utah and Arizona territories. Nevada annexed 150 miles of the west bank of the Colorado River, along with Las Vegas Valley, the Muddy and Virgin rivers, and Meadow Valley Wash. The Colorado is one big mama of a river, which had followed its own destiny for countless eons until the Bureau of Reclamation had a better idea. With a few smaller dams on lesser rivers to its credit, the Bureau of Reclamation took on the Colorado and plugged it with Hoover Dam. (For the staggering number of kilowatt-hours, irrigation acres, and miles of Lake Mead shoreline, see "Hoover Dam" in the East of Las Vegas section.) Davis Dam, 80 miles south of the Hoover and built in 1954, further controls this now-docile dragon in Nevada.

The Sierra Three
The Truckee, Carson, and Walker rivers all flow east out of the Sierra and fan out northeast, east, and southeast, respectively, into western Nevada. The northernmost of the three, the Truckee River, emanates from the edge of Lake Tahoe and flows northeast. It provides all the water for Reno-Sparks and some water for the reclamations project in Fernley and Fallon. (Derby Dam, which diverts Truckee water to Lahontan Reservoir, was the Bureau of Reclamation's first dam, built in 1905.) The rest of the river water reaches its destination at Pyramid Lake.

The Carson River, which flows north to Carson City, then east between the Virginia Range and Pine Nut Mountains, at one time spread out into the desert within the large Carson Sink. Today, a dozen or so miles west of the sink, the Carson is backed up by Lahontan Dam and then sent by canal and ditch every which way to irrigate Fallon. For years little water reached the Carson River marsh at Stillwater National Wildlife Refuge, but that's beginning to change. For a closer look at this reclamation system, see "Stillwater National Wildlife Refuge" under "Fallon" in the Central Nevada chapter.

The Walker River flows north from two forks into idyllic Mason Valley. It passes Yerington, then makes a big U-turn around the Wassuk Range and heads south into Walker Lake. Bridgeport Lake (in California) dams the East Fork early on, and Topaz Lake dams the West

Walker Lake

JOHN ELK III

Fork early on; Weber Reservoir backs up the Walker on the east side of the Wassuks, a little north of Walker Lake, its final resting place.

The Idaho Three

The Bruneau, Owyhee, and Salmon rivers flow north from the area where the Snake River Plateau protrudes into the Great Basin. They empty into the Snake, which empties into the mighty Columbia River. The headwaters of the Humboldt cascade south from the Great Basin side of the plateau. This is a very active corner of Nevada for water—a real slice of the Pacific Northwest. The Owyhee is dammed at Wildhorse, the Snake is dammed in Idaho.

THE LAKES

Man-Made

Dams are the name of this game. Lake Mead is the largest man-made lake in the country. All it took was seven million tons of cement poured 700 feet high to hold back the ragin' Colorado. Lake Mojave is no slouch, but nothin' to brag on, either: it's only restrained by an earth-filled 200-footer. Both Rye Patch (on the Humboldt) and Wildhorse (on the Owyhee) reservoirs are popular with anglers, boaters, and campers; South Fork Dam, completed in 1988, is the newest dam in Nevada, impounding 40,000 acre-feet of South Fork Creek 10 miles south of Elko; the state's newest park is there. Lahontan Reservoir (on the Carson) also has lots of campsites, in addition to the amazing network of ditches and canals through Fallon between it and the Carson Sink.

Man-Altered

The overflow from the Truckee River once drained out of Pyramid Lake and into Win-

nemucca Lake. It took only 30 years for large Winnemucca Lake to dry into a playa after the Truckee Canal diverted some river water over to Lahontan Valley. Today, more than 90 years later, Pyramid Lake has dropped to uncomfortable levels, the Fallon National Wildlife Refuge is gone, and the Stillwater National Wildlife Refuge is hanging on by a thread. But now it appears as if almost everyone—the feds, the state, the hatcheries, the power company, and the conservationists, though not the farmers, entirely—are starting to agree on how to satisfy all the various, and often conflicting, water requirements for the lakes, refuges, irrigation systems, and urban populations.

Ruby Marsh has a number of dikes and causeways around and through it; Pahranagat is less changed. Walker Lake, like Pyramid, has had its water diverted and its fishery devastated; this lake could be one of the most endangered in the West.

For sheer beauty, Lake Tahoe—logged out, fished out, dammed, silted, but now slowly returning to a fairly pristine condition—is unsurpassed. Except maybe by a few of those back-country lakes way up in the Ruby Mountains.

CLIMATE

Dry

Two generalizations apply to Nevada's weather: it's hot in the summer and dry year-round. But because the state is so big—500 miles from the southern tip to the northern, more than 300 miles wide in the northern half—and mountainous, it experiences a great variety of local climatic conditions. Still, weather patterns can be generally distinguished between the north and south state.

The prevailing winds in the north state blow either from the west or the southwest (occasionally from the northwest in the winter). Most of the fronts blowing in from the warm and moist Pacific drop their precious precipitation on the *west* side of the high Sierra, watering the long, sloping, Central Valley-facing hillsides of California. This rainshadow effect alone is responsible for the relative dryness of the Great Basin Desert: an average of seven inches of precipitation a year. Still, the Sierra don't only taketh away. They also giveth back, in the form of runoff from the

desert iguana

BOB RACE

bighorn sheep

BOB RACE

rains and snowpack. Several rivers that flow east out of the mountains supply almost all of the water demanded by the densely populated urban area of Reno-Sparks, the agricultural lands and wetlands of Fernley, Fallon, and Smith and Mason valleys, and the fisheries of Pyramid and Walker lakes.

The prevailing winds of the south state are southerlies, which, having already crossed the fierce Sonoran Desert, hold little moisture. Las Vegas is America's driest metropolitan area, receiving an average of three to four inches of precipitation a year. On top of that, the south state gets scorched seven or eight months a year. Temperatures in Las Vegas reaching 110° are not uncommon in May and September; highs can rise to 115° in July and August. Laughlin can hit 120° and usually registers over 20 days a year of the country's highest temperatures. (A record-high temperature for the state was recorded in Laughlin in June 1994: 125 sizzling degrees.) Luckily for Las Vegas and vicinity (in a historical sense, since Las Vegas was founded for its plentiful local water), the mighty Spring Mountains to the west grab some clouds and relieve them of their moisture, which then percolates into the water table. But for most of its water needs, southern Nevada relies on Lake Mead.

Wet

Other mountain ranges provide similar water-gathering services. The Sheep, Snake, Schell Creek, Ruby, Humboldt, Jarbidge, Independence, Santa Rosa, Toiyabe, Toquima, and Monitor ranges, among others, all coax a little of life's sustaining fluid from passing clouds. Many peaks are snowcapped for nine months a year, and one, Mt. Wheeler in the Snake Range, has a permanent icefield. The Rubies help swell the Humboldt River, and runoff from the Toiyabes and Shoshones collects to create the Reese River. Many lush and gorgeous basins on each side of the highest mountain ranges—Washoe, Paradise, Independence, Clover, Spring, Big Smokey, and Steptoe valleys—support farms and ranches.

Cloudbursts and thunderstorms anywhere in the state, but mostly in the south, can dump more rain in an hour than many places receive in half a year. These torrential downpours tend to be extremely localized and dangerous, giving rise to raging and roiling waves that surge down gullies and washes and drainages that might have been dry for a decade. The "wet" season is December to March; summer storms and flash floods (known in Las Vegas as "monsoon" season) occur between June and August.

Since most of the state is around a mile high, winters can be surprisingly severe. The harshest locations for this season are northeastern Nevada from Jarbidge to Ely, with temperatures regularly dropping below zero and the snow remaining for four or five months, and even longer in some places. Central Nevada is similar. The western and southern sections, from Reno to Laughlin, luck out with milder and shorter winters, one reason that around 80% of Nevada's population lives in this "sun belt."

FLORA AND FAUNA

FLORA

Creosote

The Mojave covers the southern quarter of Nevada, and the creosote bush covers the Mojave. Because of the extremely arid environment, these shrubs, which grow from two to 10 feet tall and sprout dull-green, resinous foliage, are widely scattered over the desert sand, occupying only about a tenth of the available surface. Creosote shares the Mojave floor with a variety of cacti, yucca (especially the easily recognizable Mojave yucca, also known as Spanish bayonet), and the Joshua tree, which is endemic to the Mojave. Creosote is sometimes referred to as greasewood and is closely related to saltbush, which grows at an elevation that's lower than the sagebrush zone in the Great Basin. Greasewood, saltbush, rabbitbrush, shadscale, and other plants with spiny stems and tiny leaves are highly adaptable to alkali soil; their presence generally indicates conditions unsuitable for agricultural cultivation. They grow in the 450- to 3,000-foot zone in Nevada, mostly limited to the Mojave in the south and the lowest points in the lowest valleys in the Great Basin.

Joshua Tree

This picturesque tree, also known as the tree yucca or yucca palm, is the largest species of the yucca genus. It can grow to 30 feet tall, with a stout body and boldly forking branches. It blooms bright yellow from March to May. The Joshua tree was named by Mormon pioneers, who imagined the big yucca's "arms"—imploring, slightly grotesque—to be pointing the way to the Promised Land.

Sage

Sagebrush is the state flower. It's also possibly the most memorable and enduring image of Nevada, along with neon, that travelers take home with them. The Great Basin Desert has been called a "sagebrush ocean"; the sagebrush zone, roughly 4,000–6,000 feet, could also be considered a "Lilliputian forest." Unlike shadscale and greasewood, sage grows in well-drained and minimally alkali environments. Healthy sage can grow 12 feet tall, with roots up to 30 feet deep. Tall sagebrush indicated fertile soil to farmers, promising good crops with proper irrigation. Thus, farmers considered sage a pest and cleared it with a vengeance. Emigrants cursed sage as the vilest shrub on Earth, more useless even than Humboldt River water.

It was the Indians for whom sage was the great provider. They chewed the young leaves and

bristlecone pine

JOHN ELK III

drank decoctions brewed from the buds as a general tonic. They dried, ground, and made a mud of the stems and used it as a poultice. They stripped the pliable bark from the tallest sage plants, near streams for example, and made robes, sandals, and other wear from the fiber. And they used the leaves and stems for insulation.

Covering a third of the desert surface, sage protects the earth from wanton erosion. It also gives shelter to snakes and small rodents that burrow under the bush, and feeds sage hens, squirrels, jackrabbits, and other fauna that eat the spring buds. Sheep, cattle, and pronghorn also nibble on the young leaves.

Sage has successfully resisted nearly all attempts at commercial exploitation. Except for fuel in the absolute absence of any other wood, this bitter and oily plant hasn't been found to fulfill any productive purpose. Most desert rats consider this just as well, since there's nothing quite so evocative of the desert as the silver-green sheen and pungent aroma of an ocean of sagebrush after a good rain.

Juniper

Utah juniper is the most common tree in the Great Basin. It grows on every mountain range and in some basins, too. Juniper is also the first tree that takes to a particular microenvironment; piñon follows later. Junipers grow to 20 feet and are sometimes as round as they are tall. They produce blue-green juniper berries (bitter but edible), pale green needles, and yellowish pollen cones. You'll normally see them between 6,000 and 8,000 feet.

Recent research has indicated that the Utah juniper has survived the radical climatic changes that the Great Basin experienced over the past 30,000 years. By cross-breeding with its cousin, the western juniper, the Utah juniper altered its genetic makeup and was able to live out the ice ages (the western juniper thrives in a cooler wetter climate, such as in the Sierra). Forestry paleontologists are comparing the DNA of Utah juniper seeds and twigs discovered in ancient pack rat nests with today's juniper to decipher how plants survive climate changes—as well as which local trees will live through the current global warming.

Like sage, juniper provided for many Indian needs. The Puebloans favored it as a building material, especially for the roofs of their structures. They used it as a savory firewood. They stripped, softened, and made the bark into baskets, rope, and clothing. Ronald Lanner, in *Trees of the Great Basin,* even reports that they smoked the inner bark in cigarettes. Once you learn to recognize this tree, you'll not only come to appreciate its shade, but also use it to gauge your elevation.

Piñon Pine

If juniper is the most prevalent, then piñon is the most popular tree in the Great Basin. Juniper is the lower-growing tree of the pair in the piñon-juniper zone, piñon is the higher. It's the only variety, of 100 different types of pine worldwide, that has a single needle—thus its nickname: singleleaf pine.

Piñon is a Spanish word for pine nut. The pine nut feeds small and big rodents, birds, deer, even bighorn and bear. It was the staple food for Great Desert Indians, who harvested the nuts from groves that they considered sacred and ground them into flour, which they baked into biscuits, cakes, and a type of breadstick. Today, the Paiute and Shoshone continue to celebrate piñon harvest festivals in the early fall; new subdivisions, especially in northern Nevada, have been encroaching perilously close to the groves. Actually, gathering pine nuts is a popular pastime for many non-Native Nevadans in late September and early October; be sure you're not trespassing where you're picking, then let the cones dry in the sun, and roast or boil the nuts carefully.

Singleleaf pines were the preferred tree of the *carbonari,* the Italian charcoal burners. Most of the piñon woodlands of Nevada were clear-cut to produce charcoal for the silver smelters, to fuel the steam engines at the mines, and to burn in woodstoves for heat and cooking. But because of the piñon's popularity with our fine feathered friends, seeds were widely redistributed and the singleleaf pines have made a successful comeback.

Cottonwoods, willows, aspens, sagebrush, rabbitbrush, and Mormon tea, among other trees and plants, also grow in the piñon-juniper zone.

Other Trees

Starting at around 7,500 feet and going up to 11,000 feet or so are the trees that most people relate to the forest. In the Great Basin, the higher you go (up to a certain elevation), the wetter the environment, thus the bigger the trees. Ponderosa, Jeffrey, and sugar pine, white fir, and incense cedar occupy the lower reaches of the forest; lodgepole and white pine and mountain hemlock inhabit the middle zone, at about 9,000 feet. Douglas fir, white fir, blue spruce, and Engelmann spruce top off the thick growth up to 10,000 feet. Limber and bristlecone pine trees survive and thrive at or above the usual treeline in the harshest environment known to trees of the Great Basin (for a detailed look at the wondrous ancient bristlecones, see the Special Topic "*Pinus Longaeva* Trees: Q & A," in the Central Nevada chapter.

Foraging

Foraging for edible foods, though not the cakewalk of California, the Pacific Northwest, or even Alaska, can nonetheless be enjoyed in the Nevada desert. Many of these forageable wild plants are "escaped domestics," which grow around old ranches, settlements, even ghost towns.

Raspberries and strawberries are sometimes found near remnants of civilization, though they also grow wild, mostly in damp woods or along steep well-drained slopes. They fruit in late summer (late August and early September). Wild asparagus is a good forage to stalk. It's easiest to spot in summer, when the shoots are tall; return to the spot the next spring to harvest the tender five- to seven-inch-high edibles. Roses grow above 5,000 feet in the sagebrush zone; look for five-petaled pink flowers on thorny stems in spring, and the orange-red hips in September. In well-watered areas, the hips are juicy and delicious on their own; dry and mealy hips are generally made into jams. Remove the pips and process the flesh. Finally, pine nuts are the traditional and ultimate forage in the Great Basin. Harvesting and preparing these thin-shelled, starchy seeds is almost a rite of passage for Nevadans.

FAUNA

Fish

Contrary to popular perception, Nevada is not just a great desert wasteland. In fact, nothing dispels the myth quite so forcefully as the fact that Nevada has more than 600 fishable lakes, reservoirs, rivers, streams, and creeks. (*Nevada Anglers Guide,* by Richard Dickerson, lists 162 of them, the ones with the best public access and that can take the fishing pressure without too much strain.)

The biggest fish are found in the biggest lakes. Mackinaw, a variety of Great Lakes trout, averages 20 pounds (the record is a monster 37-pounder); catch mackinaw deep in Lake Tahoe. Lahontan cutthroat, the "trout salmon" that so impressed John C. Frémont, grow to 15 pounds in Pyramid Lake; a 41-pounder is on display at the State Museum in Carson City, but it's a member of the original species, which is now extinct. The ancient cui-ui sucker fish is endemic to Pyramid. Lake Mead boasts an abundance of striped bass, and a regenerating population of the popular largemouth bass.

Seven-pound cutthroats, five-pound browns, and three-pound rainbows are fished from Topaz Lake and a number of ponds and streams in Nevada. One-pound golden trout are catchable in the lakes (especially Hidden Lake) high up in the Ruby Mountains. Rye Patch Reservoir near Lovelock was a favorite for walleye until it was drained in 1992. Comins Lake near Ely has been known to harbor big northern pike (27 pounds is the record), but it too has dried up in the drought.

gila monster

BOB RACE

Finally, one stream in Nevada, Desert Creek near Yerington, actually has Arctic grayling, a tasteless white fish well known to all anglers familiar with the lakes and streams of Alaska.

Lizards

Of 3,000 different kinds of lizards worldwide, Nevada has 26, 15 or so of them in the Mojave Desert. Only two lizards of the 3,000 are poisonous and Nevada has one of them. The **banded Gila monster** is found in Clark and Lincoln counties between the Colorado and Virgin rivers. Your chances of seeing one are a little better than of seeing a polar bear. (Well, sort of. I mean they *are* here—and you can see a polar bear in Elko.) Nevada's Gila monsters are nocturnal—most active right after dusk—though you might see one after a summer rain or on a cool day. They're also endangered.

The **chuckwalla** is nearly as common as the Gila is rare. This 16-inch vegetarian eats mostly blossoms and leaves and is found in Clark and Nye counties. The **desert iguana** is another vegetarian. The **Great Basin whiptail** is found anywhere from 2,000 to 7,000 feet. It's easy to identify, since its tail is twice as long as its body. Another tail by which to tell a lizard is that of the **zebratail,** which is banded with black and white stripes. It wags its tail as it flees, hoping to distract its predators. If a Gila, say, gets the tail, the zebratail grows another. But that would be a feat for the Gila, since zebratails are extremely fast and zig-zag when they run.

The **collared lizard** has a black-and-white band around its neck. It's generally seen around rocky terrain, hunting for grasshoppers, cicadas, and leopard lizards. It bites if handled. **Leopard lizards** are extremely common in northern Nevada, and prefer to hang around sage. They're easy to recognize, with thick spots all over their bodies and very long thin tails. If you creep quietly toward them, they'll tolerate you till you're very close before darting away. They

also bite readily and are fierce predators.

The **horned lizard** is an unusual creature of the desert Southwest. It's black and tan and grows horns on the back of its head. Small spines cover the rest of its body. Ants are its favorite food. It relies on camouflage for protection, but will puff up and hiss if threatened.

The most common lizard of Nevada is the **Western fence lizard.** It's brown with bright blue stomach patches. Like the zebratail, it can shed its tail to escape danger, then grow another.

Since lizards, like all reptiles, are cold-blooded, you'll often see them sunning on rocks in the morning and evening. They need a body temperature of 104 degrees to be in full fettle. Too much heat, however, is fatal; during the hottest part of the day, they hide in the shade of shrubs, rocks, or burrows. And, of course, they hibernate in the winter.

Snakes

Like lizards, most snakes in Nevada are found in the Mojave. Several varieties of rattlers inhabit the Las Vegas area. The **Panamint** has a wide range (from Las Vegas to Tonopah) and a bad bite. The **Southwestern speckled** likes the mountains and washes around Lake Mead. **Western diamondbacks** are easy to identify, as their name implies, and it's a good thing, too, since they're especially ill-tempered, as well as being the largest of the seven species of Nevada rattlers. The **Mojave rattler** is sometimes mistaken for the diamondback, although the latter rattler has distinctive black and white tail rings. The Mojave is less nasty but its venom is 10 times more poisonous. The **sidewinder** is a small rattlesnake (around two feet long), known for the S-curve trail its slithering motion leaves in the sand. The **Great Basin rattlesnake** has the greatest range, covering more than half the state, from 5,000 to 10,000 feet in elevation.

The **mountain king snake** is not poisonous,

SAFETY IN SNAKE COUNTRY

Though there are seven different types of rattlers living in Nevada, a couple of them extremely venomous, your chances of seeing one in the daytime are narrow, your chances of being bitten by one are slim, and your chances of having a fatal encounter are statistically nil. Two Nevada deaths have been attributed to snakebites in the last 50 years.

Rattlers are mostly nocturnal, though they do move around during the day. However, most daylight sightings turn out generally to be Great Basin gopher snakes. These are harmless guys, but they do make a hissing noise that might sound like a rattler.

The best way to protect against snakebites is by wearing tough hiking boots. Use caution when walking in rocky areas, around ledges, or near any area that might make a snake den. Try to keep night strolling to a minimum, and if you can't, be extra careful. If you bump into a snake, stay calm, stay still, and when you can, edge away. Experts recommend that you try for a soft foot-fall, so as not to disturb the snake's sensitivity to ground vibration.

In the unlikely event of a bite, stay calm, keep the bite below heart level, and ascertain if the snake was poisonous. A fang mark or two will be apparent, the area will swell and discolor, and it will hurt. Loosely bandage above and below the bite and wash it with soap and water. The old way of dealing with a snake bite, which some old—and young—codgers still subscribe to, was to take a sterilized knife, cut a quarter-inch incision between and slightly past the fang marks, then keep squeezing out the venom until you reach a doctor. The new way is to skip the cut-and-squeeze part and hightail it to a doctor.

Remember that snakes are as afraid, if not more, of you as you are of them. Because they'll sense your presence before you will theirs, they'll generally be long gone by the time you get to where they were. Caution is always the rule. But don't let the fact that you share the backcountry with snakes deter you from using and enjoying it.

likes riverbottoms and farmlands, and eats rattlers for breakfast; it's immune to the venom. Because it displays red and black bands, it's often confused with the highly poisonous **Arizona coral snake,** with its red and yellow bands. Though they're not supposed to exist in Nevada, coral snakes have been identified as far north as Lovelock and as far west as Carson City.

The **Great Basin gopher snake** is probably the most common and widely distributed serpent in Nevada and is active during the day. It's not poisonous; rather, it kills small mammals by constriction.

Desert Tortoise

The desert tortoise is the state reptile. It's unmistakable: hard shell and four fat legs, the front legs larger than the rear for digging burrows. Burrows protect them on hot summer days and when they hibernate throughout the winter. These tortoises eat grasses and blossoms in the early mornings and late afternoons. In June, females lay four to six eggs in shallow holes and then cover them with dirt. The eggs hatch in late September-early October. The tortoises can live to be 100 years old.

These days, however, most don't. In April 1990 the desert tortoise of the Mojave was listed as threatened, due to loss of habitat to agriculture, road construction, military activity, energy and mineral development, off-road vehicles, raven predation, and private collection. The tortoises are also victims of a new upper-respiratory syndrome. Clark County seems to be taking the desert tortoise situation very seriously. It has devised a plan in which 400,000 acres of critical desert tortoise habitat will be preserved around the far edges of the county, in return for U.S. Fish and Wildlife Service permission to develop 22,500 acres.

Birds

Nevada is one of the best places in the West to look for raptors—eagles, hawks, falcons, ospreys. The Goshute Mountains especially, between Ely and Wendover, are on the "flyway," or aerial highway, of up to 20,000 migrating raptors every year. In fact, HawkWatch International, P.O. Box 35706, Albuquerque, NM 87176, 800/726-HAWK, has been monitoring the migrations over the Goshutes from the Pacific Northwest and Alaska since 1979: counting the individual birds among 18 different species, capturing birds to observe their health and size, banding birds to track their movements, and assessing their data to estimate population fluctuations. Recently, HawkWatch's count was the highest in a decade; it concludes that the use of DDT and other pesticides, to which raptors are especially susceptible, is diminishing.

Both bald and golden eagles are found in Nevada. Golden eagles stay year-round, mostly in the northern part of the state; bald eagles migrate here for the winter and like well-watered and agricultural areas.

Ospreys have wingspans approaching those of eagles and are related to vultures. Since they feed entirely on fish (they're also known as fish hawks), osprey are mainly observed feeding in the Reno-Tahoe rivers and lakes on their migration south for the winter.

Accipiters include goshawks, fairly large birds about the size of ravens; sharp-shinned hawks, about the size of robins; and Cooper's hawks, similar to sharp-shins. Since accipiter habitat is mostly in forests and heavily wooded areas, HawkWatch has found their populations to be on the wane because of extensive logging in the Pacific Northwest and western Canada.

Buteos are the hawks normally seen soaring above the desert. Among them are ferruginous hawks, which live in the juniper of eastern Nevada year-round. Common red-tailed hawks prey on lizards in the Mojave. Rough-legged hawks winter in Nevada, while Swainson's hawks prefer Nevada in the summer and then fly to South America for the winter, though they're fairly uncommon these days.

Sharp-eyed birdwatchers can also spot marsh hawks, kestrels, merlins, and peregrine falcons.

Pelicans have traditionally nested in large numbers at Anaho Island in Pyramid Lake. Their numbers had fallen dramatically because of the drought, reaching an all-time low of nine chicks in 1991, after a high of 10,000 in 1986. But they recovered in 1992 and 1993, producing 1,500 chicks each year. In 1996 and 1997, the pelican population was back in the thousands.

Other shorebirds also nest at Anaho. The wildlife refuges at Ruby Marsh, Stillwater, Pahranagat Lakes, Railroad Valley, Kirch (south of Ely), and others are also prime birdwatching locales.

Mountain Lions and Bears

Predators and prey around the West are considered plentiful nowadays by experts, compared to their numbers during the first half of this century. Pronghorn, elk, deer, sheep, wild horses, and burros all have revived in the past 20 years or so. That's why mountain lions and bears have become more common in the mountains, both remote and inhabited.

Mountain lions aren't particularly shy of humans, but they're so elusive that they're not often seen. When one is, especially in a population area, it's trapped, relocated, and it makes pretty big news. Attacks on humans are rare,

desert tortoise

BOB RACE

but not unknown; in spring 1994, a mountain lion killed a woman jogging in northeastern California. Also known as cougars, panthers (or painters), and pumas, mountain lion males weigh up to 160 pounds, females 100–130. As such, they're second in size only to bears as North America's largest predators. They hunt at night, taking everything from coyotes, mule deer, and bighorn sheep to beavers and even porcupines.

Likewise, black bears are more common in Nevada than most people might think. A Department of Wildlife study a few years ago concluded that up to 400 black bears live in Nevada, 300 or so in the Sierra, and the rest in Pine Nut and Sweetwater ranges in western Nevada and up around Jarbidge in northeastern Nevada. These bears can be any color from blond to cinnamon to jet black; nearly all have a white patch on their chests. The males can be six feet long and weigh 300–400 pounds, the females five feet long and up to 200 pounds.

Coyotes

Coyotes are the west's most common predator, and therefore its contemporary symbol of defiance. Coyotes are extremely smart and patient; they've been known to take a week to kill a calf by biting off a snippet of its tail every day. They're fast, they reproduce readily and in large numbers, and they're utterly opportunistic, taking advantage of bumper crops of rabbits or vulnerable deer, even supplementing their diet with pine nuts. Coyotes have also pretty much lost their fear of humans and are occasionally seen in towns, looking for cats and dogs. They prey voraciously on domestic stock, killing an estimated 10,000 sheep and cattle a year in Nevada. The federal Animal Damage Control (ADC) hunts them all over the west, killing nearly 100,000 coyotes in 17 Western states every year.

Bighorn Sheep

The desert (or Nelson) bighorn is the state animal. It is smaller than its cousins, the Rocky Mountain and California bighorns, but has bigger horns, and is therefore highly prized as a big-game trophy. In fact, hunters have stalked this animal since records of such activities have kept track of such things; petroglyphs and pictographs, such as in Valley of Fire State Park northeast of Las Vegas, illustrate bighorn hunt-

ing. It's even believed that sheep comprised a larger part of Indians' diet than deer. More than 2,000 hunters apply for the 100 or so sheep tags distributed every year for Nevadans; 1,000 non-residents compete for a dozen out-of-state tags.

Nevada is the only state in the country that can claim all three subspecies of bighorn. Desert bighorn inhabit south and central Nevada, Rocky Mountain bighorn occupy northeastern Nevada, and California bighorn live in northwestern Nevada. An aggressive relocation program is underway; bighorn are trapped and redistributed throughout the state to ensure healthy populations.

The Desert National Wildlife Range, at 1.5 million acres, is the largest wildlife refuge outside of Alaska in the country. It was established to protect the desert bighorn, seen mostly in the Sheep Range, which stretches from just north of Las Vegas all the way up to near Alamo (along US 93). Desert bighorn have overpopulated the area around Lake Mead to the point where they can be seen grazing on the grass at Hemenway Valley Park, right in the middle of Boulder City (see "To the Dam" under "Boulder City" in the East of Las Vegas section).

Wild Horses and Burros

One of the great wildlife controversies in Nevada is over wild horses, also known as mustangs. Since passage of the 1971 Wild Free-Roaming Horse and Burro Act, the Bureau of Land Management has protected these horses and burros "as a symbol of the history and pioneer spirit of the West." This leg-

coyote

KAREN McKINLEY

islation was enacted, thanks in part to the efforts of Velma Johnson, a Reno secretary, to put an end to the brutal business of the legendary mustangers. These cowboys chased wild horses, often with low-flying airplanes, roped them from flatbed trucks, and sold them to slaughterhouses as pet-food meat. Mustanging was graphically dramatized in the classic movie *The Misfits,* written by Arthur Miller, who took the six-week cure (got divorced) at the Reno clinic in 1956 and observed mustangers working around Pyramid Lake. Possibly the most famous movie filmed in Nevada (1960), *The Misfits* captured the last performances by Clark Gable (who died of a heart attack shortly after completing the picture) and Marilyn Monroe (who died of a drug overdose under mysterious circumstances in 1962).

Since 1971, the BLM has been in charge of rounding up wild horses (see "Sights" under "Pyramid Lake" in the Northwest Nevada chapter for details). Everyone seems to agree that a definite limit to the population needs to be maintained. Ranchers insist that the horses destroy the range and pollute water sources. Herds of wild horses are occasionally found shot in remote ranching areas.

Some environmentalists note, however, that when the horses are removed, ranchers run twice the number of cattle that's appropriate for the particular area. Others claim that horses actually benefit the range, by allowing growth of shrubs and plants that provide forage for native species, such as pronghorn, bighorn, and mule deer. One expert, Joel Berger, studied horses for five years in the remote Granite Range north of Gerlach and concluded that horses account for minimal damage to the range. Still, he recommended that 90% of the wild horses be removed to protect the native species.

In a recent round-up from a 300,000-acre horse-management area east of Eureka, of nearly 1,500 mustangs, upwards of 1,250 were culled. Horses nine and younger were transported to Palomino Valley to be offered for adoption. Horses older than nine were released back into the wild. The BLM defended the process, claiming that the older horses can reproduce till they're 16 or 17 years old. But critics insist that by pulling out the young horses, the government is purposely weakening the herds.

Once the horses are removed from the range, the question is what to do with them. In 1985, for example, 19,000 horses were culled from the wild herds, but only 9,000 were adopted. Since then, the BLM has begun to cultivate the market, by matching particular kinds of wild horses to local preferences in the southern, midwestern, and eastern states. One long-discussed proposal for dealing with a saturated wild-horse market is now being tested in a $400,000 program to inject a contraceptive vaccine into 120 nonpregnant five-year-old or older mares from a herd north of Ely; the contraceptive is effective for two years. Even environmentalists and animal activists support this project. Other possibilities include sterilization, establishing large horse sanctuaries, destroying horses that aren't adopted in, say, 90 days, and selling unwanted horses for meat to supply the many people around the world who eat horse meat as well as to supply the domestic pet-food manufacturers.

In the 1992 BLM census, Nevada was home to roughly 33,000 free-roaming horses, 60% of the nation's total 54,000. But a combination of factors, including the round-ups and drought, reduced the population by more than 30% to 23,000 in 1996. The BLM plans to further reduce the number of mustangs to 19,500 by 1998.

In an agreement negotiated by the Fund For Animals and Animal Protection in 1997, the BLM admitted to major abuses in its adoption system, whereby people who adopted mustangs for $125 apiece sold them to pet food manufacturers at a profit. It turns out the BLM had lost track of 32,000 adopted horses since the program began; 90% of the mustangs adopted each year, the Fund claimed, wound up as pet food. The BLM agreed to monitor its wild-horse adoption program more vigorously.

Controversy and drought notwithstanding, it's a thrill to see free-roaming herds, which is possible in nearly any rural setting in Nevada.

ENVIRONMENTAL ISSUES

WILDERNESS

To many Nevadans, *wilderness* is a dirty word, a negative concept. Wilderness means controlled access and use: reduced grazing and logging; regulated road building, mineral exploration, and mining activity—in short, general commercial restraint of the activities that most rural Nevadans rely upon for their livelihoods. All through the 19th century, after original settlement and statehood, the term "public-domain lands" was tantamount to "anything-goes lands," with no restrictions whatsoever on grazing, mining, roadcutting, polluting. Especially since the vast majority of Nevada land is desert, traditionally considered unattractive and useless, it belonged to whomever wanted it, with no thought to preserving it in (what environmentalists think of as) its "pristine state." At the turn of the century, Theodore Roosevelt, a "preservationist" president, was elected, and Nevada became the object of some of the earliest environmental-protection and controlled-usage policies (the Ruby Mountains, for example). However, up until quite recently, only small isolated chunks of Nevada's federal lands were protected: Jarbidge Wilderness Area (1964) and Great Basin National Park (1986).

The federal government owns more than 80% of Nevada, with 70% in the hands of the Bureau of Land Management (BLM). Traditionally, mining and ranching interests have been far too strong to be overcome by any wilderness proposals. Recently, however, the mass migrations into Nevada's two urban areas, the increasing importance of tourism to the state's economic well-being, and the election of three Democrats (out of a possible four) to Congress in the late 1980s turned the tables. In 1989, 25 years after the passage of the Wilderness Act in 1964, empowering states to set aside peaks, canyons, forests, streams, and wildlife habitats in parks, the political stars were aligned properly for the federal government to designate wilderness areas in Nevada.

Original legislation proposed in 1985 by the House Interior Committee included 1.4 million acres of wilderness and recreation areas. In 1987, a bill sponsored by Congressman Harry Reid setting aside 760,000 acres of wilderness and recreation areas was passed by the House of Representatives, but was killed in the Senate by Chic Hecht, known as a booster for rural livelihoods. In the 1988 election, however, Hecht's Senate seat was taken by Richard Bryan, who supported a bill to set aside 600,000 acres. Finally, on December 5, 1989, the Nevada Wilderness Protection Act became law, designating 733,400 acres of national forest lands as wilderness areas in 14 separate locations around the state.

The largest is Arc Dome in the Toiyabe Range in central Nevada at 115,000 acres; the smallest

NEVADA WILDERNESS AREAS

SANTA ROSAS

JARBIDGE

EAST HUMBOLDTS

RUBIES

MT. MORIAH

TABLE MOUNTAIN

ARC DOME

MT. ROSE

ALTA TOQUIMA

CURRANT MOUNTAIN

GRANTS

QUINN CANYON

BOUNDARY PEAK

MT. CHARLESTON

0   75 mi

0   75 km

© AVALON TRAVEL PUBLISHING, INC.

is Boundary Peak, with 10,000 acres surrounding Nevada's highest mountain. The wilderness areas range from Mt. Rose (28,000 acres) and Mt. Charleston (38,000 acres) within an hour's drive of Reno and Las Vegas, respectively, to the remote and trackless Quinn Canyon (27,000 acres) and Grant (50,000 acres) ranges in eastern Nevada. Also included are the Santa Rosas (31,000 acres) in the northwest, East Humboldts (36,900 acres) and Rubies (90,000 acres) in the northeast (along with the long-established Jarbidge Wilderness Area), Mt. Moriah (82,000 acres) and Currant Mountain (36,000 acres) in the Ely vicinity, and Table Mountain (98,000 acres) and Alta Toquima (38,000 acres) in central Nevada.

In July 1997, the first guide to Nevada's wilderness area's was published. *Nevada Wilderness Areas And Great Basin National Park—A Hiking and Backpacking Guide* by Renoite Michael C. White. The book covers a dozen wilderness areas, plus Great Basin, with a total of 56 trips. It's indispensable for anyone wanting to explore the highest peaks and most remote ranges, as well as some of the most popular and accessible areas of wilderness in Nevada. See the "Booklist" for the publishing information.

Another guide in which some of the access and backpacking routes are covered in detail is John Hart's *Hiking the Great Basin.* For the latest government publications on the areas, contact the Humboldt and Toiyabe Forest Service headquarters (see "Information" in the On the Road chapter for addresses and phone numbers). The Toiyabe Chapter of the Sierra Club (P.O. Box 8096, Reno, NV 89507; 775/323-3162; www.sierraclub.org) publishes the *Toiyabe Trails* newsletter six times a year, covering Sierra Club activities, wilderness, water rights, and other Nevada environmental issues and publicizes group outings.

Wilderness Continued

In 1976, Congress passed the Federal Land Policy and Management Act (FLPMA), which instructed the Bureau of Land Management (BLM) to examine its land holdings (which in Nevada amount to nearly 50 million acres) to determine the areas that had potential as official wilderness. The BLM selected 100 sites encompassing a little more than five million acres to study in minute detail, out of which 52 areas and 1.9 million acres were proposed as wilderness areas. The rest of the study areas were released from wilderness consideration.

The BLM's proposals add up to more than double the existing wilderness in Nevada, and the prohibitions, in some ways, are even stricter than in Forest Service wilderness. No mechanized vehicles are permitted (including bicycles) and mining is prohibited (except if the mines existed before FLPMA). As might be imagined, the mining and environmental industries disagree over the areas and their boundaries. But spokesmen for the groups seem to indicate that they'll be able to compromise on the extent of the wilderness, which Congress will then have to pass into law. The process is expected to take years, but in the meantime, FLPMA prohibits any development in the proposed wilderness areas. They're now protected by default and will remain so until the determinations are finalized by law.

Wilderness P.S.

The Wilderness Society is urging the federal government to use $15 million from the Land and Water Conservation Fund (provided by a share of the royalties from offshore oil production) to purchase Nevada land to be protected by the Forest Service. Most of the sensitive areas are near Carson City, Reno, and Las Vegas, in the Carson Range, along the Truckee River, and in the Spring Mountains.

NUCLEAR ISSUES

Nevada Test Site

This 1,350-square-mile chunk of the southern Nevada desert is a Rhode Island-sized area that's off limits to the public—but you probably wouldn't want to go there even if it weren't. Between 1951 and 1962, 126 atmospheric tests of nuclear weapons were conducted within the Test Site's boundaries. Between 1962 and 1992, another 925 underground explosions rocked the desert (add to that another 204 tests that the federal government admitted it conducted secretly).

It all started after American scientists and military planners found that nuclear test explosions over the Marshall Islands in the central Pacific were politically and logistically inconvenient, and they went looking for a more suitable location on the U.S. mainland. Nevada already had the enormous Las Vegas Bombing and Gunnery Range, and there was nothing out there, anyway, right? The first bomb, a one-kiloton warhead dropped from an airplane, was detonated in January 1951, initiating another bizarre episode in southern Nevada history, not to mention a deadly "nuclear war" conducted against atomic veterans and downwinders that continues to this day.

About one bomb a month was tested every month for the next four years; after a two-year suspension of testing at the site (during which larger bombs were exploded again in the central Pacific), a bomb was blown off every three weeks until the first Nuclear Test-Ban Treaty was signed in the early 1960s, eliminating atmospheric explosions.

Set off just before dawn, the tests sometimes broke windows in Henderson (100 miles away). The fireballs could be seen in Reno (300 miles away). And the mushroom clouds tended to drift east over southern Utah. For most of the blasts, the Atomic Energy Commission erected realistic "Doom Town" sets to measure destruction, and thousands of soldiers were posted within a tight radius to be purposefully exposed to the tests.

In his classic *Been Down So Long Looks Like Up To Me*, Richard Fariña described it thus:

The sky changed, the entire translucent dome stunned by the swiftness of the shimmering atomic flash. The light drove their once tiny shadows to a terrifying distance in the desert, making them seem like titans. Then it shrank, the aurora crashing insanely backward, like a film in reverse, toppling, swimming into a single white-hot bulge, a humming lump, a festering core. It hovered inches above the horizon, dancing, waiting almost as if it were taking a stoked breath, then swelled in puffing spasms, poking high into the stratosphere, edging out the pale skyrocket vapor trails at either side, the ball going sickly yellow, the shock wave releasing its roar, the entire spectacle catching fire,

blazing chaotically, shaming the paltry sun.

In the echo, there was silence.

And in a less rhapsodic but no less poignant description, K.J. Evans, now Public Information Officer for the Nevada Commission on Tourism, in his story "A Hometown Grows Up" (*Nevada Day* magazine, 1987), wrote:

I recall an early morning in 1957, seated with my family around the breakfast table. Suddenly, an atomic blast lit up the sky. My mother stopped stirring the Wheatena, peeled back the curtain from the kitchen window and peered out. A faint rocking motion that failed to stir my kid brother, asleep in his high chair, accompanied the flash.

Dad arose and padded to the back door.

'A-bomb,' he grunted, and went back to blotting the bacon.

Indeed, far from disturbing the local health consciousness, at the time Las Vegas turned the blasts into public-relations events, throwing rooftop parties to view them. Moe Dalitz and Wilbur Clark planned the opening of the Desert Inn to coincide with a detonation; the former garnered more coverage than the latter. A silent majority certainly worried which way the wind blew, and a vocal minority seemed to contract a strange "atom fever": marketing everything from atom burgers to nuclear gasoline and appointing a yearly Miss Atomic Blast.

But in a recently published coffee-table book that gives a brand new dimension to the word horrifying, *American Ground Zero: The Secret Nuclear War*, author Carole Gallagher quotes a 17-year-old soldier who witnessed an aboveground explosion in 1957:

That cloud was like a big ball of fire with black smoke and some red inside, big, monstrous, almost sickening . . . It left me really sad, real apprehensive about life . . . That explosion told me I was part of the most evil thing I have ever seen in my life.

GIs were stationed as close to the blasts as was physically possible without killing them outright. Citizens in the path of the fallout wore "film badges" on their clothes to measure the amount of radiation they were subjected to. Livestock dropped dead fairly soon after the exposure. People involved with or in proximity to the tests have been dying of cancer and leukemia ever since. Today, exposed soldiers, residents of southwestern Utah, and their children are part of extremely high cancer clusters. For more than 35 years, our government steadfastly denied any connection between the deaths and the tests; the Justice Department spent untold millions of dollars fighting lawsuits brought by victims of the nuclear tests, primarily people who worked at the Test Site and people downwind of the tests in Nevada, Utah, Arizona, and New Mexico. Only in the past few years have the feds begun to consider the possibility that maybe, gee whiz, there could be a possibility of some cause and effect relationship between the two.

The Nuclear Waste Repository

Now the state is being asked to play host to yet another aspect of the nuclear industry—radioactive waste. Yucca Mountain, 100 miles northwest of Las Vegas, is the only site being considered to become the nation's permanent high-level radioactive waste disposal site.

In a power play involving the U.S. Congress, the states, the Department of Energy (DOE), and the nuclear industry, Nevada has been awarded the dubious honor of receiving spent, partially cooled, but highly radioactive fuel from nuclear weapons plants and 100-odd nuclear reactors across the country. In 1987, Congress mandated that the DOE conduct an in-depth study of the Yucca Mountain site over the next five years, with the goal of opening a repository there in 2003. In so doing, the nation put all its radioactive eggs in one basket.

Congress passed the landmark Nuclear Waste Policy Act (NWPA) in 1982. It was the U.S.'s first coherent, long-range plan to manage the 15,000 metric tons of high-level radioactive waste that has been accumulating in temporary sites at nuclear power plants across the country. The NWPA originally instructed the DOE to locate and build two repositories, one in the East and one in the West, thereby providing a regional balance and fragile compromise on the unpopular issue of rad-waste disposal. Understandably, no state wished to become home to a waste dump that would remain radioactive for 20,000 years. By 1986, more than 40 lawsuits had been filed, alleging that the DOE's selection process was politically motivated, scientifically unsound, and a violation of the NWPA.

Under pressure by an election-year Congress and nuclear utility companies, the DOE in 1986 abdicated its search for an eastern site and selected three western locations for further study—Hanford, Washington; Deaf Smith County, Texas; and Yucca Mountain, Nevada. Then, on the last day of its 1987 session, bowing to more political influence and popular protest, Congress amended the NWPA to specify Yucca Mountain as the only site to be assessed. All eyes turned to Nevada.

Not actually a peak, Yucca Mountain is a six-mile-long ridge rising 1,500 feet above the Amargosa Desert. The proposed repository lies astride the Nevada Test Site, Nellis Air Force Range, and a BLM parcel. The plan calls for a surface building complex covering 150 acres. New water wells, utilities, roads, and a railroad would be required, as well as fire, security, medical, and waste-receiving and handling facilities. The underground repository would encompass 1,500 acres, with 700 boreholes housing 24,000 canisters of spent fuel. The site would reach its legal maximum storage capacity of 70,000 metric tons in 28 years of operation.

Adjacent to Death Valley, Yucca Mountain's rainfall measures only six inches per year, 95% of which evaporates or runs off the volcanic rock surface. The DOE believes it can deposit the rad-waste 1,000 feet below the surface and still maintain a 700- to 1,400-foot buffer of dry rock above the water table. This deep "unsaturated zone" was one of Yucca Mountain's most attractive features, since no other site under consideration could offer near the protection from groundwater and deep-aquifer pollution.

The dry desert ecology also helps to mitigate federal engineers' concerns regarding the length of time it will take before the casks that hold the spent fuel inevitably corrode and begin leaking beneath the surface of Yucca Mountain. No one expects the casks not to leak! Opponents' data suggest that the chemical composition of the local water may corrode the casks more rapidly than expected, however. Indeed, DOE revealed in October 1994 that water contaminated by the underground explosions was found 1,450 feet deep, which is *below* the proposed waste site.

Other features of the site that should make it unattractive to store nuclear waste include its proximity to volcanic craters and 32 earthquake fault lines; still another fault line was discovered in January 1994, amid quotes from geologists that Yucca Mountain is less a monolith and more a big piece of Swiss cheese.

The DOE maintains that the chance of an earthquake or volcanic eruption is slight. Tunnels at the NTS have withstood shocks from weapons testing for 25 years. Above-ground structures, such as the waste-handling buildings, would definitely be vulnerable should seismic activity affect the site. And seismic activities measured at the site have bolstered critics' claims that the site is at risk from earthquakes. The worst, in June 1992, was a 5.6-magnitude quake that rocked Little Skull Mountain, which is only 10 miles from the repository, causing roughly $1 million in structural damage to the Yucca Mountain Field Operations Center. Proponents, on the other hand, contend that the sizable jolt would have done much more damage had the area been as unstable as some believe. In any event, they say the repository would be built to withstand an earthquake with a magnitude of 7.0.

The transport of 5,000 shipments of highly radioactive fuel per year to Yucca Mountain is also a major concern to Nevadans. Based on the DOE's record of accidents in its nuclear weapons transportation program, opposition groups estimate the probability of 50 transport accidents *per year* involving radioactive waste on the nation's highways and railroads. Around 250 shipments per year would pass through the

Reno-Sparks area alone, and only a few states would be spared because they are not en route from the various reactors and weapons factories where the spent fuel is now being stored.

Another concern: critics have assailed the Yucca analysis process for containing less science than public relations. A long line of independent scientists are criticizing the government for sugar-coating, white-washing, even falsifying its data. After years of resistance, DOE finally agreed to an independent study of the site. At the same time, however, the feds have accelerated their efforts to determine if Yucca will be safe for 20,000 years as the deadline nears for taking title to the canisters of nuclear waste now stored at power plants around the country.

The process for completing the dump is well underway. The new timetable calls for the Department of Energy studies to take seven years and cost $9 billion. The DOE environmental impact report (EIR) is scheduled to be completed at the end of 2001. Although once the site is approved the DOE can apply for a license to build the repository, there is reason to believe that the DOE's EIR may face lawsuits challenging whether their EIR is adequate, which would further delay the approval process.

Lately, it looks as though the tide is turning against Nevada. Bills are now starting to be passed by Congress. In late October 1997, the House of Representatives voted 307 to 120 to send the waste to Yucca Mountain—the margin was large enough to override a veto by President Clinton (an old friend of Nevada Governor Bob Miller). Earlier in the year, the Senate also voted for the Yucca Mountain legislation, 65–34, only two votes shy of overriding a presidential veto. Congress is two votes away from passing legislation that would open Yucca Mountain in the year 2002. Since presidential veto has been the critical factor in protecting Nevada from this development, Al Gore's loss in the 2000 presidential election was a blow.

Citizen Alert, a statewide environmental organization working since 1975 to assure public participation and government accountability on issues affecting the land and people of Nevada, has in recent years been focusing on nuclear waste, nuclear testing, and Native American sovereignty. A good resource for information and education about these issues, Citizen Alert publishes a quarterly newspaper. Contact: Citizen Alert, P.O. Box 5339, Reno, NV 89513; 775/827-4200; www.citizenalert.org.

MINING REFORM

Under Democrat Bill Clinton's administration, the General Mining Law of 1872, still in effect today, has come under serious fire. The law, designed 126 years ago to hasten western exploration, gives miners the right to prospect hundreds of millions of acres of land that's ostensibly owned by the government, lease it for $2.50 to $5 an acre (prices set in 1872 and never raised), and dig up the minerals on the land without paying the government any royalties.

The latest tempest over mining reform erupted when Secretary of the Interior Bruce Babbitt was court-ordered to sell Barrick Resources, a Canadian gold mining company, the 2,000 acres it claimed on the Carlin Trend in northern Nevada, worth an estimated $10 billion in gold, for a grand total of $10,000 ($5 an acre). Babbitt blasted Barrick publicly, stating that the sale was the "biggest gold heist since Butch Cassidy." Below the surface, however, were the less sensational facts. First, Barrick paid $10,000 for the "surface rights" to the claim, not to the deposit (which it already owned; it bought the claim for $62 million in 1987 from another mining company, and then developed the technology that made mining it feasible). The 2,000 acres were worth more like $50 per. Secondly, of the $10 billion in gold recovered from the mine, it's estimated that $2 billion to $4 billion will come out in payroll, and another $3 billion to $5 billion will be spent on capital equipment, sales and use taxes, state royalties, local contributions, and myriad other costs of doing business.

Besides, critics of Babbitt's position argue, other "miners" of federal property, such as commercial crab fishermen in Chesapeake Bay and lobster farmers off the coast of Maine don't pay royalties on their harvest.

Congress has long been considering reforming the antique law, by imposing a federal royalty of somewhere between 2% (Senate bill) and 8% (House bill), in addition to other fees and requirements; the 8% would put many marginal mines out of business and eat into the profits of all mines, all to flow more tax dollars into the bottomless federal-budget abyss. It's not as if the mining companies don't pay corporate taxes on their profits, like every other company in the country.

The other sticking point of the 1872 Mining Law is eminent domain. It allows mining companies to condemn private property that they want to mine and buy it for "fair market value", which is almost always less than it's worth. The law was invoked in Silver City in the early '80s and in Tuscarora in the late '80s. Intense public pressure defeated both attempts.

RANGE REFORM

Farming and ranching are no different from mining when it comes to changing perceptions of land use based on environmental values as opposed to lifestyle and economic considerations. The argument on one side goes that alfalfa farming, for example, produces one percent of Nevada's gross state product, while using more than 85% of the available water. Range-reform advocates cite over-grazing damage of the range, water pollution, and trampled streambeds and riparian habitats to argue for such legislation as raising the grazing fees on federal land, now under consideration by Congress.

On the other side, ranchers argue that so-called "federal" lands are owned and used by the *people,* more often than not third- and fourth-generation ranchers on the same land, who have a strong vested interest in the health of the land for their continued livelihoods and lifestyles. Farmers, ranchers, miners all believe that their very way of life is coming under attack and will soon be legislated out of existence by the powerful forces of urban environmentalism, which hold an almost religious conviction of returning the land to their vision of nature—an early 18th century ideal.

These are tough issues anywhere, but out here in a state that's owned almost in its entirety by the federal government, these are profoundly momentous, and divisive, concerns, which will affect the future of all Nevadans.

HISTORY

INDIANS

Prehistory

Excavation and carbon dating of artifacts discovered in a number of caves around the state have supplied evidence that primitive aboriginals occupied the region now encompassed by Nevada as early as 11,000 B.C. Bones taken from a cave near Winnemucca Lake and spear tips unearthed at Leonard Rock Shelter (south of Lovelock) attest to human presence along the shoreline of great Lake Lahontan between 10,000 and 7500 B.C. Basket remnants from the rock shelter are thought to have been woven around 5600 B.C.

At Tule Springs, an archaeological site near Las Vegas, indications are that Paleo-Indians also lived in shoreline caves at the tail end of the wet and cold Wisconsin Ice Age, and hunted Pleistocene mammals, such as woolly mammoth, bison, mastodon, and caribou, as early as 11,000 B.C. At Gypsum Cave, also near Las Vegas, remains of humans, horses, and even a giant sloth certify a hunter culture from 8500 B.C. Little is known, beyond these finds, about the earliest "Nevadans," but starting around 3,000 years ago, a picture of the local prehistoric people starts to emerge.

The Lovelock Cave was a treasure trove for archaeologists, who excavated darts and fishhooks, baskets, domestic tools, tule duck decoys, shell jewelry, and human remains dating from roughly 2000 B.C. It's known that Lake Lahontan was shrinking, and these water-based aboriginals had to evolve a new desert culture. The area's later Paiutes demonstrated similar basket-making skills, but it's unclear whether the people who used Lovelock Cave were their ancestors. Petroglyphs from around this period have been located in the vicinity (especially at Grimes Point near Fallon), but they raise many more questions than they answer about the lives of the Paleo-Indians.

Anasazi

In the southern regions, an Indian culture began to evolve around 2500 B.C. Known as Archaic

Indians, these were a foraging people who lived and traveled in small bands, built rock shelters, used the atlatl (an arrow launcher), hunted bighorn sheep and desert tortoise, and harvested screwbean mesquite and cholla fruit. By around 300 B.C., the Basket Maker culture had arrived; these people too were foragers and lived in pit houses.

Long about the beginning of the common era, natives in Nevada's southern desert began to develop the first signs of civilization. They lived in close proximity to each other in pit houses (little more than holes in the ground with brush roofs), and evidence exists of co-operation during hunting and gathering chores. By around A.D. 500, these Anasazi ("Enemies of Our Ancestors") had developed pottery and bows and arrows, begun building more sophisticated dwellings with adobe walls, learned

NEVADA COMMISSION ON TOURISM

how to mine salt and trade with neighbors, and started to bury their dead. By A.D. 800, their civilization was at its peak: they cultivated beans and corn in irrigated fields, lived in grand 100-room pueblos, fashioned artistic pots and baskets, mined turquoise, and generally enjoyed a sophisticated lifestyle in the fertile delta between the Muddy and Virgin rivers in what's now southeastern Nevada—an outpost in Las Vegas Valley was the first prehistoric architecture in Nevada. Around 1150, however, the Anasazi disappeared. No one knows for sure why, but speculation includes drought, overpopulation, disease, collapse of the economic underpinnings of the culture, or warring neighbors. Whatever, the Anasazi abandoned their pueblos and farms (one of the largest of which was uncovered in the 1920s and is now preserved at Lost City Museum in Overton).

Paiute, Washo, Shoshone

The Southern Paiutes claimed the territory that the Anasazi had fled, but they never regained the advanced elements of their predecessors' society. In fact, for the next 700 years, these Paiutes remained nomadic hunter-gatherers. Some migrated north to populate the high desert (Northern Paiute), where they encountered the Washo and Shoshone peoples. All settled into a basically peaceful existence, adapting to the arid land. (Their fishing techniques, rabbit and sagehen drives, pine-nut harvests, salt mining, foraging, tools and weapons, basket making, and shelters are graphically displayed in the Archaeology Gallery at the State Museum in Carson City.) For hundreds of years, the Washo Indians of western Nevada, the Shoshone Indians of eastern Nevada, and the Paiute of northwestern and southern Nevada developed and maintained cultures perfectly adapted to their difficult environments. Until, that is, the first white explorers from the east—harbingers from Indian hell—arrived. Within 40 years of contact, the Native American lifestyles had been destroyed. (For a closer look at precontact customs, see "Native Americans" under "People" later in the Introduction.)

EXPLORERS AND PIONEERS

1776–1841

The first white men to enter what is now Nevada were Spanish friars surveying a trail to connect missions between New Mexico and the California coast. Two expeditions, one led by Francisco Garces, the other by friars Escalante and Dominguez, explored the region, but only Garces touched the far southern tip of Nevada. Escalante and Dominguez, however, discovered a couple of large rivers running west from Utah and postulated a great waterway flowing from there to the Pacific. Thus the mythical San Buenaventura River, the one great river that flowed from the Rocky Mountains to the Pacific Ocean, was introduced into the frontier imagination. It took almost 70 years to once and for all bury the myth of this great river.

In 1819, a treaty between the U.S. and Mexico designated the 42nd parallel as the boundary between American and Spanish territories (today the borderline between Nevada and Oregon/Idaho). For the next 30 years, all the American explorers, trappers and traders, mapmakers, gold rushers, and settlers who entered Nevada were technically illegal aliens. The 1848 Treaty of Guadalupe Hidalgo, following the Mexican-American War, ceded most of the Southwest, including all of Nevada, to the United States.

In 1826, Jedediah Smith led a party of fur trappers through the same country that Garces had crossed, and spent that winter in California. In the spring, he crossed the central Sierra Nevada and discovered the Great Basin Desert—the hard way. Smith's party struggled through the sand and sage with no water for days at a time, crossed a dozen mountain passes, stumbled into Utah, and reached Salt Lake an agonizing month and a half after leaving the coast.

A year later, Peter Skene Ogden entered Nevada from the north and trapped beaver along the Humboldt River. In 1829 Ogden returned to the Humboldt, then continued south, becoming the first white man to cross the Great Basin from north to south. Meanwhile, Kit Carson and company were following parts of the route laid out by the Franciscans, thereby helping to establish and publicize the southern Spanish Trail. In 1830, Antonio Armijo, a Mexican trader, set out from Santa Fe on the Spanish Trail. An experienced scout in Armijo's party, Rafael Rivera, discovered a shortcut on the route by way of Las Vegas's Big Springs, thereby making him the first non-Indian to set foot on the land that only 75 years later would become Las Vegas.

Enter Joseph Walker. In 1833 he led a fur-trapping expedition west along the Humboldt and Walker rivers through Nevada, crossed the Sierra into Yosemite Valley, spent the winter in California, then returned east along the same route in the spring of 1834. In both directions he encountered and fired upon the Northern Paiute—the first skirmishes between the races in Nevada.

In 1841, the famous Bidwell-Bartleson party became the first emigrants to set out from Missouri and enter California. Through a combination of dumb luck and good guides, these pioneers managed to follow Walker's route along the Humboldt, Carson Sink, Walker River, and over the Sierra. With them were the first cattle, wagons, and white woman and child to enter Nevada. Their success encouraged a few more staggered wagon trains to attempt the long journey across the uncharted western half of the country and stimulated the first official map-making expedition through the Great Basin.

Frémont and the Forty-Niners

In 1843, John C. Frémont, a lieutenant in the U.S. Army's Topographical Corps, was assigned the job of exploring and mapping much of what would become Nevada 20 years later; he also hoped to finally locate that elusive San Buenaventura River. Guided by Kit Carson, he marched west through the Columbia River Basin, then cut south into far northwestern Nevada. He "discovered" and named Pyramid Lake, followed the Truckee River for a spell, turned south and "discovered" the Carson River, and continued down to the river that Joe Walker had found. Frémont's party crossed the Sierra in January, glimpsing Lake Tahoe, then traveled south through California and reentered Nevada on the Spanish Trail, camping at Las Vegas. From there they continued through Utah, crossed the Rockies, and returned to Missouri. This initial trip resulted in the naming of the Great Basin—and

John C. Frémont

NEVADA HISTORICAL SOCIETY

the denaming of the San Buenaventura. Frémont returned to Nevada a year later, this time guided by Joe Walker himself, and further mapped the country. By then, several hundred emigrants had already crossed the great desert into California.

The famous Donner incident, in which an ill-fated pioneer party became snowbound in the Sierra and resorted to cannibalism to survive, slowed emigration temporarily. But one year later, in 1847, a mass migration of Latter-day Saints settled Salt Lake Valley, advancing civilization to the eastern edge of the Great Basin. A year after that, the Americans emerged victorious from the Mexican-American War and appropriated the rest of the West; fortuitously, only two weeks earlier, the country's first major gold had been discovered at Sutter's Mill. Roughly 500 people emigrated to California from the east in 1847. But over the next five years, nearly a quarter of a million frenzied stampeders flooded the coast. Of those who took the Emigrant Trail through the vast Utah Territory, some stopped to pan the eastside creeks of the Sierra Nevada and found gold, while others settled just short of California in the verdant valleys at the base of the great range. Mormon advance parties set up trading posts to supply the travelers; the one established in Carson Valley (Mormon Station) in 1851 attracted other settlers, who turned it into the first real town in Nevada.

Genoa and Las Vegas

Over the course of the next few years, the population of the country around Mormon Station—Washoe and Carson valleys, Johntown, Ragtown—started to grow. Traders, prospectors, wagon drivers, and homesteaders moved in. In 1855 this far western corner of Utah Territory, administered from Salt Lake City, was designated Carson County and put under the direct administration of local Mormon officials and colonists. Mormon Station was renamed Genoa and became Nevada's first county seat.

Missionaries were also dispatched from Salt Lake City to civilize southern Nevada at a rest stop along the Spanish Trail known as Las Vegas, or the Meadows. They built a stockade similar to the one in Genoa, befriended the Paiute, nourished the travelers, and even began mining and smelting lead nearby. But tensions between the Mormon colonists and miners, meager rations, and the hardships and isolation of the desert caused the mission to disband.

In addition, Brigham Young, concerned with possibly going to war with the U.S. Army over autonomy, bigamy, and manifest destiny, recalled the Saints from Genoa. Their places were taken by the people who would soon become the first official Nevadans.

THE COMSTOCK LODE

Jockeying for Position

Prospectors and gold miners had been crawling all over the Carson River and its creeks for almost a decade. Chinese laborers had even been brought in to dig a canal from the river to Gold Canyon; their settlement became Dayton, second oldest town in Nevada. The prospectors were already following their noses up toward what could be the source of the promising placer pay dirt. Of the hundred or so ignorant and unwashed miners, only the young Grosch brothers, mineralogists and assayers from New York,

knew of the gargantuan silver lode under everyone's feet. But they both died suddenly one winter, and their secret was buried with them.

Meanwhile, Abraham Curry bought a ranch and opened up a trading post in Eagle Valley, between the county seat at Genoa and the lumber mills at Washoe City. And Myron Lake bought a bridge over the Truckee River in the large basin north of Washoe. Lake had dreams of a boomtown, and Curry had dreams of a capital.

An expedition led by one Lieutenant Ives powered the steamboat *Explorer* up the Colorado River all the way to Black Canyon, and a surveying team led by one Captain Simpson blazed a trail through central Nevada as an alternative to the heavily trafficked road along the Humboldt to the north. Soon, Pony Express riders were galloping over the Simpson route, passing linemen stringing telegraph wire between poles. Several new roads were cut across the Sierra into California from the east side for the settlers at Truckee Meadows and Washoe, Eagle, Carson, Mason, and Smith valleys.

Virginia City

In 1859, two Irish gold miners dug a hole around a small spring high up on Sun Mountain and struck the fabled daughter lode. The respectable quantities of gold, however, were encased by a blue-gray mud, a peculiar rock that polluted the quartz veins, fouled the sluice boxes, and diluted the quicksilver. But when a visitor to the diggings carried a bit of the mud down and had it assayed in Placerville, it was found to be nearly pure sulphuret of silver. A drunken prospector dropped a bottle of whiskey and baptized the ragged settlement on the eastern slope of Sun Mountain with the name Virginia after his home state. And a shifty, lazy, and scheming braggart made so much noise about *his* claim to the riches that the whole outfit came to be named after him: the Comstock Lode.

The Comstock is still one of the largest silver strikes in the world. And Virginia City remains one of the most authentic and colorful boomtowns in the Wild West. Such was the enormous impact of the riches, the power, and the fame of this find that within a year Nevada had become its own territory. The capital was placed in Abe Curry's Carson City, and of the territory's nine original counties, six surrounded the Comstock.

Meanwhile, trading posts were established all along the Humboldt Trail, at Lovelock, Winnemucca, and Carlin, among others. Boomtowns such as Aurora, Austin, and Unionville were mushrooming up from the desert. Gold was also discovered at Eldorado Canyon on the Colorado, a short distance from Las Vegas. But Virginia City was the lodestar, the ultimate boomtown. In 1864, a mere five years after its discovery, the Comstock had earned Nevada statehood status. It also helped finance Lincoln's Union Army. (Nevada's two new senators cast the deciding votes to abolish slavery.) And the unearthing of tons of silver affected monetary standards worldwide.

The Roaring Sixties

Abe Curry, founder of Carson City, not only got his capital, but he got the state prison and the federal mint as well. Myron Lake won a 10-year contract to collect tolls on his bridge over the Truckee at a bustling little site soon to be known as Reno. The new state's eastern and southern boundaries were pushed outward, swallowing a few chunks of Arizona and Utah territories, including 150 miles of the Colorado River. Alfalfa was on its way to becoming the star crop of Nevada agriculture. The mines of the Comstock, deepening to more than 500 feet, were greedily devouring virtually every tree within 50 miles for timber supports. And Virginia Town

was quickly turning into Virginia City, the largest and loudest metropolis between Salt Lake City and San Francisco.

Silver was located at Eureka, 70 miles east of Austin, and Hamilton, 70 miles east of that. Gold and silver were mined in Robinson Canyon, as well as Osceola, just west of the Utah border around today's Ely. The silver at Tuscarora opened up the northeast. A gold miner from Eldorado Canyon named O.D. Gass homesteaded Las Vegas Valley, squatting in the ruins of the Mormon fort. But the big news, in 1868, was the arrival of the Central Pacific Railroad—at Reno in May, Winnemucca in September, Elko in February 1869, and Promontory Point, Utah, in May, also hatching Lovelock, Battle Mountain, Carlin, and Wells as it went.

The Railroads

The transcontinental railroad across northern Nevada stimulated the building of numerous wagon roads to the north and south of it, interconnecting the whole top half of the six-year-old state. The Virginia & Truckee Railroad was laid from the mines at Virginia City to the mills at Carson City, then hooked up to the main line at Reno. Thousands of Chinese were abandoned by both railroads after construction was completed; every Chinatown in the state was hounded and persecuted out of existence over the next 15 years. The Indians as well, after numerous skirmishes and several major battles, were finally subdued, then left to fend for themselves,

Virginia & Truckee Railroad

JOHN ELK III

both on and off the few reservations set up to contain them. In the late 1860s and early 1870s, the Comstock hit the third or fourth bust of its boom-bust cycle, but in 1872, John Mackay's Big Bonanza gave Nevada a six-year $150 million infusion of cash. A disastrous fire in 1875 temporarily muffled Virginia City's boom, and although Big Bonanza silver restored it even beyond its previous splendor, the Comstock mines played out in the next few years.

By then Eureka was producing serious enough silver to rate its own railroad connection, the Eureka and Palisade, to the Central Pacific. The Nevada Central followed suit between the mines around Austin and the main line at Battle Mountain. Other shortlines were laid from mines to mills, with boomtowns in between. But the demise of the Comstock quickly forced Nevada to its knees. From a population of nearly 60,000 within a 20-mile radius of Virginia City in 1876, only 42,000 people remained in the whole state 20 years later.

Twenty-Year Bust
Between 1880 and 1900, it seemed every strike in the whole state played out and stayed out. No new ones appeared. The boomtown economy deflated into a shambles. A still-unbroken record snowfall and cold snap during the winter of 1889–90 wiped out the entire livestock industry. Silver politics became the pastime of choice: calling for the federal government to turn more of Nevada silver into circulating coins at the mint. This minor political wrangle ushered Nevada into the new century.

TWENTIETH CENTURY

The New Boom
In May 1900, Jim Butler, once a miner in Austin and at the time a rancher outside of Belmont, located some very rich rock in the wilds of south-central Nevada. Butler's silver strike at Tonopah was the first news of prosperity in a generation. Two years later, Goldfield began booming even more loudly 25 miles south of Tonopah. Prospectors fanned out from there and located the Bullfrog, Round Mountain, and Manhattan districts. Railroads were slapped into place between Tonopah and the Southern Pacific (which had re-

placed the Central Pacific). The Tonopah & Las Vegas Railroad hooked up the new boomtowns in central Nevada to a new transcontinental railroad, the San Pedro, Los Angeles and Salt Lake, that crossed the southern corner of Nevada; a new town, Las Vegas, was created in 1905 as a service station for the railroad from Salt Lake City to Los Angeles. Copper in unimaginable quantities was ripped from the earth in eastern Nevada at Ruth, smelted at McGill, and shipped to the northern Southern Pacific near Wells on the Nevada Northern Railway.

Nevada's population nearly doubled in the first decade of the 1900s. The newly established federal Bureau of Reclamation dug right in to divert Truckee River water out into the fertile desert around Fallon with the Derby Dam and Truckee Canal. Humboldt National Forest was created to manage the Ruby Mountains. The Western Pacific Railroad was laid across Nevada in 1909: from Oakland, California, across the Black Rock Desert, then along the Southern Pacific route from Winnemucca to Wells, and then along a northern route to Salt Lake City. Shortlines ran from Tonopah into California, from Searchlight to Las Vegas, from Pioche to Caliente, from Carson to Minden, from near Yerington to Wabuska, and elsewhere around Nevada. The railroads were in their prime, but they would last only one more generation. A company with the auspicious name of Nevada Rapid Transit had already built a road especially for automobiles between Rhyolite and Las Vegas in 1905. Floods in 1907 and again in 1910 knocked out hundreds of miles of track on both the northern and southern routes. And in 1913, the designation of Nevada Route No. 1 along the Humboldt, the first state auto road, spelled an end to the railroads' monopoly on automated transportation.

The Road
Also in 1913, Nevada passed its first motor vehicle law, the license fee based on the horsepower (any auto with more than 20 horsepower needed a license). In 1914, a highway between Los Angeles and Salt Lake, through Las Vegas, was begun; it took 10 years to build. The Federal Aid Road Act of 1916 allocated funds to stimulate rural road building, which sent Nevada on such a road-building binge that it had to establish a

Department of Highways less than a year later. In 1919, this state agency laid a road down on top of the defunct Las Vegas and Tonopah right-of-way, the first stretch of the Bonanza Highway (US 95).

The Federal Highway Act of 1921 invested more money in building long-distance connectors. Over the next several years, the Highway Department improved old Nevada Route #1 by widening and grading it and laying down gravel. By 1927, the transcontinental Victory (US 40) and Lincoln (US 50) highways were complete; a national exposition was held in Reno to celebrate, for which that city's first arch was erected over Virginia Street. The roads had an immediate negative impact on the railroads; the downtowns along the tracks began their inexorable migrations, relocating along the highways.

The Crash

The stock market went down and out in 1929 and took Nevada's banks with it. The Great Depression was in full swing, but three events in the next two years did more to shape Nevada's urban history than any others: divorce residency requirements were lowered to a scandalous six weeks; wide-open casino gambling was legalized; and Hoover Dam was built. Divorces and gambling combined to focus a national spotlight on Reno, Biggest Little City in the World, and biggest big city in Nevada. Unhappily married celebrities waited out their six weeks till divorce in the spotlight of newspaper society pages around the country—dateline Reno. Raymond and Harold Smith, veteran carnies and fledgling casino operators, embarked on a national advertising campaign to polish the image of gambling; their "Harold's Club Or Bust" billboards attracted the gamblers and thrill-seekers in droves. (The house advantage did the rest.) Las Vegas also hit the front pages: Best Town by a Dam Site. Construction workers from the dam flooded the Fremont Street clubs and Block 16 cribs on payday; after the Hoover Dam was topped off, many stayed. And when the first turbine at the dam turned, Las Vegas had as much juice as it would need to do what it so desperately wanted, and was destined, to do.

From the War to the Sixties

A big Naval Air Station went in at Fallon, and an Army Air Base opened at Stead Field outside Reno. When the Army Airfield was installed near Las Vegas in 1941, it supplied the growing town with a steady stream of soldiers and prompted the opening of El Rancho Vegas and the Last Frontier Hotel on what would soon be known as the Strip. Basic Magnesium began mining metals at Gabbs and built factories and a town for 10,000 people at Henderson between Las Vegas and Boulder City. After the war, Mafia money and muscle, supervised by a "charming psychopath" named Benjamin Siegel, raised up and nailed down the ultimate one-stop pleasure palace. Bugsy Siegel expanded the Las Vegas Strip, furthered the modern tourism industry, and ushered in a 20-year underworld siege of southern Nevada. Embattled state officials, caught in an unexpected squeeze play between federal heat and its growing casino revenues, slowly legislated systems of control.

Otherwise, the conservative moral sensibilities of 1950s' America did little to prevent Nevada from marching to its own unconventional drummer. In 1951, for example, Nevada welcomed the Nuclear Test Site to the state, enjoying the fireworks for 10 years (until they went underground, where they continued to go off until the most recent Test Ban Treaty of less than ten years ago). The casino-hotels kept opening one after another, year after year, and the brothels were left the way they've always been. Divorces were granted as automatically as ever and the Freeport Law, instituting tax-free warehousing, was passed.

Finally, Howard Hughes rode into Las Vegas on a stretcher and bought half a dozen of the most troublesome Mafia-owned hotels. This put the seal of corporate respectability on them and paved the way for Hilton, Holiday Inn, Ramada, MGM, and other publicly traded companies to run the industry. Nevada's gambling revenues have never looked back.

Late Twentieth Century

These days, gambling has become the country's most explosive growth industry. In 1990, only two states had legal casino gambling; in 1998 fully 24 states had it, with more lining up every day to get it. With gambling now an acceptable pastime, where do all the small-time casino customers want to go? The big time, of course: Las Vegas. In 1997, upwards of 31 million visitors (a whopping 23% increase over 1993) wagered nearly $30 billion, leaving $6 billion in pretax profits in Las Vegas alone; statewide, casinos won $7.5 billion. Growth continues every year: in 1999, 33.8 million visitors came to Las Vegas, an increase of 10.5% over 1998, and left a gaming revenue of $6.7 billion. Statewide, gaming brought in a revenue of $7.8 billion in 1998, and a full *billion dollars more*—$8.6 billion—in 1999. In addition, Nevada for the past 25 years, but especially over the last half-decade, has been the fastest growing state in the country. Also, Nevada has once again become the nation's number-one producer of precious metals (particularly gold).

These large reasons, and other smaller ones, have introduced the stress of success to Nevada. The state faces a bewildering combination of contemporary changes and challenges. Growth issues are typical: water rights and conservation; carrying capacities and social services; housing, employment, and education; utilities and infrastructure. The recent resurgence of gold and silver mining, as well as the long-established policies of grazing, road building, subdividing, and other forms of developing public lands, have put environmentalists on a collision course with the boomers. The irradiation of Nevada continues to raise pressing questions about the U.S.'s nuclear testing and waste policies, which also have a direct impact on the local debate about preservation and progress. Nevada continues to try to balance the old boom-bust propensities with the new social responsibilities, to maintain the traditions that have made and kept Nevada unique and great, while at the same time changing with the times to ensure its continued presence at the cutting edge of national morality and policy.

GOVERNMENT

Nevada's executive branch has six elected officials. The governor is elected to a maximum of two four-year terms. The current governor, Kenny C. Guinn, assumed office in January 1998, after former governor Bob Miller served nine years as governor, the longest stint in the state's history. Democrat Bob Miller assumed office in January 1989 after former governor Richard Bryan became a U.S. senator. Bryan left office in the third year of his four-year term; Lieutenant Governor Miller filled in the rest of the term, and was then elected in 1990 and 1994. The Lieutenant Governor, Attorney General, Secretary of State, Controller, and Treasurer all answer to the governor while in office and to the voters at election time. The state government's executive branch employs roughly 10,000 people.

The Nevada Legislature is one of the smallest in the country, with a 21-member Senate and a 42-member Assembly. It meets for 120 days (though it's often much longer) starting on the third Monday in January of odd years.

The Nevada Supreme Court's five justices are elected for six-year terms. Trials are conducted at nine District Courts, whose judges are also elected for six years. Municipal courts handle preliminary hearings on felonies, misdemeanors, and small claims. Most municipal judges are elected for four-year terms; some are appointed. There's no appellate level in Nevada's judicial system; to be appealed, cases travel from municipal or district court directly to the Nevada Supreme Court.

Nevada's two U.S. Senators are Harry Reid (Democrat) and John Ensign (Republican). Nevada's two Congressional representatives are Jim Gibbons (Republican) of Reno and Shelley Berkley (Democrat) of Las Vegas.

Nevada has 16 counties, plus Carson City, which is a consolidated "city-county." County governments consist of three to seven elected commissioners. Also elected are assessors, treasurers, clerks, recorders, sheriffs, and district attorneys.

City councils, headed by mayors, govern Nevada's 18 incorporated cities.

ECONOMY

TOURISM AND GAMBLING

Gross Revenues

In fiscal 1996, the taxable gross revenues from 229 hotel-casinos with earnings of more than a million dollars was $12.8 billion. In plain English, this means that visitors and locals spent nearly *thirteen billion dollars* on gambling, food, rooms, and services at Nevada's most lucrative casinos. The net profit was $1.3 billion, giving the hotel-casinos an overall 10% profit margin. Casinos are very profitable. Of the statewide total, Clark County casinos (132 locations) grossed $5.8 billion and net $2.8 billion.

In fiscal 1996, there were 40 more casinos with earnings of more than a million dollars than there were in 1993; the gross was up $3.2 billion and the profit was down 2%. In 1991, the casinos grossed $9 billion, but only net $546 million, a 6.1% profit margin.

By the end of the fiscal year ending in June 2000, Nevada had 238 casinos with net gaming win of more than $1 million each, per year. Taxable gross revenues from these large casinos came to a total of $8.4 billion; their net profit was $877 million, for a 5.7% profit margin. Of the statewide total, Clark County casinos with net gaming win of over a million dollars each (144 casinos) had gaming revenue of $6.7 billion, with a net income of $712 million. Total gaming revenues in Nevada came in at $9.5 billion for the fiscal year ending in June 2000, up a full one billion dollars from the same date in 1999, when gaming revenues totaled $8.5 billion.

Tourism is by far the state's largest employer, accounting for 35% of all jobs. (In southern Nevada it's closer to 45%.) By the end of 1999 it was taking 229,543 tourism employees to shepherd Nevada's 45.5 million tourists through the state, up from 208,233 and 42 million, respectively, the year before. Nevada is number one in the na-

CASINO CASH

Stop and think about it for a moment. Nevada casinos take nearly eight billion dollars a year from their customers. That's eight thousand million. Or eighty million hundred-dollar bills. Eight hundred million ten-dollar bills. There's always a lot of talk about how much money enters casinos in the pockets of customers, and how much money is transferred from those pockets to the slot buckets and table drops and cashier drawers and counting rooms. But did you ever wonder what the *casinos* do with all that cash?

Nevada casinos average more than $20 million in daily cash receipts. That's more than two million ten-dollar bills. What to do with it all? First, casinos employ numerous people, for three shifts round the clock, whose jobs are solely to do the hard (coin) and soft (bill) count: organizing, processing, recording, and storing the cash. These days, casinos don't even actually count the money; they weigh it, both coin and paper, on super-sensitive scales that calculate the amounts within fractions of a penny. Then,

armored cars transport the money to various banks for deposit. The casinos and banks work closely together, using high-tech computerized accounting systems to ensure the accuracy of deposits.

The banks then ship the cash, by armored car, to local central vaults, where it's counted again and stored. Any surplus cash (over and above the vaults' storage capacities) is transferred to California. Reno-Tahoe's cash is sent to San Francisco, Las Vegas's to Los Angeles. Again, high-security trucking is used for the transfers, either private armored-car companies or official Federal Reserve transportation. Occasionally, money is sent via insured mail.

At the California Federal Reserve, personnel separate out the old currency and destroy it. Sometimes new currency is added. Some of this money is sent to other regions of the country according to their cash needs, which are monitored by Federal Reserve officials. Presumably, a number of these same bills make it back into casino counting rooms.

tion in tourism jobs per capita, ninth in the number of foreign visitors. Roughly 25% of the state's labor force works for casinos directly. Tourists generate nearly $3 billion in payroll, which equates with $16,000 in revenue for every Nevadan, and more than $1,800 in taxes per capita.

Given these statistics, it's amazing to think that the state Commission on Tourism wasn't created until 1982. In 1981, Nevada spent $165,000 on promoting itself as a destination, compared to a national average of $2.5 million. By 1984, Nevada had already spent more than $3 million. By 1993, $5.8 million collected from room taxes throughout the state was designated for statewide tourism promotion. In 1999, promotion of tourism topped $138.9 million, and the Nevada Commission on Tourism estimated that the state received an additional $66 million of free publicity in newspapers and magazines throughout the country.

TAXES

Money magazine perennially ranks Nevada as having the third-lowest state tax burden in the country. The same prosperous and hypothetical family of four, which would pay $3,775 in state and local taxes in Nevada, would pay $1,694 in Alaska (number one), and $11,020 in New York (number 51). *Money* notes that Nevada's average 7% sales tax is higher than that of most states nationwide. Nevada also ranks third among 90 federal judicial districts in its percentage of IRS criminal prosecutions.

Analysts agree that Nevada has the second-highest taxing capacity in the country, while the actual taxes imposed are the third lowest. However, there's a price to pay for residents' taxes being subsidized by "export" or out-of-state taxes. Much of the General Fund is spent on tourist industry infrastructure, such as police and fire protection, parks and recreation, and visitor authorities and tourism agencies. At the same time, Nevada ranks low in spending on education and health care.

According to Census figures, the U.S. government spent $4,800 for every American in fiscal 1996. Thirteen cents of every dollar was spent in California, compared to half a cent of every dollar spent in Nevada. It's ironic that the federal government, which owns a larger percentage of Nevada than any other state, spends one of the least amounts per capita.

INCORPORATING

Nevada's corporation system is one of the most liberal in the country (it competes with Delaware). Benefits of incorporating in Nevada include no state corporate tax on profits, no state personal income tax, very little paperwork and a low filing fee ($125), and protection from personal liability and public scrutiny. In addition, a single individual can be the sole president, secretary, and treasurer. Nevada corporations can conduct their primary business out of the state. And most attractive of all, Nevada is the only state without a reciprocal agreement with the IRS to exchange tax returns, which legally ensures maximum privacy.

Madonna is the head of a Nevada corporation, Music Tours, Inc. Michael Jackson, Paul Simon, (the artist formerly known as) Prince, Chevy Chase, Rodney Dangerfield, and Diane Keaton all funnel their large incomes through Nevada corporations to legally avoid taxes and protect financial privacy; the state doesn't require income data, and it releases no information. A New York City cab company formed 50 corporations for every pair of cabs in its 100-taxi fleet; its liability is limited to two percent (unless a litigant wants to sue 50 companies). Ski resorts have done the same with ski lifts, oil companies with oil wells.

It's easy, it's cheap, and it's anonymous. It doesn't even require an attorney. The one necessity is a resident agent within Nevada who can receive mail and be served with any legal documents. Several service businesses help other businesses to incorporate in Nevada. Many incorporating companies provide such services. A good one is Laughlin Associates, 2533 N. Carson St., Carson City, NV 89706, 775/883-8484, www.laughlinassociates.com. For the price of a phone call or stamp, you receive a fat package explaining how to legally eliminate state income taxes, how to judgment-proof a business, how to protect your privacy and estate, and more.

Nevada's Secretary of State office is another

good source of information. They'll send you out a free packet of information on incorporating in Nevada, and on how to qualify to do business in Nevada. Contact: Secretary of State, 101 N. Carson St., Suite 3, Carson City, NV 89701-4786, 775/684-5708.

MINING

Mining is Nevada's number-two revenue-generating industry. Upwards of $2.7 billion dollars worth of minerals are mined from Nevada every year, $2 billion of that consisting of precious metals, mainly gold and silver. Gold is the most valuable in its economic impact, but a long list of other minerals are also mined in Nevada.

Nevada is the United States' largest gold and silver producer, producing a whopping 74% of the nation's gold and 11% of the world's gold each year. If Nevada were a separate country, it would be the third-largest gold-producing nation in the world, South Africa being first and Australia being second; as it is, Nevada's gold production brings the USA in as the second-greatest producer of gold in the world, after South Africa.

More gold has been mined in Nevada in the past five years than was mined at the height of the California, Comstock, and Klondike rushes combined. In 1999, Nevada mines produced 8.3 million ounces of gold, down a bit from the all-time record year of 1998, when 8.9 million ounces were mined. (In 1850, at the zenith of the California rush, three million ounces were produced. The Klondike, Goldfield, and Montana mines produced five million ounces between 1900 and 1910. And the Comstock produced 8.3 million ounces of gold between 1864 and 1889.) In economic terms, the 1998 price of $300 per ounce meant that Nevada gold production earned $2.7 billion in 1998; in 1999 it earned $2.3 billion, with gold prices at $275 per ounce.

North America's physically largest gold mine, the Barrick Gold Strike Mine north of Carlin, is one of several Nevada mines that each produce over 1 million ounces of gold every year. Along with Newmont Gold's mines on the Carlin Trend in Eureka County (Nevada's second-largest mine), and the Cortez Mine in Lander County in the Carlin area (the state's third-largest),

Nevada's gold mines account for 74% of all the gold mined in the U.S.

Silver is mostly produced as a by-product of gold mining, somewhere between 22 million and 28 million ounces annually. (This is opposite of Comstock production, in which gold was a by-product of the silver mining. Just under 200 million ounces of silver were wrested from the Comstock.) Today Nevada has just one mine, the Coeur-Rochester mine near Lovelock, which is a primary silver mine; in all other Nevada mines today, silver is a by-product of gold mining. Nevada is the country's largest producer of silver, with 19.5 million ounces produced in 1999, down from the high of 25 million ounces produced in 1997. It doesn't look like Nevada's slogan of "The Silver State" will change any time soon.

Mining directly employs around 12,360 workers in Nevada, down a bit from the previous 15,000; another 40,000 employees have indirect ties to the industry. However, along the "I-80 mining corridor" (between Winnemucca and

miner at consolidated Virginia mine

DOVER PUBLICATIONS, INC.

Elko), one of three employees works for a mining company. In fact, Elko, where most of Newmont's and Barrick's employees live, closer to 40% of workers are employed by the mining industry, at an average annual salary of $54,037, which gives Elko on average the highest-paid workers in Nevada (the average state salary is $27,700). The total annual payroll for all miners comes to $667 million.

Mining companies pay a large share of state taxes: in 1999 mining paid $26 million in property taxes, $14 million in sales tax and $25 million in income tax, for a total tax contribution of $65 million.

Two useful websites for further information on Nevada's mining industry are: minerals.state.nv.us and www.nbmg.unr.edu.

AGRICULTURE

In 1978 there were 2,400 farms in Nevada. Today there are just over 3,000. Half of them are under 100 acres, while the 11% of farms larger than 2,000 acres occupy 90% of Nevada's farmlands. Alfalfa is the major crop; other important crops include wheat and barley, alfalfa seed, garlic, onions, and potatoes. Hay crops as a whole account for well over half of all harvested acreage in Nevada. Nevada's total crop value came to $118 million in 1999. Farms em-

ploy 5,000 workers, one percent of the labor force.

There are approximately 1,700 cattle ranches in Nevada. Cattle production dropped dramatically in the 1980s, primarily because of bad publicity about red meat. But in the early '90s it became profitable again, primarily because of a strong ad campaign. The number of cattle on Nevada land remained generally steady throughout the 1990s, fluctuating between a low of 490,000 and a high of 530,000; in 2000, there were 510,000 head of cattle in the state. Nevada ranchers are largely dependent on public grazing lands, primarily federal Bureau of Land Management (BLM) lands, for at least part of their forage needs.

Nevada also is home to 90,000 sheep and 7,500 hogs, figures that have decreased dramatically from previous years. At one point, around the early 1930s, Nevada had 1.3 million sheep. But sheep ranching declined as it became less profitable, due in part to a reduction in demand for wool and in part to a change in consumer tastes in meat, moving away from mutton and lamb and more towards beef. In 1999 Nevada had 14,000 hogs, but by 2000 there was only one commercial swine operator left, with a count of 7,500 head. Poultry figures are so low that the Department of Agriculture quit keeping track of them.

PEOPLE

DEMOGRAPHICS

Population
According to official population statistics, Nevada's population topped 2 million for the first time in the year 2000: the 2000 figure came in at 2,059,433, up from 1999 when the estimate was 1,967,650, a growth in one year of 4.66%. A whopping 87% of Nevada's residents live in urban areas. Believe it or not, Nevada ranks fourth in the percentage of its population living in cities and towns (California is first, New Jersey second, and Hawaii third). Clark County is home to 1.3 million Nevadans—a remarkable fact considering that the county was not established until

1909—while Washoe County is home to 300,000.

Nevada has been the fastest growing state for most of the past quarter century. Clark County, for example, has grown an astounding 350% in the last 25 years. Projections conservatively estimate another 300,000 moving into the Las Vegas area in the next five years. According to the U.S. Census Bureau, Las Vegas is the fastest-growing city in the United States, gaining over 470,000 people during the 1990s, bringing the Clark County population to 1,343,540 in 1999. Reno's population has more than doubled in the past 20 years; in 1999, Washoe County's population had reached 323,670. Even though Nevada has an overall population density of only around 19 people per square mile, Truckee Meadows is filling up fast and Las Vegas's water worries are growing. With 87% of the population living in urban areas, that means that only 13% of the population resides in all the rest of the state. That's a lot of wide open, sparsely inhabited space.

Statewide, Nevada has had a growth rate over the past 15 years of nearly 50%, highest in the country. Only 20% of Nevada's residents were born here; Nevada has the lowest proportion of native-born residents in the country. Of the 80% who migrate to the state, a third of them come from California.

Health

So many elements of Nevada are extreme that it tends to attract extremists. Nevada is always either a big winner or a big loser in terms of almost every behavioral characteristic, compared state by state, that somebody cares to count. Nevada wins large, and dubiously, in the health department. Nevada ranked 43rd in 1996 in an annual comparison of state health statistics conducted by Northwestern National Life. Nevada finished 49th in total deaths from smoking and 44th from heart disease and motor vehicle deaths. It placed a miserable 46th in spending on public health.

Nevada has been distinguished by the number-one consumption of alcohol in the country for the past 15 years: 4.85 gallons per person. It also ranks number one in the most deaths from smoking-related diseases: 24% of all deaths in Nevada are caused by smoking. (By comparison, Utah checks in with 13%.) The large number of seniors who move to Nevada to retire might skew the statistic somewhat, but one of three Nevadans is a smoker. Nevada also claims the largest number of chronic drinkers in the country, twice the national average (alcohol is as good as free in casinos). Nevada's suicide rate is also two to three times higher than the rest of the country, and leads the U.S. in senior suicides. It stands to reason that Nevadans pay the third-highest hospital bills. And Nevada has the nation's 12th-highest auto insurance rates; Las Vegas's are highest in the state.

Other Vital Statistics

The transience and low economic status of Nevadans, many attracted by a boomtown mentality to low-paying hotel and casino service jobs, are evident in a number of social categories. In 1990, the income of 10% of Nevadans was below the poverty level, a figure that is probably still about the same. Nevada has the highest rate of high school dropouts in the country: 15% or one in seven kids between 16 and 19. And those who go on to higher education have the

THE NEVADA ALPHABET SCOOP

Those tall whitewashed letters on the hillsides above most of the towns in Nevada—who put them there? How? Why? When?

Similar letters are scattered all around the west. But Nevada's 30 are the most of any state. The first letter was put on a hill overlooking Berkeley, California, in 1905 by college students as an imaginative expression of school spirit. The sentiment found its way to the University of Nevada—Reno in 1913, when students constructed a huge "N" on Peavine Mountain above the campus, consisting of thousands of rocks, hundreds of gallons of whitewash (water and lime), and covering 13,000 square feet. The rage quickly spread to high-school students around the state. Elko teens assembled their "E" in 1916, the Tonopah "T" went up in 1917, and Carson City ("C"), Battle Mountain ("BM"), Virginia City ("V"), and Panaca ("L" for Lincoln County) all had their own letters by 1927. Austin high schoolers finally put up their "A" in the early '50s, and Beatty's "B" dates back to 1971.

Lately, liability worries have prevented students from maintaining some of the letters. The "R" (for Reno High) on Peavine west of the big "N," for example, is noticeably faded. In places, the task has been taken over by service clubs and alumni groups. In fact, the "SV" above Smith Valley has gone high-tech, and is now kept bright with an air sprayer powered by a portable generator. It'll take more than insurance premiums to jeopardize Nevada's 85-year tradition of sweater letters on hillsides.

second-highest loan default rate in the U.S.: more than one out of three. Voter turnouts also reflect the transience and carpetbagging nature of Nevada: 45th out of 50 with just under 50% of eligible voters going to the polls.

According to one study, Nevada's crime rate is seventh-highest in the country, and according to another, Nevada is the nation's fifth-most lawsuit-prone state (neither study takes into account the number of visitors who are in the state at any given time).

In the good-news department, only 5.4% of Nevada's population is without a telephone!

NATIVE AMERICANS

The Bands

At the turn of the 19th century, four groups of Indians lived in what is now Nevada. The small Washo tribe lived in the west-central region around Carson City, Lake Tahoe, and the eastern Sierra. The Northern Paiute made a large section of western Nevada their home, from today's Humboldt to Esmeralda County. The Southern Paiute occupied all of Clark County and the southeastern section of Lincoln County. The Shoshone were found in the east, from Elko to southern Nye counties.

The Northern Paiute (*pah* meaning "water" and *Ute* designating a Utah branch) called themselves *Numa,* and the Shoshone called themselves *Newe,* both meaning simply "the People." The name for the Southern Paiute was *Nuwuvi,* or "Peaceful People of the Land."

These different people shared many similar customs and lifestyles. They spent so much of their time gathering and preparing food in their harsh environment that they had little time or energy left to battle each other. The only time the small bands gathered into tribes was for cooperative hunting or harvesting efforts or to skirmish with neighbors or encroachers. Otherwise each band, a single-family unit or a group of no more than 100 individuals, was mostly autonomous. The resources of the local environment tended to dictate the size of bands; the Pyramid Lake Paiute, for example, was a large group with an abundant ecology. Its chiefs were famous. And the band was able to hold its own against the more warlike Pitt River bands from the north.

Bands had headmen, and shamans, who were found to possess powers of prophecy, healing, or magic.

Traditionally, all the bands in a given area would come together several times a year for pine-nut harvesting, antelope hunts, and rabbit or mud-hen drives. Celebrations during the get-togethers included sports such as archery, races, and stick games, story-telling, and music and dance; some of the dances dictated courting rituals. The Washo, in particular, held large gatherings twice a year, once in the fall at the Pine Nut Mountains to harvest the pine nuts for their winter flour, and once in the spring at Lake Tahoe to fish.

The Family

Indians enjoyed extended family arrangements, usually including the maternal grandparents. Variations might consist of two wives and a husband (the second woman was adopted if she found herself alone for some reason) or two husbands and a wife. Sketchy accounts describe the society as having very little divorce, with no words for broken homes, orphans, or child abuse. Children were loved and well cared for, assimilating into the ways of the family and band, proving themselves worthy as they went along, learning skills and morality mostly from the grandfather.

Religion

In the Indians' pure paganism everything in nature, animate or inanimate, was embodied by a spirit. Fire, fog, even rocks were alive, and required an empathy equal to that for a wolf (good influence), coyote (bad influence), or a wife or husband (either). Dreams, omens, seasonal cycles and unnatural variations, prayers, and the powers of the medicine man all figured into Native American religion—which was as integral a part of their daily routine as eating and sleeping.

Lifestyle

The never-ending search for food in the somewhat barren desert dictated daily and seasonal activities. The Indians had little need for shelter (except for shade) or clothing (except for a breechcloth and skirt) in the summer. In winter they stayed in a kind of teepee with a framework of poles and branches; grass or reed made up the roof, which had a hole in it for smoke from the fire. At that time they wore animal-skin robes, hats, moccasins, skirts, or sage-bark sandals and caps, and slept under rabbit-fur blankets. Colored clay was dabbed on as makeup and to ward off evil spirits, and bones, hooves, or traded shells provided jewelry for necklaces, earrings, or bracelets.

Mostly nomadic people, they had to carry everything during their frequent movements; a sophisticated basket technology evolved. Woven from split willow twigs, grasses, and cattail reeds (tule), conical baskets were used for transporting possessions or served as women's caps. Flat trays were used for winnowing seeds and sifting flour. Large pots were even used to cook in and to carry water-pitch from piñon pines, grasses, and mud kept them from burning or leaking. Decoys and snares were also fashioned from willow and tule twigs. Cradleboards attained a level of art. Properly shaped stones provided mortar-and-pestle tools for grinding, and drums, rattles, and flutes combined the use of baskets, skins, and grasses. In their knowledge and use of the local plants, the Indians were particularly ingenious. Everything had a use, and everything was sacred. They also fished and hunted rabbits, squirrels, antelope, mountain sheep, deer, ducks, and birds.

Contact

The first Anglo-Europeans who came into contact with the Shoshone, Paiute, and Washo Indians considered them to be slightly better than wildlife. They had no possessions, no houses, and hardly any clothes. As James Hulse writes in *The Nevada Adventure,* "The greed, brutality, and contempt of the white man destroyed much of the beauty of Indian life and prevented the Indians from entering the white man's culture." The Native Americans were on peaceful, even friendly terms with the first trappers and traders; Chief Winnemucca prophesied, and his daughter Sarah preached, that whites and Indians could live together with a mutual respect for each other and the land. But the wagon trains quickly put an end to the utopian vision. The migrating cattle ate all the Indians' grasses, loggers cut their sacred piñon pines; large areas were denuded of all the living things that the Indians used to survive.

Though the Nevada Paiute and Shoshone had no real organization for waging war, and Nevada histories are usually devoid of any but the largest armed confrontations (Pyramid Lake, Paradise Valley, Black Rock Desert, Battle Mountain), many skirmishes occurred, with some loss of life on both sides. Treaties were signed and violated and signed and violated. Within 25 years of the first wave of emigrants, the Indian spirit was broken, self-reliance was shattered, and dependence became the way of life.

Reservations

The first reservations in Nevada, Pyramid Lake and Walker Lake, were surveyed and set aside for the Paiute in 1859. Several others (Fort McDermitt, Moapa, Fallon, Owyhee) followed over the next 15 years. But as E.A. Hoaglund writes in his *Washoe, Paiute, and Shoshone Indians of Nevada,* "The early history of Indian reservations in America is generally one of confusion and mismanagement." A near total lack of direction, financing, facilities, equipment, education, understanding of the Native experience, and compassion for their cultural dislocation colored a full 70 years of white-Indian relations. The reservations were usually too small, the land too poor, and the populations too large. Also, the reservations continued to segregate the Indians from the mainstream. "The period from 1890–1934 was one of slow moral and physical decline [for the Natives]. Many left the reservations and found work on ranches or the fringes of towns."

In 1887 the Dawes Act tried to disenfranchise the reservations in an attempt to ease Indian assimilation into white culture. In June 1934, the Indian Reorganization Act began a process of redressing this tragic part of American history, by giving more money, land, cattle, and irrigation systems to the reservations. Self-government was made official by way of Tribal Councils. The 1978 Indian Self-Determination Act addressed the need for economic development. Slowly, the federal government has untangled the complex questions of Native land issues and begun to show some responsiveness to the simple question of human rights.

Self-Determination

In an interesting article in *Nevada* magazine

(August 1989), Becky Lemon and Linda Johnson explain that since the 1960s, smoke shops have been the 24 Nevada tribes' primary revenue producers. Tribes buy cigarettes at wholesale prices, which include federal taxes. But instead of the high local taxes on smokes, the Indians charge a smaller tribal tax, which is reinvested in the tribal organization. Most smoke shops also display and sell Indian arts and crafts.

But the tribes are beginning to require sources of revenue other than cigarette sales. And many have found the means. The Las Vegas Paiute, for example, have begun a large-scale resort development on reservation land 20 miles north of Las Vegas; when complete, there will be four golf courses and several hotel-casinos.

The Washo Indians, whose reservation is in Gardnerville, raise cattle and own and manage feedlots. They're beginning to develop their own alfalfa farms to feed the cattle; what they don't raise, they buy from other Indian farmers.

The Yerington Paiute own a Dairy Queen in town and have gone into the laser ground-leveling business, relied on by local farmers. The Walker River Paiute opened a truck stop and tourist center near Schurz. The Fallon Paiute-Shoshone raise small game birds for hunting. The Pyramid Lake Paiute fishery has helped Pyramid Lake regenerate into one of the top cutthroat lakes in the West. The Indians raise funds from fishing, boating, and camping licenses. And they own and operate a marina in Sutcliffe.

The Reno-Sparks Colony's smoke shop is in a small shopping center, from which it leases space to other businesses. The smoke shop opened a second location on US 395 just south of Foothill Drive in Reno.

A good way to observe Indian traditions and customs in action is to attend any of a number of powwows put on by the different tribes over the course of the year. The dancing, drumming, traditional costumes, and intensity of the participants clearly indicate the Indians' commitment to "abiding," write Becky Lemon and Linda Johnson, "by the spiritual values of balance, harmony, and oneness with nature," while at the same time "initiating modern business practices."

BASQUES

Origins

The Basque people are the oldest ethnic group in Europe. Evidence of their continuous existence dates to 5000 A.D., a full 3,000 years before Indo-European people arrived. There are roughly three million European Basques, their homeland occupying the Pyrenees Mountain provinces of France (three districts) and Spain (four districts). The true origin of these people is a mystery. Some scholars maintain that similarities exist between Basques and Iberians (early Spanish neighbors); others believe that they share characteristics with the Irish and Welsh. Some Basques contend that they're descended from the Atlanteans!

Their language is unrelated to any other in the world, although researchers have tried to match it up with all of them—from ancient Aquitanian to modern Japanese. Though the Basques were never conquered, the Spanish and French have had a noticeable influence.

LARRY PROSOR, NEVADA COMMISSION ON TOURISM

Basque festivals occur annually in most of the large towns of northern Nevada.

Basque argonauts migrated to Argentina, from where many made their way north, especially in the 1850s to the California gold rush. Following the silver exodus east to Washoe, they mined in Nevada until that work dried up. They then returned to a skill familiar from the old country: sheepherding. Basque sheepherders took to the pastoralist life of the American West readily, particularly in northern Nevada. For nearly 50 years, Basque ranchers ran the largest bands of sheep in the country. They imported relatives, friends, and neighbors to herd sheep. Contract shepherds often took payment in lambs and sheep, with which they started their own ranches. Herders remained in the backcountry alone with their flocks all through the summer. It was an arduous and lonely life, being an immigrant in a strange and barren country, barely speaking the language or understanding the strange customs in the towns. But a prevalent aspect of the Basque national character is the ability to endure: hard work, loneliness, and physical strength all add up to the measure of their self-worth.

Sheepherding was seasonal. Many newcomers were laid off in the fall after the animals were shipped to market and not rehired till spring lambing season. Some sheepherders remained on the ranches, but others drifted to the hotels run by Basques in the towns. These boardinghouses quickly became the center of Basque culture in the rural towns of Nevada. Shepherds old and young spoke their own language, played their own games, ate their own food, and kept company with their own countrymen and -women. Many married and remained in the towns, assimilating into the new culture. Some made their money and went home to Europe. Others stayed bachelors and lived out their lives at the inns. The Basque hotel was "a crucible of birth and death, joy and sorrow; a public establishment masking many private intimacies," writes William Douglass in *Amerikanuak: Basques in the New World.*

Oso Garria!

The Basque hotel is a legacy that endures. The Winnemucca Hotel, for example, is the second-oldest hotel in the state. Gardnerville's Overland Hotel dates from 1909, Elko's Star Hotel from 1911, and the Ely Hotel is from the 1920s. No traveler to Nevada should leave without experiencing a meal at a Basque hotel.

A Basque meal, especially dinner, is never taken lightly, nor is it a light meal. It consists of a multitude of courses served family-style: soup, salad, beans or pasta, french fries, and usually an entree of chicken, beef, or lamb. Make sure to try a picon punch, made with Amer (a liqueur), grenadine, and a quick shot of brandy. Few of northern and central Nevada's towns are without Basque restaurants, where you're guaranteed a fine filling meal and a social experience. Raise your glass of picon punch and toast the house: "Oso garria!"

The Basque festival is the other enduring cultural tradition. Festivities include mass, folk dancing, strength and endurance competitions, a sheep rodeo, and the consumption of enormous quantities of red wine from the bota (the festival itself is an endurance contest!). The Basques are known for their world-class wood chopping, and the contestants compete in areas of strength and will. Soka and tira are the popular tugs-of-war. Pelota is handball, of which jai alai is an offspring. Weight lifting and carrying are the real crowd pleasers. Annual festivals take place in most of the larger towns in northern Nevada. Check the events section of Nevada magazine in the summer.

BOB RACE

ON THE ROAD
SIGHTSEEING HIGHLIGHTS

Reno and Western Nevada

The best view of downtown Reno is from Top of the Hilton on the 21st floor of the Flamingo. The best overview of Truckee Meadows is the 23-mile loop on McCarran Blvd. around the perimeter of the Reno-Sparks metropolitan area. Two good "cheap aerials" of Lake Tahoe are from Llewellyn's/Peak Lounge at the top of Harvey's at Stateline and from the fire lookout in Crystal Bay on the north shore. The best views of Virginia City require a little more effort: just climb straight up Mt. Davidson. Nevada 341 up Geiger Grade overlooks Truckee Meadows, NV 431 up Mt. Rose overlooks Washoe Valley, US 50 up to Spooner Summit overlooks Eagle Valley, and NV 207 up Kingsbury Grade overlooks Carson Valley. For good views of the rest of western Nevada, you'll need an airplane.

Rancho San Rafael Park in Reno, Galena Creek Park on the Mt. Rose highway, Davis Creek Park in Washoe Valley, Mills Park in Carson, and of course Lake Tahoe-Nevada State Park are all worth some quality time.

The top museums in the area include the Historical Museum, National Automobile Museum, Wilbur D. May Museum, and Liberty Belle Saloon in Reno; the Castle and Fourth Ward School in Virginia City; the State Museum and Stewart Indian Museum in Carson City; and the Lyon County Museum in Yerington.

Casinos not to miss are the Reno Hilton, Cal-Neva, and the Peppermill in Reno, John Ascuaga's Nugget in Sparks, the Bucket of Blood and Delta in Virginia City, Carson Station and Cactus Jack's in Carson, Sharkey's in Gardnerville, and Harvey's (south shore) and the Cal-Neva (north shore) on Lake Tahoe.

Northwest Nevada

Pyramid Lake is perhaps the most beautiful desert lake in the world, so any time spent doing anything there is a major highlight. Spending a night anywhere on the lakeshore (especially at the Great Stone Mother on the east side) will more than give you the idea.

Likewise, the Black Rock Desert is the most mind-bending stretch of desert in a state that's composed of mostly mind-bending desert.

The Charles Sheldon National Wildlife Refuge hosts the most concentrated numbers of wildlife in Nevada; travel through at sunrise to see countless pronghorn antelope and birds.

Lye Creek campground in the Santa Rosa Wilderness Area north of Winnemucca is the lushest and most comfortable campground in the state.

In Winnemucca are the Buckaroo Hall of Fame, which stakes a claim to cowboy country, and a redwood tree trunk, which stakes a claim to the Pacific Ocean. South of Winnemucca is Unionville, where Mark Twain once mined silver and the Old Pioneer Garden Guest Ranch today provides idyllic accommodations. Midas is one of the great off-the-beaten-track towns in Nevada.

Northeast Nevada

In 1994 Elko was named the country's most livable small town, and after a look inside the Northeastern Nevada Museum, the Commercial Hotel, the Western Folklife Center, and the Star Dining Room, you'll know why. South of Elko is stunning Lamoille Canyon in the incomparable Ruby Mountains; a leisurely seven-day stroll along the 45-mile Ruby Crest Trail is a literal and figurative highlight.

Tuscarora offers Dennis and Julie Parks and their pottery operation and school. Jarbidge is one of the most remote towns in the Lower 48: 50 miles of dirt road in from the Nevada side, 25 miles out on the Idaho side. In a town of 28 permanent residents, the five campgrounds come as a surprise. The friendliness doesn't; drop by the Trading Post and set a spell with Rey and Marguerite Nystrom.

Jackpot brings Las Vegas to Idaho—walking through Cactus Petes, you'll think you've just gone through a space machine and emerged on the Strip. Wendover brings Reno to Utah—the Stateline casino seems like a cousin to John Ascuaga's Nugget in Sparks and the Peppermills are fraternal twins.

Central Nevada

Highlights galore are found here, so many in the Ely area alone that they can't be described, only listed: Prometheus's tree trunk, Nevada Northern Railway museum and joyride, Cave Lake State Park, McGill, Ruth, Ward Charcoal Ovens, and on and on. Great Basin National Park has the highest paved road (10,000 feet) and the second-highest peak (13,063 feet) in the state, along with the most southerly permanent ice and Prometheus's descendants.

US 50 is not the loneliest road in America, but it does cover a cross-section of Nevada like no other road. Eureka is one of the most prosperous small towns in the Silver State, thanks to gold; the Eureka Opera House is the new pride and joy, the County Courthouse and museum the old ones. Austin seems like poor relations by comparison—and proud of it. Fallon is the classic old reclamation town, with the modern water wars to prove it.

Walker Lake's water woes are equally serious, though to the untrained eye the lake is nearly as startling and spectacular as its northern sibling, Pyramid. Tonopah has the excellent Central Nevada Museum and the beautifully restored Mizpah Hotel. Goldfield is decidedly unrestored and that's its charm; the county courtroom and the Santa Fe Saloon are highlight original.

Las Vegas and the Southern Corner

The view from Stratosphere (not to mention the Big Shot thrill ride) and the new tower at the Rio, Luxor's atrium, Treasure Island's pirate battle, the two animatronic shows at Forum Shops at Caesars, the fountain show and conservatory gardens at Bellagio, the Moroccan acrobats at Desert Passage, the roller coaster at New York, New York, Paris' Eiffel Tower, the canals at The Venetian, Golden Nugget's gold nuggets, the Mirage's aquarium, Binion's million-dollar souvenir photo, the buffets at the Rio, Fiesta, Texas Staton, and Main Street Station, and the *Las Vegas Advisor* are just a handful of highlights in the biggest boomtown the world has ever known.

Northwest of Las Vegas sits Mt. Charleston, 15-20 degrees cooler than the Strip on the hottest day and snowy enough on the coldest for downhill skiing. Southwest is Buffalo Bill's, with the world's tallest and fastest roller coaster. Northeast is Valley of Fire State Park, with sandstone so colorful, so unusual, and so enormous that words fail. Southeast is the behemoth buttress of Black Canyon, called Hoover Dam, with its 60-story elevator ride to the bottom, with Lake Mead, largest manmade lake in the country, behind it. South of Las Vegas is Laughlin on the Colorado: bright casinos, cheap room and board, water taxis, and blast-furnace heat.

OUTDOORS

PARKS AND WILDERNESS

Nevada has one national park, Great Basin, which is 65 miles east of Ely near the Utah border. It encompasses a part of the Snake Range, which includes Wheeler Peak, Lehman Caves, and a fair amount of backcountry wilderness.

Nevada now has 13 official Wilderness Areas, encompassing 733,400 acres. Other than the Mt. Charleston Wilderness, less than an hour from Las Vegas, and the Mt. Rose Wilderness, less than an hour from Reno, all the areas are fairly remote, untouched, and primitive. The vast majority of the protected acreage is so underused that no permits are even required to hike, backpack, or camp on it.

Twenty-four state parks, historic sites, and recreation areas occupy nearly 150,000 acres. The largest and oldest (and one of the most spectacular) is Valley of Fire State Park northeast of Las Vegas, at 46,000 acres. The smallest is Belmont Courthouse State Historic Site, at a single solitary lonesome acre. The newest, the Big Bend of the Colorado State Recreation Area, on the shores of the Colorado River five miles south of Laughlin, opened in 1993.

In 1990, Nevada voters approved $47 million in bonds to be spent on state park and recreation areas. In 1994, the work finally began on repairing and improving the facilities at Spring Mountain, Valley of Fire, Floyd Lamb, and Cathedral Gorge state parks (in southern Nevada), reopening Kershaw-Ryan State Park (near Caliente), developing Ward Charcoal Ovens (near Ely), Washoe Lake (south of Reno), South Fork (south of Elko), and Walker Lake (near Hawthorne). Two new state parks will be created with the money: Big Bend State Recreation Area (on the Colorado River near Laughlin) and Old Las Vegas Fort. Fort Churchill is being expanded.

The Sierra Club Guide to the Natural Areas of New Mexico, Arizona, and Nevada, by John and Jane Perry, covers 82 sites in Nevada of the authors' choosing.

Cave Lake State Park near Ely

DEKE CASTLEMAN

Any way you look at it, there's a lot of outdoors in the Silver State.

Respecting the Land and People

When you're anywhere outdoors, especially in the backcountry, make it your objective to leave no trace of your passing. Litter is pollution. Whenever you are tempted to leave garbage behind, think of how you feel when you find other people's plastic bags, tins, or aluminum foil in *your* yard. If you packed it in, you can pack it out. Burying garbage is useless as animals soon dig it up. Be a caretaker by picking up trash left by less conscientious visitors. In this way, in part, you thank the land for the experiences it has provided you.

Human wastes should be disposed of at least 100 feet from any trail or water source. Bury wastes and carefully burn the toilet paper, if possible. Extreme care should be taken with fire everywhere. As you explore, remember that Nevadans are fiercely independent people who value their privacy. They can also be overwhelmingly hospitable if you treat them with respect.

SPORTS

Ballooning

Reno hosts the state's largest hot-air-balloon event the second weekend in September. For information on the Reno Balloon Race, call 775/826-1181 or visit www.renoballoon.com.

For a description of the typical commercial balloon flight, see "Ballooning" in the "Outdoor Recreation" section of the Reno chapter.

ALASKA-NEVADA COMPARISON

The number of similarities—historically, demographically, statistically, economically, even spiritually—that can be made between Alaska and Nevada are surprising. First and foremost has to do with the land. The tundra can easily be likened to the desert: vast stretches of wilderness, a handful of prevalent species, and mountain ranges from the foreground to the background. Willow on the tundra is as dominant as sage is in the desert. No trees grow above 2,500 feet in Alaska, and none grow below 4,000 feet in Nevada. The sparse forests of small black and white spruce trees in Alaska can be compared with the stands of juniper and piñon in Nevada. The state and federal governments own 85.8% of Alaska (number one in the nation) and 85.2% of Nevada (number two).

In terms of population centers, Anchorage is to Las Vegas as Fairbanks is to Reno. Juneau and Carson City, the third-largest demographic areas, are both state capitals. Statistically, Alaska is second-last in its number of state-born residents (33.3%), while Nevada is dead last (20%). Likewise, Alaska was the second fastest-growing state during the 1980s (31.1%) while Nevada was first (38.9%). Alaska's divorce rate (8.8 per thousand) is beat out only by Nevada's (13.1 per). Alaska, however, soundly triumphs in the people-per-square-mile category, with 0.7 people, as compared to Nevada's 11 (third lowest).

Historically, both Alaska and Nevada were explored, exploited, and settled because of precious minerals. The Klondike is arguably as much a household word as the Comstock. Dawson, too, has the reputation of a wild west semi-ghost town that Virginia City enjoys. Also, Dawson produced Robert Service, Canada's frontier poet laureat, while Virginia City can claim Mark Twain. And though Alaska's early attraction was gold, while Nevada's was silver, mining quickly lost its luster in both states; the real population explosions didn't occur until huge military bases were established in both Alaska and Nevada during WW II.

Economically, oil conclusively is comparable to gambling. Valdez is the Alaskan oil-economy's big-winning small town; Laughlin is the Nevadan gambling economy's.

Finally, Alaskans and Nevadans hold freedom dear to their hearts—of expression and lifestyle. They don't abide by very much official interference and they pride themselves on self-reliance. Neither Alaska nor Nevada has a state income tax. The people who gravitate to both states seem to be either rugged-individualist or boomtown types.

And getting completely carried away with this, both names have six letters—three vowels and three consonants, and end in "a." And both states have travel guidebooks written by your humble author.

For balloon rides year-round, in the Reno area try **Mountain High,** 888/GO-ABOVE, or **Dream Weavers,** 775/265-1271, 800/FUN-ALOFT. To balloon right over Lake Tahoe there's **Lake Tahoe Balloons,** 530/544-1221, 800/872-9294. In Las Vegas, try **D&R Balloons,** 702/248-7609.

Biking

Riding mountain bikes off-road and racing bikes on the streets of Nevada is a special treat. The surfaces on- and off-road are excellent; you have your choice of flat and hilly terrain; in most places you can see forever—or at least to the next mountain range; and the birdwatching is potentially exciting. As inviting as all this sounds, certain precautions are mandatory to have an experience that's not only comfortable but safe as well. In the spring-to-fall desert heat and searing sunshine, riding is best in the early morning and evening. Though it might be tempting to wear short shorts and a T-shirt, adequate protection for your tender skin is a must, as are sunglasses to cut the potentially blinding glare. Carry twice as much water as you think you'll need, and when you run out of water earlier than you'd expected, cut your ride short. Take along the tools and first-aid kit you normally carry and for God's sake wear a helmet. Your mother and the highway patrolman who'd have to scrape your cracked head off the pavement will thank you.

Boating

Boating? In Nevada? At last count, nearly 50,000 marine vessels were registered in Nevada. The state Department of Wildlife lists 27 sites for boating; eight of them aren't even reservoirs. Nevada has boating from rowboating on Jiggs Reservoir to houseboating in Lake Mead. For a complete rundown of all the lakes and reservoirs, public and private, in Nevada, along with the numerous state boating laws and regulations, and tips on water safety, equipment, waterway markers, etc., contact the Nevada Department of Wildlife, 1100 Valley Rd., Reno, NV 89512, 755/688-1500, and ask for the *Nevada Boating Access Guide.*

Fishing and Hunting

For the official word, contact the Nevada Department of Wildlife. The state headquarters is in Reno (address and phone number above under "Boating"). The Las Vegas office is at 4747 W. Vegas Drive, Las Vegas, NV 89108, 702/486-5127. In Elko, it's 1375 Mountain City Hwy., Elko, NV 89801, 775/738-5332.

For the expert look at the whole range of fishing opportunities in the state of Nevada, pick up *Nevada Angler's Guide—Fish Tails in the Sagebrush,* by Renoite Richard Dickerson. For a mere $14.95, you'll have yourself a guide to everything you'd ever need to know to enjoy a lifetime of fishing in Nevada. See "Booklist" for publishing information.

Golf

Nevada has more than 60 golf courses, with 20 in Las Vegas alone and 10 in Reno. *Nevada* Magazine publishes an annual directory and guide to all the golf courses in the state. It's available for the asking: contact *Nevada* at 401 N. Carson St., Suite 100, Carson City, NV 89701-4291, 775/687-5416, fax 775/687-6159, editor@nevadamagazine.com, www.nevada magazine.com.

Winter Sports

Thirteen **downhill ski** resorts, along with the numerous **cross-country** operations, around Lake Tahoe are covered in "Skiing" under "Other Practicalities" in the Reno chapter. The Lee Canyon Ski Resort, 45 minutes from Las Vegas, is described in the Northwest of Las Vegas section. Elko Snowbowl is listed in "Practicalities" in the Elko section.

For **heli-skiing** in the Ruby Mountains, call Ruby Mountain Heli-Ski, 775/753-6867; fees for the 2000 season are $2650 for three nights' lodging, 39,000 feet of helicopter lift, and guided ski touring.

You can **ice skate** indoors at the Santa Fe Ice Arena (at the Santa Fe Hotel-Casino), 4949 N. Rancho Dr., Las Vegas, 702/658-4991. You can ice skate outdoors at the Squaw Valley Olympic Ice Pavilion (highest year-round ice rink in the world); 530/581-7246. You can also skate on ponds and puddles around the state; Davis Creek Park in Washoe Valley, Elko City Park, and Winnemucca Sports Complex prepare pond surfaces for ice skating in the winter. In Reno, the city puts up a portable outdoor ice skating rink somewhere near the Truckee River, usually in Wingfield or Idlewild Parks.

Have **inner tube,** will slide down a snowy hill in the state.

Rent **snowmobiles** at Zephyr Cove Snowmobiles, 775/588-3833; the Reindeer Lodge on Mt. Rose Hwy., 775/849-9902; and at Eagle Ridge Snowmobile Outfitters, 14 miles north of Truckee on Hwy. 89, 530/546-8667 (they also lead guided overnight trips).

GAMBLING

Gambling and Nevada are inseparable in the national consciousness. No other state in the country is so inextricably linked to a single social, economic, recreational, and controversial activity. Indeed, the state's reputation for the past 67 years since casino gambling was legalized for good has been predicated on Americans' *image* of gambling. For nearly the entire three-score-plus period, an irresistible torrent of public censure rained down on Nevada. The media, authorities, moralists, and sore losers accused and convicted the Silver State of being a haven for the underworld, petty criminals, crooked casinos, vice run amok, and general lowlife. The height of the heat centered on the 20-year period between 1946, when Benjamin Siegel, Las Vegas's most notorious gangster, built the seminal Flamingo Hotel, and 1966, when Howard Hughes introduced corporate respectability.

Since then, Nevada's image has taken a turn

NEVADA'S CASINO THEMES

The names and themes bestowed on Nevada casinos have always reflected the prevailing local currents. The tracing and linking of these themes can serve as a looking glass into Nevada's unique heritage.

Gold fever originally brought prospectors and stampeders to Nevada, and continues to; gold reigns supreme among casino themes. The **Gold Strike Hotel** guards the L.A. approach to Las Vegas, and the **Gold Strike Inn** the Boulder City approach. Don't confuse them with the **Gold Spike** in downtown Las Vegas, which also claims the **Golden Gate.** Ironically, the **Gold Coast** near the Strip is 250 miles from any ocean; and Reno's **Gold Dust West** is decidedly east of the Mother Lode. In a similar vein (so to speak) are two casinos in Sparks: the **Mint,** which coins money; and the **Treasury Club,** which keeps money. Surprisingly, the only contemporary Nevada casino with "money" in its name was **Mapes Money Tree,** closed now for 20 years.

Thematically, gold is so strong that it has a partner: nuggets. The **Golden Nugget** in Las Vegas boasts a display of the largest gold nuggets in the world (Vegas's GN has a sister **Golden Nugget** casino in Laughlin); the Carson City **Nugget's** nugget display is a close second. Not to be outdone, John Ascuaga's **Nugget** in Sparks displays a solid-gold rooster, and the collection of memorabilia at **Sharkey's Nugget** in Gardnerville includes just about everything *but* gold. **Jim Kelly's Tahoe Nugget** at Crystal Bay could be the only brick casino in Nevada. And while there are **Nuggets,** presumably gold, in downtown Reno, Fallon, and Searchlight, **Mahoney's Silver Nugget** in North Las Vegas is an oddity of metallurgy.

But it was silver, after all, that gave Nevada its own original theme. **Silver City** provides Las Vegas with its only connection to the coin of the realm, except for the **Silver Spur,** which is more of a saloon. Appropriately, the **Silver Smith** in Wendover belongs to the longest-lasting gambling family in Nevada. Queen Victoria would feel right at home at the **Silver Club** in Sparks, given the Victorian decor inside and out, though she might feel outclassed at the **Silver Queen** in Virginia City.

The **Pioneer** casino in Laughlin reflects a prevalent theme in the state's history. The **Frontier,** for example, stands appropriately near the **Westward Ho** on the Las Vegas Strip. Casinos such as the **Mizpah** in Tonopah, the **Eldorados** in Henderson and Reno, the **Bonanzas** in Fallon and Reno, and the **Comstock** in Reno also commemorate Nevada's emergence out of the vast Far West. The **Burro Inn** and **Stagecoach** in Beatty, the **Saddle West** in Pahrump, the unusual **Jailhouse** in Ely, **Buffalo Bill's** in Primm, and the **Red Garter** in Virginia City capture the slapdash side of the scene. But the whole 19th-century Silver State spirit is per-for the bettor. Today, state gaming revenues are $9.5 billion dollars a year, of which 60% are from the gambling losses of out-of-staters. Casino employment accounts for a full 25% of the jobs in Nevada and taxes on the house profits are responsible for 40% of state General Fund revenues. And that's just from gambling; the indirect effect of the massive tourism on the state's economy is incalculable.

Though it's not often credited for it, Nevada has contributed heavily to the growing legitimacy of various forms of gambling that exist now in 48 states: lotteries, bingo, off-track betting, video gambling machines, pull tabs, card rooms, and casinos. Casino gambling was legalized in Atlantic City in 1978, the first in the country outside of Nevada—and the last until Iowa riverboats came on line in 1991. Since then, casino gambling has become available on riverboats in Illi-

nois, Indiana, Mississippi, Missouri, and Louisiana; in historic mining towns in Colorado and South Dakota; and on Indian reservations in a growing number of states. Gambling has become an accepted way to raise revenues without raising taxes, a sort of "painless user's tax." Certainly gambling is still generally considered frivolous by a great many Americans. It's also a highly addictive activity that has been called the deadliest psychiatric disorder. Yet its growing popularity shows no signs of abating. In fact, it's the most explosive growth industry in the country in the 1990s.

The Question of Honesty

In this cash-crazy business, everyone is afraid of everyone. The casinos have always been afraid of cheating customers and dishonest dealers and have evolved some of the most sophisti-

---

fectly embodied by two **Boomtown** casinos, one on I-80 just west of Reno, the other on I-15 just south of Las Vegas.

The railroad played an integral part in shaping the state—and draping casinos. **Railroad Pass** casino sits just above Las Vegas Valley on the original right-of-way to Hoover Dam. A kiddie choo-choo tools around **Ramada Express** in Laughlin. **Palace Station** and its clone, Boulder Station, in Las Vegas are fronted by Disney diesels, and Tonopah has its **Station House.** Carson Station in the capital is just down the block from the State Railroad Museum, and **Main Street Station** in downtown Las Vegas is getting up a new head of steam.

Riverboat gambling was never particularly prevalent hereabouts, but its legend is strong enough that a handful are drydocked in the desert. This has been a popular theme in Nevada since 1954, when the **Showboat** was christened in Las Vegas, nearly floating away, in fact, during a flash flood on opening day. The Reno **Riverboat** rests a significant block away from the Truckee River and **Nevada Landing** floats in a sea of sand at Jean. Amazingly, the **Colorado Belle** in Laughlin is a Nevada riverboat casino actually on a river.

Despite the absence of a coastline in Nevada, the coast is another popular theme. Las Vegas has the **Barbary Coast,** the **Gold Coast,** the **Holiday Inn Boardwalk Casino** (a la Coney Island) and **Mandalay Bay.**

The desert theme, conversely, was only too ap-

propriate, and it gripped Las Vegas in the boom days of the early 1950s. Inaugurated by the **Desert Inn,** the **Sahara, Sands,** and **Dunes** followed close behind; the Sands and Dunes have since bitten the dust. There's also a **Sands** in Reno. **Cactus Jack's** in Carson City is characteristic of the motif, as is **Cactus Petes** in Jackpot, not to be confused with **Whiskey Pete's** at Primm. Then there's the **Oasis** in Mesquite. But it took until 1989 for a **Mirage** to round out the desert theme, and what a mirage it is.

The horseshoe is one of the best-known and most popular lucky charms, and Nevada has its share: Binion's venerable **Horseshoe** in downtown Las Vegas, the **Horseshu** in Jackpot (across from Cactus Petes), not to be confused with the **Horseshoe** in Carson City (next door to Cactus Jack's).

Where there are gold and silver, there are bound to be palaces. Las Vegas claims all three of these, which run the gamut from **Caesars,** the mother of all palaces, to **Nevada Palace,** a run-of-the-mill palace. **Imperial Palace,** Nevada's only Asian-themed casino, ranks somewhere in between. Then there's **Bellagio,** which is like a Lake Como palatial estate.

Possibly the most successful and profitable casino theme is the circus. **Circus Circus** carries on its bigtop action in Reno and Las Vegas. Its **Excalibur** is without a doubt the world's most imaginative Renaissance carnival. But the **Primm Valley Resort and Casino** in Primm, with its Ferris wheel and carnie decor, is, perhaps, Nevada's ultimate amusement-park casino (so far).

cated security and surveillance technology, not to mention one of the heaviest envelopes of private muscle, this side of the Pentagon. As the benders, crimpers, hand muckers, and past-post artists of yesteryear have turned into today's sleight-of-hand artists, card counters, and computer-equipped players, the catwalks and one-way glass above the casino ceilings have given way to video cameras and recorders, in addition to all the bosses in the pit, the house guard, and outside security contractors.

The Nevada casino industry is not the most heavily regulated in the country. Atlantic City's is. But Nevada's is the most efficient and practical; New Jersey has been over-regulated to the extent that it's been difficult for Atlantic City casinos to succeed (though that's starting to change). Nevada, on the other hand, started with little to no regulation of casinos when gambling was legalized in 1931, then took more than 50 years to reach a middle ground where the regulation is sufficient to keep things honest, but also allow the industry to prosper. Mississippi, where nearly 50 casinos have opened in the past five years, copied Nevada regulations verbatim; in fact, in a few instances the Mississippi typists neglected to change the name of the state!

The Nevada Gaming Control Board, by way of its announced and unannounced inspections, owner and employee screening, and customer-complaint services, has dealt with the *state's* two main fears. The first is the house cheating the state, by under-reporting the action, skimming the cash, and other various nefarious scams. The second is the house cheating the players. Here, the conventional wisdom is that with the astronomical number of people coming, the amount of money that they're risking (and losing), and the profits that are accruing, the casinos don't *need* to cheat the players; indeed they'd be crazy if they did: they'd risk losing what amounts to a license to coin money, thanks to the house advantage.

Casino Psychology

More than 33.8 million people sampled the excitement and temptations of Las Vegas alone in 1999, a 10.5% increase over the number of visitors the year before, with numbers of visitors continuing to grow every year. Inside the casinos are a dozen different table games and scores of gambling machines, free drinks, acres of dazzling lights, expert come-ons—in short, limitless choices designed to sweep you off your feet and empty your pockets. You have nearly 70 years of marketing history and a distinct mathematical disadvantage working against you. Every inch of neon, every leggy cocktail waitress, every complimentary highball shares the same purpose: to confuse you, bemuse you, and infuse you with a sense of saloon-town recklessness. And that's where the house advantage kicks in.

The game of roulette best illustrates the house advantage. There are 38 numbers on the wheel: one through 36, plus a zero and double zero. If the ball drops into number 23 and you have a dollar on it, the correct payoff would be $37 (37 to 1, which adds up to the 38 numbers). However, the house pays only $35. It withholds two out of 38 units, which translates to a 5.26% advantage for the house. Now, this 5.26% advantage can be looked at in different ways. Over the long haul, for every $100 you bet on roulette, you can expect to lose $5.26. Or, you'll lose your bankroll at a little less than four times the rate at roulette than on a pass line bet at craps, which has a 1.4% house advantage. But don't make the mistake of thinking that for every $100 you carry into the casino you'll only lose five bucks. Anything can happen in the short run. You can win 13 bets in a row and make a bundle, or you can lose all your money in one big bet. But the house advantage guarantees that you'll be a long-term loser at almost all the games in a casino, and that the casino will be long-term winner.

The house advantage is the single most important concept to be aware of to understand

DOVER PUBLICATIONS

the well-known secret behind casino gambling. As soon as you're savvy to all its implications, and the varying percentages of the games, you'll begin to recognize the difference between a sucker bet, a break-even bet, and even an advantageous bet—which occurs more frequently than most people think. Then you can gamble in such a way that the percentages aren't so overwhelmingly unfavorable, and in that way you can make sure that your bankroll lasts as long as it possibly can against the omnipotent house advantage.

For First-Timers

If you've never learned to play, it's very wise to study up beforehand and practice, practice, practice. All these games move very fast, and if you try learning them as you play, you'll not only lose, but everybody will get very impatient with

you, which is embarrassing. *Looking like* a piker is a technique that expert players use to slow down the game (to minimize risk) and to deflect the attention of and heat from the pit bosses (to make other advanced moves). But there's no upside to really not knowing what you're doing.

It's easy and fun to learn to play. Most casinos offer free lessons in all the games at specified times of day. In Las Vegas, lessons are sometimes advertised on marquees; signs are also posted in the casinos. Or ask someone in the pit about them. In Reno, one of the dealer schools (see "Reno-Tahoe Gaming Academy" under "Sights" in the Reno chapter) is a good place to learn.

Loads of books have been written on how to play all the casino games. John Scarne's guides, though a little outdated, should be in most libraries. To really get into it, write or call for cat-

COMPULSIVE GAMBLERS

The vast majority of people who gamble do so for entertainment or recreation, to satisfy the primal urge of financial risk-taking for fun and profit. For them, losing is a sensation they can live with. But three to four percent of Americans who gamble are unable to simply walk away having had a good time. For them, gambling becomes compulsive, an addiction, a dangerous and deadly psychiatric disorder.

What makes a group of people turn to gambling for an escape, as opposed to alcohol, drugs, sex, food, TV, or crossword puzzles, is a matter of endless conjecture. A gambling disorder starts out as a euphoria derived from the initial excitement. For the particular people susceptible to it, gambling is a more satisfying sensation than any other. Whether it's the surging adrenaline of a crap game, the hypnotic trance of a video poker machine, or even the fast pace and high stakes of a securities market, as long as these people gamble, they're high. Stopping means coming down, and they need to gamble again to get back up. This dependence is particularly insidious, since the house advantage ensures that the longer they play, the more they lose. The more they lose, the more they start chasing losses. And herein lies the danger signal. Nearly all compulsive gamblers spend their own, and their families', savings. Three

out of four sell or hock valuables and write bad checks. Almost half descend to theft or embezzlement. Finally, in the terminal stages of ruin, despair, fear, and shame, an estimated 20% of compulsive gamblers attempt suicide. Then and only then, if unsuccessful, do most addicts reach a point of seeking treatment.

However, public perception of compulsive gambling is 10 to 20 years behind that of alcoholism, for example. Though the ranks of addicted gamblers have swelled in the last few years, serious treatment remains hard to come by and is often a case of too little, too late. There are 600 Gamblers' Anonymous chapters nationwide, but only a handful of primary treatment centers (one in Las Vegas). Dr. Robert Custer, considered the father of compulsive-gambling treatment, says that compulsive gambling is the "most under-researched" psychiatric disorder, and the most deadly. "No other psychiatric disorder even approaches" a 20% rate of attempted suicide, he points out. Of the 35 states with lotteries, only Iowa earmarks a share (one-half percent) of lottery revenues for a Gamblers' Assistance Fund. Ironically, by the time a compulsive gambler is ready for recovery, expensive treatment programs are often beyond his shattered resources. Governmental assistance, so far, hasn't been forthcoming.

alogs from the Gambler's Bookstore, 1 E. 1st St. (corner 1st and Virginia Streets), Reno, NV 89501, 775/825-7778, 800/748-5797, www.gamblerhome.com, or the Gambler's Book Club, 630 S. 11th St., Las Vegas, NV 89101, 800/634-6243, www.gamblersbook.com. Huntington Press, 3687 S. Procyon Ave, Las Vegas, NV 89103, 800/244-2224, www.huntingtonpress.com, will send you a "boutique" catalog of the best gambling books and software.

Attitude

Don't ever let anyone tell you differently. In a casino, it absolutely *is* whether you win or lose. You *can* beat the casino, but *not* with any one of a thousand superstitions or "systems"; not with being cool, knowing all the rituals, looking like James Bond; not even with an above-average degree of competence at the games. The gambling professionals (there are maybe a few thousand true pros—defined as people who make their entire living at gambling—mostly in Las Vegas) are part mathematician, part probability theorist, part banker, part actor, and part martial artist. They play high-level blackjack (sometimes in teams) and rarely get caught; they pounce on progressive video poker machines when the meter goes positive; they enter all the big-money gambling tournaments (often in teams) and win regularly; they factor comps into the positive expectation; and they subscribe to the unlimited-bankroll school, which holds that "money management" is a crock. They take the big losses in stride and the big wins for granted. They eat, sleep, and dream gambling theory; they spend all their time in casinos; they carry a lot of cash and and flash it when necessary; they throw big bucks at small edges; and sooner than later they go into gambling publishing, where the real money is.

The rest of us? Rank amateurs. We're supposed to be in it for the fun, the recreation value, and to some extent the dream of the once-in-a-lifetime jackpot (though that's only possible at bad-odds games such as keno and slots, which take your money a bit more slowly than a pickpocket). For us it's about spending the same money with which we'd buy tickets to a ballgame, a concert, an amusement park, for gambling. It's about maximizing our vacation budgets by taking advantage of the rock-bottom

room, food, beverage, and entertainment prices in Nevada, plus the slot club and comp systems for the freebies that accrue to players. It's about risking our gambling bankrolls for the excitement and adrenaline of the casino, the camaraderie with fellow players, the interaction with the dealers and cocktail waitresses and bosses, and seeing how our luck is running lately. It's mostly about risking the pain of losing for the fun of winning.

In this case, the way to play is to set a limit and *not go over it.* Simple as that. Never sit down to play with money that you can't spend. That's one of the sure signs of degenerate gambling. And never try to chase your losses—another sign of the onset of problematic or compulsive gambling. Be a good loser. Be a good winner. Have some fun, get some comps. Oh, and good luck.

Comps

"Comps" is short for complimentaries, also known as freebies. These are travel amenities—free room, food, drink, shows, golf, limos, even airfare—with which the casinos reward their good players and entice other players into their joints. Comps come in many varieties. The easiest to get are free parking (in downtown Reno and Las Vegas parking garages, you're entitled to three to four hours of free parking with a receipt validated at the casino cage) and funbooks (which often contain coupons for free drinks, snacks, and souvenirs). For these comps, you don't have to play; you only have to walk into the casino to get them.

The lowest level comp for players is the ubiquitous free drink. It doesn't matter if you're putting one nickel at a time in a slot machine or laying down $5,000 baccarat bets, the casino serves you complimentary soft drinks, cocktails, wine, and beer.

The value of comps increases with the value of bets. The standard equation used by casinos to determine comps is: size of average bet times number of hours played times the house advantage times the comp equivalency. In other words, say you play blackjack, making $10 bets for two hours. The casino multiplies 120 hands (60 an hour) by $10 and comes up with $1,200 worth of action. It then multiplies $1,200 by the two percent house advantage and comes up with $24—what the casino believes it will win from you on average in two hours of $10 blackjack. It then multiplies $24 by 40% (what it's willing to return in comps), so you're entitled to $9.60 in freebie amenities (in this case, probably a coffee shop comp for one).

Comps returned to big bettors enter the fabled realm of high-roller suites, lavish gourmet dinners, unlimited room service, ringside seats, private parties, limos, and Lear jets. Caesars has 10,000-square-foot apartments complete with butler and chef, private lap pool and putting green, monster jacuzzi and grand piano. The Mirage will fly you to the Super Bowl, put you in box seats at the 50-yard line, and send you to a party with the Most Valuable Player. All you have to do is bet $25,000 a hand eight hours a day over a long weekend, or have a $5 million credit line.

Comps for $25 players might include casino rate on a room (generally 50% of rack), limited food and beverage, and line passes to the show. Hundred-dollar players qualify for full RFB (room, food, and beverage, meaning your whole stay is free) at some of the second-tier joints (Riviera, Stardust, and downtown), while the first-tier places (Caesars, Mirage, Desert Inn, MGM) typically want to see $200–250 a hand for full RFB.

To enter the comp game, you must "get rated." This consists of identifying yourself to the casino cage (where you fill out a credit application and are entered "in the system," or given a file in the casino computer), or a casino host (who will also put you in the system), or a pit supervisor (typically a floorman or pit boss, who will either look you up in the system or keep track of you on his or her own). If you're in the system, you simply identify yourself to the boss, who then fills out a rating slip, which records your time in, time out, average bet size, and a few other details. The data is entered into the computer and casino marketing determines what comps you're entitled to. If you're not in the system, you call the boss over and say something like, "How long do I have to play to get a coffee shop comp for two, or a gourmet room comp for two, or a show for two, etc.?" Then, if you fulfill his requirement, he'll write you a comp.

And herein lies the weakness in the comp tracking system. It's possible to trick the casino into thinking that you're a higher roller than you really are by practicing "comp wizardry." Casinos are especially vulnerable to attack on their comp systems, because your play must be observed by pit bosses. By slowing down the game (actually playing only 40 hands an hour, instead of the 60 the casino expects to deal), betting $25 when the pit boss is watching and only $10–15 when he isn't, looking like a loser, and employing other advanced moves can greatly minimize your risk and maximize your reward in the comp game. The book *Comp City—A Guide to Free Las Vegas Vacations* by Max Rubin (see "Booklist") is the best (and only) book on the spectrum of casino comps for table game players. It's highly recommended for anyone who plays blackjack for $5 a hand and up. It's also one of the funniest and savviest gambling books ever written.

That's the upper tier of the two-tier comp system. The lower tier encompasses the vast majority of casino players, who prefer the machines to the tables. And here we enter the world of slot clubs. Almost all casinos in Nevada have slot clubs, which are similar to the frequent-flyer clubs of the airlines. Slot clubs are free to join; all you do is sign up at the slot club or promotions booth usually located somewhere on the edge of the casino. There, you're issued a slot club membership card, similar to a credit card, which you put into a slot in the gambling machine that you play. Card readers in the machine track the amount of your action, e.g., the number of coins that you play. Once you play a certain number of coins, usually 20–40, you're awarded a point. And once you have a certain number of slot club points, you can exchange them for comps, just like a table-game player. Every slot club is different, so there's a science and an art to getting the most comp value out of the various slot clubs in the various jurisdictions around the state. The best (and only) book to read for your slot club education is *The Las Vegas Advisor Guide to Slot Clubs* by Jeffrey Compton (see "Booklist").

Kids

No one under 21 can play in the casino. That's the law. People under 21 can walk through the casino, but the operative word here is *through*. Older kids on their own and younger kids with their parents must be moving along toward some destination. If you're with your kids and you stop somewhere in the casino for some reason, security guards not far behind will invite you to continue on your way. The guards will tell you that both you and the casino can be fined for having youths in a gambling area (this is so rare that you could argue the point, but it's not recommended that you get into a tussle with casino security guards).

You and your kids can stop in a gambling area only if you're standing in a line to see a show or enter a buffet that winds through the casino.

What about 19- and 20-year-olds who sit down and play? That depends on the casino. The conventional wisdom used to be that minors could play, but they couldn't win. In other words, a 20-year-old could feed the slots till he was broke, but if he hit a jackpot that required a slot host to fill out IRS paperwork (anything more than $1,200), for which he needed to see identification, the underage player not only wouldn't get paid, but he'd get the bum's rush out the door to boot. Court case after court case has upheld the casino's right to refuse to pay; in fact, if the casino did

AGEISM IN THE CASINO

L as Vegas used to be a place to get away from kids. Then, a few casinos realized that if they touted Vegas as a family destination, parents who didn't want to leave their kids home when they went on vacation would still come and gamble. These casinos created castles and pyramids, pirate battles and motion simulators, amusement parks and observation towers, to occupy the kids while the adults did what adults have always done in Las Vegas. But the casinos were in for a surprise.

The attractions appealed to everyone (we're all kids inside) and many parents abandoned the gambling to do things with their children. The casinos hated that—instead of dropping hundreds at the slots, they were dropping five dollars for a ride.

Since then, there's been a Great Retreat from the kid-friendly stance, and many casinos now actively discourage the under-21 crowd. Because of this, the family attractions are usually deserted. But I've got a radically different idea about dealing with the Las Vegas kid situation.

Loosen up!

I know plenty of kids; I'm one myself (I'm 14). My firsthand experience has been that all kids enjoy so-called adult activities, and most are mature enough to handle them. I'm not talking about drinking, smoking, or even gambling. I'm talking about entertainment. It's time the hotel-casinos started sharing the "adult" parts of the playground with their children.

My biggest problem is with the lounges. Kids are snagged by security if they so much as glance at the lounge acts while they're passing through the casino. Why? Because alcohol is served? That's ridiculous. Alcohol is served in virtually every restaurant

and showroom, even at every pool, in Las Vegas. Minors shouldn't be served alcohol, but I don't have a problem knowing it exists. Some people claim that kids would be rowdy in the lounges. Gee, do you think casino security guards would be able to handle that? It probably wouldn't happen too often anyway; most kids wouldn't want to disrupt good entertainment.

Likewise the comedy clubs. Next to lounge acts, I believe that the comedy clubs are the best entertainment value in Las Vegas. Only Comedy Max at the Maxim (16 and up) and the Comedy Stop at the Tropicana (13 and up) allow minors to attend. It's my firm belief that it should be the parents' decision, not the casinos', whether their children go to a comedy club. Are comedians vulgar? Yes, many are. Do they talk about sex? Too often, in my opinion. Why let your kids hear it? Because this is your chance to find out how mature your children really are. See how your child reacts to the raunch. Make it clear that you'd be happy to discuss anything in the routines that he or she doesn't understand. You can use these monologues to communicate with your kids.

Should we be allowed to gamble? I think the age limit should be lowered to 18. How much more irresponsible could an 18-year-old be than a 21-year-old?

Many parents bring their kids to Las Vegas once, but find there are too few activities families can enjoy together. As soon as kids are given a little more respect in Las Vegas, I predict that many of the so-called kid attractions will be a lot more crowded.

—by David Langlieb

pay, it could get fined or lose its license.

These days, with more and more kids roaming around Las Vegas, some joints check ID religiously. Others don't. A few years ago, for example, Bally's found itself in a hassle with the Nevada Gaming Commission for dealing blackjack over a several-hour period to three underage players, one of whom was said to have looked 14 years old. After hearing that the boys lost upwards of $6,000, the parents of one of them complained to the Gaming Control Board, whose agents reviewed the videotapes of the game and recommended a heavy fine. They didn't, to be sure, require Bally's to return the $6,000. What if the boys had started winning those $100 bets? My guess is the pit bosses would have been all over them, demanding to see ID and kicking them out without further ado.

THE GAMES

Wheel Games

The Wheel of Fortune (or **Big Six**) is a direct descendant of one of the most popular and crooked carnival games. The wheel is partitioned into 54 slots of different denominations: 24 $1 slots, 15 $2 slots, seven $5 slots, four $10 slots, two $20 slots, and two slots with a joker, casino logo, American flag, or other symbol. You place your bet atop the corresponding unit on the layout; the odds are the same as the denomination. For example, a $1 bet on the $20 pays $20, and the joker pays 40 to one. The house advantage starts at a prohibitive 11.1% for the even-money bet and rockets to 24% on the joker. Anyone you see playing the Wheel either thinks he's at a carnival, enjoys losing, or doesn't know any better.

Keno is a slow-paced, bad-odds, easy-to-learn numbers game for first-timers, suckers, drinkers, long-shot artists, and the walking wounded. Look at it this way: first you pick *your* numbers, then the casino picks *its* numbers. You simply mark your numbers (one to 20 of them) with the black crayon on the paper ticket according to the instructions in the ubiquitous instruction booklets, then pay the keno runner or writer. According to a recent analysis of the payout schedules on a standard eight-spot ticket for 47 keno games in Las Vegas, the "winner"

(casino with the lowest house advantage) was the Gold Coast at a 21.37% edge, four times worse than roulette! The 47th was the Sahara at 33.14%, where you could expect to lose 33 cents of every dollar bet. Why do people play? Since each keno "race" takes about 10 minutes to run, this is a good game to play in the coffee shop, or if you're killing time in a casino, or if you want to rest from other games in relative stress-free comfort, or if you want to drink, or if you're looking for a shot at a jackpot risking only a small spot. Also, keno is promotion-intensive. Progressive jackpots are enticing to many. And extra action (cars or vacations as additional prizes) often lowers the edge considerably.

Roulette is French for "little wheel." You can make a total of 14 bets on a roulette layout, 13 of which carry a disadvantage, as we've seen, of $5.26 out of every $100 bet. Though you can play roulette with regular casino checks (chips), you can also buy "wheel chips," which come in half a dozen different colors—to differentiate between players. You must specify to the dealer what denomination your personal wheel chips represent, and you *must* redeem them for regular checks before you leave the table. Roulette is an easy game to play, even if you've never been to a casino. It's also full of history, pageantry, and glamour. And if you want to cut the house edge in half, you can play at a joint that uses the European-style wheel, which has only one green zero and therefore a house edge of 2.7%. Monte Carlo and Stratosphere in Las Vegas deal single-zero roulette.

Reel Slots

Slots are also particularly popular with first-timers, as well as players somewhat intimidated by the fast pace and high pressure of the table games, and people who buy into the "one-pull-can-change-your-life" ads. They're particularly unpopular with old-timers and professionals, who consider them machines that take your money. The main problem is that you simply can't fathom the odds against you, which can be anywhere from two to 25% (state law mandates at least a 75% return on all slot machines). You can reduce the edge a fair amount by belonging to slot clubs and accumulating comp points while you play (though you're better off sticking to video poker and forgoing the jackpot idea).

In the last several years, microchips, fiber optics, video and 3-D animation, and sophisticated graphic design have helped to produce an incredible variety of slot machines. For example, progressive machines, such as Quartermania, Megabucks, Fabulous Fifties, Nevada Nickels, etc., are linked throughout the state by telephone modem, and have multiplied jackpots into the millions of dollars, competing with state lotteries. Some slot machines take tokens worth $100 and $500. The latest is interactive slot machines with bonusing features, such as the popular Wheel of Fortune game, in which when you line up certain symbols on the main slot, an attached wheel spins and awards you a secondary jackpot. The Odyssey slot machines, manufactured by Silicon Gaming of San Jose, are the most sophisticated machines to date, but new designs and tech are following at a rapid rate.

Video technology has also made an impact on the variety of gambling machines. Video poker, keno, blackjack, roulette, even greyhound racing contribute to coin-operated gambling devices' average of 65% of casino floor space and more than 50% of revenues, which means more profits for the casinos than all the table games combined.

NEVADA COMMISSION ON TOURISM

Video Poker

Video poker is especially popular (and addictive) with Nevadans and gamblers in the know. Video poker dominates locals' casinos, especially in Las Vegas and Reno. Why? Video poker could be the most successful gambling game ever devised. It's fast, like craps. Bets are as low as a nickel, like slots. Also like slots, there's the possibility of a big jackpot. There's control, like blackjack; also like blackjack, the advantage is often in the player's favor. But the most brilliant coup of all (from the joint's point of view) is that a push feels like a win. When you're dealt a pair of jacks, for example, which returns your bet, it actually feels like you've won something.

Unlike slots, it's possible to calculate the exact payback percentage of the individual machine that you're playing. All you have to do is read the payout schedules. Some variations (full-pay double bonus poker and deuces wild are the most prevalent) are actually positive, meaning that the long-term advantage rests with the player. How can the casinos offer a game in which

they're at the disadvantage? Primarily because of player mistakes—you have to play perfectly to maintain your edge against the house.

So how do you learn to play perfectly? The best way is with a video poker software program. Video Poker Tutor, for example, is programmable for almost every variation of pay schedule and wild cards, and it tutors you while you play, pointing out mistakes and calculating how much they cost you in real money. Video Poker Tutor is available from Huntington Press for $29.95; call 800/244-2224 to order.

In the meantime, *do not* play video poker without knowing 1) how to handicap the payout schedules 2) perfect strategy. Also, never play any machine game without having a slot club card in the card reader. The casino is ready and willing to reward you with comps for your play, so you should get all that's coming to you (and more if you can!).

Craps

Craps generates the most action and excitement of all casino games, for several reasons First, it's extremely fast. Second, selected bets have one of the lowest house advantages in the casino. Third, the variety of wagers, odds, and strategies gives the illusion of skill and control. Also, craps is a game in which the players, especially the shooter, have a personal connection with the primary equipment, the magical dice. And it's a *group* game, in which you can bet with or against the shooter.

Craps is a complicated game to learn completely, and the hardest to step up to the first time. Luckily, with only a partial knowledge of the rules and percentages, you can still play an intelligent and exciting game of craps. By making the most common and simple wager (on the pass or don't-pass line) and backing the bet with odds (usually single and double), you're bucking one of the lowest percentages in the house: around half a percent. This means you'll lose your money a little more slowly than the guy next to you working the field, the big six and eight, and the proposition bets.

To fully understand the game, it's necessary to spend a couple of hours reading about the bets, rules, and procedures, a couple more hours practicing with the dice and memorizing the odds, and a few more making tinhorn bets at the live action (though preferably at a relatively quiet table) while familiarizing yourself with the well-defined craps subculture.

Blackjack

Blackjack is the only casino "bank" game (played against the house) that invites various levels of skill into play (other than video poker). In fact, the house advantage itself is measured against the level of skill the player brings to the game. Blackjack is also the only casino game in which, with enough skill, the player can have an advantage over the house. Naturally, the casinos have a difficult time tolerating a game at which they can be beaten, and card counters (skilled players who can track the cards and calculate the corresponding advantages and disadvantages at a high speed and degree of accuracy) have been receiving the bum's rush since card counting was first invented in 1961, and especially since advanced and highly effective systems showed up in the early 1970s. But even if you have no interest in casing the deck, a lesser level of skill known as basic strategy can be learned in just a few hours of study and practice. Basic strategy reduces the house advantage to near, or even below, the best odds at craps.

Again, books explaining basic strategy and software to practice it by are readily available from gambling catalogs and in local bookstores. Stanford Wong's *Basic Blackjack* is best for beginners; his *Blackjack Analyzer* software is perfect for learning basic strategy.

For first-timers, 20 minutes observing a blackjack table will reveal the few rituals involved: buying in, betting, hitting, standing, busting. Any mistakes will be immediately corrected by the dealer.

PROSTITUTION

(Author's Note: In this section, the term "girls" is short for "working girls," which, though not necessarily politically correct, is a common synonym for "prostitute.")

The Early Days

It all started, in Nevada anyway, in Virginia City, where the "girl market" opened long before any grocery stores. Anywhere from 150 to 300 dens of ill repute were operating at its peak. And just as the miners fanned out from the Comstock to discover the mineral riches across the vast state, the girls followed right behind, to relieve the miners of their loads, so to speak. James Scrugham, governor of Nevada during the Roaring Twenties,

wrote, "The camps were not for wives. They just couldn't put up with the roughness. On those slopes, where many tents and shacks had no heat, the cribs had stoves. They had pictures on the walls, and maybe a bottle of sherry (whiskey was not as refined). The miners, some coming in from a day in the drifts, some coming in from months of prospecting, hands calloused, boots worn, having smelled only sagebrush and sweat—why, the poor bastards knew that the one place they could get a welcome, a smile, a bed with springs, clean sheets, the smell of perfume, was the crib. These men had it all the same. Come evening, the miners, card sharps, high-talent guys, blacksmiths took the same walk down the street of whores."

Of course, conditions back then weren't exactly conducive to sanitation and health, especially for the girls. "All night, men have pawed and used her and not one has given a damn about her feelings," wrote George Williams III, in *Rosa May—The Search for a Mining Camp Legend.* "She may start to drink hard, snuff cocaine, or take laudanum (an opium derivative), to ease the pain of her loneliness." Suicide rates, murder, and death from venereal diseases and poisons taken for contraception and infection took a heavy toll among mining-town prostititutes.

But prostitution was a frontier tradition, and in Nevada the frontier tradition refused to be tamed. The railroad towns adopted the mining-camp custom of keeping a house to satisfy the need of the crews, cowhands, sheepherders, travelers, or just to keep the single guys away from the married women and high schools. Tonopah and Goldfield had their girl markets through the 20th century's first couple of decades. Reno had its complex of cribs down by the Truckee River, and Las Vegas had its Block 16, both remaining in operation up until WW II. Ely, Elko, Winnemucca, Beatty, Wells, even the state capital at Carson City, had their dens.

Though prostitution was not technically legal, it wasn't technically illegal either. It stayed acceptable on unwritten terms refined since the towns came into existence. A modest house on the edge of town displayed a small red light near the front door. A discreet madam kept the girls off the streets and somehow prevented them from scandalizing or blackmailing the married men, bankers and lawyers, reporters and editors, politicians, even ministers, who availed themselves of their services.

World War II

Military bases sprang up in Nevada during WW II like springs on a busted bed. Stead Army Base just north of Reno and Las Vegas Bombing and Gunnery Range imported thousands of soldiers, with the same need as the miners and ministers. But the War Department quickly put a lid on it. As Gabriel Vogliotti writes in his excellent *The Girls of Nevada,* "The road to Reno [and Las Vegas] could become a coital express . . . and the town[s] could wind up with the whore district of Hong Kong. With five hundred off-duty passes a night, [the brothels] could become the pubic center of the west; this at a time when syphilis took weeks to check, and when gonorrhea could cripple a company. Moreover, the War Department had heard from the wives, who had many arguments: . . . men who were called to arms should not receive federal help in sex betrayal, the War Department should not debauch men and cheapen woman hood . . ." The base commanders insisted that Reno and Las Vegas close up the girl shops, and they never reopened, legally, anyway. Today, prostitution is officially *illegal* in Reno's Washoe County, Las Vegas's Clark County, Lake Tahoe's Douglas County, Carson City, and Lincoln County.

The New Las Vegas

Just as mining and prostitution have had a long and mutually profitable liaison, gambling and commercial sex have always gone hand in hand. After the war, when Ben Siegel and the boys started to develop Las Vegas into the greatest gambling town on Earth, it was only natural that Las Vegas should also become Pay-for-Lay Central—brothels or no brothels. I mean, all those hotel rooms! Clearly, gamblers needed sex: the suggestion of it, with girls parading around on stage and decorating the floor, generally part of the casino scenery; the mysterious, slightly sinister glamour and myth of its ready availability with gorgeous and expensive pros; and the eventual consummation—prescribed, safe, discreet—that gets the guy to sleep or wakes him up, makes him feel lucky when he wins or consoles him when he loses, keeps him around the tables a little longer, and sends him home having experienced what has been called the "Las Vegas total."

There was one complication, however. The prostitution had to be directly and carefully choreographed, from start to finish, in order to avoid any chance of offending the millions of straights that filled the hotels, of becoming so obvious or vulgar or hazardous that it menaced in any way the smooth and consistent workings of the great god Percentage.

Suffice it to say that the gambling establishment over the years has managed to juggle the law, the image, and the reality of the legions of men with the need, the legions of women—

house girls, swingers, cocktail waitresses, Lolitas, call girls, weekend warriors, and freelance street-walkers—willing to satisfy the need, and the legions of straights who might find the whole thing just a bit distasteful.

Joe Conforte

Meanwhile, in the northern part of the state, a man named Joe Conforte was openly challenging the vague mishmash of law that regulated the girl industry. By the time Conforte arrived in the 1950s, whorehouses had been around in Nevada for 100 years, and nearly 50 rules and regulations had been entered into the state statutes governing the brothel business. For example, no brothel can operate on a main street; no advertising is permitted; habitual clients can be charged with vagrancy; pimps are verboten; and all brothels must be at least 300 yards from a school or church (Vogliotti reports that Beatty townspeople "complied and moved the school"). Basically, 50 convenings of the state Legislature had tiptoed around the issue, leaving it up to the counties to decide for themselves.

Joe Conforte had fought for official *legalized* prostitution in Reno (Washoe County) for years, doing battle with a crusading district attorney who finally succeeded in jailing Conforte for a number of years on charges relating to their disagreements. (For the whole sordid tale, see Jim Sloan's *Nevada—True Tales of the Neon Wilderness*.) But after serving his time, Conforte set up shop at a ranch, just over the Washoe County line in Storey County, known as Mustang. Eventually, the allegations of paying off all the county officials started to rankle him. By then, the Mustang Ranch was Storey County's largest taxpayer, which gave him a certain influence in county politics. In 1971, Conforte convinced the commissioners to pass Ordinance 38, which legalized prostitution, making Storey the first county in the country to do so. Lyon County, next door, quickly followed suit. Finally, in 1973, the Nevada Supreme Court upheld the right of counties with fewer than 50,000 people to license brothels. They're regulated by the sheriffs, district attorneys, and health department. (Several years ago, Joe Conforte retired and left Nevada.)

PROSTITUTION TODAY

Legal

As of the year 2000, 10 of Nevada's 17 counties have legal prostitution, and there are currently 26 licensed brothels in the state. Some have two or three girls working in them, others dozens. The girls are subcontractors to the brothel, for tax purposes; the usual cut is 50–50. They pay a minimal amount for room and board and sleep where they work. The kitchen and maybe one other room in the compound (generally a house in the towns and a group of trailers outside town or at junctions) are off-limits to customers, where the girls, the manager, the house mother (so to speak, or madam), the cook, and the handyman hang out. Each girl has her own arrangements as to how much she works, her scheduled days, hours, etc. Most girls average around four to six dates per day. The good pros can earn up to $10,000 a month, a figure that's not hard to believe, if you consider the prices. Prices start as low as $60 for a "quickie," average $150 and up, and can top out in the thousands.

All legal prostitutes are checked weekly for venereal diseases, monthly for AIDS; the state health department oversees the ladies' weekly health checks. Health officials assert that there hasn't been a single case of an HIV-positive test while the girl was working at a brothel (though a dozen or so applicants have been turned away after their results came back positive). In addition, not a single customer has been infected with the AIDS virus from a prostitute in a licensed brothel.

Licensed brothels have great advantages over illegal prostitution. At a legal, regulated brothel, the client knows he will be safe, get what he pays for, be treated well, and will not get ripped off or face danger from the police or sexual exploiters such as pimps, etc.

For a guide to brothels in Nevada, pick up *The Best Cathouses in Nevada,* by J.R. Schwartz (see "Booklist"). Published in 1987, it's a bit outdated, but so far remains the only book of its kind.

Illegal

Prostitution in Las Vegas is a different story. Prostitution is illegal in Las Vegas. Both the client and woman can go to jail, and although the women are arrested more often than the clients are, clients are taking a risk when they engage in illegal prostitution. Las Vegas police spend $3 million per year enforcing anti-prostitution laws.

Nevertheless, even though it's illegal and risky, prostitution does still exist in Las Vegas. Three types of prostitutes work there. The first and most dangerous are the streetwalkers or "lounge lizards." They're not at all obvious, mostly because Metro Vice keeps them out of the tourist mainstream as much as possible. You'll occasionally see them downtown on the side streets or walking down the Strip late at night. A streetwalker who'll turn a trick in the back seat of a car or in a motel room either has a vicious pimp, regularly shares needles, has just been let out of the nuthouse or the joint, has *very* low self-esteem, or all of the above.

The second kind of Las Vegas prostitutes, call girls, advertise in sex rags found in newspaper vending machines downtown and along the Strip. The third kind, "adult entertainers," are found under about 100 pages of "Entertainer" listings in the *Yellow Pages.* The distinction between a call girl and an adult entertainer is tenuous at best. Both are illegal, neither is checked for diseases (unless she's arrested), and their prices are fairly uniform. It could typically cost around $200 for an "entertainer" to come to the client's room, but the client must understand that this price only pays for the "entertainment" being advertised—dancing or whatever. If the client also wants sex, the price could quickly escalate to $500 or more. This is not a tolerated activity in Las Vegas; police frequently set up sting operations. Metro Vice busts around 300–400 pros every month.

All arrested prostitutes are tested for AIDS, and a girl who tests positive is liable for 20 years and $10,000. About half a dozen prostitutes (two of them male) have been imprisoned on this. (Since 1988, when AIDS testing began in Las Vegas, about 140 of those arrested have tested HIV positive.) Otherwise, prostitution is a misdemeanor in Las Vegas, punishable by 30 days and a $1,000 fine.

Illegal prostitution may sometimes seem a little cheaper than in the legal brothels, but it's a lot riskier. Patronizing a legal brothel makes a lot better sense. The nearest licensed brothels to Las Vegas are the Cherry Patch Ranch and the Chicken Ranch, both situated 60 miles west of Las Vegas outside Pahrump, in Nye County. Reno has licensed brothels in closer proximity: 10 miles from Reno there's the Old Bridge Ranch, and about 40 miles from Reno there are four other licensed brothels in Mound House, just east of Carson City.

FESTIVALS AND EVENTS

What follows is a list of Nevada's major annual festivals and events. The dates given here are the dates these events occurred in 2000, but dates can be changeable, i.e. events often take place on a particular weekend of a particular month (the third weekend in June, for example), or even just sometime during a particular month, rather than on a particular date. Sometimes events' dates can be changed, or ongoing events can be cancelled. Before you use this list to make travel plans, be sure to phone ahead to check current schedules.

The statewide Nevada Commission on Tourism has current information on these and hundreds of other events around the state. They publish an excellent Calendar of Events, and also list events on their website. Contact: Nevada Commission on Tourism, 401 N. Carson St., Carson City, NV 89701, 775/687-4322, 800/237-0774, fax 775/687-5496, www.travelnevada.com. Local tourist information centers and chambers of commerce, mentioned throughout this book, also have current information on events in their areas.

January
January 15—Carson City: Winter Wine and All That Jazz: Wine and cheese tasting, music. Ormsby House, Carson City, 775/884-7477.
January 20–23—Laughlin: Laughlin Desert Challenge: 165-mile off-road race along the banks of the Colorado River, 800/452-8445.
January 22–29—Elko: Cowboy Poetry Gathering: Largest gathering in the country (reserve early); weeklong concerts, readings, workshops

and other activities. Last week in January, 775/738-7508.

February

February 3–26—Reno: Nevada Shakespeare Festival, 775/324-4198.

February 6—Las Vegas: Las Vegas International Marathon and Half-Marathon: Attracts more than 7,500 runners from all 50 states and 40 other countries for the 34th annual 26.2 and 13.1-mile races. Event includes a 5K "friendship run" the day before, and on race day an international food festival and health and fitness expo, 702/240-2722.

February 19–21—Hawthorne: Walker Lake Fishing Derby: Competition for cash prizes, on Walker Lake, 12 miles north of Hawthorne, 775/945-5896.

March

March 3–12—North Lake Tahoe: Snowfest Winter carnival: Mountain Mardi Gras with serious and offbeat ski races, outdoor parties, concerts, parades, bonfire, ice carvings, snow sculptures, polar bear swim, snowshoe races, torchlight parade. First week of March, at area ski resorts, North Lake Tahoe, 775/832-7625.

March 31–April 2—Henderson: Invitational Native American Arts Festival: Demonstrations, dance and music performances, lectures and films, outdoor Native American arts and crafts market, food vendors. Clark County Heritage Museum, Henderson, 702/455-7955.

April

April 5–9—Laughlin: Laughlin Rodeo Days: PRVA rodeo, entertainment, vendors. Special Events Arena, Laughlin, 702/298-2214.

April 6–9—Logandale: Clark County Fair and Rodeo: PRCA Rodeo, concert, entertainment, carnival, junior livestock judging and auction, juried art show, antique farm equipment displays. Fairgrounds, Logandale, 888/876-FAIR.

April 7–9—Las Vegas: NHRA Winston Drag Races: NHRA national event. Las Vegas Motor Speedway, Las Vegas, 702/644-4444.

April 15–16—Hawthorne: Loon Festival: Boat tours of Walker Lake during the loons' migration season. Third weekend in April, Walker Lake, 12 miles north of Hawthorne, 775/945-5896.

April 21–23—Lake Mead: Las Vegas Governor's Cup Regatta: Nevada State Powerboat Championship, Boulder Beach, Lake Mead, 702/393-6163.

April 27–30—Laughlin: Laughlin River Run: West Coast's largest motorcycle event featuring displays, trade show exhibits, custom bike show, concerts, 800/357-8223.

May

May 5—Las Vegas, Reno, Virginia City, Wendover: Cinco de Mayo: Large Hispanic celebrations; Las Vegas's celebration attracts thousands of Mexican nationals. This festival is often celebrated on the weekend nearest May 5. Virginia City's celebration is a Cinco de Mayo Chili Cook-Off, 775/847-0311.

May 6–7—Rachel: The X Rides: Fully-supported bicycle rides include an evening ride to Area 51 mailbox, a mountain bike ride to Area 51 gate, 775/588-9658.

May 12–14—Ely: Nevada Open Road Challenge: Car race against the clock on State Route 318 from Lund to Hiko, with pre-race activities in Ely. Third weekend in May, 775/289-8877.

June

June 9–11—Carson City: Carson City Rendezvous: Civil War re-enactment and living history camps, Mills Park, Carson City, 775/687-7410.

June 9–11—Reno: National Wild Horse and Burro Show: Wild horse adoption, mustang and burro competition in English, western and timed events; demonstrations, vendors. Livestock Events Center, Reno, 775/687-1400.

June 10–11—Gardnerville: Carson Valley Days Hot-Air Balloon Race, 775/782-8144.

June 16–18—Austin: Gridley Days and Rock and Bottle Show: Parade, entertainment, exhibits, crafts, vendor booths, barbecue, pancake breakfast, mountain bike rally, 775/964-2200.

June 17–25—Reno: Reno Rodeo: Major PRCA rodeo with a cattle drive, parade, carnival, entertainment. Third week in June, Livestock Events Center, Reno, 775/329-3877.

June 30–July 2—Elko: National Basque Festival: Entertainment, games of skill and strength, dancing, food and drink. Fairgrounds and City Park, Elko, 775/738-7135.

June 30–July 4—Fallon: Silver State International Rodeo: Parade, booths. Churchill County Fairgrounds, Fallon, 775/423-4674.

July
July 4—Most towns: Fireworks displays and other celebrations, especially in Las Vegas and Reno.
July 1–2—Elko: National Basque Festival: Traditional dances, games, food, drink, and contests of strength and skill. Fairgrounds and City Park, Elko, 775/738-7135.
July 1–31—Reno: Uptown Downtown ARTown: Summer arts festival with performances and exhibits citywide, 775/329-1324.
July 1–September 3—Virginia City: Nevada Shakespeare Festival: Piper's Opera House, Virginia City, 775/324-4198.
July 7–9—Stateline: Celebrity Golf Championship: Sports and entertainment stars compete in golf tournament. Edgewood Tahoe, Stateline, 530/544-5050.
July 8–10—Ely: White Pine 4x4 Rally: All 4WD vehicles invited; full and half-day runs in White Pine County, Ely, 775/289-6798.
July 8–15—Las Vegas: Nevada 2000: A 2,000-mile off-road race loops around the state, starting and finishing in Las Vegas, 702/457-5775.
July 11–September 3—Incline Village: Lake Tahoe Shakespeare Festival: The Bard's plays are presented on the beach with Lake Tahoe as a backdrop. Sand Harbor, Incline Village, 800/74-SHOWS.
July 14—Las Vegas: Bastille Day: at the Arc de Triomphe at Paris, 702/946-7000.
July 14–16—Fallon: Fallon All-Indian Rodeo and Powwow: Rodeo, Native American dancers, handgames, arts and crafts, dance, parade, food booths. Regional Park, Fallon, 775/423-2544.
July 21–23—Reno: Reno Basque Festival: Traditional food, dance, games, Mass, barbecue. Wingfield Park, Reno, 775/787-3039.
July 28–30—Tonopah: Jim Butler Days: Annual town party celebrates Tonopah's founding in 1900, 775/482-3558.
July 28–30—Carson City: Silver Dollar Car Classic: Street dance, custom cars, poker run, barbecue, entertainment. Mills Park, Carson City, 775/687-7410.
July 29–30—Genoa: Renaissance Fair: Arts and crafts, antiques, actors, jugglers, jousters, rapier fighters. Antiques Plus, Genoa, 775/782-

4951 or 775/782-2893.
July 31–August 5—Reno and Sparks: Hot August Nights: Hot rods, music of the '50s and '60s, dances, concerts. Reno and Victorian Square, Sparks, 775/356-1956.

August
August 1–September 3—Incline Village: Lake Tahoe Shakespeare Festival: The Bard on the beach at Lake Tahoe. Sand Harbor, Incline Village, 800/74-SHOWS.
August 1–5—Reno and Sparks: Hot August Nights: Hot rods, music of the 50s and 60s, dances, concerts. First week of August, Reno and Victorian Square, Sparks, 775/356-1956.
August 13–15—Battle Mountain: Pony Express 100: Open road race from Austin to Battle Mountain, also car show, dance, parade. Civic Center, Battle Mountain, 775/635-8245.
August 19—Virginia City: Outhouse Races, 775/847–0311.
August 21–27—Reno: Reno-Tahoe Open: Golf tournament featuring top PGA players. Montreux Golf and Country Club, Reno, 775/322-3900.
August 23–27—Reno: Nevada State Fair: Livestock exhibits and auction, creative living competition, food booths, carnival, entertainment. Livestock Events Center, Reno, 775/688-5767.
August 25–27—Yerington: Spirit of Wovoka Days Powwow: Native American dance, food, arts, crafts. Fourth weekend of August, 775/463-2350.

September
September 1–4—Sparks: Best in the West Nugget Rib Cook-Off: World-class event featuring the West's best rib cookers competing for fame and the crowd's acclaim, with entertainment and arts and crafts fair. Labor Day weekend, Victorian Square and John Ascuaga's Nugget, Sparks, 775/356-3300.
September 1–4—Fallon: Hearts of Gold Cantaloupe Festival, 775/423-2544.
September 8–10—Virginia City: Virginia City International Camel Races: Camel, ostrich, and water buffalo races, specialty acts, daily parades, food. Second weekend in September, Camel Arena, Virginia City, 775/847-0311 or 775/329-7469.
September 8–10—Reno: Great Reno Balloon

Race: A top ballooning event that draws 120,000 people. Early morning rally has been voted one of Nevada's best events. Second weekend in September, Rancho San Rafael Park, Reno, 775/826-1181.

September 14–17—Reno: National Championship Air Races: Four classes of racers, plus military displays and aerobatics. Third weekend in September, 775/972-6663.

September 15–17—Ely: Silver State Classic Challenge: 90-mile open road car race on State Route 318 from Lund to Hiko, with pre-race activities in Ely. Third weekend in September, 775/289-8877.

September 21–24—Reno: Street Vibrations Music, Metal and Motorcycles Festival: Motorcycle tours, entertainment, ride-in shows, parade, poker run/walk, vendors, concerts. Various community locations, Reno, 775/329-SHOW or 800/200-4557.

September 23–24—Genoa: Genoa Candy Dance: 80th annual arts and crafts fair featuring over 300 fine arts and crafts booths; dinner and dance on Saturday night. Third weekend in September, 775/782-TOWN.

October

October 7–8—Reno: Great Italian Festival: Grape-stomp, spaghetti-eating contest, Italian food booths, entertainment. Eldorado Hotel, Reno, 775/786-5700.

October 24–31—Carson City: Nevada Day Celebration: Parade, carnival, midway games, entertainment, food booths, arts and crafts, dance bands. Mills Park, Carson City, 775/687-4680.

October 30–November 5—Reno: National Senior Pro Rodeo Finals: Athletes 40 and older compete in traditional rodeo events. Livestock Events Center, Reno, 775/323-8842.

November

November 25—Hawthorne: Fisherman's Holiday Fish Derby: Anglers compete for cash prizes. Fourth weekend in November, Walker Lake, 12 miles north of Hawthorne, 775/945-5896.

December

December 1–10—Las Vegas: National Finals Rodeo: Top 126 rodeo contestants compete for more than $4.2 million in prize money. Thomas and Mack Center, Las Vegas, 702/260-8605.

December 2—Boulder City: Parade of Lights: Annual parade of 50 decorated boats on Lake Mead, starts at Lake Mead Marina, 322 Lakeshore Rd., off Highway U.S. 93, Boulder City, 702/457-2797.

December 3—Carson City: Victorian Home Christmas Tour: Decorated homes, historic district, 775/882-1565.

December 31—Las Vegas and Reno: Outdoor public New Year's Eve celebrations.

ACCOMMODATIONS AND FOOD

CASINOS

Nevada is one of the easiest and cheapest states in the country to travel in. Forty percent of its employees are in the service trades, 25% working directly in casinos. A casino can be a traveler's best friend. They're all open 24 hours and have lots of convenient parking, so you know right where to go for a bathroom and can get there post haste. Most have 24-hour coffee shops and bars, so you'll never go hungry or thirsty. The cashier will happily change traveler's checks and personal checks into cash, cash into coin and vice versa, and plastic to paper. There's usually a vacant motel room within walking dis-

tance. And of course they all have slots and most have table games, if you need a distraction and don't find it too oppressive or disorienting to go from white-line fever to three-reel or five-card fever. (Better is to walk around, stretch your legs, and take deep breaths.)

In interior Nevada, bona fide casinos can be few and far between. In towns such as Austin and Eureka, Battle Mountain and Carlin, Pioche and Caliente, Goldfield and Gerlach, and of course Boulder City (the only place in Nevada where gambling is illegal), you're on your own, especially late at night. But everywhere else in the state, all hours of the day and night, when you're in need of grub, caffeine, action, toilet, or just other people, casinos are a welcome sight.

Casinos are also good places to be careful around. Many people, including those who are on the road, stumble out under the influence of too much free booze, smoke in the eyes, video poker, even hysteria (from winning) or despair (from losing) or alienation (from overstaying). You've simply got to be on the defensive with everyone who's just walked out of a casino.

LODGING

There are upwards of 165,000 motel and hotel rooms in Nevada, with more being built all the time (at the end of 1999 Nevada had 165,326 rooms available, up from 149,824 rooms at the end of 1998—an increase of 10.3% in just one year). In addition there are thousands of camping and RV sites. Taken on average, Nevada lodging, indoor and out, is among the least expensive in the country, subsidized as it is by attached casinos or competing against casino-subsidized rooms.

The absolute cheapest way to spend the night is also the most satisfying and soul nurturing: to camp out somewhere in the wilds of the vast Great Basin or Mojave. Pull off the pavement onto a graded dirt road, then pull off that into the real outback; set up your tent, watch for stray cows and rattlers, and commune with the desert and the sky. If you prefer some civilization, county, state, and national park and forest campgrounds charge $0–12; a few have showers. With a tent, you can also always pull into an RV park and pay no more, usually, than $12–18 for the night, which includes flush toilets and hot showers. Often RV parks will sell showers alone for $3–5.

The bargain-basement lodging, usually in old hotels right downtown, often costs as little as $20–25 for a double. The bathroom's down the hall, you don't get Showtime, the rooms are small and the walls are thin, but they're indoors and cheap. If you're diligent and don't mind inspecting and rejecting rooms, you can often find acceptable motel accommodations, with air-conditioning, cable, and a telephone, for $25–30 for two. If you're not shopping and don't mind spending $35–45 a night (on all but the busiest weekends during high season), you can pull into most any motel in Nevada and have yourself a room.

Las Vegas, Reno, Laughlin, Stateline, Primm, Mesquite, and Jackpot have high-rise hotels, where your room can be a pretty fur piece from your car, the front desk, even the elevators. Motels are more convenient for the quick in and out; hotels are more convenient for casinos, coffee shops, room service, pools, and big rooms. The hotel scene in Reno is fairly straightforward, though still a miniature version of the wacky world of hotel rooms in Las Vegas. For a complete rundown, see the Las Vegas "Accommodations" section.

Summer is the high season, and some towns regularly sell out of rooms every night. Sunday through Thursday, you're pretty much guaranteed a room without a reservation if you check in early enough; it could be tight if it's late. On Friday and Saturday nights, it gets a little trickier. You've got a good shot at a room on Friday up till around 6 P.M. and on Saturday up till around 3. After that, every VACANCY sign in the state says NO, and at the ones that don't, you don't wanna know how much they're charging. On

camping at Red Rock Canyon

PHIL GUERRERO/B.L.M.

HOTEL-MOTEL INDOOR POOLS

John Ascuaga's Nugget (Sparks)
Caesar's Tahoe
Harrah's Tahoe
Inn at Incline (north Lake Tahoe)
Shady Court (Winnemucca)
Holiday Inn (Elko)
Ameritel Inn (Elko)
Copper Queen (Ely)

Saturday later than mid-afternoon in Nevada, if you don't have a prepaid reservation for a Saturday night anytime during the year and you're not prepared to spend the night in the car, on the road, in a casino, or in a tent, your only play is to stop at the biggest motel you can find between 5 and 6 P.M. and wait around hoping for an unpaid reservation to become a no-show; you'll have the room if you're there. Otherwise, stay put wherever you spend Friday night—if they'll have you.

FOOD

In terms of food, Nevada is a land of extremes. There's either a gluttonous abundance of eateries (Las Vegas has nearly 850 restaurants, more than 100 coffee shops, 30 buffets, and hundreds of fast-food stops) or you're doomed to yet another bacon and eggs, burger and fries, or chicken-fried steak. In the larger towns that have any variety, you might find a chow-meinery, or if you're really lucky, a Mexican restaurant. In the northern half of the state, you can usually locate some good and plenty Basque food. And in the cities, choose from Italian, French, Chinese, Japanese, Vietnamese, Korean, Mongolian, Brazilian, Salvadoran, Indian, Greek, deli, and natural food.

Buffets are great for traveling—fill up in the morning and go till dinner, or have a big lunch and two small meals before and after. They're also the nuts for children under 5; real young kids eat free, and you can have food in their mouths within 30 seconds flat of walking in if you do it right. If it's not a kid food emergency, I suggest you take a peek at the buffet before you pay to eat; just ask the cashier or hostess if it's all right. At the cheap cudfests, the way to gauge taste by sight is simple visual recognition. Don't read the labels (if there are any), and see if you can tell what the food is. If the steamtable fare looks like gloppy casseroles and starchy sauces over mystery meat and fish, and if the salads appear to be straight from 55-gallon drums, just go next door and look at another buffet. Or if the heat lamps give the food an other-worldly amber glow, find one that's a little more, you know, down to earth. If you can't recognize the food by sight, the odds are overwhelmingly against that you'll be able to by taste. Still, for $3.99 for breakfast, $5.99 for lunch, and $9.99 for dinner (on average), if your buds have been completely McDonaldized and you're looking to shovel home the volume, what the hell.

Also take a good close look at the Friday night seafood buffets, whether they're cheap or not. Here, the salmon steak, halibut, bay shrimp, steamed prawns, and clams are labeled, recognizable, even presentable, but often taste (if you can call it that) like a preposterous pile of insipid pollack.

If you're staying in Las Vegas or Reno for any length of time, it's handy to carry a hot plate and extension cord to cook your own store-bought. A full discussion of weekly rooms with kitchenettes appears under Las Vegas "Accommodations." If you're out seeing the backcountry and come into towns only occasionally, you'll probably have your camp stove, bulk dry goods, and freeze-dried food.

Drink

Always carry water! It's a desert out there. If you're hiking, have a canteen on your belt and a gallon jug on your pack. If you're driving, a five-gallon container will get you—or someone you happen upon—through almost any emergency. All supermarkets sell gallon jugs of spring water. Don't run out! You might also buy canned or boxed juices; try diluting the strong juice with half or more water: it gets the water in you, and it tastes nicely sweet.

The drinking age in Nevada is 21. If you're 21 or older, you can drink alcoholic stupefacients more readily and cheaply in Nevada than any other place in the country, if not the world. Every casino in the state and many bars remain open 24 hours and every casino in the state serves free drinks to players. The easiest way to get free beer or booze is to plop down at a video poker bar, buy in for a roll of quarters, and tip the bartender well; if you get a live one, he or she will refill your drink till you're out of quarters or are otherwise ready to leave. You don't even have to play: simply buy in, get your comp drink, and cash out at the change booth. Then go next door and do it all over again. As Max Rubin says in *Comp City,* this technique "has carried many an alkie through some desperate nights in Glitter Gulch."

If you don't even want to buy in, ask any bartender about drink specials. In Las Vegas, 75-cent draft beers, 99-cent margaritas, dollar imported beer, and dollar well drinks are all common. Most of the casino bars outside of Las Vegas offer some variation of the same.

Don't drink and drive. The life you save might be my own.

TRANSPORTATION

Getting There

Five main roads crisscross Nevada, three east-west and two north-south. Interstate 80 takes the long northern route west across the shoulder of Nevada. US 50 cuts across the shorter waist of the state, joins up with I-80 at Fernley, then splits off to Reno or Carson City. US 6 travels along with US 50 in eastern Nevada for a while, then cuts south to Tonopah and out toward Fresno in California. US 95 zigzags south, then southwest, then south, then southeast for nearly 700 miles from McDermitt at the north edge of the state to Laughlin at the south. US 93 travels between Jackpot to Boulder City for 500 miles, but in a fairly straight line.

Greyhound bus routes connect Las Vegas with Carson City, Reno, Laughlin, and Mesquite; routes heading further afield from Las Vegas include routes to Los Angeles, Phoenix and Salt Lake City, with connections to other places. Greyhound routes connect Reno with Carson City, Las Vegas, Winnemucca and Elko, and places further afield including Sacramento, Oakland, San Francisco and Salt Lake City.

Otherwise, rural bus lines are few and far between. Today, there are only three: **Ely Bus** connects Ely to Las Vegas and Reno. **K-T Bus Lines** carries passengers between Reno and Las Vegas. Public Rural Ride (PRIDE) operates between Reno and Carson City.

Amtrak operates the *California Zephyr* train between Emeryville (in the east San Francisco Bay area) and Chicago, stopping in Nevada in Reno, Winnemucca, and Elko. (Note that Amtrak no longer runs through Las Vegas.)

There are big airports at Las Vegas and Reno, fair-sized airports at Elko and Ely (each has four departures and arrivals a day), and 10 other airports attended either 24 hours a day or during daylight hours. Carson City is one of a handful of state capitals without regularly scheduled airline service.

If you're driving in, get in your car and make a beeline; having this book along will help no matter which way you go. If you're flying in, consider touching down in Las Vegas first. McCarran International is one of the easiest airports to access in the country and with a little research and planning, it can also be one of the cheapest. Reno is an hour by air from Las Vegas and nowhere in Nevada is more than ten hours or so by car.

Getting Around

The best way is with your own car. Buses don't reach half the state. Distances are long and services are few and far between. You can find yourself on gravel a lot if you're adventurous, and if your steed is trusty, you can really get out there. That's the idea, isn't it? And if you want to get back from out there, you have to treat your car right. First of all, does it have a name? Give it one. Cars, like pets, prefer familiarity. Desert driving is hot, dusty, bumpy, and can be strenuous on your car. There's a whole lotta shakin' going on out there. Make sure it's had the best fuel, fluids, tires, parts, and care. Carry plenty of spare water and fluids, spare tire and jack, flashlight and flares, spare belts and hoses, tool kit, and shovel; baling wire and Super Glue often come in handy. Don't forget a rag or two.

Common-sense maintenance consciousness is required on the road. If the car gets hot or overheats, stop for a while to cool it off. Never open the radiator cap if the engine is steaming. After it's sat, squeeze the top radiator hose to see if there's any pressure in it; if there isn't, it's safe to open. Never pour water into a hot radiator—you could crack your block. If you start to smell rubber, your tires are overheating, and that's a good way to have a blowout. Stop and let them cool off, too. In winter in the high country, a can

of silicone lubricant such as WD-40 will unfreeze door locks, dry off humid wiring, and keep your hinges in shape.

Road Courtesy
The speed limits on most of the interstates and US highways outside of the cities and towns have been raised in the past couple of years—praise be the Lord! They're now 75 mph on Interstates 80 and 15, US 95 and 93, and a few state roads. You can drive 65 mph on the interstates in Reno and Las Vegas. Most passers-

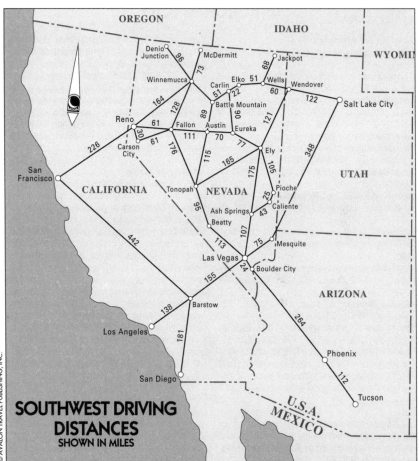

SOUTHWEST DRIVING DISTANCES
SHOWN IN MILES

through drive upwards of 80–85 mph without worrying about being noticed by the highway patrol. Since the superhighways are two lanes in each direction, road courtesy isn't much of a problem; anyone wanting to go faster than you can zip around on the left, if not the right.

Passing is generally not a problem on the two-lane highways through rural Nevada; the solid and dotted lines are well maintained and long straight stretches through the valleys are conducive to safe zipping.

There are only a few long climbs up mountains on main roads in Nevada, and here passing can be a problem. The good news is that turnouts are common. The bad news is that some flatlanders and RV drivers don't know what turnouts are for. If you're pulling a heavy load, are nervous about mountain driving, or just have a slowpoke car, please pull over and let zippety, who's sure to be behind you, doo-dah around.

INFORMATION

Government Agencies
State and federal government agencies include:

General Information (on state government agencies): 775/687-5000
Nevada Commission on Tourism: 401 N. Carson St., Carson City, NV 89701; 775/687-4322 or 800/237-0774; email travelnevada.com; www.travelnevada.com.
Nevada Division of State Parks: 1300 S. Curry St., Carson City, NV 89703-5202; 775/687-4384.
Great Basin National Park: Baker, NV 89311; 775/234-7331.
Lake Mead National Recreation Area: 601 Nevada Hwy., Boulder City, NV 98005; 702/293-8907.
Bureau of Land Management: State Office, 1340 Financial Blvd., Reno, NV 89502, 775/861-6400.
Humboldt-Toiyabe National Forest: Supervisor's Office, 1200 Franklin Way, Sparks, NV 89431; 775/331-6444.
Nevada Dept. of Wildlife: 1100 Valley Rd., Reno, NV 89512; 775/688-1500.
State Library and Archives: 100 N. Stewart St., Carson City, NV 89701, 775/684-3360.
Road Condition Report: 877/687-6237.

For chambers of commerce, convention and visitors authorities, and visitor centers, see "Information" under the specific travel chapters.

Maps
The biggest, most beautiful and informative map about the land—mountains, rivers, lakes, and elevations—is produced by **Raven Maps,** Medford, Oregon, 800/237-0798. It's available for $25 (paper) or $45 (laminated); call for a free catalog. The Nevada **Department of Transportation,** 1263 S. Stewart St., Carson City, NV 89712, 775/888-7627, also has big wall-size maps of the roads, counties, and natural features. In addition, it publishes an indispensable *Nevada Map Atlas* of 127 quadrangle maps of the state, which include all the nonpaved roads; it's now in its 15th edition. The quadrangles are also sold separately in a larger scale.

Nevada Magazine
The best general source of information about Nevada is *Nevada*. This magazine has been financed by the state government since the 1930s. With access to the hundreds of back issues (such as at the Getchell Library at UNR and the State Library in Carson City), you could write an excellent travel guide. "Getaway Hotlines" in the "Travel Planner" section in the center of the magazine has a list of nearly 100 addresses and phone numbers for statewide and local information: convention and visitors bureaus, chambers of commerce, events hotlines, and more. If you're interested in Nevada, subscribe to *Nevada*. The main office is at 401 N. Carson St., Suite 100, Carson City, NV 89701-4291, 775/687-5416, editor@nevada magazine, www.nevadamagazine.com.

Libraries
Every major library in the state has a Nevada room or a special collection of local-interest titles. But the three main libraries for researching specific aspects of the Nevada experience are the **Getchell Library** on the UNR campus, the **Dick-**

AREA CODE

I n December 1998, northern Nevada's telephone area code changed to 775. Only Clark County (the Las Vegas area) still uses the 702 area code.

inson Library on the UNLV campus, and the **State Library** in Carson City.

Money

A lot of people have found themselves suddenly broke and stranded somewhere in Nevada over the past 135 years. Of course, *you'll* never wind up in such an unenviable situation, but you might bump into someone who has. Here's how to help.

Personal checks are easy to cash in Nevada, provided you have a major credit card and a driver's license, or another valid form of photo ID. The cashier will instruct you to write a check to cash for up to the house limit, generally $200.

It's also a breeze to turn a credit card into cash. A form of ATM machine is found near every cashier cage in the state, though they work a little differently from your standard automated bank teller. Run your credit card through the slot and punch in how much cash you want. If the transaction is approved, a check is spit out from a special printer in the cage. Show your ID to a cashier, sign the check, and crisp cash magically appears. Well, not so magically. More like tragically. Consider the following. On top of the normal 12–18% interest you pay on the revolving charges, *plus* the normal cash-advance fee charged by the credit-card company, you *also* pay a special service charge of 10% or so for the cash. (This is split by the casino and the machine company.) In addition, your name and address are recorded by both the casino and machine company, and if the significance of that escapes you, Max Rubin explains it best. "You probably don't want your name on a mailing list," he writes in *Comp City,* "labeled 'Degenerate Gamblers Who Can't Control Themselves and Make Really Stupid Decisions About Money.'"

Another less-than-optimal alternative: pawn shops will hock your wedding ring or watch for less than half of what they're worth, charge a $5 transaction fee, and collect six percent interest a month (72% a year) until you buy it back.

If all else fails, get on the phone and try to find someone who cares enough about you to wire you some money, in Nevada, where you've somehow run out of your own. This can be accomplished for a reasonable fee through a bank's wire service, or for a little higher fee through Western Union.

Taxes

The sales tax varies from county to county, but falls somewhere between six and seven percent. Room taxes are higher, up to nine percent in downtown Las Vegas (now paying for the Fremont Street Experience). The entertainment tax on shows around the state totals 17%: seven percent sales tax and 10% entertainment tax. Check carefully what the tax will be on rental cars in Las Vegas. It can approach 21%: seven percent sales tax, seven percent use tax, and seven percent airport tax.

Area Codes and Time Zones

The area code for all of Nevada is 775, except for Clark County (the Las Vegas area), which is 702. For directory assistance, dial 775/555-1212 or 702/555-1212. Nevada is mostly on Pacific time, same as California, Oregon, and Washington. Note, however, that the border towns of Jackpot and Wendover keep their clocks on Mountain time, same as Idaho and Utah.

RENO AND WESTERN NEVADA

INTRODUCTION

In *Fear and Loathing in Las Vegas,* Hunter S. Thompson describes Reno as a "mom and pop store," compared to the megamall that is Las Vegas. In the last 40 years or so, Las Vegas has eclipsed Reno to the extent that when asked their impressions of Nevada, many people (especially those from the East) describe a vast desert wasteland, with the neon blaze of Glitter Gulch scorching a swath right through the middle of it. In their mental cartography, Las Vegas fills up the Nevada desert from border to border. At the very least, Las Vegas sits smack in the center of it, its capital and only city.

The fact is, Reno is the *original* Las Vegas. Las Vegas could never have become Las Vegas if Reno hadn't been Reno first. But Reno made a deliberate conscious decision *not to become* Las Vegas. While Las Vegas is arguably one of

the littlest big cities in the world, Reno is still, to those in the know, the Biggest Little City in the World.

The welcoming arch that spans Virginia Street in downtown Reno is a highly recognized civic symbol. Its attending slogan might today seem grandiose or antiquated to some, but when the arch was first installed, everybody knew that Reno could lay perfectly legitimate claim to the boast. Thus, to understand contemporary Reno, it's necessary to place its slogan in the proper historical perspective.

Reno began its life as a crude bridge across the capricious Truckee River and grew initially into a crossroads settlement for the Comstock Lode. The arrival of the transcontinental railroad gave Reno a brief bask in the local limelight; the arrival of the Virginia & Truckee Railroad from

Virginia City gave it a cut of the Comstock riches. For more than 30 years, the mainline ensured a steady flow of people, products, and progress, even after the Comstock finally played out. Even so, Reno remained a whistlestop, fighting river flooding, economic stagnation, and the day-to-day struggles of all northern Nevada railroad towns.

But then, just after the turn of the 20th century, Reno got "discovered"—as a divorce destination. Suddenly, the little outpost found itself at the center of a national controversy between social conscience and license.

On the one hand, rich and public figures or their wives graced Reno with their presence for six months while awaiting divorce decrees. On the other hand, it took another 15 years for Reno to fully embrace its growing national notoriety. But once it did, Reno wasted little time solidifying its celebrity as the country's sexiest town.

Millionaires, movie stars, socialites, and artists—unhappily married all—flocked to the Reno "clinic" to take the "cure"; throughout the nation, newspaper society pages covered them daily, rendering Reno a household word. The daily train became known as the Divorcée Special, the county courthouse as the Separator. The mayor of Reno himself set the record for the number of clients granted divorce decrees in one day. In addition, the political and financial power brokers all moved to Reno from the waning mining excitement of Tonopah and Goldfield in central Nevada. And to cap it off, a national exposition celebrating the completion of the transcontinental Victory and Lincoln highways was held in Reno, prompting the exultant residents to install an arch at the entrance to downtown with the proud slogan, "Biggest Little City in the World."

In 1927, the divorce residency requirement was reduced from six months to three, and in 1931 to a scandalous six weeks. Now, everyday people could afford a glamorous Reno divorce. That year, nearly 5,000 divorces were granted in Reno, roughly 20 every working day of the year. By then, however, the divorce trade had some competition not only from several other states, but also from little Las Vegas, the southern Nevada railroad town with aspirations to take on its big-sister city to the north.

Luckily for Reno, wide-open legal gambling and instant marriages quickly filled in the gap. Throughout the 1930s and '40s, the Smith family's national advertising campaign for Harold's Club and William Harrah's classy carpet joint kept Reno firmly in its familiar limelight. In addition, California's and Utah's "gin and syphilis" marriage restrictions (waiting periods and blood tests) triggered a boom of wartime weddings—which led to a miniboom of postwar divorces—in Reno.

By the mid-1950s, as hotels rose regularly along the new Las Vegas Strip, Reno had seen it all for more than half a century. City planners, officials, and downtown interests witnessed Las Vegas's unbridled growth (and evolving notoriety) and decided to slap a "redline" around the gambling district, content to allow Las Vegas to sustain the type of attention from which Reno was only recently recovering. While the new Nevada boomtown to the south experienced its adolescent growth pains, a mature Reno could sit back and observe from a safe distance, and concentrate on principles and values that had less to do with reputation or visitor volume and more to do with local quality of life.

By the late 1970s, however, Reno, by then a dowdy spinster, got a little jealous of its brazen still-young sibling, and officials removed the redline. A major casino boom ensued, accompanied by a substantial population increase throughout the '80s. But Reno couldn't shake a lingering ambivalence about growth, trying to protect itself from, and at the same time compete with, the Las Vegas urban situation. Reno has been attempting, over the past 20 years or so, to adopt an identity, a unifying design and marketing theme, that will remind potential visitors that Nevada consists of more than just Las Vegas and the desert.

But with its celebrated history of mining, divorce, gambling, and hospitality, its full slate of current events such as Balloon, Air, and Grand Prix races, rib and chili cook-offs, Hot August Nights and Harley-Davidson gatherings, and a surrounding wonderland of mountains, lakes, and desert, Reno would do well simply to remain what it is and always has been: the Biggest Little City in the World.

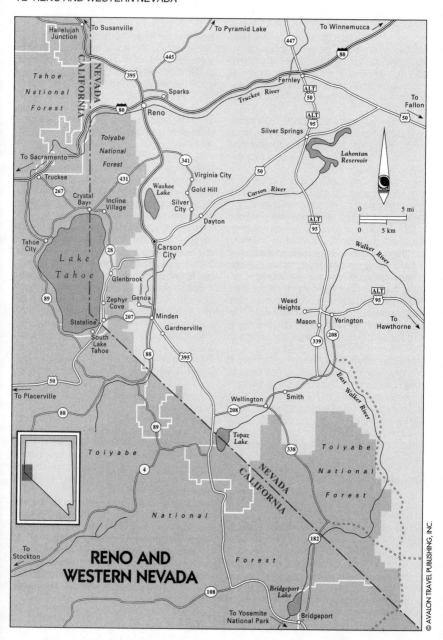

RENO AND
WESTERN NEVADA

HISTORY

Washo

It's estimated that upon contact with the first explorers from the east, 3,000 Washo Indians occupied a small territory from the Pine Nut Mountains east of Carson Valley to Lake Tahoe in the west and Truckee Meadows (where Reno and Sparks are today) to the north. Peaceful, purposeful, and private, these people disappeared into the desert and mountains when transients were in the neighborhood, so their numbers were greatly underestimated by the earliest white visitors. The Washo maintained a strong culture: loosely structured families that subsisted on fish from their own traditional sections of the Truckee River and Lake Tahoe, and pine nuts from their own groves in the forested mountains The technology for harvesting the food, especially the highly sophisticated woven-willow fish weirs, astonished even the mountain men who observed it. Small groups of families came together seasonally for rabbit or antelope drives and the entire tribe gathered on the shores of Lake Tahoe in the spring to fish and in the fall to harvest, and to partake in ceremonial, social, and athletic events.

The most famous Washo, and one of the most famous Nevada Indians, was Dat-So-La-Lee. Born in 1829, she began making baskets at a young age, using the traditional methods. She harvested the willows, then dried and cured them for a year. She dug the roots of black ferns and redbud for dyes. She used only her fingernails, teeth, and a piece of sharp rock (later broken glass) to perform the intricate weaving of the tough materials. Dat-So-La-Lee named and designed her baskets from Washo tradition and often took an entire year to complete a series. In her lifetime she created more than 250 works of art; it was said that her baskets were possessed of "perfect perspective." Her finest, known as "Migration," fetched $10,000 while she was still alive. Until she died at the age of 96 in 1925, Dat-So-La-Lee lived in Carson Valley, still making baskets with her hands and teeth, having achieved ultimate and long-lasting fame as the greatest basketmaker

NEVADA HISTORICAL SOCIETY, RENO

young Dat-So-La-Lee

in a society of great basketmakers. (Several are displayed at the Nevada State Museum in Carson City.)

The Bridge

John C. Frémont first saw and named Pyramid Lake in 1844, and followed directions given to him by the Pyramid Lake Paiute, neighbors of the Washo, through Truckee Meadows and over the Sierra via Carson Pass. Only five years later, emigrants by the hundreds were following this same trail over the Sierra, or others nearby; one passed through Truckee Meadows and up over the Sierra at Donner Summit (the route taken by the ill-fated Donner party). Ten years later, in the late 1850s, this route was so well traveled that there were several "crossings" over the Truckee River in Truckee Meadows. In 1859,

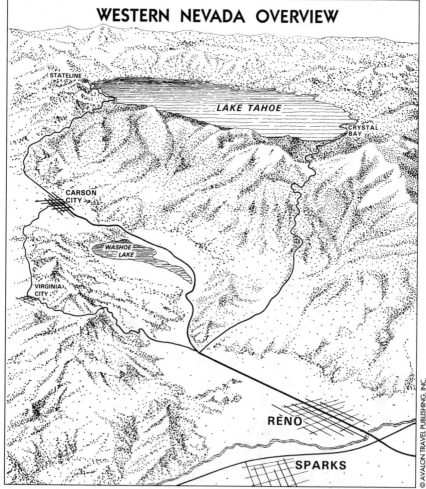

WESTERN NEVADA OVERVIEW

STATELINE

LAKE TAHOE

CRYSTAL BAY

CARSON CITY

WASHOE LAKE

VIRGINIA CITY

RENO

SPARKS

© AVALON TRAVEL PUBLISHING, INC.

NEVADA: THE BEGINNING

Here is where it all began, where Nevada became Nevada. This tiny parcel of the 36th state accounts for why and how it grew up to be what it is today. The earliest explorers, mountain men looking for furs and surveyors looking for rivers, knew this prime real estate on the western edge of the Great Desert and the eastern face of the Great Mountains. The first emigrants struggled out of the sand and sage and into the snow and cedar, following vague trails toward freedom, land, and shortly afterward, gold. Prospectors drifted east, back across the mountains, on their restless search for indications. And pioneers settled to mine the minerals, service the trails, and farm the lush valleys between the dry and the high.

The oldest towns in Nevada survive along this thin strip of the west-central state, thanks to the largest silver deposit ever unearthed, sudden statehood, and a frontier libertarianism that refuses to be tamed. These towns and their frontier ways still exist in spite of the crushing busts that inevitably followed the booms, the enormous difficulties of bringing society to such a vast, inhospitable, and lawless land, and the censure of the rest of the states for their immoralities. Only recently have the permissive policies that began in Virginia City and spread through Carson City to the rest of Nevada gained any measure of respectability in the eyes of the nation. A few generations of rugged individualists forged the desert, valleys, mountains, lakes, rivers, and minerals into a rough-and-ready civilization that remains the genetic essence of the most unusual state in the Union.

an enterprising man named Charles Fuller took the lay of the basin and selected the site of his own crossing to compete for the pioneer traffic. He invested $3,000 in a crude log bridge and toll booth, but he soon found that travelers preferred the more established crossings. In a little less than two years, a discouraged Fuller sold out to a 33-year-old New Yorker named Myron Lake.

Lake had a longer-range vision for the area and spent a financially marginal year or so of his own rebuilding the bridge and opening an inn. In 1862, Lake obtained a toll road franchise from the young Nevada Territorial Legislature

for Sierra Valley Road (now Virginia Street), which stretched in both directions from his bridge. Thanks to the boom at Virginia City, Fuller's site selection proved fortuitous, and a steady stream of travelers between California and the Comstock began filling Lake's pockets. He invested the profits in land, water rights, and commercial enterprises and by 1868 he owned most of what would soon become Reno; he also controlled a long stretch of the Truckee River, centered on his bridge and businesses at Lake's Crossing.

Meanwhile, the Central Pacific Railroad was conquering the Sierra, on its way to laying track through the rich river valley only 25 miles from Virginia City. Lake cut a deal with Charles Crocker, the construction superintendent. He donated 60 acres for a town site in return for a promise to install a passenger depot and warehouses, making the town a distribution center. In May 1868, 400 lots were auctioned; within a month more than 100 homes and businesses had been constructed. Railroad officials named the new town Reno, after Jesse L. Reno (an anglicized version of Renault), a Union general who was killed in the Civil War.

Boom and Bust

By 1870 Reno was big, brash, and bustling enough to wrest the Washoe County seat from Washoe City, a declining mill town 15 miles south in Washoe Valley. With the railroad supplying the goods daily, Reno's growing population superseded Washoe City's declining numbers, and the former won the special election by nearly 200 votes. In 1872, the Virginia & Truckee Railroad completed the connection from the mines in Virginia City to the mills in Carson City, then built a spur to the main line in Reno, further enhancing its crossroads status. Subsequently, the town really began to take shape, with brick buildings rising downtown, residential areas spreading outward, a large theater adding culture, and a new iron bridge across the Truckee.

Reno grew slowly during the Twenty-Year Depression between 1880 and 1900, but still it grew. In 1880, the population stood at an even 1,000; by 1900 4,500 people called Reno home. And this was during the same period when the state was dropping a whopping 35% of its total population as the mines played out, the boomtowns were abandoned, and the remaining residents fell on difficult times. The railroads ensured Reno's survival, if not prosperity; "the tough little town on the Truckee" certainly took its fair share of abuse. A large downtown fire kicked things off in 1879. Vigilante groups imposed their own brand of frontier justice. Anti-Chinese sentiments and policies escalated. Several killing-cold winters wiped out the majority of open-range cattle. And the omnipotence of the Central Pacific continued to manifest itself in less than positive ways. In fact, the Californians who had owned most of the Comstock Lode and ran the railroads treated Nevada as little better than a colony.

Not all the news was bad, though. The university relocated to Reno from Elko in 1886. As the population base inexorably expanded, infrastructure improvements were resolutely carried out. Residents were noted for their fierce civic pride, born of perseverance and adversity. Still, Reno struggled out of the 19th century along with the rest of Nevada—impoverished, outpaced by California, and persisting in a pioneer attitude that, though stagnant, ironically helped to usher in the 20th century.

The New Boom

The silver strike at Tonopah, the gold discoveries at Goldfield, Rhyolite, Manhattan, and elsewhere, and the big copper find at Ely brought miners, money, and upward mobility to Nevada starting right after the turn of the century. In addition, the Truckee and Carson Irrigation Project, the first federally funded reclamation program in the country, opened up land east of Reno for agriculture and settlement. Electricity arrived at the same time. The Interstate Commerce Commission began to regulate the railroad, gradually ending its stranglehold on rates and policy. And Reno began to gain a measure of national notoriety as the biggest little city in rowdy and libertine Nevada, which sponsored easy divorces and prize fights. The first "Fight of the Century" took place in Reno in 1910 between Jack Johnson and Jim Jeffries, attracting 10,000 spectators, national press coverage, and the seed of a tourist industry. Meanwhile, prostitution within Reno's Lake Street red-light district, along with abundant back-room gambling on Reno's famous Douglas Alley, continued serving the local miners, cowboys, ranchers,

railroad workers, city slickers, and train travelers. By 1910, Reno's population had more than doubled since the turn of the century to nearly 10,000. And its reputation kept pace.

To Reform or Not to Reform

The mushrooming population also brought a growing desire for respectability for Reno, and the next decade witnessed a backlash against the town's permissiveness. The country's moral majority of that time were known as Progressives. Catalyzed by women's suffrage, Progressives advocated a repressive platform of Prohibition, difficult divorce, and outlawed gambling, prize-fighting, and prostitution. The moral vacillation on the western frontier was further polarized by the imperative of sacrifice brought about by WW I. In response, Nevada increased its divorce residency requirements from six to 12 months, pushed gambling deeper underground, and even banned alcohol sale and consumption in 1918, two years before national Prohibition.

But the Roaring '20s, of course, were just around the corner, and a power struggle for the conscience of Reno erupted during the 1923 mayoral campaign. George Wingfield, who had gained his fame and fortune 20 years earlier at Goldfield and was now the most powerful behind-the-scenes mover and shaker in Nevada politics, supported E.E. Roberts, whose cam-

Fortunes changed hands over the course of a good cigar.

NEVADA COMMISSION ON TOURISM

paign theme was that "protecting people from the weaknesses of their own characters was bad for business." Roberts walked away with the election, and during his two and a half terms as mayor openly refused to enforce laws in "areas of personal choice": gambling, drinking, commercial copulating, divorcing, etc. Reno became the center of a new Wild West, with Wingfield and his cronies, especially local gangsters James McKay and William Graham, operating the backroom gambling dens, the Stockade cribs, and speakeasies. They also laundered eastern Mafia money and protected hot mobsters such as Baby-Face Nelson, and were rumored to murder their adversaries.

Roberts presided over Reno's increasing infamy as Sin Central for the country, and the state legislators followed suit, reducing divorce residency requirements from 12 months back to six, then three. When California initiated a three-day waiting period for marriage in 1927, Nevada's *no*-waiting marriages made Reno not only the divorce but also the marriage capital. The completion of the Victory Highway over the Sierra between Sacramento and Reno in 1925 and the first scheduled airline service in 1927 made the tough little town on the Truckee more accessible than ever.

1931

The crash of '29 and the terrible three-year drought it preceded rang the death knell for Wingfield's empire, as well as northern Nevada's ranchers and livestock and the state and national economies. The legislature called one more time on Nevada's old standby revenue producers. It reduced divorce residency requirements to an unheard-of and scandalous six weeks and sanctioned casino gambling once and for all. Ironically, legalizing gambling had as little impact as banning it had had, and its effect on Reno's economy was negligible for several years. But the divorce trade exploded, nearly doubling from 3,000 divorces in 1930 to roughly 5,000 one year later; the average court time required for a dissolution fell to no more than five automatic minutes. Celebrities continued to obtain highly publicized dissolutions. George Wingfield's bitter adversary from Tonopah days, Pat McCarran, entered the U.S. Senate and helped attract New Deal work projects that improved Reno's infrastructure.

Then, in the mid-'30s, a carnival veteran named Raymond "Pappy" Smith came to town and promptly made a clean sweep of the old back-alley dark-room style of gambling. With his sons Harold and Raymond Jr., he opened Harold's Club. The casino front doors swung right into the daylight of Virginia Street. He spruced up the decor, sent the cheaters, hookers, and drunks down the road, and launched a nationwide campaign advertising Nevada casinos as good clean fun. William Harrah further improved on the Smiths' innovations. By the end of WW II, Reno's population had swelled to almost 30,000, the divorce and marriage industries continued to boom, and tourists swarmed into town from California and around the country to partake of the newly respectable casino games. Reno had finally managed to unify all its disparate elements into a single attractive package.

Modern Times

Meanwhile, Hoover Dam, Bugsy Siegel, and the military were turning Las Vegas into the world's greatest boomtown. The Reno City Council observed the Las Vegas phenomenon and in 1947 passed redline legislation that prevented the spread of casinos beyond the downtown core. Warehousing, light industry, the university, Lake Tahoe recreation, and general tourism helped diversify Reno's economy. The redline lasted 25 years till the early '70s, and then gambling really took off, culminating in the construction of the Las Vegas–like MGM Grand (now the Reno Hilton) in 1978—$150 million, 26 stories, 2,000 rooms. Reno's downtown skyline also changed dramatically in 1978, known as the Year of the Crane, with seven new hotels opening, only three of them on Virginia Street. By 1980 Reno's population had crested the 100,000 milestone.

As of 1999, upwards of 177,000 people were living in the city of Reno, a whopping increase of 6.6% over just the year before, and almost 324,000 were living in Washoe County. Growth issues facing Truckee Meadows in the late '90s and early 2000s center on water, housing, pollution, local wetland preservation, further economic diversification, and pumping up visitor volume.

Two other hot-potato issues face Reno as this edition is being prepared. The first is co-existing with the railroad. In Sept. 1996, the Union Pacific and Southern Pacific railroads merged, the local result being that the length and number of trains running through downtown increased. The trains, which run above ground right through the heart of Reno, block traffic and create an objectionable noise factor for local hotels, businesses and residents. Some local officials want the UP to replace the surface track with a below-ground, open-trench trainway nearly two miles long, at a cost of $185 million. The UP says it can contribute $35 million, but that still leaves a lot of money for the city to come up with—a controversial issue, as city planners and committees argue about whether the money should be spent on this, as well as whether or not an open trench is a desirable or even viable option. A feasibility study for the open trench idea was being done in 2000, and it was looking like a trench might be unfeasible due to the presence of groundwater at a certain depth, what with the Truckee River being right there. Another suggestion is that the railway tracks could be re-routed outside of town, to bypass the city, but this option would be even more expensive. At this writing, in autumn of 2000, the railroad had been a controversial issue in Reno for four years and was no nearer to being resolved than it was at the beginning, and it was

a hot issue among candidates for city office in the November 2000 election.

The second issue centers around the renovation of downtown. The latest major wave of improvements to the Reno core kicked off in 1995 with the opening of the $50 million National Bowling Stadium, the only one of its kind in the country; it's strictly for the big national tournaments, which deliver up to 100,000 bowlers, men and women, to Reno over six-month periods. Shortly after the Bowling Stadium debuted, the Silver Legacy opened a block away, downtown's first megaresort, and the first major hotel-casino to be built in Reno in nearly 15 years. The city is now in the process of redeveloping the riverfront. After years of indecision, acrimonious debate, and a few failed initiatives as to how to "clean up" the aging core, the old Mapes Hotel, a beloved historic landmark on Virginia St. at the Truckee River was demolished and removed, and a 12-theater cinema and dining-retail complex have now been built along the Truckee, much to the consternation of a large and vocal group of dissenters, who'd rather see less commercial building and more "open space." But after having just moved back to Reno after living in Las Vegas for three years, I'm happy so long as Reno refrains from adopting the southern Nevada style of cleaning up the aging joints: imploding the whole thing and starting from scratch.

SIGHTS

ORIENTATION

The Core

The Truckee River runs west to east right through the heart of downtown Reno. First St. parallels the Tahoe-to-Pyramid waterway as it flows under Virginia Street. The intersection of 1st and Virginia, roughly where Myron Lake had his bridge and inn, is the "00" point for Reno's numbering system. Everything east and west of Virginia St. and north and south of 1st St. is labeled such. The higher the number, the farther away from downtown. The "downtown core" is a five-block stretch of N. Virginia between 2nd and 6th streets. Interstate 80 cuts an east-west swath a block

north of there, separating high-rise downtown from the mostly low-rise buildings of the University of Nevada-Reno campus on N. Virginia, which sits on a bluff overlooking downtown.

Between 2nd and 6th streets are souvenir shops, pawn shops, clothing and jewelry stores, old residence hotels, the famous Reno Arch, and 10 hotel-casinos, boasting 4,000 rooms, a score of restaurants, hundreds of gambling tables, and thousands of slot machines. Countless hordes of hopefuls disappear through the yawning entrances. Inside, they gamble, drink, and generally forget about the world. Outside though, the world awaits. Be careful when visiting downtown Reno. The sidewalks and thoroughfares are narrow and crowded. Often pedestrians stagger out of dim or flashy casinos

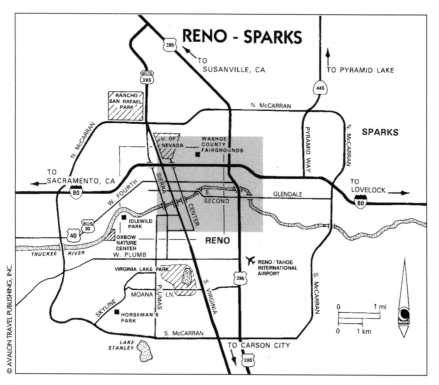

RENO - SPARKS

TO SUSANVILLE, CA

TO PYRAMID LAKE

RANCHO SAN RAFAEL PARK

N. McCARRAN

SPARKS

U. OF NEVADA

WASHOE COUNTY FAIRGROUNDS

TO SACRAMENTO, CA

W. FOURTH

GLENDALE

TO LOVELOCK

E. SECOND

IDLEWILD PARK

OXBOW NATURE CENTER

TRUCKEE RIVER

W. PLUMB

RENO

RENO / TAHOE INTERNATIONAL AIRPORT

VIRGINIA LAKE PARK

MOANA LN.

HORSEMAN'S PARK

S. McCARRAN

S. VIRGINIA

S. McCARRAN

LAKE STANLEY

TO CARSON CITY

0   1 mi
0   1 km

© AVALON TRAVEL PUBLISHING, INC.

into the bright day (or night), still in the grips of casinility, and suddenly they're in the middle of the street. More than a few people perambulate in a casino or alcohol daze. Many drivers are from out of town and don't know where they're going. Walking or driving—stay on your toes.

Truckee Meadows

US 395 drifts down from California to the northwest; several miles north of the college N. Virginia St. branches off the freeway to become Business 395. From there, the freeway turns due south at N. McCarran Blvd. two miles east of downtown (near the Reno-Sparks boundary), bypasses the business district, and reconnects with S. Virginia St. near the Mt. Rose-Virginia City intersection roughly eight miles south of downtown. Thus, US and Business 395 make a banana-shaped oblong around Reno's high-density center.

McCarran Blvd. surrounds the suburbs, making a complete 23-mile loop around Reno-Sparks. In fact, a 45-minute drive on McCarran Blvd. is an enjoyable way to get instantly oriented to the different faces of Truckee Meadows: mountains, desert, river, industry, commerce, and suburbs. There are some superb views of downtown with a variety of backdrops, and the fastest growing residential areas in Reno-Sparks are along McCarran. Since you'll be covering the compass, it's advisable to do this in midday; otherwise you'll have the sun in your eyes at one or the other end.

From downtown, head north on N. Virginia, pass the college, and take a left (west) on McCarran. You drive right by the big white-washed "N" for Nevada, maintained by UNR students, on Peavine Mountain (elev. 8,266 feet), northernmost peak of the Carson Range of the Sierra

Nevada; the Basque Monument of Rancho San Rafael Park provides a stark green contrast. From there you're into the desert—sand, sage, hills—continuing west before turning to the south and entering the newest expansion zone of Reno. The western subdivisions are the fastest growing neighborhoods in Truckee Meadows, having expanded 100% in the last 10 years. The high Sierra are close by to the west, and 4th St., old US 40, cuts between Mt. Rose on the left and the Peavine drainage on the right. The developments continue on the other side of the Truckee River, where sprawling new suburbs have taken over most of the old Caughlin Ranch.

When you cross Mayberry St., you're on the newest section of McCarran, opened in 1990. On the other side of Plumb Ln. are the southwestern foothills of Reno. At the summit is Caughlin Crest and the southern edge of the one-time Caughlin Ranch, which is now one of the largest and most expensive subdivisions in Truckee Meadows.

There, the road twists and turns down the hills to south Reno, through the ritzy Lakeridge subdivision. At the bottom of the hill, back in the basin, you go under US 395, past Virginia St., and between Smithridge Plaza and Meadowood Mall in the big shopping district of south Reno. Next up is Longley Lane; to the right (south) about a mile is Double Diamond Ranch, site of an 1,800-acre development that will eventually consist of nearly 5,000 residential units and a 200-acre golf course, the largest single housing project ever proposed in the Reno area. Just north of Double Diamond is the site of the industrial park where Lockheed is building a 400-acre research facility.

Just before Mira Loma Park you turn north. Beyond the park are most of the last wide-open spaces within the McCarran loop. Cows graze along the flat fields, backdropped by the rugged line of the Virginia Range to the east. A bit north you come to the University of Nevada-Reno's Main Agricultural Experimental Station, with green and white farm buildings, stables, barns, silos, and stock pens sandwiched between Clean Water Dr. and the Truckee River.

Cross the Truckee River and enter Sparks proper. The big white-washed "S" rests on a foothill to the east. The transition from the pastoral to the industrial is palpable. Immediately you're into Sparks's freeport zone, with its sprawling warehouses and truck yards; the overpass provides a wide view of railroad tracks, fuel tanks, and entrepôts. After passing under I-80 you're into a world of truck stops and shopping centers, then the fast-growing northeast Sparks residential area.

Just before butting up against the northern hills, McCarran Blvd. swings west. Beyond Pyramid Way, you wind up into the hills, crest a rise, and get one of the best views of downtown Reno, backdropped by the stunning Sierra. In a few miles, you're back to the corner of N. Virginia and McCarran, where you started.

DOWNTOWN

Reno-vation

The revitalization of downtown hasn't only been about the big-ticket national Bowling Stadium and Silver Legacy and Hampton Inn. Smaller piecemeal development is noticeable: the **River Walk** was completed in 1991 at a cost of $7.7 million and has been extended to two full blocks; the **Wingfield Park Amphitheater** has been in place since 1992; the **Parking Gallery** on Sierra St. across from the Riverboat, providing 640 spaces and 20,000 square feet of new retail space, was completed in summer 1993; the **Eldorado parking garage** went up in 1994, a 10-story structure with 700 parking spaces and a skywalk to the restaurant level of the hotel; the financial district has been given a half-million-dollar facelift, with cobblestone sidewalks, trees, and benches; and the **Circus Circus** and **Cal-Neva** parking garages were also built in the last few years, as was the **Century 12** cinema, facing the Truckee River at Sierra St. The **Lear Theater**, on the corner of First and Ralston Streets, is being renovated, and promises to be a fine venue for theater and other performances.

Still, the Reno core lacks a unifying characteristic, such as downtown Las Vegas's Fremont Street Experience, or even downtown Sparks's Victorian Square.

Riverfront Plaza

The $7.7 million two-tiered Raymond I. Smith Truckee River Walk, on the river side of the Riverside, was completed in July 1991. The plaza beautifies a city block between the Virginia and Sierra Street bridges with an attractive and low-maintenance granite deck, benches, shelters, and bandshell. Arts and crafts shows, performing groups, and special events, such as the popular Celebrate the River festival, are held on the plaza. In 1992, the River Walk was extended one block west toward Wingfield Park on Island Avenue.

Truckee River Bridges
The Virginia Street bridge is only eight feet upstream from where hapless Charles Fuller built his original log structure in 1859. Reno founder Myron Lake bought the span in 1861, completely rebuilt it, and collected his tolls for 10 years, until his license expired (and wasn't renewed) in 1871. In 1877 the county replaced the wood with iron, matching the railroad bridge just downriver. In 1905, the reinforced concrete bridge standing today (146 feet by 56 feet) was constructed. Now 90 years old, its design and strength have enabled it to survive numerous floods, including the horrendous flood of January 1997, which inundated 20 blocks of downtown Reno with river water.

The Center Street bridge, one block east, however, was poorly constructed when it went up

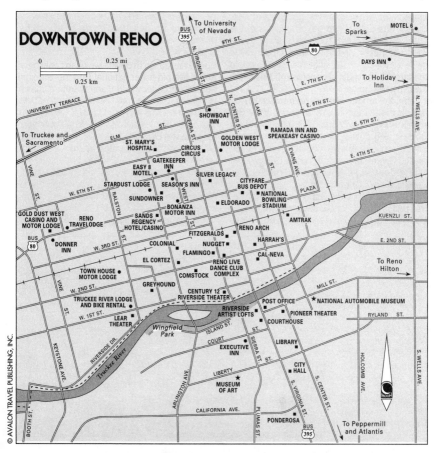

DOWNTOWN RENO

To University of Nevada
BUS 395
9TH ST.
To Sparks
MOTEL 6
80
DAYS INN
To Holiday Inn
0   0.25 mi
0   0.25 km
UNIVERSITY TERRACE
E. 7TH ST.
E. 6TH ST.
E. 5TH ST.
N. WELLS AVE.
To Truckee and Sacramento
ELM ST.
SHOWBOAT INN
GOLDEN WEST MOTOR LODGE
RAMADA INN AND SPEAKEASY CASINO
E. 4TH ST.
ST. MARY'S HOSPITAL
CIRCUS CIRCUS
GATEKEEPER INN
EASY 8 MOTEL
SILVER LEGACY
CITYFARE BUS DEPOT
PLAZA
STARDUST LODGE
SEASON'S INN
ELDORADO
NATIONAL BOWLING STADIUM
AMTRAK
KUENZLI ST.
SUNDOWNER
BONANZA MOTOR INN
SANDS
RENO REGENCY HOTEL/CASINO
RENO TRAVELODGE
FITZGERALDS
RENO ARCH
E. 2ND ST.
GOLD DUST WEST CASINO AND MOTOR LODGE
BUS 80
DONNER INN
W. 3RD ST.
COLONIAL
NUGGET
HARRAH'S
CAL-NEVA
To Reno Hilton
EL CORTEZ
FLAMINGO
RENO LIVE DANCE CLUB
TOWN HOUSE MOTOR LODGE
COMSTOCK
COMPLEX
GREYHOUND
MILL ST.
W. 2ND ST.
CENTURY 12
RIVERSIDE THEATER
POST OFFICE
NATIONAL AUTOMOBILE MUSEUM
TRUCKEE RIVER LODGE AND BIKE RENTAL
W. 1ST ST.
RIVERSIDE ARTIST LOFTS
PIONEER THEATER
COURTHOUSE
RYLAND ST.
LEAR THEATER
Wingfield Park
ISLAND ST.
LIBRARY
RIVERSIDE DR.
Truckee River
COURT
EXECUTIVE INN
CITY HALL
HOLCOMB AVE.
S. WELLS AVE.
KEYSTONE AVE.
LIBERTY
MUSEUM OF ART
Moon
BOOTH ST.
CALIFORNIA AVE.
PONDEROSA
BUS 395
To Peppermill and Atlantis

in 1926. In 1994 it was in such bad shape that the sidewalks were closed. Reconstruction commenced in fall 1996, but was interrupted by the flood. The bridge was finally completed, to the tune of $3.1 million, in May 1998.

Riverside Artist Lofts

The Riverside Artist Lofts, on the corner of Virginia and Mill Streets, on the south bank of the Truckee River, occupies the historic building that used to be the Riverside Hotel.

This is the site of the original inn at Lake's Crossing, built by Myron Lake in the early 1860s. In 1880, Lake sold the Lake House to his son-in-law, State Senator William Thompson, who renamed it the Riverside; he was the first of two dozen owners of the hotel over the next 100 years. Five years later Thompson sold it to Harry Gosse, who owned it for 40 years, until George Wingfield acquired it in 1925. The present 188-room building was completed in 1927, and remained the toniest Reno hotel into the 1970s. During the Wingfield era its Old Corner Bar was the center of almost as much political intrigue and power as the Capitol in Carson City. During Reno's heyday as Divorce Capital, the Riverside acted, in David Toll's words, "like a passenger liner on a perpetual six-week cruise."

In fact, in 1927 Wingfield engineered the secret passage (the whole discussion and vote took place at 3 A.M.) of a bill through both houses of the legislature that reduced the divorce residency requirement from six to three months to coincide with the grand reopening of his Riverside Hotel. Governor Fred Balzac signed it into law at 8 the following morning and Nevadans awoke to the news that the new divorce requirements were a fait accompli.

The Riverside was expanded in 1950. Pick Hobson bought the hotel in 1980 and made a go of it for seven years, till it closed in November 1987. Two years later, Peter Eng, a Vancouver hotel owner and former history professor at the University of Hong Kong, bought the building. Bob Stupak tried to buy it in 1996, but was rebuffed. In 1997, the 1950 portion succumbed to the wrecker's ball. The historic portion has been remodeled and is scheduled to reopen as the Riverside Artist Lofts by the time this book goes to press.

Reno Arch

Reno's main Arch, which spans Virginia St. at 3rd between Fitzgerald's and Harold's, is one of the four most famous arches in the U.S. (along with St. Louis's, Devil's, and McDonald's). Its slogan, "The Biggest Little City in the World," is arguably the most recognized in the country. The first arch was erected in 1926 to celebrate the completion of the transcontinental Victory and Lincoln highways. It cost $5,500 and read "Reno Transcontinental Highway Exposition." Afterwards, when it was decided to leave the arch standing over N. Virginia St. downtown, Mayor

Reno from the northeast

JOHN ELK III

RENO'S CLIMATE

Reno reflects the Great Basin's general climate conditions: cool, semi-arid, continental. It may not feel like it on a 95-degree day in July or an 18-degree night in January, but Reno's weather is often referred to as "mild." The average annual high temperature is 67 degrees, the low 32, with 51 days reaching above 90 degrees and nine days dropping below 32 degrees. The sun shines proudly 306 days a year (80%), with 47 days of measurable precipitation. Lying right in the middle of the Sierra Nevada rainshadow, Reno receives only seven yearly inches (half of it snow), and that's in a normal year. During much of the 1990's, western Nevada received less than half its expected precipitation. In a good year, Mt. Rose, only 20 miles south (and 5,000 feet higher), gets 200–300 inches of snow. The Sierra snowpack is critical to western Nevada's water supply: most snowmelt in the Tahoe basin runs off into Lake Tahoe, source of the Truckee River, total source of the water for the Reno-Sparks area and Pyramid Lake fisheries, and partial source for Fernley and Fallon farmers, and Stillwater Indians and wildlife refuge.

The winds come primarily from the north in the winter, from the south and southwest in the summer. The coldest and wettest month is January, with an average high of 45 degrees and an average low of 20. July and August are the hottest, driest months, with average highs around 90 degrees; average lows around 50 at night, however, make the nights not only bearable, but enjoyable. During these months humidity hovers around 20%. John Townley, in his *Tough Little Town on the Truckee: Reno,* comments that in the summer, "the valley's consumption of hand-lotion is second only to beer."

In the summer, occasional hot storms blow in from the north, bringing major cloudbursts and the real threat of flash floods. But the climate's harshest element is the wind, the famous Washoe Zephyrs which, funneling through Truckee Canyon, can reach 100 mph in April and May, and 70 mph anytime throughout the rest of the year. Yet the Zephyrs are more often gentle, gusty at worst, and are locally appreciated for blowing away the smog inversions that settle over the Meadows during the occasional calm air.

Here's a high/low temperature chart for the Reno-Sparks-Carson City-Washoe Valley area:

	High	Low
January	46°	16°
February	51°	22°
March	56°	25°
April	65°	30°
May	73°	35°
June	80°	40°
July	91°	46°
August	90°	44°
September	83°	38°
October	71°	30°
November	57°	22°
December	48°	18°

Roberts challenged Renoites to create a permanent slogan. The winning slogan was lifted from the ad campaign for the 1910 Jim Jeffries-Jack Johnson prizefight in Reno, which was "Biggest Little City on the Map." The sign consisted of nearly 1,000 bulbs and cost $30 a month to operate, which proved too rich for the Depression budget, so it was shut off in 1932. A great hue and cry erupted over the cost-saving measure, and downtown businessmen paid the electric bill to keep the arch lit for the duration.

A new improved arch was erected in 1934, reinforced with steel and lit with neon, which read, simply, "RENO." This change was again universally condemned and in 1936 the old slogan was returned to the arch (that Arch now stands outside the National Automobile Museum at Lake and Mill streets). The next time a flunky tried to monkey with the archway was in 1956, when Mayor Ken Harris proposed to change the slogan; it nearly cost him his job.

In 1963, a new arch was installed in preparation for Nevada's centennial. The fourth and current arch was unveiled in front of a jam-packed Virginia Street crowd in August 1987. It was designed by Charles Barnard of Ad Art Company, Stockton, California, who is also responsible for the sizzling light show outside the Stardust Hotel in Las Vegas. Young Electric Sign Company (YESCO) built the arch for $99,000, charging the city for the materials only. It uses 800 feet of tubing and 1,600 light bulbs.

National Bowling Stadium

This $35 million stadium, the only one of its kind anywhere, has made Reno the Bowling Capital of the World. It features 80 lanes, a 100-seat geodesic Omnimax theater (in the shape of a bowling ball), a '50s-style diner and dance hall, and the downtown visitor center. Ten major bowling tournaments sponsored by the American Bowling Congress and the Women's International Bowling Congress are already contracted to be held in Reno over the next 15 years, pumping at least $1 billion into the local economy. Ironically, Reno's main competition for bowlers comes from Las Vegas, where there are well over 400 lanes, most of which are spread among five casino-hotels. The National Bowling Stadium is at 300 N. Center St., 775/334-2600.

Reno-Tahoe Gaming Academy

This dealer and gambling school, 1313 S. Virginia St., 775/329-5665, is the oldest dealer school in the USA. The Academy offers classes for careers in the pit: 21, craps, mini-baccarat, roulette, poker and pai-gow poker, plus pit supervisor and bartender courses. The Academy offers 30 different program combinations, with classes all year round; programs of study can last anywhere from two weeks to six months, and cost anywhere from $600 to $5000, depending which games and skills are chosen. Job placement assistance and some financial assistance are available. The student dealers receive intensive training, and practice against each other, until they are proficient enough to assume "precasino break-in status" by dealing to tourists and visitors who pay $15 for a 90-minute lesson in the game or games of their choice in a behind-the-scenes gaming tour. You probably can't *learn* all the fine points of either blackjack, craps, roulette, pai-gow, etc., in an hour and a half, but if you read up a little beforehand (see "Booklist" for gambling titles that your local library should stock, or see the Gambler's Bookstore under "For First-Timers" under "Gambling" in the On the Road chapter), you can get over your first-time

shyness about the tables at this mostly realistic (for the players *and* the dealers) setting. The tour of the Academy includes a fine display of antique gaming equipment and memorabilia, some of it available for sale. The classes and the gaming tour are by appointment only.

Newlands Heights

Much of the great wealth from the Tonopah and Goldfield mines began to show up in Reno around 1908, as speculators, lawyers, bankers, physicians, merchants, and laborers migrated from the mining frontier back to civilization. The richest of them gravitated to a bluff above the Truckee River a short walk from downtown Reno. Frederic DeLongchamps, Nevada's most famous architect, designed many of the homes in this historic district, which you can reach by heading south on Sierra St., crossing the river, and taking a right on Court Street.

The house on the corner of Arlington, **247 Court,** is one of the oldest in the district, built in 1907 for the Frisch family. Roy Frisch was a cashier in George Wingfield's bank who agreed to testify against bad guys Graham and McKay in their prosecution for federal mail fraud. Frisch disappeared before the trial and was never seen again. The houses at 401, 421, 435, 457, 491, and 514 Court are all more than 80 years old. The **Hawkins house** at 549 Court, built in 1911 in the Georgian style, is at the center of a recent neighborhood controversy: the residents don't want it converted into offices, which the City Council has allowed, arguing that offices are less threatening than apartments or tearing the building down.

The house at **617 Court,** completed in 1890, was once the Queen Anne office of Francis Newlands, the powerful U.S. senator from Nevada at the turn of the century; **7 Elm Ct.** was the Newlands' house. Number **4 Elm Ct.** was built by DeLongchamps personally as a honeymoon cottage.

Follow Lee and Ridge streets around to California and take a right. Number **631 California** was George Nixon's house, built in 1906 for his move to Reno from Winnemucca. The house at **825 California** was designed by DeLongchamps for Mrs. William Johnson, Newlands' daughter and the granddaughter of William Sharon, Comstock mogul and U.S. Senator.

Downtown Parks

Three blocks west of Virginia St. along the Truckee River is **Wingfield Park,** on an island in the middle of a bulge in the river, connected to the mainland by walking bridges. The amphitheater there was completed in June 1992 at a cost of $810,000. Some concert, comedy, or gathering occurs here nearly every day in the summer, always free. In winter, the city installs an 85- by 200-foot outdoor ice skating rink—sometimes here, opposite the amphitheater, and sometimes a bit further downriver at Idlewild Park.

Surrounding the island on both riverbanks is **Riverside Park,** three acres of grass, with a playground and tennis and basketball courts. It's a good place to stroll from downtown day or night to clear your head of all the mind games and guessing games of gaming: whether or not to double down on 11 against a dealer's ace, how many Kelly units to bet with the count at plus five, whether to place or buy the six and eight, if the Giants can really beat the 49ers, and on and on and on.

Continue west along the north side of the river (or motor out Riverside Dr. and follow the signs) to **Idlewild Park.** Just under a mile from downtown, this park, originally developed for the Transcontinental Highway Exposition in 1927, is one of the oldest and prettiest city parks in the state. It boasts a large duck pond and outdoor swimming pool, picnic pavilions, baseball fields, volleyball courts, a playground, stately old trees, a rose garden, and Peter Toth's Nevada sculpture, *53rd Whispering Giant,* looking down from 30 feet to whisper something important (and different) into every visitor's ear. The kiddie amusement park opens daily at 11 A.M. May through Labor Day, weekends and holidays (weather permitting) the rest of the year. The rides are perfect for kids ages two to around seven; tickets go for 70 cents apiece (or 20 for $12). The merry-go-round, kiddie choo-choo, airplane, and octopus charge one ticket, while the roller-coaster and tilt-a-whirl charge two. It's 50 cents for popcorn to feed the duckies.

VW Beetle

One of the most unusual sights in Reno is an 18-foot tall and 30-foot wide horror-movie spider made out of a Volkswagen body and irrigation pipe. It was created by artist David Fambrough in 1978 as "fun art," and has occupied a number of locations around town. In 1994, it settled atop the six-story pink fire building just east of the Wells Street bridge near 6th Street and has been there ever since.

MUSEUMS

National Automobile Museum

In the first edition of this book I wrote, "Unless you're *seriously* into automotive history and technology, this collection of roughly 200 of the most amazing cars in the world can give you an awesome case of tired blood. If your great American love affair is *not* with the automobile, you might as well be walking through a collection of the 200 most amazing . . . printing presses, oil burners, or vacuum cleaners." This is still true. But what a difference a $10 million dream building in downtown Reno can make over a concrete-slab warehouse in Sparks, where the collection used to be housed.

The downtown museum, opened in November 1989, is about as evocative of automotives as a 100,000-square-foot building could ever be. The curvaceous design has been described as "latter-day Modern, with metallic skin colored heather-fire mist set off with chrome bands," which "might bring to mind an airflow Chrysler or a '50s dream car." And the tinted glass all around adds considerably to the effect.

Inside it's no less imaginative. The wide hallways or "streets" are interesting sets suggestive of the period encompassed by each of four galleries. The first gallery starts with the one-of-a-kind 1890 Philion and displays a Locomobile, Rolls, Cadillacs, and winds up with the 1913 Stutz. The second contains cars from 1914 to 1931, including one of the first station wagons (a sign explains the etymology of the term), plus two working cutaway engines. The third has the wildest vehicles, from the 1934 Dymaxion and 1938 Phantom Corsair to the 1954 Buick, including an unusual Airomobile, and what's probably the classiest car in the collection: a 1936 Mercedes. Gallery four has the familiar Mustangs and Chevys, along with unfamiliar European models, and some speed demons such as the Flying Caduceus, Jerrari, and 1962 Maserati (which inspired Joe Walsh's lyric "My

Maserati does one-eighty-five/I lost my license, now I don't drive"). Of course, no collection would be complete without a '59 Edsel or one of Elvis's Cadillacs.

The collection is just a small percentage of the 1,000 or so cars amassed by the late William F. Harrah. After Harrah died and his company was sold, it auctioned off nearly 75% of the cars, many of which were bought by Ralph Engelstad, owner of the Imperial Palace in Las Vegas, and displayed in the Auto Collection there. The remainder were donated to the museum foundation.

A 22-minute multimedia presentation is shown in the museum theater, in which cars roll on and off the screen (how do they *do* that?!), and two banks of 12 video screens present dazzling, though hard-to-see, effects.

Wheels Cafe is in a separate building, with outdoor seating right on the river's edge. You can partake of hot dogs, burgers, soup and salad, and drinks.

The gift shop has a great stock of auto-related paraphernalia, including models, wooden toys, books, T-shirts, knickknacks, car cups, chocolate cars, road signs, cards, stationery, magazines, and trucks. You've heard of car phones, but check out the phone cars.

The museum, 10 S. Lake St at the corner of Mill and Lake streets, 775/333-9300, is open Mon.–Sat. 9:30 A.M.–5:30 P.M., Sunday 10 A.M.–4 P.M. Admission is $7.50 adults, $6.50 seniors, $2.50 ages 6–18, under 5 free. Look for dollar-off coupons on the back of the museum brochure, available at the visitor center in the National Bowling Stadium.

Nevada Museum of Art

For more than 10 years, this museum occupied the Hawkins House, built on Court St. by Nevada banking pioneer Prince Hawkins. His family lived there until the Art Society bought it in 1978. But in early 1990, the museum (the only state-operated museum for fine art) opened in its new, spacious, and attractive building at 160 W. Liberty St., next to the Porsche Building two blocks west of Virginia, 775/329-3333, Tues.–Fri. 10 A.M.–4 P.M. (Thursday till 7), Saturday and Sunday noon to 4, admission $5 adult, $3 seniors and students. Admission is free on Fridays.

Inside, the floors and ceiling are stark black,

and the walls are bright white. The effect nicely highlights the colorful paintings and photographs in the three galleries. The front two house the changing exhibits; the back gallery has the permanent collection.

The museum store sells books, posters, prints, art magnets, jewelry, cards, pottery, T-shirts, and some sculpture.

Time and Space

The **Nevada State Historical Society Museum** at the north end of the UNR campus at 1650 N. Virginia St., 775/688-1190, is open Mon.–Sat., 10 A.M.–5 P.M. Admission is $2 for ages 18 and over, free for those under 18. This is one of the best historical museums in the state. Its walls and floor are so packed with artifacts, photographs, cartographs, and typographs that to absorb it all will take hours. In fact, you might want to leave halfway through and come back to finish.

Follow its well-organized timeline from the primitive immigrants of 13,000 years ago and the Desert Archaic culture of 8000–1000 B.C., through the Paiute, Shoshone, Washo, and Anasazi evolution, up to initial contact with Europeans in the 1820s. Learn how the earliest explorers, the first wagon trains from the east, the original settlers, and finally the Comstock strike and Pyramid Lake battles managed, in only 25 years, to disrupt, co-opt, and completely overwhelm the Native cultures. Finish up reading about the mining boom, military arrival, Pony Express, telegraph, railroad, and 20th-century politics and progress. If you still have any feeling in your feet, look through the books in the gift shop and the changing art display in the side room.

The adjoining research department houses a huge collection of historical black-and-white photographs, books, manuscripts, diaries, brochures, pamphlets, newspapers, phone books, directories, death and census records, site files, maps, even the collection of William Stewart, one of Nevada's first two U.S. senators. It's open Tues.–Sat. noon–4 P.M.

Next door is **Fleischmann Planetarium and Science Center,** where it's easy to get lost in space among the thought-provoking exhibits: globes of the Earth and moon, large relief map of the Sierra area, clouds display, and a collection of meteorites found in Nevada and elsewhere, one weighing more than a ton. Stick a nickel in the gravity well and play (gently) with the instruments in the gift shop. Admission to the main building is free. You can also catch a multimedia planetarium star show and a super wide-angle dome movie (both changeable) in the dome theater ($6 adults, $4 kids and seniors). A small permanent observatory next to the planetarium, with a 12-inch reflecting telescope, is open for free public viewing on clear Friday and Saturday evenings from 9:30 to 10:30 P.M.

Public showings are always a double feature, pairing a SkyDome large-format film with a planetarium show. Shows and schedules vary throughout the year. In summer, from the Memorial Day to Labor Day weekends, shows are every day at 11:30 A.M., 1, 2:30, 4, 7, and 8:30 P.M. The rest of the year, shows are: Mon.–Thurs. 2:30, 4 and 7 P.M.; Friday 2:30, 4, 7, and 8:30 P.M.; Saturday 11:30 A.M., 1, 2:30, 4, and 8:30 P.M., Sunday 11:30 A.M., 1, 2:30, 4 and 7 pm. Call 775/784-4811 for recorded show information, 775/784-4812 for reservations and further information, or 775/784-1-SKY for current sky and star information.

Wilbur D. May Museum and Arboretum
This amazing man (1898–1982), though physically challenged from birth, led a charmed and charming life. Heir to the May Department Store fortune, young Wilbur was already quite financially successful in his own right when, just before he left for Africa in early 1929, he liquidated all his stocks for cash and government bonds. Upon his return later that year, after the Crash, he bought everything back for 10 cents on the dollar, and it's safe to say that he enjoyed the fruits of his remarkable foresight for the 63 years left of his life. He didn't, to be sure, get fat, lazy, and bored. He was a pilot, world traveler, art and artifact collector, big-game hunter, composer (his tune "Pass a Piece of Pizza, Please" sold 100,000 copies), philanthropist (mostly for children's organizations), and rancher, living on a 2,600-acre spread outside of Reno.

And as this gem of a museum amply illustrates, May not only had money, he had excellent taste; he collected treasures during more than 40 trips around the world. Tour the replicated rooms from May's ranch house: tack room, living room,

trophy room, and bedroom. Watch the 20-minute video of his life—great travel and wildlife footage. Notice his passports, a spine-chilling shrunken head, and weavings, glass, silver, masks, ivory, pottery, from all corners of the globe. Compare all the horned, antlered, fanged, and wild-eyed creatures in the living room to the identification chart.

Relax at the indoor arboretum, with its ponds (stocked with koi) and waterfall. Then ask at the desk for the attractive brochure with the layout of the **arboretum** out back and wander through the large variety of gardens: energy conservation, xeriscape, songbird, fragrant, rock, desert, rose, and many others.

The museum, 1502 Washington St. at the south end of Rancho San Rafael Park, 775/785-5961, is open in summer Mon.–Sat. 10 A.M.–5 P.M., Sunday noon–5 P.M. (the same hours, except closed Monday, in winter); admission $3 adults, $2 children and seniors.

An extra treat for the kids is the **Great Basin Adventure** historical theme park next door, which whisks kids back to pioneer days. Hands-on "exhibits" include gold panning, mining, and flume and pony rides. There're also farm animals, a petting zoo, a dinosaur play area, and a pond. It's open 10 A.M.–5 P.M. summer only (closed Monday), 775/785-4064; $2.50 adults, $1.50 kids and seniors.

The whole complex is within Washoe County's **Rancho San Rafael Park** (see "Parks And Zoos" later in this chapter). To get there, take W. 5th or 6th to Washington, go right, and continue to the top of the hill. Or enter through the big white gate on N. Sierra directly across from the Lawlor Events Center (which is one block east on N. Virginia St.).

Liberty Belle Saloon
Any slot player with the slightest curiosity about the machines should not leave town without visiting the Liberty Belle Saloon & Restaurant, 4250 S. Virginia (right in front of the Convention Center), 775/825-1776, for its outstanding exhibit on the development of this seductive pastime. The owners, Marshall and Frank Fey, are the grandsons of Charlie Fey, 16th child of a Bavarian schoolmaster. This adventurous and industrious young man left home at 15, arrived in San Francisco in 1885, and promptly redesigned the

THE FOUNDER OF RENO

Myron Lake, like Carson City's Abe Curry, surveyed a patch of godforsaken desert in western Nevada and foresaw, somehow, a booming metropolis. They both embodied the necessary aptitudes for vision and business, faith and acuity, to triumph in such a grand undertaking. However, while Curry had a civic-minded, people-oriented, generous spirit of ambition, Myron Lake, it turned out, was interested in one thing and one thing only: Myron Lake.

Even though Curry and Lake both donated land and sold buildings to the government, almost everything Curry did is remembered with favor; indeed, Curry was appointed first superintendent for both the prison and mint after he'd finished building them. Almost nothing that Lake did, however, is remembered for any reason other than his own profit and aggrandizement.

In 1871, Lake subdivided land on the south side of his bridge for housing and the county courthouse. Naturally, people had to use Lake's Crossing to get from the town on the north side of the river to the new seat of government and south addition. Lake had already made tens of thousands of dollars by 1869 when the Central Pacific arrived, charging $1 for each horse-drawn vehicle, ten cents for pedestrians, and three cents for every pig, sheep, and horse that crossed his bridge. In fact, in 1869, county commissioners forced Lake to reduce his tolls up to 25%. But as late as 1872, Lake still charged the full toll each way for delivery wagons using his bridge.

In 1872, the Virginia & Truckee railroad bridge was built a few hundred feet east of Lake's Crossing, and people walked over it to avoid the tolls. When the county commissioners declared the railroad bridge a public thoroughfare, Lake responded by withholding taxes on his tolls. And a year later, when Lake's 10-year toll franchise was not renewed, he closed the gate and guarded the bridge with a shotgun. Lake was arrested, and though he eventually won the court battle, he lost the bridge.

But his troubles were far from over. In 1879, Jane Lake, his wife of 15 years, sued for divorce, claiming extreme mental and physical cruelty, which included beatings and threat of murder. Myron Lake in turn accused Jane of infidelity. The vicious court battle dragged on for years, and seemed to take the spirit from Lake. He died two years later, in 1884, a rich, powerful, unpopular, and unhappy man.

NEVADA HISTORICAL SOCIETY, RENO

---

first gambling machines, which had just come on the S.F. bar scene a few years earlier, revolutionizing the young industry. From his prototype three-reel Liberty Belle, more than a million similar slots have been produced. Fey also invented the five-card poker reel in 1901, and the dollar slot in 1929 (both on display).

Just walking into the Liberty Belle is a historical experience: the heavy brass doors were salvaged from William Ralston's famous Palace Hotel after the San Francisco earthquake. Buy a drink at the bar, then settle in for a long look at one of the finest collections and accompanying descriptions of antique slot machines and gaming devices anywhere.

Fey's first slot is on display, as are the first dollar slot and early five-card poker reels. Check out the original reel strips and read how the fruits—cherries, lemons, strawberries, etc.—corresponded to the flavor of gum delivered as prizes. Other pay schedules list the number of winning cigars. Don't miss the old map and big photographs of historical Reno in the front alcove.

Then head around to the side room to catch R-rated "Dakota Pearl Getting Ready for Bed" in the 1880s' moving-picture machine—with its surprise ending. The donkey fortune-telling machine also works with a nickel. Look around at the other old and unusual slots. In fact, anywhere you wander inside the Liberty Belle, even the bathrooms, is full of pleasant surprises. This is one of the best places in Reno to hang out and have yourself a truly authentic Nevada experience.

Finally, fish out some of that gambling change and buy *Slot Machines,* a gorgeous oversize coffee-table book ($29.95) by the heirs of the inventor of the machines that now earn Nevada casinos more than three billion dollars each year in profits—more than all table games combined. The restaurant here has reasonable prices on meat and fish for lunch and dinner, and a congenial atmosphere. It's always packed when there's a convention in town, and usually packed with locals most other times.

You can stop by the saloon to see the collection any time the restaurant is open. It's open for lunch Mon.–Fri., 11 A.M.–2:30 P.M. Dinner hours are Mon.–Sat. 5–10 P.M., Sunday 4–9 P.M.

Lake Mansion

While you're down in this neck of the woods, take in this restored mansion, home of Reno's founder, at 4598 S. Virginia St. on the far southern corner of the Convention Center parking lot, 775/829-1868. Myron Lake, Reno's founder, bought a toll bridge across the Truckee River in 1861, then donated land to the Central Pacific Railroad to ensure the perpetual prosperity of what was then known as Lake's Crossing. His house originally sat at Virginia and California streets: Reno's first address. You only tour the first floor and few of the furnishings are original, but in the dining room check out the painting by McClellan of Lake's bridge. And the pink bathroom off the downstairs bedroom might have contributed to the undoing of the Lakes's marriage; Jane Lake filed for divorce right after Myron bought the place in 1879. Upstairs are offices of the March of Dimes and a couple of other community organizations. The mansion is open Mon.–Fri., 9 A.M.–4 P.M.; donation optional.

THE UNIVERSITY OF NEVADA

This is perhaps one of the most attractive campuses in the country; a more idyllic ambience for upper academia is hard to imagine. In a way, this 12,000-student center of higher learning is a saving grace of Reno, making it as much of a college town as a tourist town. It's a must-stop on even the briefest Reno itinerary, if only to enjoy the refreshingly rural respite: the 200-acre campus boasts large luxuriant grassy areas, huge 100-year-old oak trees lining the walkways, pleasing old brick buildings, duck pond, gardens, museums, galleries, recreational facilities, stadium, arena, and more.

UNR perennially ranks among the top 200 universities (out of more than 1,300) in the "American's Best Colleges" issue of *U.S. News and World Report.* It's one of the least expensive schools for resident undergraduates. UNR's Mackay School of Mines is among the top five mining programs in the country, and is home to several key industry and national research groups. The Reynolds School of Journalism (named after late Las Vegan Don Reynolds, founder of Donrey Media) is the only one of 90 accredited journalism schools that meets all 12 points of accreditation; four of its graduates have won Pulitzer Prizes. Nearly 30% of graduates from the School of Medicine go on to practice medicine in Nevada. The Agricultural Experiment Station sponsors programs aimed at making more efficient use of the state's water resources.

Morrill Hall

Up the hill from 9th St. (between Center and Lake) is imposing Morrill Hall, the university's first building. The University of Nevada is a land-grant school established in 1864 along with statehood. The state legislature struggled to fund it for 10 years, until Elko took over the struggle. After another 10-year unsuccessful college try there, however, it was moved to more populated Reno. The cornerstone of the first building was laid in early 1885 and Morrill Hall, named after the Vermont senator who was instrumental in establishing the state-college land-grant system, was finished a year later.

When classes began in March 1886, there

were two teachers, 56 students, and a dozen subjects, from mineralogy, metallurgy, and mechanical drawing to Latin, Greek, and astronomy. Four-story Morrill Hall housed the entire school. In 1889, a lab building was constructed for chemistry and biology courses. The first graduating class, of 1891, consisted of three bachelors (and no married men). *Sagebrush,* the student newspaper, was started in 1893; it celebrates its 105th birthday in October 1998.

In the early 1900s, John Mackay's son, Clarence, was appointed to plan the campus, and he enlisted Stanford White, famous New York architect. White had earlier unearthed Thomas Jefferson's 1810 blueprint for the University of Virginia, which he used to enlarge the UV campus and to design UNR. (White later designed Madison Square Garden, where he was murdered by Harry Thaw, for reasons still unexplained—most recently speculated about in E.L. Doctorow's brilliant novel, *Ragtime.*) All the buildings erected around the central Quadrangle between 1906 and 1945 were in the Jeffersonian revival style: Victorian architecture with Italianate and Gothic detail.

Morrill Hall was restored beautifully in 1970, and today houses the offices of the Alumni Association as well as those of the University of Nevada Press. The press is in the basement, accessible by the entrance on the east side of the building. Stop in and see Charlotte Heatherly, supremely accommodating office manager, to pick up a catalogue of the press's scores of titles, including series on the Basques, the Great Basin, history and politics, plus novels, reprints, biographies, and references. Especially recommended are the books by Robert Laxalt (especially *Nevada*) and Oscar Lewis, plus the Great Basin's *Birds, Trees, Fishes, Shrubs,* and *Geology.* My favorite, other than Oscar Lewis's *Silver Kings,* is *East of Eden, West of Zion,* a collection of essays on contemporary Nevada.

Student Union and Library

Many of the above titles are for sale at the bookstore in the **Jot Travis Student Union,** N. Virginia and 11th, 775/784-6597, open Mon.–Fri. 7:30 A.M.–5 P.M., Saturday 9 A.M.–1 P.M. Also sold here are UNR T-shirts and sweatshirts, mugs, and souvenirs, as well as cards and other assorted items. Across the hall is the Wolf's Den,

with a Carl's Jr., Pizza Hut, TCBY, and other fast food. The **Crossroads Cafe** upstairs (and around the corner) serves three meals seven days a week ($5–8, public invited) and overlooks the pond.

Walk out the back door of the Union and across the yard to the **Getchell Library**—unmistakable for its folded roof and tall granite columns. Named after Noble Getchell, a mining mogul and university regent, this spacious place, largest library in the state with 750,000 volumes, is especially conducive to the sublime quest for knowledge, wisdom, and inspiration by the serious and dedicated students that make this college (indeed, this country) great—and is large enough to muffle the sounds of those who just want to goof around.

The Getchell has a limited selection of Nevada books among the stacks, but an entire collection of bound *Nevada* magazines can be found half in the stacks and half in the Government Publications department. The *Gazette-Journal* and Las Vegas *Sun* and *Review-Journal* are on microfilm in the reference section. The Mining Library is downstairs in the front of the building to the right. But for true Nevadaphiles, the place to go is the **Special Collections Room,** 775/784-6500, ext. 327, on the second floor. It's open Mon.–Fri. 8 A.M.–5 P.M., with additional Saturday hours of 10 A.M.–2 P.M. when the university is in session. This is one of the best collections of books, maps, and manuscripts on Nevada anywhere in the world.

The Getchell Library, 775/784-6528, is open Mon.–Thurs. 8 A.M.–midnight, Friday 8 A.M.–7 P.M., Saturday 10 A.M.–9 P.M., Sunday noon–midnight during the school year, generally 8 A.M.–5 P.M. during the summer and over vacations.

W.M. Keck Minerals Museum

Next door to the library is the Mackay Mining School (775/784-4528), with a statue of the famous and generous miner, John Mackay, who became Bonanza King of the Comstock and later endowed the university. The building, constructed in 1908, has recently been renovated for earthquake-proofing. It now rests an eighth of an inch off the ground on 66 high-tech rubber bearings and 43 Teflon slider plates.

The museum entrance is on the first floor of the building; it's open Mon.–Fri. 8:30 A.M.–5 P.M., admission free. Here you can see all the gold, silver, copper, lead, uranium, turquoise, magnesite, magnesium, mercury, gypsum, and borax that you've been hearing and reading about around the state. Not to mention the sulfides, oxides, haloids, quartzites, geodes, silicates, phosphates, psychedelic jasper, infamous black hydrocarbons (and argilite). Historical black-and-whites of many mining boomtowns grace the walls, and Mackay's own vault houses two dozen rocks from the Comstock itself. Upstairs on the mezzanine is a geological breakdown of minerals and some fossils from around the world, plus miners' tools, machines, scales, and diagrams.

PARKS AND ZOOS

Truckee River Bike Path

This is a paved cycling, jogging, and walking trail nearly the length of Truckee Meadows, right along the river most of the way. It's roughly 12 miles long, stretching between the eastern edge of Sparks (near the Vista Blvd. exit of I-80) through Rock Park (near the west edge of Sparks), Galetti Park (in east Reno), Idlewild Park (in central Reno), and finally to the Mayberry area (at Caughlin Ranch in west Reno). It's an idyllic ribbon of river, trees, and parks that snakes right through the middle of the city.

Oxbow Nature Study Area

Head west on Second St. and bear left on Dickerson Rd. just before the railroad underpass about two miles west of town. You might think you're in the wrong neighborhood to be looking for a park, with all the auto body shops, apartment complexes, used furniture stores, moving and storage warehouses, and truck lettering shops. But it's all just to enhance the surprise with a bit of relief by arriving at the portal to this unusual city park.

An oxbow is a former river channel diverted from the main flow by sediment deposition. This 30-acre park along the Truckee encompasses a large oxbow area. A flood on New Year's Day, 1997, completely changed the face of the park, and it took three years to rebuild—but the park naturalist says the re-designed park is even better now than it was before, sporting a half-mile boardwalk interpretive trail (wheelchair and stroller accessible) winding through 18 acres of interesting features including ponds and riparian (or wetlands) flora and fauna, and a large deck right out over the river, great for bird-watching. Grasses, sedges, tules, cattails, wild rose, alder, and cottonwood, along with beaver, muskrat, great blue herons, geese, and other birds, naturally inhabit this environment. (The Russian olive is an introduced tree for attracting game birds; its dominance is destructive.) The sage and rabbitbrush identify the areas that have been high and dry for some time.

Most of the year, most of what you see here are local flora and birds. The park really gets jumping from early May through late July, when 150 species of migratory birds arrive here to nest and rear their young; this park is a wetlands habitat for nesting on the Pacific flyway. Hummingbirds are usually the last to leave, in August.

You can spend an enjoyable and relaxing several hours walking the interpretive trail, leaning over the river on the deck, and looking for birds. The park and its trails are open every day, 8 A.M. to sunset; the interpretive center is open for groups by appointment, or whenever the lone naturalist is present (775/334-3808).

Rancho San Rafael

This big, beautiful, empty, 408-acre hunk of property (775/785-4319) has been owned by the city since 1979 when Reno voters approved a $10-million bond issue to buy it. Since then it's been a battleground for pro-development and pro-status-quo proponents. So far the leave-it-alone faction has emerged victorious, and a proposed golf course, supermarket, and water park have not made it beyond the drawing board. Long-range development plans are being monitored, and generally opposed, by Friends of Rancho San Rafael.

A few facilities have been installed, including picnic areas, a fitness circuit, wide open fields (which host large public events such as Earth Day and Hot August Nights and are great for kite-flying), Great Basin Adventure kiddie park, nature trail, par course, and children's play area. Enter the southern end of the park off of N. Washington St. or N. Sierra Street.

The park's biggest surprise is a one-mile hiking trail in the remote northern stretch, north of

McCarran Blvd. Head north on Virginia St., take a left at the gate (signposted), and drive to the back of the parking lot. Gorgeous view of the city from up here. The trailhead is one of the most conspicuous in the state, and leads you down to and across the Highland Ditch, then up to the big green **Basque Memorial,** with its dedication of eternal homage to the Basque sheepherder, and big board of donors and credits. A little loop trail around the back of the memorial has four explanatory signs on the Basque people.

The main trail branches off to the left of the memorial and down to the Highland Ditch flume, built in 1917 to carry water to the 73-acre farm where the planetarium now stands. Tracks and trails continue north beyond the flume up to the big whitewashed "N" on Peavine Mountain: 160 feet high, 140 feet wide, 13,000 square feet, traditionally repainted every year by freshmen at UNR.

Peavine Mountain has been at the center of a local controversy for many years. This mountain, the northernmost peak of the Sierra Nevada, was once covered with Jeffrey pine, all cut for the Comstock. It was mined briefly, and the miners, as was the custom up until recently, abandoned it without bothering to clean up behind them. Since then, especially recently, Peavine has been used as a garbage dump; all manner of trash, from old cars to couches to containers, is strewn around the mountain. Off-road drivers also consider it their private preserve. Their two and four wheelers leave scars, tracks, and deep ruts that a good rainstorm can turn into virtual irrigation ditches. The Forest Service has plowed up 20 miles of such terrain, built berms, planted wheat grass, and posted keep-out signs. To little avail. Though 100 miles of established off-road tracks are still available for use, destruction of Peavine's slopes continues unabated. Two of the abusers caused a 600-acre brush fire on the northeast side in 1992 with illegal fireworks; they were caught, tried, sentenced, and will be paying firefighting expenses and punitive fines for the rest of their lives (they were in their early twenties). Climb around Peavine if you're up for it, both physically and psychically.

Back on the nature trail at the flume, you head over to the riparian area below the ditch, with the old alder and cottonwood trees, pond, mead-ow, and signs explaining it all. You stroll around the meadow and through the group picnic area, then back up through the sage and sand to the Basque memorial. Like Oxbow Nature Area, this is an entirely unexpected and even remote little hike right outside the high-density city.

Virginia Lake Park
This 32-acre park consists of a pond surrounded by suburban houses. It's quite popular with joggers, bike riders, dog walkers, baby-sitters, hand holders, and duck feeders. Heading south on Virginia, take a right on W. Plumb, then left on Lakeside Drive. Be careful of the 15-mph speed limit here.

Other Parks
For descriptions of **Wingfield, Riverside,** and **Idlewild** parks in downtown Reno, please see "Downtown Parks" under "Downtown" earlier in the "Sights" section. Also turn to the "Vicinity of Reno" section for more information on Washoe County parks at **Davis Creek** and **Bowers Mansion** (under "Washoe Valley"), and **Galena Creek** (under "Mt. Rose"), and for information on **Washoe Lake State Park** ("Washoe Valley").

Zoos
Two zoos sit north of Reno on US 395 toward the California border. The **Sierra Safari Zoo,** 10200 N. Virginia St., 775/677-1101, is open every day 10 A.M.–5 P.M., but only from April 1 to October 31 (closed November to March); admission $5 adults, $4 children and seniors. This is Nevada's largest self-supporting wild-animal attraction, featuring 200 animals of 40 different species from aoudads to zebras, baboons to wallabies. Visitors can mingle with the tamer species. The mission statement of this zoo is "to foster compassion for and knowledge about animals and our environment by bringing people and animals together." Most of the animals, including the "big cats," have been hand-raised from birth. It's an exciting experience to actually interact with and touch the unusual animals here. To get to the zoo, drive eight miles north of Reno on US 395 to the Red Rock Rd. exit. Phone ahead if weather is questionable.

The **Animal Ark** is nearby, but less accessible, and purposely so. For the past 15 years,

Aaran and Diana Hiibel have lived on 38 acres north of Reno, where they've cared for orphaned and infirm wildlife, such as lion and tiger cubs, wolves, monkeys, and birds of prey. Animal Ark exists to provide permanent care in captivity to animals who cannot be returned to the wild, and is dedicated to helping create a bridge between humans and animals by increasing the appreciation of our natural world. Check out "Wolf Howl Night," held on the Saturday night nearest the full moon, when participants view the park, attend a short lecture on wolves, observe wolf pack dynamics firsthand, and then join in a group howl. The Ark is open to the public from April 1 to October 31, Tuesday to Sunday, 10 A.M.–4:30 P.M. (closed Mondays, and closed November to March), 775/969-3111; admission $6, children $4. To get there, take US 395 north to the Red Rock Rd. exit, turn right on Red Rock, drive 11.2 miles to Deerlodge Rd., take a right and go another mile. The Ark is on the right.

CASINOS

Silver Legacy

When the plans were unveiled in 1993, this new megaresort, a joint venture between Circus Circus and the Eldorado, was going to be a 16th-century Spanish seaport theme, complete with 2,000 rooms in three curved hotel towers, a Spanish castle inside a 200-foot-tall dome, a galleon amusement ride on a river through the property, and 60,000 square feet of casino space. It was supposed to be completed by April 1995. However, the Castillian harbor concept proved too difficult to anchor in reality, and the theme was changed to the Old West. The legend to go with the theme owes a large debt to Circus Circus's Luxor in Las Vegas: Sam Fairchild, aka "Old Silver," hit a silver lode directly under the megaresort and built a resort to end all resorts on top of it.

Opened in June 1995, Silver Legacy is downtown Reno's answer to the Las Vegas Strip. (Of course, even though it boasts 1,700 rooms, second largest in Reno, and covers two full city blocks, it would still only be the 21st largest hotel in Vegas.) Its main claim to fame is Reno's only Las Vegas-type spectacle, housed in the world's largest composite dome, with a surface area of 75,000 square feet: a 120-foot-tall mining rig, a sort of cross between a train trestle, a mining headframe, and a Mr. Magoo machine.

Skywalks connect the Legacy with the Eldorado on one side and Circus Circus on the other (the joint's a joint venture between the two). It gives its blocks a sort of subterranean feel, which might remind New Yorkers of around Grand Central Station. But you can now walk more than four city blocks in downtown Reno without stepping foot outside, by parking in the Circus garage at West and Sixth and heading over to the Eldorado at Virginia and Plaza. 407 N. Virginia St., 775/329-4777 or 800/687-8733, www.silverlegacy.com, double room rates $49–249.

Harrah's

Harrah's dominates downtown Reno, as it has for 55 years. Like Harold's Club before it (see the Special Topics "Harold's Club or Bust" and "The Pioneering Smiths" in this section), Harrah's is also the result of a Nevada gambling pioneer's success story. William Harrah arrived in Reno in 1937 and opened two ill-fated bingo parlors before beginning his steady journey to fame and

BOB RACE

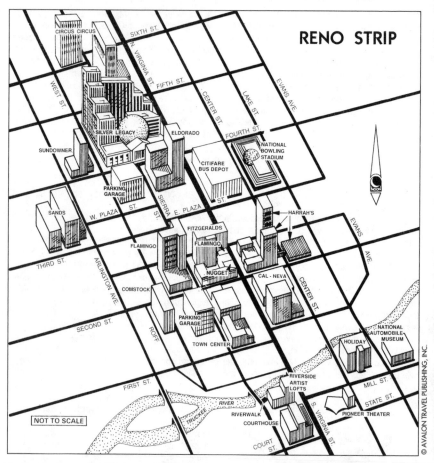

fortune by acquiring five bar-casinos before 1942. He opened Harrah's at its original location in 1946 and continued his expansion downtown, culminating in the purchase of the Golden Hotel in 1966. Harrah also bought the old Gateway Club at the south shore of Lake Tahoe in 1956. When he died in 1978, his hotels had 7,000 employees and the reputation for being the cleanest, classiest, and best managed in the gaming industry.

Holiday Corporation bought the company two years later and quickly picked up where the old man had left off. It opened a casino-hotel in At-

lantic City, expanded the Holiday Hotel in Las Vegas (now known as Harrah's), and built what was then called the Del Rio in Laughlin. When Holiday Corporation was sold to Bass PLC in 1989 for $2.2 billion, Promus Companies was spun off to oversee Harrah's five properties, along with three hotel chains (Embassy and Homewood Suites and Hampton Inns). Since then Promus has built casinos all over the country. Its big disaster was winning the contract to build a huge casino in New Orleans that fell victim to Lousiana politics and cost them untold hundreds of millions.

William Harrah built his hotels into one of the most profitable, reputable, and impeccable operations in Nevada. Harrah's hotels have consistently achieved four- and five-star ratings from AAA and rave reviews from patrons. Harrah's Reno is a perennial four-star joint. It expanded many times over the decades, and finally gained a foothold on Virginia Street in 1991 when it took over and remodeled the old bank building on the corner of Second where George Wingfield once had his offices (it's now a Planet Hollywood). A non-casino Hampton Inn opened next door in 1996. 219 N. Center St., 775/786-3232 or 800/HARRAHS, www.harrahsreno.com, double room rates $39–139.

Fitzgeralds

Like Pappy Smith and Bill Harrah, Lincoln Fitzgerald was an early Reno casino operator, who opened the Nevada Club in 1947. Fitzgeralds, named after him, opened in the boom year of 1979 and has been going strong ever since. The thing to do here is to take the escalator to the second floor and follow the footlights to "Lucky Forest." Walk by the queue waiting to sign up for something and just take in the exhibit: horseshoe, Leprechaun's cave, Ho Tei (Chinese god of good fortune), Aladdin's lamp, wishing well, blarney stone, rabbit's foot, and Abraxas (supreme Egyptian deity)—maybe some of the luck will rub off on you. Then again, so might some of the bad-luck display! Can't have one without the other—the old yin and yang of risk. 255 N. Virginia St., 775/785-3300 or 800/648-5022, www.fitzgeralds.com, double room rates $34–300.

Eldorado

The Eldorado is owned and operated by the Carano family: Don the don and assorted sons, daughters, wives, and uncles. Don Carano's great-grandfather Bernardo Ferrari emigrated from Italy and wound up as a cook in Virginia City during the Comstock boom. His daughter married Ben Carano, whose son Louis worked in Reno as a clerk for the Southern Pacific Railroad. Ben Carano invested in a 50-foot parcel on Virginia Street at 4th just north of the Arch, in 1929. The family added on to the property with land purchases over the years. Louis's son Don was born in the pivotal year of 1931, when gambling was legalized. He became a Reno lawyer,

which introduced and taught him the casino business, and he held an interest in the Pioneer and Boomtown before building the Eldorado, which opened in 1973 with 282 rooms and a 10,000-

---

THE PIONEERING SMITHS

Spokesmen for the Smith family have said over the years that they started in Reno with $600. In 1962 they cashed it in for $16,675,000 in a sale and lease-back arrangement (to a group of New Yorkers) that may become more popular among gambling operators. The total implications of the Harold's Club sale have not been lost on the others in the gambling business in Nevada. It has been obvious since the deal was worked out that the federal tax laws were responsible for the Smiths' decision to sell.

First, the price was ridiculously high for what they had—a group of buildings in downtown Reno and some speculatively held real estate around town. Second, there was no disclosure of how much cash the New Yorkers were buying—that is, how much reserve liquid assets the Smiths' corporations had and could not distribute to their owners without ruinous tax bites. The suspicion is that the Smiths sold the money to the new owners, who then would have tax advantages that would enable them to use the money. The Smiths would be able to declare their sale proceeds to be capital gains, taxable at much lower rates.

Meantime, the Smiths have leases and options that could be extended for 25 years. They continue to run the casino. They will get the $16,675,000 sale price within five years, and the documents indicate that they got $3,250,000 in cash at the time of the sale.

—WALLACE TURNER,
GAMBLER'S MONEY

HAROLD'S CLUB OR BUST

At 250 N. Virginia, Harold's Club was once the point of emanation of the modern Nevada boom, and therefore of the whole nationwide madness over gambling. Raymond "Pappy" Smith, a carnival operator, sent his son Harold to Reno to open a little roulette concession (one wheel, two nickel slots) in 1935, at a time when gambling, though legal, was still very much a Douglas Alley, back-room, scam-riddled affair. That first little excursion into legal gambling proved profitable, so the Smiths expanded, and in the process proceeded to change the face of casino gambling forever. They not only ushered gambling into the daylight of modern Virginia St. and jettisoned the old-time flotsam from their club, but they also launched a campaign to improve the image of legalized casino gambling in the national consciousness, which also, of course, reflected on the image of Harold's Club and Reno. In so doing, the Smiths set the ground rules for Nevada's incipient gambling industry, by showing the first generation of casino operators how to make gambling palatable to the middle-class masses. Without them, Meyer Lansky and Ben Siegel could never have envisioned their own resort hotel in Las Vegas. And it would've been a very different world today.

In the late 1930s, the slogan "Harold's Club Or Bust" suddenly loomed from billboards, played on radio, and appeared in newspapers all over the country, introducing locals and non-Nevadans to the novel concept that gambling was good clean fun. The Smiths implemented sophisticated safeguards against cheating perpetrated on both sides of the table, inventing them as they went along—the original eye-in-the-sky one-way-glass-and-catwalk system, for example. Harold's Club was first to offer free drinks, comps, and junkets, and to charter trains and planes for its customers. Harold's was the first to hire female dealers, during the man shortage of WW II, further enhancing casino respectability. The whole strategy worked so well that it immediately became standard casino operating procedure and has remained so ever since.

The distinctive mural above the main entrance on Virginia Street was painted in 1949 to commemorate the centennial of the Gold Rush. The Smiths were also the first to implement a sophisticated leaseback sales arrangement for the club that became popular throughout the state with casino owners (see the Special Topic "The Pioneering Smiths" in this section).

Pappy Smith, who's been called the Henry Ford of Nevada gambling, died in 1967. The Club was sold to Howard Hughes's Summa Corporation in 1970. Summa expanded the casino in 1979. When Fitzgeralds bought Harold's Club from Summa in 1988, it was the last casino property that Summa had to sell, thereby ending the 20-odd-year presence of Howard Hughes's corporation in Nevada. (Fitzgeralds also bought the Sundance in Las Vegas in 1987, thereby ending Moe Dalitz's nearly 40-year reign as that city's King of Juice.) Fitzgeralds tried to sell the unprofitable casino for years, and finally had to shut it down in 1995. It remained dark for a couple of years, until a discount store moved in. I see nothing symbolic about that.

square-foot casino. Another 129 rooms were added in 1978 during Reno's great expansion phase, and the hotel was again expanded in 1985 to 800 rooms and a 40,000-square-foot casino. The Eldorado casino has an interesting roulette table, with three separate wheels and layouts.

The Caranos partnered up with Circus Circus to build Silver Legacy, which fits snugly between them. And it expanded in 1996, adding 12-story all-suites tower, a showroom, brew pub, health spa, and expanded buffet.

The Eldorado is revered locally for its fine hotel restaurants and buffet. The Caranos also operate a $6 million winery on a 60-acre ranch in Sonoma, California, called Ferrari-Carano. 345

N. Virginia St., 775/786-5700 or 800/648-5966, www.eldoradoreno.com, double room rates $40–750.

Cal-Neva

In 1947, the Cal-Neva opened on the site of the old Fortune Club, which had occupied the southeast corner of Virginia and 2nd since the 1930s. In 1955, Leon Nightingale, a downtown bar owner, bought it from Sanford Adler, then sold it in 1957, then bought it back in 1961. Nightingale and his partners, including Warren Nelson, remodeled the club and had a big grand opening in 1962, still fondly remembered by old-timers. Cal-Neva expanded with the rest of them in 1978, and the casino now occupies nearly an entire city block (except for the defunct Virginian), even though it doesn't have any hotel rooms. Leon Nightingale mined a lot of gold from the club and donated fortunes to the university for scholarships, to the city for culture, and to private charities. He owned it until his death in 1990. Now Warren Nelson and the other original partners carry on the tradition—a rare occurrence in Nevada: the same owners for 35 years. It's said they have 150 years of gambling experience among them.

Warren Nelson has been a fixture on the Reno casino scene since the 1930s, when he started Nevada's first keno game at the old Palace Club. He adapted a Chinese lottery by giving it a horse-racing theme. The numbers represented jockeys; he played racetrack music and announced the numbers as in a race. (To this day, keno games are called "races.") A short time later, he witnessed a game in southern California played with ping-pong balls drawn from a cage and applied it to horserace keno.

Cal-Neva sports many interesting features. Trains frame the slots in the Railroad Express casino; the balcony on the second floor provides a good overlook. On the third floor is the hot and sweaty (and smoky) action, with machines galore, a rammin' jammin' pit, the poker room and sports and race books. In fact, the race and sports books account for 25% of the total casino floor space, and the managers also operate sports books at several other casinos around town.

Cal-Neva (no relation to Cal-Neva Lodge in Crystal Bay) is always in the top five revenue and profit producers among Reno-Sparks casinos. It also offers some of the best food deals in the vicinity. 150 N. Virginia St., 775/954-4540 or 887/777-7303, www.nevadanet.com, double room rates $39–150.

Flamingo Hilton

Del Webb built the 21-story, 604-room Reno Sahara on the block between Sierra and West and 2nd and Commercial and sold it to Hilton in 1981. It transformed into the Flamingo Hilton in 1989 and is now unmistakable for its pink-plumage neon spectacular along Sierra Street. The casino is bright and claustrophobic and has one of the biggest lounge stages in town. A Las Vegas-size neon sign was installed above the Flamingo portico in 1993.

The Flamingo now has a presence on Virginia St. between the Nugget and Fitzgeralds; the small Virginia St. entrance is fronted by the distinctive pink and purple plumage. You take an overhead walkway across Sierra Street and come out at front desk and coffee shop on the second floor of the main building. Top of the Hilton is the highest restaurant in town. 255 N. Sierra St., 775/322-1111 or 800/648-4882, www.flamingoreno.com, double room rates $59–219.

Holiday

The Holiday has been a fixture on the Truckee River just east of Virginia Street for thirty-something years. Since the National Auto Museum was built across the street, it's closer to downtown than ever. It recently had a $1.5 million facelift, including lights on trees along the riverbank, and of course new carpeting and slot carousels. The window seats of the Shore Room coffee shop overlook the river. 1000 E. 6th St., 775/786-5151 or 800/648-4877, double room rates $49–135.

Reno Nugget

This Nugget, one of a dozen in the state, was opened by Dick Graves, the Idaho restaurateur also responsible for the Sparks and Carson City Nuggets, in the mid-1950s. John Ascuaga worked here for Graves then, before moving over to Sparks. Jim Kelley, another Idahoan, bought this Nugget from Graves, then sold it to Rick Heaney, who owns it today. The Reno

Nugget has 200 slots and one low-limit blackjack table. At this very same table, blackjack guru Stanford Wong counted down his first deck of cards in a Nevada casino, a few days after his 21st birthday around three decades ago. The Nugget serves 99-cent margaritas, $1 draft beers, and free popcorn; the diner in the rear is a classic. 233 N. Virginia St., 775/323-0716, no accommodation.

Circus Circus

Circus Circus, with its big-top acts performed continuously throughout the day and its consistent crowds of low rollers, tourists, and kids, is the best place for cheap thrills, people watching, and free entertainment in Reno. The concept of an actual circus-in-a-casino was first imagined by Jay Sarno, who is also credited with the idea for Caesars Palace. Amazingly enough, Sarno conceived of Circus Circus as an attraction for high rollers and actually charged admission when the first Circus opened in Las Vegas in 1968. After a few years of dismal business (and some ridicule), Sarno sold out to William Bennett, an Arizona furniture mogul and Del Webb casino executive, who turned the operation into one of the largest casino companies in the world.

Today, Circus Circus Enterprises owns the original hotel in Las Vegas and Grand Slam Canyon indoor amusement park in back of it, along with the $290 million, 4,000-room Excalibur, the $300 million Luxor, Silver City, and Slots A Fun in Las Vegas, plus the Colorado Belle and Edgewater in Laughlin, and this one in Reno, opened in the boom year of 1978. The low table limits, high occupancy rates, circus acts and midway, automatic monorail shuttle between towers, and perpetual crush of crowds have become this hotel's trademarks. Circus was remodeled in 1996 and is now less of a dungeon. The new restaurant is Art Gekko, serving Southwestern cuisine. 500 N. Sierra St., 775/329-0711 or 800/648-5010, www.circus-reno.com, double room rates $29–295.

Sands Regency

Just a few blocks off the strip on Fourth St., the Sands has the classic Las Vegas-type look of a casino that's grown up piecemeal, with original (1964) low-rise motel units surrounding its first pool, towers rising above, and three or four different wings to the casino. Owned by the Cladianos family, the Sands opened a new hotel wing and an enlarged casino in 1989. The Sands is popular with locals for the franchise approach to food service: Winchells, Arby's, Baskin-Robbins, Pizza Hut, Orange Julius, Tony Roma's, and others. On the other hand, nearly three out of every four Sands overnight customers arrive on package trips from the Pacific Northwest and Canada. 345 N. Arlington Ave., 775/348-2200 or 800/648-3553, www.sandsregency.com, double room rates $49–69.

Sundowner

This hotel, farthest from Virginia Street in downtown, is casual, making no bones about its top priority: catering to a devoted clientele. The uniforms are basic western ware, and the well-worn crap table is often crowded with locals. For a break, ride an elevator to the 20th floor of the tower and catch the long view south from the big front picture windows. 450 N. Arlington Ave., 775/786-7050 or 800/648-5490, double room rates $30–159.

Peppermill

About a mile south of downtown, at 2707 S. Virginia, this is Reno's most psychedelically impressive (or oppressive—depending on your tolerance for psychoactive sensations) casino. In fact, stop by if only for a hallucination check: the place either sucks you in or spits you out. There's enough indoor neon and noise for *five* casinos, but the plush red-velvet chairs at the slots are *so* comfortable. The cocktail uniforms are unprintably sexy—with the waitresses to fill them, too. And the dealer uniforms are suitably glittery, which make the mostly women dealers sparkle. The bar is big and boisterous, and the upstairs phone booths would've made Clark Kent's day; call home and then stretch out for 40. The casino also displays at least a million dollars in silk flowers, leaves, ferns, and trees. And if you think the Peppermill is a little far out even for Reno, consider its 96-room little sister in Wendover on the Nevada-Utah border at the edge of the blinding Bonneville Salt Flats. This one doesn't pack *half* the punch! Western Village at the east end of Victoria Ave. in Sparks also exhibits the unmistakable Peppermill signature (as does the Rainbow Casino in Henderson).

The original Peppermill on this site opened in 1971 as a small motel and restaurant (a lone Peppermill coffee shop remains on the Las Vegas Strip near the Riviera). Its expansions culminated with a 632-room tower in 1986. The Peppermill expanded in 1996, adding a 300-room tower, a new sports book, and a parking garage to the tune of $60 million. In summer 1997, it unveiled the $3 million Sierra Mountain pool complex, with a 60-foot faux mountain with waterfall that hosts a 10-minute show featuring five animatronic animals and a 10,000-watt sound system. 2707 S. Virginia St., 775/826-2121 or 800/648-6992, www.peppermillcasinos.com, double room rates $49–500.

Atlantis

Like the Peppermill, the Atlantis started out as a small motel, the Golden Road, in the early 1970s, and has expanded many times since. It became a Travelodge, then a Quality Inn, then a Clarion (when the owners, the Farahi family, built a $25 million, 160-room tower in 1991), and finally an Atlantis (in 1996). A $25 million, 300-room tower was built in 1994, complete with an 18-story glass atrium and glass elevators (fun little thrill ride with a good view). The new tower makes Atlantis the seventh-largest hotel in Reno, just behind number six, the Peppermill.

Atlantis has capitalized on its location—the only lodging and gambling within walking distance of the Reno-Sparks Convention Center—to become a major player in the Reno casino firmament. The casino features a tropical setting, including a 30-foot waterfall and thatched roofing over the pits, and an underwater theme for its fancy eponymous restaurant and nightclub. 3800 S. Virginia St., 775/825-4700 or 800/723-6500, www.atlantiscasino.com, double room rates $49–159.

Reno Hilton

This memorable monstrous monument, Nevada's largest hotel casino outside of Las Vegas, was built by master financier Kirk Kerkorian in 1978 and opened as the MGM Grand. Kerkorian, a horsetrader by nature, sold both the Las Vegas and Reno Grands to Bally's in spring 1986 for a little more than half a billion dollars, a price that Bally's never recovered from. Junk-bond debt, mismanagement, and lack of vi-

sion (not to mention questionable taste in carpeting) plagued Bally's Reno for the next six years, and the company declared bankruptcy in late 1991. In spring 1992, it was announced that an offer for $78 million from Harvey's (of South Lake Tahoe) had been accepted for Bally's Reno. Being the bargain-basement price of the century, the deal immediately attracted Hilton, which eventually outbid Harvey's in bankruptcy court for the 2,001-room hotel and 100,000-square-foot casino.

Since then, Hilton has covered the two-and-a-half-million square foot hotel with 14,000 gallons of white paint, 3,000 thermal-pane and reflective bronze-colored windows and spandrel coverings, and 22-foot red-and-white-neon sign lettering. The overall effect has spruced up the Reno skyline considerably, and turned drab old Bally's into an attractive Hilton. (Coincidentally, Hilton bought the rest of Bally's, which included the Las Vegas and Atlantic City joints, in 1995 for $3.2 billion.)

As for the interior, the Hilton completed an $84 million renovation of the property, which included remodeling all 2,001 rooms, a 60-foot extension of the sports book for the addition of a bar and Johnny Rocket's Diner, and a new 450-seat buffet. The old Ziegfeld Theater has been renamed the Hilton Showroom. The 33-acre cement-lined lake created from the original quarry has been turned into a driving range, with four greens floating in the middle.

To get the full effect, approach it from the south heading up US 395, and exit at Mill St., in effect the Hilton's own driveway off the freeway. Park in one of the 5,000 spaces and walk through one of the 20 front doors into this 2.5-million-square-foot hotel, whose 2,001 rooms (including 418 suites) account for just under 10% of Reno-Sparks's total accommodations. The 100,000-square-foot casino, at one time the largest in the world, is so big that John Elway would need two tosses to get a football from one end to the other. More practically, this Alaska-size casino is so big that, even with the 1,160 slot machines, 68 blackjack tables, 10 craps tables, four roulette wheels, baccarat, Big Six, and poker tables, 275-seat race and sports book, 150-seat keno lounge, two bars, and restaurant row, you can still hear yourself think.

In addition, it could easily take you an entire afternoon to see, let alone partake of, the Hilton's restaurants, production show "Aireus," show lounge, comedy club, two movie theaters, 50-lane bowling alley, 40-shop arcade, Fun Quest arcade and virtual-reality attraction, eight tennis courts, his-and-her health clubs—and you'd never even have to step outside, except to get to the Olympic-sized swimming pool or the 452-space RV park. It takes so long to real-ly experience the place that you might as well sleep here; its one- and two-night package plans are reasonable. In the unlikely event that you get restless to leave the property, a free shuttle bus departs the south doors every 40 minutes for the 15-minute ride to the Eldora-do downtown. 2500 E. 2nd St., 775/789-2000 or 800/648-5080, www.renohilton.net, double room rates $59–200.

SPARKS

Until comparatively recently, this town, named after cattle baron and fourth Nevada governor John D. Sparks, might just as well have been called Embers, or even Ashes. Glendale, the original community here, was built up around the Stone and Gates Crossing over the Truckee, against which Charles Fuller decided he couldn't compete and Myron Lake decided he could. Sparks is the newest railroad town in northern Nevada, founded just after the turn of the 20th century by Southern Pacific. The railroad, in an effort to shorten and flatten its route through western Nevada, packed up its switching yard, maintenance plants, and most of the houses at Wadsworth 25 miles east, and moved them board by board to the new townsite on ranchland a few miles east of Reno.

By 1906, Sparks had reached a population of 3,500, almost all of whom were connected to the railroad in one way or another. Until the early '50s, Sparks remained a stolid working-class railroad town, steadfastly maintaining its rural, small-town, church-going identity as separate from Reno. Gambling, drinking, and divorce all stopped where the Sparks city line started. But the railroad shops again moved, this time to Roseville, California, in the early 1950s, and Sparks lost its main reason for being.

Enter Dick Graves, a restaurateur from Idaho, who moved into the northern Nevada restau-rant and casino scene in 1955, opening Nuggets in Reno, Carson City, Yerington, and Sparks. A young accountant with a specialty in hotel man-agement named John Ascuaga moved from Idaho to Sparks to help run the businesses. In 1960 Ascuaga, son of a Basque sheepman turned farmer, took over the Sparks Nugget, and Sparks finally saw some sparks.

After the state legislature passed the Freeport Law in 1960, warehousing and light industry began to develop in Sparks's wide-open spaces and the town took on a new identity. The popu-lation doubled from 1970 to 1986 (and now stands at around 65,000), and the physical boundaries between Sparks and Reno began to blur. Except that Sparks finally decided, in the late 1980s, to compete head-on with its step-sister next door, to the tune of a $1.7 million downtown redevelopment plan, which included street widening and improvements, a false-front facelift for the Treasury, Mint, and Silver clubs and some Victorian Avenue shops, a fountain, bandstand, gazebos, London lamps, custom bus stops, and concrete benches and iron fences. In 1998, Sparks underwent a $13 million six-block downtown revitalization project, which included a new 14-plex movie theater, lawns, gardens, fountains, a retail mall, and two large parking garages (with 700 and 900 spaces). Today the Reno-Sparks metropolitan skyline ex-tends from the Sands just west of Reno, through downtown, past the Reno Hilton, to finish off at the two-tower 28-story Nugget in Sparks, which now almost, but not quite, lives up to the richness of its name.

SIGHTS

If Reno-Sparks is one town with indistinct bound-aries, Sparks itself is actually two distinct towns in one, split in half by I-80, which runs elevated above it all. North of I-80 are the downtown and residential areas; south along Glendale Avenue and Greg Street are low sprawling warehous-es, tall round fuel tanks, and big wide truck stops. Straddling both sides of the highway is the

Nugget; I-80 runs right *over* the Nugget's casino, separating its Victorian Avenue entrance on the one side from the hotel towers on the other and giving you a strange subterranean sensation, like a *presque-vu* vibration, when you're inside gambling or eating.

Victorian Square

Sparks's Victorian Square is a successful effort at providing a unified theme for the downtown casino strip. The "Square" is actually eight blocks long and one block wide, stretching from 16th Street to Pyramid Way along Victorian Avenue. Along with all the theme pieces are two hotel-casinos, several slot joints, restaurants, and shops. The Square lights up effectively at night, catalyzing a classic Nevada-style reaction when you're blowing into town from the wild darkness of I-80 to the east. Truckers especially love Sparks and pull off at Truckee Meadows's easternmost exits for Western Village, the Alamo, and Sierra Sid's. The Square also hosts a number of popular events throughout the year, such as Hometowne Christmas, Best in the West Rib Cook-off, Hot August Nights, and Festival of the

DEKE CASTLEMAN

Arts. An open-air farmer's market takes place every Thursday evening in June, July, and August 5–9 P.M. Call 775/353-2291 for current dates of events.

The **Sparks Information Center and Chamber of Commerce** occupies a typical Southern Pacific-style depot at the corner of Pyramid and Victorian Avenues, 775/358-1976, info@sparks chamber.org, www.sparkschamber.org, open Mon.–Fri. 8 A.M.–5 P.M. year-round and 9 A.M.–5 P.M. summer weekends. It has a very well-organized and complete selection of brochures, booklets, and maps. On the left side of the depot is **Lillard Railroad Park,** with cool grass, some shade, and a monument dedicated to the "countless humble tasks" of the Chinese in building Nevada (a small but noticeable apology for the state's bitter early policies against Asian immigration). On the right are several old rail cars, including Engine No. 8, one of the last SP steam engines, which ran from 1907 till 1954; an SP executive car, retired in 1947; a City of Sparks sleeper; and a caboose that the city is trying to raise funds to restore.

Next to the train cars is the old **Glendale School.** It was built in 1864 for $1,500 and operated as a school till 1958; the late U.S. Senator Patrick McCarran, one of the most powerful politicians in Nevada history, was its most famous graduate. Originally located at the old Glendale town site in east Sparks, the school was moved in 1976 next to the Lake Mansion on the grounds of the Reno-Sparks Convention Center, where it languished unattended for nearly 20 years. But in late 1993 it was moved to its present site in Victorian Square. You can look in the windows, but you can't go inside until after its planned restoration. Next to the school is an amphitheater for concerts and plays.

Across the street and a bit south is the **Courthouse,** designed in 1931 by famous Nevada architect Fredric DeLongchamps; it also served as Washoe County's first branch library (till 1965).

Next door is **Sparks Heritage Museum,** 820 Victorian Ave., 775/355-1144, open 11 A.M.–4 P.M. Tues.–Fri., 1–4 P.M. Saturday and Sunday. The real attraction here is the enthusiasm of the old-timers who staff the museum. Get one of them talking, then settle back for some great stories—for example, how the interstate happened to be built over the Nugget casino. Also check out the artifacts: the war ration-book coupons, railroad hand tools, old typewriters and cash registers, ghost town junk, skulls and bones, a 1910 Amish doctor's buggy, a couple of crazy quilts, and a railroad room. Pick up the "Story of Sparks" brochure if you'd like to look around town at the historical buildings; City Hall on C and 12th streets and the 1904 Southern Pacific repair shops on East Nugget on the south side of the freeway are worth a drive-by.

John Ascuaga's Nugget

This two-tower hotel-casino at the east end of the Reno-Sparks skyline started out in 1955 as a 60-seat coffee shop on the north side of B St. (now Victorian Ave.) at the corner of 12th. It was opened by Dick Graves (one of four Nuggets that he opened within a few years; two of the others, in Reno and Carson City, remain, while the Yerington Nugget is gone). John Ascuaga, who'd put himself through college by working as a bellman at one of Graves's Idaho hotels, was appointed general manager. Graves retired in 1960 and sold the Nugget to Ascuaga. Business was good; three years later, the Nugget moved to a new building on the other side of B St., and Ascuaga opened Trader Dick's in the old building. By 1965, John Ascuaga had bought Graves out and the Nugget Motor Lodge, Nugget Inn, and Convention Center had come on-line.

In the early '70s, when I-80 was cutting a swath right through downtown Sparks, it threatened to install a stop sign to the Nugget's further expansion. Ascuaga negotiated with federal and state highway departments and came away with a long-term lease on all the space beneath the freeway. Subsequently, the Nugget expanded right around the support pillars. Which makes the Nugget the only casino in the world, probably, holding up a superhighway.

Trader Dick's moved under the freeway in 1973, and within 10 years all the restaurants, lounges, convention center, lower-level pavilion, lobby, and 29-story, 600-room tower (1984) had been completed. The stunning glass-walled indoor swimming pool and recreation facility on the fifth floor were completed in 1990. In 1992, the Nugget installed its new sign just west of the tower next to I-80; built by YESCO, it uses a million watts to power 25,000 bulbs in the mes-

sage marquee and 2,800 feet of neon tubing, all connected by 40 miles of wiring. It's 100 feet high by 55 feet wide and cost a cool mil. It faces east/west, so the impact is diminished a bit in the early morning and late afternoon, but at night the effects are dazzling and mesmerizing. The colors and graphics catch your eye from all over the freeway system in Truckee Meadows.

In 1994, the Nugget expanded again, with a new race and sports book in the lower level, along with Gabe's Pub & Deli, and $9 million 1,250-space parking garage with a 160-foot-long skywalk to the hotel. Another 980 rooms were added in 1996, giving the Nugget a total of 1,980 rooms.

The Nugget is the largest employer in Sparks (more than 2,500 employees), and by all accounts an enlightened one. It offers a child-care program, profit sharing, and English as a Second Language classes. The Nugget's scholarship program is locally famous; you can see the recipients' pictures on the convention-center level.

Everything about the Nugget is done with taste and style. And there are some surprises, as well. Notice the 6,000-gallon aquarium above the back bar at Trader Dick's. Also be sure to walk around to the lobby to view the 18-karat gold Golden Rooster, which weighs 206 troy ounces (17 pounds) and is worth more than $60,000. The rooster was fabricated in 1958 to grace the entrance to the Golden Rooster Restaurant at the Nugget. The Treasury Department, however, pointed out that at the time, it was illegal for individuals to possess more than 50 ounces of gold unless in an artistic form. After a few years of wrangling, the T-men confiscated the rooster, but in 1962 a jury found it to be an objet d'art and the rooster returned to the Nugget for good. 1100 Nugget Ave., 775/356-3300 or 800/648-1177, www.janugget.com, double room rates $69–114.

Other Casinos

At Victorian Ave. and 14th is the old-time **Victorian Gambling Hall,** which has three blackjack tables, two bars, and a coffee shop. Next up is **Dotty's,** a very homey little two-story slot joint. The floor of the **Mint Casino** directly across from the Nugget is often covered with the '90s' version of sawdust: empty coin rolls!

The **Silver Club** is the second largest of the

Victorian Square casino crowd. In fact, the Silver Club has a Victorian Square of its own, inside, surrounding the main pit. Upstairs you'll find pool tables, darts, the popular Rail Bar and Grill with a *big* big-screen TV, sports book, and a fine balcony for overseeing the action. 1040 Victorian Ave., 775/358-4771 or 800/905-7774, double room rates $35–69.

Farther afield is **Western Village** at the east end of Victorian Ave.—a distinctive Peppermill-style casino (see "Peppermill" under "Casinos" earlier in this chapter); 815 E. Nichols Blvd., 775/331-1069 or 800/648-1170, double room rates $39–69.

Rail City at the west end of Victorian Ave. had a facelift inside and out in 1994 and a name change (from Plantation Station) in 1996. It's still kind of a grind joint, but it's immensely popular with locals, thanks to its many promotions and giveaways, and very cheap food (the big steak dinner at $5.50 is the most expensive item on the menu). This place jumps round the clock. 2121 Victorian Ave., 775/359-9440.

Finally, **Baldini's Sports Casino** is possibly even more popular with locals than Rail City. It underwent an expansion in 1994 that doubled the size of the property, adding a steakhouse, buffet, race book, and arcade. The same half dozen video poker bars, however, keep packin'

'em in, along with blackjack, craps, and tons of slots. Like Rail City, Baldini's has unbelievable food deals (see "Snack Bars" under "Hotel Food" in the Food section). It's also the "Pepsi Historical Landmark," of all things. In December 1988, Baldini's became the first casino to award a six-pack of Pepsi each time a video poker player hit a natural 4-of-a-kind; since then Baldini's has been Pepsi's largest account in the state of Nevada. In fact, Pepsi is a kind of currency at Baldini's—you can trade in your six-pack for a "six-pack credit" at the Pepsi redemption center. It's worth a dollar cash, or you can use it for merchandise at the gift shop. 865 S. Rock Blvd. at the corner of Glendale, 775/358-0116.

Sparks Marina Park

Just off I-80 at the Sparks Blvd. exit, Sparks Marina Park, officially dedicated in October 2000, is Sparks's newest natural attraction. It's a lovely park with green areas and a man-made lake stocked with fish, a fine place for swimming, fishing and going to the beach. The lake has an interesting history: for many years it was the Helms Gravel Pit. When the New Year's Day flood occurred on January 1, 1997, the river overflowed and the pit filled with water. Later on, the city came into some money and decided to use it to create a lake and park here.

ACCOMMODATIONS

With roughly 28,000 rooms to choose from, finding a bed in Reno-Sparks suitable to your taste and take-home pay is child's play—except on weekends and holidays year-round, nearly every night in the summer, and during the many special events that happen here. On the Friday of Hot August Nights, for example, vacancy rates plummet, room rates skyrocket, blood drips from desk clerks' rabid fangs, and you have your choice of sitting up all night in a car, coffee shop, or casino. But on a Tuesday night in February, you'll be welcomed everywhere like a long-lost high roller.

Reserving a reasonable room in Reno is somewhat akin to buying an airline ticket. If you book it far enough in advance you get a Super-Saver; as it gets closer to your travel date, you'll have to spring for regular coach

fare; show up on any Saturday night and all that'll be left is first-class, one-way. Rates rise a minimum of 20 percent on Friday and Saturday nights for reserved rooms, and often up to 100 percent or a required two-night stay at the last minute. This is true for all the cities and towns in Nevada.

A reminder: always ask to see the room first, and check it out carefully. Make sure the windows open (and lock securely) and the air-conditioning works. Also, don't forget to ask about the telephone situation (if local calls are free and if long-distance access charges are imposed). Finally, be sure to ask if any coupons or funbooks are available, which often include substantial food and show discounts and gambling incentives.

MOTELS

Orientation

Except for a few scattered monoliths (Hilton, Peppermill, Holiday Inn, Atlantis), all of Reno's large hotel-casinos are found on or near Virginia Street downtown, and most of the motels surround them in six distinct clumps. If you like to step out of your motel-room door right onto the main drag, a dozen or so places are strung along N. Virginia from 4th St. to just across I-80, with a couple up the hill near the university. Four others are a block east on N. Center between 5th and 6th Streets.

East 4th St. has another dozen or so between downtown and the US 395 overpass. This is blue-collar country: heating and air-conditioning, sheet metal, refrigeration, tires, auto parts, gas stations, topless joints, truck repair, scrap metal and salvage, and machine shops. Some of the digs here are welfare motels; some are for visitors.

The motels along W. 2nd St. by the Greyhound depot are a bit more sedate; the street is wider and the neighborhood a bit more residential. A couple of blocks north on W. 4th, motels stand one after another all the way out of town. In fact, the whole two-by-three-block area just west of Virginia St. between 2nd and 5th is packed with motels.

The same is true for the east side of Virginia St. between E. 3rd and 6th on Lake Street.

South Virginia Street's motel row starts half a mile out of town and stretches past the Peppermill all the way out to the southern edge of the city.

Almost all of Reno's motels are competitively priced. The rates quoted are for two people and one queen-size bed on a summer weekday. Add $10 for a king, $20 or so for a weekend night, and nine percent sales tax.

Downtown Motels

There are plenty of motels right in the heart of downtown, near the casino action. Virginia Street motels include the **Showboat Inn,** 660 N. Virginia St., 775/786-4032 or 800/648-3960, $35–125; and the **Golden West Motor Lodge,** 530 N. Virginia St., 775/329-2192, $35–175. On Fifth Street are the **Easy 8 Motel,** 255 W. 5th St.,

775/322-4588, with rooms starting at $22; the **Gatekeeper Inn,** 221 W. 5th St., 775/786-3500 or 800/822-3504, $30–60; and **Season's Inn,** 495 West St. at the corner of 5th, 775/322-6000 or 800/322-8588, with rooms for $40–115. On the next corner, at the corner of West and 4th Streets, the **Bonanza Motor Inn,** 215 W. 4th St., 775/322-8632 or 800/808-3303, has rooms for $38–125. The **Stardust Lodge,** 455 N. Arlington Ave., 775/322-5641, has rooms for $30–85.

The quieter area near the Greyhound station is a good intermediate location—very near the downtown casinos, and yet with a more residential feel. Recommendable motels in this area include the **Truckee River Lodge,** 501 W. First St., 775/786-8888 or 800/635-8950, a nonsmoking hotel with 224 rooms for $31–220 (ask about weekly rates and bicycle rental), and the **Town House Motor Lodge,** 303 W. 2nd St., 775/323-1821 or 800/438-5660, with rooms for $29–58.

North of Downtown

The **University Inn,** 1001 N. Virginia St., 775/323-0321, opposite the university, is a bit removed from the hubbub of the downtown casino area although it's actually only a few blocks north. Its 170 rooms go for $30–150.

South of Downtown

Just south of the Truckee River is the good **Executive Inn,** 205 S. Sierra St., 775/786-4050, with rooms for $55–90 (ask about weekly rates). Further south, more removed from the downtown area, are **Best Inn & Suites,** 1885 S. Virginia St., 775/329-1001 or 800/237-8466, with rooms for $52–78, and **Motel 6,** 1901 S. Virginia St., 775/827-0255 or 800/466-8356, $36–50.

West of Downtown

The blocks just west of downtown are also a bit quieter, while still being near the casinos. Motels here include the **Gold Dust West Casino & Motor Lodge,** 444 Vine St., 775/323-2211 or 800/438-9378, with rooms for $29–109; the **Reno Travelodge,** 655 W. 4th St., 775/329-3451 or 800/578-7878, $29–89; and the **Donner Inn,** 720 W. 4th St., 775/323-1851, $30–60.

East of Downtown

La Quinta Inn, 4001 Market St., at the Plumb Lane exit of US 395 (exit 65), 775/348-6100 or 800/NV-ROOMS, has a fine reputation. Its 130 rooms go for $49–103, and there's a family restaurant right there too. Just off I-80, at the Wells Ave. exit, are a **Motel 6,** 1400 Stardust St., 775/827-0255 or 800/466-8356, with rooms for $36–50, and a **Days Inn,** 701 E. 7th St., 775/786-4070 or 800/448-4555, $29–60.

Lucky Charm?

Choosing a hotel or motel in Reno at random could be indicative of your character. Are you a tried-and-true national-chain habitual? For you there are four **Motel 6's,** one **Days Inn,** and two **TraveLodges.** Do you believe in the Law of Octaves? For you there's an **Easy 8,** and a **Super 8.** Are you superstitious? Choose from the **777 Motel,** the **Shamrock Inn,** and the **Horseshoe Motel.** Into Snow White? Try the **Hi-Ho.** Finally, for all you been-there done-that jaded winners/losers, there's the **Ho Hum Motel.**

Adventure and Romance Inns

Two motels stand apart from the madding crowd. The **Adventure Inn,** 3575 S. Virginia just south of Moana, 775/828-9000, was built by one of the owners of the Atlantis, who wanted to treat his wife to an exotic motel room without feeling degraded. Theme rooms here include the Jungle, Bridal, Roman, Adam and Eve, Tropical, Bordello, Cave, and Space suites. All come with round or heart-shaped beds, "rainforest" showers, free limo rides within 10 miles and complimentary champagne, but from there, well, you just have to *see* these rooms. Prices range from $69 up to $235.

The **Romance Inn,** 2905 S. Virginia, 775/826-1515, is similar, with in-room spas built for two, mirrored ceilings and walls, romantic lighting, and mini-refrigerators. Rates range from $69 to $180.

Weeklies

For the complete rundown on the Nevada big-city seven-day motel-room scenario, see "Weekly Motels" under "Accommodations" in the Las Vegas chapter.

Probably the largest and most comfortable weekly rooms are at the all-suites **Executive Inn:** large rooms, full refrigerator, microwave, pool, parking garage, just south of downtown, on the south side of the Truckee River. 205 S. Sierra St., 775/786-4050. Weekly rates are around $145–155.

Truckee River Lodge, 501 W. First St., 775/786-8888 or 800/635-8950, a non-smoking hotel near both the Truckee River and downtown, has a great variety of rooms available by the week, ranging from single rooms with one twin bed up to two-bedroom suites and even houses. Weekly rates range from $154 for one person, up to $406 for the largest and most luxurious accommodation, with plenty of options in between. They also rent bicycles.

Good weekly rooms downtown are available at **Castaway Inn.** The smaller, less expensive rooms, though a bit cozy, are comfortable, usable, and affordable. Great location, too: quiet and used mostly by tourists and local singles. 525 W. 2nd St., 775/329-2555. Weekly rates start at $165.

HOTELS

Downtown Budget Hotels

Most of the older hotels are convenient and adequate, if not classy. Some bathrooms are down the hall, some are in the room. Around the Greyhound depot (W. 2nd St.) are the **El Cortez,** 239 W. 2nd St., 775/322-9161, $20–60, and the **Windsor Hotel,** around the corner at 214 West St., 775/323-6171, $22–48. Each has parking available in parking lots across the street.

Big Hotels

For a nuts-and-bolts description of how to navigate your way into and out of Nevada's big-hotel room and package scene, see "Accommodations" in the Las Vegas chapter. Rate and contact information for the Reno-Sparks area's big hotel-casinos is given in the preceding "Casinos" section.

Suites

The suite on the 12th floor of the **Atlantis Casino Resort** is the least expensive of the lot, but it could cost more. The tropical theme is implemented with rattan, palm fronds, and floral prints throughout the bedroom, living room, and bar;

there's also a black-marble jacuzzi in the bedroom (and a phone in the bathroom, standard in suites).

The **Sands Regency Hotel/Casino** offers a suite on the 17th floor with a stunning view out of floor-to-ceiling picture windows. It comes complete with sunken living room, free-standing fireplace, full kitchen, and marble jacuzzi.

The **Peppermill Hotel Casino's** 16th-floor suite has three TVs, gold bathroom fixtures, velvet-bolstered bar (very comfortable), and a pool-size jacuzzi as close to the bed as you'd ever need. The large walk-in shower converts to a steam bath at the snap of your fingers.

John Ascuaga's Nugget charges similar rates for its top-of-the-line (literally: it's on the 29th floor) suite. Sauna, marble fireplace, and a jacuzzi that could fit your whole extended family. Nice desert view to the east.

BED & BREAKFAST

The **South Reno B&B,** 136 Andrew Lane, 775/849-0772, is out in the countryside about 12 miles south of Reno. There's plenty of privacy, peace and quiet; it has a large grounds with lots of lawn and trees, the owners' cattle and horses are in a field off from the house, and the swimming pool is great in summer. Upstairs room-with-bath is $75.

CAMPING

The closest place to pitch a tent to downtown Reno is at **Chism's Trailer Park,** 1300 W. 2nd Street, 775/322-2281 or 800/638-2281.

The closest places to spend the night in the Great Outtadoors are all about 30 miles from Reno. By far the best spot to pitch your tent is at **Davis Creek Park,** a Washoe County facility, 19 miles south on US 395 (see "Washoe Valley" in the Vicinity of Reno section). A 10-minute drive from there around Washoe Lake is **Washoe Lake State Park.** There might even be water in the lake.

Lookout Campground is 18 miles northwest of Reno beyond Verdi in California (see "Around Town" under "Verdi" in the Vicinity of Reno section).

Warrior Point Park is at the end of the paved road on the west side of Pyramid Lake (see "Sights" in the "Pyramid Lake" section of the Northwest Nevada chapter).

RV Parks
The oldest private campground in Nevada, having opened in 1926, right along the Truckee River just west of downtown, is **Chism's Trailer Park,** 1300 W. 2nd Street, 775/322-2281 or 800/638-2281. It's also the shadiest, with towering trees and lush landscaping. A lot of the park is occupied by permanent mobiles, but there are enough overnight sites to make it worth checking out. Also, it's the closest place to downtown to pitch a tent. There are a total of 152 spaces, but only 28 for motor homes, all 28 with full hookups; six are pull-throughs. Tents are allowed. Accessible restrooms have flush toilets and hot showers; public phone, sewage disposal, and laundry are available. The fee is $10 for tents, $18.50 for trailers and RVs.

The largest RV park in the area, not surprisingly, is **Reno Hilton KOA,** at the Las Vegas Hilton, 775/789-2147 or 888/562-5698. It's parking-lot camping; some sites overlook Hilton bay (a square pond in the original gravel pit where there's a driving range). Note that it's right on one of the two approaches to Reno-Tahoe Airport. There are 264 spaces for motor homes, all with full hookups, and 42 pull-throughs. Tents are not allowed. Accessible restrooms have flush toilets and hot showers; sewage disposal, laundry, groceries, video rentals, and heated swimming pool are available. The stay limit is 28 days. The fee is $21–26 per vehicle.

Reno RV Park, 735 Mill Street, 775/323-3381 or 800/445-3381, has four rows of parking off of two narrow alleys, all back-in sites. The park's been here 12 years and it's still the closest to downtown Reno. It's an older part of town: hospitals, medical offices, and the police station are all nearby. Security is beefy, with a high wall and gates in and out. Harrah's sends its shuttle around Friday through Monday. There are 46 spaces for motor homes, all with full hookups. Free-standing tents are allowed, but not tents that require stakes. Accessible restrooms have flush toilets and hot showers; public phone, sewage disposal, and laundry are available. The fee is $20–23 for two people; cheaper in winter. Good Sam and AAA discounts are offered, as are more economical weekly and monthly rates.

Keystone RV Park, 1455 W. 4th Street, 775/324-5000 or 800/686-8559, is on the western edge of the downtown business district, within walking distance of plentiful fast food, supermarket, ice company, even a good bookstore. The front section opened in 1993, the back (which fronts an 18-room motel) opened in 1992. It's parking lot camping, with a few trees and a little grass. The casinos are about eight blocks away, so the Keystone fills up fast for the nonstop events in Reno between Memorial Day and Labor Day. There are 104 spaces for motor homes, all with full hookups, no pull-throughs. Tents are not allowed. Accessible restrooms have flush toilets and hot showers; sewage disposal and laundry are available. The fee is $19–21 for two people. Good Sam discounts offered.

Shamrock RV Park, 260 Parr Blvd. (from I-80, take the Virginia Street exit and go north about two miles to Parr Boulevard. Turn right on Parr and drive down the hill; the park is on the right), 775/329-5222 or 800/322-8248, was new in 1985, but it's so clean you'd think it opened last week. It sits in a little bowl with earthen walls in an industrial part of town. It's big, all paved, and has trees and shrubs between wide sites. The rec hall has exercise equipment and a full kitchen. It's two blocks from the small but popular Bonanza Casino. A mile south is Rancho San Rafael Park, the largest park in the urban area. Two miles south of that is downtown. There are 121 spaces for motor homes, all with full hookups, 75 pull-throughs. Tents are not allowed. Accessible restrooms have flush toilets and hot showers; sewage disposal, laundry, groceries, rec room, small playground, and heated swimming pool are available. The fee is $20–24 per vehicle. Good Sam discounts offered.

River's Edge RV Park, 1405 South Rock Blvd., Sparks, 775/358-8533 or 800/621-4792, is an idyllic setting for an RV park, right on the Truckee River. You have immediate access to many miles of paved riverside biking and hiking trails. It's lush and well-shaded. It also happens to be right on the eastern landing route for Reno-Tahoe Airport, so big commercial airliners fly 300 feet overhead. But if you can stand an occasional jet engine or two, River's Edge is one of the nicest RV parks around. There are 164 spaces for motor homes, all with full hookups; 98 are pull-throughs. Tents are not allowed. Restrooms have flush toilets and hot showers; sewage disposal and laundry are available. The fee is $18 for two people.

Victorian RV Park, 205 Nichols Blvd., Sparks, 775/355-4040 or 800/955-6405, is at the eastern edge of downtown Sparks's business district, right off Victorian Avenue (the main drag in Sparks). It's young, clean, and paved. RVers have access to the pool and arcade across the street at the Thunderbird resort. There are 92 spaces for motor homes, all with full hookups; 46 are pull-throughs. Tents are not allowed. Accessible restrooms have flush toilets and hot showers; sewage disposal, laundry, groceries, heated pool and spa are available. The fee is $18–20 per vehicle. Good Sam, AAA and AARP discounts offered

Boomtown RV Park, I-80, Verdi, 775/345-8650 or 800/648-3790, is a large self-contained area below the casino, with wide spaces, some greenery, and its own pool. You'll never lack for knowing the time, with the Boomtown clock tower right above. Inside the hotel are: the Family Fun Center, featuring an 18-hole indoor miniature golf course, an antique carousel, a motion-simulation theater (the only one in northern Nevada), and video games galore. There is also a steakhouse, buffet, and 24-hour coffeeshop. It has 203 spaces for motor homes, all with full hookups; 132 are pull-throughs. Tents are not allowed. Accessible restrooms have flush toilets and hot showers; sewage disposal, laundry, groceries, video rentals, heated swimming pool, and two spas are available. The fee is $21–23 for two people. Good Sam and AARP discounts offered.

FOOD

Restaurants aren't nearly as numerous in Reno-Sparks as they are in Las Vegas, but food, especially in casino-hotel restaurants, is just as much a loss leader in northern as it is in southern Nevada. Restaurant prices are heavily subsidized by casino earnings, and as soon as you eat a 99-cent breakfast, a $1.99 plate of spaghetti, a $4.95 prime rib, a $7.99 dinner-buffet hog-o-rama, and a $10.95 steak-and-lobster in a fine dining room, you'll find it hard to go home to California or wherever and fork over the tab at your local restaurants. Many people come to Reno and Sparks not for the slots or tables, not for the shows or recreation, but for the food alone.

Note that things change fast around here. It's not uncommon for an entire casino to change, let alone a particular restaurant in a casino, or a particular dish in a restaurant, or a particular price of a dish. The buffets, especially, change times, prices, and themes frequently. The following listings have been selected for reliability as much as quality and value, but use them only as a, you know, guide. If the listing still exists at the time that you're counting on it, its vital statistics should be within an hour and a dollar. Always call first to make sure where you want to go is still there and what you want there is still available.

The *Reno-Sparks Menu & More,* a free magazine published seasonally and available at all the usual free-paper news racks and visitor centers, gives current news and listings for all the Reno-Tahoe area casino restaurants, plus other food news. Their two-page spread lists all the latest in casino restaurants.

CASINO-HOTEL FOOD

Snack Bars
The **Cal-Neva** takes the prize, hands down, for the best snack bar in town. The Sports Deli on the third floor in the far corner of the sports book serves a big fat frankfurter and a bottle of Heineken for $1.50; Cal-Neva claims that it sells more Heineken than any other single location in the country. Other great deals are the honkin' burgers, monster roast beef sandwiches, and fries. The Sports Deli is open 7 A.M.–10 P.M., 775/323-1046.

Baldini's at 865 S. Rock Blvd. in Sparks is nearly unbeatable for lunch and dinner specials. At Baldini's Kitchen, you can enjoy a deli sandwich and a beer or soda, or a hot dog, for cheap. Or try the spaghetti and meat sauce, double cheeseburger, or hot sandwiches with potato, roll, and beer. Baldini's Big Kitchen is open 10 A.M.–11 P.M., 775/358-0116.

The **Gold Dust West** at W. 5th and Vine is similar, with cheap specials: spaghetti, burgers with topping bar, steak and eggs, and usually a big steak special, all with salad bar. Open 6 A.M.–10 P.M., 775/323-2211.

Cafeteria-Style
The **Cal-Neva** takes another prize in this category, for its Hof Brau on the second floor. You won't believe the prices nor the volume of food, and the quality is good for a cafeteria. Entrees include a big bowl of beef stew and a pretty nice piece of prime rib (along with potatoes and

DOVER PUBLICATIONS, INC.;

vegie). Big sandwiches, and you can get the famous Cal-Neva $1.49 breakfast here too (see "Breakfast," below). Open 24 hours, 775/323-1046.

There's a fast-food court at the **Peppermill,** in the northwest wing. You have plenty to choose from: Mexican, Italian, Chinese, American, and everything (even a big prime rib dinner, baker, and vegie) is inexpensive. Very comfortable seats to boot. Open 8 A.M.–10 P.M., 775/826-2121.

The fast-food court downtown is Choices at the **Eldorado.** This is actually a step above fast food, served cafeteria style. Choose from Mexican, Chinese, Italian, and American, with a full bakery and ice cream counter. Soup, salad bar, slices of pizza, etc Open 7 A.M.–10:30 P.M., 775/786-5700.

Coffee Shops
Note that all the following coffee shops are open 24 hours.

Just as Choices is a step up, Tivoli Gardens at the **Eldorado** is head and shoulders above your usual coffee shop. With food from every continent (with Vietnamese and Thai specialties), plus wood-fired oven pizza and 24-hour breakfasts, you'll have a harder time choosing here than at Choices. Tivoli Gardens (opened 1992) looks more like a Roman plaza than a coffee shop. 775/786-5700.

The Purple Parrot at **Atlantis** points to the fact that "coffee shop" in a casino is a misnomer. Though it's open 24 hours and everything on the menu is inexpensive, the Parrot serves up everything from a bacon cheeseburger and club sandwich to halibut steak and shrimp louie. With a coffee shop comp for two, you could teach 'em a lesson easy. 775/825-4700.

The Shore Room in the newly refurbished **Holiday Hotel** at Center downtown overlooks the Truckee River. Other than that, it's basic cafe fare. Try the house special Tahoe Sandwich. 775/329-0411.

The Farmhouse coffee shop at the **Nugget** in Sparks is famous for its Awful Awful Burger, a half-pound burger served with a full pound of fries and all the trimmings. For just $3.50, it's awful big and awful good. (Both the Reno and Sparks Nuggets serve Awful Awful burgers and have since they were both opened in the '50s by

the same owner.) The Country Store is the other coffee shop at the Nugget. The Nugget actively competes with the Eldorado for the best hotel food in town; it has incredible seasonal festivals such as strawberry, rhubarb, and the BBQ Rib Cook-off. 775/356-3300.

Not surprisingly, the coffee shop at the **Alamo Truck Stop** just off I-80 at the Sparks Blvd. exit is a good place to get an honest and filling meal. The menu is tractor-trailer size, the prices are extremely reasonable, the phones at the booths are always busy, and the fried chicken is about as good as it gets. But the real treat here is the potato dishes. Bakers are available 24 hours a day, home fries are thick and hearty, and the Potatoes Piled High will hold you for eight hours easy. 775/358-8888.

Diners
Johnny Rocket's, at the Las Vegas Hilton near the race and sports book, is the only retro '50s-style diner at a hotel-casino in Reno. It ain't cheap, but it is authentic, with a black-and-white-checked floor, red naugehyde booths, and individual juke boxes at the counter and on the tables. Try the big burgers with the works, vegie burger, chili dog, chili fries, malts, shakes, floats, hot fudge sundaes, and apple pie a la mode. The fries are brought first; the waitress pulls a bottle of ketchup from her apron and fills up a paper basket. The straw act is pretty cool, too. It's open 10 A.M.–midnight, till 2 A.M. Friday and Saturday, 775/789-2000.

The diner at the back of the little **Nugget** in downtown Reno isn't retro; it's a classic. Eighteen red stools face the counter and another eighteen face the back wall. The Awful Awful burger is two meals. Every Wednesday you can get an eight-ounce prime rib with all the trimmings for a great price. Or fill up on a dollar beer and free popcorn at the bar. Nugget Diner, open 24 hours, 775/323-0716.

Breakfast
Cal-Neva's $1.49 breakfast has been voted the "Best Of Reno" and no wonder! This is the *$5.99* breakfast at Denny's. This fill-er-upper comes with two eggs, ham or bacon, hash browns, toast, and coffee, and is served at the Top Deck on the third floor. Cal-Neva serves more than a million of these eye-openers every year, which

averages roughly 3,000 a day! It's crowded on weekend mornings (try the counter if there're one or two of you), so sign up at the Top Deck on the third floor, then wander around the slots, pits, and books. From midnight to 7 A.M. this breakfast is an even better deal—only 99 cents! If the $1.49 breakfast isn't to your liking, how about a cube steak and eggs, top sirloin and eggs, oatmeal, and orange juice? Open 24 hours, 775/954-4540.

The Food Court at the **Peppermill** has a good three-egg-and-bacon deal. Open 8 A.M.–10 P.M., 775/826-2121.

The **Sundowner** serves up steak and eggs 24 hours a day in the coffee shop. Open 24 hours, 775/786-7050.

The **Treasury Club** on Victorian Ave. in downtown Sparks has some cheap breakfasts at John Juan's Mexican-American restaurant. Open at 7 A.M., 775/356-7177.

The **Silver Club** up the street from the Treasury in Sparks serves a $2.50 breakfast with a half-pound of ham and two eggs in the coffee shop. Open 24 hours, 775/358-4771.

Steaks and Prime Rib

Cal-Neva's Top Deck coffee shop (open 24 hours) and Copper Ledge steakhouse (open for dinner) serve a recommendable eight-ounce prime rib; it's thin but consistently tender and tasty. You can also get a 12-ounce cut. You'll see these advertised all over town on billboards. 775/323-1046.

The Steakhouse at **Harrah's** is highly rated by restaurant reviewers (as well as by UNR professors who like to hang out there for lunch). Downstairs from the main casino, order your sandwiches, liver, filet, or lamb 11 A.M.–2 P.M. Dinner prices are dear: peppersteak, filet, 20-ounce T-bone, salmon, sole, steak Diane, and more. Open Mon.–Fri. 11 A.M.–2 P.M., daily 5–10 P.M., 775/786-3232.

At the Steakhouse at **Western Village** in East Sparks, there's an Early-Bird Special: your prime rib or New York strip costs $9.95 with all the trimmings and fixings 4:30–6 P.M.—one of the best steak deals in town. Especially since this is a pretty fancy steakhouse. Open 4:30–10 P.M., 775/331-1069.

As always, the **Eldorado** has a fine entry in the field: its Grille and Rotisserie on the mezza-

nine. The salad bar has been judged the best in town by independent experts; *this* expert can verify that it's the biggest. Entrees are grilled or spit cooked in the open kitchen. Filet, blackened rib steak with peppercorn sauce, prime rib, and spit-roasted lamb, chicken, fish, all in the $12–16 range. You can get the prime rib, pork, lamb, or chicken, along with the salad bar, for $8.99 with the Early-Bird Special 5–6:30 P.M. (the salad bar costs $8.50 by itself and is worth it). Open 5–10 P.M., 775/786-5700.

The Steakhouse at **John Ascuaga's Nugget** in Sparks has been around a long time. More than three million steaks have been served since the joint opened in 1956. For lunch, you can get a chicken breast, Reuben, or N.Y. steak sandwich, among others, along with salmon or seafood fettucine. Dinner entrees include prime rib, steak, lamb, veal, chicken, duck, salmon, swordfish, and pasta. Open Mon.–Fri. 11 A.M.–2 P.M., daily 5–11 P.M., 775/356-3300.

Seafood

And speaking of fish, the Oyster Bar at John A's Nugget is, according to Anthony Curtis of the *Las Vegas Advisor* (who's eaten in more Nevada casino restaurants than anybody in the world), one of the best places to eat shellfish this side of San Francisco. This restaurant has been in operation for 35 years, and several of the waitresses have been there almost as long. You've never seen so many big clams in the red and white chowders, and the oyster, shrimp, and combo pan roasts are *loaded* and delicious. You can also get king salmon, prawns, scampi, oysters on the half shell, seafood cocktails, louies, cioppino, and sandwiches. Open 11 A.M.–10 P.M., 775/356-3300.

The other good casino seafood restaurant in town is Atlantis at the **Atlantis.** The theme here is underwater, and the decor is sea cave, with the tallest aquarium you've ever seen and a rippling ceiling. Half of the menu here consists of piscatory pleasures, while the other half is meat. Seafood fettuccine, king crab legs, halibut, steamed mussels and clams, surf and turf, and more. Open 5–10 P.M., 775/824-4430.

If it's Friday or Saturday night, head to the **Eldorado** for its seafood buffet (served in a crowded ballroom in the convention center; cozy it ain't), with all-you-can-eat cracked snow crab legs and peel-and-eat shrimp, half a dozen ocean entrees, big salad bar, and fancy desserts, including made-to-order cherries Jubilee. 775/786-5700.

Buffets

The best buffets in Reno, in my opinion, are found at Atlantis, John Ascuaga's Nugget, and the Reno Hilton. There's a steak buffet nightly at the Silver Club. Those at Harrah's, the Peppermill, and the Sands will fill you up with no particular joy, though no particular despair either.

The **Atlantis**'s lunch and dinner buffets have one feature that's duplicated at only two other buffets in the state (the Rio and Fiesta in Las Vegas): a Mongolian barbecue, where your vegetables and meats are stir fried on a round grill. It also has a specialty salad buffet with Caesars and hot spinach salads made to order. There's also a long salad bar, plenty of variety, and an excellent selection of desserts. Open for breakfast, lunch and dinner, 775/824-4433.

Lunch and dinner only are served at **John A's Nugget** Rotisserie buffet. The food here is consistently good, especially the salads and desserts. If you're here on Tuesday and you like chocolate, you'll think you went to heaven, since it's chocolate dessert night. Open for lunch and dinner, 775/356-3300.

The Hilton remodeled and retooled its buffet in 1994; eating there now makes you feel as if you're at the El Tovar near the South Rim of the Grand Canyon. It's the most spacious casino in town and has a large variety of salads and entrees. On a recent visit, I was impressed by peel-and-eat shrimp along with snow crab legs and claws, lobster linguini, peppers and shrimp, Szechwan scallops, pecan chicken, Grand Canyon chili, and big desserts. Open for breakfast, lunch and dinner, 775/789-2000.

There's an all-you-can-eat steak dinner buffet at the **Silver Club** in Sparks that's very popular with locals. The room is small, cramped, and tumultuous, and the buffet part is kind of ordinary (corn on the cob, baked beans, spaghetti, garlic bread, baked potato), but let's face it, the steak's the thing: all you can eat, cooked to order, fair-sized boneless New York slabs. If you get one that's not tender, juicy, and grilled to perfection, toss it and step up for another! Well, sneak it

out and feed it to the dog. Open for dinner, 775/358-4771.

Ethnic

For Mexican, Amigo's at the **Comstock** has reasonable prices and quality, with fajitas, tamales, flautas, enchiladas, and combination plates. There's also a good margarita special. Open 5–10 P.M., 775/329-1881.

The prices are roughly the same, though the quality is better, at **Pancho and Willie's** Mexican-Italian restaurant at Western Village off I-80 in Sparks. Good chips and salsa and filling entrees. It's open for breakfast on weekends (Mexican and American) Saturday and Sunday 8 A.M.–11 P.M., 11 A.M.–11 P.M. Mon.–Friday, 775/331-1069.

The **Eldorado's** La Strada is not only one of the top Italian restaurants in Nevada, but also in the country: it has been named among the nation's top 25 Italian and has won the *Wine Spectator's* Award of Excellence. All the pasta is handmade on the premises and the pizza is so good that they ought to open a take-out place. Everything is baked in wood-fired brick ovens. Start off with a little carpaccio, then go on to spaghetti marinara or other pasta dishes. The ravioli is excellent (spinach, seafood, or regular). Chicken comes picatta, marsala, arrosto, parmesana, and saltimbocca. You can also get T-bones, scaloppine, and fish. A 30-by-5-foot mural on the back wall depicts the Ferrari-Carano vineyards in Sonoma County's Alexander Valley. Open 5–10 P.M., 776/348-9297.

With La Strada right across the street, **Harrah's** had to do something different to make Cafe Andreotti a success. It succeeded. The create-your-own-pasta menu offers a selection of six pastas and six sauces. You can also try Andreotti's pizzas, pasta specials, manicotti, chicken, veal, scampi, or snapper. Or sample the calzone: a big half-moon of delicious pizza dough, bursting its seams with vegetables, cheese, and meats. Open 5–10 P.M., 776/786-3232.

The **Flamingo's** Emperor's Garden is an excellent Chinese restaurant right downtown. The food here is light, savory, and exotic, and it's available long hours. Try the minced chicken delight, any of the tofu dishes, lemon chicken, salt-baked shrimp or scallops, or the steamed squab. Open Sun.–Thurs. 11 A.M.–midnight, Friday and Saturday till 3 A.M., 776/322-1111.

Trader Dick's at **John Ascuaga's Nugget** is one of the oldest restaurants in town, featuring Polynesian (mostly Chinese- and Japanese-style) cuisine in a low-lit, South-Seas ambience; dark and leafy, it's a good place to feel enveloped by a sultry Polynesian evening. It's open for lunch, when you can get sandwiches if you're not in the mood for pork chow mein, teriyaki chicken, or stir-fried shrimp. The dinner menu lists steak, prime rib, king crab, and duck along with Chinese pepper steak, cashew chicken, and lobster and shrimp Cantonese. Have a mai tai, cha cha, chi chi, aku aku, zombie, wahine, Molokai Mike, or Rangoon Ruby at the bar, topped by the largest aquarium in town. Open Mon.–Fri. 11 A.M.–2 P.M., daily 5–10 P.M., 775/356-3300.

View

The highest restaurant in town is Top of the Hilton on the 21st floor of the **Flamingo.** The view from the restaurant and bar up here is obscured a bit by a surrounding deck. But inside it's a very comfortable and classy establishment. The bar often has piano and synthesizer entertainment and hors d'oeuvres such as crab legs. On the other side at the restaurant, try the chicken, salmon, prime rib, and filet. The Sunday brunch here is considered the best in town, by some. Open Tues.–Sun. 6–11 P.M., 775/322-1111.

LOCAL FAVORITES

Cafés

Odette's is classy and usually crowded. It serves salads, sandwiches, and quiches, and a large variety of espresso, coffee drinks, and fountain treats. For breakfast, try a vegie-brie omelette or Belgian waffle. If it's really busy, you can almost always find a seat or two at the counter. Odette's is at 4935 Energy Way, 775/857-2828, open Mon.–Fri. 9 A.M.–4:30 P.M., Saturday 10 A.M.–2 P.M. for cake pick-ups only.

Josef's Vienna Bakery, Café & Ceramic Studio takes top honors every year as the best bakery in the "Best of Reno" according to the *Gazette-Journal* voting. It bakes pastries, danishes, croissants, rolls, muffins, cookies, and breads, all served with coffee. Or have some muesli with fresh fruit and yogurt for $3. If it's clement, eat outside at the sidewalk tables. It's in the Moana West shopping center, 933 W. Moana at the corner of Lakeside Dr., 775/825-0451. The bakery is open Mon.–Fri. 7 A.M.–5:30 P.M., Sat. 8 A.M.–4 P.M., Sun. 8 A.M.–2 P.M. The café is open weekdays 7 A.M.–3 P.M., Sat. 8 A.M.–4 P.M., Sun. 8 A.M.–2 P.M.

Deux Gros Nez (Two Big Noses) is one of the funkiest little cafes in Reno, and proud of it. Above the Hermitage Gallery on California St. (look for the purple staircase), this place is not noted for its elegance or fastidiousness! But it is renowned for its excellent fresh vegetarian food, such as flavorful pasta and rice dishes and focaccia (chewy bread with pizza toppings), quiches, cakes and pies, coffee and teas, soups and sandwiches, all between $3 and $6. Deux Gros Nez is one of the last unreconstructed hippie-type establishments that remain in Reno from the good old days, but that doesn't at all deter the lawyers, bankers, and socialites from patronizing the place. Located at 249 California, 775/786-9400, open Mon.–Fri. 6 A.M.–midnight, Saturday and Sunday 7 A.M.–midnight.

Miscellaneous Faves

The **Little Waldorf Saloon,** operating since 1922, is the oldest restaurant in Reno, if not Nevada. Like Sharkey's in Gardnerville, the walls here are chockablock with photos, plus wildlife prints, big-game trophies (including a big Alaskan brown bear), ducks, birds, guns, and the like. Several big- and small-screen TVs are dotted around the room, one on each end of the *long* bar. Eggs start at $3.50; a four-egg omelette is $5.25. Burgers and sandwiches start at $5, and diner-type dinners start at $9. 1661 N. Virginia, open 24 hours, 775/323-3682.

Rapscallion has an interesting interior—lots of wood, some of it walling in very private dining alcoves, attractive bar, stained glass. Lunch is served Mon.–Fri. 11:30 A.M.–4 P.M.; sandwiches run $5–7. Dinners, served 5–10 P.M. nightly, start with escargot, calamari, or Cajun coconut prawns and continue with salads and fish and beef. Rapscallions features a whole page worth of fresh seafood daily. Good food, good prices, attentive yet unobtrusive service, very popular. 1555 S. Wells, 775/323-1211, open Mon.–Sat. 11:30

A.M.–4 P.M., daily 5–10 P.M., Sunday brunch 10 A.M.–2 P.M.

Café Soleil, serving gourmet California/Mediterranean style cuisine, is one of Reno's most popular upscale restaurants, consistently voted "Best Restaurant in Reno" in local newspaper readers' polls. The menu features tempting seafood, filet mignon, pasta and vegetarian dishes for $14–26, and there's an extensive wine list. The restaurant is up on a hill, with a good view of the city; décor features an open kitchen where you can see the food being prepared, and a big wood-fired oven is great for winter warmth. Located a bit out of town but worth looking for, it's west of downtown at 4796 Caughlin Parkway on the corner of McCarran Blvd., about 3.5 miles south of I-80; 775/828-6444. Open every night 5–9:30 P.M. (till 10 P.M. Fri.–Sat.), with Sunday brunch 10 A.M.–2 P.M.

ETHNIC

Basque

The original Basque boardinghouse and dining room is at the **Santa Fe Hotel.** Long-time residents swear by the Santa Fe, which opened in 1949. On busy nights, the big barroom in front is packed with people waiting to be seated (in waves) at the family-style tables in the dining room. The food is plentiful and hearty, the wine carafes are bottomless, and the service is feisty. For an interesting view, stand across Lake St. and see how the Santa Fe, which refused to sell out, seems an island of 1950s' Reno-Basque culture floating in the 1990s' Harrah's ocean. 235 Lake St., 775/323-1891, open for lunch ($8) Wed.–Fri. 11 A.M.–2 P.M., dinner ($14 adults, $7 children 12 and under) every night except Monday, 6–9 P.M.

With Basque food, it's a good idea to call ahead to find out what the entrees of the evening are. If the Santa Fe doesn't entice, try **Louis' Basque Corner,** just down the street from the Santa Fe. Bring an appetite and a half to this family-style gorgery to enjoy the soup, salad, beans, french fries, bread, wine, and ice cream that accompany the rotating entree, generally a choice of lamb, steak, or chicken. If you're prepared to sit at tables with strangers and have a good time, you'll leave both downtown Basque

restaurants satisfied and socialized. It's at 301 E. 4th, 775/323-7203. Lunch ($8.95) is served Wed.–Fri. 11:30 A.M.–2:30 P.M., a six-course dinner ($16.95) nightly, 5 P.M. –9.30 P.M.

Italian

Johnny's Ristorante Italiano is out W. 4th on old US 40. When you walk in, a nice little bar is on the right, and the hostess on the left leads you down a brothel-style hall—except here, the men are following their noses instead of that other anatomical protuberance (sorry, couldn't resist). The big red-leather booths are quite conducive to settling back and enjoying your ravioli, lasagna, chicken cacciatore on polenta, or seafood platter. 4245 W. 4th, 775/747-4511, open for dinner Tues.–Sat., 5–9:45 P.M.

Reno also has two other favorite Italian restaurants. **Luciano's,** 719 S. Virginia St., 775/322-7373, is open for lunch ($7–12) Tues.–Fri. 11:30 A.M.–1:45 P.M., and for dinner ($9–17) Tues.–Sun. 5–8:45 P.M. **LaVecchia,** 3501 S. Virginia St., 775/825-1113, is open for lunch Mon.–Fri. 11 A.M.–2 P.M., and for dinner every night starting at 5 P.M.

Mexican

Miguel's is one of the original Mexican restaurants in Reno, pleasing patrons for more than 30 years. It's very bright and friendly; excellent service, authentic, and inexpensive. One of the highlights of Reno. 1415 S. Virginia St., 775/322-2722. Open Tues.–Thurs. 11 A.M.–8 P.M., Fri.–Sat. 11 A.M.–9 P.M., Sun. noon–8 P.M., closed Monday.

A couple of blocks south of Miguel's is **El Borracho,** the other original Reno beanery. Relaxing interior, 11 interesting shrimp dishes (salads, cocktails, stew, brochette, ceviche), plus the usual tostadas, enchiladas, burritos and gringo specials. 1601 S. Virginia St., 775/322-0313, open 11 A.M.–11 P.M. Wed.–Mon., closed Tuesday.

Bertha Miranda's has a deservedly good reputation among locals for great Mexican food. It has two restaurants: one at 2144 Greenbrae in Sparks, 775/356-1310, and the other in Reno at 336 Mill St., 775/786-9697; both are open every day, 10 A.M.–10 P.M.

Micasa Too regularly wins "Best Mexican Restaurant" in the *Gazette-Journal* poll. There's *always* a huge crowd waiting to fill up here; luckily, the bar is as big as the restaurant, and the usual 30- to 45-minute wait is painless. Micasa Too now has two locations in Reno and another in Carson City. 2205 W. 4th St., 775/323-6466, and in south Reno at 3255 S. Virginia St., 775/824-0566. Both are open every day, 11 A.M.–11 P.M.

Chinese
Palais de Jade is the ritziest Chinese (and my wife's favorite) restaurant in town, in an extremely tasteful room done in mostly black and white, quite understated and elegant. It's won the best Chinese food category in the newspaper poll seven years in a row. All styles of Chinese food are represented, with the mu shu, cashew, and kung pao you've come to love, along with some scallop and lobster dishes and specials. The food is delicious and the service lively. Highly recommended. Located at 960 W. Moana, 775/827-5233, open Tues.–Sun. 11 A.M.–10 P.M., closed Mondays.

Soochow is the yang of Palais de Jade's yin. A plain old neighborhood Chinese restaurant out in Sparks, favored by couples with kids for the inexpensive family dinners, starting as low as $5 per person for six or seven courses. Shrimp with snow peas for $4, pork egg fu yung for $3.75, and hot-and-sour soup for $4.25 gives you the idea. 656 E. Prater, 775/359-5207, open Mon.–Sat. 11 A.M.–9:30 P.M., Sunday 4:30–9:30 P.M.

Yen Ching on West Moana falls somewhere between the Palais de Jade and Soochow in terms of price, character, and quality. Located at 565 W. Moana, 775/825-2451, open daily 11 A.M.–2:30 P.M., and 4–10 P.M.

Japanese
Ichiban downtown is a great place to take the kids, who love the spectacle of theatrical Japanese short-order chefs dicing and slicing, stirring and frying, on private teppanyaki grills (kids menu and kids drinks, too). Adults like Ichiban as well, for the pampering—hot fragrant towels and warm sake instantly do the trick. You choose steak, shrimp, scallops, chicken, lobster, or a combo thereof to be prepared with vegetables at your counter. Good location, walkable from everywhere downtown. 210 N. Sierra, 775/323-

5550, open daily 4:30–10 P.M.

The most inexpensive and fast Japanese food is available at **Kazuko's** in Plumb Lane Plaza. Its beef bowl is only $4, yakisoba, yakitori, tempura, and chicken teriyaki are in the $6–8 range. They come with rice and salad. Kazuko's miso soup is great for what ails you. Good value. 475 E. Plumb Lane, 775/329-8999, open Mon.–Sat. 11 A.M.–8:30 P.M., closed Sunday.

Kyoto is a fine little Japanese barbecue house serving yakis, tempura, sushi, and special Kyoto steak. Located at 915 W. Moana in the Moana West Shopping, 775/825-9686, open Mon.–Sat. 11:30 A.M.–2:30 P.M. (lunch) and 5 to 9:30 P.M. (dinner).

Other Asian
My own favorite restaurant in Reno is definitely **Cafe de Thai,** at the Mira Loma Shopping Center on McCarran just east of the Huffaker Hills. *Everything* here is out of this world, all concocted by chef Sakul Cheosakul, a Thai trained in his native cuisine as well as at the Culinary Institute. Try the satay or papaya salad appetizers or the hot hot Oriental sausage salad; the *tom kha kay* soup is like swallowing purity. The wok dishes are superb and reasonably priced: garlic pepper pork, peanut beef, basil chicken, and the curries are spy-cee. Vegie dishes are delicious, as is the pad Thai. Highly recommended. 3314 S. McCarran in the Mira Loma shopping center, 775/829-8424, open for lunch 11:30 A.M.–2:30 P.M., dinner 5–9:30 P.M., Sunday for dinner only, closed Mon. and Tues.

For Vietnamese, head for the **Golden Flower.** Choose from 17 different kinds of *pho* (traditional beef-noodle soup), along with the must-eat imperial rolls and shrimp stickers. Most entrees are around $8–10. 205 W. 5th St. at the corner of Arlington St., 775/323-1628, open daily 9 A.M.–10 P.M.

For Mongolian barbecue and a full Asian buffet, try **Genghis Khan** in the Sierra Marketplace. The barbecue is typical: meats, vegies, and spices all flash fried on the big round grills. The buffet has soup, standard salads, dim sum, ribs, chow mein, kung pao, sweet and sour, etc. Lunch is $7.50, dinner $12. Good deal for the amount and variety of food, with the barbecue thrown in. 3702 S. Virginia St., 775/829-8868. It's open every day for lunch (11:30 A.M.–3:30 P.M.) and dinner (4:30–9:30 P.M.).

European

Adele's, open in Reno since 1991 (the Adele's in Carson City has been there since the mid-'70s and is famous around the state), is one of Reno's finest restaurants. The sheer volume of menu choices (33 appetizers and more than 50 entrees) makes for a daunting selection, but let it be said that you can get practically anything you can imagine at Adele's. The number of fish dishes alone would make any Seattle restaurant jealous: sushi, crab cakes, clams, prawns, scallops, and cocktails, and those are just the appetizers. For dinner, try your choice of chicken, duck, veal, lamb, beef, pork, fish, sushi, and pasta, and that's just on the menu; the waiter will describe the dozen or so evening specials. Dinner entrees start at $20 and can go as high as $60, $70 or $80; steaks are around $27. Wine, dessert, and coffee drinks will stretch the dining experience to nearly 200 minutes. It's also open for lunch. 425 S. Virginia St., 775/333-6503. Open Mon.–Fri. 11 A.M.–midnight, Sat.–Sun. 5 P.M.–midnight. Dinner service stops at 10 P.M., but the bar stays open till midnight, with a late-night menu. There's live entertainment on Friday and Saturday nights, starting around 9:30 or 10 P.M.

Bavarian World's name says it all. You walk into a big German deli and grocery store, stocking everything from rye bread and strudel to a big selection of Spaten and Swiss chocolate and a lot of unusual boxed and canned foods. At the corner of Valley Rd. and 6th St. on the east side, the big festive restaurant in back, with an Octoberfest-size dance floor, is a surprise considering the plain warehouse exterior. It serves schnitzel, sauerbraten, a vegetarian potato pancake and other German dishes, all for $8–18. 595 Valley Rd. at 6th St., 775/323-7646. Open Mon. 8 A.M.–3 P.M., Tues.–Sat. 8 A.M.–8 P.M. (closing for an hour 3–4 P.M.), closed Sunday.

OTHER PRACTICALITIES

ENTERTAINMENT

Periodicals

Reno has plenty of non-gambling entertainment, and many different publications can help you plan when you want to visit, according to how you prefer to be entertained.

The daily Reno *Gazette-Journal* has a special entertainment section in its Thursday edition called "Best Bets," which covers the headliners, big-name bands, comedians, and lounge groups at the hotels, plus an up-to-date chart with listings of all entertainment, club acts and events in the area. It also has blurbs on parks, museums, outdoor activities, and local recreation. You'll often see *Best Bets* on giveaway racks. Or subscribe to the Thursday *GJ;* contact Reno Newspapers, Box 22000, Reno, NV 89520, 775/786-8744, www.rgi.com.

The weekly *Reno News and Review* is published on Thursday and distributed free on news racks around town. It covers the news scene briefly, offers up a couple of features, runs reviews of local arts, movies, restaurants, and clubs, and prints a weekly calendar of events. You can subscribe by mail for $52 per year; call 775/324-4440, www.newsreview.com.

Fun & Gaming is another free weekly, published on Thursday, distributed free on news racks, and covering the same basic territory of the other two, with a sports center section. For a copy, call 775/786-3594, funngaming@aol.com.

Casino Showrooms and Lounges

Almost all the major hotel/casinos have at least one lounge, cabaret, show bar, or bandstand with groups entertaining the masses. The Eldorado often has good groups, as do the Reno Hilton and the Atlantis. Pick up one of the entertainment tabloids (the chart listings in *Best Bets* are the best bet) and review the action.

Harrah's renamed its showroom Sammy's Showroom after Sammy Davis Jr., one of the most venerable and best-loved performers in Reno, died in 1991. Also here is the newer Outdoor Plaza, for concerts and other entertainment. Call 775/788-3773 for times, prices, and reservations.

The **Flamingo Hilton** has the 600-seat Flamingo Showroom, plus another venue called Top of the Hilton. Call 775/785-7080 for reservations.

The **Eldorado** has four entertainment venues: the Brew Brothers, Bistro Roxy, the BuBinga Lounge and the Eldorado Showroom. Call 775/786-5700 for more information.

John Ascuaga's Nugget has the 750-seat Celebrity Showroom, plus the Rose Ballroom, Casino Cabaret, and Trader Dick's. Call 775/356-3300 for reservations.

The **Peppermill** has two entertainment venues: the Convention Showroom and the Cabaret; 775/826-2121.

At the **Reno Hilton** is the 2,000-seat Hilton Showroom. The Hilton has long offered room and show packages; call 775/789-2285 for prices and reservations.

Circus Circus, of course, has continuous entertainment under the Big Top. Free circus acts are presented every day, 11 A.M.–midnight; 775/329-0711.

More Concerts & Events

Other venues for concerts and events include the **Church Fine Arts Complex,** 775/784-6847, and the **Lawlor Events Center,** 775/784-4444, both on the University of Nevada campus, and the **Pioneer Center for the Performing Arts,** 100 S. Virginia St., 775/686-6600.

Comedy Clubs

Reno has three venues for stand-up comedy. The Reno Hilton has the **Improv Comedy Club,** 775/789-2285. **Just for Laughs** is at the Sands Regency, 775/348-2200. Or you can **Catch a Rising Star** at the Silver Legacy, 775/325-7454.

Karaoke

At last count, the *Best Bets* tabloid entertainment chart had listings for 14 karaoke clubs in Reno and three more in Sparks. (See Periodicals, above.) The **West Second Street Bar,** 118 W. 2nd St., 775/348-7976, opening nightly at 9 P.M., is recommended by locals.

DANCING

Nightclubs

These places come and go almost as fast as first-run movies. Check the chart in the *Gazette-*

Journal's Thursday *Best Bets* entertainment section for all the latest.

Paul Revere's Kicks, owned by Paul Revere of Paul Revere and the Raiders fame, is one of the busiest clubs in town. The music runs the gamut from '50s to '90s (spun by a DJ), but the main attraction for rock 'n roll buffs is the collection of memorabilia that jams the walls of the club. Concert tickets, posters, photographs, even musical instruments are displayed. Also here is the Junk Rock Café: "Dance! Dance! Dance! Eat! Eat! Eat!" is the motto up over the door. The club is at the entrance of the National Bowling Stadium, 300 N. Center St., 775/322-4860; open Wed.–Sat., 9 P.M. on.

The **Reno Live Dance Club Complex** contains four dance clubs: Club 2000 for Top 40 dancing, The Blast Room with hits from the '70s and '80s, The Lounge with pool tables and a jukebox, and the downstairs Fusion Room with house, techno and trance music for rave parties. There's also The Basement downstairs, for live concerts. Thursday nights, the whole complex is open for ages 18 and up, and no alcohol is served in the building; Friday nights 9–11 P.M. ladies receive free admission and free drinks. The management emphasizes that this is a place where women are safe to relax and enjoy a night out; they have the most bouncers of any nightclub in the USA. It's on the corner of Sierra and 2nd Streets, opposite the Flamingo Hilton casino, 775/329-1950. Open nightly, 9 P.M. on.

Another popular Reno dance venue is the upmarket, lavishly decorated **BuBinga Lounge** at the Eldorado casino, which starts off each night with sophisticated jazz or piano early in the evening, followed by live music or cutting-edge DJs for dancing. Opens 4:30 pm nightly; 775/786-5700.

The **Atlantis** nightclub at the casino of the same name gets going around 10 P.M. nightly. A room-size octopus with two glowing eyeballs and light-show tentacles presides over the dance floor; lasers fire beams from inside the mouths of sharks suspended from the ceiling. Great sound, too, for the tunes spun by a DJ. Popular with the casino yuppie crowd. 3800 S. Virginia St., 775/825-4700,

For country music fans there's the **Haywire Waikiki Country Night Club,** with live country bands, country DJs, and free dance lessons

Wed.–Sat. nights. Here you can dance to all your favorite country hits, on the largest hardwood dance floor in Reno. 701 S. Virginia St., 775/337-2345. Opens nightly at 5 P.M.

OTHER ENTERTAINMENT

If you've had enough drinking, eating, and losing money, and want some routine escapism, take in a first-run flick at the **Century 12 Riverside Theater,** 11 N. Sierra St. beside the Truckee River, 775/786-7469; **Century Theaters 16,** 210 E. Plumb Lane, 775/824-3333; **Cine-3 Theatres,** 4001 S. Virginia St., 775/826-6900; **Greenbrae 8 Theaters,** 520 Greenbrae Dr. in the shopping center near the corner of Pyramid, 775/358-3456; or the **Century 14 Cinema,** 1250 Victorian Ave., Sparks, 775/353-7440. Or check out the current presentation at the giant-screen **IMAX theater** in the National Bowling Stadium, 775/334-2634.

The historic **Lear Theater,** on the corner of First and Ralston Streets facing the Truckee River, is being renovated and promises to be a fine venue for theater and other performances; 775/786-2278. There's also the **Pioneer Center**

KAREN WHITE

for the **Performing Arts,** 100 S. Virginia St., 775/686-6600. Other performing arts venues and companies in the Reno area include the Bruka Theater, 775/323-3221; the Gothic North Community Theater, 775/329-7529; the Nevada Festival Ballet, 775/785-7915; the Nevada Opera, 775/786-4046; the Reno Chamber Orchestra, 775/348-9413; the Reno Little Theater, 775/331-1877; the Reno Philharmonic Association, 775/323-6393; the Sierra Arts Foundation, 775/329-2787; and University of Nevada Performing Arts, 775/784-4046.

Keystone Cue and Cushion, 935 W. 5th St., 775/323-2828, has well-maintained pool tables, plus video slots and games, snack bar—burgers, BLTs, and beer—and a Brunswick and billiard supply shop in back. These guys know their business.

OUTDOOR RECREATION

Bicycling
Three places in Reno rent bicycles. **Truckee River Lodge & Bike Rental,** 501 W. 1st St., 775/786-8888, is near both downtown and the Truckee River. **Sundance Bike Rental** is based downtown at the Sands Regency Hotel, 345 N. Arlington Ave. at the corner of 3rd St., 775/786-0222. **Snowind Sports,** 2500 E. 2d St., is based at the Reno Hilton, 775/323-9463.

For the Truckee River Bike Path, see "Parks and Zoos" under "Sights" earlier in the Reno section. The most popular hill climb is to the top of Geiger Grade on NV 341 to Virginia City; it's a killer. Cyclists also work out on McCarran Blvd. between 4th and Skyline (though it's somewhat narrow). The streets of Reno-Sparks are in pretty good shape, but mountain bikes are preferred around town for their fat and cushiony tires.

Ballooning
One of the most popular Reno events of the year is the **Great Reno Balloon Race,** which takes place in September. More than 100 balloons take to the atmosphere from Rancho San Rafael Park, starting very early in the morning. To go up in one yourself at other times of the year, call **Mountain High,** 888/GO-ABOVE, or **Dream Weavers,** 702/265-1271, 800/FUN-ALOFT in Minden, 50 miles south of Reno. For

around $150 per person, you get a tour of the Dream Weavers balloon while it's assembled and inflated and a 60- to 90-minute ride above Carson Valley, which, according to the manager, is much more visually exciting than Truckee Meadows. You land where you land (you can't *steer* balloons); a chase crew catches up to you. This is an experience that's nothing like anything you've ever done before—but it's only for early risers. The balloons take off around 8 A.M. in the winter and as early as 6:30 A.M. in the summer to avoid being caught in warm thermals as the air heats up.

Hiking

Reno has a number of tucked-away trails in all corners of the metropolitan area, reachable (and most of them hikable) with only a little effort. For the **Oxbow Nature Study Area,** see "Parks and Zoos" under "Sights" in the Reno section. The **Rancho San Rafael Park** hike is also covered there. The **Davis Creek** and **Galena Creek** park hikes can be found under "Washoe Valley" in the Vicinity of Reno section. The major Mt. Rose trail is described under "Mt. Rose" in the Vicinity of Reno section.

Amusement Parks

The **Wild Island Family Adventure Park** is located at 250 Wild Island Court at the very east end of Sparks (take the Sparks Blvd. exit from I-80 and go north; you can see it from the freeway), 775/359-2927. Slides, pools, waves, and just all-around splashing await you during the summer season. There's also a three-story Scorpion ride, an 18-hole miniature golf course open year-round (weather permitting), kid-size racecars, and an arcade and fun center.

The water park is open every day in summer, from around Memorial Day to Labor Day. Normal hours are 11 A.M.–7 P.M., with shortened hours at the beginning and end of the season. Waterpark admission is $16.95 for everyone over four feet tall, $12.95 for those under four feet tall, free for ages three and under, seniors $4.95; after 4 P.M., admission is $8.50 for everyone.

The mini-golf course and raceway are open every day, all year round; they open at 10 A.M. on weekends, 1 P.M. weekdays, and stay open until

10 P.M. Friday and Saturday, 9 P.M. Sunday through Thursday. Golf costs $4.50 for 18 holes, $5.50 for 36 holes. Indy car rides are $4, sprint car rides $2.50.

Bungee Jumping

The Ultimate Rush, 775/786-7005, operates bungee jumping all year round from its 180-foot tower in front of the Reno Hilton. Jumps cost $25.

Swimming

Reno has two indoor public pools, one at 240 Moana Ln. (right off S. Virginia just north of the Convention Center), 775/334-2268, and one at 2925 Apollo Way in a northwestern residential area, 775/334-2203. They both have public swim times afternoons and evenings, but if all you want is a shower, call ahead and ask. They're very accommodating. Sparks has the same at **Alf Sorenson Community Center,** at 1400 Baring Blvd., 775/353-2385. Outdoor pools are found at **Idlewild Park** (see "Downtown Parks" under "Sights" in the Reno section), 775/334-2267, and **Traner Rec. Complex,** Carville Dr. right behind Washoe County Fairgrounds, 775/334-2269.

Fishing

Idlewild Park in Reno has bluegill; Virginia Lake in Reno has brown trout. The Truckee River, running from Lake Tahoe through the heart of Reno, has rainbow and German brown trout. In Sparks, the newly developed Sparks Marina Park is stocked with rainbow trout. Pyramid Lake, 32 miles north of Reno, is noted for its cutthroat trout. Lake Tahoe, a 40-minute drive from Reno, has Mackinaws, rainbow and brown trout, and kokanee salmon. Fishing licenses are available at most sporting goods stores. (State fishing licenses are not required for Pyramid Lake, but a lake permit is required; 775/476-0555.) For the latest information on area fishing, phone the 24-hour Fishing Hot Line, 775/786-FISH, for a recorded fishing report.

Horseback Riding

High Sierra Stables, 775/972-1345, in Golden Valley, about a 10-minute drive north/east of Reno. Open 9 A.M.–7 P.M. daily, year round; rides by appointment only.

Golf

The Reno area is golf heaven, with 38 public golf courses within a 90-minute drive of downtown. The Reno-Sparks area has 10 courses, and another eight courses are just to the south in the Carson Valley. Information on golf courses and golf packages is available from area visitor centers and Chambers of Commerce. For a free Reno/Tahoe golf package brochure, contact the Reno-Sparks Convention and Visitors Authority (RSCVA), 800/FOR-RENO, www.reno-laketahoe.com.

SKIING

Several downhill ski areas are within 45 minutes of the Arch, and numerous ski resorts are scattered around Lake Tahoe no more than an hour and a half from town. Cross-country trails abound. Most resorts make snow when nature falls short; call their Snow Phones for current conditions. In addition to lodging and shopping, most resorts offer equipment rentals and ski schools. You can also buy ski packages, family packages, and interchangeable lift tickets for the North Shore downhill ski resorts. Cross-country packages are available too. For detailed information, call the Tahoe North Visitors and Convention Bureau (530/583-3494 or 800/TAHOE-4U), or the Reno-Sparks Convention & Visitors Authority (800/FOR-RENO), or the resorts.

Nevada

Of all the area resorts, the **Mount Rose—Ski Tahoe** resort is the closest to Reno, on NV 431 22 miles from Reno. Mount Rose offers 1000 skiable acres. Mount Rose has Tahoe's highest base elevation (8,260 feet), summit elevation 9,700 feet, five lifts, 43 runs and trails, and a 1,440-foot vertical drop evenly divided among beginner, intermediate, and advanced trails. Snowboarders are welcome. You can also rent equipment and take classes at the ski school. Shuttles are available twice daily from several of Reno's larger hotels and casinos. Call 775/849-0704 for specific information, or the Snow Phone at 775/849-0706 for a recorded conditions announcement. Outside Nevada, call 800/SKI-ROSE; www.skirose.com.

Closer to Lake Tahoe, **Diamond Peak at Ski Incline** in Incline Village 35 miles from Reno bills itself as a family ski resort with great views of the lake. With a summit elevation of 8,540 feet, it offers seven lifts and a vertical drop of 1,840 feet, fourth-longest at Lake Tahoe. Trails are one-third advanced, half intermediate, and the rest beginner. It also offers ski school and day care. Call 775/832-1177 to reach the office, 775/831-3249 for 24-hour information, 775/831-3211 for the Snow Phone, and 800/GO-TAHOE or 800/TAHOE-4U for reservations.

Diamond Peak also is known for its cross-country skiing. Off NV 431 five miles north of Incline Village, it offers 16 trails on 35 km of groomed track, one-third advanced, half intermediate, and the rest beginner.

The **Spooner Lake Cross-Country Ski Area** is on NV 28 a half mile north of US 50, 775/887-8844, open daily 9 A.M.–5 P.M. Its 21 meadow and backcountry trails total 101 km, and include an 18 km roundtrip to Marlette Lake. Call for info on ski schools and skating lessons.

South along the lake and 58 miles southwest of Reno lies the **Heavenly** resort on the Nevada-California state line. Heavenly has a summit elevation of 10,040 feet, a base elevation of 6,540 feet, a vertical drop of 3,500 feet, 4,800 acres for skiing, 24 lifts, 79 trails, and ski school. It's open to snowboarding. Call 530/586-7000 for information, 530/541-7544 for the Snow Phone, and 800/2-HEAVEN for reservations.

Across the Border

Climb the Sierra on I-80 and take CA 267 to reach **Northstar at Tahoe** 40 miles west of Reno. The resort, with a summit elevation of 8,600 feet, base elevation of 6,400 feet, and a vertical drop of 2,200 feet, has 11 lifts and is open to snowboarders. Its trails are half intermediate, and one-quarter each advanced and beginner. It also has a ski school with more than 100 instructors and offers child-care and 65 km of groomed cross-country trails. Call 530/562-1010 for information, 530/562-1330 for the Snow Phone, 800/GO-NORTH or 530/562-1010 for reservations.

Back on I-80, take the Donner State Park exit to reach **Tahoe Donner.** Northwest of Truckee on Northwoods Blvd. off Donner Pass Rd., this resort caters to new skiers and children. With three lifts, a summit elevation of 7,350 feet, and a vertical drop of 600 feet, its trails are split fifty-fifty between beginner and intermediate. Call 530/587-9444. Tahoe Donner also offers cross-country with 32 trails and 65 km of track. Call 530/587-9484 for information.

The next resort west on I-80, also serving less-advanced skiers, is **Boreal,** just off the interstate. Take the Castle exit. It's known for night skiing, every night but Christmas Eve. It has nine lifts, summit elevation of 7,800 feet, a vertical drop of 600 feet, with nearly a third of its trails for beginners, and slightly more than half for intermediates. Call 530/426-3666. Associated with Boreal is **Soda Springs,** a resort set up for

families. On old US 40, one mile off I-80 by way of the Norden/Soda Springs exit, it's open to the public weekends and holidays, available for rental other times. It has two lifts, summit elevation of 7,400 feet, a vertical drop of 652 feet, and its trails are split in much the same proportions as Soda Springs. Call 530/426-3666.

A bit closer to Reno, three miles from I-80 on the Norden/Soda Springs exit, is **Donner Ski Ranch.** It offers skiing for all abilities; its trails are half intermediate, one quarter each beginner and advanced. It has six lifts, summit elevation of 7,031 feet, and a vertical drop of 750 feet. Call 530/426-3635 for info.

Close by sits the recently expanded **Sugar**

SKIING NEAR RENO

Bowl resort, with half its runs catering to advanced skiers and nearly a third to intermediates; snowboarders are welcome. With a summit elevation of 8,383 feet, it has eight lifts, 58 runs, and a vertical drop of 1,500 feet. Summer '94 expansion included a road and parking area for drive-in access and a new chairlift on Mt. Judah. Call 530/426-3651.

Around the Lake

The famous **Squaw Valley** resort, site of the 1960 Winter Olympics, lies 45 miles west of Reno off Hwy. 89, northwest of Tahoe City. Seventy percent of its runs are geared for beginners and intermediates. With 33 lifts, it has a summit elevation of 9,050 feet, a vertical drop of 2,850 feet, and more than 4,000 acres of terrain served by lift in its 8,300-acre spread. It also offers ski school, child care, and cross-country trails. For information, call 530/583-6985, for reservations 800/545-4350, for Snow Phone 530/583-6955.

Closer to the lake on CA 89 and one hour from Reno is **Alpine Meadows.** Serving skiers of all abilities, it has 12 lifts, summit elevation of 8,637 feet, and a vertical drop of 1,800. Its runs are one-quarter beginner, intermediate 40 percent and advanced 35 percent. Its ski schools include lessons for the disabled. No snowboarding is allowed. For information, call 530/583-4232 or 800/441-4423, for Snow Phone 530/581-8374.

Just south of Tahoe City off Hwy. 89 is Tahoe's oldest resort, **Granlibakken.** With one lift, a summit elevation of 6,500 feet, and a vertical drop of 300 feet, it's set up for beginners and families. Forty percent of its runs are beginner, the rest intermediate. Call 530/583-4242.

Farthest from Reno, six miles south of Tahoe City on Hwy. 89, or 19 miles north of South Lake Tahoe, is the 1,200-acre **Homewood.** Known for its views of the lake, half its slopes are for the intermediate skier, with plenty set aside for the advanced, and 15 percent for beginners. It offers a day-care

center, ski school, and snowboarding lessons. With a summit elevation of 7,880 feet and a drop of 1,650 feet, it has 10 lifts. Call information 530/525-2992, Snow Phone 530/525-2900, lodging 800/TAHOE-4U.

SERVICES

Drinking Water

For your internal fluid requirements (it's a desert out there), bring one- to five-gallon containers to the **Crystal Springs Water Co.,** 901 S. Center one block east of S. Virginia at Taylor (across from the Pizza Junction), 775/323-4710. It's 35 cents a gallon for purified (distilled, de-ionized) water; 30 cents for pure artesian well water. Well worth it. Crystal Springs has been serving Reno's drinking water needs since 1930.

Marriage and Divorce

The County Clerk's office is in the courthouse at S. Virginia and Court St. right at the river, 775/328-3275, www.co.washoe.nv.us/clerks/marriage.htm, open daily 8 A.M. to midnight. Bring your I.D., your betrothed, and $35 cash for your license (no blood test, no waiting period). Then get married in any one of Reno's dozen wedding chapels (prices start at $150); most are bunched up on the strip, along W. 4th, and around Court and S. Virginia.

To just get married cheaply, with no muss and no fuss, go to the **Commissioner of Civil Marriages,** 195 S. Sierra St., 775/328-3461. In Reno-Sparks, the County Clerk doubles as the Commissioner of Civil Marriages. She appoints deputy commissioners whose sole function is to marry people. Just show up at their office with your license and $35 cash 9 A.M.–6 P.M. Thursday to Monday (closed for lunch 1–2 P.M., and closed Tuesdays and Wednesdays), and in 10 minutes you're hitched. On busy days you might have to wait a little for a couple or two ahead of you.

If it ultimately doesn't work out, well, Reno acquired its slogan, Biggest Little City in the

BOB RACE

World, because of its lenient criteria for granting divorces. One (or both) of the divorcing parties must be able to prove they have been a resident of Nevada for six weeks. **Ace Paralegal,** 1000 Bible Way, Suite 39, 775/786-9985, types up the court documents for you for $150, then sends you down to the courthouse to file; filing costs another $150. **Divorce Nevada Style,** 775/747-6921, prepares and files all documents for a fee starting at $100 for a simple divorce. Fees can be higher at either place, depending on circumstances; the fees mentioned here are for a simple divorce. You don't need to come in to either place personally, if you prefer not to; they can handle the whole thing for you by mail.

Smokes

Get your cheap cigarettes at the **Smoke Shop,** 2001 E. 2nd St., just before the freeway, 775/329-0275, or **Smoke Shop III,** 11450 S. Virginia, just south of Foothill Rd., under the tallest Marlboro sign in the state, 775/852-4010; both open seven days a week, long hours.

INFORMATION

The Reno-Sparks Convention and Visitors Authority (RSCVA), 775/827-7600 or 800/FOR-RENO (800/367-7366), www.renolaketahoe.com, has their main office at 1 E. 1st St. on the corner of Virginia St., beside the Cal-Neva, on the 2nd and 3rd floors, open Mon.–Fri. 8 A.M.–5 P.M. They carry loads of useful tourist literature, brochures and other information; be sure to ask for the excellent *Travel Planner,* published annually. Call their 800 number for a recording of entertainment, casino activities, golf and ski packages, conventions, entertainment, and special events, and to access the Reno-Sparks Convention and Visitors Authority (RSCVA) hotel reservation service. A separate website, www.rscva.com, gives current information on conventions.

The RSCVA operates two visitor information centers in Reno, both convenient for picking up brochures, visitors guides, maps, and answers to questions. One is the **Reno Downtown Visitor Center** in the lobby of the National Bowling Stadium, 300 N. Center St., 775/334-2625, open 9

A.M.–5 P.M. every day. The other is the Visitor Center at **Meadowood Mall,** 5000 Meadowood Mall Circle in south Reno, 775/827-7708, open Mon.–Fri. 10 A.M.–9 P.M., Saturday 10 A.M.–7 P.M., Sunday 11 A.M.–6 P.M.

You can also stop off at the **Sparks Information Center and Chamber of Commerce** at the corner of Pyramid and Victorian Avenues, in Sparks, 775/358-1976, info@sparkschamber.org, www.sparkschamber.org, open Mon.–Fri. 8 A.M.–5 P.M. year-round and 9 A.M.–5 P.M. summer weekends.

For **University of Nevada** information, stop in at Jones Visitor Center, right on the Quad, open daily 9 A.M.–5 P.M., or call 775/784-4865. The university's campus operator and general information number is 775/784-1110.

Libraries

The **Washoe County Library** is at 301 S. Center, 775/785-4190. The Reno Library and Social Club started up in 1876; their Carnegie Library sat on N. Virginia St. right at the river. The first Reno Free Public Library opened in 1904, then moved in 1930 to the old State Building, where it remained until 1966, when the new building, on S. Center St., replaced it.

The unusual interior features spiral staircases, pools and fountains (with the inevitable coins for luck), and a veritable jungle of trees, ferns, shrubs, and plants. My mother, who's a retired librarian, says she's never seen such an attractive and comfortable facility. The magazine department is large, and the library subscribes to most Nevada newspapers. The auditorium hosts many community functions, and the upstairs walls are almost always graced with a local exhibit. The sizable Nevada shelf is to the right as you enter against the front wall; check out the murals above. The library is open Mon.–Wed. 10 A.M.–8 P.M., Thursday and Friday 10 A.M.–6 P.M., Saturday 10 A.M.–5 P.M., and Sunday noon–5 P.M.

A good place to find the Nevada books that are checked out of the Washoe County Library is at the **Truckee Meadows Community College Library,** 7000 Dandini Blvd. off US 395 about 10 miles north of downtown in the piney and sagey hills, 775/674-7600, open Mon.–Fri. 8 A.M.–9 P.M., Saturday 8 A.M.–4 P.M., Sunday 10 A.M.–3 P.M.

For the university **library** and **bookstore,** see

"Union and Library" under "The University of Nevada" earlier in the Reno section.

Bookstores

Reno's best community bookstore is **Sundance,** in the Albertsons Shopping Center on Keystone and W. 4th, 775/786-1188, open Mon.–Fri. 9 A.M.–9 P.M., Saturday and Sunday 10 A.M.–6 P.M. Occupying two storefronts in the Keystone shopping center, check out the Nevada section and the local author table next to it.

Waldenbooks has stores in Meadowood Mall, way down S. Virginia at McCarran Blvd., 775/826-5690, and at Park Lane Mall, at S. Virginia and Plumb, 775/825-7541.

Barnes and Noble opened its superstore, with more than 150,000 titles, newsstand, and coffee bar in 1995 at 5555 S. Virginia, 775/826-8882, open 9 A.M.–11 P.M. daily (Sunday 9 A.M.–10 P.M.) This is the largest bookstore in northern Nevada, with the longest hours. **Borders Books, Music & Café,** 4995 S. Virginia St., 775/448-9999, is another huge store, open the same hours.

The **Gambler's Bookstore,** 1 E. 1st St. on the corner of Virginia St., 775/825-7778 or 800/748-5797, www.gamblerhome.com, is open Mon.–Fri. 9 A.M.–6 P.M., Saturday 10 A.M.–6 P.M., Sunday noon–5 P.M.

Maps

Oakman's, 634 Ryland, 775/786-4466, open Mon.–Fri. 8 A.M.–5:30 P.M., Saturday 9 A.M.–5 P.M., is a big art, crafts, office, and drafting supply store; in the back corner are many raised-relief maps ($18) and USGS topo maps.

Also pick up **AAA's** uniformly fine maps of Reno-Sparks and Nevada at its offices at 199 E. Moana Lane, 775/826-8800, open Mon.–Fri. 8:30 A.M.–5:30 P.M. It's worth it to belong to AAA for the maps alone, to say nothing of the towing benefits, good insurance rates, and peace of mind.

TRANSPORTATION

By Road

Reno is 10 miles east of the California border. The Reno-Sparks area is served by two major highways: I-80, which crosses the country from San Francisco to New York, and US 395, which runs from southeast Oregon briefly through Nevada (from Reno to Topaz Lake), then heads south through California down to near Los Angeles.

The **Greyhound** bus terminal is at 155 Stevenson between W. 1st and 2nd, 775/322-2970 or 800/231-2222. Buses depart roughly 24 times throughout the day and night, with services south to Las Vegas (via Carson City), west to Sacramento, Oakland and San Francisco. In Sacramento there are connections heading south to Los Angeles and north to Redding, Portland, and Seattle. Eastbound buses head out I-80 to Salt Lake City, via Winnemucca and Elko. **K-T Bus Lines** operates between Reno and Las Vegas, arriving and departing from the Greyhound depots on both ends.

Ely Bus (775/289-2877 in Ely) operates a bus route connecting Reno and Ely. Buses depart Ely at 7:45 A.M. every Wednesday, arriving at the Western Village Casino in Sparks at 1:45 P.M.; cost is $63 one way, $104 round trip. The return bus departs from Sparks at 7:45 A.M. the following morning.

Public Rural Ride **(PRIDE)** (775/348-RIDE) operates buses 10 times a day, 6:30 A.M.–7 P.M., between Reno and Carson City. Fares are $3 adults, $2 youth, $1.50 seniors, including free transfers to Reno's city bus system, Citifare. In Reno, the bus operates from the local bus terminal at the corner of Center and 4th Streets downtown, opposite the National Bowling Stadium. (See the Carson City sections for bus stops on the Carson City end of the line.)

By Rail

Amtrak's cross-country rail service runs on the transcontinental rail laid through Nevada in 1869. Its *California Zephyr* passes right through the middle of downtown Reno (blocking traffic twice a day for 5–10 minutes; Myron Lake, 90 years in his grave, *still* gets a kick out of it). The depot is at 135 E. Commercial St., at the corner of Lake St. and Commercial Row, across from the north side of Harrah's parking building, 775/329-8638, or 800/USA-RAIL. The *California Zephyr* train stops in Reno once daily in each direction, heading west to Sacramento and Emeryville (in the east San Francisco Bay Area), and east to Salt Lake City, Denver and Chicago; this train stops in

Nevada in Reno, Winnemucca and Elko. Amtrak also operates several buses daily between Reno and Sacramento, to connect with other trains there, including the *Coast Starlight* train going south to southern California and north to Oregon and Washington. The depot, open 8:30 A.M.–5:30 P.M. daily, has the air of a real old downtown train station, which it is—built in 1925, it became Reno's fifth and last depot.

By Air
Nearly six million people pass through **Reno-Tahoe International Airport** every year; the airport is served by Alaska, Allegiant, America West, American, Continental, Delta, Northwest, Skywest, Southwest, Shuttle by United, TWA, and United.

Conveniently located, the airport is only a 10-minute drive from downtown; take US 395 south to the airport exit. Or catch the Bell airport shuttle every 30 minutes (on the half and hour) at the baggage-claim area, operating between the airport and the major downtown hotels, 775/786-3700, $2.45 one-way.

A Citifare bus route, Route 13, operates between the airport and the Citicenter bus depot, downtown at 4th and Center Streets opposite the National Bowling Stadium. On weekdays and Saturdays the bus departs every half hour from around 6 A.M. to 7 P.M., with hourly service continuing until around 1 A.M. On Sundays this bus route runs hourly, from around 6 A.M. to 7 P.M. Fares are $1.25 for adults, 90 cents for youth and 60 cents for seniors; call 775/348-7433 for current info.

Getting Around
Reno's local bus system, **Citifare,** operates 24 hours a day on 24 routes around downtown all the way out to the four corners of Truckee Meadows. Fares (exact change) are $1.25 cents one-way, youth 90 cents, seniors 60 cents. For info call 775/348-RIDE. All routes start and end at the CitiCenter Transit Center, 4th and Center streets.

For bicycle rentals and tips, see "Bicycling" under "Outdoor Recreation," above.

Rental Cars
Call **Alamo,** 800/327-9633, **Advantage,** 800/777-5500, **Hertz,** 800/654-3131, **Avis,** 800/831-2847, **Thrifty,** 800/847-4389, **Dollar,** 800/800-4000, **Budget,** 800/527-0700, **National,** 800/227-7368, or **Enterprise,** 800/736-8222. All of the rental-car companies operate out of the airport, which makes it convenient if you're flying in and out, though you'll have to join the throngs there if you're not.

If you don't want to deal with the airport, some of the rental companies also have offices in town. Avis has rental desks at Circus Circus, 775/785-2748, and the Reno Hilton, 775/785-2750, in addition to its desk at the airport, 775/785-2727. Enterprise has an office downtown at 4th and Vine Streets, 775/328-1671, and in south Reno at 665 E. Moana Lane, 775/826-2442, in addition to its desk at the airport, 775/329-3773. Dollar has an office downtown at the Flamingo Hilton, 225 N. Sierra St., 775/348-2812, in addition to its desk at the airport, 775/348-2800. Hertz has a desk at the Silver Legacy, 407 N. Virginia St., 775/325-7593, and an office at 1567 Vassar St., 775/785-2650, in addition to its desk at the airport, 775/785-2554. Budget has an office at 1595 Marietta Way in Sparks, 775/785-2545, in addition to its desk at the airport, 775/785-2545.

Alternatively, some companies will come to where you are to pick you up when you rent a vehicle, a convenient service.

To Tahoe
Tahoe Casino Express, 775/785-2424 or 800/446-6128, provides service between the Reno airport and Lake Tahoe's south shore casinos. Fare is $17 one way, $30 round trip.

Tours
Gray Line, 775/331-1147, offers a daily guided bus tour departing Reno at 9 A.M., heading over to Lake Tahoe with stops at Squaw Valley, Emerald Bay and South Lake Tahoe, then stopping at Carson City, then Virginia City, and arriving back at Reno at 5:30 P.M. The tour costs $49 adults, $39 ages 6–12, free for children age 5 and under, lunch included. Call to ask about their "Room and Roam" packages, which include lodging, sightseeing tours, all-day ski lift tickets and transportation.

Scenic Tours, 775/826-6888 or 800/828-7143, is a friendly, locally-owned tour company offering a similar tour, departing Reno daily and heading for Truckee, Lake Tahoe, Carson City,

Virginia City and then back to Reno. The cost of $49 per person includes breakfast and lunch; on a special promotional deal, you can save $15 if you phone their local number and book the tour yourself. Locals recommend this tour.

VICINITY OF RENO

MOUNT ROSE

About 10 miles south of downtown Reno is the intersection of Business 395 (S. Virginia St.) with NV 341 and 431. Going left on 341 leads you up Geiger Grade through the Virginia Range over to Virginia City. Going right aims you straight at the Sierra Nevada and onto the slopes of Mt. Rose (elev. 10,778 feet). US 395 now runs all the way to this intersection, having been extended by four miles from its previous southern terminus in 1996. The freeway bypasses the intersection and dumps you off right on the business route south to Carson or on Mt. Rose Highway.

Mt. Rose Hwy., too, boasts four smooth lanes for the six-mile stretch to Galena, completed in 1993 to the tune of $8 million. The road travels past Galena High School, which opened in fall 1992, and by a number of recent subdivisions. Commercial development has kept pace with the road and residential: there's now a Raley's shopping center across from the high school and a large Chevron station up the road.

At treeline, you pass through the little settlement of **Galena,** with its scattered developments, firehouse, and **Galena Forest Inn,** 775/849-2100, serving continental cuisine, with entrees in the $16–29 range. It's open every day except Monday, 5 to 9 P.M.; reservations recommended, especially on weekends.

About a mile beyond the Inn is Washoe County's **Galena Creek Park,** open 8 A.M.–9 P.M. summers, 8 A.M.–5 P.M. winters (no camping). The first turnoff (right) is into the north picnic area: tall trees, large erratic boulders, pump water, and picnic tables. At the end of the spur road is an interpretive sign at the trailhead for the Jones' Creek and White's Creek loop, a serious eight-mile hike into the Mt. Rose Wilderness Area. The first mile of this trail is a killer, but then it settles down to just plain steep torture. Pick up a trail brochure at the signpost.

Up the road a bit is the entrance to the south picnic area, right at the Galena Highway Maintenance Station. Here is the park office, Galena Creek itself, and the trailheads for the interpretive loop trail, Black's Canyon Trail, and the north extension trail that hooks up to Jones Creek—all providing an afternoon of enjoyable hiking. The loop trail meanders around the mountainside for a mile or so, coming into contact with Thomas Creek, with a couple dozen numbered signposts that correspond to descriptions in a brochure. You'll smell Jeffrey pine bark (vanilla) and tobacco bush, see the ruins of an old fishery at the creek—and generally get an education on the local ecology. Worth doing. For more information on the park, call headquarters at 775/849-2511.

Continuing up (southwest) NV 431 toward the summit, you wind around a handful of switchbacks, and then come to the **Reindeer Lodge,** 775/849-1960. This roadhouse was once as popular as it was funky, but the funk seems to have gotten the upper hand of late. Still, it's definitely a sight to see, and you can sample one of the 'Deer's thick buffalo burgers if they're making them that week.

Just beyond the Reindeer is **Christmas Tree Restaurant,** 775/849-0127, all done up in reds and greens, with a nice view of Washoe Valley, big comfy bar, and good food. This restaurant has been in the same location since 1946; the current establishment is from the '50s. The bar opens at 4:30 P.M., and dinner is served from 5 to 9:30 P.M. daily. The view, along with the mahogany-grilled steaks and chops, has kept this place in business for more than 40 years; what's more, the same family has been running it the whole time.

Three official pull-outs

are within a mile uphill from the Christmas Tree. They're all well-marked and conveniently located, so that if you're taking a scenic cruise into the mountains or over to Lake Tahoe, driving 10–15 miles an hour under the speed limit, you can easily pull over for the many commuters between Reno and Incline Village, who tend to want to go 10–15 miles an hour *over* the speed limit, and might be tailgating you with black smoke shooting from their ears.

Around a few more corners is the **Mt. Rose/Ski Tahoe** ski resort (see "Skiing" under "Outdoor Recreation," above). The first road (off to the left) up to the Slide Mountain part of the complex has a stunning view that takes in Truckee Meadows, Washoe Valley, and Eagle Valley. Looking straight across (east), you can make out the summit of Mt. Davidson, on the other side of which is Virginia City. With binoculars, you can even see the flagpole that has sat on that peak for more than 100 years. The second left is to the Mt. Rose section of the complex (actually, both sections are on Slide Mountain; the Mt. Rose part faces Mt. Rose).

Summit, Trail, and Campground

The summit of NV 431 (elev. 8,911 feet) is the highest pass in the Sierra Nevada that's kept open year-round. This area was also the hangout of Dr. J. E. Church, a researcher at the Nevada Agricultural Experimental Station at UNR at the turn of the century. Measuring the water content of the winter snowpack in order to predict the seasonal runoff started out as a hobby for Dr. Church. Over a five-year period between 1904 and 1909, Church gauged typical stretches of snow on the eastern slopes of Mt. Rose, compared them to spring and summer water levels in the rivers and lakes, and thereby established a norm for the snowpack and runoff. His methods proved so reliable and his predictions so accurate that he created an entirely new science: snow surveying. Today, farmers, power engineers, ski operators, water districts, and long-range weather forecasters rely on snow surveying to make decisions about their business.

Right at the summit is the turnoff (left) into **Mt. Rose Campground,** one of the prettiest camping spots in the state, open Memorial Day to Labor Day, depending on snow conditions. The campground is right at the summit, in a beautiful wooded mountain bowl; it's always 15–20 degrees cooler up here than it is in Reno or Carson. There are 24 campsites for tents or self-contained motor homes up to 16 feet. Piped drinking water, flush toilets, picnic tables, grills, and fire rings are provided. The maximum stay is 14 days. Reservations are accepted for some sites; call Mystix at 800/280-2267, or reserve at www.reserveusa.com. The fee is $9 per campsite. For more info, contact the Carson Ranger District, 1536 S. Carson, Carson City, NV 89701, 775/882-2766.

Only a quarter-mile downhill from there is the trailhead for the **Mt. Rose peak climb.** The sign is small, but since the "trail" is really a service road, with a road-maintenance shed and gate at the trailhead, it's hard to miss. This is a steady climb, starting at 8,840 feet, along the wide service track, through stately pines, around grassy meadows and a small kettle, then up and past an old tramway that once ferried supplies to the radio tower near the peak. At the tower, a big concrete bunker with antennae and satellite dishes around it, the view opens up to the vast west side of the Sierra, with a good look at I-80 passing Donner Lake, along with three or four reservoirs of the Truckee River water system.

You're not done with the mountain yet, though. A rough extension trail heads off to the left (south) and climbs another 500 feet up to the peak, where there's an old wooden tripod atop a pile of scree; look for the hiker's register, kept in a Tupperware container. Allow three hours roundtrip for this moderate hike.

Back on the road, just on the other side of the pass is **Tahoe Meadows.** The Ophir Creek Trail from Davis Creek Park in Washoe Valley ends here. It's also a favorite winter destination of Renoites and Incline Villagers for cross-country skiing, sledding, tubing, and snowball fights. In addition, it's a landing strip for the world-class hang-gliders that regularly fly off the top of Slide Mountain. And finally, it's the first real place to pass in 20 minutes.

From there, you start dropping down pretty fast: roughly 2,700 feet in five miles. There's a big pull-out to the right at the first good view of Lake Tahoe. But there's a much better overlook another mile down the road (to the left on a blind curve; careful). It overlooks all of Incline Village, from the ski slopes to the beach. In another few miles are the village and the lake (covered later on in this chapter).

WASHOE VALLEY

Steamboat Valley

Just past the intersection of Business 395 and NV 431 (Mt. Rose), Truckee Meadows narrows into Steamboat Valley, with the road running along Steamboat Creek at the bottom of the Steamboat Hills. This is the start of a highly active geothermal region in western Nevada; the area boasts some of the highest amounts of geothermal energy available for power production in the country. The geothermal river runs roughly from here down through Carson City (providing hot water for Carson Hot Springs) and down farther into Carson Valley (providing hot water for Walley's Hot Springs).

The big plant you see just past the intersection with Mt. Rose Highway is a Sierra Pacific geothermal power station, which draws 300-degree water from 1,000–2,000 feet deep, removes the heat to turn turbines, then returns the water. The plant, completed in 1992, cost $60 million to build and produces 24 megawatts of electricity, enough to power roughly 15,000 houses. The small power plant behind it is several years older and produces six megawatts.

Hot springs were discovered here in 1860, and when conditions were right, around 50 columns of steam could be seen rising from the area. The constant geothermal rumbling reminded the early settlers of a sound peculiar to a working steamboat.

Steamboat Hot Springs is the oldest commercial hot springs spa in the state; look for the mission-like building on the left hand side of the road. The first spa was developed here during the Virginia City mining days; later on, in 1909, Dr. Edna Carver arrived here and in succeeding years developed a therapeutic spa here, using the healing mineral waters. Today, the natural geothermal therapeutic waters remain the same, but the site has been renovated, and the water is available in clean, fresh, private tile tub rooms with single-use water. Also here are a steam room, a large outdoor tub, and a variety of healthful treatments including therapeutic massage, mud body wraps, exercise classes and chiropractic. The spa is open every day except Wednesday, noon to 8 P.M. Children under 12 are not admitted. Contact: Steamboat Villa Hot Springs Spa, P.O. Box 18106, 16010 S. Virginia Rd., Reno, NV 89511, 775/853-6600, www.steamboatsprings.org.

In another few miles, US 395 curves around the west side of Washoe Valley. Continue 2.6 miles and take a right onto Davis Creek Road.

Davis Creek Park

This is another fine Washoe County park, 20 miles south of Reno, with a campground, day-use picnic area, small lake, and extensive network of trails. Upon entering, go right at the fork

Washoe Valley landscape

JOHN ELK III

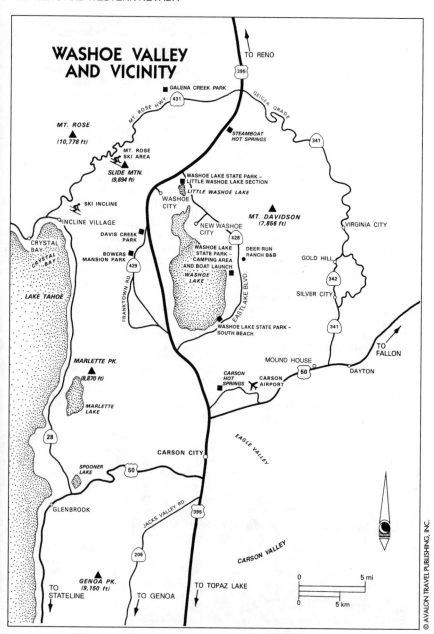

WASHOE VALLEY AND VICINITY

TO RENO

395

Galena Creek Park

431 MT. ROSE HWY

GEIGER GRADE

MT. ROSE
(10,778 ft)

STEAMBOAT
HOT SPRINGS

341

MT. ROSE
SKI AREA

SLIDE MTN.
(9,694 ft)

WASHOE LAKE STATE PARK –
LITTLE WASHOE LAKE SECTION

SKI INCLINE

LITTLE WASHOE LAKE

WASHOE
CITY

MT. DAVIDSON
(7,856 ft)

VIRGINIA CITY

INCLINE VILLAGE

DAVIS CREEK
PARK

NEW WASHOE
CITY

428

CRYSTAL
BAY

CRYSTAL
BAY

BOWERS
MANSION PARK

429

WASHOE LAKE
STATE PARK –
CAMPING AREA
AND BOAT LAUNCH

DEER RUN
RANCH B&B

GOLD HILL

FRANKTOWN RD

EASTLAKE BLVD.

342

LAKE TAHOE

WASHOE
LAKE

SILVER CITY

341

WASHOE LAKE STATE PARK –
SOUTH BEACH

TO
FALLON

MOUND HOUSE

MARLETTE PK.
(8,870 ft)

CARSON
HOT
SPRINGS

CARSON
AIRPORT

50

DAYTON

MARLETTE
LAKE

28

EAGLE VALLEY

SPOONER
LAKE

50

CARSON CITY

GLENBROOK

JACKS VALLEY RD

395

N

206

CARSON VALLEY

GENOA PK.
(9,150 ft)

0   5 mi

0   5 km

TO
STATELINE

TO GENOA

TO TOPAZ LAKE

© AVALON TRAVEL PUBLISHING, INC.

for the campground, which has 63 campsites for tents or self-contained motor homes up to 40 feet, with 19 pull-throughs. Piped drinking water, flush toilets, showers, sewage disposal, picnic tables, grills, and fire pits are provided; firewood is for sale. The maximum stay is seven days. The elevation is 5,100 feet. No reservations; the fee is $11 per site. Contact Park Headquarters, 25 Davis Creek Rd., Carson City, NV 89704, 775/849-0684. The first (south) campground is open year-round; the back (north) campground has remote walk-in sites on the pine needles.

Look up to see why they call it Slide Mountain. A 15-foot wall of mud and debris slid down the Ophir Creek drainage on Memorial Day 1983, killing one person and burying parts of Washoe Valley with tons of mud, which you can still see in places.

The day-use area is to the left at the fork, open 8 A.M.–5 P.M. A half-mile nature trail starts from the parking lot and circles the lake; it's stocked with rainbow trout and is used for ice skating in the winter. A brochure describes the sights at the numbered posts. A one-mile discovery trail loops around the whole park. A Forest Service trail heads right up and over the Sierra: 2.5 miles to Ophir Creek, another mile from there to Rock Lake, and another 2.5 miles to Tahoe Meadows. The first section of the trail gives you a close-up view of the slide: broken trees, boulders, and debris.

A two-minute drive south brings you to the Bowers Mansion county park.

Bowers Mansion Park

The 16-room granite Bowers Mansion was built for $400,000 in 1864 by Lemuel Sanford ("Sandy") Bowers, the only original Comstock discoverer ever to see any real money, though his rags-to-riches story ended in rags. Sandy, a Missouri mule skinner turned miner, staked claim to one of the most profitable of the early ore deposits on the Comstock. His next-claim neighbor was Eilley Orrum Hunter Cowan, a twice-divorced Mormon Scotswoman who ran a primitive boardinghouse in Gold Hill. They married their fortunes together and proceeded to spend the whole in the manner to which they hadn't yet and never would become accustomed. Eilley dragged a reluctant Sandy to Europe, where they bought everything in sight to furnish the house so they could hobnob with the Comstock nabobs. But Sandy died in 1867 of silicosis (miner's lung disease), and Eilley, out of her element and slightly off her rocker, began her slow decline. She expanded the house, adding a third floor of hotel rooms, along with pools, bathhouses, and other recreational attractions, and managed to make a go of running the new resort. But her 12-year-old adopted daughter Persia died in 1874, and Eilley lost the mansion right afterwards. She was reduced to reading fortunes as the "Washoe Seeress" in Virginia City and San Francisco, dying broke in an Oakland nursing home in 1903.

The mansion changed hands 11 times in the next 70 years. In 1946, the Bowers Mansion Restoration Committee began running ads in Nevada newspapers requesting the return of the Bowers's original furnishings, which could be validated against an inventory taken in 1864. Over the next 20 years the furnishings trickled in enough to fill up one room at a time. In 1967–68 the unfinished third-floor hotel rooms were torn off, the interior voids were filled with donated period pieces, and the mansion was opened in something akin to its original splendor.

Look first into the visitor center, once the root cellar, out behind the mansion. Good displays of natural and man-altered environments, including an excellent exhibit on the V flume, which transported logs, lumber, and sometimes people from the mountain forests to the valley sawmills, and Schussler's siphon, which pumped water from Marlette Lake down to Washoe Valley and back up over Mt. Davidson to Virginia City.

Then climb the short trail behind the house up into the manzanita, with benches, fences, a bridge, and steps along the way, to the family cemetery. The trail provides a great view of the back of the house, the old pool (from Eilley's original resort), the new pool, the valley road, and the Virginia Range.

Also here at Bowers Mansion Park are a park with abundant green grass, attractive picnic areas and children's playgrounds, and a large, beautiful outdoor swimming pool to rinse off the hot and dry blues; open daily 12–6 P.M. in summer, $2 adults, less for kids, lockers available.

The 30-minute tour of the mansion ($4 adults, $2 children and seniors) leaves every half-hour,

11 A.M. to 4:30 P.M., every day in summer from Memorial Day through Labor Day weekends, and on weekends during May, September and October (closed November through April); 775/849-0201.

Around the Lake

Continue south on Davis Creek Rd., then hang another right onto **Franktown Road.** Here you're right between the Sierra montane zone and the edge of the valley, watered to a verdant lushness by runoff and some irrigation. The farms, ranches, barns and stables, large trees, great views east and west, and large one-of-a-kind houses dazzle the eye. The big front yards could be golf courses and the white picket fences offset the road and private property perfectly. This few-mile drive along Franktown Rd. is one of the state's prettiest scenic valley/foothill stretches of road.

Rejoin Davis Creek Road (NV 429) and cross under US 395 onto NV 428 up the east side of Washoe Lake. Suddenly you're in the desert, with nary a tree in sight, and only the gray-green sagebrush to hold the sand in place. If you're coming from Reno, in less than an hour's driving time you've gone from city to mountain to valley to desert to lakeside. On the way to Washoe Lake State Park a mile north, notice the boulder painted like a doggie, in a similar manner to the one of Tufa Snoopy on the road to Gerlach.

Washoe Lake State Park

At the end of the eight-year drought in 1995, Washoe Lake was bone dry. Once 3,000 acres at a depth of 18 feet, it was the first time since the drought of 1937–39 that the lake had evaporated completely. Normally, it loses five feet in the summer to evaporation, and runoff puts back five feet in the spring. Even the skeletons of two-foot catfish had all but dried up and blown away. But thanks to the ferocious winters of 1996 and 1997, the lake filled up again, so high that it was contiguous with Little Washoe Lake at the north end of the valley.

On the south-east side of the lake are the **Washoe Lake Wetlands,** at the **Washoe Lake State Park South Beach.** The wetlands and south beach are great for bird-watching; a system has been set up to provide wetlands for birds here all year round, even in years when the lake might go dry. There are picnic tables and a beach here, and a fine view across the lake to Slide Mountain; day use costs $3 per vehicle.

Continue north to the main entrance. Go right into the campground (open year-round): 49 campsites for tents or self-contained motor homes up to 40 feet, with 10 pull-throughs. Piped drinking water, flush toilets, hot showers, picnic tables, grills, and fire rings are provided. It's pretty bare camping here—flat, open, a few lonesome trees, and not much else you can sage about it. The maximum stay is seven days. No reservations; the fee $10 is per campsite. Contact Park Headquarters, 4855 Eastlake Blvd., Carson City, NV 89701, 775/687-4319. Left at the entrance takes you to the day-use area ($3 per vehicle), with phone, restrooms, a boat ramp leading to the lake, and a long pier extending out over the water.

Deer Run Ranch Bed and Breakfast

This is one of the most purely idyllic public places to spend a night or two in the whole state. It's a working alfalfa ranch nestled against the Virginia Range, with a view west of the lake, highway, ranches, foothills, and Sierra, including the famous Slide. On the grounds are a natural pond, used for skating in the winter (ice skates supplied); the pond has a new pier for a new boat (so now the B&B can longer claim to be without pier). There are also a big round Doughboy, a horseshoe pit, long sled run, gorgeous gardens and orchards with walking paths, and a potter's studio where hostess Muffy Vhay turns out all the plates, bowls, and containers used at the Deer Run.

Muffy Vhay grew up on the Quarter Circle J ranch, which abuts the Deer Run property; this land has been in her family since the 1930s. She and her architect husband, David, along with their four children, built the ranch house from local Doug fir, using the hill as a berm on two sides. The two guest rooms (each with private bath) sport handmade quilts, wall-to-wall window seats with built-in magazine racks, and ranching and western decor. Breakfast is served in a guest sitting room with a fireplace, kitchenette, and bookshelves. Highly recommended. Located at 5440 Eastlake Blvd., 775/882-

3643. Rates start at $85 a night during low season and rise to $110 for the height of the summer. There's a two-night minimum on holidays and special events weekends.

VERDI

Old US 40

Get on 4th St. in Reno and head west. Quickly the four-lane city street becomes a two-lane river road in the bottomlands at the foot of the Sierra. On the other side of McCarran Blvd. is old US 40. One of the first transcontinental highways, it was completed in the mid-1920s, which was celebrated with an exposition in Reno in 1927, when the first arch was erected. You'll still find a real slice of Reno in those days, with '30s bungalow-style motels (one named Old US 40), farmhouses, and ranch land, mere minutes from downtown on an old-fashioned Sunday drive. You thread between the foothills of Peavine Mountain on the right and high Mt. Rose on the left. The big dark-wood ghost of a lodge and resort, the River Inn, just before the ramps onto I-80, had a long and illustrious run through Reno history.

This is one of the longest stretches of Old Highway 40 found along the whole 400-mile course through Nevada; it was replaced by the I-80 superhighway, section by section, from 1959 and through 1983. You can follow the original road through Mogul, but you have to get on the interstate there; beyond is a long dead end. You only have to stay on I-80 for a mile, though, and then you can take the Business 80 exit into Verdi.

History

A man named O'Neil built a bridge across the Truckee here in 1860. A sawmill was installed nearby and a logging boomtown named Crystal Peak was created by the demand for railroad ties as the Central Pacific Railroad roared toward, through, and past this point. The construction paused just long enough to rename the town Verdi, after Giuseppe Verdi, the Italian composer. Of course, in a typical frontier bastardization of the Italian pronunciation, you instead say VUR-die (one wonders what might have happened if Charles Crocker had named it Giuseppe instead).

Verdi remained an active mill and railroad town after the CP was completed. In fact, Verdi is remembered as the site of what's considered by some to be the first train robbery in the west. In 1870, seven bandits held up Train Number One and made off with more than $40,000 in payroll money bound for the Yellow Jacket mine. The robbers holed up in mine shafts on Peavine Mountain till they were tracked down and brought to justice inside of a week. Only $3,000 wasn't recovered, and some say it's still buried on Peavine.

Eventually, the area around Crystal Peak got logged out and a disastrous fire in 1928 might have doomed the town. But US 40 passed through and kept it alive with traffic. A popular truck stop that serviced the old road moved up the hill to be on the new interstate; Boomtown is a familiar sight to freeway travelers.

Today, Verdi is a ritzy bedroom community for Reno, with Franktown Road-like mansions on or near the Truckee and up in Dog Valley on the California line.

Around Town

Verdi has two bars, a country store, an antique shop, and the **Sagebrush Cantina,** a homey bar and restaurant (open 11 A.M.–10 P.M.) decorated with license plates, serving Mexican food along with burgers and sandwiches. The wild green-and-white stone castle in the middle of town is as far as the owners, the De Domenico brothers, have gotten with rebuilding the venerable **Verdi Inn.** Originally erected in 1925, it served Verdi till burning down in 1985. The rebuilding began a year later and the Inn was advertised in the *Yellow Pages* for years, since the owners of the "Gothic Western" inn believed the opening was always just around the corner. It's a shame that this building is in Washoe County instead of, say, Storey, because then someone could buy it and turn it into the brothel that it seems to want to be. Compare the Verdi Inn, with its frilly trim and feminine aspect, to the River Inn up the road, with its strong solid angles and brooding masculine presence.

Drive past town on Business 80 and stop to read the historical sign. Then take the first left after that and bear right at the fork for **Crystal Peak Park.** Right on the river, there are his-and-her restrooms, along with 15 stone barbecue grills and picnic tables.

Back in town, turn onto Dog Valley Rd. and go by the big old brick building and the school. Adjacent to the elementary school is the **Verdi Upland Habitat,** an eight-acre reserve providing a lush habitat in the transition zone between the Sierra Nevada and the Great Basin, created for wildlife that come down from the Sierras to get to the Truckee River, in the Great Basin. The **Verdi Nature Trail,** a half-mile loop trail constructed in 1998, makes a pleasant walk; the trailhead begins at the north parking lot of the elementary school. Trail maps are available at the public library in the school (open Tuesday–Friday 3–6 P.M., Thurs. 3–8 P.M., Saturday 10 A.M. –6 P.M.), and at the school office.

Continuing on past the school, big houses, old and new, move by as you enter rugged Sierra country. The pavement ends with a bang right at the **Toiyabe National Forest,** and a very rough road continues 8.5 miles north to the Forest Service campground: 21 sites, water, free.

Boomtown

Boomtown (775/345-6000 or toll-free 877/726-6686, www.boomtowncasinos.com), on highway I-80 at the Boomtown exit, has been expanding in recent years and is now a full-fledged tourist attraction, a major hotel-casino-RV park-fun center-border resort on 40 acres of developed land in the middle of 500 undeveloped acres. The operation went public in 1992; the money raised financed a massive expansion. Today, Boomtown boasts a major casino, with over 1,200 slots, dozens of tables, and four restaurants including the Silver Screen old "chuck wagon-style" buffet, Waddie's Steakhouse, and the 24-hour Tumbleweed Café with Tex-Mex dishes, wood-fired gourmet pizza and other American favorites. Tacked on to the casino is an award-winning 40,000-square-foot amusement complex, one of the best places in the area to take kids. The gorgeous carousel is 75 cents a ticket; 18 holes of miniature Ghost Town Golf is $3.50 per person, and the Dynamic Motion Theater features simulated joyrides on a roller coaster, spaceship, bobsled, dune buggy, and others for $2.50. Unlimited ride tickets are $10. There's also a ton of arcade action: air hockey, Sonic Blast Man, Kid's Adventuredome, Skee Ball, Sidewinder, Big Top Fiddlesticks, Neck and Neck, Bumper Boats, and a gift redemption center. Accommodations include 318 new rooms and suites, and a 200-space full-hookup RV park; see accommodations details in the Reno section.

A free shuttle bus operates hourly between Boomtown and downtown Reno. In Reno it departs every hour on the hour, 8 A.M. to 11 P.M., from in front of the National Bowling Stadium, on Center St. at the corner of 4th St.

VIRGINIA CITY

HISTORY

In the beginning was the word, and the word was gold. In reckless pursuit of the word, the whole wave of '49ers, the tens of thousands of gold-fevered stampeders, rushed to California, forever after known as the Golden State, entirely missing Nevada's Gold Creek and Gold Canyon and Gold Hill. But starting as early as 1851, a backwash of prospectors filtered east again to search the high desert for the precious word, and some prospectors stopped in Nevada on their way to California and stayed. At the time, this land at the edge of the eastern Sierra was referred to by the U.S. government as the western Utah Territory. The Latter-day Saints' administrators called it the Carson County Colony of the State of Deseret. The gentile (non-Mormon) settlers considered it eastern California. John C. Frémont considered it the western edge of the Great Basin Desert, which he'd explored and named only seven years previously. And the local prospectors referred to it as Washoe, after the Wa-She-Shu Indian tribe, for centuries the mountains' and desert's primary inhabitants.

Discovery of the Daughter Lode

Throughout the 1850s, a handful of hopefuls huddled over several Carson River creeks near present-day Dayton, panning a day's wages in summer and either hunkering down or heading out for the winter. Though the Grosch brothers, two young New Yorkers with a working knowledge of geology, mineralogy, and assay proce-

BOB RACE

dures, had an indication of the quality and immensity of the *silver* wealth in the vicinity, they both died suddenly in 1857, and their valuable information was buried with them. By around 1858, the placer gold in the river valley was depleted, and the prospectors fanned out. Some followed Gold Creek up Gold Canyon and settled a town called Gold Hill on Sun Mountain. A few hardcore miners, including James "Old Virginny" Finney (after whom Virginia City was eventually named), began digging *into* the ground in the spring of 1859; several feet below the surface they struck quartzite containing serious gold.

Immediately, miners began digging in nearby canyons. Two Irishmen made their way up Six-Mile Canyon on the east side of Sun Mountain and located some color. After a few days of pulling out about $12 a day, Henry Comstock, a Canadian trapper, prospector, and blowhard, accused the pair of trespassing on his "ranch." Instead of challenging the preposterous claim, the prospectors gave Comstock a piece of nearby ground. Although none of the participants realized it at the time, the Comstock Lode had been found, claimed, and named.

Silver!

The miners on Sun Mountain optimistically called their gopher hole the Ophir Mine, after the bibli-

cal land where the wealth of King Solomon was located. Yet they remained unaware of the real riches right beneath their feet. In fact, the more they dug, the more they got bogged down by a heavy blue-gray mud they'd never seen before. This mud polluted the quartz veins, settled quickly to the bottom of the sluice boxes, diluted the quicksilver—in general, seriously impeded recovery of the gold. The miners hated this mud with all their hearts. They cursed it and damned it and flung it aside . . . until, by happenstance, a visitor carried a chunk down to Placerville in July 1859 and had it assayed. The mud was found to contain $875 per ton in gold, and an incredible $3,000 per ton in pristine sulphuret of silver. The news spread immediately west and east, and a new rush began gathering steam. The Comstock Lode, Virginia City, and Nevada were about to explode onto the scene. The big bam boom had begun.

Rush and Flush

An estimated 10,000 fortune-seekers remained poised on the west side of the Sierra Nevada in early 1860 until the passes cleared of snow, then swarmed over the ragged settlement on Sun Mountain that had waited out the winter. Many of these hopefuls, such as J. Ross Browne, pre-eminent travel and mining writer of

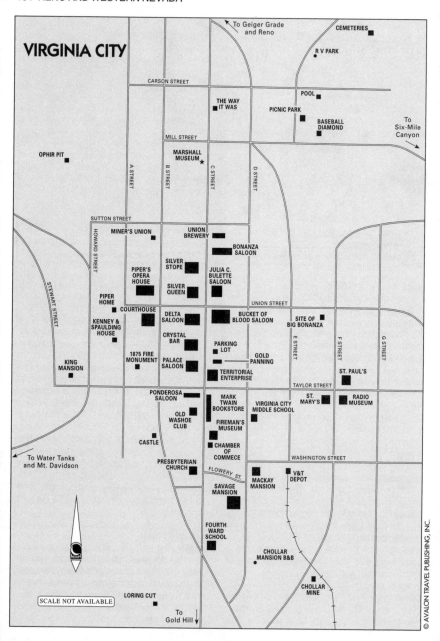

VIRGINIA CITY

To Geiger Grade and Reno

CEMETERIES

R V PARK

CARSON STREET

THE WAY IT WAS

POOL

PICNIC PARK

BASEBALL DIAMOND

To Six-Mile Canyon

MILL STREET

OPHIR PIT

MARSHALL MUSEUM

A STREET
B STREET
C STREET
D STREET

SUTTON STREET

HOWARD STREET

MINER'S UNION

UNION BREWERY

BONANZA SALOON

STEWART STREET

PIPER'S OPERA HOUSE

SILVER STOPE

SILVER QUEEN

JULIA C. BULETTE SALOON

PIPER HOME

COURTHOUSE

DELTA SALOON

BUCKET OF BLOOD SALOON

UNION STREET

SITE OF BIG BONANZA

E STREET
F STREET
G STREET

KENNEY & SPAULDING HOUSE

CRYSTAL BAR

KING MANSION

1875 FIRE MONUMENT

PALACE SALOON

PARKING LOT

GOLD PANNING

TERRITORIAL ENTERPRISE

ST. PAUL'S

TAYLOR STREET

PONDEROSA SALOON

MARK TWAIN BOOKSTORE

VIRGINIA CITY MIDDLE SCHOOL

ST. MARY'S

RADIO MUSEUM

OLD WASHOE CLUB

FIREMAN'S MUSEUM

CASTLE

CHAMBER OF COMMECE

To Water Tanks and Mt. Davidson

PRESBYTERIAN CHURCH

WASHINGTON STREET

FLOWERY ST.

MACKAY MANSION

V&T DEPOT

SAVAGE MANSION

MooN

FOURTH WARD SCHOOL

CHOLLAR MANSION B&B

SCALE NOT AVAILABLE

LORING CUT

To Gold Hill

CHOLLAR MINE

© AVALON TRAVEL PUBLISHING, INC.

his time, took a look and left. The conditions were rigorous to say the least, and only the hardiest and most committed men and women stuck it out in the early days.

During that summer of 1860, anarchy reigned supreme. Food, water, and fuel were perpetually scarce, though whiskey flowed from a dozen taps. The plushest living conditions were deplorable. Men slept in their gopher holes as much to get out of the wind as to protect against claim jumpers. Death was casual and commonplace. Several governments competed for jurisdiction. The original discoverers sold out to California speculators for a song. The mines, deepening under newly renamed Mt. Davidson (after a San Francisco silver broker), outgrew the technology available to keep them from collapsing.

In early 1861, however, a young engineer, Philip Deidesheimer, invented square-set timbering, which revolutionized hard-rock-mining support systems and allowed the Lode to be unloaded at depths whose lower limits no one would know for another 20 years. Quartz mills sprung up locally to refine the medium-grade ore. Steam engines replaced mule-powered hoisting equipment; steam pumps cleared the shafts and stopes of water. The virgin forests of the eastern Sierra across Washoe Valley began to be systematically felled, freighted, and buried within the Comstock.

THE DEVIL AND J. ROSS BROWNE

John Ross Browne was one of the most prodigious travelers, prolific writers, productive illustrators, and improbable bureaucrats of his day. Born in Ireland in 1821, by the time he was 39 years old he'd explored four continents, published three books, served as the official stenographer at the California constitutional convention, held jobs as a postal agent and customs inspector, regularly contributed articles to the popular *Harper's Monthly*, and become famous as one of the originators of the school of Western frontier humor. He was living in the Bay Area when "the cry of silver! Silver in Washoe!" was "borne on the wings of the wind from the Sierra Nevada" and "wafted through every street, lane, and alley of San Francisco."

Browne made his way on public transportation to Placerville and set off on foot over the mountains in the early spring of 1860. "In the course of a day's tramp we passed parties of every description and color: Irishmen, wheeling their blankets, provisions, and mining implements on wheelbarrows; American, French, and German foot-passengers, leading heavily laden horses, or carrying their packs on their backs, and their picks and shovels slung across their shoulders; Mexicans, driving long trains of pack mules, and swearing fearfully, as usual, to keep them in order; dapper-looking gentlemen, apparently from San Francisco, mounted on fancy horses; women, in men's clothes, mounted on mules or burros; whiskey peddlers, organ grinders, drovers, white-haired old men, cripples and hunchbacks, even sick men from their beds—all stark mad for silver."

He rested in Carson City, then took the stage to Silver City. On foot he approached Devil's Gate, and as he passed through, it struck him that there was something ominous in the sound of the name. "Devil's Gate—as in 'Let All Who Enter Here . . .' But I had already reached the other side. It was too late now for repentance."

Browne found "every foot of the canyon claimed, and gangs of miners were at work all along the road, digging and delving into the earth like so many infatuated gophers." He also observed it a bit breezy. "Never was such a wind as this! Capsizing tents, scattering the grit with blinding force into everybody's eyes, and sweeping furiously around every crook and corner in search of some sinner to smite. It was the most villainous and persecuting wind that ever blew, and I boldly protest that it did nobody good."

During his inspection of the town, his worst forebodings upon passing through the Gate were confirmed. "The deep pits on the hillsides; the blasted and barren appearance of the whole country; the unsightly hodge-podge of a town; the horrible confusion of tongues; the roaring, raving drunkards in the barrooms; the flaring and flaunting gambling saloons, filled with desperadoes of the vilest sort; the ceaseless torrent of imprecations that shocked the ear on every side; the mad speculations and feverish thirst for gain—all combined to give me a forcible impression of the unhallowed character of the place."

After a few days, poisoned by the water, parched by the wind, appalled by the brutality, and deprived of sleep and sustenance, Browne departed Washoe, to "once more get clear of Devil's Gate."

By 1863, square-set supports, stamp mills, territorial government, and polite society had ushered in the first golden age of Virginia City. Fifteen thousand residents clogged the steep eastern slope of Mt. Davidson in a boomtown the likes of which had never been seen before in the United States. Still, as the mines got deeper (to the 300-foot level) and the ore got richer, stock speculation and property litigation ran rampant, defining this early wildcat period of the development of the Comstock Lode. Thousands of claims—badly recorded according to vague laws enforced by Darwin's Theory—overlapped to the extent that the Comstock was "owned" in its entirety three or four times over. Hundreds of lawsuits clogged the territorial courts to determine rightful possession of a rat's maze of mines. Corruption in the courts became so pronounced that the distinction between judge and auctioneer was rhetorical. Speculation fever, heavy and sweaty, gripped the city. Stock certificates turned into the instant currency of the boom. The wildly fluctuating value of the famed "feet" of paydirt in one's possession turned paupers to princes and back to paupers in a single day.

Busts and Bankers

Toward the end of 1863, it seemed as if the silver edifice had reached so high that nobody could see the top of it. California capital was pouring into the mines and mills for equipment and payroll and the silver was shipped out in wagonloads to San Francisco. The *Territorial Enterprise* emerged as the trendsetter among a half dozen newspapers on the Lode; Samuel Clemens and William Wright adopted their pen names, Mark Twain and Dan DeQuille, as well as the frontier writing style popularized by J. Ross Browne.

Nevada became a state in 1864, and the five-year-old legal gridlock was unsnarled by a battery of new and unimpeachable federal appointees and elected officials. Right afterwards, however, the major mines hit rock bottom at 400 feet deep. Most of the wildcat operations succumbed to the Comstock's first bust. The stock market crashed. Mining in even the largest and most California-capitalized claims was suspended. The small-time quick-buck lawyers and scammers left town, to be replaced by the big-time big-stakes bankers and swindlers.

William Ralston, president of the Bank of Cali-

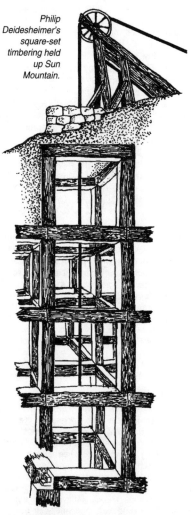

Philip Deidesheimer's square-set timbering held up Sun Mountain.

LOUISE FOOTE

fornia, dispatched his functionary, William Sharon, to Virginia City to gain control of the desperate situation. Both had been born in Ohio in the 1820s. Both had started out in the riverboat business. Both were gamblers and empire builders. Sharon immediately began consolidating the bank's interests: buying out bankrupt claim holders for pennies on the dollar; approving loans liberally and accumulating collateral; exploring the shafts, tunnels and drifts; and conducting numerous and systematic assays. He studied geology, mineralogy, and ore bodies; the hoisting, pumping, and communications mechanisms of the mines and mills; timbering and teaming and transportation; the town's water and gas systems. Driven by determination, plus a natural greed and streak of ruthlessness, by the spring of 1865 William Sharon had emerged as the ultimate expert on the Comstock, the possessor of the big picture, the maestro of the maelstrom.

For the next seven years, "Ralston's Ring" ruled the Lode. Sharon accumulated a huge monopoly of mines, mills, transportation, utilities, and stock. He unearthed bonanzas from the deepening diggings and became quite adept at manipulating the stock market to fleece the gamblers, little and large. Even the swindlers had never imagined a con game on such a grand scale. All Sharon had to do, for example, was quietly buy up the stock of an unproductive mine at $10 a share, then plant a rumor of a possible bonanza at that mine. This would drive the price up to $80, when he'd sell it off and fill the vault. In no time the vault itself was no longer large enough. In June 1867 the Bank of California moved into its new palatial headquarters at the corner of California and Sansome streets in San Francisco. The building immediately earned the subtitle "The Wonder of the Silver Age."

Monopoly—Almost

In 1867 Sharon devised a plan to monopolize the two dozen reduction mills, scattered willy-nilly between Mt. Davidson and the Carson River. He allowed the mill owners to overextend their credit with the bank, then squeezed them till they suffocated. In the meantime, Sharon formed the Union Mill and Mining Company, and his tentacles closed around the remaining independent mines on the Comstock by withholding credit unless they refined their ore at his mills. Finally, he determined to control the transportation between the mines and the mills by constructing the Virginia & Truckee short line railroad from Virginia City to the Carson River and Carson City. From Carson City the train went north to Reno, where it connected with the Central Pacific railroad.

Only John Mackay, who came to the Comstock as a common miner in 1860 and climbed the ladder to become a major stockholder in some of the larger mines, continued to produce profits for anyone outside Ralston's Ring. With his partners James Fair, James Flood, and William O'Brien, Mackay began to beat Sharon at his own game, taking control of the Bank of California's Hale & Norcross Mine from right under Sharon's nose. Their Kentuck Mine, too, paid dividends to its shareholders and enabled Mackay and Fair to play a hunch during the temporary bust of the early 1870s and quietly acquire the Consolidated Virginia Mine. They gambled again and followed a low-grade vein away from the main Lode.

Big Bonanza

Both gambles paid off in 1873 when the Consolidated Virginia Mine, 1,200 feet beneath downtown Virginia City, hit the granddaddy of all Nevada orebodies. The ore was so rich that Mackay's Bonanza Firm made an even greater fortune manipulating the stocks a la Sharon and actually opened a bank of its own in San Francisco. This act helped precipitate a run on the Bank of California; William Ralston was forced out (and drowned that same day in San Francisco Bay). William Sharon took control of the bank.

The Great Fire of 1875 destroyed 33 blocks of Virginia City, including the 10-square-block downtown. But Big Bonanza money financed the rebuilding of Virginia far beyond its previous splendor. The peak year, 1876, saw 23,000 residents (half the state's population) celebrating the city's re-emergence as if the bonanza would produce its riches forever. But within two years, the Comstock Lode had been pretty well played out. It took a few more years of gambling, speculating, and artificial stock highs and lows to convince the last die-hard investors of it. Estimates of the 20-year take (in 19th century dollars) range between $320 million and $750 million worth of precious metals, $100 million to $200 million of which had been from the Big Bonanza.

Twentieth-Century Rocks

The boomers packed their carpetbags and money pouches and blew town in search of new adventure, and Virginia City was left to die in the desert, like the hundreds of boomtowns created in its wake. But the Queen of the Comstock refused to succumb. A little further digging, a new cyanide process for recovering low-grade ore from tailings, and rising gold and silver prices all kept the Comstock on life-support systems into the 1930s. In 1935, the controlled price of gold was raised from $20 to $35 an ounce and Virginia City saw some renewed activity. The WPA paved C Street in 1937.

Around that time, Paul Smith, a mysterious New York hotelman, showed up and introduced the concept of merchandising and museums to the town. He opened the Museum of Memories in a section of the building that now houses the Bucket of Blood Saloon, hired all the local kids to scrounge artifacts from the dumps and attics, and displayed them—without much concern for authenticity (for example, an old top hat that one of the youngsters found became Sandy Bowers's own). He sold bags of sagebrush, conducted two-block walking tours to Piper's Opera House, and had the kids sell a booklet, "Drama of the Comstock," for 15 cents to the tourists who happened to pass through.

The rigors of WW II caused a suspension in the mining, and by 1950 Virginia City seemed destined to dry up, fall down, and blow away. But Lucius Beebe and Charles Clegg, bon vivant authors from New York who wrote many popular histories of the American West and its railroads, fell in love with the town. They revitalized the *Territorial Enterprise* and sent copies out to friends around the world; they also helped revive the business district. The immensely popular TV show "Bonanza" renewed the aura around the town, with Ben Cartwright forever sending Joe, Hoss, Ben Jr., and Hop Sing to Virginia City for supplies, entertainment, Doc, and the sheriff. With tourists arriving in ever-increasing numbers, the few hundred residents, many of whom had been inspired by Paul Smith as kids, began to recondition the infrastructure, facilities, and attractions. Mining, too, continued, in fits and starts. Travelers quickly rediscovered Virginia City's boardwalks, saloons, mansions, mines, opera house, churches, cemeteries, and vistas. Today more than three million visitors a year drive up Geiger Grade or Devil's Gate to capture a piece of the glory of its past.

HIGHLIGHTS

With dozens of storefronts strung along five blocks of C St., you could spend a long day just walking in and out of museums, saloons, eateries, and shops from the near end of the street to the far end, then back up the other side. And that doesn't include the mine tours, mansions, opera house, churches, train and trolley rides, and hiking around. In short, Virginia City is so full of history, adventure, excitement, and curiosities that it's too hectic to do it all in one visit. Either plan on going full bore from sunup to sundown or hit a half-dozen highlights in a casual day-trip.

For a look at the conditions in which the lowliest miners worked, the richest executives lived, and the whole spectrum of Comstockers were entertained, the top three attractions are: an Underground Mine tour, the Castle, and Piper's Opera House.

Underground Mine Tour

The heart and soul of Virginia City was the Comstock Lode. Two mine tours allow you to get under the ground and see what the miners saw. Most authentic is the tour of the Chollar Mine, the last of the Comstock's old original mines. The Chollar Mine was the fifth highest in production, producing over $18 million in gold and silver, and this tour shows you the real thing, with the square set timbering, ore, old tools and equipment, and knowledgeable, experienced guides. The Chollar claim was filed in 1859, production started in 1861, and the mine was worked for almost 80 years, until it closed in 1942. It was reopened in 1961 for tours, 100 years after its first began producing, and has been giving tours ever since.

Guided walking tours of the Chollar Mine go over 400 feet into the mountain, take 30 minutes and cost $5 adults, $2 children age 4 to 14. The mine is open every day from Easter to the end of October; hours are noon–5 P.M. from June to August, with shorter hours in spring and fall (may be 1 to 4 P.M.). The Chollar Mine (775/847-0155) is not far from the center of town; you can get there by going downhill from C St. to F St., turning right (south) on F St. and just keep going for about half a mile, or, head south from town on C St., turn left (east) onto the truck route just past the Fourth Ward School, and follow the road around.

Virginia City's other mine tour departs from the rear of the **Ponderosa Saloon** on C St. The mine tunnel snakes 315 feet from the rear end of the saloon into the Best and Belcher diggings, whose paydirt yielded 55% silver and 45% gold. Displays include gold-rich ore, the powder room where "monkeys" (young boys) worked, square-set timbering, minerals under black light, and all the heavy buckets, drills, winches, and rods the miners used to muck the rock, tunneling six to eight feet a day. The guide enumerates myriad dangers: the perpetual threats of cave-in, fire, scalding steam and water, the terrible heat and bad air, not to mention the back-breaking, head-knocking, bone-crushing work itself. At $4 per day (the equivalent of $232 today), the miners were well paid, considering that most hard-rock miners around the world earned less than a dollar a day; still, this tour is graphic evidence that the Comstock miners earned every penny. At the far end, the guide might light two candles and kill the overheads. If he blows out the candles (early-warning signal of gases or lack of oxygen), you'll be back in 1873! The only inconsistency in the authenticity is the 52-degree temperature; you could take a jacket, but don't really need one. Tours operate here all year round. In summer, from April to mid-October, they operate 10 A.M.–5:30 P.M. Winter hours, from mid-October through March, are 11 A.M.–5 P.M. daily. Tours take 25 minutes and cost $4 adults, $1.50 children, $8 family, 775/847-0757.

Locals say that the Ponderosa Saloon tour is not as authentic as the Chollar Mine tour, because although the tunnel on this tour goes *to* an authentic mine tunnel, the tunnel you walk through was never an actual mine tunnel—it was dug in the 1970s, from the rear of the saloon, for the purpose of tourism. They say the guides at the Chollar Mine are more authentic, too, often working miners. We took both the Chollar Mine and Ponderosa Saloon tours, and enjoyed them both!

The Castle

This elegant mansion, on B St. up the hill a block from C St., a little south of Taylor along Millionaire's Row, is so superlative that even guide-

bookese hyperbole fails to touch it; after this tour, the Mackay, Chollar, Bowers, and governor's mansions seem low rent. The history of this 16-room "castle" is absolutely charmed. It escaped the 1875 fire, was sold only twice in its 120-odd years with all its original furnishings, and was never refurbished. What a house full of priceless antiques! Built in 1868 by Robert Graves, superintendent of the Empire Mine, the tour is nothing less than a lesson in 19th-century European fine craftsmanship. The list is endless: English steel-cut prints, olivewood shutters, 14-foot (plus leaves) walnut dining-room table; French wallpaper, bronze statues, and gold-leaf mirrors; Italian marble fireplaces, mouldings, and alabaster urns; hand-painted Dutch vases and original wall paint; spectacular Czech rock-crystal chandeliers; Belgian linen lace; German walnut guest-room set. Notice the "fainting couch" in the living room, the rosewood headboard and the unique Czech lamp in the master bedroom, and the Heidelberg burl circassian walnut sideboard in the dining room. Everything was shipped from Europe around the tip of South America to San Francisco, by riverboat up the Sacramento River to Knight's Landing, upriver from Sacramento, and then by wagon over the Sierra. Graves lived in it only for four years, then sold it to the Blauvelys of Gold Hill Bank, who lived here for 44 years. The banker sold it to the McGuirks, whose descendants still live in the home. The castle is open daily 11 A.M.–5 P.M., Memorial Day weekend through October; $4 adults, $2 students, 775/847-0275. Leave your camera in the car; no photographing allowed.

Piper's Opera House

On the corner of B St. and Union, this is Virginia City's well-preserved, nearly restored theater. John Piper built this building in 1885, after the first two opera houses burned. It has canvas walls (for acoustics), balconies, chandeliers designed to throw patterns on the ceiling, the original round-backed chairs, the railroad spring-loaded floor (dancer enhancer), and a stage raked higher in the back—from which the terms "upstage" and "downstage" originate. Ads appear on top of the curtain. Three slotted sets (parlor, forest, and street) were rolled into and out of view by stagehands. Proscenium box seats are on one side of the stage. Signs inside tell of the performers who appeared here, who included Mark Twain, Harry Houdini, John Philip Sousa, Lily Langtry, Al Jolson, and John Barrymore, among many others. Circles and keys painted on the floor date from when Piper's was used as a basketball court and roller rink in later years.

Tours are conducted 11 A.M.–4:30 P.M. every day from May through October, and 11 A.M.–4 P.M. weekends and holidays the rest of the year, weather permitting (groups by appointment, year round). Tours, including a five-minute video, cost $2.50 adults, $1 children, $6 for families or groups. Shows are presented here year round; phone the opera house (775/847-0433) or check with the Chamber of Commerce for current schedules.

the incomparable castle

MUSEUMS

The following "museums" (the term is used liberally around here) are all on C Street.

The Fourth Ward School, at the far south end of town, was one of four public schools in the town at its peak. Built in 1876 for $100,000, it boasted many revolutionary modern conveniences: cut-stone foundation anchored with steel rods to the granite of Mt. Davidson; new-fangled heating and ventilating technology; water piped to all four floors, including indoor drinking fountains. The last class graduated in 1936. The Nevada State Museum has set up an excellent exhibit on the ground floor in the form of nine "lessons," including highlights of Comstock history; mining technology (3-D viewing machine and models of a stamp mill and hoist works, and mine shaft and stopes); entertainment on the Comstock; women and immigrants in Virginia City; and many other informative signs and exhibits. Two classrooms across the hall have also been restored; one has all the desks, blackboards, and wood stove, the other has team and class pictures and other historical black-

and-whites. Notice how large the rooms are: at its peak, the Fourth Ward School had 1,000 students. The second floor has also been restored; a theater and art gallery occupy the classrooms, and there's an excellent exhibit about Mark Twain. The building is beautifully restored, and has a great view. Your $2 will help continue the restoration. Open daily 10 A.M.–5 P.M. May through October, 775/847-0975.

The Way It Was Museum at the north end on C St. at Sutton has a large array of Comstock mining artifacts, maps, and minerals, including working scale models of stamp mills, mines, Cornish pumps (all built by J.E. Parson of Oroville, California). Three "American Frontier" videos with Charlie Jones and Merlin Olsen, about the Comstock, Piper's Opera House, and Mark Twain, alone are worth the price ($3) of admission (children under 11 free). Also check out the scale model of the underground mine workings and Jim Fair's personal stamp mill. The Way It Was is open daily 10 A.M.–6 P.M. year round, weather permitting; 775/847-0766.

BOB RACE

The **Marshall Mint Museum,** a combination museum-mineral-gold shop, opened in late 1990 on the Reno side of town across C St. from The Way It Was Museum. It's owned by Texas mine magnate Hugh R. Marshall of Marshall Earth Resources, Inc. (MERI). The collection of gold, silver, other precious metals and minerals (some under black light), and art is definitely worth seeing. Feast your eyes on ivory, turquoise, malachite, jade, and lapis lazuli creations from around the world. The gold shop displays coins, gold nuggets, silver, and books for sale. If you're at all into Comstock history, you probably won't be able to resist the Bonanza King silver medallions (all four go for just under $100). Marshall Mint coins and jewelry are minted and assembled on the premises; they also make personalized coins (you can design your own), and a series of "Angel of the Day" and "Our Lord and Savior" coins. The museum is open daily 10 A.M.–5 P.M., 775/847-0777.

The Red Light Museum, downstairs in the basement of the **Julia C. Bulette Saloon & Cafe,**named for the Comstock's most famous prostitute, is an unexpected little gem. Displays here chronicle the vices of the Comstock—sex, drugs, magic. Opium pipes and paraphernalia mingle with medicinal cure-alls, amputation saws, gruesome-looking douche kits, and patent medicines. Also check out the early 20th-century French postcards, antique condoms and vibrators, and snapshot ads for the Sagebrush Brothel in Carson City. The Chinese and Indians were into some even wilder stuff, also displayed here. It's open daily 7 A.M.–8:30 P.M., the same hours as the restaurant; admission $1, 775/847-9394.

The Gambling Museum highlights the 150-year history of gambling in the West: Indian sticks and bones (dice), Mexican monte, faro, Chinese chips, an 1800s' Hazard Wheel, chuck-a-luck, and scores of antique slots. The history of cards and the cheating devices are interesting, as are the display of old U.S. currency and clear-glass slot machines. It's open daily 10 A.M.–6 P.M. April through October, 10 A.M.–5 P.M. November through March, admission $1, 775/847-9022.

You can't go wrong at the museum in back of **Grant's General Store** next door to the newspaper office, with shelves full of old dry goods, an antique cash register, beautiful woodwork, and a barber shop replica—it's free. The "Victoriana" woodstove is one of the finest sights in Virginia City: it was fabricated for the 1904 World's Fair in St. Louis, Missouri, and embellished with silver and gold instead of the usual nickel and chrome.

The **Mark Twain Museum,** also called **The Territorial Enterprise Museum,** 47-53 South C St. in the center of town, is downstairs in the basement of the Territorial Enterprise Gift Shop. The museum displays 19th century printing technology, such as an 1894 linotype, old binding machine, and hot type cabinet. This was the press room for Nevada's oldest publication, which started up in Genoa in December 1858, moved briefly to Carson City, then in October 1860 settled down into a long and profitable run in Virginia City, with the likes of Mark Twain and Dan DeQuille keeping things lively. Mark Twain's original desk is on display, along with some of his books and journals, and there's an interesting recording telling about Twain and his times in Virginia City. The museum is open every day, 10 A.M.–6 P.M., admission $1, 775/847-7950.

The **Comstock Firemen's Museum** is in Virginia City's original firehouse, built in 1864. Not many buildings survived the big fire of October 1875, but this brick building is one that did. The old ladder trailer, 1856 Knickerbocker hand fire engine, and hose carriage are unique. The old fire extinguishers, model fire truck, helmets, and photographs, collected by the Virginia City Volunteer Fire Department, are definitely worth a good look, and a dollar or two donation. It's open 10 A.M.–5 P.M. every day, April to mid-October; 775/847-0717.

The **Virginia City Radio Museum** is on the corner of F St. and Taylor St., just behind the St. Mary's church, three short blocks downhill from C St, It looks like an ordinary house; you'll know it from the big statue of Nipper, the RCA Victor radio dog ("his master's voice"), in the front window. The museum entrance is in the rear. Whether you're a radio buff or not, this is a fascinating museum, with over 200 antique and classic radios on display, plus antique wireless (telegraph) apparatus, a ham radio room with vintage ham radios and a collection of QSL cards from around the world, and a collection of photos of famous old-time radio personalities (see how many you can identify), and several more statues of Nipper. Pride of place goes to an original, complete and authentic 1912 Spark Station, discovered in Reno in November 1999. Owners and curators Henry and Sharon Rogers will give you a guided tour of the museum, if you like. Radio buffs from far and wide contact the Rogers with radio issues, and for antique radio repair; contact Henry and Sharon Rogers, 109 South F St., P.O. Box 511, Virginia City, NV 89440, 775/847-9047, hands@radioblvd.com, www.radioblvd.com. The museum is open 11 A.M.–5 P.M. most days, April through October, or by appointment; November to March it is open "by chance or by appointment." Admission $2 adults, $1 children.

SALOONS

The **Crystal Bar,** corner of C St. and Taylor, 775/847-0464, is a quiet place to have a drink and chat. The crystal and gold-plated chandeliers are original, and many mementos line the walls. Be sure to look at the framed 1946 *Life* magazine story on America's great bars. The photo of the Crystal in its heyday is superb; notice that the Mystery Clock worked. Rumor from reliable sources indicates that the Crystal is being turned into a visitor center, and that by the time you are reading this book, you may find that this is the new home of Virginia City's Chamber of Commerce and Tourist Information Center.

The **Delta Saloon,** half a dozen doors north, 775/847-0789, is as close to a casino as it gets in Virginia City, with rows and rows of slots and video poker (there are no table games in Virginia City), the Sawdust Corner coffee shop on one side and the Delta Gift Shop on the other. Be sure to traipse upstairs (if it's open) to check out the period carpeting, wallpaper, chandeliers, plus the bright skylights, four big banquet rooms, and restrooms. The Delta is also the home of the infamous Suicide Table against the back wall. Read its description if your curiosity is killing you. An interesting shrine to the Bonanza Kings is next to it on the wall. At the opposite end of the casino is an 1880s' world globe, built at a cost of $450 of rosewood (complete with mariner's compass) for Bonanza King James Fair. It's estimated that this unique globe is now worth $100,000.

A few shops north is the **Silver Queen,**

775/847-0440, home of a 16-foot-tall lady on the wall, with a low-cut dress of more than 3,000 silver dollars, a belt of 28 gold pieces, bracelet of dimes, and 50-cent-piece ring. Here are also some old Bally's slots and a great big back bar.

The **Union Brewery,** across the street at the north end of town, was built in 1862; the exterior is original.

A few storefronts south of there is the **Bucket of Blood Saloon,** 775/847-0322. The Bucket, named after one of the hundreds of early licensed premises, is one of the most popular saloons in town, for good reason. It's light and airy, thanks to the big picture window in back overlooking Six-Mile Canyon. And it has a unique dice machine, the world's largest, which is so much fun it's addictive. Look up at the 50 old lamps, the portraits (such as of the Bowerses), and the great woodwork and brass rails.

Across the street and up the block is the **Ponderosa Saloon,** 775/847-0757, in the old Bank of California building. The highlight here (other than the mine tour; see above) is the original bank vault, with a half-inch steel-plate cage surrounded by two-foot-thick walls where Billy Sharon kept his spare change. Study the historic photos and the portraits of the early celebrities: Julia Bulette, James Finney, Henry Comstock, Sam Clemens.

South of there along the funny boardwalk is the **Old Washoe Club,** 775/847-7210, built in 1875 after the great fire. This was the local millionaires' hangout, frequented by Ulysses S. Grant, Thomas Edison, and Wyatt Earp, among others. The posh upstairs digs were accessed by the spiral staircase, still viewable in the back, which is listed in Ripley's as the longest spiral stairs without a supporting pole.

The **Bonanza Saloon,** 775/847-0655, has a big side room full of slots on a fine wood floor, plus an outdoor deck in the back with a coin-operated telescope and a large, faded, historical black-and-white photograph labeled with the features of the view.

SELECTED SHOPS AND ACTIVITIES

Virginia City offers a handful of old-time photo shops: **Silver Sadie's Old-Time Photos, Priscilla Penneyworth's Photographic Em-**

porium, Rotten Rowdie's Old-Time Photos, and **Old Time Photos.** The props and costumes turn you into practically any kind of character from the roaring 1870s that you'd like to be: barmaid, piano player, cocktail waitress, cowboy and cowgirl, gunslinger. Priscilla's prices are representative: $13.95 each for 8 by 10 glossies with one person, $16.95 for two people, $19.95 for three people, additional copies $11.95.

Bogie's Brew and Stogies sells cigar and beer collectibles, including neon beer signs and Coca-Cola memorabilia. **Stone Age** stocks fossils, minerals, petrified wood, jewelry, crystals, and gemstones. And **All Aboard** features railroad-oriented merchandise. Otherwise, nearly two dozen gift, souvenir, craft, art, western, jewelry, Christmas, leather, Indian, candy, clock, candle, and fudge shops sell a huge variety of items, including amethysts, antiques, balsa models, belt buckles, bolos, boots, brass, bullwhips, caps, cards, carvings, Christmas-tree ornaments, coins, copper flowers, cowhides, crystals, custom license-plate frames, dice earrings, dolls, fortunes, fossils, gems, glass, gold, lampshades, leather goods, minerals, moccasins, music boxes, painted plates, paintings, paperweights, peace pipes, pewter, postcards, posters, pottery, stained glass, Stetsons, T-shirts, turquoise, wallets, weavings, and Western wear.

Mark Twain Books, 111 S. C St., with an excellent selection of new, used, out-of-print and rare books about Nevada, specializes in books about Nevada, Western Americana, the Comstock Lode, Virginia City, and Mark Twain, plus Nevada travel guides, kids' books, postcards and plenty more. Come in to take a photo with the lifelike dummy of Mark Twain, and check out the good selection of books by and about Twain and his years as a journalist here in Virginia City. The building is interesting, too; this is one of the oldest buildings on C St., built in 1862. One of very few buildings on C St. to survive the Great Fire of October 1875, it survived because it is of stone and brick, whereas the other Virginia City buildings in 1875 were primarily constructed of wood. Ask for a leaflet telling the long and interesting history of the building; parts of it have been a livery stable, a bank, a hardware store and a museum over the building's long life. Bookshop owner Joe Curtis is friendly and quite a Nevada historian. They do a lot of mail-order business, too; contact

Mark Twain Bookstore, 111 S. C St., P.O. Box 449, Virginia City, NV 89440, 775/847-0454, joe@marktwainbooks.com, www.marktwainbooks.com.

A **panning for gold** operation can now be found beside the old Territorial Enterprise building. The gold mine is down a set of wooden stairs, at the bottom of a water wheel and sluice. It's $5 per person to wash out some specks of salted gold, which you get to keep. The prospector in charge is full of fascinating tidbits about the gold rush and good advice about the panning process. This is a very popular attraction, and draws a crowd of both onlookers and gold panners.

The **Virginia City Outlaws** present an enjoyable, old-timey stunt show twice daily, at noon and 2 P.M., at Union and E Streets. Admission is $3 adults, $1 children.

JOYRIDES

None of the following thrills are quite as anus-clenching as the 15-mile daredevil stunt on the flume from Lake Tahoe, or the four-mile subway trip from Sutro through the bowels of Mt. Emma to the Comstock mainline, then up the hoist to the streets of Virginia City. (Read about both at Fourth Ward School.) Nonetheless, for $3 you can take a 20-minute tour on a replica trolley that looks like an old San Francisco cable car; in warm weather they use an open-air trailer pulled by a Ford tractor. It's a great tour, full of history and inside tips. Catch it at the parking lot next to the Bucket of Blood Saloon every half-hour 9 A.M.–6 P.M.; $3 adult, $2 children, 775/786-0866. While waiting, read the various plaques that grace the Centennial Monument in the parking lot.

The same company operates another trolley which is not a tour, but simply transport around town; you can pick it up at the park 'n ride lot across the street from the Fourth Ward School and ride it around town all day for $1.

Much more thrilling is a 35-minute jaunt on the **Virginia & Truckee Railroad,** departing from the railcar depot on F St. near Washington, just south of St. Mary's Church. A steam locomotive pulls an open car and caboose down to the red Gold Hill depot through tunnel number 4. Since there are nine trips a day between 10:30 A.M. and 5:45 P.M., you can disembark at Gold Hill and catch the next train back to Virginia. It's $5.25 for adults, $2.75 for children, and definitely worth it for the relaxation in the sun, the offbeat narration, and the sensation of going through the tunnel. The V&T runs daily from Memorial Day weekend till October 1, then weekends through the end of October, with possible weekday trains in October depending on weather and passenger load (call for info). Moonlight rides are given monthly on the Saturday evening closest to full moon, June through September. For more info, call 775/847-0380. And for a closer look at the V&T, one of the most famous short lines in U.S. history, see "Nevada State Railroad Museum" under "Sights" in the Carson City chapter.

A proposal to extend the tracks another 17 miles all the way to Carson City and to refurbish more old trains would cost around $25 million; on the 1994 ballot, the residents of Storey and Lyon counties and Carson City voted on a.25% higher sales tax to fund it. Storey County residents approved the measure, but Carson City and Lyon County residents cast the majority vote against. Today, funding is being sought from a variety of sources. You can get more information on plans to restore the railroad, and how you can help recreate this icon of the American West, by contacting the Northern Nevada Railway Foundation, 3208 Goni Rd., Suite 183, Carson City, NV 89706, 775/883-7333, www.steamtrain.org.

For another kind of joyride, check out the **Virginia City Stables,** 499 North C St., 775/847-9242, offering trail horse rides, wild horse viewing rides, lunch and dinner rides, and moonlight rides.

UP THE HILL

Even on the busiest Saturday afternoon in August, walk one block to either side of C St. and you'll think you're the first to stumble upon a very well-preserved and remote ghost town.

By 1863, Virginia had segregated itself along literal lines of wealth, class, and race. Stewart, Howard, and A streets, highest on the slope of Mt. Davidson and laid out along the original location of the great vein, hosted the mansions of the richest owners and bankers. Forty feet down the hill and parallel ran B St., on which lived the mine superintendents, brokers, engineers, lawyers, and officials; some commerce was conducted on B St. as well. C St., then as now the main business thoroughfare, separated the high life from the low. Down on D and E were the prostitutes' cribs and the miners' shacks. The Chinese lived along I Street. And the Paiute squatted below them where no streets yet existed.

B Street
The **Castle** is the one mansion to see if you have time for only one (see above). Two houses

Virginia & Truckee Railroad during the Comstock heyday

NEVADA COMMISSION ON TOURISM

over along Millionaires' Row is the **A. M. Cole Mansion,** built in 1887 by an affluent druggist (not open to the public). Next door is the white two-story building that housed the original Virginia City and Gold Hill Water Company, built in 1875.

Across Taylor St. on B is the **Storey County Courthouse,** completed in 1877 at a cost of $117,000. The style is distinctively High Victorian Italianate. Notice that the life-size statue of Justice standing over the front door is not blindfolded. Justice had her eyes wide open in 19th-century Virginia City.

North of the courthouse are **Piper's Opera House** (see above), the **Knights of Pythias** building (now the Comstock House), and the **Miner's Union Hall,** all built after the big fire in 1875. Between Miner's Hall and Piper's is a little park with a gazebo, perfect for a picnic.

Above B Street

On A St. near Taylor is a historical plaque commemorating "the most spectacular calamity to befall Virginia City." On October 26, 1875, an oil lamp, knocked over in a boardinghouse near this site, burst into flames, which were spread by high winds. When the conflagration had been brought under control, 33 blocks had been leveled. Only a few buildings in Virginia City today predate the fire. The hydrant system constructed afterwards is still in use.

Also on A St. is the old **Piper House.** With your back to the fire monument it's one over to the right, the one with the beautiful square bay window, the Victorian detail, and the two black hitching posts. It was originally inhabited by John Piper of Opera House fame. The house remained vacant for many years until it was bought and completely refurbished by Lucius Beebe. The **Kenney and Spaulding Home** is the one to the left of the fire monument—light purple, with distinctive windows and doors, an attic dormer, and black hitching posts.

The **King House** at the corner of Taylor on Howard was built in 1861 by a taxman and survived the great fire. The tree in front could be as old. The house served as a rectory for St. Mary's Church for more than 60 years, and then became the Bonanza Inn gourmet restaurant. Notice the carved corbels, the wrought-iron fence, and the attractive front door with etched glass.

Next door on Howard St. is the **Shield Home,** built in 1886 after the Comstock had had its heyday, which is clear when you contrast the two.

Continue north on Howard and take the first left. Follow it up and around to the north for the site of the **Ophir Mine** adit. Signs here make it plain that this is private property. Wander around on the high slope of Mt. Davidson, past beautiful houses and the long pit where the first indications were located.

Climbing Mount Davidson

Drive or walk up Taylor St. and follow it around to the water tanks. An overgrown track behind the tanks leads to a large outcrop overlook. If you get no farther than this, you'll have a better view of town than the nine out of ten visitors who never leave C Street.

But if you want the total experience, start up the hill. Thrash through the sage, scaring bunnies and attracting flies. As you march upward, it's easy to pretend you're a prospector—with your head down and nothing much on your mind but the rocks and what they're all about. Mark your progress against the shrinking town below and the widening whitewashed "V" above. The closer you get to the "V," the more spray-paint cans you'll see.

The big flagpole on the peak comes into view once you're past the "V." It does get closer, I promise, no matter how slowly you climb. The last couple of hundred yards you scramble up the scree, on all fours if necessary. A strong hiker should be able to conquer this magnetic mountain in 60–90 minutes. Be prepared for some steep, some huffing and puffing, and some shaky knees. As you get to the top and the scenery opens up to the west and north, you'll see the beautiful two-lane paved road that comes up the other side, with a tour bus or two parked at the top and day-trippers from Reno marveling over the view.

Just kidding.

Seven poles are secured to the peak, including the original flagpost carried up here in 1864 to mark statehood, which sheared off in the wind, plus the second, a telescoping metal pole at least 60 feet high that was carried up to replace it. If you've always wondered what vertigo feels like, stand at the bottom of the pole and look up at the top. The U.S. Coast and Geodesic Survey reference plates are from 1951.

Turning in a full circle, you can just see down into Truckee Meadows to Reno, with the tall tower of the Reno Hilton to the northwest, the Pah Rah Range to the northeast, and *almost* up to Pyramid Lake in the north, depending on the haze. To the west are Mt. Rose and Slide Mountain, and you're not looking too far at them, either. Washoe Valley is down from there, with the north edge of Washoe Lake in view. Turn south for a great view of American Flat to the west of Silver City, so flat it looks man-made. With binoculars you can make out the big white ruins of the Comstock Merger Mill which used to process ore tailings; it was built in 1923 and went out of business in 1928. Closer to you, you can also see the Houston Minerals cyanide mill left over from a mining venture in the early 1980s. There's also a photo op, best of course with a long lens, of Occidental Grade, the truck route between Virginia City and Silver City that cuts out treacherous Greiner's Bend. Greiner's Pit and other recent mining signs around Gold Hill are clearly visible. East, however, is the long view: down Six-Mile Canyon past Sugarloaf onto the Carson Plains, then out to the Dead Camel Mountains, the Desert Mountains beyond them, and the big Stillwater Mountains beyond them.

But the best view of all is right down at Virginia City—the town and the tailings—and whatever vision you can conjure up of the 20-year boom of 125 years ago.

Coming down is almost as much fun as going up. You might wish you'd cut your toenails in the past few days. Your upper thighs start expressing themselves clearly: "Wait a minute. Just what is *this?*" Don't drink any alcohol on the peak; you'll be staggering and stumbling enough on the way down as it is. As you get closer to town, you'll start hearing the telltale sounds, and some great snapshots present themselves, such as the three steeples in a row—the firehouse, St. Mary's, and St. Paul's. From car door to car door it's a fine three-hour experience.

DOWN THE HILL

On the corner of Union and D streets is the site of the house of Virginia City's most notorious Angel of the Night, Julia Bulette. She occupied the prime location for a woman of her profession. Though considered by the city's proper wives a common harlot, she was the undisputed Queen of the Row, with the furs, jewels, and coin to prove it. Some of it, it was rumored, found its way back to her hometown of New Orleans and the underground railroad to help free the black acquaintances of her girlhood. Jule was murdered by a French Canadian customer out of jealousy and greed. Though a thief and killer, he was the undisputed King of the Respectable Women, who felt he did the town a big favor. Needless to say, he was found, tried, and hanged in front of a very big crowd at the edge of Virginia City, near the cemeteries.

One block south at Taylor, **St. Mary's Catholic Church** is definitely worth a visit for its stunning stained glass, huge pipe organ on the large Gothic altar, and high vaulted ceilings. The original silver bell is rung by a rope for mass on Saturday at 4 P.M. and Sunday at 10:30 A.M.; other electronically controlled bells ring on the hour. *St. Mary's in the Mountains,* a souvenir book ($5) sold in the gift shop, tells the church story, from its rebuilding after the 1875 fire to its refurbishing in 1980.

St. Paul's Episcopal Church is on the opposite corner. The original church burned in the fire, and the present building, like so many in town, dates from a year later. The pine used in construction is from the Sierra and wooden pegs hold it all together. Take a peek inside at the 123-year-old pews and wood paneling.

At the corner of Union and F streets is a big white house with green trim. Twelve hundred feet below this house is the **site of the Big Bonanza,** whose rock was so rich with silver. Two blocks downhill at I St. to the left is the area that was once Virginia City's **Chinatown;** nothing is left of Chinatown today. As you continue down Union you'll see the gas works building, the dump for the Big Bonanza, and the old Catholic hospital building. Take a right at the end of Union and go past the new high school and library; come back up Washington past big tailing dumps.

More Mansions

The **Mackay Mansion** is at D and Flowery streets, just above the Savage Mine ruins. The tour starts in the large vestibule that served as the Gould and Curry Mine office. The Bonanza King of the Comstock, John Mackay, born in Dublin, made his way to California in 1851 at the age of 20 and worked for nine years as a placer miner. He was among the first Washoe hopefuls over the pass in the spring of 1860 and quickly went from miner to timberman to independent contractor to mine owner. His Kentuck Mine made him a millionaire in 1865, and his Consolidated Virginia Mine unearthed the Big Bonanza in 1872. Mackay's generosity is legendary. In *Nevada—A History* Robert Laxalt comments, ". . . out of the billion and more dollars taken from the Nevada earth in its boom days, little of it was sown back. The exception was John Mackay. . . [whose family] became the first major benefactors to the University of Nevada." The house is open for self-guided tours every day, 10 A.M.–6 P.M. year round, weather permitting; $4 adults, children free; 775/847-0173.

The yellow **Savage Mansion** is not open to the public. The Savage brothers' claim was one of the earliest, dating from July 4, 1859. The mansion was built in 1861 for the office and residence of the superintendent. In 1879, President Ulysses S. Grant visited Virginia and stayed as a guest here; he gave a speech from the porch. This house was vacant for decades until it was restored by the Harwood family, who gave tours and rented out a few rooms. When Hugh Roy Marshall of Marshall Earth Resources mining company bought it, it became a private residence.

For a look at the **Chollar Mansion,** see "Accommodations," below.

Outskirts of Virginia City

The **cemeteries,** on NV 341 at the far north edge of town, are segregated by racial, religious, fraternal, and vocational affiliation. Pick out the Catholics, Chinese, Mexicans, Irish, English, Oddfellows, Freemasons, and firemen. The Jewish cemetery is at the bottom of the canyon, which the upper cemeteries overlook. A white picket fence surrounds it, and two Stars of David mark the entrances.

Across from the Fourth Ward School is a big pit known as the **Loring Cut** or the **Chollar Raise.** This was the site of major mining activity in the mid-1930s, when the Arizona Comstock Mining Company opened up a section of the Chollar Mine tunnels with a power shovel, creating this pit. A million and a half dollars in metals were recovered at that time. The United Mining Company reworked the pit in the early 1980s.

The **Combination Mine** is the large headframe to the southeast visible from nearly everywhere in town. This is the head of the deepest shaft on the Lode—3,250 feet. Cross the bridge on highway 341 just south of town over the V&T tracks, take an immediate left, and go a quarter mile to the structure. Beautiful views of the back of Virginia City and Mt. Davidson appear to the west, and Sugarloaf Peak, Six-Mile Canyon, and the Dayton Valley to the east. The dirt road continues east, where you'll be entirely alone.

For further enjoyable explorations, pick up a copy of the *Walkers & Hikers Guide to Virginia City and The Comstock Area* ($2.95) from the Mark Twain Bookstore on C St. The booklet, published by the Mark Twain Bookstore, details nine walks and hikes ranging from 2.1 to 10.8

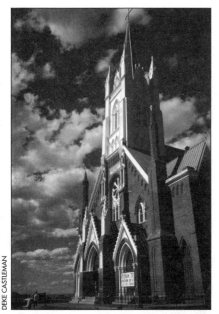

DEKE CASTLEMAN

St. Mary's is one of the most divine churches in Nevada

miles in length, with practical tips, historical information and points of interest noted for each walk and hike. Another useful booklet is the *Comstock Driving Tour/Virginia City Walking Tour,* also available at the Mark Twain Bookstore.

SPECIAL EVENTS

The second weekend in September for the past 30-something years, more than 25,000 people have gathered in Virginia City for the **International Camel Races.** The race started in 1959 as a hoax (a long Virginia City tradition), when the editor of the *Territorial Enterprise,* Bob Richards, wrote a fictitious account of the city's camel races to fill a three-inch hole in the newspaper. The following year, Richards announced the races, and in fact challenged the staff of the *San Francisco Chronicle* to compete. Camels were leased from the San Francisco Zoo and celebrity riders participated (movie director John Huston won that first competition). The races are held in a racetrack on F Street; accompanying events include ostrich races, dances, parades, food, and more.

Other special events throughout the year include a Cinco de Mayo Chili Cook-Off on the weekend nearest May 5, Outhouse Races in mid-August, and the Nevada Shakespeare Festival at Piper's Opera House during July and August. The Chamber of Commerce (775/847-0311) has information these and many other popular events held throughout the year.

PRACTICALITIES

Accommodations
Virginia City has two motels both on C St. at the far south end of town almost to Geiger Grade. The **Comstock Lodge,** 875 South C St., 775/847-0233, has 14 rooms priced from $48–65. All the rooms are done in period antiques; the room comes with coupons for a breakfast special at the Delta Saloon. The **Sugarloaf Mountain Motel,** 430 South C St., 775/847-0551, has 12 rooms for $48–58.

The **Chollar Mansion B&B,** 565 South D St., 775/847-9777, is a three-level fire-engine-red-brick 13-room 125-year-old Victorian mansion. It served as the lodging and offices of Isaac Requa, superintendent of the rich Chollar Mine. Twelve-foot-high ceilings, men's and women's parlors, and a total of 40 stairs in the house are just a few of the features befitting of Requa's station. Other structural elements are even more intriguing. The kitchen pantry was once the paymaster's booth, where an armed banker doled out the miners' four dollars a day in coin; a sliding teller's window connects to the kitchen. The company vault, with its arched brick roof, stone floors and walls, and mine-tunnel entrance, is now the wine cellar. There are two guest rooms on the main floor, a suite on the ground floor, and a two-room cottage for rent. Rates range from $75 to $125.

The **Crooked House B&B,** 8 South F St., 775/847-4447 or 800/340-6353, crookedhouse@gbis.com, is another historic bed & breakfast, built in 1870. Its four guest rooms cost $65–125.

The **Virginia City RV Park** at Carson and F Streets, 775/847-0999 or 800/889-1240, vcrvpark@compuserve.com, www.vcrvpark.com, has been here since early 1988. It's down the hill on a bluff; to get there, turn downhill at Carson Street and drive three blocks to F Street. Some sites overlook the cemetery. It's a bit cramped, but the bathrooms were recently remodeled and the showers have individual dressing rooms. The town park, with a pool and tennis courts, is right across the street. There's a large market here. Downtown Virginia City is a mere four-block walk. The park has 50 spaces for motor homes, all with full hookups; 2 are pull-throughs. Tents are allowed. Reservations are recommended through the summer (open year-round). The fees are $12 per tent site (includes a shower) and $20 for RVs (AAA and Good Sam discounts).

In Seven Mile Canyon, a mile from Virginia City, **Tyson's Canyon Ranch,** 775/847-7223, www.NevadaDudeRanch.com, offers a bed & breakfast luxury cowboy adventure, with many special ranch events including cowboy entertainment, longhorn cattle events and campfire hay rides. Three private guest cottages, each with private kitchen and romantic fireplace, cost $115–145 nightly.

Food

The **Firehouse Restaurant & Saloon,** 171 South C St. at the south end of town, 775/847-4774, is a coffee shop and bar, open 7 A.M.–4 P.M.. It serves a variety of inexpensive breakfasts and lunches. French toast $3.50, omelettes $6; for lunch there's a variety of burgers, barbecue, hot sandwiches and other good fare, all for around $6.50.

The cafe attached to the **Delta Saloon,** known as Sawdust Corner, is a justifiably popular place for breakfast or lunch 10 A.M.–3 P.M., and for dinner on Wednesday nights. It's airy, comfortable, friendly, has an authentic air, and seats 100; 775/847-0789.

The **Julia C. Bulette Saloon,** 775/847-9394, has an espresso bar up front, the museum in the basement, and a full-service bar in back that's been remodeled: two large-screen televisions, nice ceramic-tile floor, pleasant restrooms. It serves burgers and bar food.

The **Bonanza Saloon,** 775/847-0655, serves $5 burgers, $6.75 Philly cheesesteak, $4.95 soup and sandwich, and the like. It has a few slot and video poker machines and a small gift shop in front.

The **Brass Rail,** 775/847-0304, offers balcony dining out back, with a great view over Six Mile Canyon. If you prefer, dine inside, with a gargantuan Alaskan brown bear overhead. The house specialty, a pot pie and cobbler special for $8.95, is a hugely filling meal with a choice of two meat pies and four fruit cobblers. They also make breakfasts, vegetarian selections, burgers, hot and cold sandwiches, etc. Open from around 9 or 9:30 A.M. to 6:30 or 7 P.M., or as long as customers are present. (Most restaurants in town close earlier; this is one place that stays open later.)

The **Palace Saloon** has a row of eating tables between a row of stools at the bar and a row of leather goods at the emporium. Locals say the burgers here, for $4.95, are the best in town. Check out the ice-cream-and-liquor drinks at the bar.

Solid Muldoon's, 775/847-9181, serves the usual lunch offerings—burgers $5, hot roast beef or turkey $6.75, steak sandwich $7.75—and is open for dinner. Blackened prime rib, chicken marsala, halibut, scallops, and the like go for $9–12.

You'll certainly see, probably smell, and maybe even taste the fudge being slopped around on tables in the picture windows in front of **Grandma's Fudge Factory. Aunt Rosie's Fudge Store** next to Grant's General Store is similar; notice the old Coca-Cola cooler. **Red's Old-Fashioned Candies & Deli Bar** makes good deli sandwiches in the back. **Comstock Cookie Company** sells cookies, cobblers, and ice cream (try the waffle cone), along with espresso, hot dogs, and soft pretzels. The cobblers are mouth-watering at $2.50, a la mode $3.95.

Information

The Virginia City **Chamber of Commerce** occupies an old yellow train car at 131 South C St., P.O. Box 464, Virginia City, NV 89440, 775/847-0311. It's in the Virginia & Truckee car No. 13, a unique bullion car that transported the refined silver between the mills of the Comstock and the mint in Carson City between 1874 and 1893, when the mint closed. It remained in service on the line till 1939. The Chamber stocks brochures and visitors guides and sells tickets for the ride on the V&T. It's open every day, 9 A.M.–5 P.M. in summer (May to October), 10 A.M.–4 P.M. in winter (November to April). Reliable rumor has it that the Chamber office may be moving into its new Crystal Bar location by Spring 2001.

To Reno

No public transportation runs between Virginia City and Reno, but tour buses do; see "Transportation" in the Reno chapter.

By car, head north on C St. past the Way It Was Museum, the cemeteries, and **Cedar Hill,** which is noticeably scarred from the 19th-century hydraulic mining and 20th-century power-shovel pit mining. You twist and turn around the Virginia Range, until you come to 6,800-foot **Geiger Summit** and viewpoint, Geiger Lookout, both named for Dr. C.M. Geiger, the pioneer road-builder who received a franchise to build the Geiger Grade toll road in 1861. Park and stroll to the overlook for a stunning view of Truckee Meadows to the north and the Sierra Nevada to the west. It's seven miles and a seven percent grade (a 2,000-foot drop) from there down to Business 395; this is the most popular and one of the most grueling bike climbs for local cyclists, whom you'll no doubt share the road with.

You come off the Grade, meet highway 395, and then it's a straight shot north through the south end of Truckee Meadows to join up with S. Virginia St. (Business 395), roughly 10 miles south of downtown Reno. Either continue up Virginia to downtown or use the freeway a few miles north to zoom up to Sparks, then take US 80 west into Reno.

VICINITY OF VIRGINIA CITY

GREINER'S BEND

Greiner's Bend, between Virginia City and Gold Hill, is the sharpest and steepest grade in Nevada's highway system. This double-hairpin curve was the scene of bitter controversy in the late 1970s as Houston Oil and Mineral Corporation leased most of the old claims in Gold Hill. In 1978, the Storey County Commissioners granted Houston permission to mine the Con-Imperial pit that still yawns gapingly right next to the road at the bend. For months the mining continued all hours of the day and night, raising up a world of dust, noise, and vibration. The residents in the stately Victorian houses along the bend suffered, fought back, and raised enough of their own ruckus to disrupt the operation. Even other miners protested Houston's threatened use of Nevada's archaic eminent-domain law, which allows mining companies to condemn and buy property in their path (but is usually only invoked discreetly to claim remote desert or property whose owner is non-locatable). By the early 1980s, however, the value of gold had soared to $850 an ounce, with silver up to nearly $50 an ounce, and Houston was determined to mine every last speck.

The mining company cranked up a PR program and proceeded to buy the property along Greiner's Bend for great sums, donate cash and equipment to Gold Hill and Virginia City, reduce the hours of operation, offer generous settlements to avoid court battles, and employ many residents at its big new $15 million cyanide mill on American Flats down the hill. Ironically, soon after the price of gold fell quickly and Houston shut down without ever undermining Greiner's Bend. The mill operated three years, till 1983, and then closed. Today, the pit is all that remains.

GOLD HILL

As we know, the 1850s' prospectors followed Gold Creek up Gold Canyon to Gold Hill, where James "Old Virginny" Finney decided to start digging right into the ground, and a few feet down struck the Comstock. Incidentally, that's nearly the last heard about James Finney, Henry Comstock, and the pair of Irish miners on Sun Mountain. Within months of discovery, they'd all either sold out or freaked out, or both. None got rich. Comstock lived another 10 years on bragging rights alone, then blew his brains out in Montana. Old Virginny traded his claim for a horse and a bottle of whiskey, later falling drunk off the horse to his death.

Only Eilley and Sandy Bowers managed to hold on long enough to see any real wealth from their long years of deprivation and faith in the big magnet of the Comstock Lode. Eilley ran a primitive boardinghouse at the site of Gold Hill in the late 1850s and, according to legend, foresaw in her "peep stone" or crystal ball the immense riches of silver under everyone else's ignorant noses. (Possibly Eilley, educated by the Mormons, overheard and understood the Grosch brothers' guarded discussions about the silver vein.) She married Sandy Bowers, a Missouri mule skinner, and together their 20 feet of the Lode paid off enough to build their mansion in Washoe Valley, though even their story had a tragic ending (see "Bowers Mansion" under "Washoe Valley" in the Vicinity of Reno section).

After discovery, Gold Hill grew up as Virginia's "brother" city (men outnumbered women three to one until the mid-1870s), reaching the proverbial population of 10,000 at its peak. The huge Consolidated Imperial open-pit mine, just below the steep "S" curve right above Gold Hill, is the site of the discovery, as well as Sandy and Eilley Bowers' claim to fame, riches, and rags. About 100 people now live in Gold Hill.

Just below the bend is the bell tower from the Liberty Engine Company No. 1. Read the historical marker. Across the street is the big red Virginia and Truckee depot, where the V&T turns around to head back to Virginia City. Stop off at the other historical signs describing features of Gold Hill, including the Pink Victorian, the First Methodist Church, and the V&T Railroad. Also notice the amusing camel-crossing street sign.

Gold Hill Hotel

The main excitement in town is at Gold Hill Hotel, 775/847-0111, www.goldhillhotel.net, which harkens all the way to the first days of the Comstock Lode—making it the oldest operating inn, and one of the oldest buildings, in Nevada. And a fine specimen it is. Situated just below Greiner's Bend, the steepness of the bend continues past the inn and is reflected by a noticeable tilt to the floors in the original wing, which lends it a foundation of authenticity. The Great Room on the main floor, now the lounge, has a stone floor and fireplace, stucco walls with exposed brick, some period furniture, and an antique piano and organ. The cozy bar was added in 1960, built to look original; the Crown Point Restaurant was added in 1984 and decorated with black-and-white photographs of the area's mining heyday.

The four guest rooms in the 135-year-old stone structure are original; they're cute, each has its own private bath, and two have balconies over the street ($45–60 weekdays, $50–65 Friday and Saturday, $55–70 holidays and special events). Of the eight rooms in the new wing, built in 1987, four are suite size and feature stone fireplaces, wet bars, TVs, balconies, and large modern baths ($75–125). The all-wood Guest House across the road from the inn offers two one-bedroom suites with full kitchen and a sofa bed in the living room ($100–120). There's also a Honeymoon Guest House ($150–200), Miner's Lodge ($90–110) and Brewery Lodge ($150–200). All prices include continental breakfast.

The Crown Point Restaurant serves recommendable food. Lunches in the **Crown Point** dining room, served 11:30 A.M.–4 P.M., include a variety of tasty salads, sandwiches and gourmet burgers ($6–9). For dinner, there's an interesting selection of appetizers, entrees ($15–32) and special dinners for two including Chateaubriand,

beef Wellington, roasted rack of lamb Dijonaise and salmon en croute ($58–78). Unusual offerings include venison, wild boar, buffalo, elk, pheasant, duck, and ostrich. Dinner is served Wed.–Sun., 5–10 P.M.; Monday nights there's a Miner's Special Menu ($7.25), served 5–9 P.M., and on Sundays there's a Sunday Champagne Brunch, 10 A.M.–2 P.M. ($7.50–$13). Reservations are a good idea (775/847-0111).

In keeping with the historical status of the inn, lectures on a variety of aspects of the Comstock experience are presented here every Tuesday evening ($4), except during December and January; phone for topic. Adjoining the hotel is **Western Books,** a specialty bookstore with a good selection of titles on the Comstock, Nevada, western explorers, railroads, and Native Americans (it's open the same hours that the front desk is manned: roughly 8 A.M. to 10 P.M.).

Silver City

Heading down to Carson Plains, you pass two headframes. The New York Mine was established in 1913; its metal headframe contrasts with the wooden Keystone headframe, built fewer than 50 years earlier during the Comstock heyday. In a half mile you leave Storey County and enter Lyon County, and immediately pass through **Devil's Gate,** whose jagged ridges formed a natural boundary between Silver City, already a fairly sizable settlement when the Comstock was located, and upper Gold Canyon. The rock was blasted away for a wagon road, and immigrants paid a toll to travel the last stretch to Gold Hill and Virginia City. Shortly thereafter you come into Silver City, already a boomtown while Virginia City and Gold Hill were just rabbit warrens. J. Ross Browne took a coach from Carson City to the end of the line in Silver City in spring 1860 and then had to walk the rest of the way up the hill into Virginia City.

In another three miles you reach US 50; go left and three more miles bring you to downtown Dayton.

DAYTON

History

This is one of the oldest settlements in Nevada, a mere year or two younger than Genoa down the road. The little town is quite alive, but certainly has its share of ghosts. A single ghost for every *name* it's been known by over the past 140 years would keep Bill Murray and the boys distracted for a while. The 1840s' name was Ponderer's Rest, the Ponderer part for the fork in the Emigrant Trail (south to Walker Pass or west to Donner Pass) and the Rest part because it was at the end of the Twenty-six Mile Desert on the Emigrant Trail. While the gold rushers rested and pondered which fork to take, some of them took to panning a creek that flowed down the east slope of the Virginia Range into the Carson River nearby. The first gold in Nevada was discovered there in 1849, and the place became known as Gold Creek.

DANGERS OF ABANDONED MINES

There are plenty of old abandoned mines around the Virginia City area, and around other parts of Nevada, too. Although entering an abandoned mine may seem tempting, DON'T DO IT! There's only one safe way to deal with abandoned mines—stay out, and not only that, but keep a good distance!

SHAFTS—The top of a mine shaft is especially dangerous. The rock at the surface is often decomposed, and timbers may be rotten or missing. It is dangerous to walk anywhere near a shaft opening the whole area is often susceptible to sliding into the shaft, along with anyone who might be walking by.

CAVE-INS—Cave-ins are an obvious danger. Areas likely to cave in are often difficult to recognize. Even minor disturbances, such as vibrations caused by walking or speaking, can cause a cave-in. If a person is caught, he can be crushed to death, or trapped behind a cave-in without anyone knowing he is there, in which case death can come through hunger, thirst, or gradual suffocation.

TIMBER—The timber in abandoned mines can be weak from decay. Timber that is apparently in good condition may become loose and fall at the slightest touch. A well-timbered mine opening can look very solid when in fact the timber can barely support its own weight. There is a constant danger of inadvertently touching a timber and causing the tunnel to collapse. Another danger is a winze—a shaft sunk inside a tunnel. In many old mines, winzes have been boarded over. If these boards have decayed, a perfect trap is waiting.

LADDERS—Ladders in most abandoned mines are unsafe, vertical ladders especially so. Ladder rungs may be missing or broken; some will fall at the slightest weight because of dry rot.

BAD AIR—"Bad air" contains poisonous gases or insufficient oxygen. Poisonous gases can accumulate in low areas or along the floor. A person may enter such areas breathing the good air above the gases, but the motion caused by walking will mix the bases with the good air, producing a possibly lethal mixture for him to breathe on the return trip. Because little effort is required to go down a ladder, the effects of bad air may not be noticed, but when climbing out of a shaft, a person requires more oxygen and breathes more deeply. The result is dizziness, followed by unconsciousness. If the gas doesn't kill, the fall will.

WATER—Many tunnels have standing pools of water which can conceal holes in the floor; pools of water are also common at the bottom of shafts. It is usually impossible to estimate the depth of the water, and a false step could lead to drowning.

EXPLOSIVES—Many abandoned mines contain old explosives, which are extremely dangerous and should never be handled. Old dynamite sticks and caps can explode if stepped on or even just touched.

RATTLESNAKES—Old mine tunnels and shafts are among the favorite haunts of these creatures—to cool off in summer, or to search for rodents and other small animals. Any hole or ledge, especially near the mouth of a tunnel or shaft, can conceal a snake.

RESCUE—Attempting to rescue a person from a mine accident is difficult and dangerous for both the victim and the rescuer. Even professional rescue teams face death or injury, although trained to avoid all unnecessary risks. If someone needs to be rescued from an abandoned mine, call the county sheriff, who can organize a rescue operation.

RESPECT SIGNS—Fences, barricades, and warning signs are there for your safety. Mine owners have constructed these safeguards at their expense, for your protection. Disturbing or vandalizing them is dangerous.

—from pamphlet Dangers In and Around Abandoned Mines, *published by Nevada Bureau of Mines and Geology, University of Nevada, Reno*

In 1853, Spafford Hall set up a trading post, and the name changed to Hall's Station. Prospectors and miners by then had been in semi-permanent residence for several years and had already made their way up Gold Canyon. In 1855, 200 Chinese were imported to dig a ditch from the Carson River to the canyon, whereby the settlement, to the chagrin of the Americans, was designated Chinatown. Finally, in 1861, after the Comstock Lode triggered the installation of stamp mills there on the Carson River, the site was designated Dayton after surveyor John Day, who platted the town. It served the Pony Express for the 18 months of its existence, as well as the Overland Stage.

Dayton was soon designated seat of Lyon County. Fires in 1866 and 1870 reduced the downtown to rubble, and the oldest buildings date back to the rebuilding in 1871. The courthouse burned in 1909, after which Yerington took the opportunity to take the seat. Clark Gable, Marilyn Monroe, John Huston, Arthur Miller, and the cast of *The Misfits* invaded Dayton in 1960. Their legacy can still be seen at the Old Corner Bar.

Dayton has one of the highest levels of mercury soil contamination in the country. The locals, however, aren't fazed: they've been eating vegetables from their gardens for 125 years. Recent tests of Dayton residents failed to indicate elevated levels of mercury; the researchers speculated that most residents don't eat the fish or gamebirds that have been found to be contaminated. However, the children tested (who spend more time outdoors) did have slightly higher levels of blood- and urine-mercury than adults. (See "The Carson River Mills," below for more information.)

Dayton is a fairly fast-growing area. Its population has nearly tripled (to around 6,000 people) in the last decade or so. The expansion is generally east of town in Dayton Valley: two large business parks, an 18-hole golf course, new four-lane expansion of US 50 and four lanes on Dayton Valley Rd., and some large subdivisions. Growth on the west side of town is controlled by Comstock Historic District constraints. The historic district is where most of the sights are.

Around Town

Drive into town on Main St. (at the traffic light on US 50) for some photo ops at the old Union Hotel. Main Street continues to recover from its near ghost status of only half a dozen years ago; a dollhouse, antique store, mercantile, lawyer and insurance agent, surveying and engineering company now inhabit the three-block old downtown. Drive past the **Bluestone Building,** once the offices of a company that supplied "bluestone," or copper sulfide, to the stamp mills for refining silver. The building now houses a substation of the offices of Lyon County's D.A., sheriff, and court. Continue up the hill over the gravel pit to the **Dayton Cemetery,** founded in 1851 and oldest in the state. James "Old Virginny" Finney is buried here, and there's a nice overlook of town, river, and valley.

Return to town and take a left at the Bluestone Building onto Shady Lane. Halfway down the street is a one-lane bridge over venerable Gold Creek (long dry). At the end of the street is the stone **Dayton Public School,** built in 1865, one of the oldest school buildings in the state. Its last class was in 1959, and it's now the local Senior Center.

At the other end of Logan Alley is the adobe **Dayton High School** building, which rose in 1918 from the foundation of the county courthouse that burned in 1909. It too closed in 1959, and it now serves as the Community Center.

Take a right on Pike St. to complete the square tour of town. Recross the creek. The big building on the right is **Odeon Hall,** (re)built in 1870 as the meeting place of the Odd Fellows. The second floor was the town's performance center till 1930, and gave the building its name.

The extension of Main St. across the highway at the traffic light is **Dayton Valley Road.** Head down here to get a glimpse of one of the newest and fastest-growing neighborhoods in western Nevada. Cross the Carson River and drive past brand new schools and firehouse, large expensive subdivisions, airport and business park, golf course and country club, and convenience store. The four-lane road reduces to two at the far edge of the golf course; the new houses continue all the way up to the end of Dayton Valley, on five-acre lots. Comstock Rd. swings around to the left, then the pavement ends. Return the way you came.

Practicalities

Mia's Swiss Restaurant occupies the ground floor of the historic Odeon Hall, with a bar and dining room, at 65 Pike Rd., 775/246-3993. It's open for lunch Tues.–Fri. 11:30 A.M.–2 P.M. and for dinner 5–9 P.M. (closed Monday), serving Wiener schnitzel, bratwurst, and sauerbraten, along with continental dinners, such as piccata Milanese and veal Florentino, ranging from $9 to $18. Proprietors Max and Mia see to it that you feel right at home.

Back on Main St., the **End of the Trail Bar**, open weekdays 11 A.M.–11 P.M., till late on weekends, is a friendly and homey bar and restaurant run, for more than a decade, by Vita Scrivani. She serves sandwiches in the bar for lunch, and dinners in the back room. A few doors down is the **Old Corner Bar** and **Misfit Touchdown Club** restaurant (open 7–11 A.M. for breakfast, 11 A.M.–1:30 P.M. for lunch, and 5–9 P.M. for dinner). *The Misfits* movie memorabilia line the walls, banjo and piano players often fill the airwaves, and poker slots ring up the drop.

Roadrunner Cafe is in the Riverview Corners shopping plaza just west of downtown on US 50 at the corner of Gates Ave., 775/246-0205, open Tues.–Sun. 6 A.M.–2 P.M., serving road-food breakfasts and lunch.

Dayton Depot is half bar and half grill in a newish shopping center just east of downtown on the highway, 775/246-9696; open at 6:30 A.M. It has half a dozen bartop video poker machines, an arcade, and a full breakfast, lunch, and dinner menu. **Rocky's Pizza** is a pub in Sutro Square next door to the Depot. **Dayton Valley Library** is here too.

Across the street is a long-time Dayton tradition: the **flea market.** Hopping on weekends, a few booths are usually open during the week. Check out the attic treasures.

VICINITY OF DAYTON

Dayton State Park

This is a small quiet campground on the north bank of the Carson River, four miles east of Dayton on US 50 (on the right). It has 10 campsites for tents or self-contained motor homes up to 20 feet. Piped drinking water, flush toilets, picnic tables, grills, and fire rings are provided; there's a campground host in the summer (open year-round). The maximum stay is seven days. No reservations; call 775/885-5678. Pay $5 per site in the drop box, and don't wade in the river. A trail runs between the Cardelli Ditch and the Carson River. Across the highway is the site and some ruins of the old Rock Point Mill, which operated between 1861 and 1920.

Mound House

Just west of the intersection with NV 341 to Virginia City and US 50 is the site of Mound House, once a booming railroad division point for the Virginia & Truckee and Carson & Colorado lines. Originally constructed as a siding for the V&T in 1871, it served primarily as a water and fuel stop, but grew enough to merit the establishment of a post office in 1877. In 1880, the V&T began construction of the Carson & Colorado narrow-gauge from Mound House east to Fort Churchill, then south to Mina and then west to Inyo, California, and Mound House became a booming transshipment center.

The Southern Pacific bought the C&C in 1900. During the first two decades of the 20th century, gypsum was mined at Mound House, which in fact was named for the mounds of gypsum throughout the area. But by 1915, Southern Pacific had built a short line to connect the C&C to the transcontinental main line between Churchill and Hazen, bypassing Mound House. The short stretch between Mound House and Churchill was abandoned in 1934, and Mound House disappeared within a few years.

Today, Carson City has expanded all the way out to the junction for Virginia City, and all that's left of Mound House are the historical sign, the Mound House Shopping Center, remnants of the gypsum mining, and some residents who are dependent on the antiquated Mound House water system.

The Carson River Mills

Between Dayton and a little west of Carson City, along the Carson River, 12 major stamp mills processed the silver and gold ore of the Comstock Lode for decades. Dan DeQuille, in his landmark *The Big Bonanza*, estimated that nearly 4,000 tons of quicksilver (mercury) were dumped into the Carson River during the first 10 years of the Comstock. The EPA estimates that of the 7,200 tons (or nearly 15 million pounds) of toxic elemental mercury dumped in the 19th century, all of 37 pounds have been reclaimed. Fifty miles of riverbottom are known to be contaminated, 1,500 people in Churchill and Lyon counties obtain their drinking water from wells located along the contaminated stretch of the Carson, and fish and game birds contain high levels of mercury. In addition, millions of pounds of mercury are found in tailing piles in the Dayton area. They leach the metal into the soil, which has been found to be heavily poisoned.

In 1990, the Carson River was added to the EPA's Superfund list of toxic-waste sites to receive priority attention and funds, but the contamination is believed to be so vast that it's possible it will never completely be cleaned up. However, investigators from the Desert Research Institute of the University of Nevada have found a "silver lining" to the clean-up challenge: because the mercury binds with particles and then settles into the sediments at the bottom of the river and lake beds, reclaiming the mercury would yield millions of dollars in silver and gold.

Very little but the mercury remains of the big mills which, with a total of 280 stamps, processed hundreds of millions of dollars in gold and silver. But you can take a rough drive along the stretch of river where the mills once roared. A little more than 1.5 miles west of the junction of NV 341 from Silver City and US 50, take a left onto Highlands Dr. and pass through a small new subdivision. The pavement gives out immediately and then you're on a marginal 15-mph one-lane track. A huge junkyard to the left might or might not worry you about the road ahead. The road winds around for a mile until you find yourself on a dramatic cut in the hills several hundred feet above the river. The edge has washed away in places—once on both sides of the road! Good adrenaline. Other places are so rocky that only 4WD vehicles should really be crossing them, at 10 mph or even five, though the Cadillac I was following would disagree. In fact, an unexpected amount of traffic appears on this track, being so close to Carson City.

You come to a fork. Left takes you down to the river at Brunswick Canyon, right puts you through a narrow rocky gap. From there you drop down into a pretty canyon, lazy river making lazy "S" curves. It gets even more crowded with people on this end: skipping rocks, taking target practice, or just hanging out by the sluggish stream. At the mine, the road widens and smoothens, almost seven miles from the start. In another mile the pavement returns; bear right at the fork to join up with US 50 again at Deer Run Industrial Park, one block east of the road into Centennial Park. Downtown Carson City is in another few miles.

CARSON CITY

HISTORY

Abe Curry and Eagle Ranch

In 1858, Abraham V. Curry was a 43-year-old businessman who, born near Ithaca, New York, had worked on the docks in Cleveland, the hills of San Francisco, and the boomtowns of the Mother Lode. According to Doris Cerveri's fine book *With Curry's Compliments,* he and some partners were in Downieville, California, when they heard that Brigham Young had recalled his Mormon settlers to Salt Lake City to help defend Deseret against a rumored invasion by the U.S. government. Curry immediately foresaw the potential in the prime real estate at the eastern edge of the Sierra Nevada that the Mormons had abandoned.

Curry and his partners traveled to Genoa, where they found the price of land to already be both outrageous and nonnegotiable. So they continued to Eagle Valley just north of Genoa and bought 865-acre Eagle Ranch from John Mankin for $1,000. Curry put $300 down but Mankin, who was something of a crook, took the money and ran, never bothering to collect the other $700. Thus, though discovery of the Comstock was still more than a year away and the "ranch" was little more than sand and sage, Curry had found the spot where he'd make his stand. Or maybe the spot found him.

CARSON CITY

To Dayton

E. WILLIAM ST.

STATE ST.

SEELY LOOP

Mills Park

N. SALIMAN RD.

E. TELEGRAPH ST.

PINTO CT.

APPALOOSA CT.

EVAN ST.

COMO ST.

GOLDFIELD AVE.

To Riverview Park and
Carson River Park

S. SALIMAN RD.

0   0.2 mi

0   0.2 km

SIMONE AVE.

RAWHIDE WAY

N. CARSON MEADOWS DR.

S. CARSON MEADOWS DR.

PARKLAND AVE.

HACKAMORE WAY

CATALPA WAY

ALLOUETTE WAY

COUNTRY VILLAGE DR.

LINDA KAY CT.

PALO VERDE DR.

E. ROBINSON ST.

N. HARBIN AVE.

S. HARBIN AVE.

N. PRATT ST.

S. PRATT AVE.

CARSON CITY
COMMUNITY
CENTER

■ INDOOR POOL
■ OUTDOOR POOL

OXOBY LOOP

MILLS PARK LN.

CARSON CITY
LIBRARY ■

N. ROOP ST.

S. ROOP ST.

N. WALSH ST.

E. SPEAR ST.

N. ANDERSON ST.

E. KING ST.

E. 2ND ST.

E. 3RD ST.

E. 4TH ST.

E. 5TH ST.

E. CAROLINE ST.

E. WASHINGTON ST.

N. ROOP ST.

N. JOHN ST.

E. PARK ST.

CORBETT ST.

E. JOHN ST.

N. VALLEY ST.

S. VALLEY ST.

S. STEWART ST.

FALL ST.

CHILDREN'S
MUSEUM OF
NORTHERN
NEVADA

POST OFFICE
& FEDERAL
BUILDING

NEVADA COMMISSION ON TOURISM

▼NUGGET CASINO

E. ROBINSON ST.

E. TELEGRAPH ST.

▼JAVA JOE'S

■BUS DEPOT

E. PROCTOR ST.

CITY HALL

STATE ★
CAPITOL ★

★NEVADA
STATE
LIBRARY AND
ARCHIVES

CAPITOL
COMPLEX

STATE
LEGISLATIVE
BUILDING

▼ORMSBY HOUSE HOTEL/CASINO

▼ CITY CAFE BAKERY

S. CARSON ST.

To Reno

■ ROBERTS
HOUSE PARK
MUSEUM

NEVADA
STATE
MUSEUM ★

CACTUS JACK'S
HORSESHOE CLUB ▼

COURTHOUSE ■

RINCKEL MANSION ■

BREWERY
ARTS
CENTER ■

W. PARK ST.

W. JOHN ST.

W. WILLIAM ST.

W. SOPHIA ST.

W. ANN ST.

W. ROBINSON ST.

W. PROCTOR ST.

W. CAROLINE ST.

W. WASHINGTON ST.

W. SPEAR ST.

W. TELEGRAPH ST.

W. MUSSER ST.

W. KING ST.

FLEISCHMANN WAY

CARSON-TAHOE
HOSPITAL ■

GOVERNOR'S
MANSION ■

BLISS
MANSION B&B ■

MOUNTAIN ST.

W. 2ND ST.

W. 3RD ST.

W. 4TH ST.

W. 5TH ST.

S. CURRY ST.

S. NEVADA ST.

S. DIVISION ST.

S. MINNESOTA ST.

THOMPSON ST.

W. 7TH ST.

To Lake Tahoe,
Minden and Genoa

To Kings Canyon
and Spooner
Summit

© AVALON TRAVEL PUBLISHING, INC.

The State Capital

The ambitious New Yorker knew he could never be content with a ranch. He immediately began promoting the desolate (though watered and scenic) valley as the eventual site of the state capital, which he named Carson City after Kit Carson. Curry's dream required an amount of foresight usually relegated to people labeled prophets (if successful) or lunatics (if not): Nevada was not yet even a territory, let alone a state, and Eagle Valley could boast no more than a handful of residents and even fewer buildings. The local surveyor refused to plat a town site in return for ownership of "a full city block" of what at the time was desert scrub. The surveyor worked instead for an IOU (but soon became the first postmaster of Carson City).

Curry had him lay out wide city streets and a four-square-block area known to settlers as the Plaza, though Curry called it Capitol Square. Lots were sold dirt cheap to anyone who wanted them, including Major William Ormsby, a businessman fed up with Genoa. Curry used clay from the ranch to fabricate adobe bricks and constructed a few buildings in "town." He also discovered a

NEVADA HISTORICAL SOCIETY, RENO

Abe Curry—farsighted and fearless founder and philanthropist

large limestone outcrop near a warm springs on the property, which he used as a quarry; he dammed the springs and built a bathhouse, which attracted prospectors and travelers.

Prophecies Fulfilled

The winter of 1858–59 was especially severe and conditions in Carson City were still primitive at best, but Abe Curry possessed the faith of Job and he persevered. Spring arrived warm and fresh. That summer the Comstock was discovered mere miles east, and the rush was on. Thousands of frenzied miners and freighters and merchants and lawyers and scammers rumbled through Carson City's dusty (though wide) streets. Curry quickly located a claim high up on the Comstock, consolidated it with a Carson City butcher named Alva Gould, and sold his share to Californians for $2,000 (with which he traveled back to Cleveland to collect his wife and six daughters; his one son was already with him in Carson). The Californians immediately became millionaires from the mine that forever carried his name, the Gould and Curry, and proved to be the richest ore body in the early days of the Comstock.

By 1860, the town's population had grown to more than 500. By the time Congress created the Territory of Nevada in 1861, burgeoning Carson City beat out Genoa and Virginia City for the territorial capital. Curry befriended fellow New Yorker James Nye, territorial governor, and helped induce him to convene both the territorial and the new Ormsby County governments at Carson. Finally, on Halloween 1864, Nevada became a state with Carson City its capital, and Curry's rise from lunatic to prophet had been completed—in a mere six years.

Power Attracts Power

By then, Uncle Abe, as he was henceforth universally known and revered for his civic spirit and generous soul, was Carson City's major landowner, contractor, hotelier, saloonkeeper, and road builder. He couldn't be content, of course, with mere prophethood and property, and quickly made another transition to politician: he acted frequently as sheriff, delegate to an early constitutional convention, and aide to Territorial Governor James Nye. Curry also saw the fulfillment of what one imagines to be his grandest ambition—philanthropy. He donated his hastily constructed Warm Springs Hotel for the first territorial legislature; the hotel being two miles from town, he transported the legislators in his horsedrawn streetcar—Nevada's first. Next, Curry sold his second hotel, Great Basin, to the government to serve as a courthouse and legislature; the Warm Springs building later became the territorial prison, with Curry as first warden. Prison labor quarried the limestone for many of Carson City's distinctive buildings, some still standing. In 1865, Carson City received federal approval to build a branch of the U.S. Mint, and Curry not only oversaw construction of the building, but also was appointed *its* first superintendent when it opened in January 1870.

Uncle Abe resigned his commission at the mint in September 1870 to run on the Republican ticket for lieutenant governor, a campaign that he lost. He then turned his attention to building the mammoth stone roundhouse and shops for the Virginia & Truckee Railroad. The Grand Ball, held to celebrate their opening on July 4, 1873, proved to be Curry's swan song. He was compelled to surrender to Nature's final summons in October 1873 from a stroke at age 58. All in all, Uncle Abe Curry had lived one of the richest lives of any early Nevadan, and had earned and maintained a reputation for being one of the most warm-hearted, civic-spirited, generous, and honest men during those turbulent times.

Twentieth Century

The capital shared the boom-bust cycles of the Comstock over the next few decades, though never as severely, thanks to the business supplied by the burgeoning bureaucracy. Afterwards, except for the championship heavyweight prize-fight between Bob Fitzsimmons and Gentleman Jim Corbett in 1897, Carson City settled down to the peaceful and purposeful community it has been ever since. The boxing match landed in Carson City after San Francisco elders caved in to public sentiment prevalent at the time against boxing and canceled it. Carson City elders felt no such squeamishness, and the 14-round bout attracted such large numbers of visitors and publicity that the legislators, most of whom had witnessed the prize-fight phenomenon first hand, put two and two together and came up with the Nevada tradition that evolved into legal gambling and prostitution, quick divorce and simple marriage procedures, nonrestrictive mining laws, and nuclear testing, among other unusual revenue-attracting efforts over the years.

Carson City became home to the Stewart Indian School, which provided vocational and higher education to thousands of Native children from around the West for 90 years (though many

---

CURRY SHOULDERS THE SHIP OF STATE

There is something solemnly funny about the struggles of a newborn territorial government to get a start in this world. 'Instructions' from the State Department commanded that a legislature should be elected at such-and-such a time, and its sittings inaugurated on such-and-such a date. It was easy to get legislators, even at three dollars a day, although board was four dollars and fifty cents, for distinction has its charm in Nevada as well as elsewhere, and there were plenty of patriotic souls out of employment; but to get a legislative hall for them to meet in was another matter altogether. Carson [City] blandly declined to give a room rent-free, or let one to the government on credit.

But when Abe Curry heard of the difficulty, he came forward, solitary and alone, and shouldered the Ship of State over the bar and got her afloat again. He offered his large stone building just outside the capital limits, rent-free, and it was gladly accepted. Then he built a horse railroad from town to the capitol, and carried the legislators gratis. He also furnished pine benches and chairs for the legislature, and covered the floors with clean sawdust by way of carpet and spitoon combined. But for Curry the legislature would have been obliged to sit in the desert, and the government would have died in its tender infancy.

—Roughing It,
Mark Twain, 1872

people consider Indian schools such as the Stewart to be little more than government kidnapping and indoctrination). Carson City also partook of the early 20th-century booms at Tonopah and Goldfield, thanks to the railroad connection and government participation. But the excitement was short-lived. From a high of 8,000 in 1880, the capital's population dropped to 2,000 in 1930. The 1931 gambling and divorce legislation prompted gradual growth, to 4,000 in 1950, then doubling three times again over the next 30 years. Boom times revisited Carson throughout the '80s and into the '90s.

Carson City has roughly 70,000 people today. The State Prison, Gaming Commission, huge Department of Transportation, Commission on Tourism, Economic Development Department, and all the myriad state and federal agencies keep the cogs and gears turning. The Legislature meets for several months every two years.

Carson City could be thought of as the center of Nevada. The geographic center of the state is roughly 200 miles away, 30 miles southeast of Austin. Reno and Las Vegas are the financial and entertainment centers and are magnets for visitors and transplants. The claim of historic center rightly belongs to Virginia City. But Carson City is the *power* center, to which all the state looks for vision, leadership, and order (bureaucratic though it may be). And it's not only the obvious fact that Carson City is the state capital—center of *political* power. This calm, comfortable, pretty, and friendly town seems to sit atop a rare locus of *planetary* power. These emanations from the Earth certainly infused its founders and partisans with a special zeal and authority. And they continue to infuse residents and visitors, who appreciate the city's excellent size, central location, friendliness, excellent facilities, and subtle sensation of powerful forces still at play just below the surface of this capital of the most unusual state in the country.

SIGHTS

Nevada State Museum

This is Nevada's premier museum, inside the old Carson City Mint, which operated between 1870 and 1893. After the mint closed, the stone building, erected by town father Uncle Abe Curry, served as a federal office building until 1933 when it was abandoned because of neglect. Five years later, Judge Clark J. Guild noticed a For Sale sign on the building and promptly mobilized a coalition, which included his friends, local residents, Senator Patrick McCarran, Nevada philanthropist Max Fleischmann, and the state Legislature, dedicated to repairing the building and outfitting it as a museum. It opened to the public on Nevada Day (October 31), 1941; a plaque on the north corner of the mint commemorates the event and leading players. The rear wing was added in 1959.

In 1990, the front wing (in the old mint building) was closed for safety reasons. Structural engineers found an uncemented rubble foundation and sandstone block walls held together with limestone mortar; a number of thin cracks ran clear through the walls. It's all fixed now, and better than ever.

Pay your admission, then head into the mint exhibit, which illustrates the entire coining process, from depositors' bullion through ingot melting, into gold and silver "cakes," which are rolled, annealed, and cut into blanks, then washed, weighed, and coined by the likes of the museum's huge coin press into $5, $10, and $20 silver and gold pieces. The mint produced $49.2 million from 56.6 million coins in its 23 years of operation, and you can see a sample of every coin minted here in a collection donated by the First Interstate Bank (which also has a fine money museum in Las Vegas). The mint wing also houses the silver collection from the USS *Nevada*.

Beyond is the dark and cool of the walk-through ghost town, narrated by a grizzled old prospector and his mule.

On the second floor are more excellent exhibits. The Environmental Gallery is full of local fauna—great looks at a big black bear, bobcats, porcupine, big Lahontan cutthroat trout and cui-ui, and the Pyramid Lake pelicans and cormorants, plus eagles, owls, crows, falcons, hawks, and songbirds, small birds, scavenger birds, wading and diving birds, swans and geese. There's a skeletal ichthyosaur on the stairs.

The Earth Science Gallery is a geology lesson, including an underwater Devonian sea walk-around, seismograph, plate tectonics video, and

Black Rock Desert diorama. The Archaeology Gallery in the next room displays projectile points and weapon sticks such as the atlatl, shells, tools, baskets, dioramas of a native mudhen drive, Great Basin camp, Pyramid Lake scene, pine-nut harvest, salt mining, natural foods, and much, much more. The Changing Gallery is always a surprise.

The underground mine was re-created with timber, vents, and ores from once-active mines around the state. It's in the basement and has a very "low cap." It meanders through a large maze under the whole building and imparts a life-like sense of working in tunnels underground. It leads to an exit; shield your eyes from the sun!

There's a big selection of Nevada books and museum gifts in the gift shop on the second floor. The museum, 600 N. Carson St., 775/687-4810, is open 8:30 A.M.–4:30 P.M. seven days a week, $3 adult, seniors $2.50, under 18 free.

Cross Robinson St. and enter the **Carson City Nugget** casino, where you can spend a few minutes drooling over the "world's rarest gold collection"—worth a cool mil, and 70 years in the collecting. The brochure explains how these specimens, completely unchanged by human hands, formed into such peculiar and stunning shapes.

The Capitol and Legislature

The state capital building (a.k.a. the Capitol), just south of the State Library on Carson St. between Musser and 2nd, 775/687-5030, was built in 1870. Improvements, including the iron fence, were made five years later for $25,000; the library annex (now the Controller's offices) was added onto the back of the building in 1905; the two legislative wings were constructed in 1913; and the whole original structure was gutted and restored in 1977 for $6 million.

A fine museum on the south side of the second floor, in the old Senate chambers, displays a collection of Nevada artifacts. Just a few of the highlights include William Stewart's Wooten Patent Cabinet desk, an 1862 map of the Nevada Territory, the front page of the New York *Herald* from November 2, 1864, announcing admittance of the 36th state, the 36-star flag, architectural drawings of the Capitol from 1870, the silver trowel from the cornerstone ceremony, the goblets used by Abe Curry and James Nye to toast statehood, and a graphic exhibit of all the state symbols. Spend some time following the history of the building, especially the photographs of the gutted interior during restoration in 1977 and the installation of the new fiberglass dome. Whatever you do in the capital city, don't miss the Capitol room. In the old Assembly chambers down the hall is a display on the USS *Nevada*.

The Legislative Building across the plaza hosts the legislators during January and February (and often into March and April, and sometimes into May and June) during odd-numbered years. As you're wandering around the building looking for the water fountains, peek into the Assembly (south) and Senate (north) galleries. During the other 660 or so days when they're not in session, you're all alone in the public galleries in air-conditioned meditative luxury.

Brewery Arts Center

Walk south a block to King, west a block to Division, then into the Brewery Arts Center, 449 W. King, 775/883-1976, open Mon.–Fri. 9 A.M.–5 P.M., free; the art gallery and store are also open on Saturday, 10 A.M.–4 P.M. Jacob Klein swept across the Sierra in the fateful spring of 1860 with the silver-crazed hordes to establish Nevada's first brewery in Carson City. Within four years, the dividends from the beer had built this establishment, which operated first by steam and then by lager till 1948 (with a hiatus during Prohibition). A display of Carson Brewing Company artifacts can be viewed here; tours of the historic building can be arranged. The Arts Center sponsors more than 100 classes and workshops in visual and performing arts, art exhibits, crafts fairs, concerts, plays, storytellers, and other cultural programs throughout the year.

Children's Museum of Northern Nevada

It took six years of fundraising ($400,000) and another year of renovating to unveil this children's learning center at 813 N. Carson (between Ann and Washington), 775/884-2226, open Tues.–Fri. 10 A.M.–4:30 P.M., Saturday and Sunday 10 A.M.–5:30 P.M., admission $3 adult, $2 kids 3–13. The museum is one block north of the Nevada State Museum, on the opposite side of the street. There are 25 exhibits in fine arts, humanities, and science, aimed at the 6–13 age group, but fun for the whole family.

Fire Museum

Warren Engine Co. No. 1 began as a volunteer firefighting fraternity in 1863 and has served Carson City uninterrupted ever since, making it the oldest volunteer company in the West (mostly professional firefighters now make up its ranks). That first year, 20 charter members of the company raised $2000 at a fireman's ball to buy the first firefighting equipment in town: a Hunneman Engine built in the early 1800s and used by the Warren Engine Company of Boston. Later it was shipped around the Horn and worked in San Francisco and Marysville, California, before arriving in Carson City, where the company named itself for the Warrens of Boston. In 1913, on its 50th anniversary, the company bought a Seagrave fire engine, Nevada's first motorized fire truck. A new firehouse was built in the late 1950s at 111 N. Curry, with the upstairs devoted to a museum for all the memorabilia accumulated during the first 100 years. That station remained in service till 1994, when a new station was opened at 777 S. Stewart St., 775/887-2210 (then dial "0" for the receptionist), open Mon.–Fri. 8 A.M.–5 P.M., donation. Check out the 1913 Seagrave, the wild old goggles, masks, helmets, and caps, the 1870s two-wheeled hose cart, and the familiar Currier & Ives original prints of New York conflagrations. One of the firefighters will show you around; ask your guide to explain the trumpet trophies.

Historical Houses

The **Roberts House Park and Museum,** 1207 N. Carson St., 775/887-2714, is Carson City's oldest house—but the Gothic Revival-style house was not originally built here. It is believed that this is a "kit house," shipped from New England to San Francisco (possibly around Cape Horn), then transported by rail to Folsom, California (the trailhead for the Kingsbury Trail), and then hauled to Washoe City, where it was assembled in around 1859. In 1875 the house, home of James Doane Roberts and family, was moved to Carson City. Today the house has been restored and contains period furniture; guided tours include the story of who has lived in this house, and why the house is historically significant. Open Fridays, Saturdays and Sunday, 1–3 P.M., April through October; admission $1 donation.

Pick up the **Kit Carson Trail map** ($2.50) at the Nevada State Museum (see above) or the Chamber of Commerce (see below) for the historic tour of town. The flyer is beautifully illustrated and adequately written, though the tour, a bit too long to walk especially in the heat of high season, requires an accomplished navigator and careful attention to glimpse all the historic structures. You might read the map and choose the five or six houses that strike your fancy (the **Bliss Mansion**, for example, built by the Tahoe lumber magnate, or the **Stewart-Nye home,** home to both famous politicians). Or you could park on a corner with three or four of the houses nearby (around the **Governor's Mansion** at Mountain and Robinson, at Minnesota and Proctor, or at Spear and Nevada), and see them on foot. Whichever, do wander around these historic residential back streets; the stately old trees alone are worth every minute. A free pamphlet available at the Chamber of Commerce office outlines a simpler one-hour walk you can do around the historic area.

For historical reasons, you might want to make a pilgrimage to **Abe Curry's stone house** at 406 N. Nevada St., or **Orion Clemens' residence** at 502 N. Division, with its distinctive five-sided bay window. Clemens came to Nevada by Overland Stage in late 1860 to serve as secretary to newly appointed Territorial Governor James Nye. His younger brother Sam, better known to history as Mark Twain, accompanied him for the adventure.

The entire historical tour of Carson City encompasses 59 sites along the "blue line," a blue stripe painted on the city's sidewalks; 15 of the houses on the tour are "talking houses," which tell their tales on specific AM frequencies on the dial. Get all the info at the Chamber of Commerce.

Stewart Indian Museum

A visit to this campus of the Stewart Indian Boarding School is one of the highlights of Carson City. Thirty years after the complete dislocation of Nevada's Indian population, in 1890 U.S. Senator William Stewart secured federal funds to open this school, on a 240-acre campus site, with three teachers and 37 students. At that time, the federal policy was to "assimilate" Native Americans, which really meant "forced conversion" to white ways. The first students consisted of orphans, sons and daughters of tribal leaders, and children who were forcibly removed from their parents. In the early years, the school was run like a military boarding institution, with an emphasis on vocational skills and strict sanctions against observing traditional ways. Later the direction changed to academics and Native heritage.

By the time the federal government closed the school in 1980 (budget cuts during the Carter administration), nearly 3,000 students had gone through the program.

The museum is in the former superintendent's home at 5366 Snyder Ave., 775/882-6929, www.stewartmuseum.com, open daily 10 A.M.–5 P.M.; donations pay operating costs. Black-and-white photos illustrate campus life: Indian children learning academic, vocational, agricultural, and sports skills. Washo, Paiute, and Shoshone baskets, among others, are also on display. The gift shop sells jewelry, beadwork, cards, and prints. Exquisite Indian-woven blankets and rugs sell for $150–450. A large powwow is held every June; artists sell their work, 200 dancers perform, and photo ops abound.

The campus has a palpable spirit: the stunning 1930s polychrome stone buildings (dorms, classes, auditorium, gymnasium, churches, etc.), the gigantic shade trees planted as early as those downtown, the quiet. Some of the buildings now house the State Prison Administration offices, which lends a contrasting spooky air to the grounds. If you bring a picnic lunch and stay kinda close to the museum, you'll still sense the specialness of this spot, epitomizing the powerful soul of Carson City. To get there, head south on US 395 about three miles from downtown, beyond Raley's and Mervyn's, go left on Snyder Ave. (named after the 1930s' superintendent responsible for most of the stone buildings). In about a mile, just beyond two churches, go right into the parking lot.

Nevada State Railroad Museum

The brainchild of Bank of California's William Sharon, the Virginia & Truckee Railroad was installed (almost completely by Chinese labor) on the 21-mile tortuous route (dropping 1,600 feet in 13 miles) from Virginia City to Carson City in less than a year (1869). In its 81 years of operation, the V&T became the richest short line

(later connected to Reno) in the West. The Jacobsen Interpretive Center houses a number of painstakingly restored rolling stock, big and shiny and beautiful. The *Inyo* is the V&T No. 22 Baldwin steam engine, with the fireman and engineer working at the controls. The No. 4 passenger car has plush green seats and a smiling conductor. There's an incredible display of 15 model V&T engines and wood, coal, and mail cars assembled over 10,000 hours by George Lincoln Robinson of Santa Barbara. Bulletin boards display text and photos of the restoration process for Caboose No. 9, Coach No. 4, and Boxcar No. 1005, with before-and-after pictures that you won't believe.

The gift shop as you walk in sells books, T-shirts, maps, caps, and a video of the V&T ($39.95). Two engines do a loop around the grounds during the summer ($1). One is No. 8, an 1888 Baldwin steam locomotive that chugs around the grounds, a couple of times a month, at five mph ($2.50 adult, $1 children). Seven to nine volunteers man the thing. The other is a regular motor car that runs regularly ($1 adult, 50 cents children).

The museum is at 2180 S. Carson St. on the far south end of town, 775/687-6953. Open daily 8:30 A.M.–4:30 P.M.; admission $2 adults, free for ages 18 and under.

Carson Hot Springs

Head out Hot Springs Rd. (bear right when heading north on Carson St. at the Safeway north of downtown) and drive about a mile past a couple of traffic lights. Follow the road around to the right and there are the old hot springs on the left, 775/885-8844. Abe Curry built his Warm Springs Hotel next to these waters and ferried the territorial legislators to here when they met at the hotel. Today, there's a pool with 100-degree soft spring water (no sulphur odor, nor any chlorine; they drain the pool every night and fill it up again every morning, which takes a total of six hours), along with private hot tubs, masseuse, motel, RV parking, and restaurant. The facilities are open daily 7 A.M.–11 P.M.; $10 gets you use of the pool for all day (you can come and go). A private hot tub for two is $15 per person for a two-hour session. Massage is $45 for an hour and includes the use of the pool and spa. Carson Hot Springs is just the thing after coming into the big city from anywhere in outback Nevada.

Also at the site is Richard Langson's Racing Museum and Pit Stop Bar. Langson, a world-champion top-fuel dragster, displays his memorabilia, mostly photographs and models, along the walls of this comfortable premises. The restaurant has come and gone over the years. At press time, it was just coming again.

Casinos

Carson City now has two major carpet clubs and a couple of slot joints—not much gambling variety in the state capital.

The grand old man of Carson City hotels is **Ormsby House,** 600 S. Carson Street. The hotel dates back, in various incarnations, to 1859, when it was opened by Major William Ormsby, who was killed in the Pyramid Lake skirmish with Numaga's Paiute in the spring of 1860. Immediately it was sold to one John Kooser, who expanded it. In 1872 it was expanded again, and was renowned as one of the fanciest hotels between Denver and San Francisco. In 1880 the name was changed to the Park Hotel, and the hotel operated into the 1920s, when it closed. It was reopened in 1931, after legalization of casino gambling, by the Laxalts, possibly the most famous Nevadan family. Paul Laxalt, governor, U.S. senator, and close friend of Ronald Reagan, built the existing hotel in 1972, then sold it in 1975 to Woody Loftin. Loftin engineered a multimillion-dollar expansion in late 1988, which shook its financial stability; two years later Loftin

filed Chapter 11, and the Ormsby House struggled along for another year and a half, finally shutting its doors on 250 employees and owing more than $15 million to creditors. It remained closed until early 1995, when it was resurrected by a group of southern California developers. It's suffered, however, from short-bankroll problems ever since, and at press time was undergoing a management shake-up in which ex-lieutenant governor and long-time casino owner Bob Cashell was named CEO to try and revive the joint.

Otherwise, **Carson Nugget** is the main action in town. This is one of four Nuggets opened by Idaho restaurateur Richard Graves in northern Nevada in the mid-1950s; two of the others are still in operation (one in downtown Reno and the other in Sparks). It has a dozen blackjack tables, along with roulette and craps. Not unlike John Ascuaga's in Sparks, this Nugget also boasts bingo, a big race and sports book, steakhouse, oyster bar, lunch and dinner buffet (no breakfast), and 24-hour coffee shop; the only thing it's missing are the elephants. Being the main action, it's always crowded with locals and some visitors, which gives it the typical air of casino excitement.

Carson Station is the other main casino, which has been completely revamped and improved since its old Mother Lode Casino days. This is also a popular joint, especially at night when there's usually some jumping live entertainment. Carson Station has plenty of black-

Some of the V&T's superbly restored rolling stock is on display at the State Railroad Museum.

jack (with Las Vegas rules-the trend in northern Nevada these days), craps, roulette, keno, a sports book, coffee shop, and a good snack bar. The gift counter has a good selection of newspapers.

Cactus Jack's right downtown is not to be confused with Cactus Petes in Jackpot or Whiskey Pete's in Primm. It was opened in 1971 by Pete Piersanti of Cactus Petes fame (Jackpot); he sold it in 1989. The neon Senator out front waves cash (but is a bit too red for comfort). Inside is perhaps the most compact casino in the state, where the horseshoe bar is the largest feature, followed, in descending size order, by a U-shaped snack bar, tight aisles of slots, a four-table pit (three blackjack and one Let It Ride; one bj table is often shut down to host bingo of all things, right in the pit), a two-teller cage, and a mini-sports book.

Right next door is the **Horseshoe Club,** not to be confused with the Horseshu across from Cactus Petes in Jackpot nor Binion's Horseshoe in downtown Las Vegas. It too is a slot haven-newer and darker than Jack's, and way less tightly packed, with some of the best snack bar prices in the state.

Slot World, 3879 Highway 50 East, 775/882-SLOT, 1.5 miles east of downtown on US 50, is a slot machine casino open 24 hours, with a bar and a restaurant, the Caravan Café, open 6 A.M.–10 P.M.

The **Best Western Piñon Plaza Resort,** 2171 Highway 50 East, 775/885-9000 or toll-free 877/519-5567, www.pinonplaza.com, 2.5 miles east of downtown on US 50, is one of Carson City's newer casinos. It's large and luxurious, with facilities including a full service casino, the Fiesta Lounge with live entertainment, sportsbook and sports bar, a state-of-the-art bowling center, a steakhouse and saloon, plus swimming pool, sauna, Jacuzzi, exercise room and a 148-room Best Western hotel. This resort was voted the "Best of Carson" in 12 categories in a *Reno Gazette-Journal* poll.

PRACTICALITIES

Accommodations

Be sure to have reservations if you're planning to stay in Carson City on a Friday or Saturday night, when every room in town is usually booked up.

A good room-dining-gambling package that's been around forever is at the **City Center Motel** (room) and the **Carson Nugget** (food and gambling). For $46, you get a room for two, two buffet dinners, four cocktails, four dollar tokens, and some miscellaneous coupons–a very good deal. You can get a second night for an additional $37. Call 800/338-7760 and ask for the "Good Times Package." The City Center Motel is at 800 N. Carson St., 775/882-1785; prices for "room only" are $28–54 for the 78 rooms.

The **St. Charles Hotel,** a three-story red-brick building right downtown at 3rd and Carson streets, was built in 1862 and was central to city life for a hundred years. After decades of neglect, it had turned into a run-down downtown hotel and bar called the Pony Express. But then Bob McFadden bought it for $750,000, renovated it and installed antiques in the 27 rooms to the tune of $200,000 (including $40,000 of Redevelopment Authority money), and renamed it the St. Charles. And he didn't stop there: he also opened Vittles restaurant next door, McFadden's Bar next door to that (have a friendly drink in the comfy little lounge, complete with sofas, in the back room), and a mini-mall across the street on the opposite corner, with an antique shop and a sandwich shop so far. There are 27 rooms here; seven rooms share a bath. The St. Charles rents rooms only by the week; prices are $49–129 per week. 310 S. Carson St., 775/882-1887.

First place to try if you're looking for a potentially inexpensive room is the **Frontier Motel,** 1718 N. Carson, 775/882-1377, with rates as low as $25 a night–and as high as $179! Also try the **Pioneer Motel,** 907 S. Carson, 775/882-3046, $28–70. Rates at **Carson City Inn,** 1930 N. Carson, 775/882-1785, **City Center Motel,** 800 N. Carson, 775/882-5535, **Best Value Motel,** 2731 S. Carson, 775/882-2007, and **Downtowner Motor Inn,** 801 N. Carson, 775/882-1333, all start at around $30. For slightly more uptown digs, head for the **Super 8 Motel,** 2829 S. Carson, 775/883-7800, $42–61; **Nugget Motel,** 651 N. Stewart, 775/882-7711, $45–55; the **Mill House Inn,** way down at 3251 S. Carson, 775/882-2715, with rooms for $45–75; or the **Hardman House Motor Inn,** 917 N. Carson, 775/882-7744, $62–99.

The **Best Western Piñon Plaza Resort,** 2171

Highway 50 East, 775/885-9000 or toll-free 877/519-5567, www.pinonplaza.com, 2.5 miles east of downtown on US 50, is one of Carson City's newer casinos (see Casinos, above). Its 148 spacious, luxurious rooms range from $50–150, and there's also an RV park here (see RVing and Camping, below). If you're a golfer, ask about their "Golf Getaway" packages, starting from $55 per golfer midweek.

For a truly exceptional place to stay, check out the **Bliss Mansion Bed & Breakfast,** 710 W. Robinson St., 775/887-8988 or 800/320-0627, opposite the Governor's Mansion. Built in 1879, this magnificent State Historical Landmark was completely renovated and restored in 1994, and is decorated with Victorian museum-quality furniture and art. The four upstairs guest rooms, each with private bath, are $175 per night; reservations required, adults only.

RVing and Camping

Camp-N-Town RV Park, 2438 N. Carson (US 395), Carson City, NV 89706, 775/883-1123, is aptly named: it's right in downtown Carson City, a 15-minute stroll to the Capitol, State Museum, and casinos, and across the street from a large shopping center. It's relatively quiet for such a central location, behind the 49er Motel. And it's shaded by the tall trees that help give downtown Carson its charm. It has 74 spaces for motor homes, all with full hookups; 38 are pull-throughs. Tents are not allowed. Restrooms have flush toilets and hot showers; public phone, sewage disposal, laundry, groceries, game room, bar, and heated swimming pool are available. Reservations are recommended for summer weekends; the fee is $18.50–22 for two people.

Comstock Country RV Resort, 5400 S. Carson Street (US 395), Carson City, NV 89701, 775/882-2445, has a great location just south on US 395 past the intersection with US 50. There are 163 spaces for motor homes, all with full hookups; 133 are pull-throughs. Tents are allowed. Restrooms have flush toilets and hot showers; public phone, sewage disposal, laundry, groceries, game room, and heated swimming pool and spa are available. Reservations are accepted; tent sites are $18, RV spaces $24.

The **Piñon Plaza Resort RV Park** is beside the Piñon Plaza Resort Casino, 2171 Highway 50 East, 775/885-9000 or toll-free 877/519-5567,

2.5 miles east of downtown on US 50. RV spaces are $19–21, with AARP, AAA and Good Sam discounts available. No tents allowed. Prices include use of the pool at the hotel.

Three public campgrounds are within easy striking distance of the capital. **Dayton State Park** is 13 miles east on US 50 (see "Vicinity of Dayton" under "Vicinity of Virginia City" section). **Davis Creek** and **Washoe Lake State** parks are 15 miles north in Washoe Valley (see "Washoe Valley" under "Vicinity of Reno").

Food

Carson City has a large range of restaurant fare for a town its size, from the 89-cent breakfast special at the Horseshoe to the $50 chateaubriand at Adele's.

For the cheapest food around, patronize the snack bar at the **Horseshoe Club** downtown, 775/883-2211. Good breakfast, lunch and graveyard specials; open 24 hours. **Cactus Jack's** Coroner Café, 775/882-8770, has been remodeled and the prices are a little higher since.

Perhaps the best place in the whole state to get breakfast or a true old-fashioned blue-plate-special diner meal is at the **Cracker Box,** 402 E. William (Hwy. 50 one block east of Carson St. downtown), 775/882-4556, open 6 A.M.–2 P.M. daily. This is the real deal, with an eight-seat counter and tables for 50 in a squat green-and-white box of a building. The grill cooks are straight out of the '40s, the waitresses out of the '60s, and the patrons run the gamut from the lowliest proles to the uppiest pols. The basic breakfast has the thickest meatiest bacon this side of Macon, a big pile of home fries with bits of pepper and onion, and large eggs cooked *exactly* the way you order them; the orange juice is freshly squeezed (and comes in two sizes: "not very small" and "huge!"). The egg dishes are the mainstay, but the menu also bursts with burgers, hot sandwiches, and daily specials, all in the $3 to $8 range. It's a classic.

Heidi's, 1020 N. Carson St., 775/882-0486, serves big breakfasts and diner lunches to crowds of locals and passers-through at good prices. Its long north and south walls are now graced by detailed trompe-l'oeil murals: the south wall's is a V&T steam engine with cattle pusher pulling out of the Engine House (a historic stone building constructed by Abe Curry and torn down amid controversy in 1992); the north wall's is a view of the desert from inside the Engine House. Heidi's also has branches in Reno, Minden, and South Lake Tahoe. The same folks run the popular **City Cafe Bakery,** 701 S. Carson, 775/882-2253, which is a little bit of San Francisco in Carson: six kinds of brewed coffee, along with espresso and cappuccino, big sandwiches, muffins, rolls, and breads (honey wheat, rye swirl, sourdough).

Juicy's hamburger joint, corner of Winnie and N. Carson by Launderland, 775/883-5600, has some of the best burgers in western Nevada. The burger-and-fries will ensure that you don't think about food for at least a few hours. Eat in air-conditioned and house-planted comfort, or take out for a picnic at Stewart Indian Museum and campus.

Nick's Pizza is also a good place to fill up. Get big fat thick and cheesy slices, or a big 10-incher. The 16-inch Grecian special goes for $16: feta, garlic, red onion, and fresh tomatoes. Small Greek salads $3, large $5. Nick's is at 303 N. Carson right downtown, 775/885-8008.

Right next door to Nick's is **Garibaldi's** Italian restaurant, 775/884-4574, open Mon.–Fri. 11:30 A.M.–2:30 P.M., nightly from 5 P.M. It's a cozy little room, with an eight-seat bar, about a dozen tables, six ceiling fans, and all-wood decor. For lunch, the pasta (homemade) is in the $8–10 range (the vegetarian lasagna is down to earth; the spaghettini with shrimp and capers in a lemon-rosemary sauce is orbital), or try the meat pies (rabbit and vegetables, for example) or the veal-meatball sandwich for $8. Dinner pastas run $11–15, and the eggplant, veal, chicken, Italian sausage, N.Y. steak entrees are $12–19.

Station Grill and Rotisserie, 1105 S. Carson next to J.C. Penney's, 775/883-8400, open Mon.–Sat. 11 A.M.–10 P.M. (on Saturday from 5 P.M.), has an open kitchen, murals of fruits and veggies, echoing stone tiles, and great food. The $9 rotisserie chicken (with soy and lime) is the play here, or you can get California-style wood-fired pizza ($8), grilled ravioli or cioppino ($10), along with blackened shrimp, leg of lamb, and other interesting dinner entrees. For lunch, the Grill serves mesquite-grilled burgers turkey enchiladas, pizza, and smoked chicken and avocado salad in the $8 range.

Red's Old 395 Grill, 1055 S. Carson St.,

775/887-0395, is a fun barbecue restaurant with great décor and great food, very popular with locals. Lunch and dinner are served every day (dinners $10–13), both inside and out on the barbecue patio.

The **Nugget,** 775/882-1626, has lunch and dinner buffets, a Saturday breakfast buffet and Sunday brunch buffet. The Nugget's oyster bar features white chowder, crab sandwich, seafood cocktails, combo pan roast, and louies. Its Steakhouse has entrees in the $9–17 range. The coffee shop is open 24 hours; you can call the above number and be connected to a recording about the changeable specials in the coffee shop and steakhouse.

For some of the best Mexican food anywhere, pull up an appetite at **El Charro Avitia,** 4389 S. Carson, 775/883-6261, open Mon.–Thurs. 11 A.M.–9 P.M., Friday 11 A.M.–10 P.M., Saturday 5–10 P.M., Sunday 5–9 P.M. El Charro, opened in 1978, is one of four cantinas run by the Avitia family: Bishop and Ridgecrest, California, and Kailua, Hawaii. The seafood enchiladas, burritos, and gorditos are worth the drive from Tahoe or Reno. Or try the Taco Nacionales, with chicken, cream cheese, and almonds. The tamales are stuffed with barbecued pork, the mini-fajitas are a steal, as are the three-item combos, and the guacamole shrimp cocktail is to die for. You won't be disappointed by anything at El Charro (which means a *vaquero* with fancy duds and moves to match).

Other good Mexican restaurants include **Mi Casa Too,** 3809 N. Carson St., 775/882-4080, voted Best Mexican Restaurant by locals in the local newspaper poll; the **Café del Rio** at the St. Charles Hotel, 302 S. Carson St., 775/885-9088; and **Tito's,** 444 E. William St. (Highway 50), 775/885-0390, all serving lunch and dinner.

For Chinese food, try **Ming's Chinese Restaurant,** 202 Fairview Dr., 775/841-2888, or the **Panda Kitchen,** 2416 Highway 50 East, 775/882-2666. For Japanese, try **Yamacho's,** 3747 S. Carson St., 775/884-2366. All serve lunch and dinner.

For the finest dining in Carson, where the power brokers broker their power, head for **Adele's,** 1112 N. Carson St., 775/882-3353. This gourmet restaurant is in the 19th-century house of Nevada Supreme Court Justice Murphy, and is extremely elegant in all its Second Empire appointments (read about it on the dinner menu). Inside, the bar is in the living room and several tables are in the dining room, with Victorian-style carpet, stained-glass windows, and fine lamps. "Lite" meals served in the bar—clams, oysters, sandwiches, omelettes—start around $10. Full-blown dinners in the dining room start at $18.50 and go up to $50; they're far too numerous to even mention. Suffice it to say that practically anything you want that's in season is available at Carson City's finest restaurant.

Parks

Mills Park, four blocks east on US 50 from US 395, is an excellent city facility with lots of recreation choices: big green shady lawn for stretching out and daydreaming, picnic tables and barbecues, tennis courts, horseshoe pits, indoor and outdoor pools next door at the community center with a big water slide (variety of hours; 775/887-2242), and the Carson and Mills Park Railroad (775/887-2523), a one-mile, 15-minute ride in toy passenger cars behind a 100-year-old steam engine on Carson & Colorado Railroad 30-pound track. The train runs from 11 A.M.–4 P.M., on weekends from mid-April to Memorial Day, weather cooperating, and every day from June to September; the ride costs $1.25, and a snack bar is open whenever the train is running.

Carson River Park is on both sides of the Carson River, about four miles outta town. Heading south on US 395 from US 50, take a left (east) on E. 5th and drive right through the middle of the grounds of the state maximum-security penitentiary. Just the sight of the pen, roasting in the desert within high cyclone barbed-wire fencing and with gun towers in the corners, would be an effective deterrent to every boy between 15 and 25, the prime crime time. Cross Edmonds, take a right on Carson River Rd., and head across the green valley down to the lazy river. Cross the little bridge and explore the network of dirt roads along it. Turn right (south) onto Mexican Dam Rd. and in about 1.5 miles you'll come to **Mexican Dam.** You can't go onto the dam itself (it's private property), but there's a fine one-mile trail along here, called the **Mexican Dam Ditch Trail.**

On the way to the river, you'll pass the **Silver Saddle Ranch Park,** operated by the BLM

(775/885-6000); they may have gotten a sign put up, by the time this book is published. The park is on the south side of Carson River Rd., a quarter-mile north of Mexican Dam, between the river and Prison Hill; another section of the ranch is on the east side of the river. The intention for this park is that it remain undeveloped; you can walk down to the river on the old farm roads and just enjoy the quiet, open space. Open every day, 8 A.M.–dusk.

Alternatively, if you don't turn onto Carson River Rd., you can continue straight ahead on East 5th St. until you come to **Riverview Park,** a lovely riverside park with a wetland area, exercise stops along a trail, and people walking their dogs.

Centennial Park is one of the largest municipal recreation facilities in Nevada. It's off US 50 east of town to the south, along Centennial Drive. It boasts several softball and soccer fields, many pleasant and shady picnic sites, tennis courts, and a public golf course with driving range and clubhouse. This is the place for a long walk after a soak at Carson Hot Springs and a meal at Garibaldi's, and before hunkering down for some craps at Carson Station.

Services and Information

The **Chamber of Commerce,** 1900 S. Carson, downstairs in the building next door to the Railroad Museum, 775/882-1565, www.carsoncitychamber.com, is open Mon.–Fri. 8 A.M.–5 P.M. Pick up local maps, handouts, and a copy of the Kit Carson Trail map and brochure ($2.50) of historic houses and sites around town; the solid blue line on the sidewalks downtown is the walking tour, the dotted blue line on the map is a driving tour. Another free pamphlet outlines a simpler one-hour walk around the town's historic district. If you're from out of state, collect a free fun book for the casinos. The chamber sells some books, T-shirts, and souvenirs. It also answers general questions about the area, offers relocation and starting business packets, and brochures on area lodging, dining and special events.

Upstairs in the same building, the **Carson City Convention & Visitors Bureau,** 1900 S. Carson St., 775/687-7410 or 800/NEVADA-1, www.carson-city.org, open the same hours, is another good place for visitors to ask questions.

Call ahead and they'll send you a visitor packet.

The **Nevada Commission on Tourism,** in the historic brick Paul Laxalt State Building at 401 N. Carson St., 775/687-4322 or 800/237-0774, www.travelnevada.com, has information on the entire state of Nevada. The two offices mentioned above are the places to go for information about Carson City; this is the place to come for information on the rest of the state. This state office's goal is primarily to promote tourism in Nevada's rural areas. Here you can pick up brochures on all of Nevada and its territories, events around the state, the Nevada Scenic Byways brochure, regional brochures, Great Basin National Park brochures, and a good state map. The office is open Mon.–Fri., 8 A.M.–5 P.M.

In the same building are the offices of *Nevada* magazine, 775/687-5416, www.nevadamagazine 167.com.

The **Carson Ranger District** office is at 1536 S. Carson St., a block north of the Railroad Museum, 775/826-2766; open Mon.–Fri. 8 A.M.–4:30 P.M., Saturday to noon. The staff is extremely helpful, with good literature, maps and information on Mt. Rose, Lake Tahoe, and the Humboldt-Toiyabe National Forest, the national forest which comprises all the national forest land in Nevada, in many different places. The office also sells maps and a number of useful books and other items, unusual for a Forest Service office. Ten percent of the sales goes back to the Carson District for recreation and wilderness programs.

Ormsby Library, 900 N. Roop next to Mills Park, 775/887-2247, opens at 10 A.M. Mon.–Sat, staying open till 6 P.M. Fri., Sat. and Mon., till 9 P.M. Tues.–Thurs. **Bookcellar** is at 1202 N. Carson St., 775/885-7772.

If you've been camping nearby and need a shower, call the **Community Center pool,** 851 E. William, 775/887-2290, and ask politely. Or use the excellent facilities at **Carson Hot Springs** (see "Sights," above).

If you're serious about your maps (and if you're a serious traveler, how can you not be?), head to **Room 206** of the Nevada **Department of Transportation** building, 1263 S. Stewart St., 775/888-7627, for the graphics and cartography department. Beautiful huge prints grace the foyer; beautiful huge maps are for sale upstairs. Pick up the catalog, plus mileage and public transportation maps free; huge state maps, poster-size city maps, enlarged area maps and quad maps (one inch to one-half, one, and two miles), plus the excellent *Nevada Map Atlas* are available.

At the **Gaming Commission,** 1919 E. College Parkway, 775/687-6500, you can buy a number of publications about the casino and slot industry, including thick printouts of regulations and lists of locations. But the booklet *Gaming Nevada Style* is free and explains most of it in English.

Transportation

Public Rural Ride **(PRIDE)** (775/348-RIDE) operates buses 10 times a day, 6:30 A.M.–7 P.M., between Carson City and Reno. Fares are $3 adults, $2 youth, $1.50 seniors, including free transfers to Reno's city bus system, Citifare. In Carson City, PRIDE bus stops are at the Wal-Mart on the south end of town, at the Nevada Department of Transportation (1263 S. Stewart St.) in the center of town, and at the K-Mart on the north end of town.

Greyhound and **K-T** long-distance buses depart from the Carson City bus depot at the minimart of the Frontier Motel, 1718 N. Carson St., 775/882-3375. Direct buses go to Reno, Las Vegas, South Lake Tahoe, Sacramento and Los Angeles, with connections to other places.

Unless you've got a private plane or are chartering one, you won't need information about the Carson City Airport; no regularly scheduled flights service the capital!

Carson City has three rental-car companies: **Enterprise,** 1001 S. Carson St, 775/883-7788; **Hertz,** 3660 S. Carson St., 775/841-8002; and **U-Save Auto Rental,** 2001 Hwy. 50 East, 775/882-1212. You can also call the Toyota dealer, 3659 S. Carson St., 775/882-8211, to rent their vehicles. Check with all four to get the best price.

To Lake Tahoe

You can levitate to Tahoe on four-lane US 50, which exits US 395 three miles south of Carson City. It's nine miles to **Spooner Summit** (7,146 feet), where there's a pull-out with a picnic area on the downbound side of the road, and trailhead access to the new **Tahoe Rim Trail** on both sides of the road. It's then another mile to the intersection with NV 28 north to Sand Harbor, Incline Village, and Crystal Bay. Or stay on US 50 south for 15 miles to get to Stateline.

LAKE TAHOE

INTRODUCTION

This immense lake is the dazzling crown of west-ern Nevada. Its air is so crisp and clean, its water is so clear and colorful, its mountains are so craggy and close, and its people are so crowded and condoized that the crown's gemstones are either splendor or spectacle, beauty or vanity. It's as if Mother Nature has created a perfect optical illusion: do you see the white setting or the black development? For example, you can swim and sunbathe in seclusion, hike and climb so far and high that you just have to reach up to kiss the sky, and sleep for free among the pine needles and longtail weasels, as if you're Sam Clemens in 1861. Or, you can get your instant tan under sunlamps in December, strut from blackjack to video poker with Lady Luck herself on your arm, and then take the elevator to your two-bathroom, three-telephone, four-TV, five-star suite, com-plete with butler, bar, and choice of pillows, as if you're Donald Trump in 1998. This perfectly bal-anced pendulum swings only, of course, on the *Nevada* side of Tahoe, between the south wall of Harvey's (at Stateline) and the north wall of Cal-Neva (at Crystal Bay), with stunning Lake Tahoe State Park in between. With all the wilderness, you never have to step indoors if you don't want to, and with all the high-rise hotel-casinos, you never have to step outside. But you're a winner either way. Because you get to keep the crown.

The Setting

Lake Tahoe, 12 miles wide, 22 miles long, with 72 miles of shoreline and averaging 1,000 feet deep, is the largest alpine lake in North America and the tenth-deepest lake in the world. Tahoe's 122 million acre-feet are enough to cover all of California with a foot of water, and its 40 trillion gallons of water could supply every human on the planet with a shower a day from January through August. Its water clarity is rivaled only by Crater Lake in Oregon and Lake Baikal in Siberia, and you can clearly see a dinner plate sitting 75 feet beneath the surface. Its greatest depth is 1,645 feet, and Tahoe drops 1,400 feet straight down

from the shoreline at Rubicon Point (in California). The great depth and volume of water and its constant movement from lake bottom to top pre-clude Tahoe from ever freezing.

Tahoe's watershed encompasses 520 square miles, including more than sixty inlets from trib-utaries, and a single outlet, the Truckee River. The river drains the lake at Tahoe City, where a dam regulates the water flow. The top six feet of the lake is reservoir, which supplies water for the Reno-Sparks metropolitan area, Fallon agri-cultural irrigation, and Pyramid Lake fisheries. The river flows north through Truckee, California, then cuts east through Reno, then finally empties into Pyramid Lake at Nixon, nearly 100 miles northeast.

The lake's denizens consist mainly of big mackinaw trout; the largest mackinaw caught in recent memory was in 1974 and weighed in at 37.5 pounds. Kokanee trout (a variety of land-locked sockeye salmon) are smaller, both in numbers and size. And there's some talk of try-ing to reestablish the great Lahontan cutthroat trout in Tahoe and its spawning areas.

Of the lake's 72 miles of shoreline, 29 are in Nevada; of its 122,200 acres of surface area, 31,700 are in Nevada. The vast majority of recre-ational opportunities—beaches and picnic areas, marinas and launching ramps, golf courses and stables, camping and skiing—are in California. The casinos, of course, are only in Nevada.

Geology

The lake lies in a huge bowl, almost completely surrounded by the granite Sierra Nevada (on the west) and the granite Carson Range (on the east). During the Oligocene (about 25 mil-lion years ago), the immense Sierra were up-lifted: tilt, faults, and erosion caused massive slippage along the new slopes, sinking the land and creating the Tahoe Basin. Five million years ago, volcanic activity at the north end sealed the basin. Rainwater and snowmelt filled it.

During the Wisconsin Ice Age 10,000 years ago, the vast Lake Valley Glacier marched into the area, extending feeder ice rivers into the

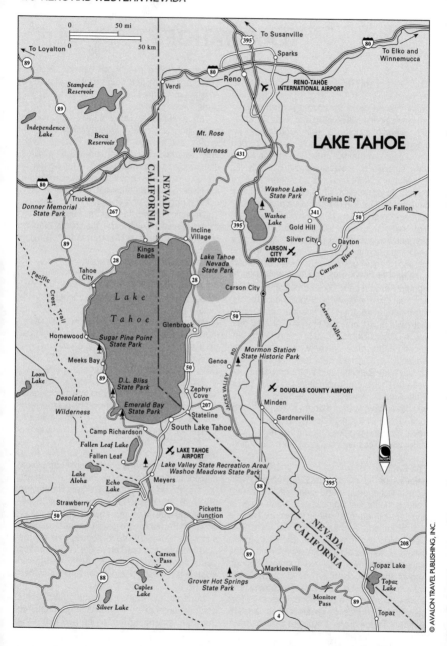

© AVALON TRAVEL PUBLISHING, INC.

TAHOE RIM TRAIL

The Tahoe Rim Trail is a magnificent 150-mile trail encircling Lake Tahoe. Following the ridges and mountaintops that circle the lake, the trail winds through national forest, state park and wilderness lands, passing through a variety of vegetation zones and providing spectacular views. The trail passes through thick conifer forests and wildflower-filled meadows, and skirts the shores of pristine alpine lakes. The trail offers something for everyone, with stretches ranging from easy to difficult, a number of loop trails, and an average grade of 10%. Hiking, horseback riding and skiing are allowed on all parts of the trail; mountain biking is allowed on specified portions.

The idea of a trail circling Lake Tahoe was dreamed up in the early 1980s by the Forest Service Recreation Officer at Tahoe, and the non-profit Tahoe Rim Trail Association (TRTA) was organized in 1981. The trail was designed to link up with 50 miles of the Pacific Crest Trail that travels along the west side of the Tahoe wilderness. Work on the trail, performed entirely by volunteers, began in 1983, and a year later, the TRTA had attracted 50 members. By 1988, 1,500 members had helped clear 30 miles of the trail, working strictly between May 1 and October 15. At the end of summer 2000, all but 4.5 miles of the trail were completed, with the last section scheduled to be completed by September 2001. The TRTA has scheduled a trail-completion celebration for September 22, 2001, and they are looking for a new slogan to replace their "Done in 2001," which will become outdated once the trail is completed.

You can easily do a part of the trail by beginning at any of 10 trailheads, or if you are ambitious you can do the whole circle and become a member of the "150 Mile Club." Camping is permitted along most of the trail, allowing extended trips into the solitude of backcountry and wilderness regions; the numerous trailheads give day users abundant opportunities to do smaller portions of the trail and explore the beauty of the mountains. On the Nevada side, trailheads include the Spooner Summit trailhead (Hwy 50), the Kingsbury trailhead (two miles north of Hwy 207) and the Ophir Creek and Mt Rose trailheads (Hwy 431). California-side trailheads include the Brockway trailhead (Hwy 267), the Tahoe City trailhead (1/8 mile north of Hwy 89), the Barker Pass trailhead (Blackwood Canyon Rd, four miles south of Tahoe City), and, on the south side of the lake, the Big Meadow trailhead (Hwy 89), and the Echo Lakes and Echo Summit trailheads (Hwy 50).

Trail maps are posted at the trailheads, but users are urged to carry maps with them on the trail. A detailed map is available at the Tahoe Rim Trail Association's office in Stateline for $10; it can also be mail-ordered, or ordered over their website.

There's lots of opportunity for involvement with the Tahoe Rim Trail Association. You can join a trail construction or maintenance party, buy a TRT T-shirt, volunteer in a variety of capacities, or "Adopt a Mile," among other possibilities. Contact: Tahoe Rim Trail Association, 297 Kingsbury Grade, Suite C, P.O. Box 4647, Stateline, NV 89449, 775/588-0686, fax 775/588-8737, tahoerimtrail@aol.com, www.tahoerimtrail.org.

---

lake, including one that carved out Emerald Bay. Eventually the glacier retreated, the ice melted, and the lake level rose hundreds of feet, forcing an outlet through the porous volcanic seal at the northwest end—now the Truckee River.

HISTORY

There Goes the Neighborhood

Washo Indians gathered on the northern shoreline each spring for at least 5,000 years to harvest the teeming trout, partake in leisurely water sports, and ceremoniously thank the spirits for their benevolence and abundance. The Washo spoke a Hokan dialect, separating them ethnologically from their Paiute neighbors, members of the Uto-Aztecan linguistic group. The Washo name for the lake was Da Ow A Ga, meaning "Edge of the Lake"; it is generally considered the forerunner of the name Tahoe. Another possibility for its etymology, however, is the Spanish word *tajo,* meaning "sheer cliffs." At contact, there were an estimated 3,100 Washo people. In *Rabbit Boss,* Thomas Sanchez's sprawling novel about this tribe, two Washo men first laid eyes on *them* (whites) by witnessing an episode of Donner Party cannibalism. Intense.

Pyramid Lake Paiute drew a map for John C. Frémont in 1844; he followed the Truckee River and spied the lake, which he named Bonpland,

SAM CLEMENS VISITS TAHOE

BOB RACE

Sam Clemens arrived in Carson City on the Overland Stage in July 1861 with his brother Orion, who had been appointed Secretary to James Nye, governor of the new Nevada Territory. Sam, in his self-appointed position as secretary to the Secretary, quickly found that he "had nothing to do and no salary." Heeding the call of the wild, he and a friend therefore set off on the Bigler Toll Road up to Lake Tahoe.

At this time, from their encampment, they could hear "a sawmill and some workmen" at Glenbrook, "but there were not fifteen other human beings throughout the wide circumference of the lake." They posted notice of their timber ranch and felled a few trees to inaugurate it.

They found a small skiff and rowed it upon the water—"not merely transparent, but dazzlingly, brilliantly so." They fished, read, smoked, hiked, and heard no sounds "but those that were made by the wind and the waves, the sighing of the pines, and now and then the far-off thunder of an avalanche. The view was always fascinating: "the eye never tired of gazing, night or day, calm or storm; it suffered but one grief, and that was that it could not look always, but must close sometimes in sleep."

Still, they never required any paregoric to effect such a sleep. For there was "no end of wholesome medicine" in the life they led for those few idyllic weeks on the shores of Lake Tahoe. "Three months would restore an Egyptian mummy to his pristine vigor and give him an appetite like an alligator," Clemens enthused in *Roughing It*. He did, however, qualify his statement, lest any readers infer any exaggeration, with "I do not mean the oldest and driest mummies, of course, but the fresher ones."

after a famous French explorer-scientist. Both California and Nevada approved the name Bigler, after the third California governor, but the head federal cartographer vetoed the choice simply by leaving it off the official map. He then consulted an expert in the Washo tongue, who suggested Tahoe.

By this time, word of the area's incomparable beauty had been carried far and wide by the traffic between the Comstock and the California coast. The lake's first resort and the insatiable logging and fishing industries were established at Glenbrook in the mid-1860s. By 1870, only 500 Washo could be counted. By the 1890s, the lake was nearly fished out, and 50,000 acres of forest had been cut (out of the total 51,000): half a million cords, 750 million board feet. Most of this lumber was manhandled into the lake,

pulled by steamer to Glenbrook or Incline, railroaded to Spooner Summit, then shot down flumes to mills at Washoe Valley and Carson City. Delivered to Virginia City first by freighters and then by the V&T Railroad, the forests of Tahoe were killed, then buried in the monumental maze of square-set tunnels far below Mt. Davidson.

Recent Developments

Meanwhile, luxury hotels began opening to cater to the kings and queens of the Comstock. A narrow-gauge short line reached Tahoe City from the transcontinental stop at Truckee in 1900, and the first automobile arrived in 1905. Paved roads reached the lake in the 1930s, transforming this playground of the rich into one for everybody.

Still, the Tahoe Basin managed to maintain a

kind of pristine second-growth remoteness well into the 1950s, with a total year-round population of under 3,000. But then Tahoe's development began in earnest with several water, power, and subdivision schemes. Small reasonably priced hotels attracted more and more visitors and private ownership of more and more shoreline encouraged an influx of residents. Harvey Gross and Bill Harrah built casinos at South Shore, land values skyrocketed, and the 1960 Winter Olympics at Squaw Valley completed Lake Tahoe's rise to a world-class year-round vacation and recreation destination. After the Olympics, development began to spiral out of control.

Finally, in 1965, the League to Save Lake Tahoe was formed, which spurred the creation of the joint Nevada-California Tahoe Regional Planning Authority in 1969. The planners now have a very tight rein on growth, enforcing what could be the strictest development restrictions in the United States. The TRPA set ecological "thresholds" to hold the line on the deterioration of the environment—water and air pollution, traffic congestion, forest management, and development. A complete moratorium on building permits was in force in the mid-'80s; since then only a small amount of construction has been allowed.

Needless to say, this has created a large-scale controversy. Developers and people who own "unbuildable" lots harbor resentments, often litigious, against the TRPA. Environmentalists, on the other hand, are rabid about the thresholds, to the point where some are calling for the creation of a Sierra Nevada National Park. Unlike most such battles, so far the hard-line control-growthers hold the stronger cards.

The Drought

Lake Tahoe is the main reservoir for the entire Truckee River water system: Reno-Sparks municipal water, Sierra Pacific hydro-electric water, California and Nevada Fish and Game water, U.S. Fish and Wildlife water, Pyramid Lake Paiute fisheries water, and (some) Truckee-Carson Irrigation District water. The dam at Tahoe City (6,229 feet) regulates the six feet of reservoir water above the lake's natural rim (6,223 feet). The drought, in its ninth and last year in 1995 (with a one-year respite in '93)

greatly diminished the winter snowpack in the Tahoe Basin, which supplies more than 60% of Lake Tahoe's water. The lake level dropped below its natural rim in July 1991, and except for a brief trickle in spring 1993 and 1995, not a drop of H_2O flowed into the Truckee River. Downstream storage (Donner Lake and Stampede, Boca, Prosser, and Independence reservoirs) fell to precipitously low levels in the summer. Finally, the lake dropped to its lowest level (6,220 feet) in recorded history.

But a couple of wet winters (1996–97) replenished the rez, and in fact filled it a little too full. In January 1997, lake water started pouring over the dam, out of control. The Truckee River flooded over its banks for most of its 100-mile length, submerging downtown Reno under up to five feet of water in some places and causing hundreds of millions in damage. But that's life in the desert.

Scientists at Reno's Desert Research Institute have studied tree stumps found in 25 feet of water at Baldwin Beach. Their rings indicate that they lived 200 or so years, and carbon-dating puts them living 5,000–6,300 years ago. This could mean that large old trees once grew along the shores of a lake much more depleted by drought than today. Tree rings and pack rat middens (crystallized balls of vegetation the rats assemble for nests using urine as an adhesive) support a theory that the eastern Sierra have sustained a number of 30- to 40-year droughts (the latest believed during the 15th and 16th centuries). The researchers postulate that since instruments began to keep records within the last 100 years, our climatic cycle could be much wetter than the norm. Meaning that the nine-year drought might only be the beginning and the heavy winters of 1996 and 1997 were brief respites.

"The Most Beautiful Drive in America"

Shoreline roads go all the way around Lake Tahoe. The full 72-mile circle can be driven in about 2.5 hours, but you could easily spend a very enjoyable day doing the drive, stopping off at many beautiful places all along the way. A free pamphlet called *The Most Beautiful Drive in America* outlines the many attractions of the drive; it is available at all area chambers of commerce and visitor centers.

STATELINE/SOUTH LAKE TAHOE

South Lake Tahoe could be the quintessential California-Nevada bordertown, a representation not only of the strange glue that binds the two together, but also of the discrete elements that differentiate each from the other. The California side of town is an elephantine freeway exit ramp, taffy-pulled into an elongated frontage road. Literally hundreds of low-rise motels, fast fooderies, service stations, shopping centers, and apartment, condo, and professional complexes all jut up like warts from one continuous Brobdingnagian asphalt parking lot, cars crawling all over it like so many Lilliputians. On the Nevada side of the border are the half dozen or so pleasure palaces, as contained and vertical as the California side is widespread and horizontal. These temples of temptation engorge themselves with the offerings and sacrifices of the vast hedonistic polyglot, who are then disgorged, most of them empty-handed, to sweep back across the border, regroup, and return to pay homage another day. Beyond the high-rises north along Nevada's east shore is the wilderness, naturally—the cathedrals are all that stand between the masses and the great unknown.

Harvey's

Harvey Gross's Wagon Wheel was the first bona fide casino at South Lake. Gross was a meat wholesaler in Sacramento who supplied the beef to the restaurants and resorts at the lake in the 1940s. Gambling on growth, he and his wife Llewellyn bought some property near the California state line across from two existing slot joints. They started in a one-room log-cabin saloon with six slot machines, three blackjack tables, and a six-stool snack bar, and quickly added a dozen more slots and a gas pump out front—the only one at the time on the old Lincoln Highway (US 50) between Placerville and Carson City.

Harvey's grew steadily, quietly, for 30 years. Then, in August 1980, a bomb placed on the property in an extortion attempt exploded, causing extensive damage but no loss of life. (The whole fascinating story of the bomb is recounted in *Nevada—True Tales From the Neon Wilderness* by Jim Sloan; see "Booklist"). Harvey Gross died in 1983, and the hotel was owned solely by his family until early 1994, when Harvey's went public. Also in 1994 Harvey's celebrated its 50th anniversary on July 18 by burying a time capsule containing Harvey's, Lake Tahoe, and Nevada memorabilia, along with 1990s products such as a cellular phone, and a Tahoe water sample and analysis. The capsule will be reopened in the year 2044.

Today, Harvey's is a 740-room hotel, largest on the lake; the $87 million Lake Tower was completed in 1992. The casino is also monumental at 88,000 square feet; a wooden "path" helps you to navigate the casino easily. On the back wall of the poker room is the world's largest **hand-tooled leather mural,** commissioned by Harvey Gross in 1946. It re-creates a scene from Virginia City at the height of the Comstock, taking some liberties with the characters and setting. Read the description of the damage it sustained during, and the restoration it received after, the bombing incident.

Unusual for a Nevada hotel-casino, the front desk is on a level lower than the casino, under a two-story chandelier, so you don't have to lug your suitcases by the blackjack pit. Harvey's has nine restaurants, plentiful bars and lounges, and a tunnel under US 50 that connects with Harrah's.

Harrah's

Harrah's is one of the country's top-10 hotel-resorts, earning five stars from Mobil and five diamonds from AAA (until 1991, when it dropped to four diamonds for the first time since AAA began its ratings in 1977). This is luxury pure and simple: each room has two full bathrooms, with a phone and TV in each, along with a mini-bar and great mountain or lake views from the picture windows. The 65,000-square-foot casino has 1,800 slots and 170 table games; each pit area has a different theme, such as the Sports Casino and the Classic Rock Casino (where the tables are named after rock stars and the big sound system plays, you guessed it, classic rock). The health club has an indoor pool, hot tubs, and complete exercise facility. The retail shops were remodeled in 1993 and are now the Galleria, and the lounge was remodeled in 1994. The kids' arcade was tripled in size and is now a "family fun center." Finally, in a rare microcosm of this schizophrenic town, the hotel-casino is in Nevada, the parking lot in California.

Tahoe Horizon

This hotel-casino opened in 1965 as the Sahara, built by Del Webb, who at the time owned the Sahara and Mint hotels in Las Vegas. Webb, a Phoenix contractor, first arrived in Las Vegas in 1946 to build Bugsy Siegel's fabulous Flamingo. In 1951, he was hired to build the Sahara in return for 20 points in the hotel. By the time Webb opened the Sahara Tahoe, he was one of the largest hotel-casino operators in the state. The name was subsequently changed to the High Sierra. Gradually, the Del Webb Corp., still based in Phoenix, divested itself of its Nevada holdings; when it sold the High Sierra to a Kentucky real-estate investor, William Yung, for $19 million cash in early 1990, the sale ended a highly successful 44-year run.

Yung's Wimar Tahoe Corp. changed the name to Tahoe Horizon and spent $12 million on remodeling. It shows in the marble, brass, and glass. The Horizon has the brightest and airiest casino on the lake.

Caesars Tahoe

Like Caesars Las Vegas, Caesars Tahoe is a fine carpet club. This hotel is the newest in Stateline (opened in 1980) and has 440 rooms; the casino is only vaguely reminiscent of Caesars Las Vegas, with Corinthian columns, an 18-foot-tall statue of Augustus Caesar that greets you as you enter, and whatnot. The indoor pool is something to see: rock borders, a big rock waterfall with a tunnel you can swim through, and poolside dining at the Primavera Italian restaurant. The 13th Planet Hollywood restaurant opened here in July 1994, with appearances by Arnold Schwarzenegger, Bruce Willis, and Luke Perry; it was the first Planet Hollywood to open in a casino. Since then, Planet Hollywoods have opened in the Forum Shops at Caesars Las Vegas in July and Harrah's Reno in September 1994. Caesars also has four other restaurants and a buffet.

Bill's

This casino (owned by Harrah's and named after Bill Harrah) is low-roller heaven for Tahoe. You can't exactly call it a sawdust joint, but you can call it a *popcorn* joint—help yourself to free popcorn toward the rear of the casino. It has a McDonald's, a gang of old mechanical slots (one of Harrah's trademarks); it also has a gaggle of $3 blackjack tables, even on the weekends (also one roulette and one crap table).

Round Hill Pines Beach & Marina

The Round Hill Pines Marina is on a half-mile-long sandy beach two miles north of the casinos and half a mile north of the Round Hill Shopping Center. Facilities include a large deck area, heated swimming pool, tennis court, volleyball courts, horseshoe pits, barbecues, a deli and bar. Activities include water skiing, fishing, parasailing, and private lake tours. H2O Sports, 775/4155 or 775/588-3055, rents Sea-Doos, kayaks, Sea Cycles and paddle boats. Guided two-hour Sea Doo Excursions to Emerald Bay depart in the morning. Also here are the Don Borges Water Ski School, 530/541-1351, and Mile High Fishing Charters, 775/588-4155 or 530/541-5312.

Outdoor Activities

The *Tahoe Star,* a 54-foot luxury yacht operated by Harrah's, offers cruises on the lake including an Emerald Bay Cruise ($18, children $9), a Historic East Shore Cruise ($18, children $9), and a

---

DON'T DROWN IN LAKE TAHOE

Every year, an average of three people drown in Lake Tahoe, and another ten or so don't drown only because they get rescued. Though it looks tame and inviting, Tahoe is cold and clear and has strong currents, a potentially deadly combination. The average surface water temperature is no more than 60 degrees; near the shoreline it warms up to 68 degrees—still cold. Numbness is an immediate danger and hypothermia can set in after 20 minutes in 60-degree water. The clarity of the lake renders distance and depth deceptive, which can get you into trouble fast. And strong currents can result from heavy runoff from snowpack-fed creeks. People are swept out from the shore—and they don't last long in the cold water.

In addition, Tahoe doesn't give up its dead. The lake is so cold that it prevents gases from forming that would raise the body to the surface. Take common-sense precautions about going into Lake Tahoe if you want to come out again.

Sunset Cocktail Cruise to Emerald Bay ($26, or $18 excluding cocktails; no children). Phone 775/586-6505 or 800/729-4362 for reservations.

You can fly a hot-air balloon right over Lake Tahoe with **Lake Tahoe Balloons,** 530/544-1221, 800/872-9294, or **Balloons Over Lake Tahoe,** 530/533-7008.

The Shore Line Bike Shop, 259 Kingsbury Grade, 775/588-8777, rents mountain bikes, mountain boards, inline skates and off-road and in-line skateboards in summer, skis and snowboards in winter. Electric touring bikes can be rented from Leif and Jana's, based at the Horizon Casino, 530/573-5524.

Sierra Nevada Adventures, 888/831-4591, offers a variety of mountain bike tours including the Flume Trail, the North Flume to Diamond Peak, the Tahoe Rim Trail, the Tyrolean Downhill and the Northstar at Tahoe Mountain Bike Park; shuttle services to nearby mountain bike trailheads are available for groups not requesting guide services. The same company also offers morning and sunset kayak tours at Sand Harbor.

Sleigh rides, hayrides and carriage rides are offered by the Borges Family, departing from near the casinos; 775/588-2953 or 800/726-RIDE.

Several fishing guides are available around the lake, including Tahoe Sportfishing, 775/586-9338 or 530/541-5448, O'Malley's Fishing Charters, 775/588-4102, and Mile High Fishing Charters, 775/588-4155 or 530/541-5312.

Stateline Accommodations

Caesars Tahoe, 55 Hwy. 50, 775/588-3515 or 800/648-3353, has 440 rooms ranging from $89 to $225 a night.

Harrah's Tahoe Hotel Casino, Hwy. 50, 775/588-6611 or 800/HARRAHS, has 532 rooms that range from $179 to $269 a night.

Harvey's Resort Hotel & Casino, Hwy. 50 and Stateline Ave, 775/588-2411 or 800/HARVEYS, has 740 rooms that range from $119–209 weekdays, $169–299 weekends.

Horizon Casino Resort, Hwy. 50, 775/588-6211 or 800/322-7723, has 539 rooms that range from $69 to $200 a night.

And the **Lakeside Inn & Casino,** Hwy. 50 at Kingsbury Grade, 775/588-7777 or 800/624-7980, has 124 low-rise motel rooms that range from $59 to $99 a night.

The **Pine Cone Resort,** in Nevada right on the highway about five miles from the state line, just north of Nevada Beach, 775/588-6561, has condo-like rooms, with kitchenettes and fireplaces, for $85–95 in summer, $75–85 off-season. The road's a bit noisy in the daytime but quiets down in the evening.

For motels and other information on the California side, see "Information," below.

Stateline Food

Harvey's: Downstairs on the tunnel level at Harvey's is El Vaquero Mexican restaurant, open 5–10 P.M. daily. Upstairs in the casino, the Sage Room steakhouse opens nightly at 6 P.M., just as it has for nearly 50 years. Harvey's also has a Classic Burgers with half-pounders for $6 and a steak sandwich for $7; the curly fries are good. The Pizzeria serves pizza such as Hawaiian, Greek Goddess, garlic chicken, and fajita, as well as delicious minestrone, and Caesar salad. Harvey's also has a buffet, coffee shop, and snack bar. Or try the Seafood Grotto, serving lunch and dinner.

The top of the lot is the four-diamond Llewellyn's, named after Harvey Gross's wife. This reasonably priced gourmet room on the 19th floor has the best lake views of all the restaurants at Stateline, with two-window alcoves and three levels of tables. If you're in the mood for the view but not an elaborate meal, relax in the Peak Lounge and order up an appetizer, salad, or bowl of soup. Llewellyn's also hosts a Sunday champagne brunch.

Harrah's: There's an excellent deli, the North Beach, in the southwest corner of the sprawling casino. Cafe Andreotti's, with Italian cuisine, is open Wed.–Sun. 5:30–10 P.M. Friday's Station steakhouse on the 18th floor with a lake and mountain view opens daily at 5:30 P.M. On the other side of the top floor is the Forest Buffet, with concrete tree trunks and brass-leaf branches, and a gorgeous panorama to the south. Harrah's answer to Llewellyn's at Harvey's is the Summit on the 16th floor, open Wed–Mon. at 5:30 P.M., a beautifully appointed room with balcony dining, mountain views, and everything a la carte.

Bill's Roadhouse Cafe has some of the least expensive food at a casino at Stateline. This place is casual, cramped, and crowded on weekends.

Caesars: This place has the Broiler Room steakhouse, Primavera Italian restaurant poolside, the Empress Court for Chinese, a 24-hour coffee shop, and the Roman Feast buffet serving breakfast, lunch, dinner and a Sunday champagne brunch.

Nero's at Caesars is Stateline's hot spot, opening at 8 P.M. with live music nightly. By the way, according to Mario Puzo in *Inside Las Vegas,* Emperor Nero was not fiddling while Rome was burning. He was shooting dice and losing.

Information

The **Tahoe-Douglas Chamber of Commerce Visitor Center** is directly across the parking lot from the Shell station on the ground floor at the Round Hill Shopping Center about a mile north of Stateline, 195 Highway 50, P.O. Box 7139, Stateline at Lake Tahoe, NV 89449, 775/588-4591, info@tahoechamber.org, www.tahoe chamber.org. This is an attractive and highly useful little place, with fine exhibits, pretty photographs and posters, tons of information and brochures on everything from casinos to nature trails to ski packages to weddings, coupon booklets, and a reservation service; it also sells T-shirts, books, and video postcards. Open Mon.–Fri. 9 A.M.–6 P.M., Sat.–Sun. 9 A.M.–5 P.M.

The California strip of US 50 west of the border is lined with motels; for more information, contact the **Lake Tahoe Visitors Authority,** 1515 Ski Run Blvd., South Lake Tahoe, CA 96150, 530/544-5050, www.virtualtahoe.com; open Mon.–Fri. 9 A.M.–5 P.M. To make reservations or request free materials, call toll-free at 800/AT-TAHOE. Its "Lake Tahoe Travel Planner" has a good amount of useful information, including a lodging guide.

Also on the California side is the **South Lake Tahoe Chamber of Commerce,** 3066 Lake Tahoe Blvd., South Lake Tahoe, CA 96150, 530/541-5255, sltcc@sierra.net, www.tahoeinfo .com, with heaps of useful brochures, magazines, etc. It's open Mon.–Sat., 8:30 A.M.–5 P.M.

Another excellent source of information about the California side of the lake is Kim Weir's *Northern California Handbook.*

EAST SHORE

Nevada Beach

This large U.S. Forest Service beach, day-use area, and campground, only two miles north on

US 50 from Stateline (and take a left at Elk Point), is one of the most popular beaches along the lake. Open May 1 through mid-October, its parking lots are spread well apart, which spreads out the people, too. There's a $5 per vehicle entrance fee for day use.

Nevada Beach Campground is one of the most popular beaches and campgrounds on Lake Tahoe; this place fills up fast. Make reservations as far in advance as possible (up to 240 days); if you don't have a reservation, you can show up at 9 A.M. to see if someone left early. Checkout time is officially 2 P.M., but many campers spend a few extra hours on the beach and then leave. A good method is to pay the $5 for the day, hang out on the beach, then every so often take a walk through the campground to see what's vacant (see the campground host to pay for first-come first-served sites). The camping is under the trees, shared equally by tenters and RVers. The beach is a two-minute walk. There are 54 campsites for tents or self-contained motor homes up to 45 feet. Piped drinking water, flush toilets, picnic tables, grills, and fire pits are provided. There is a campground host. The maximum stay is 10 days. Reservations are recommended (877/444-6777); for more info call the park office at 775/588-5562. The fee is $18–20 per campsite. It's open May 1 through mid-October.

A pretty walk or aerobic run from here is north up Elks Ave. to Elk Point, a fairly exclusive residential neighborhood overlooking Zephyr Cove.

Round Hill Beach Resort

Another little ways up the round on the left is a Forest Service sign for this marina; you twist and turn down to the beach, where it's $6 to park (check in at the snack bar). There's a small beach area and you can rent Sea-Doos. Sit on the deck or stroll out the dock; this is mostly a boat zone.

Zephyr Cove

This is an action-packed small marina a few miles north of Nevada Beach on US 50; its long pier is home base for the MS *Dixie II* paddlewheeler and *Woodwind II* sailing vessel. You can also arrange sailing and fishing charters, sailboarding, jet-skiing, parasailing, horseback riding, and marrying. There's also a bar and grill, resort, and RV park and campground.

The original *Dixie* started her illustrious career on the Mississippi in 1927 and was brought to Tahoe in 1947 to become a floating casino. Legal squabbles over ownership prevented the *Dixie* from fulfilling that mission, and she sank under mysterious circumstances in shallow water off Cave Rock in 1949. The boat was raised in 1952, but didn't start tour cruises until 1972. The *Dixie I* made an estimated 17,000 trips on the lake in 22 years, but repairs necessary to pass the 20-year Coast Guard inspection in 1993 would have cost nearly $2.5 million. Instead, the owners decided to dry dock *Dixie I* and build *Dixie II* from scratch.

The *Dixie II* at 151 feet long is 37 feet longer than its predecessor, with a carrying capacity of 550 people (compared to the *Dixie I's* 360). It cost $4 million to build, at a shipyard in LaCrosse, Wisconsin, and was shipped to Tahoe in four pieces in spring 1994. The main deck has a dining area for 200 and the galley; the upper deck is also enclosed for dancing and cocktails (and the captain's cabin). The "hurricane deck" is open-air, and hosts the snack bar and pilot house. A variety of cruises depart from the cove year-round, starting at $20 for the two-hour Emerald Bay trip, up to $45 for the 3.5-hour dinner-dance excursion. Call 775/588-3508 for info and reservations.

The 55-foot *Woodwind II* catamaran sails from Zephyr Cove with up to 50 passengers, several times daily, from March or April through October, weather permitting. Eastern Shoreline and Happy Hour cruises cost $22 adults, $20 seniors, $10 ages 3–12; the Sunset Champagne Cruise costs $28. Phone 775/588-3000 or toll-free 888/867-6394 for reservations and current info. The same company also operates a 41-foot, 30-passenger trimaran, the *Woodwind I*, departing from Camp Richardson on the south side of the lake and cruising to Emerald Bay.

Zephyr Cove Resort Marina, 775/588-3833, rents open bow runabouts, ski boats, cruisers, deck boats, pedal boats, canoes, kayaks, electric Sunkats, water skis, wetsuits and more. Reservations are a good idea.

Hop a horse at **Zephyr Cove Stables,** 775/588-5664: one-hour ride $25, two-hour $45, rides plus meals $35–40.

A snack shop offers burgers, and a bar and

grill restaurant overlooks the pier. A free shuttle runs back and forth to the casino area. Finally, after an exciting day on the water with your honey, why not get married at Lakeside Chapel, 775/588-5366?

In winter, the **Zephyr Cove Snowmobile Center,** 775/588-3833, is the largest snowmobile touring center in the USA, with over 100 Ski-Doo Touring E snowmobiles, including single ($89) and double ($119) rider machines. Tours depart five times daily.

Then spend the night in one of Zephyr Cove Resort's rooms, 778/588-6644. The resort was built in the early 1900s and much of the original architecture and charm remain. A variety of accommodations includes six rooms in the lodge that sleep from two to six; there are also bungalows, cabins, cottages, studios, and chalets. Rates start at $60 and ascend to $260.

You can also camp or park an RV across the highway from the lodge at **Zephyr Cove RV Park,** 775/588-6644, a rustic campground under the pine trees. There are 105 spaces for motor homes, all with full hookups; 7 are pull-throughs. There are also 75 tent sites. Restrooms have flush toilets and hot showers; public phone, sewage disposal, and laundry are available at the park.

Reservations are recommended for the summer, especially on weekends. The fee is $16 for tent sites ($100 for the week), $25 for RV sites ($150 per week). If you need a shower you can grab one for $3.

Note: Discount coupons for Zephyr Cove's many attractions are ubiquitous. Get $5 off horseback rides and motorboat rentals, $4 off the *Dixie* cruises and **Whirlwind** rides, $4 off T-shirts, and 2-for-1 soft drinks or beer at the Sunset Bar and Grill.

Lake Tahoe-Nevada State Park

Continue north on US 50 four miles to **Cave Rock,** one of Tahoe's legendary landmarks. One tunnel through it dates from the early 1900s, another dates back to prehistory, fashioned by the Great Spirit with a spear. This is one of only three tunnels (that you can drive through) in the whole state; the others are on I-80 east of Carlin and the new airport access in Las Vegas. Just before you reach the tunnel there's a turnoff for a parking lot, lakefront picnic area, and a boat launch, with Cave Rock towering overhead. Day use fees are charged at Cave Rock beach: $5 per vehicle, or $1 for bike-ins and walk-ins.

In another four miles is the Glenbrook historical marker. Glenbrook was the site of the first non-Washo settlements at Lake Tahoe, dating from 1860. Friday's Station opened that year a few miles above Glenbrook along the Placerville Road to Genoa over Kingsbury Grade. A year later, A.W. Pray established a sawmill at Glenbrook, and in 1862, the Lake Bigler Toll Road connected Friday's Station to Carson City by way of King's Canyon, the route US 50 follows today. Finally, in 1863 Tahoe's first hotel was constructed at Glenbrook. Glenbrook is a small residential area with a country club.

Just beyond is the intersection of US 50 and NV 28. A right onto US 50 crests Spooner Summit and heads down to Carson City. Go left to continue north up the east shore of the lake.

Almost immediately, you enter Lake Tahoe-Nevada State Park. It preserves three miles of shoreline, plus a 10-mile-long stretch of the wooded Carson Range, and adjoins Toiyabe National Forest. There's a lot of wilderness to explore here, with elevations between 6,200 and 8,900 feet, on several high-country trails. Most flora is second growth, at most 120 years old: pine, fir, cedar, and aspen to 7,000 feet, red fir and lodgepole pine above. Countless birds and rodents live here. The black bear population is increasing hereabouts as well.

Turn right into Spooner Lake parking lot; $5 to

park, $2 to bike in, or $1 to walk in. Stroll down to the lake; an easy 2.3-mile nature trail circles the lake, taking about an hour; keep an eye out for birds and wildlife. A hundred feet to the left is a post that marks the five-mile trail through North Canyon to Marlette Lake, which still supplies water to Virginia City, just as it has for 120 years; the moderate 10-mile round-trip trail takes about 4–6 hours to traverse. Fishing is not allowed at Marlette Lake, due to hatchery operations. The trail continues 11 miles to the far trailhead at Hidden Beach; it has become part of the Tahoe Rim Trail. The Hidden Beach to Twin Lakes trail, a moderate five-mile round trip hike, takes around four hours.

Fishing at Spooner Lake is catch-and-release only; the lake is stocked with trout.

In summer, activities at Spooner Lake include hiking and mountain biking on the **Flume Trail.** This ride, an exciting singletrack 1600 feet above Lake Tahoe, is one of the most scenic rides anywhere, providing spectacular views of Lake Tahoe; the trail follows the path of an historic flume line that once provided water to the silver mines of Virginia City. Most mountain bike parties begin at Spooner Lake; take North Canyon Rd to Marlette Lake dam (six miles, 800 foot gain) and follow the historic flume line 4.4 miles to Tunnel Creek Rd. From there you can return to Spooner Lake, a 21-mile round trip, 3–5 hours; descend 1600 feet (2.5 miles) to Highway 28, a 13-mile one-way trip, 3–4 hours; take a backcountry loop back to Spooner Lake (24 miles

Memorial Point

round trip, 4–6 hours; or a different backcountry loop back to Spooner Lake via the Tahoe Rim Trail, 22 miles, 2000 foot gain. Nevada's Division of State Parks published a pamphlet with a basic map and information about these trails, called *Lake Tahoe Nevada State Park Backcountry;* look for it at the state park office, 775/831-0494 or at the Incline Village/Crystal Bay Visitors and Convention Bureau.

You can bring your own bike and use the Flume Trail Shuttle Service ($10 for one person, $15 for two) to bring you back up to Spooner Lake, or rent a bike for $37.50, from the Spooner Lake Outdoor Company, 775/749-5349. The same company also offers guided Flume ride trips including mountain bike rental and shuttle service back from Incline Village, every day June through August, weekends September and October. Sierra Nevada Adventures, 888/831-4591, also offers Flume Trail mountain bike trips.

In winter, Spooner Lake has 101 km of groomed cross-country-skiing trails spread over 8,000 acres with skiing for beginners up to experts. The lodge is right off Hwy. 28, open daily 8:30 A.M.–5 P.M. Trail fees range from free (under 7 or over 70) to $15, and ski rentals from $4 to $15. Lessons are also available. Call 775/887-8844 for conditions or 775/749-5349 for more info.

Spooner Lake does not have facilities for camping, but **Spooner Lake Cabins**, 775/749-5349 or 888/858-8844, spoonerlake@pyramid .net, www.spoonerlake.com, offers self-contained cabins with fully-equipped kitchens for $79–85 in summer and fall, $130–175 in winter.

Eight miles north of this area is **Sand Harbor,** the main beach in the park. An arm of land, crowded with pines and boulders, juts into the lake. On the south side lies a gorgeous crescent beach—long, sandy, and sunny. Because of the spit, and the prevailing winds and currents, the swells here are occasionally high enough to surf (foam boards are best; fresh water is not as buoyant as salt). The term often used to describe the water temperature is "bracing." Sand Harbor beach is a fine place to watch bathers try to ease into the lake—an inch a minute! The water reaches its highest temperature during the last two weeks of July: 68° on the surface. So you might as well just screw up some courage

and plunge—the water isn't getting any warmer, no matter how slowly you slice it. Morning and sunset kayak tours of Sand Harbor are offered by Sierra Nevada Adventures, 888/831-4591; single kayaks $45, doubles $75.

The north side of the spit is a different lake entirely: calm, clear, rugged with rocks, little beach. Known as Diver's Cove, it's a great spot for snorkeling and boulder hopping.

Sandy Point at the end of the spit has an excellent three-quarter-mile nature trail with interpretive displays in summer (left of the first parking lot). It takes an easy half-hour and is well worth the time for the close look at the lake ecology. Pick up free handouts at park headquarters near the entrance.

Sand Harbor has a wheelchair-accessible boardwalk, three large parking lots, bathrooms, group picnic facilities, lots of water fountains, and no concession stands. This is good for limiting litter, but bring everything with you, except bottles (prohibited). Get there early on weekends. It's open daily from 8 A.M. on, closing at 9 P.M. June to August, 7 P.M. May and September, 5 P.M. October to March. Entrance costs $6 per vehicle, $12 for boat launching, or $1 for walk-ins.

During the summer Sand Harbor is the site of a fine music and drama festival in an excellent venue with a new $2 million outdoor stage. Held every summer since 1978, the North Tahoe Fine Arts Council sponsors four days of music in mid-July and a **Shakespeare Festival** during the entire month of August. Call 800/74-SHOWS to order tickets and for current details; you can also buy tickets at the Incline Village Visitors Center.

Another mile and a half brings you to **Memorial Point overlook** and parking lot. From here, it's just under a mile to the state park's **north trailhead,** which is unmarked but obvious at a fire track between two posts. You can also park a quarter mile farther on the north side of the trailhead just beyond the park boundaries, but here you're competing with cars to Hidden Beach (see below) and from the south residential section of Incline Village. The trail starts climbing quickly up the granite slopes of the Carson Range. It's an hour to Tunnel Creek Station (one and a half miles), another hour (one mile) to Twin Lakes, and one more hour to Hobart Creek

Reservoir, where you loop back past Red House camping area to Tunnel Creek. Or walk across the park down to Spooner Lake, 16 miles, at least 10 hours. Two hike-in campgrounds, Marlette Peak and North Canyon, are available in the backcountry; each has around 10 campsites, all first come, first served; 775/831-0494 for info.

Hidden Beach is a half-mile-long stretch of prime Tahoe shoreline, where nude bathing and skinny-dipping are de rigueur. The U.S. Forest Service in 1992 bought 41 acres hereabouts for $7 million from The Trust for Public Land, which acquired the property from William Bliss. Since 1982, The Trust has bought up and protected nearly 11,000 acres of Tahoe real estate, at a cost of nearly $90 million. How to get to Secret Harbor is kind of a secret, but here's a hint: grab a parking space near other cars on the stretch between the north edge of the state park and the south edge of Incline Village, then bushwhack through the under- and overgrowth down to the lake.

INCLINE VILLAGE

Drive around town. Head up Ski Way to the town's own (public) ski area, or down Country Club Dr. past the Hyatt Regency. Go right on Lakeshore Dr. to check out one of the most valuable and scenic two-mile stretches of real estate in Nevada. Tool around the town's own golf courses, tennis clubs, beaches, and ski resorts, then stop in at the Chamber of Commerce for some super-slick local brochures. If you haven't quite gotten the idea that Incline Village is, well, prosperous, consider this: for a town of just under 8,000 year-round residents, there are more than two dozen real-estate agencies and *300 agents*, five banks, and four title companies. Incline Villagers make up three percent of the population of Washoe County and pay 10% of the total property tax the county collects.

This area has been inclining upward since 1874, when the Great Incline Tramway was completed on Incline Mountain (it started at Tramway Dr. at the far south end and oldest part of town, then passed through what's now the Ponderosa Ranch). This high-wire act rose 1,400 feet in elevation in only 4,000 feet of distance, for a straight-up grade of 35%. Two 12-foot wheels

powered by a 40-horsepower steam engine hoisted log-loaded flat cars up to the summit, where they were shot down a flume, milled in Washoe Valley, and freighted to Virginia City. The empty car going down counterbalanced the loaded one going up, using technology that was later employed in San Francisco's cable cars.

By the early 1890s, the Comstock was dead and every single tree within 10 miles of the incline had been cut down. The operation ceased; the post office at Incline Village closed in 1895. The north shore of Lake Tahoe remained remote through the 1950s, when the only life at Incline was a small trailer park (where Burnt Cedar Beach is today).

Then, in 1960, a real-estate investor from Oklahoma started up Crystal Bay Development Company, bought 9,000 north-shore acres for $25 million, and designed a development for 10,000 people. The original layout is still very much intact, with mansions on the lake, chalets on the mountainsides, and condos on the flats, all surrounded by dense forest, thanks to strict tree-cutting regulations. The commercial zones stretch in a thin line along NV 28 and down Southwood Blvd., designed to prevent congestion and preclude the establishment of a town center.

The town of Incline Village is still privately owned. The "local government" is known as the Incline Village General Improvement District (IVGID), which manages the beaches, ski resort, golf course, rec center, and forests. (The beaches are open only to local homeowners and their guests, who pay $5.) A movement has been gathering steam over the past half a decade to secede from Washoe County.

Incline is said to have the best weather on the lake: 300 days of sunshine a year,\ and the least accumulations of snow. Still, the population more than doubles in the balmy summer months. The Village has more outdoor-related stores-outfitters, ski and ski-repair, sportswear, camping, running shoes, cycle, fishing, and the like—than anywhere in Nevada, and the majority of residents and visitors are decked out in sweats, warm-ups, bike shorts, ski suits, sailing gear, and Vuarnets. Which all makes it a little interesting to think that Incline Village is still in Nevada and not California, and in Washoe County to boot. It's as far away from Gerlach as it could

TREES ARE STILL DYING FOR THE COMSTOCK

Only 100–125 years ago, 50,000 acres of virgin forest around Lake Tahoe, mostly sugar and Jeffrey pine, cedar, and some fir, were clear-cut, then milled, shipped, and buried forever in the shafts, drifts, stopes, and tunnels of undermined Mt. Davidson. The big Jeffreys were what the loggers were after, and they took them all, leaving only a few firs, which provided the seeds of today's forest. The second-growth fir has regenerated the lake's forests, but they are completely lacking in diversity, age, size, and therefore health. Furthermore, these young trees have overpopulated their habitat, and fir, unlike pine, is extremely drought intolerant, which has left most of the forest susceptible to attack by fir beetles. Since most of the lakeside is also thickly settled, fire, which thins the forests naturally, has been suppressed, and conservation policies strictly inhibit logging activities. Combine all these factors and you'll understand why so many of Tahoe's trees are dead or dying.

Though some tree die-off is beneficial to the health of the forest, the recent ravages are unprecedented. Tahoe National Forest officials estimate that between 25% and 33% of the trees in the 200,000-acre Tahoe Basin are dead or dying, and half the forest, roughly four million trees, is in grave danger from the drought and insects. Of course, the danger is only relative to people, houses, and to some extent wildlife. The natural cycle of a forest is growth, decay, fire, and regeneration. Indians found it not inconvenient to live with fire, simply moving their settlements to escape the danger. White settlers, however, built houses that couldn't easily be moved out of the way of the flames and therefore saw forest fires as destructive. For the last 100 years, the lack of fire has been the one element preventing the forest from recovering its health.

On the other hand, it's possible that the beetles are doing fire's work for it by thinning the forest. The insects also supply food for birds and other predators. Soon, predator populations will increase and eliminate the beetles. Then it'll rain. And a new forest will emerge. Nature could be providing a cycle to cope with the human suppression of fire.

Since late 1995, California and Nevada forestry crews have cleared 11,000 acres of fire hazards, but that's only 25% of the highly susceptible areas. Even so, the danger of wildfire mounts, since the dead trees that fall to the forest floor increase the danger. "Defensible space"—landscaping maintenance and clearing dead trees from privately owned land to protect houses—is the buzzword of the day, but homeowners have been slow to clean up, which threatens their own, and their neighbors', property.

possibly be—in every sense but one: the people are uniformly friendly and helpful, which makes Incline, same as Gerlach, a great place to visit.

The Ponderosa Ranch

"Bonanza" made its debut on NBC in September 1959, sponsored by Chevrolet. The show became the most popular and successful television program ever, eventually reaching 88 countries in 12 languages for a total of 400 million viewers—and this in the youth of the medium. It rendered Virginia City a household word, its effect on the ghost town's revival incalculable. It became as much a myth of its own as the myth of the American West itself: God's country, where a man is a man, his word is his bond, reason and justice prevail, and the good guys always wear white and win.

Some scenes for the show were filmed on location around Lake Tahoe, which gave Bill and Joyce Anderson the idea to buy ranch property near the north shore, call it the Ponderosa, reproduce the sets and props of the show, and charge admission. Immediately, the lines separating the global myth of the Cartwright family's ranch from the Ponderosa tourist attraction blurred into oblivion. In fact, even the writers and directors began believing it to be the mythical Ponderosa and filmed there frequently. The cast simply remained in costume to interact with the hordes passing through the gate. It was truly a unique episode in the history of television technology and its effect on consciousness. Not to mention one of the most brilliant marketing coups in Nevada history.

The Ponderosa Ranch celebrated its 30th anniversary in 1997. Though "Bonanza" has been off the air for a while, the place still packs 'em in between April and October, at $9.50 a whack, which could mean that "Bonanza" and the Cartwrights are now genetically imprinted for succeeding generations.

The Ponderosa Ranch, 775/831-0691, www.ponderosaranch.com, is open mid-April through October 31, daily 9:30 A.M.–6 P.M. (last tickets sold at 5 P.M.), $9.50 adults, $5.50 kids 5–11, hayride $2. From Memorial Day weekend through Labor Day, entertainment includes daily live Wild West shows, haywagon rides and guided horseback rides (stables 775/831-2154). Another attraction is an "authentic" Old West town, with lots of fun attractions.

Casinos

Of the five casinos on the north shore, one is in Incline, the other four in Crystal Bay. No other hotel-casinos in Nevada are so close to forest and lakeside. The state line on the north shore has a much less "religious" feel to it than the south shore, but a lot more "reverence." This tiny corner of the state would be California but for the casinos. Where else can you walk away from a crap table and into some manzanita?

Hyatt Regency, on Country Club Dr. and the corner of Lakeshore, has 20 more rooms (460) than Caesars Tahoe. But you'd never know it from the outside. The casino, along with its faux pine-tree trunks and blinking needles, has high-limit games and a big-money atmosphere (though a high-roller friend of mine claims the Hyatt really sweats the $100 player). It also competes with Caesars (Las Vegas) for the most beautiful people—gamblers and dealers—in Nevada, which is perfect as the only action in Incline.

The **Tahoe Biltmore** and **Crystal Bay Club** are right on NV 28 a block before the Placer County, California, line. Both are homey compared to the places at the other end of the lake. Between them they have two dozen blackjack tables, and a couple of crap and roulette.

Jim Kelley's **Nugget** is a slot shop, as classy in its way as the Hyatt is in its. This could be the state's only red-brick casino, which fits in nicely at the lake. It's definitely the state's only seasonal casino, closing its doors between mid-January and mid-May.

But the *pièce de résistance* of north shore is the **Cal-Neva.** The nine-story hotel building sits on a narrow head of land at the edge of Crystal Bay; each of the 220 rooms has an impressive view. It's the only hotel-casino in Nevada that qualifies for the title of "lodge," with features such as a real log exterior, stone vestibule, and stone flooring. The lodge part of the Cal-Neva is in California; the state line runs smack down the center of the huge stone hearth (as well as through the middle of the swimming pool outside). Known as the Indian Room for the poignant display of and by the Washo, the lobby has a fireplace burning real wood, massive granite boulders topped with a big bobcat, wooden cathedral ceiling, and big-game trophies; take some time to absorb the graphically presented story of the Washo. Peek out the back door to see the Washo bedrock mortar in a stone boulder on the deck. The round barroom is also one of a kind. The round room is paneled in carved wood (below) and mirrors (above), with an attractive stained-glass dome overhead.

The Cal-Neva opened over Memorial Day weekend 1926, making it among the top 10 most venerable hotels in the state. Supposedly, it operated as an illegal casino till 1931, when gambling was legalized in Nevada. Prohibition made barely a dent in its patrons' alcohol consumption. Frank Sinatra owned it in the 1960s when, legend has it, Marilyn Monroe met President Kennedy there (this is apparently apocryphal; Guy Rocha, state archivist, has thoroughly debunked the myth and insists that Kennedy never visited the Cal-Neva). The Gaming Commission revoked Frank's license for allowing Chicago's Sam Giancana, inscribed in the Black Book of undesirables, to stay and play on the premises.

After that, the Cal-Neva (which has no connection to the Club Cal-Neva in downtown Reno) went into a slow decline, till it was closed in 1983 by the state for gaming violations. It reopened three years and $11 million later. The latest owner, Chuck Bluth, reduced the casino by 30% (possibly the only casino in Nevada that's *shrunk* in the past 25 years) to re-create the original lodge. Today, the Cal-Neva is once again a true Tahoe resort.

In the past few years, the casino has been shrinking and the resort facilities have been expanding. Weddings and honeymoons now account for 30% of the Cal-Neva's business, same as the casino.

Accommodations

The **Hyatt Regency Lake Tahoe Resort & Casino,** 111 Country Club Dr. at Lakeshore Blvd., 775/832-1234 or 800/233-1234, has it all: private beach, tennis courts, health club, bike and nature trails, boat rentals, golf, and 458 rooms that go from $185–235 (suites $500–850) off season, up to $245–320 (suites $600–1200) high season (June to September, and the Christmas season).

The **Cal-Neva Resort,** 2 Stateline Rd., Crystal Bay, 775/832-4000 or 800/CAL-NEVA, has 200 rooms for $85–269.

The **Tahoe Biltmore Lodge & Casino,** 5 State Route 28, 775/831-0660 or 800-BILTMOR, offers 92 rooms from $39–129.

Inn at Incline, 1003 Tahoe Blvd., 775/831-1052 or 800/824-6391, is on Tahoe Blvd. (NV 28) just south of Country Club Drive. Its 50 mini-suites range from $59 to $135 a night, and it has a surprise in the basement: indoor swimming pool, hot tub, and sauna.

In Crystal Bay, the **Crystal Bay Motel,** 24 State Route 28, 775/831-0287, has 18 rooms for $35–85.

All the Tahoe guides and travel planners list vacation rentals, apartments, and condos. But there is one special place in Incline Village, the only bed and breakfast on the east (and part of the north) side of the lake. **Haus Bavaria,** 593 N. Dyer Circle (P.O. Box 9079, Incline Village, NV 89452), 775/831-6122 or 800/731-6222, is a two-story stucco-and-wood chalet built by a German couple in 1980 to be a B&B. There are five guest rooms upstairs, each with a private bath, and a large sitting room with a woodstove. Breakfast is served by owner Bick Hewitt, a transplanted San Diego airline worker, who also provides passes to Incline's private beaches and indoor recreation center. Rates are $95–225.

Crystal Bay Food

Starting from the north end, **Soule Domain** is on Stateline Rd. right on the California-Nevada border, west across the street from the Biltmore's parking lot, 530/546-7529. Open nightly 6–10 P.M., this is one of two non-casino restaurants in Crystal Bay. In a cozy log cabin complete with fireplace (real wood burns in the winter), wood fence, and shake roof, Charlie and Steven Soule

serve non-traditional American/Italian fare, with appetizers such as garlic ravioli with lamb and olive filling, shrimp scampi, softshell crab, shiitake mushrooms, and escargot; salads include Caesar, Greek or spinach, and an interesting grilled lamb and goat cheese. Entrees include fresh vegetables in a pastry shell with Swiss cheese, herbs, and roasted garlic in a tomato cream sauce, fresh pasta of the day, rock shrimp (with sea scallops or with lobster and scallops), sliced chicken breast, vegan sautee, curried cashew chicken, New Zealand lamb, and filet mignon.

The other non-casino restaurant here is the **Border House Brewing Company,** between the Crystal Bay Club and the Cal-Neva, 775/832-2739, open for lunch, dinner, and late bar. The Border House was built in 1927, around the same time that the Cal-Neva went up. Since then it's been a lodge, boarding house, casino, and even a brothel (read about it on the menu). They serve all kinds of home-brewed beers, plus appetizers (seared ahi or baked brie and roasted garlic), wood-fired pizzas, rack of lamb, filet mignon, wild game and seafood.

The **Crystal Bay Club** has a 24-hour coffee shop with snack-bar specials such as $1.50 hot dogs and Heineken and 99-cent breakfasts. It also features the Crystal Bay Steak and Lobster House in a quiet, uncrowded, and attractive room with big booths and an open kitchen, opening at 6 P.M. daily.

At the **Cal-Neva** is the Lakeview Room, with big picture windows overlooking Tahoe, open 7 A.M.–10 P.M. There's also a snack bar in the video arcade where you can get Polish dogs, pizza, and nachos.

The **Biltmore** coffee shop is open 24 hours, and has a renowned $1.99 breakfast special with two eggs and meat. Daily specials include all-you-can eat spaghetti for $3.95, prime rib for $7.95, plus changing specials for each day of the week. The Biltmore also has the Pub and Grill and Aspen Cabaret, with 60 beers on tap, 30 different microbrews, finger food, darts, and pool tables.

Incline Village Food

The following restaurants are listed from north to south along Tahoe Boulevard.

The butcher counter at **Village Market** in the Village Center on Southwood sells good sandwiches. The **Grog n' Grist** on the corner of

Southwood and Tahoe Blvd., 775/831-1123, is a local lunch legend, sometimes cranking out 500 sandwiches a day from its big bustling deli counter in the rear.

In the Christmas Tree Center is **Mofo's Pizza and Pasta,** 775/831-4999. Open daily 11 A.M.–10 P.M., it does subs, mini-pizzas, chicken wings, and entrees such as lasagna and pasta primavera.

A great place for breakfast and lunch is the **Wildflower Cafe,** 775/831-8072: eggs, burgers, and specials served on huge plates full of hearty food. This homey place has been a locals' favorite since 1984. Open 7 A.M.–2:30 P.M. Recommended.

T's Rotisserie,, 901 Tahoe Blvd., 775/831-2832, is tucked away in the little shopping center beside the 7-Eleven store and the Incline Cinema, but it's often full of locals who pack in for the delicious, inexpensive fare including unique rotisserie roasted chicken and beef, big burritos, soft tacos, tostadas, Yucatan style and soy lime chicken, beef tri tip, salads and salsas. You can phone in "to go" orders. Open daily 11 A.M.–8 P.M., Sunday noon–8 P.M.

The only chain fast-food in Incline is a **Subway,** on Village Blvd. just uphill from Tahoe Blvd., 775/831-3370.

Azzara's in the Raley's shopping center is great for Italian. Everything is delicious, and a bargain to boot. Open 5–11 P.M. Tues.–Sun., 775/831-0346.

Hacienda de la Sierra, 931 Tahoe Blvd., 775/831-8300, is the favorite for Mexican, with medium prices, tasty food and attractive décor. Open nightly, 4–10 P.M.

The **Hyatt,** 775/832-1234, has the 24-hour Sierra Cafe, an upscale coffee shop with a salad bar and seafood buffet weekends. There's also Ciao Mein Trattoria, open for dinner Wed.–Sun. 6–10 P.M. with Italian pastas and Chinese entrees. The real fancy dining is across Lakeshore Dr. at the Lone Eagle Grill, 775/832-3250, right on the lake. Lunch and dinner are served; there's also a Sunday champagne brunch 10:30 A.M.–2:30 P.M. If the food prices are too dear, you can always sit and have a drink and enjoy the view.

Information and Miscellany

The **Incline Village/Crystal Bay Visitors and Convention Bureau** is at 969 Tahoe Blvd. near the south end of town, 775/832-1606 or 800/GO-TAHOE, www.gotahoe.com. It's open Mon.–Fri. 9 A.M.–5 P.M., Sat.–Sun. 10 A.M.–4 P.M. (closed major holidays). It has a friendly, helpful staff and all the brochures and information you'll need, including everything from hiking trails and outdoor activities to restaurants and resorts.

The library is just north of the Christmas Tree Center, set back from the road a little, 775/832-4130. A sign points the way. Open Mon.–Fri. 10 A.M.–6 P.M., Sat. 10 A.M.–5 P.M., this is a branch of the excellent Washoe County library system and has an admirably thorough Nevada shelf (against the right-hand wall). Also check out (so to speak) the historical black-and-white prints of Tahoe scenes through the years. It's very bright, often crowded, and has good long hours.

For a convenient and comfortable hike above Crystal Bay, take Stateline Rd. on the north edge of the Tahoe Biltmore parking lot toward the water tower, then curve around to the right beyond the fire station and go up the hill. At the fork in the road, pull off to the left, and stroll up the beautiful two-lane gravel fire road to the lookout. When you're done, follow Lakeview Rd. to Tuscarora and take a right. Some incredible houses up here: chalets, cabins, domes, A-frames, many with stone facades and fireplaces. Tuscarora runs into Lakeview and then returns down the hill to Tahoe Boulevard.

For a pamphlet outlining 17 other good hikes, ranging from easy to strenuous, ask the Incline Village/Crystal Bay Visitors and Convention Bureau for their free Trail Map to the North & East Shores of Lake Tahoe.

CARSON VALLEY

Driving south on US 395 from Carson City, you go up and over a hump, which demarcates the south edge of Eagle Valley. At the top of the hump is the cutoff (right) to Jacks Valley and Genoa (see below). If you continue on the US highway, you descend to large and bucolic Carson Valley, which is irrigated by the West Fork of the Carson River and creeks running down the western face of the Pine Nut Mountains. This valley is unusual for Nevada, in that it is almost square, as wide as it is long.

At the narrower northern end of the valley on the west are some foothills that separate Carson from Jacks valleys. The foothills don't last long, though, and just south of them the whole thing opens up. From then on, it's Carson Valley from the base of the Sierra all the way to the base of the Pine Nuts—big and flat compared to what you've traveled through since Reno. US 395 travels in a ruler-straight line down the western side of the valley, passing ranch after ranch, beautifully green with alfalfa in the summer, and then cuts southeast to pass through Minden and Gardnerville. These two contiguous towns are also hemmed in by ranches on all sides, and several times a year traffic is halted for cattle drives crossing the highway.

Just southeast of Gardnerville the valley starts to close in a bit and the highway starts to climb into the Pine Nuts, sacred mountains to the Washo. You keep climbing into the juniper and piñon and cooler air of the range, the trees big and the slopes thickly forested (for Nevada). Then you drop down to an intersection: for Yerington turn left; Topaz Lake lies south just over the next rise. Beyond Topaz Lake is another author's state.

GENOA

Introduction

A mile and a half past where US 395 intersects with US 50, take a right on Jacks Valley Road. Covering the three miles to Genoa, you'll easily see why the first settlers in what is now the state of Nevada chose this spot to set up shop. You head straight toward the sheer eastern scarp of the **Carson Range** of the Sierra Nevada. **Duane Bliss Peak** (8,658 feet) is dead ahead and **Genoa Peak** (9,150 feet) is to the south. In a couple of miles you turn south and parallel the mountains. **Jacks Valley** sits a bit above broad Carson Valley. Interestingly, just on the other side of the big rock walls to the west at road level is the very bottom of Lake Tahoe. Say a little prayer that the mountains don't burst, because the lake water would probably create quite a flood, taking your car along for the ride. If this happens, steer *with* the wave, and bail out just before crashing into the Pine Nuts.

Genoa (pronounced juh-NO-uh) is the oldest town in Nevada, settled by Mormons in 1851 after an advance party had established a trading post here a year earlier to service the Emigrant Trail. The first settlers returned to Salt Lake City extolling the valley's scenic, agricultural, and commercial virtues. Brigham Young assigned a mission to colonize this western outpost of the Utah Territory. The settlement, known as Mormon Station for its first five years, was the site of the first house, first public meeting, first written records, first land claim, and first squatter government in what would soon be Nevada.

In 1855, Young dispatched a prominent Mormon judge, Orson Hyde, to administer the colony, along with another 100 settler families. By then, the fertile surrounding valleys had already been homesteaded by gentiles, and Mormon Station, which Hyde renamed Genoa (in honor of the birthplace of Christopher Columbus), was thriving. But in 1857, all the Mormons were recalled by Brigham Young to help defend Salt Lake City from an imagined invasion by the U.S. government, and Genoa began its downhill slide from prominence.

The Latter-day Saints expected to be paid for their property, which was quickly claimed by gentile residents. After years of failed attempts to be reimbursed for the land, structures, and businesses, Orson Hyde finally placed a curse on gentile Genoa. "You can pay [$20,000] and find mercy, or despise the demand and perish!"

It's arguable that the curse succeeded; since

JOHN ELK III

Genoa

then, Genoa has suffered some serious set-backs. When Abe Curry tried to buy a plot of land in Genoa, he was sent packing, so he went off to start his own town. Immediately after the discovery of the Comstock, Curry's Carson City, with a much more advantageous location to serve the Lode, eclipsed Genoa. The *Territorial Enterprise,* established in Genoa in 1858, moved to Carson City, then Virginia City. And although Genoa became the seat of Douglas County in 1861, the post office moved into Carson City the same year. Next, in 1879, some Genoa boys played a prank on a town resident, Lawrence Gilman, who immediately bought a plot from homesteader John Gardner at the southern end of Carson Valley, and moved there in a huff. Gilman's new settlement, Gardnerville, proved a much better location to serve the farmers of Carson Valley and the miners on their way to strikes farther south. A bad avalanche hit the town in 1884, and a flood in 1891.

In 1910, a fire consumed most of what was left of Genoa and in 1916, Minden took away the

Douglas County seat. The curse seemed to fade after that. In the late 1940s, the state rebuilt the original Mormon station and fort. That attraction (and others), along with the beautiful setting, historical significance, and mushrooming tourism, have turned Genoa into a popular destination, especially as a day-trip from Carson City, 12 miles north. And today, Genoa is actually a grow-ing suburb of the capital, with large new houses surrounding the historical center of town.

However, some residents still fear the effects of living under Orson Hyde's 130-year-old hex. One local tried to organize a curse-lifting cere-mony to coincide with the unveiling of a new his-torical marker at the Mormon fort in 1991. But no-body seemed to know how to do it.

Candy Dance
Genoa is also the scene of one of the oldest an-nual events in Nevada, the Genoa Candy Dance. This dentists' delight originated in 1919 when the town was trying to raise funds to install lights on the streets of the town. The fundraiser started out as a dance and midnight dinner, and even-tually turned into a bake sale after the Genoa matriarchs mixed up batches of fudge to sell by the pound to the partygoers. The candy proved to be the star of the show, and the Candy Dance tradition began. Now having celebrated its 80th year, the proceeds from the Candy Dance pay for most of Genoa's town services.

The Candy Dance takes place the third week-end of September. An arts and crafts fair is held Saturday and Sunday 9 A.M.–5 P.M.; up to 300 vendors set up booths with candy, food, and crafts at Mormon Station, the town park, and the Volunteer Fire Department. On Saturday night, a buffet dinner is held at the old fire station (next to the country store) and the dance takes place at the town hall (next to the old fire de-partment).

More than 4,000 pounds of candy—plain, nut, and mocha fudge; almond roca; nut brittles; dipped chocolates; divinity; mints; almond clus-ters (35 different kinds altogether)—is sold dur-ing the two-day fair. For more information, call 775/782-8696.

Sights
First stop should be at the **Genoa Courthouse Museum** across from the park, 775/782-4325,

open May to mid-October, 10 A.M.–4:30 P.M. every day; free admission. The building, a courthouse from 1865 to 1916, then a school till 1956, has been a museum since 1969. Eye-catching artifacts in the eclectic collection include: model stamp mill, beautiful Washoe baskets, nine-inch "escape" keys from the replica prison cell, luxurious burgundy velour furniture in the pioneer parlor, and valuable first-day issues displayed in the original post office. Upstairs is the courtroom—can you figure out what the women are doing and what the judge is thinking? Snowshoe Thompson, legendary Scandinavian mail carrier, gets a display case, as does the Ferris wheel, invented by George Ferris, who grew up in a house still standing in Carson City. An entire

room is devoted to the Virginia & Truckee Railroad. From the museum book rack, pick up a copy of the *Genoa-Carson Valley Book* ($3), 100 pages of coverage of this whole neck of the woods.

Stroll across the road to **Mormon Station State Historic Park,** 775/782-2590, the site of Nevada's first permanent non-native settlement, The stockade replicates one built by the earliest settlers to keep livestock—it's doubtful they were much afraid of the timid Washo. A small museum displaying relics of pioneer days is housed in a replica of the original 1851 trading post; take some time to read the signboards and check out the copy of the *Territorial Enterprise* from January 1, 1859, published here before it moved

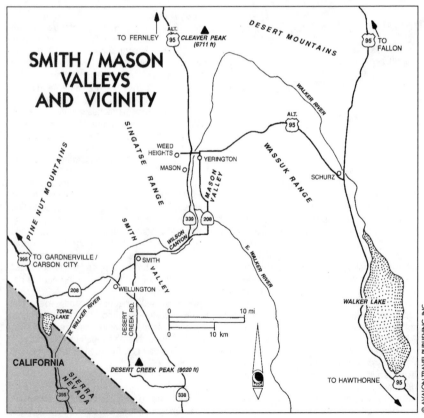

SMITH / MASON VALLEYS AND VICINITY

© AVALON TRAVEL PUBLISHING, INC.

on to more silvery press rooms. The museum and park are open May through mid-October, every day 9 A.M.–5 P.M.; donation.

Down the road in town is **Genoa Bar,** which accurately claims to be Nevada's oldest operating thirst parlor (since 1863). Have a beer and read the newspaper story about the place—more than you ever wanted to know, including the names of the first two bartenders.

South of the courthouse is the old **Masonic Hall,** built in 1862, and added onto in 1874. The **Genoa Country Store,** built in 1879, is one of the great country stores in Nevada, with an interesting assortment of cards, bottles, flags, hats, and jams, plus a wooden Indian, Coke and beer, and a soda fountain with ice cream, frozen yogurt, and snacks. The **Volunteer Fire Department** was built in 1960, but the old **Town Hall** next door is more than 100 years old; the bell tower and porch were added in 1977.

You can view a colorful variety of architecture in a three-block stretch across town. The subdivision on Genoa Ln. features big new pastel gingerbread-and-gable houses with stone facades and fireplaces. Across the road are old farmhouses fronted by large valley shade trees and white picket fences. Continue across Main St. and up Nixon St. where you're immediately in the Sierra with their stately pine trees and soft needles, chalets and cabins. Follow Genoa St. around to the south, then take a right onto Carson St. up the hill to the water tower. Park here and hike up into the Sierra on the fire road.

Practicalities

Genoa boasts two bed and breakfasts. **Genoa House Inn,** Nixon St. (P.O. Box 141, Genoa, NV 89411), 775/782-7075, was built in 1872 and is a National Historical Place. It features three guest rooms upstairs, one with a jacuzzi, the other with a bi-level shower stall, and one downstairs. Linda and Bob Sanfillippo run the inn; he's the Genoa town maintenance man and she's famous far and wide for her homemade cinnamon rolls. Rates are $105–145.

Just up the street from the Genoa House is the **Wild Rose Inn,** 2332 Main St. (P.O. Box 256, Genoa, NV 89411), 775/782-5697. This three-story Queen Anne Victorian was built in 1989 as a B&B by Sandi and Joe Antonucci. All five guest rooms have private baths. One is on the

main floor. Three are on the second floor, which features a circular plan in which none of the rooms share a wall—very private and quiet. The third floor has the inn's suite, with an full, twin, and trundle bed, sitting room, and long bath. Rates are $110–150.

The rates at both B&Bs include the use of Walley's Hot Springs (see below).

The Pink House, 775/783-1004, is unmistakable. Serving dinner Tues.–Sun. 6–10 P.M. (bar opens at 5 P.M.), the restaurant and bar are in a two-room guest cottage and bunkhouse on the property of the actual Pink House, around the corner on Genoa Lane. This is one of, if not the, oldest houses in Nevada, having been built in 1855 on a site up the hill a piece at today's Mill St. by Captain John Reese, the earliest non-Mormon settler at Mormon Station, and therefore Nevada. A man named Johnson bought the original structure in 1870 and moved it, using wood planks, a winch, and manpower, to its present location. He also painted it pink. The house changed hands only twice before Walt and Nora Merrell bought it in 1971 and opened the restaurant and bar; new owners took over in 1994. The menu is full of meat, king crab and halibut, chicken, and "the best rack of lamb in Nevada," according to the host. All are in the $15–20 range. Dinners come with a mountain of other food: onion soup, Caesar or spinach salad, and baked potato.

The **Inn Cognito,** 202 Genoa Lane, 775/782-8898, serves dinner and drinks every night except Tuesday; the bar opens at 5 P.M., and dinner is served from 6–9 P.M. (until 10 P.M. Friday and Saturday nights). Make your reservations early for this extremely popular restaurant, one of the finest in western Nevada. The meals here are slightly more expensive than the Pink House's. Try the veal dish of the evening, calamari amondine, scallops pommery, or any one of the many daily specials. Save room for dessert, included. Dinners run around $17–40.

Walley's Hot Springs

This splendid resort is just over a mile south of Genoa on NV 206/Foothill Rd. (P.O. Box 158, Genoa, NV 89411), 775/782-8155 or 800/628-7831. The springs have hosted a hotel since 1862. David and Harriet Walley opened a $100,000 spa at springs along a fault whose water reached 160° F. In 1895, after falling into disrepair, the resort was sold for $5,000. The original hotel burned in the 1920s, and was rebuilt in the late 1980s with no expense spared and attention paid to every last detail. Today, it's a beautifully landscaped, luxurious, and reasonably priced hotel-spa.

Cabins can be rented for $85 to $105. The rates include use of six mineral pools, large heated swimming pool, separate steam rooms and saunas, and weight rooms. You can also get a massage, play tennis, take exercise classes, or just use the facilities for the day ($20); open every day, 7 A.M.–10 P.M.

The restaurant and bar are in a large and beautiful stone and wood lodge. The restaurant is open for dinner Tues.–Sat., 5–9 P.M., and once a month for Sunday brunch.

To Lake Tahoe
Continuing south on Foothill Rd., just beyond Muller Ln. (the next left) is the historical sign for **Kingsbury Grade.** This is the location of the original toll road over Daggett Pass to Lake Tahoe, completed in 1860 by D.D. Kingsbury and J.M. McDonald. Surrounding today's intersection of the Grade and Foothill Rd. about a mile south of the sign is the small suburb of **Mottsville,** near the site of the ranch of Israel Mott, who began homesteading Carson Valley in 1851. His wife, Eliza, was the first white woman to settle in Nevada.

The toll road ($17.50 one way!) shortened the trip from Placerville to Virginia City by 15 miles, and is still the only connection (11 miles) between Carson Valley and the lake. You head immediately up into the Sierra and get a beautiful buzzard's-eye view of lush Carson Valley. Stately pine trees escort you up to Daggett Pass (7,334 feet), where you start the steep descent to the lake,

Henry Fredrick Dangberg
NEVADA HISTORICAL SOCIETY, RENO

accompanied by advance-guard condos of the South Lake Tahoe area suburban sprawl. At the intersection with US 50 at Kingsbury Center, go left three-quarters of a mile to the Stateline skyscrapers, or right to Round Hill Beach, Zephyr Cove, and the north shore.

To Minden/Gardnerville
The next left is Centerville Rd. (NV 756), which heads east to join with NV 88 at **Centerville,** with a few ranch houses and the Valley Bar at the corner. Centerville Rd. curves around to the left (north) and runs up the valley, with **East Peak** (9,591 feet) on the west overlooking Gardnerville.

MINDEN AND GARDNERVILLE

Lawrence Gilman, a refugee from the curse of Genoa, in 1879 bought nearly eight acres of land on the East Fork of the Carson River from John Gardner, who'd homesteaded the southern Carson Valley since 1861. He moved a building there from Genoa and opened the Gardnerville Hotel. He also opened a blacksmith shop and saloon, which served the local ranchers, and the miners and freighters heading from Washoe to the doings at Esmeralda (Aurora, Bodie, and the borax country south). In the 1880s, a number of Danish immigrants settled in Gardnerville; their Valhalla Hall became the social center of the valley. Then, at the turn of the 20th century, Basque sheep ranchers swelled the ranks, both human and ungulate, of Carson Valley, doubling the number of sheep in the valley from fewer than 10,000 in the late 1890s to more than 25,000 in 1925. Basque boardinghouses flourished in Gardnerville and their legacy is alive today.

In 1905, the Virginia & Truckee Railroad extended its line from Carson City down to southern Carson Valley to service the farmers and freight their produce to market. The right-of-way was provided by Henry Fredrick Dangberg, a rancher in residence from the early days of Mormon Station who owned 36,000 acres. Dangberg was the first to grow alfalfa in Nevada and he married Margaret Ferris, sister of Carson City's George Ferris, who invented the Ferris wheel. Dangberg Senior died in 1904, and Dangberg Land and Livestock Company, run by his three sons, established a town to capitalize on the railroad depot. They named it Minden for their father's birthplace in Westphalia, Prussia.

A tidy little town with square blocks and a central plaza was laid out around the V&T depot. Within 10 years, Minden scooped the county seat from Genoa, and got a $25,000 courthouse in 1915. Gardnerville got the high school the same year. Minden developed its residential aspect while Gardnerville developed its businesses. In the 1930s, both towns claimed a combined population of only 500. But in the 1960s, the area got an economic boost when Bently Nevada, maker of electronic instruments, moved into the old Minden flour mill and creamery buildings.

Only two miles apart, Minden and Gardnerville have grown contiguous over the years, with most of the action strung along both sides of US 395 for several miles. A major subdivision called Gardnerville Ranchos south of the towns was one of the fastest growing neighborhoods in western Nevada, doubling its population to nearly 8,000, in the 1980s. Modern times caught up to the twin towns in late 1991, when the mail was delivered to houses for the first time.

It's worthwhile to wander the thin strip of back streets on each side of the highway; you'll get an instant sense of Minden's tranquil European charm and Gardnerville's 100-year farm-to-market tradition.

Sights

Starting at the north end of Minden and heading south on US 395, you pass the Carson Valley Inn; at the stoplight, notice the big **flour mill** and **butter company** buildings, now occupied by the Bently Nevada Corporation, along with its several buildings behind. Don Bently heads Bently, which produces rotating and vibration-

monitoring and measuring machinery. Don Bently was named Nevada Inventor of the Year in 1983, and ten years later was awarded the Vibration Institute's Decade Award.

Continue down to the **C.O.D. Garage** and the rest of the brick buildings on Esmeralda St. in old downtown Minden. The garage is the oldest continually operating car dealership in Nevada, founded in 1910 as a Model-T dealer by Clarence O. Dangberg (C.O.D.), who immediately hired Fred "Brick" Hellwinkel as his mechanic. In 1916, the Minden Inn was built nearby, and Dangberg built a parking garage for its patrons, complete with a newfangled semi-automatic "car shampooer." He also became a Goodyear tire distributor, and in 1919 replaced the Model Ts with Buicks and Chevrolets. In the 1920s, the C.O.D. Garage expanded to a full block between Esmeralda St. and the US highway. In the 1930s, Brick Hellwinkel began taking shares in the business in lieu of pay, eventually achieving ownership. Today, Brick's sons Danny and Don run the "garage," which is now the oldest family-franchise Chevy and Buick dealership in America. The Union 76 sign on Esmeralda makes for one of the great art-deco photo ops in Nevada.

Follow Esmeralda St. north again a few blocks, past **Minden Park**, laid out by H.F. Dangberg across from his house for the pleasure of his workers. The **courthouse** is at the top of the street at the corner of 8th.

Heading south into Gardnerville, you pass the old high school building (which later became the junior high), built in 1915. The Carson Valley Historical Society spent several years restoring the building, which is now the **Carson Valley Museum and Cultural Center,** 775/782-2555. Inside you'll find the East Fork Artists Coop art gallery, a children's art museum, natural history and agricultural exhibits, a Basque exhibit, and an exhibit on the Washo tribe. Outside are picnic areas. The museum is open daily, 10 A.M.–5 P.M. in summer, 10 A.M.–4 P.M. in winter.

Casinos

The big action in the twin towns is at **Carson Valley Inn,** Hwy. 395 in Minden, 775/782-9711, opened in 1984. The popularity of this joint has been reflected in a decade's worth of almost continuous expansion, from a small casino on the highway to a classy hotel, with blackjack, craps, roulette, lots of slots, sports book, plus two bars, Katie's 24-hour coffee shop, Fiona's steak and seafood restaurant (in the building next door), Michael's steak and seafood restaurant (in the casino), kids arcade, wedding chapel, RV park, and a new motor lodge. It's definitely the biggest action of any kind between Reno and Mammoth Lakes on US 395.

Sharkey's on US 395 in Gardnerville, 775/782-3133, is as small as the Carson Valley Inn is large, and as unusual as CVI is typical. In fact, Sharkey's ranks right up there with the most interesting casinos in the state. Milos "Sharkey" Begovich learned the gambling business at his parents' boardinghouse in the California gold country. He worked as a pit boss at Harrah's Tahoe in the 1950s and '60s, and one night ran up a lucky streak on a blackjack binge at Harvey's, across the street, into six digits. He used the money to buy a stake in the Tahoe Nugget, which he operated for five years, then sold in 1969. He used that money to buy the Golden Bubble in Gardnerville and changed the name to Sharkey's Nugget. It's mostly slots, with three blackjack tables and keno.

But the gambling is secondary to the real attraction here. Every inch of wall space is packed with paintings, prints, posters, and photographs of gambling, horse racing, boxing, movies. Check out the huge woven back side of the one-dollar bill, and the large-format b&w's of the 1910 Johnson-Jeffries fight in Reno. Stroll around to also look at the rooms full of antiques and saddles. You can't help being an oblivious tourist in this place—leaning over slots, bumping into people, getting the amused glance from some and the cold eye from others. Sharkey's one-of-a-kind memorabilia collection, his legendary generosity, and his huge prime-rib dinners can all be observed in the coffee shop behind the casino. First, look at the long line of commemorative and appreciative plaques in Sharkey's name on the left wall as you walk into the dining room. In the Rib Room is a fantastic collection of portraits of American Indians—handsome and dignified—by F.K. Young of Sparks. In an ironic twist, George Custer peers out over them all from the corner above the door. If you're going to eat here, the prime rib is famous far and wide (see below).

Heritage Tours

Heritage Tours, the creation of a fifth-generation Carson Valley native and her daughter, offer fun and informative tours of the Carson Valley, visiting more sites of interest than you would have thought would be here, with plenty of interesting stories. Tours operate year-round, with a minimum of two persons; cost is $20 per hour for tours for one to five persons. Contact Laurie and Shannon Hickey, 1456 Foothill Rd., Gardnerville, NV 89410, 775/782-2893.

Practicalities

The **Carson Valley Inn,** 1627 Hwy. 395, Minden, NV 89423, 775/782-9711 or 800/321-6983, has 153 rooms for $49–159. Next door is the **Carson Valley Motor Lodge,** same phone numbers, with 76 rooms for $39–109. Behind the Inn is **Carson Valley RV Resort,** same phone numbers. It's parking lot camping, but is surprisingly quiet for being so close to the highway. There are 59 spaces for motor homes, all with full hookups; 26 are pull-throughs. Tents are not allowed. Accessible restrooms have flush toilets and hot showers; public phone, sewage disposal, laundry, groceries, and gas are available. The stay limit is 14 days during the summer months. Reservations are accepted; the fee is $16 (Good Sam, AAA, and seniors-over-50 discounts available).

Other motels in Minden include: **Holiday Lodge,** 1591 US 395, 775/782-2288 or 800/266-2289, $30–48; and **Minden Best Western,** 1795 Ironwood Dr., 775/782-7766 or 800/528-1234, $39–98.

Gardnerville motels include the **Westerner,** 1355 US 395, 775/782-3602 or 800/782-3602, at $30–43 the least expensive of the bunch; **Sierra,** 1501 US 395, 775/782-5145 or 800/682-5857, $32–64; and the **Village,** 1383 US 395, 775/782-2624, $32–48.

The **Jensen Mansion B&B,** 1431 Ezell St., Gardnerville, NV 89410, 775/782-7644, is the local bed and breakfast. It's in one of the great public mansions in northern Nevada, built in 1910 in a combo Southern Colonial and New England architectural style. It has 12-foot ceilings, a huge Great Room, and four guest rooms on the second floor. Now under new ownership, it's expecting to re-open in 2001; call for current info.

Minden-Gardnerville is Basque-food country, with one of the most famous and oldest (1909)

Basque restaurants in the state. **The Overland Hotel,** 691 Main St., 775/782-2138, has been in Basque hands for decades. Lunch is served 12–2 P.M. ($12) and dinner 5–10 P.M. ($16), closed Monday. No menus—just choose between a few entrees and then watch the food pile up on the table.

Also try the **J&T Bar and Restaurant** down the street at 760 S. Main, 775/782-2074, for a Basque family-style experience: open Mon.–Sat. for lunch 11:30 A.M.–2 P.M., dinner 5–9 P.M. ($17).

Sharkey's coffee shop is open 24 hours: bacon and eggs and omelettes, burgers, club sandwiches, big plates of delicious beef stew and dinner rolls for a mere pittance, veal, and shrimp. Sharkey's is famous for prime rib. Recommended.

Fiona's belongs to the Carson Valley Inn and is therefore just as classy: pleasing little tropical atrium with a koi pond, high ceilings, and impressive stonework. It's open for dinner Tues.–Sun. 5–9 P.M., and for Sunday brunch 9 A.M.–2 P.M. The play here is the salad bar, nearly as nice as the one at the Eldorado in Reno. Otherwise, the menu is full of the usual steak and seafood, with some interesting chicken (Cajun, pecan, or teriyaki) and pasta plates, mostly in the $14–20 range.

Petrello's Italian Restaurant, at the corner of US 395 and Esmeralda in downtown Minden in the historic district, 775/782-4410, is in the same league as Fiona's. It's open for lunch Tues.–Fri. 11:30 A.M.–2:30 P.M., dinner nightly 5–9 P.M. ($10–23), and Sunday brunch 9 A.M.–2 P.M. ($4–10).

Outdoor Activities

Four golf courses grace the Carson Valley: **Carson Valley Golf Course,** 1027 Riverview Dr., south of Gardnerville, 775/265-3181; **Golf Club at Genoa Lakes,** Jacks Valley Rd., Genoa, 775/782-4653, listed among the Best Courses in America in 1995; **Sierra Nevada Golf Ranch,** 2901 Jacks Valley Rd., Genoa, 775/782-7700, in the Sierra Nevada foothills on a former cattle ranch; and the **Sunridge Golf Club,** 1000 Long Dr., Carson City, 775/267-4448, five miles south of Carson City at the north end of the Carson Valley.

A well-established glider-ride company, **Soar Minden,** 775/782-7627 or 800/345-7627, has been taking people soaring since 1978. The scenery is breathtaking, and there's no engine noise to interfere (though the wind does whip up pretty good). Their most popular flight is the Mile High flight ($125/200 for one/two people); other popular flights include the Lake Tahoe View flight ($95/160), the Emerald Bay Excursion ($210/275), and an aerobatic experience ($175). Introductory flying lessons are $150. Soar Minden operates out of Douglas County Airport, three miles north of Minden. To get there, heading south from Carson City or north from Minden on US 395 and turn east on Airport Road. Soar Minden's office is at 1138 Airport Rd., at the entry to the airport parking lot; look for the sign saying "glider rides."

You can also take a hot-air balloon high above Carson Valley, with views of Tahoe and the Sierra. Contact **Dream Weavers Hot Air Balloon Company,** 775/265-1271 or 800/FUN-ALOFT. Dream Weavers flies out of Lampe Park in Gardnerville; flight times are just after sunrise.

Information

The Carson Valley Chamber of Commerce and Visitors Authority, 1512 US 395, Suite 1, Gardnerville, NV 89410, 775/782-8144 or 800/727-7677, www.carsonvalleynv.org, has information on the entire Carson Valley. It's open Mon.–Fri., 8 A.M.–5 P.M.

To Topaz Lake

The first major intersection south of Gardnerville on US 395 is at Riverview Drive. If you go right, you can wander around **Gardnerville Ranchos,** the fastest growing development in Douglas County. You roll past the Carson Valley Country Club and Basque restaurant, then wind around this unusual suburb. The Ranchos, first subdivided in 1955 as affordable housing for Lake Tahoe's south shore service employees, now accounts for almost half the population of Carson Valley, and a third of the county. The population has grown nearly 15% every year for 10 years, and in 1989 claimed a full third of all real-estate transactions in Douglas County. Between the Ranchos and US 395 are **Dresslerville** and the Washo Indian Tribe Reservation. The tribe's smoke shop is on US 395 about a mile south of Riverview Drive.

From there, US 395 cuts southeast up and

over the wide southern edge of the Pine Nut Mountains, parallel to the California state line and the Sierra Nevada just a few miles east. You cruise through the juniper and piñon for 15 miles or so, then drop down out of the Pine Nuts toward Topaz Lake. High **Antelope Peak** (10,241 feet) stands out behind the lake in the southern distance. And **Antelope Valley** spreads out east and south of the lake, edged on the east by the rolling **Wellington Hills.** The awesome Sierra of Mono County, California, rise like a wall to the west.

TOPAZ LAKE

This undiscovered little gem, like its famous big sister to the north, sits half in Nevada and half in California. It's also fringed by the mighty Sierra, and has a state line lodge just across the Nevada border on the US highway. Unlike Tahoe, however, Topaz is a man-made water-storage basin, which impounds water from the West Walker River for recreation and irrigation of farms in Lyon County's Smith and Mason valleys. It's also more of a treeless desert scene than forested Tahoe. So in a sense, Topaz Lake is a hybrid of Lake Tahoe, Pyramid or Walker lakes, and Lahontan or Rye Patch reservoirs.

The Walker River Irrigation District, created in 1919 to manage the river, built a feeder canal from the West Walker River into a dry lake bed, renamed Topaz Lake, in 1921. An outlet tunnel was dug in the rim of the lake, allowing the river to continue on its way through Smith and Mason valleys and into Walker Lake. The Army Corps of Engineers built a rock-face wall in 1937 that added 15,000 acre-feet of storage for a total of 60,000. At its deepest, Topaz Lake is 100 feet.

Topaz Lake Park

Topaz Lake Park is one of two county parks with a campground in Nevada (this is a Douglas county park; Davis Creek Park is a Washoe County facility). It's a big spot, with a mile of beachfront. The RV sites are up the slope a little, and there's a grassy playground for the kids. There are 140 campsites for tents or motor homes up to 35 feet; 29 spaces have water and electric hookups and 13 are pull-throughs. Piped drinking water, flush toilets and showers, sewage disposal, picnic tables, grills, and fire rings are provided. The maximum stay is 14 days. Tent sites cost $8 and are first come, first served; RV sites cost $10 and can be reserved up to a year in advance. It's usually full on the weekends with anglers; the lake is stocked twice a year with trout. Call 775/266-3343 for information on the park and fishing, or 775/782-9828 for camping reservations. To get there, from the intersection of US 395 and Highway 208, drive south on US 395 to the lake. At the sign, turn left and drive one mile (the last little bit is dirt) to the campground.

Topaz Lake Lodge and RV Park

This resort (P.O. Box 187, Gardnerville, NV 89410), 775/266-3338 or 800/962-0732, provides all the indoor recreation, accommodation, and supplies. Open year-round, the Lodge's casino has a good-size pit with a half dozen blackjack tables, plus crap and roulette tables. The long bar upstairs has a great view of the lake, the Wellington Hills, and Desert Creek Peak beyond. The 101 rooms at the lodge cost $39–58. The RV park next door has full hookups, plus showers and cable TV. The general store is open 24 hours; use your Shell card for any and all purchases. Check out the trout trophies hanging on the front wall: four- to five-pound browns and a seven-pound cutthroat (the average fish weighs three pounds and is 18–20 inches long). Trout are caught mostly between January and March, and the Lodge sponsors a trout derby from New Year's Day through the middle of April.

The Lakeview coffee shop is open 24 hours, and there's a buffet Friday and Saturday nights 5–9:30 P.M. There's also a non-smoking steakhouse, open for dinner Friday, Saturday and Sunday nights, 5:30–9:30 P.M. There's also a service bar and a big dance floor.

The RV park is next to the lodge. It has 36 spaces for motor homes, all with full hookups; 6 are pull-throughs. Tents are not allowed. Accessible restrooms have flush toilets and hot showers, and public phone, sewage disposal, groceries, and heated swimming pool are available. Reservations are recommended for summer; the fee is $17.

To get there take US 395 18 miles south of Gardnerville; it's three miles beyond the intersection of 395 and NV 208 east (38 miles to Yerington).

TO YERINGTON

Return north three miles north to the intersection with NV 208 and go east (right). The route skirts the southern edge of the Pine Nut Mountains, at the north head of Antelope Valley. The road and the West Walker River converge at **Wellington,** a village that dates back to territorial days. It served as a stage stop for Aurora and as a service town for **Smith Valley,** which spreads out east before it. Check out the Mercantile in the big red barn, the cozy Wellington Inn, and some of the stone ruins dotted about town.

NV 208 turns northeast beyond Wellington, running now along the southeast rim of the Pine Nuts. At **Smith,** the road turns due east through the middle of Smith Valley, settled as early as 1859 by a group of ranchers, three of whom happened to be named Smith. The Pine Nuts finally fade off to the north, and the Sierra are left behind. The low, rugged volcanic hills ahead are the **Singatses,** and all of a sudden you're aiming straight for **Wilson Canyon,** where the West Walker has cut a sharp and steep path through them. The 500-foot-sheer colorful rock wall at the right-hand entrance to the canyon is known as the **Bulkhead;** the polychromatic face on the other side of the canyon is equally impressive. This canyon comes up on you without warning, and unexpectedly you're twisting through the bottom of one of the most spectacular canyons west of Jarbidge and north of Red Rock.

In two miles Wilson Canyon, named for David Wilson, an early settler in the area, opens onto broad and lush **Mason Valley.** Mason Valley and Smith Valley to the west are often considered two halves of a single geographical unit. The big **Wassuk Range** rises from the eastern edge of the valley. The **East Walker River** travels north out of the Sierra and the southern Wassuks, joins up with the West Walker in the middle of Mason Valley, flows clear around the head of the Wassuks, makes a near U-turn south, and finally empties into Walker Lake.

Once out of Wilson Canyon, almost immediately is a fork in the road. A left puts you on the road north to Mason. Going straight, the road also takes a hard left after a few miles. Both travel straight up Mason Valley toward the **Desert Mountains** at the north end, with Cleaver Peak standing in the way (6,711 feet). This peak is probably not named after Ward, June, Wally, and the Beav, though it's fun to think so. In around 10 miles is Yerington.

YERINGTON

INTRODUCTION

Jedediah Smith explored this valley, out where the Walker River flows, in 1827. John C. Frémont camped near the site of Yerington in 1845 on his quest for the mythical San Buenaventura River in 1845; he crossed Wilson Canyon into Smith Valley. As early as 1854, Hock Mason and two brothers were driving cattle from Arkansas to California and paused at the banks of the Walker River for a few days. Mason must have liked what he saw; he returned in 1859 to homestead the valley. Others were attracted by the elements, and by 1870 Mason and Smith valleys were settled, and supplied much of the beef and produce consumed in the mining boomtowns north (Virginia City) and south (Aurora and Bodie). The area also hosted a mini-mining boom of its own, sending the local "bluestone" copper ore to the boomtown mills to be used in the refining of silver and gold.

A saloon near the geographical center of the valley constructed entirely of willow was called the Switch. Its whiskey was so stiff that it earned the nickname Pizen. "Pizen Switch" proved too negative for the growing population, who renamed it Greenfield in 1878. In 1890, the residents again changed the name to Yerington, after the general manager of the Virginia & Truckee Railroad, in an attempt to attract a division point on the new Carson & Colorado. This proved too optimistic. Henry M. Yerington bypassed his namesake town by a dozen miles, locating his own new town, Hawthorne, on the south shore of Walker Lake.

In the late 1880s, word spread that a local Paiute Indian, Jack Wilson, embodied the qualities of an Indian messiah. Also known as Wovoka, the religious teachings of this charismatic healer, prophet, and pacifist were known as the Ghost Dance. Wovoka envisioned the imminent disappearance of white people and all land reverting to the Indians. His influence extended as far as South Dakota, where Sioux Ghost Dancers, counting on the protection of the prophecies, were massacred at Wounded Knee. Born in Smith Valley, Wovoka lived the last 20 years of his life in Yerington, preaching pacifism and brotherhood until his death in 1932 at age 72.

In 1898, Smith and Mason valleys escaped the clutches of Esmeralda County and were tacked onto Lyon County, to which they more rightly belonged. In 1909, Yerington assumed county-seat duties after a disastrous fire in the then-seat, Dayton. From 1911 to the early 1930s, the Yerington area witnessed renewed copper mining, and the Nevada Copper Belt Railway ran from Wabuska on the Southern Pacific mainline through Yerington, Wilson Canyon, and up around the west side of the Singatses to Ludwig, four miles southwest of town.

The giant Anaconda Copper Mining Company prospected the area in the 1940s, and initiated full-scale production in the early '50s. It built Weed Heights, a model company town, right on the other side of the Singatses from Ludwig, and dug a gargantuan open pit, surrounded by flat-top mountains of tailings. At one point, 11,000 tons of ore a day were mined and milled, making Yerington the largest copper producer in Nevada. The mine closed in the early 1970s, throwing 500 people out of work and decimating the local economy, leaving Weed Heights high and dry and the huge pit to slowly fill up with rainwater.

Today, Yerington is a friendly and leisurely little farm community of 2,500 slow-moving souls. Back off the accelerator *before* you approach the town, so you'll be prepared to creep behind a pickup truck traveling eight mph so the driver can wave at all the neighbors and stop to talk to a few, or to let a couple of unconcerned kitties cross the main drag between the casino and the motel, or to shoot the breeze yourself with a local strolling alongside your vehicle. You'll continually return to the word "leisurely," and it's a special feeling to quickly and unconsciously adopt the sensuous pace of people who have time to visit with friends and strangers, to chew and taste their food, and to

understand that the slower you move through your life, the longer your life lasts. You might find yourself lingering a few hours more than you'd originally anticipated. Or a few days. Luckily, there's not much to do here! Except breathe and enjoy.

SIGHTS

The **Lyon County Museum,** 215 S. Main St., 775/463-6576, is open Thursday–Sunday 1–4 P.M. all year round, with additional Saturday hours of 10 A.M.–4 P.M. April through October. Open since 1978, this large and comprehensive museum overflows with exhibits, from an interesting Chinese collection (check out the carved walnuts) and Paiute baskets, blankets, arrows, water bottles, and cradle boards to a complete sheriff's office, barber shop, and pioneer kitchen and closet. The mine exhibit room tells most of the story, with photos of Weed Heights in 1954 and the mine in '64 and '72, plus the sulphuric acid plant, leaching vats with the deep and beautiful blue copper solution, the concentrator, flotation machines, and more. A display case holds chrome, nickel, and silver-plated copper products: faucets, padlocks, eye hooks, slide bolts, mirror handles, chains, screws and screwdrivers, bullets, knives, etc. There's an interesting collection of antique Walker River Irrigation District water machines, and don't miss George Washington's personal strongbox and its story by the door.

Be sure to explore the out buildings. The schoolhouse has a nice lunch-pail exhibit, old vehicles surround the blacksmith shop, and in the shop next to the country store there's a good desert wildlife exhibit. It includes a six-panel panorama of the Pine Nut Range and a wonderful relief model of Mason and Smith valleys, constructed between 1977 and 1981 by freshmen earth science students at the high school. This is the perfect place to pause and pay your respects to the Yerington pace and past; admission is free, but leave a buck or two.

As you enter town from the west, take a right just before the car dealership at the sign for the Yerington Paiute Colony; 100 feet on the left is a **monument to Wovoka,** revered spiritual leader who lived most of his life in Yerington or the nearby valleys.

Check out the photogenic old school building (1912) at the corner of Littel and California a block east of Main St. along public-school row.

There are two casinos in town. **Dini's Lucky Club,** 45 N. Main, 775/463-2868, is owned by Joe Dini, six-time speaker of the Nevada Assembly and a 16-term Assemblyman (since 1966). His joint has lotsa slots, a blackjack table, and a poker bar. Ask inside about the breakfast special (see below for Giuseppe's restaurant). **Casino West,** a few doors away at 11 N. Main St., 775/463-2481, is owned by the Masinis, who have a 1,000-acre ranch and a couple of unusual homes just south of Wabuska. The casino has three blackjack tables and one crap, an attractive coffee shop, a video poker bar with TVs all around, another smaller bar with a stone wall and big-screen TV. There's also a 12-lane bowling alley, with video games and air hockey.

For a good view of the area, take E. Bridge St. from the intersection with Main, go two miles, take a right on Mackenzie Lane, and a left past the cemetery. The pavement ends, then you climb the hill behind town past the dump—nice peaceful views of the town, its water tower, rich Mason Valley and the Walker River, and the sheer eastern scarp of the Sierra Nevada.

For a view of a different kind, head west on Bridge St. past the Indian colony; you can see **Weed Heights** above and straight ahead. Go north (right) on Alt. US 95 and take the first left on a paved road up into the hills. Go past the guard station and up into the suburb. Contrary to what you might suspect, Weed Heights was named for Clyde Weed, Anaconda vice president of operations. There are also recreation facilities (rec hall, swimming pool, driving range, miniature golf, tennis, and a park) and an observation parking lot.

PRACTICALITIES

Accommodations
Yerington has four motels. **Casino West,** 11 N. Main downtown, 775/463-2481 or 800/227-4661, with 79 rooms is the largest; expect to pay $38–58 for one of them. **In Town Motel,** 111 S.

Main, 775/463-2164, has 18 rooms at $35–45. And the **Ranch House,** 311 W. Bridge, 775/463-2200, has 15 rooms at $29–41. **Copper Inn,** 307 N. Main, 775/463-2135, has 12 rooms at $35–45.

Greenfield RV Park is only a few years old, with young trees and new grass at every site. It's adjacent to a mobile home park. Dairy Queen is next door, the new Warehouse Market superstore is across the street, and downtown Yerington is a short walk away. There are 40 spaces for motor homes, 24 with full hookups, all pull-throughs. Tents are allowed on a separate grassy area near the laundry. Restrooms have flush toilets and hot showers; public phone, sewage disposal, and laundry available. Reservations are accepted; the fees are $8 for tentsites and $15 for 2 RVers. Good Sam discount available. Contact Greenfield RV Park, 500 W. Goldfield Avenue, Yerington, NV 89447, 775/463-4912. To get there, traveling south on Alt. 95, take a left at the intersection of Highway 339 onto Goldfield Avenue, and drive five blocks. The park is on the left.

Food
Both **Dini's** and **Casino West** have coffee shops. Dini's is open 6:30 A.M.–10 P.M. Casino West's opens at 5 A.M. for coffee, serves breakfast starting at 6, and closes around 10 P.M. Dini's also has **Giuseppe's,** a weekend dinner house, open 5–10 P.M. Friday and Saturday nights. It serves steaks ($13–16), fish and lobster ($10–18), and Chinese dishes ($6–9).

Information
Stop first at the **Mason Valley Chamber of Commerce,** next door to the museum at 227 S. Main, 775/463-2245, open Mon.–Fri. 8 A.M.–5 P.M. It hands out a good little information packet that includes a map, some historical flyers, and lists of businesses. Here you can learn that Lyon County is one of the largest agricultural and livestock production areas in Nevada, growing high-protein alfalfa, onions, garlic, barley, and oats, and raising beef and dairy cattle and sheep on 50,000 cultivated acres.

BOB RACE

NORTHWEST NEVADA

PYRAMID LAKE

North of Sparks for a little more than 30 miles, you drive through sandy valleys hemmed in by desiccated hills where the most color in the country is found in the names—**Pah Rah Range, Hungry Valley, Dogskin Mountain.** Then you round a bend, crest a rise, and there, confronting startled eyes, is a hallucination. A huge lake stretches before you, its stark desert setting unlikely, its turquoise water improbable, and its stone pyramid, rising out of the depths, as perfect as Cheops. Its shorelines are smooth and treeless, its inlets gentle and graceful, its beauty strange and unsettling. And there's not a house, condo, cabin, motel, hotel, restaurant, nor even a parking lot in sight. As you descend to its edge and reach a tentative, unbelieving hand toward it, the cool clear water finally convinces you that it's as real as you are, and not a desert mirage after all.

Pyramid Lake has been called the most beau-tiful desert lake in the world. It's one of the largest freshwater lakes in the western United States: 27 miles long, nine miles wide, 370 feet at its deepest, 3,789 feet above sea level, with a water temperature fluctuating between 75° F in summer and 42° in winter. Its source, the Truckee River, leaves Lake Tahoe, travels 105 miles—down the east face of mighty mountains, through thirsty cities, and across reclaimed desert—then trickles into the southern delta of the lake, which has no outlet. Large Anaho Island juts up off the eastern shore slightly south of the pyramid, providing breeding grounds for the majestic American white pelican and other shorebirds. Jagged pinnacles stand sentinel over the northern end, where hot springs drain into the lake and a steam geyser vents from a rusty wellhead. Great Lahontan cutthroat trout grow to 15 pounds, and the endemic cui-ui sucker fish haunt the ancient depths. Nearly half a million acres of lake and surrounding desert are enclosed by the Pyramid Lake Reservation, a sacred area managed and preserved by its traditional Paiute caretakers.

HISTORY

Pyramid Lake is the larger vestige (Walker is the smaller) of great Lake Lahontan, which covered much of the western Great Basin only 50,000 years ago. Glacial incursions during the ice ages of the previous two million years touched Nevada only in the high ranges, but the accompanying cold wet climate created and supported this giant prehistoric body of water. An incredibly complicated inland sea, with its digitated branches spreading between, around, and over the basins and ranges, Lahontan stretched from McDermitt in the north and Honey Valley in the west to Hawthorne in the south and the Stillwater Range in the east. Its surface spread for 8,600 square miles at an average depth of several thousand feet (75 times larger and 10 times deeper than Pyramid Lake).

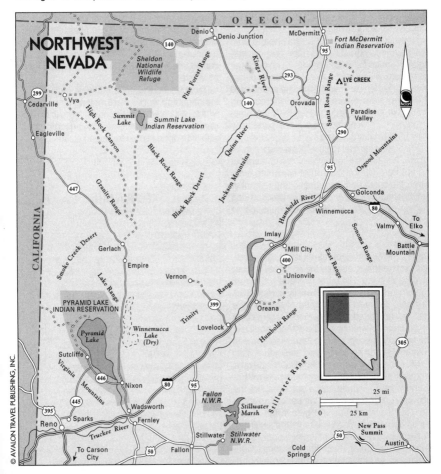

The climatological warming and drying trend that's prevailed since the last ice age, which ended roughly 15,000 years ago, has been shrinking the vast lake, smaller and shallower, shallower and smaller, down to this "minor" remnant. And unless a new ice age arrives, it'll continue to shrink until sometime in the not-too-distant future, when the Truckee River will echo the fate of the Humboldt and Carson rivers, which both disappear, white and sour, into a desert playa that was once an improbable turquoise lake.

Lovelock and Paiute Peoples

Paleo-Indians of the Lovelock period 11,000 to 4,000 years ago dwelled in lakeside caves, wore pelican-skin robes, chipped arrowheads from obsidian, carved fishhooks from deer antlers, and fashioned fishnets, baskets, even duck decoys from willow and tule reeds. It's undetermined whether the Lovelock people abandoned the area, were driven away by encroaching Paiute, or evolved into the Paiute. Many similarities exist between the two cultures, particularly their basketmaking styles.

The Paiute term for themselves is Neh-muh, or Numa. A nomadic people, the Numa gathered at Ku-yui Pah (Cui-Ui Waters) at spawning time, when the cui-ui and the gigantic and Lahontan cutthroat trout (actually a kind of landlocked king salmon—averaging 30–35 pounds) were easiest to catch.

Contact

John C. Frémont, famous explorer, surveyor, and cartographer, entered the northwest corner of Nevada in late 1843, heading due south from eastern Oregon. He lingered briefly at High Rock Canyon, camped at the base of the Granite Range, and skirted the Black Rock Desert, about which Frémont wrote in his diary, "Appearance of the country is so forbidding that I was afraid to enter it." He and his party marched south in early 1844 along the edge of the Fox Range, beyond which they climbed a hill where "a sheet of green water . . . broke upon our eyes like the ocean . . . For a long time we sat enjoying the view [of the lake] set like a gem in the mountains." Frémont named the lake for the smaller of its two islands, which "presented a pretty exact outline of the great Pyramid of Cheops." Continuing south, Frémont and his men encoun-

tered Paiute in a village near present-day Nixon. There, they were served up a feast of "trout as large as the salmon of the Columbia River . . . the best-tasting fish I had ever eaten." The explorers went on to name and map the Carson and Walker rivers, then crossed the Sierra into California.

Only 15 years later, in January 1859 just before the discovery of the Comstock Lode and the establishment of Virginia City, an estimated 1,700 Numa congregated at the lake to fish and socialize. Chief Winnemucca was there with 300 of his clan; his son Numaga (Young Winnemucca) and his 300 Kuyui Dokado (Cui-Ui Eaters), whose territory encompassed the lake, hosted the gathering. At the same time, roughly a thousand white settlers and prospectors occupied traditional Numa land in what would soon be western Nevada.

Troubles between the nomadic Indians and the migrating whites were well underway. The Numa had determined the newcomers to be disrespectful people. Whites took prized ground with little or no regard for Indian claims or sub-

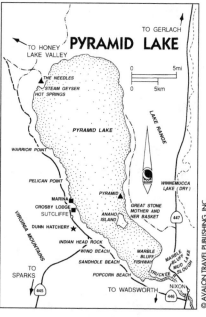

sistence. They killed the game, felled the trees, wasted native food. They practiced indiscriminate violence against the Indians along the Humboldt River Trail. And they disrupted the natural order and sacredness of things, without giving anything in return. Still, the Northern Paiute, a strong, industrious, and peaceable people, knew the futility of waging war on the whites. In 1855, Chief Winnemucca had negotiated the Treaty of Friendship with federal Indian agents, in which it was agreed that tribal laws would be invoked to punish criminal acts by Paiutes, and white justice would likewise deal with breakers of its own law. This treaty also defined territories, which were further delineated by the agents in 1859 as a precursor to the Pyramid Lake reservation. These agreements managed to keep the two peoples friendly for five years. Until the discovery of the Comstock Lode.

Pyramid Lake War

The vast horde of fortuneseekers bound for Washoe in the spring of 1860 knew little, and cared less, about the five-year-old Treaty of Friendship. Thousands of them overran prime Numa pinenut land in the Virginia Range and cui-ui spawning grounds along the Truckee River. Tensions mounted. Finally, an unfortunate spark touched off two pitched battles in the brief Nevada Indian wars. In May 1860, traders at Williams Station on the Carson River kidnapped and abused several Numa women. The Indians avenged the crime by killing the traders and burning the station. The incident spread hysteria and bloodlust through Washoe, and a ragged troop of volunteers set out on an ill-conceived, ill-prepared, and ill-fated retaliatory expedition.

Numaga, six-foot-four, fluent in English, son of great Chief Winnemucca (The Giver), spoke eloquently against engaging the whites in a fight. He led his Kuyui Dokado to meet the irregulars and sent a rider with a white flag to arrange a powwow. But the excited avengers shot at the rider and then blindly chased the Paiute into a ravine, where the Indians turned and slaughtered them. A month later, a force of regular troops from California pursued the Kuyui Dokado and exacted two Indian lives for every white life lost.

The Reservation

Two years later, Territorial Governor James Nye

met with Chief Winnemucca near the site of the second battle, where they exchanged gifts and spoke of peace. But another 12 years passed before President Grant in 1874 proclaimed Pyramid Lake and the surrounding desert an official reservation. Thereafter, a typical combination of unfortunate factors inhibited economic development. The continual replacement of Indian agents precluded consistent government relations. Federal appropriations proved remarkably insufficient. "Entrymen" (white squatters) appropriated prime agricultural acreage—at the big bend of the Truckee River, for one. Then the Central Pacific Railroad placed a division station at the southern edge of the reservation at Wadsworth in a 600-acre land grab that is still, after more than 120 years, in dispute. At the time, however, a quarter of the reservation's Indians were coaxed to Wadsworth to work as laborers and housecleaners.

After the diversion of the Truckee River in 1905 at Derby Dam to irrigate farmland around Fernley and Fallon, the water supply to the lake diminished systematically, depleting its fisheries and causing frequent irrigation problems for the Indian farmers and ranchers. The lowered inflow created a silty, swampy delta where the river joined the lake, preventing the big Lahontan cutthroat from spawning. That, along with massive overfishing, rendered the trout almost extinct by the 1930s, further exacerbating the financial instability of the reservation. (In 1975 the Paiutes began to stock the lake with purebred cutthroat, and today 15-pound trophies are not uncommon.)

Water Controversies

The depth of the lake dropped continually throughout the 20th century; the surface level has been reduced nearly 100 feet in 85 years. Diverting the river for reclamations and urban growth upstream has sidetracked much water from reaching the lake and increased the amount of pollution finding its way there. In addition, during periods of long-lasting drought such as occurred in the 1990s, the surface level of Lake Tahoe, source of the Truckee, falls below its natural rim. With all flow of Tahoe lake water into the river cut off, river water is prevented from replenishing the system's reservoirs in California, as well as Pyramid Lake at its terminus.

CUI-UI FISH

The endangered cui-ui (kwee-wee) is a sucker fish that lives only in Pyramid Lake. These fish are *old,* in every sense of the word. A prehistoric species, cui-ui inhabited Lake Lahontan for tens of thousands of years; as the inland sea slowly evaporated, these fish of the deep were able to survive at the bottom of the little Pyramid Lake remnant.

Cui-ui grow as large as seven pounds and can live 40 years. They spawn between the ages of 12 and 20, as early as April and as late as July, when they lumber upstream as far as 12 miles west to lay their eggs. In the old days, before the Derby Dam water diversion lowered the lake level, the Paiute spearfished and snagged them at the mouth of the delta during the spawn.

The WPA's *Nevada—A Guide to the Silver State* reported, "Now that the flow into the lake has been curtailed by upstream storage, the fish runs have practically ceased. Cui-ui schools circle through the shallows near the river mouth, searching in vain for spawning grounds, and pelicans step in and gorge themselves."

The cui-ui were nearly extinct by the 1940s. They managed to recover slightly in 1952 with one of the largest spawning runs (120,000 fish) in recent history. But compared to the millions of cui-ui that spawned in olden days, the population was decimated, prompting the federal government to list the fish as an endangered species in 1967. Another large run was recorded in 1969 (110,000 fish), but so few fish spawned in the '70s that tribal members voluntarily stopped eating them in 1979.

In the early 1970s, federal courts directed that water in Stampede Reservoir be used exclusively to benefit the cui-ui. A small pulse of fresh reservoir water is released as early as January to tickle the spawning instinct; the pulse reaches its peak by April, which helps the fish reach the spawning grounds. The fresh water also incubates the eggs and helps the microscopic larvae to swim back to the lake.

Only a handful of cui-ui spawned between 1976 and 1982, and a census in 1984 counted only 150,000 of them. No cui-ui spawned between 1987 and 1992.

The Marble Bluff dam and fishway were built in 1976 to stop the erosion of the riverbank, which threatened the stability of Nixon, just upstream. The dam also protects critical cui-ui spawning habitat. Some cui-ui will use the three-mile clay-lined fishway, which resembles an irrigation canal with a number of terraces known as ladders, but many won't. (These suckers are hard to domesticate.) During large spawning runs, the fish jam the entrance to the fishway and some are smothered before they can be gathered onto a large elevator platform, which raises them up to the river and washes them into it. In 1993, after one of the wettest winters and springs in the century, so many fish struggled onto the elevator that it couldn't lift them, and 3,000 died. Officials had to load nearly 5,000 cui-ui into trucks, drive them past the fishway, and drop them back into the river.

After the failure of the fish elevator three years earlier, the federal government in 1996 allocated $2.5 million to redesign the Marble Bluff dam, fishway, and elevator. The project was underway in August 1997.

Two good water winters—1995 and 1996—and an astounding winter in 1997 have improved things considerably for Pyramid Lake and its cui-ui. In August '97, the lake was up 14 feet from three years earlier. At an elevation 3,809 feet above sea level, the lake hasn't reclaimed the high water mark of the early '80s (3,820 feet), but its current level still is one of highest since the early years of the century.

Aided by high water and other factors, more than 250,000 cui-ui spawned in the spring '97 run (a 50-year high). The Cui-ui Recovery Team now estimates the total cui-ui population at between four and six million, four to six times more than estimates from the 1993 census. John Jackson, director of water resources for the tribe, says downlisting the cui-ui's position on the Endangered Species List from endangered to threatened is under consideration.

Recently, members of the tribe have been able to get a taste now and then of this favored traditional food. An agreement with U.S. Fish and Wildlife allows the tribe to harvest and consume a small number of cui-ui, whose gills are removed and sampled by USF&W to test fish health and water quality. The tribe distributes the harvested cui-ui to elders and others on the reservation.

The Truckee-Carson-Pyramid Lake Water Rights Settlement Act (a.k.a. the Negotiated Settlement) was signed into law in November 1990. It settled nearly all the major water conflicts in western Nevada, allocating 90% of Truckee River water and 80% of Carson River water to Nevada (the rest to California). It allowed Westpac Utilities (the Reno-Sparks water company, a division of Sierra Pacific) to store 39,000 acre-feet of its own water in Stampede Reservoir, which is controlled by the Pyramid Lake Paiute, for drought or emergency conditions. In exchange, the Paiute received $25 million for the Pyramid Lake fisheries program, plus $40 million for economic development. In addition, conservation plans in the municipal water district were to be implemented, including the controversial retrofitting of all the houses in the Reno-Sparks area with water meters. Enough water rights were to be purchased to maintain 25,000 acres of Lahontan Valley wetlands and to improve the spawning potential of Pyramid Lake trout and cui-ui. The Army Corps of Engineers was mandated to prepare a plan for the rehabilitation of the lower Truckee River to restore natural spawning grounds.

The only major player along the Truckee-Carson water system that was not directly included in the Negotiated Settlement was the Truckee-Carson Irrigation District (TCID). Though the farmers of Fallon and Fernley would certainly disagree, Elmer Rusco in an article in the *Nevada Public Affairs Review* (1992, No. 1) wrote that the Settlement "does not worsen the situation of the TCID but simply confirms what existed before its passage." However, in another critical defeat for the Fallon farmers in June 1994, the federal Interior Secretary of Water and Science ruled that unclaimed water from the Truckee River (the overflow that isn't shunted off to reservoirs, ranging from 200,000 acre-feet in a dry year to more than a million acre-feet in a flood year) cannot be diverted to the reclamation project; it must be allowed to run its course into Pyramid Lake. (For the farmers' point of view, see "Heading South Through the Farmland" under "Vicinity of Fallon.")

One of the first concrete accomplishments of the Negotiated Settlement was the Truckee River Operating Agreement, a pact that allows the tribe, the TCID, and various state and federal agencies to achieve the goals of the 1990 settlement by storing and exchanging each other's water throughout the lakes and reservoirs of the Truckee watershed. Prosser, Boca, Stampede, Independence, and Marlette reservoirs, in addition to Lake Tahoe, fall under the agreement.

The improvement of water quality on the lower Truckee is the goal of yet another working agreement that evolved from the Negotiated Settlement. The water-quality agreement calls for the tribe and Sierra Pacific Power Company to work together to purchase water rights in the watershed from the TCID and others. New ownership is viewed as a first step toward protection, enhancement, and rehabilitation of the entire river. Where the West and water are concerned, however, things move slowly.

While the deluge of January '97 left the reservoirs along the Truckee brimming and raised the level of Pyramid Lake to a 15-year high, it took scant pressure off the region's water users. With the drought years of the last decade still fresh in people's minds, water-conservation measures remained in effect, partly because such measures are mandated by the Negotiated Settlement.

Since 1975, the Paiute have operated the Dunn Hatchery at the lake. The hatchery has stocked Pyramid and Walker lakes with native cutthroat trout and have helped the cui-ui to spawn.

Friends of Pyramid Lake was founded in 1982 to unite citizens concerned about the lake's future. The group produces a newsletter and organizes forums, field trips, and other educational activities to increase awareness of the challenges, and the pleasures, of one of the most beautiful desert lakes in the world, and also organizes an annual triathlon at the lake. For more information, contact Friends of Pyramid Lake, P.O. Box 20274, Reno, NV 89515-0274, 775/323-6655.

ANAHO ISLAND

Anaho Island floats in Pyramid Lake like a giant sombrero, with a wide brim and a high crown. For centuries this 600-foot-tall island provided a breeding ground for the largest colony of American white pelicans in the United States.

Because these birds—clumsy and comical on the ground, majestic and dignified in the air—have such sensitive nesting instincts, they have long been considered a symbol of the wild country, a measure of its wildness. Predictably, the numbers of nesting pelicans on Anaho Island have dropped dramatically in recent years, almost to the point of disappearance.

Pelicans could be the easiest birds in the world to recognize. Their creamy white feathers, black-tipped wings with 10-foot spans, and huge orange bills cause them to stand out in the crowd of cormorants, herons, terns, ducks, geese, gulls, hawks, owls, and smaller species that, several months a year, call Anaho home. For thousands of years, tens of thousands of these creatures have migrated to Anaho from Southern California and western Mexico in the spring to set up housekeeping in this makeshift pelican city. A pair of pelicans settle into a nest, barely a hole in the ground softened perhaps with some dry grass and sage twigs. Into it the female lays two eggs, incubating them for a month with the webs of her feet. The male flies off every day to bring back a fish dinner. After hatching, the chicks mature quickly, reaching flight growth in two months and full growth (15–20 pounds) by migrating time in the fall.

Contrary to common conception, pelicans do not store fish in their large beaks. (The pouch stretches or contracts to control body temperature.) They swallow the fish (traditionally tui chub and carp from Winnemucca Lake—now dry—just east over the Lake Range), then regurgitate and redigest them. Pelicans, in fact, are the true bulimics of the animal kingdom, vomiting their food in the face of intrusion or danger. They're so skittish that fast-growing chicks confronted by chronic emotional distress can't hold their food down and will starve to death. Adult pelicans, startled by noise, will abandon their nests, leaving their eggs to fry in the hot desert sun, if the gulls don't eat them first. Unprotected days-old chicks, too, will quickly succumb to starvation, exposure, or predation.

In 1913, President Woodrow Wilson signed a bill preserving Anaho Island as a bird sanctuary, and today it's a 750-acre national wildlife refuge. In 1948, 10,000 pairs of pelicans nested here; by 1968, only 5,000 were showing up. In 1988, an all-time-low 350 pelican couples arrived to breed, from which a mere 50 chicks matured.

Since then, the numbers have improved dramatically. The solution was simple: a big inflow of water into the lake (and the Stillwater marsh country 60 miles southeast, traditional feeding grounds for the pelicans). Nature saw fit to end the drought in 1995 and supply the area with all the fresh water it needs—until the next drought.

FISHING & BOATING

Fishing season for cutthroat trout is from October 1 to June 30. Record cutthroat are generally 15–20 pounds. Fishing permits cost $6 a day, or $32 for the season; boating fees are the same. (If you're going to fish from a boat, it's therefore $12 per day, or $64 for the season.) If you buy a fishing permit, you don't pay the reservation's $5-per-vehicle day use fee. (Otherwise, for non-fisherfolk visiting the lake, there's a $5-per-vehicle day use fee or camping fee.) If you catch a cui-ui, you have to release it unharmed immediately; the penalty for being caught with an endangered species is a $10,000 fine (and very bad publicity). Fishing and boating permits are available at the Pyramid Lake Marina and at the Pyramid Lake

pelican

Store, near the entrance to the reservation.

You can bring your own boat, or rent one at the Pyramid Lake Marina. Two small locally-owned companies operate fishing charters on the lake. Lex Moser of **Pyramid-Tahoe Fishing Charters,** 775/852-3474, comes highly recommended by locals, who say his trips are a lot of fun. He offers fishing trips on Pyramid Lake from mid-October to mid-May, and on Lake Tahoe from early May through late October. George Molino, owner of the Pyramid Lake Store, operates **Cutthroat Charters,** 775/476-0555, with fishing trips on Pyramid Lake from October 1 through June 30.

VISITOR PERMITS & FEES

A day use fee of $5 per vehicle is charged for those visiting the lake and/or the marina. You can camp anywhere around the lake; the camping fee of $5 per vehicle *includes* your day use fee. Additional fees are charged for fishing and/or boating on the lake (see Fishing & Boating, above). Permits can be purchased at the Pyramid Lake Store, just inside the boundary of the reservation if you're coming from Reno, and at the Pyramid Lake Marina, where permits are available at both the store and the ranger station.

SIGHTS

The Road from Reno
The four-lane strip north through Sparks on Pyramid Way (NV 445) continues into the **Pah Rah Hills,** over a rise, then down into residential **Spanish Springs Valley.** Spanish Springs, like East Dayton, Mt. Rose Highway, and Gardnerville Ranchos, is an area slated for dramatic development over the next ten years. A regional growth plan approved by the Sparks city and Washoe County governments calls for subdivisions that will house an additional 15,000 people by the year 2005. And the urban spread northward doesn't stop here, either: Palomino, the next valley north, could host an even more controversial development of 1,700 homes, a business park, and three commercial centers.

North of Spanish Springs is one of the most dangerous stretches of road in western Nevada;

a number of roadside crosses mark the sites of fatal accidents, many involving drunken teenage drivers on their way home from partying at the lake. It also passes a growing number of large secluded homes of varying architectural styles.

Wild Horse and Burro Placement Center
Eight miles north of Sparks, just beyond the last Spanish Springs intersection (Chevron station), the speed limit steps up to 55 mph. Shortly, Spanish Springs narrows into **Palomino Valley.** The Bureau of Land Management operates the **Palomino Wild Horse Placement Center** here, with large and extensive fenced corrals, bales of hay, barns, and administration buildings.

An estimated 23,000 wild horses roam free in Nevada, roughly 5,000 more than the bureaucracy and its scientists claim is optimum for a thriving ecological community. Periodically, the BLM undertakes to thin the herds, by using helicopters (sub-contracted) to move groups into large wing-shaped traps or by fencing off water holes. Once caught, the mustangs are segregated by gender and trucked to Palomino Valley (or to centers in Susanville, California, and Rock Springs, Wyoming). There, the horses are corraled, vaccinated, fattened up a bit, freeze-branded with a distinct ID, and generally introduced to life in captivity. Horses older than three years are sent to sanctuaries in Texas and South Dakota, according to the BLM. Younger horses are put up for adoption by any American. The market is generally east of the Mississippi.

The BLM charges an adoption fee of $125 per horse (four-horse limit) and reviews the horse's care for one year. These and other controls are supposed to prevent the horses from being exploited or simply sold for dog food. If everything is satisfactory, the adopter is given title to the horse. Since the wild-horse law was instituted in 1971, 52,000 horses have been processed through the program. That's the good news. The bad news? Wildlife activists have long claimed that many of the horses—those supposedly sent to refuges as well as the ones that are adopted—are actually sold to pet-food manufacturers, and that BLM employees either turn a blind eye or personally profit from these sales. The BLM vociferously denied it for years, but in 1997 information uncovered by the Associated Press told a different story: in recent years, BLM lost track of 32,000 of the horses that it adopted out and up to 90% of the horses rounded up by BLM went to the slaughterhouse. Though the Bureau disputed the report, The Fund for Animals and Animal Protection Institute of America sued BLM, which settled by agreeing to tighten the reins of the adoption program.

Burros are much harder to catch (mostly by water trap, though sometimes by individual roping), but much easier to place. Burros have been known to bond even more closely with humans than dogs, and they make excellent pets. Nevada's 1,500 burros are only occasionally thinned.

The Palomino Center, 775/475-2222, is open Mon.–Fri. 8 A.M.–4 P.M. Although the gates are locked on weekends, you can still drive around the perimeter and see the horses inside the fence. Notice the alfalfa farms just north of the center.

Crossing into the Reservation

Just inside the boundary of the reservation at mile 23 is the **Pyramid Lake Store,** 775/476-0555, open every day 6 A.M.–7 P.M. (6 A.M.–6 P.M. in winter). Here you can stock up on last-minute fishing and boating supplies, pay your $5-per-vehicle day use or camping fee, and buy fishing and boating permits. **Cutthroat Charters** operates fishing charters from the store through the Oct. 1-June 30 season. Boat storage in a fenced compound can be arranged for a fee.

A little beyond the store you get your first unforgettable view of the lake—big, blue, rocky, and treeless, with a strange and desolate beauty that no words can prepare you for. The near-perfect tufa pyramid catches your eye same as it did Frémont's in 1844, when he named the loch for the rock. Anaho Island rises unmistakably just south (right). At the fork, go straight to Sutcliffe, or hang a hard right to Nixon.

The West Side

Just under three miles north (left at the fork) is the settlement of **Sutcliffe** (also spelled Sutcliff). Take a right at Sutcliff Dr., drive past a few homes and a playground, and you'll come to **Crosby's Lodge,** 775/476-0400. The expanded

bar has slots, video poker and large screen TV. The lodge, grocery store/gift shop, and gas pump are open 7 A.M.–8 P.M. most days, opening a bit earlier (6:30 A.M.) on Saturday and Sunday, closing a bit later (9 P.M.) on Friday and Saturday nights. The bar usually stays open later, depending on business—it stays open "until the bartender is tired of everybody," which might take until the next morning if they're having a good time. Four cabins, and additional kitchen-equipped trailers, are available for $32–112; a house is available for $80 a night, and RV spaces with full hook-ups are $14.

Go down the hill and around the corner from Crosby's for the **Pyramid Lake Marina,** 775/476-1156, where there's a ranger station, mini-mart, small museum, and RV park. Stop off at the ranger station or mini-mart and pay $5 per vehicle for a day use permit, which applies to everyone visiting the lake, even if they're just passing through. The ranger station is open every day, 7 A.M.–5 P.M. Next door, the store is open daily 6 A.M.–6 P.M., open later in summer. It's similar to Crosby's, but bigger and brighter. There's also a snack bar.

The centerpiece here is definitely the exhibit walk, through half a dozen rooms full of wildlife and historical photography, and informational displays about the tribe and the lake, with video, artifacts, and maps. Spend an hour or so here and come away with a much deeper understanding of the whole Tahoe-Pyramid water system, both contemporary and geologic. The explanation of Lake Lahontan, as well as the climatic evolution from its time till now, are excellent. Also be sure to check out the photos of those big Lahontan cutthroat, which no less an expert than John Frémont himself declared the best-tasting fish of all.

Since the floods of January 1997, the Pyramid Lake Marina no longer offers mooring slips for boats. The slips were removed when high water threatened to snap the cables tethering the floating dock to the lake bottom. A second boat ramp has been constructed to ease congestion. You can rent boats at the marina for $12–40 an hour, or $55–110 for six hours. Store your own boat at the marina for $25 a month.

Also here at the marina is a 44-site **RV park** with a laundromat, flush toilets, showers, and a dump station ($5). All RV spaces are pull-throughs, with full hookups. Tents are not allowed. Camping fees are $15 a day, $86 a week, and $275 a month. Dry camping along the lakeshore costs $5 a night; this covers your $5-per-vehicle day-use fee, too.

Also visit the **Dunn Hatchery,** 775/476-0510, up the hill from town, to learn about the Paiute tribe's Pyramid Lake fisheries. It's open Mon.–Fri. 8 A.M.–4:30 P.M. Tours are given 10 A.M.–noon or 1–3 P.M. Mon.–Fri., or on weekends around 1 P.M. (For large group visits, make arrangements by calling their main office, Pyramid Lake Fisheries, at 775/476-0500, open Mon.–Fri. 8 A.M.–4:30 P.M.) First examine the displays on prehistory, history, tufa, fishing, and past problems and future solutions in front of the main hatchery. Then a Paiute employee will show you around the work area. These hatcheries are considered among the most advanced and successful in the world. A million cutthroat (and a handful of cui-ui) are planted yearly in Pyramid and Walker lakes. Pregnant fish are captured and artificially spawned at the Marble Bluff fish-

biking on Pyramid Lake

DEKE CASTLEMAN

way. The fertilized eggs are brought to the hatchery and incubated; they hatch in one to four weeks. The fry are then "ponded" in 60 small or three large freshwater tanks. After a year, they're planted in the lakes. You'll see the numerous ponds, the incubation chambers, and the rock-filtration room.

Then head around to the back building to check on the much more specialized and intimate cui-ui hatchery. This operation provides a graphic representation of how difficult it is to artificially breed these ancient suckers. The good spawning runs of the mid-'90s (see the Special Topic "Cui-Ui" in this section) make the breeding program a little less critical.

(The **Numana Hatchery,** 775/574-0290, on NV 447 about 10 miles south of Nixon and eight miles north of Wadsworth, also grows cutthroat trout and gives tours. If there are just a couple of people, you can show up any day from 8 A.M.–4:30 P.M., visit the visitors' center and see the fish. Large groups must make tour arrangements at the main office, Pyramid Lake Fisheries, 775/476-0500.)

Two miles north of Sutcliffe is **Pelican Point,** with a boat ramp, good beach, Sani-Huts, and probably several tents right on the water. Farther north on the pavement (NV 445), you pass many turnoffs and dirt roads down to the shore—the sites aren't exactly "secluded" (little shade, no facilities), but there's plenty of opportunity to be by yourself on the beach. The pavement runs out in eight miles at **Warrior Point Campground,** which has a phone (might work), picnic shelters, drinking water, barren campsites, and little else. Day use or camping fee is $5 per vehicle.

The gravel road north starts out fairly well graded—35–40 mph. In another half mile is a flat site on an attractive inlet; two miles from there is one of the few forested and green areas on the lake. Horses graze in the grass.

Honey Lake Valley
In six-plus miles is a fork. Bearing left delivers you, in 30 dusty miles, to Honey Lake Valley. Honey Lake, a true playa lake that can go from flooded to dry, represents the western remnant of great Lake Lahontan. The valley is famous for the Sagebrush War between Nevadans and Californians. In 1850, the eastern California state line

was designated at the 120th meridian, but no official survey was conducted. In 1861, the western boundary of the new Territory of Nevada was established as everything east from the crest of the Sierra Nevada. But everything between the crest and the 120th, including Honey Lake Valley, fell into dispute.

In 1862 the sheriff of Plumas County, California, entered the valley to collect taxes but the residents, who considered themselves citizens of Roop County, Nevada, showed him the business end of their guns. During the next year a battle was waged in the courts with injunctions, fines, and contempt citations flying back and forth between the two counties. The hostilities inevitably escalated. When a Nevada judge and sheriff were arrested near Honey Lake by Californians from Quincy holding a Plumas County court order, a larger posse of Nevadans, led by Isaac Roop of Susanville, freed the officials. Shortly, armed avengers arrived from Quincy, and the two camps shot at each other for the better part of a day. Four of the men were wounded. Reinforcements from Susanville surrounded the Californians, who surrendered. In 1864, the official boundary survey awarded this western edge of the Great Basin to California.

The water in and under this valley (and other valleys between here and Reno) has for years been coveted by Westpac and urban developers. But so far, all the plans for its importation by pipeline have been saddled by controversy, and as of this writing, the likelihood of a pipeline between Honey Lake Valley and Reno-Sparks is very low.

The North Side

The right fork cuts northeast, and the road slows down to 25–30 mph. In roughly 13 miles, with a few sandy stretches near the end are the **Needles** and the **Hot Steam Well**. The huge Needles are rugged igneous masses thickly veneered with "tufa," formed by the precipitation of calcium carbonate from the lake water onto the rock. Researchers dug the well to explore geothermal effects, then capped it. Over the years the cap rusted shut, then blew out, and now a tall beam of steam streams into the atmosphere, and a seam of hot water teems into the lake. You used to be able to top off a temporary dam if you brought a shovel and sit in a sandy hot tub behind it, with the

rugged tufa formations towering over your head. Then you could run down to the lake for a cold plunge, or soak in the spot where the hot and cold waters mingle, for a tingle.

Sadly, the north side of the lake is now inaccessible to the public. Tribal officials closed the area for liability reasons in 1996 after a climber fell from one of the tufa Needles and was killed. Ongoing vandalism and litter problems also contributed to the closure. Apparently, a group of "Reno teenagers" who visited the area over the 1996 Labor Day weekend spray-painted graffiti on some of the formations (tufa is too fragile to be cleaned) and left garbage scattered around. Shards of glass were found in some of the hot pools. Such problems had been occurring for some time, but the tribe finally had enough. The area remains closed permanently, officials say, except to authorized tribal members. In addition, Tribal Chairman Mervin Wright said archaeologically sensitive sites around the lake, mostly on the south and east sides, also may be closed in the near future. Plans call for concentrating public use within the already developed "recreational zone" on the southwest shore near the marina, he said.

Indian legends about Pyramid Lake abound. One of them attributes the lake's creation to a young man who went away from his family and returned accompanied by a mermaid. This was considered very bad magic by the elders who were highly mermaphobic (which is not, contrary to popular conception, a fear of Ethel Merman), especially since the unusual couple was accompanied by a river of water. The family pleaded with the young man to carry the mermaid back to where he found her and take the river with them. When they refused, the people fled. But the couple, and the water, followed. Finally, the young Indian and the mermaid were compelled to remain at the edge of the river as their people continued north to their village. Soon the river water had created a large lake, at the north end of which the Indian, the mermaid, and their babies dwelled. The mermaid mother cast a spell on the babies to retaliate for their exile: if any Numa glimpses the "water babies," he will fall sick and die. When the area was open, if you listened very hard, you could almost hear the whimpering of the water babies. During very special occasions, you could also spot them near the shore at dusk.

The South and East Sides

South of Sutcliffe on NV 446 toward Nixon are a number of signposted beaches: Wino, Sandhole, and Popcorn, plus Indian Head Rock. Then you pass the southern edge of the lake and reach NV 447. In 1997, Congress designated NV 447 through the reservation as the **Pyramid Lake National Scenic Byway,** the first federally recognized scenic highway in Nevada.

At the junction of NV 446 and 447, just southwest of Nixon, the **Cultural Center and Museum,** 775/574-1088, occupies a striking circular stone building representing a traditional kiva. The displays here are not as extensive as those at the museum at the Pyramid Lake Marina, but they do have a few exhibits. Cultural events are presented here; phone for current schedules. The museum is open Mon.–Fri. 8 A.M.–4:30 P.M., Saturday 10 A.M.–4:30 P.M.; the hours may be changing, so phone ahead before you make a special trip out here.

When you reach NV 447, take a left. Cross the Truckee and head into **Nixon,** a tiny town on a green spot where the Truckee River sloughs off into the lake. Houses, health and senior centers, and a road maintenance station in town give way to farm and ranch land north of Nixon;

stone mother and basket

BOB RACE

the river is lined with tall cottonwoods. Nixon's new Paiute school, the Pyramid Lake Junior and Senior High School, dreamed of for 20 years and opened in September 2000, is the pride of the town.

NV 447 aims straight at **Marble Bluff,** but at the last possible moment veers around it lakeside. Before that, though, a paved road to the left leads down to the **Marble Bluff Dam** and **Pyramid Lake Fishway,** 775/574-0187. There's not much to see here unless you have an appointment for a tour; call their main office in Reno, 775/861-6300, to make arrangements.

On the other side of NV 447 before it rounds Marble Bluff is **Mud Lake Slough,** which once diverted the overflow from the Truckee River into Winnemucca Lake just a bit northeast. After rounding the bluff, you look down on the dried-up old lakebed.

Five miles north of the fishway, a sign points left toward the pyramid. The road starts out promising, but quickly turns as rough as the wild tufa formations alongside it—15–20 mph. In five miles, passing Anaho Island, you're in the middle of some serious tufa territory—strange calcareous rocks, bleached white or dull beige or dark brown, much of it striated and honeycombed. In two miles bear left to the **pyramid**—450 feet high. Camp on the beach up from the unmistakable **Great Stone Mother and basket.**

Straight across is Sutcliffe, with its green-dot trees, white-dot trailers, and bright-dot lights at night. Gnats swarm but don't seem to light or bite—you get used to them quickly. Creamy white pelicans and chocolate brown cormorants sun themselves on rocks. The beige mountain ranges, silver-green sage, bleached tufa, and green fields are all offset by the impossible blue of the water. Sunsets across the lake are exquisite—orange to red to purple. If you're lucky the moon will be going down directly over the pyramid, against whose sheer walls the waves, driven by the wind, lap. The Great Stone Mother watches through her grief. You can't help but feel the power of the place.

According to one myth, the pyramid represents the spearhead of the Great Father, whose sudden knifing through the surface indicated the end of a long period of drought and famine. Another holds that it's a giant cap placed over a licentious woman. But that sounds suspiciously like a legend connected to Anaho, to which a Paiute maiden was exiled for immorality. Nearby, the Great Stone Mother continues to mourn for her lost children, rotten kids who drove each other away. Her tears filled Pyramid Lake; the basket at her feet remains empty. Many legends, in fact, describe ancestors disappearing around the lake. A huge serpent, embodying a lake spirit, is said to live in its depths. It swallows swimmers in a swipe—which explains why the bodies never return to the surface. The spirit's moods can turn the glassy-smooth surface into an angry sea, and the color from bright azure to deep purple to dark and brooding gray. Camping at night on this beach, the looming shadow of

the Great Father's trident, the Stone Mother sitting awake, and the spirit's restless whispers wafted by the winds are splendid stimuli for fantastical, mystical, or just plain scary stories of your own.

INFORMATION

For further information about Pyramid Lake, the reservation and the businesses or other features found here, a good resource is the **Pyramid Lake Paiute Tribal Council,** 775/574-1000. The office is open Mon.–Fri., 8 A.M.–4:30 P.M.

NORTH OF PYRAMID LAKE

Winnemucca Lake
Back on NV 447 heading north, you'll see the **Lake Range** on the west and the dry bed of Winnemucca Lake on the east. Known as Little Lake of the Cui-Ui by the Paiute, this transient body of water came and went often throughout the ages, since its depth was dependent on the overflow of the Truckee. In 1876, for example, a gravel bar partially blocked Pyramid Lake from the mouth of the river, which emptied much of its mountain and desert water into Winnemucca Lake to a depth of 85 feet. After the Derby Dam diversion in the early 20th century, Winnemucca Lake received a continually diminishing supply of water. In the mid-1930s, the WPA's *Nevada* reported that "it is only in wet years that it contains any water," though "many geese and ducks live in the bordering tule marshes." Since then, the lake has dried up completely, leaving only a few tufa sculptures and a long playa. See if you can imagine a big blue lake out there. The **Nightingale Mountains** rise up from its extinct eastern shoreline.

This road is pencil straight; you can put it on autopilot for both the accelerator and steering wheel. Twenty minutes north, the tufa begins appearing on the west side of the road; keep an eye out for **Tufa Snoopy.** Thirty miles north of Marble Bluff you can clearly make out the old shoreline at the north edge of Winnemucca Lake. The **Selenite Range** picks up where the Nightingales leave off; Mt. Limbo's **Purgatory Peak** rises to 7,382 feet. North of it, **Kumiva Peak**

scrapes the sky 900 feet higher. About 40 miles north of Nixon, you'll pass a turnoff with sign pointing right to Empire Farms, a company which dries and packages dehydrated garlic and onions. Burns and Phelps, another local company, grows garlic for seed in the area.

The valley narrows as it ushers you into **Empire,** a thin strip of green along the highway backed by the southern edge of the great **Black Rock Desert.** Giant mineload trucks haul dusty, chalky-white salt into the U.S. Gypsum plant here, passing flatbed 16-wheelers hauling out heavy loads of sheetrock. The mine is a little east up in the Selenite Range. The mine and mill employ around 125 people.

On the corner of NV 447 and Empire Road is Empire Distributing Company grocery store and a Mobil station. Take a left onto Empire Rd. passing the sheetrock plant. Empire is a shady, breezy, comfortable company town four blocks wide and four long. Cruise up and down the streets to get a glimpse of company housing, the community pool and park, a nine-hole golf course (free and open to the public), and tennis and basketball courts.

Just beyond Empire is the green oasis of **Gerlach,** huddled directly below distinct **Granite Peak,** more than 9,000 feet tall, the southernmost peak of the Granite Range. But first, the road cuts across the Black Rock playa, which stretches northeast toward the horizon, flat as a mackerel and dry as July.

GERLACH

Gerlach, at first glance, is a tiny town that serves as a division point for Southern Pacific Railroad as it chugs through northwestern Nevada. (The sign going into town lists the population at 350, but locals say the entire population of Gerlach, Empire, and the outlying ranches probably doesn't add up to that. The figure on the sign hasn't changed as long as anyone can remember, and folks insist there are only about 100 people on the Gerlach General Improvement District's tax rolls.) But as soon as you stop to consider that Gerlach is the largest settlement in an area of probably 10,000 square miles, from Reno to the south and Lakeview, Oregon, to the north, from Susanville, California, to the west and Winnemucca to the east, the town takes on a much greater significance. Gerlach, in fact, claims the only gas station, slot machines, restaurant, and motel in Nevada's vast northwest corner. It's also the gateway to the famed Black Rock Desert, where the world's land speed record was set in 1983. And it's a friendly, comfortable town in its own right, boasting the best ravioli in the state, a surprising variety of house architecture, a cool pottery ranch, and one of the most dramatic views imaginable of a railroad snaking across a desert. Gerlach's clever motto, "Where the Pavement Ends and the West Begins," could very well be no brag, just fact.

History
This area was settled by Indians for its good spring water, wild food, and plentiful shelter. More recently, pioneers paused at the springs here, marking the end of the Black Rock Desert and the beginning of the arduous journey through High Rock Canyon.

Louis Gerlach began ranching in this area around the turn of the 20th century. A few years later, the Western Pacific Railroad laid tracks along the northern route out of Winnemucca, crossing Desert Valley and the Jackson Mountains, then skirting the edge of the Black Rock and Smoke Creek deserts (then crossing Beckwourth Pass north of Reno and dropping down into Oakland). Gerlach was founded as a rail division point in 1906, named for the ranch.

The most exciting times in Gerlach are the land-speed record-setting events on the Black Rock playa, which happen every so often. It all started in October 1983, when Project Thrust was rained out of the Bonneville Salt Flats on the other side of the state near Wendover. Driver Richard Noble and his team of Brits relocated their rocket-car operation to the Black Rock Desert northeast of Gerlach. They set up a 10-mile straightaway on the flat cracked-mud playa (another dry lakebed of vast Lake Lahontan), with a 10-mile overrun—in case the braking parachutes failed to deploy. Noble cranked up the Rolls Royce Avon engine (with afterburners) of *Thrust II,* the rocket car, and attained a speed of 633.606 mph, finally breaking Gary Gabelich's 13-year record of 622.407 mph, set at Bonneville in 1971. The residents and racers adopted each other, and a great time was had by all. In fact, a second record was set when a crew member towing an outhouse to the raceway hit 70 mph, establishing a world speed record for portable toilets.

Gerlach's rush over speed was rekindled in summer 1997 as Noble the Brit and former record-holder Craig Breedlove (407 mph in 1966) of the U.S. made plans to face off on the Black Rock playa in the first-ever head-to-head challenge for the land-speed record. By August '97, the Noble and Breedlove camps had received permission from the BLM to construct a dozen parallel 15-mile tracks on the playa. Plans called for the teams to leapfrog from track to track in a succession of speed trials throughout September (or until the start of rainy season, whichever came first).

The BLM imposed a series of conditions on the racers intended to address complaints from the Paiute tribe about possible damage to cultural sites, environmentalists over possible impacts to wildlife, and history buffs concerned about the proximity to nearby emigrant trails. The ever-popular Black Rock simply isn't as remote as it was in 1983. In the '90s, the speed with which your permit is issued can be as important as the speed of your vehicle. Breedlove blamed the failure of his attempt at Noble's record in 1996, in part, on a last-minute appeal that postponed his run into the windy season. His hopes, though luckily not his brains, were dashed when a gust lifted the nose of his *Spirit of America* rocket car

BOB RACE

Thrust II *is 54 feet long, 12 feet wide, and weighs 10 tons. It's the first car ever to use two turbojets (manufactured by Rolls Royce); each produces 110,000 horsepower, which is roughly equivalent to* the power produced by 1,000 Ford Escorts; the powerplant is similar to the one in the F-4 Phantom jet. It has a pencil-thin fuselage with the two engines mounted on either side of the cockpit.

(clocked at 677 mph), sending him careening through the world's fastest—and longest!—U-turn. Setting a record requires a car to make one run down the track, refuel, and return within 60 minutes. Official speeds are averaged from the elapsed time, minus the midway pit stop. So even though he exceeded Noble's record by over 40 mph, Breedlove's 1996 time didn't count.

A month before the 1997 event, the Breedlove and Noble camps were downplaying any hint of a personal or international rivalry as hard as the media was playing it up. Their respective representatives said both men were eyeing the record—and the 741.4 mph sound barrier—not each other. The fact that both teams ended up in the Black Rock at the same time, however, seemed designed to boost public and corporate (read: sponsorship) interest in the event. The pressure was on to burst through the Mach 1 sound barrier (750 mph) by a land vehicle in '97 to coincide with the 50th anniversary of Chuck Yeager's first supersonic flight.

Breedlove, a 62-year-old grandfather, was set to pilot *Spirit of America,* which boasts a single jet engine with afterburners from an F-4 fighter that can deliver 48,000 horsepower. Incidentally, that's more horse than all the formula racers in the 1995 Indy 500 combined. Noble (also in his 60s and now an organizer and front man) enlisted Andy Green, a Royal Air Force pilot, to take the wheel of Thrust II, a sinister-looking twin-jet design. Resembling a jet fighter without wings, the thing looked capable of accelerating to Mach I and more.

Craig Breedlove's team began test runs on the Black Rock on Sept. 6, two days before Noble's. *Spirit of America* was clocked at 330 mph before engine problems delayed further runs till Sept. 19, when Breedlove hit 381 mph. After more technical (and financial) problems, Breedlove's car was clocked at its top speed of 531 mph on Oct. 12.

Noble's team arrived at the Black Rock with the 10-ton *Thrust II* on Sept. 8 and the race was on. The first run was made on September 8; on September 10 the car reached speeds of 428 and 517 miles per hour. For the next two weeks, problems with the suspension, power converter, hydraulic system, computer, and weather postponed the British team's quest. On September 22, *Thrust II* completed two runs at 618 and 653 mph, but they didn't count toward breaking the record because they weren't within an hour of each other. The next day, Green revved the car up to 693 and 719 mph, but again missed the record books on the same technicality as the previous day. On Sept. 25, it finally became official: two runs of 700 and 728 mph within an hour of each other set the new land-speed world record at an average of 714 mph, 80 mph faster than the previous record.

But Noble's team didn't rest on its laurels, not by a long shot. On October 14, 1997, one day before the 50th anniversary of Chuck Yeager's breaking of the sound barrier in a jet, *Thrust II* achieved supersonic speeds of 760 and 764 mph, breaking the sound barrier on land for the first time in history. When the speed of the rocket car exceeded Mach 1, it let off a light sonic boom; much of the noise was absorbed by the acoustically soft desert. It didn't, however, set a new record—the runs were 61 minutes apart!

Around Town

Drive into Gerlach, passing five bars. Tooling around the residential streets, you'll notice all the different **architecture:** single wides, double wides, peeling wood-frames, ranch houses, barns, a lone two-story house, even a modern log cabin. **Sunset Blvd.** has the community center and post office; W. Sunset has the sheriff's substation and courthouse. Look for the old water tower, built in 1909 and listed in the National Register of Historic Places. The **high school** is the home of the Gerlach Lions. The graduating class averages six students a year.

Planet X

John and Rachel Bogard maintain a pottery lifestyle, known as Planet X, 775/557-2500, in an old farmhouse and a complex of studios and three galleries. The whole rustic affair sits on a 200-acre ranch first settled in the 1880s and resettled 20 years ago by John and first wife. The desert ware exhibited and sold include cups, bowls, plates, pitchers, and vases, many painted with colorful desert panoramas or black-and-white forest scenes. The showrooms are also decorated with sixties-style posters announcing parties, exhibitions, sales, and classes held throughout the years.

These days, things occasionally get so busy that the Bogards hand out fliers with the most frequently asked questions—and answers—about their little oasis of art in the vast aridity of northern Nevada. When asked a question he's answered a thousand times, such as, "Why do you call the place Planet X?" John says, "Quick, Rachel, get him a flier." Before she returns with one, he answers. "Look around," encompassing the valley and surrounding mountains in a one-armed sweep. "Doesn't it look like Planet X?" It is, one supposes, a world apart from the greenery of his native Berkeley and Santa Cruz.

Bogard's printed replies sometimes come in multiple choice. Question: Why did you move out here? Answer (pick one or more): a) Low overhead; b) Hot springs; c) Had no other place to live; d) My truck broke down here; e) The federal witness protection program put me here. A similar playfulness can be found in Bogard's pottery. Check out his huge suspended decanters, some bearing images of trilobites skittering in the mud of some primordial ocean.

Except for propane refrigeration, Planet X is solely solar. John sold solar systems around the valley for awhile through his sideline, Planet X Power and Light, but no more. "The people who need it the most—the ones who find solar attractive because they live beyond the grid—can't afford it," he said. You can also ask John about his passion for landsailing.

To get there, take the Planet eXit at the fork just north of Gerlach (left) and go eight miles on NV 447. You can't miss it (the address is 8100 Hwy. 447). Stop in and check out this exquisite pottery—excellent souvenirs for travelers and Nevadans and gifts for non-Nevadan friends and family. Open every day from around 10 A.M. on.

Spirit of America *is 44 feet long, 8 feet wide, and weighs 4.5 tons. It's powered by one 48,000-horsepower GE engine with an afterburner.*

Hot Springs

Unless someone has bought Gerlach Hot Springs ($150,000 asking price) and fixed it up, you'll find it closed, despite the sign that stands on the right side of the road just past and opposite the Jalisco Bar in town (to attract interest from potential buyers). The opening of the springs on Memorial Day 1991 was a proud day for little Gerlach, and folks here still haven't shaken the bitter disappointment that took over when the springs closed several months later. It seems that the contractor who designed the filtering system thought he was building a swimming pool and didn't take the spring's mineralized water into account. In just a few months, the very expensive filters clogged up—in the words of the Gerlach General Improvement District's Don Wardle "harder than cement"—with silica.

Though the contractor had been recommended by the county, a clause in his contract kept the town from forcing him to correct his mistake. Apparently another clause protected both the contractor and the county from legal action, or so the dispirited townsfolk claim. Options to reopen the springs explored by the town have proved too expensive or unworkable. So there it sits, a sad reminder to the elderly ladies of the Hot Pool Committee who raised more than $90,000 for the project with eight years of bake sales and barbecues and who even carried cinderblocks to help raise the bathhouse with heated floors.

In autumn 2000, the hot springs had still not reopened, and locals doubted that it ever would. For someone with a lot of energy and $150,000, the springs may be a good investment. After all, it comes with almost five acres of prime Gerlach real estate.

Practicalities

The reason that **Bruno's Country Club** in Gerlach, 775/557-2220, has been called the "social center of northern Washoe County" can be summed up in a single surprising word: ravioli. These big fat fatties, swimming in old-country meat sauce and covered with home-cured imported cheese, go for a bargain $8.85. Bruno's starts serving breakfast every day at 5 A.M. and finishes dinner at 9 P.M.

The adjoining bar has video poker and black-jack and reel slots, along with photographs of the racers and local artwork. The bar also serves as the front desk for **Bruno's Motel**, 775/557-2220, which has 40 units for $30–55, next to the Texaco.

Just up the street, the **Black Rock Landing Saloon** is another fun place to eat, have a beer or cocktail, and hang out. **Joe's Gerlach Club** next door and the **Miner's Club** next to Bruno's cafe round out the licensed premises.

Gerlach made a splash in the Reno newspaper in 1992 when two Washoe County sheriff's deputies showed up to enforce some law and order in unruly Gerlach (or that's the way the paper made it sound). Between Empire and Gerlach, there are six bars for fewer than 400 people. After 80 years generally outside the clutches, suddenly townspeople started getting busted for DUI at a very accelerated rate: 35 arrests in 14 months. (It's a two-hour ride to jail in Reno.) Note that the deputies' jurisdiction covers 3,500 square miles around this corner of the state. Unless you're driving drunk around town, you're definitely on your own out here.

Speaking of which, **Bruno's Texaco** station is at the south end of town, last gas till Eagleville (80 miles) or Denio (110 miles). You can pick up local brochures here.

Sixty miles north of Gerlach, the **Soldier Meadows Guest Ranch & Lodge,** Soldier Meadows Rd., Gerlach, NV 89412, 530/233-4881, www.soldiermeadows.com, is a working cattle ranch with a 600,000-acre range. Guests can go horseback trail riding, or ride out with the cowboys to join them in their ranch activities; the ranch is popular with hunters, too. The ranch lodge has 10 guest rooms. Lodging alone costs $45 per person, per day, or $75 per day with all meals included; horses are another $50 per day.

FROM PAVEMENT TO PRONGHORN

By taking the left fork just north of Gerlach, you continue on NV 447 northwest toward Eagleville and Cedarville in California, where you cut back due east to Vya and the Sheldon Antelope Refuge. (The right fork takes you past the Black Rock Desert and up to High Rock Canyon; see below.)

Just beyond Planet X, a turnoff (left) heads out onto the **Smoke Creek Desert,** which on topo maps appears to be a southern extension of the Black Rock. If you have an older map, you might expect the pavement of NV 447 to run out, but it doesn't. Instead, you twist and turn through the juniper forest of the granite **Buffalo Hills,** then cross broad **Duck Flat.** You then thread your way through the south end of the **Hays Canyon Range,** which hugs the western boundary of Nevada. A sign demarcates the Lassen County (California) line, 56 fast, easy, and scenic miles from Gerlach. You drive north between the eastern foot of the big **Warner Mountains** and the western edge of well-watered **Surprise Valley.** Scattered ranches lead you into **Eagleville,** with big Eagle Peak looming over the sleepy picturesque little farm town.

The surprises in Surprise Valley start in Eagleville, which boasts venerable whitewashed, wood-framed buildings, but is not quite as sleepy as it was a few years ago when the windows of most of the town businesses sported "Closed" signs. Jill and Joe Barnett, who bought the **Eagleville General Store & Stockroom Cafe,** 530/279-2121, a few years ago, seem to have sparked a local resurgence. The building, a frontier classic, has been in continuous operation (except for two years) since 1888. The couple moved to the valley from Susanville on the back side of the Warners to retire and, typically, they haven't stopped working since.

Open 7:30 A.M.–6 P.M. every day, the store has groceries, some camping supplies, a deli counter, and a gas pump out front. The Stockroom Cafe is open Sundays, 7:30 A.M.–8 P.M., with dinner beginning at 5 P.M., serving home-style meals emphasizing local beef, but also scampi, lasagna, barrel-roasted chicken, and meatloaf. The store/cafe is town central, says Jill, who welcomes phone calls from people with questions about fishing, hiking, and camping in the Warners and in Great Basin, just across the state line. She can also be contacted at her web site: www.modoc-marketplace.com/eagle.

The big annual event here is the **Eagleville Volunteer Fire Department Picnic,** a 52-year-old tradition held the last Saturday in July. The menu is—you guessed it—beef (it's what's for dinner in these parts), cooked slow in an underground pit the night before. Everyone who stops by is welcome. In 1996, the town served half a ton of beef to a crowd of 1,000. **Cockerell's High Desert Guest Ranch,** 530/279-2209, about eight miles north of Eagleville and eight miles south of Cedarville, has three guest rooms for $70 single, $85 double. Meals are not served here, but there's a kitchen where guests can do their own cooking.

Between Eagleville and the next town north, **Cedarville,** rows of tall poplars and ranches nestled one after another lend an air of long civilization to Surprise Valley. The rich stretch at the base of the Warners, however, gives way to Lower and Middle Alkali lakes down on the playa, and then the bare Hays Canyon Range over the state line. Not only does the view provide a fine contrast between the two states, but the name Surprise Valley itself is telling. This kind of agricultural strip on the wet edge of a basin between two ranges would surprise only Californians. It's exceedingly typical in Nevada.

Cedarville

A Surprise Valley resurgence is even more evident in bustling Cedarville, 18 miles up the road from Eagleville. A handful of new businesses, many run by recent arrivals to the valley, have sprouted in the last few years, providing a mix of old and new (age). The town saddle repair shop, for example, sits between the eclectic Great Basin Books (Modoc County's one and only) and an acupuncturist who moved to town from Ashland, Oregon, in 1997. The **Jothi Marga** spiritual center, offering weekly meditations and other activities, also operates the **Jothi Surprise Valley Natural Foods Co-op,** in the center of town.

Historic buildings line the streets of Cedarville. The one that houses the bookstore faces the old drugstore, built in 1890 by a man who claimed to be the only white survivor of Custer's Last Stand.

Great Basin Books, 530/279-2337, book wood@pacbell.net, is a good source for information about the town and surrounding area. It's open 10 A.M.–5 P.M. most days, including weekends. For information about the area's natural beauties and local hot springs, stop by the Modoc National Forest's **Warner Mountain Ranger District** office, 385 Wallace St. a block off Main St., 530/279-6116, open Mon.–Fri. 8 A.M.–4:30 P.M.

Town events include the **Cedarville Squirrel Shoot** in early April where local ranchers team up with local hunters to help keep the ground squirrel population in check. The rodents' prolific population is a problem around these parts, and their burrow holes can trip and cripple a horse. Professional bull riders and their mean mounts are the draw at the **Modoc Super Bull Rodeo** held in mid-June at the **Modoc County Fairgrounds**, 530/279-2315. The town airport hosts the **Pancake Fly-In Breakfast** in mid-July, which draws pilots and hand-built planes from around the tri-corners region where California, Nevada, and Oregon meet. The **Modoc County Fair,** held at the Modoc County Fairgrounds the last three weeks of August, is always a whooping good time. Every Friday, July through September (or until the first frost), there's a **farmer's market** next to the health clinic. The restaurant across from the bookstore holds outdoor exhibits of **local art** over the Memorial and Labor Day weekends.

Most travel-related services—gas, auto parts, food, and lodging—are located along the highway. Restaurants include the popular **Country Hearth Restaurant & Bakery,** 530/279-2280, serving breakfast, lunch and dinner; it's open Mon.–Sat. 6 A.M.–9 P.M., Sunday 7 A.M.–2 P.M. and 5–8 P.M. For snacks and casual fare, **Susan's Frosty Deli & Pizza,** 530/279-6284, serves up pizza, burgers, fries and ice cream specialties; open every day, 11 A.M.–9 P.M. in summer, till 8 P.M. in winter. The **Cedarville Café & Saloon,** 530/279-6363, serves full breakfast, lunch, and dinner, with changing dinner specials such as prime rib, grilled salmon, and pasta dishes; open every day except Monday, 6 A.M.–8 P.M.

Inns along the main drag include the refurbished 14-room **Drew Hotel,** 530/279-2423 ($31 single, $42 double) and the **J. K. Metzker House B & B,** 530/279-2650 ($65 single, $75 double). Half a mile west of town on Highway 299, on the right, is **Sunrise Motel & RV Park,** 530/279-2161, with motel rooms for $40 single, $49 double, RV spaces with full hookups for $15 a night, and tent spaces for $10. The **Modoc County Fairgrounds,** 530/279-2315, offers space for tent and RV camping in summer, unless there's a special event going on at the fairgrounds (such as the rodeo in mid-June or the county fair in August).

It's wise to top off the gas tank and check all your fluids, belts, and hoses before heading east on Rt. 299. As you leave Cedarville for the Sheldon Refuge you'll see a sign stating "Next Services 100 miles." On Rt. 299, you quickly descend into the basin. In eight miles, at the Nevada border, the pavement immediately, without any ceremony, ends, and there won't be any more for at least the next 70 miles.

Surprise Valley Hot Springs

Five miles east of Cedarville on Rt. 299, the **Surprise Valley Hot Springs & Resort,** 530/279-2040 or 877/927-6426, warmh2o@ hdo.net, www.svhotsprings.com, offers overnight accommodation, therapeutic massage, and relaxing soaking in tubs supplied from artesian mineral water coming out of the ground at 208°F.

Day use, by advance appointment only, costs $10 per person for a two-hour soak. Half-hour, hour and 1.5-hour massages are $36–69. They also offer accommodation: deluxe villas with full kitchen are $105 a night, standard villas with microwave and fridge are $85 (double occupancy). Each villa has its own private hot tub. "Fly & Soak" packages are available for those with small airplanes, who can fly in to the Cedarville airstrip. Plans are in the works for a new RV park here at the springs, which may be completed during 2001; plans are to give each RV pad its own private hot tub.

Advance reservations are essential, whether for day soaking or overnight visits, because they are often full up.

To the Sheldon Refuge and Range

The road (8A) is good—graded and drained gravel, comfortable even at 45–50 mph. You climb into the northern Hays Canyons where, 11 miles from the state line, a steep shortcut forks off to the left, twisting and turning over **Fortynine Mountain** (not recommended for trucks or motor homes), while main 8A heads right, also climbing through the juniper over a summit, then dropping down into Long Valley. At the first junction, signs point right (south) to Gerlach (84 miles) and straight ahead to the Sheldon Refuge. In a mile is a second intersection, sometimes labeled **Vya** on maps. A right turn keeps you on 8A through the southern part of the Sheldon Range; straight ahead on 34 leads north to the refuge. This road, too, with its signs and road number, is well graded. It ought to be, with the Vya Highway Maintenance Station around the bend. Though a sign at the gate says "No Services," it's comforting just knowing that it's there. The original winding shortcut rejoins 34, and in a mile a sign points right, 21 miles to the refuge.

It's a straight shot northeast, cutting a diagonal across **Long Valley.** After a wide bend north, the road narrows and roughens. A final fork to the right at the Department of the Interior sign takes you up, way up, **Bald Mountain,** with a fine view of aptly named **Mud Lake** in the valley. A dozen switchbacks, at 10–15 mph, deliver you to the summit, where you drop a bit down to the high plains of the Charles Sheldon National Wildlife Refuge.

THE BLACK ROCK DESERT

In *Hiking the Great Basin,* John Hart observes that, overall, the Great Basin Desert is not generally referred to as "the desert." "That word," he writes, "is reserved for sections that stand out as barren among the barren, wastes among wastes," among which the "Black Rock Desert, at least one million acres in extent, is second only to the Great Salt Lake Desert." In short, this is a desert's desert, a landscape of unique barrenness and beauty, solitude and plentitude, danger and freedom. It's a vision so forbidding that as eminent an explorer as John C. Frémont, on his way to discover Pyramid Lake, was afraid to approach it. Yet thousands of westbound pioneers crossed it in awe and agony, on the Lassen-Applegate Cutoff from the main Emigrant Trail. And it was the scene of Nevada's fiercest fighting between Indians and white settlers. Today, the Black Rock, largest playa in North America, is a magnet for rockhounds and history buffs, hikers and pilgrims, landsailors and hotrodders, UFO nuts and other nuts. Doug Keister, author and photographer of a book called *Black Rock: Portraits on the Playa,* says, "I see the playa as the world's largest stage. It's so pure and clean that anything you put on it becomes significant."

Indeed. Drive down onto the playa (a broad mud plain, another dry lake bed of ancient Lake Lahontan) and accelerate for miles without bothering to steer (but only after you've checked on conditions in Gerlach—you're looking for dry dry dry, because when wet the playa is an impassable sump). The edge of a shimmering lake that you seem to be hurtling toward is always just ahead. But wait! What's that black thing out there? Looks like a motorcycle, or maybe it's one of those jet cars on a collision course! Nah, it's too big and standing still—a cow! What's a cow doing on a silt bed, halfway between nothing and nowhere? But the black thing keeps looming bigger and bigger until you pass it at 65 mph and oh.

A beer can.

Then the surface starts feeling like thin ice, which you're always just about to crack through and fall deep into a dense mud bog. Now the other cars' tracks are racing up to you, crossing under you in a flash, then disappearing behind you—while you're standing still. Even the illusions are on a grand scale.

The Black Rock encompasses a million acres, split into two forks by the encroaching thrust of the Black Rock Range, the volcanic outcrop that gave a bearing to an estimated 30,000 emigrants who crossed the desert between 1849 and 1870. Because of its remoteness and hard surface, the Black Rock section of the Emigrant Trail is the best preserved in the west, and conservation groups want to set aside large tracts as a National Conservation Area, with interpretation and a visitor center.

To get onto the Black Rock, take the right-hand fork just north of Gerlach and continue on the paved road that travels along the upper edge of the playa; in several miles an obvious entrance ramp presents itself. Late spring through fall is the safe season for cruising the cracked desert; winter it's too muddy. The first time you get out there you'll understand exactly why the root of playa is "play," and you'll be hooked.

The best descriptions of this country, and its unlimited hiking potential, are found in *Hiking the Great Basin.* For a group experience, contact the **Reno Gem and Mineral Society,** 480 S. Rock Blvd., Sparks, 775/356-8820, a hobby club which holds monthly meetings and conducts monthly field trips. If you're soloing, be careful! This place is treacherous, and people die out here every year. It's very easy to get lost, and if your car breaks down, you might be in serious trouble. If you're planning to explore the Black Rock in any depth for an extended period, it's recommended that you carry detailed topo maps and a compass; five gallons of water per person per day and emergency food for a week; sunblock, first-aid kit, warm clothes, and some portable shade; two spare tires, tools, a hand winch, rope and chain, shovel, axe, extra gas, belts, hoses, and fluids; and a CB radio. Many people actually tow an extra car in. Finally, don't forget Session Wheeler's classic *Black Rock Desert*.

The paved road, NV 34, continues northeast, leaving Washoe County and entering Pershing

County. Ten miles past the first access to the playa is a second. The road cuts north for a bit and then back west, reentering Washoe. Sixteen miles out of Gerlach the pavement ends, and you can kiss it goodbye for many a long mile.

HIGH ROCK CANYON

After the pavement ends, the gravel road starts out relatively smooth, and you can run 50 mph for a short while. This is ranching country, with alfalfa fields, ranch houses under big cottonwoods surrounded by cypress windbreaks, and frequent cattle guards. The road slows you down to

---

BURNING MAN CONTINUES TO GROW

The Black Rock area is the scene of a huge yearly event called Burning Man. A 40-foot, 1,500-pound wood sculpture is erected in the area each year over Labor Day weekend. The Man symbolizes "a mockery of the busyness of society." In other words, an enormous amount of energy and money are invested in transporting the materials to the Black Rock Desert, attracting an audience, erecting the statue, and celebrating (the busyness of) life. Then the Man is burned. The symbolism is about construction and destruction, ambition and futility, and just plain getting wild on the playa.

What started as a fringe event by a bunch of fringe characters has evolved into a spiritual celebration for modern times. Whatever Burning Man has become, it certainly has grown in terms of the number of people it attracts—in 1998 the gathering attracted an estimated 15,000 participants, in 1999 it was up to 24,500, and in 2000 the count came in at just under 26,000. In recent years the village that springs up on the playa outside Gerlach over Labor Day takes its place, temporarily, as one of the ten largest towns in Nevada, complete with its own constabulary (the Black Rock Rangers), village lamplighters, cafe district, and fire and sanitation departments.

The event takes place on BLM land (that's the federal Bureau of Land Management) in the midst of the scorching desert. There's a hefty admission fee, part of which goes to the BLM. Ticket prices increase throughout the year, so it pays to buy tickets well in advance.

Organizers promote the festival as an experiment in temporary community, where participants can shed the fetters of society and stretch the ordinary limits of life. Each year at the festival there are drugs, naked bodies, raves, mud parties and big art. But organizers put a lot of effort into trying to make Burning Man a peaceful experience, and although police are present, citations are rare. The most serious complaint after the 1997 Burning Man gathering was that quite a mess was left behind, which took several months to clean up. Nowadays, participants are required to take away everything they brought in, and volunteers stay for weeks to return the Black Rock Desert to its pristine condition. After a while, no trace can be found in the desert to show that the event ever took place.

Burning Man takes place every Labor Day weekend (late August-early September), about 12 miles from Gerlach.

Contact:
Burning Man
 P.O. Box 884688
San Francisco, CA 94188-4688
Burning Man Hotline:
(415/TO-FLAME)
www.burningman.com

about 35 as it grows narrower and twisty turny. Short stretches of pavement on bridges over creekbeds give you just enough time to say "Ahhh" before it's back to rough riding. A few miles past the second access to the playa is a turnoff (right, signposted) onto another gravel road for Summit Lake Indian Reservation, Rainbow Opal Mine, and Soldier Meadows Ranch B&B.

As you get deeper into the Granite Range, the road deteriorates further, down to 25 mph in places, then back up to 40 on a long flat smooth stretch. Just before the end of the straightaway, 35 miles from Gerlach, is a second main fork in the road: NV 34 veers off to the west toward Vya, while a very ugly road runs northeast to High Rock Canyon. You can get up to 20–25 mph on this one-lane primitive dirt road for about a mile and a half, and then it turns dire: chuckholes, washboards, grass in the middle of the lane, sage scratching both sides of the car. It gets worse. You creep across stretches with big rocks in the road, up and down deep gullies and washes, and thick sand. Five or ten miles an hour max. Then it gets worse. Only if you have a high-clearance 4WD vehicle should you even consider taking this little canyon excursion.

After a while, you come to an intersection. Bearing left you'll enter **Little High Rock Canyon.** There's a very narrow jeep track into this canyon–better hiking than driving. The left fork leads to more creeping toward the main show. Finally, two hours and 15 miles from the turnoff, three hours and 50 miles from Gerlach, you reach the BLM-brown sign for High Rock Canyon.

It's still another couple of hard miles to the start of the long series of canyons that make up High Rock. But then there you are, three hours and 17 miles from the fork, at 800-foot-high sheer walls of polychrome volcanic rock. The dark basaltic rock near the top of the walls is from the last volcanic activity, somewhere around 15 million years ago, when massive lava flows obliterated the landscape and laid down a uniform layer of tuff. The bright red band below the dark rock is the fine layer of soil that was turned red when the hot lava flowed over it. The beige bands below are ash deposits from earlier volcanic eruptions. Adding to the Kodak potential

are the lichens growing on the rock—chartreuse, sageleaf green, rust. Those majestic birds with the huge wingspans soaring on the updrafts are golden eagles; you might also see falcons, hawks, and great horned owls.

John Frémont, as usual, made the first recorded passage through High Rock Canyon in 1843, and described it in his diary. In 1846, the Applegate brothers, following Frémont's directions, blazed a trail through the canyon, which Peter Lassen, in 1848, used to lead a wagon train from near Winnemucca on the main Emigrant Trail to Goose Lake in the northeast corner of California.

A pull-out in the middle of the first (and most spectacular) canyon has firewood, campfire rocks, and a cozy carbon-covered cave. Driving through, you almost think there are two canyons, one under the high rock walls and the other under the sage towering over the road. You can look straight out of the car window and see the root structure of the shrubs.

The road slows down to about one mile an hour, because of the rocks, dips, ruts, creek crossings. It's kinda dusty, too. This is both the High Rock road, and the high-rock road. Actually, "road" is a bit too optimistic a description; it's really a jeep track, no place for anything but a high-clearance, heavy-duty-suspension, 4WD vehicle. (Me? I had a 4WD '91 Ford Tempo, which required $600 of front-end and drive-train repairs when I got home. And I don't even like canyons.)

Getting out is no less painful. The grass you drive over is taller than the car. You cross creeks, four-wheel over hillocks, and hope that nobody comes in the opposite direction (nobody does). You might feel like one of the long-distance automobile pioneers in the first decade or two of the century, who had to rely on directions from people who didn't know what they were talking about, maps that lied deliberately to get them to come through towns, and roads that were probably in even worse condition than this one.

If you're really into this country, you can carry the appropriate topo maps, which will let you know about side trips to historical sights, such as cabins, pioneer graffiti, and old emigrant camping grounds. Along the main track is a lone cabin, where there's a pullout if it gets dark and you need to stop for the night, or if you want a break from the psychic tension and physical pounding you get from the trail. The surface improves around 25 miles from the entrance to the canyon; it's back up to 20 mph, with some cattle around.

At the next fork in the road, go straight; you'll have to open and close a wire gate behind you. From there you climb up to Stevens Camp, the only place on the road with potable water. At Stevens you cut around to the northwest and drive for another little while at around 25 mph, till you come out on NV 8A—wide, smooth, 45 mph, a bit slippery and washboardy from the gravel, but it might as well be black velvet compared to the past 35 miles. Phew!

Take a left; Vya is 20-odd miles west. At Vya bear right, and head north up Long Valley to the entrance to Sheldon National Wildlife Refuge.

SHELDON NATIONAL WILDLIFE REFUGE

Like the American bison, pronghorn once roamed the west in the millions, but within 100 years of the first mountain men entering Nevada, overgrazing, hunting, disease, and deliberate poisoning had decimated their numbers to the verge of extinction. One pocket of pronghorn holdouts remained in the far remote corner of northwestern Nevada. In the early 1920s, Edward Sans, state director of predator control and a representative of the U.S. Biological Survey, began a campaign to carve a pronghorn refuge out of the large ranches in that corner of the state. He lobbied the Washoe County Commissioners, the federal land agencies, and the New York conservation societies and big-game clubs. The Boone and Crockett Club donated $10,000 for the effort, in return for naming the refuge after its leading member, Charles Sheldon, a hunter, explorer, and writer who had studied and reported on the pronghorn over the years.

By 1928, ranch land had been purchased and President Herbert Hoover set it aside as a refuge. Audubon Society experts and money managed the 34,000 acres until 1933, when the young refuge was officially taken over by the federal Department of Biology, forerunner of the Fish and Wildlife Service. Edward Sans was appointed director. By 1937, seven additional parcels had been acquired, expanding the refuge

to 575,000 acres. Since then, programs have been implemented to manage the antelope, mule deer, and burros. The highway across the refuge was completed in 1962; bighorn sheep were introduced in 1968.

Sights

Today, the pronghorn at the refuge have regenerated to a winter population of 3,500. They are more dispersed in summer, as they range widely for food and water. In the spring and summer many antelope leave Sheldon for the Hart Mountain Refuge across the border in Oregon. Best time to spot them is in the morning and evening, though because they feed during the day (a boon to hunters), you might see them anytime. Early in the morning, especially, you can see hundreds of these graceful and skittish creatures all over the park. They're very fast and they'll keep a distance between themselves and your car, but when they feel safe, they'll resume their camel walk, their bouncing over the sage as if on springs, bobbing their heads back and forth and flashing their white rumps.

The western **ranger's residence** is a little past Bald Mountain summit: a beautiful stone house built in 1934 and a shop next door. Pick up a map and a brochure (if there are any) at the information signpost where you enter the refuge, coming in from US 140.

Continuing east, it's one fine dirt road, though narrow. You can go about 35 mph, but you'll probably want to poke along at 25. At the top of a gentle grade, you get a nice overlook of **Swan Lake Reservoir**. If the pronghorn are out at all, there could be scores of them on the flats south of the lake. Then you turn north, into unusual country for Nevada: high volcanic plains, vast and rolling, good for spotting wildlife. Little humps above the plateau carry names such as Sage Hen Hills, Round Mountain, and Blowout Mountain; flattop crests are called Bitner Butte, Big Spring Butte, and Gooch Table. You cruise along, then around, Rubble Ridge and come to **Catnip Reservoir** and a primitive **campground** (firepit, picnic table, outhouse, no fishing). You leave Washoe and enter Humboldt County, a little beyond which is a junction. Route 34 ends and 8A, the southern route which forked off at Vya, rejoins; if you've come up through High Rock Canyon and headed around via Vya, you've just completed 300 degrees of a circle.

You enter Humboldt County as 8A climbs a low rise between Fish Creek Table and Fish Creek Mountain. There's no sign, but a change in county road crews is evident as you're forced to slow to 20–25 mph. Razor-sharp shards of obsidian glisten on the roadbed. Locals say the road eats tires, so watch it. But in five miles is US 140, the Winnemucca-to-the-Sea Highway, which means pavement, glorious pavement.

Going left brings you, eventually, to Lakeview

and Medford, Oregon, and finally to Crescent City, California. But those are other authors' states. Instead, take a right toward Denio. A half mile east is a turnoff to **Big Springs Reservoir Campground.** Beyond, the road descends to Virgin Valley, where a long, straight, flat plateau points at the road like some cosmic freight train— the Nevada Road Atlas calls it **Black Ridge,** the USGS two-degree map **Railroad Point.** US 140 runs along Thousand Creek and then leaves the Sheldon Refuge. The Pine Forest Range is straight ahead.

PRONGHORN ANTELOPE

The pronghorn *(Antilocapra americana)* is unique. It's endemic to North America and is not related to any other antelope, or deer, or elk, or goat, or sheep, or elephant. Its name is derived from its horns, which are pronged like the tines of a fork. But these "horns," which grow to be about a foot long and only on the males, are more like antlers, as they're shed after mating season in the fall, and regenerate completely by the next July.

Pronghorn bucks stand three feet high and weigh between 100 and 150 pounds. The does have tiny button horns slightly longer than their ears; females weigh 80 pounds max. Both males and females are reddish-brown, with a black band from the eyes to the nose, white throat and stomach, and a white rump patch whose hairs bristle when the animal senses danger. The horns and hooves are jet black.

The rut is quite a bit more vicious than is normally known in ungulates, always bloody and occasionally deadly. A dominant buck will acquire three to eight does in his harem. The does give birth in the spring, usually to twins, but sometimes to single kids. The kids weigh four to six pounds at birth, and it takes only a week for them to be able to run 20 miles at a clip, fast enough to outrun a coyote or bobcat.

Special glands give off an odor repugnant to flies and mosquitos. Two pointy hooves, as opposed to the usual four, provide firm traction and good protection against predators. The resolution of their eyes, extremely wide-set and sharp, has been compared to eight-power binoculars. But mostly these animals are *fast,* having been clocked in a dead run at close to the speed limit! Big livers store abundant glucose for bursts of speed and long-distance endurance.

But two fatal flaws quickly doomed the pronghorn after the arrival of settlers. First, they're diurnal, and move about in the light. Second, they're as curious as cats and want to get to the bottom of anything out of the ordinary, such as a red flag waved by a hunter. In addition, the pronghorns' vast western grazing and watering habitat was fenced; they were killed en masse by hunters, settlers, even trains; they were poisoned to eliminate wolves and bears. By 1913, when Charles Sheldon estimated their numbers, fewer than 15,000 pronghorn remained. Today, pronghorn in the Antelope Refuge number approximately 3,500, the largest concentration of this unique animal in the world.

KAREN McKINLEY

Heading toward Denio on US 140, about 10 miles north of Denio you'll come to a sign pointing out the turnoff to the **Virgin Valley Campground and Hot Springs.** Another sign advertises the Royal Peacock Opal Mine, with recreational opal mining for a fee. A good gravel road takes you one mile to the campground—and back into the refuge—past the Dufurrena Ponds. The free campground has about eight loosely defined spaces with fire pits and tables, pit toilets, and a tap for drinking water. The ponds offer fishing for bass and perch; state regulations apply.

A group called Friends of the Refuge has done an excellent job fixing up the place. The stone-rimmed hot pool has a fresh gravel bottom and the adjacent showers, in an old stone building, are clean and in good repair. At about 85 degrees F, it's more of a warm springs, really, but welcome nonetheless. A colony of guppies lives in the lightly mineralized water. Some are fantails with orange, yellow, and blue spots, just like the ones you had in your aquarium as a kid.

All in all it's a nice place, marred only by the halogen lights outside a nearby ranch house and the minimal privacy afforded by the open campsites. In summer, you'll fall asleep to a serenade given by bullfrogs, which load the two dozen or so ponds in the area. While you're out and about, check out **Thousand Creek Gorge,** visible on the left on the drive in to the campground. A two-mile hike or drive from the Virgin Valley Campground leads you to the mouth of the gorge and a trail that meanders past ponds and willows in the shade of redrock walls 300 feet high. Signs of wild burros are everywhere. You might think you're in Moab around sunset as the evening light burnishes the cliffs a coppery gold.

Looking for more amenities? Driving eight miles farther into the refuge on the same road brings you to the **Royal Peacock Opal Mine,** 10 miles in from the highway. The RV park here, open May 15 to October 15, offers tent camping for $4 per person, 18 RV sites with full hookups for $15, and four fully-furnished trailers for $40 a night, to which you need bring only your food (reservations suggested). Hot showers are available to non-guests for $3 per person, and there's a laundromat, gift shop and rock shop, too. You can dig for opals here at the mine, for a fee: $65 per day to dig in virgin ground, $25 per day to dig in the tailings, and you keep all the opals you find. This is a working mine; the black fire opals found in this valley are Nevada's state gemstone, and other types of opals are found here, too. Contact: Royal Peacock Opal Mine, P.O. Box 165, Denio, NV 89404, 775/941-0374 (winter 775/272-3246), maestes@ctnis.com, www.royalpeacock.com.

Camping in the Refuge

There are approximately a dozen primitive camps in the refuge, most of which have vault toilets. The campsite at Virgin Valley has public hot springs and a tap providing drinking water. The other campsites have no drinking water. No camping reservations are accepted. All sites are free. Contact: Sheldon National Wildlife Refuge, P.O. Box 111, Lakeview, OR 97630, 541/947-3315.

ALONG US 140

Back on US 140, in a few miles is Denio Junction where a truck stop, **Denio Junction Service,** awaits, 775/941-0371. It has gas, a cafe, bar, grocery store, slots, and 10 motel rooms for $45–50. They also offer RV parking: RV spaces with full hookups are $5 a night, but if you don't need hookups, there's no charge for parking RVs (just make sure to park out of the way). The store and café are open every day, 8 A.M.–9 P.M.

If you're hankering for tasty road food in a quaint diner, head north into Oregon 24 miles to **Fields Station,** 541/495-2275. It may be out of your way, but the place has most things travelers need: meals, gas, rooms, propane, and supplies. It has three motel rooms ($30 single, $40 double, $55 with two beds), plus an older house ($75 a night for the whole house, or the same prices as the motel rooms, if you share). Five RV spaces with full hookups are $7.50 a night; cheaper in winter, when the water is turned off. The café is open Mon.–Sat. 8 A.M.–6 P.M., Sunday 9 A.M.–5 P.M., longer hours in summer. A chat with the Northrops, the ranching family that runs Fields Station, is worth the drive.

Denio

Denio is three miles north of Denio Junction.

Aaron Denio started out from Illinois in the early 1860s, settled in Winnemucca, and then roamed north to the Oregon border to ranch. The town, junction, and summit are named after him. Denio's post office opened in 1898 in Oregon and remained there for 50-odd years until it moved into Nevada. The town today looks a bit like Logandale, near Overton in Clark County: a few houses along the road, fronted by large stockyards, backed by green fields of feed. Stop off at the **Diamond Inn Bar** for refreshment and a chat; there's a post office and a community center, which houses the public library. The hotel and mercantile are ghosts, and a cattle guard marks the state line.

As you head back toward the junction, big bare **Black Mountain** broods over the road on the west; across the valley (kind of a northern extension of the Black Rock Desert) are the golden peaks of the **Bilk Creeks.**

To US 95

US 140 runs south for a while between the Bilk Creek Mountains on the east and the **Pine Forest Range** on the west. It's possible, though improbable, that the western mountains were once forested; today there's not a single solitary tree to be seen for 25 miles. The naming of this range seems more likely to have been the height of frontier sarcasm.

Shortly the Winnemucca-to-the-Sea Highway veers off to the southeast across the upper Black Rock Desert, leaving the Pine Forests behind to pine for the forests, and then cut between the Bilk Creeks to the north and the **Jackson Mountains** to the south. The **Quinn** (an 1800s' spelling of "Queen") **River** meanders along this stretch on its way southwest to its sour sink in the Black Rock Desert. The **Kings River** joins the Quinn north of where US 140 turns and runs due east across the huge **Desert Valley.** Then you skirt the southern edge of the **Double H Mountains** and cross over into the long **Quinn River Valley.** Aiming straight at the **Santa Rosa Mountains,** US 140 joins US 95—billboard junction. McDermitt is 42 miles north; Winnemucca is 31 miles south.

If it's getting late and you're looking for a comfortable campground for the night, make a beeline for the Lye Creek Forest Service facility, roughly 45 minutes away in the heart of the Santa Rosas (see below). Or if it's real late and you want the nearest facilities, head 12 miles north for **Orovada,** a small farm and road service stop in the morning shadow of craggy Sawtooth Mountain. Here you'll find houses with satellite dishes, farm-machinery sales and service, triple trailer trucks loaded with bales of green hay, and a highway maintenance station. **Orovada Store** at the Texaco station sells gas, groceries, and supplies; open every day, 6 A.M.–9 P.M. The **Rocky View Inn,** 775/272-3337, has a café, a bar, and a six-room motel (rooms $30–40).

THE SANTA ROSAS

Ten miles south of Orovada is the junction with US 140, beyond which the road sneaks between the main Santa Rosas (left) and the **Bloody Run Hills** (right), whose namer is anonymous and whose name is unexplained. You crest a minor summit, **Palisade Hill Pass** (4,900 feet), and drop right down into **Paradise Valley,** one of the most classically beautiful basins in Nevada.

Paradise Valley

The valley itself, pointing north like a shaft from the Humboldt River into the spearhead Santa Rosas, attracted homesteaders even before Winnemucca was on the map. It also, therefore, attracted the hostility of Paiute and Bannock bands of whose territory the area was a part. Several skirmishes in the early 1860s between Indians and farmers attracted the avenging cavalry from Fort Churchill. They established Fort Winfield Scott right in Paradise Valley, which was subsequently transferred north to the Quinn River Valley after Colonel McDermit was killed in the summer of 1865.

Life for both peoples settled down thereafter, and a hotel was built in the town of Paradise Valley in 1866. The post office was established in 1871. The valley, then as today, supported gardens and ranches (mostly cattle, plus sheep for a while). Surrounded on two sides by the rugged, snowcapped, granite Santa Rosas and on the third by the ruler-straight **Hot Springs Range** with proud stands of trees dotted among the fields, the valley and town grew, peaking at several hundred residents who serviced the agricultural economy.

Today, this idyllic little town is as classic as its namesake valley. The wide shady lanes, beautiful houses on large lots, and falling-down abandoned businesses make great subjects for black-and-white photographs. **Paradise Bar and Mercantile** is the main action in town. The bar is one of the funkiest in Nevada, with soft couches and easy chairs, electric fans, and no slot machines. The ice cream parlor next door is a fine place to sit and chat with anyone else who's around over a Coke in souvenir Coca-Cola glasses. In 1995, the ice cream parlor next to the bar was expanded to include a small grocery and deli. You can also stop in at the Humboldt-Toiyabe National Forest's **Paradise Valley Ranger Station,** 385 Main St., 775/578-3521, to check on current conditions at Lye Creek Campground, road conditions in the mountains, and to buy a map of the Santa Rosa Ranger District. The ranger station is open Mon.–Fri. 7:30 A.M.–4 P.M.

There are some accommodations on NV 290 a few miles south of town. **Stonehouse Country Inn,** 775/578-3530, is in a wooden country house built by a lumberman in the 1940s. The inn has six guest rooms; two can accommodate large groups or families. Four of the rooms have private baths, and the other two share one. Rates are $75–95 a double, and include a continental breakfast. They will prepare a special dinner for an extra fee. The menu? Beef is prominent, of course. Amenities include a large-screen TV, big screened-in verandah, large dining room, and commercial kitchen. The big grounds feature a canvas wigwam with fire pit and smoke hole, barn, corrals, horseshoe pit, trap and skeet range, and a half-mile-long dirt landing strip. Bring your own horses and ride into the Santa Rosas. Reservations six months to a year in advance are usually required to secure a room during holiday weekends.

Into the Mountains

Make a dogleg through town heading east and travel three miles to the end of the pavement. It's a little hard to tell right away that the road beyond the pavement is dirt, until you enter the national forest (typically not a tree in sight). There, your speedometer drops as fast—50, 40, 30, 20—as your altimeter rises. It gets steep, twisty, and even a little exhilarating. Great views—if only you could look! You climb climb climb, past massive, weathered granite outcroppings, cliffs, and walls standing guard over one of the all-time great stretches of off-pavement road in Nevada. You finally crest **Hinckey Summit** (7,867 feet)—beautiful views on all sides, great hiking in every direction. You rock and roll down toward Martin Creek and take a left (at road sign 087) just before the turnoff (right) to the USFS Guard Station. It's another 1.5 miles farther down to **Lye Creek Campground.**

This lush and plush campground has 13 sites. Some have been converted to double sites, al-

ghostly storefront in old downtown Paradise Valley

DEKE CASTLEMAN

lowing more campers to utilize the existing space. Single sites go for $6; doubles cost $8. Most of them are right along the creek. Potable running water, accessible toilets, picnic tables, grills, and fire rings are provided. There's a 14-day stay limit. Reservations are recommended for the group sites in summer; contact the Santa Rosa Ranger District in Winnemucca, 775/623-5025, ext. 111. (Only the group sites can be reserved; individual campsites are first come, first served.) For general information about the campground, call the Paradise Valley Ranger Station, 775/578-3521.

Lye Creek has some unusual vegetation for 7,000 feet in Nevada: lots of willow, aspen, mountain mahogany, even mint and fennel, and no conifers. For an easy hike, follow the spur road up over the gully into the high country, with **Granite Peak** (9,732 feet) awaiting the hale and hardy just to the south. The road and campground should be open from late May till mid-October, depending on snowfall. Ordinary vehicles can make it to Lye Creek Campground, but once you leave the campground going up towards Granite Peak, you'll need four-wheel drive.

Back on the loop road where Lye Creek flows into big Martin Creek, take a left and continue your adventure north through the Santa Rosas. The road prowls through the high country, crisscrossed by old sheep trails. In a little under three miles, go left at the fork (signposted to US 95). Keep prowling. The big peak straight ahead is **Buckskin Mountain,** with a dramatic slide on its west flank. You climb and climb up to **Windy Gap** (7,380 feet), which comes as something of a surprise—be sure to make the turn! There's quite a view looking down onto the Quinn River Valley; gazing farther west, you'll again know why this physiography is called Basin and Range. Five miles of hairpin turns and a stint in the canyon deliver you to the boundary of the National Forest. Three miles from there are the ruins of a fairly recent mercury mill. Finally you get down and dusty again in the desert and after a while you arrive back at the pavement, 23 miles and an hour and a half from the campground and 39 miles from the last pavement in Paradise Valley.

McDERMITT

History
In the early 1860s, the Winnemucca-to-Boise stagecoach stopped at Quinn River Station near the border of Nevada and Oregon. In the summer of 1865, in response to Indian unrest, military personnel patrolled the area; their bivouac was called Quinn River Camp. Colonel Charles McDermit, commander of the Nevada Military District, and his troops engaged the Indians on several occasions; McDermit was shot and killed on August 7, 1865. A post was immediately established and named Camp McDermit. Occupying 2,000 acres, its dozen buildings (including a hospital) typically surrounded a square. In 1870, Sarah Winnemucca, daughter of great Chief Winnemucca, led a group of 500 Indians from the squalid Truckee River reservation to the camp and begged the Army to feed them. Subsequently, another several hundred Indians arrived from southern Oregon. Educated in California and fluent in English, Spanish, and three Indian dialects, Sarah spent her life crusading for humane treatment of her people. She served in the McDermit hospital for a time.

The name of the camp was changed to Fort McDermit in 1879, after which it operated for another 10 years. The longest-lived active Army fort in Nevada, it was also the last of the state's posts when it was converted into an Indian reservation in 1889. Somewhere along the way the name of the fort, the reservation, and the little service town next to it was altered, by post office officials or mapmakers, to the more common spelling of McDermitt.

Sights and Practicalities
Today, the **reservation** covers 34,650 acres, most in Nevada, the rest in Oregon. The town rests in the shadow of the Santa Rosas. Of the 800 members of the Fort McDermitt Pauite-Shoshone tribe, roughly half live here. The 13-mile loop road travels back into a pretty, well-watered canyon shaded by large old trees. Small farms sprout vegetables and alfalfa; ranchers raise horses and some cattle. A historical marker commemorates the life of Sarah Winnemucca. The smoke shop is in a big green building just off US 95 at the south end of the circle drive. A small stone remnant of the origi-

nal fort, which served as the jail, still stands in the tribal compound—administrative offices, senior center, and gymnasium.

In 1992, the McDermitt tribe was awarded $300,000 in grants to study the possibility of locating a temporary high-level nuclear waste dump (MRS, or "monitored retrieval storage facility") on its land. The facility was supposed to store spent fuel rods from nuclear reactors in aboveground containers for anywhere from 10 to 40 years. But the deal fell through, so life up in this corner of Nevada will stay pretty much the same.

Visitors are welcome to attend a sun-dance ceremony held annually on the reservation in late July or early August. The Paiute-Shoshone adopted the sun dance from the Great Plains tribes such as the Sioux, Cheyenne, Kiowa, and Comanche. To honor the sun/creator, warriors would (and still do) insert bones or sticks through two slits cut into their chest. In one version, buffalo skulls are attached to the bones by cords and dragged around until the weight rips the fasteners from the dancers' flesh, a mind-altering process that can take hours. In another version, a group of dancers are tethered in the same manner to a tall pole. The dancers circle the pole under the mid-day sun, using their body weight to break free. The tribe also stages a three-day "All-Indian" rodeo Fri.–Sun. over Father's Day weekend. Phone the tribal administration office, 775/532-8259, for more information.

In town (250 residents), the pink **Ore-vada Club** on the street called "the Lane" by the locals is the oldest active building (1880). The locally owned **Say When Casino,** 775/532-8515, has served border traffic for decades. The casino houses the full complement of nickel, quarter, and dollar slots and video poker, along with a two-table blackjack pit. The coffee shop and bar here, like the casino, are open 24 hours.

Across the street from the Say When is the **McDermitt Service Station and Motel,** 775/532-8588, with a gas station and a mini-mart with an interesting old-fashioned candy counter. The cashier serves as the front desk clerk for the motel; its 23 rooms go for $39–60. The same owner runs the **Snack Stop** across the parking lot, open seasonally (summer), serving burgers, chicken, milkshakes and the like.

Across the street and south two blocks, the **Diamond A Motel,** 775/532-8551, has 10 rooms for $27–38.

Mitchell's Stateline RV Park, 541/522-8101, is across the street from the state line on the Oregon side, catty corner from the post office. Pull-through RV spaces with full hookups are $15, tent spaces $10.

The **Desert Inn Bar,** 775/532-8009, has antiques, gifts, and souvenirs for sale, including Native American art and craft creations from the reservation. It's open every day, 10 A.M. till whenever.

The **McDermitt Mine** (still labeled on most maps as Cordero), 11 miles southwest of town, was one of the largest producers of mercury in the world, till it shut down in the late 1980s.

The McDermitt Branch of the **Humboldt County Library** is at the south end of town.

To Winnemucca

US 95 south from McDermitt to Winnemucca is a long road straight down the eastern edge of Quinn River Canyon, with a string of ranches running green along the bottomland and the big Santa Rosas rising tan to the east. Roughly 11 miles south of McDermitt, a dirt road turns off (left) toward Buckskin Canyon, the north end of the loop road through the mountains across Hinckey Summit and down to Paradise Valley. In another 18 miles is Orovada, and 12 miles south of there is the junction with US 140.

From there, you cross Palisade Hill Pass and follow the Bloody Run Mountains along the western edge of Paradise Valley. In the distance are the northernmost peaks of the **Sonoma Range** straight ahead and the **East Range** to the west of them, **Grass Valley** in between. Shortly the road crosses some anomalous and slightly mysterious sand dunes, which could be creeping east on a secret mission for Lawrence of Arabia. The Bloody Runs give way to the **Krums,** beyond which **Winnemucca Mountain** sits in lonely splendor at 6,400 feet just north of town. US 95 drops down to the Humboldt River Valley, snaking its way back and forth, traveling almost as far north and south as it does east and west—a long, lazy stream. For a break, pit stop, or picnic lunch, turn off (left) into **Pioneer Memorial Park,** conveniently situated for southbound travelers just before the urban brouhaha and foofaraw—after days or weeks in the northwestern Nevada wilderness—of Winnemucca, City of Paved Streets.

EAST ON INTERSTATE 80 FROM SPARKS

TRUCKEE CANYON

Just beyond the Pyramid Way exit is the Southern Pacific tank farm, with 46 tanks full of aviation fuel, diesel, gasoline, and heating oil. The farm was installed in the mid-1950s; in 1987 the state Environmental Protection Division discovered a fuel plume, three to five feet thick, atop groundwater 100 feet under the tanks. It's estimated that between four million and 40 million gallons of oil spilled during operations or were leaked through faulty tanks. A low estimate of 10 million gallons makes the spill as big as the one from the Exxon *Valdez.*

In 1988, the spilled oil began to show up in the Helms Pit, a 20-year-old gravel-excavation operation 120 feet deep and covering 78 acres. The bottom 25 feet or so were below the water table, which allowed the pit to act like a half-mile-wide recovery well, since the fuel plume, 750 feet wide and nearly a mile long, was carried by groundwater into the pit and trapped there. Roughly six million gallons of water were pumped from the pit daily and skimmed of fuel; the pumping and cleaning cost the nine tank-farm companies involved in the suit well over $6 million. But it prevented the leak from spreading to the river and into the water table.

In 1995, the companies settled a suit brought by the state Environmental Protection Division for $10 million, the largest such settlement in Nevada history. The city of Sparks received a $5 million settlement, part of which it used to make a park and lake out of the pit, which became filled with water thanks to the flood of January 1, 1997. The pit, now a man-made lake stocked fish, is now the prime attraction of the Sparks Marina Park; read more about it in the Sparks section. You can see the park on the north side of the interstate, just off I-80 at the Sparks Blvd. exit.

Just east of there, the big "S" for Sparks sits on a hillside to the left and the Purina tower rises on the right (this plant makes breakfast cereal). Beyond that, you leave the urban area behind and enter narrow Truckee River Canyon. The Southern Pacific Railroad tracks are just to the south between the highway and the river. At the entrance to the canyon on the right, right on the river, is one of four Reno-Sparks wastewater treatment plants that take municipal and industrial water, purify it, and return it to the river.

The Truckee River Canyon

This is a highly scenic 25-mile stretch that most people barely notice thanks to the 65-mph speed limit and the good pavement. But the fast and comfortable ride on the superhighway today is inversely proportional to the agonizing travel along the Truckee River for the pioneers of 145 years ago. One emigrant's diary described the ordeal: "The backbreaking first stage of the arduous climb over the mighty Sierra Nevada was so rough, broken, and steep that wagons had to travel in the streambed of the crooked river—in places crossing ten times in a mile. The water softened the oxen's hoofs, rough stones wore them down, and traveling was torture." In addition, the gale-force Washoe zephyrs provided additional pain: head winds.

Truckee Canyon was one of the roughest sections over which the Central Pacific Railroad laid tracks along its whole route. In 1919, US 40 road builders had a little easier time, since they could make partial use of the railroad grade. Five years later, the newly created Nevada State Highway Department awarded one of its first contracts to a Reno construction company to grade and gravel an eight-mile stretch west of Fernley, for $45,000. By 1927, US 40 through the entire canyon had been improved, and it was completely paved by 1934.

Work on I-80 occupied the last half of the 1950s; when the highway through the canyon was completed in 1959, it was the most expensive ($10 million) section of road in the whole state. The superhighway was designed to handle 2,000 cars *an hour,* an extremely forward-looking goal for 1959, when 4,000 cars passed *daily.* Today, nearly 22,000 cars are accommodated daily by I-80 through Truckee Canyon, taking 25 minutes for a trip that 100 years ago required three grueling days.

Lockwood, Mustang, McCarran, and Megawatts

At Exit 22 is the small settlement of Lockwood, with a subdivision on the river and the old Mustang Ranch on the hill. The road into the hills beyond the water tank goes to the main garbage dump and landfill for western Nevada. It collects roughly half a billion pounds of garbage a year.

At Exit 23 are one of the largest auto wrecking yards and the remains of what was the largest brothel in the state of Nevada until it closed down in summer 1999. Writers have been making wild comparisons between the two for nearly three decades and for a while during the summer of 1990, the fate of the latter finally equalled that of the former: federal bankruptcy court junked the pink pleasure palaces, after arguing successfully in federal bankruptcy court that Joe Conforte, owner of the famous brothel, owed $13 million in back taxes. The Ranch reopened after a dramatic series of events in which the IRS ran the brothel for a brief time, then auctioned it off to Joe Conforte's lawyer's brother for 10 cents on the dollar. But the Mustang finally closed in summer 1999 and was not expected to reopen—although some still speculate that it may someday be revived.

If you're down here for a look, or even for something else, go right at the fork. Just past the Mustang is another legal brothel, the **Old Bridge Ranch,** owned by Joe Conforte's nephew, David Burgess, and his wife Ingrid. Recently, the Burgesses have borrowed a chapter out of Uncle Joe's story, filing for bankruptcy protection against the IRS, which claims they owe nearly $1 million in back taxes.

Beyond the Ranch is, in fact, an old bridge across the Truckee. This side of the river is Storey County, one of three counties in the United States where brothel prostitution is truly legal. On the other side is Washoe County, one of thousands where it's not.

An enormous effort was required to cut the highway through McCarran Hill near the **Patrick** exit (28). Two hundred and thirty feet of hillside were excavated, 750,000 cubic yards of material. The resulting passage is spectacular. Off the exit is a frontage road below some of the leftover rubble and above the McCarran Ranch, occupying this prime river acreage since 1875. Five-term Senator Patrick McCarran was the most influential representative to Washington that Nevada has ever produced.

At Exit 30 is Sierra Pacific Power Company's **Tracy Station Power Plant,** opened in 1963, producing 330 megawatts of electricity from gas and oil. Note the holding ponds where wastewater is held until it's cool enough to return to the river (still a degree or two warmer than normal).

Just east of there, at Exit 33, is the Eagle Picher **diatomaceous-earth processing plant.** Diatoms are single-celled algae that grow in water and moist soil. When they die, their silica shells accumulate and over millions of years transform into a variety of materials, including limestone, petroleum, diatomaceous earth, and its more highly refined state, diatomite. Diatomaceous earth is best known for its use in swimming pool filters, but also commonly appears in absorbents, insulation, and filler. Diatomite, a fine chalky powder, is used in explosives and abrasives.

Derby Dam

At Exit 36 take a right at the top of the exit ramp and drive about a mile to the tiny underpass beneath the railroad tracks. Nine feet wide and eight feet high, it's just big enough for a pickup with camper—great for a picture with your vehicle "wedged" underneath. Take a right onto the gravel road and drive a few hundred yards to the gate. If you're in the mood for a walk, climb through the gate and stroll about a quarter mile to the Derby. This dam, topped off in 1905, was the first one constructed by the new U.S. Bureau of Reclamation, and was the forerunner of such great dams as the Hoover, Grand Coulee, and Shasta. Down here, though, are just the murky Truckee and diversion ditch—an excellent habitat for mosquitoes. This dam diverts water to the Truckee Canal, which runs 35 miles through Fernley to Lahontan Reservoir, and from there to Fallon farms and Stillwater National Wildlife Refuge.

A little beyond the dam, highway builders dug a canal 1,500 feet long and 100 feet wide to straighten the Truckee, enabling them to eliminate a dangerous curve in the original road. A little farther ahead you cross into Lyon County.

Wadsworth

Past Painted Rock, a stretch with another major road cut, the canyon opens up onto Dodge Flat, and the Truckee River makes a big turn north. Some pretty farms and ranches spread out from the river here. Exit 43 is the turnoff for NV 447 to Pyramid Lake through Wadsworth, a sleepy remnant of what was a thriving 19th-century railroad maintenance town. The maintenance facilities, and most of the town as well, were moved board-by-board to Sparks in 1905.

Drive into town and pause at **Wadsworth Antiques** to read the historical sign outside of the old Tonopah and Goldfield railcar (built in 1870 and sitting right here for the past 50 years). Stop for groceries at the store or for spirits at Wadsworth Inn, then take a left. Go right at the fork onto Ackley Street. A little past the white church with green trim and weather-vaned steeple is an unusual footbridge across the Truckee. Continue around onto School St. where the old building remains a memorial to the time, from 1868 to 1905, when you really got your Wadsworth. The big trees, old houses, and well-tended gardens also conjure the 120-year history. Back on NV 447, take a left toward the highway. The Nevada Cement Company plant, opened in 1964, is on the left. The highway passes overhead, as do the railroad tracks under a bridge built in 1936. Beyond is Fernley. The Paiute's **I-80 smokeshop and campground** are right off Exit 43.

FERNLEY

Fernley was founded in 1905 as part of the Newlands Reclamation Project, which once irrigated as much as 60,000 acres of desert between Fernley Valley, hemmed in on four sides by the Truckee, Virginia, Pah Rah, and Hot Springs mountains, and Lahontan Valley 30 miles east. Up until the early 1960s, Fernley remained a small trade center for the local ranchers and farmers, as well as the terminal of a branch line of the Southern Pacific that ran up the west shore of Pyramid Lake and on into Sierra logging areas. The arrival of Nevada Cement Company in 1964 improved the town's economy (though deteriorated its air) and completion of the high-speed freeway to Reno drew it closer into a suburban orbit.

Today, Fernley also finds itself an "alternative crossroads" town. Downtown is intersected by two branch roads to major routes US 95 and US 50. (The "real" highways cross in downtown Fallon.) In addition, reader Dave Embry, a true Nevadaphile, points out that Fernley is a good base of operations for northwestern and west-central Nevada, compared to the higher prices and lower vacancies of Reno-Sparks, especially on weekends. So whether you're passing through on a shortcut or just looking for a different place to go or stay, check out friendly Fernley. It's a good alternative.

Truck Inn

This is more than one of the biggest truck stops in the state. It's almost an entire Fernley suburb. Opened in 1982, the Truck Inn occupies a 40-acre lot, 35 of them designated for tractor-trailer parking. Consolidated Freightways has a terminal here. There are also a 26-unit RV park, holding corrals for livestock in transit, a motel, two casinos, spa, barbershop, dentist, repair shops, truck wash, scales, maxi mart, bar with live entertainment, coffee shop, and phones in the bathrooms and at the truckers' counter in the diner. Check out trucker haul of fame, the trucker memorabilia covering the walls. A couple of recent high-tech additions are the telephone-debit-card machine and computerized truck scheduling in the maxi mart. If you just want the quick in and out, stop off at the Winner's Corner mini-mart with Exxon station just off the exit ramp. Truck Inn, 485 Truck Way, 775/351-1000, has 53 motel rooms for $27–43. RV spaces are $10 a night, with weekly and monthly rates available.

Accommodations

Other than the Truck Inn, as you come into town from Wadsworth or the west, the first motels are the **Lazy Inn,** 325 Main St., 775/575-4452 or 800/682-6445, $30–60, and the **Lahontan Motel,** 135 E. Main St., 775/575-2744, $30–45. At the east exit (48) are **Super 8,** 1350 W. Newlands, 775/575-5555 or 800/800-8000, $42–65, and the **Best Western-Fernley Inn,** 1405 E. Newlands, 775/575-6776 or 800/528-1234, $50–80.

Food

If you're hungry, there are a few options. On Main St. downtown is the venerable **Herrera's,** open Mon.–Sat. 10 A.M.–10 P.M. This is a very homey cantina, with food and prices to match. Try the Caldillo (cahl-DEE-yo) soup, with beef, potatoes, and jalapeños, a meal in itself. The cheesy tamales or enchiladas will clear your sinuses. Across the street are the **China Chef** and **Fireside Lounge.** On the same side of Main and down the block is **Moe and Mary's Wigwam Cafe,** open 5 A.M.–9 P.M., another venerable and popular Fernley eatery, serving breakfast till 11, a good salad bar for lunch and dinner, and big portions of everything.

For quickie road food, try the coffee shops at **Sturgeon's** (open 6 A.M.–midnight) and the **Truck Inn** (open 24 hours). In Fernley Plaza next to Sturgeon's are a pizza place and a barbecue joint. **McDonald's,** opened in 1992, is nearby. For a picnic, stop at **Fernley Desert Park** just south of downtown on Alt. 95.

Other Practicalities

A couple of interesting knickknack shops are worth a browse: **Picky Pat Rat** next to Herrera's, and **Halfa Crown** across from the Wigwam.

There's a poker table at the **Truck Inn,** as well as two blackjack tables and one crap table. There are also two blackjack tables at **Sturgeon's,** and lotsa slots at both.

The **library** is behind the Fernley Complex on the east end, open Monday, Wednesday, and Friday 10 A.M.–5 P.M., Tuesday 10 A.M.–8 P.M., and Saturday 10 A.M.–2 P.M.

FROM FERNLEY

To Fallon

Alternate 50 cuts off I-80 at Exit 48, Fernley's eastern exit (take the west Exit 46 if you want to go through town). It's 15 miles or so east on Alt. 50 along the Southern Pacific tracks, which run between the Dead Camel Range to the southeast and the Hot Springs Mountains to the northeast, to **Hazen,** named for William Hazen, who settled here after the Civil War. It became a station for the railroad at the turn of the century; one side line of the railroad continued east to Lahontan Valley, another branched off south to Mina, where it connected with the Tonopah & Goldfield short line. Hazen merited a post office in 1904 when it sprang up to house workers on the Newlands project. Today, all that's left is a

blip on the map, where you'll find a gas station and store. Check out the antique soda chest.

A few miles east of Hazen is the intersection with US 50 and then it's a nine-mile straight shot into Fallon.

To Fort Churchill

At Exit 46, Alt. 95 runs halfway through Fernley, then takes a right and heads due south toward Yerington. Before leaving the Fernley area behind, you pass the high school, airport, and cross over Truckee Canal. Then it's up and over the eastern edge of the Virginia Range and down to **Silver Springs** (see "Lahontan Recreation Area" under "Fallon" in the Central Nevada chapter) at the intersection of US 50, with Lake Lahontan just east. In another eight miles is the **Carson River,** shaded by big cottonwoods; it's just a trickle of water in the summer on its way to impounding in Lake Lahontan. Just before the river is a turnoff for Fort Churchill.

FORT CHURCHILL

At the sign, turn onto the gravel road to this state historical monument, an extensive, well-preserved skeleton of the first and largest Army base built in Nevada, in 1860, right after the two Pyramid Lake skirmishes. The 1,400-acre post protected Overland Route travelers and miners in the mushrooming boom camps. Fort Churchill was also briefly a Pony Express station, a recruitment center for Civil War volunteers, and a telegraph station. Completion of the transcontinental railroad rendered the fort obsolete; it was forsaken in 1871 and auctioned for $750.

Over the next 60 years, the site served briefly as an Indian school, but mostly as a supply of building materials for local construction. In the 1930s, 200 acres were transferred to the state. The National Park Service restored the site a bit, and the CCC built a visitor center and headquarters. Fort Churchill became a State Historic Park in 1957.

Today, this 1,200-acre park, in a beautiful little valley next to the Carson River in what was once Bucklands Ranch, has an interesting visitor center, with displays on the Pony, telegraph line, Pyramid Lake War, and 1860s' military life.

ruins at Fort Churchill

DEKE CASTLEMAN

There's also a large-scale model of the post in its prime. Portraits of General Sylvester Churchill, James Nye, and Abe Lincoln grace the walls. The center is open 8 A.M.–4 P.M. daily, year-round.

Outside a couple of signs point out the wave-cut terraces of Lake Lahontan on the hillside across the valley, and the different buildings of the fort. A walking trail also starts here and goes down to the ruins.

You can drive on the loop road around them, passing the quaint John C. Frémont picnic area. A left turn leads into the **Fort Churchill Campground.** The trees here are as tall and full as in any campground in the state. There are 20 campsites for tents or self-contained motor homes up to 24 feet. Piped drinking water, vault toilets, sewage disposal, picnic tables, grills, and fire pits are provided. The maximum stay is 14 days. No reservations; the fee is $10 per site.

A recent addition to the park is an area called the Carson River Ranches, stretching about 7–8 miles along the Carson River and giving the park an additional 3,000 acres, with about 4–5 miles of new hiking trails. Horses are not allowed in the rest of the Fort, but the new Carson River Ranches area has two equestrian areas. Carson River Ranches also has two primitive campgrounds, each equipped with vault toilets, picnic tables and grills, but no water; camping costs $3 per vehicle.

Contact: Fort Churchill State Historic Park, Silver Springs, NV 89429, 775/577-2345.

TO YERINGTON

Five miles south of the river is **Weeks,** a tiny settlement of historic and modern buildings. The old two-story wood hotel was once Buckland's Station, which serviced stage passengers, soldiers at the fort, and local ranchers. Weeks is still a ranching center, so take care not to trespass.

You drive south through Churchill Valley for another several miles till you come to **Wabuska,** a Washo word meaning "white grass." Wabuska once served as a railroad junction town, where the Southern Pacific branch line to Mina, the Carson and Colorado Railroad from Carson City to Hawthorne, Sodaville, and into California, and the Nevada Copper Belt Railway from Ludwig (above Yerington) all intersected. Today, you cross the Southern Pacific tracks here; there's also a derelict roadhouse and some light industry.

From Wabuska, it's another 15 miles through **Mason Valley** and **Walker River** country, with the **Singatse Range** on the west and the northern **Wassuks** far to the east, to Yerington (see "Yerington" at the end of the Reno and Western Nevada section). This is one of the prime agricultural valleys in Nevada, and you can say what you will about resource conservation, reclamation and irrigation, alfalfa farming and cattle ranching, lake levels and fisheries. But when the sun is bathing the mountains in alpenglow, the big cottonwoods lining the road are casting long gray shadows across the wide green fields, and the desert rims the valley in a golden frame, it's a divinely inspiring sight.

TO LOVELOCK FROM FERNLEY

Interstate 80 passes through the little "beak" of northern Lyon County, then crosses into the remote northeastern stretch of Churchill County, which contains the forbidding **Carson Sink**. The transition is unmistakable. A vast stretch of flat barren land extends into the southern distance where the Carson River loses its banks, peters out, and disappears into the desert. Mud cracked and alkali-encrusted, the occasional hardy shrub and small-pools of briny water atop pervious soil surrounded by clumps of saltgrass render the whole scene, depending on how thirsty you are, reminiscent of random margarita glasses, salt clinging to their rims, on a colossal white bar.

Carson Sink occupies nearly half the distance from Lovelock to Fallon. A part of it was known to pioneers on the Emigrant Trail as Forty-Mile Desert, a dreaded and dangerous dash from Humboldt River water at Lovelock's Big Meadows to Carson River water at Ragtown. The massive wall of the **Stillwater Range** rises on its eastern edge, and the **Trinity Range** borders it to the west.

By contrast, you can drive right past the humble **Humboldt Sink** without really noticing. It might as well have been swallowed by the Carson Sink. But it wasn't. The **West Humboldt Range,** entering the foreground in front of the mighty Stillwaters, separates the sinks. This is the bitter end of the Humboldt River, which meanders in a trickle through the vast Great Basin and surprised trappers, disgusted emigrants, and guided railroad and highway builders. It was one of the most important rivers in the West for exploration, migration, settlement, and transportation. Still, you enter Humboldt River territory without really noticing it, either.

In fact, it's likely that you won't notice much of anything along this stretch of I-80, which is precisely why these 120 miles from Fernley to Winnemucca rank among the deadliest sections of superhighway in the country. The 14 miles in Lyon County place third in the nation for fatalities; the other 100 or so miles to Winnemucca are in the top 20. According to officials, the monotony of the scenery causes boredom and fatigue and lulls drivers into a seemingly secure daze. Three out of four accidents are one-car rollovers, when a daydreaming driver suddenly becomes mindful that he or she is drifting off the road, then overcorrects in a panic and winds up end over end in a ditch.

The solution? Simply alert your consciousness that this is by no means a long dull ride. Look at all the sensational phenomena around you. Imagine the colossal forces that could tilt the Stillwaters 5,000 feet into the air. Picture the leading edges of the Carson and Humboldt rivers pushing toward each other for hundreds of miles through desert with one ultimate goal—to join—but each disappearing just short of the other. And right when you start thinking that the color green was washed out of nature's palette while you weren't looking, you crest a ridge around mile 87 and ahead of you is lush Lovelock Valley.

The Rest of the Way into Lovelock

For thousands of years, the Humboldt River carried its muddy water west toward the dead end of its own sink, spreading out into wide and shallow channels before dying a dry death. Rich silts and soils were deposited on the broad river plain; Indians, explorers, and pioneers knew the fertile delta as Big Meadows. A few emigrants traveled no farther than the Big Meadows, terminating their cross-country trek here to farm and settle, as early as 1861. As upstream homesteaders diverted more and more river water, however, fecund Lovelock Valley found itself in danger of being swallowed by the sink. But the Rye Patch Dam was completed in 1936 and provided a bounty of irrigation water—until the drought.

At Exit 105, you come into Lower Lovelock Valley, south of town and east of the interstate. I-80 crosses the valley from southwest to northeast, passing Lovelock, which sits smack in the center; Upper Valley is north of town and west of the highway. Stands of poplars dot the land, shading ranch houses and alfalfa farms. Except in the fall, when the farmers burn the alfalfa fields and a dense gray pall settles over everything, it's a bucolic sight.

If you're bypassing Lovelock, there's a good view from the highway of the uniquely round **Pershing County Courthouse.** But a stopover in town is worthwhile, especially to break up this dangerous and numbing drive on I-80 between Fernley and Winnemucca.

LOVELOCK

INTRODUCTION

Lovelock (pop. 2,280) is a pleasant old farming community, with big houses and trees surrounded by well-kept lawns, neat green alfalfa fields, and the rugged West Humboldt Range hemming in the valley to the south, the Trinity Range to the north. The town is named after George Lovelock, a Welsh quartz miner who came to California by way of Australia and Hawaii in 1850, at age 26. He worked for a while in San Francisco, Sacramento, and Oroville, then homesteaded a ranch in Humboldt County, Nevada, in 1861. In 1866 he bought 320 acres at Big Meadows and took title to the oldest water rights along the Humboldt River—just in time to donate 85 acres to the Central Pacific Railroad in return for naming the new railroad town after him, plus other terms that the railroad never fulfilled. "Uncle George" kept busy for the next 40 years with agricultural, mining, and business ventures, raising eight children, and voting Republican. He died at age 83 in 1907 after a three-day bout with pneumonia—reportedly the first sick days of his life—that he caught while out in the country, prospecting.

The rich land and good grass attracted cattlemen and ranchers; by the early 1900s reservoirs on the Humboldt irrigated 8,000 acres. But the supply of river water, never dependable, seemed to diminish year by year as settlers for several hundred miles to the east diverted more and more of the precious Humboldt. Finally, in 1933 the Bureau of Reclamation lent the Lovelock Irrigation District $1 million—$600,000 to buy upstream water rights and $400,000 to build Rye Patch Dam. The dam was completed in 1936, and its reservoir, when full, provides irrigation water to 40,000 acres of the Lovelock Valley. Almost all the farmland is cultivated for grain to feed livestock. In addition, the Lovelock Seed Company is one of the top alfalfa seed growers in the world.

Edna Purviance is Lovelock's claim to Hollywood fame. She grew up in town, then moved to San Francisco, where she was discovered by Charlie Chaplin. They appeared in 40 movies together and she was the leading lady in Chaplin's famous *The Tramp*. They were lovers on and off for decades, but never married. She remained on the Chaplin payroll till she died of cancer in 1958 at age 62.

In 1919 Humboldt County was halved, and Lovelock became the seat of new Pershing County, named after the famous WW I general, and last of 17 counties created in Nevada. Pershing encompasses 6,000 square miles, roughly twice the size of Connecticut. Mining supports a large segment of the economy these days, with a large diatomaceous-earth mine and plant and several gold and silver mines nearby.

SIGHTS

Marzen House

The commercial district stretches between Exits 105 and 107 of the interstate. Start your tour of Lovelock at the **Pershing County Museum** and **Chamber of Commerce.** As you come off I-80 at Exit 105, take a left toward Lovelock. You'll see a blue sign for Visitor Information; take another left, just before the Lovelock Inn, onto a little gravel driveway around back to the **Marzen House,** 775/273-7213, open daily 1:30–4 P.M. (closed Monday). Stroll around this restored house, built by Colonel Joseph Marzen, a German farmer and rancher who moved to Lovelock in 1876 and proceeded to become the area's major grain and livestock producer. Originally the Big House on Marzen's 3,400-acre ranch, the museum is packed with an amazing collection of memorabilia, much of it affectionately labeled with the names of the donors. Noteworthy are the pump organ from Unionville, a 1923 atlas, an early 20th-century carpet sweeper, a big map of Lake Lahontan, which once covered the area, and a great wide-angle shot of downtown Lovelock in 1913. Upstairs, rooms are devoted to agriculture, mining, stock certificates, and much more. Chat with the friendly volunteer, help yourself to Chamber of Commerce handouts, and leave a small token of appreciation.

Downtown

Continue east along Cornell Ave., old Highway 40, to 8th St.; take a right and go one block down to Broadway, the old business street along the tracks. Go left by the Bernd Hotel, Lovelock's oldest (now a rooming house), Ranch House and Walks Place bars, and the abandoned Red Depot. Cross Main St. to the old railroad depot and assay office, both closed and boarded up. Felix's Bank Club, once the main casino in town, is also boarded up at the corner of Cornell and Main Street.

Take Main St. back across Cornell for the **Pershing County Courthouse,** one of only two round courthouses in the country. A park with picnic tables and a jungle gym is in back, between the courthouse and library. Also here is the Lovelock Memorial Swimming Pool, with two diving boards, one fairly high, and a kiddie pool.

To the Tufa

Head north (right) on Central a mile through irrigated farmland, take your first left onto Pitt, and go by aptly named **Lone Mountain** in one-half mile, just past where the road curves around. Take a right onto the unmarked gravel road and kick up dust for a mile, till you come to the long line of low tufa formations. Park and get out into the desert a little by hiking the few hundred yards to and around the calcareous remnants of Lake Lahontan, familiar formations in northwestern Nevada. Hawks and owls peer down from atop the towers. Take winding Lone Mountain Rd. back to town past the mountain and cemetery.

Tufa with Petroglyphs

Seventeen miles south of town is **Leonard Rock Shelter** which has tall tufa with petroglyphs; excavations in the early 1950s by UC Berkeley archaeologists recovered artifacts at the rock's base that were later carbon-dated to approximately 4000 B.C.

PRACTICALITIES

Accommodations

Interstate 80 through northern Nevada wasn't completed until 1983, and Lovelock was one of the last towns to be bypassed; for a long time the traffic light at Main and Cornell was the only one on the highway between New York and San Francisco! This also accounts for the dozen or so motels along Cornell Ave.; until a mere ten years ago, all the interstate traffic had to drive right by them.

Starting from the west side of town, the **Lovelock Inn,** 55 Cornell, 775/273-2937, on the west side next to Marzen House, advertises "quiet luxury" and has a heated pool, $39–65. The **Cadillac Inn,** 1395 Cornell, 775/273-2798, offers 12 rooms for $20–42. **Sturgeon's Ramada Inn Casino,** 1420 Cornell, 775/273-2971 or 888/234-6835, has 74 rooms for $36–75. Two motels are on Dartmouth Ave.: the **Covered Wagon** at 945, 775/273-2961, $27–45; and the **Sierra** at 14th St., 775/273-2798, $20–42.

The **Lazy K Campground and RV** is at 1550 Cornell, 775/273-1116; from exit 105 off Interstate 80, go north to Cornell Street, then take a right (east) for a mile to the campground. The Lazy K was a KOA for years, till it closed in 1994. Friendly proprietor Ron Kiel reopened it in 1995 and has been restoring it to its prior glory. It's

NEVADA HISTORICAL SOCIETY, RENO

George Lovelock

THE ROAD TO LOVELOCK CAVE

Lovelock Cave was discovered by teenagers in 1887, though it was not explored until 1911 when guano miners excavated 250 tons of bat scat, uncovering numerous Indian artifacts in the process. The 160-foot-wide by 40-foot-deep cave, created by Lake Lahontan, served as a shelter for aboriginal inhabitants around 2000 B.C., and was the first Great Basin site to be excavated by archaeologists. The artifacts—which include baskets, textiles, and the famous Loveland cave duck decoys—are exhibited at museums around the country.

The route from downtown Lovelock to Lovelock Cave has been declared a "cultural back country byway" by the state. Begin at the Marzen House Museum on the southwest side of town. Drive northeast through town and then turn right on Main Street. Go two blocks and turn right on Amhearst. After the park the road becomes South Meridian or State Road 397. The first half of the 20-mile route takes you through irrigated fields. After crossing the Humboldt River, the road changes to dirt. This byway is at its best is summer and early fall.

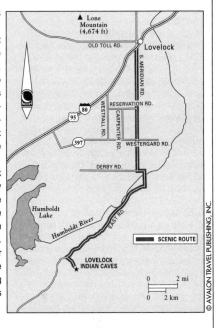

right off the freeway, but luckily, the large trees and landscaping hold down the noise—'cause this is the only camping in Lovelock. There are 49 spaces for motor homes, 30 with full hookups and 27 pull-throughs. There are 12 tent sites in the trees. Restrooms have flush toilets and hot showers; laundry, groceries, snack bar, and playground are available. The fee is $12 for tents, $22 for RVs.

Food
Sturgeon's is at the west end of town, 775/273-2971. There's a stuffed mountain lion on display (shot in 1970 on Mt. Tobin). Two blackjack tables operate at night, or try your luck at the video poker bar. Catch a bite anytime at the 24-hour coffee shop, which has surprisingly good and reasonable food.

McDonald's has finally made it to Lovelock, opening in the summer of 1994. This pretty much completes Mickey D's march across northern and western Nevada: since 1992, McDonald's have opened in Tonopah, Fernley, Hawthorne, and now Lovelock.

Information
Pershing County Chamber of Commerce, P.O. Box 831, Lovelock, NV 89419, 775/273-7213, is open Mon.–Fri. 9–11 A.M., or sometimes 10 A.M.–noon. **Pershing County Library,** just north of the courthouse, is open Mon.–Fri. 10 A.M.–5 P.M., also Wednesday 7–9 P.M., and Saturday 10 A.M.–3 P.M.

EAST FROM LOVELOCK

Rejoin I-80 at the east end of town. Back on the highway, the mini **West Humboldts** (6,000 feet) bump along low-slung, though rugged, until the maxi **Humboldt Range** (9,000 feet) takes over from behind. Just north of town is another **Eagle Picher diatomaceous earth** mill; the mine is 20 miles east. At Exit 119 is **Oreana,** an old mining center, once known for lead and tungsten, now just a few houses and warehouses. The side road east of Oreana climbs into the Humboldts; in about eight miles is a fork. A right turn points you toward the big **Coeur Rochester Mine,** whose cuts crisscross the southern Humboldts. A left turn takes you off the pavement, through **Limerick Canyon,** and down into Buena Vista Valley (see "Unionville," below).

Rye Patch State Recreation Area

Take Exit 129 toward Rye Patch Dam. (A small **Travel Centers of America (TCA) Truck Stop** is on the eastbound side, 775/538-7504.) Built in 1936, the dam's 22-mile-long reservoir when full covers 11,000 surface feet, impounds nearly 200,000 acre feet and supplies irrigation water for 40,000 acres of reclaimed Humboldt River bottomland.

However, in fall 1992 Rye Patch was providing no irrigation water for any acres at all, having been drained in mid-July of the last of its stored water, leaving more than a million fish to rot in place. The die-off caused considerable controversy; fish and game officials claimed it would set back the state's fisheries program at the reservoir at least 10 years. Ironically, the Nevada state-record walleye (15 pounds) was caught at Rye Patch four months earlier.

Thanks to the big winter and plentiful runoff in 1993, state wildlife officials restocked the reservoir with 50,000 trout, along with hundreds of thousands of walleye and bass fry. But then the winter of 1994 was bone dry, and the farmers drew down Rye Patch again. This time, however, they left 2,000 acre feet to save the fishery; commercial fishermen netted a bunch of fish and carried them by truck to Lake Lahontan. Nowadays, the lake is at a healthy level again, and is an attraction for anglers, being annually restocked with walleye, bass and crappie. Fishing, swimming, boating, water skiing and jet skis are popular activities on the lake, and there's also fishing in the river, below the dam.

Near the entrance to the reservoir is the guard station (unmanned); pay up if you're staying for the day ($3 per vehicle) or camping ($8 per campsite). The first left past the guardhouse goes down to a shaded picnic area on the north bank below the dam. The dam is 800 feet long, 72 feet above the riverbed, and 500 feet thick at the base. A 110-foot concrete spillway is at one end, the rest is earthen fill.

The recreation area has two campgrounds. The **River Campground,** just downriver from the spillway, is well shaded and relatively quiet. It has 22 campsites for tents or self-contained motor homes up to 30 feet. Piped drinking water, flush toilets, showers, sewage disposal, public phones, picnic tables, grills and fire rings are provided. The **Boat Ramp Campground,** on the reservoir near the dam, has a boat launch ramp. A little swimming beach on an inlet nearby has 24 developed campsites, with running water, showers, flush toilets, a fish cleaning station, picnic tables and grills provided. The maximum stay at either campground is 14 days. No reservations; all campsites are first come, first served. In addition to the boat ramp near the dam, there's another boat ramp 10 miles north up the lake, called the **Pitt Taylor** boat ramp.

Camping outside the developed campgrounds is allowed here, too: you can camp anywhere you like around the lake. If you have a boat this is a great option—you can take your boat anywhere on the 22-mile-long lake that you want to, pull up on the shore and set up camp.

Contact: Rye Patch State Recreation Area, 2505 Rye Patch Reservoir Rd., Lovelock, NV 89419, 775/538-7321.

Humboldt River Ranch

Nevada is the seventh largest state in the U.S. and one of the least populated. But lest you think that private land is abundant and inexpensive, consider this. State, local, and federal governments, along with the railroads and large ranching corporations, control 96% of Nevada dirt. And most of the remaining 4% of ownable acreage is found in the cities and towns. Rural desert property with adequate access and water rights is hard to come by. But if you're at the Rye Patch exit off I-80, look east across the freeway at the foothills of the Humboldt Range to get a glimpse of one of the largest rural subdivisions in the state, with all the necessities and more.

Humboldt River Ranch is a 10,000-acre subdivision. Two thousand fee-simple lots come in ten, five, 2.5, and 1.5 acres; each has its own water right. The Ranch runs a resort for owners just before the entrance to Rye Patch State Recreation Area, with cabins, a rec building, and a 15-acre campground with a mere 15 sites right on the Humboldt River. Today, there are only a few dozen homes on the ranch (most people who live here commute to Lovelock or the prison), but in the next few years, Humboldt River Ranch promises to be one of the hottest rural developments in northern Nevada—and I'll be building my retirement house high up in these hills. Lots range from $14,000 to $19,000—ground-floor prices. Call Devco Properties in Reno at 775/323-7377 for more information.

Imlay

East of Rye Patch is a big mining operation that's dismantling an even bigger red mountain. This is **Florida Canyon Gold Mine.** Opened in 1986, this mine is one of many all over northern Nevada recovering microscopic gold, making Nevada the foremost gold-producing state in the country. Here, it takes hundreds of tons of earth to produce (by cyanide leaching) one ounce of gold.

If you feel like paying further respects to the crusty old river above the reservoir, take Exit 145. Imlay sits at the head of the Humboldt Range, parallel to the top end of Rye Patch Reservoir, with the nondescript **Eugene Mountains** to the north. Follow the frontage road left past Imlay village one mile to the historical sign. This is roughly the site of Lassen Meadows, terminus of the trail blazed by Oregon's Applegate brothers in 1846. Two years later, Peter Lassen established a similar route from here through Black Rock Desert and High Rock Canyon to his ranch in northeastern California; his trail was somewhat more treacherous than the Humboldt Trail to the south, and many emigrants suffered mightily on it. Take a right, and go just under four miles on a washboard gravel road to the river—a very pretty and quiet picnic or camping spot.

To Unionville

Back on the highway, the big peak to the west is **Majuba Mountain.** Contrary to legend, Majuba is not a Swahili word meaning "Missing Teeth" or "Gap-Tooth Grin," and was not given to the peak by a visiting Mombasan dentist in the 1870s. Rather, it's named after the Boer Victory over the British at Majuba Hill, South Africa, in 1881.

The Humboldts trail off at Exit 149, **Mill City. Burns Bros.** is on the westbound side of this exit, 775/538-7306. This truck stop burned down in 1989 and was rebuilt by early 1991. This is a surprisingly extensive operation out here in the boonies of northern Nevada, worth a look if you need gas, groceries, 22-inch tires, or a shower, or have a bad slot or video poker jones.

Also from Mill City, paved NV 400 runs south straight down **Buena Vista Valley** along the east face of the ubiquitous Humboldt Range. **Star Peak** (9,834 feet) is obviously named and unmistakable—one of the finest-shaped mountains in the state. At 3 P.M. on weekdays, a school bus travels down this road, dropping kids off at the far-flung ranches. Pause at the historical sign for **Star City,** a ghost town located four miles west in a dramatic bowl on the skirts of Star Mountain. Established in 1861, at its peak in 1864 it boasted 1,200 residents and two hotels. The main Sheba and DeSoto mines eventually produced $5 million in silver. Here George Hearst made his original fortune, getting in on ore worth as much as $2000 a ton and mining stock that at one point sold for $600 a foot. *Borrasca* (the final bust) however, had reduced the city to an eternal ghost by 1868.

In a few miles the pavement ends. You take a right and head three miles up into the Humboldts to Unionville.

UNIONVILLE

Sam Clemens arrived in Carson City in July 1861, eager to assume his duties as secretary to his brother Orion, who was secretary to the territorial governor, James Nye. He soon found that he had "nothing to do and no salary" and was free to create his own diversions. At that time, the large mines of Virginia City were in their first bonanza frenzy, and "cartloads of solid silver bricks, as large as pigs of lead, were arriving from the mills every day. I would have been more or less than human," he wrote later in *Roughing It,* "had I not gone mad like the rest."

News of new strikes in the vicinity fairly shouted from the banner headlines day after day. And by the time Clemens was good and delirious with silver fever, the strike at Esmeralda had begat a boomtown, Aurora, complete with half a thousand claims and intense manipulations of stocks, in which the Clemens brothers had invested. But the cry of "Humboldt" was also then selling newspapers before the ink had it in mind to dry. So just before Christmas 1861, Clemens and three partners put together a grubstake—wagon, two horses, and 1,800 pounds of provisions—and started off through the sand and sage for the rich diggings in newly created Humboldt County, 200 miles northeast.

Two weeks later they pulled into Unionville, which consisted of 11 cabins and a liberty pole. They erected a crude shelter, headed off to prospect in the hills, finally located and claimed a ledge with indications, and set about to dig down to the vein, which they estimated to rest at 150 feet. They went at their rock with picks and shovels, then crowbars, then dynamite, then *more* dynamite, until their hole had reached the

ALEXANDER VON HUMBOLDT

As you've probably gathered by now, the area around Winnemucca is Humboldt Land. You've got your Humboldt County, your Humboldt Mountains (plus your East and West Humboldt mountains), your Humboldt National Forest, Humboldt Sink, Humboldt Mining District, Humboldt Trail, and of course your Humboldt River. So who was Humboldt, anyway, and how did his name become attached to so many important features in northern Nevada?

The first white man known to have stumbled on the river was Peter Skene Ogden in 1829, and his humble name for it, Ogden River, stuck at least until 1833, when Joseph Walker followed its entire length west through Nevada, and continued from there into California. But it appeared on Bonneville's 1837 map as Mary River. John C. Frémont, the Great Labeler of the West, designated it the Humboldt River in 1844 in honor of Alexander von Humboldt. And the Humboldt River it has remained.

Alexander von Humboldt was born in Berlin in 1769. He received a college education in mining technology and advanced quickly in his field. At the age of 27 he inherited a substantial sum of money, with which he embarked on a scientific expedition that ranged from Venezuela, Cuba, and Colombia to Mexico and the United States. He collected botanical, zoological, geological, and astronomical data, studied Pacific Ocean currents, the Cuban plantation economy, and pre-Columbian cultures. He climbed to 18,000 feet in the Andes, surveyed the headwaters of the Amazon, followed ancient Inca trails in Peru, and sipped mint juleps with James Madison in Washington, D.C.

Humboldt settled in Paris in 1808 and began publishing the reports and results of his travels and inquiries. The subsequent 30-volume, 12,000-page encyclopedia earned him an international reputation as a "one-man institution," at the same time that it ruined him financially. Humboldt then embarked on several years of diplomatic missions for Frederick William III of Prussia, traveled through Siberia at the invitation of Czar Nicholas I, and finally settled down to a position as lecturer and author in Frederick's court in Berlin.

For the last 30 years of his life, Humboldt concentrated on his five-volume *Kosmos,* an epic survey of the Earth and universe. In it, he attempted to determine, through scientific knowledge, man's place in the cosmic order.

Alexander von Humboldt died in Berlin in 1859, at the age of 90. Frémont did northern Nevada a great service by naming the country after such an illustrious and erudite figure.

BOB RACE

12-foot level. Next they tried tunneling through their hill and "had blasted a tunnel about deep enough to hide a hogshead in" before returning to the drawing board.

By then, however, the rush had arrived, and Clemens and his partners quickly fell victim to another epidemic: speculation. They traded their own feet for feet in 50 other mines that had been prospected, staked, claimed, but "never molested by a shovel or scratched by a pick. It was a beggar's revel! There was nothing doing in the district—no mining, no milling, no income—and yet a stranger would have supposed he was walking among bloated millionaires. We had not less than 30,000 feet in the 'richest mines on earth'—and were in debt to the butcher. But we never touched our tunnel or shaft again. We had learned the *real* secret of success in silver mining—not to mine the silver ourselves, but to *sell* the ledges to the dull slaves of toil and let *them* do the mining! On such a system the Humboldt world had gone crazy."

In short, Unionville was a mouse that roared. Clemens moved on to greater adventures. Still, by 1863, three distinct sections of town had emerged, strung along two-mile-long Buena Vista Canyon, named for its rare beauty. Upper Town was known as Dixie, Lower Town as Union, and the middle district as Centerville; the name finally settled on Unionville when it became clear that the north would win the Civil War. The town became a stop on the stagecoach routes in and out of Virginia City, got hooked up to the telegraph line, and assumed administrative duties for huge Humboldt County. The county "courthouse" was kept in a saloon, in a corner where "the rain didn't come any thicker than it did outside."

The Arizona mine began producing rich silver ore that year, which restimulated speculation in Branch, Grand Mogul, Sultan, and Universe mine stocks. The *Humboldt Register* recorded all the details for posterity. A public school and the first church in the county were built. But construction of the Central Pacific Railroad through Lovelock and Winnemucca on the *other* side of the Humboldt Mountains in 1868 signaled the beginning of the end for Unionville's boom. Five years later, Winnemucca wrested the county seat for itself. In all, roughly $5 million in ore was recovered from the Buena Vista district's

mines. By the end of the 1870s, *borrasca* had emptied the town, save for a hundred or so residents content with life in the pretty canyon whether the mines were producing or not. And in this way, Unionville has survived extinction for more than 100 years.

Sights

Today, Unionville is one of the most attractive villages in Nevada. Beautiful houses—of stone, brick, and wood, with decks, porches, and cared-for yards shaded by ancient poplars and apple trees—line the south side of Main St. for nearly two miles to the top of the canyon, where a 4WD track continues into the Humboldts. Ruins of the general store, stage depot, and Odd Fellows building are scattered along the north side of the street; even the remains of Sam Clemens's cabin, behind the Pershing County Youth Center, still stand. "We built a small, rude cabin in the side of the crevice and roofed it with canvas, leaving a corner open to serve as a chimney, through which the cattle used to tumble occasionally, at night, and mash our furniture and interrupt our sleep," he wrote later, after working as a reporter for Virginia City's *Territorial Enterprise* and adopting the pen name Mark Twain.

Approximately two dozen inhabitants reside in Unionville year-round. **Ernst's Thrift Store** (arts and crafts, souvenirs, antiques) is at the beginning of town on the right. Stop in for a chat with the town's oldest-timers: Ernst's mother, Sadie, was born in Unionville in 1892, and her son Bob lives there still.

Lew and Mitzi Jones operate the **Old Pioneer Garden Guest Ranch B&B,** 775/538-7585, on property that once belonged to Thomas Jefferson Hadley, the blacksmith. The inn was built in 1864; the Joneses' farmhouse, with more rooms, dates from 1863. Lew and Mitzi have decorated the entire place with period furniture from across the West and Europe. Some of the pieces were acquired from historical buildings from the region that have since been demolished. The cupboard doors in the Hadley kitchen, for instance, came from the Old Golconda Hotel. As you descend the stairs to the library/rec room, check out the weathered, double ox yoke on your left, a relic from one of the many emigrant trails that traversed the Black Rock Desert. The Hadley House can sleep about 13 people in various combinations. When it fills up, five additional guests can be accommodated in the Jones' ranch house. There's another room off the barn where horse lovers can sleep near their best friends. Rider and mount can keep an eye on each other through a window connecting the room and the stall next door. Another house on the 155-acre spread has three rooms perfect for families or groups. Lew has added four more rooms in yet another old house located on the north end of the property. Many famous and near-famous actors, writers, and artists stay here. Reservations are essential for weekend stays since the place usually fills up. Arrangements a year in advance are needed for holiday weekends. Quiet reigns during the week, however, when you usually have the run of the place. Nearby trails and roads are excellent for riding, biking, and hiking. The horse boarding facilities here are first rate. Double rooms are $85.

Check out the **mailboxes** of the Knoops and Moheas. Then park at the top end of town and go for a stroll in the mountains to join the jackrabbits, chukars, mule deer, maybe even a bobcat.

Kyle Hot Springs

Straight across Buena Vista Valley toward the **East Range** is this old, somewhat dilapidated hot pool. It's 11 miles from the intersection of NV 400; heading south, take a left on the ranch road (instead of a right up into Unionville). You can see the hot spring the whole way: a small light-brown patch to the left of the road up in the hillside. Drive eight miles, by ranches and across the valley, to the Spaulding Canyon fork and keep right. In another two miles is a second fork;

go left. One more mile brings you to the pool. The hot water is in a concrete pool, surrounded by some stone ruins, a lot of corrugated sheet metal and other trash, and a white sulphury residue—but with a fine view of the valley and mountains beyond. Bring everything, especially cold water and firewood.

The springs are a party spot for teenagers from Lovelock and Winnemucca. Their all-night revels drove the last caretaker away, which is why the place has fallen into its current state of disrepair. The owner lives out of state, and the sheriff's department says it doesn't have any jurisdiction on private property. Your best bet is to visit on a weekday when school is in session.

Back to Lovelock

Heading south through Buena Vista Valley on the unpaved extension of NV 400, you cut through the southern Humboldt Range. Heavy equipment, old and new, marks the many mines nearby, and then you begin climbing **Gold Mountain** steeply, with a good overlook of the country. Just beyond the pass (6,204 feet), you arrive at the pavement. The fork to **Rochester** veers off (hard left), while the road continues straight down **Limerick Canyon,** between Gold and Lone mountains. The speed limit, even on the pavement, is 35 mph—for good reason; the washboard asphalt can knock you right off any one of the sharp corners if you're going too fast. In eight miles you're down from the mountains at Oreana, where you meet up with the Humboldt River, the highway, and the railroad—22 miles and an hour from where the pavement ends at the Unionville/Kyle Hot Springs junction.

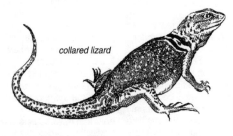

collared lizard

BOB RACE

LOUISE FOOTE

WINNEMUCCA

INTRODUCTION

Winnemucca has always been an overnight stop on a variety of long-distance journeys. A traditional crossroads for Indians, mountain men, pioneers, and miners, the site of Winnemucca was originally named French Ford after a Frenchman, Joe Ginacca. Ginacca began a ferry service across the river for pioneers along the Emigrant Trail who opted to take the secondary Applegate-Lassen Cutoff into northern California and Oregon. By 1865, minerals had been located all around the area, a small hotel stood near the ferry stop, and a bridge was built to ease the crossing. French Ford kept growing as a supply center for the trail and local mines and ranches and was a logical stop for the Central Pacific Railroad, which arrived in fall 1868. Railroad company officials promptly renamed it Winnemucca, in honor of the famous Paiute chief.

After several years of steady growth, a battle erupted between Winnemucca and declining Unionville for the Humboldt County courthouse. Unionville put up a good fight. A writer for the Unionville *Silver State* wrote, "The principal production of Winnemucca consists of sand hills, vapid editorials, and a morbid hankering for the county seat." But Winnemucca gained the courthouse in 1873.

A large Chinatown sprouted after the railroad was completed, and Basque shepherds settled around Winnemucca to labor on ranches and herd sheep. As usual, the Chinese were hounded away and little remains of their time here, but the Basque influence is still evident in the town's restaurants and cultural events. George

Nixon, a telegraph operator on the Central Pacific, opened his first bank here and began a financial empire that stretched to Tonopah and Goldfield and a political career that stretched to Washington. In September 1900, Butch Cassidy's gang rode into town and stole $32,000 from Nixon's bank. Some disagreement exists as to whether Butch himself was in attendance (but probably not).

Winnemucca maintained a passable level of prosperity in the early 20th century, thanks to the railroad. The construction of three highways—US 40, Winnemucca-to-the-Sea Highway, and I-80—reinforced Winnemucca's status as a crossroads town. The population, however, remained steady at no more than 3,000 until the mid-1980s. At that time, Winnemucca's population and economy, like Battle Mountain's and Elko's, exploded in conjunction with a large new surge of mining activity—gold, silver, dolomite, and specialty limestone—in the area. Since then, the population has more than doubled (the 1999 population figure was 8,860), and Winnemucca has visibly burst its small-town boundaries, spreading north into Paradise Valley and south into Grass Valley.

Even so, by all reports and personal experience, Winnemucca has retained its old-time homey and friendly feeling for the newcomers, as well as for the visitors continuing to pass through town as they've done for at least the past 145 years or so. It's also still a service center for a large chunk of northern Nevada, mostly the ranching and farming country from Lovelock to Denio and McDermitt to Battle Mountain. Winnemucca has been making a name for itself as the Buckaroo Capital of the country, with the

Buckaroo Hall of Fame located right downtown (see below). And locals feel they have now hit the retail big time after getting a Kmart in 1996 and a Wal-Mart in 1998.

SIGHTS

Downtown

At the main intersection downtown, on the corner of Winnemucca Blvd. (locally known as Main St.) and Melarkey St., is an eight-foot-diameter cross-section of a **redwood tree trunk,** which washed ashore in Crescent City, California, in 1964. The townspeople there thought it appropriate to present a slice of it to the people of Winnemucca to mark the beginning of the Winnemucca-to-the-Sea Highway, which ends in Crescent City. The grassy square it stands in front of was until very recently the **Nixon Opera House.** This historic building was built in 1907 by George Nixon, who wanted to leave Winnemucca a memorial when business compelled

him to move to Reno. It served as a theater and community center for nearly 80 years, till it was condemned in 1984. In 1991 the state Legislature earmarked $582,000 and townspeople raised another $300,000 for its restoration. Then it burned to the ground in July 1992. Arson. Now there's a hole in the heart of Winnemucca that will take a long time, if ever, to fill.

On the corner of "Main" and Bridge St. is the **East Hall** of the Convention Center, which houses the **Chamber of Commerce,** 30 W. Winnemucca Blvd., Winnemucca, NV 89445, 775/623-2225, chamber@winnemucca-nv.org, www.winnemucca-nv.org. May to September it's open 8 A.M.–noon and 1–5 P.M. Monday to Saturday, 9 A.M.–4 P.M. Sunday. Winter hours, from October to April, are the same except that it closes at 4 P.M. Pick up 10 pounds of xeroxed histories, town practicalities, brochures, and tabloids. You can also buy books, postcards, and T-shirts (check out the tees; they're always interesting and attractive).

While you're here, stop in to see the **Bucka-**

roo Hall of Fame and Western Heritage Museum, open weekdays 8 A.M.–4 P.M. This collection of cowboy art and gear is the outgrowth of the Western Art Round Up, held in Winnemucca every Labor Day weekend since 1982. Inductees to the Hall of Fame must have been born in the 19th century and worked as a cattleman within a 200-mile radius of Winnemucca. Many legendary local cowboys are commemorated here, as is the buckaroo lifestyle. For more info, contact Carl Hammond, Buckaroo Hall of Fame, 30 W. Winnemucca Blvd., Winnemucca, NV 89445.

To get to **Riverview Park,** head north on Bridge St. and go under the freeway and across the river. This is an old well-shaded part of town and a fine place to have a picnic or just a drink and watch the river flow.

From the Convention Center, walk north on Bridge St., the main business district, toward the venerable **Winnemucca Hotel.** This is the site of the first bridge across the Humboldt, around which old downtown Winnemucca grew up. The Winnemucca Hotel is the oldest building in the city, built in 1863, one year before Nevada became a state. If you're not planning to come back later for a drink or meal, stop in at this old Basque bar, restaurant, and rooming house; notice the collection of international currency above the bar, and the old cash register.

On the other side of Winnemucca Blvd., **St. Paul's Catholic Church** is at the corner of 4th and Melarkey. Built in 1924, it has elements of baroque, Romanesque, and Spanish mission in the architecture.

Across the street at 49 W. 4th St. is the building that houses the Winnemucca city offices. Built in 1921, this was the first federal building erected in Winnemucca. It housed the post office, which had a large, fine "Cattle Roundup" mural, painted in 1942. When the post office moved in the 1990s, it took the beloved mural along! You can see it in the new post office location, 850 Hanson St. at the corner of Grass Valley Rd., 775/623-2456; open Mon.–Fri. 8:30 A.M.–5 P.M.

From the city offices corner, go south a block and west a block to the **Winnemucca Grammar School** at the corner of 5th and Lay, built in 1927, worth a look from the outside. A block or so south on Lay St. is **Railroad St.,** once the town's commercial center. A couple of original bars are down the block. At the corner of 6th and Bridge

is the **Shone House,** built in 1901 by Thomas Shone, who was the keeper of the Station Toll House; the old frame rooming house has been restored to its original two-story splendor, complete with a verandah shading the sidewalk and a balustraded porch on the upper floor.

Heading south across the tracks on Bridge St., make a left onto Haskell, go two blocks to Mizpah, and take a right into **City Park:** big, green, shady, kiddie playground, two tennis courts, and an indoor pool—all right across the street from Humboldt General Hospital, in case you overexert yourself.

You can do a fine walking tour around town by following the route shown in the pamphlet *Take A Walk Through History,* which you can pick up for free at the Chamber of Commerce office.

The Chamber also has a flyer with information about the **Bloody Shins Trail,** a BLM trail about three miles east of town. At an elevation of 4,540 to 5,200 feet, it has hiking, mountain biking and equestrian loop trails for beginners (seven miles), intermediates (12 miles) and advanced (24 miles). Another BLM trail, the Blue Lakes Trail, is further afield. Further information on both trails is available at the BLM's Winnemucca Field Office, 5100 Winnemucca Blvd., Winnemucca, NV 89445, 775/623-1500.

Special events are held May to September at the **Humboldt County Fairgrounds,** on the north end of town. Events include a Mule Show and Races (May), ICRA Roping (June), Junior Rodeo and USTRC Grassroots Team Roping (July), Nevada All-Around Working Cowhorse Championship USTRC—Northwest Finals (August) and Tri-County Fair and Stampede (Labor Day weekend, September). For information, contact: Humboldt County Fairgrounds, 50 W. Winnemucca Blvd., Winnemucca, NV 89445, 775/623-2220, Winnemucca@desertline.com.

Humboldt Historical Museum

Take Melarkey north under the freeway, then over the river and railroad tracks up to **Pioneer Park.** Take a left into the parking lot of the **Humboldt Historical Museum,** 775/623-2912, open weekdays 10 A.M.–noon and 1–4 P.M., Saturday 1–4 P.M. (donation recommended), and have a little visit with Pansilee Larson, the delightful curator. The building was originally St. Mary's Episcopal Church (1907), which stood on 5th St. till it was moved to 4th in 1917, then up to its present location in 1976 onto city-donated land. The old church houses Winnemucca's first piano (from the Winnemucca Hotel), a square grand piano brought to Winnemucca in 1868, Indian relics from Lovelock Cave such as projectile points, Paiute handicrafts, an Edison talking machine, paintings of the Jungo Hotel and Golconda School, posters of Charlie Chaplin and Edna Purviance, and a scrapbook from *The Winning of Barbara Worth,* starring Gary Cooper, Ronald Coleman, and Vilma Banky, filmed 30 miles west of Winnemucca at the edge of the Black Rock Desert in 1926.

The new rear building boasts a beautiful floor, a wall-length mural of what downtown Winnemucca looked like around the turn of the century when Butch's gang robbed the bank, plus a pump organ from Paradise Valley, couches from Unionville, and an original, hand-inked, mint-condition survey map of Winnemucca from 1867. The antique auto collection includes a 1901 Merry Oldsmobile, the county's first car.

An old grain store in the grounds serves as a thrift shop to raise funds for the Historical Society.

Casinos

Red Lion Inn, 721 W. Winnemucca Blvd., 775/623-2565, is an interesting little place. It's like a midget casino—with everything that the big ones have except in miniature: red and blue border neon outside and upside-down pyramid lights above the main entrance; lotsa slots; four blackjack tables and a roulette wheel around a tiny pit; little lounge right in the middle of the floor with a big-screen TV; little coffee shop with salad bar; even mini chandeliers lighting the place—all stuffed into a space the size of Harrah's Tahoe ladies' room.

The **Model T** casino and truck stop at the west end of town on Main St., 775/623-2588, has six blackjack tables, including one offering multiple action. The Model T also has plenty of slots (even some 10-centers), a good coffee shop, and a lounge with country-western groups playing 9 P.M.–3 A.M. Wed.–Sunday. There's also a three-story motel. Jump out of the first-floor back-corner room windows right into the pool. The room comes with a free breakfast at the coffee shop.

Winners, right downtown on the corner of

Winnemucca Blvd. and Melarkey, 775/623-2511, is the biggest casino, the only one with a crap table. Its big lounge has high-tech duos and trios playing Top 40 nightly, usually with some energy and a good beat.

Legends lounge and casino, 775/625-1777, owned by Winners, is the newest gaming house in town with 104 slots and three tables—two offer blackjack and one features Let It Ride. The complex also has a Holiday Inn Express motel and a 24-hour Denny's coffee shop inside.

Sundance Casino, downtown across from the Chamber of Commerce at Bridge and Main, 775/623-3336, is, except for the only poker table in town, all slots, including a video poker bar.

PRACTICALITIES

Accommodations

Twenty-two lodging houses offer a little more than 1,000 rooms in Winnemucca, so you shouldn't have too much trouble finding a suitable one. But pay close attention to all the changes that the rates can go through: summer and winter, weekend and weekday, two people in one bed or two beds, etc.

The **Red Lion Inn & Casino,** 741 W. Win-

from left to right: Sarah Winnemucca, Chief Winnemucca, Natchez, Captain Jim, and the photographer's son

NEVADA HISTORICAL SOCIETY, RENO

nemucca, 775/623-2565 or 800/633-6435, is the largest, with 104 rooms at $59–164.

Scott Shady Court, 400 1st St., 775/623-3646, has a cozy setting off the main drag, and a big luxurious indoor pool. The motel stands on part of the Scott family's old dairy farm, converted to the original campground and cabins in 1928. One of 70 rooms goes for $35–75.

Motel 6, 1600 W. Winnemucca on the far west end of town, 775/623-1180 or 800/466-8356, is next, with 103 rooms at $39–52. Next up on W. Winnemucca is the **Model T Hotel Casino,** 1130 Winnemucca Blvd., 775/623-2588 or 800/645-5658, with 75 rooms in the $45–65 range. Across the street is the **Best Western-Gold Country Inn,** 921 W. Winnemucca, 775/623-6999 or 800/346-5306, with 71 rooms at $79–104.

Some of the least expensive Winnemucca motels include: **Bull Head,** 500 E. Winnemucca, 775/623-3636, $33–50; **Cozy Motel,** 344 E. Winnemucca, 775/623-2615, $30–40; **Budget Inn,** 251 E. Winnemucca, 775/623-2394, $25–55; **Ponderosa,** 705 W. Winnemucca, 775/623-4898, $28–59; and **Scottish Inn,** 333 W. Winnemucca, 775/623-3703, $32–75.

RV Parks

Hi-Desert RV Park, 5575 E. Winnemucca Blvd., 775/623-4513, is one of the larger and nicer RV stopovers for Interstate 80 travelers, with grassy sites and good shade. The game room has a pool table, video games, and a TV; a weight room and hot tub are by the pool. A casino shuttle provides free 24-hour transportation to downtown. There are 137 spaces for motor homes, all with full hookups. There are 80 pull-throughs and 11 tent sites. Accessible restrooms have flush toilets and hot showers; laundry, groceries, video rentals, game room, and heated swimming pool are available. Reservations are recommended June through September; the fees are $17 for tents, $24 per vehicle, and $3.50 for non-campers to take a shower. Good Sam, AAA and AARP discounts.

Winnemucca RV Park, 5255 E. Winnemucca Blvd., 775/623-4458, has been in the same location, about a mile east of downtown Winnemucca, for more than 20 years. The trees are mature, there's plenty of grass (nice tenting area), and the spaces are spacious. There are

132 total spaces for motor homes, 84 with full hookups; 74 are pull-throughs. Tents are allowed. The fee is $22.50 for two people in an RV, $17 in a tent. Good Sam and AAA discounts.

Model T RV Park, 1130 W. Winnemucca Blvd., 775/623-2588, is in the parking lot of the Model T Casino, lending a somewhat urban setting for this RV park. There are 58 total spaces for motor homes, all with full hookups, all pull-throughs. No tenters need apply. Restrooms have flush toilets, hot showers; laundry, convenience store, and seasonal pool are available. The fee is $22 per vehicle. Good Sam and AARP discounts.

Food

Winnemucca Hotel, 95 Bridge St., 775/623-2908, is the second-oldest hotel still operating in Nevada today. The back bar is also one of the most beautiful in the state, with a large display of international currency above. Rooms are for rent (mostly to boarders) and Basque food is served family-style: lunch noon–1 P.M. Mon.–Fri. ($6), dinner 6:15–9 P.M. Mon.–Sat. ($13).

For Basque dining, also try the **Martin Hotel,** Railroad and Melarkey, 775/623-3197, open for lunch 11:30 A.M.–2 P.M. Mon.–Sat, and for dinner nightly 5–9 P.M. (till 9:30 P.M. on weekends). Lunch costs $5–9. The full family-style dinner costs $18 including wine and dessert; an a la carte menu is also available, from which you can select dinners from $6–18. This is a sprawling old hotel, with a cozy bar up front, the dining room on the side, and a small all-purpose room in the rear. Good Basque food, too.

A newer Basque restaurant in Winnemucca is **San Fermin,** 485 W. Winnemucca Blvd., 775/625-2555. The steak, I'm told by a correspondent who's compared, is not quite as big as the one you're served at the Star in Elko, but the accompanying dishes are all better than any other in Nevada. A young Basque/Basque-American couple, Jesus Flamarique and Alicia Garijo, have reinvigorated this cuisine with culinary news from the "Old Country." Together they run a top-notch operation. It's open for dinner Monday to Saturday, 5–9:30 P.M., with family-style dinners for $15–18. Hard-core traditionalists should be warned that each party gets its own table and that there's smoking in the bar only.

The Griddle, 460 W. Winnemucca Blvd.,

775/623-2977, opens every day at 5:30 A.M. and closes around 1:30 P.M. Mon.–Fri., around noon on the weekends. This is the best and most popular coffee shop in town—the food (try the huevos rancheros) is fast and friendly, though the waitresses are a tiny bit bashful. It's also one of the oldest restaurants in Winnemucca, having been owned by the Aboud family since 1961.

Winners, Model T, and **Red Lion** casinos all have 24-hour coffee shops. **Grandma's,** the fine dining room in Winners, is open for dinner nightly from 5–10 P.M. **Jerry's,** 1195 W. Winnemucca, 775/623-2990, serves up 24-hour road food without a casino attached.

The Bakery, 227 S. Bridge St. across from the chamber, 775/623-3288, has been a local institution since 1935. It moved to its present location in 1946; the oven installed at that time is still as good as new. It's open from 4 A.M. until 5:30 or 6 P.M. Tues.–Sat.; closed Sunday and Monday.

Winnemucca has its share of fast food: Round Table and Pizza Hut, Arby's, A&W, Taco Time, and Subway, all on Winnemucca Boulevard. **Route 66,** 329 E. Winnemucca, 775/623-2763, has a fountain and grill; the food is a step up from the usual galloping grub: burgers, sandwiches, chicken, etc.

Good, cheap Mexican food can be found at **Los Sanchez,** 1105 W. 4th St., 775/625-2000. Giant burritos start at $5 and combo plates run up to $7. It's open 9 A.M.–9 P.M. for breakfast, lunch, and dinner. For breakfast, try the machaca and eggs. **Las Margaritas,** 47 E. Winnemucca Blvd., 775/625-2262, is another good Mexican restaurant, open daily 11 A.M.–10 P.M.

Other Practicalities

Note that Winnemucca seems to be a siesta-type town: lots of businesses close for lunch between noon and 1 P.M. For five businesses that don't close for lunch, in fact *never* close for *any* reason, take Baud St. down to the corner of 2nd at the Red Apple, then continue down the alley and around to the right. You'll see "the Line"—**My Place, Pussycat, Simone de Paris, Penny's Cozy Corner, Paradise Cafe** and **Villa Joy's Oriental Massage.** Penny requests that you don't leave your diesels running in the parking lot, and if you're hauling cattle, please park elsewhere.

Park Cinemas, 740 W. Winnemucca Blvd.,

775/623-4454, opened in 1986 and remains the only theater between Sparks and Elko. It shows first-run features weeknights and matinees on weekends.

Winnemucca has a fine **library,** at the corner of 5th and Baud, 775/623-6388, open nice long hours. The Nevada section is in its own room in solid wood cabinets—great for anything from browsing to serious research. Sheri Allen, a fifth-generation Humboldt County resident, has been head librarian for more than 25 years; her great-grandfather was the first mayor of Winnemucca.

Humboldt County Hospital is located at E. Haskell and Mizpah, 775/623-5222.

Transportation

The **Greyhound** office is at 665 Anderson St., 775/623-4464.

Amtrak, 800/USA-RAIL, blows through town once daily in each direction. The mini-depot is located at 209 Railroad Street.

TO BATTLE MOUNTAIN

Heading east again on the interstate from Winnemucca, Paradise Valley stretches far and wide to the north, the Santa Rosas bordering it on the west and disappearing toward the left-hand horizon (see "The Santa Rosas" in the North of Pyramid Lake section). The road hooks around the top of the big **Sonoma Range** through its northern badlands, then turns southeast. There's a **rest area** on the westbound side at Exit 187, Button Point. The minor-in-size though rich-in-ore **Osgood Mountains** point a finger at Golconda, exit 194.

Golconda

Golconda, named by railroad officials for an ancient city in Hyderabad, India (which was famous for wealth derived from its diamond cutters), was known to emigrants for its hot springs. Joe Ginacca, one of the Frenchmen of French Ford (later Winnemucca), began digging a canal from here, hoping to channel the local water 90 miles west to Mill City, where he planned to build large reduction factories. (The canal, 15 feet wide and three feet deep, was dug as far as Winnemucca, then abandoned as unworkable.)

Some mining excitement occurred around the turn of the 20th century but went the way of the canal in a few years.

In the 1930s, however, the Getchell Mine, 20 miles north of Golconda, began producing gold in record amounts, then took a turn mining tungsten during WW II. Though the original Getchell closed in 1967, the area remained rich in ore. At the beginning of the new mining boom of the 1980s, the Pinson Mining Company opened a pit a few miles south of the old operation, and installed what was called "the most modern gold plant in the world." Today, the Getchell Mine has been reopened by FirstMiss Gold, and with the Rabbit Creek and Chimney Creek mines nearby, nearly 1,000 miners are working the neighborhood.

The most distinctive sight in Golconda is the old schoolhouse, its red roof visible from all around town. The headgates of the old canal, installed 125 years ago, are still visitable a couple miles east of town along the river.

The road to **Midas,** past the big mines, cuts out from this exit. This is supposed to be the better of the two 50-odd-mile gravel roads to this remote little former ghost town. For a description of the route from the Tuscarora side, see "North of Elko" in the Northeast chapter. As you leave Golconda on the road to Midas, you'll pass **Water Hole No. 1** with a bar, casino, cafe, store, post office, and gas station. Though the sign out front advertises a motel, don't bother asking for a room. The place rents only to miners from the area on a long-term basis.

To Valmy

Leaving Golconda, the highway makes a short but steep climb up **Edna Mountain** to **Golconda Summit** (5,145 feet). There's a **rest area** at the top, and you can catch a glimpse of **Osgood Peak.** Then you cruise along Edna's shoulder for awhile, and drop down her thigh into **Pumpernickel Valley,** with **Buffalo Mountain's** skirts hemming it in on the southeast, and the broad Humboldt River valley opening wide on the northeast.

As you head southeast, the skyscraping stacks of Sierra Pacific Power Company's huge **Valmy Power Plant** are visible a few miles north. This 500-megawatt generator, completed in 1985, burns nearly two million tons of Utah coal annually.

Valmy

This little settlement at Exit 216, named for a famous battle site in France, is famous in its own right for an unusual combination of factors, which includes the post office, Greyhound, and Bruce Springsteen. Originally a railroad siding, in 1932 a 19-year-old pilgrim found his destiny here. Eugene DiGrazia, known before he died as the "Mayor of Valmy," lived in and developed Valmy for 58 years and held many longevity records to prove it. He was the most senior postmaster in the country, with 56 years of service. He also operated the Shell station for 56 years, and the Greyhound depot for 54. But possibly DiGrazia's greatest claim to fame was the frame, on the cover of a 1981 Springsteen album released in England, of a very young-looking Bruce sitting under the old Valmy Auto Court neon sign one lonely night, with a '65 Ford Fairlane convertible (Utah plates) at the gas pump—the Boss's representation of classic Americana. Eugene DiGrazia died in 1990, and progress did in the old Valmy's. **Valmy Station,** an undistinguished mini-mart, cafe, and bar, now sits on the site of the old auto court and gas station. (The Springsteen album cover was taken to the home of one of Di Grazia's relatives.)

Valmy Station Motel, 775/635-5511, has six rooms for $33 a night, with weekly rates available. They also operate the **Valmy Trailer Court** across the highway on the eastbound side, with spaces with full hook-ups for $150 per month (monthly rental only).

The **Round Trip Cafe,** a.k.a. Gene's Golden Grill, opens, according to the waitress, "when we get the energy," and closes "when we get tired." (In other words, when the miners show up and when the miners go home.)

The Rest of the Way to Battle Mountain

Battle Mountain, the mountain, sits alone and square southeast of the road, its **Antler Peak** rising to 8,236 feet. The tail of the **Sheep Creek Range** points off to the northeast. The long **Shoshone Range,** still running north all the way from just this side of Tonopah, sits dead ahead to the right and left. Battle Mountain, the town, squats in the middle of the northern edge of the **Reese River Valley,** extending north all the way from the south side of Austin.

BOB RACE

NORTHEAST NEVADA

BATTLE MOUNTAIN AND VICINITY

History

Emigrants were attacked near this spot by Shoshone in 1861; the pioneers regrouped and counterattacked the Indians in the hills southwest of town. The mountain was named for the battle and the town was named for the mountain. But it could just as easily have referred to the mining-men battling the mountains themselves, wresting minerals from the reluctant earth.

The Central Pacific, fresh from Winnemucca, arrived in 1869, coinciding with a rush to Copper Canyon nearby. Mining and the main line attracted three more railroads and even a phony navigation company. The Nevada Central ran a spur line straight down the Reese River Valley 90 miles to the old mines at Austin. The Battle Mountain and Lewis Shortline ran 12 miles to Lewis, operating a total of a year and a half. Western Pacific arrived around the turn of the 20th century. And the Reese River, a suitably

long but unsuitably shallow waterway, provided clever eastern promoters the means to bilk unwary investors with stock in the only steamship company in Nevada's history—and a crooked one at that.

A new boom erupted in the late 1960s, when the Duval Company reopened the Copper Canyon operation, initiating a resurgence of mining in the area, for gold, copper, silver, turquoise, iron, mercury, and barite. (Battle Mountain is the barite capital of the world.) And after coveting the county seat for 110 years, in 1980 Battle Mountain, at one end of long thin Lander County, finally usurped the courthouse from Austin, at the other end.

The McCoy/Cove Mine, operated by Echo Bay Minerals south of town, has been in operation since the 1980s and for a number of years was the major employer in town, employing 500 people and recovering millions of ounces of silver, along with hundreds of thousands of ounces of gold. Several other gold and silver mines in the vicinity also helped sustain Battle Mountain's population at around 7,000 residents. By late 2000, however, after several major mine layoffs, the town's population was down to 3,600 people, and a third of the houses in town were up for sale. Nevertheless, unlike many places in Nevada where the mining boom-and-bust cycles mean the birth and death of towns, here in Battle Mountain, both the growth and decline in population have been accomplished without compromising the graciousness of its traditional small-town character. Battle Mountain remains a pleasant small town with a slow pace of life.

Unlike other towns along the Humboldt River, Central Pacific, US 40, and I-80 corridor, downtown Battle Mountain hasn't budged for 120 years. Front Street still fronts the railroad yards, with most of the businesses (and no vacant storefronts) lining the opposite side of the thoroughfare.

Around Town

Like Fernley, Lovelock, Carlin, and Wendover, Battle Mountain has two exits off I-80, on the east and west ends of town (Winnemucca, Elko, and Wells have three). Heading east into Battle Mountain from Exit 229, you pass the inevitable smoke shop and head downtown to the main intersection, Front and Reese. Take a left and cross the tracks. At the corner of N. Reese and N. 1st is the **VFW Park.** It's shady and has picnic tables and kids' apparatus—a pleasant place for a stretch, a bite, or a rest.

On the south side of town, the **Lander County Courthouse** is at Humboldt and S. 3rd. At Broad and 6th (NV 305 toward Austin) is the **Civic Center,** with the Chamber of Commerce office and library. The **Chamber of Commerce,** inside the Civic Center building at 625 S. Broad St., P.O Box 333, Battle Mountain, NV 89820, 775/635-8245, battlemtncc@hotmail.com, www.theonramp.net/battlemountain, is open Mon.–Fri. 9 A.M.–5 P.M. in summer, 8 A.M.–4 P.M. in winter. In the lobby of the Civic Center is a rack of brochures, both local and statewide. The **Library** next door, 775/635-2534, is open Monday 11 A.M.–5 P.M., Tuesday noon–6 P.M., Wednesday 2–6 P.M., Thursday 4–8 P.M., Fri-

day noon–4 P.M., Saturday 10 A.M.–2 P.M., closed Sunday.

The **Trail of the 49ers Interpretive Center,** 453 N. 2nd St., 775/635-5720, is a tribute to the pioneers who traveled through this area heading west. It is estimated that from 1828 to 1869, around 200,000 immigrants passed through here, with a particular swell around 1849 with the California gold rush. The immigrant route followed the Humboldt River, much as Highway I-80 does today. You are invited to live the experience with the immigrants, here at the center. Open Mon.–Fri. 10 A.M.–5 P.M., Saturday noon–4 P.M., or by appointment; donation.

Battle Mountain has a **Museum site** in town on Broyles Ranch Rd., opposite the Gold Strike Lanes bowling alley, off I-80's exit 231. For a long time the town had the land for the museum, but no museum to put on it. But in October 2000, the historic **Old Ranch Cookhouse** was being moved onto the site, and work was to begin to make this the home of the town's new museum. The town was all excited about it; phone the Chamber of Commerce to see how progress is coming, or stop by.

Check with the Chamber of Commerce for current info on **gold mining tours** in the area. Barrick, Newmont and Cortez are the major mines here, and there are also a number of smaller mines.

Other attractions include the **Battle Mountain Swimming Pool,** 560 Altenburg Ave., 775/635-5850, open June through August, and the **Iron Place Gym,** 720 S. Broad St. opposite the Civic Center, 775/635-3352, where walk-ins are welcome.

Events

Battle Mountain's major annual event is the **Pony Express** open road car race, with cars racing down NV 305 from Battle Mountain to Austin. It's held every summer, usually in June; the Chamber of Commerce has details.

At the **Human Powered Vehicle** bike race held in October 2000, it appeared that two world speed records were broken. (At this writing, official confirmation of breaking the world record was being eagerly awaited.) Canadian Sam Wittingham, of the Varna bicycle team from Vancouver, Canada, clocked in at a speed of 72.41 miles per hour, beating the previous world record

NORTHEAST NEVADA

© AVALON TRAVEL PUBLISHING, INC.

of 68 mph. A woman from the same team also apparently set a new female world record, clocking in at 53 mph. It is expected that this will become an annual event; call the Chamber of Commerce for details.

Accommodations

Coming in from the westside exit (229), you pass the **Broadway Colt Service Center,** with minimart, truck stop, cafe, and motel. The motel, **Best Inn & Suites,** 650 W. Front St., 775/635-5400 or 800/343-0085, offers 70 rooms for $39–69, continental breakfast included. Next up is the **Big Chief Best Western,** 434 W. Front, 775/635-2416 or 800/528-1234, with 58 rooms for $38–50. Downtown along Front St. are the **Owl Club,** 8 E. Front, 775/635-5155, with rooms for $35–40, and the **Nevada Hotel,** 36 E. Front, 775/635-2453, with six rooms for $17–27. The **Bel Court Motel,** 292 E. Front, 775/635-2569, has nine rooms for $20–30. And the three-story **Comfort Inn,** 521 E. Front at the east exit, 775/635-5880, has rooms for $56–60.

Broadway Flying J RV Park, 650 W. Front St., 775/635-5424, has 96 spaces for motor homes, all with full hookups; 79 are pull-throughs. Tents are allowed. Accessible restrooms (in the truck stop) have flush toilets and hot showers; public phone, laundry, and groceries are available. Tent and RV spaces are $15; non-campers can shower for $5.

Nature-loving campers will like the **Mill Creek camping area,** 19 miles south of Battle Mountain off NV 305, heading towards Austin. It's a small, shady, secluded little camping area beside Mill Creek, with trees and a footbridge across the creek. There are no hookups, and no running water, but the price is great: it's free!

Food and Casinos

The **Owl Club** is the main action downtown, 72 E. Front, 775/635-2444. The dining room is open 24 hours—save room for a piece of pie. The casino has lotsa slots, a three-table blackjack pit, and three big screens.

The **Nevada Hotel** on the same block, 36 E. Front, 775/635-2453, has a diner (open 7 A.M.–9 P.M.), slots, and blackjack.

The **Hide-A-Way,** 872 Broad Street, 775/635-5150, specializes in steaks and seafood.

For a real local-color scene, try **Donna's Diner,** 150 W. Front St. a bit west of town, 775/635-5101, open 5 A.M.–9 P.M. every day. Check out the 64 different burgers ($4.50–6), and the baked potatoes are good, too. Another spot for local flavor is the tiny **Mickey's Mouse House,** 156 S. Scott St., 775/635-5551, a cute little coffeehouse with just one table inside and one table outside.

For Mexican food, locals rave about **El Aguila Real,** 254 E. Front St., 775/635-8390, with delicious medium-priced Mexican fare, open 11 A.M.–9 P.M. every day.

The **Broadway Colt Restaurant,** 650 W. Front St. at the Broadway Colt Service Center at the far west end of town, 775/635-5424, open 24 hours, is a nice, bright, airy coffee shop serving good food, with daily specials. The casino next door has expanded from two rows of slots to more than 100 machines.

Mama's Pizza is next door to the Comfort Inn on the east side of town, 515 E. Front, 775/635-9211, open 11 A.M.–9 P.M., Sunday till 8 P.M. **McDonald's** has arrived in Battle Mountain; as you might expect, you can't miss it. **Pack Out,** 212 W. Front St., 775/635-2525, is a locally owned burger stand.

Other

For sundries, magazines, prescriptions, and whatnot, stop in at **Mills Pharmacy,** 990 Broyles Ranch Rd., 775/635-2323.

Battle Mountain is a good place to do your laundry! There are two big laundromats—you'll see the billboards on Front St.—one of which is open 24 hours.

CRESCENT VALLEY

Beyond Battle Mountain to the east, I-80 runs straight across the long Reese River Valley, then cuts abruptly north between the north rim of the Shoshones and Stony Point at the southeast tail of the **Sheep Creek Range.** At Exit 244 is the huge Argenta barite mine, which has produced more than 60,000 tons of barium sulfate, used as filler for linoleum, rubber, and plastics, as a mud for sealing oil wells during drilling, in paint pigments, rat poison, drying agents, and water softeners.

Continuing east, broad **Boulder Valley** gives

Cows quench their thirst at the waste-water pipe at Chevron's geothermal plant in Whirlwind Valley.

DEKE CASTLEMAN

way to the **Tuscarora Mountains.** At **Dunphy,** the river and the railroad turn south while the highway continues east—one of the few sections of I-80 in northeast Nevada that does not closely parallel the track and trickle. **Rest stops** are on both sides of the highway at Exit 258. In three miles is Exit 261, NV 306 to Whirlwind Valley, Beowawe, and Crescent Valley. It's a relief to leave the numbing, hypnotic interstate and drive into Whirlwind Valley, along an irrigation ditch with two long rows of old windbreak cottonwoods shading pastoral alfalfa farms (one of which is the historic Horseshoe Ranch, established in 1869, and once owned by Dean Witter). In a few miles is Beowawe.

Beowawe and Whirlwind Valley

Pronounced bay-oh-WAW-wee, the name is a Paiute or Shoshone word meaning "Gate." Reader Jan Roberts of Washington, possibly the world's foremost living expert on this area, says that Beowawe actually translates more closely into "Great Posterior," or something even earlier. Somewhere along the line, the translators removed the cultural color. The prehistoric locals maintained camps at Beowawe and the geysers and hot springs area. Later, with the coming of the Central Pacific Railroad tracks, a modern village (hotel, depot, siding, etc.) was established at the present-day site of Beowawe; the village supplied local ranches and mines in the area. The village remains just that, albeit less active now than in the past, with a crossing

and siding, a highway maintenance station, a justice court, and a branch of the **Eureka County Library** (open Monday 10 A.M.–2 P.M.).

Less than a mile south of town on NV 306 is a distinct (though signless) turnoff to the right (a stop sign does face the dirt road at the intersection). Welcome back to dust. You go up a Shoshone Range hill, veer hard to the right over the crest, and descend fast into beautiful **Whirlwind Valley.** In a little more than two miles is a surprising intersection; go straight on wide, smooth, clay **Geyser Highway.** Continue five miles on this outstanding (except where it crosses private land, delineated by cattle guards) road to the sinter terrace—half a mile long, 100 feet wide, 150 feet above the valley floor.

The Beowawe geyser group was one of at least three dozen geyser areas on Earth, only a handful of which were as large and active as these once were. The Indians who occupied the area before the coming of white men were very aware of the geyser area. Who the first non-Indian to "discover" the geysers was is lost in the geothermal mists of history. However, Albert Evans appears to be the first non-Indian to publicize the place (in the February 1869 issue of *Overland Monthly*). Evans's description of the geyser area also provides us with an earlier place-name (one that he hinted preceded his visit) for the geyser area: Volcano Springs. Although popularized in 19th-century railroad tourist guidebooks, the Beowawe geysers never received formal attention by the U.S. Geological

Society as, for example, Yellowstone's geysers did. Nor did they receive the protection: the National Park Service considered, then dismissed, three different proposals to establish a national monument at the site in the 1930s. Likewise, preservation of the geysers as a state park in the 1930s, 1950s, and 1970s was doomed by a variety of problems, including a lack of adequate funding and disagreements on how to develop the site.

Finally, the forces of industry arrived. Geothermal energy explorations took place between 1959 and 1965, and in those six short years nearly all the active geysers were eliminated. A few, located on the valley floor, survived, one of which still erupted as high as 10 feet. But even those diehard geysers have since disappeared, along with several beautiful hot pools and springs. A few hot springs and steam vents remain on top of the terrace, a token reminder of what was once one of the world's best geyser areas (before the geothermal explorations, about 50 active thermal springs were located on top of the sinter terrace, with a handful more near its base). Dr. Donald E. White of the USGS (who unofficially investigated the geyser area between 1945 and 1958), noted that more than half of the 50 thermal springs were active geysers, erupting as high as 30 feet. Jan Roberts has copies of Dr. White's maps and slides showing the extent of the activity and the damage done by the engineers. During the years 1959–65, several geothermal test wells were drilled on and near the sinter terrace; four wells were drilled on top of the terrace where most of the geysers were located. The wells diverted hot water away from the geysers and hot springs, which caused their deactivation. Bulldozers and concrete finished off the rest.

Today, a pipeline snakes from the **Beowawe Geothermal Power Plant,** built in 1985, to an injection well located at the foot of the terrace. The two wells that supply the hot water to the plant are inside the fence around the plant, which uses 2,500 gallons of 320-degree water a minute to produce 11.5 megawatts of electricity. Big power lines running out of the plant hook up to the Sierra Pacific grid, which directs the electricity to Southern California Edison. Cows congregate around the waste-water pipe to quench their thirst.

The Soul of the Shoshone

West and south of Whirlwind Valley, Crescent Valley has been the scene of a 25-year-long disagreement between Shoshone ranchers Mary and Carrie Dann and the Bureau of Land Management over the sovereignty of 800 acres of Dann ranch land and, incidentally, 55 million acres of land in central Nevada. The Western Shoshone Nation claims the land is tribally owned and immune from government regulation and fees, while the BLM insists the land is federal. The dispute erupted in 1992 when the BLM rounded up horses and cattle from Crescent Valley that it believed to be grazing illegally, while the Dann sisters and their supporters accused the Bureau of stealing their livestock. BLM personnel were armed and the protestors were not; the feds took at least 160 horses, but not without an altercation.

To Cortez and Beyond

Retracing your route to the pavement outside Beowawe, head right (south) on NV 306 13 miles to the little settlement of **Crescent Valley,** home to miners at several active gold mines and a large mill in the area. The pavement continues south down Crescent Valley toward **Cortez Canyon** under **Mt. Tenabo** in the **Cortez Range.** A sign for Cortez Gold Mine points left and the pavement ends; you head straight across the valley toward the big mine and mill. Large ore trucks come and go. Another fork points right, and you drive to the intersection where a sign directs you six miles into the mountains to the ghost town of **Cortez.**

High on a shoulder of Mt. Tenabo, take a left at the sign to the ruins. Cortez was discovered by prospectors from Austin in 1863. One of the original locators, Simeon Wenban, managed not only to hang on to the property but also to consolidate the major mines in 1867. Cortez reached 1,000 in population and produced $10–15 million in silver by 1895. Some later excitement visited the area in the 1920s and '30s, but not since. Today, you'll find stone and brick ruins terraced on the hillside, a few cabins staring into infinity with vacant windows, the smell of sage, and the buzzing of huge horseflies.

Return to the "main" road and take a left. In five miles, take another left. This road heads due east across **Horse Creek** and **Denay** valleys; continue east till you meet up with NV 278—then go right to Eureka, left to Carlin. (As usual, don't try this unless you have a current edition of *Nevada Road Atlas*.)

To Carlin on Interstate 80
As you leave Lander and enter Eureka Coun-

ty, the interstate runs along the river, then crosses it at a concrete mine. You start climbing and climbing up to **Emigrant Pass.** There's a rest area with no view, but climb the hill behind to stretch your legs. Exit 279 is the western entrance into Carlin.

CARLIN

Carlin, like Lovelock and Wells up and down the road, is a graphic representation of the transitions in mobility technology over the last century. The first settlers in Carlin were Chinese, who grew vegetables for railroad workers and emigrants in this small scenic valley. After the transcontinental line was completed, the Central Pacific crews changed here and Carlin quickly developed into the archetypal railroad town: a line of shops, stores, dinner houses and saloons, a hotel or two, depot, and telegraph office stretched for a few blocks along Main St., right across from the switching and maintenance yards, repair shops, and an ice warehouse for keeping produce chilled.

But as the railroad's days were numbered by automobile traffic, so were downtown's. US 40 coaxed some businesses a few blocks north to the old highway; likewise, I-80 has pulled services farther north still, to its exit ramp. The town straddles the three routes in such a way that

traveling in a straight line from the tracks to the superhighway—three blocks—is like traveling 120 years through time.

Around Town
Cruise into Carlin from the west on old US 40 (Chestnut St.) and take a right on 4th St. directly toward the big C on Buckskin Mountain. Cross the six sets of railroad tracks and take a left on Main Street. Most of this old district is defunct, except for the Triple H restaurant and casino, the Overland Bar, the Colonial Hotel (established 1911; now a rooming house), and the City Club (local watering hole). You can also cruise in, or back out, from the west exit of I-80 on **Bush Street,** the country road into Carlin (no trucks).

The **Chinese Gardens Nature Study Area** at the west end of town, south of Chestnut St. and the Carlin-Eureka highway, is a remnant of Carlin's history. In 1868, Chinese workers, far from their homeland where they had tended crops,

railroad trestle over the Humboldt with palisades in the background

DEKE CASTLEMAN

CAPITAL PUNISHMENT NEVADA STYLE

The first hanging of a woman in Nevada occurred in July 1851 on Gold Creek near the present site of Dayton. A Mexican woman named Juanita murdered a prospector named Jack Cannon for insulting her. A kangaroo court found Juanita guilty in 30 minutes, and a bloodthirsty mob strung her up. It appears that at least one of the vigilantes mildly disapproved of the lynching and left this verse:

At first content with hanging men
Who classed the rogues among,
At last they halted not for sex
And then a woman hung.

It's possible that other women were executed for capital crimes before Nevada became a state, but only one woman has been hanged as a result of due process in Nevada since 1864. Elizabeth Potts was sent to the gallows, along with her husband Josiah, for the murder of Miles Faucett in June 1890. One version of the crime holds that Elizabeth Potts married Faucett in San Francisco during a period of estrangement from her husband Josiah, and then murdered number two after he followed her back to Elko County when she reunited with number one. Another version states that the argument between the Pottses and Faucett concerned a debt.

Whichever, the Pottses buried Faucett under the basement of their Carlin home, then moved to Rock Springs, Wyoming. George Brewer and his family bought the Potts house, which they quickly perceived as haunted. Investigating, George Brewer dug up the basement and found Faucett's corpse, dismembered and charred. The Pottses were extradited to Elko, tried, and hanged. This event too was immortalized in verse:

Faucett's ghost rattled and clattered
And made an awful din,
For in that house in Carlin
The Potts had done him in.

---

were sent ahead to prepare the land for the Central Pacific Railroad. The Chinese workers planted their vegetable gardens in the Carlin meadows, beside the Humboldt River. These gardens gave the town its first name: Chinese Gardens. Today, the Chinese Gardens Nature Study Area, dedicated in 1992, offers trails shaded by thickets of trees, with picnic areas and a pond. It's open 6 A.M.–10 P.M. every day; free admission.

An enjoyable (and unique in Nevada) climb is up and over the footbridge that crosses the railroad tracks; this is the literal highlight of Carlin.

Practicalities

Up at the I-80 exit, **Best Inn & Suites of Carlin,** 1018 Fir St., 775/754-6110 or 800/626-1900, offers 60 rooms for $44–98. Also here are a **Pilot** truck stop-convenience store, 775/754-6384, a **Subway** sandwich franchise, and a complex including a Texaco station, **Burger King,** sports bar, and a small casino.

The **Cavalier Motel** on the southeast corner of 10th and Chestnut, 775/754-6311, has 17 rooms for $32–48. A mini-mart next door sells liquor; the **café** there is open 4 A.M. to midnight.

Chin's Restaurant, 923 Bush St., 775/754-6674, is a block south of the Cavalier Motel. It's open Mon.–Fri. 11 A.M.–9 P.M., Saturday noon–9 P.M., closed Sunday. Everything here is pink: the tablecloths, the pole paint, the take-out menus. The food is good, plentiful, and reasonable.

The **Hungry Miner,** 521 Chestnut St., 775/754-2444, serves up old-fashioned home-made cooking every day from 7 A.M.–10 P.M. in summer, closing an hour earlier, at 9 P.M., in winter. Homemade soup is served daily throughout the winter, and they boast that their food is "seved fresh to your likin's."

The **Triple H,** on the corner of Main & 6th, is a new place in an old building, housing a restaurant, bar, and casino with three banks of slots. The restaurant here is open for breakfast, lunch and dinner.

Sharon's is on NV 278 between Bush and Chestnut streets, and that's not a steeple on the roof supporting the red light.

Palisade

Take Bush St. back to the west end of Carlin Valley, past two churches, the archery range, and ranches. Go left on NV 278, following the Humboldt and tracks toward spectacular **Palisade Canyon,** and feast your eyes on some of the finest views on the whole main line through northeastern Nevada. The river and the railroad pass through a narrow gap with sheer walls, high and dark, looming above like Scylla and Charybdis. This gap gave the town its name, after the palisades on the Hudson River in New York, when it was founded in 1868 as a stop on the Central Pacific Railroad. Palisade got a big boost in 1875 when the **Eureka and Palisade Railroad** began servicing the 84 miles between the main line and the rich silver mines of Eureka. But the town began a slow decline after the mines played out in 1885, accelerated by ferocious floods in 1910. The Eureka and Palisade shut down in 1938, taking most of Palisade town with it. But not in the least disturbing the view.

Take a right at the road across from the historical sign, 10 miles southwest of Carlin. You skirt the hillside under which the railroad tunnels and come around to an unparalleled view of the tunnel, trestle, town, and palisade. Beautiful sunset shot. Stretch your legs and have a picnic under the century-old trees on the edge of town.

NV 278 continues south along the track's right-of-way through **Pine, Garden,** and **Diamond** valleys, along the **Cortez, Simpson Parks,** and **Roberts** mountains on the west, and the **Piñon, Sulphur Spring,** and **Diamond** mountains on the east (see "North to Carlin" in the Eureka section for a description of the road heading north out of Eureka).

Interstate 80 continues east, crossing the Humboldt River immediately before it passes under the Independence Mountains, through one of the three tunnels in Nevada (the others are at Cave Rock at Lake Tahoe and on the I-215 airport arterial in Las Vegas).

ELKO

INTRODUCTION

The Elko area's history generally parallels that of all the towns along the Humboldt River. Peter Skene Ogden blazed the trail in the 1820s that the emigrants from the east followed to California; miners created a demand for goods that the railroad fulfilled; when cars came into their own, the long-distance highway followed the railroad right-of-way, which the superhighway ultimately replaced.

Elko itself was founded at the same time the Central Pacific arrived in the area: very late in 1868. The company laid out a townsite for a division point and sold lots for $300; the origin of the name "Elko" is obscure, but is believed to be a lyrical form of "elk."

Immediately, Elko turned into a major supply and freighting center for the eastern Nevada mining boom—from Tuscarora, 52 miles north, to Hamilton, 140 miles south. It also became the seat of huge new Elko County (which remains today larger than Massachusetts, Connecticut, and Rhode Island combined), and site of the first University of Nevada. Elko suffered the inevitable boom-bust cycles throughout the rest of the century and lost the university to Reno. Cattlemen grazed large herds on public lands around the county, but the mercilessly severe winter of 1889–90 wiped out most of the stock. Soon afterward, the Basque sheepherders showed up.

Clashes between the buckaroos and Basques over public grazing lands occasionally became violent and necessitated state and federal legislation to control matters. The arrival of the Western Pacific passenger trains in 1907 helped lift Elko from its doldrums, and the Victory Highway (US 40) began delivering more travelers in the early 1920s. In addition, Elko was selected as a stop on the transcontinental airmail route. At first administered by the feds, when the routes were turned over to private carriers, Valmy Airlines (a forerunner of United) made the first commercially scheduled airmail flight, from Pasco, Washington, to Elko.

When gambling was legalized in 1931, Elko started up its casino industry in the venerable Commercial Hotel. Newton Crumley, who'd owned hotels in Tonopah and Goldfield, and a saloon in Jarbidge, had bought the Commercial

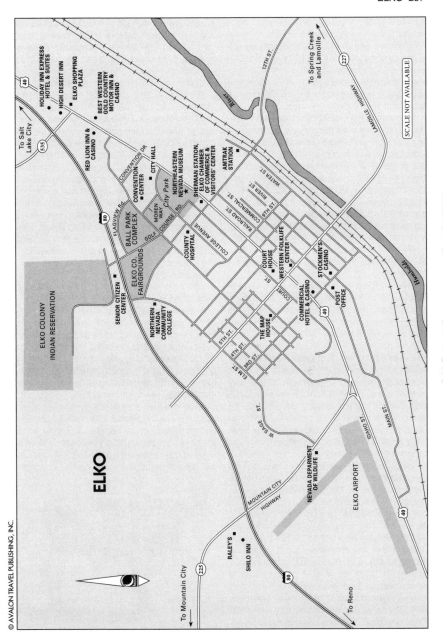

ELKO

© AVALON TRAVEL PUBLISHING, INC.

SCALE NOT AVAILABLE

To Salt Lake City

To Spring Creek and Lamoille

To Mountain City

To Reno

HOLIDAY INN EXPRESS HOTEL & SUITES
HIGH DESERT INN
ELKO SHOPPING PLAZA
BEST WESTERN GOLD COUNTRY MOTOR INN & CASINO
RED LION INN & CASINO
CONVENTION CENTER
CITY HALL
City Park
MOREN WAY
GOLF COURSE RD.
BALL PARK COMPLEX
FLAGVIEW Rd.
CONVENTION DR.
SHERMAN STATION, ELKO CHAMBER OF COMMERCE & VISITORS CENTER
NORTHEASTERN NEVADA MUSEUM
AMTRAK STATION
WATER ST.
RIVER ST.
HIGH ST.
COMMERCIAL ST.
RAILROAD ST.
COLLEGE AVENUE
COUNTY HOSPITAL
ELKO CO. FAIRGROUNDS
SENIOR CITIZEN CENTER
ELKO COLONY INDIAN RESERVATION
NORTHERN NEVADA COMMUNITY COLLEGE
COURT HOUSE
WESTERN FOLKLIFE CENTER
STOCKMEN'S CASINO
COURT ST.
COMMERCIAL HOTEL & CASINO
POST OFFICE
THE MAP HOUSE
6TH ST.
5TH ST.
4TH ST.
3RD ST.
ELMS ST.
W SAGE ST.
NEVADA DEPARMENT OF WILDLIFE
ELKO AIRPORT
IDAHO ST.
MAIN ST.
MOUNTAIN CITY HIGHWAY
RALEY'S
SHILO INN
LAMOILLE HIGHWAY
Humboldt River

six years earlier. The Crumleys followed the lead of Raymond and Harold Smith of Reno by making the new gambling accessible and acceptable to the masses. But the Crumleys went an important step further and began to book big-name acts to do the floor show in the lounge. A rousing success, this began the tradition of headliners and floor shows in casinos.

Since then, Elko has prided itself as a can-do sort of town. The people of Elko managed to relocate the railroad tracks from between Commercial and Railroad streets downtown to out by the river—something that no other town along the northern Nevada main line, not even Reno, has managed to accomplish. When Elko wanted a community college, it got one. Kids' parks? No problem—the town raised the money and built them with volunteer labor. Downhill skiing? Someone bought a hill, dug a well for snow-making machinery, and put in a rope tow. Museum? Convention center? Cowboy gatherings? Yup—they're all here.

In the past ten years, however, Elko has really taken off. The resurgence of gold mining around here doubled every number in Elko's demographics between 1987 and 1990; mining now accounts for nearly 60% of the economy, with gambling and ranching filling in the rest. Elko embraced the boom with its customary aplomb. Housing? It takes 60 days to approve a new subdivision and another few months to complete one; the houses are filled before the paint's dry. Doctors? At one point, a $10,000 reward was offered for anyone who coaxed a physician to Elko. In 1993, Elko was named the "best small town in the United States" by Norman Crampton, author of the *The 100 Best Small Towns in America*. According to the U.S. Census, Elko County ranks first in Nevada for average household income, at $38,000 a year; this puts Elko in the top 8% of the country.

For a town with such a big aura, Elko is still, well, small. The metropolitan area has roughly 34,000 people; there are 42,000 in the county (that's a little less than three for every square mile). Projections in 1994 put Elko's population at around 30,000 by the year 2000; this estimate was exceeded three years early.

Elko is the largest town between Salt Lake City (237 miles east) and Sparks (nearly 300 miles west), and between Las Vegas (400 miles south) and Twin Falls (173 miles north)—an area roughly comparable in size to New England. It's is the fourth most populated locale in Nevada, behind Las Vegas and Reno and their vicinities, and Carson City. It has regularly scheduled air, rail, and bus services, an interstate passing by, one of the finest museums in the state, the Cowboy Poetry Gathering, and some of the most irresistible outdoor recreation anywhere. It also has the most legal brothels in the country. And in one of the stranger twists in local mythology, Hunter S. Thompson, master of hallucinatory journalism, published a cover story in *Rolling Stone* called "Fear and Loathing in Elko," in which Thompson smashes into a herd of sheep on I-80 outside of town and rescues Judge Clarence Thomas and two prostitute companions whose car was totaled by the same sheep. This unlikely team proceeds to have a string of wild and drunken adventures as dark and mean as the inside of Thompson's head. (Anyone interested should see the January 23, 1992, edition; a more twisted view of northern Nevada you will never read.)

Anyway, this booming town has a brash, modern, frontier energy all its own. It's easy to slip into Elko's strong stream of hustle and bustle, which seems to keep pace with the cars and trucks on the superhighway, the freight and passenger trains chugging right through town, and the planes landing at and taking off from the airport. Yet Elko also has a warm, homespun vitality to it. Coming into Elko after a long drive from any direction is like stepping up to a blazing campfire on a cold desert night. And you seem to return to Elko again and again, after playing around for a while in the Rubies or up around Jarbidge, or just passing through on your comings and go-

BOB RACE

ings. So get to know Elko. Within and around it is everything you could need or want from a major Nevada town.

SIGHTS

Northeastern Nevada Museum

This remarkable museum, at 1515 Idaho St. toward the east end of town, 775/738-3418, is open Mon.–Sat. 9 A.M.–5 P.M. and Sunday 1–5 P.M. It is one of the largest, finest, and most varied collections in the state, so plan to spend at least an hour or two perusing the highly informative and artistic exhibits and displays, musing over the many books in the gift shop, and schmoozing with the friendly volunteers and staff.

The Ruby Valley Pony Express Cabin out front was built in 1860. Relocated from Ruby Valley, about 60 miles south, it's now the oldest structure in Elko. Inside the museum, sign the guest register and go into the room on the right, with rotating art and photo exhibits, an old mud wagon, and Bing Crosby's Levi tuxedo (one of two ever made). There's also a Basque display and video, and a display case of photos of downtown, with an emphasis on the Commercial and Stockmen's.

On the other side are big exhibits on local wildlife (birds, bighorn, bobcat, badger, black bear, beautiful butterflies), mining and minerals, railroads, and buckaroos, along with a pioneer kitchen, type shop, and schoolroom. The Chinatown display is exotic, with its abacus, game book and chips, and salt-glazed stoneware, as are the Indian baskets, points, and beads. A new wing, the Wannamaker Wildlife Wing, dedicated in August 1999, is impressive, with animals from around the world beautifully displayed. Another highlight is an exhibit of the Spring Creek Mastodon bones.

But perhaps the most relevant piece in the place is the display on mining, which features the Newmont Company's promo slide show about microscopic gold mining along the Carlin Trend, so rich and extensive that some say it won't be mined out till the year 2030. Watch how the ore is blasted, scooped, hauled, dumped, vibrated, separated, crushed, limed, conveyed, ground, pulped, thickened, settled, leached, cyanided, charcoaled, stripped, steel-wooled, retorted, acid-treated, inductothermed, poured, and bricked—all to recover microscopic specks of gold; it requires up to 100 tons of paydirt to process a single ounce. Marvel over the 100-ton dump trucks with their 10-foot-diameter tires that dwarf good-sized truck drivers, and all the equipment that is used to make Nevada the number-one gold-producing state in the nation.

The gift shop sells historical and local-interest books, Basque and local cookbooks, along with some art and jewelry.

Admission is: adults $5, seniors and youth (ages 13–18) $3, children (age 12 and under) $1; free for everyone on the last Sunday of each month.

Sherman Station

Next door to the museum is the historic Sherman Station, another very interesting place to visit. This group of five historic buildings, built of logs at various times between 1880 and 1903, was part of the historic homestead of Valentine and Sophie Walther, who homesteaded 600 acres on Sherman Creek in Huntington Valley, about 60 miles south of Elko, in 1875. The main house, a large two-story, 4,800-square-foot structure, is full of interesting historic exhibits, and also houses the Elko Chamber of Commerce and visitors' center. The other, smaller buildings are a historic blacksmith shop, schoolhouse, creamery (now housing a cowboy emporium), and stable (home to a company offering carriage tours of Elko). Sherman Station, 1405 Idaho St., 775/738-7135 or 800/428-7143, is open year-round, Mon.–Fri. 9 A.M.–5 P.M. and Saturday 9 A.M.–4 P.M., with additional Sunday hours in summer, 11 A.M.–3 P.M.

Around Town

Between Sherman Station and the Northeastern Nevada Museum is the large and shady **Elko City Park;** around it are picnic facilities, a childrens' playground, tennis courts, ball fields, Convention Center, swimming pool, community college, fairgrounds, city hall, public schools, and cemeteries. Take Court St. (one block north of Idaho) back downtown to view a number of **historic houses.** Mostly brick, with big lilac trees blooming and perfuming in mid-May, the oldest is on Court St. near 4th, refurbished and now inhabited by Chilton Engineering. The map store next door on the corner was the first schoolhouse in Elko, built in 1869; buy topo maps here.

Drive north of town up the bluff through a nice residential neighborhood to the interstate; coming back to town, the Ruby Mountains stand out—high, jagged, snowy. Continue down to the river; the footbridge over it at South Water and 9th streets could have been designed by a 15-year-old thrasher.

Make sure to stop off at **J.M. Capriola's,** one of the largest cowboy outfitters in the state, on the corner of Commercial and 5th, 775/738-5816, open Mon.–Fri. 8 A.M.–5:30 P.M., Saturday 9 A.M.–5:30 P.M., closed Sunday. Guadalupe S. Garcia was born in 1864 in Sonora, Mexico, and moved to San Luis Obispo, California, when he was three; there he did a long apprenticeship at a saddlery. He moved to Elko at age 32, where he proceeded to become one of the West's most renowned saddle makers, winning every award in the book, outfitting American celebrities, international *vaqueros,* and local buckaroos by the thousands. Guadalupe died in 1937 in Monterey, California, but not before Joe Capriola completed his apprenticeship with Garcia and opened this shop. Downstairs, ranch and Western wear, boots, and hats are sold; check out the artwork on the stairway and the tools of the buckaroo trade upstairs, where craftsmen handmake saddles, bits, and spurs.

Western Folklife Center

The Pioneer Saloon opened in 1868, and the Pioneer Hotel was built in 1912 on the same site, at the corner of Railroad and 5th streets, at a cost of $50,000. In 1981, the hotel was gutted and renovated for $2 million.

In 1991, the Western Folklife Center (WFC), sponsor of the Cowboy Poetry Gathering, received a grant generous enough to buy the Pioneer Hotel and move lock, stock, and barrel from Salt Lake City to Elko, where the Poetry Gathering had been held since 1985. The ground floor houses a gift shop full of tapes, CDs, and

COMMERCIAL HOTEL

This classic Nevada establishment, third oldest hotel in the state, began its long life as the Humboldt Lodging House in 1869, opened by a man named Crocker. At the time, it was a typical boomtown "lodge"—crudely slapped together with cheap wood on a 25-foot lot. It had a few rooms, a cafe, and the all-important bar. A short while later, Crocker sold the whole Humboldt for $300.

For the next 25 years, the hotel passed through many hands, was occasionally remodeled and expanded, and greatly increased in value. One owner, Billy Mahoney, an affluent sheep rancher from near Mountain City, bought the Humboldt in 1899, completely renovated it, adding a concrete facade and side wings, and renamed it the Commercial Hotel. He sold it in 1904 to L.L. Bradley and R.H. Dunn.

Ten years later, the Commercial again changed hands. William Doyle bought the hotel, already nearly 50 years old (along with the Bradley Opera House), for $500,000. Eleven years after that, in 1925, Doyle sold it to Newton Crumley, late from Jarbidge.

In 1931, immediately after the legalization of gambling in Nevada, Crumley went into the casino business. His operation was such a success that in 1937 he added the 200-seat Commercial Lounge, described as "Elko's first sophisticated cocktail lounge." Newton Crumley Jr. had an inspiration to book big-name entertainment in the lounge to attract customers to fill up the seats and spill over into the casino. In April 1941, Ted Lewis, his jazz orchestra, and his Rhythm Rhapsody Revue stage show played an eight-day engagement. The response was so overwhelmingly positive that Crumley immediately booked Sophie Tucker, "Last of the Red Hot Mamas," followed by Paul Whiteman's jazz orchestra and revue.

During the next several years, the Dorsey Brothers, the Andrews Sisters, Lawrence Welk, Ozzie Nelson's Orchestra, Ray Noble's Orchestra, even Chico Marx appeared at the Commercial, earning an astounding $12,000 a week. By the mid-'40s, these acts began their tours in Elko, and from there went on to appear at the Golden Hotel in Reno, and the El Rancho and then the Desert Inn in Las Vegas. Thus the Commercial Hotel became the birthplace of Nevada's claim as the "Entertainment Capital of the World."

the Humboldt River near Elko

books of cowboy poetry and music, and other ranching and Indian items, as well as posters from more than a decade of Poetry Gatherings, cowboy guitars, photos of the festivals, and songbooks full of the music of Gene Autrey, Roy Rogers, and Dale Evans from the heyday of cowboy culture. The old mahogany bar has been restored for functions, workshops, and performances, which spill over to, or in from, the Music Hall next door. Now that the WFC is home for good in Elko, it can present year-round programs; call for current info.

The Center is at 501 Railroad St., 775/738-7508 or 800/748-4466, tbaer@westernfolklife.org, www.westernfolklife.org. Admission to the center is free. The gift shop is open Tues.–Sat. 10 A.M.–5:30 P.M. Administrative offices on the third floor are open Mon.–Fri. 9 A.M.–5 P.M.

Cowboy Poetry Gathering

The reason this popular event takes place the last weekend in *January,* when the tempera-tures up here at a mile high barely get above zero and the snow is measured in feet, is because it's the only time of year that cowboys can all gather indoors and recite their rhymes and reasons. Held every year since 1985, the idea developed when folklorists rediscovered the art form of cowboy poetry in the late '70s, and the Western Folklife Center in Salt Lake City began sponsoring it. Working cow persons from all over the West (they come in both major genders) along with an audience that now numbers almost half the population of Elko and leaves more than $5 million in Elko, converge on northeastern Nevada to participate in five days of poetry reading, yodeling, music, workshops, seminars, art exhibits, demonstrations, partying, and more partying. Events also include demonstrations of buckaroo handicrafts such as leather and silver work, horsehair braiding and more.

The large formal events take place at the 900-seat convention center; smaller informal gatherings are held at the Pioneer Hotel, home of the Western Folklife Center. The after-reading get-togethers can crowd more people into Stockmen's than a lone *charro* might see in a lifetime. One aspect that is immediately noticeable is that these are the real *hombres,* instead of the barstool types; the gathering is consciously "high cowboy and low glitz." A verse like this sums it up: "There ain't nothin' fancy about 'em, and their writin' will show it/Just a man doin' what he loves, bein' a cowboy and a poet."

Tickets go on sale October 1 (call the 800 number above, or write WFC, 501 Railroad St., Elko, NV 89801; $20 for a pass to the entire event or $8 a day). Cowboys and ranchers interested in participating should send samples of their work to WFC by June 15.

This event is not only important for Elko, or Nevada, or cowboys and ranchers. It's important for its contribution to rural and small-town American culture, which is seriously threatened by urbanization, industrial water rights, corporate agriculture, environmentalism and, of course, the federal bureaucracy.

Casinos

The **Commercial Hotel** downtown at 345 4th St., 775/738-5141, has been around for nearly 130 years, which makes it the third oldest hotel in

"IN 45 YEARS"
by Peggy Godfrey

*I've learned to see the mountains
as more than stone and mud
Come to know my neighbors
as more than flesh and blood
I've grown to see the work I do
as more than passing time
Poetry means more to me
than getting words to rhyme.
I'm now aware each day is more
than getting on with life
I see myself as more than just
my role as mom or wife
Life offers me a framework
like bones stripped bare and white
What I can do is flesh them in
with muscle, love, and light.*

(Author's Note: Peggy Godfrey is a rancher in Colorado and a perennial star of the annual Cowboy Poetry Gathering held in Elko in January. "In 45 Years" is reprinted with permission from *Write 'Em Cowboy*, Elliot Publishing. To order *Write 'Em Cowboy*, send $10 to Peggy Godfrey, 19157 Cty Rd. 60, Moffat, Colorado 81143.)

the state (behind the Gold Hill and the Winnemucca). The White King on display here is the largest polar bear exhibited in Nevada (which isn't saying much) and probably the country (which is). This guy stands 10 feet four inches and weighs more than a ton. Too bad he had to be killed. The Commercial used to feature a fascinating series of portraits (by Lea McCarthy, 1958) and biographies of two dozen of the Wild West's most famous gunfighters, but now only a few portraits (*sans* bios) hang in the coffee shop. Of the two casinos downtown, the Commercial is more the sawdust joint, with six blackjack tables, one Caribbean stud, and lots of nickel slots and video poker.

Across the plaza is **Stockmen's** (not to be confused with Stockman's, in Fallon), 340 Commercial, 775/738-5141, which has old downtown carpeting, a big pit with craps, roulette, and black-

jack, a popular sports bar, and a good dining room (see below).

The **Red Lion Casino,** on the east end of town at 2065 Idaho, 775/738-2111, is the big fancy joint in Elko. This place is more a big-city's gambling house than a town's, with its long luxurious pit (including two each crap and roulette tables, plus lots of blackjack), comfortable sports book, big lounge with dance floor, gourmet restaurant, buffet, and foxy cocktail uniforms.

The Red Lion also runs a charter airline service, called the **Casino Express,** on Boeing 737s from all around the country, the closest thing to an old-fashioned junket as you'll find in Nevada these days. Casino Express delivers to the Red Lion thousands of "green-button" people a month, who pay upwards of $150–200 for two or three nights and round-trip airfare. You have to show somewhere around $350 in cash to qualify; there's no gambling requirement, but your play is monitored once you get here, which will affect your future junket prices. The planes are cramped and crowded, but there's some action: $500 is given away. Reports are that it's a pretty good little getaway.

Across the street is the **Best Western Gold Country Motor Inn & Casino,** 2050 Idaho St., 775/738-8421, with three blackjack tables, some slots, and a big 24-hour coffee shop.

Mining
Witness first-hand what's igniting Elko's boom with a visit to two of the larger working gold mines in the area. There are ten mines in all leaching microscopic gold from northeast Nevada rock. **Barrick Goldstrike Mines,** 775/934-9274, offers tours of its operation twice a day, beginning at 8 A.M. and 1 P.M., every day from mid-May through mid-August. Tours begin at the Northeastern Nevada Museum and take around four hours, including the bus ride out to the mine. Space is limited, and the tours are popular; call for reservations at least 48 hours in advance. Children must be age six or older, and be accompanied by a parent. Long pants and closed-toed shoes are required; cameras welcome.

Newmont Gold Company, 775/778-4068, offers mine tours from 9 A.M. to noon on the second Tuesday of each month, mid-April through October. Reservations are first-come, first-served; it's a good idea to reserve at least a week ahead. Children 12 and older are welcome, accompanied by an adult. Transportation is provided.

Both of these tours are free—what a deal!

Local Art

Desert Gold Gallery, 2170 Idaho St., 775/738-1553, open 10 A.M.–5 P.M. Tue.–Fri. and 11 A.M.–3 P.M. Saturday, features the work of local artists. The gallery also offers art classes.

ACCOMMODATIONS

Being the biggest town for several hundred miles in every direction and a boomtown to boot, Elko can be a tough place to get a room, especially in the summer and on weekends year-round. Still, Elko has more than 1,800 rooms, so if you call even a day or two in advance, you'll probably be able to come up with an adequate place to stay in your price range.

The biggest hotel in town is the **Red Lion Inn & Casino,** 2065 Idaho, 775/738-2111 or 800/545-0044. It has 223 nice big rooms, which go for $79–99. A block east is the next largest lodging in Elko, the **High Desert Inn,** 3015 Idaho, 775/738-8425 or 888/EXIT-303, with 171 rooms at $69–109 and an indoor swimming pool. Across the street from the Red Lion is the **Best Western Gold Country Motor Inn & Casino,** 2050 Idaho, 775/738-8421 or 800/621-1332, with 151 rooms at $59–104. **Best Western Elko Inn Express,** 837 Idaho, 775/738-8822 or 800/528-1234, has 49 rooms at $49–69 and an outdoor pool. **Ameritel Inn Elko** is at 1930 Idaho, 775/738-8787 or 800/600-6001, with 109 rooms at $69–150 and an indoor pool.

The **Motel 6,** 3021 Idaho, 775/738-4337 or 800/466-8356, at the east end of Idaho St. is tried and true, with rooms for $42–50; even though it's the fifth largest lodging in Elko with 123 rooms, it fills up fast. Reserve early. The back rooms at **Towne House Motel,** 500 W. Oak St., 775/738-7269, at the corner of Idaho and W. Oak on the west side, are far enough off Idaho to be relatively quiet. Attentive managers, too; $32–42. The **Centre Motel,** 475 Third St. across Idaho from the Commercial on 3rd St., 775/738-3226, has a fine location and is amazingly quiet in the bargain. Great TV sets,

and from the windows you get good neon—the Commercial, Stockmen's, and the Thunderbird; $35–50. The **Elko Motel,** 1243 Idaho St., 775/738-4433, is also a good deal at $32–45; the rooms are old and small but clean.

The **Shilo Inn** is at 2401 Mountain City Hwy. in the Raley's shopping center, 775/738-5522 or 800/222-2244; its 70 rooms ($69–99) are all suites, with microwave, fridge, and wet bar; there's also a fitness center with steam, exercise equipment, and an indoor pool (with three indoor pools, Elko has the most of any town in Nevada).

Other places to try include: **Budget Inn,** 1349 Idaho St., 775/738-7000, $35–75; **Park View Inn,** 1785 Idaho St., 775/753-7747, $44–60; **Manor Motor Lodge,** 185 Idaho St., 775/738-3311, $30–60; and the **Thunderbird Motel,** 345 Idaho St. right downtown, 775/738-7115, $39–89.

Bed & Breakfasts

The friendly **Once Upon A Time B&B,** 537 14th St., 775/738-1200, mjohnson@elko-nv.com, operated by Michael and Madeline Johnson, is walking distance to downtown. The three guest rooms are $65–95, including full breakfast.

Ranches

Ranch accommodation in the area is available at Red's Ranch in Lamoille, and at the Ruby Crest Ranch in Spring Creek. See those sections, further along, for details.

RV Parks

Double Dice RV Park, 3730 E. Idaho St., 775/738-5642, is a full-scale urban RV park atop a hill in East Elko (the Daily Free Press newspaper offices are next door). The park has its own bar and lounge, complete with video poker, slot machines, and sandwiches and burgers for sale (or catch the shuttle down the hill to town). The Double Dice makes its showers available to non-campers: $3 for 20 minutes. There are 140 spaces for motor homes, all with full hookups, and 55 pull-throughs. Tents are allowed. Reservations are recommended in summer. The fees are $13 for tent sites and $22 for RV sites. Good Sam discounts.

Best Western Gold Country RV Park, 2050 Idaho St., 775/738-8421 or 800/621-1332, is right in the thick of the urban action at the east end of Elko; the RV park is behind the Best Western Gold Country motor inn. There are 26 spaces for motor homes, all 26 with full hookups. Tents are not allowed. Laundry and heated swimming pool are available. Reservations are recommended; the fee is $22 up to two people. AARP discounts.

Cimarron West RV and Trailer Park, 1400 Mountain City Highway, 775/738-8733, is a busy little complex just up the street from the airport and down the street from the Raley's shopping center. There are 12 spaces for overnight motor homes, all with full hookups (there are a total of 73 spaces, but 61 are occupied by permanent residents). No tents are allowed. Here you'll find a full-service mini-mart with ice-cream parlor and slots, 24-hour restaurant, video rentals, gift store, Texaco service station, and drive-thru car wash. Reservations are recommended (without reservations, especially in the summer, forget about staying here). The fee is $17 per night.

Valley View RV Park, 6000 E. Idaho St., three miles east of town, 775/753-9200, is open all year and has 100 pull-through spaces that can accommodate motor homes up to 50 feet long. Facilities include laundromat, showers, children's playground, dog walking area, barbecue areas, and there's plenty of grass and trees. Tents are allowed. RV spaces with full hookups cost $15, tent spaces $8; weekly and monthly rates also available.

Camping is available at the **Eagle's Nest Station** ranch, 15 miles south of Elko; see Tours, further along, for details on the ranch and the activities held there.

FOOD

Not surprisingly, the main theme in this cow town is beef—at coffee shops, diners, burger joints, steakhouses, and Basque restaurants.

Basque

Of the four Basque dinner houses in Elko, three are strung along Silver St., one block south of Idaho behind Stockmen's. The **Star Hotel Basque Restaurant,** 246 Silver St. at the corner of Silver and 3rd, 775/753-8696, is the oldest. It opened in 1910 as a Basque boardinghouse with 11 rooms (built for $11,000); business was so brisk that another dozen rooms were added in 1913. Since then, the Star has been owned by a succession of Basque innkeepers, the latest since 1989. Typically, the seating is family style, and the food bowls full of soup, salad, beans, veggies, fries, and bread are bottomless; entrees include selections such as trout, pork, lamb, steaks, even bacalao or salted cod. It's open for lunch Mon.–Fri. 11:30 A.M.–2 P.M., dinner Mon.–Sat. 5–9:30 P.M.

The **Nevada Dinner House** at 351 Silver St., half a block east between 3rd and 4th, 775/738-8485, offers Basque dining with regular restaurant seating. Open for lunch Tues.–Fri. 11 a,.m.–1:30 P.M., dinner every night except Monday, 5–10 P.M.

Biltoki, 405 Silver St., is half a block east on the corner of 4th, 775/738-9691. This is the least expensive of the three, with the most specials: lomo, beef tongue, lamb stew, along with lamb chops, Spanish omelette, and the usual steaks, with full dinner costing around $11–20. Open for dinner every night except Wednesday, 4:30–10 P.M.

Toki-Ona (Come To This Place), 1550 Idaho St. across from the museum, 775/738-3214, is open every day, 6 A.M.–9:30 P.M., serving breakfast, lunch and dinner.

Mexican

In the Raley's plaza is **9 Beans and a Burrito,** 2503 Mountain City Hwy. #120, 775/738-7898, economical and popular with locals, especially at lunchtime. It's open Mon.–Sat. 7:30 A.M.–9:30 P.M., Sun. 8:30 A.M.–8:30 P.M.

La Fiesta at 780 Commercial St., 775/738-1622, is another local favorite, serving lunch specials and dinner. Topping the menu in price is steak and lobster. Open every day, 11 A.M.–10 P.M.

Dos Amigos, 1770 Mountain City Hwy., 775/753-4935, is another Mexican restaurant popular with locals. And don't forget **El Guadalajara,** 1900 Idaho St., 775/777-3043, yet another good Mexican place.

Hotel Food

The **Stockmen's** and **Commercial** casinos downtown, 775/738-5141, each have a 24-hour coffee shop.

The Red Lion Inn & Casino has the 24-hour

Coffee Garden Restaurant & Buffet, the only buffet in town, with buffets for breakfast, lunch and dinner. Lunch and dinner themes are different every day; on Friday, the dinner buffet features multiple seafood choices. The breakfast special goes 24 hours: two eggs, bacon or sausage, and biscuits and gravy. The Red Lion is at 2065 Idaho St., 775/738-2111,

Misty's, also at the Red Lion Inn & Casino, is the first-class dining room hereabouts. Try out appetizers such as shrimp royale and crab cakes, a Caesar salad for two, or treat yourself to a filet mignon Diane or angel pasta pescatore with shrimp and lobster. Open 5–10 P.M. weekdays, 5–11 P.M. weekends.

JR's Bar & Grill, in the Best Western Gold Country Motor Inn & Casino, 775/738-8421, features the only rotisserie-grilled meats in town, plus an array of tasty meat and pasta dishes. Have breakfast, lunch, or dinner at this local favorite. Open 24 hours.

Other Local Favorites

For a slightly exotic combination of Chinese and buckaroo, try the popular Elko Dinner Station, 1430 Idaho, 775/738-8528. It serves chow mein, fried rice, moo goo and egg foo, steaks and seafood, and special dinners synthesizing the two. Open 11 A.M.–9:30 P.M., closed Monday.

Savary, 217 Idaho across from Zapata's, 775/738-0488, offers "casual fine dining" in a house with a long history that's described on the menu. It's a comfortable place, with five dining rooms, three fireplaces, bar and lounge area. The eclectic menu offers a wide range of choices; the emphasis is on fresh foods, with a Mediterranean and Southwestern flair. Open for lunch 11 A.M.–2 P.M. ($6–11) and dinner 5–9 P.M. ($9–20), every day except Sunday.

If you're tired of road swill or are simply a coffee snob, Cowboy Joe serves espresso and sweet snacks at two locations. Cowboy Joe's Downtown, 376 5th St., 775/753-5612, is open Mon.–Fri. 5 A.M.–6:30 P.M., Saturday 5:30 A.M.–6:30 P.M., Sunday 6:30 A.M.–3 P.M. The other Cowboy Joe, 2130 Idaho St., 775/753-3900, is open Mon.–Sat. 6 A.M.–6 P.M., Sunday 8 A.M.–4 P.M. Both shops carry unique gifts and souvenirs.

Other

Elko is well represented by fast-food franchises: Arby's, Burger King, McD's, Pizza Hut, Round Table, Subway, and Wendy's, mostly on the newly developed east side of town, which might actually remind you a little of Las Vegas. If it does, you can make this comparison: Elko is to Las Vegas what Winnemucca is to Reno.

For cheap cigarettes, head up 5th toward the freeway, go right on ITC Street, then right again on Sunset, into the Elko Indian Colony and Te-Moak tribal administration offices. The smoke shop here is open weekdays 9 A.M.–5 P.M., Saturday 9 A.M.–4 P.M.

ENTERTAINMENT AND INFORMATION

The action, as you'll quickly discover, is at the three big hotels. Nevada-style entertainment started right here in the Commercial Hotel; check the Round Up Room for your dancing and listening enjoyment. Stockmen's also has the country, and can get swingin' with the right players and audience. The Red Lion Inn lounge, Club Max, has a big dance floor and bar bands that can get the rock 'n' roll crowd movin' and groovin'.

Speaking of moving and grooving, five brothels huddle in a two-block area around S. 3rd between River and Water three blocks south of Idaho: Mona's II in a 100-year-old house, along with Sue's, P.J.'s, Inez's, and Mona Lisa's a bit down Douglas.

The Crystal Theater five-plex is at 676 Commercial St. at 7th, 775/738-5214. There's also the newer Cinema 4, 1145 Connolly Dr., 775/778-6606.

Elko SnoBowl is Elko's new ski and winter recreation area, six miles north of town via 5th Street, 775/738-4091. With a north-facing slope, a base elevation of 6,200 feet and a maximum elevation of 6,900 feet, it offers good skiing even when there's no snow in the valley. The ski hill is served by two rope tows and a chair lift. Saturday ski lessons are offered for children and beginners; more advanced skiers can try the expert run. Sledding and snow tubing are also popular. Skiers can compete in the SnoBowl Fest in February. A Snack Shack is open during ski season. A shuttle bus leaves hourly, on the hour, from the end of 5h St.

Special Events

Elko is a lively community with enjoyable events happening throughout the year; the Chamber of Commerce should have details on all of them.

The **Cowboy Poetry Gathering,** 775/738-7508 or 800/748-4466, takes place in the last week of January (see more information above). In April there's the **Spring Creek Ranch Hand Rodeo,** 775/753-6295. June brings the **Golf Tournament and Mining Expo,** 775/738-4091, and the **Lamoille Country Fair,** 775/753-6410. In July there's the **National Basque Festival** held on the Fourth of July weekend, 775/738-7991; the **Silver State Stampede Rodeo,** 775/738-3118, and **Art in the Park,** 775/738-1553. **Elko Days** is celebrated in July/August, 775/778-3556. In September, the **Elko County Fair, Livestock Show and Parimutuel Horse Racing** provide entertainment for Labor Day weekend, 775/738-3616, and there's also the **Kiwanis Buckaroo Breakfast,** held in Elko City Park. October events include the **Nevada Day Parade,** 775/753-7991, and **Octoberfest,** 775/738-4187. In December are the **Nurses' Bazaar,** 775/738-5414, the **Christmas in the Nighttime Skies** fireworks show, 775/738-8011, and the **Parade of Lights,** 775/778-3556.

Information

Started in 1907, the **Chamber of Commerce,** 1405 Idaho St., 775/738-7135 or 800/428-7143, chamber@elkonevada.com, www.elkonevada.com, is Nevada's oldest. It's open Mon.–Fri. 9 A.M.–5 P.M. and Saturday 10 A.M.–4 P.M., with additional Sunday hours of 11 A.M.–3 P.M. in summer (Memorial Day weekend to Labor Day weekend). Located in the historic Sherman Station, the office has a goodly amount of information, brochures, and free newspapers. The town boosters working here are a friendly, efficient, and busy bunch. Much of their work involves sending out relocation and employment information to people (hundreds of requests come in each day) eager for a stake in Elko's continuing economic boom. Requests were coming in so fast and furious that they finally had to start charging ($5) to offset the skyrocketing printing and

mailing costs; they recommend viewing their website, which displays a lot of the same information.

The **library,** Court and 7th Streets, 775/738-3066, is open Mon.–Thurs. 9 A.M.–8 P.M., Friday and Saturday 9 A.M.–5 P.M. A big wall of bookcases is full of Nevadana; ask the librarian to open them up for your edification.

The **Bookstore,** in the Rancho Plaza Shopping Mall, 1372 Idaho St. at 13h, 775/738-5342 or 800/580-5342, is the area's primary book source, with a large selection of new and used books, magazines, paperbacks, local-interest and Louie L'Amour books. Open Mon.–Fri. 9 A.M.–5:30 P.M., till 5 P.M. on Saturday, closed Sunday.

For maps, check out **The Map House,** 421 Court St., 775/738-3108, chilton@chiltoninc.com, carrying USGS maps, Rand McNally maps and others.

The **U.S. Forest Service** office, 2035 Last Chance Rd., 775/738-5171, www.fs.fed.us/htnf, is open Mon.–Fri. 7:30 A.M.–4:30 P.M. Stop here to check on road conditions in the Rubies and up around Jarbidge, and to pick up maps, information sheets on trails, camping, and fishing, and to get personal recommendations; information and maps are available especially for the Ruby Mountains, Mountain City and the Great Basin National Park. **Elko General Hospital,** 1297 College Ave., 775/738-5151, was founded in 1921 and has a 24-hour emergency room.

Tours

City Slicker Tours, 775/738-5642, based at the Double Dice RV Park in Elko, offers all kinds of trips and tours in the surrounding area, including Elko, Landers, Eureka and White Pine counties. To mention just one example: their half-day tour of Lamoille and the Lamoille Canyon costs $45, with lunch included at O'Carroll's Bar & Grill in Lamoille. They also offer a number of full-day tours ranging further afield. Operated by Marv Churchfield, a rancher whose family has lived in the area since 1891.

Eagle's Nest Station, 775/744-4370, 15 miles south of Elko, offers wagon rides in summer, sleigh rides in winter, meals, cowboy music and poetry, and a log art gallery. Lunch rides and sunset steak supper rides are also offered (minimum four persons). Transport is available from Elko, to bring you out to the ranch and take you back to town, with magnificent views along the way. The Eagle's Nest is open year round, except for a short time in spring and fall if there are muddy conditions. Camping is also available here on the ranch, except during fire season: $8 per night, $10 with shower, $15 with shower and ranch tent.

Guide Service

For full-service summer horseback pack trips, fishing and hunting trips, photography, or backpacking, call Bill Gibson of **Elko Guide Service,** 775/744-2277. Gibson and his guides have a lot of experience in the outdoors around Elko, and are licensed to operate on the federal lands in the vicinity.

Other local licensed outfitters serving the Rubies and beyond include **Nevada High Country Outfitters & Jaz Ranch** in Lamoille, 775/777-3277; **Ruby Valley's Secret Pass Outfitters,** 775/779-2232; **Humboldt Outfitters** in Wells, 775/752-3714; and **Hidden Lake Outfitters** in Ruby Valley, 775/779-2268.

TRANSPORTATION

By Bus and Train

The **Greyhound** depot, 775/738-3210 or 800/231-2222, is at 193 W. Commercial St. Three eastbound and three westbound buses a day pass through.

One **Amtrak** train comes through daily in each direction. They stop at two shacks on either side of the tracks. Get there via the 12th Street overpass, and follow the signs. If you're getting off late at night, hike up to the bridge and take a right to Idaho St.—something will be open. Call 800/USA-RAIL (800/872-7245) for schedules and fares.

By Air and Rental Car

The **Elko Air Terminal,** on Mountain City Highway at the west end of town, is open 5:30 A.M. to 9 P.M. The airport is also known as Jess Harris Field, after an Elko County sheriff and aviation pioneer of the 1920s. Historical black-and-white photos and captions line the wall behind the luggage carousel. The men's room has wonderfully high sinks for us long-legged dudes. Regularly scheduled air service is provided by **Delta Connection-SkyWest Airlines,** 775/738-5138 or 800/453-9417, connecting Elko with Reno, Salt Lake City, and Ely/St. George. Sunrise Airlines, 888/252-8646, offers daily round trip service between Elko, Ely and Las Vegas. Then there's Casino Express Airlines, 775/738-6080 or 800/258-8800, with economical round-trip excursions to/from Elko (originating in other places, or outbound from Elko), with flights serving 90 locations in the USA, with more than 60 flights a month (see Casinos, above).

Avis, 775/738-4426 or 800/831-2847, **Enterprise,** 775/753-2333 or 800/325-8007, and **Hertz,** 775/738-5620 or 800/654-3131, are the three options for rental cars in Elko.

THE RUBY MOUNTAINS

Head south down either 5th or 12th streets in Elko; they join across the river and become NV 227. A bit south of town, you crest the **Elko Hills** at Elko Summit (5,773 feet) and head east toward the northern Ruby Mountains, sometimes called the "Alps of Nevada." You go by **Spring Creek,** Elko's southeastern suburbs. The area features an 18-hole, par 71 golf course and 19th Hole Bar and Restaurant, a trap and skeet club, and the Horse Palace Event Center. The 62,000-square-foot Horse Palace, built in 1976 to entertain prospective home buyers in the new suburb, hosts rodeos, horse shows, concerts, and other local events.

The majority of commuter traffic turns off on the three Spring Creek exits, and one to Pleasant Valley. Then it's just you, the ranchers, and the Rubies. In another five miles is the turnoff (right) to Lamoille Canyon. Instead, take a detour first into **Lamoille,** a wonderfully picturesque valley town nestled right into the western base of this rugged and gorgeous range.

LAMOILLE

Lamoille Valley originally provided an alternative route to the denuded Fort Hall main stretch of the California Emigrant Trail. Pioneers cut south from Starr Valley near Wells, traveled along the western foot of the East Humboldts on a well-worn Shoshone trail, availed themselves of Lamoille Valley's water and forage, then rejoined the main trail near Elko. The first homesteaders settled here in 1865, and within a few years a small village grew up around the farms and ranches. The post office arrived in 1883, but it took another 50 years for an actual road to reach the valley. Even then, Lamoille continued to hang on to its isolation for yet another 30-odd years, until 1965, when Lamoille Canyon was developed as a scenic area by the Forest Service.

Around Town
A favorite place in Lamoille is the **Pine Lodge,** on NV 227 as you enter town, 775/753-6363. The lodge was built in 1947 and has been expanded over the last 10 years into the operation of today. It has three hotel rooms, at $55 each. Next door is the restaurant and bar, in a beautiful cabin representative of its stunning setting; check out the trophies and fantastic wildlife photography. The restaurant, a steak-and-seafood dinner house, is open Tues.–Sun. (closed Monday); it opens at 3 P.M. and dinner is served 5–10 P.M.

The Presbyterian church in Lamoille has a most heavenly location.

DEKE CASTLEMAN

Also in town is **O'Carroll's Bar & Grill,** 775/753-6451. Food is served every day, 8 A.M.–4 P.M.; the bar stays open till 11 P.M. **Swisher's General Store,** 775/753-6489, is open every day, 8 A.M.–7 P.M.

The **Presbyterian Church** on the corner where the pavement runs out has a fine steeple and stained glass and might be the most heavenly located house of worship in the state—very close to God.

Red's Ranch, Country Lane, P.O. Box 281406, Lamoille, NV 89828, 775/753-6281, offers ranch accommodation on a beautiful Lamoille ranch. Activities include horseback riding, swimming, hiking and skeet shooting, and there's a spa; in winter, Ruby Mountains Heli-Skiing ski trips operate from the ranch. It has 10 rooms, each with private bath; reservations required.

THROUGH THE RUBIES

Heli-Skiing

The Rubies are a mighty range, 100 miles long, with nearly a dozen peaks over 9,000 feet. They can receive 400 inches of snow in the upper elevations, and are snow-patched year-round. In 1976, three partners from Alta, Utah, were granted permission by the Forest Service to operate a heli-ski service in the Rubies, and a year later they were in business. Joe Royer, the youngest and most energetic of the three, subsequently took over the whole operation. Today, **Ruby Mountain Heli-Ski,** P.O. Box 281192, Lamoille, NV 89828, 775/753-6867, www.helicopterskiing.com, is still owned by Joe and Francy Royer. They offer three-day ski packages, Mon.–Wed. or Fri.–Sun., which include lodging at Red's Ranch, all meals, ski rental, helicopter rides, guide service, and a guarantee of 39,000 vertical feet of skiing. With a maximum of 16 skiers, flying in groups of four guests per guide, they do an average of seven runs a day in fairyland frosting. The season runs from late January through early April. Make your reservations far in advance; for the 2000–2001 season, package prices were $2,650 per person. With a 1,500-square-mile terrain, 3,000 vertical feet of virgin deep powder, and a chopper ride to the best conditions, this is the ultimate in skiing.

Picnicking and Camping

Driving up Forest Service Rd. 660, **Powerhouse** (6,200 feet) picnic area at the mouth of Lamoille Canyon has one group site and four single-family picnic tables, BBQ grills and pit toilets. There's no water, however. Day use fee is $4 per vehicle.

Thomas Canyon Campground (7,600 feet) has 40 paved sites; 30 have tent pads, there are five double-family sites, and four pull-throughs. Facilities include picnic tables, barbecue and firepits, vault toilets, and pump water. The campground is officially open late May through October, but they try to keep a loop open all year, depending on climate conditions. The campground is situated in a spot in the canyon where downhill is due west, and the sun setting beyond the valley turns the rugged ridges a distinct ruby hue (the mountains, however, were named for its garnets). Sunrise is right over the cirque, imbuing the canyon with golden and magic light. Single campsites cost $12, double sites $18. Reservations can be made in summer; for reservations phone 877/444-6777. For further information, contact: U.S. Forest Service, Ruby Mountains Ranger District, 140 Pacific Ave., Wells, NV 89825, 775/752-3357.

Terraces, at 8,400 feet on the other side of the road (left), is for picnickers only; it has picnic tables, barbecue and firepits, vault toilets and potable water. $4 parking fee per vehicle.

Twenty-nine miles from Elko up 660 is **Roads End** picnic area (8,800 feet) and the trailhead for Island Lake and the Ruby Crest Recreation Trail. The area has one picnic site, water, and toilets; no fee.

Trails

The **Island Lake Trail** heads off north for two miles to 9,672 feet; the trailhead is just off to the right at the fork near the entrance to the parking lot. The 40-mile **Ruby Crest Trail** heads off south from the far edge of the parking lot; looking up at the top of the mountain, you'll see a prominent V-shaped saddle just down to the left of what can only be called "Bald Eagle Crest." That's Liberty Pass.

The trail starts out in forest primeval, and you start heading up fast into the cirque. You cross three creeks on nice Forest Service bridges,

LAMOILLE CANYON, THE "YOSEMITE OF NEVADA"

If you go back a mile toward Elko from Lamoille and turn left up Lamoille Canyon, you'll be on the Lamoille Canyon National Scenic Byway. a 13.5-mile road that takes you straight into the heart of the Ruby Mountains. These metamorphic mountains occupy a sacred place in the hearts of most Nevada hikers, climbers, skiers, photographers, picnickers, and writers. Wettest of the high ranges, they combine the best aspects of the nearly 250 other discrete ranges in the Great Basin—long (100 miles) and thin (10 miles), tilted, and geologically labyrinthine—with dramatic features all their own. Glacial ice has played a large part in their erosion, with U-shaped valleys, cirques, kettles, valley-bottom moraines, and glacier-swept cliffs. This rain-maker range also supports lush vegetation, including a large alpine tundra. In addition, the 8,800-foot level is accessible by car, and you can follow a good trail, through some of the most beautiful mountain country in the West for days.

After long debate and some controversy, in 1989 the Ruby Mountains were designated one of 14 official wilderness areas in Nevada, fourth largest with 90,000 acres. The Ruby wilderness area, which along with the East Humboldt wilderness area comprises 25percent of the local U.S. Forest Service ranger district, is mostly in the higher elevations of the mountains.

Lamoille Canyon Road runs around Ruby Dome (11,249 feet), highest peak in the range. Massive skyscraping outcrops loom high overhead on both sides of the canyon in two continuous lines up the road; four-score rock sculptors would be kept busy for 10 lifetimes carving the busts of all the U.S. pres-

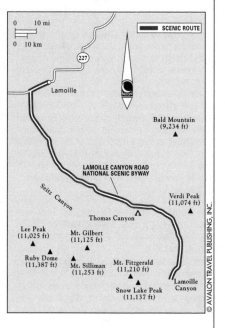

idents, vice presidents, and secretaries of the interior on the faces of these cliffs. Explanatory signs along the way describe the glacial features.

In the winter, the road often closes to cars but is alive with snowmobilers and cross-country skiers.

then pass **Dollar Lakes** (9,600 feet). Before you know it you're at **Lamoille Lake** (9,740 feet), where signs point the way. A hiker in fair shape can make it here in 40 minutes. From there you keep going up, twisting and turning toward the pass. **"Bald Eagle Crest"** defines itself into beak and head, shoulders, wings, and, even in late August at the end of the heat and sun, some snow patches that you could imagine to be the wing tips. Finally, another 40 minutes above Lamoille Lake, you reach **Liberty Pass,** at 10,450 feet, and get to see the other side. Which predictably is even more beautiful than the side you just climbed. **Liberty and Favre Lakes** await

those with more time and energy, as does **Harrison Pass,** 30 miles and several days from the parking lot.

The hiking season starts around June 15 and lasts roughly 12 weeks. Weekdays you'll meet a few other people, but weekends you're fending off crowds, especially on the first few miles. Backpackers, however, can leave the crowds far behind on any number of explorations to high-country lakes (many filled with trout) and isolated canyons.

For detailed and up-to-date information on campgrounds, hiking trails, and road conditions in the Rubies, call or write the U.S. Forest Service: Ruby Mountain Ranger District, 140 Pacific Ave., Wells, NV 89825, 775/752-3357. Office staff will send you a copy of *A Guide to the Ruby Mountain Ranger District* (very informative) and all kinds of other brochures and pamphlets about the area.

Towards Harrison Pass

To go across the Rubies by car, you head back down Lamoille Canyon—don't coast unless you *want* to get up to 85 mph on the winding road— then backtrack along NV 227 toward Elko through Spring Creek. Take a left at the sign for Jiggs. This road, NV 228, is nicely paved for 25 miles, through the **Te-Moak Indian Reservation,** across White Flats and Mound Valley, with the Rubies rising high and stark to the east and cows playing chicken with your front bumper.

South Fork Reservoir

The **South Fork State Recreation Area** is at the South Fork Dam, 16 miles south of Elko on NV 228. The dam, constructed between 1986 and '88, is made up of a million cubic yards of earth, which dammed South Fork Creek roughly 10 miles from the Humboldt River. The reservoir, when full, stretches 3.5 miles, covers 1,650 surface acres and impounds 40,000 acre feet of water. The reservoir is surrounded by 2,200 acres of wildlife-filled meadowlands and rolling hills. Swimming, boating, fishing, hunting, wildlife viewing, camping and picnicking are popular activities here. The Nevada Department of Wildlife stocks trout and bass; the park is known for its trophy-class trout and bass fishery. Facilities include a campground, trailer dump station, boat launch, and picnic area. The 24-site campground, with showers and running water but no hookups, is on the reservoir shore, about two miles from the dam; camping costs $8, maximum 14 day stay. Or you can camp anywhere else you like around the park, outside the developed campground; this costs $5 per night, and you can come to the campground to shower. Day use of the park costs $3 per vehicle. The park is open year round, but winter access may be difficult due to extreme cold and snow. Access is off NV 228, roughly 10 miles south of the intersection with NV 227. Contact: South Fork State Recreation Area, HC 30 353-8, Elko, NV 89801, 775/744-2010.

Twelve miles south of Elko and half a mile from the South Fork reservoir, the **Ruby Crest Guest Ranch,** HC 30 Box 197 #13, Spring Creek, Elko, NV 89815, 775/744-2277, also the home of the Elko Guide Service, offers a wide variety of activities including horseback trail riding, summer horseback mountain pack trips, fishing and hunting trips, sightseeing and photography trips, and nature tours. Winter activities include cross country skiing, snowmobile trips, ice fishing and chukar hunting. Ranch vacations are a specialty, with accommodations ranging from a room at the ranch, to rustic log cabins at the base of the Ruby Mountains, to tent camps.

Jiggs & Harrison Pass

Roughly 20 miles south of the turnoff to the South Fork State Recreation Area is **Jiggs,** a tiny settlement that was once the center of a large ranch in Mound Valley. It was homesteaded in the 1860s by Texans, and was originally known as Mound Valley, then Skelton, then Hilton. In fact, the local ranchers were still arguing over a proper name for the place in 1918, when some anonymous post office official with a slightly zany streak finally labeled it Jiggs—either after Jiggs, a character in the comic strip "Bringing Up Father," whose characters were involved in an endless and fruitless feud, or, after tiring of the bickering, for the slang expression "the jig's up."

A few miles past Jiggs, bear left (a sign here might warn, "Travel Not Recommended"—call the U.S. Forest Service office in Elko, 775/738-5171, to check road conditions if it's before or after the season) and start climbing up to **Harrison Pass** (7,247 feet). Here the road meets the far end of the **Ruby Crest Trail,** with **Pearl Peak** (10,847 feet) to the south and **Green Mountain** (10,680 feet) to the north. From there you drop down pretty fast into Ruby Valley.

Ruby Marshes

Take a right (south) to visit **Ruby Lake National Wildlife Refuge,** open every day from an hour before sunrise until two hours after sunset. This is an unusual sight for the Great Basin Desert—a freshwater bulrush marsh, host to a large variety of birds, fish, and mammals. Within the 38,000-acre refuge, created in 1938, is a network of ditches and dikes built to manage

the Ruby Mountains

DEKE CASTLEMAN

the riparian habitat. More than 200 species of birds, including trumpeter swans, canvasback and redhead ducks, cranes, herons, egrets, eagles, falcons, and small birds are found in the refuge in a normal year, along with five types of introduced trout and bass.

The water is collected up on the porous slopes and peaks of the southern Rubies, then is flushed out at the bottom from more than 200 springs into **Ruby Lake.** Ruby Lake, and **Franklin Lake** farther north, once covered 300,000 acres 200 feet deep in this valley, but are now down to fewer than 3,000 acres, lowest level in 30 years. In 1986, before the drought, the largest bass harvest on record occurred, with 300,000 fish caught; by 1992, the catch was down to a few thousand. In 1994, after eight years of drought, the normal 6–7 feet of water was down to two feet. Precipitation returned, however, during the winters of 1995–97 to what passes for normal and so did lake and fish catches. Refuge officials say both are at normal levels now—"normal" including quite a bit of fluctuation in this desert environment.

Take a left at **Bressman's Cabin** onto the causeway to see the birds and birders, fish and fishers. Make the big loop around the marsh and rejoin the road at the south end of the East Sump.

Heading south on county road 767, the **South Ruby Campground** (6,200 feet) has 35 gravel sites, water, toilets, and an RV waste dump ($4 fee). Most sites have tent pads; $10 per night

($8 in winter). Near the Gallagher Fish Hatchery, sites are on a rise overlooking the marsh. Campsite reservations can be made in summer; for reservations phone 877/444-6777. For further information on this campground, contact: U.S. Forest Service, Ruby Mountains Ranger District, 140 Pacific Ave., Wells, NV 89825, 775/752-3357.

Two miles south of here is **Shantytown,** a small settlement that dates back to the 1940s, when the BLM leased half-acre parcels hereabouts for $5 a year. In 1967, the BLM sold off the parcels for $499; they now go for around $30,000. Shantytown has no services.

Heading back north, the **Wildlife Refuge Headquarters** is open weekdays 7 A.M.–4 P.M., Mountain Time. Brochures describing the refuge, wildlife, and fishing and boating regulations are available in a rack on the front of the office; they'll send you some brochures, if you like. Call or write for further information: Ruby Lake National Wildlife Refuge, HC 60, Box 860, Ruby Valley, NV 89833, 775/779-2237.

Rather grandly named, **Harmon's Ruby Lake Resort** is on the main Ruby Valley road, one mile north of the Harrison Pass junction. It's not a "resort" a la Las Vegas or Lake Tahoe, but it is a friendly place with a few amenities, including a store, gas station, bar, café, trailer spaces and rooms for rent. The six rooms, each with private bath and sharing a community kitchen, are $30 a double. The 10 trailer spaces, all with full hookups, are $15. It's not a good setup for tents, but if tenters show up they won't be turned away; cost is $10 for tents. Public showers are $4. The café is open the same hours as the bar: noon to 9 P.M. every day. Contact: Harmon's Ruby Lake Resort, HC 60, Box 725, Ruby Valley, NV 89833, 775/779-2242.

Continuing north on the gravel road you pass

Franklin Lake, then travel a long way back to the pavement. NV 229 forks 15 miles east to connect with US 93, or 33 miles north to join I-80 at Halleck. You can also get back by traveling on a gravel road for 11 miles north to Deeth, 12 miles east of Halleck on I-80.

NORTH OF ELKO

TUSCARORA

Leaving Elko on NV 225, you start heading northwest, past the new homes being built among the foothills north of I-80; the paint is barely dry on the street signs up here. You climb up the **Adobe Range,** ascending steadily toward **Adobe Summit** at 6,540 feet. The big **Independence Mountains** come into view as you descend from the pass, turn north, and zoom up the long straight road through the high desert and low sage. In a few miles is **Sage Corners:** store, cafe bar. Here you turn off the main road onto NV 226 toward Tuscarora. You skirt the north face of aptly named **Lone Mountain** (8,567 feet), which you just passed the east edge of. The road narrows as it negotiates **Taylor Canyon,** following a creek through the hills.

Taylor Canyon Resort
This is a friendly rest stop on the way to Tuscarora, Midas, and all points north. The resort, 775/756-6500, has a cafe, bar, laundromat, showers ($2), gas pump, RV parking ($15 a night full hookup), and cabins for rent ($30 a night). For $5, you can pitch a tent on grass in a shady park.

The area is popular with hunters seeking antelope and huge mule deer bucks. The Nevada record for a mule with an irregular rack was taken here not long ago. The monster dressed out at well over 200 pounds. It was impossible to count all the tines in the photo on the wall of the resort bar. Pretty **Willow Creek Reservoir** west of Tuscarora and nearby **Jacks Creek** draw anglers angling for bass and trout, respectively. The state-record bluegill was caught at Willow Creek in 1997—1 pound, 13.5 ounces. And the

locals didn't even know the lake had bluegill! Miners heading out to the Ken Snyder Mine at Midas stop by on their way to (for coffee) and from (for beer) work and to chat with Tom, Gary and Joyce. Just how friendly is this place? There's a pot of coffee on a timer in the laundromat so the miners can refill their thermoses at 4:30 A.M. on the way in from Elko. You can fill up, too. Leave a donation.

Just past the resort, you take a left onto the inevitable gravel, aiming straight at Tuscarora across **Independence Valley** on the lower slopes of **Mt. Blitzen** (8,130 feet). It's good gravel, 45 mph, and you can see anybody coming at you, thanks to the doorbell dust plumes. Climb into the hills, then follow the sign to the right into town.

History
The Beard brothers, Steve and John, had a placer operation all to themselves in the area in the mid-1860s, but when the railroad reached Elko, prospectors joined them. Shortly thereafter, several thousand Chinese joined the prospectors, after they were abandoned by the railroad upon its completion. They were hired to dig flumes to bring water to the mines. A man named Weed is credited with discovering the Young America silver vein in 1871, about three miles north up Mt. Blitzen from the original town site, and the boom was on. The town, named after a Civil War gunboat, itself named after an Iroquois tribe, relocated to the lode and reached a population of 5,000 in two years. The patient and industrious Chinese took over the placer mines abandoned by the whites, grew vegetables, and harvested sage by the ton to feed the smelters on the hill; it's estimated they recovered upwards of $3 million in gold. In 1874, a larger vein, the Grand Prize Bonanza, was discovered, which triggered a huge rush. By 1880 Tuscarora had a greater

VICINITY OF ELKO

OWYHEE

DUCK VALLEY
INDIAN RESERVATION

MOUNTAIN
CITY

HUMBOLDT
NATIONAL
FOREST

JARBIDGE

JARBIDGE
WILDERNESS

WILDHORSE
CROSSING

WILDHORSE
REC. AREA

CHARLESTON

WILDHORSE

JACK CREEK
CAMP

JACK CREEK

226

225

TUSCARORA

WELLS

DEETH
230

ANGEL
LAKE C.G.

231

ANGEL LAKE

ANGEL
CREEK C.G.

225

HALLECK

93

ELKO

SPRING
CREEK

227

LAMOILLE

229

SOUTH FORK
STATE PARK

228

THOMAS CANYON

CARLIN

80

TRAILHEAD

LAMOILLE CANYON

RUBY MOUNTAINS

HUMBOLDT
NATIONAL
FOREST

JIGGS

RUBY VALLEY

TO EAST HUMBOLDT
NATIONAL FOREST

RUBY VALLEY

HARRISON PASS

REFUGE
HEADQUARTERS

RUBY LAKE NATIONAL
WILDLIFE REFUGE

RUBY LAKE

SHANTYTOWN

N

0   10 mi

0   10 km

© AVALON TRAVEL PUBLISHING, INC.

population than Elko. And its Chinatown was the largest in the country.

In 1884, a major fire ripped through Tuscarora, and many Chinese departed. Shortly after, *borrasca* (the big bust) arrived, the town shrank even more, and only the famous Dexter gold mine continued to produce till the turn of the century. Roughly $50 million was removed in the first 15-year frenzy. The stalwarts hung in through the early 1900s, but by the end of 1920, only the recluses remained.

In the mid-1960s, a ceramics professor from southern California happened to visit and fell in love with the semi-ghost town. A refugee from tenure (which he viewed not as lifetime security but as a lifetime sentence), Dennis Parks and his young family later moved up to Tuscarora and bought two houses and a Land Rover for $4,500. This raised the population to around 15 and lowered the average age to around 50. Parks then proceeded to establish a pottery studio, business, and school. Today, 20-some years later, the operation is famous not only in Nevada, but also throughout the international potters' networks.

The town's idyllic isolation, however, was shattered in the mid-1980s when Horizon Gold Shares, a Denver mining company, reopened the Dexter Mine. Over the next several years, Horizon expanded the pit to 800 feet long, 400 feet wide, and nearly 150 feet deep—precipitously close to the town. Residents claim that the blasting damaged the old foundations of the historic buildings and sent chunks of rock and waves of dust into and through the town. And though the residents owned their homes, the mining company owned the mineral rights to the land underneath them.

Horizon made offers to buy out the residents, but at rates that Dennis Parks called "insultingly low." Horizon kept digging, and it looked as if either the pit was going to swallow Tuscarora, or the tailings were going to bury it. Finally, though, Horizon ran out of room, and the Tuscarorans steadfastly refused to sell. So the mining company packed up and moved on to brighter horizons. Gone are the leaching ponds and gone is the dust, gone are the trucks and trailers and miners. The tailings, however, remain; the company contoured them a bit according to law. The pit, too, isn't going anywhere; a spring and three wet winters have turned it into the town

swimming hole. What was once a source of aggravation and an eyesore is now a great place to cool off on a hot summer day.

Sights

The road to Tuscarora is kept open all winter so the mail can get through. The two chimneys sticking up as you head into town are about all that's left of Nob Hill, Tuscarora's ritzy section during the boom years. Chinatown was down the hill from there. Drive up to the massive, 100-year-old chimney from an old smelter up on the hill, still standing as tall and proud as a boomtown and as useless as a ghost. Play around up there and hike beyond into the tempting hills. Come back down to town, park at the post office, and start your tour on foot.

In back of the post office is the old **hotel,** built in the 1880s with 10 rooms and moved from Palisades to Cornucopia and finally to Tuscarora, which houses Dennis and Ben Parks's pottery showroom, 775/756-6598. Track down Dennis or his wife Julie—usually found at their home up the street with the red-and-white flag—to take you around. (Ben stays next door when he isn't teaching ceramics at Great Basin Community College in Elko.) Dennis will explain the unusual ceramic techniques that have earned him some fame: firing with old crankcase oil, whose impurities give the glazes a nice blush; using sage ash and some local clay; and starting the oil with Kingston charcoal briquettes. And Julie will greet you with real Dixie hospitality. Even though she hasn't lived in her native North Carolina for more than 20 years, she still has the most delightful Southern style in northern Nevada.

Five bedrooms in the hotel—three upstairs, two down—accommodate the international crew of students who come from as far away as New York, Europe, and New Zealand for one of eight two-week seminars between May and August. The dome out back is the students' studio—interesting acoustics! Possibly Dennis will take you to his studio, where he works in splendid privacy. It's decorated with a stunning series of plates with different abstract representations of Taylor Canyon—the view outside his picture window on the other side of the valley. There's also a series of profiles Dennis did as a guest artist in Poland. In fact, it seems as if he's constantly commuting to Eastern Europe.

Dennis continues to do the guest-artist circuit, traveling frequently to Eastern Europe, Russia, Japan, and Korea to demonstrate his techniques. His book, *A Pottery's Guide to Raw Glazing and Oil Firing* (1980, Scribners and Sons), may be back in print in the near future. Meanwhile, Ben Parks is developing a following for his own clay creations. When Nevada hosted a state governors conference in 1996, Governor Bob Miller asked Ben to create a series of 50 pieces to serve as official gifts for his fellow chief executives. Ben's whimsical cowboy boot series earned him a nickname at home—Tuscarora's only Zen bootist. The November 1997 issue of *Bon Appétit* magazine has a photo spread of decorative dinner plates made by Ben, Dennis, and four other Western potters.

Tuscarora is also home to artists Ron Arthaud and Gail Rappa who, like Ben, teach art at the community college in Elko. Looking for an inexpensive place to work, the couple purchased the town's only substantially intact brick building in 1996, which Ron is restoring—brick by crumbling brick. The vintage 1870s' two-story structure on Weed St. was once the home of a prosperous Tuscarora merchant and later an assay office. When it's finished, Ron and Gail plan to live and work in the main house and convert two old mining shacks on the property into studio/galleries. The shack that currently serves as Gail's studio houses a hydraulically powered ore shaker that Ron wants to put back in working order. It's a wonder he finds time to paint his truly splendid impressionist oils of Tuscarora and its relics. Gail creates antique-looking clay dolls and exquisite jewelry of sculpted stone, silver, and brass. Their work is popular in the Mendocino, California, and Sante Fe, New Mexico, galleries where it's currently displayed; you can also find their work displayed at the Western Folklife Center in Elko. Stop by and say hi, and ask to see their work. And ask Ron what it's like being a 19th-century mason in the 21st.

MIDAS

Pass the turnoff to Tuscarora and drive by hay fields and a ranch house or two on the 45-mile gravel road to Midas. The road is exceptionally well maintained for another 12 miles (40–50 mph), but starts getting bumpy (15–25 mph) as it ascends toward a low pass over a spur of the Tuscarora Mountains. Watch out for commuting miners tooling along in their company four-wheel drives at speeds of up to 70 mph. For the next dozen or so miles, hills and curves obscure the dust plumes that signal oncoming or overtaking traffic. Don't be surprised to find a big dusty truck filling your rearview mirror or windshield as you round one of the many blind curves. Still, the road is passable for careful drivers in all but the lowest or longest vehicles.

Once over the pass, both the visibility and the road improve, and the speedometer finds its way back up to 45 mph. Willow Creek Reservoir appears on the right. Just past the dam, the road descends through green meadows beside Willow Creek, a tributary of the Humboldt via Rock Creek. A picturesque canyon with interesting rock formations is the gateway to Squaw Valley. BLM signs point the way to defunct mines and still functional ranches. One of the ranches, the sprawling IL, was once owned and occasionally visited by crooner/actor Bing Crosby, who was known to down a few with the locals in Midas.

After 20 more miles, you'll pass the large Squaw Valley Ranch (started in the 1880s) in the distance on the left. Eight miles farther a large sign on the right points the way to the Ken Snyder Mine. In another mile is the right turn to Midas, clearly marked.

History

Prospector James McDuffy founded the Golden Circle mining district in 1907 after he located good pay dirt on the flanks of the Owyhee Bluffs near the Elko/Humboldt county line. Prospecting with his two young sons, McDuffy was looking for—and located—the source of the promising placer deposits miners had come across in the area years before. McDuffy took the name from a "perfect circle of malipi" (a rock associated with gold) that he believed surrounded a mineral belt three miles long and one mile wide.

In its first few months of life, the town that boomed near the mines also bore the name Golden Circle or Gold Circle, writes Dana R. Bennett in her history of the town, *Forward with*

Enthusiasm, Midas 1907–1995. But later that year when townsfolk applied to the federal government for a post office, the agency refused to approve another office in the state beginning with "Gold." Locals placed three other names in the hat: Mint, Porphyry (a common rock in the area), and Midas (the name of one of the larger mines). Of the three, the ever-efficient feds probably chose Midas, Bennett writes, because the name was already on the books, though not in use. Conveniently, the name had been abandoned a few years earlier by a short-lived boomtown in central Nevada.

By September 1907, 12 square miles of claims had been staked in the Gold Circle Mining District with Midas as the hub. The Battle Mountain newspapers described Midas as "first-class in every respect" with nine lodging houses, 11 saloons, five grocery and general stores, two lumber yards, two assay offices, two real estate offices, one bakery, two news and confectionery stores, two butcher shops, two feed stables and several restaraunts. Soon the town boasted a modern water system. (The system was still serving residents in 1997.)

By 1909, the population had stabilized and remained at about 150–300 through the peak production years of 1916–21. Though it never rivaled Tonopah or Virginia City, Gold Circle District led ore production in Elko County regularly in the teens and '20s. Then the inevitable decline began and the population fluctuated between 25 and 150, depending on mining activity. The population hit an all-time low in 1954, and Midas began appearing on maps as a ghost town. From 1907 through 1965, 129,000 ounces of gold and 1.6 million ounces of silver, worth more than $4 million, were taken from mines like the Midas, Elko Prince, Rex, and Esmerelda.

Midas may rise yet again. In 1992, the Franco-Nevada and Euro-Nevada mining corporations started Midas Joint Venture, buying up many of the old claims and grouping them under the name Ken Snyder Mine. Exploratory drilling began, and several bodies of microscopic gold and silver ore were located. The most promising claim, the Rex-Grande, is believed to hold more than 2.5 million ounces of gold. Moreover, the company believes there is enough silver in the ground to reduce the cost of removing the gold to $74 an ounce! With a workforce of about 50 miners—most bused in from Elko and Winnemucca—Midas Joint Venture expects to be around until at least 2007. Many locals believe the new mine will have little impact on the town, but some think they smell the scent of another boom.

Sights

Tall cottonwoods planted in 1913 line Main Street, a wide, shady, ten-block, gravel boulevard that retains hints of the town's former glory. Tidy summer homes—a few quite new—rub elbows with leaning mining shacks and several double- and single-wide mobiles. Dozens of fan-shaped tailing dumps on the steep hillside mark the early mines. Here, as in Tuscarora, many of the homes belong to deer hunters from Reno and Vegas. Hunters can be credited with the rediscovery of many of Nevada's ghost towns. Exploring Nevada's backcountry in the '50s and '60s, they found the deer big, the views grand, and the land cheap. Some returned to buy property and erect hunting camps, and many of those camps eventually became retirement homes. At the end of town, Main Street turns back into a mountain road as it winds through spectacular Midas Canyon.

Lower Main Street is where you'll find the two remaining Midas businesses. **Midas Gold Circle Bar,** 775/529-0439, is a friendly place to have a beer. Owner Don Mellen bought the bar in '54—when the population numbered three—after spending several years prospecting around the area. He sold several claims to Midas Joint Venture in the early '90s. After 42 summers, he moved to Midas permanently in 1996. Mellen, who publishes a sporadic newsletter, *The Midas Touch,* is a good source of information about hunting, fishing, and prospecting around Midas. If you're here on July 4th, stop by the Gold Circle for a picnic out back and dance to a live band with the cowboy, cowgirl, or miner of your choice. Wave to the king and queen of the Midas Independence Day parade as they pass by on Main Street.

Two doors up Main is the **Midas Saloon and Dinner House,** 775/529-0203, owned by Les and Bev Matson. Part of the old building was built around the turn of the century in Golconda, where it served as a railroad office. It was moved lock, block, and stairwell to Midas in the '40s and has been a bar ever since. The saloon is postcard quaint with a recent red-and-white paint job and a 1920s' gas pump outside (non-working). Les used to own and skipper fishing boats in Kodiak, Alaska, which he doesn't miss at all. "It got to where I thought I was going to drown every time I went out," he says, reflecting on the hectic pace of Alaska's big-money king crab and salmon fisheries. (The desert can be cruel, but at least you can't drown in a sea of sage.) The closest Les gets to a salmon these days is when he throws one on the grill, and hungry travelers are better off for it. Les's cooking is legendary from here to Las Vegas, and his place has been written up in *Nevada* magazine three times. His King Midas prime rib dinner goes for $18, rack of lamb for $25, chicken piccata, $17, cheeseburger, $7. When Les can get live lobster, so can you; the price isn't posted. It's not cheap, but that's not the point. Call ahead if you want something special; reservations are a good idea on weekends. Breakfast (starting at 4 A.M.), lunch and dinner are served every day except Thursday, when they make their shopping run into Elko; Thursday it's dinner only, served 5–7:30 P.M.

There's no lodging in Midas, but if you ask around somebody probably will let you pitch a tent or park a self-contained RV somewhere.

Stop and talk to Dan Bennett if he's at home. His place (with a big half-circle driveway out front) is at the top of Main on the left just before the road makes the first S-turn into Midas Canyon. Dan used to hunt deer up the canyon in the '50s. He fell in love with the place and started bringing his family up on holidays, winter and summer. Those vacations were the seeds of *Forward with Enthusiasm* by Dana Bennett, Dan's daughter. Dana, now a state historian, grew up on campfire tales spun by the likes of the late Willie Wilcox, who was born in Midas in the '20s. Dan bought the property in the early '60s with dreams of retiring there. The dream became reality in 1992, and Dan and his wife have put together a cozy home and quiet life away from the hustle-bustle of Reno. In 1995, Dan and Dana created Friends of Midas, a non-profit group dedicated to raising money for the preservation of Midas and its history. Donations and federal funding have helped Friends of Midas restore the town cemetery and research the identities of the people who are

believed to lie in 40 or so unmarked graves at the site (the grave markers, most of them wood, fell victim to the elements and vandals). Looking to preserve the 1928 schoolhouse, for example, the group cut a deal with Midas Joint Venture, which wanted to buy the building for office space. The mining company restored the school, used it for two years, and returned it to the town in 1999 following construction of a new office building. The residents want to turn the building—you can't miss it on the left as you leave town—into a community hall and museum.

While you're there, ask Dan to show you the mining and blacksmithing museum he's put together in a shed next to the house. A tunnel at the back of the shed snakes 200 feet into the adjacent hill. Dan thinks it was used to hide a still operated by a previous owner, but he's laid track into the opening to give people a sense of what the old mines were like. The shed out front houses hundreds of relics, including an old forge once used by Midas miners and craftsmen. Across the road, he's fixed up a miner's shack with furniture and other household items to give people a glimpse of how a wage miner lived when he wasn't mucking for gold. If he's got the time, ask him for a tour. Dan says he'll gladly answer questions about the area and its history if you e-mail him through Friends of Midas: MidasFrnds@aol.com.

THE OWYHEE LOOP

If you want to get to Wildhorse Reservoir, Mountain City, and Owyhee by pavement, from Tuscarora, get back on NV 226 and return to NV 225, then go north (left). The pavement, in fact, is relatively new, and it's a smooth ride the 33 miles to the reservoir along the eastern flank of the Independence Range. Halfway up the road is one of the most creative mailboxes in the state, made of chain, sheet metal, and concrete boots, overlooking the north fork headquarters of the pastoral PX Cattle Company spread. Just north of the PX is the southern access road to Jarbidge (67 miles) via Charleston. In another 10 miles is the Wildhorse Reservoir.

To take the alternative (dusty) road north to Owyhee, get back on NV 226 and go left (north), past the historical sign for Tuscarora and the highway maintenance station, with the one-room pink-cinderblock schoolhouse next to it. You begin to travel up the east side of gorgeous Independence Valley, with the Tuscaroras on the left and the Independence Range on the right; **Jacks** and **McAfee** peaks, both over 10,000 feet, loom ahead in the Independences. This is spectacular ranch land—a lot of cattle, a lot of water, a lot of green, and a lot of canyons into Humboldt National Forest. You start climbing past **Jack Creek** (where the pavement ends) to **Chicken Creek Summit** (6,441 feet), then drop down along several long "S" curves. A fork in the road points you left to Owyhee and right to Mountain City.

To Mountain City

The right-hand fork puts you on a narrow twisty-turny gravel road (30–35 mph) through the southeastern foothills of the **Bull Run Mountains,** with the northwestern Independences off to the right. In eight miles you enter Humboldt National Forest property and climb through the aspens, at 10–15 mph in places. Two miles northeast is **Maggie Summit** (6,167 feet). Then you drop down real fast, though at a slow speed on the rough road. In another three miles you enter Timber Gulch at the beginning of a small, beautiful ranching valley. A few ranches along is **Hutch Creek Manor** with the creative and amusing Auto Parts Gang—Gold Pan Sam, Tex, Dolly, and friends—fronting the driveway. After several miles of bucolic hill and dale, you twist and turn out of the valley and arrive back on the NV 225 pavement. Mountain City is five miles north, Wildhorse Reservoir is about 15 miles south.

To Owyhee

Back at the Jack Creek Fork, taking a left leads you to one of the most bucolic ranching valleys in the state. The road is rutted—washboard, chuckholy, dusty, narrow—but it's worth every minute of it. When you come to a sign for Wilson Reservoir to the left, go straight through the posts onto private land owned by the Petan Company. **Wilson Peak** is on the right, **Bull Run Creek** runs through the valley, and the view west is long and wide. Watch for cows. Cross Bull Run Creek and come into a breathtaking basin with an incredible canyon running back up into the Inde-

pendence Range, all national forest land. Climb up out of the bottomland; the road gets a little rougher. Eventually you come to another intersection, where a hard left goes off to **Sheep Creek Camp,** a campground that marks the entrance to Duck Valley Indian Reservation (see "Owyhee," below).

Wildhorse

If you've come up NV 225 on the pavement, you'll first encounter the **Wildhorse Reservoir.** Just as you reach the southern end of the reservoir, you pass **Wildhorse Resort,** 775/758-6471. Tent camping costs $10, RV sites with full hookups are $12.50, and the 16 cabins are $52.50 each; also here are a café, bar, gas pump, small store, laundry and showers.

Four miles up the road is the turnoff into the **Wildhorse State Recreation Area,** which consists of 120 acres on the northeast shore of Wildhorse Reservoir. Turn in. The first right on the paved access road goes to one of the campgrounds: gravel pads, picnic tables, and firepits, plus pit toilets and sinks. The second right enters the other campground, this one with some of the best public showers in the state. The road continues down to the boat launch on the reservoir behind the dam. This is an idyllic camping spot, with a beautiful view across the reservoir at the Independence Range, especially at sunset. And those showers! Overnight camping is $10 per site ($12 with boat); day use costs $3 per vehicle ($5 with boat). Altogether there are 33 spaces, six restrooms, and two showers. The park is open year round, but access may be difficult due to extreme cold and snow in winter; Wildhorse Reservoir often has the coldest temperatures in Nevada, in winter. The park is on NV 225, 67 miles north of Elko. Contact: Wildhorse State Recreation Area, HC 31, Box 265, Elko, NV 89801, 775/758-6493.

Just north of the state park is the **Dept. of the Interior campground,** a very primitive affair. Next to that is the **Shoshone Duckwater campground,** where the facilities are halfway between the state park's and the federal's: grill, garbage cans, and pit toilets in concrete outhouses. Camping is $4 a night on asphalt pads. There's a boat ramp here and no mention of fees. The store at the entrance has been closed since 1995.

From there, you approach **Wildhorse Dam,** built in 1969 by the Bureau of Reclamation. Now you're in **Owyhee River** country, with its many forks flowing north into the Snake River drainage system, eventually reaching the Pacific via the Columbia River watershed. This renders the area more Idaho than Nevada. Just south of the dam is a national forest campground, **Wildhorse Crossing:** 18 single family sites and three group sites. In the bottom of the Owyhee River Canyon, the sites have grills, tables, running water, and outhouses; $6. (The U.S. Forest Service office in Elko, 775/738-5171, is the resource for current info.)

You pass the dam and wind through the canyon, with a score of twists and turns; finally the canyon widens and ranches spread out on the east. The road across the Bull Run Mountains from the valley above Tuscarora joins up with NV 225 a few miles north of there. About two miles south of Mountain City, a mile-long dirt road goes to the Rio-Tinto pit (see below).

Mountain City

Mountain City consists of half a mile of houses and businesses along the road and river; Mountain City U.S. Forest Service Ranger Station is the most official building in town, except for maybe the post office. This is the site of an early but short-lived boom in silver and gold. A town of a few thousand burst from the earth in 1869, produced a million dollars in silver, then disappeared again in 1880.

A geologist and latter-day prospector, Frank Hunt, began re-surveying the area in 1919, convinced that a great ore body still lay beneath the mountains near Mountain City. Hunt made a careful and thorough geological study of the area, finding metamorphic rock specked with copper in among the granite. Tracing the outcrop, he defined the outline of his imagined ore body. He staked a thousand claims, which totaled nearly three square miles of mineral rights, and then began to sink a shaft in the middle of it.

For years he carried rock from the bottom of the hole up rickety ladders to dump. Eventually, he convinced a man named Ogden Chase to become a partner, after which Hunt dug and Chase hauled the rock up a windlass. Next they

incorporated, printing two million shares of stock, selling them for a nickel apiece—the instant currency of the prospecting business. Ten years passed while Hunt and Chase dug their shaft, papered Elko with mining shares to meet expenses, and notched a decade's worth of misadventures on their shovels.

Finally, in 1932, Hunt struck the lode at 227 feet deep. The paydirt, assayed in Salt Lake City, proved to be 40% pure copper. The stock certificates, many of which locals had long disposed of as so much scrap paper, rocketed to $40 a share. Anaconda Copper Company bought out Chase and Hunt, the latter 60 years old and ready to enjoy his fortune. Anaconda's **Rio-Tinto Mine** was active for another 12 years, producing $23 million in copper, and a second boom for Mountain City. Recently, a third boom has visited the area, with some small gold mines nearby.

First things first: Mountain City is on Mountain Time, so turn your clocks ahead an hour. **Chambers Motel,** 775/763-6626, has 11 rooms for $30–45. **Mountain City Motel,** 775/763-6617, has 14 rooms for $28–60; it also has seven RV spaces in back ($25 full hookup). **Hilltop RV Park,** 102 Davidson St. right in town, 775/763-6621 or 775/763-6629, offers tent and RV spaces for $10 per night.

Mountain City Steak House & Casino, 775/763-6622, is open Tues.–Sat. 7 A.M.–9 P.M., closed Sunday and Monday; it has nine slots, juke, and bar. The portions and prices are Alaska size. The **Miner's Club** bar, 775/763-6625, is open 10 A.M. till whenever, every day except Tuesday. Contrary to the sign outside, the cafe is closed—permanently. Across the street is the **Trailer Bar;** there's no name, but you can't miss it. If you do—and you weren't trying to—look for the '57 Studebaker pickup parked out front. It rarely moves.

Tremewan's General Store, 775/763-6621, is open Mon.–Sat. 8 A.M.–6 P.M. and has a little of everything, even microcassette tapes (which saved my hide once when I broke a tape right outside, a disaster in my business not unlike getting a hole in your gas tank). **Reed's Golden Rule,** 775/763-6616, is the catch-all store in town, selling Chevron gas, groceries and much, much more. Motto: "We sell everything from baby clothes to horseshoes."

Owyhee

If you've come up NV 226 through the dust, you finally get to glorious pavement on the south edge of Owyhee. Farms usher you along into town. The big "O" is on the hill directly ahead of you. Right when you come into the reservation you start heading northeast back toward NV 225. When you hit the pavement you turn due east, cross the Owyhee River, and meet up with the main road; Owyhee is about a half mile north of the junction.

Coming into town, you pass the **Presbyterian stone church,** complete with steeple and bell. Next is the Crawford Gymnasium and **Owyhee High,** home of the Braves. Across the street is a Texaco station and the **Feather Lodge,** 775/757-3080, with seven rooms for $38 single, $48 double. Then you come to "downtown," with the Dept. of Interior police station, tribal headquarters, tribal court, and the municipal center, all in old stone buildings. The $4 million **Indian health-service hospital,** largest building in town, serves nearly 3,000 Native Americans in the area, half of whom live on the reservation.

Up the street from there is **Chet and Lou's general store.** That's what the faded sign out front says anyway. Inside it's J & W's, which has a small selection of snacks and drinks and a little cafe. The friendly owners appeared to have just set up shop in the old BIA residence hall in 1997. If you want the unofficial lowdown of what's happening at the reservation, this is where to

get it. Short version: Politics is culturally universal. The store and cafe are open 8 A.M.–8 P.M. summer, 8 A.M.–7 P.M. winter.

The **Duck Valley Indian Reservation** is situated in a 10- by 25-mile valley, half in Nevada, half in Idaho, but mostly outside the Great Basin in the Columbia Plateau. It was created in 1877 on a site selected by a Shoshone leader for its beauty and fertility. After a five-year struggle to hold onto the land through hard winters and a typical string of broken promises, conditions began to improve. The land was augmented twice through the years, and today the reservation remains "free of exploitation and under [tribal government] control." Nearly 1,400 people live on the 298,819-acre reservation. Though closely related culturally and linguistically—and now by a century or more of intermarriage—Pauite and Shoshone share the reservation uneasily. One problem is that the land traditionally belonged to the Shoshone, who now find themselves outnumbered by the Pauite.

THE ROAD TO JARBIDGE

Just across from the entrance to Wildhorse State Recreation Area is the north access road to Jarbidge. (Another 10 miles south is the turnoff for the southern access route.) Jarbidge is the most remote town in Nevada—50-odd miles on gravel roads to get there from here.

bouncing into your own private Idaho on the road to Jarbidge

DEKE CASTLEMAN

On this northern route, the road starts out comfortable, 35–40 mph. In six miles you drive by Gold Creek and the abandoned site of old **Gold Creek** mining town, now the North Fork Cattle Company, in a big green meadow. Ranches continue for a couple of miles, and then the national forest property begins. At the fork, bear left; a right leads to the unmistakable green-and-white Forest Service ranger station. The road narrows and slows, to 30 mph. In another few miles is **Big Bend Campground:** 13 family sites, two group sites, picnic tables and barbecue, plenty of wood and water, two outhouses, under aspens; $6.

Bear right just after the campground, then twist and turn all the way down into **Meadow Creek** gulch, at the bottom of the **Mahogany Mountains.** This is gorge country—the hills get higher, the canyon gets closer, the walls sheerer, the dust denser, the rock rockier. Huge outcrops and high palisades tower above and big trees reach for the sky as the road runs along way down at the bottom. It's inspiring to think that this little creek could gouge such a giant gorge.

Twenty-four miles in, the road crosses the **Bruneau River,** with its own gorgeous gorge. Then you start a climb, out of the canyon, which is one of the longest and steepest in the state. Another fork appears; go right. In four miles you're still climbing, steeply, in first gear. Four miles *later* you're still climbing, the G's actually pushing you back into your seat! Finally, the road levels out, with the **Jarbidge Range** rising up to the southeast and the vast **Snake River Plateau** stretching off into infinity. You know for sure that you're not in the Great Basin and Range any longer: no basins, no ranges, only greatness. Vastest vistas this side of the Tibetan highlands.

You drift through the high plains and then enter **Diamond-A Ranch** country. The road straightens, widens, and quickens, but the relief is brief. A road forks off to the right to the beautifully situated ranch, tucked in beneath rimrock at the bottom of Buck's Creek, with huge old trees and photogenic ranch houses—a classically pastoral scene. The road heads down into **Buck Creek Canyon,** 15 mph, and more sheer walls gouged by creek water. You enter Idaho 44 miles from Wildhorse, peering ahead at a stunning V-shaped canyon. A bridge across the **Jarbidge River** leads you smack into a canyon wall; luckily, a road runs right and left along it. Someone finally painted a sign right on the rock with Jarbidge in big red letters and black arrows pointing right.

You cruise along Jarbidge River at the bottom of Jarbidge Canyon for eight miles. Erect stone sentinels seem to guard the canyon from above like chessmen, a fantastic gallery of natural statuary. In another three miles you pass the **Mahoney Ranger Station** and finally arrive at Jarbidge town, roughly 55 miles and nearly three hours after setting out on this quest from the Wildhorse campground.

Sleep in the Barn at Jarbidge.

DEKE CASTLEMAN

JARBIDGE

Jarbidge is an Anglicized version of *ja-ha-bich,* or *tsaw-haw-bitts* (sah-HAH-bits), the Shoshone name for a mountain ogre who caught Indians, carried them home to his lair in a giant basket, then ate them. Eventually, the Indians tricked the ogre into entering a deep canyon and sealed it shut, trapping him forever. According to legend, the Shoshone then left and have never returned.

Prospectors had been traipsing around the Jarbidge Range for many years before the turn of the century, looking for the Lost Sheepherder's Ledge, a legendary lode known only to a shepherd who died before he had a chance to exploit it or even divulge its location. But in 1909, a man named Dave Bourne found gold where a stream empties into the Jarbidge River just south of the present-day town limits. Within two years a boomtown of 1,500 huddled at the bottom of the canyon. The remoteness of and dangerous access to the new strike attest to the mobility and determination of this enduring group of Nevada boomtowners, even well into the 20th century.

In 1916, the last stagecoach robbery in United States history occurred outside of Jarbidge. The stage carried several thousand dollars in payroll money for the local miners. The driver was shot dead, the money never recovered.

The inevitable fire destroyed Main Street in 1919, but in the early 1920s Jarbidge had rebuilt sufficiently to become the largest gold producer in the state and had recovered somewhere between $10 million and $37 million (few accurate records remain) in bullion by the early 1930s.

A handful of hardy souls have lived in this remote village over the recent decades. Remote it was and still is! Jarbidge is only accessible by gravel roads. Two from the south, Nevada-side, are 50-odd and 60-odd miles long. The one north into Idaho twists 18 miles to pavement, then another 50 miles to the nearest town. The Idaho road is kept open all winter for mail service, but the other two are snowed in up to eight months out of every year. Residents shop for supplies in Twin Falls, Idaho, nearly 100 miles away; the clocks are set on Mountain Time. During the long winters, Jarbidgites must travel nearly 80 miles to get back to Nevada—and that's only to Jackpot, right on the Idaho border. Jarbidge finally received phone service for the first time in 1984.

Even so, today there are roughly three dozen residences in Jarbidge that are occupied at some point during the year, with 28 or so permanent residences—quite a surprise if you're expecting only the ruined remnants of a ghost town. Of course, there are also around 50 abandoned places of all sorts.

Still, it's not all *that* remote. Tons of visitors show up every season, many from nearby, some from far away (Europeans, especially, often think of Jarbidge as a quest). An inordinate number of people have been heading to Jarbidge of late to be married by the local justice of the peace. And a number of people, it seems, would like to live here, or at least buy property. In the summer of 1997, there were three places for sale; the least expensive was asking $90,000. High? Maybe. But when you consider that Jarbidge is never going to get any bigger, maybe not. Jarbidge is completely surrounded by the Humboldt National Forest, a tiny private atoll in a vast federal ocean, and it's about as far removed from any rat race as you could ever hope to get (short of the hermit-in-a-cave option). In short, Jarbidge is a wonderful place to visit, and you might even want to live there.

Around Town

Note that the speed limit on Main Street, which runs a half mile through town, is 10 mph. *Creep* through unless you want the whole town mad at you. Also, Jarbidge, like Owyhee and Jackpot, is on Mountain Time; set your watches ahead an hour.

First stop should be at the **Trading Post**— Best Little Storehouse in Jarbidge, 775/488-2315, open 9 A.M.–6 P.M. seven days a week year-round. Run by Rey and Marguerite Nystrom, one-time almond farmers from Chico, California, this little store sells the daily necessities, some eclectic collectibles, three books by local authors (*I'd Rather Be In Jarbidge* by Donald Mathias, *Gold Fever* by Helen Wilson, and *A Place Called Jarbidge* by Donald Mathias and Valerie Berry) and one by an out-of-town author (*Nevada Handbook* by what's-his-name), and dispenses an interesting fact sheet about the town and vicinity. Sign the guest book and visit awhile—Mrs. Nystrom might be the easiest person with whom to strike up a conversation this side of, well, Helen Wilson next door! But be careful of the dog under the table—especially if it moves. (If the Nystroms are away on a fishing trip, a supply run to Mountain Falls, or some other outing, there'll be a sign on the door telling customers to track down Joan or Larry Hawker to open the place up.)

For eight years, the Nystroms lived in the rooms behind the store, and the townsfolk kinda got used to the convenience of that, calling, for example, at 9 P.M. to ask "Are you still up? I need some aspirin (or Copenhagen or ice cream or pick one)." But a few years ago the Nystroms moved up the creek into a mobile home they had shipped down from Boise (a wild tale in itself), so the residents had to change their whole way of life.

Now that the Nystroms have the Trading Post up for sale (they did move here to retire, after all), people are wondering what sort of changes are coming next. Rey Nystrom welcomes questions about the area from visitors. Call or e-mail him at jarbidge@aol.com.

The **Bear Creek Woodworks & Gallery,** 775/488-2336, features the work of its owner, master carpenter and wood craftsman Randy Knight, as well as the creations of other local artists.

The work of prominent nature photographer and clay artist Beverly DeGero can be seen at the Trading Post and at the Bear Creek Woodworks & Gallery. While you're in town, you might give her a call, 775/488-2369. She and her husband moved a few miles down the road from Jarbidge in 1994. The couple entered into an agreement with the Nevada Nature Conservancy to preserve the pristine quality of their 160-acre former homestead by placing it in a lifetime trust. They'll soon be launching the **Deer Creek Retreat Center and Earth Art Institute** on the property, where artists can stay and work while learning about the ecology of Jarbidge Canyon.

Next door is the old **jailhouse,** and next door to that is **Helen Wilson's** home. Helen is an effusive and sprightly lady over 90 who's lived in Jarbidge on and off since 1910. Stop in to say hello (if she's home, generally between May and October; she winters in Southern California), to hear entertaining stories within a time frame of four-score years ago up till next week, and buy a copy of *Gold Fever.* If you do drop by, make sure you have time to sit a spell, because if there's one thing Helen hates, it's having a good story cut short. That ancient alligator handbag hanging in the window? It's the very same one that was stolen in the famous Jarbidge stagecoach robbery of 1916, or so claimed the man who sent it to Helen in 1996. Note the knife slash across the front. If it's not hanging up any more, she'd love to show it to you, and why stop there? If she's up to it—and she usually is—she'd love to show you the **Community Hall** (once the Commercial Club, built in 1910 and restored in 1965) and her photographs of the area and the wonderful letters she receives from people around the world who've read her book, *Gold Fever,* and and and . . .

Across the street is the main action in town, the **Outdoor Inn,** 775/488-2311, and adjoining **Tired Devil Cafe,** both of which open at 8 A.M. daily; the cafe closes at 11 P.M., while the bar sometimes never does. This is where you make arrangements to stay down the road at the Barn or to rent one of the three apartments or four motel rooms next door to the cafe. The bar and restaurant are brand new, rebuilt in 2000, after a fire totaled the previous building in November 1999. The Outdoor Inn sports a piano, juke box, slots, walls covered with graffiti, and business cards on the ceiling. It also boasts a big-screen TV for watching football, football, and more football. The prices at the cafe are good and so is the food. A BLT at the Tired Devil has been described as one where the waitress-cook-owner "slaps the bacon on to sizzle and slices the homemade bread before calling into the darkness of the bar for someone to 'go down to the Trading Post and get me some tomatoes.'" The Outdoor Inn closes after deer season (first part of November) and opens again in early May, in time for the Cinco de Mayo party on May 5, snow conditions cooperating.

On the other side of the street is the other action, the **Red Dog Saloon** with another interesting bar. It's open all year round, serving bar food; it's owned by the same folks as the Outdoor Inn.

Up the road is the **Sinclair gas station and**

Take a pack trip into the Jarbidge Wilderness.

garage, operated by Larry and Gwen Allen. Larry once made it into the Guinness Book of World Records: he took the engine out of a running Volkswagen bug, replaced it with another engine, and got it running again—in a record three and a half minutes. Needless to say, Larry's busy fixing up a lot of Jarbidge junkers.

Finishing your tour through town, you pass the Jarbidge **historical sign** and **schoolhouse** behind it, and the **fire department.**

Accommodations

The Barn at the north end of town is just that, refurbished of course, with 10 rooms starting at $35; register at the Outdoor Inn, 775/488-2311. The Barn closes along with the Outdoor Inn in early November (but the phone number still works). The owners of the Outdoor Inn also rent out apartments and motel rooms year-round in the building right next door to the Outdoor Inn; four motel rooms are $55 each, or you can rent an apartment with full kitchen for $75 a night.

Tsawhawbitts B&B, 5 Main St., 775/488-2338, was once a getaway estate for the Fawcett family of Fawcett publishing fame. An avid hunter, old man Fawcett loved coming to Jarbidge to stalk mule deer and antelope to add to his collection of big-game trophies. The estate was also used to host rustic parties and hunting junkets for Fawcett friends, business associates, and clients. Fawcett sold the place to Chuck and Krinn McCoy after his wife died in the late '80s. The McCoys moved to Jarbidge in 1989

and host hunters in the fall, cross-country skiers in the winter, and travelers all summer long. The Carriage House rents for $100 a night for four people, $212 for eight. The Party House can accommodate four guests for $150 a night. Rooms come with a full gourmet breakfast. Floods nearly washed away the main house in 1995. A Jarbidge cat operator saved the day when he plunged a dozer into the torrent and bolstered the foundation with boulders.

Camping

The U.S. Forest service operates two campgrounds in Jarbidge Canyon: the Jarbidge and Pine Creek campgrounds. Camping is free at both, and sites are first come, first served. The U.S. Forest Service office in Wells, 775/752-3357, is the resource for current info on these campgrounds.

Jarbidge Campground, a quarter mile south of town, has one group site, four single sites, plus a group of benches around a firepit for picnics; no water is available.

Continuing through Bonanza Gulch, you'll reach **Pavlak Campground** just beyond the bridge across the river, near the site of the old Pavlak post office, with room for three sites. (This is not a Forest Service campground; you may or may not still find it there.)

A bit south of Pavlak, the left fork leads up to the southern gravel road into Jarbidge from NV 225 out of Elko. The right fork continues along the canyon. Following this road, you come to the **Pine Creek** campground. With several large campsites and one outhouse (though no drinking water), this camp fills up in the late summer and fall during deer season.

Two other informal camping areas past Pine Creek, **Urdahl** and **Mexican Camp,** were isolated by a washed out road in 1997. Also wiped out by flooding was **Fox Creek Camp.** Fox Camp has been added to the Jarbidge Wilderness and is off limits permanently to vehicles. A trail hugs the creek (one mile roundtrip) into a little canyon where you'll be all alone with your thoughts.

Pack Trips, Hiking, Fishing, and Hunting

The 65,000-acre Jarbidge Wilderness Area was carved out of the Humboldt National Forest in 1964. It remained the only official federal wilderness area in Nevada for 25 years, until the passage of the Wilderness Bill in 1989. But of Nevada's 14 wilderness areas today, it remains by far the wildest and least accessible, plus the second largest.

The Jarbidge Mountains form a sort of diamond, with eight peaks higher than 10,000 feet. More than 125 miles of trails are passable June 15-Oct. 1, though heavy weather can descend at any time. Covering the myriad outdoor recreational opportunities in the vast and untamed wilderness around Jarbidge is beyond the scope of this edition. Luckily, a spiral-bound book, *I'd Rather Be In Jarbidge* by Donald Mathias, has 140 pages of detailed coverage of history, fishing, hunting, backpacking, and camping in the wilderness area. It's for sale ($11.95) at the Northeastern Nevada Museum in Elko, at the Jarbidge Trading Post, or write to 331 East Meda Ave., Glendora, CA 91740. You can get brochures, maps, and a report on current conditions from the U.S. Forest Service office in Wells; the Forest Service office in Elko may have information, too.

The Smith family leads weeklong dude pack trips between June and September into the high and remote Jarbidge Range, and guides hunters in the fall. The going price in the year 2000 for a week-long pack trip was $1,500 per person (10% discount for groups of 6–10 people). The five-day expeditions terminate with a parade down Main Street in Jarbidge on Friday, providing all the excuse the townsfolk need

for a regular party, which repairs, of course, to the Outdoor Inn for a night of Virginia reels and banjo playing. It's quite an event for visitors too.

The Smiths also offer a real Western experience at their **Cottonwood Ranch** spread about 70 miles northwest of Wells. It's a working horse ranch with a ranch lodge with five guest rooms (soon to be seven). Guests are welcome to take part in all the ranch activities; there's lots of horseback riding, three horse drives each year (June, July and September), cattle drives, and elk trips in the elk mating season. The guest rates of $200 per person, per day, include lodging, three meals a day, and all ranch activities. There's a 20% discount for kids age 16 and under, and a 10% discount for groups of 10 people or more. Contact: Contact: Cottonwood Ranch, HC 62, Box 1300, Wells, NV 89835, 775/752-3604 or 800/341-5951, www.guestranches.com/cottonwood.

Lowell Prunty, 208/857-2270, from across the border in Idaho, is another popular local guide who specializes in leading trips into the Jarbidge Wilderness.

AROUND TO JACKPOT

Head north out of Jarbidge along the canyon. In about 12 miles is **Desert Hot Springs,** 208/857-2233, Idaho. In the 1800s, this site was the headquarters of the Wilkins Ranch, run by Miss Kitty Wilkins. The hot springs were known then, and are still sometimes referred to by the old-timers, as **Kitty's Hot Hole.** New owners bought the resort in 1994 and changed the name from Murphy's Hot Springs. Today, the hot springs has a gas station, lodge and cafe, bungalows, camping, along with a big, warm swimming pool, three private rooms with hot tubs (two twin and one double), and the creek running right through the middle of it. Good hiking, too. The swimming and soaking are $4—great for rinsing off 70 or so miles' worth of northeast Nevada dust. Camping is $5 for tents, $15 for RVs with hookup. You also can rent a variety of cabins: $25 with one double bed, $35 with two, $45 with three. The owners are marketing spring water bottled at the site under the name Purity Sweet for a dollar a quart. They also run a shuttle for rafters and kayakers floating the Jarbidge and Bruneau rivers. At high water in May and June, the 90-mile trip through the canyon is said to be spectacular.

From there, you climb up, then more up, finally way up above Jarbidge Canyon. At the top, back in the high country, three miles from the hot springs is pavement, blessed pavement, your first in more than 70 miles. Again, this is glorious country for travelers accustomed to the Great Basin roller coaster. Here, you cut across the extreme southeast corner of wild Owyhee County, Idaho, atop the Snake River Plateau—thousands of square miles of rolling boundlessness. In some places on the plateau, the horizon is so far in the distance that you can barely distinguish the land from the sky. Only two paved roads traverse the whole county. You can see for at least a million miles, and if you think that's an exaggeration, come up here yourself and dispute it.

After crossing into and traveling through Twin Falls County for a while, the road suddenly narrows to one lane and crests the **Salmon Dam,** topping an astounding canyon, with a campground hugging the shore of the reservoir. Back in civilization, a few ranches go by and then you enter **Rogerson,** which consists of a few houses and the Salmon Dam Saloon; there's no directional sign, but go right at the stop sign and

---

BORDER TOWNS

A unique feature of the Silver State is that gambling houses tend to prosper most at her outer edges, hugging the state line so tightly that no sooner does the highway traveler pass the silver and blue point-of-entry marker than he is instantly blinded by the glare of 10,000 colored light bulbs. It's said that night pilots often navigate by the light of these commercial beacons and rumored that Nevada is the only state whose shape is discernible from outer space, thanks to her iridescent outline.

—RICHARD MENZIES,
NEVADA MAGAZINE, June 1984

---

bear around to the left for the junction with US 93. There at the corner is a gas station-mini-mart-cafe-motel-RV park.

It's 18 miles south, mostly along the gash in the earth above Salmon Creek Reservoir, to get back to the Nevada state line and Jackpot.

JACKPOT

INTRODUCTION

For all intents and purposes, Jackpot belongs more to Idaho than to Nevada. The town's very founding (1956) took place less than two years after Idaho banned slot machines. It's in the same U-shaped corner of northeastern Nevada as Jarbidge, outside of the Great Basin, where Salmon Falls Creek and tributaries drain north into the Snake system. A major share of Jackpot's business arrives from Twin Falls (50 miles north, closer to Jackpot than Wells), Pocatello, and Boise. And at last count, Jackpot was paying out at least five million dollars a year to Idaho suppliers, four million to Idaho resident employees and a million in Idaho payroll taxes,

half a million to Idaho Power Company and nearly a quarter million to Idaho Telephone Company. It's also within Idaho's Mountain Time Zone, an hour later than the rest of its own state.

In one respect, however—border-town gambling—Jackpot is pure Nevada. Its name means "the cumulative payoff." Almost every street name in town has to do with casino games. And Jackpot is booming like only a border town in Nevada can. So it might be that in one sense Jackpot is an iron filing clinging to the massive Idaho magnet. But in another sense, Jackpot itself might be the magnet, drawing in the entire southern half of Idaho, and beyond.

History

An establishment a little north of present-day Jackpot called Twin Springs consisted of a frame "hotel," bar, and Nevada girls. After a border survey, Twin Springs was found to be in Idaho, so it moved—lock, stock, and barn—two miles south. Later, it somehow proved to be in Idaho still, and was shut down.

Senator Estes Kefauver's exposure of the connection between organized crime and gambling was so successful that every state (except Nevada, of course) with previously legal slot machines—chicken-hearts every one—banned them. Shortly thereafter, Don French of Garden City, Idaho, opened a slot club called the Horseshu right on the border. The same year, 1956, Pete Piersanti, who owned Cactus Petes cafe and slot joint at Mineral Hot Springs 12 miles south of present-day Jackpot, relocated across the street from the Horseshu. The Elko County Commissioners referred to the tiny settlement as Unincorporated Town Number One for three years. In late 1959, the state Gambling Commission approved nonrestricted gaming licenses for the Horseshu and Cactus Petes, and the town's name was changed to Jackpot. Thus Jackpot became the only town in Nevada that I can think of founded entirely on gambling. (Laughlin, one of the only towns in Nevada younger than Jackpot, and about as far away from Jackpot as it's possible to be in Nevada, was founded on fishing and *grew up* on gambling.)

But Jackpot did not appear on maps or road signs until the early 1970s. Carl Hayden, a roving reporter for the Salt Lake City *Tribune,* retired in Jackpot and became a one-man PR department for the Horseshu and Cactus Petes, and therefore the town. One of Hayden's first campaigns focused on sign- and map-makers. He then began to send out folksy press releases promoting special events and publish visitor handouts. Carl Hayden remained number-one publicist for Petes and Jackpot until August 1992, when he died at 84; he was fondly eulogized in obits throughout the West.

Hayden did a great job. Jackpot today is northern Nevada's gambling boomtown, competing, figuratively, with the likes of Laughlin and Wendover. With an occupancy rate, like Laughlin's, nearing 100%, and with Cactus Petes pretending, quite successfully, to be a Las Vegas casino, Jackpot has definitely hit the jackpot.

SIGHTS

Roll south through the center of town on US 93, by Holiday Inn Express, Barton's 93 Club, Cactus Petes and the Horseshu, the Star, and Four Jacks. Head east (left) down Progressive St. to the grammar and high schools (the street's named after a type of slot-machine jackpot, not a type of education). Before the high school was built, teenagers had the choice of being bused 68 miles each way to and from Wells or to go to school in Idaho, whereby they had to drive 18 miles from Jackpot just to get to the bus stop. Gurley Drive (named for one of the original partners in Cactus Petes) is the ritzy section of Jackpot; it has actual houses. On the north side of town, take Ace Drive across from the 93 Club in back of town to the Jackpot Municipal Golf Course. You'll notice that the residential section is made up almost entirely of four-plexes and single- and double-wides.

For an overlook of Jackpot, park at the back of the Star Motel and hike 10 minutes up the hill behind town by the water tanks. The municipal building, fire department, and community hall are on the street behind the Horseshu's and Barton's parking lots, all there is to the west side of Jackpot.

Casinos

A mere 10 minutes wandering around **Cactus Petes** will put you right into a Las Vegas time warp. The casino itself is now 30,000 square feet, expanded in 1990 from 10,000. It houses three pits, with 24 blackjack, two crap, and two roulette tables, a keno lounge, sports book, poker room, six-station cage, slot club, slot and poker tournaments, $5 video poker, gourmet room, showroom, country-and-western lounge, convention center, and a respectable 420 hotel rooms (you can see the 10-story tower from miles around). The one thing Petes doesn't have (anymore) is the post office, which moved to a new building in the fall of 1990.

Owner Craig Nielsen also owns the **Horseshu** across the street, with six blackjack tables and a crap table (quarter stakes Sun.–Thurs.), and good video poker in the bar's back room. Craig Nielsen grew up in Twin Falls and ran his father's construction business when he came out of college. His father had points in Petes, and when he died in 1971, Craig began to manage his family's share. Eventually, he bought out the other owners and owned the whole thing outright by 1988. In the process, he upgraded, expanded, upgraded, and expanded it, taking Petes from a truck stop to a casino that would make the Las Vegas Strip proud. In 1993, Nielsen went public with Petes, issuing 2.4 million shares of stock for $26 million, and in early 1994 he opened Ameristar riverboat casino in Vicksburg, Mississippi. He's also involved in the ill-fated Reserve casino in Henderson.

Barton's Club 93 also dates back to the founding days of the town, and is still run by the Barton family. In 1990 they expanded and remodeled, doubling the size of the casino. Barton's "slotspitality" extends to its blackjack tables which, unlike Petes and the Horseshu, offer Las Vegas rules (double down on any two cards). The "sunken" pit has 12 blackjack tables, along with a crap and roulette table. The 93 Club added another 140 slots in 1996, bringing the total to well over 500.

The **Four Jacks** at the south end has a bar, motel, slots, and an 1890, $50,000 Ragola nickelodeon in the coffee shop, one of only 18 ever made.

At the far north end of town, just up the hill from Cut Rate Liquors, is the **West Star Resort** hotel and casino, with 75 rooms and 100 slot machines.

PRACTICALITIES

Accommodations

It's a good idea to reserve a room in Jackpot as far in advance as possible. Package tours from Alberta, Saskatchewan, Montana, and Idaho pour into Jackpot, and reservations made early are essential to compete for one of the town's roughly 750 rooms.

Jackpot's most amazing lodging bargain vanished when **Barton's Club 93**, 775/755-2341 or 800/258-2937, closed its motel annex across the street from the big house a few years back. Barton's has since built a new 60-room complex—the Sandstone—which houses its most expensive rooms ($50 Sun.–Thurs., $60 weekends). The old Hillside wing (40 rooms) sells

rooms for $35–45. Barton's also runs an **RV park** across the street with bathhouse and showers; amazingly, this place is free. Pull in, hook up, and have a ball.

The Four Jacks Hotel Casino, on the south side of town, 775/755-2491 or 800/251-6313, has 60 rooms for $20–45.

Cactus Petes Resort/Casino, 775/755-2321 or 800/821-1103, has rooms starting at $59 in the Diamond Peak Tower Sun.–Thurs., going up to $125 for suites with hot tubs. In their Granite section, rooms are $69–79 Sun.–Thurs., suites $125–175. Weekend rates are higher in both sections: add $20 to the rooms and $50 to the suites.

Rooms at the **Horseshu Hotel Casino,** 775/755-2321 or 800/821-1103, go for $29–49; rooms with Jacuzzi are $49–69.

West Star Resort at US 93 and Poker St., 775/755-2600 or 800/665-0643, has 75 rooms for $40–65. Or there's the **Covered Wagon Motel,** 1601 US 93, 775/755-2241 or 800/838-1241, with 85 rooms for $20–40.

Cactus Pete's RV Park, 775/755-2321 or 800/821-1103, has one section directly behind the casino, next to the airport, and another section south of the hotel. The section behind the casino has 52 spaces for motor homes; all 52 are pull-throughs, with full hook-ups. The other section has 15 spaces, all with full hookups. The water in both sections is shut off during the winter, but water is available at the office. Heated swimming pool, hot tub, and two tennis courts are available to campers. Tents are not permitted. Reservations are recommended; this place fills up fast in the summer. The fee is $10 per vehicle.

Spanish Gardens RV Park, corner of Gurley St. and US 93, 775/755-2333 or 800/422-8233, is right off the main highway, but a security wall, trees, and grassy areas buffer the impact. It has 27 spaces for motor homes, all with full hookups; 11 are pull-throughs. Tents are allowed. Laundry and cold-storage game lockers (for hunters) are available. Reservations are recommended during summer and fall. The tenting fee is $8 for the first two people and $2 for each additional camper; RV spaces are $13.50.

If you're planning to tent it somewhere out of town and want to rinse off, follow the blue tourist information signs to the **Rec Center,** where you can swim and shower as long as you want for $2. There's also a bank of brochure racks.

Food

Head either to Cactus Petes or Horseshu's 24-hour **coffee shops,** where food is cheap and plentiful. Petes also has a **buffet** three meals a day. The Horseshu's 24-hour **Frontier Kitchen** is good and economical; good choices here include the prime rib, the 14-ounce T-bone, or fajitas and other Mexican dishes.

The **Coyote Cafe** snack bar at Petes is recommended: selections include great big sandwiches (try the chicken fajitas or smoked turkey and cream cheese), baked potatoes, and burgers.

The **Plateau Room,** with a certified master chef, is the fine dining at Petes. The room is intimate, with six booths and five tables and a three-seat service bar.

The **Gala Room** hosts the dinner and cocktail shows, Sunday brunch, and headliners at Cactus Petes. The lounge at the north end of Petes casino has live music nightly.

Note: For several years now, on Wednesday nights from 5 to 11, all food at Cactus Petes (and that was *all* food—from the snack bar to the Plateau Room, from the coffee shop to the dinner show) has been half-price. Incredible! Make sure to check it out if you're in Jackpot on a Wednesday evening; word is you need reservations for the Plateau Room a week in advance.

The **Four Jacks** serves breakfast 24 hours a day, plus lunch and dinner specials. An everyday dinner special built around a slab of mesquite-grilled prime rib goes for $10.95.

The **Paradise Cafe** at the Club 93 is open 24 hours. Their dinner buffet is served Wed.–Sat. from 5–10 P.M.; on Sundays the buffet is served 2–9 P.M.

To Wells

Just a few miles south of town, still in southern Idaho plateau country, is a rest stop on the river, alternately known as the Little Salmon River and Salmon Falls Creek. A few miles south of that, the country starts looking again like Great Basin Desert, with distinct **Gollaher Mountain** (8,153 feet) off in the eastern distance, and **Middlestack Mountain** (8,104 feet) closer to the road. Soon you come to **Mineral Hot Springs** (abandoned), then **Contact,** just a few-house town from a once-thriving copper region. A 1939 photo in *Nevada Highways* magazine showed Contact with a gas station, garage, and cafe.

The sage-scrub country on both sides looks raw and unexplored, states writer Sam Felton in an article published by the *Elko Free Press,* but the area has a ranching history that dates to the 1880s. The first big herds were brought here on the hoof from Texas by John Sparks and Andrew Harrell and a crew of black cowboys. They came for the native Great Basin rye grass that grew so tall "a cowboy could bend down from atop his horse and pull up a blade . . . to pick his teeth," according to one old-timer Felton interviewed. By the winter of 1889–90, 160,000 cattle were grazing on area ranches, setting the stage for a disaster. Overgrazing and an unusually severe winter that year resulted in a die-off that broke many outfits. Harrell's operation survived, but when he died in 1907, his 11,000 acres eventually became part of the vast Utah Construction Company. Between 1914 and the late '40s, the Old UC, as it was known, owned 38 ranches in Nevada, Idaho, and Utah totaling 3 million acres. At its peak the UC had 50,000 head of beef, 42,000 sheep, 3,000 horses, and 232 year-round employees. The UC was one of the unintended victims of World War II. With most of its cowboys off fighting, the lack of experienced hands crippled the operation, which was sold off to speculators from Denver, split up, and resold.

China Mountain on the east (8,229 feet) and **Ellen D** on the west (8,613 feet) surround Contact. At the south foot of Ellen D are some badlands—a series of big rocky mounds. These give way to a few miles of buttes, which look, briefly, a little like the Idaho plateau again. The big **Snake Mountains** cut in from the west, and the **Windemere Hills** join in on the east about 20 miles north of Wells. Twelve miles north of Wells, US 93 crosses the Fort Hall stretch of the Emigrant Trail. Finally look down **Town Creek Flat** at Wells, crouching at the northern edge of the prominent and pretty **East Humboldt Range.**

WELLS

INTRODUCTION

A spot a little northwest of the present-day town of Wells was once a famous camping site on the Emigrant Trail. Called Humboldt Wells for the dozen springs providing fresh water and grass, it was the easternmost source of the Humboldt River. The Central Pacific established a division point nearby, around which the town, shortened to Wells, slowly grew up. You can easily trace the evolution of the business district, from 7th Street at the railroad tracks to 6th Street along old US 40 to the developing exit ramps on I-80. Wells seems to have embraced each transition in a concerted effort to keep up and grow with the times.

Mining and ranching have also long contributed to the local economy. The WPA's *Guide to Nevada* has a story about the brutal winter of 1889–90, when most of the cattle froze or starved to death. "Wealthy stockmen went bankrupt almost overnight, and some were forced to begin all over again as cowboys. A Negro camp cook, looking over the dismal scene, exclaimed, 'Lawd, how your snow done equalize society!'"

Wells has also suffered its share of diversity in the past 15 years or so. In the early 1980s, a con man named Michael Wilwerding set up shop in Wells, claiming he could revert used tires back to oil. He got all kinds of tax breaks and state aid money, and even produced a small amount of oil. But the site turned out to be primarily a dump for highly toxic liquid wastes, and Wells received the first Superfund money in Nevada to clean up the mess. More recently, Sierra Pacific proposed to develop a $4 billion, eight-plant, 250-megawatt, coal-fired power complex nearby, but the deal fell through.

Still, Wells has rebounded admirably, and in the past few years a new shopping center at the west exit of I-80, a Flying J truck stop at the east exit, an industrial park, and a subdivision south of town have been built.

Wells is not only a crossroads town, hosting the intersection of I-80 and US 93. It is also a border town of sorts. Technically, Jackpot, 68 miles north on US 93, gets the travelers right after they enter Nevada from Idaho, and Wendover, 60 miles east on I-80, gets 'em from Utah. But Nevada border towns in general, and the above two specifically, exist for one reason: gambling. Room rates are high, vacancy rates are low. Wells's accommodations are cheaper and decidedly more available. Also, as a junction town, Wells has excellent travelers' and truckers' facilities. So if a casino at a real border town isn't your final destination, it might be worth it to drive the extra 60–70 miles to Wells—the nearest junction town to two borders.

DAVID HURST

the Old Bank of Wells

SIGHTS

Start out at the "historic district" on 7th St. along the tracks, the most abandoned and intact railroad row on the entire original Central Pacific line. The **Bullshead Bar** on the corner opened as a log hut on Christmas Eve 1869; the last incarnation still stands, though it's closed. Since the last edition of this book, **Quilici's,** an interesting old general store—at the same location since the late 1880s and owned by the Quilici family since 1928—closed.

The **Wells Bank,** across Lake and up the block, opened in 1911; Morris Badt, Wells's first merchant (1876) was its original president. The **Nevada Hotel** on 6th St. is also a relic, turned into a movie theater until it closed. The **Coryell Residence,** at the corner of 9th and Lake, is the oldest house in town, and an old house on the other corner was built out of railroad ties.

A lot of the downtown area is being renovated now, including the historic **El Rancho Hotel.** There is also now an art gallery. A free brochure has been published to lead you on a self-guided walking tour of the downtown historic district, with plaques identifying the various historic buildings; pick one up at the Chamber of Commerce or at area businesses.

Between Lake and Clover streets and 4th and 1st, is the municipal, educational, and recreational center of town. The city park provides picnic tables and grills, playgrounds, tennis, baseball fields, basketball courts, and a heated swimming pool.

Casinos

The **Old West** and **Luther's** bars downtown have slots. The **4-Way** truck stop has a gang of slots and a three-table blackjack pit. The **Ranch House** casino is still closed. The new kid on the block is **Lucky J's Casino** at the Flying J truck stop on the south side of the interstate at US 93: two blackjack tables and some slots.

Metropolis

Metropolis was once the center of an ambitious agricultural experiment. In the reclamation frenzy following the Truckee-Carson Project in the first decade of the 20th century, a New York company, Pacific Reclamations, bought 40,000 acres north of Wells, partly from the Badt family, partly from the government. It dammed Bishop Creek and built canals, then sold irrigated land for $75 an acre, unirrigated for $10–15. It also set up an office in Salt Lake City to attract pioneering Mormons.

Farmers arrived and started farming. Southern Pacific Railroad built an eight-mile spur from the main line at Wells; the first train arrived at the new two-story depot in October 1911. Three months later, the New Year was greeted at the Metropolis Hotel—three stories, 50 rooms, marble-tiled lobby, barbershop, bank, and billiards. The following year, a two-story school went up, and the town's water system went in. Turkey red wheat grew to shoulder height, yielding 30 bushels an unirrigated acre!

For a decade or so, Metropolis was a model company city. The company, on the other hand, proved less successful. Water rights were its Waterloo. Local ranchers and farmers filed suit, and the courts decided against the company, which quickly went under, bankrupt by 1920.

Even so, Metropolis rolled right along on its own for a while, until a few seasons of drought, grasshoppers, and rabbits did their dirty work. Some stalwarts hung on even after the train stopped running in 1925. But by 1942, the post office closed, and Metropolis was a ghost.

Today, the photogenic front frame of big Lincoln School is all that's left here at Nevada's only *agricultural* ghost town.

To get there, take a left on 8th when you cross over the tracks, and follow it around by the railroad overpass (which doesn't quite pass over anymore). The pavement starts up again and runs along the tracks for awhile. Follow the road as it curves around to the right, then to the left, then right, then left. The pavement gives way to 45-mph gravel, just slippery enough to be fun. Cross the cattle guard, and turn onto an unmarked gravel road to the left; you'll see the ruins on the right.

California Trail

The California Trail Historic Back Country Byway, beginning 25 miles north of Wells off US 93, consists of 96 miles of gravel roads in the extreme northeast reaches of Elko County. An information kiosk near the Winecup Ranch, four miles off the highway, tells of the trail's history, when over 200,000 emigrants passed this way heading for California in the 19th century. The 96-mile-long byway follows the emigrants' route for over 40 miles. Trail markers are placed along the way to show visitors where the actual trail was; trail ruts can still be seen in many places.

The BLM Field office in Elko, 775/753-0200, has information on the route.

PRACTICALITIES

Accommodations

The old hotel downtown, the **Old West Inn,** 455 6th St., 775/752-3888, is pretty inexpensive, with 20 rooms for $18–22. The **Lone Star Motel,** 576 6th St., 775/752-3632, and **Shell Crest Motel,** 426 6th St., 775/752-3755, advertise rates from $24–39. The **Best Western Sage Inn,** 576 6th St., 775/752-3353 or 800/528-1234, was remodeled a few years ago and charges $45–80. The **Rest Inn Suites,** 1250 E. 6th St., 775/752-2277 or 800/935-5768, is the new kid on the block, across from the 4-Way next to Motel 6; all 57 rooms are mini-suites with microwaves, fridges, hair dryers, and remote-control TVs, $37–49.

Mountain Shadows RV Park, 807 S. Humboldt Ave., 775/752-3525, is one of the coziest, cleanest, and friendliest RV parks on the interstate through northern Nevada. Dick and Chickie Smith took it over in 1993 and improved the bathhouse and laundry, planted trees, and spruced up the landscaping. There are 38 spaces for motor homes, 33 with full hookups and 13 pull-throughs. Tents are allowed and non-campers can take showers for $5. Reservations are recommended Memorial Day to Labor Day, especially for pull-throughs. RV sites cost $19.50; tent sites are $14 (10% AARP, AAA, Good Sam, and senior-citizen discounts). Open March 1 through November 15.

Crossroads RV Park, 734 6th St., 775/752-3012, open April to October, has 24 RV spaces with full hook-ups. Tents are not allowed.

Eight miles west of Wells, the **Welcome Station** at I-80's Exit 343, 775/752-3808, is open May to November and offers 35 spaces. Tents are allowed. RV sites cost $17, tent sites $14.

For campground camping, see "Angel Lake," below.

Food

The **4-Way** at the east exit has a 24-hour coffee shop, with the usual road food and a 40-item salad bar. On the other side of the interstate, **The Cookery** restaurant at the Flying J truck stop, 775/752-2405, is also open 24 hours and has an all-you-can-eat breakfast, lunch and dinner buffet. Also at the east exit ramp to Wells is a **Burger King.**

Burger Bar at the west end of 6th St., corner of Humboldt, 775/752-3210, serves burgers, pizza, milkshakes and the like; the specialty of the house is a ham and turkey croissant melt with fries. Open Mon.–Sat., 10 A.M.–9 P.M.

The **Old West Café** at the Old West Inn, 455 6th St., 775/752-3888, serves all three meals, with good home cooking.

For groceries, stop at **Stuart's Food Town,** 647 Humboldt Ave. at the west exit ramp, 775/752-3215, open Mon.–Sat 7 A.M.–9 P.M., Sunday 8 A.M.–8 P.M.

Other Practicalities

Wells is a good place to wait for the sun to go down if you're heading west. The interstate aims directly toward the fiery orb, setting into your very eyes, and everything other than the blinding sun is shadows. Scary driving for 20 minutes or so.

The **Chamber of Commerce** is at 395 6th St. at the corner of Lake St., in the Kelly Kreations building; 775/752-3540, coc@wells-snv.com, www.wellsnv.com. Open Mon.–Sat. 7 A.M.–4 P.M. When the office is closed, you can pick up extensive tourist information in the lobby area; it's accessible 24 hours, seven days a week.

You can also stop in at **City Hall,** 279 Clover Ave., 775/752-3355, and read the bulletin boards and rifle the info rack. Next door, the **library,** 775/752-3856, 196 Baker St., is open Monday, Tuesday, Wednesday, and Friday 11 A.M.–5 P.M., Thursday 1–5 P.M. and 7–9 P.M.

The **Forest Service** office for the **Ruby Mountain Ranger District,** 140 Pacific Ave., 775/752-3357, is open Mon.–Fri. 7:30 A.M.–4:30 P.M. Pick up maps, trail guides, and general information on the Rubies and East Humboldts, read the proclamation by Teddy Roosevelt naming Ruby National Forest in 1906, and check out the picture of Hole in the Mountain Peak.

The two **brothels** are on the far north end of the railroad tracks, visible from all over the east side of town. Go up Lake to 10th, take a right, then another right down to the **Hacienda,** and **Donna's,** with the big sign on the roof.

Events

Many events take place in Wells all year round; the Chamber of Commerce has details. On Memorial Day weekend, **Senior Pro Rodeo** is a four-day event with contestants competing for points towards the National Finals in Reno. The **Wells Annual Fun Run Car Show,** held the last weekend of July, includes street dances, drag races, burn-outs, show-and-shine, and fireworks. In November are the **Chariot Races,** in which 40–60 teams (rider, horse, 100-pound chariot) run around the chariot track on the west end of town. The Chariot Races handles bets in the form of "calcuttas"—usually the night before the races, teams are "auctioned off" to "buyers" who, if their team wins, win the pot.

EAST HUMBOLDTS

Angel Lake

The 12-mile road from Wells to Angel Lake makes a lovely drive, especially in spring when the fields along the way are full of wildflowers. It's so pretty that it has been designated an official scenic route: the **Angel Lake Scenic Byway.**

Go under Wells's west exit ramp, then take a right at the sign. A paved road climbs up into the East Humboldt Range above **Clover Valley,** with beautiful high views down onto the lowlands, and beautiful low views up at the highlands. Pretty **Angel Creek Campground** is seven miles along in a little gully. The campground loop road, too, is paved: 18 campsites for tents or self-contained motor homes up to 40 feet, piped drinking water, vault toilets, picnic tables, grills, and fire rings provided. Angel Creek Campground is private, shady, and 15 minutes from Wells; camping costs $11 per site ($9 in winter). They try to keep this campground open all year, depending on snow conditions; the running water is turned off in winter.

Another steep mile and a half up, a trail goes left four miles to **Winchell Lake.** The road twists and climbs for another two miles, then ends at the **Angel Lake Campground** (8,378 feet) alongside a pretty alpine lake at the bottom of the cirque: 26 campsites, half a dozen outhouses, and a large picnic area share the bowl. Camping costs $12 per site; day use $5. The lake itself is over a small rise (you could almost spend the

whole night without knowing it's even there). This campground is open only in summer, from around mid-June to early September, depending on snow and weather conditions.

For both Angel campgrounds, contact Ruby Mountain Ranger District, 140 Pacific Ave. (P.O. Box 246), Wells, NV 89835, 775/752-3342.

Look east; several ranges disappear into the distance. Look south and up; **Chimney Rock** stands out prominently. **Grey's Peak** is 10,674 feet.

A trail up to **Grey's Lake** and beyond leaves from the horse-unloading parking lot at the east end of the cirque. This trail receives little to no maintenance and peters out frequently. Take along *Hiking the Great Basin* by John Hart for a good trail description.

Clover Valley

US 93 runs south from Wells along the magnificent eastern scarp of the East Humboldts. Ten miles south, NV 232 makes a loop west of the highway through luxuriant Clover Valley, which competes with Washoe Valley's Franktown Road at the eastern base of the Sierra for the number-one spot on Nevada's list of the most prime real estate.

You start out heading west toward a hump in the middle of the valley that looks like a hound dog with his chin on the floor and his haunches in the air. Then you turn south and drive through a truly bucolic scene—venerable trees towering over two-story, 100-year-old ranch houses with horses, cows, and goats grazing in the greenery, and creeks, defined by shrubs, snaking away from the sheer mountain walls.

Hole in the Mountain

About six miles from the highway is a distinct right turn onto a narrow 4WD track up into **Lizzie's Basin,** below the East Humboldt's highest mountain (11,276 feet). The phenomenon from which the peak derives its name accounts for one of the strangest and most compelling summits in the west. Roughly 300 feet below the peak is a large (30- by 25-foot) natural window in the weak and thin marble of the mountaintop. This cyclopean eye, staring east and west, was known as Taindandoi ("Hole In The Top") to the Shoshone, and Lizzie's Window to the early settlers, named after the first local to mention the hole.

As you cruise along Clover Valley, especially at sunset, the light shining through the window below the peak is a superlative sight in a land full of superlative sights. The pavement, oddly, runs out after about 15 miles, right where the road turns east again to meet up with US 93. But it's only for a mile, at 40–45 mph. Ely is 121 miles south.

TO WENDOVER

Back on I-80 heading east out of Wells, you cross broad **Independence Valley** and then climb the wall ahead of it, the **Pequop Range.** When you crest the summit (6,967 feet–highest point on I-80 in Nevada), you'll be looking ahead at the **Toana Range.**

The Oasis exit (378) puts you on NV 233. **Oasis** is just that, a tiny settlement dedicated to travelers through the desert. A ranch hereabouts in the 1880s was called Oasis; in the 1930s, there was a telephone and a Red Cross station on old US 40. A two-story hotel and gas station were built in 1946 to accommodate servicemen en route to and from Wendover; the hotel was renovated in 1982. Today, Oasis has a population of roughly 25, what might be the smallest post office in the country (with antique postal boxes), a cafe (with reputedly delicious pies), a gift shop full of crafts and souvenirs, and a gas station. A new paint job helps Oasis stand out on the north side of the highway. To get in touch, call 775/478-5113.

If you head northeast on NV 233, the first place you'll come to is **Cobre,** the division point between the Southern Pacific main line and the Nevada Northern from Ely. Farther along, 24 miles from Oasis and I-80, is **Montello,** in pretty Tecoma Valley just east of the big Toano Range. With a population of only around 100, Montello is not big, but it's very friendly. At one time, Montello was a railroad town, where crews were changed on the trains to/from Ogden, Utah; there was a round house here, opposite where the motel is today, and the town had a population of 5,000. Now, however, the crews are changed in Elko, and Montello has only a skeleton crew of about five railroad workers. Today, Montello is a cattle ranching community. There are only four ranches, but one of them, the Gamble Ranch, is a huge million-acre ranch ex-

tending all the way from I-80 up into Idaho. Otherwise, most of Montello's residents are retired; some of the younger people work in casinos in Wendover, about 50 miles away.

Montello has one **motel.** The sign out front says "The Pilot," but nobody ever calls it that— they call it simply "the motel." It's operated together with the **Montello Gas & Grocery,** 775/776-2451; the 10 motel rooms cost $25–38. For food, check out the **Cowboy Bar,** 775/776-2466; try the huge Cowboy Burger with fries, for $5.60, comes highly recommended. Food is served every day, 5:30 A.M.–8 P.M.; the bar stays open later. The **Saddle Sore Bar,** 775/776-2564, is planning to start serving food one of these days, and they also operate a laundry.

Around 20 or 25 miles outside Montello, the **Sun Tunnels** is an unusual attraction. Built by a European sculptress, at summer solstice the tunnels turn pink inside at sunrise; a number of Europeans come out to see it.

Back on the interstate, I-80 drops down into **Goshute Valley,** then climbs again into the Toanas. From there, you descend into **Pilot Creek Valley,** with climactic Pilot Peak rising to 10,714 feet above it.

Pilot Peak

Named by Fremont in 1845, this is one of the most beautiful and historic mountains in Nevada. Pioneers along the Emigrant Trail focused on it during their brutal 50- to 90-hour ordeal of crossing the blazing Great Salt Lake Desert. Finally arriving at Pilot's base, just over the Nevada line, they found water and grass, the knowledge of which sustained them during the three-day desert dash to the mountain, and the presence of which replenished them for the next leg to Humboldt Wells.

Pilot is a classically conical mountain, wooded across the waist, with a long and tapered *bajada* beckoning to the salt flats in the southeast. It also slopes off to the northwest, pointing to California and the promised land. As it stands there, tall and alone, it seems a proud mountain— proud of its handsomeness, proud of its heritage of hospitality, and proud of its unique location, providing, more so than all of the hundreds of Great Basin peaks, a hopeful and nourishing welcome to travelers of past and present, to the golden sands of Nevada.

The Curve and the Flat

Beyond, you cross a small rise on the edge of **Leppy Peak,** known as Three-Mile Hill. Then you round a bend, and there, directly east, is the town of Wendover, clinging tentatively to the edge of the great white **Bonneville Salt Flats.** Do not fail to pull over at the summit to check out the view, preferably through binoculars. The salt flats, which stretch all the way to the horizon, are absolutely level—flat as a mackerel, flat as a dance floor, so flat that the dark gray stripe of highway across them is visibly arched! This is one of the few places in the world where you can so clearly observe the foxy curvature of our mother, Earth.

WENDOVER

INTRODUCTION

Wendover sits on the western side of what was once Lake Bonneville, which covered a large area of northwestern Utah to a depth of 1,000 feet. The lake had no outlet, and as it shrank, and then disappeared (except for what is now the Great Salt Lake), it deposited a smooth layer of salt and other minerals in the lowest point of the Bonneville basin—where the salt flats are now—roughly 16,000 years ago.

The Central Pacific bypassed this area by 30 miles to the north in the late 1860s, but the Western Pacific pushed a railroad across the salt flats in the early 1900s. Wendover was founded to supply water to the railroad (piped in from Pilot Peak springs, 25 miles west), the only stop with water on the main line for 100 miles.

In 1914, the anonymity of this sleepy railroad village, with its roundhouse, saloon, and railroad-tie cabins, was lost forever. Speedsters discovered the advantageous features of the flats; one Teddy Tezlaff set the first land-speed record driving a Blitzen Benz just under 142 miles an hour and put Wendover in the media and on the map.

Highway 40 arrived in the mid-1920s, the start of Wendover's destiny as a travelers' oasis. William F. Smith, a young entrepreneur, opened a gas station and garage to service the border traffic, and over the next several years added a cafe and bungalows. In 1931 the state issued him one of the first gambling licenses, which has been in the family ever since; today his son, Jim Smith, holds the license.

Wendover Air Force Base was created in 1940. At 3.5 million acres, it was one of the largest in the world. Pilots, navigators, and bombardiers learned their skills over this range, and the crew of the *Enola Gay,* which dropped one atom bomb on Japan, trained here.

Potash (potassium chloride) has been mined from the flats over the years for use as fertilizer; magnesium chloride, a by-product of potash processing, is used in refining sugar beets. And speed freaks have kept coming back with hotter and faster wheels. Jet cars such as the *Meteor, Green Monster,* and Craig Breedlove's famous *Spirit of America* set and reset records; Breedlove was the first to break the 600-mph mark. (The first jet car, the *Flying Caduceus,* is on display at the National Automobile Museum in Reno.) Gary Gabolich's *Blue Flame* set a record in 1970 of 622 mph, which held for 14 years, until Richard Noble broke it on the Black Rock Desert. Weather permitting, racing takes place every year for a week in August and a week in September (see below).

Today, Wendover, like Jackpot, is a booming border town. Straddling the Utah state line, Wendover's backyard is a shimmering, carbon-arc-white expanse of earth, so white that even in the summer's scorching heat, the surface remains cool. Another weirdness is that the heat waves and blinding silver reflection do strange things to radio and TV signals. Another: the bases of telephone poles on the flats become permeated with salt water; when the water evaporates, the salt crystals expand, swelling and splitting the poles. Fierce thunderstorms are caused by the rising heat, but then everything dries and brightens in a matter of minutes. Against such a backdrop, the big hotels, bright lights, and Wendover Will are as inviting to modern-day travelers as Pilot Peak, on the western horizon, ever was to the pioneers of the past.

SIGHTS

Welcome Center

Exit I-80 in central Wendover and take a left. The **Nevada Welcome Center** is near the corner of Wendover Blvd. and US 93 across from the Peppermill, 775/664-3414, open 9 A.M.–5 P.M. five days a week (days changeable), wendovercc@lnet.com, www.wendover.org. Outside is a **peace memorial** to the 509th Composite Group, dedicated in April 1990. Inside is a whole wall devoted to the 509th, a group of nearly 2,000 military personnel at Wendover Air Force Base involved in top-secret preparations for delivering the bomb to Japan, with Paul Tibbets as pilot and commanding officer. Other exhibits cover the speed records and races, discuss desert wildlife, and display statewide tourist information. Since this center opened in early 1990, Wendover has boasted three welcome mats for travelers: Pilot Peak, courtesy of Mother Nature, this center, courtesy of the Commission on Tourism, and Wendover Will, courtesy of YESCO and the Smith family.

Museum

The white state line is painted across Wendover Blvd. between the Stateline and Silver Smith; Wendover Will points at it with two moving arms. As in South Lake Tahoe, the big hotels are on the Nevada side, and the low-rise services line the main street of the state next door (Utah). On the east side of town is the **Bonneville Speedway Museum,** 801/665-7721, open daily 10 A.M.–6 P.M. between June 1 and September 15, weekends 10 A.M.–6 P.M. the rest of the year; $2. This museum has a collection of antique vehicles, from an 1870 carriage to a 1963 Silver Cloud. Extensive photos, captions, trophies and newspaper clippings document the races, racers, and racing cars—Golden Rod, Blue Flame, Green Monster, and Mormon Meteor, to name a few. Hood ornaments, pianos, dolls, and antique cash registers round out the exhibits.

Speedway

To drive on the **salt flats,** take I-80 into Utah, get off at Exit 4, then head five miles northeast. Obey the signs carefully if you don't fancy digging your wheels out of the mud or walking out for a tow truck, and watch for jet cars whizzing around at 500 mph.

Three weeks of official races are held on the flats. **Speed Week** has occupied the third week in August since 1948; 350 cars and motorcycles participate. **World of Speed** is a month later, with 100 cars and bikes. The **Bonneville Salt Flats World Finals,** held in October, is when the really fast cars come out. The race course has to be prepared from scratch every year, as "temporary Lake Bonneville" inundates the flats with six inches of water from November to May. The water's movement levels the desert, and a landplane scrapes the surface (clearing an area 80 feet wide, 10 miles long, between black spray-painted lines). This leveling of irregularities is important, I'm told, for vehicles traveling 350 mph or so on the ground.

The whole speedway encompasses 28 square miles: 3,700 feet wide and 13 miles long, of which about half is normally used in speed trials. The speedway is managed by BLM, which works closely with the Utah Salt Flats Racing Assn. (801/785-5364) and Southern California Timing Assn. (714/783-8293).

Airport

Heading west back into Nevada, take a left onto 1st St. (the last street in Utah) and cross the tracks. Bear left at the fork and head for the old tower, hangars, big buildings, and huge runway. The Air Force sold the airport to Tooele County in 1977 for $1, giving little Wendover the most amazing small-town airport anywhere: 3.5 miles of concrete runway, plus a third of a million square yards of concrete parking apron. Drag races are held at the airport in summer.

Casinos

Start where it all started in Wendover, at the Smith properties right at the state line. The **Stateline** casino, 775/664-2221, is Wendover Will's joint. This hotel not only has everything, it's all in very fine taste, as well: three crap and roulette tables, two dozen blackjack tables, a comfortable and classy sports book (downstairs), couple of snack bars, dinner buffet and weekend brunch, gourmet restaurant, and a big lounge. The Stateline did a $60 million expansion, adding 241 rooms, restaurants, an atrium, and additional gambling space.

The grand reopening was in September 1997.

Take the spiral staircase behind the front desk to the walkway over Wendover Blvd.—nice view. The **Silver Smith,** Stateline's sister hotel, 775/664-2231, is in the same classy vein. The casino is a casino is a casino. A small showroom puts on headliners and mini-revues, and there are also a snack bar, deli, and dinner buffet and weekend brunch.

The exterior of the **Peppermill,** 775/664-2255, is understated and pleasing; inside is the largest casino in Wendover. It has 1,000 slots and a single-zero roulette wheel. It also has the same red-and-blue-neon, silk-flower decor that it's famous for. The Cabaret bar is similar to the Reno Peppermill: high stage above the bar, video poker within and along the perimeter, even a dance floor. In 2000 the Peppermill was planning to enlarge, and construction was underway.

The Peppermill bought Mac's Casino in the mid-'90s and transformed it into the **Rainbow,** 775/664-4000, a scaled-down version of the Peppermill in Reno with a rain forest motif and lots of neon. The Rainbow has 1,000 slots, 20 tables for blackjack and craps, a restaurant and buffet. Two new towers give it a total of 298 hotel rooms.

The **Red Garter,** 775/664-2111, has expanded: the old part of the casino is still dark, small, and usually jammed with people having a good time; the new wing is big, bright, and airy, with a bunch of slots, a snack bar and real bar. The casino has a 106-room hotel; a hallway leads to the Super 8 motel desk.

PRACTICALITIES

Note that Wendover is on Mountain Time; move your watches ahead one hour.

Accommodations

Wendover has more than 1,500 hotel and motel rooms, and there are another 540 on the Utah side to accommodate the overflow (Motel 6, Western, Bonneville, Heritage, Salt Flat Inn, and Days Inn). The big show is between the **Stateline** and the **Silver Smith,** 100 Wendover Blvd., 775/664-2221 or 800/848-7300, with 740 upscale hotel rooms between them, for $29–175. **Nevada Crossing,** 1035 Wendover Blvd., 775/664-2900 or 800/537-0207, has another 137

rooms at $29–95. At the **Peppermill,** 680 Wendover Blvd., 775/664-2255 or 800/648-9660, rooms go for $26–200. And then there's the **Super 8 Motel,** 1325 Wendover Blvd., 775/664-2888 or 800/800-8000, with 74 rooms for $30–80.

Wendover KOA Campground, is just south of the Red Garter at 651 N. Camper Drive, 775/664-3221; take exit 410 off Interstate 80 to Wendover Blvd., then turn right and go approximately a half mile to Camper Drive and turn left. This big bustling RV park is on the southern edge of town, between the back doors of the Red Garter casino and the front doors of the desert. The handy casino shuttle will pick you up and drop you off. It's the only place in town to pitch a tent. Proprietor Mike Cappa also has seven cabins for rent, each sleeping four people, for $29; one larger cabin sleeping six costs $39. There are 140 spaces for motor homes, 72 with full hookups and 85 pull-throughs. Tents are allowed and showers are for sale to non-campers for $5. Mini-mart and gift shop, heated swimming pool, playground, tetherball, volleyball, basketball, horseshoes, miniature golf course, rec room with slot machines and video games, meeting room, and bike rentals are available. Reservations are recommended, especially for the cabins. Camping fees are $17–21 for RVs, $16 for tents. Good Sam and KOA discounts.

The other RV park in Wendover is **Stateline RV Park,** 775/664-2221. This RV park, though in Utah, is connected to the Stateline casinos, just on the other side of the parking terrace. The park is graveled and has a few small trees. Overnighters get the use of the hotel's heated swimming pool and two tennis courts. Campers also are provided with the casino funbook and a discount coupon for the Wendover Golf Course. There are 56 spaces for motor homes, all 56 with full hookups; no pull-throughs. Tents are not allowed. Reservations are recommended. The fee is $17–19 per vehicle (10% Good Sam discount). To get there, take exit 410 off Interstate 80, go left and drive a mile on Wendover Boulevard. Just across the Utah state line, go right on 1st Street and continue for one block.

Food

The **Stateline, Peppermill, Rainbow,** and **Red Garter** all have 24-hour coffee shops. The breakfast special at **Nevada Crossing** is best: $1.99

for two eggs, bacon, and hash browns, served 24 hours (a holdover from its truck-stop bygone days).

Wendover is a snack bar kind of town. All five major casinos have at least one snack bar, and they're all good and cheap. The one in the sports book downstairs at the Stateline is the most comfortable.

The **Peppermill** has three buffet meals a day, while the **Stateline** and **Silver Smith** both have a dinner nightly and weekend brunches. The Rainbow casino has the new **Rainforest Buffet.**

The Stateline offers fine dining in the **Salt Cellar,** open Sunday and Tues.–Thurs. 6–11 P.M., Friday and Saturday till 11, closed Monday. Appetizers include delicious king-crab quesadillas and mussels; entrees include linguini, prime rib, salmon, veal, lobster fettucine, venison medallions, and steaks.

Over the Rainbow at the Rainbow also is open 24 hours, with a daily breakfast special. Dinner starts at $8 and climbs to $19 for steak and lobster. There's a good selection of dinner pasta dishes.

In the Crossroads Shopping Center at the west end of town is **Chinatown Restaurant,** 775/664-3262, open daily 11 A.M.–11 P.M., serving typical Chinese-American specials and family dinners.

Information

For details on the **Welcome Center,** the place for touring info about the area and the state, see "Sights," above.

Wendover Library, the coolest and quietest oasis in town, is across from KOA on Camper Dr., open Mon.–Wed. noon–6 P.M., Thursday and Friday noon–5 P.M., Tuesday 1–5 P.M. and 6–8 P.M. Nice mineral display, good water fountain, and you'll find the *Salt and Speed* booklet prepared by University of Utah's Jesse Jennings.

TO ELY

Alternate 93 runs 60 miles south to where it rejoins Main 93. Just south of town, the Utah Air Force testing range must have a bunch of unexploded ordnance that could go off with just a little vibration or contact, which would explain the Danger Zone signs on the barbed-wire fence every 100 feet along the road for miles.

About 15 miles south of town is the turnoff for **Blue Lakes,** frequented by local scuba divers. You can see the lakes from the highway; they look a mile away, but after five miles of the very rough (20–25 mph) dirt road, they still look a mile away. In three more miles, they're still another mile. You might make it all the way in a low-clearance vehicle, but I didn't. Got stuck in a wash, had to shovel and struggle and sweat for a while. One of those cases where the eyes are bigger than the tires.

You travel over **White Horse Pass** (6,550 feet), right through the middle of the White Horse Range, part of the **Goshute Mountains,** then cross **Antelope Valley,** heading toward the **Antelope Range.** After climbing them, you drop down into **Steptoe Valley,** a straight shot south between the **Schell Creek** (east) and **Cherry Creek** (west) ranges; the latter drops off, and then the **Egan Range** starts up. You're coming into Pony Express country here, and cross the trail (signposted).

At **Schellbourne** is a bar, cafe, and motel; a rest area across the road has a Pony Express trail marker, and a historical sign commemorating this junction. From here it's another 40 miles in a straight line due south to Ely.

CENTRAL NEVADA

INTRODUCTION

Covered Wagons to Volkswagens
In the early 1920s, the US 50-Lincoln Highway Association was actively competing against the US 40-Victory Highway Association for automobile traffic across Nevada. The northern Victory Highway had the edge: it was the first and always the more popular route for travelers, after Peter Skene Ogden and Joseph Walker pioneered it in the 1820s and '30s. It came to be known as the Emigrant or Humboldt Trail, and was used by the vast majority of pioneers who crossed Nevada in the 1840s and '50s. The central route, however, had its advocates. Jedediah Smith had blundered across it in 1827, almost dying of thirst, on one of the bravest and most desperate explorations of the American West. After Smith's horror march, however, it was nearly 30 years before a trail was surveyed through central Nevada by Howard Egan, then mapped by Captain James Simpson four years later, in

1859. The Overland Stage, Pony Express, and transcontinental telegraph all used the shorter central route. But the Central Pacific Railroad opted for the Humboldt Trail, which put an end, as early as 1870, to passage through the central state on long-distance public transportation.

Rough wagon ruts were developed between the major towns along both trails, but when the newfangled horseless carriage necessitated actual roads and when the new breed of automobile adventure traveler began to go *distances* on them, constructing statewide highways was an idea whose time had come.

Immediately, every town wanted a highway. Savvy promoters began publicizing routes through *their* towns, whether or not the road to and from was maintained, had services, or even provided the most direct line from the last town to the next. Soon, individual boosters formed associations with neighboring towns and counties. These routes, in pre-road-map days, still often followed three points on a square to get from the first to the fourth. Finally, government sur-

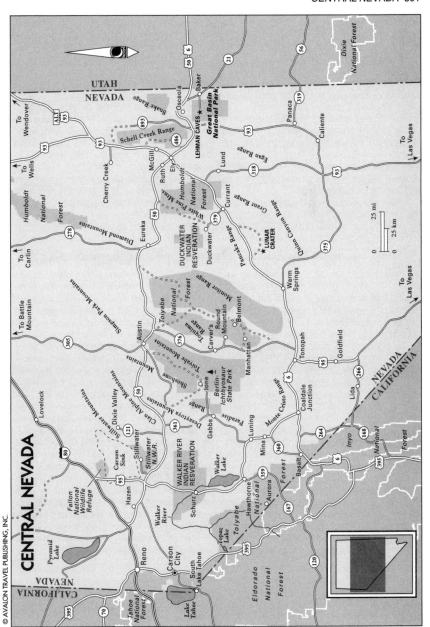

© AVALON TRAVEL PUBLISHING, INC.

CENTRAL NEVADA

veyors stepped in and brought some order and logic to the routes. Like the railroads before them, the highways made or broke the fortunes of many small towns in Nevada.

Defense Highway

The Victory Highway (US 40) followed the tortuous river route through northern Nevada, 400-odd miles between Utah and California, by way of Elko, Winnemucca, and Reno. The Lincoln Highway (US 50) followed the telegraph through central Nevada 370 miles by way of Ely, Eureka, Austin, Fallon, and Lake Tahoe. The competition between the two was sometimes good-natured and sometimes heavy-handed.

In the early years of long-distance auto travel, the Lincoln Highway held its own against the Victory Highway. In June 1931, a one-day traffic count at the junction of the two roads in Fernley revealed 181 cars turning onto the central route and 141 cars taking the northern route. But then the battle heated up: the Victory Highway Association installed signs designating its road the "Main Line" across Nevada, and the Lincoln Highway Association set up shop at Jim Smith's gas station in Wendover to try to divert westbound traffic to the central route.

The signs proved more successful than the service station; a traffic count in 1939 at Wendover showed that of nearly 3,000 cars, a few more than 700 turned south, while the rest continued on US 40 west across northern Nevada. More significant, of 2,000 cars with out-of-state license plates, only 500 headed for the central route. A year later, US 40 was designated a national defense highway, which gave it priority over other roads in the state in terms of expenditures for improvements.

The Lincoln Highway Association now realized it couldn't beat 'em, so it joined forces with the victorious Victoryites, along with Utah and Wyoming road associations, to promote the central route across the U.S. West, as opposed to the southern route (New Mexico and Arizona) and the northern route (Montana and Idaho).

Eventually, the multistate organization expanded into Nebraska, Iowa, and California, and named the lengthening route the "49er Trail." The interstate highways' time had come.

The Interstate System

The Highway Act of 1956 called for the improvement of the national defense highways and construction of connecting interstates for a total of 41,000 miles of transcontinental superhighways. Interstate 80 was designed to follow the US 40 route across the 49er Trail. That introduced a new form of competition, now among the half-dozen or so towns along the new highway in northern Nevada; each town promoted itself as the best service stop for the high-speed tourists and travelers.

It took more than 25 years for I-80 to be completed through Nevada while, in the meantime, US 50 traffic continued to decline. In 1983, the last stretch of superhighway was completed, finally bypassing Lovelock. Only three years later the old Lincoln Highway's fortunes had plummeted to the point where Eastern writers and editors were calling it the country's loneliest road.

The completion of I-80 and the dubious publicity might've set back a lesser foe. Indeed, the story goes that *Life* magazine ran an article admonishing travelers as to the lack of services on US 50 through Nevada, suggesting they avoid the road entirely. (However, a reader several years ago did some extensive research, and found that the article didn't appear in *Life* at all, but in *Trailer Life!*) Wherever it appeared, the article inspired a lighthearted and extremely successful advertising campaign by the Nevada Commission on Tourism. Far from being apologetic about it, the state publicists actually celebrated US 50's remoteness, challenging adventuresome drivers to get off the beaten interstate and *rejoice* in the loneliness. The magazine editors hadn't planned it, but they had given an unwitting shot in the arm to the 65-year-old traffic competition between the central and the northern routes across Nevada.

ELY

INTRODUCTION

Explorers Jedediah Smith and Howard Egan, mapmaker James Simpson, the Pony Express, and the transcontinental telegraph all passed through this neighborhood between 1827 and 1861. In 1863, small-scale gold and silver mining began in the Egan Range, while it was still part of Utah Territory. In 1866 Nevada's eastern boundary was moved one degree east, which incorporated the Egan District. A year later, Treasure Hill on Mt. Hamilton created a stir, attracting the "requisite 10,000" (more likely half of that) boomers. When White Pine County was carved out of vast Lander County in 1869, Hamilton became the county seat. *Borrasca,* the final bust, came to Treasure Hill in 1878. Hamilton's courthouse burned in 1885. And the county seat transferred to Ely in 1887.

Copper Copping

Ely had been settled for 15 years or so around small gold mines in the canyons west of the village. It boasted a stagecoach station, a post office, a few supply houses for the local ranchers, and mills for the nearby mines. Becoming the county seat fully doubled the population—to 160 people.

It had long been known that major copper deposits were there for the taking, but the task, especially during Nevada's Twenty-year Depression (1880–1900), remained too unwieldy. Gold and silver could be mined and refined with hand tools and small machines and hauled away in the form of valuable bullion on mule trains. But copper meant *tonnage:* every 60 pounds of raw copper required dumping 25,000 pounds of tailings and smelting 6,000 pounds of ore and was worth roughly $10. Only big bucks could buy and bring in the giant equipment required for mining, crushing, smelting, and shipping the astronomical quantities of paydirt, ore, and refined copper.

Typically, however, it was a couple of little guys who got the ball rolling. David Bartley and Edwin Gray, copper miners from California, ap-peared in September 1900, secured a grubstake, and started digging into a hill in the Egan Range just up from Copper Flat. They went 300 feet in and 200 feet down and discovered the richness and vastness of the deposit.

In 1902 Mark Requa, son of renowned Comstock superintendent and Eureka railroad builder Isaac Requa, took a $150,000 option on the claim, raised money from Eastern financiers, and by 1904 had organized the Nevada Consolidated Copper Company. Requa laid out a townsite east of Ely, calling it (naturally enough) East Ely where he planned to build the big copper smelter. He also surveyed a railroad, Nevada Northern, from East Ely to the mine, growing deeper six miles northwest, as well as from East Ely 90 miles north to the Southern Pacific main line at Cobre (Spanish for "Copper"), 30 miles east of Wells. He even managed to refine the first copper ore. By 1906, however, Requa had been bought out by the eastern investors. Within two years the original mine had been opened into a pit and the immense smelter had been located at McGill, 12 miles north of Ely, instead of at East Ely, much to the chagrin of local land speculators and developers. The Nevada Northern Railroad operation, however, remained based in East Ely, and track connected it with the pit at Ruth, the smelter at McGill, and the main line at Cobre.

A Billion, Then *Borrasca*

Thus began Nevada's longest-lived and most prolific mineral venture, lasting a full 70 years. In 1909 six million dollars' worth of copper left White Pine County; by 1926, profits from the operation were recorded at nearly $50 million. Meanwhile, Utah's Kennecott Corporation had taken over production, and the pits kept growing. The granddad Liberty Pit expanded to more than a mile long, half a mile wide, and 700 feet deep. The dizzying descent to the bottom eventually required 14 miles of track. In 1940, the WPA *Guide to Nevada* predicted that the "copper supply can be mined profitably for another 50 years." In the mid-1960s the mine hit the billion-dollar milestone. But the ore started to thin, profits began to sag, and new pollution regulations finally shut

HWY. 50 VS. HWY. 93: LONELY VS. EXISTENTIAL

US Highway 50 may be "the loneliest road in America," but loneliness, by definition, can only be felt in relation to other people. You might feel a bit forlorn on US 50, as cars from the other direction whiz by occasionally and as you pass or are passed by another car in your lane every so often. However, since US 50 is an east-west road, the scenery provides plenty of company as you cross a dozen mountain ranges and valleys, several quite imposing. Ely, Eureka, and Austin are perfectly spaced, an hour apart, for services and the human connection. And though it's a major haul from Austin to Fallon, the desert is so vast and the sky so boundless that it's as easy to become part of it, and expand into it, as it is to disregard it and contract into yourself. It's really a matter of choice. Wanna be lonely? Fine. But the road certainly doesn't require it of you.

But if US 50 can be lonely, then US 93, the other long road through central Nevada, can catalyze a deep existential aloneness. Since US 93 is north-south road, you drive through seemingly endless straight valleys, with the same few mountain ranges hemming you in for a hundred miles at a stretch like some sort of police escort. Wells, Ely, and Caliente are a long two hours apart, and talk about deserted! You can drive for hours at a time and not see another car on either side of the road. No choice there. You really are on your own. And after you've traversed the nearly 500 miles from

Jackpot, even if your sanity is still intact, you're dumped right into the heart of psychedelic and mind-altering Las Vegas. US 50 gets the ink, has the history, and is a fine and dandy alternative to the mile-blurring impersonality of I-80. But for that bittersweet cosmic abandonment, it doesn't hold a candle to US 93.

---

the mine down in 1979. The WPA guide was only off by 10 optimistic years.

The smelter closed a couple of years later, and the railroad ceased operation for good in 1982. Ely's population, which had peaked in the late '50s at 12,000, dropped by the mid-'80s to just over 7,000. Unemployment in the county reached a depressed 25%.

Recovery

But in 1986, local politicians, the Chamber of Commerce, and the newly formed White Pine

Historical Railroad Foundation convinced Kennecott to donate the railroad property and equipment to the town; the trains have been running and the yard has been a museum since 1987. In addition, Great Basin National Park was created 70 miles east, and a new state prison was built just outside of town. A few gold and silver mines are operating in the area. Los Angeles Power and Water influence extends all the way out here; it owns the main line from Cobre to McGill, which it plans to use to deliver coal to the White Pine Power Project, a 1,500-megawatt power plant near Cherry Creek, 45 miles north of Ely.

A big new copper mine, BHP Mining, created an economic boom when it opened here in 1996; when it closed in 1999, it created somewhat of an economic bust. Today, Ely has a population of around 4,500 souls.

Ely has certainly benefited from the US 50 Loneliest Road campaign. But this town is much more than merely a stop on an old 3,000-mile highway (from just west of Washington, D.C. to Sacramento), 10% of which crosses Nevada. Intersecting US 50 here is another east-west highway, US 6, as well as the north-south US 93, one of the longest roads in the Americas. Its route through eastern Nevada, more than 500 miles from Jackpot to Boulder City, seems to have as much claim on Ely as US 50. Indeed, there's so much to do in and around Ely—copper pits, working railroad museum, Kennecott company town (McGill), Cave Lake State Park and

Duck Valley, charcoal ovens, the Schell Creeks, Lehman Caves, and Great Basin National Park—that this is not a place just to pass through on any road. Here is one of Nevada's preeminent destinations all by itself.

SIGHTS

Orientation

Ely has the most road numbers per highway sign in Nevada. US 6 and US 50 run together from the Utah border 75 miles east through town, where US 6 cuts southwest (to Tonopah) and US 50 continues west (to Eureka). From the south, US 93 joins up with 6 and 50 just before Connors Summit over the Schell Creeks, and all three routes run together till the big intersection in East Ely. You might want to study a map, then drive around town a bit to get your bearings

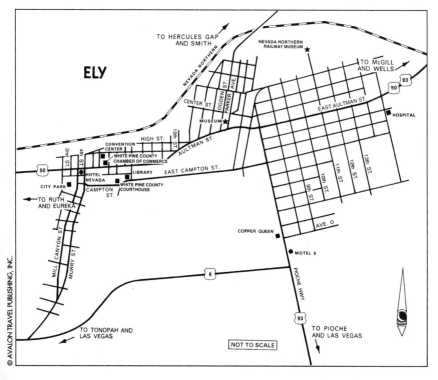

© AVALON TRAVEL PUBLISHING, INC.

and sense of direction.

If so, start out on the west side, driving south of downtown on Murry St. through pretty Murry Canyon, site of Ely's original settlement. US 6 intersects at the top of the hill, from where you can drive east (left) to US 93, then north back into town. Or just return on Mill St., one over from Murry. Then take a right (east) on Aultman (US 50 West) and cruise through the 1880s' townsite. The central square is a nice place to relax and watch Ely go by: little duck pond and fountain, big trees in the park, and the students coming and going from White Pine Middle School, built in 1913, right across Aultman.

Continue to the intersection with 6/50 East and 93 South. Here, Aultman turns into East Aultman, in East Ely on the townsite laid out by Mark Requa for the smelter and railroad in 1906. The depot is at the top of 11th, at A Street.

Be sure to take a drive around downtown Ely on Aultman St to see the murals in Ely's downtown mural project. By autumn 2000, five murals had been completed, and there may be more, by the time you are reading this book.

Finish up your driving tour by heading north on Ogden St. at White Pine County Museum, through the 'burbs, and out into the west side of Steptoe Valley in back of town. In three miles the pavement ends, and two miles from there is **Hercules Gap,** a natural passage through the Egan Range between Steptoe and Smith valleys. Two miles north of the gash is a state maximum-security penitentiary, opened in 1989, which has a national reputation for the degree to which it educates its inmates.

In Town

The White Pine County **Chamber of Commerce,** 636 Aultman, Ely, NV 89301, 775/289-8877, www.elynevada.net, open Mon.–Fri. 8 A.M.–5 P.M., stocks an abundance of brochures, visitor's guides, maps, and answers to questions. Go around the corner to the **Bristlecone Convention Center,** 150 6th St., 775/289-3720, where there's a framed display of the cross section of a bristlecone pine. The 4,900-year-old tree, "Prometheus," was cut down by the National Forest Service and the bark dated in 1964; recorded history is traced through the rings all the way back to 1450 B.C., when Moses led the exodus out of Egypt, and beyond to 3000 B.C.,

when the pharoahs built the pyramids. The whole story of Prometheus, which when cut down was determined to have been the oldest living creature on the planet, is recounted in Jim Sloan's excellent *Nevada—True Tales from the Neon Wilderness* (see "Booklist").

White Pine County Public Museum is at 2000 Aultman, almost to East Ely, 775/289-4710, open weekdays 9 A.M.–3 P.M., weekends 10 A.M.–2 P.M., donation. Opened in 1959, this is an eclectic and fun museum. Outside is Nevada Northern rolling stock, along with the original Cherry Creek depot, which was transported to the museum in 1991 and is slowly being restored. Inside is crowded with an array of items—everything from a petrified dinosaur footprint to an 1891 bicycle. Highlights include a big map of the county with corresponding black-and-white photographs, 1917 xylophone, mine-timbering model, 1876 cannon from Taylor, and a beautiful display of wood artistry—bowls, boxes, candle holders—by a late Elyan, A. Earl Preston. Study the schematic of the Ruth copper mine—what a pit! The museum displays a large collection of dolls, more than 300 types of minerals, early 20th-century furniture, and much more. A great introduction to Ely, you can also pick up maps and brochures here, plus buy postcards, souvenirs, and books.

Also check out the gallery of historical black-and-white prints in the hallway between the **Jailhouse** casino and restaurant. Some great shots of Riepetown, Cherry Creek, and Hamilton, plus an interesting retrospective series on William Curto: eight frames of the evolution of his drayage company between 1912 and 1972. Curto lived to be 99 years old.

Casinos

The main action in Ely is at the corner of Aultman and 5th. The **Hotel Nevada** dates from the early 1920s, and was once the tallest building in the state. Sit down at one of four blackjack tables or nourish the hungry slots with your pocket change. The bar is especially lively at times.

Across the street, the **Jailhouse** is all machines; the restaurant here (see the Food section, further along) is highly unusual and worth a look. Up the block is the **Collins Court.** It opened in the spring of 1992 and shut down not long thereafter, the owners bailing out the back door at midnight.

Out on the Pioche Hwy., the **Copper Queen** has slots, both vertical and horizontal, but no table games. It's the only casino in the state that shares a room with the motel pool. Chlorine Queen. There's no craps in Ely. In fact, there isn't a crap game for nearly 500 miles in eastern Nevada between Jackpot and Las Vegas on US 93 (Wendover is on *Alt.* 93 and Mesquite is on I-15).

The **Holiday Inn Prospector** opened out on the Pioche Hwy. in 1995 with 50 slots in the lobby and a cafe.

NEVADA NORTHERN RAILWAY

Museum

This "museum" encompasses the entire Nevada Northern railyard, 1100 Ave. A in East Ely (P.O. Box 150040, East Ely, NV 89315), 775/289-2085, www.nevadanorthernrailway.net. The tour, one of the most thrilling in the state, takes you through the most complete and authentic working remains of any short line railroad in the country, if not the world. And then you get to ride on it!

When the Nevada Northern suspended operations in 1982, the company and workers at first thought it was temporary; layoffs had happened several times before. So they just left everything the way it was, figuring it would start up again, sooner or later. After three years, though, the workers received their severance

*1910 Baldwin steam engine (old No. 40)—
Ghost Train of Ely*

checks, which made it final. Yet all the equipment still sat there like the day they'd walked away from it. By then the townspeople had started to come out of the shock of the loss and began a campaign to take over the operation.

Kennecott was prevailed upon to donate the depot, administration and dispatch office buildings, freight warehouse, yard, and even the 1910 Baldwin steam engine (Old No. 40). Later it also threw in 32 miles of usable track, all the machine shops, roundhouse, rolling stock, McGill depot, and the buildings along the entire Cobre route. The whole donation has been conservatively estimated at $45 million. Altogether there are over 30 buildings here from the 1906–1907 era, including an old water tower and sand and coal bins.

The museum is open from mid-May to mid-September. Hours are Mon.–Fri. 8 A.M.–4:30 P.M., Saturday and Sunday. 9 A.M. to 7 P.M. Tours are given at 11 A.M. and 2 P.M., Wednesday to Sunday, and cost $3 for everyone ages five and up. You start out at the old depot, built in 1907 for $12,000 with local sandstone (from Currie). Check out the ticket office and big historical black-and-white photos. The depot is actually separate from the rest of the museum. It's state owned and operated, and so far has received $100,000 worth of restoration; another $180,000 will complete the job of restoring the depot to its original 1907 appearance. Sean Pitts, late of the White Pine Public Museum, is the curator.

From the depot you walk by the freight barn (oldest building in the complex, dating from 1905), past the bus barn and master mechanics offices, and then into the engine house, where most of the equipment is stored: locomotives, cabooses, a passenger coach, a rotary steam-driven snowplow, a steam crane, and track-repair cars. Next stop is the rip-track building, or car-repair shop. Here is the home of the 1910 Baldwin steamer (Ghost Train, or Old No. 40). This steam engine was restored in 1939 and almost immediately retired after Nevada Northern passenger service was discontinued, having transported nearly five million people over a 35-year period. It was as good as new, but the steamer was mothballed in the coach shop and not used for 45 years (except when brought out for special occasions), till it was resurrected in 1985 for the tourist train rides. Your guide helps you up into the cab and explains the valves, gauges, faucets, pipes, boiler, and controls with which the engineer and fireman get the danged thing stoked and rolling. Behind the Ghost Train are a converted flatcar, a Pullman sleeper, and a passenger car (used for the food concession).

Finally, you wind up in the transportation building, which has a small gift shop. By now you're itching to fire up a train and light out for the territory.

The Rides
At this writing, nearly every Saturday and every other Sunday between mid-May and mid-September, the No. 40 and the No. 93 (restored in 1993) steam engines or the diesel No. 109 pull passengers on the Keystone and Hiline routes. The Hiline diesel was brought out for a trip to McGill 11 miles north every other Saturday from May 24 until August 30 in 1997. (Schedules may change from year to year, so call ahead.) The Keystone ride parallels Aultman Street a bit up the hill, for a great view of downtown and Ely's red-light district. Then it parallels US 50 through Robinson Canyon and passes through Tunnel No. 1, blasted out in 1907. The canyon broadens into Lane Valley, where the train goes by the Lane City ghost town, site of the original strike in 1869. The steamer then runs up to the copper-tailing mountains just this side of Ruth, then turns around. The 14-mile roundtrip takes 90 minutes and uses a ton of coal and 1,000 gallons of water.

The Hiline trip is a relaxing ride as the train rocks gently to and fro on its trip north toward McGill along a low eastern rise of the Duck Creek Range above Steptoe Valley. The locomotive switches from the front to the back of the train, then pushes the passenger cars ahead of it till the end of the track just before McGill—stand at the front of the open car in front of the train at this time!

Each of these train rides takes approximately two hours. Tickets cost $16 for adults for the steamers only ($14 seniors, $12 ages 6 to 18, free for kids under 6 years), $12 (seniors $10, kids $8) for the diesel only, and $18 for both (seniors $16, kids $8). A snack bar in the last car sells drinks and munchies. The museum also offers a variety of special event train rides, including a 4th of July Fireworks and Barbecue

Train, Sunset at Steptoe, and Ely After Dark; call for current information, schedule and prices. Advance reservations are required.

You can also charter the equipment for special runs. You can even rent the engines by the hour and receive instruction on driving the damn things. Advance reservations are definitely required, and you must do it on days of operation. Call or write for schedules and reservations.

The gift shop is in the transportation building, open 8:30 A.M.–4:30 P.M. weekdays, museum hours on weekends. It sells mostly T-shirts, railroad books, videos, and odds and ends, and munchies for the train trips.

Finally, you can join **The Nevada Northern Endowment** and help preserve and restore this unique piece of history by becoming a member of the White Pine Historical Railroad Foundation; write P.O. Box 150040, East Ely, NV 89315, or call 775/289-2085.

VICINITY OF ELY

Ruth
Head out US 50 west through downtown and into Robinson Canyon; shortly you see the mountains of overburden (tailings) from the copper pits. This was the site of one of BHP Mining's copper pits, which is no longer operating. In a few miles take a left at Keystone Junction, between more mountains of waste, then another left into the little settlement of Ruth. Go a mile, then turn hard right onto the partially paved road and climb up and over the pit past Silver King mine—a real moonscape up here. BHP has installed historical black and whites and rock samples around the overview, complete with descriptions and explanations.

Continue another mile for the Old Ruth town site. Above the town is a NASA tracking station on the slopes of Kimberly Mountain. In another couple of miles is the intersection with US 6; take a left and head back to town.

You can look at such massive lacerations in the Earth in several different ways. Certainly the ore from these pits supplied thousands of tons of copper and supported several communities for three or four generations. Certainly it's a big blight of a hole, surrounded by mountains of waste that will take hundreds, if not thousands, of

a busy day at the Liberty Pit at Ruth

WHITE PINE HISTORICAL SOCIETY

years, if ever, to regenerate and blend in a natural way into the landscape. But look at it from that kind of long-range perspective for a little lesson in geology at work.

These mountains were formed by miners, a trainload or truckload at a time, which is something of a fast-forward unnatural "uplifting." The "ranges" were formed so recently that you can just start to see the effects of water, wind, and sun on shaping them. Water running down the steep smooth slopes digs channels that eventually become canyons. The silt and sand wash down to eventually fill the "basins" at the bottom. Plants begin to grow. In some places the heat and chemicals combine to petrify the sand into sandstone, and in time erosion might contour the geology into a geography not unlike, for example, Cathedral Gorge.

Certainly this area is not "pretty" now; neither was Cathedral Gorge a million years ago when it was just the swampy remains of an exposed lake bed. But if you view the Ruth overburden as geological process rather than static scenery, you can come away with an entirely different aesthetic.

Garnet Hill

At the intersection of US 50 and NV 485 to Ruth is a historical sign (etched in stone) commemorating the copper mines' billion-dollar milestone in 1964, Nevada's centennial year as a state. Just beyond the sign on the right is a turnoff onto a rough gravel road (15 mph) up to Garnet Hill. Follow the road up the hill for at most a half

mile, or even park on the highway and walk up to save wear and tear on your ride. You'll see faint trails up the canyon; at the peak you can start your search. Try hounding light-colored soil for the reddish crystals, or break up the pink rhyolite to expose these deep-red manganese-aluminum garnets. Note that this has been a popular hound hill for years, so you might wind up enjoying only the exercise, the fresh air, and the view.

McGill

East Ely was supposed to be the site of the big smelter and the central company city for the copper country. For a couple of years promoters, developers, and real-estate speculators did their best to bring it about. But land prices quickly skyrocketed out of reach and company officials clashed with Ely residents over water rights from Murry Canyon. So the smelter was built on a bluff on the Duck Creek Range's east slope overlooking the McGill ranch, 15 miles north of Ely. The miners already lived at settlements (Ruth and Kimberly) near the big pits. So the Nevada Consolidated Copper Company decided to build the company town below the smelter instead of in East Ely, which was left with only the railroad.

McGill, the ultimate orderly town, by 1910 had 2,000 residents. Nevada Con owned everything, controlled everything, and supplied everything, extending what appeared to be unlimited credit. This worked both ways: employees had to work to pay back the company, and the company had to keep them working to collect. Steam from the smelter was piped through the houses for heat. Company officials lived in big houses in the Circle on the hill just below the smelter. Workers were housed along ethnic lines—Greektown, Japtown, Austriatown—and discrimination was policy. The inevitable Ragtown, two miles north, with saloons, dance halls, and brothels, was tolerated for only a few years, then shut down by the company in 1915. The jail, symbolically, was next to the saloon. A big rec hall was built and a swimming hole was surrounded by a park. Workers' children could take jobs as soon as they became teenagers. For 70 years, McGill existed for the company and the copper.

Then the mines shut down. The smelter operated for a few more years, working on ore from other places. Today, McGill hangs on, still a quiet, orderly company town, only now without the company. The smelter has been dismantled and removed. A lone surviving smelter smokestack, built 750 feet tall according to EPA pollution specs in the 1970s, was knocked down over Labor Day weekend 1993 at the annual town picnic.

McGill might be down, but it's by no means out. The **McGill pool** is still the recreational focus for the town (and in fact the county) between Memorial and Labor days. Kennecott built it way back when; the water comes both by pipe and from a hot spring bubbling up on the far side of the hole. The deep end by the diving board was dredged in 1990; today it's probably around 15 feet deep. After the season, the pool is drained as much as possible, but it's never entirely empty, and it never freezes. It's open 11 A.M.–8 P.M. daily, admission is 75 cents 14 and under, $1.25 over 14, season's passes are sold to residents. Big trees and barbecue grills surround the pit.

Most of the houses remain well cared for, especially up on the hill. New sidewalks were installed downtown in fall 1994. **Marie's Cafe** on 4th St. is open Mon.–Sat. 7 A.M.–8 P.M. The **Frosty Stand** on the south side of 4th St. serves ice cream, snacks, sandwiches, and beer.

The **McGill Bar** is the focal point with its massive, cherry and mahogany Brunswick back bar and built-in liquor cabinet. The back bar is well over 100 years old. It was shipped to San Fransisco, railroaded to Caliente, and hauled by wagon (it fell off three times) to Ely. It was put into service in one of the hotels, where it sat until 1943. That's when the owner of the McGill Bar bought it for $4,000. Photos of 145 servicemen and women sent from town to WWII fill up a big wall in front (read the article from a 1981 *L.A. Times*).

Nearby **Basset Lake,** once a settling pond for the mill, may not offer shade or other amenities, but it is home to a population of big northern pike. The standing state record (24 pounds; 51 inches) was taken from the lake.

Success Summit Loop

Continue north on US 93 six miles past McGill, following the long white pipeline running for nine miles from Duck Creek Reservoir parallel to the highway along the lower slope of the Duck Creeks. The pipeline delivered nearly 300 million gallons of water to the smelter and still supplies all the town's water. Kennecott still owns the pipe and the water and in 1994 threatened to shut off the flow to the town in order to redirect it to a 3,500-acre project to restore Steptoe Valley (covering mill waste with dirt and vegetation). After an uproar in the town, the company decided to use non-potable water for the restoration. The original pipe, built in 1907, was replaced with the metal pipe in 1929. It delivers 380 gallons of cold pure water to McGill per minute.

Take a right on NV 486 and head through **Gallagher Gap,** on the other side of which the road cuts south. Beautiful **Duck Creek Ranch** is three miles off to the right, and **Bird Creek** Forest Service campground is off to the left, up into the Schell Creeks. This is a classically beautiful eastern Nevada ranching valley, with **Timber Creek** Forest Service campground four miles east, and **Berry Creek** campground five miles east from the junction at the end of the pavement. The road now turns rocky and rough (20 mph, some places 10). In a few miles you come to an unmarked fork in the road—go right. You descend into Boneyard Canyon, then up to aptly named Success Summit (you haven't slid off the road, hit a cow, ruined your suspension, had a flat tire, gotten lost . . .). Great views, too. This is where Nevada's largest elk and deer herds are found, so keep an eye out for them; they are most often seen in early mornings and evenings, or at night. Now you switch back about a dozen times and descend, along Steptoe Creek, to **Cave Lake State Park** where, after 25 miles and a couple of hours, is pavement, smooth, silky, quiet, luvvy-duvvy pavement.

Cave Lake State Park

This is one of the most beautifully situated parks in Nevada. Perched high in the Schell Creeks (7,300 feet), the emerald lake is backed by a sheer slope and stocked with rainbow and brown trout. German brown trout and albino trout from this lake have repeatedly set state records. An earthen dam maintains the lake depth at an average 20 feet, 60 feet at the deepest. Two campgrounds combine for a total of 36 sites. The main camp at the lake has 20 sites, along with toilets, running water, and dump station. The Elk Flat camp across the road was completed in 1990 and competes with Wildhorse State Recreation Area for the best public showers in Nevada; campsites are $12 nightly per vehicle, first come, first served. With more than 100,000 visitors to this park yearly, these sites fill up fast! But a spot somewhere is usually available. Call 775/728-4467 for further info.

A trailhead at the main entrance leads to a five-mile interpretive trail, which winds through the piñon-juniper forest to meet up with Cave Creek Rd., and is popular with hikers and mountain bikers. A small cave yawns across from the sign that marks the park entrance. Even if you don't have several hours to spare on yet another rough gravel road making the loop over the summit and down through the Duck Creeks, be sure to at least come this far. You won't be disappointed, or even inconvenienced.

Ward Charcoal Ovens

Coming down from Cave Lake, take a left (south) onto US 93/50/6 and go a few miles to the historic sign for the Ward Charcoal Ovens. Take a right (west) onto a good gravel road (40 mph) and go six miles to Cave Valley Road. Turn left and enjoy the view of the ovens lined up in the desert, hemmed in by a digitated ridgeline.

For thousands of years, man has known that charcoal, the residue of campfires, burns at a much higher temperature than mere wood. The ancient Egyptians used the pit method to produce charcoal. They filled a pit with 100 cords of wood, covered it with sod, and let it smolder for two to three weeks; this created 3,000 bushels of charcoal. Some time later, the mound method, which piled wood in a conical mound with vents, improved production. When brick kilns were invented in 1820, they were the first technological breakthrough in the charcoal industry in 2,000 years.

The Ward Mining District was discovered in 1872 by Thomas Ward. A San Francisco company began digging in 1875. These six charcoal ovens, the largest in Nevada, were built in 1876 to supply the smelter attempting to refine the complex lead-silver-copper ore. The mills shut down in 1879, a big fire razed the town in 1883, and the post office closed in 1887. Only a quarter-million dollars in silver was reportedly recovered. The kilns, however, having been built by a master mason, survived it all, plus another 100 years of the elements, vandalism, practical jokes, shelter for cattle, sheep and horses, and Ely teenage partying.

Each oven is 30 feet high and 25 feet wide at the base, with a door, window, and chimney hole. Thirty acres of piñon and juniper were cut into 35 cords of wood and stacked in the kilns; the openings were shut with iron doors and a fire was started. By controlling the fire with small vents around the base of the ovens for roughly 12 days, tenders charred the wood to perfection and then smothered the fire by closing all the vents. Each oven yielded 300 bushels of charcoal.

For now, this is an otherworldly scene, with six large one-eyed jacks standing guard over history, speaking a silent language that only Gary Larson can understand. In the near future, however, it won't be so cosmic. At press time, Nevada State Parks was constructing a campground nearby. There were already tables, toilets, and grills. Water was on its way, and so were camping fees in the range of those currently being charged at Cave Lake. Plans are also afoot to put a reservoir in the area.

Take Cave Valley Road almost all the way back to Ely.

PRACTICALITIES

Accommodations

Nearly two dozen lodging houses offer more than 650 rooms at quite reasonable rates. Most

Six one-eyed jacks stand guard over Ward.

DEKE CASTLEMAN

of the older and less expensive places are bunched along Aultman between 3rd and 15th streets; some newer ones are on US 93 South (Pioche Highway).

The six-story **Hotel Nevada,** 501 Aultman St., 775/289-6665, is among the oldest hotels in the state, and has an appropriate exterior with neon slot machines and a big die-cut Unknown Prospector, a combination of the two most enduring and recognizable images of the state's regional identity. This hotel also has some of the best rates in town. Rooms start at $20/25 a single/double; higher-priced double rooms cost $38 and $48. The fifth and sixth floors are nonsmoking.

Across the street is the **Jailhouse,** 500 Aultman St., 775/289-3033 or 800/841-5430; it added 22 rooms in 1996, and now offers a total of 61 "cells" at $39–65. There's also now a weight room and jacuzzi.

The **Ramada Inn/Copper Queen Casino,** 701 Avenue I, 775/289-4884 or 800/851-9526, has an interesting lobby. Walk around the front desk; the slots stand between it and the pool/jacuzzi. Have a drink downstairs in the barroom, or walk upstairs and lounge on the deck. This is the only casino in Nevada that has a pool in the middle of it; I call it the Chlorine Queen. Rates for the 65 rooms are $72–77. **Motel 6,** 770 Avenue O, across from the Copper Queen, 775/289-6671, is the largest joint in town with 100 rooms for $38–40.

The **Four Sevens,** 500 High St. right behind

the Jailhouse, 775/289-4747, was the newest motel in town, until the Holiday Inn was built; it has 40 rooms at $35–40. The **Holiday Inn,** 1501 E. Aultman, 775/289-8900, was completed in early 1995 with 61 rooms and the Prospector Casino, $52–85.

Steptoe Valley Inn Bed and Breakfast at 220 E. 11th St., just up 11th St. from the Nevada Northern depot, 775/289-8687, was built in 1907 as the Ely City Grocery. It was completely restored in 1990 by Jane and Norman Lindley, who paid careful attention to all the Victorian details: paint, wood trim, tile, marble, fixtures, glass, etc. The inn features a library, lounge, and upstairs verandah. Five guest rooms named after Ely pioneers go for $86–99 with a full breakfast; all have private baths and balconies. The Inn closes in January and February.

Other motels include: **El Rancho,** 1400 Aultman, 775/289-3644, $28–48; **Grand Central,** 1498 Lyons, 775/289-6868, $32–36; and **The Shakespeare Inn,** 1550 High, 775/289-2512, $25–35.

RV Parking

Valley View RV Park, 65 McGill Highway, 775/289-3303, opened in 1976 and is now one of the most mature RV parks in Nevada—and the tall trees, lush grass, and double-wide RV sites are there to prove it. It's quiet, friendly, and convenient to US 93 heading northbound from Ely. There are 83 spaces for motor homes, all with full hookups, and 12 pull-throughs. Tents are allowed. Accessible restrooms have flush toilets and hot showers; public phone, sewage. Reservations are recommended spring through fall, especially for the pull-throughs. RV sites are $18, tent sites $14. Good Sam discounts.

West End RV Park, 50 Aultman St., 775/289-2231, is on Ely's main drag, a three-minute walk from the Nevada Hotel and the Jailhouse Casino. The trees are large enough to shade the whole park. Sometimes West End fills up with long-termers, but you should try your luck if you want to be right in the thick of things. There are 11 spaces for motor homes, all with full hookups, but no pull-throughs. Tents are not allowed. The fee is $12 for two people.

Holiday Inn/Prospector Casino RV Park, 1501 E. Aultman St. on the east side of town, 775/289-8900, has 21 spaces with full hookups (six spaces are pull-throughs) for what must be the best price in Nevada: the first two nights are absolutely free, and succeeding nights are $7. Guests are welcome to use the swimming pool at the Holiday Inn next door, and receive drink coupons, a free $1 roll of nickels for use in the casino, and a 10% discount at the casino restaurant, open daily 6 A.M.–10 P.M. No tents allowed. All the spaces are first come, first served; the park often fills up by early afternoon.

KOA of Ely, three miles south of Ely on the Pioche Hwy., 775/289-3413, is the largest RV park in all of eastern Nevada. Mature cottonwoods rim the perimeter and Chinese elms line the sites. Ward Mountain of the Egan Range broods directly behind the park, which sits up above the valley a little, so at night you can look down at the lights of town. There are 100 spaces for motor homes, most with full hookups; 38 are pull-throughs. Tents are allowed (a separate grassy area). Groceries, playground, and volleyball are available. The fee is $20–25 for RVs, $15–18 for tents. KOA and Good Sam discounts.

Food
Hotel Nevada has a 24-hour coffee shop; the **Jailhouse** coffee shop is open daily 6 A.M.–9:30 P.M.

A new sensation (for most of you) awaits at the **Jailhouse Dining Room:** cellblock dining behind bars; 775/289-3033, open for dinner 5–9 P.M.

Try the Inmate Special, chicken Alaska (with crab) for $16.50. It also serves prime rib, ribs, halibut, shrimp, Cajun and teriyaki chicken, all around $16. The dining alcoves are designated by cell numbers, completing the theme. This is a great example of a negative cell.

Locals rave about the wonderful dinners served at the **Steptoe Valley Inn B&B,** 220 E. 11th St., 775/289-8687. The B&B serves dinners on Thursday, Friday and Saturday nights; cocktails hour starts at 7 P.M. and dinner is served at 7:30 P.M. There's just one seating each evening, and one set meal (phone for the menu of the evening); three-course dinners are $25, four-course dinners $35. Closed January and February.

For Mexican food, try **La Fiesta,** on Highway 93 North, about two miles north of Ely, at the Fireside Inn, 775/289-4112, open 11 A.M.–10 P.M. every day. Here you'll find lunch specials for $5 and combo dinners starting at $7.75, with entrees going up to $17 for lobster and shrimp. Recommended.

The **Copper Queen,** on Pioche Hwy. near town, has **Big J's,** 775/289-4884, open 6 A.M.–10 P.M., well-known for its home-baked bread, big steak dinners, and Sunday buffet brunch. The dining room and lounge were tastefully remodeled in 1990, though the banquet room in back was wisely left alone. Recommended.

Silver State Restaurant, 1204 Aultman, 775/289-2712, is as classic a '50s diner as you'll ever see, right down to the orange vinyl booths and counter seats. No slots, no credit cards, no change for the laundromat, no checks accepted; just good coffee shop grub, along with Mexican (served 2–9 P.M.) and steaks.

Shy Simon's, 905 E. Aultman, 775/289-4162, is good for pizza.

Fast food in Ely used to be represented by a lone McD's, with a big play area, near the corner of Pioche Hwy. and US 6. The burger giant has been joined by Arby's, and Taco Time.

Finally, for a real old-fashioned treat, stop in at **Economy Drug,** 7th and Aultman, 775/289-4929, open Mon.–Fri. 9 A.M.–7:30 P.M., Saturday 9 A.M.–6 P.M., and pull up a stool at the soda fountain. Milkshakes, floats, ice-cream sodas, freezes, and splits start at $1, and they use real milk, ice cream, and soda.

Entertainment and Information

The **Central Theater** is at 145 W. 15th in back of Grand Central Motel, 775/289-2202. If you get the chance, see a movie here, just for the experience of walking into the cavernous room. This is one of Nevada's few remaining movie houses that someone forgot to turn into a 16-plex!

A girl of your choice (if not of your dreams) at the **Stardust Ranch** will happily supply a memorable half-hour or so. She's up at 190 High St. at 1st, 775/289-4569, at the west end of town.

The **Chamber of Commerce** is at Aultman and 6th, 775/289-8877 (see "Sights," above). The **library** is next to the courthouse on Campton, 775/289-3737, open Mon.–Thurs. 10 A.M.–8 P.M., Friday 10 A.M.–5 P.M., Saturday 10 A.M.–4 P.M. *Big* Nevada section, two of everything; glance through *White Pine Lang Syne* by local historian Effie O. Read (1965).

For a map unique in Nevada, stop in at the front office of **Valley Motors,** 807 E. Aultman in East Ely, 775/289-4855: a score of USGS two-degree maps (1:250,000).

Transportation

Ely Bus (775/289-2877), with a terminal at 426 Campton, operates two long-distance bus routes. Buses depart for the Reno area at 7:45 A.M. every Wednesday, arriving at the Western Village in Sparks at 1:45 P.M.; cost is $63 one way, $104 round trip. The return bus departs from Sparks at 7:45 A.M. the following morning. On the other route, buses depart for Las Vegas at 7:45 A.M. on Tuesday and Friday, arriving at the Las Vegas Greyhound station at 12:15 P.M. The return buses depart from Las Vegas the same afternoon, at 2:30 P.M. The Ely-Las Vegas buses cost $44 one way, $79 round trip.

GREAT BASIN NATIONAL PARK

INTRODUCTION

The 77,000-acre park, officially designated in October 1986, is the only national park in Nevada. It was carved out of 80-year-old Humboldt National Forest and surrounds 65-year-old Lehman Caves National Monument. National Park status was first proposed in 1922, when Lehman Caves was designated a National Monument, but the idea was heartily defeated by a powerful lobby of mining and ranching interests from the remote area. A second movement gained momentum in the late 1950s, but local opposition this time included miners, cattlemen, loggers, hunters, and even the Forest Service. A 28,000-acre Scenic Area was the result of a compromise on the 150,000-acre park proposal; the paved road up to 10,000 feet on Wheeler Peak was laid right afterward, in 1961.

Finally, in the mid-1980s, after Kennecott closed and unemployment in White Pine County reached 25% (same number as the population decline), the White Pine Chamber of Commerce resurrected the issue. This time the political climate was favorable, and another broad compromise was worked out: boundaries were drawn to exclude private mining land, grazing was permitted, and the 174,000-acre park proposal was whittled to its present 77,000 acres.

The nation's 47th national park and one of the smallest, Great Basin receives an average of 90,000 visitors a year. It gets crowded on weekends during the short peak season, and late arrivals can be turned away from the cave and campgrounds. (All the park's campgrounds are first come, first served, but you can make advance reservations by phone for the cave tours—a wise idea—for summer weekends.) But many visitors treat the park as a detour, just a day-trip, and view the caves, drive to the peak overlook, and then are on their way. Since it's extremely remote from urban areas and interstate highways, there's little of the carnival atmosphere that pervades many other national parks, especially in the West. For anyone used to the circuses at Yosemite, Grand Canyon, and Yellowstone (among other) national parks, this place most of the time seems like solitude personified.

Great Basin National Park was created to preserve and showcase a preeminent example of the vast Great Basin ecosystem, which covers parts of five states and occupies nearly 20% of the land area in the continental United States. And indeed, the Snake Range packs a more diverse ecology into a discrete mountain range than any of the other 250 ranges in this vast western desert. All five Great Basin life zones occur in the roughly 8,000 feet from the valley to the peak, second-highest point in Nevada. The range contains the only permanent, glacier-like ice in the state. It boasts a large forest of 3,000- to 4,000-year-old bristlecone pines, the oldest living creatures on the planet. Within the quartzite limestone are corridors of caverns that have been carved by God and water for millions of years. What's more, the major attractions are eminently accessible: a road to 10,000 feet, highest in Nevada, day-trip trails to the peak, ice, and bristlecones, and rough 4WD tracks to the most solitary backcountry. The air is fresh,

the views are grand, and the vibe is reverent in this hallowed temple of peaks, trees, caves, and wilderness.

Tiny Baker (pop. 55), five miles from the park entrance, is the nearest settlement; see the Practicalities section, further along, for services available in Baker. Ely, the largest town nearby, is a full 70 miles away by road.

SIGHTS

From Ely

Head east out US 93/50/6, past Comins Lake and the cutoffs for Cave Lake State Park and the Ward Charcoal Ovens. Then you start to climb up into the piñon and juniper of the **Schell Creeks.** Right over **Connors Pass** (7,780 feet), the very big **Snake Range** comes into view. **Wheeler Peak** towers 3,000 feet above treeline, with permanent snow dropping down from the peak (13,063 feet). For a short distance, as you cross **Spring Valley** toward the Snakes, you're heading right at Wheeler Peak.

At Majors Junction, US 93 cuts south (right) at the fork, and you follow US 6/50 left. But before you do, stop off at **Major's Station roadhouse,** 775/591-0430. With cold beer and slots, Majors is a popular hangout for local ranchers and visiting hunters. Notice the elk-crossing road sign right outside the front door. The Schell Creek elk herd started as transplants from Yellowstone. They've flourished in the area and the state now releases tags to hunt them. The restaurant here is open every day: 7 A.M.–10 P.M. in summer and autumn, 8 A.M.–7 P.M. in winter. They also offer camping here: 11 RV spaces with full hook-ups are $10 a night or $50 a week, tent sites are $5.

Continuing east, you drop into Spring Valley between the Schell Creeks behind and the Snakes ahead. The road up Spring Valley is an afternoon's scenic drive of its own.

A "short" cut goes right at the sign for **Osceola.** This very rough gravel road is passable, though just barely, with a low-clearance vehicle. You climb and climb straight up into the Snakes, and go by the cemetery and old gold pit. Some rusty mining junk is lying around near the top, and headframes still stand. Placer gold was discovered here in 1872, and hydraulics were used to sluice out the nuggets and dust. *Arrastras,* primitive grinders, were employed in the early days. Later, a small stamp mill was built. In order to supply more water for the sluicing, a ditch was dug in 1889 around the mountain from Lehman Creek on the west side of the Snakes. The cost, $100,000, was never paid back in gold, as Osceola declined a year or two later, having produced $2 million in its 20 years. The rough road rejoins the highway on the east side of the mountains.

If you don't take the Osceola detour and stay on the main highway, you make a big loop north, through the low point of the Snakes, **Sacramento Pass,** at 7,154 feet. To the north **Mt. Moriah** rises to a peak 1,000 feet lower than Wheeler's. Nevada's fifth-highest peak, Mt. Moriah is now a designated Wilderness Area, one of the 14 created in 1989. It's 82,000 acres, and features the one-square-mile rolling-tundra Table at 11,000 feet, which is bordered by bristle cones. Hampton Creek Trail is a steep 15-mile round-trip hike to the summit of Mt. Moriah (4WD required); Hendry's Creek Trail is a 23-mile round-trip backpack up to the Table. For complete descriptions to and instructions for these trails, see *Nevada Wilderness Areas* by Michael White.

Turn off US 6/50 at the boarded-up **Y Truck Stop** onto NV 487. High country, low sage. Take a look-see around **Baker** (see below for practicalities). At a site just north of Baker, archaeologists have discovered the ruins of a settlement of the Fremont Indians, who were based in central and southwestern Utah around the time the Anasazi were predominant in southern Nevada. The Fremonts had the largest population of any native civilization in the area before and after, about 10,000 at its height. The Baker site is

the ice field in the cirque of Wheeler Peak

LARRY PROSOR, NEVADA COMMISSION ON TOURISM

believed to be a western outpost of the agricultural Fremont. Like the Anasazi, they too disappeared from their western frontier around 1270, because of a 20-year drought in the area. Three pit houses, pottery, arrowheads, and artifacts have been found.

Now double back to the road up to the park. Keep an eye peeled for Sherman's whimsical roadside art gallery that extends from Baker to the park entrance. On the left is "Horse with No Name," a skeletal horse at the wheel of an old jalopy; on the right is "It's All Downhill From Here," a bony bike rider with flame-red hair, and several others. On the way back you'll want to track down Doc, a retired locksmith in Baker, just to hear him talk about his work.

Visitor Center

The park visitor center is open every day from at least 8:30 A.M. to 5 P.M., with the possibility of longer hours from Memorial Day to Labor Day. Contact the center with any questions about the park: 775/234-7331, www.nps.gov/grba, or write to Superintendent, Great Basin National Park, 100 Great Basin National Park, Baker, NV 89311-9700.

Buy your tickets for the cave tour as soon as you enter the center, if you haven't already bought tickets in advance by phone. Allow time to study the exhibits on park flora, fauna, cave formations, and to enjoy the three-dimensional Landsat thematic image. You could easily spend an entire hour just looking at the books, slides, and videos.

Borrow a trail guide from inside and take the nature walk on the side of the visitor center. Stop off first at **Rhode's Cabin** to see the historical exhibit on the caretaking of the national monument. Then stroll the trail, stopping to read about juniper and piñon, mountain mahogany and mistletoe, limestone and marble, and cave entrances.

In front of the visitor center and down the hill slightly are some trees planted by Ab Lehman himself more than 100 years ago. The giant apricot trees flesh out a ton of very fine fruit—sweet, juicy, healthy—somewhat late in the season, perfectly ripe the second week of August. Help yourself; they're better than candy. The Park Service is cloning the apricots, and you'll also see apples, pears, peaches, and plums. An irrigation ditch off to the side is the only remnant, along with the fruit trees, of Lehman's homestead.

Various activities are centered around the visitor center; check the bulletin board or with a naturalist when you arrive. Next door to the visitor center is the gift and coffee-shop concessionaire, open April through October. Tonia Harvey operates the joint, Lehman Caves Gift and Cafe, 775/234-7221. The food is gratifyingly good, and Tonia's done a great job stocking the place with quality artwork, books, T-shirts, and the like. Quite a bit of her inventory comes from Nevada, some from the immediate area: silver and turquoise jewelry by Jan Everitt of Austin and Erman Blossom, a northern Paiute from Pyramid Lake; T-shirts by Virginia City's Tom Gilbertson, etc. On the cafe side, breakfast and lunch are served, and her homemade soups are distinctive and well-seasoned. Try the "incredible ice cream sandwich," a double scoop crammed between a giant pair of oatmeal cookies ($3.75),

easily big enough for two or three people. The Great Basin Natural History Association operates a bookshop in the visitor center that benefits the park, 775/234-7270.

Lehman Caves

Five hundred million years ago, nearly everything, everywhere, for all time, had been under water. Nevada's sea was shallow, teeming with skeletoned creatures. The bottom turned into a graveyard for the little bones, which accumulated for eons, pressurizing into limestone. By 150 million years ago, the sea was out and the sandy desert in. Eventually the sand petrified into sandstone, which was metamorphosed into quartzite. Uplifting, tilting, and stretching 70 million years ago created the Snakes, mostly from quartzite, with a little limestone coming to rest at the eastern base of the range. Some molten granite was burped up near the joint, superheating the limestone into marble. Seepage dissolved the marble, opening up large caverns and long aqueducts for underground streams and lakes and springs. Then the water table dropped, leaving the caves high and dry. Now the seepage began to dissolve the surrounding limestone, depositing calcite, drop by drop, drip by drip, speck by speck, until the . . . things . . . started to grow, imperceptibly, inexorably, one-hundredth of an inch a year. Today, countless megazillions of calcite dribbles later, this is the classic Old Man Cave, with the ornate and incredible stalagmites, stalactites, helictites, aragonites, columns, shields, draperies, bacon, popcorn, and soda straws to prove it.

Enter Absalom Lehman, in 1885. The legend is obscure, but Ab discovered the cave, explored it, altered it, and fostered it. The cave concessionaire changed a few times after Lehman's death in 1891, and the area became a national forest in 1909, achieving national-monument status in 1922. Additional changes have been made over the years, including entrance and exit tunnels and trail improvements.

Park Service personnel are putting together a proactive management strategy to protect the caves. The installation of a lighting system years ago resulted in unnatural algal blooms on some formations. Another problem is lint from visitors' clothing, which attaches itself to the cave walls—look closely at some of the formations and you'll see a fuzz coating. There is now a program in place to clean algae and lint from the cave on a regular basis.

The Park Service has also completed a resource survey on 30 other caves and rock shelters scattered throughout the park between the 8,000- and 12,000-foot level. A permit system allows people to visit some of the caves, while keeping others off limits. Contact the park's Resources Management department, 775/234-7270, for a permit to visit wild caves.

Lehman Cave Tours

Cave tours are of varying lengths; options include a 30-minute tour ($2), a 60-minute tour ($4) and a 90-minute tour ($6). In summer, tours usually depart from around 7:20 A.M. to 4:30 P.M. every day (call for details); in winter, tours usually depart around four times daily. You can reserve space on a tour in advance, which is a good idea if you're planning a weekend visit. Call 775/234-7331, ext. 242, and put the admission fee on your credit card.

This is an excursion to the *inside*—inside the studio of a sculptor who's learned a thing or two during her 20-million-year career, and inside your own head, where the most dramatic macros and the infinite, intricate micros take their weird effects. Don't bother with the prosaic public names—West Room, Lake Room, Inscription Room, Palace and Talus rooms. Instead, let the formations trigger whatever's in the mind's eye. Me? At first I saw the usual root crops—yams, rutabagas, turnips, carrots. But then it all changed to every kind of dentition known to horror-movie set designers, enclosed by every kind of gaping, twisted, dripping mouth. Next I started seeing a series of priapistic erections that would make even Rasputin blush. Then everything started looking like a nose or a tongue. Or skeletal, with the proper anatomical jointing and articulation. Or my own neurological reflection—nerves, dendrites, synapses. Then it was clubs clobbering and points piercing. Haunted houses after a few hundred years. Spiked torture racks from New Guinea. Jonah in the whale. Suddenly everything struck me as funny. The caricature snake faces, cartoon zoo animals, *Fantasia* flowers. What finally got to me were the eyes . . . and this was all *before* the hallucinogenics took effect.

Hatted rangers lead cave rats into the bowels of the Snakes.

NEVADA COMMISSION ON TOURISM

TRAILHEADS AND CAMPGROUNDS

The park has four developed campgrounds: the **Baker Creek, Lower Lehman Creek, Upper Lehman Creek,** and **Wheeler Peak** campgrounds. The charge for staying at any of these is $7 a night, and all sites are first come, first served. All have drinking water during the warm months, and some have flush toilets. The Upper Lehman Creek campground has one handicap-accessible site, and the Baker Creek campground has two. The park also has primitive camping facilities along Snake Creek and Strawberry Creek Roads; campsites have fire grates, picnic tables and pit toilets, and are free of charge.

An excellent guide for this remote backcountry is *Hiking and Climbing in Great Basin National Park* by Michael Kelsey. Another book with a good chapter on Great Basin Park is

PINUS LONGAEVA TREES: Q&A

Are bristlecone pines really the oldest living beings on Earth?

In 1964, only six years after Edmund Schulman of the Arizona Tree-Ring Research Group published an article in *National Geographic* announcing the discovery of bristlecone pines, a scientist doing research on Wheeler Peak found the tree called Prometheus, later determined (when it was felled by the Forest Service) to be 4,900 years old. This ancient organism was older, by more than 1,000 years, than the most giant California sequoia. It predated the pyramids in Egypt by 1,200 years. In fact, Prometheus when it was cut down was only a bit more than 700 years younger than the date that the Old Testament gives to the birth of the world.

How do they live so long?

In his excellent and lyrical *Trees of the Great Basin*, Ronald Lanner comments that in the case of the bristlecones, "Adversity breeds longevity." Because these trees inhabit such a harsh environment—at the highest elevations, on exposed and rocky slopes, bearing the full brunt of the elements—they enjoy a suitable lack of competition; only limber pine and Engelmann spruce keep these timberline ancients company. Also, since the bristlecone stands are somewhat sparse, fire presents less of a danger to their lives. Finally, these slow-growing trees produce an extremely dense wood, which is highly resistant to infection, parasites, and decay. Carol Muench, in a 1967 article in *Nevada* magazine, expresses the ironic truth that sometimes the "most tormented of species lives the longest."

LOUISE FOOTE

How do they die?

A very little at a time! Even 3,000-year-old trees continue to be active reproductively and bear cones. Incredibly, the inexorable forces of erosion finally overtake their mountain habitat and expose the root system, which dries out and rots or becomes susceptible to fungus or parasites. The upper limbs connected to the lower roots then die off, one by one. Next, the wind and rain scour off the bark, leaving a bleached and polished trunk. Still, 90% of a bristlecone pine can be dead while, in Lanner's words, "a single sinuous strip of living bark connects the occasional live limb to the occasional live root." Also, an old bristlecone can stand for 1,000 or so years after dying off completely.

What does science learn from the mighty memories of these trees?

Thankfully, scientists have developed core-sampling techniques that enable them to "read" the rings without having to cut down the whole tree to do it. (Prometheus wasn't so lucky.) Bristlecones are sensitive to drought conditions, which restrict their ring formation. In this way these trees provide dendrochronologists a natural calendar of climatic events dating back to nearly 9,000 years ago, using long-dead trees. When you consider that scientific weather records have only been kept for the last 100 years, it becomes clear that the bristlecones add immeasurably to our knowledge. In addition, the trees can help us measure the action of erosion itself. Lanner writes, "Exposed roots of trees of known age have been used to estimate rates of mass wasting—the geological process that wears away mountains." And it's all right there to see, a mere half-hour walk from the parking lot at Wheeler Peak Campground in Great Basin National Park.

Nevada Wilderness Areas by Michael Rose (see "Booklist").

Baker and Johnson Lakes

Baker Rd. leaves the main park road just below

the visitor center and heads south, then west, up to 7,000 feet. It's a good gravel road, 25 mph, through piñon and aspen, past massive stone outcrops. A little less than three miles from the main road is **Baker Creek Campground.** Three loops contain 32 sites (two wheelchair-accessible), with outhouses and running water (boil first). The choice spots are under big evergreens right on the creek. This campground is open from around May 15 to September 15.

A little more than three miles from the campground is **Baker Lake and Johnson Lake Loop Trail.** Both lakes are five miles from the trailhead, with a mile between, over Johnson Pass (10,800 feet) of Pyramid Peak (11,921 feet). Much of this area in the central and southern part of the park is generally accessible to high-clearance vehicles on dirt roads in from NV 487 near Garrison, Utah.

A well-graded gravel road heads into the southeast corner of the park from south of Garrison. At the end, a 1.7-mile trail brings you to **Lexington Arch,** a six-story natural limestone arch. Ask at the visitors center about the **Big Wash** hike. No permits are required for backcountry hiking or camping, but the Park Service strongly encourages you to fill out a voluntary backcountry registration form.

Lehman Creek and Wheeler Peak

Just below Baker Creek Rd., down from the visitor center, take a left onto Wheeler Peak Rd., and go up up up this mountain toward the peak. **Lower Lehman Creek Campground** at 7,500 feet has 11 sites, mostly used by trailers and RVs, and pit toilets. **Upper Lehman Creek Campground,** just up the road at 7,800 feet, has 24 tent sites on three levels of the slope. The upper Upper campground is on a creek; the trailhead for Wheeler Peak Campground leaves from here. The lower Upper campground is open year-round, the upper approximately May 15 to September 15. Both have drinking water available (in winter, water is available at the visitor center, if not at the campsites).

Continue climbing up this extraordinary road (RVs or vehicles over 24 feet not recommended). At around 8,500 feet are a couple of curves; then the peak, from treeline to summit, takes your breath away. At 9,000 feet the views, if possible, get better. Pause at the Serene Overlook, gazing right up into the glacial cirque. Keep climbing and climbing, with the peak ahead and the vast valley behind, till you get to the end of the road at the parking lot for the trailheads and the loop through **Wheeler Peak Campground.**

The campground is 13 miles from the visitor center at a breath-catching 10,000 feet. It has 37 sites and pit toilets, open usually June through September.

Warm up your hiking boots on the **Theresa Lake** and **Stella Lake** trails, which you can do in an aerobic hour or a lethargic two. The grades are easy and the lakes are pretty and the peaks are mighty.

After acclimating on this loop, head up to the **bristlecones** and the **ice field,** two to three hours roundtrip, though not especially strenuous. Signs point the way at the forks with the other trails. An interpretive trail circles the bristlecone sanctuary, where these ancient beings cling to life with the most tenacious yet precarious grip in God's Great Kingdom. The reverence here is palpable, and you'll unconsciously adopt a light step and a hushed tone as you move in awe through this divine forest. But don't be shy about caressing the trees—the barkless wood, polished for hundreds of years by the elements, invites touch, and not a hint of a splinter will you notice. The bottlebrush needles, likewise, are soft and sensual, surprisingly young feeling. The living parts of the trees are vital and triumphal, but even the dead parts are beautiful and immortal. This forest is exquisite proof that wood is one element that can remain aesthetic long after death, one which does not automatically demand to be buried.

Past the temple of the pines, the trail becomes steep and rocky and will tickle your ears with the bunches of scrunching underfoot. Tune in to this rock concert! In no time you enter the cirque, a hall of the mountain kings. It might be stretching it a bit to call the permanent snowpack here a "glacier"; there's not a touch of blue to it. But the parkies hereabouts are a little sensitive about their glacier. One of the many political skirmishes in the effort to name the area a national park was over whether the icefield was a true glacier. Ranchers and miners opposed to the park called it a snowfield. Park supporters rallied behind the little patch of ice. If Wheeler was the site of Nevada's only extant glacier, then it needed protection, right? According to the parkies, it has now been determined that Wheeler's ice does move, so a glacier, they say, it is. But anyone who's spent any time in Alaska or the Yukon might think it looks more like an ice cube.

Stella Lake, Great Basin National Park

JOHN ELK III

But you can certainly imagine the big river of ice that carved out this cirque, though it's about time the Park Service got some dump trucks up here to clean up all this scree and debris! (Just kidding.) Great echo toward the north wall. And the lone pillar between Wheeler Peak on the right and Jeff Davis Peak on the left ought to be called Sore Thumb Pinnacle. Maybe it was just my imagination, but it seemed to be swelling as I walked around below it.

Wheeler Peak Trail branches off from near Stella Lake and climbs 3,000 feet in four miles—steep, high, exhilarating. This trail is open all year, but in winter you'll need winter gear (i.e., cramp-ons) to traverse it.

PRACTICALITIES

Accommodations

The tiny town of Baker (pop. 55), five miles from the park entrance, has a couple of options for accommodations and a bite. The **Silver Jack Motel,** P.O. Box 166, Baker, NV 89311, 775/234-7323, has seven rooms at $37. The motel stays open April through October. If you're curious what time it is back home in Tokyo or Moscow or Berlin, a clock on the wall behind the counter, next to the one with Baker time, will tell you. Check out the gift shop and art gallery here. The Great Basin T-shirts, among other things, are original. Doc Sherman's copper, wood, and what-have-you sculptures are prominently displayed.

Owner Bill Roundtree makes metal sculptures of western themes and his wife does the T-shirts. Both have a self-described twisted sense of humor, which is what it takes, they say, to make a living out here. Three blocks up NV 488 toward the park, turn left to find End of the Trail . . . er, operated by the same owners; it's a two-bedroom mobile home with a view, renting for $62 a night. The same owners also run **The Bunkhouse,** a cabin with kitchenette on the ranch, for $57 per night. Contact the owners at the Silver Jack Motel for info on all of these.

A **Thrift Store** is next door to the Silver Jack. Owner Barbara Sand offers notary and photo-copying services and a chance to browse through and buy the second-hand stuff she's collected. She also rents out spaces across the road to tent and RV campers, $5 self-contained.

Also in Baker, the **Whispering Elms Motel & RV Park,** 775/234-7343, has motel rooms for $32. Their RV park, with trees and big lawns, offers RV spaces for $17, tent sites for $10. Even if you're not staying there, you can stop by for a shower, for $5.

The **Border Inn,** 13 miles east of the park entrance on US6/50, smack on the Utah-Nevada line, 775/239-7300, has 29 motel rooms for $31–40, plus a restaurant, bar, slots, showers, laundry, and gas. The gas pumps are in Utah where transportation taxes are lower, which makes the gas here about 15 cents cheaper than in Nevada. Everything's open 24 hours a day.

Hidden Canyon Guest Ranch, 775/234-7267, P.O. Box 180, Baker, NV 89311, is a lovely ranch down Big Wash Rd., about 15 miles south of Baker. Open in summer (June through September), by reservation only, it offers horseback riding, hiking, fishing and Western activities. Packages including lodging, all meals, activities and tour guides cost $125 per person, per day ($85 for ages 5–11). Lodging alone is $48 in tent cabins or in nice, big teepees. Camping is $9 per person, or $35 per family, in your own tent or small RV (long RVs cannot negotiate the road). In autumn and winter, the ranch opens for pheasant hunting; hunting packages are available including rustic lodging and meals, or hunters can rough it, or come out just for day hunting; phone for details.

Food and Services
Do not leave the area without having breakfast, a burger, or a burrito at the **Outlaw** in Baker, 775/234-7302. It starts serving when someone shows up hungry, stops serving when everyone has been fed, and closes up when the last reveler has gone home. Bacon and eggs are $4.95, burgers (beef or buffalo) will run you $5–6. Dinner choices, mostly around $10–12, include a pasta dish that changes daily, steak and shrimp for $18.95, and baby back ribs for $13.95. Great food, and a fine place to eat, lounge, laugh.

Across the street is **T&Ds,** 775/234-7264, with a country store, restaurant and lounge. The store is open daily, 10 A.M.–6 P.M. The restaurant is open for lunch and dinner most days from 11:30 A.M.–8 P.M.; closed Tuesdays, and opening at 5 P.M. Wednesdays.

The **Border Inn,** 13 miles east of the park entrance on the Utah-Nevada line, serves three meals, 6 A.M.–10 P.M., and has a gas station.

Baker no longer has a gas station, so be sure to gas up your car before you get here.

EUREKA

FROM ELY TO EUREKA

Heading west beyond the Ruth moonscape, you cross **Copper Flat** and start nosing northwest up into the **Egan Range** until you hit **Robinson Summit** (7,607 feet). Then you drop down into **Jake's Valley,** approaching the **White Pine Mountains.** Right where the road cuts northwest heading up to Little Antelope Summit is the turnoff left (south) to Hamilton.

Hamilton
It's 12 miles to the site of this once-booming mining camp at 8,000 feet on Treasure Hill in the rugged White Pine Range. The surface deposits here, unearthed in 1867, were so rich in silver that they added up to $15,000 a ton. The WPA guide reports that "a couple of men . . . threw up a little rock house to shelter them from the bitter winds, only to find their walls held $75,000 worth of ore." As in Virginia City, thousands of claims were staked with no rhyme, reason, or reliance on any law. White Pine County was quickly cleaved off vast Lincoln County, Hamilton became the seat in the same breath, and the courthouse was hastily erected—all to *begin* to record the claims and counterclaims and to manage the initial litigious chaos.

The indications were so promising in the first two years that the total worth of mining stocks was listed at $70 million. Freighters from the White Pine District up to the Central Pacific main line at Elko were robbed nearly every day of the week. Even the primitive appalling conditions of high and remote Hamilton couldn't discourage the proverbial 10,000 miners, promoters, lawyers, con men, gamblers, merchants, and camp followers from settling atop what they considered a second Comstock Lode.

The boom lasted four years. By 1872 the mines had bottomed out, at only 30 feet deep. But the uproar had been so fulsome that its mere echo kept Hamilton vital for another dozen years. Several fires, labor strikes, runaway inflation, and the harsh living conditions hastened *borrasca.* After the courthouse burned in 1885, Ely took over as White Pine County seat. Ghost-town scavengers cleaned the place out by the 1950s, and the new breed of miners and prospectors once again set up shop in the early 1980s.

Over the Mountains and through the Woods
You crest **Antelope Summit** of the White Pine Range at 7,433 feet, and descend into forked **Newark Valley.** To the south, **Mt. Hamilton,** at nearly 11,000 feet, is the centerpiece of this part of central Nevada's Humboldt National Forest. Traverse the east fork of Newark Valley, then head up to **Pancake Summit** (6,521 feet) of the Pancake Range. This northern tip of the Pancakes is actually a short stack compared to the **Diamond Range** west of it, with Diamond Peak soaring to 10,600 feet. After crossing the west fork of Newark Valley, you cut north straight up into the southern Diamonds, till you hit **Pinto Summit** (7,360 feet) and head up into Eureka.

HISTORY

Silver was discovered in 1864 in a little bowl between the Fish Creek Range and the Diamond Mountains by prospectors fanning out from Austin 70 miles west. But the lead content of the ore proved such a hindrance that it took six years and several false starts to develop an efficient method of smelting and refining the monetary mineral. Within a year, five blast furnaces were superheating the ore, and by 1872, another 10 were operating. The furnaces from this "Pittsburgh of the West" emitted enough lead and other toxic fumes to lay the little canyon low, spreading sickness and death to wildlife and people—especially infants.

In 1873, the state Legislature created Eureka County from a section of next-door Lander County; Eureka has been the county seat ever since. In 1875, the Eureka and Palisade Railroad was constructed to connect the Eureka smelters with the Central Pacific main line in Palisade, just south of Carlin. Eureka became the freighting and supply hub for a large part of central Nevada. The next few years saw the peak of the boom, when the smoggy city boasted 100 saloons and 25 gambling establishments; 8,000 people gave it Nevada's second-largest population for a short while.

In the late 1870s, the Italian immigrants who supplied charcoal for the smelters became disgusted with wages—13 cents for a bushel of charcoal—and working conditions. The nearby piney-green hills had long been denuded, and

the charcoal burners had to travel more than 40 miles to find trees to satisfy the smelters' voracious 200,000-bushel-a-year appetites. They formed the Charcoal Burners Association, went on strike, and demanded a three-cent-per-bushel raise. For a month, tensions escalated, until a group of miners, led by a deputy sheriff, confronted the *carbonari* near Fish Creek, killing or wounding a dozen and arresting a score. This incident, along with water flooding the mines and two extensive downtown fires within a year, signaled the beginning of the end for Eureka's boomtown days. By 1891, all the smelters had closed. But for its troubles, Eureka in 15 years had produced $40 million in silver, $20 million in gold, and more than a thousand tons of lead.

The railroad shut down in 1938, but county administrative duties, agriculture in Diamond Valley to the north, traffic along the Lincoln Highway/US 50, and occasional flurries of mining have helped Eureka maintain some stability in the 20th century. The huge Newmont and Barrrick Gold Strike mines near Carlin in the far northern part of the county has provided additional revenues and local gold mining helps bolster the economy. Homestake Mining, famous for the century-old still-producing Homestake mine in South Dakota, has reopened the Ruby Hill mine southwest of town, taking over where Atlas Gold Bar left off in 1994. The company has erected a 7.8-acre subdivision northwest of town to house the 125 (one-third of them local) employees it will take to operate the Ruby Hill project. The local economy is gearing up for a mini boom.

The old brick buildings (Eureka is by far the brickest town in Nevada) and black slag heaps in town are reminiscent of the trials and tribulations that Eureka has overcome: fire, flood, smelter smoke and lead fumes, a labor war, smallpox, bitter winters, mining accidents, lack of fresh food, and the boom-bust cycles stimulated by mines and railroads. Its colorful past, extensive historical walking tour, excellent museum, beautiful county courthouse, and pretty countryside make this hilly, hardy, and high town (6,500 feet) a perfect stop for stretching out, gassing up, washing off, chowing down, and wandering around—in short, an effective antidote for the cultivated lonelies of US 50.

SIGHTS

Eureka is only two blocks wide and five blocks long. You won't get lost here.

Museum

Coming into town from the east, take a left on Ruby Hill Ave. and go one block to the corner of Ruby Hill and Monroe to the **Eureka Sentinel Museum,** 775/237-5010, open every day 9 A.M.–5 P.M. May through October, Tues.–Sat. 9 A.M.–5 P.M. November through April; donations accepted. In newspaper offices built in 1879 after one of the disastrous fires, most of the displays and descriptions are done in newspaper style.

Read all about Eureka's early days: discovery of the stubborn ore, the new blast-furnace technology, the Eureka and Palisade Railroad, foreign talent, and the Fish Creek War. Don't miss the colorful style of a courtroom reporter: a certain "female slightually on the rampage" was fined by the judge who "perorated his remarks with an invitation to pungle $40."

In the back of the museum is an entire room in which the Eureka *Sentinel* was published between 1870 and 1960, with the attending memorabilia and machines: 1919 Linotype, paper cutters, punches, staplers, presses, editor's and proofreaders' desks, and posters pasted on the wall, some of which date from the peak period in the 1880s.

Courthouse and Vicinity

Now head back to the **County Courthouse** on the corner of Main and Bateman, 775/237-5262, open Mon.–Fri. 8 A.M.–noon and 1–5 P.M. This building was completed in 1880 for $55,000; the attached county jail cost an additional $15,000.

The courthouse is a handsome companion for the Eureka Opera House across the street; it was restored as part of a $3.3 million restoration and beautification project, completed in 1999, that has placed street lights, wood and iron benches, flower pots, and sidewalks the length of town. The courthouse is open to the public for tours, with a helpful and friendly staff.

Right next door to the courthouse is another brick building that has served as the post office and a Farmer's and Merchant's Bank. During the "bank holiday" in 1933 during the Depression, the front doors of all banks in the country had to remain locked after closing on the stated day, but this one in Eureka managed to sidestep the stipulation by remaining open 24 hours a day, every day, until the bank holiday ended.

Eureka Opera House

Directly across the street is the Opera House. This historic building was constructed of completely fireproof materials in 1880; its first public event was a masquerade ball on New Year's Eve 1881. Many pop stars of the late 1800s played this palace. The first silent movie was shown here in 1915. The name was changed

compositor's desk at the Eureka Sentinel Museum

LARRY PROSOR, NEVADA COMMISSION ON TOURISM

to the Eureka Theater in the 1940s. The last movie was shown in 1958. The building also housed a store, saloon, and bowling alley at different times. It closed to the public in 1978.

In 1991, Eureka County officials voted to spend $2.3 million to restore the Opera House as a banquet and convention facility. The old timber supports were shored up, the basement was enlarged and an underground spring diverted, and original artwork was restored. The Opera House reopened in October 1993. In 1994 the building won an honor award from the National Trust for Historic Preservation; it is the only building in Nevada to have won this award, so far. (This is one of three historic opera houses left in Nevada; the others are the Piper Opera House in Virginia City and Thompson's Opera House in Pioche.)

The Opera House now has a permanent fine arts collection in the meeting rooms and gallery space, with works by artists from the Great Basin area. The art can be seen on weekdays when the Opera House is open, on weekends by appointment, or whenever there's a function or event going on.

The Opera House presents an eclectic lineup of entertainment, bringing in one major cultural event per month, year round. The Grand Hall seats 325 people, including a rare horseshoe-shaped balcony with 64 seats. For info about upcoming performances, contact the Opera House: P.O. Box 284, Eureka, NV 89316, 775/237-6006, www.eurekaoperahouse@eurekanv.org, www.eurekacounty.org. You can tour the Opera House Mon.–Fri. 8 A.M.–5 P.M., other times by previous arrangement; call and talk to director Wally Cuchine.

Along Main Street

Eureka's last great fire was in 1879, when most of Main St. was burned; lots of buildings were built right after that, of brick and stone, a good reason why there have been no more great fires since.

Along with all the historic restored sites, Eureka is a great town for wandering in and out of the stores on Main Street. Start at **Tommy-knockers**, 775/237-5556, where owner-artist Judy Klindt creates stained glass. Her work is mostly special order (for example, the beautiful windows in the McGill Methodist Church), but some smaller pieces are for sale. Judy also sells some jewelry, Indian weavings, small antiques,

and tasteful knickknacks. Notice the classy display cases, typical of an artist who came to Eureka from Southern California to get away from it all for a year, and so far has stayed for more than 20. Tommyknockers is in an old bank building, with what could be the oldest vault in Nevada still inside. Another shop, the **Hanging Tree**, 775/237-5017, open every afternoon except Thursday, sells ceramics and craft supplies.

Then head down to **Raine's**, a wonderful old-fashioned general store selling everything from oranges to Wrangler's, 775/237-5296, open 9 A.M.–7 P.M., Sunday 9 A.M.–6 P.M. Check out the trophies high up on the walls, especially the Nevada bighorn (a big one as you walk in) and the pronghorn.

Farther along, you pass the most unusual **Masonic Temple** extant. Built in 1880, this is the last Masonic temple with an underground meeting room. (For privacy purposes, meetings on the first floor were forbidden.)

Around Town

Climb the hill on the east side of town behind the elementary school for the view and the community pool. The Catholic and Presbyterian churches are up here, a few blocks from **graveyard flat**, also known as Death Valley.

Back down the hill, cross Main and Buel streets and take a right on Spring. The first building on the left is the old **Methodist Church**, refurbished into a private residence in 1982 by Frank and Carol Bluess. Next door is the **Parsonage House**, built in 1886 and renovated in 1986. A pleasant little park with big shade trees and picnic tables lies half a block west (and across the creek) from the Parsonage.

You can also see the sites of the **Richmond Consolidated Smelter** on the south (west) end of town, and the **Eureka Consolidated Smelter** on the north (east) end. Both are no more than black slag heaps.

A free *Self-Guiding Tour of Eureka* booklet gives descriptions of 47 historic sites whose identifying numbers correspond to the numbers in the brochure. It's a fine resource for taking a really close historical look around. You can pick up the tour booklet at the Opera House, at the courthouse or any other county building, and at most of the businesses in town; most town businesses have a selection of brochures about the town and the area.

The **Eureka County Swimming Pool,** 200 Sheridan St., 775/237-5216, two blocks west of the auto parts store, is an indoor swimming pool open year round. It's open every day except Monday; phone for hours.

If you happen to have your shotgun along, check out the **Perdiz Sport Shooting Club,** 775/237-7027, two miles south of Eureka in Windfall Canyon. As you approach town from the east, you'll see a sign proclaiming, Sporting Clays—Two Miles. Take a left. The fully automated course has 10 stations with five clay rounds. Each station fires a clay target that mimics the flight pattern of chukar, sage hen, and other game birds. The club hosts three shooting contests each year: the Gold Country Blast April 5–6, the Nevada State Duck Unlimited Shoot June 21–22, and the Eureka Walk About Aug. 1–3.

PRACTICALITIES

A hotel and three motels account for less than 100 rooms in Eureka. In small communities like this, where accommodation is limited, it's always best to call in advance for reservations. All the town's restaurants are on US 50, called Main St. as it goes through Eureka.

On the southwest corner of Main St. and Ruby Hill is the **Jackson House Hotel,** 775/237-5518—built in 1877, burned in 1880, rebuilt, renamed, vacant for decades, restored, and reopened. The bar is bright and airy for a bar; in fact you can even sit outside on the verandah, have a beer, and watch the world go by—one of the great things to do not only in Eureka, but Nevada as well. Next door to the bar is a restaurant. Upstairs are nine hotel rooms, again beautifully restored in the style of a historic inn, which it is. Most of the rooms and bathrooms are big, have lots of wood, heavy quilts, cable TV, and carpeted floors. You can sit on the balcony and overlook Main St. and the courthouse. Rates are $79 to $119.

The **Best Western Eureka Inn,** 251 N. Main St., 775/237-5247, has 41 rooms and two suites, with prices from $69 to $119. It's quite luxurious accommodation, for a historic mining town. Otherwise, there's the **Ruby Hill Motel,** 775/237-

5339, with 11 rooms at $28–38; **Sundown Lodge,** 775/237-5334, with 27 rooms at $31–45; and the **Colonnade Hotel,** Clark and Monroe, 775/237-9988, www.thecolonnadehotel.com. The Colonnade, an historic 1880 hotel, was closed for restoration at this writing, but is expected to be restored and open again by early 2002.

On the southwest side of town is **Eureka RV Park,** renting spaces for $10 per night. **Silver Sky Lodge & RV Park,** 775/237-5034, on the left side of US 50 as you are driving east out of Eureka, has spaces for $15 per night with full hookups.

Food

DJ's, 775/237-5356, on Main St. at the far south end of town, is a drive-in restaurant with a dining room attached. It's moderately priced, serving breakfast, lunch, and dinner, with a large variety of foods on the menu, ranging from drive-in style food to full dinners. You can go to the walk-up window for burgers, chicken, burritos, tacos and the like, then eat at picnic tables around the side. Open 11 A.M.–9 P.M. every day.

The **Jackson House Bar & Restaurant** in the Jackson House Hotel is a gourmet restaurant with a big-city selection of dishes—the chef was trained in New York. Dinners are in the $20 range. Open Tues.–Sun., 5–9 P.M. Across Main, the **Owl Club & Steak House,** 775/237-5280, serves everything from burgers to lobster, with prices about the same as at the Jackson House. It's open long hours, from 5:30 A.M.–9:30 P.M. every day.

Opposite the Owl Club is the **Eureka Café,** 775/237-7165, serving a full selection of Chinese and American foods, with lunch and dinner specials daily. It's open every day, 11 A.M.–10 P.M. The **Cowboy Bar & Grill,** 775/237-5353, is another medium-priced place, serving a cowboy selection from burgers to prime rib. It's open for dinner 5–9 P.M. Thursday, Friday, and Saturday nights.

Information

The Opera House is the best place to go for information about Eureka town and county (see the Opera House, above); museum director Wally Cuchine is very helpful. The **Eureka County Library,** kitty-corner from the back of the courthouse on Monroe, 775/237-5307, is open Mon. 4–8 P.M., Tues.–Thurs. noon–5 P.M., and Fri. 10 A.M.–4 P.M.

NORTH TO CARLIN

Almost immediately upon leaving Eureka, you drop down out of the Diamond Mountains and head north, into cultivated Diamond Valley, where US 50 swings around again to the west. Right at the curve in the road is the junction with NV 278 north to Carlin (92 miles). You turn northwest and run up the west side of Diamond Valley, with **Whistler Mountain** rising 8,147 feet to the west, and big **Diamond Mountain** (10,614 feet) fading to the east. This is a busy ranching and agricultural valley, full of farmhouses in the middle of green fields, irrigation rigs, long and tall rows of baled hay under big hay shelters. The civilization continues to about 15 miles north of Eureka, beyond which is fenced range, cattle ruminating in the sage.

The well-paved road cuts west across a shoulder in the southern **Sulphur Spring Range**, skirting east of **Hope Mountain** (8,411 feet), turning north, and cresting **Garden Pass** (6,685 feet). The compact **Roberts Mountains** come into view in the west, mostly consisting of **Roberts Creek Mountain** at 10,133 feet.

You head north into **Garden Valley**, and then the landscape opens up into interconnecting **Horse Creek** and **Pine Valleys**. The **Cortez Mountains** come into view, with **Mt. Tenabo** standing 9,162 feet tall, and a turnoff to the ghost town of Cortez (see "Crescent Valley" in the Battle Mountain and Vicinity section) by way of JD Ranch and Buckthorn. The **Sulphur Springs Range** usher you mile after mile on the east. It's open range up here; watch for cows.

At the top of Pine Valley, **Pine Creek** materializes and accompanies you past **Pine Mountain** (8,132 feet) in the Piñon Range, and through the north foothills of the Cortez Mountains. You're back in civilization here somewhat: alfalfa country, with trucks hauling hay and school bus stops on the side of the road. It even looks a lot like Crescent Valley, one valley west on the other side of the Cortezes, with long rows of big windbreak trees protecting the fields of green.

A little more than 80 miles from Eureka, you go by the turnoff to Palisade (see "Palisade" in the Carlin section).

TO AUSTIN

Back on US 50 heading west, you've passed the turnoff for NV 278 to Carlin, and the road has curved around toward the setting sun. You go through **Devil's Gate** in the **Mahogany Hills,** then cut due west across broad **Antelope Valley.** The **Simpson Park Mountains** are on the north side, curving around to the southwest, on the other side of **Bean Flat.** The road runs by the north face of the **Monitor Range,** where **Summit Mountain** and **Antelope Peak** both rise to a little over 10,500 feet, and then across big **Monitor Valley.**

You pass the cutoff to Belmont, an excellent graded and gravel road (45–50 mph) straight down Monitor Valley between the big Monitors and Toquimas. Finally, after keeping company with the Simpson Park Mountains for many miles, you start climbing into them, up to **Hickison Summit** (6,594 feet). Some outstanding **petroglyphs** have weathered the ages up here, and are now protected as part of the BLM **Hickison Petroglyph Recreation Area.** The ancient rock carvings are visible in a shallow sandstone draw (pun intended) on the north side of the highway. A half-mile trail loops through sage and pine, passing dozens of the drawings, some of which date back 12,000 years.

From there, you drop down south into **Big Smoky Valley,** and 12 miles east of Austin pass NV 376, which runs 117 miles straight down the valley to Tonopah (see below).

US 50 cuts north into the Toiyabes over **Scott Summit** (7,195 feet) with **Bob Scott Campground,** a Forest Service facility, right there on the right. It has picnic tables, fire rings with grills, single-leaf piñon and juniper, 10 sites, and flush toilets all high up and comfortable in these beautiful mountains. There's no fee. Bring your own drinking water. The spigots scattered liberally throughout the campground may not be working. An interesting historical sign about surveyors—railway, military, water, and wagon routes—is across the road.

After Scott Summit, it's a little strange to *continue* climbing, to 7,484 feet at **Austin Summit.** Then you drop down a six-percent grade into Austin, which sits at 6,575 feet.

AUSTIN

INTRODUCTION

Austin's history reaches back to the days of the Pony Express. Silver was discovered in May 1862 by a recently retired rider in a small canyon in the Toiyabe Mountains, just up the hill from Reese River Valley, along the route of the express mail service. The "Rush to the Reese" got underway in early 1863, and by spring of that year a thousand claims had been staked in newly named Pony Canyon and on nearby hills. By summer, Austin, named after the Texas hometown of one of the original locators, was a bona fide boomtown.

Virginia City's International Hotel was dismantled board by board, hauled across the desert, and re-erected in downtown Austin. Lander County was created around Austin in 1863; it was so big that it occupied almost the entire eastern half of the territory. Eventually, Eureka, Elko, White Pine, and Nye counties were carved out of it (Lincoln County wasn't even part of Nevada yet). The *Reese River Reveille* went from a weekly to a daily in a matter of months. Three quartz mills started up almost immediately. Prospectors fanned out into the far northern, northeastern, and eastern reaches of the territory, returning to town for supplies. Their indications triggered rushes to Belmont, Tuscarora, Hamilton, Eureka, Pioche, and later Tonopah and Goldfield.

Austin dogged Virginia City's output ounce by ounce in silver and history for the next 10 years. Roughly $50 million in gold and silver were recovered from the Reese District during its heyday, which lasted until around 1873. The Nevada Central Railroad, arriving in 1880, proved a bit late.

Austin is home to a number of classic Nevada legends, such as the Gridley Flour Sack that raised $250,000 for the Sanitary Fund (the Civil War's version of the Red Cross); the Sazerac Lying Club immortalized in Oscar Lewis's 1954 *The Town That Died Laughing;* and the Reese River Navigation Company, a phony steamship line.

Like everywhere else in Nevada, Austin experienced the long, melancholy decline of resources and population until quite recently, with this latest resurgence of mining. Turquoise and barium are abundant, in addition to the gold and silver.

Today, Austin has fewer than 300 residents, with no doctor, no pharmacy, and no barber shop. But it's still as central to Nevada's history as any other town of any size in the state. Its location, in addition, is 12 miles from the exact geographical center of Nevada. But Austin sits nearest to the heart of Nevada in *attitude.* Austin takes pride in offering the kind of personal liberty whereby "a person can do just about anything he sets his mind to so long as he doesn't step on anybody else's toes." With just 250 inhabitants in town, and two hours from Fallon and Tonopah and more than an hour from Eureka and Battle Mountain, stepping on anybody else's toes isn't easy.

SIGHTS

A two-minute drive at 10 mph along Main Street near the bottom of Pony Canyon takes you past almost everything. The town park is on the east edge of town as you come in on US 50; turn left on Nevada Street. Here you'll find kids' apparatus, outdoor pool (with the locker room in front), and some big trees with picnic tables underneath.

Bikes and Rocks

Coming from the east into town, the first business you reach is also the newest. Rick Crawford of **Tyrannosaurus Rix Mountain Bike and Specialties** (known as **T-Rix**), 775/964-1212, www.t-rix.com, is trying to lead Austin to its rightful place in the mountain biking world: the top. This corner of the Toiyabes is chock full of all the things post-pavement pedalers demand: lung-searing hill climbs, heart-stopping downhills, and killer views. Problem is, no one knows it, even though Austin straddles US 50, the most direct route from California to the mountain biking

SAZERAC LYING CLUB

Fred Hart, editor of Austin's *Reese River Reveille* from 1873 to 1878, frequently found himself without anything "of a startling nature in the line of news" to print. This was a not uncommon predicament for editors of small frontier-town dailies, and it partially accounts for the tradition of 19th-century western journalism, which incorporated elements of exaggeration, fantasy, satire, ribaldry, and just plain fiction, to fill up the column inches. Mark Twain, its most famous practitioner, summed it up with, "Never let the facts get in the way of a good tale."

One night, Hart, making his reporter's rounds, stopped into the Sazerac Saloon, where old-timers gathered to drink, smoke, and storytell. He overheard a description by one of the regulars about silver bars he had once seen in Mexico, which made a pile "seven miles long, forty feet high, and thirteen feet wide." The next day, strapped as usual for hard news, Hart printed a notice of the formation the previous night of the Sazerac Lying Club, which had unanimously elected Mr. George Washington Fibley as president.

It didn't take long for other Nevada and California newspapers to begin reprinting tall tales from the *Reese River Reveille* attributed to the Sazerac Lying Club, and from there news of the Austin institution spread far and wide. One story recounted the reason that a stage from Belmont had been delayed. Uncle John Gibbons, the driver, was en route when he seemed to be approaching a "thick bank of dark clouds," which in fact turned out to be a flock of sage hens. "'But boys, that was more sage-hen obstructin' that road than I had reckoned on, and when them thar leader horses struck into them thar sage-hen, they was throwed back on the haunches just as if they had butted clean up ag'in a stone wall. As far's you could see thar warn't nothin' but sage hen; you

could about see the top of the pile of 'em.'" Uncle John unhitched one of the horses and rode back to the station for help.

The hostler grabbed an axe, ready to "chop a road through the sage-hen." But a prospector there said, "'See here, boys, don't you think we could blast 'em out quicker'n we could chop through 'em?'"

The prospector "went up the hill and got his drills and his sledges and a lot of giant-powder cartridges and some fuse, and the rest of the blastin' apparatus, and then the whole raft of us started back for the place where the stage was; and when we got thar—well I wish I may be runned over by a two-horse jerkwater if there was a sage-hen in sight as far's a man could see with a spy-glass. I hope you fellows is contented now you know what kept the stage late the other night.'"

This tale somehow made its way to Germany, where it was printed by the *Karlsruher Zeitung.* The article was forwarded back to Austin, where a German-speaking resident translated it into English.

"In Austin, Nevada, America, there is a society whose object is competitive lying . . . The lie which took the premium this year was told by Uncle John Gibonich. He said that while riding post across the Valley of the Smoke there arose from the earth a flock of geese so numberless that they blocked the road and shut out the light of day. And in order that the blockade might be raised, and the royal mails pass on their way, it was deemed useful to telegraph for a corps of sappers and miners from the Government barracks, who mined a tunnel through the mass of geese, and the post proceeded on its way."

—Adapted from
The Town That Died Laughing , by Oscar Lewis

mecca of Moab, Utah. Rick can rent, sell, or build you a bike. Rick also offers guided off-road bike tours of the Toiyabes. The refreshments served here, including espresso, latte, frozen or hot cappuccino, yogurt and other refreshments, are especially popular with European visitors longing for a good European-style coffee. The store is open every day, all year round.

Rick opened up shop in 1996, and a year later he was organizing his first American Mountain Bike Association race, T Rix Lost World Chal-

lenge, Aug. 23–24, 1997. Since then, the event, held for a full weekend each August, has blossomed into the annual Claim Jumpers Mountain Bike Festival, a family event including a 27-mile mountain bike cross-country race on Saturday, a downhill race on Sunday, plus free racing and activities for children, barbecues featuring home-made ice cream, open swimming and a live band.

4 M's Gems, 775/964-1346, is a retail outlet for a local turquoise miner, Mitch Cantrell. This store sells rocks and old bottles; Mitch also arranges rock hunting to his mine and wildlife-viewing excursions. **Nevada Blue Rock & Gem,** 775/964-2063, owned by Pancho and Joan Williams, carries a large selection of jewelry and gifts. Across from the courthouse, **The Trading Post,** 775/964-1348, has an extensive collection of rocks, old bottles, jewelry and gifts. There's a display of handmade dolls for sale in the office of the **Mountain Motel.**

Gridley Store

You can't miss this stone building on Main Street on the right coming into town from the east. The store was opened in 1863 by Rueul Gridley, whose name lives on in conjunction with a 50-pound sack of flour. Gridley paid off a losing bet by carrying the flour from his store to a bar across town, and then auctioning it off for a donation to the Sanitary Fund. The highest bidder auctioned it off again, then again, and again. Nearly $10,000 was raised by the end of the afternoon. From there, Gridley took the sack to Virginia City and repeated the process, then on to California and eventually the East Coast, raising $250,000 for Civil War relief. Gridley himself died penniless six years later. The house next to Gridley's store was originally the town brothel.

Up the hill from the store is **Austin RV Park and Baptist Church** (see below), along with most of Austin's residential neighborhood (the other side of the canyon lives in shadows half the year). Also up here is the Austin school, built in 1926. Less than 10 students graduate each year.

Down Main, across from the old courthouse, a historical sign tells about Austin's three striking churches, all visible from this point.

Churches

The Catholic church is the oldest in the state, the Episcopal church has been in continuous use since 1878, and the Methodist church has been in continuous use since 1866, though it hasn't been a church for a long time (today, it's the town hall). Another classic Austin tale involves a Reverend Trefren, who announced his intention to build a church for his parishioners in Austin and asked for donations. Immediately, stock certificates encompassing hundreds of feet of mining claims poured into the hat. Trefren had a minister's faith, a miner's tongue, and a

manipulator's talent. He immediately named himself president of the Methodist Mining Company, using his wildcat stock certificates as assets. He then issued shares in his own company and printed a brochure explaining how he would invest any initial capital in producing silver, the dividends of which would build a house of worship to the everlasting glory of Methodists and God. He had maps drawn, assay certificates notarized, and illustrations of the workings produced; he carried a fancy display case full of precious metals. Then he traveled back to his home territory of New England to sell to the Yankees. Trefren raised tens of thousands of dollars, and though his mining venture quickly collapsed, the church still stands.

Stokes' Castle

To get to this curious attraction, which could only be found in Austin, take a left on Castle Rd. at the west end of town, and follow a precipitous road about a half mile around to the back of the hill. This rare, three-story, stone "castle," built by mining baron Anson P. Stokes, has stood here like a sentinel for over 100 years. Incredibly, it was only occupied for a month or two in the summer of 1897. Still, it's a fine place to have a picnic, or stretch your legs in the piñon forest uphill, with a great overlook of Reese River Valley. You could camp here in a pinch.

PRACTICALITIES

Accommodations

There are a total of 39 rooms in Austin, none of which could be considered anything but utilitarian. Actually, things have improved some on the Austin lodging scene in the past few years: the Pony Canyon and the Lincoln Motel now have phones in the rooms.

The **Lincoln Motel,** 728 Main St., 775/964-2698, has eight-by-ten-foot rooms with a queen bed; you can sit on the toilet, wash your hands, shave, and brush your teeth all at the same time; $29–45. The rooms at the **Mountain Motel,** 902 Main St., 775/964-2471, occupy a single-wide trailer, with walnut paneling and gas heat; there are no phones in the rooms here, but the new owners seem to have fixed the crazy angles the rooms used to lean at. The Mountain is also the only inn in Austin that offers non-smoking rooms; $32–45. There are 10 rooms at the **Pony Canyon Motel,** 775/964-2605, not a whole lot fancier than the others, $34–52.

You can rent the two-bedroom **Pony Express House,** 775/964-2306, for $35 a night (one room) or $70 a night (both rooms). The house is historic, built in the late 1860s. This is a "bed and fix your own breakfast."

Austin RV and Baptist Church on the right as you enter town, 775/964-1011, set at 6,900 feet, is the only RV park in Nevada that's connected to a church. The retired minister's wife, Donna White, leases the parking-lot RV park from the church (there are too many potential conflicts of interest for the church to be in the campground business); still, the RV office doubles as the Sunday school. Fee collecting is somewhat on the honor system (read the signs on the information board and drop the night's payment in the drop box on the front of the office). There are 21 sites, $17 for RVs (20 and 30 amp service available). Tent campers can use the large grassy area, $10. Hot showers and laundry facilities are available.

Food and Information

Austin has two places to eat, each with unique charms. **Toiyabe Café,** 775/964-2220, is open 6 A.M.–9 P.M. April–October. They close an hour earlier in the off-season. For breakfast try the green chile and Swiss or Spanish omelette, or bacon and eggs for. Lunch and dinner fare includes good soup and burritos, burgers, steak sandwich, and fish, beer and wine available.

The **International** cafe on the west side of town is in the second-oldest hotel building in Nevada (though lodging is not available). It's open 5:30 A.M.–9 P.M. and has good food. For a tasty filling meal, try the twice-baked potatoes with broccoli, bacon, and cheddar cheese for $3.95. Your basic burger runs $4.25, add 50 cents for cheese.

The new **U.S. Forest Service station,** on the west side of town overlooking the junction of NV 305, 775/964-2671, is open 7:45 A.M.–4:30 P.M. weekdays. It sells detailed maps ($2) and can advise you on hikes and the like.

The **Austin Chamber of Commerce,** 775/964-2200, has a large rack of brochures in the foyer of the courthouse; the chamber office upstairs is open most weekday mornings. Track down Wally Trapnell or Joy Brandt of the chamber for the latest Austin info. You can pick up brochures from the rack downstairs in the courthouse whenever the courthouse is open—Mon.–Fri. 8 A.M.–5 P.M.

To Fallon

For the continuation of the trip description for the 111 miles east from Austin to Fallon, please see "To Fallon" in the South of Austin section later in this chapter.

SOUTH OF AUSTIN

THE TOIYABES

Like the Ruby Mountains in northeast Nevada, the Snake Range in eastern Nevada, and the Spring Mountains in southern Nevada, the Toiyabe Range is the preeminent stretch of mountains in central Nevada. "Toiyabe" is a Shoshone word, variously translated as "Black Mountains," for the thick piñon, juniper, and mahogany cover, and "Big Mountains," for their length, height, steepness, and ruggedness. From Toiyabe Peak near Austin to Mahogany Mountain opposite Carver's, this mansard roof tops the exact middle of the state in a thin straight line more than 10,000 feet high for 50 miles. The southern slope extends for another 20 miles, tapering off into two squat legs (with feet), while the upper range elongates for another 50 miles, rising to a head at mystical Mt. Callaghan. Austin, at 6,500 feet one of the highest towns in Nevada, rests below the neck.

Three peaks at the southern waist and up near the shoulder tower over 11,000 feet, with Arc Dome the highest at 11,788 feet. Another four peaks in the range rise over 10,000 feet. Big Smoky Valley accompanies the steeper eastern scarp from up near Austin to the bottom. The top of mighty Mt. Jefferson of the Toquima Range right across the valley actually looks down

the Toiyabe Range

JOHN ELK III

200 feet at the crown of Arc Dome. This is one of the finest mountain scenes in the state. Reese River Valley faces the wetter western wall. Numerous creeks converge at the trough on the west side of the range to create the mud-puddle Reese River and fertile ranch land.

Frémont appears to have been the first non-Indian to set foot in Big Smoky Valley (1845); he named it after the late summer haze that partially obscured it. He followed it for three days, camping at Birch Creek, the hot springs, and Peavine. James Simpson passed along its northern edge in 1859 as he surveyed the central alternative route through the territory. After Austin attracted its horde of fortune seekers in 1863, prospectors crawled all over the Toiyabes, finding some minerals within the granite intrusions. Toiyabe City, Kingston, Canyon City, Geneva, Amador, and Yankee Blade all sprouted and withered at the finds.

Today, Arc Dome is the largest Forest Service Wilderness Area in Nevada at 115,000 acres. *Hiking the Great Basin* by John Hart covers a baker's-dozen hikes here in detail, including two for Arc Dome, several from Twin Rivers, Jett Canyon, and the 65-mile Toiyabe Crest National Recreation Trail. *Nevada Wilderness Areas* by Michael Rose covers seven hikes here, including two Twin River loops, Cow, Tom's, and Jett canyons, and the Toiyabe Crest Trail. If internal combustion is more your style, the roads down Big Smoky from Austin to Tonopah and up Reese River Valley from Ione Canyon to Austin

provide two of the most breathtaking scenic cruises not only in Nevada but throughout the West.

Heading South
As you turn south on NV 376, 12 miles east of Austin, the first ridgeline you see is defined by Toiyabe Peak (10,793 feet) and Bunker Hill (11,474 feet). About 15 miles south of the junction is a turnoff into **Kingston.** In the late 1960s, a developer attempted to transform the ranch land around present-day Kingston into a town like Venice, California, with cobblestone streets, outdoor cafes, and upscale boutiques. It didn't happen. Today there's a little gold mining going on, supported by a small settlement; still, it's the third-largest population center, behind Battle Mountain and Austin, in Lander County.

You drive on pavement past the town and continue to where, predictably, the pavement ends on the way into **Kingston Canyon.** In another couple of miles is Kingston Canyon Forest Service campground, with 12 sites right on the creek at the lush bottom of the canyon, with big trees, and fat gooseberries in August; $7. A half mile up the canyon is a small fishing pond; another half mile presents the trailhead to the Toiyabe Crest Trail. One more half mile brings you to the Forest Service station. And from there, the road travels right over the Toiyabes in the shadow of massive Bunker Hill, to connect up with the Reese River Valley road into Austin.

Continuing south on NV 376, you pass Sheep

Canyon, Crooked Canyon, and Toiyabe Range Peak (10,960 feet), with a few 8,000- to 9,000-foot "hills" in between. Ten miles from the Kingston junction is **Smokey Joe's** gas station (Shell) and mini-mart: clean restrooms, friendly service, and food.

South of there is a line of sheer granite walls, and I mean *straight* up and down. The valley just below is lined with ranches. The bottomland below that is another alkali bed of another ice-age lake. Roads head up into Summit Creek and Ophir Creek and Twin River below Toiyabe Range Peak (10,805 feet) to the old mining sites. Directly across the valley to the east in the Toquima Range loom **Mt. Jefferson's** three summits, all over 11,000 feet.

Carver's

Just beyond Darrough's Hot Springs (private, no sign) is Carver's. Jean and Gerald Carver homesteaded in the area in the early 1940s, then built a small restaurant and bar called, naturally enough, Carver's, halfway between Austin and Tonopah in 1947 right after the state road was cut. They served auto travelers and truckers, along with miners from the Round Mountain district just down the road. Twenty years later, as the mining continued in fits and starts, enough people had settled nearby that the name Carver's started showing up on state maps. And 20 years after that, when Round Mountain Gold cranked up the mining in earnest, Carver's found itself a full-fledged boomtown. The place that gave the town its name is now owned by the folks who run the International back in Austin. Retired now, Jean and Gerald are still nearby.

Today, Carver's consists of a big highway maintenance station, cafe, two gas stations, small shopping center, LDS temple, and firehouse. The **Jumping Jack Motel,** 775/377-2566, is the only motel between Austin and Tonopah. It has only 17 rooms, and sometimes fills up with vendors for the gold mine, so it's a good idea to phone ahead for reservations. Rooms are $35 single, $40 double.

The newest place on the strip is **Scott Stop USA,** 775/377-2100. Scott Stop is a veritable roadside empire with a Chester's Chicken joint, video rental counter, gas station, Western Union office, grocery store, and U-Haul franchise tucked under its pre-fab roof. Bertie and Larry Berg own

the **Napa Auto Parts** store, 775/377-2301, a few hundred yards down on the left next to the Boyer family's **D&S Shopping World,** 775/377-2490. Get your tourist info at D&S, along with horseshoes, pig feed, flowers, fishing license, guns (real and toy versions), and Western-style shirts with pearl snaps; closed Sunday. **Scissors Salon** next door will do your hair. Also, be sure to stop in and have a look at the **Full Moon Saloon** to have a direct experience of why the words "bar" and "barn" are so similar. The Full Moon is party central for Big Smoky Valley, and serves lunch and dinner.

At Carver's the road turns to the southeast, aiming right at Round Mountain, where Round Mountain Gold Corporation's miners dig for gold and pile up overburden at one of the largest operations along a major road in Nevada. At the turnoff, the road to the right leads to **Hadley,** one of the largest company towns in Nevada. It's occupied by roughly 500 miners and their families, who pay $50 a month for their mobile homes. Here there are a 24-hour day care center, an elementary and junior high school, medical clinic, swimming pool and rec center, and nine-hole golf course.

The Round Mountain Golf Club, 775/377-2880, operates the longest nine-hole course in Nevada. William Howard Neff, a top golf course architect from Utah, designed the par-36 course, which boasts three lakes. The course has a country club, cafe, lounge, cart rentals, and one of the best pro shops north of Las Vegas. There are two par fives, one 571 yards and the other 538. The course is open to the public; green fees run $10 for nine holes and $15 for 18. There's a paved airstrip 300 yards away (par 3?).

ROUND MOUNTAIN AND VICINITY

Round Mountain

Round Mountain is the name of the town, the hill it sits on, the circular tailings piling up around the pit, and the company doing the digging. All these "Round Mountains" provide an excellent history of the different forms of gold mining that have been practiced around the West over the last 140 years.

Placer gold (waterborne deposits of sand or

gravel containing minerals eroded from original bedrock), which washed down from ledges in the Toquimas into this valley, was discovered by prospectors from Goldfield in 1906. The gold occurred in small high-grade veins that could be dug out with hand tools and hoisted up with gasoline engines. Later, dry-wash machines worked the surface gravel deposits. A million dollars was recovered by the initial individual operators. In 1914, a larger syndicate laid a pipe across Big Smoky Valley from Jett Canyon in the Toiyabes to sluice the gold out of the lower-grade ore. In the mid-1920s, the Nevada Porphyry Gold Mine Company installed a dredge, which became the largest gold-gravel washing operation in the state's history.

A number of companies tried their hands at mining Round Mountain over the next couple of decades, till large equipment was installed in 1950. Huge power shovels scooped the paydirt into equally huge hoppers, which funneled it onto long conveyor belts. These belts, 36 inches wide and miles long, traveled at three miles an hour to stockpiles. From there, the ore was weighed and sent to crushers and washers, which could handle 500 tons an hour.

A lull in the mining quieted the area and nearly evacuated the town in the 1960s. But in the 1970s, a number of gold and oil companies began developing the lode; by 1977, the mine was processing 7,000 tons a day. In 1985, Echo Bay Ltd. bought in and began an extensive expansion, culminating in 1991 with a system that could handle 135,000 tons of ore every day. In 1983, the mine produced 92,000 ounces of gold leached from 3.6 million tons of ore at a cost of $265 per ounce; in 1990, the mine produced 432,000 ounces of gold from 16 million tons at a cost of $174 per ounce.

Today, the open pit is 8,000 feet long, 7,200 feet wide, and 1,200 feet deep; the miners will dig another 400 feet deep. This microscopic stuff is mined on a scale that seems more like copper than gold; it takes 300 tons of ore to produce one ounce of gold. Twenty-eight-yard shovels, 23-yard excavators, 10,000-gallon water trucks, 190-ton dump trucks working at the bottom of the pit are dwarfed by its magnitude. But when those dump trucks come barreling by, with tires as tall as your house, and you think that it takes two full loads to make just one ounce of gold, you

get a forcible impression of what "microscopic gold" really means. Still, say what you will about the ugliness of open-pit mines and the toxicity of the sodium cyanide leaching solution on the one hand, and the land use, employment, and economic benefits on the other: when you come right down to it, it's just a bunch of guys playing in the dirt.

You can't just waltz in and tour the operation, but you can tell from the size of everything as you drive by on NV 376 and 378 that this place means business. As you drive up NV 378 past the round mountain surrounding the pit, the colorful overburden is eye-catching: grays, reds, pinks, purples, even blues. The town of Round Mountain is up the hill past the pit and has a grand total of five, if that many, actual houses. The few dozen dwellings are mobile homes.

Manhattan

After gold was discovered in the shadow of Bald Mountain in the Toquimas in 1906, a rush from Goldfield got underway. The first excitement, financed by San Francisco capital, was prematurely aborted by the great earthquake that year, but Manhattan recovered in 1910. Successful placer operations necessitated the building of a large mill in 1912. Then rich paydirt was discovered in the lower levels of the hard-rock mine in 1915, and the mill had to be reconditioned. In the late 1930s, advanced gold-mining technology arrived in the form of a great gold dredge, an Alaska-size contraption that looked like a cartoon cross between an oversized houseboat and a crane. An endless conveyor on the dredge circulated dozens of steel buckets that scooped the gravel, conveyed it to the top end, and dumped it onto a revolving screen. The screen separated the larger rocks (shunting them off to the tailings piles), from the golden gravel, which was sifted by the screen onto riffles. There, quicksilver (mercury) gleaned the gold, forming an amalgam. The riffles were cleaned and the amalgam was further processed into bullion, which was assayed and shipped to the mint. The dredge operated for eight years. Manhattan produced $10 million in gold over its 40-year run. Houston Minerals started up the process again in the late '70s after gold was set loose to find its own worth on the international market, and Round Mountain Gold continues to run a comparatively small operation.

Today, Manhattan is a big-city name for a tiny, though attractive, village in a lovely canyon in the lower Toquimas. Driving up on NV 377, you pass the Manhattan pit. Old headframes overlook the pit from the hill above; the company production plant is behind the pit on the other side. Manhattan town is up the road, with abandoned shacks, old houses, big trees, and a couple of bars. **Miner's Saloon** has video poker, bar food such as polish sausage, collectibles such as rocks, bottles, and jewelry, and apple trees outside. **Manhattan Bar** is darker, more rustic. Around 60 people live in Manhattan year-round. NV 377 continues past the water tank near the top of the canyon. There the pavement ends, and you drive over to the east side of the Toquimas 12 miles to Belmont.

This is a fun road, full of ups and downs, twists and turns, 30 mph. At the first fork, bear left. At the second fork, go right to hook up to the main gravel road from the original right fork off NV 376 just north of Tonopah. In a few miles you come to pavement, pass the big stack from the Belmont-Monitor mill, then cruise into Belmont.

Belmont

Silver indications were uncovered high up on the sunrise side of the Toquimas in 1865, in the lee of big Mt. Jefferson. The site, blessed by wood, water, and stone, was so attractive that after several initial names for the site, Belmont, meaning Beautiful Mountain in French, stuck.

The rush was so great that 2,000 people lived in and around Belmont within a year. The mines and mills began producing millions of dollars of silver, and the state Legislature decided to move the Nye County seat from Ione to Belmont in 1867.

The courthouse, however, remained in a rented storefront for 10 years until a two-story building was completed in 1876. Ironically, by then the Belmont boom was as good as dead; the $22,000 courthouse opened the same year that the mines produced $11,000 worth of silver. Belmont continued to decline until most of the last 150 people left were county administrative employees. In 1905 the seat moved to Tonopah.

Still, Belmont had produced $15 million in silver during its 15-year heyday. Some excitement returned in the early 1900s on the aural edge of the Tonopah noise, but it was short-lived. Fire, vandals, ghost towners, and entropy took their toll for the next 60 years, until the state stepped in to stabilize the courthouse building and protect the town as a park. Belmont was also declared a National Historic District, which eliminated further scavenging.

Today, Belmont's restored beauty is reminiscent of Unionville's a couple of hundred miles northwest. Fewer than 10 residents are full-time. Old and new houses are full of character and surrounded by well-tended yards. The courthouse (no entry) presides over it all. The ruins, too, are picturesque, but be aware that tramping in, around, and through them is trespassing, and

Dick Ashton's Belmont Saloon is open only on weekends, but it is worth scheduling your visit around.

DEKE CASTLEMAN

the locals are very protective about their town. In fact, the town's only paid employee is a caretaker (he'll no doubt check you out in his Jeep).

The **Belmont Saloon,** which has been called the Queen of Nye County Ghost Towns, has been owned by Las Vegas refugee Dick Ashton since 1979. It's open only on weekends. But you can get a good look through the front windows, at the bar, taken from the ruins of an 1880s hotel up the street, 1940s jukebox, denim bar-stool covers, sardine-can ashtrays, '50s refrigerator, potato-sack ceiling, and the infamous "jug mug" atop the 1905 cash register.

Continuing on the Monitor Valley road for 17 miles brings you to a sign for **Pine Creek Campground;** follow the sign to the left and drive another 2.5 miles to the USFS camp. There are 26 sites and no fee. Catch trout in the stream. This is also your entrance to the 38,000-acre **Alta Toquima Wilderness Area,** containing the three-peaked Mt. Jefferson, at 11,941 feet the sixth highest mountain in Nevada. The Pine Creek Trail travels just under 14 miles to the South Summit and the ridgeline that connects it to the Middle and North summits. See *Nevada Wilderness Areas* by Michael Rose for all the details.

THE TOQUIMAS AND MONITOR VALLEY

Spencer Hot Springs

Just after you turn south onto NV 376 from US 50 a dozen miles east of Austin, a dirt road immediately heads off east (left) toward the Toquima Range. The dirt starts out rough (30 mph and a lane and a half) and gets worse (15 mph and a lane). Roughly halfway across the valley, a left turn (distinct though unsignposted) leads up to Spencer Hot Springs. This is a fine spot—with the Toiyabes stretching into the background and the Monitors reaching into the foreground and the big desert valley spreading out at your feet—for a hot soak. These springs are not only quite civilized and not too far off the beaten track, but also expertly "developed." The big pool at the top ledge is sandbagged, tastefully tiled with slate, and offset by a little wooden deck. Toward the road a bit is a big galvanized tub. Hot water flows from a pipe. Put the pipe in

the tub to regulate the temperature. Then lie back, breathe deeply, and offer up a prayer of thanks for your nerve endings.

Toquima Cave

Back on the main dirt track to the Toquimas, you travel in a ruler-straight line due southeast across Big Smoky Valley to where the mountains close in around you and then you climb up into them. At **Pete's Summit** (7,900 feet), a turnoff to Toquima Cave is signposted: picnic tables, firepits, parking. Take the trailhead through the forest about a quarter mile. You start seeing a big red outcrop, and then arrive at a 15-foot cyclone fence installed by authority of the Antiquities Act of 1906. The "cave" behind the fence is more of an overhang but has primitive pictographs of mostly circular designs, such as suns and ripples, buns and nipples. Carbon from fires clings to the walls and ceiling. Frankly, it's not even worth hopping the fence.

Diana's Punch Bowl

Back again on track, you drop down pretty quick through **Sam's Canyon** into **Monitor Valley** and meet up with the good gravel road from US 50 just east of Eureka to Belmont and Tonopah. Take a right (south) and drive through the front yard of Monitor Ranch. Nice spread.

Speeding along at 45–50 mph affords some thrills and chills, you hope without the spills, on the roller-coaster road. The first left leads down to the site of **Potts,** which has stone, wood, and adobe ruins, plus a cold and delicious spring gurgling up from a pipe. You can see the Punch Bowl out there in the desert to the southeast— one big white mound, a roadcut winding to the top, a little steam maybe coming off it like warm breath. R.O. Livestock owns this property and in the past has been averse to hosting uninvited members of the public. But in 1997, word was the good folks at the R.O. had loosened up about allowing people on the property to visit the punch bowl. Just be quiet and conscientious, good rules to go by anywhere. And if you insist on getting naked, try not to spook the cattle.

Anyway, proceeding on your best behavior, you see that this big ol' hole is unique among natural hot springs formations: a cone-shaped bowl 50 feet across and 40 feet deep, with a hot pool at the bottom, not quite bubbling, but almost.

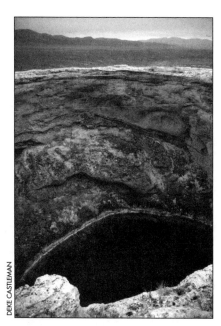

Diana's Punch Bowl—one of the strangest of geothermal phenomena in Nevada.

Around in back a creek runs out of the bowl. You can set up a pretty idyllic campsite in the grass by the creek, cow dung notwithstanding. Put up your tent and then go soak. The water is perfect, exact body temperature, and pretty soon you can't tell where your skin leaves off and the water starts up. All the while, Diana's weird boob looms, circular and steaming, overhead. Ultimately, you (and R.O.) own this part of Monitor Valley for the night. Just you, the water, stars, dark, fear, and bliss.

TO BERLIN-ICHTHYOSAUR AND BACK

The Mighty Reese River
Back on US 50 west, you drop down out of Austin onto the **Reese River Valley** flats, heading toward the **Shoshone Range**, still in national forest. Here you cross the raging Reese River. This perfect description appears in David

Toll's well-written *Complete Nevada Traveler:* "The Reese at floodtide has barely the breadth of a man's wrist and the depth of his fingers. Stagecoaches forded it at a full gallop with only the suggestion of a bump, and in the dry season the Reese is even less spectacular." This one is from Jim Andersen's affectionately funny article in *Nevada* magazine: "The Reese River is a river in the same sense that Stokes Castle is a castle; you have to use a little imagination."

Still, it was a well-known and surveyed river in the 1860s, and appeared on all the contemporary maps to flow confidently north from south of Austin in the Toiyabes to Battle Mountain and the Humboldt River. It provided a perfect apparition for starting up a paper business, calling it the Reese River Navigation Company, and selling phony stock in it to unsuspecting investors. Great joke.

Pony Express
Just beyond the Reese are markers for the Pony Express Trail. US 50 generally parallels the Pony Express Trail through central Nevada, but this stretch, between Austin and Carson City, is full of reminders of this 18-month adventure that helped open up the West.

Pony expresses had been known as mail and message relayers since the time of Genghis Khan (1203–27), who is generally credited with inventing the system: small jockeys riding flying ponies between stations every 25 miles or so. Several pony expresses were established on the East Coast to carry correspondence and news in the 1820s and '30s. But the idea for the express route from Missouri to California originated in the imagination of California Senator H.M. Gwin on a cross-country ride to Washington, D.C., in 1854. The tensions of pre-Civil War politics in the following years prevented the government from acting on Gwin's proposals, so he turned to the freighting firm of Russell, Majors, and Waddell, which ran the Overland Stage from St. Joseph, Missouri (western terminus of American railroads), to Salt Lake City. At Gwin's urging, the partners, against their better bottom-line judgment, accepted the challenge. Within two months they had recruited several division agents, built nearly 200 stations in the remote, barren, and dangerous 700-mile stretch between Salt Lake and Sacramento, bought 500 horses,

DEKE CASTLEMAN

and hired a score of riders. The first 10-day run from St. Joseph to Sacramento was completed on April 3, 1860.

The efficiency, bravery, endurance, and dedication of the employees are legendary. In Nevada, each rider completed a 33-mile route, with a fresh horse every 10 miles. Riders carried a pistol, a Bible, and the *mochila,* or padlocked mailbag. The stations, in Sir Richard Burton's eyewitness words, were "about as civilised as the Galway shanty—or the normal dwelling place in Central Equatorial Africa." Maintaining fresh horses, food, water, and security at the lonely stations was a continuous life and death struggle. Several riders and many stationmasters were killed on the warpath.

But the miracle of delivering mail from St. Jo to Sac in 10 days, the singlemindedness of the operation to open up the West (even in the face of the financial ruin of the company), and the romantic vision of the Pony riders stirred the collective imagination of the entire nation. That the Pony was logistically able to operate year-round proved that telegraphs and railroads could do the same, and prompted the government to invest in those evolving technologies. Ironically, completion of the transcontinental telegraph line along the Pony's route in October 1861 spelled its immediate demise: the incredible land-speed records set by Pony Express riders across the West were still no match for the miraculous dispatch of communications through the wire.

Modern-Day Pony

If US 50 is truly lonely on this stretch, try driving 10 mph for a ways to get a feel for the one-horsepower speed of the "XP" riders. From the Reese River Valley, you climb up to **Mt. Airy Summit** (6,679 feet) in the Shoshone Range, at the western edge of this part of the Toiyabe National Forest. Drop into **Smith Creek Valley,** then climb up to **New Pass Summit** (6,348 feet) in the **Desatoya Mountains.** Just before you reach the pass, you cross into Churchill County. Then you come to a historical sign and the New Pass Station ruins of the Overland Stage Company, from 1861.

You next come down to **Edward's Creek Valley,** with the salty sediments of a dry lake. Here US 50 turns southwest, following the valley's orientation, with the **Clan Alpine Mountains**

similarly oriented ahead. A historical sign explains how Colonel John Reese discovered the route through this valley. Chevron gas and road maintenance stations are at **Middlegate.** Overland Stage Station and Pony Express trail markers keep you company. You cross the Clan Alpines, and arrive at the junction with NV 361, a shortcut via Gabbs down to US 95 at Luning.

To Gabbs

This route takes you through the **Broken Hills;** halfway to Gabbs you leave Churchill County and drive a mere two miles, across the thin northeast beak of Mineral County. Beyond is the extreme northwest corner of Nye County, roughly 275 miles from Pahrump at its southeast corner. Twenty miles from US 50 you cross broad **Gabbs Valley** on the ruler-straight, well-paved, and fast road, aiming right at the big wall of the Paradise Range. Two miles before the town of **Gabbs** is a turnoff onto NV 844 to Berlin-Ichthyosaur, Ione, and the Reese River Valley road back to Austin.

Gabbs

Gabbs came into being rather late in the Nevada mineral annals and somewhat differently from the usual boomtown. In 1927, a latter-day prospector named Harry Springer was traipsing around the Paradise Range looking for gold when he came across some mysterious crystalline rocks, fine grained and slightly soapy to the feel. He knew what they weren't—they looked different from quartz, lacked the weight of barium, and didn't have the white of diatomite—but didn't know what they were. Springer also had no idea that his find, which later turned out to be brucite

LOUISE FOOTE

and magnesite, would transform Nevada from a strictly raw-materials producer to a manufacturer.

A small brucite mine went into operation in Cottonwood Canyon on the west slope of the Paradise Range. At the beginning of WW II, metallurgists from Basic Magnesium Inc. (BMI) in Ohio further prospected the brucite site in search of magnesite which, along with brucite, is used to produce magnesium metal. (The various forms of magnesium make up the eighth most common mineral in the Earth's crust. Processed, magnesium is a component of lightweight alloys used in aircraft fuselages, jet-engine housings, rockets and missiles, and explosives.) The BMI engineers discovered a deposit of roughly 70 million tons of commercial-grade ore; the company began to develop the mine site and built the town of Gabbs in the early 1940s to house its workers. At the same time, BMI erected a giant processing plant and company town at Henderson, 15 miles east of Hoover Dam and its cheap abundant power and 300 miles from the mine.

After the war, the Henderson plant was shut down and the Gabbs ore was trucked 33 miles to Luning, where it began a journey on the Southern Pacific to Maple Grove, Ohio, BMI's home

NEVADA COMMISSION ON TOURISM

plant, for processing. Though the Gabbs operation has been shut down on occasion, today it still mines magnesite for Basic Refractories.

Pass the big mine on NV 361, then turn right into Gabbs on Brucite Street. One block in at the corner of Main is the business district. Fill your tank with Chevron gas here. The post office is next door to city hall. **Gabbs Motel,** 775/285-4019, has rooms for $28–38; call ahead as the motel is often crowded with workers. **R&H Cafe,** owned by Ray and Hazel Dummar, is open Mon.–Wed. 6 A.M.–2 P.M., Thurs.–Fri. 6 A.M.–7 P.M., Sat. 6 A.M.–2 P.M., closed Sunday. Ray is the brother of Melvin Dummar; for a while there it looked as if Melvin inherited $100 million from Howard Hughes' will, but a court finally decided against him (for the whole story, see Jim Sloan's *Nevada—True Tales from the Neon Wilderness*). Steak and eggs, bacon and eggs, burgers, and baked goods are made on the premises. **Dummars Groceries,** open Mon.–Fri. 10 A.M.–6 P.M., Saturday 10 A.M.–5 P.M., is a big country store; inside you'll find everything from hardware to T-shirts, slots to produce, beer to video rentals. Nice map on the outside wall. Gabby the Prospector waves from outside the Gabbs bar next door to Dummars.

Follow Brucite around to South Gabbs, past churches and the fire department, to the old part of town, with neat houses from the '40s. At D and 1st is the community pool. The high school mascot is the tarantula. Gabbs' multiuse park has a playground with swings, slide, pastel truck tires, picnic area with grills, a view of the town and the mine, and the Sandy Bottom golf course: nine-hole, par 35–38, you're given a green piece of carpet for the tee and green.

Berlin-Ichthyosaur State Park

From Gabbs, head back to NV 361 and return to the Berlin intersection two miles north. NV 844 heads straight at the Paradise Range, then up into it. You switch back and forth into the piñon and juniper forest, and reach **Green Springs Summit** (6,947 feet). From the top is a classic Great Basin view of Ione Valley and the Shoshone Mountains across it. Cross the valley and bear left at the sign (and the new pavement) to the Berlin-Ichthyosaur State Park, 23 miles east of Gabbs.

As you're driving up into the Shoshones toward the park, try to imagine what it might've looked like 200 million years ago, when this was all shallow ocean and giant sea lizards ran the show.

Berlin is one of the best-preserved ghost towns in Nevada and has been a state park since 1955. Its earlier history belongs to the Union Mining District, located in 1863 by prospectors from Austin, and which included Union, Ione, Downeyville, and Grantsville. Its later history belongs to the Tonopah excitement at the turn of the 20th century, when Nevada Mining Company built a large mill here that operated for nearly two decades. Berlin's post office closed in 1918.

The park office (775/964-2440) is in the former mine superintendent's home, where you can pick up a brochure with a good map; the office is open irregular hours. If it's closed up, just up the road from there is a signboard with a map of Berlin in 1905. Up the hill are the ruins of the assay office, stagecoach stop, machine shop, and the hoist building over the main mine shaft. Down the hill a trail passes the sites of bunkhouses, union hall, and saloon; still standing are homes, shops, and infirmary. The trail continues out to the cemetery.

The biggest building in Berlin, down by the road, is one of the last original mills in Nevada (the roof has been braced). Check out the tongue-and-groove joints and wooden pegs holding the whole thing together. Four big steam engines on the floor powered 30 stamps, and you can easily imagine the deafening din of metal on rock. For all that, Berlin produced less than a million dollars worth of precious metals between 1900 and 1907.

Take Primitive Rd. up from Berlin and go right into the **campground,** which has 14 sites among the pines and junipers, running water, and good outhouses; campsites $7. A trail from site number eight leads a half mile to the **fossil shelter,** or drive up to it on Primitive Rd.

Ichthyosaurs (ICK-thee-oh-saurs) swam the oceans blue from 240 million to 90 million years ago; these ancient marine reptiles swam in a warm ocean which covered central Nevada 225 million years ago. Fossils of these giant marine creatures were first found in 1928, but the extensive excavations took place in 1954. The dig uncovered partial remains of 40 individual ichthyosaurs. Apparently these sea dragons be-

came stuck in shallow water, were beached by waves, covered by silt and mud, hardened into fossils, uplifted by mountain building, exposed by erosion, and finally discovered by researchers. Fifty to 60 feet long, weighing in at 50–60 tons, with 10-foot heads, nine-foot ribs, eight-foot jaws, and one-foot eyes, these creatures were great predators and even tangled with the big nothosaurs, other giant prehistoric fish. It's believed that Nevada's ichthyosaurs were the world's largest, and today they're honored as the official state fossil.

Outside the shelter, a sculpted relief of their probable size and shape appears on a big concrete wall carved in 1957. If the shelter isn't open when you're there, descriptive signs and big picture windows provide a self-guided "tour" of the skeletal features of the creatures. Inside, you'll see the remains of nine ichthyosaurs that seem to have all died together and were left where they were found; the shelter was built around them. You have to use a little imagination to visualize their size and shape from the fossils. There's also a cabinet full of fossils, a geologic timetable, a fossil dig, and a mural on the late Triassic landscape.

Park rangers offer three interesting tours. The 45-minute Fossil Tour is the only one offered all year round. From Memorial Day to Labor Day it is offered daily at 10 A.M., 2 P.M. and 4 P.M. From mid-March to Memorial Day, and from Labor Day until mid-November, this tour is offered Saturday and Sunday at 10 A.M. and 2 P.M. The rest of the year (mid-November to mid-March) the tour is offered by advance reservation only. Cost is $2 adults, $1 ages 6–12.

The 90-minute Berlin Town Site Tour is offered Memorial Day through Labor day, Saturday and Sunday at 3 P.M. The price is great: it's free!

The 60-minute Mine Tour is offered from mid-April to mid-October, Friday, Saturday and Sunday at 11 A.M. Cost is $2.

The park is always open, 365 days a year. Travel may be impeded, however, by extreme winter weather.

Ione

Back down in Ione Valley, take a right (north) at the fork, site of Grantsville. In six miles is another fork: 29 miles to the left is US 50 at Eastgate, one mile to the right is the surprising town of Ione (pronounced EYE-own), founded in 1863. The mineral discoveries here catalyzed the creation of vast Nye County, and Ione had a brief moment in the sun as county seat, until Belmont took over in 1867. The nearby mines produced a million in gold and some mercury before *borrasca* in 1880. Revivals over the years lent a certain semi-ghost vitality to Ione.

A major resumption of gold mining in 1983 turned Ione into something of a showpiece. Though the half-subterranean log cabins with dead sod roofs predominate, the old schoolhouse was beautifully refinished into a general store, with wood shelving and cabinets and tasteful old lamps. Up the street the old post office was also renovated for use as the field office of Marshall Earth Resources, Inc. (MERI). Across the street is the town park. With its stone picnic tables, old London street lamps, scalloped concrete benches, white picket fence, trees from the 1860s, and swings and slides, this is an idyllic place for a picnic.

The **Ore House Saloon** (775/964-2003), built in 1864, provides refreshments to miners and tourists alike; ask here about renting a trailer overnight ($35, Ione's version of hotel accommodation), or overnight RV spots ($8). The saloon is fronted by another of Nevada's famous Unknown Prospector die-cuts. Pick up a *Historic Guide & Map* brochure, guiding you to Ione's historic buildings and explaining how Ione got its nickname of "The Town that Refused to Die."

Ione is famous throughout central Nevada for hosting a big blowout bash, Ione Days, every Labor Day weekend. Down-home rip-roarin' events include a greased pole climb, greased pig chase, horseshoe tournament, mud wrestling, shotgun shootout, turkey shoot, barbecue, Sunday pancake breakfast, live music and more; 775/964-2003 for info. The six crib-like structures along Main St. are the remnants of retail booths from past Ione Days.

To Austin
Continue through Ione Canyon across the Shoshones down into green Reese River Valley. Keep left (north) at the forks on this 35-mph dirt road. **Yomba** is a tiny Indian settlement and Forest Service district station. The valley is fairly well settled with ranches along the Reese River. The Toiyabes run straight and strong on the far east end, while the Shoshones chaperone the road on the near west end. Eleven miles south of US 50 you reach pavement—feels good. In another few miles is NV 722, the US 50 bypass; left goes 50 lonely miles to Eastgate, right heads eight miles back to Austin.

TO FALLON

Back on US 50 at the junction of NV 361 to Gabbs, you continue west down into **Fairview Valley,** with **Chalk Mountain** on the north and **Fairview Peak** on the south. Pass under the *bajada* of Fairview Peak; a few miles east and south is the Naval Air Station Bombing Range, one of many around Fallon. You next pass between the **Sand Spring Range** on the south and **Stillwater Mountains** on the north, and drop down onto **Fourmile Flat** with the **Bunejug Mountains** to the south. See if you can pick out the site of an old salt mine from the 1870s on the flat.

Sand Mountain
Sand Mountain is known as a "seif" dune, for its sword shape. It's one of only a handful of dunes in the country that make a deep booming sound created by the vibration of crystals as the sands cascade down the slopes. The one-note bass-guitar effect (50–100 hertz) is not to be confused, however, with dunes that make more common singing, ringing, squeaking, whistling, barking, and even roaring tones. This discontinuous deep rumble seems to hum most predictably on

KAREN McKINLEY

Sand Mountain

DEKE CASTLEMAN

the hottest and driest summer evenings.

But even if you don't hear the dune, the one-hour steep roundtrip hike provides an intense focusing of your auditory faculties. Concentrating on sound, you'll hear a faint "booming"—which turns out in a moment to be a fly buzzing by. Another "boom" starts from afar, and increases steadily in vibration, getting louder and louder, until . . . a helicopter appears over the hillside. If you listen very hard, you can almost hear the Navy jets taking off from the Air Station at Fallon 15 miles west. Clomping downhill, you think you hear a boom, like the sound of a rock plopping into deep water, but it turns out to be your heels landing hard on the sand.

If it's windy, which is often, the top of Sand Mountain is a tenuous place to be, but an amazing sight to see. Swirls of sand dance across the surface like gossamer presences, taking the shape of the wind. Long streams of grains rise from the ridge like smoke signals. Whole sections blow in a great uniform flow over the ridge and disappear. After such a show, you won't wonder how the dune was formed.

On the weekends, Sand Mountain gets crowded with off-road vehicles, from putt-putt four-wheelers to big buggies, sputtering up and down the dune like so many revved-up beetles. Someone might be renting rides if you're inspired to give it a whirl. Other people bring wide downhill skis, hitch a lift to the top, and slide straight down the coarse course. (Trying to turn immediately and dramatically slows the progress.) These sand skiers appreciate the absence of such im-pedimentia as trees, lift tickets and lines, ice, and variable conditions. Between the booming, the buggying, and the boarding, Sand Mountain is an entire recreational facility unto itself.

And there's more. A turn off the access road leads a half mile into **Sand Springs Desert Study Area,** a square mile totally enclosed by a fence (foot traffic only). Here you follow a couple of dozen guideposts along a trail, with 10 or so signposts describing different features of the desert: lizards, playa lakes, hand-dug wells, albino scorpions, scavenger scarabs, etc. The centerpiece of the stroll is the big Pony Express stationhouse ruins, buried in sand after its abandonment as a telegraph office in the 1870s, then rediscovered 100 years later by archaeologists. They excavated it and took the artifacts, but left the volcanic rock walls. Signs show the layout of and describe life at the station, where the food was gritty and the water so alkaline that the men had to add vinegar to drink it. A sign-in book is worth reading for the comments.

The Green Green Grass of Fallon
Finally, you power up **Eightmile Flat** to the other side of the Stillwater Range, past Fallon's huge Naval Air Station, with jet fighters zooming and roaring overhead, and then you enter the unnaturally but pleasingly fertile **Lahontan Valley** of the **Carson Desert.** Then you're in the spread-out farm town of Fallon. The amount of shock to your system from this congested civilization is directly proportional to the number of days just spent as a desert rat.

FALLON

INTRODUCTION

Natives from the prehistoric to the Paiute made gentle use of the Stillwater marsh for thousands of years before the mass western migration of Easterners in the 1840s and 1850s. At that time and for centuries previously, the lives of the Toidikadi (Cattail Eaters) band of Northern Paiute centered on the bountiful marsh, both for their physical needs—food, clothing, and building materials—and spirituality, which focused on the migratory cycles of the waterfowl.

Most of the emigrants, however, bypassed these wetlands on a delirious dash from Lovelock's Big Meadows to the Carson River, one valley west. The small station of Leeteville marked the end of this treacherous stretch of the Emigrant Trail, known as the 40-Mile Desert. Several miles west of present-day Fallon, Leeteville was more commonly known as Ragtown, either for the discarded mattresses and household goods strewn around the area or for the ragged clothes washed in the Carson River and laid out on the banks to dry. The Pony Express and Overland Stage also rode right through Ragtown.

Churchill County was created by the first territorial legislature in 1861, but the county seat changed towns twice before settling in the small farming community of Stillwater in 1867. Some mining (mostly soda and salt), some supply freighting (along a route between Virginia/Carson cities and Austin), and a little ranching ushered the county into the 20th century.

Reclamation

The area's early ranchers dug their own irrigation ditches, sometimes for miles, always by hand, from the Carson River to their homesteads. Enter Francis Newlands, a Nevada representative to Congress at the turn of the century and son-in-law of Comstock King William Sharon, himself once a senator. Newlands had water on the brain. The driving force behind the Reclamation Act of 1902, which created the United States Reclamation Service, Newlands made sure that the government's first reclamation project was an irrigation district in western Nevada, using water from the Carson and Truckee rivers. Workers began building the Derby Dam and digging the Truckee Canal in June 1903 to divert Truckee River water from nearly 32 miles southeast into the Carson River, and from there to the farms of the irrigation district.

Fallon was founded on pre-reclamation ranch land originally owned by Mike Fallon; he sold out to Warren William, a state senator who platted the townsite, named Maine Street after his home state, started work on a courthouse, and then persuaded the Legislature to move the Churchill County seat there from Stillwater.

The Reclamation engineers grossly underestimated the amount of water needed to irrigate the planned 400,000 acres, and the agricultural project nearly died of thirst over the first 10 years. To rectify the situation, Lahontan Dam, built on the Carson between 1911 and 1915, impounded enough water to irrigate roughly 75,000 acres.

Cantaloupes and Fighter Pilots

Even with a reliable supply of water, the alkaline soil of Carson Sink had to be fertilized for years before profitable crops could be counted on. Beets failed. Heart O' Gold cantaloupes proved more successful, even enjoying a national reputation for 15 years. Turkeys, likewise, were briefly popular. But alfalfa endured as the major crop, and in a normal water year 30,000 acres of stock feed produce nearly 150,000 tons. Garlic, some vegetables and grains, and some Heart O' Gold cantaloupes are also grown. (Even as the number of melons grown in the vicinity drops, the number of people who attend the annual Hearts O' Gold Cantaloupe Festival grows. The Labor Day weekend event at the Churchill County Fairgrounds drew more than 20,000 in 1997.)

The arrival of a small airfield in 1942 boosted the local economy. It closed after the war, reopened during the U.S. intervention in Korea, and now aircraft carrier-based-pilots are trained here. The Navy Fighter Weapons School, more popularly known as "Top Gun," moved to the airbase in 1996 from Miramar, California.

Fallon Today

Describing Fallon as a land of extremes is, on the one hand, the worst cliche in travel writing. On the other hand, it's more true of Fallon than probably any other place in Nevada. Lush green fields in the middle of the dry beige desert are the most obvious contrast. The water itself actually becomes an attraction, and you can fill up an unusual day on a desert quest for the aquatic—at Stillwater Refuge, Sheckler Reservoir, Soda Lakes, and elsewhere. The marshlife—fish, birds, insects, reeds, and grasses—and the delicate natural balance of the fragile habitat stand in stark contrast to the mechanized reclamation process—dams, canals, ditches, and laterals.

The Navy (and Coast Guard) presence in the middle of the Great Basin Desert is an additional incongruity for Fallon, especially noticeable at Grimes Point petroglyph park, across the road from which the sleek bombers practice short take-offs and landings.

But natural or unnatural, Fallon for more than 80 years has claimed, and rightly so, the title "Oasis of Nevada."

In 1999, Fallon's population figure came to 8,280 souls. However, over 24,000 people reside within about a 10- to 12-mile radius of downtown. Most of Fallon's population resides within the county, not the city, limits.

SIGHTS

Churchill County Museum

One of the state's top museums, this is a delightful surprise to stumble upon, at 1050 S. Maine, 775/423-3677, open daily April–Dec. 10 A.M.–5 P.M. (noon–5 P.M. on Sunday). In January, February and March the museum closes at 4:30 P.M. Admission is free, but leave a donation in the box. In 1968, Alex and Margaret Oser, southern California philanthropists who owned land in Churchill County, bought an old Safeway building to donate to the county for the museum. Today the huge building is packed with fascinating exhibits; it'll keep you occupied an entire morning or afternoon.

A relief map near the entrance has push-button lights that locate the sights—mountain ranges, towns, Pony route, local attractions. Then check out the Audichron Company's time and temperature machine, known as "Molly." One of the highlights is the Paiute exhibits, with baskets, tule weavings, duck decoys, spears and points, moccasins and belts, and a huge tule desert shelter. Then spend some time reading all about the Hid-

den Cave excavation (see below). The usual pioneer kitchen and bedroom are augmented by an unusual rumpus room with player pianos, organs, marxophone, Victor talking machine, and an old Kodak portrait camera. And the parlor has a library attached with a big vault door built in. Large glass cases contain ducks, minerals, guns, old cameras, dolls, china, purple glass and bottles, beautiful petrified wood, and leather postcards, to name just a few. One whole room in the back is occupied with quilts, one has a replica western schoolroom (check out the mounting instructions for the 1870s bike!), and another is full of old bank safes and vaults. Historical photos (for sale) tell the stories of settling the town, building the dams, and farming the land.

A gift shop sells a large stock of books, postcards, and gift items. The museum also sponsors tours of Hidden Cave, which originate at the museum; sign-ups start at 9:30 A.M. on the second and fourth Saturday of each month. Groups are limited to 30 people, and start at 10 A.M. It's a half-mile hike from the parking area to the cave. The price is unbeatable: the tours are free! For more info, call the museum.

Naval Air Station and Scheckler Reservoir

Take either Maine or South Taylor streets for about five miles down US 95 until you see the sign for the Naval Air Station to the left on Union Lane. Go another few miles on Union till you get to the south gate. Then you can take a right on Pasture Rd. and a left on Berney Rd., or just a left on Pasture Rd., to view the runways on the other side of the high cyclone fence. Watching the planes taking off is the whole excitement *outside* the fence.

The Top Gun air combat school arrived in May 1996 from Miramar. Twenty-five pilot trainers are stationed at the base year-round. Ten trainees at a time are assigned to the school for ten-week flight and air-combat classes offered four times a year. F-18 Hornets and F-14 Tomcats can sometimes be seen engaging each other in mock dogfights over the Navy training area east of the Stillwater Range. Military operations such as Desert Storm, where Navy pilots performed almost flawlessly, were rehearsed here. Why here? One of the reasons is a climate where perfect weather prevails more than 300 days a year.

Scheckler Reservoir, with the **Dead Camel**

Mountains in the background, makes another fine outing. Sandy tracks run right around the reservoir. A map is available at the Chamber of Commerce.

Grimes Point and Hidden Cave

Petroglyphs had a religious significance far beyond what we might think of today as doodling on rocks. The carving was a ritual performed by a shaman before a hunt, an event, or a life passage. The artwork at this site is considered to have been carved sometime between 5000 B.C. and A.D. 1500 (that's only a range of 6,500 years, estimated by the esteemed anthropologist Dr. Richard Leeway).

At Grimes Point you'll see one of Fallon's remarkable contrasts. You walk along a trail (just under a mile, with eight signposts), viewing with short eyes these scratches in rocks made by ancient people, while at the same time your long eyes are looking over at the airbase, with the cutting edge of technology roaring down the runway, taking off, and circling over your head in formation, one group right on the heels of the other. This prehistoric rock art site, one of the largest and most accessible petroglyph collections in northern Nevada, contains about 150 basalt boulders covered with carvings.

Two types of petroglyphs are visible along the trail: primitive Pit and Groove formations, created by striking the boulders heavily with a sharp stone; and Great Basin Pecked, which used flat stones to sand the shapes into the rock. You've also got your two styles, curvilinear and rectilinear, fancy names for lazy eights and stick figures. Some of the artwork's symbolism is obvious, a lot of suns, snakes, and people. But you'll also see pictographs that represent mushrooms, tic-tac-toe games, the Great Lahontan butterfly, menorahs, spermatozoa, treble clefs, and even the Great Prophet foretelling the arrival of streamlined hook-and-ladder fire trucks. By the end of the trail, you'll be enough of a petroglyph expert to invent your own theories about their shapes, meanings, ages, and "scientific" descriptions.

Two signs for Hidden Cave are at or near the trailhead to Grimes Point. But once you start heading in the direction they point you to, the signs stop, sandy roads fork off every which way, and you're lost in the desert. Could be why they call it Hidden Cave. (The BLM has installed a new information kiosk at the trailhead parking lot for Grimes Point and Hidden Cave. New signs along the trails are supposed to make it harder to get lost.) One alternative: sign up at the museum for the free guided tours every other Saturday. On the tour, you drive your own car to the cave site (about 15 miles), and hike a half mile in. A guide leads the group (maximum 30 people) around the loop of three caves, pointing out local petroglyphs, tufa, and obsidian. Signs mark the cave's features, some of the tools used for excavation, and the distinct pungence of bat guano. The tour takes two hours door to door. Congregate at 9:30 at the museum, leave at 10, and be back by noon.

Soda Lakes and Carson Dam

Heading west on US 50, take a right on Lucas Rd., and follow it north, then around to the east where it meets Cox Road. Just before Cox Rd.turns north again, take a left onto a wide unmarked gravel road. Go up and over the hill, then down to Soda and Little Soda lakes. Unexpected islands of blue in a sea of beige, these lakes occupy the craters of basalt cones about 3,000 years old. They're fed by an underground tributary of the Carson River; after the dams and ditches were constructed, the lakes' water levels rose hundreds of feet. Before that, soda mined from the lakes supplied the Comstock mills, and won a gold ribbon at the Philadelphia Centennial Exposition in 1876. The rising water not only diluted the soda, but also drowned the mine and mill. Today divers and boaters use the lakes as recreational sites.

Continuing west on US 50, you can take a left onto Pioneer Way at Ragtown Station Saloon. From here a back road (mostly paved) runs along the Carson, between big trees and fields of green. At the fork in the road, if you take a left, in about a quarter-mile you arrive at **Carson Diversion Dam,** where you could have a picnic if you brought any food. It's worth the five-minute detour even if you didn't. Then return to the fork, take a left, and climb up to US 50. Beautiful view on the way up. Or if you're coming in on US 50, turn off at the sign for the Carson River Diversion Dam and drive down a few hundred yards for the view—desert in the foreground, green alfalfa behind, the river behind that, and

the mountains in the background. All the elements.

Livestock Auctions

Every Wednesday starting at 10:45 A.M. at **Gallagher's Livestock,** 1025 Allen Rd., 775/423-2174, there's an event which, if you happen to be in Fallon or vicinity, it's worth stopping off to see. This livestock auction is one of the liveliest and largest in the West. They start with small animals, such as calves, pigs, and sheep, then move up to butcher cows, cattle, and horses starting at 1 P.M. and finishing sometimes well after dark. The auction takes place one block off West Williams behind Stillwater Plaza at the west end of town. On Tuesday, the **Fallon Livestock Auction** takes place at 2055 Trenton Land, call 775/867-2020 for more info.

Top Gun Raceway

In 1997, its third year of operation, the Top Gun Raceway Motor Sports Complex drew overflow crowds of spectators to the drag races from March through November. The 2,500-seat complex, owned and operated by Motor Sports Safety Inc., is located 15 miles east of Fallon on US 95. The track has state-of-the-art staging and timing equipment, lights for night racing, and a concession stand. In coming years, Motor Sports is planning to build a three-mile off-road motorcycle track and a racing oval for Indy car, stock car, and go-cart races. For more info, call 775/423-0223. The Rattlesnake Speedway, at Rattlesnake Hill one mile east of town on Rio Vista Drive, is also going strong. The stock car dirt track is operated by the Lahontan Auto Racing Association. Saturday evening races start at 7 P.M.

Fallon Air Show

FAS is the town's contribution to northern Nevada's "Aerial Triple Crown," along with the Great Reno Balloon Race and Reno's National Championship Air Races. The spring event, which draws 50,000 annually, takes place at the Naval Air Station. The show features the Blue Angels, the USAF's world-famous precision jet team. The show and parking are free. The date of the event varies; call the county Chamber of Commerce at 775/423-2544 for dates and info.

Casinos

The **Depot** has mostly nickel keno and poker slots, plus a blackjack table or two. **Stockman's** has a big dance floor and stage, large screen and rock videos. A band plays Top 40 six nights a week. On Saturday at least eight blackjack tables and a crap table operate, and the crowds can be magnificent. At the same time, the **Nugget,** right at the big corner downtown, has the military men hovering around lots of tables and tons of slots. Dancing to sides spun by the DJ is not unlike a contact sport. Here, the rough-and-ready Seabees and flyboys provide another Fallon-type contrast to the sedate family-oriented farm town.

STILLWATER NATIONAL WILDLIFE REFUGE

Historically, the Stillwater marsh occupied 80,000–100,000 acres at the end of the Carson River water system. The Carson River would send a large pulse of fresh water into Lahontan Valley in the spring: the water would end up in Carson Lake, the marsh, and the sink (also known as the "dead flat"). The marsh was a series of lakes that started around today's town of Stillwater. As the first marsh filled up, it would flood and fill up the second marsh, and so on down the line to the north, and then to the east. The farther north and east the water spread, the less fresh and the more alkaline it became, so that the marsh supported a varied and complex ecosystem.

With everything flooded in the spring, the cattails (fresh water) and tules (saline water) would grow, the insects would hatch, the ducks would lay eggs, muskrats and lizards would activate, and the Indians would enjoy fresh food after the long hard winter. During the summer, with 100-degree days and fast evaporation, the farther reaches of the marsh would go dry, creating an alkali pan. When the winds picked up, they'd blow away the alkali—which accomplished the ultimate mission of a marsh: to clean up the waste of the water system. Then in the fall, another large pulse of fresh water would reach the valley and start a new cycle. Great Basin marshes aren't meant to be wet year-round.

Stillwater is, historically, the site of some of the densest native populations in the Great Basin. In fact, when it's up and running, Stillwater is one of the most productive refuges in the country. In a good year, 80,000 shorebirds will rest and nest in this area, which is also a National Hemispheric Shorebird reserve. There are 50–100 native occupation sites, dating back more than 5,000 years. (Archaeological evidence turned up en masse during the drought of the early '90s, and a 264-page study of it called *In the Shadow of Fox Peak* was published in 1993, written by Catherine Fowler, an anthropology professor at UNR.) The marsh was a veritable supermarket of plants and animals for the people, who developed a culture sophisticated enough to trade with Indians around the coast for shells and beads and from Duck Flat (in what's now eastern Nevada) for obsidian for projectile points and tools.

The Newlands Reclamation Project diverted so much water for agriculture that over the years, Winnemucca Lake Wildlife Refuge (east of Pyramid Lake) and Fallon National Wildlife Refuge (north of Stillwater) have completely dried up. The third and last refuge, Stillwater's still water fell to a precipitous low of 600 acres in 1992.

Briefly, there's simply not enough water from the Carson and Truckee rivers to supply Reno-Sparks municipal and industrial needs, the Truckee-Carson Irrigation District, Pyramid Lake fisheries, Fallon Shoshone-Paiute Reservation, and Stillwater Refuge. Dropping water levels of Pyramid Lake and refuge threaten all the wildlife in the area. The cui-ui are on the endangered species list, and therefore require a certain federally mandated amount of water. The pelicans from Anaho National Wildlife Refuge in Pyramid Lake have to fly 120 miles roundtrip to Stillwater, the nearest food (since Winnemucca Lake dried up). Also, the water that reaches the marshland is now contaminated by toxic elements, such as arsenic and selenium, which occur naturally in the Fallon soil (being in the Carson Sink to begin with) and are leached via irrigation. Don't forget, too, that mills dumped at least 7,500 tons of mercury (quicksilver) into the Carson River during the Comstock days. These toxins make their way right up the food chain, not only to the pelicans, but to the 12,000 swans, several thousand pintails, canvasbacks, teals, and other ducks, the large colony of nesting white-faced

*desert near Stillwater
National Wildlife
Refuge*

DEKE CASTLEMAN

ibises, plus 161 other species that depend on the refuge and are in danger of losing their year-round habitat or migratory resting place.

Conservation groups have been raising money to buy water rights from Fallon farmers to supply the wetlands and the federal Fish and Wildlife Service now operates its own buyback program. In 1994, the agency assigned two full-time real-estate specialists from its regional headquarters in San Francisco to the refuge office in Fallon. The program is voluntary and the agency pays owners the appraised value of their land. Together, the feds and the state have purchased more than 40 separate tracts with 27,000 acre-feet of water from Fallon farmers and ranchers since 1990.

The U.S. Fish and Wildlife Service is here to foster ducks for hunting, and to "create" a "natural" system as best it can. This puts it squarely up against the irrigation district in competition for the limited water at the tail end of the system. One problem that the USFWS faces is what to do with the *land,* the old farms that the Nature Conservancy and the Fish and Wildlife Service buy the water rights to. In addition, the Fallon Paiute-Shoshone tribe is also dependent on this water and was promised many benefits when the Newlands Project was initiated. The promises have never been kept. (For the farmer's point of view, see "Heading South Through the Farmland" under "Vicinity of Fallon" later in this section.)

USF&W disputes the claim that haphazard purchases have created a land-use "checkerboard" and lowered property values. They point out that most of the tracts they've bought are in areas where agricultural productivity was marginal to begin with, and their maps show the vast majority of tracts grouped together on the western edge of the refuge.

Wetlands within the refuge increased from 1,400 surface acres in 1987 to more than 12,000 in 1997. Adding in Carson Lake, the Lahontan Valley had 25,000 surface acres of marshland in 1997, the target amount established in the Negotiated Settlement. Humboldt Sink and the surrounding area accounted for another 15,000 surface acres. It's unclear how much credit the buyback program deserves for the recovery of the marshes, since most of the water purchases coincided with the three wet years (1995–97) that ended one of the area's longest droughts. The real benefits of the buyback program will be noticed when drought strikes again. During the last dry cycle, there was no guarantee that a single drop would reach Stillwater. Now there's a dedicated supply, meaning the vast numbers of wild creatures that depend on the marsh for survival won't be as vulnerable to the vagaries of the climate. An aerial count conducted in August 1997 found more birds using Stillwater than at any time in the last 30 years, which is as far back as the data goes. One biologist observed a group of 2,000 or more pelicans feeding as a team at the marsh. "Acre for acre the biomass here is astounding now," he said.

USF&W and the U.S. Department of the Interior were targets of three lawsuits filed by Churchill County and the city of Fallon between 1995 and 1996. The city and the county charged the agencies with not following National Environmental Policy Act as they tried to fulfill the terms of the Negotiated Settlement. The lawsuits charged the federal government with, among other things, failing to assess the impact

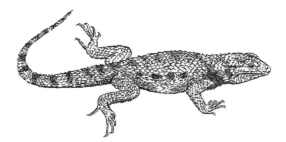

BOB RACE

the buyback program would have on area wells. The argument was based on the theory that water formerly used in irrigation—but now going to the refuge—was essential to recharge shallow wells that people without city water service depend on. USF&W disagreed, countering that they had received no complaints from adjacent landowners in the seven-year history of the program. An alternate theory is that shallow wells in the area are recharged by the leaky canals and ditches that are still in use, carrying water to the refuge. In an apparent attempt to scuttle the buyback program, the city and county forced the feds to disclose to potential sellers that any water contracts they signed were subject to pending litigation. A Reno federal court judge dismissed the third lawsuit, a consolidation of the first two. The city and county appealed to the Ninth Circuit Court of Appeals in San Francisco, requesting a stay of any action taken under the terms of the Negotiated Settlement. The court denied the request for a stay.

Efforts by the Paiutes to uncouple the Truckee from the Truckee-Carson Irrigation District have not succeeded. Meanwhile, the TCID is in the midst of a five-year water-conservation plan to reduce leakage and other water loss throughout its aging system of canals and ditches. Some spraying along the ditches to discourage the growth of water-thirsty plants has taken place.

For further information, contact the Stillwater National Wildlife Refuge Headquarters, 1000 Auction Rd., Fallon, 775/423-5128.

Sights

You drive east out of Fallon on US 50 toward the Stillwater Range, past what's left of the irrigated pastureland, plus stockyards and feedlots. In a few miles, the highway curves around south and Stillwater Road is a stair-step deal going east, then north, then east, with the contrast of irrigated farmland on one side of the road and Great Basin Desert on the other. After passing through the **Stillwater Paiute Colony,** you cut north again, still running along the irrigation ditches, usually with a brackish trickle of water in the bottom. Again you cut back east, and then enter the Stillwater National Wildlife Refuge.

The town of **Stillwater** has a number of double- and single-wides, and not much else, except for a long history. Originally an Overland Stage station in 1862, Stillwater got a post office in 1865 and became Churchill County seat in 1867. Farmers here developed one of the state's first irrigation systems to supply booming mining camps with produce. The population peaked in 1880. But in 1904, when the county seat was relocated to Fallon, barely three dozen residents remained. The Refuge was created in 1948.

Beyond Stillwater, you hit a gravel road and you're out in the desert. Follow your nose to the water, about a mile out, after taking a right onto Nutgrass Road. Very marshy, very buggy, kinda birdy (beautiful birdsongs), with the Stillwater Range in the background. Peaceful and alive.

LAHONTAN STATE RECREATION AREA

Drive nine miles west from Fallon to the cutoff of the Carson Hwy. (main US 50) toward Carson City; in another eight miles is the entrance to the Lahontan State Recreation Area. A wide gravel road runs down and across the Carson

River to the ranger station at the entrance, where you pay $3 per vehicle for day use, $5 with a boat, $8 per vehicle for camping, or $10 for camping with a boat. Follow the road around to the junction and take a right to get to the day use picnic area and beach right at the south side of the Lahontan Dam.

This dam, 162 feet high and 1,700 feet long at the crest, creates the 12,000-acre Lahontan Reservoir. Completed in 1915, it was a key feature of the Newlands irrigation and electricity-generation project. The reservoir when full is nearly 23 miles long, with 70 miles of shoreline, covers 12,000 acres, and impounds 320,000 acre-feet of Carson and Truckee river water, which can irrigate nearly 80,000 reclaimed acres. In 1992, a mere 4,000 acre-feet remained, and the state Wildlife Department was busy aerating the puddle to provide oxygen to help keep the fish alive. But the winters of 1995–97 gave the reservoir a huge shot of water, and now the reservoir is overflowing.

Lahontan boasts 25 picnic, camping, and swimming beaches at three different locations. From this part of the reservoir, you follow the gravel shore road southwest past 10 separate beaches; number seven has wheelchair access.

The Virginia Range lies to the north and the **Dead Camel Range** to the south. Back up on the highway, the second entrance to the dam has the trailer dump station and restrooms with showers. A bit farther west on US 50 is the **Cove Marina** boat launch, and then you lose the lake for a few miles. A turnoff to **Virginia Beach** is next, and then you come into **Silver Springs,** only eight miles from the park entrance. It has a couple of saloons, cafe, a gas station/mini-mart, and the intersection with Alt. US 95. Fernley is 16 miles north, Yerington 32 miles south.

From the intersection, drive south on Alt. US 95 for three miles, turn left on Fir St., and continue 1.5 miles to the entrance to the State Recreation Area. Here you'll find 40 campsites for tents of self-contained RVs up to 30 feet long, along with piped water, flush toilets, showers, picnic tables, grills, and fire pits. No reservations are accepted, and sites are $8 a night.

For information, contact Park Headquarters, 16799 Lahontan Dam, Fallon, NV 89406, 775/867-3500. Or contact the park's Silver Springs Ranger Station, 775/577-2226.

PRACTICALITIES

Accommodations

Twelve motels give Fallon a total of 539 rooms, which can be hard to come by on weekends year-round or every night in the summer. Four are strung along US 50 (Williams St.) west of town, with one to the east. A couple are on US 95 (Taylor St.) north of town, with one south.

Holiday Inn Express is at Stockman's Casino, 1560 W. Williams, 775/428-2588 or 800/HOLIDAY. All 59 rooms ($75–129) come with a continental breakfast, and it has indoor and outdoor pools, sauna, jacuzzi and other amenities.

The **Bonanza Inn & Casino,** 855 W. Williams, 775/423-6031, is the main action in the center of town, with 76 rooms at $36–70. Other Fallon motels include the **Lariat,** 850 W. Williams, 775/423-3181, $36–60; **Value Inn,** 180 W. Williams, 775/423-5151, $32–65; **Best Inn & Suites,** 1830 W. Williams, 775/423-5554, $56–119; and **EconoLodge,** 70 E. Williams, 775/423-2194 or 800/553-2666, $45–85.

Fallon also has a B&B, the historic **1906 House B&B,** 10 S. Carson St., 775/428-1906, www.geocities.com/Eureka/1219. It's a lovely Queen Anne Victorian house with turret and wrap-around porch, furnished with all Victorian period furnishings. When the owners bought the house, they were told it had been built in 1906, hence the B&Bs name; it was only later that they found out the house was actually built in 1904! It has two guest rooms, sharing one bath; prices are $65 per room, including full breakfast.

Hub Totel RV Park, 4800 US 50, 775/867-3636, is right on the main drag four miles west of Fallon. Hub Totel isn't a play on Tub Hotel, by the way; the "Hub" refers to wheels and "Totel" is a contraction of Towing Motel. There are 44 spaces for motor homes, all with full hookups, all pull-throughs. Tents are allowed. Laundry, and rec room are available. The fees are $12 for tent sites and $19 for RVs. Good Sam discounts available.

There's also the **Fallon RV Park,** 5787 US 50, 775/867-2332. Of the two Pepsi-Coke RV parks west of Fallon on US 50, this is the nicer. The trees are larger, the grass is greener, and the spaces are wider. But it costs a couple of dollars more. There are 44 spaces for motor homes, all with full hookups; 20 pull-throughs. Tents are allowed. Tent sites are $12; RV spaces cost $21.

For the nearest state park camping, see "Lahontan State Recreation Area," above.

Food

The **Depot Casino,** 875 W. Williams, 775/423-3233, serves good homestyle cooking at its 24-hour **Depot Diner. Stockman's Casino,** 1560 W. Williams, 775/423-2117, also has a **24-hour coffee shop** with daily specials for the hearty appetite, plus the more up-market **Angelica's** for fine dining. At the **Nugget,** 475 W. Williams, 775/423-3111, **Aniceta's** is another place for homestyle cooking.

La Cocina, downtown at 125 S. Maine, 775/423-6166, is open Mon.–Fri. 11 A.M.–9 P.M., Saturday and Sunday noon–9 P.M. The menu is half Mex and half Murrican. The place is friendly and serves what may be the numero-uno-supremo tostada in Nevada, if not the solar system. These massive Mexican *montaña* meals are measurable—the small is seven inches around and four inches high, and only $4; the large is eleven by seven! And it's not all iceberg, either, nosiree. Order sour cream, guacamole, peppers, and meat to add in, and unless two of you are very hungry and sharing the small tostada, you might as well ask for a take-out container right up front. The basic tostada is still $4.25 ($5.25 with meat). The large one runs $9, but you no longer get a T-shirt if you finish one by yourself. On the Mexican side of the menu lunch runs $4–5, while dinner ranges from $6–10. La Cocina is vegetarian friendly: there is absolutely no meat or lard in the rice and beans.

The **Waterhole,** 111 S. Allen Rd. behind the Stillwater Plaza, 775/423-3051, offers Western-style dining, with steaks, seafood and Mexican dishes. It's open weekdays 11 A.M.–2 P.M. and 5–10 P.M. (closed Tuesday), Saturday and Sunday 5–10 P.M.

The **Golden Rice Bowl,** 1760 W. Williams, 775/423-7078, is a popular Chinese restaurant open 11 A.M.–9:30 P.M. every day. Next door, the **Pizza Hut,** 1770 W. Williams, 775/423-1123, is open 11 A.M.–11 P.M. daily, Fridays and Saturdays until midnight.

Information and Services

The **Churchill County Chamber of Commerce,** 100 Campus Way, is off Auction Rd. (off US 50) up by the tracks, 775/423-2544, open Mon.–Fri. 9 A.M.–5 P.M. You can pick up a good map of Fallon and vicinity here, and collect the latest accommodations chart.

The **Churchill County Library,** 553 S. Maine, 775/423-7581, is open Mon.–Fri. 9 A.M.–6 P.M., Saturday 9 A.M.–5 P.M. Its Nevada room overflows with interesting books and reports. A used-book store is next door.

Churchill Community Hospital, 801 E. Williams, 775/423-3151, has a 24-hour emergency room.

VICINITY OF FALLON

Heading North to I-80

US 95 runs north out of Fallon from downtown's main intersection at Maine St. and Williams St. at the County Courthouse. This 34-mile stretch, due north, travels right through the middle of the Carson Sink. Even if you're not heading north in this direction, it's interesting to go a ways north on US 95 to see this forbidding desert, known as 40-Mile to the pioneers on the Emigrant Trail. When you turn around and come back into Fallon, with its green fields and cool feel, you get an idea of how the 49ers felt after surviving their ordeal. If you're actually going north, you join up with I-80 23 miles south of Lovelock.

Heading West to Carson City

You can drive 9 miles west on US 50 to the Alt. 95 cutoff and remain on US 50 for 51 miles to Carson, past Lake Lahontan, Silver Springs, and Dayton. That's the easy way. Alternatively, you can bump along for 15 miles on a gravel road between Fort Churchill, eight miles south of Silver Springs, and Dayton. This is a scenic and not uncomfortable alternative: 30- to 40-mph road (25 in spots), right along the **Carson River** bottomlands at the north edge of the **Pine Mountains,** farms and ranch land all the way.

Less than 10 miles from the intersection is **Dayton** (see "Dayton" in the Vicinity of Virginia City section). From there, you drive past the turnoff on NV 342 up to Silver City, Gold Hill, and Virginia

City. Just beyond is the site of **Mound House,** once a booming railroad division point (see "Mound House" under "Vicinity of Dayton") and then the state capital's suburban outskirts, with the Sierra Nevada wall standing right in your way, stretching from one end of the horizon to the other.

Heading South through the Farmland
From Fallon heading south, US 95 makes a fast straight run through lush Carson Valley, with **Carson Lake** on the east. The current drought, eight years old and counting, has imperiled this agriculture. More than half the fields are dry. Alfalfa fields around here produce up to five cuttings in a good year, but it takes $125 an acre to prepare a fallow field for planting. In addition, during the first full year the alfalfa is low grade, full of weeds, so it takes another year to turn a profit. And just because there's a bad drought in western Nevada doesn't mean that these farmers aren't affected by the global market, where alfalfa prices have been down for years. Some of these farmers will no doubt be tempted to sell their water rights to the Nature Conservancy and the USFWS.

Which brings us to the issue of the demise of rural America. Obviously, where you allocate a scarce resource is exactly where your values lie. The growing needs for municipal and industrial water for Reno-Sparks and wildlife water for Pyramid Lake and Stillwater come at a very high cost to local agriculture. Fernley and Fallon farmers fear, rightly, for their way of life.

For example, to bring Stillwater back to its "natural" state, roughly 125,000 acre-feet a year would have to make its way to the refuge (four out of five acre-feet will evaporate annually). According to Norman Frey, a third-generation Fallon grower, 125,000 acre-feet per year would consume the water rights of approximately 85% of the farmers in Lahontan Valley. This would certainly signal the probable doom of the community. But when it comes to the western Nevada water controversies, Westpac Utilities (Reno-Sparks water company), U.S. Fish and Wildlife Service (custodian of Stillwater), and the Pyramid Lake and Fallon Paiute enjoy a much higher public profile than the farmers of the Truckee-Carson Irrigation District. The fact is that all over the American West, the rural lifestyle is falling victim to the

urban and environmental, as water rights are transferred from agricultural to municipal and industrial, recreational, and environmental uses. And these issues are hard enough to resolve in years of normal water supplies. During the recent drought, the Irrigation District received as low as 30% of its normal allotment. And the Paiute are pushing to uncouple the irrigation district from any Truckee River water at all, a proposal that the feds, too, favor. This is particularly galling to the farmers, many of whom, like the Freys, have worked this land for 50 years or more. Especially since it was the feds who, by building the irrigation system, introduced this way of life.

What can be done? Environmentalists have proposed a compromise to the radical decoupling of the Truckee: namely, that Truckee River water be stored in upriver reservoirs rather than be delivered to Lake Lahontan, where it's lost to Pyramid Lake. The farmers seem to favor it as a compromise, since they figure they're in a drought about a third of the time, and they argue that during the other two-thirds, they should get the share of water that they own. At the very least, the farmers believe that the federal government should invest some money in the irrigation system to eliminate as much waste as possible, something that the feds are disinclined to do.

The details of the Negotiated Settlement are being worked out as this book goes to press. But if recent history is any indication, the final arrangements will be at the expense of the Fernley and Fallon farmers.

And then what? Well, as you travel south from Fallon to Walker Lake, you'll be driving through desert that's dotted with military danger areas, where fighter pilots engage in low-flying tactics and bombing target practice. The farms are failing and the Naval Air Station is expanding. Could it be that within a generation, Fallon will be a military zone?

To Schurz
You skirt the eastern edge of the **Desert Mountains,** gently hemmed in on the east by the **Blow Sand Mountains.** There you enter the Walker River Paiute Reservation. The **Terrill Mountains** and **Calico Hills** usher you the rest of the way to the town of Schurz.

WALKER LAKE

INTRODUCTION

Thirty miles long and three to eight miles wide, this pristine high-desert limnological lodestar is actually just a piddling pond left over from ancient Lake Lahontan, which once covered 8,400 square miles of western Nevada and eastern California; Pyramid Lake, 100 miles north, is the other remnant. In addition, the health of Walker Lake is in serious jeopardy these days, experiencing problems similar to, though worse than, Pyramid Lake. Still, this is deep-blue relief for eyes accustomed to the beige basins and gray ranges that surround it for scores of miles. And it's been a welcome sight since the earliest explorations: while seeking the mythical San Buenaventura River, which was widely assumed to run through the vast western desert to the sea, both Jedediah Smith and Peter Skene Ogden came across the lake in the late 1820s; Joseph Walker himself stumbled upon the lake, dying of thirst, in 1833.

Walker was with an 1830s fur-trapping expedition into the Rockies, led by Captain Bonneville, who was later immortalized by New York columnist Washington Irving. Walker continued west with the main party to Salt Lake, then took a small group on a little side trip along the Humboldt and Carson rivers and over the Sierra into California. Walker then led his men back across the Sierra, but couldn't find the Carson River. They got lost in the desert south of Hawthorne—for three days without water. At last they sniffed out the lodestar. From Walker Lake it was a quick hike up the Walker River to the Humboldt and points east.

Walker surfaced again in 1843, when he led Capt. John Frémont's mapping expedition to California, *still* looking for the San Buenaventura. They sur-

veyed Walker's river and lake, and Frémont naturally named them after the guide. That same year Joe Walker led one of the first parties of emigrants across the Sierra.

Water Water Everywhere

Walker Lake is the terminus of Walker River, which flows down from the Sierra in two forks. The East Fork originates up around Walker, California, runs down through Antelope Valley, and is impounded by Topaz Lake (60,000 acre-feet) before traversing Smith Valley. The West Fork's source is up around Bridgeport, California, where it's impounded by Bridgeport Lake (44,000 acre-feet), then flows down a valley south of the East Fork till they join up in central Mason Valley due south of Yerington. From there, the Walker River runs north on the west side of the Wassuk Range, cuts around the top, then turns south on the east side of the Wassuks. Weber Reservoir impounds 13,000 acre-feet for use by the Walker River Paiute. Beyond that (theoretically), the river empties into the lake.

Farmers around Bridgeport and in Antelope Valley (43,000 cultivated acres), in Smith and Mason valleys (80,000 acres), and on the Walker River Paiute Reservation (2,100 acres) divert the river water for agriculture. In 1919, a lawsuit between two large cattle companies in eastern California resulted in the allocation of the Walker River; the total amount of water allocated to farmers amounted to more than is carried by the river in a normal year. One hundred percent of the river water fulfills only 86% of the water rights. (Over-allocating river water in the early 20th century was a common practice.) It wasn't until as late as 1970, when it secured the lake's right

walkin' Joe Walker
NEVADA HISTORICAL SOCIETY, RENO

to floodwaters from the river, that the state of Nevada moved to end the over-allocation of Walker River.

Walker Lake immediately started to shrink. Since 1930, it's dropped more than 100 feet, at least 25 of those in the last ten years. In fact, Walker Lake received only a pittance of water from the river between 1986 and 1997. (It got roughly 4,500 acre-feet in 1993, but only when the Walker River Irrigation District was court ordered to release enough water to flush trout spawning grounds of mud and silt that accumulated when the farmers drained Bridgeport Lake in 1990. The water reached Weber Reservoir, and the Paiute released most of it for the sake of the lake.) Walker Lake didn't even get a drop of water in spring 1994, after the Walker watershed reached 140% of its normal snowpack in the ferocious winter of 1993. In the past 64 years, Walker Lake has risen only 11 times.

Walker River carries an average of 406,000 acre-feet, of which the farmers along the way are entitled to 200,000. It's estimated that riverbank trees and other flora drink up another 103,000; that leaves 103,000 acre-feet for the lake. But Walker Lake loses 136,000 acre-feet, or 3.7 feet in elevation, every year to evaporation alone. As the lake level drops, dissolved solids, such as minerals and salts, become more concentrated and kill off the microscopic zooplankton that feed the fish, and algae increase, depriving the lake of oxygen. In 1994, during the eighth year of the drought, officials estimated that the life expectancy of all the fish in Walker Lake was somewhere between two and five years.

However, fresh water was once again able to reach the lake during the wet winters of 1996—97, enough to raise the lake level 10 feet by June 1997. Half of that amount came during one warm spell early in 1997. The Walker Lake Working Group (WLWG) estimates that the influx of water added four years to the life of the lake, should drought conditions return and no water reach the lake at all, as happend for nine straight years in the late '80s and early '90s. The WLWG says the message the group is trying to send is that

everyone has to be a conscious and conservative water user to ensure that Walker Lake survives.

Recreation

For all that, the lake is still *there,* and it still has fish in it. The north quarter of the lake is owned by the Walker River Paiute, the middle half by BLM, and the south quarter by the Army Ammunition plant. Speed-boat races, fishing and derbies, water-skiing, swimming, and camping are the main sports on the lake.

Sportsman's Beach is 15 miles north of Hawthorne, along the west shore below US 95; 17 sites, outhouses, tables and shelters, free. **Walker Lake State Recreation Area,** 775/867-3001, is two miles south at **Tamarack Point.** It has 12 picnic sites, outhouses, and the lake's only boat ramp.

Camping on the lake is available at the **Desert Lake Campground,** US 95 at Walker Lake, 775/945-3373. Open from March through November, the campground has 25 sites with full hook-ups. Tents are allowed.

Best fishing for the two- to three-pound cutthroat trout stocked in the lake is in March and April. Fishing derby prizewinners are generally four to six pounds. Like many lakes, Walker is no exception when it comes to giant serpents. Cecil is the 80-foot-long monster that hides in the lake's ancient depths. Although he's less than benign in Paiute legends, to the children of Hawthorne, Cecil is friendly and is always well represented in local parades. You can also see representations of Cecil in the Mineral County Museum in Hawthorne (see "Sights" under "Hawthorne," below).

Loons visit Walker Lake twice a year. Roughly 700 in April and 1,000 in October drop in to eat and mate on their migrations. The Nevada Division of Wildlife conducts loon tours, boat trips out onto the lake to see and hear the loons, every year in April. For information, contact the Nevada Division of Wildlife, 380 W. B St., Fallon, NV 89406, 775/423-3171; open Mon.–Fri. 8 A.M.–5 P.M.

The **Wassuk Range** fringes the lake's west shore, with **Mt. Grant** rising 11,245 feet off the southwest corner; the road is chiseled between the range and lake.

WALKER RIVER PAIUTE RESERVATION

Unofficially established in 1859, the reservation was officially granted 300,000 acres in 1874 by President Ulysses Grant. The Nevada Paiutes (known as Agai Dicutta, or Trout Eaters) were also given all of Walker Lake, known as Agai Pah (Trout Lake). A few years later the Indians began to farm alfalfa and raise cattle. Eventually the land was parceled among the members. They opened a school and clinic and employed tribal police. They adopted a constitution and centralized tribal government. In the late 1800s, the Paiute fished the native Lahontan cutthroat trout from Walker Lake and sold it to the settlers at Hawthorne for 15 cents a pound. In 1906, the reservation land was reduced to allow mining in the Wassuk Range on Walker Lake's western shore, leaving the northern quarter of the lake to the Paiute.

Today, the Walker River Paiute still farm and ranch, lease land for mining, and operate a cement plant and the Four Seasons Market just south of town. The market is where you get the permits you need to fish ($5), boat ($8), and camp ($5) at the Weber Reservoir located on the reservation six miles west on the road to Yerington. The Walker River Travel Center, new in 1992, closed in 1997. No one seems to know when, or even if, it will reopen. Over the years the reservation acreage has been chipped away for mining and recreation, but the Paiute people continue to maintain a strong tribal organization and unity. The tribe celebrates its Pine Nut Festival in September, drawing thousands of participants from around the West, and hosts a rodeo in June.

The small town of **Schurz** at the junction of US 95 and Alt. 95 has a small store, gas station, historical sign, and the Tribal Administration Building, where artifacts, crafts, and pictures are displayed.

TO HAWTHORNE

Walker Lake Village
The small village of Walker Lake lies between the road and the lake; some locals live up on the slope of the Wassuks. The speed limit drops to 45 here; beware. The **Buffalo Stop Mini-Mart** marks the entrance to the little resort. Take a left onto Cliff House Rd. at the sign for the motel. The **Cliff House Restaurant and Motel** are down the road toward the lake. The restaurant has been well known for nearly a quarter-century for its fine food and views. The bar opens at 3 P.M., and dinner is served in the 48-seat dining room starting at 5 P.M.; closed Tuesday. The prawns and crab are renowned, the lobster is Australian rock, and the beef is milk-fed center cut. Make dinner reservations at 775/945-5253.

The motel rooms are on the beach (though the water is pretty far away these days, especially when you compare it to a dozen years ago when the motel had to be closed because of flooding). The rooms go for $38. Some people like to rent all 12 rooms to have their own little private beach. For room reservations, call 775/945-2444 daytime, 775/945-5253 evenings.

A gravel road runs around the east side of the lake, stretching south from Schurz. Northeast of Hawthorne you drive five miles on pavement, turn left at **Thorne,** where a military spur line connects to the Southern Pacific track, then go up the east shore on gravel. Hawthorne sprawls into **Soda Spring Valley** beyond the southern tip of the lake, between the Wassuks on the west and the **Gillis Range** on the east.

HAWTHORNE

INTRODUCTION

In 1881, the Carson and Colorado Railroad, managed by H.M. Yerington, chose a spot near Walker Lake's southern tip to serve as its freighting station for nearby mines and boomtowns. In doing so, Yerington deliberately snubbed a town 57 miles northwest, which had recently renamed itself Yerington to flatter the manager into locating the station there. Possibly as a practical joke against the town of Yerington, which until the renaming had been called Pizen Switch, the new town was named after an assistant manager of the railroad, W.A. Hawthorne. Once the railroad had been installed, the town layout was modeled after Sacramento's. Lots were sold at an auction for $100 apiece.

Hawthorne's fortunes were directly proportional to the boom-bust cycles of the railroad, mines, and county politics. Aurora had been in decline for a decade and Hawthorne replaced it as Esmeralda County seat in 1883, only to lose it 20 years later to booming Goldfield. But it regained the seat when Mineral County was cleaved off Esmeralda in 1911. The Southern Pacific took over the Carson and Colorado in 1904, and its new track bypassed Hawthorne by seven miles. Possibly in another joke, the new station was named Thorne. A fire in 1926 nearly finished off the town, leaving fewer than 200 residents. But in a strange quirk of fate, the Naval Ammunition Depot in Lake Denmark, New Jersey, also went up in flames that same year, necessitating its relocation from the major East Coast population center to some remote location in the West. Thanks in large part to the tireless efforts of Nevada Senator Tasker Oddie, Hawthorne was selected as the site.

Subsequently, Hawthorne's fortunes rose and fell with the country's war involvements. During WW II, the barracks town of Babbitt was built to accommodate the sixfold increase in population; after the war, the population dropped and Babbitt became a plywood ghost town. (Today, no more buildings are left in Babbitt.) US 95 ensured a steady flow of traffic, and in the '70s and '80s Hawthorne expanded its travelers' services: casinos, lodging, restaurants, and Walker Lake recreational opportunities.

SIGHTS

Hawthorne is completely surrounded by thousands of thick concrete bunkers and pillboxes. Like sand creatures out of Frank Herbert's *Dune,* these magazines take the shapes of whitehead-like pyramids, stubby worm segments, camouflaged caterpillars, and long gray slugs. They're filled with bullets, bombs, grenades, mortars, mines, depth charges, missiles, and other conventional ammunition and ordnance, steadied

and readied for when the Army calls. Ironically, this depot of death and destruction has for the last 65 years stabilized Hawthorne's previously precarious existence; the very same arsenal that moment by moment could conceivably wipe Hawthorne off the face of the Earth finally put it on the map for good; the Hawthorne Army Ammunition Plant provides stable employment for about 300 residents.

Hawthorne is just a short drive from a number of attractive places, including Walker Lake, mentioned above. It's also a short drive from the eastern gateway to Yosemite, the historic ghost town of Bodie, and Mono Lake, across the border in California. Lovely desert mountains surround the town, and the nighttime skies are alive with stars. The town's memorial rose garden features many rows of roses landscaped with paths, benches to rest on, and a babbling fountain. The views from the top of Lucky Boy Pass are spectacular, spanning 50 miles from north to south and showing the unique beauty of a desert lake.

Museum

If you happen to be passing through at the right time on the right days, be sure to stop in at the **Mineral County Museum.** This is a big barn of a building, with numerous interesting historical displays. First check out the big painting of Hawthorne's history commissioned for the country's bicentennial: everything from Cecil the Serpent to chromate-green bombs. Also for the bicentennial, the townspeople created a quilt now on display. The post office exhibit displays a letter from 1883 with a two-cent stamp, and a letter addressed to H.M. Yerington, the big cheese around here in the early years. The locksmith exhibit has keys from the Gold Hill Jail. There's a new apothecary exhibit from Golden Key Drugs. There's lots of mining equipment, including a three-piston stamp-mill crusher, and lots of stories, including how the collection of Spanish-mission bells was discovered. Recommended.

The museum is at 10th and D streets, on the right just as you enter town from the north, 775/945-5142. From April to November the museum is open Tues.–Sat. 11 A.M.–5 P.M.; in winter, from December to March, it's open Tues.–Sat. noon–4 P.M. Admission is free; donations are welcome.

Around Town

Coming into Hawthorne on US 95 from the north, you can go into what used to be the army base and is now run by a civilian contractor; turn right at the guardhouse. This is the big surprise of Hawthorne: the big old officers' houses now occupied by residents, the tree-lined streets and wide grassy strips, the golf course and country club. A great place to shut off the glare of the road and desert for a respite.

For a different view of Hawthorne, take a left at McDonald's on the truck bypass, and drive a couple of miles or so around the back side of town.

Casino

The **El Capitan** is the big casino in Hawthorne, with plenty of slots, four blackjack tables, a crap table, and free coffee. It opened in 1943 during the boom years of WW II, and locals owned it all the way up to 1989, when International Gaming Technology bought it. IGT sold the El Cap several years later to Summit Casinos, which also owns the Silver Club in Sparks, the Topaz Lake Casino, one in the Caribbean, and which would be the perfect corporation to buy, finish restoring, and reopen the Goldfield Hotel. An exhibit case displays memorabilia from the El Cap over the years near the side entrance of the casino.

PRACTICALITIES

Accommodations

Hawthorne has nine motels and a hotel, for a grand total of 265 rooms. The big action is at the **El Capitan Resort & Casino,** 540 F St., 775/945-3321 or 800/922-2311, with 103 low-rise rooms across the street at $26–40. The next largest is **Best Inn & Suites,** 1402 E. Fifth St., 775/945-2660 or 800/528-1234, with 39 rooms at $60–80. If you're looking for the inexpensive, try: **Rocket Motel,** 694 Sierra Way, 775/945-2143, $22–25; **Monarch Motel,** 1291 E. Fifth., 775/945-3117, $28–50; **Holiday Lodge,** Fifth and J, 775/945-3316, $26–32; **Hawthorne Motel,** 720 Sierra, 775/945-2544, $22–25; **Covered Wagon Motel,** 1322 Fifth St., 775/945-2253, $25–40; and **Sand N Sage Lodge,** 1301 E. Fifth St., 775/945-3352, $30–45.

Scotty's RV Park, Fifth and J Streets, 775/945-2079, has 18 spaces for motor homes, all with full hookups; 17 pull-throughs. Tents are not allowed. The fee is $14 per vehicle. Just down the street is the **Frontier Overnight RV Park,** 5th and L Streets, 775/945-2733, with 27 spaces for motor homes, all with full hookups; all pull-throughs. Tents are not allowed. The fee is $13. The Frontier has been here since 1977. It's got some trees and fairly wide spaces.

Food and Drink

Maggie's, 758 E. Main, 775/945-3908, serves breakfast, lunch, and dinner every day from 6 A.M.–9 P.M. Maggie bakes all her own breads, biscuits, pies, etc.; in fact, just about everything on the menu is made from scratch. This place has the best salad bar for miles around; the all-you-can-eat soup and salad bar costs just $5.50 anytime, and is included when you come for dinner. Breakfast here runs $3–8, lunch $4–8. Dinner is $7–15 on the restaurant side, $11–24 on the steakhouse side, including the all-you-can-eat soup and salad bar. Local favorites are the honey-dipped fried chicken and the chicken-fried steak. You can dine outside on the patio. Maggie's won the state's Governor's Tourism Award in 1996, Business of the Year in 2000, and many other awards.

The Idle Hour, 1302 5th, 775/945-3716, is a popular steak house. **Happy Buddha,** 570 Sierra Way, 775/945-2727, and **Wong's,** 923 5th, 775/945-1700, serve Chinese.

The **El Capitan** casino has a coffee shop open 6 A.M.–2 A.M. Sun.–Thurs., 24 hours on weekends, with daily lunch and dinner specials.

Joe's Tavern is across the street from the El Cap. It's a bar, dance hall, casino (slots and one bj table), and general hangout owned by the Viani family. Joe Viani was a beloved Hawthornite and state assemblyman; Joe Junior now runs the joint. Check out the mining artifacts, the bell from the Candalaria schoolhouse, the big scale, and the resolution noting the passing of longtime Nevada resident Grandma Julie Viani. There could be live entertainment weekend nights.

The **Texaco Truck Stop,** on US 95 about half a mile south of town, is open 24 hours, serves food and has showers available.

For a splash, the locals go out to the **Cliff**

House Restaurant on Walker Lake, 12 miles north of town on US 95; for details, see the "To Hawthorne—Walker Lake Village" section, just before Hawthorne.

The **Walker Lake Country Club,** 775/945-1111, open 8 A.M. until dark, has a bar serving simple snacks like hot dogs and chili. The green fees at the nine-hole golf course run $8 for nine holes and $14 for 18 holes. Add $2 on weekends. It's at the Army base, about three miles north of Hawthorne, between town and Walker Lake.

Information

The **Mineral County Chamber of Commerce,** 932 E St., 775/945-5896 or toll-free 877/788-LAKE, will gladly supply you with fact sheets, business directories, and the like. It's open Mon.–Fri. 8:30 A.M.–5 P.M.

The **library** is at 1st and A, 775/945-2778, open Mon.–Thurs. 10 A.M.–7 P.M., Friday 10 A.M.–6 P.M.

Stop in at **Gun and Tackle,** 898 Sierra Way, 775/945-3266, to ask about fishing and recreation on Walker Lake.

VICINITY OF HAWTHORNE

Aurora

Gold was discovered in the midst of these stray volcanic peaks (the Brawleys) just east of the southern Wassuks in 1861, several years before the California-Nevada border here had been clarified. Both territories claimed the rich mining town, and both established county seats and municipal administrations, on each side of town. In 1864, when the new state was surveyed, Aurora was placed inside Nevada, and the Mono County offices had to move to Bodie, the notorious camp next door.

Sam Clemens stopped off at Aurora to try his luck, suffered a series of setbacks, and consoled himself by submitting freelance correspondence to the *Territorial Enterprise*. At his darkest moment, a letter arrived from Virginia City, offering him a job as the newspaper's city editor for a princely $25 a week. There Sam Clemens became Mark Twain.

Aurora rivaled Virginia City in size and population just before statehood, but the former's heat was about to dissipate, while the latter's was just warming up. Aurora produced more than $20 million in gold in roughly seven years, till *borrasca*. But it kept hanging on; the WPA guide reported in 1940 that "Aurora shows signs of coming to life, maintaining a remarkable resistance to complete abandonment." Until right after the war, that is, when a contractor from Southern California dismantled the deserted brick buildings. Scavengers grabbed the rest.

To get there from Hawthorne, continue straight on Main St. (NV 359) at the intersection where US 95 turns left. This is the highway around the eastern slope of the Wassuks on **Whiskey Flat** and through a small saddle in the **Anchorite Hills** to California and Mono Lake. You'll see a turnoff on a gravel road to **Lucky Boy Pass,** up to which you start climbing immediately. Dow Corning ran a silicate mine up here, and you might find it hard to imagine big semis full of minerals barreling down off this grade. Finally you come to the pass at 8,000 feet elevation, where you can see for miles into the East Walker River Valley. From there, you head down to the Aurora Crater and around to Aurora town site. Little remains.

TO TONOPAH

Back on US 95, the highway runs 24 miles to the junction of NV 361 to Gabbs. If you're going this way, NV 361 is well paved, and provides a straight shot into the **Gabbs Valley Range.** The road turns east to crest **Calvada Summit** (6,130 feet), then turns north again to cross **Petrified Summit** (6,246 feet). Sheer sandstone walls and jagged ridges up here. Also up here is the Santa Fe gold mine, with big dumps and a plastic water pipe feeding the operation. From there it's a straight shot through **Gabbs Valley** into Gabbs.

Luning and Mina

Back on US 95, the road runs 24 miles to Luning, through the long tail of Soda Spring Valley, between the Gillis Range on the north and the **Garfield Hills** on the south. The Southern Pacific Railroad tracks run right through town, which has been settled since the 1870s. The area produced silver through the 1890s, then copper and lead in the early 1900s.

US 95 cuts south from Luning, still along narrow Soda Springs Valley, with the **Gabbs Valley Range** keeping it company on the east. Eighteen miles from Luning is the town of **Mina**, at the end of the Southern Pacific's Hazen branch. The town, in fact, is a creation of the Southern Pacific Railroad, which built its own settlement rather than deal with an unscrupulous landowner from Sodaville, a few miles south. Mina was once a major rail junction for the Southern Pacific, Tonopah and Goldfield, and an S.P. narrow gauge to California.

Before the Tonopah and Goldfield Railroad reached the Southern Pacific at Mina nearby, **Sodaville** was the most important town between Reno and Tonopah. Here, all travelers and freight transferred to stages and wagons for the 70-mile ride to Tonopah, a ride so dusty that a joke survives to this day about a man who had to take a shovel at the end of the ride to distinguish fellow passengers from his wife. The ride *from* Tonopah was made more bearable by the presence of warm springs at Sodaville. But the birth of Mina ensured the death of Sodaville.

Strung out along the highway, Mina's business district consists of a gas station and mini mart, two motels, a cafe, bar, brothel, and RV park. **Sue's Motel** is on the highway; **Jackson's** gas station and market is next door. The other motel, with the bar and café, is across the road at the **Silver King**, 775/573-9703. At the southern edge of town, the **Sunrise Valley RV Park**, 775/573-2214, offers shady RV spaces with pull-throughs for $18; ask for Good Sam and AAA discounts. Tents are allowed, and there's a small store on the premises. Three miles south is **Billie's Day and Night**. The sign out front advertises massages and all-night parking for truckers (the parking is free; staying inside all night will cost thousands).

Mina is also the home office of **Desert Lobster**, 775/573-2464. Yes, you read that right, and if owner Bob Eddy has his way, the town may become the center of a new Nevada industry-lobster ranching. A former cattleman, Eddy turned to wrangling Australian red-claw lobsters in 1994 after selling the family spread near Austin. Two years of research, three years of trial and error and $300,000 later, Eddy's gamble is on the brink of fruition. He breeds the beasts in four fiberglass tomato bins sunk into the

ground right beside US 95. Each bin will hold a thousand marketable seven-inch lobsters (six to a pound for $18). A freshwater species related to the crayfish, red claws top out at a pound in two years, but Eddy says the money is in the smaller ones, which are cooked like shrimp. Three small tanks nearby are rearing pens for the quarter-inch-or-less-long youngsters. The operation is one big balancing act, he says, and it took him awhile to get the hang of it. You can't overfeed the critters or they die, because excess food sours the water. Underfeed them and they'll eat each other. Water temperature must be a constant 75–85 degrees or they won't grow and breed. Eddy mixes water from a warm spring and cold spring located side by side on the property he leases south of town near the defunct Mule Station restaurant. Eddy thinks he's over the hump now; the second-generation lobster reached breeding age. If you start seeing blinking neon Desert Lobster signs in Las Vegas, Reno, and Tahoe, you'll know Bob Eddy made good. His goal is to franchise the business so he can retire and fly his gyrocopter.

Salt and Borax Country
Five miles south is the **Tonopah Junction** at a site once known as Rhodes. This is the center of numerous surrounding salt marshes, with Rhodes Salt Marsh on the left a bit north of the intersection. Prospectors from Aurora and Bodie drifted south into this neck of the desert in the early 1860s and discovered the Rhodes, Teels, and Columbus salt flats. Soon, freighters were snaking toward Aurora, Virginia City, and Austin full of salt used in refining silver ore. This is the time and place in Nevada history during which camels, imported from North Africa, were used to cross the 100 miles of arid land to the mills. A few years later, silver was discovered at **Candalaria,** due south of the Tonopah Junction in the Candalaria Hills, which eventually produced more than $20 million worth of silver, gold, and copper.

NV 360 heads southwest from the junction with US 95. A dirt path five miles down the road heads west (left) to **Marietta,** where borax was first mined on a large scale. Frank ("Borax") Smith, a salt miner in Columbus, spotted borax in 1873 at Teels Marsh, which soon became the most important borax mine and mill in the world. Borax previously was used in pharmaceuticals and mined exclusively in Europe, and the development of these large deposits overwhelmed the small market. But Smith was a promoter as well as a miner, one of the first American industrialists to recognize the value of a full-scale advertising campaign. Subsequently, borax became a household word as an abrasive cleanser. The operation here lasted for 20 years until a more profitable type of borax was discovered in Death Valley, California, to which Smith relocated his mines and mills and went on to further popularize the product with the outlandish 20-mule-team wagons. Borax is still used today, but its primary use is in fiberglass. Secondary uses include glass and ceramics, pharmaceuticals and cosmetics. Soap accounts for a mere 15%.

In another four miles, a road cuts off east (right) to Candelaria, which produced $20 million worth of gold, silver, and copper through the 1870s. Take the seven-mile paved road to the ghost town past vast tailing piles that are being revegetated by the Candelaria Mining Company. Owned by the Kinn Ross Company, a subsidiary of Arman Hammer's Occidental Petroleum, Candelaria Mining has been mining gold and silver in the area since the late 1970s. The mill and office complex look prosperous and somewhat ominous standing behind a huge sign warning unauthorized visitors not to approach. The mine was shutting down in 1997; the only activity was the reclamation work on tailing piles you pass coming in. The ruins of the bank and mercantile, both built of native stone, look impressive even without most of their doors and some of their walls (the bank is the one with the tall steel doors). Two shacks of rock and wood built into the hillside slouch nearby. Just up the road on the left is the mill, or rather its sprawling stone foundation. A dozen other foundations, poking through the scrub, are visible from the road. This would be a fun place to explore if it weren't for the no-parking and no-trespassing signs everywhere.

Back on US 95, it's 14 miles to **Basalt,** at the junction with US 6, which continues west over **Montgomery Pass** (7,132 feet) in the **White Mountains. Boundary Peak,** at 13,143 feet, is the highest spot in Nevada.

US 95 from Tonopah Junction runs 21 miles southeast to **Coaldale Junction.** The Candalaria Hills on the west give way to the Columbus Marsh. The **Monte Cristo Range** is on the east. These unusual volcanic mountains sport layers of ash and lava atop floodplains and lake beds in a maze of gullies and soft rounded hills reminiscent of badlands. The treeless slopes are amazingly colorful, with pastel purples, browns, yellows, even whites, and a pink so fiery that it glows any time of day. The highway follows the crescent-shaped range south by Coaldale, then east to **Blair Junction** with NV 265 to Silver Peak, then north along its eastern leg halfway to Tonopah.

At Coaldale Junction, US 95 splits off from US 6 west, which goes into California past Boundary Peak. This is the second-largest "town" in Esmeralda County (behind Goldfield). It boasts a motel, cafe, and bar with slots and gas, open 24 hours. From here it's six miles to Blair Junction, from where it's 21 paved miles to **Silver Peak,** on the edge of Clayton Valley in the Silver Peak Range. This boomtown had one of the most up-and-down cycles of all the mining camps in the area, producing nearly $9 million in silver during its heyday. Thirty-four miles east of Blair Junction, across Big Smoky Valley, is Tonopah, just inside the Nye County line.

TONOPAH

INTRODUCTION

Jim Butler

The boom at Austin in the mid-1860s sent prospectors into the rugged and remote desert south through Big Smoky Valley. The discoveries at Ione prompted the state legislators to designate it the seat of new Nye County. A bigger boom at Belmont, 50 miles southeast, was reason enough to move the county seat only three years later.

Through the last two decades of the 19th century, mining all over Nevada was a bust. One particular miner took to hay ranching in Big Smoky Valley near Belmont. Jim Butler was born at the Mother Lode in California and had been a prospector and miner from Austin to Hamilton and back for decades. In the first spring of the 20th century, Butler left his ranch to inspect a mine optimistically called the Southern Klondike, 100 miles south of Belmont. Legend relates that he camped near a spring he knew called Tonopah (Shoshone for "Small Water"). Next morning, Butler awoke to discover that his burros had wandered away. He found them up on what was soon to be called Mizpah Hill. There, he noticed likely looking quartz floaters. Following them up the hill to the vein, he packed a few samples in his saddlebags. Another legend tells a different story: that he was led right to the vein by Indian prospectors. Whichever, Butler continued to the Klondike diggings, which didn't interest him; he showed the rock to the miners there, but it didn't interest them.

Lazy or Shrewd?

Butler then returned to Belmont, where he was faced with two challenges: getting the rock assayed and baling hay. He showed the rock to a young lawyer from New Jersey, Tasker Oddie, who sent it to Walter Gayhart, principal of Austin High School and a backyard assayer. When the results of Gayhart's testing reached Belmont, Butler and Oddie found themselves owners of some very valuable, silver-rich rock.

Here, legend again overcomes fact. One story claims that Butler was a lackadaisical miner and rancher who hung around Belmont all summer to watch his hay grow. Butler's wife Belle, so the story goes, had to drag him back to Tonopah to stake a few claims. But a better version might be that word of the valuable ore started to get around, and Butler deliberately delayed his return, using the hay harvest as an excuse, to diffuse the rush and maintain personal control of the property, of which only he knew the location. In the fall, he snuck off with his wife and Tasker Oddie and laid out the ground.

The Year of 112 Handshakes

Whatever the truth, as soon as Butler showed up at Tonopah, miners immediately descended on the place wanting a piece. Butler and Oddie worked out an amazing system of verbal leases, wherein the leaseholders would pay 25% in royalties for the right to work the ore till the end of the year. Out of the 112 handshake agreements

Jim Butler

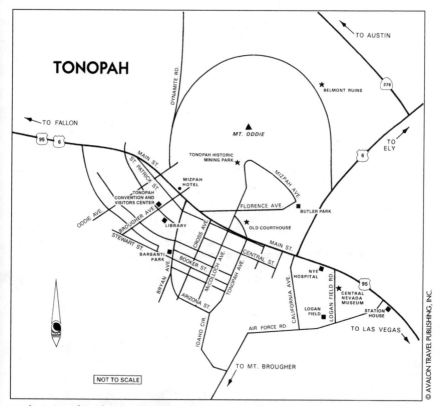

TONOPAH

TO AUSTIN

376

BELMONT RUINS

DYNAMITE RD.

TO FALLON

95 6

MT. ODDIE

TONOPAH HISTORIC MINING PARK

MIZPAH HOTEL

TONOPAH CONVENTION AND VISITORS CENTER

MAIN ST.

ST. PATRICK ST.

MIZPAH AVE.

TO ELY

6

FLORENCE AVE.

BUTLER PARK

ODDIE AVE.

BROUGHER AVE.

LIBRARY

CROSS AVE.

OLD COURTHOUSE

STEWART ST.

MAIN ST.

BARSANTI PARK

BRYAN AVE.

BOOKER ST.

McCULLOCH AVE.

TONOPAH AVE.

CENTRAL ST.

NYE HOSPITAL

95

CALIFORNIA AVE.

LOGAN FIELD RD.

CENTRAL NEVADA MUSEUM

ARIZONA ST.

IDAHO CIR.

LOGAN FIELD

STATION HOUSE

AIR FORCE RD.

TO LAS VEGAS

MOON

TO MT. BROUGHER

NOT TO SCALE

© AVALON TRAVEL PUBLISHING, INC.

made, not one formal contract was signed and not one lawsuit was ever filed. Times were hard that first winter, with everything, especially water, scarce. But by the spring of 1901, the rush was on and all the boomtown rats arrived to serve the feverish miners, who were trying to recover every last cent of silver from their leased holes before the deadline arrived at the end of the year. On New Year's Eve, the miners surfaced, brushed off, and celebrated both their own prosperity and the beginning of Nevada's most promising silver strike in 25 years. On January 1, 1902, a Philadelphia mining venture paid Butler more than $300,000 for all the leased property, incorporated the Tonopah Mining Company, and hired Oddie as general manager.

Jim and Belle Butler bought a big ranch at Inyo, California, and moved there in 1903. Butler

invested his fortune in property and hotels around central and southern California. Tales of his generosity, simple lifestyle, and fancy French car and chauffeur are legendary. Belle died in June 1922, and Jim followed her that December.

The Fall and Rise

The silver bonanza (along with the gold strike in Goldfield) initiated a resurgence in mining activity that, from Tonopah's good location, reached all corners of the state. It also created men who would attain the highest positions of power, both statewide and nationally, over the next 50 years. Tasker Oddie, George Nixon, George Wingfield, Key Pittman, and Patrick McCarran—governors, senators, financiers—were all closely identified with Tonopah-Goldfield.

The heyday years were heady until the mines

began to play out around 1915. Nearly $150 million worth of silver had been removed. Tonopah's population fell to under 2,000, and mining ceased completely at the start of WW II. The Tonopah-Goldfield short line stopped running in 1947.

Bonanza Highway (US 95) traffic, the Army Air Base south of town, and the Nye County seat kept the town alive into the early 1950s. Howard Hughes himself was an admirer of, frequent visitor to, and sometime investor in Tonopah in the 1950s, before his years as the world's most famous recluse. When Hughes married Jean Peters in March 1957, he did it in Tonopah. Also, when he set up shop on the ninth floor of Las Vegas's Desert Inn and proceeded to spend $300 million between 1966 and 1969 on Nevada hotels, casinos, airports, TV stations, and land, a large part of the $10 million with which he bought mining property was centered on Tonopah and Round Mountain.

Finally, in the mid-1970s, the price of gold was deregulated and the oil embargo was taking its toll on the black-gold companies, which saw an opportunity in the yellow-gold business. Houston Oil bought up the Hughes property around Tonopah and began a new mining boom.

Also, Anaconda Copper Company opened a large molybdenum mine and mill 25 miles north of Tonopah in the San Antonio Range in 1979. At its peak, the mine employed 450 people and processed up to 22,000 tons of ore a day, producing a million pounds of moly a month. Though the moly boom lasted only a few years (Anaconda shut down worldwide in the early '80s), the impact on Tonopah was significant. The landmark Mizpah Hotel, named after the boom's most valuable mine, was refurbished. A modern hotel-casino, Station House, opened. The town got its first supermarket, the Warehouse. A subdivision and parks were built, and the community recreation center went up. In 1999 an Australian company, Equatorial North America, came in and starting mining copper, which they are still doing today.

Tonopah These Days

Today, the departments of Energy and Defense maintain the super-secret Tonopah Test Range, which is within the Nellis Air Force Range, whose northern border is only a few miles southeast of town. The Stealth fighter F117A, along with So-

viet MiG jet fighters bought from defecting pilots, was test-flown here. The Air Force moved the Stealths to New Mexico in the early 1990s. Though the military has only a marginal impact on the local economy according to most people, Tonopah may be the only place in the world where shopkeepers smile when sonic booms shake windows around town. If the old merchants were still around, the din would probably remind them of the heady days when silver mines rumbled just two blocks off Main Street.

Of Nevada's several crossroads towns, Tonopah is the greatest. Austin, 117 miles north, might be more centrally located, but Tonopah has the roads. In a state that measures 400 miles from Reno to Wendover, 470 from Jackpot to Boulder City, and 710 miles from Laughlin to Denio, somehow Tonopah seems within only 200 miles of everywhere. NV 376 runs up Big Smoky Valley right into Austin, from where it's 90 miles into Battle Mountain—only 200 miles of traveling on good roads to fan out into northern Nevada. US 95 runs 200 miles into Las Vegas. US 95 and 395, with a few twists and turns on back roads, travel 234 miles into Carson City. US 6 runs 167 miles right into Ely, and NV 375 cuts south from US 6, for 190 miles to Caliente. Thus Tonopah makes a natural trip-breaking stop, usually for lunch, or dinner, or the night, whatever direction is your destination. It's a vital, energized town as well, with lots to see and do nearby.

SIGHTS

Central Nevada Museum

This large and varied museum, just off US 95 on the south end of town near Logan Field, 775/482-9676, is open daily 9 A.M.–5 P.M. in summer, winter hours Mon.–Sat. 11 A.M.–5 P.M.; donations gratefully accepted. Start out by wandering around the extensive outdoor mining exhibit: ten-crusher stamp mill, sheave wheel, double-deck hoisting cages. Also follow the boardwalk around the replica townsite, complete with headframe, pump station, wagon shed, shops, shacks, tent cabins, and outhouse. Many engrossing displays await inside as well. Check out the big Nevada flag, great black and whites of central Nevada towns and big color

Tonopah, mining town

DEKE CASTLEMAN

prints of abandoned mines, aerial views of Tonopah and maps of the state, purple bottle collection (manganese in the glass reacts to sunlight), animal-horn chair, lots of Shoshone artifacts including baskets, mining materials including minerals and an assay office, Tonopah's first organ, a bootlegger's still from Prohibition days, big old safe from the Belmont Courthouse, barber chair from Goldfield Hotel, gas meter and street lamp from old Tonopah, and more. Note the display concerning the early Tonopah Army Air Force Base, and the photos of the Stealth bomber.

The research room is available for modern-day digging, and for sale in the gift shop are books, historical journals, postcards, and possible gift items. After an hour or so here, you'll have a much better appreciation of the history of the town, and central and southwestern Nevada, which is sure to color the rest of your visit to Tonopah and beyond.

The 70-acre **Tonopah Historic Mining Park** on Mizpah Ave. is open every day, 10 A.M.–5 P.M. Free tours of the park are offered every Saturday at 10 A.M. The tour starts with a 15-minute video about the town's mining past. Afterward a member of the mining park committee will take you up to the site and lead you on a one-hour walk around the Silver Top and Mizpah mines. Three other big mines—the Desert Queen, Montana Tonopah, and Northern Star—are located within the park, but are deemed too difficult or dangerous to approach. These mines pulled

$150 million in silver out of the ground before they closed. You get to go inside the Mizpah and Silver Top hoistworks and warehouses, where spare parts and cases of core samples sit gathering dust pretty much the way they have since the mines shut down. The tour offers a close-up look at the snaking stopes and cracks where the lease miners removed the ore in their hustle to make their fortunes before their agreements with the mine owners expired. On the way over to the Mizpah you'll walk right across an exposed two-foot-wide vein of silver ore just like the one Jim Butler found in 1900. Curiously it was never mined. Peer into the 100-foot-deep crater of the Glory Hole site of a 1922 cave-in caused by mining too near the surface. No one was killed, but only because the collapse occurred at night. Miners returned to work the next morning to find the assay office in splinters at the bottom of the pit.

Round Mountain Gold and Echo Bay mining companies donated the land to the city. Four years ago, townsfolk formed a committee to look into the possibility of turning the site into a tourist attraction. The state legislature appropriated a total of $200,000 to get the area fixed up. The Forest Service came up with $15,000 to build some restrooms. Committee members have painted many of the buildings and fenced off the stopes. By 1998, they hope to have a visitor center, snack bar, picnic area, and a self-guided interpretive walk at the park. Later if they can swing it, they'd like to open part of one of the mine shafts for underground tours.

The park also offers an excellent view of downtown Tonopah. Look across Main at the Silver Queen Motel and you'll see that the upper wing of the inn is built on the huge tailing pile from the Silver Queen Mine. The motel swimming pool sits above the old shaft.

Around Town

For a great view and to figure out the lay of the land, turn onto Air Force Rd. near the Station House, and drive one and a half miles away from town and up **Mt. Brougher** till you get to the No Trespassing chain—enough room to turn around. From up here, the overview of the little high-desert bowl of the **San Antonio Mountains** in which Tonopah sits reveals the unmistakable evidence of a boomtown, with its haphazard layout, piles of tailings, and headframes across the way on **Mt. Oddie.**

On the way down head to the left past the public school complex, past **Barsanti Park** with its tennis courts, swimming pool, and kids' playground, and wind down over to Brougher Avenue. Take a left and drive up to the old **K.C. Hall,** built in 1907 by Jim Butler's lawyer, George Bartlett. Later it was turned into a center for the Knights of Columbus. Around the corner on Stewart St. is the **Castle House,** one of the oldest buildings in town (1906) and Tonopah's own haunted house. The Mixpah is haunted too, but it's a hotel. The owners of the Castle House say their ghost, George, is friendly, but a little shy, only making himself heard when rooms are painted or furniture is moved. It's been said that the wife of the original owner, Arthur Raycraft, Tonopah's first banker, held seances in the tower room with a crystal ball. As for the ghost at the Mizpah, visitors staying on the fifth floor have reported a "diaphanous young lady dressed in red" who is said to be the spirit of a woman who vanished 80 years ago under mysterious circumstances.

Near the corner of Brougher and Summit streets are the Chamber of Commerce/convention center and the library (see below).

Brougher St. joins Main right at the five-story bank and **Mizpah Hotel.** The Mizpah started life as a one-story saloon and grill on this location in 1905. A year later, it was hitched up to a team and dragged to another location to make way for the big hotel. The Mizpah opened in 1908, with all the mod cons, including electricity, private baths, and an elevator. Jack Dempsey, a laborer in the silver mines, took a job as a bartender-bouncer in the bar. He watched Wyatt Earp, still formidable in his fifties, down a few there. During the town's long decline, the Mizpah was sold several times; new owners installed the rooftop sign and remodeled the lobby in the early '50s. It was completely renovated in the late '70s, with no expense spared to re-create the splendorous appointments of its heyday.

Around Mount Oddie

Wander around the other (east) side of town, by taking Florence Ave. (behind Silver Queen Motel) to McCullough, continuing up to near the **Mizpah Headframe.** Located and named by Belle Butler (according to legend), the Mizpah was the richest of the Butler properties. **Butler Park** is up here, near the corner of Valley View and Mizpah Circle—picnic tables, bathrooms, a pleasant place for getting out of the car. Come back on Florence to go by the **County Courthouse,** built for $55,000 in the mid-aughts on land donated by the Tonopah Mining Company.

Heading out US 6 east of town, you go by the bowling alley. In a half mile, take a left on Ketton Rd. and creep up to the foundations of the **Belmont,** a state-of-the-art, 500-ton silver-cyanide mill that operated from 1913 to 1923. This is another good place to get out of the car and explore.

Cemetery

Ask at the Chamber of Commerce for directions to the Old Tonopah Cemetery. Opened for business in 1901, the cemetery is the final resting place for more than 300 early residents of the town, including the victims of the "Tonopah Sickness." To this day, no one knows what caused the epidemic that took the lives of more than 30 local miners during the winter of 1901–02. The outbreak caused a mass exodus from Tonopah that winter. Also buried are the 14 victims of the Tonopah Belmont Fire in 1911. Another is Nye County Sheriff Tom Logan, killed in a shoot-out at a brothel in nearby Manhattan. In 1911, a new cemetery was established a mile west of town when the old one became hemmed in by mines and the burgeoning boomtown.

Casinos

The big-town casino is at the **Station House** (775/482-9777) on the south end of town. This hotel-casino was built in 1982 in the midst of the latest boom in Tonopah, next to the Warehouse Market, Tonopah's first supermarket, which opened in 1981. The casino is cramped and crowded with slots, a small blackjack pit, and a mini-craps. A nice display of antique slot machines sits downstairs by the restrooms.

The Banc Club restaurant/bar/casino (775/482-5409), 360 N. Main St. on the west end of town, has slot machines and occupies a building that was once the Bank of America building. (Locals say it would have been named "The Bank Club," since it's in the old bank, except that Nevada law prohibits using the word "bank" in the name of a casino!) The site is the site of the old Tonopah railway depot, which burned down in 1981.

PRACTICALITIES

Accommodations

Tonopah has nearly 500 motel rooms, enough to accommodate most everybody at any time (except on the very busiest Saturday nights and during Jim Butler Days, the town festival that takes place the last weekend in May), and inexpensive enough that you don't have to worry about getting a good deal anywhere you go. All are located along Main Street from one end of town to the other.

The **Mizpah,** 100 Main St., 775/482-6200, is the centerpiece both of the town and the accommodations. The restored rooms remain magnificent, with brass beds, big wooden furniture, mock kerosene lamps with floral patterns on the bulbs, a w.c.-type toilet with pull chain, solid brass bathroom fixtures, all the way down to the ceramic shell soap dish. The original elevator lifts you there, with brass handrails, mirrors, and fancy molding. Best of all, the rates are no less reasonable than most of the motels in town, starting at just $28.

The **Sundowner Motel,** 700 Hwy. 95, 775/482-6224, with 94 rooms is the largest lodging in Tonopah, $27–34. Next largest is the **Silver Queen Motel,** 255 Main St., 775/482-6291 or 800/210-9218, with 85 rooms at $31–45. The

Tonopah Motel, 325 Main St., 775/482-3987, has 20 rooms at $27–33. Next up from there is the **Golden Hills Motel,** 826 Main St., 775/482-6238, $24–65. **OK Corral,** down by the Sundowner at the south end of town, 775/482-8202, charges $29 and up for one of its 54 rooms. The **Clown Motel,** 521 N. Main St., 775/482-5920, is one of the newest, with 31 rooms starting at $27. **Jim Butler Motel,** 100 S. Main St., 775/482-3577, has 25 rooms at $31–55. The **Station House,** 1100 Main St., 775/482-9777, has 75 rooms priced at $33–80. The **Best Western Hi-Desert Inn,** 323 Main St., 775/482-3511 or 877/286-2208, is the most expensive lodging in town, with 62 rooms at $49–89.

Station House RV Park, 775/482-9777, is in the back-side parking lot of the Station House hotel/casino. It's not exactly shady, private, or quiet. It has 20 spaces for motor homes, all with full hookups. Tents are not allowed. Reservations are recommended, especially during the summer. The fee is $12 per vehicle.

The **Twister Inn RV Park,** 1260 Kenton Rd. half a mile east of Highway 6, 775/482-9444, has 13 RV sites for $14. Tents are not allowed. Good Sam and senior discounts available.

Food

If you've been traveling around southern Nevada for a while, you'll appreciate the choice of food in Tonopah: one Mexican restaurant, a 24-hour coffee shop, hotel snack bar, steakhouse, pizza, a deli and a McDonald's (heading north into Tonopah, the first thing you see of the town are the Golden Arches themselves).

The **El Marques,** across from the Tonopah Motel, is open Tues.–Sun. 11 A.M.–9 P.M., with $5–9 Mexican dinners, and a pleasingly dark and cool room.

The **Station House** has surprisingly good food at its 24-hour coffee shop. At the snack shop you can get tacos, burritos, burgers, chili, hot dogs, root beer floats, and milkshakes, and nothing is more than $5. **The Banc Club** also has a coffee shop, open 7 A.M.–10 P.M. daily.

The **Mizpah** has two restaurants: Cirelli's Deli and the Jack Dempsey steakhouse. The menu here tells you that Jack Dempsey worked the mines around Tonopah and was a frequent participant in drilling contests and prizefights. He won his first boxing title in 1919 and became the heavyweight champion of the world in 1926, beating Gene Tunney. It's a comfortable room where you can order broiled salmon for $12, filet mignon for $17 and a selection of pasta dishes from $7 to $14.

The **Silver Queen** restaurant, 257 Main St., 775/482-3084, offers good family dining, serving everything from sandwiches to steaks.

Cisco's Tacos, 702 N. Main, 775/482-5022, is popular with the locals for its cheap good food, serving up ribs, tacos, pizza and the like.

Services and Information

The **Tonopah Convention and Visitor Center** at 301 Brougher St. (P.O. Box 408, Tonopah, NV 89049), 775/482-3558 or toll-free 877/866-6724 (877/TONOPAH), www.tonopahnevada .com, is open Mon.–Fri. 8 A.M.–5 P.M.

Down the street on Summit is the **library,** oldest one still active in Nevada (since 1912), with a new library extension built in summer 2000; 775/482-3374. The **Nye General Hospital** is on the south side of town, 775/482-6233. Tonopah has two **laundromats:** one at the Station House, and another at the Texaco station.

US 6 TO ELY

On the south side of Tonopah, take a left (east) onto US 6. Heading toward this extremely remote section of central Nevada, you pass the bowling alley, the airport, and the entrance to the Tonopah Test Site. The flats of **Ralston Valley** give way to the southern edge of the **Monitor Mountains,** with the scene around the national forest sign *completely* devoid of trees. **Stone Creek Valley** leads to a convenient pass between the **Kawich Range** on the south and the **Hot Creek Range** on the north. At **Warm Springs Junction,** the mini mart and bar are defunct, though the creek and springs are as bubbly, sulphury, and toasty as ever; follow the white-bordered stream around back and up the hill for the pool. US 6 cuts northeast beyond here, while NV 375 (the newly designated "Alien Highway") heads southeast to join NV 318 at Hiko (see "Alamo and Ash Springs" in the Northeast of Las Vegas section).

You drive along **Hot Creek Valley,** with the otherworldly **Pancake Range** hemming in the road to the east. In 25 miles is **Sandy Summit** (6,030 feet). A few miles past is the turnoff to the BLM **Lunar Crater** loop road.

Lunar Crater

Volcanism is one of Earth's most dramatic processes, and Nevada rests on one section of the most active belt of volcanoes in the world: the Pacific Ring of Fire. The Pancake Range is an excellent example of volcanism at work in Nevada, both recent and long past. During the Oligocene Epoch, 40 million years ago, a colossal episode of volcanism obliterated the existing Nevada landscape. Through fractures, fissures, and vents, an unimaginably titanic disgorgement of white-hot steam, ash, and particulate spewed up from the depths, burying the surface under thousands of feet of ash-flow sheets. The topmost sheet transformed the landscape into a single uniform layer. The **Lunar Cuesta (Field)** is an illustration of the welded tuft or fused volcanic rock that resulted from this cataclysm.

But the cinder cones, lava tongues, craters, and maars at Lunar Crater are manifestations of much more recent volcanism, only a few thousand years old. Take a right onto the Lunar loop road and drive three miles. Turn left at the sign to **Easy Chair Crater.** It's clear how this highbacked hole got its name. A 100-yard trail from the parking area leads up to the viewpoint. This could be a recliner—for the Man in the Moon; a sign points out some geology and the direction of lava flows. Within the turn of a neck and the roll of an eye is some amazingly diverse topography: pancake buttes, mashed-potato mounds, craters, cones, the cuesta floor, and the mighty Quinn Canyon Range in the background. The Apollo astronauts trained in this 140,000-acre lunar landscape.

Back on the good dirt road (35 mph, one lane), you drive another few miles and climb up to **Lunar Crater,** 420 feet deep and nearly 4,000 feet in diameter. This is a typical maar, formed when the violent release of gases reams an abrupt deep crater with a low rim. Unlike the crater behind it, which is the peak of a small cinder cone, no magma was ejected with the gases. But the old lava and ash flows were exposed by the explosion; the descriptive sign points them out. Camping at the bottom of the crater you're sure to fall into a deep sleep.

Sometimes it's hard to find any shade in Toiyabe National Forest.

DEKE CASTLEMAN

Continuing the next eight miles toward The Wall, you drive on the east side of the loop along dry Lunar Lake. You won't wonder where or what The Wall is, and it needs no description here. Suffice it to say that Pink Floyd's eponymous double album is not only apropos, but essential.

The loop ends on the old US 6 asphalt; pick a convenient spot to four-wheel up to the highway. North of the highway is **Black Rock Lava Flow,** the most recent basalt ooze in the area, covering 1,900 acres. The lava cooled so fast that it's specked with green, red, and black glass.

Railroad Valley

US 6 continues northeast beyond the Pancakes through Railroad Valley, where oil was discovered in 1954 by Shell geologists. It was the first commercial-quantity oil located in Nevada. Previously, scientists thought the geology of the Great Basin was unfavorable for oil deposits, as they suspected that the "oil traps" were susceptible to the instability of the local earth. But steady (though small) production for the last 40 years or so has proved the early theory incorrect. From 1954 till the mid-'80s, Nevada produced fewer than 400,000 barrels annually. But in the mid-'80s, oil companies explored Nevada more thoroughly, looking for domestic reserves. Since then, they've drilled wells in Pine Valley (south of Carlin) and Grant Canyon (one of the gashes in the Grant Range off Railroad Valley). Nevada's production topped four million barrels in 1990 from 52 wells. One well in Grant Canyon gurgles up 6,000 barrels a day. Most of this oil is

processed into diesel fuel, kerosene, stove oil, and asphalt.

The **Quinn Canyon** and **Grant** mountains escort the road toward the intersection at **Currant.** Both these ranges are new wilderness areas (27,000 and 50,000 acres, respectively), and have been described as "true wilderness, a virtually trackless limestone massif capped by eight-mile-long Troy Peak." The ponds and springs at the western base of the long ranges make up the **Railroad Valley Wildlife Management Area.** In 1934, nearly 140,000 acres here were set aside as a migratory bird refuge, and as at Ruby Lake in northeastern Nevada, wells, dikes, and spillways have been built to control the water in the marsh. Gravel roads lead from US 6 into four management sections.

At Currant is the turnoff for the **Duckwater Indian Reservation.** Beyond is an unexpected canyon along Currant Creek. Currant Mountain, a 36,000-acre Wilderness Area since 1989, is "one of the most impressive mountain masses in the Great Basin," according to John Hart. It's also one of the least known and accessible, and entirely trailless.

To Ely

Currant Summit reaches 6,999 feet; there's a beautiful view from the top across **White River Valley** at the **Egan Range.** White River country is lush, with bucolic alfalfa farms. The intersection of NV 318, the shortcut between Ely and Las Vegas (50 miles shorter than US 93 through Caliente) is next. At **Ward Mountain Summit** (7,300 feet) is a Forest Service campground, and in three to four miles you enter Ely.

GOLDFIELD

INTRODUCTION

When Tonopah was still less than two years old and already the biggest boomtown Nevada had seen for a generation, Jim Butler grubstaked two young prospectors who'd seen rich ore on a small ledge about 25 miles due south. Just like Butler, they staked 20 claims, mined their first paydirt, and managed a small return. Unlike Butler, whose bread and butter was silver, the two miners had a fever. This was *gold,* by god, in the Silver State.

These guys dug in with a vengeance all winter long and finally attracted some expert attention in the late spring. Again like Butler, they proceeded to lease their remaining claims. One of these claims was the Combination, most profitable of all.

The mushrooming tent camp was at first named with a pun: Grandpah. When George Wingfield moved in with George Nixon's money, the boom was on. By then the ore had been found to be so rich that $5-a-day miners could "high-grade" $250 a day worth of nuggets—in shoes, secret pockets, hollow ax handles, and body holsters—then sell it to fences for cash. The town was laid out in September 1903, and with everyone so loaded, real estate prices quickly went through the roof.

The post office opened in January 1904 and the Goldfield *News* came off the hastily imported press in April. Large stone buildings were put up over the summer and the Tonopah-Goldfield Railroad arrived in September. The ore kept growing purer and the cash-$10 and $20 coins—heavier. When the mine owners ran out of patience with high-grading employees, they attempted to install changing rooms, which the miners resisted.

A national prizefight in the summer of 1906 was promoted by Tex Rickard, a well-known character from the Klondike-Nome rushes in Alaska five years earlier; he made so much money on this event that he was able to leverage it all the way to promoting prizefights at Madison Square Garden. The famous Nelson-Gans bout went a brutal 42 rounds. The publicity was priceless, and prizefights have been big business in Nevada ever since.

By 1907 Goldfield had surpassed the milestone 10,000 people. The one-two boom—silver in Tonopah and gold in Goldfield—was heard clearly around the country.

The Powers that Be

By the turn of the century, the violence between individuals in mining boomtowns had been replaced by corporate clashes between organized labor and company-hired goon squads. Goldfield's catalyst was a confrontation between labor (represented by the emerging International Workers of the World, or Wobblies) and management over high-grading and reduced wages. It came to a head when Wingfield and his owner cronies persuaded Governor Sparks to ask President Roosevelt to send in the Army to "maintain order and protect property." The military presence allowed the corporations to hire scabs and break the union. The federal troops were replaced by a new law-enforcement unit that became the state police. And the owners' power was complete.

Goldfield became the seat of Esmeralda County in 1907 (to the dismay of Hawthorne; but when Mineral County was carved out of Esmeralda in 1911, Hawthorne was made seat). The peak of the boom occurred in 1910, with just over $11 million in production and a population estimated at 15,000–20,000, largest in Nevada by far. But *borrasca* wasn't far behind. A flood in 1913 took the starch out of the town, Goldfield Consolidated closed in 1919, and the great fire of 1923 made it a near ghost.

Today, the population is roughly 400, though you're likely to find only a handful in town at any given time. Most of the residents mine gold in the desert, or work on the highway, at the air base, or in Tonopah. Several stone buildings, including the grand old fenced-in Goldfield Hotel and the high school, are remnants of the heyday. Still, the energy from that heyday was so strong that Goldfield is not a near-ghost town, but a near-ghost *city.*

AROUND TOWN

Roll along US 95 into town, which rests in a bowl between **Columbia Mountain** of the **Goldfield Hills** on the east and the **Montezuma Range** on the west.

You can't mistake the **Goldfield Hotel,** built in 1908 for a cool half mil. It boasted 150 rooms and 45 suites with baths. Every room had a telephone, which was part of an ingenious fire-alarm system. The hotel possessed the first electric elevator west of the Mississippi. There were a pool and a billiard parlor, a separate gaming room for ladies, and the dining room was 40 by 80 feet. Opening night dinner featured oysters, caviar, filet mignon, vegetables from the hotel nursery, and ice cream; the cost, $2. The hotel passed through several hands before it finally closed for good in 1946; it's also changed hands several times since, but has never reopened. In 1986, a San Francisco investment company began to renovate the place, but never finished. Today, inside you'll find a construction job half-completed, and boxes and boxes of hotel supplies awaiting somebody else to come and tackle what appears to be one of the hardest jobs in Nevada.

The hotel, courthouse, high school, and several other stone buildings in town survived the big fire; some have historical markers on them, including the **Southern Nevada Consolidated Telephone Company** (1906–63). The huge

high school is not an editorial comment on the American public education system, but rather a statement about the transience of boomtowns, no matter how permanent they appear during the boom.

The county **courthouse,** built in 1907, still serves all 1,300 residents in Esmeralda County, smallest in Nevada. You're welcome to tour the building, respectfully; if the courtroom is locked up, ask at the clerk's office to go inside. Do, it's worth the trouble to see the best preserved courthouse in the state, thanks to the original 1905 Tiffany lamps on the bench, the original brass, leather, and wood furniture and fixtures (100 seats), the judge's chambers behind, and the bighorn head overseeing it all.

Practicalities

The **Mozart Club** serves cocktails, three meals with a small salad bar, and has slots—a pleasant rest stop.

The must-see attraction here is the **Santa Fe Saloon.** A sign points the way from the highway—at 5th Ave., past a school, headframe, Joshua trees, single-wides, satellite dishes, and pavement, all in four blocks. If the Santa Fe Saloon could speak English, it would tell you the whole long story of Goldfield. Which is not to say that it can't *talk;* anyone with eyes and a sense of history can understand its language. The sign and front door will take you back 85 years, to when Goldfield was only a few years old and this club was one of the requisite couple of

Goldfield High School

dozen, competing against the likes of George Wingfield's hotel and Tex Rickard's saloon. The original wooden floors speak of muddy boots and shiny boots, dress shoes and spike heels, brooms and mops. The back bar is one of the most lived-in in the state. The front page of the April 18, 1906, Goldfield *News* does speak English, with the big headline about the San Francisco earthquake. But the best tale, the house special, is the magnificent, pieced-together black-and-white historical photo of Goldfield at its peak: biggest, richest, most powerful, and fanciest town in all of Nevada. The saloon won't speak about surviving the devastating fire in 1923, which razed 50 blocks, and it will only briefly mention the US highway that was pushed through town four blocks away. The old cribs out back are there to stimulate your X-rated imaginations, and speak volumes about that one-of-a-kind rapacious lust for gold. Last but not least, in fact the ultimate manner in which the Santa Fe Saloon symbolizes Goldfield, is that you can count on its being open! It's one of Nevada's quintessential soul survivors.

Stop in for a drink and a chat, and try your luck at the Jolly Joker antique poker-pinball machine (oldest in the state). Check out all the history on the walls. T-shirts are for sale ($8.50). Someone interesting is sure to be sitting at the bar.

The Santa Fe also has four motel rooms next door; $30 s, $36 d, 775/485-3431.

BOB RACE

LAS VEGAS AND THE SOUTHERN CORNER

INTRODUCTION

It's all here, it's all for sale, and it's all legal (what's not might as well be). You can fly into town in a private Learjet. You can stay in a penthouse suite so opulent it'd make Liberace flinch. You can gorge yourself on every kind of food for practically nothing; happy hour goes on 24 hours a day, every day. You can cruise the Strip in nearly any kind of car made, next to god- and goddess-like escorts. Other companions-for-rent will come to your room and, well, you know. You can funnel into a deep trance state with a roll of dirty nickels (and a video poker machine) or you can go for an adrenaline overdose with pristine five-hundred-dollar chips (and a craps table).

Las Vegas turns the pun "nothing succeeds like excess" into a truism. Billion dollar hotels. Twenty-five-hundred-room pyramids. Pirate bat-

tles on the Strip. Twelve-hundred-foot-tall towers. A thousand miles of neon. Slot machines in the supermarkets. Traffic jams of cosmic proportions. Free liquor, for God's sake! Did someone say out of control? This is the cheapest place in the world to go on a bender, a runner, a wingding, a spree, a bacchanalian binge of any kind.

Of course, Las Vegas is also the easiest place in the world to develop an addiction, get divorced, commit financial suicide, generally fling oneself off the cliff of self-control. Without normal moral restraint, this town will squeeze you dry. It's all limbs—long, lean, and sexy—that unchecked, taper into tentacles, boldly stepping right over the line beyond which beauty turns grotesque. Las Vegas is all flesh—bejeweled, bedazzling surfaces and voluptuous, irresistible curves; the

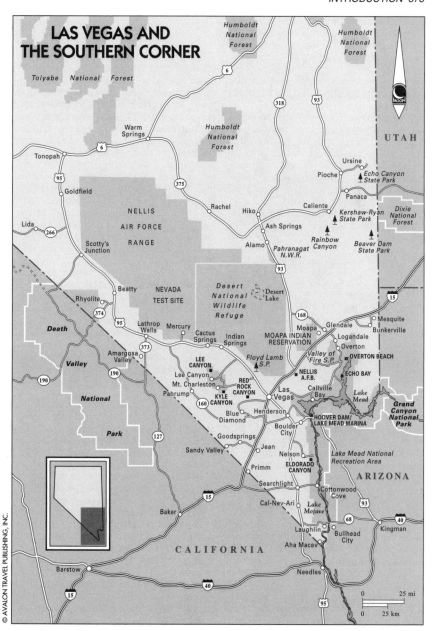

LAS VEGAS AND THE SOUTHERN CORNER

Toiyabe National Forest

Humboldt National Forest

Humboldt National Forest

MOON

UTAH

Warm Springs

Tonopah

Humboldt National Forest

Ursine

Pioche

Echo Canyon State Park

Goldfield

Panaca

Dixie National Forest

Lida

Rachel

Hiko

Caliente

Kershaw-Ryan State Park

NELLIS AIR FORCE RANGE

Scotty's Junction

Ash Springs

Rainbow Canyon

Beaver Dam State Park

Alamo

Pahranagat N.W.R.

Beatty

NEVADA TEST SITE

Desert National Wildlife Refuge

Desert Lake

Rhyolite

Death

Lathrop Wells

Mercury

Cactus Springs

Indian Springs

Glendale

Mesquite

Bunkerville

Moapa

Logandale

MOAPA INDIAN RESERVATION

Overton

Amargosa Valley

LEE CANYON

Floyd Lamb S.P.

Valley of Fire S.P.

OVERTON BEACH

Valley

Lee Canyon

RED ROCK CANYON

NELLIS A.F.B.

ECHO BAY

Mt. Charleston

Pahrump

KYLE CANYON

Las Vegas

Callville Bay

Lake Mead

Grand Canyon National Park

National

Blue Diamond

Henderson

HOOVER DAM/ LAKE MEAD MARINA

Goodsprings

Boulder City

Sandy Valley

Jean

Nelson

Lake Mead National Recreation Area

ELDORADO CANYON

ARIZONA

Primm

Searchlight

Cottonwood Cove

Baker

Cal-Nev-Ari

Lake Mojave

Laughlin

Bullhead City

Kingman

Aha Macav

CALIFORNIA

Barstow

Needles

0   25 mi

0   25 km

lascivious seduction and wet and wild consummation are those of a would-be queen in the presence of the King. But without discipline, Las Vegas is every bit as cold and dry as the desert night, sharp and dangerous as a butcher knife, and mercenary as a perfect prostitute after the job is done and she's been paid and it's time for you to leave.

At the same time, Las Vegas likes to portray itself as the pleasingly plump girl next door. Sin City has embraced family fun. Theme parks, roller coasters, high-tech arcades are all the latest rage. Youth hotels and babysitting services proliferate. Now that gambling has exploded nationally, to compete Las Vegas has transformed itself into Disneyland in the desert.

Or has it? Could it be that Las Vegas instead is now the Mecca of gambling, the imperative destination of pilgrims from little casinos all around the country? Is it just that Las Vegas, in its craven and voracious appetite for expansion, is now seducing the next whole generation of worshippers, supplicants, tithers to the almighty house advantage?

Gambling is the U.S.'s biggest growth industry, and is expected to remain so into the foreseeable future, since state after state has embraced it as a painless tax and a job producer. But then what? Las Vegas is the only city in the country that lives almost exclusively in the present. That Las Vegas has no past is apparent to even the most casual observer (the railroad? the Mafia? the small casinos?), but the future, in fact, is no less obscure. When gambling inevitably goes down (because it's grown too fast to be managed properly, because the industry is bound to suffer a massive shake-out, because scandals, labor troubles, security problems, even smoking issues will plague casinos, because federal regulations and taxation will become oppressive, because the casinos will begin to drain local economies and investors will abandon casino stocks and the moral tide will turn against gamblers once again), when the age-old gambling pendulum swings from universal acceptance to absolute prohibition, where will that leave Las Vegas?

The details are anyone's guess. But whatever happens, the odds are that Las Vegas will not only prosper. It will prevail. You can bet on it.

THE LAND

The most famous and flamboyant resort city in the world spreads out over a small harsh low-desert valley in an unlikely corner of the American Southwest. Some of the most inhospitable terrain imaginable provides a patented hospitality to more than 34 million visitors a year and another million-plus locals, and the numbers keep growing. Las Vegas is an oasis of greed and neon, but especially air-conditioning. After all, sitting as it does in the middle of the minor Mojave Desert, with the northern edge of the great Sonoran Desert and the southern edge of the even greater Great Basin Desert hemming it in on all sides, Las Vegas is one of the hottest and driest urban areas in the United States. Repellent country. (And magnetic.) A hard land. (And soft.) Everywhere you look is another contradiction.

For example, Las Vegas is one of the country's most remote cities. Yet refer to any map of the southwestern United States and you'll soon realize that Las Vegas is a perfectly situated playground. Located almost precisely in the geographical center of California, Nevada, Arizona, and Utah, Las Vegas is only a five-hour drive from Los Angeles (272 miles), and less than a two-hour flight from Phoenix (285 miles), Reno (446 miles), San Francisco (570 miles), and Salt Lake City (419 miles).

Las Vegas's biggest market is within driving distance, but commercial and charter aircraft, one right after another, fly between Las Vegas and a big city in Hawaii, three big ones in western Canada, and a dozen of the same in the Midwest. Several a day from East Coast cities from Miami to Boston. There are even several nonstop flights from Europe each week. The world is getting smaller, and Las Vegas is getting bigger.

All these people, all this attention, are zeroing in on the heart of Las Vegas, which is situated in the heart of Las Vegas Valley, a relatively flat 18- by 26-mile strip oriented northeast to southwest, cutting diagonally across Clark County in southern Nevada. The Spring Mountain Range to the west, which includes Charleston Peak, highest point in the area and eighth highest in the state (11,910 feet), and Sunrise and Frenchman's peaks to the east rise sharply from the smooth, gently sloping valley floor. Ten miles southeast of town is the low point of Las Vegas Valley, known as the Vegas Wash, which drains the valley's meager surface water into Lake Mead. Other nearby topographical features of note include Valley of Fire State Park, Red Rock Canyon, and the interminable desert.

Climate

Though Las Vegas is now a large city with every amenity you could possibly want or imagine, it is still located in the center of an otherwise dangerous land. For at least half the year, the single most important miracle of technology that makes the Mojave bearable, let alone livable, is, as I've said, conditioned air. Summer temperatures fluctuate between lows in the 80s and highs that often reach 115° F. And Las Vegas keeps getting warmer. Why? Locally, the building and population boom has its thermal counterpart: during the day, heat from the sun is absorbed by concrete and asphalt, then released at night. The hot air rises till it meets, and is trapped by, cooler air, creating a "heat island."

The summer of 1994 set a couple of all-time records: the hottest summer of the century and the hottest recorded temperature in Nevada ever (125° F in Laughlin on June 29). The average temperature for June, July, and August was 92.2°, four degrees higher than normal. The average low temperature was 80°, and another record was set for the warmest low temperature: 90°. In short, trying to do *anything* outdoors in the summer sear, other than roasting yourself to a golden crisp on a poolside chair, is problematic.

Wintertime temperatures are mild, averaging 45° F, occasionally dropping into the 20s at night, and often hovering daytime in the 60s. Las Vegas's mean annual temperature is a comfortable 67°. To say this city is a year-round destination is a laughable understatement. Las Vegas has no off-season, period. Even the slack weeks between Thanksgiving and Christmas of only a few years past are now booked solid, and prices don't come down anywhere near what they used to.

Las Vegas has the least precipitation and lowest relative humidity (20%) of all metropolitan areas in the country. Average local rainfall is only 4.19 inches annually, fairly evenly distributed by month throughout the year, with the most rain in January and August, the least in May and June. It's a desert out there, dry as Death Valley sand, and during the summer you'll know every snack bar, Coke machine, and water fountain in your sphere of operations. Cyclonic storms in summer are accompanied by cloudbursts that can drop an inch in an hour, rendering the danger of flash flooding real and worrisome—locals call it the "typhoon" season. Winds that carry in the summer storms have been known to shift all the sand from the west side of town to the east, and vice versa. But any time of year, the winds can be so strong that a giant 30-foot flag on W. Tropicana stands proudly at a perfect right angle to the pole; you have to hang on tight to Caesars Palace's people movers so as not to get blown off; and miniature golfing at Scandia Fun Center is a riot.

WATER

History

Underneath the valley is a major system of artesian aquifers. Groundwater has been tapped at levels as shallow as 40 feet and as deep as 1,000 feet. This underground lake is recharged by rain running off the ranges. Before the drastic depletion of the reservoir between the early 1900s and the 1940s, artesian pressure forced this water up into the valley as a series of springs, creating an oasis. The first Spanish explorers stumbled upon this life-saving lea and named it *Las Vegas,* "the Meadows."

Because of the conservative growth policies of the original Las Vegas Land and Water Company and a rapidly increasing population, the wildcat Vegas Artesian Water Syndicate began tapping into the artesian system almost immediately after the railroad town was founded in 1905. The Company watered only the 40 blocks of the town it had planned; the Syndicate dug wells for everybody outside the perimeter. By 1911, 100 artesian wells had been drilled, and the "mining" of Las Vegas Valley water was fully underway. For the next 25 years, acute water crises were a way of life for Las Vegans; throughout the late '30s and most of the '40s, water shortages, inadequate pressure, broken mains and clogged sewers had turned the acute crises into a chronic condition. The problem was only alleviated in 1948 by piping water from new Lake Mead behind Hoover Dam.

Though it quenched the immediate thirst, the expense of piping Lake Mead to Las Vegas, and the less than optimal water quality, initially discouraged dependence on it. Nearly 20 years later, only 20,000 acre-feet per year was used. But 20 years on in 1987, Las Vegans were using 130,000 acre-feet yearly, out of their 300,000 acre-feet-per-year allotment (one acre-foot is equivalent to 325,872 gallons, about what the average single family house uses in two years). And only five years from then, in 1992, the remaining water allotted to Nevada (between 58,000 and 106,000 acre-feet, depending on how return-flow is calculated) was finally allocated to the Southern Nevada Water Authority.

The Present and Future

That's it, folks. No more Lake Mead water is available for Las Vegas backyard swimming pools, fruit trees, fountains, man-made lakes and bays, volcanoes, golf courses, New England lawns, etc. What's more, in times of drought, Lake Mead allotments are substantially reduced.

Which is why, for the past few years, Las Vegas water officials have been eyeing the water in Lincoln, Nye, and White Pine counties, nearly a million acre-feet. In a plan hatched secretly in the traditional fashion of Western water schemes, suddenly Las Vegas was filing hundreds of claims to "unappropriated" water north and east for a couple of hundred miles and proposing to dam the Virgin River and pipe the water into town which, predictably, touched off a flurry of fury that has yet to subside. Of course, that was just a ploy, a shot in the dark, even a smokescreen for the real water games: redivvying up "the law of the river," or the 70-year-old allocation of Colorado River water among seven Western states and Mexico.

Nevada is allocated the least amount of water of the eight separate entities, two-thirds less than Wyoming and New Mexico. The imperative for changing the compact is the change in demographics over the past seven decades—from an agricultural to a primarily urban population. Indeed, the damming of the Colorado way back when was to provide irrigation water for farmers, at a time when you could count Las Vegans by the hundreds and Los Angelenos by the thousands. It's a very different world now, and the Las Vegas Valley Water Authority has taken to wheeling and dealing downstream water rights, such as paying Arizona farmers not to grow crops in exchange for future water credit.

Conservation? Yeah, right. This is Las Vegas we're talking about. More than 120,000 hotel rooms (with thousands more being planned and constructed each year), which means 120,000 showers, not to mention jacuzzi suites and megapools, plus the spas, backyard pools, and showers of all the houses (being built at a rate of about 15,000 a year). Or lakes around the Mirage, Treasure Island, and Bellagio, not to mention canals at the Venetian. Or the lakes that the most exclusive gated-community mansions are built around. The vaguest stirrings of the concept of conservation are barely noticeable to the trained observer; in fact, Las Vegans have the highest rate of water consumption in the country (therefore the world), though they live in the driest spot on the continent: roughly 300 gallons per person per day. That's twice as high as Phoenix, four times as high as Philadelphia.

Meanwhile, experts disagree vocally on how many years Las Vegas and vicinity can expect to maintain water in the taps given the current growth rates and the finite amount of O and H_2. Most prognosticators seem to agree that Las Vegas will run out of water sometime between 2006 and 2014—but Las Vegas, true to form, will have found more by then.

HISTORY

UP TO THE NINETEENTH CENTURY

Paleo-Indians

Early human habitation in Las Vegas Valley varied with the climate. Although excavations around Tule Springs in eastern Las Vegas Valley have uncovered 11,000-year-old hearths, fluted arrow and spear points, scrapers, and scarred and charred animal bones, experts consider the era between 7000 and 3000 B.C. too arid for settlement in the area. After 2500 B.C., however, the climate changed to nearly what it is today: cool and damp enough, relatively speaking, to support an evolving Indian society. Known as the Archaic or Desert period, this era hosted a forager culture, whose members adapted to the use of resources such as the desert tortoise, bighorn sheep, screwbean mesquite, canyon grape, and cholla fruit. They built rock shelters and roasting pits and used the atlatl (a primitive but remarkably efficient arrow-throwing stick), mortars and pestles, flaked knives, and hammerstones. These Archaic Indians could be considered the behavioral ancestors of the later Paiute people.

The Anasazi

Whether the Archaic people evolved into or were absorbed or evicted by the Basket Makers is unclear, but around 300 B.C. , a new people appeared in the Las Vegas area. Also hunter-gatherers, these early Basket Makers were more sophisticated than their predecessors in only one respect. They lived in pit houses: three- to four-foot-deep excavations with mud floors and walls, brush roofs supported by strong poles, and a central fireplace. By about A.D. 500, the Modified Basket Maker period had arrived; within a couple of hundred years, these Anasazi (Navajo for "Enemies of our Ancestors") were settled permanently in the fertile river valleys of what is now southeastern Nevada. They cultivated maize, beans, squash, and cotton, wove intricate baskets, fashioned handsome black-and-white pottery, constructed large adobe pit houses, and hunted with bows and arrows.

As their agricultural techniques became more refined and their population increased, the Anasazi entered the peak of their civilization: the Classic Pueblo or Lost City period (850–1050). They lived in a sizable urban metropolis known as Pueblo Grande, in the fertile delta between the Muddy and Virgin rivers (roughly 60 miles northeast of Las Vegas, near present-day Overton). The Anasazi were intricately linked to trading centers throughout the Southwest, and travelers carried back not only products but new agricultural and technological information, along with religious and social ideas. During the population explosion of the Lost City eriod, Las Vegas Valley supported an outpost of Lost City Anasazi— its only known prehistoric architecture.

By the year 1050, Pueblo Grande had become Nevada's first ghost town. The Anasazi simply packed up and headed out, dispersing throughout the Southwest. They probably returned to the center of their civilization, becoming the ancestors of today's Hopi and Zuni Indians.

Why would such a sophisticated and successful civilization abandon a major city? Theories include stress from overpopulation, natural disasters (such as several seasons of drought followed by flooding, which would strip the topsoil), and encroachment by the Southern Paiute. One eminent archaeologist insists that the swampy river bottomland was a prime breeding ground for malarial mosquitos; after too many deaths, the people simply moved. A recent, provocative theory holds that the disintegration of this extensive Southwestern society coincided with the collapse of Mexico's vast Toltec empire. Deprived of primary trading links and suffering urban and ecological stress, the Anasazi confederacy unraveled.

The Paiute

For the next 700 years, the nomadic Paiute occupied the territory in southern Nevada abandoned by the Anasazi. These Indians called themselves Tudinu, "Desert People," and spoke an Uto-Aztecan variety of the Shoshonean language, which indicates that they probably arrived from the northeast. The Paiute had some contact with the Anasazi, but the Paiute seem to

Anasazi petroglyphs

DEKE CASTLEMAN

have been peaceful; there's no evidence of confrontation between the immigrants and emigrants.

The Paiute knew the land and its resources and developed a successful culture. They cultivated squash and corn and traveled seasonally to hunt and harvest wild foods. They roamed on foot in small flexible family units. They had no chiefs, only heads of families. No formal structures linked the families, though annual spring and fall game drives and pine-nut harvests united bands for several days.

Contact

The Paiutes' first contact with Europeans occurred in 1776, when two Franciscan friars were establishing both ends of the Old Spanish Trail. Father Silvestre Escalante blazed the eastern end of the trail from Santa Fe, New Mexico, to the southwestern corner of Utah. From the other end, Father Francisco Garces traveled through California and Arizona. Garces encountered southern Nevada Paiute, who by all accounts treated him hospitably. But it was another 50 years before further Paiute-European contact.

Before Mexico gained its independence from Spain in 1822, the Spanish government had enforced strict laws against trespassing. After independence, the first wave of eastern fur trappers and mountain men penetrated the previously unknown Southwest. In 1826–27, famed trader and explorer Jedediah Smith became the first Anglo-European explorer to travel through

what is now southern and central Nevada, and he too made contact with Paiutes. Three years later, Antonio Armijo, a Mexican trader, set out from Santa Fe on the Spanish Trail. An experienced scout in Armijo's party, Rafael Rivera, discovered a shortcut on the route by way of Las Vegas's Big Springs, thereby making him the first non-Indian to set foot on what would become Las Vegas—and at the same time decisively sealing the doom of the southern Nevada Paiute. Within 25 years of contact, the Paiute were a broken people, and dependence became a new way of life.

The Trail and the Fort

By the time John Frémont, legendary surveyor and cartographer for the Army Topographical Corps, passed through Las Vegas Valley in 1845, the Old Spanish Trail had become the most traveled route through the Southwest. Las Vegas by then was a popular camping spot, the nearest grass and water to the Muddy River, a withering 55-mile march to the northeast. Frémont's exploration preceded by only three years the mass migration, in 1847, of persecuted Latter-day Saints, led by Brigham Young, to Salt Lake Valley, at that time still claimed by Mexico. Only a year later, however, the Mexican-American War and subsequent Treaty of Guadalupe Hidalgo wrested control of the vast Far West into American hands. Utah Territory was created, colonized, and administered by Young and his disciplined followers.

By 1854, the section of the Old Spanish Trail from central Utah to Los Angeles had been so tamed by Mormon guides and wagon trains that it came to be called the Mormon Trail. A monthly mail service and regular freight trains traveled between Salt Lake City and the coast. Only the 55 miles from the Muddy River to the Las Vegas Springs remained risky; it became so littered with abandoned emigrant implements and pack-animal skeletons that it was labeled "Journada de Muerta." Las Vegas constituted exquisite relief from the harrowing desert, and its name became synonymous with refreshment and hospitality.

In 1855, Brigham Young dispatched a party of missionaries to establish a community at Las Vegas. The ill-fated colony was plagued from the start. A vast desert surrounded the Meadows; the climate proved almost unbearable; millable timber had to be hauled from 20 miles away; and the isolation sapped what little morale existed. Still, the missionaries erected a fort, dug irrigation ditches, cultivated farms, and managed to befriend some Indians. They might have succeeded, but the colonists' reports of lead deposits nearby prompted Young to send a party of miners to Las Vegas to extract and refine the ore. The missionaries' meager rations were soon stretched to the breaking point by the miners' demands. As was so often the case in early Nevada settlements, deep-seated tensions between miners and Mormons often erupted into bitter disputes—even at Las Vegas, where the miners *were* Mormons. Their disagreements, compounded by the other problems, finally caused the mission to be abandoned in 1858, leaving the second ghost town in Nevada.

The Mines and the Ranch

Soon after the Mormons abandoned the mission, discovery of the Comstock Lode triggered a backwash of miners and migrants east from California. The Latter-day Saints' lead mine, Potosi, was reprospected and found to average $650 in silver per ton, attracting hundreds of fortune seekers. Some enterprising growers sold produce to the new locals. Many prospectors fanned out from Potosi, and discovered gold along the Colorado River. Among the gold miners was Octavius Decatur Gass who, in 1865, took his small stake and high hopes to Las

Vegas and built a ranch house and a blacksmith shop inside the decaying Mormon stockade. The Gass family irrigated 640 acres, and raised grain, fruit, vegetables, and cattle. By the mid-1870s, Gass had bought up or inherited most of the homesteaded land in the Meadows, and he owned the rights to most of the water.

Gass was an enlightened and active pioneer, who treated the local Paiutes with respect and generosity and extended hospitality to all who desired it. Stanley Paher, in his outstanding *Las Vegas*, writes, "Most travelers had come to Las Vegas dirty, weary, and in need of provisions, some even with sick children, but they left refreshed, clean, and happy." Gass traveled extensively to fulfill his duties as justice of the peace and legislator from Pah-Ute County, which encompassed Las Vegas, in newly formed Arizona Territory.

In May 1866, the U.S. Congress extended Nevada's boundaries to include Pah-Ute County, renamed Lincoln County, a move that Gass bitterly contested, especially when back taxes were levied on the new Nevadans. In the mid-1870s, Gass found himself overextended, and took a loan from Archibald Stewart, a wealthy Pioche rancher. When he couldn't repay the loan, Stewart foreclosed and took Gass's Las Vegas Ranch. In 1884, Stewart was fatally shot by a ranch hand. Stewart's wife, Helen, managed the ranch for another 20 years, till the advent of the railroad.

THE TWENTIETH CENTURY ARRIVES

In the early 20th century, William Clark's San Pedro, Los Angeles and Salt Lake Railroad merged with E.H. Harriman's Oregon Short Line, and track from Salt Lake City to Los Angeles was completed, the first railroad line across southern Nevada. The right-of-way ran through Helen Stewart's 2,000 acres, and in preparation, she hired J.T. McWilliams to survey her property, which she subsequently sold to the railroad for $55,000. McWilliams discovered and immediately claimed 80 untitled acres just west of the big ranch. Thanks to its strategic location and plentiful water, Las Vegas had already been designated as a division point for crew changes, a service stop for through trains, and an eventual site for repair shops. McWilliams platted a town site on his 80 acres and began selling lots to a steadfast group of Las Vegas sooners. In 1904, tracks converged on Las Vegas Valley from the southwest and northeast. In January 1905, the golden spike was driven into a tie near Jean, Nevada, 23 miles south of town.

By the time the first train had traveled the length of the track, McWilliams's Las Vegas town site, better known as Ragtown, boasted 1,500 residents, brickyards, weekly newspapers, a bank, an ice plant, a tent hotel, and mercantiles. In April 1905, with the start of regular through service, the San Pedro, Los Angeles, and Salt Lake Railroad organized the subsidiary Las Vegas Land and Water Company, platted its own town site, and bulldozed all the desert scrub from a 40-block area. The railroad advertised heavily in newspapers on both coasts and transported speculators and investors to Las Vegas from Los Angeles ($16) and Salt Lake City ($20)—fares deducted from the deposit on a lot. The company was immediately buried in applications for choice lots. Railroad officials knew a gift horse when it smiled, and they quickly scheduled an auction to pit eager settlers against Los Angeles real estate speculators and East Coast investors—gamblers all. It's fitting that the real Las Vegas (the old town site shortly dried up and blew away) was founded on the principles that would sustain it to the present.

Boomtown Rats

In two scalding days of auctioneering on the site of today's Plaza Hotel, 1,200 lots sold for a cool quarter of a million. Immediately, the proud new owners searched out the stakes marking property boundaries sticking out from the desert sand and erected makeshift shelters. Hotels, saloons, gambling halls, restaurants, warehouses, banks, a post office, and school were built in Las Vegas's first month on the map. The Las Vegas Land and Water Company lived up to its commitment to grade and gravel city streets, construct curbs, and lay water mains, hydrants, and pipes, but only within the boundaries of the railroad's own town site. The nightlife and red-light district centered on the infamous Block 16, between Ogden and Stewart, and 1st and 2nd. By the time revelers rang in 1906 at the Arizona Club in Block 16, Las Vegans already numbered 1,500.

This boom resonated for the first year or so, until initial euphoria gave way to the dismal demands of domesticating a desert. Service policies of the railroad management were conservative and bureaucratic. Flash floods tore up track and delayed trains. The usual fires, conflicts, and growing pains of a new company town dampened local optimism. Even so, William Clark's new Las Vegas and Tonopah Railroad reached the boomtown of Beatty in late 1906, furthering Las Vegas's ambitions as a crossroads.

From 1906 through 1909, the issue of dividing vast Lincoln County in two raised the political climate almost as high as when Arizona's Pah-Ute County became Nevada's Lincoln County in 1866. The distance from Searchlight, the county's southernmost settlement, to Pioche, the county seat, was 235 miles—a serious hardship for far-flung citizens needing to appear at the county courthouse. Furthermore, Pioche was without a bank; all county funds were deposited in Las Vegas. Worse, Lincoln County officials had already amassed a $500,000 debt. After the hotly contested 1909 election, officials supporting division pushed a bill through the state Legislature. Named for the railroad magnate, Clark County officially came into existence in July 1909.

Further cause for celebration that year arrived on the heels of the railroad's decision to construct a large maintenance yard at Las Vegas. Then disaster struck: an enormously destructive flood on New Year's Day, 1910, ripped up more than 100 miles of track, plus trestles and buildings, curtailing train service till May.

The hot little railroad town rebounded quickly. When completed in 1911, the locomotive repair shops created new jobs. The population doubled to 3,000 between 1911 and 1913, two years marked by growing prosperity and progress. A milestone was reached in 1915, when round-the-clock electricity was finally supplied to residents.

Fits and Starts

But the 10-year crescendo of the first boom had climaxed, and Las Vegas went into a slow but steady slide. In 1917, the Las Vegas and Tonopah Railroad suspended operations; hundreds of workers were laid off and left. By 1920, the population had dropped to 2,300. A year

THE BLOCK 16 RED-LIGHT DISTRICT

At the turn of the century, red-light districts were common in small towns and large cities throughout the country. They were confined and adequately policed. By the time Las Vegas was founded in 1905, Nevada's own tradition of flesh peddling in boomtowns was nearly 50 years old, as old as the state itself.

Las Vegas's original sex market, known as Block 16 (downtown between 1st and 2nd and Ogden and Stewart streets), was typical. A mere block from the staid and proper First State Bank, the Block was established in 1905 by conservative town planners working for the San Pedro, Los Angeles, and Salt Lake Railroad, as the predictable by-product of the company's liquor-containment policy. Immediately after investors bought Block 16 lots at the railroad's town site auction, saloons erupted from the desert downtown, with hastily erected cribs out back. Within a year or so, rooms upstairs from the bars were added, all in a "line" facing 2nd Street. The Block, sleepy and deserted during the daytime, woke up at night, when its well-known vices, gambling and whoring, temporarily banished the dried-up small-town desolation.

In a twilight zone not quite illegal, Block 16 was not quite legal either. In the earliest years, barkeeps operating brothels were required to buy a $500 license. Later, regular raids and shakedowns helped finance local government. The 40 or so "darlings of the desert" were required to undergo weekly medical exams; at $2 per, the city physician held a plum position! Law and order were maintained by the steely eyes and quick fists of six-foot-three, 250-pound Sam Gay; the one enduring character from the Block, he went from bouncer to five-term sheriff.

Even with an occasional spirited campaign to eliminate it, Block 16's activities were barely interrupted by the state's 1911 ban on gambling. It also managed to survive the tidal wave of red-light-district shutdowns nationwide during the Progressive years of this century's second decade. The Block fared well during the tricky years of Prohibition, with booze provided by bootleggers from the boonies of North Las Vegas. And even during the federal years of Boulder Dam and the New Deal, amorality thrived, and Block 16 housed more than 300 working girls without undue interference.

Ironically, the relegalization of wide-open gambling in 1931 foreshadowed an end to the Line and kindled the strong and enduring opposition to blatant prostitution of casino operators, who felt that it could do Las Vegas—and therefore gambling—no good. Still, to the dismay of local boosters, the prosaically named Block began to gain a measure of fame as word spread about this last holdout of the Wild West, and tourists to the dam site and Lake Mead visited Las Vegas to rubberneck the saloons and casinos and bordellos.

What finally killed Block 16 was WW II. The War Department had many reasons to want open prostitution closed, not the least of which included VD epidemics and the vocal opposition of military wives. The commander of the Las Vegas Aerial and Gunnery Range simply threatened to declare the whole city off-limits to servicemen, and local officials immediately revoked the liquor licenses and slot-machine permits of the casinos on Block 16. These fronts financed the prostitution, which by itself could not finance the fronts, and the Block's illustrious 35-year alternating current finally ran out of juice.

Today, what was once Block 16 is a parking lot for Binion's Horseshoe. Near the corner of Ogden and 1st is a 20-foot-tall bronze statue of old man Benny Binion, sitting atop his trusty steed, presiding over all the human drama and lust that transpired and expired under his feet so many years ago.

---

later, an elderly William Clark sold his interest in the railroad to Union Pacific, which closed the Las Vegas repair shops, eliminating hundreds more jobs and residents. Up until the late 1920s, Las Vegas remained at its lowest and remotest.

By 1931, the Great Depression was in full swing. The Volstead Act, enforcing the Temperance Movement's pet pitbull Prohibition, had entered its second decade. Nevada's economy was faring only marginally better than the nation's, thanks in large part to vice-starved visitors flocking to the state's libertarian attractions: prevalent bootlegging, prizefights, quickie three-month divorces, liberal prostitution laws, and ubiquitous backroom gambling. But when Governor Fred "Ballsy" Balzar signed legislation that legalized gambling and cut the divorce waiting period to six weeks, Nevada found itself the country's undisputed "Sin Central." Even so, it took the state's largest population center, Reno, many years to accept front-room gambling as respectable; Las Vegas, on the other hand, benefited from a fortuitous event that dovetailed perfectly with the new state-sanctioned sin-centered excitement.

Hoover Dam

The key to Las Vegas's resurrection lay just 40 miles away, at the Colorado River. By 1924, the Bureau of Reclamation had narrowed locations for a dam on the Colorado to Black and Boulder canyons, east of Las Vegas. Anticipation alone began to fuel noticeable growth. By the end of the decade, Las Vegas had long-distance phone service, a federal highway from Salt Lake City to Los Angeles, regularly scheduled airmail and air-passenger services, more than 5,000 residents, and one of the world's most colossal engineering projects about to begin just over the next rise.

More than 5,000 workers labored for five years, often inventing and installing the necessary technology as they went along, to finish Hoover Dam by 1935. Las Vegas benefited not only from the influx of workers and their families, but also from the massive worldwide publicity of the monumental undertaking. The *Las Vegas Review-Journal* adopted for its masthead the slogan, "Everybody knows Las Vegas is the best town by a damsite."

The New Boom

Though an expected exodus of dam builders put late-1930s Las Vegas in the doldrums, secondary effects foreshadowed the area's commercial eruption in the early '40s. First, 20,000 people attended the dedication ceremonies of Hoover Dam in September 1935, with a speech by President Roosevelt and a parade down Fremont Street. Second, the dam, and Lake Mead filling up behind it, quickly became major tourist and recreational destinations. Hotels and casinos began springing up to accommodate the expected horde of visitors. Third, with the dam completed and ready to supply endless water and power, the federal government, gearing up for WW II, began again focusing its attention on southern Nevada.

In 1940, with the population at 8,500, city of-

ficials teamed up with the Civil Aeronautics Agency and the Army Air Corps to expand the original airport into a million-acre training school for pilots and gunners. Over the next five years, the Las Vegas Aerial Gunnery School trained tens of thousands of military personnel; the school eventually expanded to three million acres. In 1942, a monster metal-processing plant, Basic Magnesium, was constructed halfway between Las Vegas and Boulder City—large enough to eventually process more than 100 million tons of magnesium, vital to the war effort for flares, bomb housings, and airplane components. At its peak in 1944, BMI employed 10,000 factory workers, many of whom lived nearby in housing projects at the new town site of Henderson. Las Vegas's population doubled in five years, from 8,500 in 1940 to 17,000 in 1945.

Benjamin Siegel

Right after the war ended, while the rest of the U.S. entered an era of prosperity, moral decency, and babies, Las Vegas entered an era of organized crime. The 1920s, '30s, and WW II had witnessed the evolution of the underworld from a loose agglomeration of family businesses into a unified illegal empire. In 1919, New York City street toughs were poised to exploit the prohibition of alcohol. Boyhood buddies Benjamin "Bugsy" Siegel, tall, handsome, and fearless, and Meyer Lansky, a genius for figuring, planning, and manipulating, hooked up with Frank Costello and Charlie "Lucky" Luciano. Together they developed organized crime's signature m.o.—disciplined gang action, strong-arm persuasion and ruthless revenge, and careful financial accounting patterned after big business.

In 1938, Lansky dispatched Bugsy to Los Angeles to consolidate the California mob and to muscle in on the bookmakers' national "wire" in Las Vegas. That accomplished, he bought into several downtown Las Vegas casinos, and began to implement his vision of an opulent hotel-casino-resort in the desert—the highest-class casino for the highest-class clientele. Over the next several years, Siegel managed to raise a million dollars for his Flamingo Hotel.

Bugsy hired the Del Webb Company of Phoenix to put up the Flamingo, and construction began in 1946. But building materials were scarce after the war, and Siegel's extravagance was limitless, matched only by his inability to stick to a budget. Overruns, faded by his old pal Lansky, finally reached a healthy (or unhealthy, as it turned out) five million bucks, and the project began to exact a heavy toll on Siegel's already questionable nerves, not to mention his silent partners' notorious impatience. According to conventional mob history (which is based more on legend and hearsay than any other type of American history), at a meeting of the bosses in Havana on Christmas Day 1946, a vote was taken. If the Flamingo were a success, Siegel would be reprieved and given a chance to pay back the huge loan. If it failed . . . *muerta.* But according to Robert Lacey in his exhaustive biography of Meyer Lansky, *Little Man,* Siegel was killed by his local Las Vegas associates for being a madman who might endanger Nevada's role as the gamblers' promised land.

The hotel opened the next day. Movie stars attended, headliners performed, but the half-finished hotel—miles out of town, rainy and cold the night after Christmas—flopped. Worse, the casino suffered heavy losses, which the bosses suspected to be further skim. In early January 1947, the Flamingo closed. It reopened in March and started showing a profit in May, but Siegel's fate had been sealed. In Virginia Hill's Beverly Hills' mansion in June 1947, Benny Siegel was hit. Before his body was cold, Phoenix boss gambler Gus Greenbaum had taken over the Flamingo.

The Desert Heats Up

So began 20 years of the Italian-Jewish crime-syndicate's presence in Las Vegas. And 10 years of the biggest hotel-building boom that the country had ever seen. It also triggered an increasing uneasiness among state officials who quickly moved to assume further regulatory responsibilities from the counties, which had overseen the casinos since gambling was legalized in 1931. And then the feds began to apply their patented pressure.

In November 1950, the Committee to Investigate Organized Crime, led by Tennessee Senator Estes Kefauver, came to town. The Kefauver Commission revealed beyond any shadow of a doubt that Las Vegas had completed its transition from a railroad company town to a gambling company town. The biggest gamblers—criminals in every other state in the country—were in charge. On the 20th anniversary of legalized gambling in 1951, the state, the feds—everyone—publicly woke up to the questionable histories of the people waist-deep in counting-room gambling revenues.

The Kefauver hearings triggered two additional, unexpected, though typical, events. First, it created a media hysteria that flooded the rackets divisions of police departments around the country with funds and guns to wipe out the illegal gambling operations within their jurisdictions. This, of course, engendered a large migration to Las Vegas of expert casino owners, managers, and workers, all sticking a thumb into the perfectly legal, largely profitable, and barely policed pie. Black money from the top dons of the Syndicate and their fronts and pawns poured in from the underworld power centers of New York, New England, Cleveland, Chicago, Kansas City, New Orleans, Miami, and Havana. In an eight-year period between 1951 and 1958, 11 major hotel-casinos opened in Las Vegas, nine on the Strip and two downtown, all but one generally believed to be financed with underworld cash.

Two months after Kefauver blew through town, another type of federal heat fell down on Las Vegas. The Atomic Energy Commission conducted its first above-ground nuclear test explosion in the vast uninhabited reaches of the old gunnery range, which now encompassed the Nellis Air Force Base and the Nuclear Test Site. For the next 10 years, nearly a bomb a month was detonated into the atmosphere 70 miles northwest of Las Vegas. For most blasts, the AEC erected realistic "Doom Town" sets to measure destruction, and thousands of soldiers were posted within a tight radius to be purposefully exposed to the radiation. Locals worried which way the wind blew, and seemed to contract a strange "atom fever"—marketing everything from atomburgers to cheesecake frames of Miss Atomic Blast. But mostly, Las Vegans reveled in the AEC and military payrolls, in a notoriety approaching cosmic dimensions, and in the neon-fireworks-thermonuclear aspects of the whole extravaganza.

The Diatribe

But of all the heat—local, state, federal—felt in Las Vegas in the 1950s and '60s, the strongest came from the media. A bandwagon of invective, everything from "corrupt, vile, venal, and immoral" to "gang-controlled, crime-ridden, whore-ridden, and rotten" was unleashed into the public consciousness by the scandal-obsessed press. Known as the Diatribe, it started when Ben Siegel's contract expired in the spring of 1947, gathered steam with the Kefauver investigation in 1950, gained momentum when the Thunderbird Hotel's license was removed in 1955 (because of hidden underworld ownership), and was already out of control when, according to Gabriel Vogliotti, in his brilliant and incisive *Girls of Nevada,* "In 1963, Nevada was hit by the book that would start the change in its gambling, its laws, and its history"—*Green Felt Jungle.* "It remains the greatest excoriation of an American state in the English language." The front-cover copy on the Pocket Book edition reads, "The shocking documented truth about Las Vegas . . . lays bare a corrupt jungle of iniquity." Vogliotti notes, "It became a worldwide bestseller, [and a] desk manual for American editors."

Even so, during this period, Las Vegas was sucking up gamblers, tourists, migrators, movie stars, soldiers, prostitutes, petty crooks, musicians, preachers, and artists like a vacuum cleaner. Between 1955 and 1960, the city's population mushroomed from 45,000 to 65,000 (a 44% jump), with another 20,000 people living in Henderson and Boulder City.

Howard Hughes

Enter Howard Hughes—through the back door, at midnight, incognito, with a tractor-trailer full of Kleenex, and an entire floor of the Desert Inn reserved for him and his faithful LDS advisers. By the time this part of Las Vegas history was transpiring, Hughes had been a recluse for five years and had a paranoid aversion to germs and a well-developed craving for codeine and valium. His legendary idiosyncrasies notwithstanding, the man's command of highest finance was still quite intact in 1966 while he perched on the ninth floor of the Desert Inn. The story of his official entry onto the scene is pure Las Vegas, and combines all the divergent elements of the Hughes myth. Apparently, Howard grew so comfortable at the DI that he didn't feel like moving out in time for Christmas, when the hotel needed the ninth-floor suites for its high rollers. Hughes

had just sold his interest in TWA for a cool half-*billion* dollars, and had to spend some. So he paid Desert Inn owner Moe Dalitz $13 million for the hotel—and he didn't have to move.

But he moved his cash in a big way, embarking on the most robust buying binge in Nevada history. When the dust finally settled, Hughes's Summa Corporation owned the Landmark, Silver Slipper, Sands, Castaways, and Frontier hotels, in addition to the Desert Inn. He also acquired most of the available acreage along the Strip, $10 million worth of mining claims, the North Las Vegas Airport, a TV station, and an airline. In all, Hughes dropped $300 million.

And suddenly, according to conventional chronology, Las Vegas was swept clean of its entire undesirable element by the huge broom of corporate respectability. Although Hughes ultimately contributed nothing to the Las Vegas skyline or industrial sector, the presence alone of the master financier added an enormous degree of long-needed legitimacy to the city's tarnished image. Hughes's investments stimulated an unprecedented speculation boom. Also, the special dispensations Hughes received from the Nevada gambling industry regulators paved the way for the Nevada Corporate Gaming Acts of 1967 and 1969, which allowed publicly traded corporations to acquire gambling licenses. (Before Hughes, every stockholder in a casino had to be individually licensed, which effectively eliminated corporations, with their millions of stockholders.) Hilton, Holiday Inn, MGM, and others quickly secured financing from legitimate sources to build their own hotels. Best of all for Las Vegas, the Diatribe ended, and the mob story finally passed out of the spotlight.

But Did it Really?

Actually, some original connections continued to play themselves out. In 1973, for example, past owners of the Flamingo pleaded guilty to a hidden interest by Meyer Lansky from 1960 to 1967. In 1976, the Audit Division of the Gaming Control Board uncovered a major skimming operation that amounted to a full 20% of slot revenues at the Stardust. In 1979, four men were convicted in Detroit of concealing hidden mob ownership in the Aladdin, which had been funded with $37 million of Teamsters' money. Also in 1979, casino and hotel executives of the

JOHN ELK III

the Strip today

Tropicana became embroiled in an underworld-related scandal. Finally, by the mid-'80s, Tony "the Ant" Spilotro, the Chicago mob's ruthless enforcer on the Las Vegas streets, had been killed in a power struggle of the Midwest mob, and experts agreed that Las Vegas was as free of mob involvement as was apparently detectable.

Las Vegas Today

In early 1980s, the emergence of Atlantic City as the East Coast's casino center, along with the deep recession of the early Reagan years, considerably reduced visitor volume and gambling revenues. A terrible fire at the MGM Grand (now Bally's) left 84 dead and nearly 700 injured; the Grand closed from November 1980 to July 1981. A fire at the Las Vegas Hilton in February 1981 took another eight lives. Las Vegas staggered through the rest of the 1980s, until one monumental event rang out the old decade and rang in the new: the Mirage opened in November 1989 and launched the biggest boom this world has ever seen.

More than 20 major hotel-casinos have opened since the Mirage, giving Las Vegas a total of more than 120,000 hotel rooms, the most of any city in the world. More than 30 million visitors have been showing up annually since 1995, and the influx shows no signs yet of slowing. Visitor numbers skyrocketed to over 34 million in 1999. Las Vegas can also lay claim to nine of the ten largest hotels in the world (the Ambassador City in Jomtien, Thailand, is the only non-Las

Vegas hotel on that list). Meanwhile, the population of the Las Vegas Metropolitan Statistical Area (MSA) now stands at 1.3 million (the whole state only surpassed a million people in 1987.) Las Vegas has remained the fastest growing city in the country for nearly a decade now, with roughly 5,000 people a month exchanging out-of-state for Nevada drivers' licenses. Las Vegas also continues to issue more building permits (per capita) than anywhere else in the country, averaging 1,500 a month.

Since 1998, five new mammoth resort casinos, averaging close to 3,000 rooms a piece, have thrust themselves onto the Vegas skyline, and there are no fewer than half a dozen new megaprojects in some stage of development. When Mirage Resorts debuted Bellagio, their $1.4 billion monument to extravagance, excess, and decadence, it was the first in a new wave of destination casinos that strove to present themselves as first-class luxury hotels where gaming comes secondary. Signature chef restaurants supplant all-you-can eat buffets in these pseudo-sophisticated monstrosities that envelope themselves in the trappings of wealth and privilege. Don't be fooled. Every major complex, however new, still boasts tens of thousands of square feet devoted to jangling slot machines, short-skirted cocktail waitresses plying you with free drinks, and high-stakes tables. The Venetian has risen from the rubble where the Sands fell (in November 1996), boasting over 3,000 rooms, every one a 700-square-foot suite, along with gondola-plying canals, a giant shopping mall, and a vast non-gambling entertainment center. Just south of Bally's is Las Vegas' version of Paris, a 2,900-room French-themed upscale Hilton (Hilton acquired Bally's for $3.2 billion in 1995), complete with a 50-story half-scale Eiffel Tower. The Aladdin has received a $1.4 billion face-lift that includes a 2,500-room Arabian Nights–themed resort and casino complex that rubs shoulders with its new neighbor Desert Passage, 500,000 square feet of elaborately detailed retail space. And Mandalay Bay, a 3,000 room Circus Circus affair that evokes the South Pacific, has gone in where the Hacienda went down (in January 1997).

And that's just for starters. The latest market segment that Las Vegas hopes to fill in the next few years is the luxury niche. Recently launched are an exclusive non-casino Four Seasons, a 400-room companion hotel to Mandalay Bay; a Seven Circle, a 400-room hotel surrounded by the three golf courses at Summerlin; a Ritz-Carlton (currently being built next to the MGM Grand); and a Hyatt and Grand Bay, two 400- to 500-room hotels at Lake Las Vegas, the most exclusive development in southern Nevada, located just east of Henderson. All these hotels charge upwards of $250–300 per night for a room.

And it doesn't stop there. A handful of other hotels are on the drawing boards. Plans have been completed for a 3,000-room Planet Hollywood megaresort. Plans for a San Francisco-themed joint have been floating around for a while; it's rumored to be going in where the Frontier now sits. We hear that Black Entertainment Television has gone into partnership with Hilton to build a 1,000-room joint. Plus a gaggle of locals' casinos are planned for the suburban neighborhoods where the Las Vegans (heavy gamblers themselves) live and play. And those are the ones most likely to succeed. Another half dozen are too speculative to mention.

SIGHTS

ORIENTATION

The city of Las Vegas huddles around the intersection of the three main highways that bisect southern Nevada: I-15, which hacks a wide gash from northeast (Mesquite) to southwest (the state line); US 95, which slices a thin slash northwest (Beatty) to south (Laughlin); and US 93, which cuts a thick wedge northeast (Caliente) to southeast (Boulder City). Together they make a huge "X" through central Las Vegas, like some cosmic bull's-eye, or the mark on a map that pinpoints Buried Treasure—Dig Here.

Similarly, Main St.–Las Vegas Blvd. and Fremont St.–Rancho Rd. make a smaller, rougher "X" downtown, which delineates the cardinal sectioning of the city. The corner of Main and Fremont streets in the heart of downtown, at the Plaza Hotel, is ground zero: all street numbers and directions fan out from here. Everything east and west of the Main St.–Las Vegas Blvd. artery is labeled thus.

North and south are a bit trickier. Fremont St. (all of which is technically *East* Fremont, since it dead-ends at Main) separates north from south until it intersects Charleston (which runs due east from there, unlike Fremont, which cuts south). East of the corner of Fremont, Charleston then separates north from south streets.

The west side is even more vague. Here the Las Vegas Expressway (a.k.a. Oran K. Gragson Expressway, a.k.a. US 95) defines north and south, even though it's not itself a street. To further complicate matters, US 95 is a major highway that runs north-south from Canada to Mexico, but in Las Vegas cuts due east (south) and west (north).

Thoroughly confused? Actually, five minutes spent comparing these notes with any street map will make all this plain as the neon night. And if it doesn't? Many visitors never venture half a block in either direction of Las Vegas Blvd. South between Sahara and Tropicana, more popularly known as the Strip. For that matter, some never even step out of Caesars Palace, Circus Circus, or the MGM Grand.

Most tourists, however, do manage to find their way between the Strip and downtown. One good reason to know your way around a little is that rush hour throughout Las Vegas extends from about 6 to 10 A.M. and 3 to 7 P.M., and is

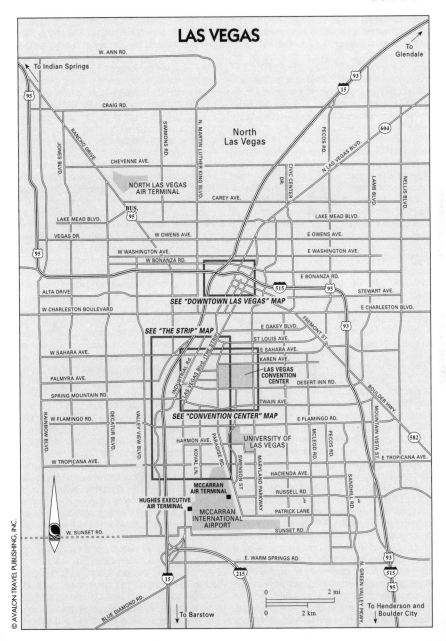

LAS VEGAS

To Glendale

To Indian Springs

W. ANN RD.

CRAIG RD.

North Las Vegas

NORTH LAS VEGAS AIR TERMINAL

BUS. 95

SEE "DOWNTOWN LAS VEGAS" MAP

SEE "THE STRIP" MAP

LAS VEGAS CONVENTION CENTER

SEE "CONVENTION CENTER" MAP

UNIVERSITY OF LAS VEGAS

MCCARRAN AIR TERMINAL

HUGHES EXECUTIVE AIR TERMINAL

MCCARRAN INTERNATIONAL AIRPORT

RANCHO DRIVE

JONES BLVD.

SIMMONS RD.

N. MARTIN LUTHER KING BLVD.

CIVIC CENTER DR.

PECOS RD.

N LAS VEGAS BLVD.

LAMB BLVD.

NELLIS BLVD.

CHEYENNE AVE.

CAREY AVE.

LAKE MEAD BLVD.

LAKE MEAD BLVD.

VEGAS DR.

W OWENS AVE.

E OWENS AVE.

W WASHINGTON AVE.

E WASHINGTON AVE.

W BONANZA RD.

E BONANZA RD.

ALTA DRIVE

STEWART AVE.

W CHARLESTON BOULEVARD

E CHARLESTON BLVD.

FREMONT ST.

E OAKEY BLVD.

ST LOUIS AVE.

E SAHARA AVE.

W SAHARA AVE.

KAREN AVE.

PALMYRA AVE.

DESERT INN RD.

SPRING MOUNTAIN RD.

INDUSTRIAL Rd.

LAS VEGAS BLVD., THE STRIP

BOULDER HWY.

TWAIN AVE.

RAINBOW BLVD.

DECATUR BLVD.

VALLEY VIEW BLVD.

W FLAMINGO RD.

E FLAMINGO RD.

MCLEOD RD.

PECOS RD.

MOUNTAIN VISTA ST.

W TROPICANA AVE.

E TROPICANA AVE.

HARMON AVE.

KOVAL LN.

PARADISE RD.

SWENSON ST.

MARYLAND PARKWAY

HACIENDA AVE.

SANDHILL RD.

RUSSELL RD.

PATRICK LANE

W. SUNSET RD.

SUNSET RD.

E. WARM SPRINGS RD.

N. GREEN VALLEY PKWY.

To Barstow

BLUE DIAMOND RD.

To Henderson and Boulder City

0   2 mi

0   2 km

© AVALON TRAVEL PUBLISHING, INC.

MOON

particularly brutal on Las Vegas Boulevard. In addition, almost all weekend long, every weekend of the year, women have been known to go through menopause and men have grown beards sitting in traffic on the Strip. You should quickly learn to use Paradise and Swenson roads (a long block or two to the east) and Industrial Rd. and the freeway (a block west) as alternatives to traffic jams of monumental proportions.

Note: Watch for speed bumps, which erupt from most parking lots and some side streets; a few, like at the airport, are so wide that they're painted yellow and used for crosswalks. Also, slow down for flashing yellow lights and speed-limit signs at school zones; Nevadans take these 15-mph limits quite seriously, as do the police and courts (fines up to hundreds of dollars). Also, make extra certain to turn on your headlights at night, especially downtown and on the Strip. You'll notice more unlit cars in Las Vegas than anywhere else you've ever been.

Finally, take extra care driving around this town. So many drivers are visitors in rental cars, or locals in a daze from the casinos, or visitors and locals full of free booze, that Las Vegas has some of the highest accident and car-insurance rates in the country.

LIGHT SHOWS

Las Vegas and light shows are synonymous. Glitter Gulch downtown is so bright that you can't tell day from night. The five-mile-long stretch of neon art against the black desert sky along the Strip is, of course, the famous cliche. Long neon tubing, in brilliant reds, whites, blues, and pinks, borders the edges of shopping centers, car washes, apartments, and restaurants. And it's not just the designs and colors and size and intensity of the lights. Like a psychedelic simulation, they're all moving—flickering, twitching, blinking; turning on and off; running up and down and across; shooting through space and back again; starting at the bottom, speeding to the top, and exploding. The latest and brightest rage is electronic billboards—programmable colors, graphics, dissolves and splashes, and animated effects. And topping it all off are the huge, square, black-on-white marquees, advertising everything from buffets to burlesque, from baccarat lessons to Bloody Marys. And all the outside glass reflects the effects in a cosmic double exposure.

As you pan back from this garden of neon and look through a wide-angle lens at the suburban sprawl, Las Vegas's other light show twists into focus. Miles-long row upon row upon row of harsh halogen street lamps illuminate the way to countless subdivisions, trailer parks, cul-de-sacs, and parking lots like runway beacons to the desert. And when you look back and down at the sprawling valley, that's what you're left with: a single row of amber streetlights, burning from one end of the horizon to the other, as far as the eye can see.

Outside, at least, you have some perspective against which to measure this massive ion icon. Once inside the casinos, however, the light show closes in on top of you, and there's no escaping the border neon, million-bulb chandeliers, flickering ceiling and wall fireflies, slot spots, alternately flashing floor, stairs, and railing beacons, and facing mirrors stereoscoping it all into infinity.

Of course, the natural color of the place is sun-scorched drab-desert sandy beige. But the ultimate color, one that's lacking from both the natural and man-made palette, but that underlies every visible color in the Las Vegas spectrum, is green.

Fremont Street Experience

The greatest light show of them all, in Las Vegas and arguably the world, is known as the Fremont Street Experience. Picture this: It's nighttime in downtown Las Vegas, and splashy neon signs illuminate what looks like a street carnival in Glitter Gulch. A crowd of bystanders mills around, waiting. People stream out of the casinos onto Fremont Street to join the throng—everyone peering or pointing skyward, in anticipation. Suddenly, somewhere, someone flicks a switch and Glitter Gulch's whole flamboyant facade is simply shut off. For a moment, from Fitzgeralds to the Las Vegas Club, it's dark on Fremont Street! But then a multi-sensory high-fidelity kaleidoscopic fanfaronade kicks on. A cheer goes up from the neck-craners as a colossal overhead graphic-display system delivers state-of-the-art animation and acoustic effects via two million lightbulbs and 540,000 watts of sound.

The whole high-tech hullabaloo consists of a four-block-long, 90-foot-tall silver canopy supported by 16 columns and 43,000 struts, 2.1 million polychromatic lightbulbs, and 208 concert-quality speakers. In addition to the canopy, FSE has a pedestrian mall, complete with food and merchandise booths, along Fremont Street from Main to 4th and a 1,500-car parking garage. The main attraction, of course, is the collection of four different six-minute musicals, performed on the hour between 6 and 11 P.M.

Fremont Street Experience, three years in the making, went on line in December 1995. Much of the technology was invented as the project went along. It's now the largest electric sign in the world, 50 times the size of the world's second largest sign (the Las Vegas Hilton's). Don't miss it. For a recording of all the special events scheduled for the promenade in conjunction with the light show, call 702/678-5777.

And the Fremont Street Experience is quite protective of its status as the largest, loudest, most illuminated downtown feature. As of this writing, the Fremont Street Experience is suing its neighbors the Mermaids and Le Bayou casinos, claiming that their amplified announcements compete too fiercely with the mall's own audio system and, as such, are a detriment to visitors' experience of the light show.

Animatronic Shows
Three free shows, two at the Forum Shops at Caesars and one at Sam's Towns, combine animatronics (moving statues) with lasers, film and video, and dancing waters; both shows are presented every hour on the hour 11 A.M.–11 P.M. The **Festival Fountain** in the original wing at the Forum opens with laser lightning and stereo thunder that awakens Bacchus, god of wine. He introduces Plutus, who infuses the dancing waters with merry-go-round music; Venus, who blots out the sun and conjures laser constellations on the ceiling; and Apollo, who strums his fiber-optic lyre strings. Finally, Bacchus bows out with a burp.

The **Atlantis** show in the new wing of the Forum Shops debuted in August 1997. It's qualitatively superior to the Festival Fountain show that, after all, is five-year-old technology. There

are four animatronic characters (the king of Atlantis, his son and daughter, and a monster); the movements of the son and daughter are more fluid and lifelike than the Festival statues. The special effects, as well, are more fully rendered: steam and mist, 20-foot flames, 30-foot dancing waters, and 18 overhead screens projecting 70 mm film.

The third show can be seen at Sam's Town in the spectacular Central Park indoor atrium. The **"Sunset Stampede"** is presented at 2, 6, 8, and 10 P.M. The dancing waters flare over 100 feet high, synchronized with lasers and a stirring sound track. The animatronic wolf steals the show.

Fire Shows
Is there anybody who hasn't heard that the 54-foot man-made **volcano** that fronts The Mirage erupts every 15 minutes nightly (as long as it's not too windy) from 8 P.M. to 1 A.M. in the summer (starting at 6 P.M. in the winter)? Flames spew from the crater, big speakers roar, and red water flows down the slopes.

Next door at Treasure Island is the by-now also-famous **pirate show.** Twenty stuntmen manning two 60-foot-tall ships duke it out nightly (again, weather cooperating) every 90 minutes starting at 4 and continuing through 11:30 P.M. The pirate pyrotechnics are truly amazing, and this whole outdoor extravaganza is an absolute must-see. Arrive 30 minutes early for a good viewing spot.

Sky Parade
Las Vegas's newest free spectacle, the Sky Parade, happens every two hours starting at noon Mon.–Thurs. and 1 P.M. Friday and Saturday in the new Masquerade Village wing of the Rio Hotel-Casino. Singers, dancers, stilt-walkers, and bungee swingers, all decked out in outrageous Mardi Gras-style costumes, perform on the main stage, while parade floats—riverboat, teacup, hot-air balloon, swan gondola, and giant interactive two-aced head—circle the casino suspended from a track on the ceiling. You might feel like Hunter S. Thompson at Circus Circus in 1970, pop-eyed from the Big Top bedlam overhead in the midst of which high-stakes players gamble oblivious to the ambient madness.

Best Views

The "cheap aerials" have improved dramatically over the last few years. Before, your best overviews were found at the **Centerstage Restaurant,** in a tinted dome in the front of Plaza Hotel, with seats looking straight down Glitter Gulch; and the **Ranch Steakhouse** on the 24th floor of the Horseshoe hotel tower, complete with a outdoor glass elevator.

These days, you can get really high on the panoramas. Seen from all over the valley is the observation pod at the top of the Stratosphere Tower (850 feet in the air). The best way to take it all in is to eat at the **Top of the World** restaurant on the 106th floor, a 360-seat and 360-degree revolving restaurant. You can hop a ride on the high-speed double-decker elevators to the top for $6, or you can make a reservation for dinner at the restaurant ($15 minimum) and ride up the special-guest elevator for free. And as long as you're up there for the view, you might as well ride the Big Shot (see below).

An even better view—lower, closer, more central—awaits at the top of the new Rio hotel tower on the bi-level decks outside the **Voodoo Cafe** restaurant and bar. It's free just to ride the outdoor glass elevator for the view.

The newest aerial highlight to hit the Strip is Paris's Eiffel Tower Experience. Eight dollars buys you the right to be whisked up 50 stories in a glass elevator, to an observation deck offering jaw-dropping views. At a lower elevation, but still affording an excellent panorama, the Eiffel Tower Restaurant hovers 100 feet above the Strip and features a piano bar and Parisian fare that doesn't come cheap.

The closest overlook ("cheap aerial") of downtown and the valley is on East Lake Mead Dr. halfway up the Sunrise peaks on the way to the lake. For the expensive aerials, see "Tours" under "Transportation" in the Practicalities section later in this chapter.

DESERT SHOWS

Ethel M's Desert (and Dessert)

That's Ethel *Mars,* as in Mars bars (along with Milky Ways, 3 Musketeers, and M&M's). The Mars family of Las Vegas is consistently ranked in the top five richest families in the world by Forbes, with around $9 billion worth of assets. If you feel like taking a ride after lunch or dinner, head out to this chocolate factory and cactus garden (way out E. Tropicana, right on Mountain Vista, left on Sunset Way, quick left onto Cactus Garden Dr.). The inside tour (self-guided, free) takes you past big picture windows overlooking the bright factory, with workers and machines turning and churning, then out into the tasting room. Sample a nut cluster, caramel, butter cream, or liqueur candy, so rich that one piece is a whole dessert. Outside is an enjoyable 2.5-acre cactus garden, with indigenous desert flora: purple pancake and horse crippler, hedgehog and saguaro cacti, yucca, cholla, Spanish bayonet, and 345 other species. Check out the Home Demonstration Garden for ideas on starting one, then make your purchases at the Cactus Shoppe. Ethel M's is open daily 8:30 A.M.–7 P.M.; it makes the chocolate weekday mornings; 702/458-8864 or 435-2655 (chocolate shop).

Las Vegas Demonstration Gardens

More than 1,000 varieties of plants and rock gardens are on display at this two-and-a-half-acre botanical garden at 3701 W. Alta Dr., 702/258-3205, just south of Valley View Blvd.—the most beautiful desert landscaping in the city. The Las Vegas Valley Water District, which supplies most of Las Vegas with its water, has designed and created the Desert Demonstration Gardens as a means of instructing people in the art of xeriscaping, or the conservation of water through efficient landscaping. Here you can inspect more than 1,000 species of plants in 11 themed gardens; it'll quickly dispel the mistaken belief that desert landscaping is limited to cactus and rock. The gardens also host a variety of wildlife, including nighttime visits by one or more kit fox searching for a meal, numerous birds feeding on the insect life, and three varieties of lizard (side-blotched, whiptail, and desert spiny). The gardens average 1,000 visitors a week; when you visit, don't forget to sign the guest register, as the funding for this beautiful xeripark depends on the number of visitors that make it through its doors.

The most common thing to do here is to take the 20-minute self-guided tour, but the gardens also have an amphitheater where classes and other community events are held. The resource center also offers xeriscape-design workshops, landscaping classes and lectures, irrigation workshops, experts to answer all your landscaping questions, and group tours. Free pamphlets and information sheets are available on a number of xeriscape subjects.

MUSEUMS

The Old Fort

This tiny museum is the oldest building in Las Vegas and a true "soul survivor." The adobe remnant, constructed by Mormon missionaries in 1855, was part of their original settlement, which they abandoned in 1858. It then served as a store, barracks, and shed on the Gass/Stewart Ranch. After that, the railroad leased the old fort to various tenants, including the Bureau of Reclamation, which stabilized and rebuilt the shed to use as a concrete-testing laboratory for Hoover Dam. In 1955, the railroad sold the old fort to the Elks, who in 1963 bulldozed the whole 100-year-old wooden structure (except the little remnant) into the ranch swimming pool and torched it. The shed was bought back by the city in 1971.

Since then a number of preservation societies have helped keep the thing in place. A tour guide presents the history orally, while display boards give it to you visually. The Old Fort is at the corner of Las Vegas Blvd. N and Washington (in the northwest corner of the Cashman Field parking lot), 702/382-6510; it's open daily 8 A.M.–4 P.M., free. Your special effort to visit this place will not go unrewarded—it's immensely refreshing to see some preservation of the past in this city of the ultimate now.

Lied Discovery Children's Museum

This museum features 130 exciting, thought-provoking, and fun exhibits. Highlights include a human-performance area with ski, baseball, and football machines to test athletic skills; a money display to teach about savings accounts, writing checks, and using ATMs; and telescopes atop the eight-story science tower. At the What Can I Be exhibit, kids can look at and play with career ideas. A radio and TV station, newspaper office, bubble machine, space shuttle display, and 120 other attractions, along with a museum store and restaurant, are all contained in the 40,000-square-foot facility. The museum is within the Las Vegas Central Library building, 833 N. Las Vegas Blvd., 702/382-3445, open Tues.–Sun. 10 A.M.–5 P.M. Admission is $5 adults, $4 for kids and seniors.

Las Vegas Natural History Museum

Across the street from the Lied is this wildlife museum, which displays a large collection of stuffed animals in realistic dioramas: North American predator species, African prey species, a whole room full of birds, another whole room full of dinosaurs and hands-on exhibits such as a fossil sandbox, and a live shark exhibit. Two leopard sharks and a banded cat shark swim in a 3,000-gallon aquarium; they're fed shrimp and squid Tuesday at 10 A.M., Thursday at 4 P.M., and Saturday at 2 P.M. Kids chosen from the crowd help feed them. A new exhibit depicts wildlife found within 100 miles of Las Vegas with mounted animals in dioramas, murals, and landscapes. The museum is at 900 Las Vegas Blvd. N, 702/384-3466, open daily 9 A.M.–4 P.M., admission $5 adults, $2.50 children 4–12.

Southern Nevada Zoological Park

This could be the "wildest" place in Las Vegas, a very personal little zoo, with an offbeat charm and a lot of heart. Lion, tiger, cougar, monkeys, bird boutique, fine arts gallery, petting zoo with pygmy goats—all just off a busy street in northwest Las Vegas, with Siegfried and Roy's mission-style mansion just around the corner (4200 Vegas Dr. at Valley). The zoo is located at 1775 N. Rancho Dr., 702/648-5955, open daily 9 A.M.–4:30 P.M.

Marjorie Barrick Museum of Natural History

This museum on the university grounds is a good place to bone up on local flora, fauna, and artifacts. First study the local flora in the arboretum outside the museum entrance, then step inside for the fauna: small rodents, big snakes, lizards, tortoises, gila monster, iguana, chuckwalla, gecko, and spiders, beetles, cockroaches, the most extensive collection of birds in Nevada, even a 10-foot polar bear. Wander through the art gallery into some graphic Las Vegas history, such as the famous painting of Frémont at Las

Nevada desert transportation has taken various forms, including experimental camel trains in the 1850s.

DOVER PUBLICATIONS, INC.

Vegas Springs in 1844, the view of Las Vegas Creek both in 1900 and 1978, and Miss Atomic Blast 1957. Display cases are full of native baskets, kachinas, masks, weaving, pottery, and jewelry. There are also Mexican dance masks, traditional textiles of Guatemala, and an extensive exhibit of Tom and Jerry cels, backgrounds, and musical scores (donated by creator Chuck Jones). The centerpiece is a rough skeleton of an ichthyosaur, a whale-sized marine dinosaur (Nevada's state fossil). The museum, 702/895-3381, is open Mon.–Fri. 8 A.M.–4:45 P.M., Saturday 10 A.M.–2 P.M., donation. To find it, drive onto the UNLVcampus on Harmon St. and follow it around to the right, then turn left into the Museum parking lot (signposted).

Nevada State Museum and Historical Society

This is a comfortable and enjoyable place to spend an hour or two studying Mojave and Spring Mountains ecology, southern Nevada history, and local art. Three changing galleries might be exhibiting anything from photography of the neon night or black-and-white desert to Nevada telephone technology. The Hall of Biological Science shows interesting exhibits on life in the desert: butterflies, cholla and cactus, reptiles, and the bighorn sheep centerpiece. Also learn here how the Spring Mountains (Mt. Charleston) are a "biological island surrounded by a sea of desert." The Hall of Regional History contains breezy graphic displays

on mining (*big* photos of Tonopah and Goldfield) and atomic testing, and eye-catching photos of nuclear tests, blasts, holes, Hoover Dam construction, politics, ranching, Indians (big tribal map of Nevada). The museum is in the back of Lorenzi Park, off Twin Lakes Dr.; open daily 9 A.M.–5 P.M., admission $2, 702/486-5205.

Liberace Museum

Liberace embodies the heart and soul of Las Vegas, in life and in death. Born in Wisconsin in 1919, third of four children in a musical family, Walter Valentino Liberace (who legally assumed the one name, Liberace, in 1950, and was known as "Lee" to his friends) was a prodigy pianist at age seven, a concert boy wonder at 14, and first played Sin City at 23. From then on, he was a one-man walking advertisement for the extravagance, flamboyance, and uninhibited tastelessness usually associated with the town he loved so much. Like Las Vegas's surface image, Liberace's costumes began as a means of standing out; then he had to keep topping himself with increasingly outrageous gimmicks. Along the way, he became one of the most popular entertainers of all time: "Mr. Showmanship" racked up six gold records.

The Liberace Museum is the most popular tourist attraction in Las Vegas, outside of the casinos. You can bet the rent that at least two tour buses will be parked out front, with hundreds of retirees paying tribute to the man who, his passable playing and uncontrollable clothing notwithstanding, was possessed of a certain charisma, generosity, and genuine rapport with his audiences that inspired mass displays of devotion.

The main building preserves Liberace's costumes: Uncle Sam hot pants, suits made of ostrich feathers, rhinestones, and bugle beads, and capes customized from 100 white fox skins (75 feet/23 meters long, $700,000) or 500 Black Glama minks (125 pounds/57 kilograms, $750,000). Also on display are the world's largest rhinestone (50 pounds/23 kilograms, $50,000) and a grossly ornate rolltop desk from his office. The library building on the other side of the Tivoli Restaurant houses family photos, miniature pianos, silver, china, cut glass, gold records, and historical data. Across the parking lot the piano and car gallery contains several antique pianos, Liberace's 50,000-rhinestone Baldwin, his million-dollar mirror-tiled Rolls, custom rhinestone car (with matching toolbox), and a 1940s English taxi, among others.

A gift shop in the main building sells Liberace albums, tapes, videos, postcards, 8x10 glossies, song books, autobiography ($30), and doll ($300). The museum, at 1775 E. Tropicana just east of Maryland Pkwy., 702/798-5595, is open Mon.–Sat. 10 A.M.–5 P.M., Sunday 1–5 P.M. Admission is $6.95, $4.95 seniors and children under 12—steep, but tax-deductible as a contribution to the non-profit Liberace Foundation For Creative and Performing Arts.

Madame Tussaud's

Over one hundred celebrities with fixed waxen smiles await the visitor at this spin-off of the infamous London Museum. The likenesses are truly amazing; in some instances the wax figure looks more alive than the real thing—this is particularly true of the aging rock stars. Set in five different theatrical settings ranging from sports arenas to concert venues, the museum provides a nice diversion before hitting the slots and attempting to win your own fame and fortune. The museum, located at the entryway to The Venetian, 702/702/367-1847, is open 10 A.M.–10 P.M. daily.

Guinness World of Records Museum

This small museum on the Strip features photographic, typographic, video, audio, and slide-show exhibits of world records: the tallest, fattest, oldest, and most-married men; longest-necked women; smallest bicycle; videos of dominoes; slides of the greatest engineering projects; and an informative display of Las Vegas firsts and foremosts, among others. The Guinness Museum is located at 2780 Las Vegas Blvd. S, behind Arby's just north of Circus Circus, 702/792-0640, open daily 9 A.M.–7 P.M., $4.95 adults, $3.95 seniors and students, $2.95 for children 5–12 and free for children under 5.

Elvis-A-Rama Museum

Elvis has definitely not left this building. Only in Las Vegas, or maybe Graceland, will you find a museum devoted to $3.5 million dollars worth of Elvis memorabilia. This quirky spot, featuring Elvis' customized purple Lincoln, his army uniform, and his peacock jumpsuit (among other things), rates high on the kitsch factor, but can be a kick for true Elvis fans. Concert footage, photos, and costumes chronicle the King's life from the early beginnings to his washed-up Vegas days. Be sure to time your visit to catch a live Elvis tribute performance, daily at 11 A.M., noon, 2 P.M., 4 P.M., and 5 P.M. The museum is open daily 10 A.M.–7 P.M. and is found one block off the Strip behind Fashion Show Mall at 3401 Industrial Rd., 702/309-7200. Admission is $9.95, $7.95 seniors.

Imperial Palace Auto Collection

IP owner Ralph Engelstad acquired much of this collection, once owned by Bill Harrah, when Holiday Inn Corp. bought Harrah's and sold off the majority of Harrah's cars in the early '80s. Among some real interesting cars here are the custom 1928 Delage limousine built for King Rama VII of Siam (Thailand) and the 1948 Chrysler convertible with the cowhead-and-horn emblem. The 1947 Tucker has a third-eye headlight that turns with the steering wheel, and the 1955 Mercedes sports car comes with factory-fitted luggage. You'll ho-hum over all the Rolls-Royces, Cadillacs, and Duesenbergs, but Hitler's bulletproof Mercedes parade car will raise some eyebrows, as will the half-dozen prototype motorcycles. Of course, the curators couldn't forget the 1954 Chrysler Imperial! Some of these cars are restored by prison convicts in a program introduced by the administrator of the collection;

some "graduates" of the program are hired once paroled. Walk through the Imperial Palace casino past the elevators and go all the way to the back; other elevators whisk you up to the collection, on the fifth floor of the parking structure, 702/731-3311. It's open daily 9:30 A.M.–11:30 P.M.; free coupons to the cars are ubiquitous (even at the entrance to the hotel), so you probably won't have to pay the $6.95 adult admission, $3 and up or 12 and under.

Nevada Banking Museum

All large industries should follow First Interstate's lead and provide such graphic, informative, and free displays of historical tools of their trades.

The exhibits trace banking in Nevada, from checks written before statehood to consolidation in 1981 of 16 original Farmers and Merchants, and Nation banks into First Interstate Bank of Nevada. The main display exhibits currency issued by local Nevada banks in the early 1900s. No less thought-provoking are the collections of letterheads, passbooks, liberty bonds, CDs, financial statements, silver commemorative bars, gaming tokens and chips, Carson City coins, and old teller machines. Don't miss this one. Located at 3800 Howard Hughes Pkwy., in the landmark First Interstate building, off Sands Ave. at the corner of Paradise. Open banking hours, 702/385-8011.

HOTEL-CASINOS

DOWNTOWN

Plaza

Start your tour of downtown Las Vegas at **Jackie Gaughan's Plaza,** a 1,000-room hotel-casino (second largest downtown) with a stunning location facing Glitter Gulch. This is the "zero-zero" point, where the original town site auction was held in 1905, and from which all street numbers and directions emanate, as well as the site of the original art-deco Union Pacific railroad depot. The Amtrak depot is tucked away in the back; a large railroad mural is painted on the wall between the depot and casino. The Greyhound station is next door. The Centerstage Restaurant presides over it all. Best nickel video poker in Las Vegas; penny slots provide the locals an easy place to cash in their jars of copper. 1 Main Street at Fremont, 702/386-2110, 800/634-6575, double room rates $40–90.

Las Vegas Club

Across the street on the northwest corner of Main and Fremont is this venerable casino, which was opened by southern California gamblers right after gambling was legalized in 1931. A 224-room hotel tower was added in 1980, and as part of downtown's expansion boom triggered by the Fremont Street Experience, a 200-room tower, new casino wing, and two new restaurants were opened in late 1996. The Las Vegas

Club also advertises the most liberal blackjack rules in town. You can double down on any two, three, or four cards. You can split and resplit any pairs, and surrender half your bet on the first two cards. And you win on any six cards that don't bust. Great for advanced basic strategy. The Las Vegas Club also displays a large collection of sports memorabilia. 18 East Fremont St., 702/385-1664, 800/634-6532, double room rates $45–150.

Golden Gate

Miller's Hotel, across the street on the opposite corner of Fremont and Main from the Las Vegas Club, was the first downtown establishment to receive water in 1905. The Nevada Hotel replaced the Miller, the Sal Sagev (Las Vegas spelled backwards) replaced the Nevada, and the Golden Gate replaced the Sal Sagev in the bad old 1950s. The Gate introduced a 49-cent Fisherman's Wharf-type shrimp cocktail in 1959, only raising the price once, in the early '90s, to 99 cents, and has dished up more than 30 million of these crunchy crustacean cocktails. It's the best, and most venerable, meal deal in Vegas. The Gate has been restored to its original condition; it's the only place in town where you get the feeling you're staying in a real old-fashioned downtown hotel. The rooms are small but tasteful, comfortable, and affordable. 1 Fremont St., 702/382-6300, 800/426-1906, double room rates $35–80.

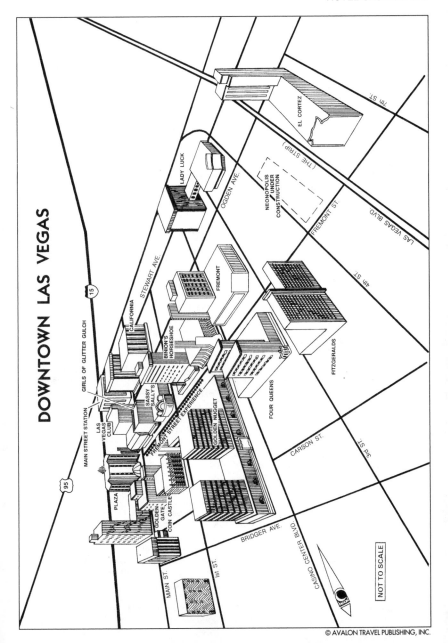

DOWNTOWN LAS VEGAS

© AVALON TRAVEL PUBLISHING, INC.

Golden Nugget

More Hollywood than Las Vegas ever since Steve Wynn (Las Vegas's top celebrity owner) bought, renovated, and expanded it, the Golden Nugget is once again downtown's centerpiece, as well as its largest hotel (with 2,000 rooms spread over two and a half blocks). It started out as a classy joint in the mid-1940s, but by the time Wynn acquired a controlling share in the early '70s (at that time one of the only Nevada casinos that was publicly owned), the Nugget's beauty had faded. No longer. The exterior features polished white marble and brass trim. The lobby showcases marble and etched and leafed glass. The highlight here is the 61-pound, 11-ounce gold nugget (displayed around the corner from the front desk by the boutique entrance)—largest in public view in the world; right under it is the second largest, both found in Victoria, Australia. Scattered about in the showcase are also a couple dozen fist-size Alaskan nuggets; the eagle's jaw is particularly gaspworthy. The buffet is one of the best in town; Lillie Langtry's serves the most expensive Chinese food this side of Moongate at the Mirage (also a Steve Wynn joint). One of two downtown production shows, *Country Fever,* boasts the hottest band on any stage in town. And the pool is the biggest and best downtown. 129 East Fremont St., 702/385-7111, 800/634-3454, double room rates $65–350.

Binion's Horseshoe

Across Fremont again is the city-block Horseshoe Hotel, which was opened in 1951 by Benny Binion, a bootlegger and boss gambler in Texas before achieving a certain legitimacy in Nevada. Benny Binion died in 1990 at the age of 85. His son Jack now runs this joint and two more in Mississippi. The Horseshoe is the quintessential old-time gambling hall, with low-limit blackjack, one of the top two poker rooms and the largest crap pit (14 tables) in town, food comps literally for the asking, and no house limit ($250,000 bets at the crap tables are not uncommon). The Horseshoe also sponsors the World Series of Poker ($10,000 buy-in for the finals and a one-million-dollar first prize).

The old Mint Hotel next door was acquired by the Horseshoe in 1988; the connecting casinos provide an interesting contrast between the Wild West motif of the early 1950s and the glitz of the mid-'60s. Have your picture taken in front of a hundred $10,000 bills, one of the world's great displays of money and the best freebie souvenir in Las Vegas. Ride the glass elevator to the Ranch Steakhouse on the 24th floor for the view.

The famous $2.75 ham-and-eggs breakfast is served in the coffee shop. The two snack bars serve some of the best and cheapest counter food anywhere (try the real turkey breast sandwich, $2.99; the bean soup of the day, which comes with a big slab of cornbread, $1.49, has seen more than one desperate local through some hungry times). 128 East Fremont St., 702/382-1600, 800/237-6537, double room rates $45–70.

The Fremont

Across Casino Center Blvd., the Fremont epitomizes the old downtown carpet joint—a wonderfully long and narrow row of table games, crowded noisy slots, with red neon border lighting heightening the effect. Stand at one end and watch the players watch the cards, the dealers watch the players, the floormen watch the dealers, the pit bosses watch the floormen. The black nippleless eye-in-the-sky watches you. The Fremont opened in 1956 and was the tallest building in Nevada at the time. It embodied a combination of Strip classiness and downtown sensibility. It weathered the Allen Glick skimming scandal in the late 1970s and was added to the Boyd Group's properties in 1985. Its seafood buffet is popular, and the Second Street Grill gourmet room is a real sleeper—excellent California-Hawaiian cuisine and rarely longer than a 15-minute wait even without reservations. 200 East Fremont St., 702/385-3232, 800/634-6182, double room rates $35–85.

Four Queens

Across Fremont from the Fremont, the Four Queens opened in 1965, named for the owner's four daughters; it declared bankruptcy in 1995 and was taken over by the management team that rescued the Riviera from a similar fate a few years earlier. Most of the good things to say about the Queen have been removed in the past little while: the largest slot machine in the world, the great coupons, jazz in the lounge. It'll come back, and I'll have nicer things to say about it when it does. 202 East Fremont, 702/385-4011, 800/634-6045, double room rates $60–200.

Fitzgeralds

Fitzgeralds started out as the Sundance Hotel, built in 1980 by Moe Dalitz when he was 84 years old. At 33 stories (400 feet tall), it was the tallest building in Nevada for 14 years, until the Stratosphere Tower surpassed it. The Fitzgeralds group, which also owns Fitzgeralds in Reno, bought it in 1987. The casino was completely remodeled in 1996, and now has two interesting views of the Fremont Street Experience: one from the wall of windows fronting the McDonald's on one side, the other from a unique second-story balcony, complete with patio furniture. Holiday Inn runs the hotel part of the Fitz. 301 East Fremont St., 702/388-2400, 800/274-LUCK, double room rates $50–100.

El Cortez

This hotel opened in late 1941 at the corner of Fremont and 6th, at a time when the downtown sidewalks stopped at 3rd. It had 71 rooms and a Wild West motif to compete with the first Strip resort, the El Rancho Vegas. Bugsy Siegel and the Berman brothers owned it for a while in the mid-1940s. The hotel changed hands a few times, until Jackie Gaughan acquired it in the early '80s. Though it's been expanded, the casino wing at the southwest corner of Fremont and 6th is original, more than 50 years old—ancient history in Las Vegas, and the oldest original casino in Nevada. The king crab, steak, prime rib, and lobster dinners in Roberta's restaurant are good and cheap. 600 East Fremont St., 702/385-5200, 800/634-6703, double room rates $25–60.

Lady Luck

This casino at the corner of Ogden Ave. and 3rd St. has grown from a tiny slot joint (opened in 1964) into a major downtown property. It's a comfortable place to gamble—bright, airy, with big picture windows on two sides. Its funbook is one of the best in town: show an out-of-state ID and get a giant hot dog (free), plus gambling coupons, dining discounts, and a free room night. The Lady is also the best joint for low-limit comps. Put up $1,000 in the cage and bet $50 a

Fremont Street

hand for eight hours for a comped suite and meals. The Burgundy Room is recommendable and the prime rib specials in the coffee shop are usually top notch. 206 N. 3rd St., 702/477-3000, 800/523-9582, double room rates $45–120.

California

This is the original Boyd Group casino, opened on the corner of Ogden Ave. and 1st St. in 1975, the same year that Sam Boyd, the late elder statesman of Las Vegas, organized his friends and family into the Boyd Group, now the Boyd Gaming Corporation, which runs Main Street Station, Sam's Town, the Stardust, the Fremont, and Joker's Wild and the Eldorado in Henderson. The California caters almost exclusively to the Hawaiian market and has a noticeably relaxed aloha vibe. This joint added 120 new rooms in 1994, but the hotel is still booked solid 365 nights a year. The Pasta Pirate is one of the best restaurants downtown, with a venerable filet mignon special; the Redwood Bar and Grill is also excellent, with a venerable 16-ounce porterhouse special. A million-dollar overhead pedestrian walkway connects the Cal with Main Street Station, across Main Street. 12 Ogden Ave., 702/385-1222, 800/634-6255, double room rates $50–70.

Main Street Station

This joint has gone through a lot of changes over the years. The last incarnation named it Main Street Station, as it was opened in early 1992 by Bob Snow, the owner of the popular Church Street Station in downtown Orlando, Florida. Snow sunk millions into stained-glass, brass, marble, and hardwood appointments, plus a collection of antiques unequaled in Nevada casinodom. Unfortunately, Main Street Station lasted only eight months before it went into receivership. Boyd Corp. bought it a couple of years later, then finally got around to reopening it in November 1996. Main Street Station could be the most aesthetically interesting and attractive casino in Las Vegas. While you're

checking it out, have a meal in the gorgeous and top-notch buffet, a beer in the microbrewery, and a cigar and cognac in the smoking car in the Pullman Grill steakhouse. 200 N. Main, 702/387-1896, 800/465-0711, double room rates $35–60.

UPPER STRIP HOTELS

Stratosphere

Stratosphere Hotel, Tower & Casino, which opened in April 1996 and occupies the site of the old Bob Stupak's Vegas World, is the tallest building west of the Mississippi, the tallest observation tower in the United States, and the ninth tallest building in the world. It boasts the world's two highest thrill rides, a revolving restaurant on the 106th floor, 1,500 rooms, a shopping mall, a showroom and lounge, six restaurants and several fast-food outlets, and a 97,000-square-foot casino with some of the best odds in

LAS VEGAS HOTEL CHRONOLOGY

1904—Ladd's Hotel
1905—Hotel Las Vegas, Miller's Hotel
1932—Apache Hotel
1941—El Rancho Vegas, El Cortez
1942—Last Frontier
1946—Flamingo
1948—Thunderbird
1950—Desert Inn
1951—Horseshoe
1952—Sahara, Sands
1954—Showboat
1955—Riviera, Dunes (closed), New Frontier
1956—Fremont, Hacienda
1957—Tropicana
1958—Stardust
1965—Four Queens
1966—Aladdin, Caesars Palace
1968—Circus Circus
1969—Landmark (closed), International Hilton
1970—Royal Las Vegas
1971—Union Plaza
1972—Holiday
1973—MGM Grand (Bally's)
1975—Continental, California, Marina (closed)

1977—Maxim, Golden Nugget
1979—Sam's Town, Barbary Coast, Imperial Palace, Vegas World
1980—Sundance (Fitzgeralds), Las Vegas Club, Lady Luck
1984—Alexis Park, Paddlewheel
1986—Gold Coast
1988—Bourbon Street, Boardwalk, Arizona Charlies
1989—San Remo, Mirage
1990—Rio, Excalibur
1992—Main Street Station
1993—Luxor, Treasure Island, MGM Grand
1994—Boomtown, Fiesta, Casino Royale, Boulder Station
1995—Hard Rock
1996—Barley's, Stratosphere, Monte Carlo, Main Street Station, Orleans
1997—New York–New York, Sunset Station
1998—Reserve, Bellagio
1999—Venetian, Paris, Mandalay Bay, Four Seasons
2000—Aladdin, Suncoast

Las Vegas. You'll see signs all over the joint insisting that the better odds—98% return on dollar slots, positive video poker, good two-deck blackjack, single-zero roulette, and 100X odds at craps—are "certified."

Take the escalator upstairs, mosey through the mall, then catch the high-speed double-decker elevators up to the observation pod, where the 360-degree view of Las Vegas Valley and environs will take your breath away. The Top of the World restaurant makes a complete 360-degree revolution once every 80 minutes or so. The roller coaster and the Big Shot will take a few years off your life, but they're worth it! 2000 Las Vegas Blvd. S., 702/380-7777, 800/99-TOWER, double room rates $40–250.

Sahara

Milton Prell, one of the most congenial of early Las Vegas hotel magnates, put together a $5 million stake in 1952 and hired the Del Webb Construction Company, which built Bugsy's Flamingo, to build the Sahara, at the corner of the Strip and Sahara Avenue. Webb retained 20 points in the hotel, which began his long and profitable stint in the Nevada casino business. He gained a controlling interest in 1961 and went on to build hotels in Tahoe, Reno, and Laughlin. Paul Lowden, who also owns the Santa Fe in Las Vegas, and the Pioneer in Laughlin, bought the Sahara from Webb in 1982 for $50 million. He added a third tower and convention center in 1988 and a fourth tower, with 600 rooms, in 1991. Then Bill Bennett, CEO and chairman of the board of Circus Circus for more than 20 years, bought the Sahara from Lowden in 1995 after being forced out of Circus. Since then, Bennett has renovated the Sahara, adding a Moroccan facade, casino wing, new buffet, and parking garage. The latest Circus Circus-inspired influence is Speed—the Ride, a roller coaster that wraps its way around the building and climbs over 200 feet above the Strip. The Sahara makes for an excellent conventioneer's hotel, being a very short ride to the convention center. 2535 Las Vegas Blvd. S., 702/737-2111, 800/634-6666, double room rates $50–150.

Circus Circus

This is the big brother of the one in Reno, and the kissin' cousin of the Colorado Belle and Edge-

water hotels in Laughlin—all, however, the poor relations of Excalibur, Luxor and Mandalay Bay at the south end of the Strip. It was opened in 1968 by Jay Sarno, best known as the originator of the Caesars Palace concept, and thus the trendsetter for themed hotels. This property, however, was unsuccessful until William Bennett took over in 1974. Bennett turned Circus Circus Enterprises into one of the most profitable hotel-casino companies in the world, before resigning under some pressure from stockholders and managers in 1994.

Circus also owns Slots-A-Fun next door, and Silver City across the street. The eponymous casino is *always* packed, as you might expect, since it offers cheap rooms, rock-bottom food prices, and caters to families. Free circus acts are presented continuously throughout the day and evening, and the well-known mezzanine midway offers every kind of dime-tossing, quarter-pitching, ball-rolling, hoop-ringing, balloon-busting, clown-drenching, camel-chasing, milkcan-downing, and rubber chicken-propelling carnie come-on known to man. Grand Slam Canyon, a five-acre indoor amusement park behind the hotel, features another midway, kiddie rides, and the world's largest indoor roller coaster (see "Entertainment" later in this chapter). 2880 Las Vegas Blvd. S., 702/734-0410, 800/634-3450, double room rates $40–200.

El Rancho

Across the street sits the El Rancho, built in 1948 as the Thunderbird. This hotel was the fourth to open on the Strip, and the first to have its license revoked by the Nevada Tax Commission, for having a hidden interest by Jake Lansky, brother of the infamous Meyer Lansky. Some of the biggest names in Las Vegas have tried their luck at owning this place, including Del Webb, Caesars World, E. Thomas Parry, Major Riddle, and finally Ed Torres, who owned it for 10 years before closing the joint in July 1992, which is how it remains. Torres could be the last of a breed; he reportedly held points in Meyer Lansky's Riviera Hotel in pre-Castro Havana in the 1950s. The El Rancho was bought in 1993 by Las Vegas Entertainment Network, a shadowy company that in five years has managed to install a plywood fence around the property, so it remains the only dark casino on the

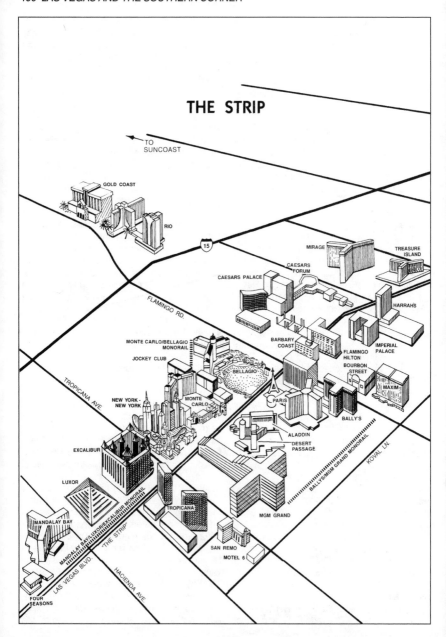

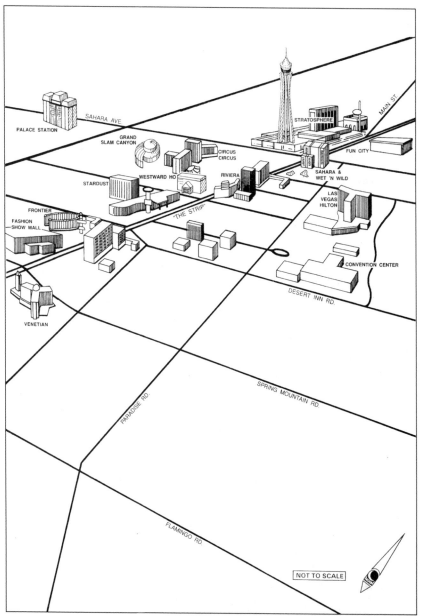

NOT TO SCALE

© AVALON TRAVEL PUBLISHING, INC.

Strip. The unconfirmed rumor at press time is that it has yet again changed hands and plans are being to level it and put condominiums in its place.

Riviera

The Riviera was the first high-rise on the Strip, starting out in 1955 with nine stories. It weathered a celebrated connection with the Chicago underworld and a succession of front men, a couple of bankruptcies, and a number of expansions. Today, the Riv is a masterpiece of tacked-on towers, leap-frogging cubes of rooms, and a maze of casino wings. Its casino is among the largest in the world at 125,000 square feet. And a magnificent casino it is, bright, open, and airy— for a maze! The Riviera has the most concentrated shows in town, with the big production revue "Splash," along with "La Cage" female impersonators, a comedy club, and "Crazy Girls," featuring the dirtiest dancing on the Strip. 2901 Las Vegas Blvd. S., 702/734-5110, 800/634-6753, double room rates $65–200.

Las Vegas Hilton

Kirk Kerkorian opened this huge hotel over the July 4th weekend in 1969, but had to sell out to Hilton a short while later to extricate himself from a financial jam. Hilton added another 1,500 rooms in 1973; Elvis made his comeback in the 2,000-seat showroom, performed there exclusively up until his death in 1977. You can see this three-wing three-ring monolith from all over the east side, and as you get closer, if you think the gargantuan gambler gobbler is growing, look again: it's really you shrinking! Everything about the place makes you feel small. The 46 video screens in the sports book are an overwhelming spectacle even for Las Vegas; among the eight restaurants is Benihana, itself consisting of three dining rooms and four bars, set in a veritable Japanese village with three-story palace, lush gardens, stone lanterns, waterfalls, running streams, and nightly special effects. Le Montrachet is no slouch either, and the buffet features king crab legs (cold). The Nightclub lounge is one of the largest (and rockinest in town). Star Trek: The Experience is a virtual reality adventure sure to appeal to Trekkies and kids. All in all it's a splendid sensation to be so humbled by this Hilton. 3000 Paradise Road, 702/732-5111,

800/732-7117, double room rates $100–300.

Westward Ho

This place claims to be the largest motel in the world with 1,000 rooms, none up more than one flight of stairs. It is a sprawling affair, which stretches from the Strip sidewalk all the way back to Industrial Rd. a good half-mile west. The casino is famous for its excellent video poker and snack bar, which serves cheap sandwiches and a legendary strawberry shortcake ($1.50). 2900 Las Vegas Blvd. S., 702/731-2900, 800/634-6803, double room rates $40–60.

Stardust

Since its inception in 1955 till quite recently, the Stardust has stepped gingerly through a minefield of high explosives. It all started in the feverish dreams of Anthony Cornero, who embarked on a crusade to build the biggest and most lavish hotel in the history of the world. He actually raised $6 million, personally selling stock in the company, and had the hotel half-completed when he dropped dead from a massive coronary while shooting dice at a Desert Inn crap table. Cornero's story alone could be the basis for a novel; the Stardust's subsequent story easily suffices as a sequel. Max Factor's brother, Jake the Barber, fronted the cash to finish the hotel for Sam Giancana and the Chicago mob, which pulled the strings for nearly a quarter century until state gaming regulators discovered that "owner" Allen Glick was running a massive slot-skimming operation for the Midwest syndicate. When the Boyd Group bought the Stardust in 1985, Las Vegas was finally free of the old-time mob influence. The recent movie, *Casino*, with Robert DeNiro and Sharon Stone and directed by Martin Scorsese, based on a book by Nicholas Pileggi, chronicles a part of this era.

The Stardust sign—188 feet tall, with 26,000 bulbs and 30 miles of wiring—*says* Las Vegas more clearly than any other image in town. *Enter The Night,* the production show, is one of the best in town. And Ralph's Diner is a fun place to eat. 3000 Las Vegas Blvd. S., 702/732-6111, 800/824-6033, double room rates $40–350.

The Frontier

The Last Frontier was the second rancho-style resort to open on the Strip, in 1942, a year after the El Rancho Vegas. It was Las Vegas's first real tourist-attraction hotel, all done up in Plush Pioneer. Last Frontier Village was a theme park next door, an entire town site filled with authentic western artifacts collected over the years by Doby Doc Caudill. The Little Chapel of the West, for example, was built for the Village in 1942. In 1955, the Last Frontier closed on the morning of April 4, and the New Frontier opened the same day next door. The New had a Stardust-like outer-space theme, about as different from the Last as it was possible to be. In 1967, the New Frontier was abandoned, and 10 months later the Frontier was ready to open. Howard Hughes watched the new hotel go up from the window of his penthouse suite across the street in the Desert Inn and bought it just before opening day. Hughes's Summa Corporation sold the Frontier in 1988 to the union-busting Elardi family. It appears that the Frontier's days are once again numbered, as this is the proposed sight for the new San Francisco–themed casino.

The Elardis built a 14-story Atrium Suites tower that's unique in Las Vegas: open to the sky and overlooking a horticulturally pleasing lagoon, creek, and courtyard, all the accommodations are two-room suites with wet bars and mini-fridges that are reasonably priced. The food at the Frontier is uniformly good and cheap, with a $2.99 steak and eggs and good specials at Margarita's. The Seafood Grotto has "creekside" dining. 3120 Las Vegas Blvd. S., 702/794-8200, 800/421-7806, double room rates $40–90.

Desert Inn

Once one of the most exclusive and venerable hotels in Las Vegas, the DI could tell you some stories. In the late '40s, Wilbur Clark spent his whole $1.5 million bankroll on his dream hotel, but came up $3 million short of completing it. In walked Moe Dalitz, boss gambler from Ohio and Kentucky, with the rest of the money. Dalitz ran the hotel for 17 years until he sold it to Howard Hughes for $13.2 million cash; it was the first major hotel Hughes bought during his four-year Las Vegas whirlwind in the late '60s. Hughes's Summa Corp. sold it in 1988 to Kirk Kerkorian, who sold it to ITT in 1993 for $160 million cash, which Kerkorian used to help finance his billion-dollar MGM Grand. ITT spent roughly half a billion renovating and expanding the DI since,

adding several new buildings in 1997 that contain some of the most exclusive hotel suites in town.

For years the DI remained a small resort that catered to high rollers and VIPs. Yet what was by many accounts the most luxuriant resort in Las Vegas, now sits empty and quiet awaiting its implosion date. As noted in their sad final press release, "The Desert Inn closed its doors for good on August 28, 2000."

LOWER STRIP HOTELS

The Venetian

The Sands opened in 1952 and was *the* in place in Las Vegas for glamorous entertainment throughout the freewheeling '50s. Frank Sinatra and Dean Martin owned points; they and their Rat Pack friends and colleagues performed in the Copa Room and relaxed in the health club. Howard Hughes bought the Sands in 1967 (and cut off Sinatra's credit). In 1988, Hughes's Summa Corporation sold the Sands to Sheldon Adelson of the Interface Group, a trade-conference company that at the time sponsored Comdex, Las Vegas's largest convention. Interface added a million square feet of convention center, before imploding the Sands in November 1996 to make room for the Venetian.

Hold onto your hats, because the Venetian is big and plans on getting bigger. The original plans call for two 3,000-suite towers. That's right: a 6,000-suite joint, a full 1,000 rooms larger than the MGM Grand, currently the largest hotel in the world. (They've only completed one 3,000-room tower, so we'll see if the second is ever built.) Each suite is 700 square feet, with a sitting room, large bedroom (two queen-size beds), and large bathroom (shower stall and tub, phone next to the toilet). Gondolas ply canals, passing the Campanile and Clock towers and the Rialto Bridge and dramatic reproductions of Venetian art grace the walls and ceiling. A peek at the sumptuous Baroque hotel lobby alone merits a visit. It features a 200,000-square-foot casino (that's huge), the 1.6-million-square-foot Sands Convention Center (second largest in the U.S.), a 140-store mall, and an entertainment-dining complex. Are you hungry? Wolfgang Puck and Piero Selvaggio are only two of the six signature chefs gracing the kitchens of The Vene-

Harrah's

JOHN ELK III

tian's 13 dining establishments. The price tag for the whole schmear? A mere $2 billion. 3355 Las Vegas Blvd. South, 702/414-1000, 888-2-VENICE, double room rates $110–1,000.

Harrah's

This hotel went up on the Strip in 1972 as the Holiday Inn, one of the first major hotel chains to build in Las Vegas after Hughes had paved the way for corporate casino ownership. It opened with 1,000 rooms; a 735-room expansion, put into service in late 1989, rendered it the largest Holiday Inn in the world. The name was changed in 1992 to Harrah's and a complete remodeling transformed the hotel into the "Ship on the Strip," with a riverboat facade. Of course, the riverboat bit got old after four years so Harrah's spent another $250 million renovating it again. It now sports an elegant yet generic French Quarter front, with Mardi Gras decor throughout. The Carnival Court Plaza features Ghirardelli's Old-Fashioned Chocolate Shop and On Stage, Harrah's logo shop. La Playa, an indoor and outdoor bar, opens onto the plaza. The Ranch House restaurant is a gorgeous steakhouse with big picture windows overlooking the Strip and the buffet shares an equally beautiful view. 3475 Las Vegas Blvd. S., 702/369-5000, 800/HAR-RAHS, double room rates $60–375.

Imperial Palace

With nearly 2,700 rooms, the IP is one of the largest hotels in the world, though you'd never

know it by looking at the facade on the Strip. The hotel-casino and parking structure completely fill the narrow slice of land it occupies between Harrah's and the Flamingo. The Asian theme consists mostly of dragons; the Las Vegas influence is noticeable in the skimpiness of the cocktail waitress uniforms. The IP is Nevada's largest employer of disabled people, and consistently wins awards and praise for its personnel policies. The big news here, however, is the automobile collection (see "Imperial Palace Auto Collection" under "Museums" earlier in this chapter). The casino is a sprawling affair on the ground floor; upstairs are the showroom, with the venerable *Legends in Concert,* the unique multi-tiered sports book, and the restaurant row. The steakhouse, Embers, has a good reputation, well deserved. 3535 Las Vegas Blvd. S., 702/731-3311, 800/634-6441, double room rates $50–300.

Flamingo Hilton

This is the house that Bugsy built, in 1946, with millions of mob dollars. It wasn't the first hotel on the L.A. Highway (contrary to public perception, Bugsy no more invented the Strip than Bugs Bunny invented the cartoon); the western-themed El Rancho Vegas and Last Frontier preceded it by half a decade. But it was the first gangster hotel, with architecture direct from Miami and a market targeted right at Hollywood. The fabulous Flamingo opened the sluice gates to a flood of black money from all around the country and changed the course of Las Vegas history forever. Kirk Kerkorian bought it during the Hughes whirlwind to use as a training facility for the core staff of his megalith International (now Las Vegas Hilton) Hotel. In 1970, shortly after the International opened, Kerkorian found himself in a cash crunch, partially due to the Flamingo's shady past: the SEC wouldn't approve a public stock offering Kirkorian needed to pay off the International unless he turned over the Flamingo's financial archives, (which he refused to do). So Kirk had to sell both of his hotels to Hilton for half of what they were worth. Since then, Hilton has erected five massive towers, expanding the hotel to 3,600 rooms, fifth largest in town. Bottom's Up, the Strip's only topless afternoon show with performances at 2 P.M. and 4 P.M. Monday–Saturday, plays in the main showroom; Forever Plaid is performed in the little theater. The Flamingo Room has one of the best salad bars in town. The 15-acre pool and water park in the central courtyard rivals the one at the Tropicana.

Don't come here looking for any evidence of Bugsy. The last vestige of him, the Oregon Building where he had his office and suite, was torn down in 1994 to make room for the water park and a timeshare tower. A small shrine, however, stands on the side of the pool area. 3555 Las Vegas Blvd. S., 702/733-3111, 800/732-2111, double room rates $75–300.

The Barbary Coast

Between the Flamingo Hotel and Flamingo Ave. sits this small hotel-casino owned by Michael Gaughan, son of Las Vegas gaming pioneer Jackie Gaughan (who owns the El Cortez, Gold Spike, and Plaza downtown). It opened in 1979 and now has 200 rooms and a early 20th-century San Francisco feel. The 30-foot Tiffany-style stained-glass mural, "Garden of Earthly Delights," is advertised as the world's largest; the stained-glass signs are also works of art. Even the McDonald's marquee is tasteful. The Strip Western Union office is here, as is Michael's, one of the most exclusive gourmet restaurants in the world. Michael Gaughan and his partners also own the Gold Coast and the Orleans. 3595 Las Vegas Blvd. S., 702/737-7111, (888) BARBARY, double room rates $60–250.

Treasure Island

This $450 million 3,000-room hotel is a scaled-down version of its sister hotel next door, the Mirage. Though Treasure Island and the Mirage have the same number of rooms, TI does it in half the space, which makes this place twice as crowded, if that's possible. Add to it the hordes that make up the audience for the pirate show six times a night and what you have here is gridlock central on the Strip. It gets so ferocious that on a busy Saturday night, foot traffic slows, stalls, then stops completely for a total of 15 minutes at showtime. Which is too bad, because the show is an absolute must-see, so you'll have to wade in and out of the belly of the beast at least once during your Las Vegas experience. Hold onto your valuables! This is the second most popular venue for pickpockets in Las Vegas (Strip buses are first).

The inside of the casino is pretty classy, what you can see of it beyond the people, that is. Attention to detail is meticulous; no expense was spared. You won't find the showstopping aquarium or tiger habitat of the Mirage, but check out the Gold and Battle bars, Buccaneer Bay restaurant, and solid-bronze-skull door handles. Cirque du Soleil's "Mystere," featuring some of the most amazing feats of human acrobatics in town, plays here. 3300 Las Vegas Blvd. S., 702/894-7111, 800/944-7444, double room rates $65–300.

The Mirage

A hundred-acre site, with nearly a half mile of Strip frontage. Spaces for 3,100 cars, and hundreds of all-weather speakers serenading the parking lots. More than 3,000 rooms in three 29-story, Y-shaped, gold-mirrored wings. Fifty-four-foot-high man-made mountain-fountain, from which a volcano erupts every half-hour after dark: flames, steam, lava. Surrounded by waterfalls, lagoons, grottoes, and a thousand or so giant palm trees. Three-million-square-foot building. Nearly 100-foot-high glass-domed atrium, sprouting royal and canary palms, banana trees, elephant ears, orchids, and humidified by a computerized misting system. Front desk backed by a huge aquarium: 20,000 gallons, 53 feet long, six feet deep, with sharks, rays, wrasses, groupers, surgeonfish, puffers, angelfish, and triggerfish. Rich tropical casino decor: carved

THE WORLD'S LARGEST HOTELS

1. MGM Grand, Las Vegas—5,005 rooms
2. Ambassador City, Jomtien, Thailand—4,631 rooms
3. Luxor, Las Vegas—4,476 rooms
4. Excalibur, Las Vegas—4,032 rooms
5. Circus Circus, Las Vegas—3,774 rooms
6. Flamingo Hilton, Las Vegas—3,652 rooms
7. Mandalay Bay, Las Vegas—3,221 rooms
8. Las Vegas Hilton, Las Vegas—3,174 rooms
9. The Mirage, Las Vegas—3,049 rooms
10. The Venetian, Las Vegas—3,036 rooms
11. Monte Carlo, Las Vegas—3,025 rooms
12. Bellagio, Las Vegas—3,010 rooms
13. Paris, Las Vegas—2,916 rooms
14. Treasure Island, Las Vegas—2,900 rooms
15. Opryland USA, Nashville—2,884 rooms
16. Bally's, Las Vegas—2,832 rooms
17. Imperial Palace, Las Vegas—2,700 rooms
18. Harrah's, Las Vegas—2,700 rooms
19. Aladdin, Las Vegas—2,600 rooms
20. Rio, Las Vegas—2,569 rooms

teakwood, bamboo, thatch, marble, rattan. White Bengal tigers in a show-biz habitat from Siegfried and Roy's $90 per-person extravaganza. Nine dolphins cavort in a million-gallon saltwater pool. Japanese, Chinese, French, Italian, steak and seafood, and buffet restaurants. Slots, table games, monumental sports book. Nearly 5,000 employees.

The Mirage kicked off this latest Las Vegas boom in November 1989; since then over 25 major hotel-casinos, at a cost of nearly $10 billion, have opened around town. And there's no end in sight. In 1999, Mirage Resorts (including Bellagio, Treasure Island, the Golden Nugget and a handful of non-Vegas casinos) joined forces with MGM Grand and its sister property, New York–New York, to create MGM MIRAGE, a corporation of monstrous proportions and influence. 3400 Las Vegas Blvd. S., 702/791-7111, 800/627-6667, double room rates $90–450.

Caesars Palace

Since it opened in 1966, Caesars has earned its place as one of the most famous hotels in the world. Start your tour from the 20-foot statue of Augustus Caesar, hailing a cab, at the driveway to the main entrance; beyond are 18 fountains spewing 35-foot-high columns of water in front of 50-foot-tall Italian cypresses. Pause at the four-faced and eight-armed Brahma nearby to light some incense and kneel in meditation on the prayer cushions. Grab one of the two people movers (the south one, next to the Mirage, forces you to go through the Forum Shops).

Once inside, wander through the sprawling Roman and Olympic casinos with their characteristic low and high ceilings. Stroll past Cleopatra's Barge dance lounge and a replica of Michelangelo's *David*. Peek into Empress Court (the most expensive Chinese food you will ever see), and Primavera restaurants; La Piazza is the most upscale food court in town and the Palatium is one of the fanciest buffets (the food is okay). Check out the NASA-esque sports book, and if you wander around far enough, you might even stumble into the hotel lobby.

The **Forum Shops at Caesars** connects to the Olympic Casino. This is the most profitable retail real estate in the country (the average mall earns around $300 per square foot, while the Forum earns $1,200). The original $100 million 250,000-square-foot wing opened in summer 1992; it was doubled in size at a cost of $250 million in summer 1997. Nearly everything for sale is Italian designer, French chic, American yuppie, or just plain dear, guaranteed to raise the eyebrows of even the highbrows. Get your designer sunglasses for $700, your burlap coffeesack jackets for $400, and your silk suits for the mid-four digits. The fine art galleries have some of the finest art within 400 miles.

The restaurant food here is divine. You've got Spago, the Palm, Bertollini's, Stage Deli, Boogie Diner, Chinois (Wolfgang Puck's Chinese restaurant), Cheesecake Factory, and the Caviarteria.

The mall itself is also is a visual and sensual extravaganza; what Caesars is to casinos, the Forum is to malls. The details are exquisite and Roman: columns and arches, railing-lined balconies, statues, marble floors, and a Mediterranean sky that changes from sunrise to sunset in three hours. The main entertainment is at the Festival Fountain and the Atlantis Fountain (see "Animatronic Shows" under "Light Shows," above). 3570 Las Vegas Blvd. S., 702/731-7110, 800/634-6661, double room rates $100–350.

Bellagio

The Dunes, which consisted of 164 acres of sprawling casino, two hotel towers, courtyard bungalows, and a golf course, was built in 1955. It traveled the rocky road of Las Vegas's thirty something hotels until 1992, when the whole bankrupt property was sold for the fire-sale price of $75 million to Steve Wynn of Mirage Resorts. Wynn proceeded to take down the casino and tear out the bungalows, and the first tower was imploded in a huge public explosion that coincided with the opening of Treasure Island up the street.

When the dust settled, Bellagio was born, Mirage Resorts' $1.4 billion monument devoted to all the luxury money can buy. Before you even set foot in Bellagio, you are treated to one of the best free shows Las Vegas has to offer: The Fountains. More than one thousand fountains dance in the 12–acre lake in front of Bellagio. The water ballet is choreographed to everything from Opera to Broadway hits, with jets of water soaring more than 200 feet into the air. The show takes place Monday–Friday every 30 minutes 3 P.M.–6 P.M. and Saturday–Sunday noon–7 P.M.; daily 7 P.M.–11:45 P.M. the show is increased to every 15 minutes.

Bellagio strives to be a first-class retreat, attracting everyone from high-rollers to non-gamblers interested in buying Gucci bags and dining in top–notch restaurants. Judging from the hotel's occupancy rate and celebrity guest list, it has succeeded. And it truly is a stunning, beautiful affair. Make your way to the lobby and turn your eyes upward to enjoy the extraordinary glass parasol chandelier *Fiori di Como* created by famed glass sculptor Dale Chihuly. While gazing upward, an overwhelming floral scent will undoubtedly draw you to the 13,500 square foot conservatory garden, where a staff of 115 horticulturists cultivates a floral display worthy of a Royal wedding.

Everything about Bellagio carries a high price tag, catering to the "it's expensive, but I'm worth it" crowd. Via Bellagio's retail district carries Prada, Armani, Giorgio, and Tiffany & Co., while

the restaurant selections include chef Julian Serrano's five-star Picasso, chef Marc Poidevin's Le Cirque and chef Mark Lo Russo's acclaimed seafood restaurant Aqua. In a theater designed to emulate Paris' Opera House, Cirque de Soleil's newest production, "O," takes place on a $90 million stage. With over 3,000 hotel rooms and a rack rate starting at $225 a night (families with children will be encouraged to find accommodations elsewhere), Bellagio has raised the bar for grand-scale indulgence. 3600 Las Vegas Blvd. S., 702/693-7111, 888/987-3456, double room rates $225–1,600.

Bally's

This hotel was built by Kirk Kerkorian a few years after he built and sold the International to Hilton. Originally called the MGM Grand, it was the largest hotel in the world at the time. It was also the last hotel to be built from scratch in Las Vegas for 16 years, until the Mirage opened. In 1980, a terrible fire raged through the Grand, killing 84 people. A couple of years later, it was sold to Bally's.

Today, Bally's is the 15th largest hotel in the world, with 2,814 rooms. It's still a giant, but a giant *among* giants. Its land area totals more than 70 acres, with 3.25 million square feet. Just under 3,000 rooms occupy two towers, one of them 26 stories. Its huge casino, along with six restaurants, full resort facilities, 40-store shopping mall, two showrooms, and two lounges, conspire to eliminate any reason to leave. A giant is still a giant.

Bally's teamed up with MGM Grand to build a $25 million mile-long monorail that has connected the two properties since 1995 (free). The long-running Donn Arden extravaganza, "Jubilee," plays in the theater; with a cast of 100, "Jubilee" features the largest congregation of beautiful bodies on any stage in town. Finally, Hilton Hotels bought Bally's in 1995 for $3.2 billion. 3645 Las Vegas Blvd. S., 702/739-4111, 800/634-3434, double room rates $100–1,000.

Paris

When Hilton bought Bally's, it inherited a vacant lot just south on the Strip, along with three-year-old plans to build a 3,000-room $785 million megaresort. Thus, on September 1, 1999, Paris made its entree onto the Strip, giving Las

Vegas another new landmark of colossal proportions: The Eiffel Tower. Using Gustav Eiffel's original 1889 drawings, architects took painstaking care—even going so far as to match the paint color and lighting system—to ensure that this half-size replica mirrored the original City of Light's tower, save for the 85,000-square-foot casino sprawled beneath its legs. Other signature Parisian touches are a replica of the Arc De Triomphe and the Pont Alexandre III, along with facades of the Paris Opera House and the Louvre.

Featuring no fewer than eight French restaurants, the creators seem confident that France's renown for gastronomic *savoir-faire* will draw diners. On Sundays, Paris hosts a jazz brunch from 11:30 A.M.–2:30 P.M. with live performances and Caribbean cuisine at Tres Jazz restaurant located in the crossover between Bally's and Paris.

Guests at Paris may enjoy the two-acre rooftop swimming pool and a 25,000-square-foot European spa, as well as Le Théâtre des Arts,with 12,000 seats. 3655 Las Vegas Blvd. S., 702/946-7000, 888/BONJOUR, double room rates $150–1500.

Aladdin

This hotel, between Bally's and the MGM Grand on the Strip, was opened on New Year's Day 1966 by Milton Prell, who'd sold his points in the Sahara a few years previously to Del Webb. Prell was a personal friend of Elvis's (Priscilla and the King were married in Prell's private suite in 1967)—the Aladdin's 15 minutes of fame. Prell suffered a heart attack shortly thereafter, and the Aladdin was sold to a succession of owners who drove it right into the ground. A Las Vegas developer, Jack Sommers, bought it out of receivership in 1994 and got it back on its feet, only to close it in November 1997. In August of 2000, it reopened with $1.4 billion dollars worth of cosmetic surgery and 2,567 rooms. With its completely revamped 1,001 Arabian Nights ornamentation comes a 50-foot tall lamp bar where you can drown your sorrows should all your wishes not be fulfilled in the 100,000-square-foot casino.

And they haven't even finished building. A state-of-the-art health spa and salon is slated to open in December of 2000, and a 12,000 seat showroom is scheduled to open in January of 2001. Other new additions include the London Club, a European high-limits gaming facility run by London Clubs International, that includes a five-star restaurant. 3667 Las Vegas Blvd. S., 702/736-7114 or 877/333-WISH, double room rates $100–800.

Blending seamlessly with Aladdin's décor, the newest shopping extravaganza to hit the Strip is **Desert Passage**, 500,000 square feet of retail shops, restaurants and performance space. Two "gates" lead into the shopping area: India Gate and Morocco Gate. Exotic music wafts overhead as you shop your way into the "Lost City," where belly dancers and acrobats perform regularly in front of the central fountain and food court. En route, you'll pass the Merchant's Harbor, where torrential rainstorms occur every 15 minutes in front of Ben & Jerry's ice cream store. Or you may have a veiled women apply a henna tattoo to your hand before you make your way into Banana Republic. Soon to be unveiled are a Theater of Performing Arts that will be able to host 7,000 people, making it the largest indoor theater in the United States, as well as a 1,400 seat nightclub. Whether you're a shopper or not, a visit to the Desert is a kick.

MGM Grand

Kirk Kerkorian likes building the largest hotels in the world. In 1969 when he built the International, in 1973 when he built the original Grand, and in 1993 when he opened this megalith, they were all the largest. But this one takes the cake. With 5,005 rooms worth of guests and 8,000 employees, the Grand is larger than most towns in Nevada. It also boasts a 16-valet-lane porte cochere, a 171,000-square-foot casino, a 15,000-seat arena, a 1,200-seat theater, seven major restaurants, plus a buffet, coffee shop, and fast-food court, a convention center, a double-Olympic-sized pool, a giant video arcade, big day-care center, 9,000-space parking garage, 90 elevators, and a 33-acre amusement park, complete with six rides, four theaters, and a dozen eateries. Still going? Well then head to Studio 54, where the bold and beautiful shake their groove thang until the wee hours of the morning. It's best to tackle the Grand after a full night's sleep; by the time you're done with the place, you'll be ready for bed again.

The notable eateries include Emeril Lagasse's

New Orleans Fish House (very creative, unusual, and expensive seafood), the original Brown Derby steakhouse (relocated from L.A.), Mark Miller's Coyote Cafe (serving hot nouveau Southwestern cuisine), and Tres Visi (Italian).

After being open for a full four years, in 1997 the Grand underwent a complete renovation—nothing lasts forever! The most highly-touted new visitor attraction is the ultimately depressing Lion Habitat. Smack dab in the middle of the casino, the "habitat" has thick glass walls that allow gamblers to gawk at lions and cubs as they pace around their living room. Well-coiffed handlers routinely feed the lions bits of steak right up against the window for maximum viewing pleasure, while lion roars are piped over the speakers. The attraction is free, and you may wander through the glass tunnel for a better look at the felines. At the end of the tunnel is a gift shop where you can buy any size of stuffed MGM lion you desire. 3799 Las Vegas Blvd. S., 702/891-1111, 800/929-1111, double room rates $75–300.

Tropicana

When the Trop opened in 1958, it was the ninth hotel on the Strip, the fifth to open in three years, and the most expensive up to that time, costing $15 million. It was initially so exquisite that it earned the nickname "Tiffany of the Strip." After the early mob owners were forced out, a series of new owners oversaw the deterioration of the Trop's aura, until Ramada Corporation bought it in 1979, and gradually reinvested the property with much of its original glory. (It's now owned by Aztar Corporation, a spinoff of Ramada.) More than an acre of the stunning five-acre centerpiece, the Island Waterpark, is water: three swimming pools, one 75 by 300 feet; glass doors slide shut in winter, transforming one side into an indoor pool, creating the town's most delightfully *humid* public room. There's also a water slide, and the lush landscaping makes it easy to pretend you're at a resort in Polynesia.

The casino's main pit is under a magnificent 4,000-square-foot leaded stained-glass dome (which the engineers had to suspend on pneumatic shock absorbers to account for building vibrations from the air-conditioning; the ceiling remains stationary and the building vibrates around it). The 425-foot people mover between the tow-

THE FOUR CORNERS

For more than 30 years, the Tropicana alone occupied the far southern end of the Las Vegas Strip. Built in 1957 and expanded in the '60s, '70s, and '80s, it wasn't until 1989 that the Trop got any company—and competition—on its corner, when the 300-room San Remo opened next door (since expanded to 700 rooms). In 1990, the massive 4,000-room Excalibur arrived across the street, and in 1993, both the 2,500-room Luxor (since expanded to nearly 4,500 rooms) and the 5,005-room MGM Grand were built at the Tropicana's intersection on the Strip. In June 1996, the 3,000-room Monte Carlo opened and six months later, in early January 1997, the 2,035-room New York-New York joined the crowd.

Today, this corner boasts four of the ten largest hotels in the world. Altogether, the seven hotels combine for more than 21,000 hotel rooms, 50 restaurants, 15,000 slot machines, 12 showrooms and theaters with a total of 23,000 seats, and a "population" at any given of approximately 75,000 employees, guests, showgoers, conventioneers, and sightseers. By comparison, those 75,000 people would make up the fifth-largest town in Nevada, larger even than the state capital at Carson City.

ers passes through a bright tunnel full of macaws, parrots, and coral aquariums. The glass-elevator ride to the top of the Island Tower is fun. The Trop is also known for its Sunday brunch, Mizuno's teppanyaki restaurant, and "Folies Bergere," the longest-running and one of the last true Las Vegas-style extravaganzas. 3801 Las Vegas Blvd. S., 702/739-2222, 800/634-4000, double room rates $60–200.

Monte Carlo

This gorgeous $350 million 3,000-room megaresort, built by Circus Circus, opened in June 1996. Modeled after the opulent Place du Casino in Monaco, the Las Vegas version of Monte Carlo replicates its fanciful arches, chandeliered domes, ornate fountains, marble floors, gas-lit promenades, and Gothic glass registration area overlooking the lush pool area. And it all took 14 months—from groundbreaking to grand opening—to put together. Amazing.

Within Monte Carlo are: a beautiful casino that combines European elegance and American informality; five restaurants, a microbrewery, and a fast-food court; Circus Circus's signature high-tech arcade; a big bingo parlor upstairs; a waterpark consisting of adult and children pools, Jacuzzi, and a wave pool and "lazy river" combo; and the Lance Burton Theater, a 1,200-seat showroom featuring world-class illusionist Burton, which is modeled after European opera houses and is one of a kind in Las Vegas. 3770 Las Vegas Blvd. S., 702/730-7777, 800/311-8999, double room rates $60–200.

New York–New York

Andy Warhol would have been proud: this is the singlemost monumental piece of pop art the world has ever seen. This $460 million 2,000-room megaresort sets a new standard for thematic accomplishment in Las Vegas. The miniskyline recreates a half-size Statue of Liberty and Empire State Building, along with the Chrysler, Seagrams, and CBS buildings, the New York Public Library, New Yorker Hotel, Grand Central Station, and Brooklyn Bridge, among others. A Coney Island-style roller coaster runs completely around the property. The interior is no less realized thematically than the exterior. Everywhere you look there's a clever replica of another New York icon: New York Stock Exchange, New York Racetrack, New York Public Library.

The pièce de résistance is the simulation of Greenwich Village. Narrow, crooked, and of course crowded reproductions of Bleecker Street, Hudson Street, Broadway, and others all frame the Village Eateries area. The floors are brick, with faux manhole covers inset here and there. Multi-story townhouses line the streets, complete with brown stone, fire escapes, and ivy trellises. The roller coaster rumbles overhead like an elevated commuter train.

The most realistic thing about New York–New York is the cramped space. The owners, MGM Grand and Primadonna Resorts, stuffed a big megaresort into a postage-sized lot, much like Manhattan is a huge city jammed into a 200- by 12-block island. For comparison purposes, Monte Carlo next door occupies a 66-acre parcel; New York–New York fills 20 acres. Get ready for a high-population density! 3790 Las Vegas Blvd. S., 702/740-6969, 800/NYFORME, double room rates $100–250.

Excalibur

A stroll through this 4,000-room hotel (each one redecorated in 1999) is a lesson in medieval architecture and culture: 14 spires, with turrets and parapets in the battlements, and cones topped by steeples and spikes. The drawbridge crosses the moat, beyond which a cobblestone foyer is draped with velvet, satin, and gold heraldic banners, and a three-story-high fountain sports lion heads and stone frogs. Upstairs is the medieval village, where magicians, jugglers, mimes, court jesters, belly dancers, contortionists, even a harpist entertain on the floor and various stages. Knights, lords, maidens, serfs, ladies-in-waiting, gypsies, even wenches provide the service in appropriate uniforms. Downstairs on the Fantasy Faire level, turret pitch, flagon toss, great racing knights, topple the towers, knock out the knaves' teeth, and William Tell darts make up the Renaissance midway. Eat at The Steakhouse at Camelot, Sir Galahad's, Sherwood Forest Café, even Robin Hood's Snack Bar. Not quite in keeping with Excalibur theme, WCW's Nitro Grill just opened on the casino level and features both planned and spontaneous visits from wrestling stars. Better yet, take the kids to the Tournament of Kings hosted in King Arthur's Arena. (See "Panorama and Pageantry" under "Food" later in this chapter for a description of this dinner show.)

Finally, there's the anomalous casino, with its neon, stained glass, gold-capped columns, huge wood beams, and the most lethal-looking chandeliers you've ever seen. Bottom line? Excalibur is fun, silly, both totally larger than life and attentive to the merest details, inviting of exploration, an amusement park with rooms and a casino. 3850 Las Vegas Blvd. S., 702/597-7777, 800/937-7777, double room rates $60–200.

Luxor

Luxor is by far one of the most dramatic architectural influences on the Las Vegas Strip (designed by Veldon Simpson, who also designed MGM Grand and Excalibur). You can't help but pick it right out of the lineup of hotels on the Strip: a sleek bronze pyramid in the midst of stark gray boxes. And the closer you get, the better it looks, until you're standing right at the base of one of the walls, staring straight up into infinity, and you get the idea of what those old Egyptian mathematicians had in mind.

This 30-story pyramid-shaped Circus Circus property opened in October 1993. Since then Circus has added another 2,000 rooms in two ziggurat towers (with 4,500 rooms, it's now the second largest hotel in Las Vegas, third in the world), a shopping mall, a 1,700-seat showroom, and a large and luxurious spa. The futuristic Egyptian dance club, "Ra" frequently tops the polls as the best place to dance in Vegas. Pulsating music, flashing strobes and expensive drinks all round out the experience.

The pyramid's interior occupies 29 million cubic feet of open space, the world's largest atrium. The casino is round, roomy, and airy (the ventilation system is world-class). On the second-floor attractions level you get the full effect the enormous atrium. (Also see "Theme Parks And High-Tech Attractions" under "Entertainment" later in this chapter for a description of the three high-tech entertainment options.) Also upstairs, the video arcade is on two levels, with interactive race cars, small motion simulators, state-of-the-art video, and a roomful of air-hockey games. If you have time to see only two casinos in Las Vegas, this is the second. 3900 Las Vegas Blvd. S., 702/262-4000, 800/288-1000, double room rates $65–350.

Mandalay Bay

The Hacienda opened in 1956. It was so far off the beaten Strip that it did its own thing through the 1960s. But after the original owners died, Chicago-mob front-man Allen Glick added it to his stable of hotels in the 1970s, then sold out to Paul Lowden, who also once owned the Sahara and now owns the Santa Fe. Lowden sold the Hacienda to Circus Circus in 1995, completing the casino giant's Miracle Mile, which stretches from the Excalibur past the Hacienda property all the way to the corner of Russell Road. A convenient monorail connects the Luxor and Excalibur to Mandalay Bay.

Circus imploded the Hacienda on New Year's Eve 1996 and constructed a 3,000-room homage to Polynesia in its place. While of course it has the requisite wedding chapels, casino floor and

lounges, the real fun of Mandalay Bay lies in all the somewhat gimmicky extras. In the lobby, hundreds of fish writhe in a 3,000-gallon circular tank. And don't miss "Shark Reef," a colossal aquarium filled to the gills with over 100 varieties of sharks, as well as rays, reptiles and fish. Need more water? Mandalay Bay boasts an 11-acre water park with four pools, hot tubs, a lazy river, and a continual "wave" for body surfing.

Since its debut, Mandalay Bay has been earning rave reviews for its eccentric dining and entertainment options. Cocktails, dinner and dancing await behind the wall of fire at Rumjungle: provided, that is, that you can get in the door—there's always a long line. Slam frozen vodka shots at Red Square next door and contemplate the irony of a Soviet restaurant set in defiantly capitalistic Vegas. For more sedate, but equally delicious, dining options, choose Wolfgang Puck's Trattoria del Lupo or Charlie Palmer's Aureole. Big name acts and Creole cuisine are the main draw at the House of Blues. 3950 Las Vegas Blvd. S., 702/632-7777 or 877/632-7000.

Literally on top of Mandalay Bay, occupying floors 36 through 39 but maintaining a completely separate identity, is the Four Seasons Las Vegas. While many of the larger, gaudier Vegas resorts claim that they are classy, this is the real deal. One of the few non-gaming hotels on the Strip, the Four Seasons offers 400 pricey (rates start at $250 and keep climbing) guest rooms, a Charlie Palmer steakhouse and a private, lushly landscaped swimming pool. 3960 Las Vegas Blvd. S., 702/632-5000, double room rates $200–600.

LOCALS' CASINOS

You might've heard that people who live in Las Vegas don't gamble—that they never go near the Strip or downtown and they'd never be caught dead inside a casino. Yeah right, and I keep telling Madonna to stop calling me. Locals, casinos, which cater to the residents, are some of the busiest and most successful in Las Vegas. They're also proliferating at an equal pace to the population. In fact, the latest trend is for five-star hotel and resort companies to throw up ultra-posh 400- to 500-room hotel-casinos in the expensive subdivisions: Seven Circle in Summerlin, the Hyatt and Grand Bay at Lake Las Vegas, and the Ritz-Carlton at Mountain Spa.

Locals' casinos combine neighborhood locations, plenty of parking, excellent restaurants, good gambling, and exemplary service. Neighborhood casinos attract the locals with full-pay video poker opportunities, active promotional campaigns (such as paycheck cashing, drawings for cash, cars, even houses, and direct-mail offers like restaurant and show discounts during slow periods), and strong slot clubs. Many of the savviest out-of-towners frequent the locals' casinos for the best deals in town.

Locals' casinos congregate in three parts of town. The "Boulder Strip" consists of the Showboat, Boulder Station, Sam's Town, the brand new Sunset Station, and several small joints farther down in Henderson. The "Rancho Strip" claims Texas Station, the Fiesta, and Santa Fe. The westside casinos include the Rio, Gold Coast, Orleans, Palace Station, and Arizona Charlie's. On the eastside is the Hard Rock.

Showboat

The "Boat," out on E. Fremont just down from the venerable Green Shack restaurant, is one of a half-dozen baby-boomer hotel-casinos that opened in the '50s that haven't been imploded yet. Dating from 1954, this riverboat-type casino out among the creosote on the Boulder Highway was far enough away from the mainstream that it could steer its own course along the tricky current of Las Vegas hotel competition. The Showboat eventually found its niche with bowling and bingo and has enjoyed mostly smooth sailing ever since. The Showboat underwent a complete renovation in 1995 and is now highly decorative and colorful. The bingo room is the fanciest in town and the bowling alley is the largest in the country. 2800 E. Fremont, 702/385-9123, 800/826-2800, double room rates $40–150.

Boulder Station

This hotel, which opened in August 1994, is the fraternal twin of the west side's Palace Station, the original locals' casino. The parent company, Station Casinos, took the highly successful Palace Station formula and improved on it. The decor is a bit upgraded, with rich hardwood and brick floors, stained glass galore, and much higher ceilings. The restaurants serve the same great

food at great prices, and even have fast-food outlets on the side that dispense the same great food at even greater prices. The Broiler has what could be the best salad bar in town. Boulder Station caters to the locals in many other ways too. It was the first casino to attach a movie theater to it (an 11-plex at that); it also has Kid's Quest, a large, efficient, and convenient child-care center (see "Child's Play" later in this chapter). 4111 E. Fremont, 702/432-7777, 800/683-7777, double room rates $55–100.

Sam's Town

This hotel, another Boyd Gaming property (along with the Stardust on the Strip, the Fremont and California downtown, the Eldorado in Henderson, and a few casinos in Mississippi), opened in 1979 way out on Boulder Highway, almost to Henderson, with a hundred or so rooms. It remained a small eastside-locals' casino with a country-and-western theme for the next 15 years. In July 1994, Sam's Town unveiled its spectacular $100 million expansion. The centerpiece is a nine-story glass-roof atrium full of live foliage, a rock waterfall, babbling brooks, and animatronic wildlife. The laser-dancing-waters-western-music show (free) is presented nightly at 2, 6, 8 and 10:30. The Final Score sports bar has more diversions than the Bureau of Reclamation. Sam's is surrounded by two 500-space RV parks. Make an effort to get out to Sam's Town to see the atrium and show, and while you're out here, have a steak at Diamond Lil's or a burger at Ralph's Diner, and check out the Western Emporium, selling every country consumable under the sun. 5111 E. Fremont, 702/456-7777, 800/634-6371, double room rates $55–300.

Texas Station

Texas Station is another Stations casino, following in the highly successful footsteps of Palace and Boulder Stations: sprawling parking lots, big casino and small hotel, seven restaurants and six bars; this one also has a 12-screen movie complex. The theme is in the details. The custom carpeting is full of wagon wheels, ten gallon hats, cow skulls, lone stars, and cattle brands. The deli sells barbecue brisket sandwiches. The cashier's cage is behind a Bank of Texas facade. A longhorn Cadillac sits 15 feet above the Texaco bar on a gas station hoist. And a 200-pound relective disco armadillo rotates above the Honky Tonk Dance Hall. Here we also have one of the top buffets in town (see "Food" later in this chapter) and a big 12-plex movie theater. 2140 N. Rancho Dr., 702/631-1000, 800/944-7444, double room rates $40–90.

Fiesta

Fiesta could be the quintessential locals' casino: tons of parking, food specials galore (late-night cheap eats for $2.99, and like Texas Station across the street, one of the best buffets in town), promotion crazy (especially if you have lots of slot club points), and jam-packed with video poker. Indeed, Fiesta calls itself the Royal Flush Capital of the World, and apparently has the goods to prove it. Fiesta also has a drive-up sports betting window—you don't even have to get out of the car to lay a wager on your favorite team. 2400 N. Rancho Dr., 702/631-7000, 800/731-7333, double room rates $60–150.

Santa Fe

The original "Rancho Strip" joint, the Santa Fe owned the northwest market for nearly four years, and still packs in the local residents. Santa Fe is the only casino in Nevada with an ice-skating rink attached; there's also bowling, bingo, and a 16-screen movie theater directly across the street. Sunday brunch at the Ti Amo Italian restaurant is the best brunch value in Las Vegas ($12.95—highly recommended); the buffet is good enough (some seats overlook the rink); and there's usually some passable entertainment in the lounge. 4949 Rancho Blvd., 702/658-4900, 800/872-6823, double room rates $40–75.

Rio

This hotel opened on W. Flamingo across I-15 in late 1990 with 400 suites. Then, the Rio's claims to fame were its stunning sign, which finally beat out the Stardust's for best neon in Las Vegas, its sandy beach by the pool, and its cocktail waitress uniforms. All three are still famous, but today the Rio is perhaps the most exciting casino in Las Vegas. A second tower was added in 1994, a third tower was completed in early 1995, and a fourth, stand-alone, 42-story tower opened in early 1997, giving the Rio a total of 2,250 suites—all the rooms are

mini-apartments, with a large bedroom-sitting area, floor-to-ceiling picture windows, and luxurious his and hers dressing areas. The Rio's Carnival World Buffet was the first, and is still one of the best, of the new-style "mini-food-city smorgasbords. The other restaurants—13 in all—are equally fantastic, right down to the sports book deli. There's also a free show, the Sky Parade, in the new casino Masquerade Village casino wing (see under "Light Shows," above). And Danny Gans, one of the great impressionists performs five nights a week in the stunning, circular Copacabana Showroom, (complete with 360-degree interactive video screens). 3700 W. Flamingo, 702/252-7777, 800/PLAYRIO, double room rates $60–350.

Gold Coast

Next door to the Rio is this Coast Hotel (sister to Barbary Coast and the Orleans), opened in 1986 by Michael Gaughan. In its first five years of operation, the Gold Coast expanded three times, most recently in 1990 with a 10-story, 400-room tower. Locals love this place for its distance from the Strip, along with its big bowling alley, bingo parlor, first-run movie theater, ice cream parlor, video poker payouts, and meal deals, especially the $7.95 one-pound T-bone with a veritable ton of carbohydrate sides, served 24 hours in the coffee shop. The sports book is wise-guy central, and the slot club boasts more than 300,000 members (almost all locals), largest in Las Vegas. In addition, the Gold Coast has a popular lounge from which live big-band music emanates day and night, and has a dance hall and saloon, featuring the largest dance floor in town. 4000 W. Flamingo, 702/367-7111, 888/402-6278, double room rates $50–80.

Sun Coast

Michael Gaughan's latest Coast property opened in 2000. Four hundred rooms, a 64-lane bowling alley, a 16-screen movie theater and day care for the tykes make this new venture popular with locals and visiting families alike. 9090 Alta Dr., 702/636-7111, 887/677-7111, double room rates $60–90.

Orleans

Another fine locals' casino from Coast Hotels, the Orleans opened in December 1996 to rave reviews. The Orleans seems to be trying to compete with the Rio, and is doing a fair job of it. The showroom features headliners, two lounges offer live big band, jazz, and zydeco bands, there's a big bowling alley upstairs, the buffet serves up some great Cajun and Creole, and the video poker machines are often monopolized by the professionals taking advantage of positive situations. The Orleans is unique among locals' casinos in that it has 800 hotel rooms; locals don't often need rooms, so the Orleans has trouble keeping them all filled, which means great deals. And if you're thirsty, a (strange) line-up of eight stainless-steel water fountains awaits on the second floor. 4500 W. Tropicana, 702/365-7111, 800/675-3267, double room rates $75–100.

Palace Station

Palace Station is a very popular casino with both locals and visitors, off the Strip about a mile west on Sahara Avenue. The parking lot is always packed. Palace Station lays claim to having the largest (though not tallest) sign in town—and therefore the world. It offers consistently excellent room deals, consistently has the best dinner deals in town along with a great 99-cent margarita, and its Feast Buffet is a perennial favorite. A 12-story tower was completed in 1991. 2411 W. Sahara, 702/367-2411, 800/634-3101, double room rates $45–350.

Arizona Charlie's

Opened in 1988, Charlie's services the western suburbs, on Decatur Boulevard a half-block north of Charleston. It was overhauled in 1994, and now has a seven-story tower (400 rooms total),

three restaurants, saloon, big sports book and deli, and, of course, great video poker. The new casino decorations and names have finally added a little slice of Alaska to Las Vegas; Arizona Charlie, after all, made his name and fortune as a saloon owner and impressario in Dawson during the Klondike. The Sourdough Cafe has the best steak and eggs breakfast special ($2.49) in town. 740 S. Decatur Blvd., 702/258-5200, 800/342-2695, double room rates $40–75.

Hard Rock

The world's only Hard Rock Hotel and Casino opened in March 1994 and has been in a world of its own ever since. It's definitely the hippest (in a rock 'n' roll kind of way) casino in Las Vegas. The small casino features tons of pop memorabilia, slot machines have guitar-neck handles, table-game layouts are customized with rock lyrics and art, and the casino employees all look like they're straight off the set of a soap opera. There's the requisite logo shop, a cool pool area with sandy beach, only 300 rooms (thousands are turned away), and a 1,200-seat concert venue. For a little non-gaming night action, there's Baby's, a cutting-edge, hipster nightclub that flies D.J.'s in from around the country to spin the latest in electronica and house music in an underground den of retro-cool. Dining options include a pricey steakhouse (A.J.s), a recommendable Italian eatery (Mortoni's) and a Mexican restaurant boasting Nevada's best tequila bar (Pink Taco). If you're under 55, you'll want to at least see the Hard Rock, if not hang here. 4455 Paradise Ave., 702/693-5000, 800/HRD-ROCK, double room rates $100–250.

ACCOMMODATIONS

With over 70 major hotels and over 200 motels, Las Vegas boasts a grand total of 120,294 places to sleep indoors. But if that makes it sound easy to find the one perfect room with your name on it, think again. More than 34 million visitors occupy those 202,000 beds every year; that's roughly 88,000 a night. In addition, every weekend of the year either sells out or comes close to; long weekends and holidays (especially New Year's Eve, Valentine's Day, Memorial Day, 4th of July, Labor Day, and Thanksgiving, along with international holidays such as Cinco de Mayo and Mexican Independence Day, and Chinese New Year's) are sold out weeks in advance; special events, such as concerts, title fights, the Super Bowl, the Final Four, and the National Finals Rodeo, are sold out months in advance; and reservations are made for the biggest conventions (Comdex, Consumer Electronics, Men's Apparel, Broadcasters, etc.) a year ahead of time.

In short, this town fills up fast—especially the top hotels, the best-value hotels, and the cheapest motels. What's more, the crowds are relentless; Las Vegas rarely gets a break to catch its breath. There are some minor quiet times, such as the three weeks before Christmas and a noticeable downward blip in July and August when the mercury doesn't see fit to drop below 90 degrees. Also, Sunday through Thursday when there aren't any large conventions or sporting events are a little less crazy than usual; almost all the room packages and deep discounts are only available Sunday through Thursday. Weekends are deal-less. In fact, most of the major hotels don't even let you check in on a Saturday night. You can stay Friday night of Friday and Saturday, but not Saturday by itself.

Of course, unless you're a travel writer with a laptop or a sybarite with a lapdance, your hotel or motel room is where you'll spend the *least* time during your stay in Las Vegas. One way to look at accommodations in Las Vegas is to remember the old travelers' axiom: eat sweet, pay for play, but sleep cheap. Otherwise, as always, it's best to make your reservations far in advance to ensure the appropriate kind, price, and location of your room. So it's wise to plan well in advance, be well informed, and use good travel common sense.

HOTELS

Orientation

Basically, Las Vegas hotels congregate in three locations: downtown, the Strip, and off-Strip. Downtown, there are ten major hotels and a couple of minor ones in a two- by five-block area on Fremont and Ogden streets between Main and 5th. The Fremont Street Experience unifies the majority of these hotels into one multifarious attraction, which has revitalized downtown, raising visitor volume and casino profits that had declined due to the juggernaut of megajoints on the Strip. Downtown's rooms are uniformly less expensive, the food is also cheaper with no loss of quality, the gambling can be more positive if you know what you're looking for, and the cast of characters is far more colorful. (You'll find rate and contact information on Downtown casino hotels in the preceding "Hotel-Casinos" section.)

The Strip has the biggest, newest, most themed, and most crowded hotels. Twelve of the 15 largest hotels in the world are along a four-mile stretch on Las Vegas Blvd. South between Sahara and Tropicana avenues. These hotels are self-contained mini-cities, and though you never have to leave them, you're also somewhat captive in them: it's often hard to find your way out; the distance from your car to your room can be daunting; the distances between the hotels can be prohibitive; and the lines to do anything—eat, drink, play blackjack, see a show, or catch a cab—can drive you to distraction. But if you want to be right in the thick of the rammin' jammin' gambling-joint action, the Strip's your bell ringing. (You'll find rate and contact information on Strip casino hotels in the preceding "Hotel-Casinos" section.)

The off-Strip hotels have the popular casinos, but they often have a minimum of rooms. A Nevada ordinance requires new casinos to open with a minimum of 200 hotel rooms, and that's all they often have. They're mostly for out-of-towners who particularly like them and for relatives of locals who live nearby. But you can often find good room deals at them, because even with so few rooms, the locals' casinos often have trouble filling them. Most visitors want to be in the thick of the neon—on the Strip or downtown.

Rates

No two people pay the same amount for a seat on the same airline, and no two people pay the same amount for a hotel room in Las Vegas. If you have to fly somewhere at the last minute, and can't arrange for any advance purchase, charter, or discount fares, you'll pay retail for your seat, often upwards of four, five, even six times more than someone who reserves a week in advance. The same holds true of reserving a hotel room in Las Vegas, but here it's not a matter of time. It's more a matter of juice (who you know). If you have to call hotel reservations for your room, you'll pay top dollar (if you can even get a room). That's because the hotel reservations departments are set up to ream the sucker off the street via the rack rate, which is one of the most expensive room rates that's charged. (Probably the most expensive rate is the convention rate; never tell a hotel reservations agent that you're coming for a convention!)

How does the Las Vegas room system work? First, Las Vegas hotel room rates change minute to minute, and the range of rates can be spectacular. Imperial Palace, for example, charges $300 a night for a standard room during the gargantuan Comdex convention in November, and $30 a night for the same room on selected dates starting a week later, between Thanksgiving and Christmas. A number of variables determine the rates for a room, but it mainly boils down to the great free-market motivator of supply and demand. When it's crowded, rooms are expensive. When it's slow, rooms are given away.

Another factor that comes into play is the operative through which you secure your room. There are four or five different departments within the hotel, as well as a number of outside agents, that are allocated rooms to sell (or give away); the system is large and complex. Depending on whom you book your room through, your rate on any given day of the year can range from free (room comps issued by the casino) up to top-dollar (last-minute reservations through the front desk).

The best way to get a free or deeply discounted room in Las Vegas is to stay where you play. If you play table games with an average bet of at least $25, you should be able to get the "casino rate" (usually a 40–50% discount off the rack rate) for any room in Las Vegas (except for the high-roller casinos, such as Caesars, Mirage, The Venetian, Bellagio, and MGM Grand, where an average bet of $50–100 is required. That same bet at the medium-priced casinos, like the Stardust, Frontier, Maxim, and downtown joints, should get you a free room). If you play slots or video poker, it behooves you to join the slot club at the casino that sees most of your action. The more slot club points you accumulate in your account, the more free rooms (and other free stuff) you're entitled to. Two excellent books cover the room situation in detail. *Comp City* by Max Rubin shows you all the tricks if you're a table game player; *The Las Vegas Advisor Guide to Slot Clubs* by Jeffrey Compton is for slot and video poker players (see "Booklist").

Other departments also handle rooms. Sales and marketing control blocks of rooms for special events (slot tournaments, sporting events such as prize fights or the Super Bowl, conventions, and wedding parties). And rooms are blocked off for the use of travel packagers and wholesalers. Discounts on rooms can often be obtained by finding a good "package," either one that the hotel itself is offering or that a tour-and-travel packager has put together or that a travel wholesaler is advertising. Look for package deals (often air-room, but sometimes room only) advertised in the Sunday travel supplement of the newspaper of the largest city near you. If you can get ahold of the *Los Angeles Times* Sunday "Calendar," that's where most Las Vegas hotels advertise their deals. Travel clubs, such as

See the "Las Vegas Major Hotels" chart in the "Further Information" section (at back of book) for hotel addresses and phone numbers. See also the preceding "Hotel-Casinos" section.

the Entertainment Book, often contain 50%-off coupons for Las Vegas hotel rooms. Your travel agent might have a connection with some discounted room deal, but don't count on it. Because Las Vegas rooms are relatively inexpensive to begin with, travel agents don't make too hefty a commission for booking them. Other discounts might be offered by the hotel, such as corporate, AAA, military, or senior.

Also, most Las Vegas hotels have a variety of rooms at different rates. At the older joints, two classes of rooms are standard: "garden" (low-rise motel-style rooms from the '50s and '60s; cheaper) and "tower" (newer high-rise; more expensive). Some offer mini-suites and suites (though these are often reserved for room comps and upgrades by the casino). "Casino rate" is another discount, generally 35–50% of rack, that's given to gamblers whose action doesn't quite merit a fully comped room, but is good enough for half off.

Bottom line, however, is that because casino profits subsidize the other revenue-producing departments, Las Vegas hotels can afford to discount their rooms 20%, 40%, 60%, up to a whopping 80% at times over the standard rates at *all* other resort destinations around the country.

Reservations

The complete rundown on what Bob Sehlinger, in his excellent *Unofficial Guide to Las Vegas,* calls "the wacky world of Las Vegas hotel reservations" is way beyond the scope of this book. Suffice it to say that booking a room at a major Las Vegas hotel can be as simple as calling the 800 reservations number, agreeing to pay rack rate, and guaranteeing arrival with a credit card number. In this scenario, all you have to worry about is getting the kind of room you want at the location you desire at the price you're willing to pay. One word to the wise here: it's always wise to make a few calls to Las Vegas hotels *before* you make a final determination on the dates of your vacation to find out if something is going on in town (convention, event, holiday) for which you'll be reamed for your room. (You can also call the Las Vegas Convention and Visitors Authority at 702/892-0711 and ask what conventions are scheduled for the dates that you'll be in town.)

However, for those of you who like to get the best deal humanly possible on everything, and are willing to travel during the low seasons, Sunday through Thursday, and maybe even play a little to see if you can win your room, the booking of Las Vegas hotel rooms will send you straight to bargain-hunter heaven. There's no doubt about it: the supply of Las Vegas hotel rooms is up, and it's going even higher. When the demand is low, they're givin' 'em away.

Las Vegas room reservation services come and go (and sometimes take your money with them), but one that's been in business for 15 years is **Las Vegas Travel,** 702/794-2061. Mitchell Group, the program director, claims that Las Vegas Travel is the largest room wholesaler and reservation service that sells rooms only in the Las Vegas market, with an availability of 500 rooms daily in all the top hotels. Call Las Vegas travel to see what kind of room deals they're offering when your dates are firm.

Specials

As previously mentioned, the last two weeks in July, the first two weeks in August, and the period from after Thanksgiving to just before Christmas are the (relatively) slow seasons in Las Vegas. These are the only times of year when Las Vegas's 101,000 hotel rooms are readily available—so available, in fact, that the hotels nearly bribe you to stay in them, to keep the casinos busy and the profits flowing. If you can come to Las Vegas the first or second week of December, and you do a marginal amount of research, such as checking the *L.A. Times* Calendar section or ordering the December issue of the *Las Vegas Advisor* (see "Information," below), you'll be hard pressed to spend more than $10 a night for a room.

In general, Sunday through Thursday, rooms are much cheaper than Friday and Saturday. Downtown is uniformly less expensive than the Strip. Always ask if the hotel is featuring any discounted packages or specials. If you're a slot player, sign up for every slot club you can, if only to get on casino mailing lists; you'll be amazed at the discounts that show up in your mailbox, even if you don't play.

MOTELS

Orientation

Many travelers, including myself, prefer motels to hotels. Since you'll be spending very little time in your room, the quality of amenities isn't particularly critical. A bed, shower, TV, heater/air-conditioner, and a good lock on the door are the salient features; the rest is luxury. Price is another consideration, since motels are generally 25–75% less expensive than hotel rooms. Distance is also a factor; at a motel you can pull a car right up to your door and don't have to navigate large parking lots or garages, crowded casinos, slow elevators, and long halls.

On the other hand, most Las Vegas motels tend to be older, less hygienic, and more run-down than their high-rise counterparts. They're also generally in funkier neighborhoods. They have thinner walls, flimsier beds, smaller bathrooms, and shabbier carpet. You need a little sense of adventure to stay in them.

Downtown—East Fremont

Glitter Gulch fills up Fremont St. from Main to 4th, but beyond that, and on side streets, bargain-basement motels are numerous. Dozens of places are bunched together in three main groupings. It's not the best part of town, but it's certainly not the worst, and security is usually seen to by the management (but check). Generally speaking, the motels along Las Vegas Blvd. N and E. Fremont are the least expensive. Motels between downtown and the Strip on Las Vegas Blvd. S are slightly more expensive and in a slightly better neighborhood.

East Fremont between 7th St. and the big Showboat Hotel has the most motels, grouped sometimes one right next to another, or separated by car dealers and bars. On the other side of the Showboat the motels are a little farther apart. It's a few minutes' drive to the downtown casinos, and an excursion to the Strip, but the venerable Showboat is on one end and Sam's Town and Nevada Palace on the other, so it's not too far to just gamble. Also, this is RV country, with RV parks lining the highway past motel row, and big parking lots at the casinos. And with so many possibilities out here, it's a good stretch to cruise if you don't have reservations and most No Vacancy signs are lit. Two reliable standards in this neighborhood, with rooms generally under $50 are **Lucky Cuss,** 702/457-1929, and **Ponderosa,** 702/457-0422.

Downtown—North

Las Vegas Blvd. N from Fremont to Bonanza, along with N. Main and the north numbered streets from 6th to 13th are also packed with motels one after the other. Stay on the lighted streets. It might be a little unnerving to deal with the front desk person through bars, but Glitter Gulch is very handy if that's where you want to spend your time, and these rooms can be amazingly reasonable, if a room is not where you

Excalibur

JOHN ELK III

want to spend your money. Weekly rates here, especially without kitchenette, could be as little as $15 a night. Both the **Golden Inn,** 702/384-8204, and the **Travel Inn,** 702/384-3040, offer the basics with rates starting at $35 for a double room with two beds and climbing to $100 during peak seasons.

Downtown—South
The motels on Las Vegas Blvd. S between downtown and the north end of the Strip at Sahara Ave. have the most convenient location if you like to float between downtown and the Strip, or if you're getting married in one of the wedding chapels that line this stretch of the boulevard. It's also brighter and busier. You're right on the main bus routes. Most of these motels also offer weekly room rates, with or without kitchenettes. The **High Hat,** 702/382-8080, has been around for several years and offers double rooms for $35–95.

Upper Strip
Several good-value motels congregate on Las Vegas Blvd. S between Vegas World and the Sahara; these places are also good to try for weekly rooms with kitchenettes. These are handy places to stay in the summer with kids, who'll be able to run right over to Wet 'n Wild. They're also within walking distance (though these blocks are very long) to the Sahara, Riviera, and Circus Circus (and Grand Slam Canyon). **Fun City,** 702/731-3155, is within walking distance of the Sahara and offers clean doubles for $35–100.

Lower Strip
Motels along the lower Strip, between Bally's below Flamingo Ave. and all the way out to the Hacienda at the far south end of the Strip, are well placed to visit all the new big-band casino resorts, but have prices that match the cheaper places north of downtown. A friendly and well-situated motel across the street from Treasure Island is the **Tam O'Shanter,** 702/735-7331, where doubles range from $40–70.

Convention Center
Another group of motels clings to the south side of the Convention Center, on Paradise and Desert Inn roads, as well as the west side, between Paradise and the Strip on Convention Center Drive. If you're attending a convention here and plan well in advance, you can reserve a very reasonable and livable room at any of several motels within a five-minute walk of the convention floor; most of them have plenty of weekly rooms with kitchenettes, which can save you a bundle. It's a joy to be able to leave the convention floor and walk over to your room, and back again if necessary—the shuttle buses to the far-flung hotels are very often crowded, slow, and inconvenient. Even if you're not attending a convention, this is a good part of town to stay in: off the main drag but in the middle of everything.

Rates
Like hotel rooms, motel room rates have more ups and downs than an elevator operator. During the summer, the price will be 10–20% higher. Weekend rates can be double weekdays; on holidays they can go up by another 25%. Conventions? Forget it. Sometimes a reservationist will leaf through the Las Vegas Convention and Visitor Authority's schedule of conventions to see if there are any in town at the time of your arrival before quoting a price. Occasionally he or she will ask you if you're coming to town for a convention. Again, deny it with authority. Often the rate quoted beforehand is for one type of room but when you arrive, only a more expensive room is available. Most motels have refundable key deposits (usually $5). Always add the nine percent room tax to the price (ten percent downtown).

WEEKLY MOTELS

An affordable way to get your fill of Las Vegas is to take a motel room by the week. Most motels give sizable discounts for these rates; many con-

For a listing of motels in geographical sequence, starting downtown and heading north, see the "Las Vegas Motels" chart at the back of the book (under "Further Information").

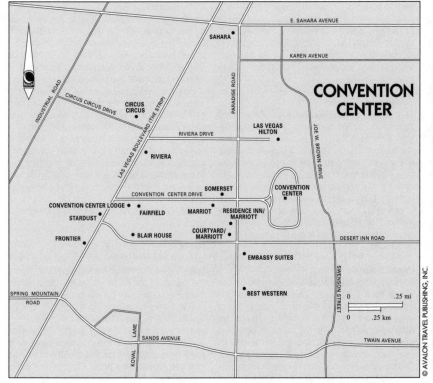

tain refrigerators or entire kitchenettes. This can save you a lot of money in both lodging and food costs, allowing you to spend it on other pleasures of the senses. The only challenge is *finding* one. Several factors conspire to make the search difficult. First, not all the motels have weeklies. And those that do often allot a limited number of their total rooms for the discounted rate. Second, every winter a flock of snowbirds migrates to Las Vegas, some of whom squat till it gets hot. It's not uncommon to hear in early December that the Desert Paradise Motel, for example, won't have a weekly room available till the Ides of March, or that Tod Motor Lodge is taking applications to be put on a waiting list, or that Hop's will be full forever. Third, with several hundred people moving to Las Vegas every week to start a new life, these newcomers often wind up monopolizing the few vacant weeklies.

Where there's life, though, there's hope (in fact, hope is quite a profitable product in this town). If you plan to eat all your meals in restaurants and don't need a refrigerator or stove, you can get weeklies for as low as $99, and you'll have a fairly easy time locating one. You can also bring your own hot plate and cooler (don't forget an extension cord or two) for your coffee, tea, hot cereal, and sandwiches. The more prepared you are the better—bring all the kitchen stuff you'll need: pots, plates, cups, silverware, spices, toaster oven, sponge, dish soap, can opener.

Once you land a room, there are several variables you'll need to hear about from the management. Be sure their week is as long as yours. Some Las Vegas motels have redefined "week" into six nights. It's true. Something having to do with Saturday night rates. The telephone situation can also be tricky. Some motels charge 25 cents for local calls; some have free local calls but don't offer long-distance; where available, long-distance might need to go through the front desk. Find out if the room is cleaned every day, or every week, or at all; sometimes linen is extra. Always look at the room first. Make sure the heat or air-conditioning works; it's never a bad idea to have a small space heater or fan just in case. Make sure the windows lock and there's at least a chain on the door; a deadbolt is even better. If there's a kitchenette, test the stove/oven, and see that the refrigerator is cold. You might have to take the room regardless of its flaws, but if you point them out to the front desk, you might be able to bargain down the price a little. Or another room might appear.

Use the "Las Vegas Weekly Motels" chart in the "Further Information" section (at back of book) to call around for availability and reservations. Most motels with weeklies operate on a first-come, first-served basis. In this case, ask about the price and amenities, and whether a weekly room is available *today*. Management doesn't really know if people are going to leave, except from day to day when it happens. Some, however, will hold a room for you. Another possibility is to take your chances and breeze into Las Vegas, grab a room for one night, then get on the phone the next day. Best time to call is around noon. In this case, it's wise to arrive on a weekday, when rooms are readily available and rates are 20–50% lower than on Friday or Saturday. With diligence and luck you'll find a weekly and wind up saving a substantial amount of dough by the weekend, which you can then blow in some other way.

Budget Suites, 702/732-1500, and **Holiday Royale,** 702/733-7676, are "mini-suites," with a sitting room, a bedroom, and a kitchen. They're a little more expensive than the run-of-the-mill weekly, but they're much more comfortable and spacious. Holiday Royale's rates run in the $150–250 range, while Budget Suites offers a weekly rate of $300–350. Fun City, (mentioned above in the "Upper Strip" section) offers week-

ly rooms in the $200 range. Most have a linen option, so be sure to ask about what you need to bring when you make your reservations. Also, most require deposits, of which a portion is non-refundable. So get all the financial details up front to avoid surprises or unpleasantness at the end of the week.

Other options. The convenience stores stock free apartment-advertising books in racks near the door; these have short-term and furnished listings that could be worth a look. Also look under the Executive Suites listings for completely furnished monthlies (expensive). For longer term, pick your location and review the apartment books. Most rental complexes have a variety of payment choices: month to month, six-month leases, etc. They can also help with renting furniture.

If you're staying at a hotel for an extended period of time (a week, or even just the typical three or four nights), you can always request, and almost always get, a mini-refrigerator delivered to your room at no extra charge. If you're asked for a reason, just say you're on a special diet (with a refrigerator in your room, you will be!). Cereal and milk in the morning is a breeze. The sandwiches at snack bars around town are big enough for two meals for a moderate eater, and you can usually take home something from dinner. A simple thing like a fridge in your hotel room will improve the quality of life measurably, by saving you time and money.

YOUTH HOSTEL

It's hard to beat this place for budget accommodations. The Las Vegas International Hostel has accommodations for 60 people in four-bed dorms and six private rooms reserved for couples. The hostel has a common kitchen and RV room; each dorm has its own bathroom with shower. Check in between 7 A.M. and 11 P.M. You get your own key and you can come and go as you please. A bed for the night is $12 with a membership card, $14 without; private rooms

Turn to the "Further Information" section (at back of book) for a chart of Las Vegas weekly motels. Most of these motels operate on a first-come, first-serve basis, so call and ask if a room is available *today*.

are $26 with, $28 without. Beds are usually available but it's not a bad idea to reserve. The hostel has a good location at 1208 Las Vegas Blvd. S, L.V., NV 89104, a bit north of Vegas World right on the bus line, 702/385-9955.

CAMPING AND RV PARKING

Camping

The nearest government tent campgrounds to Las Vegas are at Red Rock Canyon (20 miles west of Las Vegas; see "West of Las Vegas," below), Callville Bay on Lake Mead (around 20 miles east of Las Vegas; see "East of Las Vegas below), and up on Mt. Charleston (40 miles north of town; see "Northwest of Las Vegas below").

Casino RV Parking

Four casinos have attached RV parks: Circus Circus, Boomtown, Showboat, and Sam's Town. Other casinos allow RVs to park overnight in their parking lots, but have no facilities. Below are descriptions of both.

Circusland RV Park, 500 Circus Circus Drive, 702/734-0410 or 800/634-3450, is a prime spot for RVers, especially those with kids, who want to be right in the thick of things, but also want to take advantage of very good facilities. The big park is all paved, with a grassy island here and a shade tree there. The convenience store is open 24 hours. Ten minutes spent learning the Industrial Road back entrance will save hours of sitting in traffic on the Strip. The park has 370 spaces. All have full hookups (20-, 30-, and 50-amp receptacles); 280 are pull-throughs. Tents are not allowed. Accessible restrooms have flush toilets and hot showers; there's also a laundry, game room, fenced playground, heated swimming pool, children's pool, spa, and sauna, and groceries are available. The fee is $17–25 for two people.

Boomtown RV Park, 3333 Blue Diamond Rd., 702/263-7777 or 800/588-7711, opened in May 1994. It's the second largest RV park in Las Vegas, with 460 spaces, all with full hookups (20-, 30-, and 50-amp receptacles), of which 260 are pull-throughs. It's also the nicest in Las Vegas. The spaces are ample, providing room for two RVs where most other parks would squeeze four, maybe five. Each has a pine tree

and a verdant square of grass. There's also a two-acre grassy picnic area and two pools, one for adults and the other for children, complete with a play apparatus and fountains. There's also a rec room and groceries. Accessible restrooms have flush toilets and hot showers. To top it all off, this place is a bona fide Las Vegas-style bargain: the fee is $15–20 per vehicle (Good Sam discount available). Tents are not allowed. Maximum stay is 14 days. Reservations are recommended September through April.

Sam's Town has two RV parks, one on Boulder Hwy. south of the casino, the other on Nellis Blvd. east of the casino. The Boulder park is open year-round, the Nellis park is open September through May. **Sam's Town Boulder RV Park,** 5225 Boulder Highway, 702/456-7777 or 800/634-6371, is one small step above a parking lot, with little shade. But it's fairly roomy and is only a two-minute walk across the auto parking lot to the casino.

It has 291 spaces, all with full hookups (20-, 30-, and 50-amp receptacles), of which 93 are pull-throughs. Tents are not allowed. Accessible restrooms have flush toilets and hot showers; there's also a laundry, limited groceries, heated swimming pool, and spa. The maximum stay is 14 days. The fee is $14 for two people.

Sam's Town Nellis RV Park, 4040 S. Nellis Blvd., 702/456-7777 or 800/634-6371, has 207 spaces for motor homes, all with full hookups (20-, 30-, and 50-amp receptacles), of which 14 are pull-throughs. It's mostly a gravel parking lot with spacious sites, a heated pool, and a spa; the rec hall has a pool table and kitchen. This is the snowbird park, which closes down in the summer. The minimum stay to qualify for the snowbird rate ($335) is three months, the maximum stay is six months. Tents are not allowed. The fee is $16 for two people.

Non-Casino RV Parks

Twenty private RV parks are sprinkled throughout the city, but ten of them are for long-term stays and are a little rough for overnighters. The three best of the visitor RV parks are described below (in order of preference). These are a bit more expensive than the casino RV parks.

Las Vegas KOA, 4315 Boulder Highway, 702/451-5527, is a well-established RV park/campground, pleasantly rustic around the edges. The trees, oleander, and pool area are large and the sites aren't at all cramped. A little less than half the spaces are taken up by residential units, but the rest are reserved for transients. Tenters are welcome here, the closest place to downtown and the Strip to pitch a little A-frame or dome (60 tent spaces). Boulder Station is right up the street on the same side. A casino shuttle runs back and forth to the Strip. There are 180 spaces, most with full hookups (20-, 30-, and 50-amp receptacles), all pull-throughs. Accessible restrooms have flush toilets and hot showers; there are also a laundry, groceries, game room, playground, two heated swimming pools, wading pool, spa, and RV wash. The fees are $22 for tenters and $24–26 for two RVers.

Oasis RV Park is at 2711 W. Windmill, 702/258-9978 or 800/566-4707, directly across the interstate from Silverton. (Take the Blue Diamond exit, three miles south of Russell Road, and go east to Las Vegas Blvd. South. Turn right and drive one block to West Windmill, then turn right to the park.) Opened in January 1996, Oasis's 707 spaces make it the second largest in RV park in all of Nevada. All have full hookups (20-, 30-, and 50-amp receptacles); roughly 500 are pull-throughs. Five rows of towering date palms usher you from the park entrance to the cavernous clubhouse, 24,000 square feet of it. Each space is wide enough for a car and motor home, and comes with a picnic table and patio. The horticulture is plentiful, though it needs a few years to mature. Be sure to grab a map from the front desk; this is Nevada's easiest RV park to get lost in. Tents are allowed. Accessible restrooms have flush toilets and hot showers; there is also a laundry, grocery store, bar and lounge, arcade, exercise room, putting course, and heated swimming pool. Maximum stay is 30 days. The fee is $12–27 per vehicle.

Boulder Lakes RV Resort, 6201 Boulder Hwy., 702/435-1157, is a mile south of the corner of Tropicana Avenue and Boulder Highway. A long and winding road leads from the highway to this large residential park, of which a portion is reserved for overnighters. There are 417 total spaces here, 75 held for overnight motor homes, all with full hookups (20- and 30-amp receptacles). There are no pull-throughs. Tents are not allowed. Accessible restrooms have flush toilets and hot showers; there are also laundry facilities, limited groceries, rec hall, and 4 heated swimming pools. The fee is $18 for two people.

FOOD

Think of dining Las Vegas style and you're likely to conjure up free hot dogs, 99-cent shrimp cocktails, $1.99 breakfast specials, $3.99 lunch buffets, and $4.99 prime rib dinners. True, Las Vegas deserves its reputation for "meal deals"—good food at rock-bottom prices. But it also boasts enough gourmet, ethnic, trendy, themed, celebrity-chef, meat-and-potatoes, and hole-in-the-wall restaurants to delight the most sophisticated and discriminating tastes. From the snack bars at Binion's Horseshoe and the Westward Ho to the French restaurants at Bellagio and Paris, from the vast buffets at the Rio and Main Street Station to the nouvelle cuisine at Spago and Napa, Las Vegas is both a gourmand's hog heaven and a gourmet's kingdom come. Although the latest trend has been for signature chefs to bring their palate-pleasers to the new luxury resorts. Las Vegas is quickly accruing more sought-after dining establishments than any other U.S. city.

Most major hotels have a 24-hour coffee shop and a buffet, along with some combination of Italian, Japanese, Chinese, Mexican, steakhouse, and fast food. Non-casino restaurants around town are proliferating so fast (keeping pace with the population growth) that even such a leading light as Anthony Curtis, who publishes the *Las Vegas Advisor,* who has lived in Las Vegas for 20 years, and has eaten more restaurant meals here than anyone alive, can't keep up with them. Best of all, menu prices, like room rates, are consistently less expensive in Las Vegas than any other major city in the country.

Why? Because almost all Las Vegas hotel-casino food and beverage departments lose money. Food, like every other hotel amenity, is a loss leader for the casino, where the real profits are accrued. And the non-casino restaurants have to compete with the casino restaurants, so they're forced to hold the line on prices.

At first glance, you can easily believe that the casinos take a loss on their buffets, 99-cent breakfasts, $5 prime rib, $7 steaks, and $10 lobsters. But the prices in the gourmet and ethnic restaurants, and even the coffee shops, might surprise you if you've always heard that casino restaurant food is dirt cheap. How do casinos lose money on $15 chicken dinners, $12 Mexican meals, $10 spaghetti, and $6.95 bacon and eggs? Easy. They lose it on comps. At any given time in any casino restaurant, perhaps only 50–75% of the patrons in a restaurant are paying for their food. Oh sure, the comped customers risked their money at the tables and machines and probably spent way more than $10 for the spaghetti dinner they're scarfing in the coffee shop, but the gambling losses are the price of admission for the entertainment, and the free food is part of the bargain.

Of course, don't feel too sorry for the casinos that have to give away all that food to attract players. That's why the prices on the menus are so high. The casinos have it wired from every which way: by charging big-city prices, the comped customers feel they're getting their money's worth in food for the losses they've sustained; the paying customers help subsidize the comped customers; and the casino can write off comp expenses at retail, even though they're paying wholesale. Pretty slick, ay?

If you're comped meals to reward you for your casino action, by all means, teach 'em a lesson! Make 'em lose all the money you can in the food and beverage department. If you're not comped and you don't mind paying retail prices for your restaurant food, none of this should affect you. But if you're not comped and you're still looking to help the casinos lose money on food, the meal deals are your ticket.

MEAL DEALS

The *Las Vegas Advisor* is a 12-page newsletter that's come out every month for the past ten years or so. It takes an objective look at most Las Vegas consumer choices: gambling promotions, room rates, entertainment options, best values, and dining specials. The following are the perennial favorites culled from the past 50 or so issues.

99-Cent Shrimp Cocktail

The Golden Gate restaurant downtown began serving a San Francisco-style shrimp cocktail in 1955, and more than 30 million have been served since (that's roughly 4,000 tons of the crunchy little crustaceans). The price up until a few years ago was only 49 cents, but it's still a number-one value at 99 cents (served 24 hours a day at the Deli in real cocktail glasses with countless shrimpies and delicious cocktail sauce). In fact, it's the oldest meal deal in Las Vegas—appropriate for the oldest hotel in Las Vegas. It goes great with a draft beer ($1); a piano player serenades the Deli patrons. At the Deli, open 24 hours, 702/385-1906.

$1 Bacon and Eggs

Most places, you can't even get a cup of coffee for a dollar anymore. But at El Cortez, a dollar buys you two eggs, two strips of bacon, toast, hashbrowns *and* all the coffee you can drink. It's worth coming back for. Open 24 hours, 702/385-5200

$7.95 Porterhouse

This might be the best meal deal in Las Vegas. This giant 16-ounce slab of red meat is served 24 hours a day in the Monterrey coffee shop at the Gold Coast casino on W. Flamingo. It comes with salad, crisp potatoes, onion rings, baked beans, rolls, and a glass of draft beer (must be 21 or older). It's not advertised anywhere, not even on the Gold Coast marquee, so it's not particularly well known, but it is featured prominently on the coffee shop menu, so you don't have to ask the waitperson if it exists. Best of all, it's served 24 hours a day. Polish one off at 8 A.M., then go out and run a marathon. Open 24 hours, 702/367-7111.

$5.95 Steak and Shrimp

It's not on the menu, but if you ask for it at Mr. Lucky's coffee shop in the Hard Rock Hotel, they'll be happy to serve it to you. Twenty-four hours a day you can enjoy an eight-ounce steak, three grilled jumbo shrimp, salad, roll and a potato for less than six measly bucks. Open 24 hours, 702/693-5000.

$2.50 Bean Soup

The snack bars at the Horseshoe downtown serve some of the best and least expensive snack bar food anywhere. But the best value of the all the values is the bean soup of the day for $2.50. This is a hearty bowl, full of beans (split pea, black, red, etc.) and chunks of baked ham, accompanied by a big slab of cornbread. Open 24 hours, 702/382-1600.

Mini-food Cities

The Carnival World Buffet at the Rio launched the new wave of Las Vegas buffets in early 1993: little buffets within the big buffet, each "serving island" featuring a different ethnic preparation—in the Rio's case American, Italian, Chinese, Mexican, Mongolian barbecue, burger and fries, steaks cooked to order, fresh seafood and sushi, ribs, salads, and dessert. For the same $14 (dinner), you can get a plate of fried chicken and a drink in the coffee shop. Since then, a handful of casinos have jumped into the buffet fray, and you can now be wowed by the spreads at Fiesta and Texas Station (up on Rancho Blvd.), Main Street Station (downtown), and Sunset Station (in Henderson).

Free Drinks

The most common comp of them all (other, perhaps, than free parking) is free drinks to all players. Got a nickel? Sit at a slot machine and wait for the cocktail waitress to happen by. Don't wanna wait? Head over to Palace Station and get yourself a 16-ounce margarita for a mere 99 cents, or go to Slots A Fun for an imported beer in the bottle for 75 cents (popcorn is free at Slots A Fun, too).

CASINO RESTAURANTS

Buffets

In an article for the *L.A. Times* travel supplement, Anthony Curtis asks, "What is it about the Las Vegas buffet? Why is it that eating too much is the thing to do on a Las Vegas vacation?" He answers it incisively: "For 50 years Las Vegas has been synonymous with excessive gambling, drinking, 24-hour carousing, and of course eating. Yet while not every visitor is inclined to dive headlong into booze, blackjack, and all-nighters, culinary greed has never seemed tangled in formidable moral issues."

The Las Vegas buffet was inaugurated in the late 1940s, when the El Rancho Vegas put out a big spread between midnight and 4 A.M. to keep patrons in the casino after the late headliner show. A lavish feast, it cost $1, and it was called a "chuck wagon." The chuck wagon caught on and soon all the big casinos laid out major midnight smorgasbords. In the mid-1950s, weekend chuck wagon hours were extended to encompass breakfast, the forerunners of today's Saturday and Sunday champagne brunch. By the late 1960s, the chuck wagon was served at most of the major casinos for all three meals. It wasn't until the early '80s that chuck wagons became buffets. And today, Las Vegas is the buffet capital of the world.

Las Vegas buffets are one small step up from fast food in quality, one giant leap down in price, and in a class all their own worldwide in quantity. For the cost of satisfying a Big Mac attack, you can shovel home, on average, 23 choices of chow. Breakfast presents the usual fruits, juices, croissants, steam-table scrambled eggs, sausage, potatoes, and pastries. Lunch is salads and cold cuts. Dinner is salads, steam-table mook, vegetables, and potatoes, and usually either a baron of beef, shoulder of pork, leg of lamb, saddle of mutton, breast of turkey, whole rotisserie chicken, or barbecued ribs.

Prices are standard, with a few extremes at either end: breakfast $5–10 ($5.49 at Circus Circus, $11 at Aladdin); lunch $7–12 ($10 at the Mirage); dinner $8–15 ($8 at Circus, $12 at Treasure Island). Quality has less to do with price than you might imagine. If you're really starving and must have food *now,* go to the nearest buffet and load up. You can also buffet shop, simply by walking in and sneaking a peek. Otherwise, plan ahead and try to be at the right place at the right time. And those with young children, don't forget. The buffet is your best friend in Las Vegas (see "Food" in the Out and About section in the front of this book).

Buffet times and prices are quite changeable, so it's wise to check the buffet listings in the free visitors guides or the Weekend section of Friday's *Review-Journal.* Generally, breakfast is served 7–10 A.M., lunch goes 11 A.M.–3 P.M., and dinner 4–10 P.M., give or take a half hour.

The best buffet in Las Vegas is, without a doubt, the **Village Seafood Buffet** at the Rio. Traditionally, seafood buffets were dished up one night a week, always Friday. But a few years ago, seafood night began to change. Monday at one buffet, Wednesday at another, Thursday, Saturday—you needed a photographic memory to hit the right joint on the right night. But then the Rio opened Old Reliable: in its own room. Here, you have an incredible choice of seafood preparations. The Mongolian barbecue grills up whitefish, scallops, shrimp, mussels, and calamari with assorted vegetables and sauces. At the American station you can load up on seafood salads, snow crab legs, oysters on the half shell, peel-and-eat shrimp and, for example, seafood gumbo, grilled salmon, blackened scallone, broiled swordfish, oysters Rockefeller, poached roughy, steamed clams, and lobster tails. Then come the ethnic ocean entrees, such as seafood fajitas, squid chow fun, kung pao scallops, cioppino, and seafood canneloni. The Village Buffet also has the best selection of the highest-quality after-dinner goodies in town. The pies come in chocolate cream, coconut cream, coconut pineapple, lemon meringue, key lime, apple, blueberry, pecan, cherry, peach, and more; there's also assorted pound cakes, cheesecakes, pastries, tortes, mousses, chocolate decadence, and cookies. It's expensive at $26.95 for dinner, but it's worth it. 702/252-7777.

As for the best regular buffet, a lot of people still vote for the Carnival World at the **Rio,** the original big buffet. Carnivores swear by the Festival Buffet at the **Fiesta,** which features a Mongolian barbecue and one of the largest open-pit barbecues in the west; if you can grill it, you'll find it at the Fiesta (702/631-7000). The Market Street Buffet at **Texas Station** is a perennial favorite; it has a Texas chili bar with a dozen different concoctions, along with cooked-to-order fajitas, pizza, and wokked Oriental (702/631-1000). Probably the most attractive is the Garden Court at **Main Street Station;** the quality here seems superior to the others as well (702/387-1896).

Other interesting buffets are found at the **Orleans,** which features good Cajun and Creole dishes (702/365-7111); **Las Vegas Hilton,** where you can get all the cold king crab legs

you can eat (702/732-5111); **Treasure Island,** for peel-and-eat shrimp (702/894-7111); and **Golden Nugget,** where the bread pudding is world renowned (702/385-7111).

Breakfast

The 24-hour 99-cent bacon-and-eggs breakfast, once a southern Nevada staple, is now extinct. Typically, the **Horseshoe** has a great breakfast: a big slice of ham steak, two eggs, potatoes, and coffee served 4 A.M.–2 P.M. for $4.50.

As for steak and eggs, the best one is available 24 hours a day at **Arizona Charlie's** in the Sourdough Cafe: a six-ounce sirloin for $2.49. Another good 24-hour steak and eggs is found at the **San Remo** next to the Tropicana on East Tropicana for $5.95.

Steak Specials

Just about every casino coffee shop in town serves a steak or prime rib special for somewhere between $4.95 and $7.95. Just read the large print on the hotel marquees and billboards around town. Or look at the ads in the visitors guides. Some specials aren't advertised at all and aren't even listed on the menus, so you'll have to ask about them. Again, as with the buffets, if you're hungry and near a coffee shop and want a slab, check out the special. But if you want to put in a little effort, have a great meal, and take home a story about it, head straight for Ellis Island's $2.95 sirloin or the **Gold Coasts** porterhouse (see "Meal Deals," above.) go to the Hilton. The **San Remo** and **Lady Luck** have good prime ribs; the Pasta Pirate at the **California** downtown has a great $9.95 filet mignon, while the Redwood Grill there has an excellent porterhouse for $12.95.

Panorama and Pageantry

Top of the World: The 360-seat 360-degree restaurant, on the 106th floor of Stratosphere Tower over 800 feet above the Strip, makes a complete revolution once every 75 minutes or so. The view of Vegas defies description, and the food is a recommendable complement. Try the charbroiled portebella mushrooms, pan-seared peppersteak, or lobster linguine, and be sure to save room for Chocolate Stratosphere, which is nearly as tall as the tower. Entrees average $28. Open Sunday–Thursday 6–11 P.M., midnight Friday and Saturday, 702/380-7777.

In the running for "Best View," Paris' **Eiffel Tower Restaurant** hovers 100 feet above the Strip. The bilingual culinary staff masters delicate French culinary feats, while a romantic piano bars rounds out the Parisian experience. Located on the 11th floor of the Eiffel Tower, 702/739-4111.

Voodoo Cafe: It's a mini thrill ride to the top of the newest Rio tower on the glass elevator. The Rio contends that the restaurant is on the 51st floor and the lounge is on the 52nd floor, even though they're really on the 42nd and 41st floors, respectively; Rio management dropped floors 40–49—something having to do with an Oriental superstition. Whatever the hell floor they're on, the Voodoo double-decker provided the greatest view of the Strip extant: lower, closer, and more central than the Stratosphere's. The food and drink are expensive and a bit tame, but the fun is in the overlook, especially if you eat or drink outside on the decks. Open for lunch and dinner, 702/252-7777.

Ranch Steakhouse: Another glass elevator delivers you to the top of the Horseshoe tower downtown; they say it's the 24th floor and it is. Before Stratosphere opened, this was the best view in Las Vegas, and it's still fine. Steaks are the play here—filet, porterhouse, N.Y.—and the prime rib is as thick as a Michener novel (a little on the fatty side, in my experience—both the meat and the Michener). Most of the people up here are comped. Entrees average $16–22. Open 5–11 P.M., 702/382-1600.

Benihana: This spectacle of a restaurant, at Las Vegas Hilton, consists of a cocktail lounge out front, with musical waters, a Las Vegas tradition, and an animated bird show with stuffed-animal entertainers, reminiscent of Chuck E. Cheese. Hibachi tableside and *robata* barbecue rooms feature similar menus, with dinners $15–35, mostly meat, fish, and veggies. For just the show, though, sit in the lounge

and sip some steaming *sake* (performances on the hour starting at 5:30 P.M.). Open 5:30–10:30 P.M., 702/732-5755.

Centerstage: This restaurant is a combination steakhouse and coffee shop, a very effective concept for its location. Without a doubt the room with the best neon view in town, the Centerstage sits in a tinted dome looking straight down Glitter Gulch, with the lighted Plaza Hotel tower soaring above. When you make reservations, specify seating at a front-window table. Open 5 P.M.–midnight, 702/386-2512.

Ristorante Italiano: This room at the Riviera is known for its wall-length mural behind glass and its veal: osso buco, saltimbocca, piccata, and scaloppine ($18–20). Pasta $11–12, chicken $15–16, steaks $25, lobster $35. Open Fri.–Tues. 5:30–11 P.M., 702/794-9363.

Kokomo's. This Continental restaurant sits under hut-like canopies within the rain forest of the Mirage's domed atrium. It's slightly noisy from the casino and the waterfalls, but the hubbub quickly becomes part of the unusual atmosphere. Try the Dungeness crab cakes ($16), salmon ($18), filet mignon ($16–22), prime rib ($18–28), or lobster tail ($34). Open 11 A.M.–2:30 P.M., 5:30–11 P.M., 702/791-7111.

Next door to Kokomo's is **Moongate,** which replicates a Chinese village square, with a big lilac tree in the middle, pagoda roofs, scalloped walls, and great curves. The food is as pleasing as the environment, and the prices are reasonable. Satay beef, mu shu pork, tea-smoked duck, and strawberry chicken all go for $14, and scallops, shrimp, and lobster are under $20. Open 5:30–11 P.M., 702/791-7111.

All the world's a stage, or rather a movie set, at Warner Brother's **Stage 16** restaurant in The Venetian's Grand Canal Shoppes. Diners may choose to enjoy execute chef Todd Sicolo's vanilla-seared shrimp or lobster strudel in one of several recreations of their favorite movies—ranging from

BOB RACE

Batman's Gotham City to Rick's American Café in Casablanca. After dinner drinks are meant to be enjoyed in the retro-stylish Velvet Lounge. Open daily 11 A.M.–1 A.M., 702/414-1699.

Pound on the table with your goblet while you eat medieval-style (i.e., without utensils) and cheer for the jousting knights on horseback at Excalibur's **Tournament of Kings**. Shown twice nightly at 6 P.M. and 8:30 P.M., $37 buys you a Cornish game hen, all you can drink soft drinks, and the chance to hiss at fire-breathing dragons and listen to Merlin recount a somewhat modified legend of King Arthur. While a bit hokey, the horsemanship is impressive, and kids will love the noise and excitement: a definite family winner.

Caesar's version of the dinner show is the 3-hour spectacle **Caesars Magical Empire.** Enter into one of the chambers of the gods, where a wizard is your entertaining host during the three-course meal. The food is decent and the wine is plentiful at this $76 per person affair. Illusionists, invisible piano players, and ghosts are the highlights of the evening and after dinner you may explore the Spirit Bar and enjoy more magic shows. A more intimate, gourmet experience may be had by making reservations (702/731-7436) in the Séance room where the dinner show ranges from $125–200 per person. It ain't a deal, but it is worth it for the experience and the story, especially in a group. Open nightly 4:30–9:30 P.M., 702/731-7333.

Gourmet Rooms

While 5 years ago, there were only two four-star/diamond restaurants in Las Vegas, this category is quickly proliferating. Bellagio alone boasts seven James Beard award–winning chefs: **Picasso** is among only 18 restaurants in North America to win the Mobil Five-Star Award. Under the tutelage of chef Julian Serrano, the kitchen dishes up amazing twists on Mediterranean French cuisine. Pablo's artwork fittingly graces the walls and Pablo's son designed the carpet and furniture for the rustically sumptuous restaurant. Open Thursday–Tuesday 6–9:30 P.M., 702/693-7111.

When Las Vegas' first five–star dining establishment closed, the Desert Inn's Monte Carlo room, maitre d' David Orvin sought out a second home where he could take his passion for leg-endary service to a new level. And he feels right at home in the Luxor's **Isis**. Egyptian artifacts, intimate booths and a ceiling landscape of desert stars set the stage for chef Bradley Aug's classically traditional fare with an emphasis on fresh seafood. Open Thursday–Monday 5:30–11 P.M., 702/262-4773.

Mandalay Bay's **Aureole** is as remarkable for its architecture and catwalk-entry as for chef Charlie Palmer's seasonally inspired American cuisine. The Zagat guide decried that Palmer's NYC restaurant featured the best American food in the country—all the more reason to bring it to Vegas. Sweet tooths' will want to save room for the warm chocolate peanut butter liquid-center torte, with caramel-pecan ice-cream and peanut brittle, one of Aureole's signature decadent desserts. The four-story wine cellar is a sight to behold, and the wine selection covers virtually every continent on the globe. If what you want isn't in reach, a black-garbed acrobat with climbing gear will scale the tower to find the appropriate bottle. Open nightly 6–11:30 P.M., 702/632-7401.

Downtown, **Hugo's Cellar** at the Four Queens is perhaps the best gourmet room for the money. The cellar location, though right off the casino, is well insulated from the upstairs hubbub; all the ladies receive a red rose upon entering. The salad is brought around on a cart and prepared tableside, sherbet cones are served between courses. The house appetizer is the Hot Rock, which you have to see to believe. Entrees are $20–30—try the duck, snapper, or tournedos. Open 5:30–11 P.M., 702/385-4011.

Many Las Vegas veterans consider **Michael's,** a dark little room at the Barbary Coast, to be the best restaurant in Las Vegas. The entrees are $30–70 and strictly a la carte; a party of two will run up a $200 tab without trying. But the intimate surroundings, the quality of the food, and the *show* put on by the wait staff is more than worth it. This restaurant is not advertised anywhere and is run almost exclusively for the high rollers at the Barbary and Gold coasts, but reservations are taken starting at 3:30 P.M. when the count of comped customers has been taken. Open 6–11 P.M., 702/737-7111.

Other gourmet rooms of note include **Gatsby's** at MGM Grand, **Napa** at the Rio, **Seasons** at Bally's, **Postrio's** at the Venetian, and **Le Cirque** at Bellagio.

Steakhouses

Perhaps the essence of the Las Vegas steakhouse can be experienced at Circus Circus's aptly named **THE Steakhouse.** Wind your way through the permanent crowds of grinds and kids toward the buffet and tower elevators; cow portraits lead to the meat locker where sides of beef hang. The split-level dining area surrounds the grill, which lends an authentic, slightly smoky air to the room. Chicken for $12, top sirloin for $15, filet $20, surf and turf $20. Open 5:30–11 P.M., 702/794-3767.

Similarly, the large mesquite grill and line area of the **All-American Bar and Grille** at the Rio Hotel faces the downstairs dining room; upstairs are additional tables, along with a quite unusual collection of antique slot machines. Order your meat—top sirloin for $14, N.Y. for $18, filet for $19—and then choose your sauce: béarnaise, dijon, peppercorn, mushroom, horseradish. The prime rib could be the largest cut you've ever seen—you won't be able to finish it, and you'll need a trailer to carry the thing out. Open 11 A.M.–11 P.M., 702/252-7777.

Gallagher's Steakhouse at New York–New York has been an institution in New York City since 1927, and is considered NYC's oldest steak house. You'll understand the reputation after sampling their famed dry–aged beef, as well as their notable seafood selection. Open nightly 4–11 P.M., 702/740-6450.

The Ranch Steakhouse at the Horseshoe is covered above under "Pageantry and Panorama"; **Redwood Bar and Grille** is covered above under "Steak Specials." **William B's** at the Stardust has a good reputation with the locals. **Billy Bob's** at Sam's Town has excellent meat, along with some less expensive specials; big food at Billy Bob's. Also try **Embers** at the Imperial Palace and the **Broiler** restaurants at Palace and Boulder Stations.

Seafood

For variety and quantity in food fish, head straight for the Village Seafood Buffet at the Rio (see above under "Buffets").

Emeril's New Orleans Fish House: Bring your credit cards to Emeril's, in the MGM Grand, because this place is expensive and worth every dollar. The menu changes when award-winning celebrity-chef Emeril Lagasse feels like it, but appetizers have included smoked trout wontons, ragout of duck pastrami, sushi with softshell crab roll and salmon tartar, and spiced artichoke stuffed with assorted boiled shellfish (all in the $8–14 range). The lobster comes in cheesecake, a dome (covered with baked puff pastry), sauce, Creole gazpacho, and a "study" (variations on the theme). There's also Louisiana softshell crab with crawfish jambalaya, oyster stew with Andouille sausage, salmon tartar, tuna steak with fresh foie gras, potato-crusted Gulf pompano with lump crabmeat, along with Louisiana campfire steak and Mississippi chicken (entrees average $26 or so). Did someone say dessert? How about praline cheesecake, peanut butter-chocolate pie, bread pudding with whiskey sauce, or the house special banana cream pie with banana crust (averaging $10)? You've probably gotten the idea that Emeril's is exotic—especially for Las Vegas. Open 11 A.M.–3 P.M., 5:30–10:30 P.M., 702/891-7777.

The Bellagio brings San Francisco's renowned seafood haven, **Aqua,** to Las Vegas with flair. To celebrate the opening, two paintings were commissioned by Robert Rauschenberg and everything about the restaurants speaks to great taste: both literal and figurative. Chef Mark Lo Russo adds an amazing, if rather expensive ($70 for a five-course menu), French influence to traditional seafood cuisine. The restaurant is found off the botanical conservatory near the lobby, 702/693-7223.

Buzio's: The Rio, with 13 restaurants, is known for both its variety and quality of food offerings, and Buzio's is its seafood showcase (unlike the seafood buffet, which is its seafood pig-out). First, it's a beautiful room that overlooks the pool area and has a seaworthy canvas ceiling; there's also an oyster bar for informal counter seating and quicker service. Secondly, the fish: fresh oysters, lobster, clams, and catch of the day from all over the world; pan roasts, stews, cioppino, and bouillabaisse; salads and louies and cocktails; all served with bread fresh baked on the premises and soup or salad. This place gets hectic, so make reservations and arrive early. Open 11 A.M.–11 P.M., 702/252-7697.

Second Street Grill: "American contemporary with a Pacific Rim flair" is how the Grill describes its food, and its menu is a successful combination of international influences. You can get steaks, chops, and veal (there's a $10.95 porterhouse that's a bargain), but the play here is the denizens of the deep: Mongolian seafood pot, ahi sashimi, Maryland crab cakes, seared sea scallops to start; then wok-charred salmon with king crab hash, pound-and-a-half of king crab legs in a ginger-lime sauce (skip the sauce), and the usual Chilean sea bass, swordfish steak, etc. The Grill is a sleeper of a downtown restaurant and you can almost always get a table even on a busy night without a reservation. The *Las Vegas Advisor* coupon book has a 50% off coupon for the whole meal. Open Thurs.–Mon. 5–10 P.M., Friday and Saturday till 11 P.M.

Delis and Food Courts

Stage Deli: For a little slice of New York, stop in at the Stage Deli in your wanderings around the Forum Shops at Caesars, which serves specialty meats and desserts flown in from the Big Apple daily. Allow a few minutes to choose from the more than 300 menu items, such as brisket, stuffed cabbage, knishes, kishka, potato pancakes, chicken soup with matzoh balls, "skyscraper" sandwiches (literally 10–12 layers) named after celebrites, and egg creams. You'll spend $7–12 for entrees. There's also a Stage Deli fast food counter at the MGM Grand next to the race and sports book. Open daily 7:30 A.M.–11 P.M., 702/893-4045.

DIVE!: Hollywood meets Vegas at this upscale sub shop, designed and owned by director Steven Spielberg. Special effects include portholes, working periscopes, depth charges, and a simulated submerging sequence complete with a wall of water. Twenty subs (of the sandwich variety) are accompanied by fries in wrought-iron holders with dipping sauces; DIVE! also serves pizza, pasta, pot pies, huge salads, rich desserts, and fancy drinks. This place is great for kids and large groups. Entrees average $12. Open 11:30 A.M.–10 P.M., Friday and Saturday till 11, 702/369-3483.

La Piazza: La Piazza is to fast-food courts what Caesars is to casinos, which is fitting, since it the fast-food court at Caesars. You can get deli, Mexican, Chinese, pizza and Italian, burgers, beer and wine here; there's also a salad bar where you pay by the plate. The dining area overlooks the casino. Open daily 8:30 A.M.–11 P.M., 702/731-7731.

Other casino fast-food courts are found at the Riviera, O'Shea's, MGM Grand, New York-New York, and Monte Carlo.

Other casino delis are found at Luxor, Flamingo Hilton, and the Horseshoe.

Italian

One of the best hotel restaurants in Las Vegas is **Pasta Pirate** at the California Hotel downtown. The dinner salad comes with baby shrimp ($3) and the filet mignon, with a baker, veggies, garlic bread, and glass of wine, is only $9.95. Designer pasta is an alternative: first "you picka you pasta, then you picka you sauca," as the menu instructs. Huge kids' plates of spaghetti are under $5. The grill is out front, and those cooks move. The decor is early rustic—vents, pipes, shelves—plus neon. Open 5:30–11:30 P.M., 702/385-1222.

Pasta Pirate at the California is not to be confused with **Pasta Palace** at Palace Station on W. Sahara. The Pasta Palace frequently has a pizza and beer special, and the pasta dishes are all less than $10. For example, try the ravioli fra diavolo ($9.95); you'll be hard pressed to finish it. Open 4:30–11 P.M., 702/367-2411.

Alta Villa at the Flamingo Hilton is a little more expensive than the eateries above, but less than the ones below. The stone floor and ivied trellis set the mood. The play here is the appetizers: delicious minestrone ladled from a big kettle in the dining room, good salads, risottos to die for, and filling eggplant Florentine. With a glass of house burgundy, you should be full enough to skip the forgettable entrees. Open 5:30–11 P.M., 702/733-3111.

For expensive Italian casino restaurants, try **Ristorante Italiano** at the Riviera (covered above under "Pageantry and Panorama"). Another excellent place to head would be **Tre Visi** and **La Scala** at the MGM Grand. Tre Visi offers "patio dining" adjacent to the public corridor through restaurant row that leads to the arcade and the amusement park, along with a dining room in back. Tre Visi's menu changes frequently; get your pizza and sandwiches (as well as a traditional breakfast) on the patio. Entrees average $13 at Tre Visi. La Scala is the fancy dining room off the side, where the entrees average $28. Tre Visi is open 9–1 A.M., 702/891-7220; La Scala is open 5:30–11 P.M., 702/891-7393.

Andiamo's at the Las Vegas Hilton, **Trattoria del Lupo** at Mandalay Bay, **Osteria del Circo** at Bellagio, **Bice** at Desert Passage, **Stefano's** at the Golden Nugget, **al Dente** at Bally's, and **Antonio's** at the Rio round out the choices for expensive Italian casino restuarants.

Asian

Empress Court at Caesars Palace is the fanciest, most exotic, and most expensive Chinese restaurant you'll ever eat in. Try the bird's nest (not a soup), $13–19 depending on side dishes, or the shark fin (also not a soup), $16–24, also depending on what goes along. Open Thurs.-Mon. 6–11 P.M., 702/731-7731.

Moongate at The Mirage is in a beautiful setting: footbridge over a brook, tranquil courtyard in front, and a rounded entry. Here, the shark's fin is in a soup ($30); the rest of the menu is the usual kung pao, mu shu, Peking duck, and nutty chicken. Next door is the equally elegant and expensive **Mikado**. Open 5:30–11:30 P.M., 702/791-7111.

Voted one of the Zagat guide's favorite restaurants in Vegas, **China Grill** is another one of Mandalay Bay's architecturally arresting designer restaurants. Signature specialties include lamb ribs and exotic twists on traditional Chinese favorites. Open nightly 5:30–11 P.M., 702/632-7404. After hours, usually around 1 A.M., the lights go down and the deep house starts pumping, when China Grill transforms itself nightly into the **Red Dragon Lounge**. More traditional, expensive, and classic is China Grill's next-door neighbor, **Shanghai Lilly**. Here Cantonese and Szechwan creations reign supreme and the décor is understated and elegant. Open nightly 5:30–11 P.M., 702/632-7409.

Benihana at the Las Vegas Hilton is covered above under "Pageantry and Panorama."

NON-CASINO RESTAURANTS

Las Vegas's Oldest Restaurants

Green Shack: The oldest continuously operating restaurant in Las Vegas closed its doors to the public in 1999, to the regret of many locals and is worth mentioning for its historic value alone. The Green Shack opened as the Colorado in 1929, when Jimmie Jones sold fried chicken from her two-room house. In 1932, she bought a barracks from Union Pacific, hauled it to her house, and called it the Green Shack. This barracks is still the dining room, having hosted chicken dinners, birthdays, anniversaries, weddings, divorces, wakes, and hearty parties for more than 65 years—ancient history for Las Vegas. The bar and kitchen have since been added, but the Shack was run by Jimmie Jones's great-nephew until the bitter end.

Fong's: In 1933, J.S. Fong opened the Silver Cafe at 106 N. 1st St. next to the Silver Club. He advertised American food, with 25-cent breakfasts and 35-cent dinners, and was the only Las Vegas cafe serving Chinese food, by request, till 1941. In 1955, the Silver Cafe changed its name to Fong's when it relocated to the present site on East Charleston. You can't miss it: big neon pagoda-roof signs grace the entrance. Inside are mandarin-size red booths, large paintings, and a rock shrine, along with the same American and Chinese food this family has been dishing up for decades. Open Tues.–Sun.11:30 A.M.–11 P.M., at 2021 E. Charleston, 702/382-1644.

El Sombrero: This adobe restaurant has been in the same location since 1951, when it was opened by Clemente Greigo; his nephews José and Zeke Aragon are now in charge. The best thing about El Sombrero is that this stucco cantina, with six booths, six tables, and a completely Mexican jukebox, looks its age and has certainly seen it all, but retains its baby-boomer vitality and devotion to service and quality. Small dinners are $5, combo dinners are $6.45, and the service is no-nonsense! Open 11 A.M.–10 P.M., Sunday 3–10 P.M., at 807 S. Main, 702/382-9234.

The Venetian: Not to be confused with the palatial new casino, this restaurant began as the Pizzeria Restaurant, down the block from the Green Shack, in 1955, one of the first pizzerias in Las Vegas. It moved to its present site in 1966 and changed its name to the Venetian Pizzeria; the Pizzeria was eventually dropped, though the pizza is still served in the bar or with a dinner. The Venetian is very popular, always full of locals, wins awards, and has interesting interior and exterior murals of Venice and authentic Italian hospitality. Spaghetti dinners are $15, chicken $20, veal

$25, fish $25, with five pages of wine on the menu. Open 24 hours, at 3713 W. Sahara, 702/876-4190.

Golden Steer: You wouldn't recognize it from the unremarkable exterior, but this steakhouse, in the same location since 1962, is one of the most popular and elegant restaurants in Las Vegas, usually jammed with locals and visitors in the know. In the front room is the spectacular woody, glassy bar surrounded by comfy living room furniture. The three dining rooms are no less inviting. And the food? Well, the filet mignon is truly the Aristocrat of Tenderness, and the N.Y. pepper steak is the best in town. Dinners start at $17. Reservations a must at prime time. Open 4:30–11:30 P.M., at 308 W. Sahara, 702/384-4470.

Breakfast

Poppa Gar's: "Poppa" Garland Miner goes about as far back as anybody in the Las Vegas restaurant business—50 years! He started out at the Round-Up Drive-In on the Strip in the early 1940s, then took over the food service at the El Cortez in 1945. After a few years he moved up Fremont St. to Bob Baskin's, where he and Bob put out the victuals till 1965, when he moved to his present location. The walls are covered with historical and personal photographs. Open Mon–Fri. 5 A.M.–9 P.M., Sat. 5 A.M.–2 P.M., 1624 W. Oakey, 702/384-4513.

Coffee Pub: This is the power breakfast joint on the west side, with an ambience and menu that you might expect to see more at a ski resort or a mountain retreat than the Las Vegas flatlands. Big hearty breakfasts are served indoors or outside on a patio with spray misters. Open 7 A.M.–6 P.M., 2800 W. Sahara, 702/367-1913.

Bagelmania: Thanks to snowbelt sunbirds (and the Jewish Mafia), Las Vegas is a great town for bagels, lox, matzo brie, and designer cream cheese. This is one of the best. Open 6:30 A.M.–5 P.M., Sunday till 3, at 855 E. Twain, 702/369-3322.

Bagels N' More: Jewish deli with the best homemade corned-beef hash this side of the Hudson River, and fancy-schmancy omelettes.

Jamie's: Classic diner with great food and cheap prices. Open Mon–Fri. 7 A.M.–8 P.M., Saturday 7 A.M.–6 P.M., Sunday 7 A.M.–4 P.M., at 2405 E. Tropicana, 702/435-8100.

Brazilian

Yolie's Steakhouse: The only place in Nevada to get marinated meat, mesquite-broiled, *rodízio*-style—sliced continuously from the skewer onto your plate by the waiter in the fashion of a true *churrascaria* (Brazilian house of meat). Sausage, turkey, brisket, lamb, pork, along with salad, soup, and sides, come for a set price of $28.95. The room is soft and inviting, the bar is big and comfortable, and the service attentive. Recommended. Open Mon–Fri. 11 A.M.–3 P.M., daily 5:30–11 P.M., at 3900 Paradise, 702/794-0700.

Chinese

Chin's has garnered both "the highest acclaim" and the "best Chinese restaurant in the city" from two impeccable sources. Eggrolls are $5, other appetizers up to $14, vegetable plate $8, and chicken, seafood, pork, and beef dishes start at $15. Open 11 A.M.–9:30 P.M., at the Fashion Show Mall, 702/733-8899.

Golden Wok: Many local Chinese frequent the Golden Wok. It has a typically varied menu, with spicy Szechwan dishes and fresh Cantonese-style vegetables, $7–12. Lunch buffet for $6. Open noon–9:30 P.M., at 4670 S. Eastern, 702/456-1868.

Bamboo Gardens: Don't let the humble setting in a storefront in a Flamingo Avenue strip mall deter you: this little hole-in-the-wall has some of the most original Oriental preparations anywhere. The clams dou chi are out of this world; also try the Mongolian lamb, firecracker beef, and Hunan eggplant. The Szechuan string beans over steamed rice is a meal in itself. Open 11 A.M.–10:30 P.M., Sunday 5–10 P.M., 4850 W. Flamingo, 702/871-3262.

Cathay House: Sitting right on the edge of the bluff out Spring Mountain Avenue overlooking the Strip, Cathay House has the view and the food to go with it. This is *the* spot for a dim sum lunch (if you're not an dim sum expert, you'll take your chances; you won't get any help from the help). Dinner dishes include orange beef, cashew scallops, garlic chicken, crystal shrimp, shark's fin soup, and Szechuan pork. Open 11 A.M.–11 P.M., 5300 W. Spring Mountain, 702/876-3838.

Continental/French

Pamplemousse: The name is French for "grapefruit," but it might as well mean "ultimate."

The French cuisine is so fresh that the menu is spoken, not printed: your waiter describes the nightly fare in detail (be sure to ask about prices to avoid suprises). Specialties include bay scallops sauteed in grapefruit roux, medallions of veal with baked apple, rack of lamb, and filet mignon. The small house, converted into a country inn, only seats 70, so reserve as far in advance as possible. Entrees average $21. Open 6–10 P.M., at 400 E. Sahara, 702/733-2066.

Andres: This award-winning French restaurant is downtown in a strange neighborhood, but once you're inside the converted house, you'll forget all about the outside world. Plan on a couple of hours and a couple hundred dollars to enjoy a full meal at chef Andre Rochat's joint, including a bottle from the extensive wine list. Goes good with salmon tartar with cucumber salad, macadamia-crusted sea scallops, sauteed duck, rabbit loin, and the like. The vegetable-medley accompaniment is always excellent, and the fruit tarts for dessert are recommended. Entrees average $30. Open 6–10 P.M., at 401 S. Sixth, 702/385-5016.

Renata's: You wouldn't expect to find a fine Continental dining room attached to a bowling alley in Green Valley, but in Las Vegas nothing is as it seems. It's worth the effort to find this place, which serves imaginative combinations of food, such as salmon with lentil salsa, prawn salad, chicken in a tequila cream, even meat loaf with mashed potatoes. Also, Renata's isn't as expensive as the other fancy rooms, with entrees in the $17–22 range. Open Mon.–Sat. 5–11 P.M., at 4451 E. Sunset, Henderson, 702/435-4000.

Italian

Battista's Hole In The Wall: Family-style meals (antipasto, garlic bread, minestrone, all-you-can-eat pasta on the side, and all-you-can-drink red wine) start at $10.95 for spaghetti and meatballs and go all the way up to $30 for cioppino. Classic Italian restaurant decor. Walking distance of the Strip next to the Barbary Coast near the corner of Flamingo Avenue. Open 4:30–11 P.M., at 4041 Audrie, 702/732-1424.

Carluccio's: This is Liberace's old restaurant, and the decor (glittery ceiling, bar designed like a grand piano) remains to prove it. The food is workman-like Italian, with the usual pasta in red or clam sauce, eggplant parmesan, chicken, veal, and beef plates. Try the crab-stuffed shrimp. Workman-like prices too: two can escape for under $20. Open Tues.-Sun. 4:30–10 P.M., at 1775 E. Tropicana, 702/795-3236.

North Beach Cafe: This place gets some buzz from the locals, for its great service and light Italian fare. Try the linguine with your choice of shellfish or chicken cognac. The swordfish preparation is also recommendable. Entrees run in the $10–18 range. Open 5–11 P.M., at 2605 S. Decatur, 702/247-9530.

Bootlegger: Cozy, family-run for a long time, great service, reasonable, and tasty food; try the pizzas, calzone, veal saltimbocca. There's also a variety of vegetarian and low-calorie selections. Lunches are $4–7, dinners $9–17. Bootlegger also has a call-in joke line at 702/736-8661. Open Tues.-Sat. 11 A.M.–10 P.M., Sunday 4–10 P.M., 5025 S. Eastern, 702/736-4939.

Japanese

Ginza: This Japanese restaurant is always occupied by at least several tourists from Tokyo. Ten a la carte dishes, in true Japanese style, will run $40. Open 5:30 P.M.–1 A.M., at 1000 E. Sahara, 702/732-3080.

Osaka: A close second to the Ginza. Open Mon.–Fri.11:30 A.M.–3 P.M., daily 5 P.M.–midnight, at 4205 W. Sahara, 702/876-4988.

Tokyo: At the yearly Consumer Electronics Show, the Japanese exhibitors were lined up out the door and down the block, waiting to get in here to eat. Open Mon.–Fri. 11:30 A.M.–2:30 P.M., daily 5 P.M.–1.A.M., at 953 E. Sahara, 702/735-7070.

Mexican

Ricardo's has a well-deserved reputation for the best (and most) Mexican food in Las Vegas. A single tamale a la carte ($4.95) will fill you up, and a seafood enchilada ($10) is good for at least two-and-a-half meals. Open 11 A.M.–11 P.M., Sunday open at noon, at 4930 W. Flamingo, 702/871-7119.

Doña Maria's is much lower-key than Ricardo's, with just as good and inexpensive food. The tamale with green enchilada sauce ($3) is a lip-smacker. This restaurant moved into a new building at the corner of Charleston and Las Vegas Blvd. S in late 1990—much bigger, brighter, more colorful, and higher prices to go along. But still fine. Open 8 A.M.–midnight, at

910 Las Vegas Blvd. S., 702/382-6538.

Viva Mercado's: A perennial local favorite, the Mercado brothers feature traditional Mexican and Southwestern cooking with no animal fat or lard used in the preparation. The langostino enchiladas are prime; also try the steak with stir-fried cactus. The ceviche is recommendable, as is the build-your-own fajitas. Entrees are in the $8–15 range. Open 11 A.M.–10 P.M., till 11 P.M. Friday and Saturday, at 6182 W. Flamingo, 702/871-8826.

Lindo Michoacan: Viva Mercado's is the favorite on the west side; Lindo Michoacan is the eastsiders' choice. It's a bustling noisy open restaurant that stuffs lots of people into two open rooms. Try the steak cilantro, chicken with cactus, camarones rancheros, and tequila shrimp. You'll pay $8–15 for entrees. Open 11 A.M.–11 P.M., at 2655 E. Desert Inn, 702/735-6828.

El Sombrero is covered above under "Oldest Restaurants."

Vegetarian

Slim pickin's in this pig town. **Wild Oats** grocery stores are in two locations, one east and one west. Both stores have cafes, which serve good wholesome food (some meat) and have big salad and soup bars. Cafe open 10 A.M.–7 P.M., at 6720 W. Sahara, 702/253-7050, and 3455 E. Flamingo, 702/434-8115.

Shalimar Indian food has a number of vegetarian dishes. Open 5:30–10:30 P.M., at 3900 Paradise, 702/796-0302.

Vietnamese and Thai

Saigon Restaurant, with its classically plain Vietnamese interior, could be right out of San Francisco. The incomparable Imperial rolls are $3, and try the long-simmered beef-noodle soup, and satay. Open 10 A.M.–10 P.M., at 4251 W. Sahara, 702/362-9978.

Thai Spice: The best Thai restaurant in town, the soups, noodle dishes, and traditional curries, pad thai, mee krob, and egg roll are all well-prepared and cost $7–14. Tell your waiter how hot you want your food on a scale of one to ten. Open Mon.–Sat. 11:30 A.M.–10 P.M., at 4433 W. Flamingo, 702/362-5308.

ENTERTAINMENT

With a dozen arenas and concert halls hosting everything from headliners to prizefights and rock 'n' roll to rodeos, plus nearly 20 Las Vegas-style revues, more than 50 lounges with Las Vegas-style combos performing every night of the week and some afternoons, at least a dozen discos, nightclubs, and country-western saloons, another dozen topless or bottomless bump-and-grind joints, regiments of private exotic dancers, a handful of comedy clubs, along with new high-tech motion simulators, virtual reality, and interactive video, plus laser shows, dancing waters, people-watching, cruising, bargain movies, themed amusement parks, local theater, dance, music, and art performances and exhibitions—the only way to arrive in Las Vegas and not be entertained is in a coffin.

HEADLINERS AND PRODUCTION SHOWS

The only hotels with showrooms where the major headliners appear are Aladdin, Bally's, Bella-

THE PERILS OF TRAVEL WRITING

One time, in spring 1994, I was reviewing a magic show at the MGM Grand. It was about four months after the Hollywood-themed joint'd opened, and there was this simulated Oz right inside the lion's-head entrance at the corner of the Strip and Tropicana. I paid my $4 and walked down a winding yellow-brick path, passing silly cornfields and mannequin munchkins and wax witches. Then I came to the entrance to a castle, where the magic, I supposed, took place.

I happened to be early, so I stood at the gate feeling dubious. Other Oz-bound pilgrims collected behind me; when they asked me if I knew anything about the show, I just shrugged. Finally the doors opened and we were ushered into a tiny theater, 85 seats in the round, no stage, no backstage— strange. Even more skeptical now, I claimed a seat in the corner by the exit door, in case I had to beat a hasty retreat.

The lights went down and the sound system came up. Thunderclaps, laser lightning bolts, drum roll, fanfare of brass—and then a tall man dressed all in black swept through the exit door, brushing me with the corner of his cape. In the center of the theater, on the floor, this guy proceeded to do old tricks with playing cards, scarves, cigarettes, and the like, warming up for the bigger magic. Soon enough, he and a bikinied assistant, Wanda, pushed a coffin through my door, and in short order she was run through with swords to tepid applause. Then it was out with the coffin and in with—yup—

the guillotine. Rolling it in, the near-naked Wanda oversteered and bumped my chair, knocking my knee. She leaned over and whispered, "I'm sorry! Y'alright?"

"Unh," I replied.

I knew the damage had been done when it came time to pick a victim out of the audience to lend a neck, and Wanda came right for me. The next thing I knew, I was having intimations of mortality.

I mean, we've all seen this trick done a hundred times, but when it's you who's the object of guillotine magic, trust me, your mind's eye quickly betrays you. Me, I remembered a scene from the French Revolution. Just before dropping the blade, the black-hooded executioners whispered into the noblemen's ears, "You're free! Get up and run!" Then whack! Off came the head, which rolled into a basket. But the body responded to the instilled hope, and the executioners used to bet on how far the headless runners would get. (The record was two full blocks.)

Anyway, there I was, on my hands and knees, a turtle without a shell, wondering if a rusty contraption from a low-rent magic show would hold up for one more trick. Suddenly, I heard a click, sensed a whiffet of wind on the back of my neck, and damned if that contraption didn't go wrong! The blade sliced right through my skin, my spine, and out my Adam's apple, and the last thing I heard was a soft gasp from Wanda before I was decapitated.

Killed instantly. Never felt a thing.

gio, Caesars Palace, Mandalay Bay, and MGM Grand. MGM Grand has both a showroom (700 seats) and an arena (15,000 seats). The showroom hosts acts such as Randy Travis, Rita Rudner, and Carrot Top; the arena has the giants, such as Elton John, Bette Midler, Barbra Streisand, and the Rolling Stones.

Lesser lights appear in rooms at the Hard Rock, a 1,400-seat concert venue called the Joint; mostly rock and pop.

Unless the performer is a perennial sell-out, such as Cosby or Copperfield, you should be able to get into any show that's in town when you are. Check out the stars as soon as you settle in, and make reservations immediately. If you'd like to know who's going to be performing in the upcoming three months, subscribe to the *Las Vegas Advisor* (see "Information," below), which publishes a complete list of headliners and lesser lights three months in advance.

PRODUCTION SHOWS

This is the classic Las Vegas-style entertainment, the kind that most people identify the Entertainment Capital of the World with. An American version of French burlesque, the Las Vegas production show has been gracing various stages around town since the late 1950s. Of course, most of the shows have been updated over the years; only "Folies Bergere" is a throwback to the naughty old days of the French imports. ("Jubilee" fits in halfway between "Folies Bergere" and the contemporary shows like "Enter the Night" and "EFX.")

The shows fall into several categories; burlesque, extravaganza, illusion, superstar imitators, and female impersonators. The sets are lavish, the costumes dazzling, the special effects surprising, and the exposed mammaries curious. Then there are the specialty acts: magicians, jugglers, comics, daredevils, acrobats and aquabats, musclemen and musclewomen, marionetteers, and indescribable gimmicksters.

The big shows, since they're so expensive to produce, are fairly reliable, and you can count on them being around for a while. They do, on occasion, change: "Lido de Paris" at the Stardust closed in 1991 after 38 years, "City Lites" at the Flamingo closed in 1994 after 14 years,

"Starlight Express" at the Las Vegas Hilton closed in late 1997 after finishing four of its five-year run, and "MADhattan" was retired from New York–New York in recent years. The smaller shows come and go with some frequency, but unless a show bombs and is gone in the first few weeks, it'll usually be around for at least a year or so. Consult the casino directly for show time information and pricing.

"Folies Bergere"
"Folies" epitomizes the old-fashioned excess of the extravaganza: elaborate song-and-dance production numbers with performers costumed in anything from the skimpiest five-ounce G-string to the most outrageous 20-pound headgear; taped music accompanies some combination of nostalgic tunes (in this case, 150 years worth), cabaret classics, and the requisite can-can (which, in fact, is the highlight of the show). The GI generation will fully appreciate "Folies"; others might find it slow and dated. At the Tropicana, Fri.-Wed. 8 and 10:30 P.M., $45–55, 702/739-2411.

"Jubilee"
Donn Arden took the old-time French burlesque and pumped it full of steroids. Full many years, "Jubilee," and Arden's other productions, were the most extravagant and expensive on Las Vegas (and Reno) stages. But Arden died in 1993 and shows such as "Siegfried and Roy" and "EFX" have upped the ante by tens of millions of dollars. Still, this remains an exciting show, if only in terms of the sheer volume of gorgeous flesh—a cast of 100, with 60 to 70 bodies on stage at any given time. The sets are imaginative, the song and dance is entertaining, and images of the show will stay with you a long time. At Bally's, Sat.–Thurs. 8 P.M., Tues.–Thurs. and Saturday 11 P.M., $49.50-66, 702/739-4567.

"Mystere"
Bob Sehlinger, in his excellent *Unofficial Guide to Las Vegas*, says it best, "Whimsical, mystical, and sophisticated, 'Mystere' is much much more than a circus. It combines elements of classic Greek theater, mime, the English morality play, Dali surrealism, Fellini characterization, and Chaplin comedy. It's at once an odyssey, a sym-

phony, and an exploration of human emotions. The sensitive, the imaginative, the literate, and those who love good theater and art will find no show in Las Vegas that compares with 'Mystere.'" My sentiments exactly! At Treasure Island, Wed.–Sun. 7:30 and 10:30 P.M., $75, 702/894-7722.

"O"

Bellagio likes to do everything bigger, better, and more extravagant, and "O" is no exception. The most expensive show to hit the Strip since "Siegfried and Roy," Cirque de Soleil's latest Vegas incarnation involves a $90 million dollar set, 74 artists and a 1.5 million gallon pool of water. The title comes from the French word for water, "eau," and is pronounced like the letter "o." The production involves both terrestrial as well as aquatic feats of human artistry and athleticism. It truly needs to be seen to be believed, and if you can stomach the splurge it's worth it. In a word, it's breathtaking. At Bellagio, Fri.–Tues. 7:30 and 10:30 P.M., $99–110, 702/796-9999.

Blue Man Group

Bald, blue and silent (save for homemade musical instruments). Who knew that this combination would be one of the hottest things to hit the Strip in years? Hip, ground-breaking, thought-provoking and hilarious, this unlikely trio of performance artists from New York City is definitely not what you expected. Paint, neon, twinkies, music: it's all there and then some. Long-time Vegas veterans Penn & Teller were the first to suggest to the Blue Man Group that they take their successful, if eccentric, New York act to the Vegas Strip. I'd like to thank Penn & Teller and encourage anyone with a quirky sense of humor to see this outrageous show. At the Luxor, Wed.–Sat. 7 and 10 P.M., Sun.–Mon. 7 P.M., $55–65, 702/262-4400.

"Siegfried and Roy"

Hold onto your wallets—this show costs $95 a ticket, more than most competitors, save "O," by more than 20 percent. Is it worth it? I don't know. Three people can see "Forever Plaid" for the price of one admission; two can see "EFX" (in the bargain seats). But the Mirage fills its 1,500-seat theater every night that S&R appear, and have for the past seven years, so something

Siegfried and Roy statue at the Mirage

must be happening here. In fairness, "S&R" is a great show. The sets, staging, and special effects are overwhelming. The tricks are larger than life, incorporating elephants, tigers, and a dragon, and the cast of more than 70 provides a major measure of majesty. Toward the end of the show (before the white tiger advertisement), you truly won't know what's real and what's illusion. See for yourself. At the Mirage, Fri.–Tues. 7:30 and 11 P.M., $95, 702/792-7777.

"EFX"

No doubts here: "EFX" is worth every penny of the $72 ticket price (there's also a $49.50 option for the farther-away seats that's a great deal, since no seat is unsatisfactory). This show, which cost upwards of $40 million to stage, is a technological and theatrical triumph; it admirably achieves the ambitious context that it attempts to create. Unlike "S&R," there's no sense of "seen one, seen them all"; this is a seamless mosaic of stunning sets, costumes, choreography, music and, of course, effects. Highly recommended.

At the MGM Grand, Tues.–Sat. 7:30 and 10:30 P.M., $52 and $72, 702/891-7777.

"Splash"

If it's relentless variety that you're after, this is the show for you. "Splash" combines the usual song and dance production numbers with the most specialty acts of any show in town: ice skating couples, performing birds, comedians, jugglers, motorcycle daredevils (cover your ears!), trained sea lions, break dancers, and a water ballet in a 20,000-gallon tank. This show will leave your head spinning. At the Riviera, nightly at 7:30 and 10:30 P.M., $45–56, 702/794-9301.

"Danny Gans—The Man of Many Voices"

Danny Gans is an impressionist par excellence, and he does roughly 65 characters during his 90-minute show—everyone from Elvis, Frank, and Dino to Dr. Ruth, Homer Simpson, and Kermit the Frog. He not only does the voices, he does the moves, gestures, and facial expressions too; his comedic timing is impeccable. The show is a breathtaking performance by a virtuoso entertainer and his tight three-piece band. Gans only performs five times a week, so seats are at a premium; reserve early. At the Rio, Wed.–Sun. 8 P.M.; $68–90, 702/702/252-7777.

"Michael Flatley's Lord of the Dance"

In this follow-up to "Riverdance," the immensely successful Irish tap dancing sensation that swept the nation, Michael Flatley is the reigning Lord of this popular dance craze. The story revolves around elaborately costumed re-tellings of Irish folk tales, but the real show is the amazing style of dance that is at once not tap, not ballet, but something utterly its own. The music is infectious, and overall this is a toe-tapping, foot-stomping, rollicking good show. At New York–New York, Tues., Wed., and Sat. 7:30 and 10:30 P.M., Thurs.–Fri., 9 P.M., $59 mid-week, $68 weekends, 702/702/740-6815.

"Legends in Concert"

This is a long-running and fun superstar-impersonator show, where look-alike performers pretend to be major entertainers dead and alive. There's a rotating roster of celebrities—Madonna, Blues Brothers, Buddy Holly, Michael Jackson, Roy Orbison, Marilyn Monroe, Janis Joplin, Cher, and others—but the Elvis impersonator always closes the show with a rousing patriotic finale. If the Liberace character is on the schedule, he'll blow you away. (One time, Kenny Rogers, who lives in Las Vegas, appeared as himself on stage and everyone in the audience commented how realistic the impersonator seemed!) It's a little strange watching imitators, but if you can suspend your disbelief, this show will leave you singing and dancing. At the Imperial Palace, nightly 7:30 and 10:30 P.M., $29.50, 702/794-3261.

"American Superstars"

This is the other celebrity-impersonator show. It's a little less polished and effective than "Legends," but it has its charms. The Charlie Daniels fiddle-sawing character burns down the house; the Michael Jackson character is great; and the dancers are some of the sexiest in town. Look for discount coupons in the freebie mags. At the Stratosphere, Fri.–Wed. 7 and 10 P.M., $27, 702/382-4446.

"Forever Plaid"

"Forever Plaid" is the story of the Four Plaids, a quartet modeled after the four-part guy groups (like the Lettermen) that had a brief heyday in the late '50s and early '60s. The Plaids do parts or all of 30 oldies, such as "Catch a Falling Star," "Love is a Many Splendored Thing," and "Sixteen Tons"; a rousing version of "Matilda" gets the audience belting out the chorus. The show is held together by song and dance, clever shtick, and engaging characterizations. At $21.95, this is the best cheap show in Vegas. At the Flamingo Hilton, Tues.–Sun. 7:30 and 10 P.M., $25, 702/733-3333.

Showroom Darwinism

The trend in Las Vegas showrooms has turned to reserve seating, where good seats come by buying them as far in advance as possible. This eliminates the vagaries of the old system, whereby you make reservations for the show, a maitre d' signs you in, a captain seats you, and the waitperson serves you drinks and collects the admission. About half the showrooms now offer reserved seating; ask when you make your reservations; it'll determine how early you'll need to show up.

If your seats are reserved, show up any time before showtime and you'll be ushered in and seated; no tipping is necessary, since your seats are predetermined. If the show is still on the old system, seating begins 60–90 minutes before show time. You're greeted by the maitre d' and escorted to your table by a captain. Here you enter into a Darwinian domain: "survival of the tippest." To begin with, it's not absolutely necessary to tip; no seats are in Siberia. At worst you'll be sandwiched into a banquet table on the floor right in front of the stage with the other low rollers. Preferable, though, is to get a booth on the first or second tier near the center. Many of these prime booths are reserved for the casino's high rollers and you can't get them short of hundred dollar tips. But if you're one of the first in line and you hand the maitre d' a $10 bill, you'll probably do a little better than if you're late and don't flash the cash.

Occasionally two drinks per person come with the price of the ticket, but that's the old way. The new way is for people to bring in their own drinks from a bar right outside. If a server brings you free drinks, both will be brought all at once; a couple of bucks for a tip is fine. One idea is to order a bottle of wine, which won't turn flat or warm while you wait for and watch the show.

If you want to see a show but don't have reservations, you can try arriving just before show time. You might have to split up, but single leftover seats can be great. Also, if you're solo, this is a fine way to avoid waiting by yourself for an hour and a half till show time. Otherwise, strike up a conversation with the people who'll be stuffed in all around you.

Some hotels accept reservations months ahead, others only a few days before the show. Many hotels give priority to their own guests, so you might pick your hotel by the show you'd like to see, especially if it's included in a package deal. Otherwise, be persistent. If you can't get reservations, you could show up at show time and hope for a no-show. Or, consult your bell captain or motel manager, who might have the necessary juice, or at least a suggestion.

A few shows still offer dinner at the earlier performance (typical meat-and-potatoes banquet food), which isn't that much more expensive than the cocktail show, so be sure to ask for details when you make reservations. "King Arthur's Tournament" at Excalibur is performed twice a night (6 and 8:30 P.M.), and both are dinner shows—where you have to request silverware. Get into the Round Table swing of things and use your hands.

LOUNGES

Lounges are another Las Vegas institution: several dozen of the major hotels have live entertainment in bars usually located right off the casino. These acts are listed in the tabloids and magazines, but unless you're familiar with the performers, it's potluck. Some groups are hot; others absorb more energy than they supply. But it's generally a good value, since there's no cover and rarely a drink minimum.

The "good old days" of the late '50s and '60s, when up-and-coming stars earned $10,000 a week to hone their acts in the lounges on their climb to the showrooms, are over. Gone are the comedians doing a fourth show at three in the morning; gone are the singers sitting in with their friends in other lounges; gone is the Rat Pack, any one to six of whom could invade a performance and treat the crowd to a night it would never forget. The stars and singers all work the headliner rooms, comedians appear at the clubs, and the novelty acts are incorporated into the extravaganzas.

Interestingly, GenXers have been known to worship at the altar of the lounge. Las Vegas lounge acts of days gone by are what the Cocktail Nation fad is all about. The Vegas icons are Keely Smith and Sam Butera (Louis Prima is long dead), but there's a veritable subculture of hip Las Vegas twenty- and thirty-somethings who're really into the fringe and cult entertainment scenes of the '50s through the '70s. It's all quite retro and ironic, but these youngsters have a hold of some wild old music, movies, and personalities, and weirdness.

For the rest of us, the show lounges of yesterday have been turned into the keno lounges of today. The show lounges of today are mostly meant to be Muzak to the slots.

COMEDY

Four comedy clubs operate nightly in Las Vegas. **Catch a Rising Star** at the MGM Grand, 8 and 10:30 P.M., $14, 702/891-7777; **An Evening at the Improv,** Harrah's, 8 and 10:30 P.M., $16, 702/360-5111; **Riviera Comedy Club,** 8, 10, and 11:45 P.M., $18, 702/794-9433; and **Comedy Stop,** Tropicana, $16, 702/739-2714.

The best comedy deal, if it's still around when you are, is the **Comedy Funhouse** at the Four Queens downtown (in the Royal Pavilion on the second floor; ask for directions to the elevator). The show consists of an emcee and two top-flight stand-up comedians; it's an hour and a half of yuks for the cost of one drink: $3.50. Shows are at 7:30 and 9:30 P.M.

THEME PARKS AND THRILL RIDES

MGM Grand Adventures

This 33-acre amusement park in back of the largest hotel in the world has four main rides, a few kiddie rides, four theater presentations, fast food, and a few retail shops. Kids 5–12 will love it, teenagers on their own will figure out how to have fun, but the rest of us, well, you can also walk around the park for free. The best of the mini-thrills is **Over the Edge** flume ride: a 60-foot steep drop and a big splash at the bottom. Ten seconds. The **Grand Canyon** rapids ride isn't bad: some twisting and turning and splashing. The **roller coaster** lasts all of 60 seconds, yawn. How long has it been since you've played in bumper cars? A while? It'll bring back memories—and get out some aggression.

The big thrill is the **SkyScreamer,** a cross between a bungee jump and the world's largest swing set. You don an elaborate harness, a cross between a paratrooper rig and a Roman charioteer's breastplate, which hooks in the back to a cable. Then you're hoisted, horizontal, to the top of a 220-foot tower. That's high—especially when you're hanging prostrate by a thread. At the signal you pull your own rip cord and free fall 100 feet gut-wrenchingly fast. The first step's a doozy! Finally, you scream through the sky in an 80-mph arc, careening out and back like a stick figure at the end of a 450-foot pendulum. One, two or three can ride on the same cable. It runs about $18 per person, and lasts three minutes.

The best show on the lot is the Dueling Pirates; the slapstick is funny, the stunts are great, the special effects are diverting, there's even a plot and character development! The rest of the shows are take-'em-or-leave-'em. Might as well see them if you've paid.

In case you get hungry, there's Coney Island Hot Dogs, Kenny Rogers' Roasters, and the same pizza, Japanese, Burger King, and ice cream as inside the hotel.

The admission price structure allows you to enter and see the park for free; if you walk fast you can see it in 10–15 minutes. Though you might have more fun reading the public notices in the newspaper, you can check out the scenery along the way and be able to say you've been there. To ride the rides and see the shows costs $12.95, and this price does not include the Skyscreamer. This changes occasionally, so check first; if there's *any* kind of discount offer, such as $5 off after 3 P.M., jump on it. Summer hours have been 11 A.M.–6 P.M., winter hours 10 A.M.-6 P.M., but again, check before you make your plans, as there are often closures following Labor Day until spring, 702/891-1111 for info.

Top of the Tower

Up here are the two highest thrill rides in the world. The roller coaster is tame for a ride, but being 900 feet above terra firma gives an entirely new dimension on quick turns and sudden drops. It's worth the $5 just to get off the ride laughing.

The Big Shot is something else entirely. The seats are flimsy affairs that are bolted in groups of four to the four sides of the needle at the top of the tower. Attendants cinch down the rubber restraints tightly over torsos, heads sticking out like so many terrified turtles. Then you wait, sitting there while the ride is readied, anticipation building, adrenaline pumping, trepidation flowing, anuses clen—And WHOOSH! You're launched 160 feet up the needle, squeezed by gravitational forces equal to four times your weight—heads flattened, spines compressed, butts squashed—until you reach the apex of the ascent, where all is calm, all is bright. Hey, great view! Look at the—OOOPH! All of a sudden you drop like a rock, but you don't weigh a thing. It's the zero-gravity segment of the show, folks, and for a harrowing split second, it's almost as if the

CHILD'S PLAY

Activities

MGM Grand Adventures, Grand Slam Canyon, Wet 'n Wild, the midways at Circus Circus, Excalibur, Treasure Island, and New York–New York, the pirate show at Treasure Island, the dolphin tour at The Mirage, the Attractions level at Luxor, the free light and sound shows at Sam's Town and the Forum Shops, the 3-D motion simulators at the Forum Shops, even ice-skating at the Santa Fe, bowling at the Showboat or Gold Coast, and some of the museums around town—no matter how you slice it, there are a lot of things for kids of all ages to do in Las Vegas, the new Babysitting Capital of the World. And that's without even mentioning the video arcades.

Most of the major hotels have some sort of video arcade. The best is Sega Virtualand at Luxor, though it's not cheap; just the racers and the rides will set you back $12 for each kid, and that'll fill up five minutes. But there's a whole room of air hockey and rooms full of quarter video games. Another good one is in the Cyber Station level of the Forum Shops. MGM Grand, of course, has the largest; the interactive motorcycle racing is good fun, and only a buck.

Day-trips should definitely include **Red Rock Canyon, Spring Mountain Ranch,** and **Bonnie Springs/Old Nevada;** it's only a 20-minute car ride from the Strip to Red Rock. It's 30 minutes to **Lake Mead** and 45 minutes to **Valley of Fire** and **Mt. Charleston.**

Kids in the Casino

It's permissible for your kids (in fact, anyone under 21) to cut through the casino, with the emphasis on the cut. They can't watch you feed slots or play cards, nosiree. They *can,* however, stand in a restaurant line that extends into the gambling area. If you keep your kids moving toward some noncasino destination, you won't draw any heat. Slow down or stop, and the security guards will be all over you.

Casino Day Care

The MGM Grand has a big day-care center for guests only. It's not cheap, but it's worth every penny! It closes at midnight. The Showboat, Gold Coast, and Sam's Town offer three hours of free babysitting for casino customers.

Baby-Sitting Services

Two services send sitters to your hotel room: Nanny's and Granny's, 702/364-4700, charges $9–15 an hour with a four-hour minimum; Vegas Valley Babysitters, 702/871-5161, charges $50 for a four-hour minimum.

---

ride has plummeted but you're still at the apex, floating with the angels. Then—UNH! You're bounced back up, but this second time it's only about twice your weight, and dropped back down, like half a rock. Finally, the ride quivers to a halt and, knees knocking, you slip from your seat, check to see that all your body parts are in place, and chatter incessantly to no one in particular about thrust and free fall and angels. The feeling stays with you for hours. The rides run from 10 A.M. to 11 P.M., $6 apiece.

Manhattan Express

Manhattan Express is the roller coaster that circles New York–New York. You catch the ride inside the building, at the back of the video arcade on the second floor. Your car begins its chug toward the top, 17, 18, 19, 20 stories above the backstreet of New York. And then you're over the top and diving down a 75-foot drop. It's a great rush, but merely the warm-up sensation for the big 55-degree 144-foot fall, reaching speeds of 67 miles per hour. Then you hang a quick left behind the Statue of Liberty at the corner of Tropicana Avenue and the Strip, with unbelievable views of lions, castles, tropical islands, and pyramids. The first loop is a 360-degree over-the-head somersault. Then comes the one-of-a-kind "heartline twist and dive," the half-curl, barrel-roll, upside-down rigamarole that's unique to Manhattan Express. Finally, the car is put through a dizzying succession of high-banked turns and camel-back hills, plus a 540-degree spiral, before the brakes are slammed on and you roll slowly through the casino roof and into the station. Hoo wee! The ride covers nine-tenths of a mile of track in 3 minutes and 50 seconds, and it's a bumpy, neck-jarring ride.

Manhattan Express runs from 10 A.M. to 10 P.M. Sun.–Thurs., till midnight Friday and Saturday. It shuts down during periods of rain and high winds. You must be 46 inches tall to ride. It's a steep $10 a shot.

Grand Slam Canyon

The big pink dome behind Circus Circus has been through a number of changes since it opened in August 1994, and now can be called an amusement park. The main adult attractions are the roller coaster (largest indoor coaster in the world; pretty rough) and flume ride (big drop, big splash; you walk around wet the rest of the day). The other rides and midway games are geared toward children 2–8, with eight or so kiddie rides. The price structure here changes about once a month; these days, admission is $5, which includes one ride, or you can buy a ride-all-day wristband for $12 adult, $9 kids 4–9, 3 and under free. Call 702/794-3939 for the latest dope.

Speed: The Ride

So you want to go fast? The Sahara's latest foray into the roller coaster market brings us this jaw-dropping high-speed adrenaline producer. Opened in 2000, the ride wraps its way around the Sahara Hotel, curls in a loop, and climbs over 200 feet above the Strip. You pause at this vantage point for one breath-taking moment and then hurtle back the way you came, backwards. Speed is found in front of the NASCAR Cafe at the Sahara Hotel. Open daily 10 A.M.–10 P.M. (until midnight Fri.–Sat.), $6, 702/734-7223.

Amusement Parks

Even if you're in Las Vegas for only a day or two in the summer, it's hard to resist an interlude at **Wet 'n Wild,** 2600 L.V. Blvd. S next to the Sahara, 702/737-7873, open May–Aug. 10 A.M.–8 P.M., September and October 10 A.M.–6 P.M.; $25.95 adults, $19.95 kids 3–12. (Look for $2 discount coupons everywhere.) The thrills and spills and chills are nonstop and never-ending: the Blue Niagara is the beast along the Strip—six stories high and 300 feet of "blue innerspace"; the 75-foot-long Der Stuka right next to it gives you the sensation of free fall; the Wave Pool has four-foot-high surf, or float around the third-of-a-mile Lazy River; Hydra-Maniac, Banzai Boggan, Raging Rapids, Bubble Up, and Flumes

will keep you, your kids, and your granny wet and wild all day long.

Scandia Family Fun Center, 2900 Sirius Rd. right next to the freeway (catch it off Valley View), 702/364-0071, open 10 A.M. to at least 11 P.M. year-round, is a bit hotter and drier than W&W, but offers some variety for the kids. A creative 18-hole miniature golf course is $4.50 per person, race cars and bumper boats are $3.50 per person. It also has automated pitching machines, video arcade, and snack bar. Its Super-Saver coupons are good value. Miniature golf, on a good Las Vegas-style windy day, is hilarious.

HIGH-TECH ATTRACTIONS

Luxor's Theaters

Three theater presentations on the Attractions (upper) level follow a thin plot line in which the heroes are an archaeologist who discovers an ancient Egyptian civilization directly below Luxor and teams up with a local developer to preserve it for posterity and peace. The bad guys are a military agent who's trying to secure the area for the government and a mad scientist who wants to exploit the magical powers of the ancient technology. Theater One, "Search for the Obelisk," consists of two high-impact motion simulators: the first is a freight elevator that gets sabotaged and becomes a runaway; the second is a high-speed chase through the vast subterranean temple. Both are a pretty good thrill. Theater Two, "Luxor Live?," combines ultra-high-resolution large-screen video (after a while you *forget* it's video) and a stunning 3-D segment worth the whole price of admission. Theater Three, "Theater of Time," is your basic IMAX large-format film on a 70-foot-tall movie (steeply tiered seating).

If you want the whole experience, by all means follow the story from beginning to end and buy the package for a $2 discount. If you're just into the tech, you could probably skip the IMAX and get away with $5 for the motion and $4 for the 3-D. But do check out at least one of the attractions up here; this is state-of-the-art entertainment, especially for Las Vegas. Call 702/262-4000 for current times and prices.

Speedworld

The most extensive and sophisticated virtual-reality attraction in Las Vegas has opened at the Sahara. The $15 million 40,000-square-foot Speedworld consists of two 3-D motion theaters (depicting an Indy race and an off-road race), along with 24 three-quarter-scale Indy-race-car simulators, each in its own private bay. The cars are mounted on hyper-sensitive hydraulic platforms, surrounded by 20-foot-wide, 133-degree, wrap-around screens of the race course and 15 speakers powered by a 16-channel sound system. Your car accurately responds to the slightest pressure on the gas and brake pedals and the slightest turn of the steering wheel. The screen displays the track whizzing by as you speed around it. The sound effects include the roar of acceleration, the screech of rubber against pavement, even the crunch of metal against metal (or retainer walls in high-speed collisions). The 3-D motion show costs $5, the race costs $8 (the race is 8 minutes long). You view a four-minute instructional video that orients you to the simulator. You can choose the Las Vegas Motor Speedway track or the Strip Grand Prix (so far the Strip isn't available), a 760-horsepower Pro car or a 350-horsepower Lite car, and automatic or manual transmission. If you're the kind that has to experience all the latest high-tech thrill rides, this is the new one for you (it's open Mon.-Thurs. 10 A.M.–10:30 P.M., Fri.–Sun. till midnight).

Cinema Ride

The newest type of motion simulator combines seats that move in synchronization to the action with a three-dimensional screen. You climb into a compact theater, then go for a three-minute thrill ride on a computer-generated animated chase. There are half a dozen different software packages, of which a couple are showing at any given time. Cost is $4, a dollar more than the motion rides at Excalibur, but considerably less than those at Luxor and the MGM Grand theme park. Cinema Ride is on the basement arcade level at the Forum Shops at Caesars. Hours are weekdays 11 A.M.–11 P.M., till midnight Friday and Saturday.

Race for Atlantis

This is the most sophisticated digital thrill in Las Vegas (and possibly anywhere in the country): state-of-the-art motion simulation, 3-D computer graphics, and an oversize dome-shaped IMAX film format. Located in the new wing of the Forum Shops at Caesars, you enter a five-story lobby with a 30-foot tall statue of Neptune battling a sea dragon to buy your tickets ($9.50), then climb some stairs and follow a corridor around to the Heavens Room. This is a 6,000-square-foot antechamber with a cloud-simulating fog machine, otherworldly sculpture, lightning and thunder, and a bridge with fiber-optic cables. From there you're ushered into an inner sanctum for a five-minute pre-show orientation to the headgear and plot. The headset comes with a personal sound system and special goggles that receive a synchronized infrared signal from the IMAX projection system that enhances the 3-D effects. Then it's into the theater. You strap in, don the headset, and the ride begins. The hydraulics are tight for the 27-seat six-axis platforms. The 3-D is downright psychedelic. The screen is ten times larger than in a typical theater. The immersion in the virtual space is total: vents even blow air to further simulate motion. If you can only catch one of the digital thrill rides in Las Vegas, this is the one.

Theater of Sensation

The Venetian has hopped on the cinema ride bandwagon, offering four 3-D motion rides and one 3-D non-motion ride for the easily queasy. The adventures are presented in two different theaters and run the gamut from "Escape from Venice," where a gondola ride goes awry, to "Red Hot Planet," a Martian encounter. The one non-motion ride is "Blue Magic," an underwater snorkeling adventure shot in the Bahamas. Open daily, 10 A.M.–11 P.M. (until midnight Fri.–Sat.), multiple ride packages exist depending on how many movies you want to experience, ranging from $6–17.

Star Trek: The Experience

After more than two years in development, the Paramount-Hilton Star Trek attraction opened in early January 1998. It's a combination museum, motion simulator, and interactive show. Buy your tickets ($19.95) up to three days in advance from ticket windows in the Hilton's futuristic Space Quest Casino. You enter a Star Trek museum, winding around a long corridor (which doubles as the line for the ride); check out the Star Trek timeline, exhibits and displays, and clips on video monitors large and small. With four television series and eight movies produced over the past 30-some years, the range of depth of the Star Trek universe is amazing. The "ride" consists of five separate environments (including two motion simulators); the premise is that you've been kidnapped by Klingons and beamed onto the bridge of the Enterprise; it's up to the crew (ten live actors) to get you home.

HEALTH AND FITNESS

Health Clubs

Las Vegas Sports Club, 3025 Industrial Rd., 702/733-8999, open 24 hours, is a 65,000-square-foot club with indoor/outdoor pool, Nautilus, basketball court, steam room, jacuzzi and cold plunge, snack bar, and a very accommodating policy of welcoming walk-ins. It's $15 for full use, only $10 with a room key from any hotel or motel in town. Excellent deal—highly recommended.

Also check the *White Pages* for the **Las Vegas Athletic Club,** with four locations that welcome visitors for a daily or weekly fee.

A number of the hotel health clubs are open to the public. Caesars, Tropicana, Riviera, and Desert Inn welcome nonguests. The going rate is $15–20.

Sports

Las Vegas has 20 golf courses, tons of tennis courts, four casino bowling alleys, a water park right on the Strip, several bike-rental companies, and even a casino ice-skating rink. And that's just in the city. Within 30 miles are downhill skiing, scuba diving, hiking and climbing, river rafting, horseback riding, fishing, and parachuting. A good guide for bicycling, running, golf, and the rest of the outdoor stuff is Bob Sehlinger's *Unofficial Guide to Las Vegas.*

Teams

The closest to major league is the **Las Vegas Thunder,** an International Hockey League team that plays in the Thomas and Mack Arena on the campus of UNLV. 702/798-7825.

The San Diego Padres' Triple-A team, the **Las Vegas Stars,** plays at Cashman Field during baseball season (702/386-7200) and has for nearly 15 years.

The town has cooled considerably in its ardor for the UNLV college basketball team, the Running Rebels, whose one-time coach, Jerry Tarkanian, was possibly the most famous Las Vegan of his era. Tarkanian's replacement, Rollie Massimino, also departed under extenuating circumstances (a secret $350,000 bonus to his contract negotiated by controversial ex-college president Robert Maxson was ruled illegal; UNLV then paid Massimino $1.8 million to quit). The Rebels play at Thomas and Mack Arena on campus; for tickets during the season, 702/739-3276.

Also at the university arena is the **National Finals Rodeo,** the Super Bowl of the rodeo circuit, which takes place the first week in December, one of the largest sports events of the year; 702/731-2115.

LAS VEGAS CULTURE

The **Allied Arts Council** is the local arts agency that glues together the music, dance, theater, and visual arts of this rapidly expanding city. Before visiting, send for a free copy of its classy black-and-white magazine, *Arts Alive,* if you want to get beyond the "Strip tease" and into the entertainment that many of the enormously talented locals present to each other. Write 3750 S. Maryland Pkwy., Las Vegas, NV 89119. Or call 702/731-5419 to see what's going on.

SEX

Well, fellas, prostitution is illegal in Las Vegas. The nearest legal brothels are 60 or so miles west over the Nye County line in Pahrump. But "adult entertainers" are perfectly legal, and there are 130 pages of them listed under "Entertainers" in the *Yellow Pages.* In addition, flyers dispensed in newspaper racks around town contain suggestive photographs and telephone numbers of men and women who will come to your hotel room and do a private strip-tease. I don't know for sure, but I've heard a rumor that something more than getting naked to music goes on in these encounters, and I believe it. Why? First of all, for people who just want to *look,* most hotels have pay-per-view X-rated in-room movies, and there are two dozen strip joints, some totally nude, listed in the *Yellow Pages.* Second, vice cops with 20 years on the force are routinely quoted as saying that not one of the entertainer services they've staked out has ever been legitimate. I'll let you come to your own conclusions, but remember, commercial copulation is illegal in Las Vegas.

Topless clubs have lately come out of the shadows: now there's even dirty dancin' right on Fremont St. downtown, at Herb Pastor's **Topless Girls of Glitter Gulch.** This place advertises free admission and no cover, which is true, for the 20 seconds after you walk in until a waitress puts the heavy hand on you for high-priced watered-down drinks. **Olympic Gardens,** 1531 Las Vegas Blvd. S, 702/385-8987, is the classiest strip club in town for both male and female strippers; it has become a preferred spot for many bachelorette parties.

A different breed of cat club, locally known as "sex-tease" establishments, is strictly sucker bait for unsuspecting tourists. Cab drivers drop you off at Alley's, Nasty's, Tabu, Black Garter, and Expose, among others, where girls (often underage) in skimpy costumes explicitly promise the availability of you know what, right after you buy a bottle of champagne (non-alcoholic, which they don't tell you) for anywhere from $100 to $6000 (depending on how drunk or desperate you are). But just before the moment of truth, burly bouncers boot your butt through the back door. Sex-tease clubs basically offer one thing: three- and four-figure bottles of sparkling cider. Amazingly, they're extremely hard to eradicate. A fail-safe way of determining if you're in a sex-tease club is by asking for a real alcoholic drink. These places can get standard business licenses, but they cannot get liquor licenses. If all they have is "champagne," you're probably in the wrong place.

OTHER PRACTICALITIES

INFORMATION

Information Bureaus

The **Chamber of Commerce,** 3720 Howard Hughes Parkway., 702/735-4515, open weekdays 9 A.M.–5 P.M., has a bunch of brochures and general fact sheets to give away, and sells maps and some books (*Las Vegas Perspective* on area statistics, updated every year), and has a computerized phone line.

The **Las Vegas Convention and Visitors Authority,** 3150 Paradise Road, 702/892-0711, also dispenses flyers and brochures and sometimes coupons in its visitor info center right inside the front door of the Convention Center. One of the LVCVA's priorities is filling up hotel rooms—call its reservations service at 702/386-0770. You can also call 702/594-6559 for convention schedules (critical when making plans to come to Las Vegas), 702/225-5554 for an entertainment schedule, and 702/226-5030 for a job hotline. The LVCVA's website is pretty good: www.lasvegas24hours.com. The LVCVA is planning a major expansion in 2000.

Huntington Press's *Las Vegas Advisor*

This 12-page monthly newsletter is a must for serious and curious Las Vegas visitors. The *Advisor* takes a close and objective look (no advertising or comps accepted) at every particular of consumer interest in the Las Vegas firmament, from an entire megaresort to a shrimp cocktail. It also tracks important local trends, local and national gambling news, new gambling publica-

tions and products, Las Vegas restaurants, shows, theme parks, meal deals, gambling promotions, tournaments, entertainment options, coupon opportunities, and probably its most valuable information, Las Vegas's Top Ten Values. A year's subscription ($50) includes exclusive coupons worth up to $800. One trip to Las Vegas and two coupons more than pay for the annual sub price. *Advisor* subscribers have an industrial-strength edge over the tens of millions of Las Vegas visitors *and* locals. Highly recommended. To subscribe, call 800/244-2224, or write to Huntington Press, 3687 S. Procyon Ave., Las Vegas, NV 89103, 702/252-0655. Twelve issues are $50 per year, or get a $5 sample issue.

Visitors Guides and Magazines

Nearly a dozen free periodicals for visitors are available in various places around town; racks in motel lobbies and by the bell desks of the large hotels are the best bet. They all cover basically the same territory—showrooms, lounges, dining, dancing, buffets, gambling, sports, events, coming attractions—and most have numerous ads that will transport coupon clippers to discount heaven.

Today in Las Vegas is a 32-page weekly mini-mag bursting its staples with listings, coupons, 20 pages of restaurants, and a good column on free casino lessons. For a sample copy, write or call Lycoria Publishing, 3225 McLeod Dr. No. 203, Las Vegas, NV 89121, 702/385-2737.

Just as good for listings, though with very few

coupons, is the 48-page weekly *Tourguide of Las Vegas,* available for $2 Wednesday from Desert Media Group, 4440 S. Arville #12, Las Vegas, NV 89103, 702/221-5000.

What's On provides comprehensive information, plus articles, calendars, phone numbers, and lots of ads—recommended. Its Las Vegas maps are by far the best of the lot. Send $2.50 to Las Vegas Magazine, 610 S. 3rd, Las Vegas, NV 89101, 702/385-5080.

The 150-page *Showbiz Magazine* spotlights performers and has listings and ads for shows, lounges, and buffets, plus television and movie times; get a complimentary issue by calling 702/383-7185.

Libraries

The **Clark County Library** main branch is at 1401 E. Flamingo, 702/733-7810. The Nevada section is on shelf seven against the front wall.

The Las Vegas Public Library main branch is at 833 Las Vegas Blvd. N, 702/382-3493, open Mon.–Thurs. 9 A.M.–9 P.M., Friday and Saturday 9 A.M.–5 P.M., Sunday 1–5 P.M. The architecture looks like that of a playground, with cones, cubes, and a 112-foot-tall cylinder. Inside, the big picture windows and interesting layout provide big bright rooms full of books, magazines, and research materials. Upstairs is a fine young people's section.

The **James Dickinson Library** at the university is an odd, initially confusing, and very red structure. Study the two buildings, one rectangular and the other circular, with tunnels connecting them, from outside, then wander around inside a bit to get your bearings. The rectangular building houses the circulation desk (first floor); periodicals, video, audio, and computer labs (second floor); and Special Collections (fourth floor). Go through the tunnels on the second and third floors to the round building for reference and the stacks.

Special Collections, on the fourth floor of the Dickinson library, 702/895-3252, includes hundreds of computer entries under Las Vegas—everything from Last Frontier Hotel promotional material (1949) and mobster biographies to screenplays for locally filmed movies and the latest travel videotapes. And that's just what's catalogued. Ask the supremely solicitous staff to help you find photographs, manuscripts, theses, records, archives, phone books, diaries, private collections—all on Las Vegas and environs. If this place had a kitchen and shower, I could live here.

Also in Special Collections is the **Gaming Research Center,** largest and most comprehensive gambling research collection in the world. It covers business, economics, history, psychology, sociology, mathematics, police science, and biography, all contained in books, periodicals, reports, promo material, photographs, posters, memorabilia, and tape.

Bookstores

Las Vegas is not renowned as a literary town. In fact, the word "book" around here, 90% of the time, is a verb. One books reservations, rooms, tickets, criminals; "to book" also means to accept and record wagers. "Book" as a noun generally refers to the room, counter, or big board where wagers on sports events and races are recorded. Probably the only place in town where bookmaking has anything to do with publishing is at the **Gambler's Book Club,** open Mon.–Sat. 9 A.M.–5 P.M. This cramped space is crowded with all the books on every form of wagering extant, from craps to video machines, from jai alai to dog racing. It also has a large case devoted to Mafia books and biographies, lots of local fiction, history, travel guides, books on probability theory, casino management, gambling and the law, magic, and a room in the back full of used books. Eavesdrop on the animated discussions around you! And be sure to pick up the annual tabloid catalog. But beware! If you're at all into print media about the local passions, this place will clean your pockets faster than the Wheel of Fortune. It's at 630 S. 11th St. near Charleston, 702/382-7555 or 800/522-1777 to order the free catalog.

The only bona fide bookstore on the Strip is **Waldenbooks** in the Fashion Show Mall, 702/733-1049, open mall hours. Waldenbooks is also at the Meadows Mall, 702/870-4914, and has a superstore across the street from the Boulevard Mall, 702/369-1996. **B. Dalton** also has a stores in the Meadows Mall, 702/878-4405.

Barnes and Nobles are found at 567 N. Stephanie in Henderson, 702/434-1535 and at 2191 N. Rainbow Blvd., 702/631-1775.

Borders has three stores in Las Vegas: 2323 S. Decatur, 702/258-0999 1445 W. Sunset Rd., 702/433-6222; 2190 N. Rainbow, 702/638-7866.

Bookstar is at 3910 S. 702/392-7882.

Traveling Books and Maps, 4001 S. Decatur at the southwest corner of Flamingo, 702/871-8082, is a good travel bookstore, full of guides, narratives, maps, atlases, accessories, globes, even some clothing items.

Readmore Books and Magazines is found in four locations around town; they carry an amazing amount of magazines—no reason to go anyplace else for them. **Amber Unicorn,** 2202 W. Charleston, 702/384-5838, is a great used bookstore, with some excellent deals on classic Nevadana—unless *I've* bought them all already.

Maps

Front Boy sells state-by-state Rand McNallys, raised-relief maps of Las Vegas and southern Nevada ($15 each), and United States Geological Survey topographical maps in different scales ($5). Ask for the stunning USGS Landsat photo of Las Vegas and Lake Mead ($5). Front Boy also sells a street-map book of the city ($18.95), and poster-size maps of Las Vegas, the U.S., and other places. At 3340 W. Sirius, 702/876-7822, open Mon.–Fri. 9 A.M.–5 P.M.

Traveling Books and Maps (see above) carries maps of most countries, states, and Las Vegas, as well as hiking, trail, and USGS topo maps.

SERVICES

In emergencies, if you need the police, the fire department, or an ambulance, as always in the U.S., dial 911.

If you need a doctor, call the **Clark County Medical Society,** 702/739-9989, to get a referral. For a dentist referral, contact the **Clark County Dental Society,** 702/733-8700. In a dental emergency, you'll need to contact the emergency room of a hospital to see if there's a dentist on duty; a friend of mine was unable to get into a dentist's office in Las Vegas for some emergency work and had to fly home to Seattle to get it taken care of.

University Medical Center, 1800 W. Charleston Blvd. at Shadow Lane, 702/383-

2000, has a 24-hour emergency service with outpatient and trauma-care facilities. **Sunrise Hospital,** 3186 S. Maryland Pkwy., 702/731-8000) also has an emergency room.

If you need to fill a prescription in the wee hours, try **White Cross Drug,** 1700 Las Vegas Blvd. S., 702/382-1733), near the Stratosphere Tower and is open 7 A.M.–1 A.M.

GETTING MARRIED IN LAS VEGAS

More than 120,000 marriages are performed in Las Vegas every year. In Nevada, there's no waiting period, no blood test, and the minimum age is 18 (16 and 17 need a notarized affidavit of parental consent; under 16 needs a court order). All that's required is a license. Simply appear at the County Clerk's office, 200 S. 4th St. downtown, 702/455-3156, or 455-4415 after 5 P.M., weekends, and holidays, with your money ($35), your ID, and your betrothed. It's open Mon.–Thurs. 8 A.M.–midnight, and 24 hours Friday, Saturday, and holidays. Then, if you want no-frills justice-of-the-peace nuptials, walk a block over to 136 S. 4th St. to the office of the Commissioner of Civil Marriages, open same hours as above, where a surrogate-J.P. deputy commissioner will unite you in holy matrimony for another $30. No appointments, no waiting, just "I now pronounce you . . ." and it's done.

But a more traditional setting, with flowers, organ music, photographs, and a minister, awaits at the renowned wedding chapels of Las Vegas. All the major hotels have at least one, and if you're having a big party or simply want convenience to your room, this is the way to go. Most of the small private chapels are grouped around the courthouse, or on Las Vegas Blvd. S between downtown and Sahara Avenue. Within a 10-block stretch are a dozen or so; wander in, talk to the receptionist, tour the facilities, and if you're lucky you might be able to observe a ceremony or two in progress. Within an hour you'll have a good impression of the Las Vegas wedding industry: the concept lovely, the execution a matter of taste.

You have your choice of ceremonies: "civil" means no mention of God, "nondenominational" uses the word. You can also supply your own text—much depends on the minister. The basic chapel fee is $40–60, and $35 is the recommended donation to the minister. Spring for a $5 silk boutonniere and $45 bouquet, and throw in $50 worth of snapshots, plus the limo ride to the courthouse for a license or back to your hotel ($25 toke to the driver—worth it for the stories alone). You can really start to add up a tab by arranging to have live organ music, having an audio- or videotape made of the wedding, renting tuxes and gowns, buying rings, cakes, garters, and wedding certificate holders, all right there on the premises.

Then there are the wedding chapels at the casinos, where you can combine the ceremony, a night or two in the honeymoon suite, the reception, rooms for the out-of-town guests, etc. I hear the best casino wedding chapel is at Treasure Island, where for around $500 you get the works: room, officiant, photographer, videotape, and more.

The spring wedding season starts in February, around Valentine's Day, and continues through June, the monster month. New Year's Eve is the biggest wedding night of the year. Weekends are always busiest. Most chapels like to book weddings at half-hour intervals, so even without reservations, you can probably squeeze "a beautiful ceremony" into an available slot. But to reserve in advance, contact the Las Vegas Convention and Visitors Authority, 3150 Paradise Rd., Las Vegas, NV 89109, 702/892-0711, for its list of two dozen marriage parlors.

Chapels

The granddad of all the wedding chapels, in fact the oldest building on the Las Vegas Strip, is the **Little Church of the West,** 3960 Las Vegas Blvd. S, 702/739-7971. This historic chapel opened in 1942 at the Last Frontier Village, the Western theme park next to the Last Frontier Hotel. The Last Frontier's architect and manager, Bill Moore, designed it as an exact, half-size replica of a famous church built in Columbia, California, in 1849, with redwood walls and gas lamps. The Las Vegas version remained in place for almost 40 years, even after the village was

dismantled, and the Last Frontier Hotel was reincarnated as the New Frontier, then came back again as the Frontier. Finally, the chapel was moved to its present grassy and shady location, next to the Hacienda Hotel, in the early 1980s.

Wee Kirk o' the Heather (702/382-9830) and the **Hitching Post** (387-5080) have been operating since the late 1940s; they both moved to their present locations, 226 and 231 Las Vegas Blvd. S, in 1959. The **Little White Chapel,** 1301 Las Vegas Blvd. S, 702/382-5943, has been in the same location since 1954; Joan Collins and Michael Jordan were married here (not to each other).

The **Candlelight,** 2855 Las Vegas Blvd. S, right in the heart of the Strip, 702/735-4179, is probably the most popular chapel, with a 24-hour-a-day conveyor belt of ceremonies. **L'Amour Chapel,** 1903 Las Vegas Blvd. S, 702/369-5683, has red velvet love seats in the chapel, a store full of wedding gowns for rent or purchase, and the world's only drive-up wedding window! A call button summons the minister on duty, who leans out the window and shouts the ceremony as "The Wedding March" blares from overhead speakers. "We are gathered here together at the drive-up wedding window . . ."

The quintessential Las Vegas glam wedding can be yours at **The Elvis Chapel,** 727-C S. 9th St., 702/383-5909. The King will sing your wedding song, and it's up to you to select which era of Elvis you most relate to.

TRANSPORTATION

By Air

Las Vegas is one of the easiest cities in the world to fly to. The number of airlines keeps fares competitive, and charter companies can bring airfare down even more. Package deals can be an especially good value, if you're only staying the usual three or four days, but you might have to do your own research to get the best deals. A good way to start is to look in the Sunday travel supplement from the largest daily newspaper in your area, where many of the airlines, wholesalers, packagers, and hotel specials are advertised. Also, look in the travel supplements of the L.A., Chicago, Dallas, and New York newspapers if you can; though the advertised tour operators and wholesalers might not serve your area, sometimes you can get in on the air-only or room-only part of their packages. Given the popularity of Las Vegas, it's best to make your reservations as early as possible: last-minute deals are few and far between, and you'll pay through the nose to fly to Vegas on a whim. Unless your travel agent specializes in Las Vegas, don't count on him or her to help much. Las Vegas prices are so cheap that agents don't make much money on selling it, and therefore don't have much incentive to stay up on the deals, which change with the wind.

McCarran International Airport reportedly handles a greater percentage of passengers per capita than any other airport in the world. The wide-eye rubbernecking that this town is famous for kicks in the moment you step into the terminal, with its slots, palm sculptures, maze of peoplemovers, escalators, elevators and, of course, advertisements full of showgirls, neon, and casinos.

Las Vegas Transit buses now serve the airport. You can catch one of two buses, the 108 that runs up Swenson (the closest it comes to Las Vegas Blvd. is the corner of Paradise and Sahara), the 109 runs east of that, up Maryland Parkway. To get to the Strip, you have to transfer at the large cross streets onto westbound buses that cross the Strip. Both buses wind up at the Downtown Transportation Center; if you're headed downtown, stay on the bus till the end of the line. The buses ($2 exact fare) run from 5 A.M. to 1 A.M.; be sure to ask for a transfer so you can switch buses at no charge. The Strip bus runs 24 hours a day. Call 702/228-7433 for more information.

You can take a **Gray Line** airport shuttle van to your Strip ($4.50 one-way), downtown ($5 one-way), or outlying ($6 one-way) destination. These shuttles run continually (you shouldn't have to wait any longer than 20 minutes) throughout the day and evening; you'll find them outside the baggage claim area. You don't need reservations from the airport, but you will need reservations from your hotel to return to the airport. Call 702/384-1234 24 hours in advance to reserve a spot on an airport-bound shuttle.

A taxi ride should run no more than $9-12 to the Convention Center and south and central Strip hotels, $12-15 for upper Strip hotels, and $15-18 for downtown.

By Train

Amtrak's **Desert Wind** does not stop in Las Vegas any longer. This run was discontinued in spring 1997. There's talk of starting up a gambler's train from L.A., but at press time, it was just talk (won't happen during the life of this edition, I predict). So for now, you can't get to Las Vegas by train, unless you hop a freight train.

By Road

Las Vegas crowds around the intersection of I-15, US 95, and US 93. The interstate runs from Los Angeles (272 miles, four to five hours at 65 mph) to Salt Lake City (419 miles, six to eight hours). US 95 meanders from Yuma, Arizona, on the Mexico border, up the western side of Nevada, through Coeur D'Alene, Idaho, all the way up to Golden, British Columbia. US 93 starts in Phoenix and hits Las Vegas 285 miles later, then merges with I-15 for a while, only to fork off and shoot straight up the east side of Nevada, and continue due north all the way to Jasper, Alberta.

The **Greyhound depot** is right next door to the Plaza Hotel (south side), at 200 S. Main St.; 702/800/231-2222. These buses arrive and depart frequently throughout the day and night from and to all points in North America, and are a reasonable alternative to driving or flying. Advance purchase fares are extremely inexpensive, and with extended travel passes you can really put the miles on.

By Bus and Trolley

Citizen Area Transit (CAT), the public bus system, is managed by the Regional Transportation Commission and is financed by a .25 percent cut of the sales tax and passenger fares. CAT services a couple of dozen routes all over Las Vegas Valley between 5:30 A.M. and 1:30 A.M.; only the Strip buses run 24 hours a day. All buses depart from and return to the Downtown Transportation Center (DTC), at Stewart Street and Casino Center Blvd. behind the post office. The fares are $1.50 for adults, $1 for children 5–17 and seniors over 65, and $2 for the Strip buses. Call 702/228-7433 for recorded information on fares, times, and routes; stay on the line to talk to a CAT representative who can help you plan your route through the city.

Bus service has improved considerably over the past few years, and we no longer hear as many complaints about them. (Watch your wallets and purses, however; the Strip buses are the number-one sphere of operations for pickpockets.) Another way to get around, besides your own two feet, is on the local trolleys (702/382-1404). These custom vehicles travel up and down the Strip like the buses, but they pull right up to the front door of the hotels, passing every 30 minutes or so from 9:30 A.M. to 2 A.M., $1.50, exact change. They also tool around downtown. Both lines terminate at the Stratosphere, so you can now connect from the Strip to downtown on the trolley. It's a good alternative to public buses, especially from Friday afternoon to Sunday night.

By Taxi

Except for peak periods, taxis are numerous and quite readily available, and the drivers are good sources of information (not always accurate) and entertainment (not always politically correct)—the information is often more on the entertainment level. Of course, Las Vegas operates at peak period most of the time, so if you're not at a taxi zone right in front of one of the busiest hotels, it might be tough. They cost $2.20 for the flag drop and $1.50 per mile ($3.70 for the first mile); it's also 35 cents per minute waiting time. That's why it's wiser to take the surface streets from the airport to where you're going, rather than the freeway, which is several miles longer.

Cab companies include **Ace Cab,** 702/736-8383, **Checker,** 702/873-2000, **Western,** 702/382-7100, **Whittlesea,** 702/384-6111, and **Yellow,** 702/873-2000.

By Limo

With a local fleet of more than 200 limousines, **Bell Trans** can handle anything you might dream up. Its rates are most reasonable too: $35 an hour for a standard limo (seats five), $40 for a stretch (one-hour minimum, seats six, TV,

VCR, tape deck, unstocked bar), and $80 for a superstretch (one-hour minimum, seats six, real leather, moon roof, two TVs). Bell also does the airport limo transfers; 702/385-LIMO.

Presidential Limousine, 702/731-5577, charges $49 an hour for its stretch six-seater, and $75 an hour for the superstretch eight-seater; both include TVs/VCRs, mobile telephones, champagne, and roses for the ladies.

By Rental Car

Renting a car provides an opportunity to experience some real thrills while you travel around town. If you're visiting Las Vegas for the first time on a package deal at a Strip hotel and don't plan on going off the beaten track, you probably don't need a car; just ride the Strip buses or trolleys or grab a cab. But if you've been here before and want to peel out a little, or see more of stunning southern Nevada, why not do it in the style to which you've always wanted to become accustomed? You can rent everything from a Corvette to a Cadillac, from a Fiero to a 4WD Bronco, from a Subaru station wagon to a 16-passenger van. Check with your insurance agent at home about coverage on rental cars; often your insurance covers rental cars (minus your deductible) and you won't need the rental company's. If you rent a car on most Visas or MasterCards, you get automatic rental-car insurance coverage.

Rental car rates change even faster than hotel room rates in Las Vegas and the range can be astounding. In 1996, a weekly rental on a mid-size car from Alamo on Wednesday, November 9, was $149.50; a day later, near the beginning of the 125,000-participant Comdex convention, a weekly on the same car was $398.50. When you call around to rent, be sure to ask what the *total* price of your car is going to be. With sales tax, use tax, airport fees, and other miscellaneous charges, you can pay upwards of 21%

over and above the quoted rate.

Generally, the large car-rental companies have desks at the baggage pick-up room at the airport. Those that don't have courtesy phones there; they send their shuttles out to get you, and bring you to their properties, most around the corner of Paradise Rd. and Harman Avenue.

Allstate, 702/736-6147, has pickups, 4X4s, and passenger and cargo vans. **Rent-a-Vette,** 702/736-8016, rents Corvettes, Ferraris, Jaguars, BMWs, and Lexus. **Rebel Rent-A-Car,** 702/597-1707, rents mopeds and motorcycles. **Lloyd's,** 702/736-2663, rents Corvettes, Cadillacs, Lincolns, and vans. **Sunbelt,** 702/731-3600, rents convertible BMWs, Jaguars, Miatas, and Mustangs. **Hertz, Dollar, Payless, Enterprise, Thrifty, Budget,** and **Alamo** all rent cars in Las Vegas; call 800 information for their nationwide reservations systems.

Tours

The ubiquitous **Gray Line,** 702/384-1234 or 800/634-6579, offers tours of the city, Hoover Dam, and Grand Canyon. City tours last three hours; tours beyond the area are all-day affairs. Gray Line will pick you up at your hotel and return you to it at the end of the tour. Tours run from $28 (city tour) to $189 (Grand Canyon). Reservations can be made by telephone at any hour.

Ray and Ross Transport, 702/646-4661 or 800/338-8111, covers the same general territory, with city, Hoover Dam, Colorado River, and Laughlin tours. The four-hour city tours goes for $18.35. Hotel pickup and return are included.

Key Tours, 702/362-9355, offers trips from Las Vegas to Laughlin, a gambling town that is about 90 miles from Las Vegas on the Colorado River at the Arizona state line, from $5 a person and a four-hour Hoover Dam tour for $15.

Grand Canyon

Las Vegas is the gateway to the Grand Canyon, and a handful of **flightseeing companies** offer excursions from McCarran Airport. Some deals are air only: the planes don't land. Other longer excursions fly over the city, Boulder City, Hoover Dam and Lake Mead, and the West and South rims, and land at the canyon airport. From there, ground transportation covers the 12 miles to the South Rim services where, depending on the tour, you have from two to four hours for sightseeing, photography, hiking, lunch, the museum, or an IMAX movie.

These flights have become controversial lately, for two reasons. First, the feds, prompted by complaints from hikers and campers, are considering discontinuing Grand Canyon flightseeing altogether, reasoning that they disturb the "natural peace" of the national park. Operators, on the other hand, wonder how one would quantify "quiet" and argue that flightseeing has much less impact than hiking and camping, since flightseers don't touch the canyon at all. Second, fatal crashes of the small aircraft are not uncommon. Meanwhile, the flights go on and here are the vitals.

All the tours depart from the Grand Canyon Tour Center at the Scenic Airline center near Koval and Reno streets. They all pick you up and drop you off at your hotel.

Scenic Airlines, 702/638-3300, provides a 90-minute roundtrip flight to the West Rim for $200, a two-hour flight to the South Rim and back (doesn't land) for $150, and an eight-hour roundtrip excursion with a two hour coach tour of the South Rim and a buffet lunch for $230.

Sundance Helicopter, 702/597-5505, does a 10-minute helicopter tour of the Las Vegas Strip for $72 per person, as well as a thrilling two-and-a-half hour ride over Las Vegas, Hoover Dam, and Lake Mead, then halfway down into the Canyon to land on a private plateau. The chopper ride is a once-in-a-lifetime experience; $300 per person.

NORTHWEST OF LAS VEGAS

FLOYD LAMB STATE PARK

Roughly 15 miles north of Las Vegas on US 95, drive past the Las Vegas Shed Company, noticeable for its 100-foot-tall antenna, turn right at Durango Road, and follow the signs around to this oasis in the desert. The park is open 8 A.M.— 8 P.M. daily and it costs $5 to get in, 702/486-5413; signboards at the entrance detail the history of the area and present information on Desert National Wildlife Refuge, desert wildlife, and news clippings about the park.

Some of the oldest and most complete and well-known archaeological evidence in the country was discovered at this water hole, originally known as Tule Springs. Between 14,000 and 11,000 B.C., giant ground sloths, mammoths, prehistoric horses, American camels, and condors all congregated around the tules; perhaps as early as 13,000 B.C., but definitely by 11,000 B.C., humans were present, hunting the big game.

Tule Springs shows up in the early history of Las Vegas, but it wasn't until 1941 that there was any development here. The property was purchased by Prosper Goumond, who owned a casino on Fremont Street. Over the next 15 years, Goumond turned the springs into a self-sufficient ranch and dude ranch. He built the big hay barns, water tower, pump house and well, foreman's house, root cellar, and coops, stables, and storages. He also welcomed dudes to the ranch, especially socialites waiting out their six-week residency for a divorce, and built guesthouses, a bathhouse and pool, and gazebo. Activities included fishing, canoeing, swimming, tennis, horseback riding, trap shooting, hayrides, and dances.

Goumond died in 1957 and the city bought the property in 1964 to use as Tule Springs Park. The name was changed in 1977 to honor Floyd Lamb, a state senator who was later convicted of taking a bribe in a federal sting operation. The city transferred ownership to the state shortly thereafter.

Stop off first at the park office (the first building

on the "Authorized-Vehicles-only" road by the yellow fire hydrant) and pick up a brochure, which identifies all the buildings in the historic area, including the adobe hut (in ruins behind a cyclone fence) built in 1916 by Burt Nay. Then explore the lush grounds: domesticated peacocks by the foreman's house, the occasional roadrunner scurrying by, big cottonwoods, oleanders, screwbean mesquites, and tules surrounding four ponds. The largest, Tule Springs Lake, is stocked with catfish during the summer and rainbows in the winter. Fishing is definitely the main activity here, being the nearest fishing hole to Las Vegas. Picnicking is also popular, with sheltered tables all around the ponds, and a group picnic area with volleyball at the back end of the park. The Las Vegas Gun Club takes target practice right on the other side of the park fence—the marksmen almost always aim in the other direction.

In 1999, Las Vegas Assemblywoman Kathy Von Tobel attempted to change park's name back to Tule Springs. This move was prompted both both because Lamb's name was somewhat tainted in the eyes of some residents due to his being forced to resign his office in 1983 after being convicted of attempted extortion, as well as because it relates to the geographic features of the park. As of September of 2000, however, the name remains the same.

GILCREASE WILDLIFE SANCTUARY

Named for William Gilcrease, a kindly gent in his late 70s and owner of the property, Gilcrease Wildlife Sanctuary contains five acres dedicated to the care and rehabilitation of wildlife of all kinds. Bill can be seen rambling around the sanctuary at all hours, usually talking to or nurturing one or another of the animals. The Sanctuary has been in operation since the late 1970s and has been the headquarters for the Wildwing Project since 1992.

The Wildwing Project, headed by Lisa Ross, is the only licensed nonprofit organization in southern Nevada that rehabilitates ill, injured, and orphaned wildlife and birds of prey. The project works include putting on various educational programs in connection with the schools in Clark County. All donations and proceeds raised by the Sanctuary go to feed, house, and purchase medical supplies for southern Nevada's injured and orphaned wildlife while under the care of Wildwing.

The Sanctuary is open daily 10 A.M.–3 P.M. A tax-deductible donation of $5 gets you inside. It's located at 8103 Racel Road. To get there, go north on US 95 just past Las Vegas Shed Co. with the huge antenna, turn right on Durango Rd., turn right on Racel Rd., and turn right on Silk Purse Road. For additional information, call the Sanctuary at 702/645-4224.

BOB RACE

MT. CHARLESTON AND THE DESERT NATIONAL WILDLIFE REFUGE

Another five or so miles north on US 95 is NV 157; turn left (west) and head straight into Kyle Canyon, one of many short, narrow, and sheer gashes in the massive Spring Mountain Range, which hems in Las Vegas Valley to the west for 50 miles. Most of this range, well placed for Las Vegans, is administered by the Bureau of Land Management, but the elevations above 7,000 feet are managed by the Las Vegas Ranger District of the Toiyabe National Forest, under the designation of the Spring Mountains National Recreation Area. Within that is the 43,000-acre Mt. Charleston Wilderness Area. The picnic areas, campgrounds, trails, overlooks, and ski slopes accommodate nearly a million visitors a year. Some commercial logging is conducted on this Forest Service land, and the nearly 30 inches of precipitation grabbed by the Springs' high peaks are extremely important for the watersheds of the Las Vegas Valley to the east and Pahrump Valley to the west.

Being high and wet, and surrounded by low and dry, the Spring Mountains approximate "a garden island poking out of a sea of desert." In fact, the local flora and fauna have become biologically isolated; 30 species of plants are endemic. Additionally, these mountains support a system of five distinct life zones; ascending from Las Vegas to Charleston Peak in terms of altitude is the equivalent of traveling from Mexico to Alaska in terms of latitude. Good roads take you up to 8,500 feet, within 45 minutes of downtown Las Vegas, and it can be 20 to 30 degrees cooler here.

Kyle Canyon

A little more than 10 miles from US 95, NV 157 climbs into the forest and gets canyony. First stop is **Mt. Charleston Hotel**, 2 Kyle Canyon Rd., 702/872-5500 or 800/794-3456, which has a large lodge-like lobby complete with roaring fireplace, bar and big dance floor, and spacious restaurant. Built in 1984, this is one of the most romantic spots in southern Nevada, a perfect place to propose (you can then return to Las Vegas and get married an hour or two later). Two arcades house slots and video games. The lodge has 63 rooms, which start at $59 during the week, and go up to $200 for a suite on a Friday or Saturday. At press time, a golf course was being built near the hotel.

Beyond the hotel, NV 157 continues another four miles. You first pass **Kyle Canyon Campground** at 7,100 feet. This is the lowest of five high-mountain campgrounds in the vicinity, roughly 5,000 feet higher in elevation than downtown Las Vegas (and usually at least 20 degrees cooler). It's also the closest, a mere 45 minutes away. It has big sites, fairly far apart. Most are shaded by tall pines, with plenty of greenery in betweenery. Here you'll find 25 campsites for tents or self-contained motor homes up to 40 feet. Piped drinking water, vault toilets, picnic tables, grills, and fire pits are provided. There's also a campground host. Reservations are accepted for the multi-family sites, the rest are first-come first-served. The fee is $10 for single family, $20 for multi-families. The maximum stay is 16 days. It's open May through

September, depending on snowfall. Contact Toiyabe National Forest, 2881 S. Valley View, Las Vegas, NV 89102, 702/873-8800. For reservations, call 800/280-CAMP.

A little farther along is **Mt. Charleston village**, with a few residences and a U.S. Forest Service district office. Next to it is **Fletcher View Campground**, with 12 sites (it can accommodate self-contained motor homes up to 32 feet). This one is smaller and more compact than the Kyle Canyon Campground down the street, just one road in and out. Sites are a little closer together and a bit shadier. If both campgrounds are full, Kyle RV area is across the road, just a parking lot with room for about a dozen rigs. No reservations are taken; the fee is $10.

The road ends at **Mt. Charleston Lodge**, 702/872-5408 or 800/955-1314, the main action on the mountain. This is a funky alpine operation, with rustic cabins and a restaurant. The cabins come in two sizes, basic (one bed and a hide-a-bed, $125–150) and deluxe (two kings and a hide-a-bed, $190–220). The bar is open 24 hours and the restaurant closes at 9 Sun.–Thurs. and 10 Friday and Saturday. Pull into the parking lot above the lodge for the half-mile Little Falls Trail is easy going, the three-quarter-mile Cathedral Rock Trail is moderately steep, with sheer drops but great views, and the North Loop Trail covers nine hard miles to the peak. (See *Hiking Las Vegas* by Branch Whitney, or *Nevada Wilderness Areas* by Michael White, in the Booklist for all the hikes in the Mt. Charleston Area.)

Backtracking on NV 157 to just before the hotel, NV 158 heads off to the left and connects in six miles with NV 156, the Lee Canyon Road. **Robbers Roost** is a short easy hike to a large rock grotto that once sheltered local horse thieves. A mile north is **Hilltop Campground**, at 8,400 feet. Hilltop was completely renovated in 1994 and has new asphalt pavement complete with curb, new picnic tables and grills, wide staircases from parking areas to uphill tent sites, and Mr. Clean restrooms. This aptly named campground is situated high up on a bluff; a few sites have a fine view over the valley floor, but little shade. Other sites have more shade but less view. It's also cooler and breezier than the two campgrounds down in Kyle Canyon. There are 35 campsites for tents or self-contained motor homes up to 40 feet. Piped drinking water, flush toilets, picnic tables, grills, and fire rings are provide, and there's a campground host. Reservations are accepted for the multi-family sites, the rest are first-come first-served. The fee is $10 for single family, $20 for multi-families.The maximum stay is 16 days. It's open May through September, depending on snowfall.

Up the road you'll find the access for the southern loop of the **Charleston Peak Trail**, and two picnic areas—**Mahogany Grove** is for groups, reservations required; **Deer Creek** is a quarter-mile stroll in from the road. In another couple of miles is **Desert View Trail**, a brief enjoyable nature walk with incomparable views of the surrounding desert.

National Desert Wildlife Refuge

Drive out US 95 past the Kyle Canyon turnoff to Mt. Charleston. The road leading into the refuge is easily missed, so keep a sharp eye. About three miles after you pass the Kyle Canyon turnoff (but before you get to the turnoff for Lee Canyon), you'll see a sign on the right side of the road indicating the turn for the Desert National Wildlife Range.

Turn right and drive four miles down this well-graded dirt and gravel road to the **Corn Creek Field Station**, at the entrance to the refuge. Stop at the kiosk; pick up maps and a brochure. If you're planning on traveling into the interior of the refuge, sign the guest book and trip log. If you're just out for the day, take a tour around the Field Station and surrounding springs.

Archaeologists have found evidence of campfires at the dunes site to the north between 4,000 and 5,000 years ago. Around the turn of this century, this area housed a way station on the Las Vegas & Tonopah Railroad. The area was named for Corn Creek Springs, which feeds the small stream and ponds in this beautiful desert oasis. Today, Corn Creek Springs, with its lush environment, three spring-fed ponds, woodland, and pasture, is a fantastic place to have a picnic, view wildlife, or just stroll amidst quiet and clean air and meditate on the beauty of a very unusual desert oasis. More than 240 species of birds have been observed at the springs, including a great blue heron and a pair of red-tailed hawks. Well cared-for trails entwine the springs and surrounding environs. Early mornings and evenings are the best time to spot rabbits, squirrel, an occasional mule deer, coyote, badger, and fox ranging about the field station.

The refuge was established in 1936 to protect the overhunted desert bighorn sheep. It encompasses approximately 1.5 million acres (2,200 square miles) of the Mojave Desert, making it the largest National Wildlife Refuge in the Lower 48. About half the Refuge overlaps the Nellis Air Force Bombing Range, which is prohibited to public access. Only native wildlife and the Air Force are permitted entry.

If you go into the refuge, drive only on designated roads; no unlicensed off-road vehicles are allowed in the Range. All camps (except backpack camps) must be located within 100 feet of designated roads. Camping within a quarter mile or within sight of any waterhole or spring is prohibited for protection of the wildlife. There is no potable no water on the refuge, so you must bring your own. In an emergency, spring or storage water can be used, but it must be boiled or purified first. Campfires are permitted in designated camping areas. Only dead and down wood may be used for fires and no wood may be removed from the range for any reason. All firearms and other weapons are prohibited and shooting is outlawed.

Just past the entrance kiosk, a sign shows mileages along two routes through the Refuge from this junction. Alamo Road, the longest route, wends up a wide playa on the western slope of the Sheep Mountains, skirts the edge of the Nellis Air Force Range, and rambles for 72 miles through some fairly scenic Joshua forest before dropping down to the 3,000-foot-level and exiting at Pahranagat National Wildlife Refuge Headquarters on US 93. Mormon Well Road, the shorter of the two routes and by far the more scenic and historic, climbs slowly to an elevation of 6,500 feet and ends 47 miles later at US 93 about halfway to Pahranagat.

About four miles up Mormon Well Road, the surrounding mountains offer the best bighorn habitat in the entire range. The precipitous terrain allows these desert bighorn a quick escape from predators, and the shrub-covered ledges offer good forage. Bighorn visit this area early and late in the year when it is cooler. However, since there are no watering holes nearby, the sheep descend to lower elevations to drink at numerous springs and catch basins. During the hot dry summer months, the sheep move to the northern portion of the range, closer to perennial springs. Their coats blend well with the rugged terrain, so watch the high crags and pinnacles for movement or their telltale white muzzle.

About a mile farther you come to ancient roasting pits used by natives to slow-cook their meat and vegetables. Agave was placed in a bed of hot coals and limestone cobbles, then covered with vegetable material or earth and left to slowly roast.

Some 17 miles from the junction, you come to Peek-A-Boo Canyon. Watch for the natural cave located at the mouth of the canyon. In another 11 miles is a road to the left leading to Mormon Well Spring and the Mormon Well Corral. This road, closed to vehicles, is worth the short third-of-a-mile hike to visit the spring and corral, which served as a stopover during the old horse and buggy days and was later used to water livestock. The old corral on the north side of the spring is listed in the National Register of Historical Places. Storage facilities have been installed at the spring to ensure an adequate water supply for wildlife during the summer when the local springs dry up. Make your visit short to avoid keeping mule deer, bighorn sheep, and other wildlife from this critical watering place.

A little beyond Mormon Well Spring you come to an established picnic area. Stop for lunch, relax, and enjoy the scenery. This rest area is at 6,000 feet, so the weather is generally cool in the summer. After a leisurely lunch, continue north on Mormon Well Road for another 14 miles to where it joins US 93, or return to US 95 the way you came. Either way is an enjoyable trip, and going back the same way you came will seem like an entirely new trip.

Lee Canyon

Hang a left onto Lee Canyon Rd. (NV 156). It's 3.5 miles to the end of the road. Just before you get to the parking lot for the Las Vegas Ski and Snowboard Resort, you'll pass two campgrounds. **McWilliams Campground** is 1,500 feet higher (8,500 feet) than the ones at Kyle Canyon. Here, the trees are still tall but sparse and there's less undergrowth, so there's more space between sites. It's less in the canyon, so the sky is bigger. The sites are all off one large loop; the ones in the middle are most private. There are 40 campsites, one flush toilet and 4 vault toilets, piped drinking water, picnic tables, grills, fire rings, and a campground host. The maximum stay is 16 days. Reservations are accepted for the multi-family sites, the rest are first-come first-served. The fee is $10 for single family, $20 for multi-families. It's open May through September, depending on snowfall. Slightly up the hill is **Dolomite Campground,** similar to McWilliams but with 31 sites; the ones at the back (and highest point) of the campground are prime.

Finally you come to the ski resort. Only 45 miles (and 6,500 feet) away from sizzling Sin City, "Ski Lee" has been operated since 1962 by the Highfield family. With the advent of snowboarding, they changed their name in 1995 to The Las Vegas Ski & Snowboard Resort, and in 2000 they added a terrain park and half-pipe for hot-doggers. Base elevation is 8,500 feet and the top of the chairlift is another 1,000 feet higher—thin air. But cliff walls towering above the slope protect skiers from biting westerlies. A beginner chairlift (and ski school) feeds the bunny slope; three double chairlifts ferry skiers to the intermediate Strip and to runs called Keno, Blackjack, and Slot Alley that cover 40 acres. Get here early on the weekends!

Also here are a day lodge with a coffee shop and lounge, a ski shop that rents equipment (702/645-2754), and a ski school. The slopes are open daily 9 A.M.–4 P.M. from Thanksgiving to Easter, and snow machines ensure packed and groomed slopes all winter. There's also night skiing on Saturday 4:30–10 P.M., along with a a ski school, rental shop, coffee shop, and cocktail lounge in the day lodge. Lift tickets are $28 for all day, $21 kids and seniors. Call 702/645-2754 for general information, 702/593-9500 for snow conditions, 702/486-3116 for the road-conditions report, and 702/646-0008 for the Lee Canyon bus schedule (it leaves from the Santa Fe casino down in the valley).

Down the mountain a bit from the ski area are plentiful places for tubing, sledding, snowmobiling, and cross-country skiing. The best Nordic is on north-facing slopes, in open meadows above 8,000 feet (2,438 meters). Scott Canyon, Mack's Canyon, and the Bristlecone Pine Trail are popular. Next nearest skiing to Las Vegas is Brian Head, Utah, four hours away.

TO BEATTY

Cold Creek Road

Continue up US 95 past the turnoff for Lee Canyon. Just before Indian Springs, you'll see a prison on the left. The left turn is Cold Creek Road. Follow it 13 miles west as it takes you up 6,000 feet. During the gentle climb, you'll see barren desert become beautiful forests of Joshua tree and pinion pine as you enter the Toiyabe National Forest. Look for mustangs along the road. The first junction you come to, turn off to the right for the Willow Creek camping area (three miles) and 4WD road over Wheeler Pass (seven miles). Willow Creek campground has several campsites with grills, picnic tables, and centrally located chemical toilets, but no drinking water (drink from the stream at your own risk). The stream is stocked with small trout, affording endless hours of adventure and excitement for young anglers and hungry adults.

Back at the junction, continue toward the mountains on the paved road past a unique community of mountain homes. There's no power, phone, or water service up here; all residents employ generators, have water wells, and use cell phones or two-way radios for communication—if they communicate with the outside at all!

Soon the pavement ends; it's a passable four-mile dirt road to the Bonanza Trail. Passenger vehicles should take it slow and use low gear. In winter this road is covered with a blanket of snow (passenger vehicles not recommended during the snow season). When you reach the Bonanza trailhead parking area, you'll have a spectacular view of the valley. From here you can hike four miles through high mountain country to Bonanza Peak or 14 miles to Lee Canyon over the top of Bonanza Peak (see *Hiking Las Vegas*.)

On some mornings or evenings, you may get lucky and see one of the large herds of elk coming down into the lowlands to forage breakfast or dinner. If you stay till the evening, you may even be luckier and catch a spectacular fireworks show as the Air Force conducts occasional nighttime bombing runs on the valley floor below. These bombing exercises are not scheduled for public viewing, so it's mostly up to luck, but they happen about three or four times a month, according to local residents.

Two Springs and Mercury

Fourteen miles north of the Lee Canyon turnoff is **Indian Springs,** with its Air Force emergency runway (for Nellis Air Force Base and the Test Site), high-security prison, gas stations, mobile homes under trees, and no-name casino, which has good food and live entertainment on Sunday mornings. The casino is also an official Southern Nevada Bikers Checkpoint and there are usually lots of friendly bikers stopping off for some chow, rest, or just to check in on a "put."

Next up is **Cactus Springs,** a deserted wide spot along US 95. A bar and deli here have been closed since the Big Bang. On the west side of the highway at the south end of "town," a small grove of trees shelters a stinky little spring for which the place is ostensibly named. Most of the sparse population here seem to be desert misfits who want to be left alone. But just north of the spring, surprisingly, sits a temple: the **Goddess Temple of Sekhmet.** A plaque reads, "Welcome to the Goddess Temple of Sekhmet. I'm so happy you have come to visit me. I am the Goddess of fertility, the desert, and much more. Fire is my element and the sun is my messenger. Come closer and I may whisper one of my more than 10,000 names to you . . . perhaps." According to the sign, this information was channeled by Sekhmet to Patricia, keeper of the temple. All are invited to pray, meditate, and appreciate this space and time.

The temple is 15 feet in diameter, one story tall, with a set of interlocking rings for an open roof. Inside are various shrines, offerings, and the constant scent of burning incense. The temple has parking and porta-potties, but no running water. This site is definitely worth a visit!

In another 19 miles is the turnoff to **Mercury,** the guarded entrance to the Nevada Test Site. This was the scene in the past of numerous "peace camps," where demonstrators maintained a presence to protest the underground testing of nuclear weapons. The 712th bomb was exploded 2,100 feet underground in March 1992 with a payload of 150,000 tons of TNT, more than 150 times the punch of the first test, aboveground, on January 27, 1951. But a nuclear test ban is currently in effect and is expected to remain so for the foreseeable future, and few demonstrations are staged these days. Mercury, which you can't visit without permission or on a tour, is slowly becoming a ghost town, as test site workers are laid off because of the lack of business, and the Yucca Mountain waste repository is still at least 10–15 years away.

In 24 miles is Amargosa Valley.

Amargosa Valley

Amargosa Valley technically extends from about 10 miles north of Beatty at Springdale, where the Amargosa River rises from springs and flows southeast to the California line, to where it sinks and becomes lost in Death Valley east of Pahrump. The water of the Amargosa often contains salt, soda, sulfates, and other minerals that give it a nearly red color and make it poisonous to animals.

The Amargosa Desert, which runs the length of the Nevada-California border for that same distance, contains no permanent lakes, no living streams, and is almost destitute of life except for grass growing near a few springs and a few hardy two-legged desert rats.

A post office was established here in 1901, but was closed in 1904. The name, Amargosa, was adopted by the defunct Las Vegas & Tonopah Railroad in 1906 (also called Johnnie Siding), to serve as a shipping point for the nearby Bullfrog or Johnnie Mining District. When another town was founded nearer the Bullfrog Mine, the entire population of Amargosa moved to the new site in one day's time. Today, the Amargosa Valley consists of a few scattered homes running up the Nevada-California border. The Valley's main claim to fame is its famous Big Dunes. The post office has been restored to serve the valley's few residents.

Big Dunes

Also known as the Amargosa or Beatty Dunes, these huge mounds of sand can be easily seen to the west while driving up US 95. Turn on Valley View Blvd., or Amargosa Farms Road as it is more commonly known, and drive two miles west till you come to a dirt road heading off to the right toward the dunes. The road is right next to a sign that reads, "Country Store 7 miles." Follow the level dirt road approximately two miles or as close to the dunes as you feel comfortable. If you stay on the traveled road you won't risk getting stuck in the sand. If you do get stuck, let about half the air out of your tires and you'll have sufficient traction to drive out of the sand back to harder road.

These dunes are one of the best-kept secrets in Nevada, but they have been used by the locals ever since way back when. It's the backyard to Amargosa Valley and Beatty and the locals bring their ATVs, bikes, dune buggies, and anything else that'll get them out to the dunes to play. The complex covers about five square miles, of which the dunes cover more than half, rising 500 feet from the valley floor to the highest peak.

This is BLM land. Visitors are limited to the access roads. No off-roading is allowed—yeah right. Primitive camping is allowed, but you won't find any water, toilets, or even garbage receptacles. Pack it in, pack it out. One or two signs warn that the dunes protected the Big Dunes scarab beetle habitat. In mid-1970s, an entymologist who wanted to get his name in the books did a study on the beetles, which live in the transition area between the dunes and the creosote that borders them. The entymologist found that this particular beetle, indigenous to the Big Dunes area, has a bigger penis than all other scarab beetles. True story.

The prevailing winds from Death Valley keep these dunes moving northward at the rate of a few inches a year, which qualifies them as "primary" dunes—dynamic, active and constantly moving—as opposed to "secondary" dunes, which are anchored in one area by vegetation. In the next few hundred thousand years, Big Dunes will cover the town of Beatty.

Warning: These classic crescent dunes have a gentle slope on the windward or eastern side and a sharp drop-off on the leeward side, which creates a dangerous situation. People rush up the windward slopes in their ATVs and dune buggies and crest the top, expecting to find a gentle slope down the other side. They are a bit surprised when they find themselves airborne for 40–50 feet due to the sharp drop-off on the leeward side of the dune. Know what's on your dune's backside before you go rushing up the front!

BEATTY

No other town in Nevada more embodies the word "hot" than Beatty. *Thermally* speaking, it

gets so sweltering here that even the thermometer complains. Beatty is also in the middle of that uneasy border zone where the Mojave overlaps the Great Basin, and where a tiny triangle of Death Valley National Park edges into Nevada. In a word, it's a desert out there. *Thermodynamically* speaking, not too far away is the Tonopah Test Range, where you never know what Air Force streak is burning across the sky at any given time, loaded with some explosively hot hardware. And *thermonuclearly* speaking, Beatty is an exposed flea on the unprotected underside of the Nevada Test Site, where ordinary fission for 40 years unleashed a sizzle of cosmic dimensions. In addition, U.S. Ecology runs a "lukewarm" nuclear dumpsite about 10 miles south. Also, a major gold boom has been underway for half a decade, with all the attending fervor. You don't have to hang around Beatty for too long before you start to feel an intensity that skirts the edge of hyperthermia, a particular edge that exists nowhere else.

History

In the mid-1890s Montillus Beatty settled in a small abandoned ranch near the Amargosa channel; he had a Paiute wife and little else. The man liked it hot and for recreation camped in the middle of Death Valley in the middle of the summer. The watered ranch site expanded into a rest stop for travelers between Las Vegas and Goldfield, and when the Bullfrog strike was unearthed a few miles west in 1904, the campsite expanded into a town. Beatty became a supply center for the booming mines. Rhyolite ran near the red zone on the temperature gauge for several years, during which both the Las Vegas and Tonopah, and Goldfield and Bullfrog, railroads arrived in Beatty, which thought of itself as a big railroad center, no less than the "Chicago of the West." Big brick buildings were constructed in Rhyolite as if its ore were as rich and widespread as Goldfield's. But the boom quickly petered out for good in 1910, after producing only $2 million in gold. While Rhyolite was dust-to-dusting, Beatty was surviving as a water stop for the railroad. Then US 95 was routed to make a turn in town. Along with the test site and local prospecting Beatty's viability was ensured.

Today, two tangents keep the local flame intact and local tempers often intemperate; one of them focuses a national laser beam on Beatty. The first is a gold mine on the edge of the Bullfrog Hills a couple miles south of town toward Rhyolite and Death Valley. The hills have been all but taken down, terrace by terrace, and the multicolored tailings stretch halfway to Beatty. Beatty isn't booming quite as loudly as it did a couple of years ago at the peak of the mining, but it nearly doubled in size then, and will probably stay that way for some time.

In addition, Yucca Mountain, proposed site for the Department of Energy's nuclear waste repository, is already generating its own heat, mostly of the bureaucratic kind. The Department of Energy has to prove to the Nuclear Regulatory Commission that it can build a repository by 2003 for 70,000 tons of high-level waste from bombs and nukes, with a half-life of 10,000 years, that would guarantee the safety of 500 generations, at a cost of $1–3 billion—and that's just for the study. To say nothing of the political bombshell, or the lengthy arguments between environmentalists and engineers in court. (See "Nuclear Issues" in the Introduction for further coverage.)

Sights

Beatty sits in a fairly green bowl surrounded by rugged, crumbly, polychrome slopes. The Bullfrog Hills are west; southeast are the multicolored Bare Mountains. Yucca Mountain is one range east of there, and the Amargosa Desert is south.

Across from the Exchange Club at the traffic light downtown is the Department of Energy's **Yucca Mountain Info Center,** worth a look for the maps, booklets, and a view of the DOE's public relations department, trying to sell 70,000 tons of high-level nuclear waste. Just down the street from there is the **Beatty Visitor Information Center** in the old post office building, open daily 10 A.M.–5 P.M., which is really a visitor center for Death Valley, operated by the Death Valley Natural History Association. This is where you are introduced to Beatty's main claim to fame, the gateway to the newest national park in the country, Death Valley. And just down the street from there is **Beatty Chamber of Commerce Visitor Center,** 775/553-2424, open daily 9 A.M.–5 P.M. Inside are the usual brochures about the town and the national park, as well as a display on Rhyolite, one of the most photographed ghost towns in the West.

Casinos

Wander around the **Exchange Club** at the main intersection downtown, built in 1906; slots, bar, coffee shop. Though the casino has been thoroughly modernized, the bar is the same one that was shipped from San Francisco in 1905.

South on US 95 a few hundred yards are the **Burro Inn,** which is more of a regular casino than the Exchange with a small blackjack pit, and a few motels and bars. North on the highway a mile or so is the sprawling **Stagecoach casino,** the only joint between Reno and Las Vegas with a digital message marquee and 9 A.M.–6 P.M. video poker and blackjack machines; there are also a crap table, roulette wheel, and three blackjack tables. Great place to stretch your legs in Beatty.

Bullfrog Mining District

As you head west out of Beatty along NV 374, you come upon the Bullfrog Mine immediately on right. This mine is part of the Bullfrog Mining District, which has had one mine or another producing gold continuously for 90 years. The name Bullfrog comes from the Original Bullfrog Mine, discovered by Frank "Shorty" Harris and Eddie Cross on August 9, 1904, in a range of hills about five miles northwest of Beatty. The current Bullfrog mine is an open-pit and underground gold mine, owned by Barrick Gold Corporation, one of the largest gold-mining operations in the world. The body of ore being mined these days was discovered in the fall of 1986 as part of an exploration program focusing on areas peripheral to the old mines in the Bullfrog district. In eight years of operation, the mine has produced 1.9 million ounces of gold (worth in excess of $600 million dollars).

One day a year, in April, the Barrick Bullfrog Mine hosts an open house and the public is invited to tour the mine, both the underground and open-pit portions and the processing plant. Lunch is served and a seminar on gold mining is given. There's no charge for this visit. Call 775/553-2900 to find out more about where and when this interesting tour takes place.

Rhyolite

To get to Rhyolite, head four miles west of Beatty on NV 374. Go past all the gold mining, turn right at the sign, and go up the hill. On the left is the Ghost Museum, which perfectly symbolizes the ghost town: it's rarely open. But information is tacked to the front of the building about the artists (primarily a Belgian sculptor named Andre Peters) and the artwork. There are ghosts doing the "Last Supper" (which looks like a police line-up in Hades), and a ghost holding a bicycle; there's "Icara," Venus of Nevada; "Desert Flower" is a car-bumper sculpture of twisted chrome; and a mosaic graces a telephone pole. This could be the most modern art in Nevada.

The Rhyolite you see now—stark, vacant, and desolate—was once the third largest city in Nevada. Rhyolite had a peak population of be-twen 5,000 and 10,000 people during is boom years (1905–1911). The Rhyolite Bottle House, one of a few such left in the world, was com-pleted by Tom Kelly in 1906, at the same time that the first school in town opened. More than 50,000 bottles were reportedly imbedded in the adobe walls of the original house, some of which were medicine bottles, but most were Busch beer bottles carried here by Kelly. The bottle house was restored in 1925 by a movie com-pany and has been lived in, on and off, over the years. Today a large part of the house is missing, so if you try to count the bottles, you'll come up somewhat short.

Up the hill from the Bottle House stands what was one of the finest jails in all of Nevada during its time. Rhyolite was not a notoriously bad city like Pioche, but a few residents just couldn't seem to stay on the straight and narrow. This was a mining town, after all, a hard-living, hard-working, hard-drinking kind of place with 50 sa-loons, a red-light district, and as many as 10,000 people. There was bound to be trouble from time to time.

The other buildings left include the school, which had three classrooms on the ground floor and another classroom and a big auditorium on the second; the First National Bank, a magnificent three-story concrete-block structure with plate glass and a locally mined granite facade; the town's largest mercantile store, the HD & LD Porter, dated 1906; and, farther up the hill, the re-mains of the John S. Cook Bank Building, the finest and most expensive structure in town.

At the top of the hill is Rhyolite's pride and joy, the train depot. Rhyolite was one happy town when the first train arrived on December 14, 1906. The railroad meant commerce, and com-merce meant unparalleled growth and stability. The irony was that those who had jounced and jiggled into Rhyolite by whatever form of trans-portation was available, from mule to auto, before the railroad arrived could now leave in luxury. Which they did, for the unbelievable happened. By 1907, Rhyolite was looking at *borrasca*.

The San Francisco earthquake of 1906 shook the finances of the west, and the capital neces-sary to locate and produce more gold was with-drawn from the city. If the financial panic of 1907 hadn't scared off investors, things might have been different. But U.S. currency had to enter the city in order for gold to come out of the ground. When the money stopped coming, the mines stopped producing, and the Queen of Nevada's mining cities died.

Practicalities

Beatty has five motels with a little more than 200 rooms. The 44 rooms (38–68) at the **Ex-change Club,** 604 Main St., 775/553-2333, were remodeled in 1993; they're big, pastel, and con-tain a desk, clock radio, and mini-fridge. Rec-ommended. The **Burro Inn,** Hwy. 95 S., 775/553-2225, is the largest lodging in town with 62 basic rooms at $35–50. Both the **El Portal,** 426 Main, 775/553-2912, $28–45, and the **Stagecoach,** Hwy. 95 N., 775/553-2419 or 800/4BIGWIN, $25–48, have pools. Also try the **Phoenix Inn,** 775/553-2250 or 800/845-7401, at $35–50.

The Exchange Club, Burro Inn, and Stage-coach all have 24-hour coffee shops—the Burro Inn's is an experience.

The Beatty library, on the corner of 4th and Ward streets, 775/553-2257, is open daily 8 A.M.–4:45 P.M. It has an up-to-date selection of Nevada titles, just as you walk in the door, sec-ond shelf on the right; also look at the big atlas of technical maps for the repository site—biological, geological, paleoclimatic, geochemical, demo-graphic, and 30 others.

Bailey's Hot Springs, 775/553-2395, open 8 A.M.–8 P.M., is highly recommendable. His and her bathhouses are built over the natural pool, with wonderful 105-degree water. A soak costs $3 per person per half-hour, but other than miner prime time 5–8 P.M., nobody watches clocks too closely. Just north of Bailey's, a historical marker points out Nevada's southern boundary before 1867.

WEST OF LAS VEGAS

SPRING MOUNTAIN RANCH STATE PARK

Not far from spectacular Red Rock Canyon (see page 464) is Spring Mountain Ranch State Park. Watch for wild burros along the stretch of NV 159 between Red Rock Canyon and the state park; it's easy to tell the males from the females. Some might be very friendly, but don't feed them. Not only is it bad for the burros, it's against the law.

Pay at the gate ($5 per carload) to enter the state park, nestled at the base of the Wilson Cliffs, sheer buff-colored sandstone bluffs still within the official confines of Red Rock Canyon. The area's cooler temperatures, plentiful water, bountiful land, and gorgeous setting have attracted travelers since the 1830s. By 1869 a ranch had been established with a stone cabin and blacksmith shop (both still standing). Three generations of Wilsons owned the land from 1876 till 1948, after which it was sold several times, once to Vera Krupp (ex-wife of a German industrialist) and once to Howard Hughes. The State Parks Division finally acquired the 528-acre ranch in 1974; by then it was worth more than $3 million.

The long green lawns, bright white picket fences, and New England-style red ranch house make an idyllic setting for picnics, football or frisbee tossing, daydreaming, and snoozing, as well as for concerts, musicals, and kids' events put on in summer. Stroll around the grounds, and up to the reservoir, which waters the ranch via gravity-fed pipes. The main ranch house doubles as the visitors center; pick up a self-guiding tour brochure. Concerts and plays are held here during the summer. Sunsets are incomparable.

Admission to Spring Mountain is $5 per carload. The park is open daily 8 A.M. to 7 P.M. The ranch house is open Saturday and Sunday 10 A.M.–4 P.M. Walking tours of the old ranch are conducted at noon, 1, 2, and 3 P.M. Call 702/875-4141 for more information.

Bonnie Springs/Old Nevada

A half mile south of the state park is this commercial complex, 702/875-4191. Originally a cattle ranch, it now features a motel, cocktail bar and restaurant, petting zoo, and stables, along with a Western themed village. During the summer, and weekends and holidays year-round, a mini-choo-choo picks you up at the upper parking lot and brings you down to the village and zoo area (free). The village, Old Nevada, and petting zoo open at 10:30 A.M. year-round and closes at 6 P.M. in the summer and 5 in the winter; the restaurant and bar are open daily 8 A.M. to 11 P.M.

Admission to Old Nevada is $6.50 adults and $4 children under 12. Inside are a saloon, opera house, jail, gift shops, and snack bar; a melodrama, hanging, and the Deputy Jesse Posse Show are performed at regular intervals. The petting zoo (free) has chickens, goats, rabbits, deer, burros, sheep, llamas, raccoons, squirrels, birds, buffalo, cattle, pigs, coatimundis, fox, bobcat, and more. Sign up for horseback riding at the bar: $16 per person per hour, no children younger than 6.

A big spring-fed pond with ducks and geese fronts the restaurant. Read the menu on the labels of bottles on the tables. Breakfast on the green bottles runs in the $4–6 range; lunch on the white bottles features burgers, grilled cheese corn dogs, and the like. For dinner, on the brown bottles, you can get steaks, fish, and chicken for $10–15. The ambience is rustic, bordering on funky, but the big fireplace makes it comfortable. The bar has the most expensive wallpaper in the state: dollar bills. Thousands of them.

TO PAHRUMP

South of Bonnie Springs you leave BLM's Red Rock Canyon Recreation Area and pass **Blue Diamond,** a tiny town that houses workers of James Hardie Gypsum. Gypsum is a particular salt laid down in the tidal-flats era between the sea and desert; it's used as the "rock" in sheetrock, and in drywall and plasterboard. At the junction of NV 159 and NV 160, a left turn (onto

159) brings you back to Las Vegas in 35 miles; a right turn (onto 160) takes you up into the juniper slopes of the southern Spring Mountains, past Potosi Mountain, site of the original (1850s) Mormon lead mine and smelter, and up to Mountain Springs Summit (5,493 feet), which provided a cool and watered camping spot on the Old Spanish Trail one night west of Las Vegas. A few hundred yards over "the hump to Pahrump" is **Mountain Springs Saloon,** a classic little bar that seems to have been around forever, providing the social scene for the little settlement on the summit. Stop off to read the interesting signs, especially the road report on people and cars dead and injured. Watch the first step out of the bar—it's a doozy!

From there the road descends the west side of the Spring Mountains. At the bottom of the grade you'll come across a paved road heading off to the right back up into the Spring Mountains. This road follows a wash into **Lovell Canyon,** a picturesque and beautiful canyon on the west slopes of the mountain range. As you head up the winding road, you round a bend and drop down into the wash, running along a canyon floor alive with flora and fauna. Somewhere to the right as you head up the canyon, you'll see a heavily rutted dirt road that leads up into the back end of **La Madre Pass,** which is the only trail over the Spring Mountains to Red Rock Canyon at the west end of Las Vegas. This is strictly a 4WD trail and not recommended for the weak of heart or the low of clearance.

Another four miles up the canyon you come to the end of the pavement. In addition to exploring historic sites and old ranches, you can enjoy mountain springs, hiking, picnicking and primitive camping in this little-known canyon loop. Four-wheel-drive vehicles are recommended to complete the loop over Lovell Summit and down **Trout Canyon** back to NV 160. Lovell Canyon, however, can be explored with no problem in a regular passenger vehicle.

Cathedral Canyon

A project begun in 1972 by a former Clark County District Attorney is one of the most unusual sites in southern Nevada. As you drive out NV 160 toward Pahrump, you come to a road to the west (left) marked "Tecopa." This is the Old Spanish Trail Highway. Drive three miles west on

this road till you come to another sign marked "Cathedral Canyon" and turn right. Though the terrain is desolate and sun-baked and dry, you suddenly come upon a small picnic area with tables, barbeque grills, chairs, and a suspension bridge over a very deep arroyo. Say what?

The arroyo was created by the rare rains that fall on the flood plain above, then drain into the gorge. Over centuries, these floods gradually carved a miniature canyon, sculpting fantastic and strangely beautiful crevices along the rim of the caliche hardpan.

Take a walk across the suspension bridge, which is hung by cables from steel girders. Looking down, you'll see crevices and caves sheltering stained-glass windows, oil paintings, and images from many different religions. You can also see a walkway into the canyon, which leads you to a more intimate encounter with this unusual "cathedral," enhanced by ex-DA Roland Wiley. Once there, sign the guest book and continue to wander through the canyon, following the fenced path. Climb up a few of the alcoves to get a closer look at some of the art that decorates this anomalous marvel. At night, classical symphonies and arias pour forth from hidden speakers, filling the canyon with eeriness. Necklaces of colored lights adorn niches, caves and crevices, adding to the surreal surroundings.

Wiley's purpose in creating this experience is summed up in his dedication. "I wanted to leave something for everyone of all faiths to enjoy and be inspired by to seek new ways to fulfill their own lives while they, too, are on this earth." To find out more about Wiley's arroyo, call 702/727-5800. There are no entrance fees, but donations are accepted.

The Highway

In broad Pahrump Valley, NV 160 travels a ruler edge for 35 miles northwest to the city limits. It's recommended that you pay close attention to the speedometer on this inviting stretch of road. Otherwise, you might look down and notice that you're cruising along at 105 mph. It isn't very good for gas mileage, but it *does* give you a graphic idea of the relativity of time. You've never seen the tenths digit on the odometer clickclickclick by so fast, and you've never seen the minute digits on the clock flash by soooooooooo slow. The otherworldly Joshua tree

RED ROCK CANYON—ANTIDOTE TO LAS VEGAS

West of Las Vegas, stretching across the sun-setting horizon and hemming in the valley, are the mighty and rugged Spring Mountains. Smack in the center of this range is Red Rock Canyon, a multicolored sandstone palisade so close to Las Vegas that it competes with, or better yet complements, the electrified cityscape. Less than 15 miles from the world's greatest concentration of indoor recreation await 196,000 acres of outdoor splendor—as dramatic a contrast as imaginable. The transition from city and suburb to expanding sprawl and then wilderness, is unforgettable. A mere 10 miles from downtown Las Vegas on W. Charleston Blvd., you're on open road through the outback Mojave; the view—thick stands of Joshua trees, backdropped by the precipitous Spring Mountain walls, with Red Rock Canyon standing sentinel—has been known to leave even National Geographic photographers speechless. In 20–30 minutes you take a right into the Bureau of Land Management's southern Nevada showcase.

Start with the enormous expanse of the semicircle scenery, swallowing crowds and dwarfing climbers. Then superimpose the gorgeous colors of the sandstone—yellow, orange, pink, red, pur-ple—all overlaid by the stalwart and tempered gray of older limestone. Then add the narrow, steep-walled canyons, moist, cool, lush gashes between the cliffs for wonderland hiking, and the contoured, inviting boulders that have turned Red Rock Canyon into an international climbing destination. Finally, tack on the cooperative year-round climate, close proximity to the city, and the excellent visitors center, and it's safe to say that the 28 million or so tourists who don't make it to Red Rock Canyon every year simply don't see Las Vegas.

Red Rock Canyon clearly reveals the limestone formed when most of Nevada lay under a warm shallow sea, and the massive sand dunes that later covered this desert. Chemical and thermal reactions "petrified" the dunes into polychrome sandstone; erosion sculpted it into strange and wondrous shapes. When the land began faulting and shifting roughly 100 million years ago, the limestone was thrust up and over the younger sandstone, forming a protective layer that inhibited further erosion. Known as the Keystone Thrust, the contact between the limestone and sandstone is as precise as a textbook illustration and accounts for the

PHIL GUERRERO/B.L.M.

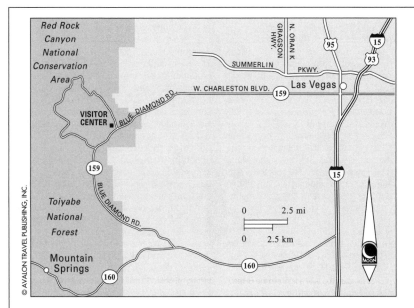

bands of contrasting colors in the cliffs. Except for the spectacular canyons carved from runoff over the past 60 million years, the 15-mile-long, 3,000-foot-high sandstone escarpment today remains relatively untouched by the march of time.

The BLM visitor center (open daily 8:30 a.m.–4:30 p.m. except Christmas Day; 702/363-1921) is situated near the beginning of the Scenic Loop road at the lower end of the wide oval that encompasses all this glowing Aztec sandstone. Take a while and orient yourself to the area at the center's excellent 3-D exhibits of geology, flora and fauna, and recreational opportunities, then walk along the short nature trail out back. The 13-mile loop road is open 7 a.m.–dusk and features half a dozen overlooks, picnic sites, and trails leading to springs, canyons, quarries, and tinajas (tanks). With any luck, you'll see hikers and climbers dotted along the rock to demonstrate the amazing scale of the fiery walls. And if you're riding a real lucky streak, they'll be wearing red! A nice long lens for your camera would be helpful. Across the highway is 13-Mile Campground, which charges $10/night for individual sites and $25/night for group sites.

You can easily spend an entire day exploring the edges of the loop road. Be sure to stop at both Calico Vista points, with humongous 6,323-foot Turtle Head Mountain leaning high and limy over the Calico Hills. A short trail from the second vista gets you into the territory. Another trail enters Sandstone Quarry, where red and white sandstone for Southwestern buildings was mined from 1905–1912. Absorb the view of the Madre Mountains, a dramatic limestone ridge line of the Spring Range, then swing around south past the White Rock Hills, Bridge and Rainbow mountains, and Mt. Wilson. Hikes enter Lost Creek, Icebox, and Pine Creek canyons. You could then spend another six days hiking around the 16- by 10-mile park, or devote a lifetime to climbing the 1,500 known routes up the red rock. The whole park, in fact, is a favorite rock-climbing destination for international climbers, who appreciate the cooperative clime. The Canyon's website (see below) has a map of the area's hiking trails.

For more details, call the Visitor Center (702/363-1921) or the BLM District Office, 4765 W. Vegas Dr. (P.O. Box 26569), Las Vegas, NV 89126, 702/647-5000, or visit the website: http://www.redrockcanyon.blm.gov/maps.htm.

forest zips by in a blur. When you decelerate to 65 mph, it feels like you're running in place, but you *will* be able to read all the billboards advertising fireworks, real estate, construction firms, mobile homes, pest control, carpet service, fence installers, landscapers, and new subdivisions that welcome you into Nye County and Pahrump (pronounced per-RUMP), elevation 2,700 feet.

The population of Pahrump is now at 25,000 and growing at the rate of 300–400 a month. It's fast becoming a big bedroom community feeding Las Vegas. Early morning and evening commuter traffic makes the drive over Mountain Springs Pass and along NV 160 sometimes quite dangerous. It is becoming known, alternatively, as the "suicide road" or "the widowmaker." Stay alert out here.

Wheeler Pass

About a mile after entering the Pahrump city limits, if you turn right off of NV 160 onto a dirt road marked Wheeler Pass Road, you can follow it up the gently sloping alluvial fan onto the backside of the Spring Mountains and Bonanza Peak. In a little more than four miles, the road drops down into a deep wash and makes a "Y" junction. Take the left fork; the right is too steep for passenger vehicles. On the other side of the wash these two roads rejoin and continue up toward Wheeler Pass, paralleling the left side of the wash, which becomes deeper and deeper.

You soon enter pinion pine and juniper foothills. The views of the distant mountains cut a great swath across a sparkling blue sky. You soon reach a point where the road drops down into the same wash and climbs back up the other side. Passenger vehicles are well advised not to proceed any farther. From this point forward, the country belongs to 4WD and high-clearance vehicles, which can continue up the road and over Wheeler Pass, then drop down into Cold Creek and Willow Creek on the eastern slope of the Spring Mountains. As for the rest of you, as you return the way you came toward Pahrump, you should venture up the wash to the **Tecopa charcoal kilns.**

In 1875, when mining was at its peak in the Tecopa-Death Valley area west of Pahrump, one J. B. Osborne, who ran a smelter in Tecopa, hired Nehemia "Red" Clark to build some kilns to supply vitally needed charcoal for his smelting

furnaces. Wheeler Pass, with its large groves of trees, provided the closest and most likely site. Red built three large beehive-shaped kilns, which measured more than 30 feet in height. The pines and conifers growing on the Spring Mountains were transported off the mountain by mule and horse, roasted into charcoal in the kilns, then carried by ox-drawn wagons to the smelter in Tecopa. It took 35 cords of wood for a kiln to produce 50 bushels of charcoal, enough to reduce a ton of ore into lead and silver. The trip from the kilns to Tecopa took five days. Abandoned in 1910 when the mines went dry, the kilns have all but fallen apart. However, in the past few years, volunteers have helped to begin stabilizing the remaining intact kiln.

As you drop down on the first road that cuts across the wash, instead of continuing across the wash, turn and follow the dirt road going up the wash. In about five miles you come across the remains of the kilns, standing like giant sentinels in the center of the wash road. Take time to explore the area. Small caves are scattered across the limestone hillsides, bedecked with green ferns and moss in their cool and shallow depressions. Early nomadic Indians used many of these caves for shelter and a number of the higher ridges are littered with artifacts of their visits. You can still catch the scent of charcoal in the cool mountain air, even though it's been nearly a century since the kilns were used.

If you continue up Wheeler Wash past the kilns, you'll come across remains of an old stageline building that once serviced a freight and passenger line that traversed Wheeler Pass. Storms have almost completely destroyed the station, but the remains are still haunted by the ghosts of intrepid pioneers and prospectors who braved these harsh lands to find their fortunes.

PAHRUMP

This valley was well known to aboriginal Paiute Indians as an oasis in the desert, where water and wild grapes were so plentiful that they named it Pahrump, which has been translated variously as "Abundant Water," "Big Springs," and "Cow Piss on Flat Rock."

The Indians cultivated corn, melons, and squash; an early settler, Joseph Yount, established the Manse Ranch in 1876, and his produce and dairy supplied prospectors, who mined gold in the Johnnie district in the 1890s. Further settlement occurred in the 1930s when farmers from the San Joaquin came to plant cotton, the area's main cash crop for nearly 50 years. The road between Las Vegas and Pahrump was paved in 1954; electricity arrived in 1963; and the planned Calvada community started up in the early '70s.

Pahrump had its Nevada-style moment in the harsh spotlight in the mid-'70s when one Walter Plankinton opened the Chicken Ranch brothel in town, initiating a chain of events that included extortion, conspiracy, intimidation, arson, attempted murder, and other felonies, implicated the local sheriff's department, district attorney, and judge, and eventually involved the FBI, federal courts, and racketeering convictions (that is, if you can believe everything you read in Jeannie Kasindorf's *Nye County Brothel Wars*—and you probably shouldn't).

Today this town of 20,000 year-round residents, a large percentage of whom are retirees, is one of the fastest-growing places in Nevada. Every other storefront is a real-estate office, in between mobile-home and double-wide lots; scattered about are a disproportionate number of construction companies advertising custom homes and cabinets, along with RV parks, homesites, mini-storage, well drilling, and pipe and pump sales. It's not incorporated, so anything goes in the name of business, which accounts for the haphazard layout of the commercial district. What's more, Pahrump is in the far southwestern corner of big Nye County, 165 miles from the county seat in Tonopah, and fully 276 miles from Gabbs in the northwest corner, and another 270 miles from the northeast corner just south of Preston.

Pahrump is also a border town with a twist: not only is it near the California line, it's also right over the Nye County line, where brothel prostitution is legal, making it a *particular* sort of bedroom community to Las Vegas, 65 miles east. It now also boasts Nevada's only winery. Late night radio talk show listeners will also recognize Pahrump as the home to the infamous Art Bell, whose programs on alien abductions and Martian cities, lend an extra-terrestrial quality to this Nevada town. All this renders Pahrump surprisingly exotic, even by southern Nevada's standards, definitely worth

a fast gas-guzzling run through the desert to check out Las Vegas's back door.

Sights

Stop off first at the **Chamber of Commerce,** on NV 160 on the west side of town in the Pahrump Station shopping center, 775/727-5800, open Mon.–Fri. 9 A.M.–4 P.M., to pick up information about businesses in the area. The buildings occupying old downtown Pahrump now house the **Humane Society,** 775/727-6203, open Mon.–Sat. 10 A.M.–4 P.M. The Thrift Shop is in the old General Store, and the little red school building is now "Nevada's best cathouse." The humaneness here is poignant: the society hates to destroy any animals, so the facility is more like a boarding kennel than death row. Leave a donation for food. To get here, turn left on NV 372 at the Valley Bank and go a block or so, past the propane store, to the gravel road on the left. A sign there points the way to the Thrift Shop.

Saddle West is the main casino in Pahrump right on Hwy. 160, 775/727-5953, with four blackjack tables, lotsa slots, and a big showroom in back, with a stage, dance floor, and plenty of room for socializing. The second casino is the **Mountain View,** on Pahrump Valley Rd. near the corner of Calvada Boulevard, 775/727-7777, with 16 bowling lanes, slots, and a comfortable sports book. There's also a baby-sitting service for casino/bowling patrons, 9:30 A.M.–9:30 P.M., free (tips appreciated). The newest joint in town is **Terrible's Town Casino,** right at the stoplight (you can't miss the huge flag), 775/751-7777. It opened in July 1996, with table games, a full contingent of slot and video poker machines, and a Kenny Roger's chicken outlet.

Pahrump Valley Winery

This is it, the only commercial winery in Nevada's history. Jack Sanders (the oenophile) and Peggy Saner (the marketer), two refugees from the San Francisco Bay Area fast lane, got it into their heads to open a winery in Pahrump. They bought 10 acres on the low slope of the Spring Mountains just southeast of town, and built a stunning white building with cobalt blue roof tiles, complete with tasting room and gift shop, restaurant and bar, winery, and observation tower. The winery opened in summer 1990, and has since bottled thousands of cases of vino. The grapes have been grown in California so far, but vines are planted and are expected to produce their first wine soon.

Lunch is served daily noon–3 P.M., dinner 5–9 P.M. Wed.–Sun., and tours are conducted 10 A.M.–4:30 P.M. daily. The tour (free) takes you through the wine-making room, with its stainless-steel and polyurethane barrels, hand bottler and corkers, and cool temperatures. You're then taken upstairs to the winery observation window and bar, then up again to the tower for a fine overlook of the valley and town. The tour ends at the bar in the gift shop, where you taste the latest batch of Sauvignon Blanc, Chardonnay, Symphony, Desert Blush, Cabernet, and Burgundy. Have your name or desired message typed right on the label (three-bottle minimum). The winery is one of the first buildings you see (on the right) when you blow into town from Las Vegas. For more information, 775/727-6900 or 800/368-WINE.

BOB RACE

Brothels

Except for the Mustang Ranch outside of Reno, the **Chicken Ranch** in Pahrump is probably the most famous brothel in Nevada. In fact, historically, it's one of the most famous in the country. It opened in the 1840s in La Grange, Texas (immortalized in a ZZ Top song of the same name), at a time when chickens, instead of money, were traded for tricks. It lasted 130 years there, but closed in 1973; the play *Best Little Whorehouse in Texas* was based on the place. In 1976 Walter Plankinton unleashed the wrath of the Nye County powers-that-be by reopening it just outside of Pahrump (see above); today, Plankinton is long gone, but the rest of the operation is still going strong. To get there, coming into town from Las Vegas, take a left off NV 160 onto Homestead Rd. two miles into Nye County and go six miles to the Ranch. Or call 775/727-5721 (382-7870 in Las Vegas) to make alternate arrangements.

Next door is **Sheri's Ranch,** 775/727-5916. Sheri's claim to fame is Lora Shaner, a beautiful

lady who was one of the madames there for half a decade. A journalist by trade, Lora's job, natural curiosity, writing talent, and compassion all combined to produce the only book ever written from the inside of the legal brothel industry in Nevada. Published in 1999 by Huntington Press, it's titled "Madam: Chronicles of a Nevada Cathouse," and has been met with solid reviews.

One other brothel also does business in the area. Continue north on NV 160 past Pahrump. Five miles from US 95, take a left on Crystal Boulevard, and it's about 2.5 miles to **Madame Butterfly's,** a sort of geisha house with baths, massage, sauna, manicures, Japanese language classes, and whatever else tickles your fancy. Call 775/372-5699. The three brothels in the area have given rise to the bad pun, "A Hundred Dollars Pahrump."

Practicalities

Pahrump is said to disappear during the day; it's so spread out over the large valley between the Spring Mountains to the east and California to the west that you can only tell it's a good-sized town of 20,000 at night, when the lights tell the tale. There's also no really concentrated downtown. It's dispersed from the Clark County line all the way to the Calvada tennis and sports center, a distance of three or four miles.

Three places in town combine for 175 total rooms. **Saddle West,** 122 S. Hwy 160, 775/727-1111 or 800/GEDDYUP, has 63% of the rooms, with 110 at $30–90. **Pahrump Station,** Hwy 160, 775/727-5100 or 800/329-7466, is a Days Inn, with 45 rooms at $39–85. Pahrump Station, also has an RV park. **Charlotta Inn,** 1201 S. Hwy 160, 775/727-5445, is the least and expensive and smallest of the three at $28–34 for one of its 17 rooms.

For food, both the **Saddle West** and **Mountain View** have 24-hour coffee shops. **Archie's,** on Hwy. 160 in the Valley View Plaza on Hwy. 160 on the east side of town, 775/727-4300, open Mon.–Sat. 10 A.M.–8 P.M., is a sandwich and fast-food outlet. **Joe's Pizza,** in the same plaza, 775/727-7477, open Mon.–Sat. 11 A.M.

to 10 P.M. and Sunday noon–8 P.M., serves the usual dough, sauce, cheese, and toppings. **The Cotton Pickin' Cafe,** off NV 372 behind the Waterhole bar, 775/727-8811, open 6 A.M.–10 P.M., is a small but popular diner with a bar attached.

A good place to pass an hour in Pahrump is at the **library,** on the west end behind the sheriff's office. It has a good Nevada and local interest shelf. The town park and swimming pool are right behind the library.

ASH MEADOWS NATIONAL WILDLIFE REFUGE AND VICINITY

Ash Meadows National Wildlife Refuge is unique to the planet. The surface discharge point for a huge underground aquifer that liberates 10,000 gallons of water every minute into 30 different springs and seeps, it's home to more than 20 plants and animals found nowhere else on Earth. Ash Meadows is so important it has been designated as one of the 15 "Wetlands of International Importance" in the United States.

To reach this unique refuge, continue through Pahrump on NV 160 to Belle Vista Road, turn left, and head up into the pass. About 24 miles along Belle Vista, you come to the dirt road into Ash Meadows. Turn right and follow the signs that guide you around the Refuge and to Refuge headquarters. As you progress toward HQ, passing through meadows and springs, note the green mineral deposits throughout the area. In spite of a close resemblance to cyanide, this mineral is actually non-toxic and highly useful. Called zeolite, it's heavily mined throughout the Amargosa Desert for such purposes as cat litter and landscaping, and for its unique ability to absorb deadly radiation.

Once at Refuge headquarters, the staff, when available, are always happy to answer questions, discuss refuge management, or arrange guided tours (with advance notice). Call Beth St. George, Ash Meadows Outdoor Recreation Planner, at 775/372-5435 for more information. If no one is there, pick up a pamphlet describing the Refuge and take a short stroll along a recently completed wood-planked walkway to Crystal Spring. Take the time to walk among the tules, rushes, and spring-watered growth, but don't step off the walkway (swimming and wading are not allowed in the spring pools). The Refuge is home to one-of-a-kind three-foot-tall poppy flowers that have tap roots reaching 10 feet down into the desert soil to find water. It's also home to the entire known population of a water beetle that survives in creeks smaller than the length of a football field. Ash Meadows is also the sole home to the unique Devil's Hole pupfish, whose ancestors swam around the feet of mastodons and saber-tooth tigers.

The best times to visit the refuge are spring and fall, when the temperatures are pleasant and the variety of wildlife affords the most advantageous viewing opportunities. In spring, the Ash Meadows pupfish, which inhabits many of the springs and pools, turn silvery blue and dart around the spring pools defending territories and laying eggs on the algae and sand. Also in spring, you'll see a plethora of migrating shorebirds that rest and feed here. Winters in the refuge can be sunny and mild, or windy and wet, depending on the vagaries of Mother Nature, but it's still the best time to catch a glimpse of long-legged herons and egrets hunting for fish at the water's edge, a dozen different species of ducks and goose diving for food, and even a few bald eagles that spend the winter here.

The clear blue springs are the Refuge's most stunning sites. Both Peterson and Crystal reservoirs are easily accessible and good places to view ducks and other water birds. If you're up for a hike, you can walk to Horseshoe Reservoir or Lower Crystal Marsh; the latter is particularly good for shorebirds in late summer. Longstreet Spring, harboring pupfish, is four miles north of Refuge headquarters. The remains of frontiersman Jack Longstreet's stone cabin are also located at this site.

Two kinds of mesquite grow here; one with corkscrew-shaped and the other with string-bean shaped pods. Wild grapes and saltgrass also flourish near the water.

Death Valley National Monument

Devil's Hole is a holdover from tens of thousands of years ago when much of the area was covered by Ice Age lakes. At the time, a tiny little-known breed of fish called the pupfish existed throughout the area. As the waters receeded, much of this "fossil water" (so called because it's thousands of years old) seeped deep into the groundwater system (all of the springs in the Ash Meadows NWR are fed by this huge underground reserve of fossil water). Springs eventually erupted in this area, where the underground fossil aquifer comes close to the surface, which managed to preserve the few remaining pupfish from that era. The pupfish you spot today are the direct progeny of those ancient ancestors.

Devil's Hole had its first recorded visit by William L. Manly in 1849 when he conducted his exploration party through this section of Nevada. In later years, a tent station, with sleeping tents and a saloon, was established at the site by "Dad" Fairbanks, a freighter who ran between Las Vegas and Beatty. The springs eventually became a source of water for the mining town of Greenwater, California. Today, Devil's Hole is a non-contiguous portion of Death Valley National Park located in the middle of Ash Meadows NWR. The limestone crevice, which is open to sunlight, contains a deep warm-water spring, the top 60 feet of which is inhabited by the entire natural population of the Devil's Hole pupfish. These inch-long fish, an endangered species, live in one of the most restrictive and isolated environments of any animal in the world.

Mom's Place and Death Valley Junction

After leaving Ash Meadows NWR HQ, turn left and proceed west to NV 373. From that intersection, make a short detour to the left (south), which will take you to the Nevada/California state line. Just before crossing into California, stop at **Mom's Place,** a gas station (the only one around for quite a ways), snack bar, and source of local information. Across the street sits the **Longstreet Inn and Casino,** although you may wonder just how it manages to stay alive in this barren and lonesome part of the world.

Continue down NV 373 half a mile and cross into California (the road becomes CA 127). Seven miles south on CA 127 you come to the small Amargosa Vally town of **Death Valley Junction,** famous as the gateway to Death Valley.

The town, while looking ramshacke and disjointed, has a rich history, some of which is in the restored and historic Amargosa Hotel, where a museum is being developed. At one time Death Valley Junction was the headquarters of the Pacific Coast Borax Company. Wild mustangs can often be seen standing in the shade of the town's many deserted buildings. The main action in Death Valley Junction is **Marta Becket's Amargosa Opera House.** Becket abandoned a promising career in New York as a dancer to pursue obscurity in this tiny hamlet after she laid eyes on the old opera house. She moved out here, restored the building (hand-painting all the wall murals), and began staging dance and theater performances October through May each year. Though they're in California, these shows epitomize a Nevada do-your-own-thing spirit (and draw most of the audiences from Vegas). They're very popular, and during the peak winter months, reservations are suggested. Tours of the opera house, conducted by Marta, can also be arranged in advance. For more information, call 619/852-4441.

Johnnie

Back on NV 160, past Belle Vista Road heading north to US 95, you come to the remains of an old mining town named Johnnie at the foot of Mt. Montgomery. The name of this dot in the desert commemorates Ash Meadows Johnnie, an Indian for whom the nearby defunct Johnnie Mine was named. It was gold, or the promise thereof, for which a few miners and their families braved inhospitable desert canyons and washes in the late 1890s to establish a life at the Johnnie Mine area north of Pahrump. The old townsite, about three miles southwest of the Johnnie Mine, and other mines are marked today by a few weathered remains scattered among the sides of the desert arroyos. A drive up a little side road into the area is worth a trip, but be sure to take care to obey the "No Trespassing" signs, because the district continues to be worked. It's said that some properties have shown some considerably rich ore.

Crystal

Continuing north on NV 160, about five miles before it intersects US 95, turn at the intersection of Clark Drive for Crystal, its three legal brothels, RV park, and Shortbranch Saloon. You've got the Cherry Patch, currently closed for remodeling, Madame Butterfly's, and Mabel's, though the latter two are really one and the same brothel. A graded dirt airstrip with an airsock is across from Mabel's. The so-called **Southern Nevada Brothel Museum** is in the bar attached to the Cherry Patch. However, it's nothing more than newspaper clippings about Nevada brothels pasted on the wall.

SOUTHWEST OF LAS VEGAS

Southwest of Las Vegas means I-15 toward California. I-15 cuts between the southern edge of the Spring Mountains and the western edge of the McCullough Range. Las Vegas is expanding in this direction, though not as quickly as it is east, west, and north, mainly because the development is industrial rather than residential. In the past few years, a new exit and interchange opened on I-15 at Russell Rd. (one exit south of Tropicana); a new hotel (Silverton), a new RV park (Oasis), and a new factory outlet mall (Belz) opened at the Blue Diamond Interchange, one exit south of there.

Silverton

This was a sister hotel to the original Silverton on I-80 just west of Reno. The owners employed the same M.O. down here as they did up there: opening a hotel on the superhighway, on the outskirts of town, far enough away to entice motorists and truckers off the interstate, but close enough to be accessible to the millions of other visitors. This Silverton has 300 rooms, a medium-size casino with a central pit of table games and a ton of slots and bonus video poker. The coffee shop serves a huge strawberry shortcake for $1 (frozen strawberries, but good enough to make a special trip out here); the buffet features old-style chuck-wagon fare: ribs, fried chicken, corn on the cob, mashed potatoes, gravy. Silverton also has a big RV park (see above under "Accommodations").

Silverton is at 3333 Blue Diamond Rd. at the I-15 interchange, 702/263-7777 or 800/588-7711. Rooms go from $25 to $85.

JEAN

It's an uneventful 25 interstate miles to the casinos of Jean. **Nevada Landing** is one of Nevada's half-dozen riverboat-themed casinos. It's big and red, and sports giant brass and cut-glass chandeliers, massive wood-looking beams, a ton of slots, a big gift shop, a 24-hour coffee shop, buffet, and Oriental restaurant. The cavernous central room has the big pit in the middle, surrounded by slots, bars, and halls leading off to the hotel rooms. Its monumental sign stands on two tall poles, with a million-bulb message marquee and the name displayed on top in tractor-trailer-size letters. Nevada Landing is at 2 Goodsprings Rd., Jean, 702/387-5000 or 800/628-6682; rates for the 303 rooms start at $25 Sun.–Thurs. and go all the way up to $45 Friday and Saturday. Only 25 minutes from Las Vegas, this is a good cheap alternative if needed.

Gold Strike Hotel & Gambling Hall across the highway has the same frilly Western falsefront exterior as the Gold Strike Inn near Boulder City, both of which might have been conceived by Liberace and painted by Zsa Zsa Gabor. It's big and red, and sports giant brass and white-globe chandeliers, massive wood-looking beams, a ton of slots, a 24-hour coffee shop, buffet, and steakhouse. The cavernous central room has the big pit in the middle, surrounded by slots, bars, and halls leading off to the hotel rooms. Its monumental sign stands on two tall poles, with a million-bulb message marquee and the name displayed on top in tractor-trailer-size letters. Sound familiar? Just like Nevada Landing? They're both owned by Circus Circus. Gold Strike is at 1 Main St., 702/477-5000 or 800/634-1359; it's a much larger hotel with 813 rooms, but the rates, not surprisingly, are the same.

Nevada Landing and Gold Strike both serve 24-hour 99-cent bacon-and-egg breakfast specials at their coffee shops. Once a staple of southern Nevada casinos, the 24-hour 99-cent special is now all but extinct. Coffee is all of 25 cents extra. This is a great play if you want to get out of Las Vegas first thing Sunday morning to beat the L.A.–bound end-of-the-weekend traffic, but want to catch some breakfast before you go. Sit at the counter and you'll be on your way in 20 minutes.

Welcome Center

There's a Nevada Commission on Tourism Welcome Center in Jean, right behind the Gold Strike, 702/874-1360. It has good information, some displays, freebie magazines by the dozen, and even some useful coupons. Stop in, sign the guest register, ask directions and questions, and you'll be loaded for bear when you reach the Big Glow.

GOODSPRINGS AND VICINITY

At the Jean exit is NV 161, which climbs gently to the northwest up from the valley floor toward Goodsprings. Drive seven miles to Goodsprings Cemetery (on the right), which contains graves both old (from the late 1800s) and new. Head-stones in the well-kept neatly fenced plot mention a several names prominent in the early development of southern Nevada. In another half mile is the town of **Goodsprings,** with a history dating back more than 100 years. It was named for an early prospector, Joseph Good, who camped at Potosi Mountain at the southern end of the Spring Mountains. Its history begins with the discovery of silver-lead ore in 1868. However, the town did not come into prominence until after the discovery of gold in those hills in the early 1890s. The district ultimately was Clark County's heaviest producer with a total yield of $31 million. But the heyday of the town occurred during WW I when the mines helped meet wartime needs for lead and zinc. The peak population was 800. Today you can still see some of the town as it was then. The railroad spur is gone. The mill is dismantled, but its concrete foundations remain. The old hotel fell victim to fire a few years back, but a number of the old buildings still hang in there. The ramshackle Pioneer Saloon still stands; and Desert Treasures sells gifts.

Goodsprings, though a shadow of its former self, is not a ghost town. People still live here and a few old-timers can still be found. Most residents, however, are newcomers who commute to Las Vegas to work, but prefer living in this quiet desert town, where dogs can run loose in the streets and kids can't get into too much trouble.

The main road through town, Esmeralda, turns into Coyote, which then becomes Reimann Road, which then continues through Goodsprings and joins another paved road that goes to Sandy Valley by way of Columbia Pass.

Columbia Pass to Sandy Valley

At the top of Columbia Pass (elevation approxi-mately 4,500 feet), the two-lane asphalt road is excellent, as are views both forward and back. Old and new mines can be seen to the left and right. The speed limit on this winding road is 35 mph and you don't want to go any faster. In fact, you'll probably want to go a lot slower, and there are plenty of places to pull over and let others by. Numerous roads to the left and right climb back into enticing mountain canyons. Caves and mines dot the hillsides. Be careful if you explore these places; this is dangerous country.

Sandy Valley

You roll down Columbia Pass and come to the southern edge of Sandy Valley, a broad, flat, expansive community at the southern end of Mesquite Valley. The sign says Welcome to Sandy Valley, A Place For A Better Tomorrow, but the spread-out town appears to be a sleepy community where a better tomorrow means leav-ing well enough alone today. It's clearly a com-munity that cares little for appearance and a great deal for comfort, convenience, and isola-tion. It's not on the way to or from anyplace. You have to want to come here to find it. While ex-ploring the town, I drove by a coyote standing brazenly in the road, casually watching me as if to say, "What the hell are you doing here?" The state line cuts through part of the town. Sandy Valley has a large number of sand and gravel op-erations—makes sense, given the town's name.

Of the great mines in Mesquite Valley, in-cluding the Shenandoah, Sultan, Hoodoo, Green Monster, and Old Timer, the Keystone was the largest, with its own stamp mill. A town, Key-stone, soon grew around the mine and mill, which was erected in 1893, and of the eight min-ing towns in Mesquite Valley, only Keystone struck a lively note in history. Somewhere along the line, the name of the town was changed to Sandy. Sandy grew up around the mill, but never achieved much in the way of size or importance, and died by 1910. Attempts to resurrect it over the years have been fruitless. A few buildings, a cemetery, and the ruins of an old mill remain to mark the place.

To save having to go back the same way you came, find Quartz Road, a main street through the heart of Sandy Valley, and go northwest till you come to Kolo Road. Turn right and begin a zig-zag course generally northeast. More specifically, from Quartz Rd., zig left on Onyx, zag right on Osage, zig left on Nickel, zag right on Papago, zig left on Marble, zag right on Cicchi, zig left on Gold, zag right on Shoshone, zig left on Diamond, zag right on Tuskegee and then, for relief, keep going straight ahead. The paved road ends a short distance down Tuskegee. Keep on going. The dirt road is well graded. After about six miles, stop, take a break, and enjoy the quiet stillness and the expansive view of Sandy Valley behind you. The plain around you is covered with Joshua and yucca. Continue on your way up a gentle climb up out of Sandy Valley to join up with to NV 160. Pahrump is 12 miles west.

PRIMM

Thirteen miles west on the interstate is Primm, Nevada, right at the state line. This is the newest name in Nevada; it was approved in 1996 by the state and national Geographic Place Names committees. Prior to that, it was known as "State Line," which caused some confusion with Stateline at Lake Tahoe. But now that it's Primm, everything's proper.

There are three hotel-casinos here, all owned by the Primm family, which explains the name. Ernest Primm homesteaded 400 acres out here in the 1950s, starting with a gas station. Hard work and perseverance led to success, and the Primms opened their first casino, Whiskey Pete's, in the 1970s. Today, Gary Prime, Ernest's son, rides herd on a little casino empire; his company also owns 50% of New York-New York in Las Vegas.

Whiskey Pete's, on the westbound side of the highway, features a castle-like exterior, with turrets and battlements and cones and banners. Strange. Inside, the castle is a large casino with a watered-down Western theme (diluted in the last expansion), along with 777 rooms, three restaurants (including the excellent and inexpensive Silver Spur Steakhouse), showroom, and Bonnie and Clyde's "Death Car" (complete with bullet holes) and Dutch Schultz's gangster car. A monorail connects Whiskey Pete's with Primadonna across the interstate; it runs every 10 minutes or so, 7 A.M.–1 A.M., depending on the weather.

Primm Valley Resort and Casino, formerly known as Primadonna, is the second Primm hotel, with 659 rooms. Outside is a Ferris wheel (it's free, but it runs infrequently if at all). Then step into this uniquely themed casino, sort of a combination of Barnum and Bailey's, Alice in Wonderland, the Wright brothers, Grimm's Fairy Tales, Around the World in Eighty Days, and Washington Crossing the Delaware. You simply have to see it all—the flying dragons, boxing rabbits, cancan girls, mermaids, barnstormers, trained bears on bicycles, to name but a few—to believe it. An eight-lane bowling alley is nearby, $1.75 a game. Primm Valley Resort and Casino also has a showroom and three restaurants.

The newest Primm complex, **Buffalo Bill's,** opened in August 1994 with 618 rooms and expanded thereafter to reach 1,242 rooms in 2000. The big thrill here, and I do mean *big* thrill, is Desperado, the world's tallest and fastest roller coaster. This $10 million monster rises 209 feet, then drops 225 feet at 60 degrees, reaching speeds in excess (depending on conditions) of 80 mph. For a second or two, you know how astronauts feel. The rest of the ride is no slouch, either: another 155-foot spiral drop, three minutes total. You board inside the casino in the attractions wing; the fare is $3 (a huge bargain), and hours (weather depending) are 10 A.M.–10 P.M., till midnight on Friday and Saturday. The other thrill ride here is **Turbo-Drop,** which is like an upside Big Shot (the ride at the top of the Stratosphere Tower), except that this one sits on the ground. You're lifted to the top of a 200-foot tower, then not only dropped like a rock, but actually thrust down at negative g's. You bounce once, then it's over. It's a 10-second thrill, a bit steep for $5.

Other attractions at Bill's are the architecture (like an old stamp mill) and interior design (fully rendered Western theme, complete with animatronic prospectors—and a vulture—who do a song and dance from a big tree inside the central circular bar). There's a water logride through the casino (same hours and price as Desperado), a motion simulator, a movie theater, a buffalo-shaped pool with two good-size water slides, and a 6,500-seat arena, Star of the Desert, which puts on headliner shows occasionally throughout the year.

The Primms are also doing big business at the **Dry Lake Store,** just over the California border on the eastbound side of I-15—the closest place Las Vegans can buy California lottery tickets. And boy, do they buy lottery tickets. Dry Lake is regularly the California lottery's number-one sales outlet. To get there, keep going past Primadonna.

Practicalities

The central number for all three casinos is 800/FUN-STOP. Room rates are no less reasonable than at the Jean casinos: as low as $23 Sun.–Thurs. and $43 weekends. Primadonna has an RV park; opened in 1993, the few trees are still small, but the park is large. It has 198 spaces for motor homes, all with full hookups, of which 157 are pull-throughs. Tents are not allowed. Accessible restrooms have flush toilets and hot showers; public phone, sewage disposal, laundry, groceries, rec room, playground, heated swimming pool (open year-round), and spa are available. The maximum stay is 60 days. Reservations are accepted and recommended (October-May). The fee is $12 per vehicle. Contact Primadonna RV Village, 702/382-1212 or 800/248-8453. From I-15, take the Stateline exit

(exit 1) and drive east two blocks on the exit road. The park is on the east side of the Primadonna Casino.

The same is true for food prices at the various outlets. All three casinos have a buffet. The one at Pete's charges $3.95 breakfast, $4.95 lunch, and $6.95 dinner; the one at Primadonna is the same (except no breakfast). The one at Buffalo Bill's is a dollar more (and worth it). Primadonna and Pete's have good cheap steakhouse; Las Vegans drive the 40 miles to get steak and seafood at Whiskey Pete's Silver Spur (in the $9–14) range. Ribs and chops at Primadonna's Skydiver are in the $7–9 range. A big bowl of ice cream at Pete's snack bar is 65 cents. Bill's has Mexican (Baja) and Italian (Prima Restorante) restaurants; the Prima (upstairs from the casino) has a good oyster bar.

The Primm properties have one of the best funbooks in Nevada. Get ahold of one and do everything for free or half-price. The crowds are ferocious on the weekends, when it seems as if half of Southern California is here. But weekdays you should have the place pretty much to yourself.

EAST OF LAS VEGAS

The old road east out of Las Vegas is Boulder Hwy., which is the extension of Fremont St. from downtown. You can hook up with Boulder Hwy. by heading east on Sahara, Desert Inn, Flamingo, and Tropicana (then take a right). The new road east is I-515, which has been extended as far as a little past Henderson. US 93 and 95 travel along with I-515 till it ends, then continue over Railroad Pass and down into Eldorado Valley. There, US 95 turns off south toward Laughlin and Needles, California, while US 93 continues east into Boulder City.

HENDERSON

History

Only four years after the completion of Hoover Dam, the Germans commenced raining terror down on England in the form of bombs whose deadly incendiary properties were attributed to magnesium, till then a little-known metal. In ad-

dition, lightweight magnesium was discovered in various components of downed German airplanes. A year later, Allied scientists and engineers had analyzed the qualities of this metal, and geologists had located huge deposits near Gabbs, Nevada. Since vast amounts of electrical power are required to process magnesium, a site halfway between Hoover Dam and Las Vegas was selected for the magnesium processing plant, and in September 1941 construction commenced on a massive factory known as Basic Magnesium. More than 10,000 workers spent only a few months erecting the plant, the town, and the transportation systems necessary to aid the war effort. By early 1942, 5,000 people lived in "Basic," and by 1943, 16 million pounds of magnesium had been produced. By 1944, so much magnesium had been shipped from Basic that the government had a surplus; with the war in Europe winding down, the plant was closed.

For the next few years, this metal-heavy town

was on the verge of becoming yet another ghost in the Nevada desert. But then the federal government agreed to turn over the property and facilities to the state. The town, renamed to honor Albert Henderson, a local politician and judge who was pivotal in the takeover negotiations, received a new lease on life. By the early 1950s, the huge manufacturing complex had been subdivided to accommodate smaller private industry, and by the early 1980s, Henderson claimed half of the entire state's nontourist industry output. The town made the national news in May 1988 when a huge explosion leveled Pacific Engineering, which manufactures ammonia perchlorate, the oxydizer in solid rocket fuel, and Kidd's Marshmallow company next door (subsequently relocated a safe distance away).

Henderson is aesthetically . . . uh . . . interesting—with its huge industrial complex set off from fast-growing residential and commercial districts. It's not only fast growing, it has plenty of room to expand; a little less than half of the space within the city limits remains undeveloped. In early 1994, Henderson joined the Nevada 100,000 Club, an exclusive group of towns with more than 100,000 residents (now three, to be exact, along with Las Vegas and Reno). Henderson is one of the fastest-growing cities in the fastest-growing state in the country. Reflecting this accelerated growth are a handful of new casinos strung along Boulder Hwy. and around town, with plans for more. Finally, its excellent location is undeniable—only 15 minutes from the lake, and close enough to Las Vegas to enjoy the benefits, while far enough away to outdistance the disadvantages.

Along Boulder Highway
Boulder Station and Sam's Town are covered under Las Vegas casinos. Down the road a little ways, just north of Tropicana, are **Nevada Palace** and the **Longhorn**. Nevada Palace, 702/458-8810, is a small locals' joint with a tradition of good cheap grub. The **Longhorn**, 702/435-9170, is another small locals' casino, with the usual good video poker, $1 blackjack, a 24-hour $1.95 breakfast special, and lots of parking.

On Sunset Rd. near Boulder Hwy. is **Tom's Sunset**, 702/564-5551, serving the many Hendersonites with coupons and dining specials. South of there is the **Skyline**, 702/565-9116,

with one whole long roomful of breakeven video poker machines, a 99-cent margarita, and a good $1 shrimp cocktail. The coffee shop is a five-room maze; or sit at the counter and have a good prime rib special.

Finally is **Joker's Wild,** just before the intersection with Water St., 702/564-8100, a Boyd Group property. This is a fairly new full-service casino with no hotel, with blackjack, Caribbean stud, craps, roulette, a coffee shop, buffet, and lounge with a large screen.

Around Town
Turn right into Henderson on Water St. at the big signs for town off Boulder Hwy., or go left from the end of the Expressway on Lake Mead Dr., then take a right on Water Street. Either way, you'll go right by the old BMI plant, now housing the big chemical companies, such as Timet ("Making Our Lives Better Through Titanium Technology"), Pepcon, Kerr McGee, Chemstar, and many others, as well as small manufacturing and construction companies.

Downtown are two main casinos and one minor casino. The **Eldorado,** 140 S. Water, 702/564-1811, is a typical Boyd Group property (like the Stardust, California, Sam's Town, Joker's Wild, etc.): a large, bright, classy joint, with a large pit full of blackjack, crap, and roulette tables, along with a sports book, keno, bingo, a couple of bars, a 24-hour coffee shop, and Mariana's Mexican restaurant. The 80-foot old neon marquee in front, big letters stacked vertically spelling GAMBLING with a star on top, dominates downtown. There's a new waterfall out back.

Next door the **Rainbow Club,** 122 S. Water, 702/565-9776, is as claustro as the Eldorado is agora. With its low mirrored ceilings, startling neon border lights, and crowds around the slots and video poker, the Rainbow has the unmistakable signature of a Peppermill. The 24-hour coffee shop serves a 99-cent breakfast special around the clock.

The **Post Office Casino** is in back of the Rainbow at 120 Market St., 702/565-0300, in the old Henderson post office building. This is basically a slot and video poker joint, with a post office annex (private) attached, where you can mail your postcards of Henderson to everybody back home.

Past downtown on Water St. are the convention center, library, and park; Water runs around to the left and joins Major St., which heads right back out to Boulder Highway. The **Chamber of Commerce** is right at 100 E. Lake Mead Dr. right at the corner of Boulder Hwy., 702/565-8951, open Mon.–Fri. 8 A.M.–5 P.M.

Clark County Heritage Museum

As you continue east on Boulder Hwy., the next attraction is this extensive and fascinating museum, 1830 S. Boulder Hwy. two miles beyond Henderson, 702/455-7955, open daily 9 A.M.–4:30 P.M., admission $1.50 adults, $1 for 55-plus and 15-minus. The main museum exhibit is now housed in the new pueblo building. The fine displays trace Indian cultures from the prehistoric to the contemporary and chronologize white exploration, settlement, and industry: Mormons, military, mining, ranching, railroading, riverboating, and gambling, up through the construction of Hoover Dam and the subsequent founding of Henderson.

The old depot, which used to house the collection, will soon be reopened, if it's not already, with the railroad exhibit, which used to be in the old caboose. Also be sure to stroll down to the Heritage St. historical residential and commercial buildings: the **Townsite House,** built in Henderson in the 1940s; the 1890s print shop; the **Babcock and Wilcox House,** one of 12 original residences built in Boulder City in early 1933; and the pièce de résistance **Beckley House,** a simple yet stunning example of the still-popular California bungalow style, built for $2500 in 1912 by Las Vegas pioneer and entrepreneur Will Beckley.

Out back are an unrestored ghost town and a mining and railroad display. The gift shop sells some interesting items, such as books, magazines, minerals, jewelry, beads, pottery, textiles, even Joshua tree seeds.

Railroad Pass

Highway 93/95 continues southwest up and over a low gate between the River Mountains and the Black Hills known as Railroad Pass (2,367 feet), named for the Union Pacific route to Boulder City and the dam. **Railroad Pass Hotel and Casino** sits at the top, at 2800 Boulder Hwy., 702/294-5000, with a full-service and red casino, coffee shop and buffet, and $29–39 rooms. Just beyond is the junction: US 95 cuts right (south) down to west of Laughlin, and US 93 heads straight (east) into Boulder City.

BOULDER CITY

In 1930, when Congress appropriated the first funds for the Boulder Canyon Project, the Great Depression was in full swing, the country was embarking on its first massive reclamation effort, the dam was to be one of the largest single engineering and construction tasks ever undertaken, and urban architects were increasingly

Boulder City

DEKE CASTLEMAN

leaning toward the social progressiveness of the Community Planning Movement. Boulder City was born of these unique factors and remains, nearly 70 years later, the most unusual town in Nevada. In July 1930, the Commissioner of Reclamation, Dr. Elwood Mead, hired Saco R. DeBoer, a highly regarded 35-year-old landscape architect from Denver, to develop the Boulder City Master Plan. DeBoer set the gov-

ernment buildings at the top of the site's hill, within a greenbelt of parks. The town radiated out like a fan, with the main commercial and residential sections concentrated around three through streets that converged symmetrically at the handle. Secondary roads conformed to the contours of the land, and parks, plazas, and perimeters enclosed the neighborhoods in pleasant settings.

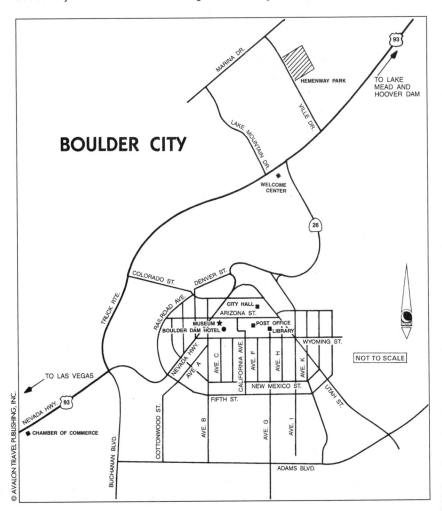

the Black Canyon colossus

LAS VEGAS NEWS BUREAU

Construction of the town began in March 1931, only a month before work commenced at the dam site. The increasing influx of workers, most of whom were housed in a cluster of temporary tent cabins known as Ragtown, forced the government to accelerate the building. Most of De-Boer's more grandiose elements (neighborhood greenbelts, large single-family houses) were abandoned in favor of a more economical and expedient approach (dormitories and small cottages). Still, Boulder City became a prettified all-American oasis of security and order in the midst of a great desert and the Great Depression. The Bureau of Reclamation controlled the town down to the smallest detail; a city manager, answerable directly to the federal Commissioner of Reclamation, oversaw operations, and his authority was near total.

After the dam was completed, the town master plan was further dismantled, as workers left and company housing was moved or torn down for materials. For a while thereafter, Boulder City seemed in a little danger of turning into a ghost, but visitors to the dam and Lake Mead had a different idea, and the town became a service center for the recreation area. For 30 years the federal government owned the town and all its buildings, but in early 1960, an act of Congress established Boulder City as an independent municipality. Officials drew up a city charter, the feds began to sell property to the long-time residents, and alcohol sales were allowed for the first time in Boulder City. Gambling, however, remains disallowed—the only town in the state

with laws against it. Boulder City today might be far from the government's squeaky clean and DeBoer's grandly green. But it retains an air of its own—especially in contrast to the rest of southern Nevada.

Sights

Coming into Boulder City on Hwy. 93 (Nevada Hwy.) is more like entering a town in Arizona or New Mexico, with Indian and Mexican gift shops and a number of galleries, as well as crafts, jewelry, antique, and collectibles stores along the downtown streets, and no casinos.

Continue into town to the **Boulder City/Hoover Dam Museum,** 444 Hotel Plaza, 702/294-1988, open 10 A.M.–4 P.M., donation. Inside are interesting black-and-white prints from the '30s, such as the Six Companies' rec hall, and high scalers working high up on the canyon walls. Also look for the high-scaler bosun's chair. And pick up Dennis McBride's excellent book on Boulder City. Upstairs is a small theater where "The Story of Hoover Dam," an outstanding 28-minute documentary of the dam construction, is shown.

Across the street at 1305 Arizona St., 702/293-3510, have a look around the 65-year-old **Boulder Dam Hotel,** restored in 1980. Though its elegant dining, private baths, and air conditioning were rarities in southern Nevada in the early '30s, the hotel over the years has fallen into disrepair. In late 1993 Boulder City's Chamber of Commerce, arts council, and historical society raised $560,000 and bought the place; the

Chamber of Commerce subsequently moved in. Plans were also in the works to house a city history museum, art gallery, and boutiques. The lobby looks exactly the same as it did in 1933 when it was constructed, as you can see for yourself in the black and whites. The fine dining room is open noon–9 P.M.; three sets of double French doors open onto the al fresco patio, with a view of the distinctive white brick and gumwood exterior. Downstairs in the cellar is the bar, a subterranean affair with a stone wall in back of the bar, where 1930s celebrities and dignitaries drank and gambled, both of which were illegal in the government town; in fall 1997, the bar was open on Monday nights for the football game.

After visiting the hotel, make sure to pull out your walking tour brochure and stroll up Arizona St., then down Nevada Hwy., to get a feel for the history and design significance of downtown. Then continue on the residential and public-building walks to get an intimate glimpse of De-Boer's imagination—as modified by government work. You can also head back toward Henderson on Nevada Hwy. to the Frank T. Crowe Memorial Park (named for the chief dam engineer, immortalized in *Big Red*), and take a right there onto Cherry St. to see the fine row of original bungalows from the '30s.

Practicalities

Boulder City has a handful of motels, all strung along Nevada Highway (US 93) as you enter town. From west to east are: **Starview,** 1017 Nevada Hwy., 702/293-1658, $25–75; **Nevada,** 1009 Nevada Hwy., 702/293-2044, $30–55; **Sands,** 809 Nevada Hwy., 702/293-2589, $37–50; **Flamingo,** 804 Nevada Hwy., 702/293-3565, $27–60; **Desert Inn,** 800 Nevada Hwy., 702/293-2827, $30–90; **El Rancho,** 725 Nevada Hwy., 702/293-1085, $60–150; and **Super 8,** 704 Nevada Hwy., 702/293-8888 or 800/800-8000, $40–50.

Canyon Trail RV Park, 1200 Industrial Road, Boulder City, 702/293-1200, is the only RV park in Boulder City. It's mostly residential, with permanent mobiles, but there're plenty of overnight spots. There's no shade and precious little greenery, but craggy sandstone mountains rise from the rear of the place. It has 156 spaces, all with full hookups, or which 86 are pull-throughs. Tents

are not allowed. The fee is $15 for two people (Good Sam discount). To get there, from the traffic light in Boulder City, take the truck route one block to Canyon Road. Turn left on Canyon Road, drive to the end, and turn left on Industrial Road. Drive half a block and turn right into the RV park.

Coming into town from Las Vegas, you'll pass **McDonald's, Wendy's, Pizza Hut, Texas Chicken & Fixins,** and **Baskin-Robbins.** Downtown are the dining room in the **Boulder Dam Hotel,** the **Koffee Korner,** open 5 A.M.–2 P.M., and **Carlos** Mexican restaurant, open Tues.–Fri. 11 A.M.–9 P.M., Saturday and Sunday 11 A.M.–9 P.M.

The **Chamber of Commerce,** 1305 Arizona St. in the Boulder Dam Hotel, 702/293-2034, open Mon.–Fri. 9 A.M.–5 P.M., has all the local brochures and can answer questions about the town, the dam, and the lake.

To the Dam

To get to the dam (eight miles away), cut off to the left on the truck route (at Buchanan Blvd.) before town, or continue through town along Nevada Hwy. to join up with it. At the junction of the truck route with Nevada Hwy. is a state Commission on Tourism **Welcome Center,** 702/294-1252, for all the visitors coming in from Arizona over the dam. Pick up your handful of brochures and visitors guides; if the center is closed, read the signboards out front.

At the corner of US 93 and Ville St. (at the Texaco station), take a left and go two blocks to **Hemenway Park.** Don't be surprised by all the signs about bighorn sheep. In the summer, these wild creatures (the state animal), which are normally extremely skittish and retiring, come down from the hills for water and grass at this park.

In a mile or so you enter **Lake Mead National Recreation Area,** and arrive at the junction of US 93 and NV 166 (Lakeshore Dr.). Taking a left on the state route brings you right to the **Alan Bible Visitor Center,** 702/293-8906, and park headquarters for the recreation area. Named after a popular Nevada U.S. senator, this modern facility is open daily 8:30 A.M.–5 P.M., has a 15-minute movie on the lake and flora (shown 9 A.M.–4 P.M.), and sells postcards, videos, books, and maps. Pick up the free Lake

Mead NPS map, and buy K.C. Publications' as-usual excellent souvenir book, *Lake Mead-Hoover Dam,* by James Maxon, or the *Lake Mead Auto Tourguide* (1971).

Across Lake Shore Drive from the visitor center is a parking lot for the trailhead to the **U.S. Government Construction Railroad Trail.** The 2.6-mile one-way route follows an abandoned railroad grade along a ledge overlooking the lake. It passes through four tunnels blasted through the hills and ends at the fifth tunnel, which is sealed. This is an enjoyable level stroll that anyone can do.

Another trail to consider in Boulder City is the **River Mountain Hiking Trail,** a five-mile roundtrip hike built originally by the Civilian Conservation Corps in 1935 and recently restored, with good views of the lake and the valley. The trailhead is on the truck bypass, just beyond the traffic light in downtown Boulder City, on the left as you're heading toward the dam.

On the way to the dam, up the hill from the visitor center, is the **Gold Strike Inn,** 702/293-5000, with 155 rooms going for $19–29, standard at these hotels. Don't be put off by the exterior design and color scheme. The casino is surprisingly big and busy (and red), with an excellent antique slot and cash register display as you walk in, a long pit, a big theater upstairs that shows the "Story of Hoover Dam" (at 11, 1, and 2:30), a steakhouse, and a big gift shop.

On the other side of the Gold Strike you enter some wild canyonlands in the rugged mountains above the Colorado River, with a massive parade of supernatural superstructures: cosmic-erector-set towers; alien electrical generators, transformers, and capacitors; neuro-planetary high-tension cables and inductive coils—in short, *the grid*—like some alien invasion force straight out of the imagination of George Lucas. Cycline fencing keeps the humans away.

HOOVER DAM

The 1,400-mile Colorado River has been carving and gouging great canyons and valleys with red *(colorado)* sediment-laden waters for nearly 10 million years. For 10,000 years, Indian, Spanish, and Mormon settlers coexisted with the fitful river, which often overflowed with spring floods and then tapered off in the fall to a muddy trickle. By the turn of the 20th century, irrigation ditches and canals had diverted some of the river water into California's Imperial Valley, west of its natural channel. But in 1905, a wet winter and abnormal spring rains combined to drown everything in sight: flash floods deepened the manmade canal and actually changed the course of the river to flow through California's low-lying valley. For nearly two years engineers and farmers fought the Colorado back into place; the Salton Sea, which had been 22 square miles, grew to 500 square miles, and remains today more than 200 square miles, nearly 95 years later. But the message was clear to the dam-building, river-diverting, nature-conquering federal overseers: the Rio Colorado had to be tamed.

Enter the Bureau of Reclamation, established only three years earlier, the brainchild of Nevada Senator Francis Newlands. Over the next 15 years, the bureau began to "reclaim" the West, primarily by building dams and canals. Its first was Derby Dam, a few miles east of Reno; it also built Lahontan Dam, a few miles west of Fallon. By 1920, Reclamation had narrowed the possible dam sites on the Colorado from 70 to 2, Boulder and Black canyons. It took another three years to negotiate an equitable water distribution among the affected states (and Mexico) and another six for Congress to pass the Boulder Canyon Project Act, authorizing funds for Boulder Dam to be constructed in Black Canyon (the dam's name was eventually changed to honor Herbert Hoover, then Secretary of Commerce).

The immensity of the undertaking still boggles the brain. The closest civilization was at a sleepy railroad town, 40 miles west, called Las Vegas, and the nearest large power plant was in San Bernardino, more than 200 miles away. Tracks had to be laid, a town built, men hired, equipment shipped in—just to prepare for construction. And then! The mighty Colorado had to be diverted. The project began in April 1931. Workers hacked four tunnels, each 56 feet across, through the canyon walls. They loosened, carried off, and dumped thousands of tons of rock every day for 16 months. Finally, in November 1932, the river water was rerouted around the dam site.

Then came the concrete.

Over the course of the next two years, eight-cubic-yard buckets full of cement were lowered into the canyon (five million of them) till the dam—660 feet thick at the base, 45 feet thick at the crest, 1,244 feet across, and 726 feet high—had swallowed 3.2 million cubic yards, or seven million tons, of the hardening stuff. The top of the dam was built wide enough to accommodate a two-lane highway. Inside this Pantagruelian wedge were placed 17 gargantuan electrical turbines. The cost of the dam surpassed $175 million. At the peak of construction, more than 5,000 workers toiled day and night to complete the project, under the most extreme conditions of heat and dust, and danger from heavy equipment, explosions, falling rock, heights, etc. (An average of 50 injuries per day and a total of 94 deaths were recorded over the 46 months of construction.)

The largest construction equipment yet known to the world had to be invented, designed, fabricated, and installed on the spot. Yet miraculously, the dam was completed nearly two years *ahead* of schedule. In February 1935, the diversion tunnels were closed, and Lake Mead began to fill up behind the dam, which was dedicated eight months later by President Franklin Roosevelt. A month after that, the first turbine was turned, and electricity started flowing as the water was finally controlled.

Today, the Colorado River system has several dams and reservoirs, storing roughly 60 million acre-feet of water (an acre-foot is just under 326,000 gallons, about as much water as an average American household uses in two years). California is allotted 4.4 million acre-feet, Arizona gets 2.8 million, Nevada 300,000, and Mexico 1.5 million. Hoover Dam, meanwhile, supplies four billion kilowatt-hours of electricity annually (enough to power half a million homes).

Sights and Tours

In 1977, the Bureau of Reclamation decided to build a new and improved visitor center to accommodate the 700,000 visitors the dam receives yearly (more than 32 million visitors have taken the tour of the most heavily visited dam in the country). Estimates in 1983 tagged the cost at $32 million. Well, in what turned out to be one of the biggest federal boondoggles in recent memory, the 44,000-square-foot visitor center and five-story 450-car parking garage (wedged into a ravine in the mountain) cost upwards of $120 million and were finally completed and opened in the summer of 1995. Construction of the visitor center weathered three presidential administrations, four regional directors of Reclamations, five Congressional elections, and 213 episodes of "Roseanne." Financed over 50 years, the new visitor center is expected to cost $435 million when all is said and done. Luxor cost only $375 million. Who pays? Customers of the power companies that receive their electricity from the dam. In fact, the cost overruns came to light only after two Nevada utilities complained about the precipitous climb in their electric bills.

Anyway, it's a pretty nice visitor center. It has some exhibits, a movie on the Colorado River, and elevators that take you into the bowels of the dam. Buy tickets for the 35-minute dam tour ($6, open 8:30 A.M.–5:30 P.M. Memorial Day to Labor Day, 9 A.M.–4 P.M. winter), then get in line and wait (arriving as early as possible will shorten the waiting time in line). Eventually you'll take the 75-second elevator ride to the bottom of the dam (it's like descending from the 53rd floor of a skyscraper). Tunnels lead you to a monumental room housing the monolithic turbines. Next you step outside, where a hundred necks crane to view the top of the dam. Next you walk through one of the diversion tunnels to view a 30-foot-diameter waterpipe. The guides pack hours of statistics and stories into the short tour. For more info, call the visitor center at 702/293-8321.

River Tours

Black Canyon Rafting Company, 702/293-3776 or 800/696-RAFT, offers river trips Jan. 9–Nov. 30 (changeable, call first). The tours leave from the Expedition Depot (next to McDonald's at 1297 Nevada Hwy. in Boulder City) at 9:30 A.M.; you're bused to the restricted side of the dam, where you board rafts that can hold 32–42 people, for a 3.5-hour ride through Black Canyon down the Colorado 12 miles to Willow Beach. You're served lunch, then driven back to the depot (arriving around 2:30). The cost is $89.95 per person.

The *Desert Princess* is a 250-passenger Mississippi-style sternwheeler that cruises Lake Mead out of Lake Mead Marina, 702/293-6180. Daily 90-minute cruises leave at 11:30, 1:30, and 3:30 ($18 adults, $9 children); a two-hour dinner cruise departs at 5:30 Friday and Saturday ($30/$17); a three-hour dinner-dance cruise departs at 7:30 P.M. Friday and Saturday ($49); and a two-hour brunch cruise departs at 9:30 A.M. Saturday and Sunday ($26/$14). Lake Mead Marina is off US 93; take a right at the sign just before the Alan Bible Visitor Center.

Back to Las Vegas

Head back toward Boulder City from the dam, but take a right at the fork onto NV 166 (Lakeshore Dr.). In a couple of miles you come to **Boulder Beach,** a typical Lake Mead settlement, with trailer parks, marinas, picnic areas, and a two-mile-long beach. Colorful Fortification Hill stands out on the other side of the lake; a basalt formation, the reddish rocks around the base are known as the Paint Pots. Continue north on Lakeshore Dr. between the lake on the east and the rugged River Range on the west. In another seven miles the road curves around left (west), where it turns into NV 147 toward Henderson. But take a right (north) on NV 147 and cross **Las Vegas Wash,** an amazing little creek that drains Las Vegas Valley into the Colorado River system. At the intersection with North Shore Dr., follow NV 147 around to the left (west). This turns into Lake Mead Blvd., passing behind and through Frenchman's and Sunrise mountains, to enter Las Vegas from the northeast.

LAKE MEAD NATIONAL RECREATION AREA

Hoover Dam began detaining the Colorado and Virgin rivers in 1935. By 1938, Lake Mead was full: three years' worth of river water braced by the Brobdingnagian buttress at Black Canyon. Largest man-made lake in the West, Lake Mead measures 110 miles long and 500 feet deep, has 822 miles of shoreline, and contains 28.5 million acre-feet of water (or just over nine trillion gallons), a little less than half the water reserved along the entire Colorado River system. The reservoir irrigates 2.25 million acres of land in the U.S. and Mexico and supplies water for more than 14 million people. Nine million people each year use Lake Mead as a recreational resource;

it's the fourth most visited Park Service-managed area in the country.

For all this, Lake Mead is only a sidelight to the dam's primary purpose: flood and drought control. In addition, Lake Mead is only the centerpiece of the 1.5-million-acre Lake Mead National Recreation Area, which includes Lake Mojave and the surrounding desert from Davis Dam to the south and Grand Canyon National Park in the east, all the way north to Overton—the largest Department of Interior recreational acreage in the country, outside of Alaska.

And recreation it certainly provides. **Swimming** is the most accessible, and requires the least equipment: a bathing suit. Boulder Beach, only 30 miles from Las Vegas and just down the road from the Alan Bible Visitor Center, is the most popular swimming site. For **divers,** visibility averages 30 feet, the water is stable, and sights of the deep abound: the yacht *Tortuga* rests at 50 feet near the Boulder Islands; Hoover Dam's asphalt factory sits on the canyon floor nearby; the old Mormon town of St. Thomas, inundated by the lake in 1938, has many a watery story to tell; Wishing Well Cove has steep canyon walls and drop-offs, caves, and clear water; Ringbolt Rapids, an exhilarating drift dive, is for advanced divers only; and the Tennis Shoe Graveyard, near Las Vegas Wash, is one of many footholds of hidden treasure.

Boating on the vast lake is even more varied. Power boats skip across the surface, houseboats putter toward hidden coves, and sailing and windsurfing are year-round thrills.

For **anglers,** largemouth bass, rainbow, brown, and cutthroat trout, catfish, and black crappie have been the mainstays for decades. These days, though, striped bass provide the sport. Five marinas in Nevada provide camping, restaurants and bars, fishing supplies, and boat rentals. Two of these offer showers, houseboats, and motels.

Recreation is also abundant at **Lake Mojave,** created downstream by Davis Dam in 1953. This lake backs up almost all the way to Hoover Dam, like an extension of Lake Mead. The two lakes are similar in climate, desert scenery, vertical-walled canyon enclosures, and a shoreline digitated with numerous private coves. It offers excellent trout fishing at Willow Beach on the Ari-

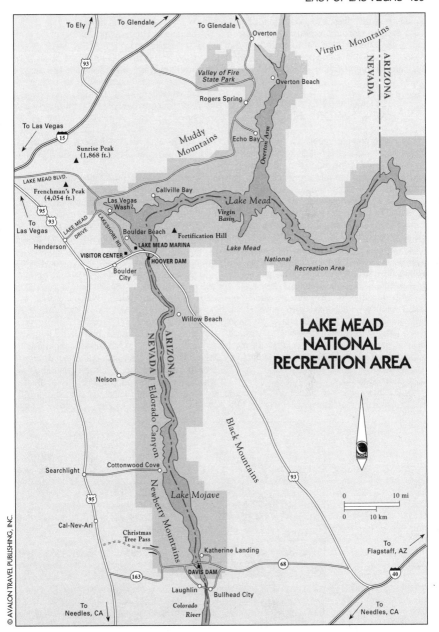

LAKE MEAD NATIONAL RECREATION AREA

zona side, where the water, too cold for swimming, is perfect for serious angling. Marinas are found at Cottonwood Cove just north of the widest part of the lake and at Katherine Landing just north of Davis Dam.

LAKESHORE AND NORTHSHORE ROADS

Three roads provide access to the NRA: one urban loop road that connects to two lakeside drives. NV 147 is the loop road; the northern section is called Lake Mead Boulevard, the southern section Lake Mead Drive. Lake Mead Blvd. runs east through North Las Vegas (pick it up off I-15 or Las Vegas Blvd. North, climbs into the Sunrise Mountains, and enters the rugged Lake Mead Recreation Area. Lake Mead Drive runs northeast through Henderson (pick it up off I-215 or Boulder Hwy.) and passes Lake Las Vegas, the most exclusive subdivision in southern Nevada. From Lake Mead Blvd., take a left at the stop sign onto NV 167 toward Callville Bay and Overton, or a right onto NV 166 toward Lake Mead Marina and Boulder Beach. From Lake Mead Drive, take a right onto NV 167 toward Callville Bay and Overton or just follow the road around to the left (NV 166) for Lake Mead Marina and Boulder Beach.

Lakeshore Road

From the intersection of US 93 and Highway 166 just past the Alan Bible Visitor Center, turn left on Highway 166 and drive one mile north. You'll come to **Hemenway Campground,** the closest camping on the lake to Las Vegas, Boulder City, and Hoover Dam. It's a sprawling campground that's rarely full, with 158 campsites for tents or self-contained motor homes up to 35 feet. Piped drinking water, flush toilets, sewage disposal, picnic tables, grills, and fire rings are provided. The maximum stay is 30 days. No reservations; $8 per site. For information, call the National Park Service, 601 Nevada Highway, Boulder City, NV 89005, 702/293-8990.

About a mile north on Lakeshore Road is **Lakeshore Trailer Village,** which is mostly for permanent mobiles and trailers, but has a compact area near the entrance dedicated to transient RVers (register at the office near the entrance). There are 75 spaces for overnight motor homes, all with full hookups, of which 23 are pull-throughs. Tents are not allowed. Laundromat and groceries are available. Reservations are not accepted (except for Memorial Day, July 4th, and Labor Day weekends). The fee is $14 for two people. Contact: Lakeshore RV Park, 702/293-2540.

You turn right off Lakeshore Road into the entrance and right to the trailer village. If you take a left at the entrance, you enter **Boulder Beach Campground,** a sprawling and somewhat rustic campground with plenty of shade under cottonwood and pines. There are 140 campsites for tents or self-contained motor

Lake Mead

DEKE CASTLEMAN

homes up to 35 feet. Piped drinking water, flush toilets, sewage disposal, picnic tables, and grills are provided. There is a campground host. The maximum stay is 30 days. No reservations; $8 per site. It's a three-minute walk down to the water (by car, a half-mile drive north on Lakeshore Drive). They don't call it Boulder Beach for nothing: the bottom is rocky and hard on the feet (bring your sandals). But the water is bathtub warm, 80 degrees or so all summer long. Sheltered picnic tables and restrooms are available waterside.

Seven miles beyond Boulder Beach is **Las Vegas Bay Campground.** Turn right into the Las Vegas Marina, then take your first left; the campground is about a mile down the spur road. The campground sits on a bluff over the lake; it's not quite as shady or large as Boulder Beach. Also, you've got to climb down a pretty steep slope to get the water, but even when you get there, there's no real beach here. There are 86 campsites for tents or self-contained motor homes up to 35 feet. Piped drinking water, flush toilets, picnic tables, grills, and fire pits are provided. There is a campground host. The maximum stay is 30 days. No reservations; $8 per site; contact: National Park Service, 601 Nevada Highway, 702/293-8906. The marina is a bit of a trek (a mile and a half by vehicle). It has a convenience store, restaurant, and bar. It's also home to the sternwheeler Desert Princess, which offers a variety of sightseeing and food cruises around the lake.

Continuing north you follow Lakeshore Road around to the left (southwest), then take a right onto Northshore Road (NV 167). In another few miles, go right at the intersection with Lake Mead Blvd. (NV 147). In another seven miles is the turnoff for Callville Bay.

Callville Bay

From the highway, you rock and roll four miles down to the marina, which is green from oleanders, Russian olives, yucca, palms, and pines. Callville Bay is the site of Callville, founded by Anson Call in 1865 in response to a directive from Brigham Young. Callville flourished briefly in the 1860s as a landing for Colorado River steamboats and an army garrison, but the post office closed in 1869. The stone ruins of Call's warehouse today rest under 400 feet of Lake Mead water and 10 feet of Lake Mead silt.

As you come into the marina, the first left is to **Callville Bay Trailer Village,** most of which is occupied by permanent mobiles and trailers. There are only six spaces for overnight motor homes, all with full hookups and three pull-throughs. Tents are not allowed. Laundromat and groceries are available at the marina. Reservations are recommended, especially on weekends. Contact Callville Bay Trailer Village, 702/565-8958. The fee is $17 for two people; register at the Administration office by the marina. RVs can also park without hookups at the campground across the way. (Better yet, drive another 30 minutes to Echo Bay, the best RV parking on the lake.)

Callville Bay Campground is a little farther down the access road. A beautiful grassy area greets you at the entrance, with stone picnic benches under shelters and a restroom. The sites closer to the front have the taller shade-giving oleanders; those toward the rear are more exposed. A half-mile trail climbs from the dump station near the entrance to a sweeping panorama of the whole area. There are 80 campsites for tents or self-contained motor homes up to 35 feet. Piped drinking water, flush toilets, picnic tables and grills are provided. There is a campground host. The maximum stay is 90 days. No reservations; the fee is $8. Contact the National Park Service, 601 Nevada Highway, Boulder City, 702/293-8990.

Continuing toward the marina, you'll encounter the visitor center in a gray trailer in the upper parking lot, open Fri.–Sun. 10 A.M.–2 P.M. Pick up the requisite ton of brochures and check out the photo of Callville's stone ruins and the geology poster. Volunteers answer your questions and sell you books about the desert. Restrooms are next door. A sign at the edge of the lower parking lot points down to a swimming area in a little inlet (no lifeguard).

The marina has a grocery store with snack bar (bacon and eggs $4–5, burgers $4, sandwiches $5) and a bar-restaurant with a wall of big

LOUISE FOOTE

picture windows overlooking the lake. Down at the boat launch you can rent houseboats (from about $250 a night between November and May up to $500 a night between June and September). You can also hop on Forever Resorts' Lake Mead tour boats. Callville attracts the lion share of the crowds from Las Vegas, and has no beach to speak of. It's worth it to drive another 24 miles to Echo Bay.

Back on NV 167, continue east. It's rugged country out here, with the Black Mountains between you and the lake and the dark brooding Muddy Mountains to the left. In a while is the **Redstone Picnic Area,** just a big old pile of Aztec sandstone in the middle of nowhere, with picnic tables, pit toilets, and a one-mile trail through the monoliths, complete with interpretive signs. Just past Redstone, the road turns north and aims straight toward the east edge of the Muddy Mountains. The turnoff to Echo Bay, 24 miles from Callville, is on the right.

Echo Bay

You rock and roll four miles down Bitter Spring Valley to Echo Bay. This resort has a similar layout to Callville Bay, but is much larger. The first left is to **Echo Bay Trailer Village** the best RV park on Lake Mead's Nevada side. Spaces are nice and wide, with telephone-pole stumps separating them. Every site has a tree or two. And there are no permanents: all the mobiles and trailers are across the way, and this lot is only for RVs. There are 35 spaces for motor homes, all with full hookups, but no pull-throughs. Tents are not allowed. Restrooms have flush toilets and hot showers; public phone, sewage disposal, laundry, and groceries are available. Reservations are accepted; contact Echo Bay Trailer Village, Overton, NV 89040, 702/394-4066 or 800/752-9669. The fee is $9 per vehicle in winter, $18 per vehicle in summer. Register at the front desk of Echo Bay Seven Crowns Resort.

Or go left into **Echo Bay Campground.** There's an upper and a lower campground. The lower campground overlooks the houseboating area and is closer to the marina action, and has 20-foot tall oleander bushes that give much-needed shade to the sites in the hot summer afternoons. There are 155 campsites for tents or self-contained motor homes up to 35 feet. Piped drinking water, flush toilets, sewage disposal,

picnic tables, and grills are provided. The maximum stay is 90 days. No reservations; the fee is $8. Contact the National Park Service, 601 Nevada Highway, Boulder City, 702/293-8990.

A little past the campground turnoff is a self-service information center, open daily 8 A.M.–4 P.M. Outside is a desert garden with labeled plants; inside are displays on fishing (including record catches) and the town of St. Thomas, inundated by Lake Mead in June 1938.

Continue down toward the marina; just before the big boat-repair building is the right turn into the lower campground. You pass the boat buildings and Park Service administrative offices and residences, then come to Echo Bay's Seven Crowns Resort, 702/394-4000. Rooms at the inn are $45 in winter and $69, $79, and $89 in summer depending on the room's size and view. The restaurant next door is open 8 A.M.–8 P.M. (an hour earlier and later on weekends), serving bacon and eggs and omelettes for $4.75, salads and sandwiches for $6, and steaks, chicken, fish, and stir-fries for $10–15. The windows overlook the parking lot.

The store and Texaco gas station are open daily 8 A.M.–5 P.M. You can rent houseboats, a variety of fishing and ski boats, and Sea-Doos, too.

But the great thing about Echo Bay is the beach: the best and most easily accessible beach on the Nevada side of the lake. There's no shade to speak of, but it's a sandy beach (unlike the rocks at Boulder Beach), and you'll pretty much own the place. The bay is shallow for a long distance out, so the swimming is safe (no lifeguard).

Overton Beach

Back on North Shore Rd., you continue north for a little ways, skirting the east edge of the Muddies. In less than a mile is **Rogers Spring,** which bubbles up clear and warm in a wash that runs east from the Muddy Mountains into Roger's Bay in the Overton Arm of Lake Mead. The warm turquoise pool, which is outlined by towering palms and old sturdy cottonwoods, overflows into a bubbling creek which meanders down a tree-lined course toward Lake Mead. The high mineral content of the water gives the pool a beautiful blue color and makes its depth deceptive. Transplanted tropical fish dart in the shallows and thrive in its warm waters. This spring has long been a favorite camping spot of southern Nevadans; in fact, it was originally developed by the Civilian Conservation Corps in the 1930s under the direction of Col. Thomas W. Miller, the same colonel who was instrumental in developing the first facilities at nearby Valley of Fire State Park. The National Park Service has plans, when the money is available, to develop some 250 campsites with water, sewer and power. For now, there're only chemical toilets and picnic shelters. A sign cautions swimmers not to put their heads in the water. The trailhead for a mile-long trail to an overlook is across the bridge over the stream.

A mile up the road from Rogers is **Blue Point Spring,** from where you have a grand view of Lake Mead on one side and the back of Valley of Fire on the other.

In another mile is the turnoff to **Overton Beach,** a three-mile straight shot to the top of Overton Arm of Lake Mead. Overton Beach is the farthest resort from the dam. The best fishing on Lake Mead is up here, thanks to its location three miles from both the Muddy and Virgin rivers (which dump a lot of fish food into the lake). **Overton Beach RV Park** is on the right. Every one of the 54 spaces has a view of the lake and is a two-minute walk to the water. There are 12 pull-throughs. Tents are allowed. Restrooms have flush toilets and hot showers ($1 for noncampers); public phone, sewage disposal, laundry, groceries, gas dock, marina, and swim beach are available. Reservations are accepted; the fee is $15 for two people. Contact Overton Beach Resort, 702/394-4040.

The marina has a convenience store and cafe, selling the usual groceries, sundries, and T-shirts, along with $2 hot dogs at the snack bar. The beach is a bearable combination of stone and sand. The eastern entrance to Valley of Fire is less than a mile west of the turnoff to Overton Beach; instead of going right to the lake, you take a left onto NV 169. This intersection is 93 miles from Las Vegas.

Virgin Basin

Just above the Overton Beach, two rivers, the Virgin to the northeast and the Muddy to the northwest, empty into Lake Mead. The Virgin Basin is a widening of the Virgin River just before it merges with the reservoir. It's a primary habitat for numerous species of wildlife, including mammals, waterfowl, birds of prey, fish, and reptiles and amphibians. In the fall and spring, for example, numerous migrating species use the Virgin Basin as a resting place on their way. Some species, including numerous bald eagles, spend the winter in the Virgin Basin. Because it's accessible only by boat, the Virgin Basin is well protected and offers wildlife a habitat safe from most human intervention. If you're careful, the basin provides an excellent opportunity to view and photograph wildlife in one of the few wilderness river areas left near the lake. To get there, you have to boat in from the Overton Arm. Most of the time there isn't enough water in the Virgin River below Riverside (just south of Mesquite) to float anything but an innertube.

VALLEY OF FIRE STATE PARK

At this stunning piece of Olympian sculpture, the gods had miles of fire-red rock to carve, and 150 million years to fill in the details. Like Red Rock Canyon, this valley, six miles long and three to four miles wide, is another spectacular ancestral hall of the Navajo Formation, a continuum of Mesozoic sandstone that stretches from southern Colorado through New Mexico, Arizona, Utah, and Nevada. Its monuments—arches, protruding jagged walls, divine engravings and human etchings, all in brilliant vermilion, scarlet, mauve, burgundy, magenta, orange, and gold—more than any other characteristic are representative of the great American Southwest.

The highest and youngest formations in the park are mountains of sand deposited by desert winds 140 million years ago—the familiar, by now, Aztec sandstone. These dunes were petrified, oxidized, and chiseled by time, sun, water, and chemical reactions into their psychedelic shapes and colors. Underneath the Aztec is a 5,000-foot-deep layer of brown mud, dating back at least 250 million years, when uplift displaced the inland sea. The gray limestone below represents another 200 million years of deposits from as long as 550 million years ago, from the Paleozoic marine environment.

This stunning valley was venerated by Indians, as evidenced by numerous petroglyphs

Elephant Rock is only one of nature's countless bizarre carvings at Valley of Fire State Park.

JOHN ELK III

in the soft rock, and was part of the old Arrowhead Trail through southern Nevada. It was originally included in lands set aside by the federal government for construction of Boulder Dam in the 1920s, then donated to the state in 1931 as a state park. Nevada had little money to spend on development, so the feds sent in the Civilian Conservation Corps, which built the road, campgrounds, and some cabins.

Meanwhile, Nevada designated Valley of Fire a state park in 1935, one of the four original Nevada state parks. Eager locals jumped the gun and held an unofficial celebration on Easter Sunday 1935 for the completion of the road, which is how Valley of Fire came to be considered Nevada's first state park.

Sights

A turnout near the entrance to the park has a self-service fee station: $4 admission for cars, $1 for bicycles. Here is also an information shelter with a description of **Elephant Rock,** one of the best and most photographed examples of eroded sandstone in the park. A short trail leads to it. Continue west past signs for the Arrowhead Trail and petrified logs to the **Cabins,** built for travelers out of sandstone bricks by the CCC in 1935. Farther in, the **Seven Sisters** are stunning sentinels along the road.

The **visitors center** has a truly spectacular setting under a mountain of fire. Outside is a demonstration garden and inside is the finest

set of exhibits at a Nevada state park. Signboards by the front window describe the complex 550-million-year-old geological history of the view. You can spend another hour reading all the displays on the history, ecology, archaeology, and recreation of the park, along with browsing in the changing exhibit gallery and at the bookshelf by the information desk. Don't miss the colorful signboard of the most popular features in Valley of Fire: Cobra Rock, Indian Marbles, Grand Piano, Beehive, Balancing Rock, Mouse's Tank, Duck Rock, Rock of Gibraltar, Silica Dome, Limestone Hoodoos, and more. And don't forget to pick up a map of the park. For info, contact Valley of Fire State Park, Box 515, Overton, NV 89040, 702/397-2088.

From the visitor center, take the spur road to **Petroglyph Canyon Trail,** and dig your feet into some red sand. A trail guide introduces you to the local flora. **Mouse's Tank** is a basin that fills up with water after a rain; a fugitive Indian, Mouse, hid here in the late 1890s. The spur road continues through the towering canyon and peaks at **Rainbow Vista,** which has a parking area and spectacular overlook.

The road used to dead-end here, but in summer 1994, the state opened a new four-mile extension all the way to Silica Dome. This is one of the most fun roads in Nevada, not only for its incomparable views, but for its twists and turns and ups and downs; a maniac on a motorcycle could catch *big* air—before being arrested by a ranger. The rare red-rocky and riotous relief will rally you to rants, raves, and high crimes of alliteration. Finally, you arrive at **Silica Dome**, where you can park your car and marvel, open-mouthed, at the walls and pillars and peaks of sparkling white rock.

Heading west again on the through road, NV 169, you come to a quarter-mile loop trail to fenced-in **petrified wood,** the most common local fossil. On the other side of the highway, another spur road goes to the campgrounds and the high staircase up to petroglyphed and sheer **Atlatl Rock.** This is the tallest outdoor staircase in the state, more than 100 steps up to the face of the rock. You'll wonder how whoever inscribed the face got up and stayed up here.

Atlatl Rock is between the two separate and prosaically named campgrounds. **Campground A** is the larger; thus it's more crowded with RVers; three walk-in campsites are in the rear of the campground. Sites here have gravel pads for tent camping, picnic tables under shelters, barbecue grills, and running water; the restrooms have showers. **Campground B** is more compact and scenic; the back campsites, under the fiery red cliffs, are the most spectacular in Nevada. Together the two combine for 51 campsites for tents or self-contained motor homes up to 30 feet. Both have piped drinking water. Campground A has flush toilets and shower, Campground B has vault toilets. Campground A is open year-round, Campground B is closed for 2–3 months every summer (to regenerate). Picnic tables under ramadas, grills, and fire rings are provided. The maximum stay is 14 days. No reservations; the fee is $10 per vehicle.

The loop road continues back to the highway, though the pavement ends. It's hard red gravel, bumpy and rocky, but it's not too far back to smooth sailing.

Take a right and continue west to the **Beehives,** worth a look. From here you can turn around, return to the east entrance, and take a left on NV 169 up to Overton. Or you can head to the west end of the park and back to Las Vegas (55 miles). Or you can take a 28-mile detour on a BLM Back Country Byway Trail, winding up on Northshore Road near Echo Bay.

BITTER SPRINGS BACK COUNTRY BYWAYS TRAIL AND BUFFINGTON POCKETS

The Bitter Springs Back Country Byways Trail to Buffington Pockets and beyond is a worthwhile scenic trip through brightly colored red and tan sandstone bluffs. The 28-mile drive is a challenging adventure that can be made in a dependable vehicle with decent ground clearance. However, you should stay on the main road and avoid side trips into the many canyons unless you have a 4WD vehicle. The beginning of the Bitter Springs Byway is 4.5 miles east of the Valley of Fire exit on I-15; follow the sign for Bitter Springs to the left (south).

You start out cutting through the foothills of the Muddy Mountains, then travel through several dry washes and past numerous abandoned mining operations, before ending up on Northshore Drive. Along the way you have the opportunity to view lush streams that provide a strong contrast to the surrounding desert and access for viewing geologic formations that are very rare for this region of Nevada. Frequent evidence of the borax mining that was once a dominant economic force in the region is obvious everywhere. Landforms are colorful, complex, and add to the feeling of isolation. Among the more striking scenes you'll encounter is Bitter Ridge, a sweeping arc that cuts for eight miles across a rolling valley. Geology buffs will appreciate the features of this tilt fault with its rugged vertical southern face looming several hundred feet off the desert floor.

Moving past rolling landforms of red, brown, black, and white, you drop into Bitter Valley, where burnt-red buttes stand like silent sentinels in the middle of the desert floor. These formations are rare, as are others found near the western edge of the Byway after driving across creosote flatlands and through a gray limestone canyon. Emerging from the canyon, you'll be captivated by the sight of the brilliantly colored sandstone hills of Buffington Pockets and Color Rock Quarry.

Continue to wind through a field of sandstone boulders; you'll soon arrive at the entrance to Hidden Valley, tucked away a short distance from the road up a deep, winding, boulder-choked canyon. Confined within the valley's walls, which soar hundreds of feet into the desert sky, are numerous sandstone windows, arches, and spires. Stop and take a short hike up into the valley. Early humans were apparently awed by the grandeur here, as demonstrated by an unusually high concentration of pictographs and petroglyphs marking various sights.

Remnants of mining man can be seen when you come across the remains of the American Borax mining operation. Several mine buildings still stand, and the ground is marked by 30-foot-deep cisterns that once held water. Mine tunnels and adits (horizontal passages) are also abundant in the area, along with the debris generally associated with old mining districts. Be very careful around the old mines. Cave-ins, rattlesnakes, and other dangers lurk in dark corners and around unseen bends. Obey all signs and fencing that have been installed for your protection.

There are no services along this isolated road, so make sure your vehicle is in good repair and running on sound tires, and don't forget to let a responsible person know where you're going and when you'll be back. Just in case. Maps of this area are available from the local BLM office. Ask for the Nevada Back Country Byway guide for Bitter Springs Trail.

MOAPA VALLEY

Over a rise awaits the Muddy River Wash, at the outlet of Moapa Valley. Lake Mead terminates here and a thin strip of rich agricultural green escorts the road up the river valley. The Anasazi Indians were farming successfully here a thousand years ago, and built the Pueblo Grande de Nevada, or Lost City, on the fertile delta between the Muddy and Virgin rivers. Paiute replaced Pueblo, and when the Mormons began to colonize the valley in 1864, the Paiute were still there. The Saints' efforts were successful, and today this well-tended plot is their legacy. Settlement extends the six miles north, up the irrigated green Moapa Valley, surrounded on three sides by crew-cut buttes, to Logandale.

Overton

Overton is a compact agricultural community whose downtown is strung along several blocks of NV 169, also known as Moapa Valley Blvd.

and Main Street. The main action in town is at **Sugars,** 702/397-8084. The restaurant serves $4.75 bacon and eggs, $3–5 burgers (including the Sugar Burger: cheeseburger and polish sausage). There's also a sports bar with bartop video poker and sports memorabilia, some from the Moapa Valley Pirates. The **Inside Scoop,** 702/397-2303, has 32 flavors of Dreyers and sandwiches for $3, baked potatoes for $2.50, and nachos for $3–4. A nice big map of Moapa Valley graces the side wall. You can also stop at the Red Rooster Bar, Pizza Plus, and the Chevron station.

If you take a right at the sign, across the street from Foodtown, you'll come to **Overton Community Park.** It has a playground with swings and slides, picnic tables under shelters with grills, big trees, basketball courts, and a baseball field.

Fun & Sun RV Park, 280 N. Cooper, Overton, 702/397-8894, has 112 spaces, 66 of which are pull-throughs. Tents are not allowed. Restrooms have flush toilets and hot showers; public phone, sewage disposal, laundry, rec room, and heated swimming pool and spa are available. Reservations are accepted; the fee is $13.75 for two people.

On the south end of town, a sign points the way to the main attraction, the Lost City Museum.

Lost City Museum

A glimpse of the Anasazi ("Enemies of Our Ancestors") legacy is found at the Lost City Museum, just south of the small farming town of Overton, 50 miles northeast of Las Vegas. The museum houses an immense collection of Pueblo artifacts, including an actual pueblo foundation, and a fascinating series of black-and-white photos covering the site's excavation in 1924. In an incisive article in *Nevada* magazine, (November 1976), David Moore makes the point that the "Lost City" wasn't so much lost as simply overlooked; Jedediah Smith sighted and cited the site during his travels through southern Nevada in the 1820s, and another expedition reported these "ruins of an ancient city" in the *New York Tribune* in 1867. But it was Nevada Governor James G. Scrugham, a mining engineer who, in 1924, initiated the official dig. Some of the Anasazi ruins were drowned by Lake Mead, but even today, the Overton-Logandale area of the delta remains one of the country's "finest bottomless treasure chests of ancient history," according to Moore. Residents who rototill their yards or replace septic tanks uncover scads of shards: in 1975 an entire ancient village was revealed by workmen digging a leach line.

The exterior of the museum, reminiscent of an adobe pueblo, was constructed by the CCC in 1935; climb down the log ladder into the authentic pit house in front. Stroll around back for petroglyphs, more pueblos, picnic tables, and a pioneer monument.

The museum is open daily 8:30 A.M.–4:30 P.M., $2 adults, 18 and under free; write Box 807, Overton, NV 89040, 702/397-2193.

Logandale

If you head north on NV 169 from Overton, you pass a string of ranches on your way into Logandale. On the site of St. Joseph, one of the original (1865) Mormon towns in southern Nevada, this ranching village is mostly east of the road nearer the Muddy River. Along the road are the post office, a grocery store, cows, and **Marc's Kountry Kitchen,** 702/398-3577, open Mon.–Sat. 11 A.M.–10 P.M., serving burgers, spaghetti, ribs, and homemade pies.

Glendale and Moapa

You cross the Muddy River and continue north for another few miles, till the road dead-ends at the interstate. Head west for a couple of miles and get off at the Glendale exit. At the bottom of the ramp, take a right (away from town) toward the Arrowhead Market; across the street is a dromedary in a small pen. It's just standing there, with a hump, a long neck, and a very sweet face, for public view. Down the frontage road is **Glendale Motel, cafe, grocery store,** and **bar,** 702/864-2277, charging $30–35 for the night. The restaurant serves $4 burgers and $2 shakes and malts. The lounge has bartop video poker and a pool table.

Take a right at the corner onto NV 168 and drive north, crossing the Muddy River again and passing BJ's restaurant and bar, a hardware store, school, and district court. The power plant on the edge of town belches white smoke into the purple sky toward the orange orb. Go up the road a few miles and take a left into the Moapa Paiute Reservation. The tribal store is behind the administrative offices. Alfalfa fields abut the small settlement.

MESQUITE

Thirty miles east of the Glendale exit of I-15 is Mesquite, on the Arizona border. A 13-mile spur road (NV 170) leaves I-15 10 miles west of Mesquite and drops fast into Virgin Valley, heading straight toward the high Virgin Mountains. The road crosses the Virgin River at Rancho Riverside, then continues along the Virgin River Valley, through dairy land, past Bunkerville, another Mormon settlement from the 1870s, and into Mesquite through the back door.

This border town is quickly turning itself into Nevada's answer to Palm Desert (that's in California), at the center of a major population and economic boom. For years, Mesquite was known for, and dominated by, the Peppermill Hotel-Casino, first gambling in Nevada for westbound travelers along I-15. From a population of 900 in 1980, Mesquite, thanks to the Peppermill, added 1,000 people in the 1980s, closing out the decade with nearly 1,900. Between 1990 and 1997, Mesquite exploded, with the population more than tripling, to 6,500. Projections for 2000 and beyond suggest that Mesquite will soon be home to over 20,000 residents. New commercial centers were thrown up along Mesquite Blvd., with names such as Sun Valley Plaza, Mesquite Business Park, and Mesquite Plaza. Condos, town homes, and custom houses popped up in developments named Rising Star, Rock Springs, Ventana, Silvercrest, and Las Palmas. A new post office was built; it was supposed to take into account potential growth over the next decade, but has already run short of post office boxes. In the past few years, three hotel-casinos have opened: the Virgin River, Player's Island (now the Casablanca), and Rancho Mesquite. In addition, Arnold Palmer designed a country club centered around two new 18-hole championship golf courses. What we have here is yet another Nevada border boomtown, centered around gambling and resort living, right in the middle of its making.

Museum

Housed in one of two known surviving buildings from the National Youth Administration (1941), exhibits at the **Desert Valley Museum,** 31 W. Mesquite Blvd. across from the Chalet Cafe, 702/346-5705, open Mon.–Sat. 9 A.M.–4 P.M., include Indian petroglyphs, petrified logs, pioneer artifacts, an antique slot machine, and basketball trophies from 1915 and 1916.

Casinos

The Peppermill went through a management reorganization in 1993 and emerged known as **Si Redd's Oasis Hotel-Casino,** 702/346-5232 or 800/621-0187. The Peppermill core casino remains, stylistically the same as the ones in Reno, Sparks, and Wendover with a predominance of red and blue border neon and millions of dollars of silk trees, flowers, and ferns. But the place underwent a $100 million expansion completed in 1995, which added Peggy Sue's Family Fun Center, a 300-room hotel tower and 60 upscale suites, new casino space, and a parking garage across the street, connected by a pedestrian walkway over Mesquite Boulevard. The Oasis offers all the usual casino hysteria, including bingo and sports book, plus a steakhouse, buffet, coffee shop, diner, arcade, and miniature golf. The Oasis also owns Arvada Ranch, nearby in Arizona, with three golf courses, horseback riding, hunting, and target shooting.

Virgin River, 702/346-7777 or 800/346-7721, is on the other (east) side of town. It's smaller and more crowded, with the usual games, plus bingo, a two-screen movie theater, buffet and coffee shop, and 724 rooms. A 300-room tower is going up behind the hotel, and the new country club is across the street.

In July 1994, Player's International (Merv Griffin's casino company) opened Player's Island across from the Oasis on the west part of town, with a view east of the Virgin Mountains. Spending $85 million, Player's put up a gorgeous property, with 500 rooms, an attractive casino, lounge, showroom, coffee shop, buffet, steakhouse, and large pool area. The piece de resistance was an extensive European-style health spa, complete with warm and hot pools, watsu pool, mud baths (Virgin River mud), steam room and sauna, and all kinds of massage and skin therapies. Very upscale and luxurious. Player's marketed their Island hard, especially in Las Vegas, but to no avail. A little more than a year later, the hotel-casino had lost so much money that it was put up for sale. In March 1997, Player's Island was sold to the Black family, owners of the Virgin River across town, for a bargain-

basement $30 million. Since then, the name has been changed to the **Casablanca,** but the address and phone numbers, 600 Mesquite Blvd., 702/346-7529 or 800/896-4567, remain the same.

While all this was happening, in February 1997, Holiday Inn came to town and built a $35 million 215-room hotel-casino with a 45,000-square-foot casino called **Rancho Mesquite,** up the hill from the Virgin River at 275 Mesa Blvd., 702/346-4600 or 800/346-4611.

Accommodations

Mesquite's lodging situation has been growing as fast as the rest of the town. There are now nine hotels and motels with a total of 3,000 rooms.

The biggest joint is the **Oasis,** 1137 Mesquite Blvd., 702/346-5232 or 800/621-0187, with 1,000 rooms at $39–69. Next largest is **Virgin River,** 915 N. Mesquite Blvd., 702/346-7777 or 800/346-7721, with 724 rooms at $22–50. Then there's **Casablanca,** 600 Mesquite Blvd., 702/346-7529 or 800/896-4567, with 500 rooms at $45–125. **Rancho Mesquite,** 301 Mesa Blvd., 702/346-4600 or 800/346-4611, has a 215 Holiday Inn rooms at $49–128. There's now a **Budget Suites** at the east exit, 702/346-7444, with 67 suites (two rooms and a kitchenette) going for $35–130 a night and around $250 a week.

The little digs include: **Desert Palms,** Mesquite Blvd., 702/346-5756, $27–50; **Mesquite Springs,** 580 Mesa Blvd., 702/346-4700 or 800/319-2935, $45–69; and **Valley Inn,** 791 Mesquite Blvd., 702/346-5281, $30–50.

Rvers have three parks to choose from in Mesquite. **Oasis RV Park** has 91 spaces for motor homes, all with full hookups; 30 are pull-throughs. Tents are not allowed. There's a laundromat, grocery store, game room, and heated swimming pool. Reservations are accepted and recommended. The fee is $12.50 per vehicle (Good Sam discount available). Contact Oasis RV Park, Mesquite, 702/346-5232 or 800/621-0187.

Virgin River RV Park is small, sparse, and clean—separated from the hotel parking lot by a low retaining wall. Register at the front desk of the hotel. It has 47 spaces for motor homes, all with full hookups, but no pull-throughs. Tents are not allowed. A laundromat and heated swimming pool are available. Reservations are accepted and recommended; the fee is $10 per vehicle. Contact Virgin River RV Park, Mesquite, 702/346-7777 or 800/346-7721.

Casablanca RV Park has what could be the widest parking spaces in the state, wide enough to fit a big motor home, slide-out, and car. Or two cars and a motor home. Or a trailer, pickup truck, and car. The RV park is all asphalt with young trees, but has a fine view of the Virgin Mountains across the Virgin Valley. There are 45 spaces for motor homes, all with full hookups; 16 are pull-throughs. Tents are not allowed. Reservations are accepted and recommended. The fee is $16.20 daily for people under 50, and $12.96 weekdays for people over 50. Contact: Casablanca RV Park, 930 Mesquite Blvd. (P.O. Box 2737), Mesquite, 702/346-7529 or 800/896-4567.

Food

The Oasis and Virgin River have three-meal buffets and 24-hour coffee shops; Carollo's is also open 24 hours. Mesquite also has a McDonald's (across from the Oasis) and a Burger King (near the Virgin River).

The Virgin River has a couple of breakfast specials: two eggs and bacon or sausage for $2.22 or ham and eggs for $2.79, 24 hours a day. A cart in the sports lounge sells good hot dogs for $1.25 that come with sauerkraut and chili—a meal in itself.

The fine dining in Mesquite is at the Redd Steakhouse in the Oasis. Early-bird beef, poultry, and seafood specials are served 5–7 P.M. in the $11–15 range. Steaks, veal, king crab, chicken, seafood, and surf and turfs regularly go for $17–21.

In Peggy Sue's Fun Center, also at the Oasis, you'll find Baskin-Robbins and Peggy Sue's Diner, which serves coffee shop food ($5.50 bacon and eggs, $5 burgers, sundaes and banana splits $1.50–2.75) dressed up by bright red metal-flaked Naugahyde and stainless-steel counter stools and chairs.

If you don't want to eat with a casino full of slots clanging in your ear, try the venerable **Chalet Cafe,** in the middle of town, open daily 6 A.M.–10 P.M. It's cozy and local, and serves $4 bacon and eggs, $3–5 sandwiches, $10 eight-ounce N.Y. steak, and shakes and malts for less than $2.

OUT FROM MESQUITE

Whitney Pockets (Gold Butte)

A huge and virtually unpopulated slice of Clark County lies between the Overton Arm of Lake Mead and the Arizona border, extending from I-15 on the north to Lake Mead on the south. This large thumb of land remains much as it was when this region was first settled in the late 1800s. Desert explorers will love finding this butte's lesser-known places. The landscapes range from barren desert washes to pine-covered mountain peaks. Exploration in this area is better done during the cooler fall, winter, and spring; travel in this remote area during the summer isn't such a hot idea.

Start out from Mesquite, where you'll need to fill up on gas, water, and vittles. In the winter it's best to begin this trip early in the day so you don't have to return over unfamiliar roads in the dark. Once you begin this backcountry trek, the goal of the trip, Whitney Pockets, will take another good hour. You're not likely to meet another vehicle on this outing, so take normal backcountry precautions. Tell a responsible person where you are going and when you expect to return. Make sure your vehicle is in good repair and has a full tank of gas. Take a good spare, working jack, basic tools, and at least a gallon of water per person. A shovel, flares, matches, spare water, snacks, and warm clothing are also advised. And don't forget to carry a flashlight and spare batteries.

Passenger vehicles should have no trouble reaching Whitney Pockets, as most of the road is paved and in good repair. However, venturing beyond Whitney Pockets would best be accomplished with a high-clearance 4WD vehicle. However, if you have a decent off-road vehicle, you can reach such interesting places as the Grand Wash Cliffs, Wolf's Hole, or the Colorado River opposite Pearce's Ferry.

To reach Whitney Pockets from Mesquite, drive south along NV 170 to just before the bridge across the Virgin River by Riverside. There, turn on the asphalt road and head south for a few miles, following the Virgin River, before turning southeast toward a range of hills and a low summit about nine miles from the bridge. As you follow the river, you'll have excellent views of the river, fields, pastures, and thickets of trees and tules that provide excellent habitat for songbirds, waterfowl, and small animals.

About five miles after turning southeast, you come across a fork in the road at a spot called Spring Ranch. Follow the left fork to reach Whitney Pockets. The right fork, which climbs the alluvial fan to Key West Mine and the Key West Springs, is for 4WD only. Continue down the left fork across the base of the Virgin Mountains till you reach Whitney Pockets. The eroded sandstone is reminiscent of formations in Valley of Fire and Red Rock Canyon. Beautiful shapes are carved into numerous niches, small canyons, and sheltered overhangs. The colorful sandstone, ranging from white to bright red, contrasts sharply with the surrounding desert, inviting you to stay a while; there are many inviting places to camp or have a picnic.

The BLM has an excellent recent Back Country Byway map of the Gold Butte area. It's available from the Las Vegas District Office at 4675 West Vegas Drive, P.O. Box 26569, Las Vegas, NV 89126, 702/647-5000.

Virgin Canyon

The Virgin River remains the only wild river left in southern Nevada. It ends in Lake Mead across from Overton, creating a silted marshland where waterfowl prowl for fish, frogs, and mud-turtles. The headwaters of the Virgin River, one of the main tributaries feeding the Colorado River and Lake Mead, are in Utah's Dixie National Forest, where winter ice and snow and summer rainstorms feed the 300-mile long river. Occasionally violent deluges flood out the valleys below Dixie, ripping out forests and sending enormous walls of water sweeping through canyons that are six feet wide and 300 feet deep at Zion National Park.

By the time the Virgin reaches the Virgin River Canyon, or Virgin Gorge as it has come to be known (in the far northwest corner of Arizona; I-15 runs through it), its waters are somewhat tamer, but during heavy rain years, they can still get cantankerous and dangerous. During calmer times of the year, many people have explored sections of the Virgin River in canoes, kayaks, on foot and swimming, depending on the time of year, the speciality of the explorer, and the nature of the terrain.

Some of the most beautiful parts of the Virgin River Gorge are accessible by driving up I-15 past the Nevada-Arizona border to the area near the Arizona-Utah border. A public campground is just off I-15 above Exit 18 to Beaver Dam Mountains Wilderness and the Paiute Wilderness. Much of the Virgin River Gorge is still pristine and explorable. Contrary to what a few old-timers maintain, the construction of I-15 has made the gorge more accessible to the average visitor.

Among some of the treasures you'll find in the gorge are extensive hikes to places where ancient Indians carved petroglyphs in rock wall. When you get tired, you can relax on soft sandy river banks under salt cedars and watch the happy birds hunting fat insects or contemplate what these rock walls have seen during the last 50 million years. Caves abound along the river banks. Inside some of them you will find large trunks of trees, pounded inside caves by the force of a raging torrent in times past. In some places the granite walls are polished smooth by water levels of thousands of years ago. In other caves, high up on the face of the cliffs, you can see where campfires of ancient natives blackened the ceiling. Deer and other small game abound in the gorge, one of the few wild places left in this kind of country.

NORTHEAST OF LAS VEGAS

AROUND SOUTHEASTERN NEVADA

Heading out of Las Vegas northeast on I-15, there's not much to look at, just desert held by the military. In 25 miles is the turnoff onto US 93 north, a fast, straight, and scenic stretch of two-lane blacktop. The road runs somewhat west toward the **Las Vegas Range,** then turns north through **Hidden Valley** between the Las Vegas and **Arrow Creek** ranges. All along to the east is the **Desert National Wildlife Refuge** (see "Mt. Charleston and the Desert National Wildlife Refuge" earlier in this chapter).

After the Las Vegas Range peters out, the mighty **Sheep Range** comes into view on the west, mostly within the Desert National Wildlife Refuge, and the **Meadow Valley Range** keeps you company on the east. At the cutoff to Caliente through Kane Springs Valley is the original Nevada state boundary, once but no longer commemorated with a historical marker. The **Delamar** and **Pahranagat** (per-RONNA-gut) mountains usher you into the Pahranagat National Wildlife Refuge. The scenery suddenly goes all greenery, and the walls close in. You wind through a small canyon till the hills open up, and you know you've reached an oasis. This is only a couple of hours away from Las Vegas, but it sure feels remote.

Pahranagat National Wildlife Refuge

This Refuge sits at the south end of a verdant little valley called Pahranagat Valley 100 miles northeast of Las Vegas. Pahranagat, an appropriate appellation, is an Indian word meaning "land of many waters." At the upper end of the valley, some 30 miles north, Hiko Springs bubble up from a deep underground aquifer and flows southward to a small lake called Nesbitt Lake, part of the Key Pittman Wildlife Refuge. Here more springs join to feed Nesbitt and Frenchy Lake, farther south. Just below Frenchy Lake,

Crystal Springs and Ash Springs both rise to join this parade of deep aquifer water clearing the surface and flowing southward. All this water, when not being used to irrigate the farmlands in Pahranagat Valley, eventually winds up in the National Wildlife Refuge.

The Refuge consists of two main lakes. The northernmost lake is called Upper Pahranagat. It's approximately 2.2 miles long and a half mile wide, and covers 450 acres. It's surrounded by tall trees, brush, and grasses. More birds than you can count use this lake for a winter camping ground and permanent habitat: numerous species of duck, geese, quail, great blue heron, occasional swans, frequent pelicans, owls, various raptors (mostly red-tailed hawks), and a large variety of small birds.

Overflow waters from Upper Pahranagat Lake are carried about four miles south to form Lower Pahranagat, which is 1.4 miles long and a half mile wide, and covers 275 acres. During the summer, irrigation usage reduces the water in both lakes. By the end of September the lakes are very low and often dry. From October to March, when irrigation ceases, the lakes become full again.

The first turnoff (left) is for the Refuge's administration offices and maintenance shops; a signboard there has park brochures. The next turnoff left is down to Upper Lake. Follow the old road along the eastern shore, where you'll find numerous primitive campsites that are easily reached by vehicle, including RVs. Overnight camping is allowed; the sites have picnic tables, grills, port-a-pot-

BOB RACE

You can canoe on Upper Pahranagat Lake.

ties, big cottonwoods, and birds birds birds. Boating on the lake is restricted to non-motorized boats (canoes, rafts, etc.) and is free.

The old road loops around back up to US 93; Alamo is four miles north.

Alamo
The small town of Alamo was settled in the late 1800s by farmers, cattlemen, and miners. One of the first settlers, George Richard, moved to this area now in 1883 from Salt Lake City at the request of the Mormon Church. Miners were drawn to this area by the ore found at Mt. Irish, Delamar, and other nearby sites. Farmers and cattlemen were drawn here by the lush vegetation produced as a result of the numerous freshwater springs that dotted the area.

For 80 years, the community grew slowly, with the certainty that comes from a continuous water supply, into a luxurious and relatively isolated farming and ranching center. Things began to happen, though, during the early 1950s when the U.S. government did a lot of a-bomb testing on Jackass Flats, some 60 miles to the west, over the mountain from Alamo. The atomic explosions rocked the town. One resident recalls everyone rushing to outside to watch for the telltale mushroom cloud and wait to see whether the wind would carry any of it over the town.

The residents were asked by the government to wear radiation badges, which they mailed to the Atomic Energy Commission weekly. Today the residents are happy the testing has ended. They worry slightly about the noise from Air Force jets as they fly, making occasional low-altitude passes, over the valley.

Take a left on First St. and mosey down to the Lincoln County annex, then back up Broadway, taking in a few old homes and buildings. Alamo has a new middle turning lane, big cottonwoods, wide alfalfa fields, Alamo Garage and Cafe (Chevron; 24-hour towing), and Meadow Lane Motel (775/725-3371; 15 rooms; $25–40). The big action these days is Del Pueblo, a combination grocery store, Exxon station, and restaurant with high-backed booths. A buffet is served for lunch ($6) and dinner ($7)—mostly fried this and that, a little salad bar, and fruit for dessert.

Just south of Alamo is a beautiful serifed **"P"** for Pahranagat on a very steep slope to the east. At the top of the slope is a sheer wall just above the

"P," just below is also a near-vertical drop-off. Quite an effort is obviously invested in making this one of the most spectacular town letters in Nevada.

Look for the turnoff for **Richardville Rd.,** the bucolic scenic route through the farm country a bit north of Alamo.

Ash Springs
In another seven miles is Ash Springs, just a small service stop, with Sinclair gas and groceries. The RV park and pools have been closed for several years. At the north end of town, directly across the highway from the R Place Texaco station, is a small dirt road marked by a sign that says No Trespassing. Ignore the sign. No one knows why it's there—maybe to keep the popular spot from becoming *too popular.* But the springs are for public enjoyment. Drive 50 yards up the dirt road, park, and walk down to the small, man-made, gravel-bottom, warm-spring-fed, wading pond and miniature lake. There are picnic benches, grills, and refuse bins, but no toilet facilities or drinking water. Swing out on the rope attached to a tree limb and drop into the main pond. This is an excellent place to relax and have a little picnic.

Five miles north of Ash Springs is a three-way junction: US 93 cuts northeast across the Pahroc Range heading toward Caliente; NV 318 runs north to Hiko, Lund, and Ely; and NV 375 heads northwest toward US 6 at Warm Springs and Tonopah.

NV 375 TO WARM SPRINGS

On the south side of NV 318 at its three-way junction with NV 375 and US 93 is Crystal Springs. The site was once a Paiute village, and served as a resting place for California-bound travelers. It was first settled by white men in the 1860s as a result of nearby silver discoveries. The settlement was declared the seat of Lincoln County in 1866, though it never had a population of more than a few dozen, and most of those were transient miners. Hiko became the county seat in 1867, and now nothing remains but the spring itself and a few surrounding cottonwoods.

At the junction of US 93 and NV 318, take a left toward Hiko, then another left onto NV 375. You start out heading southwest over the **Mt.**

Irish Range, site of the Pahranagat Mining District (a few miles north). Stretch your legs and whatever else at **Horney's Rest Stop** just before **Hancock Summit** (elev. 5,592 feet). After a couple of soft downhill curves, the road cuts northwest like an arrow through Tikapoo Valley. This is lonely open-range country. Last time I was on it, the only two cars I saw between the junction and Rachel were a Lincoln County sheriff (and I didn't even *need* him) and a big brown UPS van. (Nevada Department of Transportation officials say the highway only draws about 50 vehicles a day on average, though a great deal more show up twice annually when Rachel holds "UFO Friendship Campouts" for tourists looking for flying saucers.)

The road climbs up a bit into the Timpahute Range of the **Worthington Mountains,** not, as is generally believed, named after Cal Worthington, then over **Coyote Summit** (elev. 5,591 feet). Then you continue down down down into the big fertile Sand Spring Valley, with ranches, old farmhouses, and the town of Rachel. (Read more about the town of Rachel in the special topic "The Extraterrestrial Highway").

Beyond Rachel

Coming out of Sand Spring Valley, you climb up and over some foothills of the **Quinn Canyon Range** at Queen City Summit (elev. 5,960 feet). That's **Reveille Peak** standing at nearly 9,000 feet atop the Reveille Range across the big valley. The road cuts due north up **Railroad Valley** between the Reveilles and the Quinn Canyons. A good gravel road starts here, goes by **Nyala,** and past another dirt road that heads right into the heart of the Quinn Canyons at **Adaven,** an old mining town whose name is Nevada spelled backwards. Just below **Black Beauty Mesa,** NV 375 cuts due west through **Hot Creek Valley** up toward the **Hot Creek Range,** where Rawhide Mountain tops out at 9,169 feet. Right at the base of this range ends NV 375 at US 6 and derelict **Warm Springs** (no services). Tonopah is 50 miles west.

NORTH ON NV 318

Hiko

A few miles north of the intersection with US 93 and NV 375 on NV 318 is Hiko (HY-ko). This is a small ranching hamlet spread along the highway for a mile or two behind range fencing. The silver strike in 1867 at Irish Mountain, 15 miles north of Hiko, was a flash in the pan compared to the silver strike in the Highland Range at Pioche in 1871. Amost overnight the population of Hiko moved to Pioche, as did the county seat, where it remains today. Hiko rests in the center of a pretty little basin with a string of ranches, a post office, the state's **Key Pittman Wildlife Management Area,** and Nesbitt Pond. A sign here warns that the next gas is 100 miles away in Lund.

Named to honor Key Pittman, a former U.S. Senator from Nevada known for his vigorous support of monetary legislation designed to assist the silver-mining industry of the West, Key Pittman Wildlife Management Area comprises two lakes, Nesbitt and Frenchy. The WMA is managed by a resident ranger, Bart Tanner, who is headquartered at his home in Hiko, 775/725-3521. The lower lake, Frenchy, is usually dry about half the year since it's used to supply irrigation water for the farms in the area. Frenchy Lake is reputedly named after an old sourdough miner who worked the old Logan Mines up in the Mt. Irish mountains to the west. North on NV 318 just under five miles is Nesbitt Lake, a beautiful lake that does not go dry. It's surrounded by tules, tall cottonwoods, and oak, and is inhabited by an abundance of wildlife (birds, small animals, etc.). When you come to the entrance to Nesbitt Lake, stop, open the cattle gate, drive in (close the gate behind you so you don't let grazing cattle out onto the road), then take a leisurely drive around the lake. You can park at several shady areas at the beginning of the road around the lake. Non-motor boats are allowed on the lake. There are no fees for picnicking or camping in this lush oasis.

Mt. Irish Archaeological Site and Logan

Directly across from Nesbitt Lake is a barbed-wire gate to a dirt road leading 18 miles up into the Mt. Irish Range and the Mt. Irish Archaeological Site. The range and site are rich with ancient petroglyphs and other Indian artifacts. Up here you'll also find the remains of the old mining town of Logan. This is a dirt road and pretty isolated, so be sure to take water, a digging tool, a spare tire, and other desert survival equipment in case you get a flat or get stuck. It's

THE EXTRATERRESTRIAL HIGHWAY

While the federal government wishes everyone would go away, in April 1997 the Nevada Department of Transportation designated the desolate 92-mile stretch of NV 375 the "Extraterrestrial Highway," putting up four signs to that effect at a cost of $3,300. During the ceremony, Nevada Gov. Bob Miller quipped that some of the signs should be placed flat on the ground "so aliens can land there." Governor Miller also commented that the designation shows Nevada has a sense of humor. This is UFO country, folks, and the town of Rachel is its headquarters.

It all seems a little unlikely, when you cruise in from a remote stretch of state highway, that this tiny hamlet of 100 souls, a leftover development of the aborted MX missile project of the early 1980s, has been garnering almost as much publicity over the past few years as Las Vegas has. Rachel is in the center of a controversy that encompasses two Air Force facilities, government secrecy and security, military land grabbing, UFOs, toxic waste, and a 35-year-old computer programmer from Cambridge, Massachusetts.

It all started in 1989, when Bob Lazar, a former engineer at the Los Alamos labs in New Mexico turned Nevada brothel owner, told a Las Vegas newsman that he'd been working on extraterrestrial aircraft at a top-secret Air Force facility near Rachel known as Papoose Lake. His story, though yet to be confirmed, launched a media feeding frenzy that turned up Papoose Lake and a second previously unknown Air Force installation, Groom Lake

(also known as Area 51), in the far northeastern corner of the vast 3.5-million-acre Nellis Air Force Range.

Meanwhile, UFOnauts from around the planet descended on Rachel, convinced that the answers to all their questions rested somewhere in the alkali flats of dried-up Groom Lake.

All the hoopla attracted the attention of one Glenn Campbell, a young computer programmer from the East. He made the pilgrimage to the now infamous "black mailbox" (29 miles south of Rachel serving the Medlin ranch), a landmark where UFO enthusiasts gathered to wait for ET. Campbell never caught a glimpse of any transgalactic spacecraft, but he did see fighter jets galore, taking bombing target practice over the nearby desert and simulating dogfights in the big sky. But it wasn't until the Air Force, under media scrutiny from around the world, denied that Groom Lake even existed that Campbell found his true calling.

Meanwhile, the Rachel townsfolk lined up on both sides of the UFO uproar, some claiming to have seen and been visited by them, the rest convinced that any extraterrestrial worth his higher intelligence wouldn't be bothering with a dusty village in an unfriendly desert on a backward planet. But Pat and Joe Travis, owners of the Rachel Bar and Grill, changed the name to the Little A-Le-Inn (pronounced just like "alien") and redecorated it in an alien motif, with a giant wooden saucer outside and extraterrestrial trinkets (bumper stickers, doormats, cigarette lighters, and T-shirts) for sale in-

---

a long walk back. Passenger vehicles can easily make the 18 miles to Logan, but avoid going off this road. All other access roads are strictly 4WD.

Continuing North

NV 318 runs northeast from Hiko through the **Hiko Range** along a route cut by the once-wet **White River**. You leave the **Mount Irish Range** behind on the west and come into a basin hemmed in by the **Seaman Range** on the west and the **North Pahroc Range** on the east. For a little while you head directly toward **Fossil Peak** (6,486 feet), southernmost bump in the Seamans, then zig to the east. In about

15 miles, you come to **White River Narrows.** The White River isn't, but it is narrow; this is a state archaeological site. The walls, though not especially high, are sheer and pillared, and the road winds through them for a couple of miles.

From there the road continues north into big **White River Valley.** Here you leave Lincoln County and enter the far northeast corner of Nye County, about as far away from Pahrump as you can get. There's a turnoff on a gravel road for **Gap Mountain** (7,045 feet elevation), which is one of the southern peaks of the **Egan Range. Hot Creek Campground** is seven miles in from the highway; this is the southern access side. Try an Alien Burger or a Beam Me Up, Scotty (made from Jim Beam, 7UP, and Scotch). There are also 13 motel rooms here that go for $25–35 apiece.

Down the block from the Little A-Le-Inn is a single-wide trailer with a sign: "Area 51 Research Center." This is Glenn Campbell's publishing and public relations outfit, where he cranks out a newsletter and meets with visiting media, whom he guides to vantage points overlooking Groom Lake, described in his manual, *Area 51 Viewer's Guide.*

According to what's been pieced together from the sketchy reports of local eyewitnesses, ex-Groom Lakers, and government whistle-blowers, the Groom Lake installation has field tested top-secret aircraft since the 1950s, including the U-2 spy plane, the Stealth series, the Manta craft used in the Gulf War, and the rumored Aurora speed demon, which can fly at 5,000 miles an hour. Reports say that the three-mile long runway is the longest in the world. In the past year or so, some former employees of the base have filed a class-action suit, claiming that the Air Force's mishandling of toxic materials affected their health. Finally, the Air Force has applied for an additional 4,000 acres of land surrounding the base for security; this would effectively seal off all known vantage points of the facility that doesn't exist.

Current thought is that, as a result of the notoriety received by Groom Lake and Area 51, the Air Force has surreptitiously moved whatever was

© AVALON TRAVEL PUBLISHING, INC.

there to a more secret location, but maintains the illusion of security at Groom Lake to keep the curiosity and interest focused there where it can do no harm, rather than somewhere else where the truth may accidentally be discovered.

road to the state Wayne E. Kirch Wildlife Management Area. Beyond that to the west is the mighty **Grant Range,** with Troy Peak rising 11,268 feet, within a Forest Service Wilderness Area.

In another seven or so miles, the road skirts the edge of the Kirch Management Area; there's a turnoff onto the northern access road. You continue up White River Valley, the big Egans ushering you along to the east. Just under 200 miles from Las Vegas is a turnoff onto a 30-mile gravel road to **Currant** on US 6, a shortcut to Duckwater and Eureka. Then you leave Nye County, enter White Pine County, and cruise into Lund.

Lund and Preston
Lund is one of the prettiest and well-kept little towns in central Nevada. It's named after Anthony Lund, a president of the Mormon church around the turn of the 20th century when the town was founded. Today, it's a typical farm and ranching center, the residential streets extending one block on each side of the highway, with a tractor dealer, rodeo grounds, and two schools (slow down to 15 mph on school days) in the middle. You first come to **Carter's Country Store,** 775/238-5260, open Mon.–Sat. 7:30 A.M.–9:30 P.M., with Texaco gas and the noisiest ice-cream machine in the whole state; there's a telephone booth outside and the post office is next door.

Up the street is **White River Valley Pioneer Museum,** open daily. Stop in and have a chat with the dedicated local senior volunteer, and look around at the interesting stuff: old stock certificates, Valentines, typewriters, irons, quilts, and the first piano in the valley; old photos, including those of Lafayette Carter, one of the town elders, who donated the building. Out back is a log cabin full of cream separators, life-saving skis, and rusting equipment. A great place to stretch your legs, rest your eyes, and sign the guest book.

The main action is at **Lane's** cafe, store, fuel, public scale, and motel on the north side of town. The cafe is open 6 A.M.–9:30 P.M. every day but Christmas. The motel, 775/238-5346, has 15 rooms that go for $38 d.

A few miles north of Lund is the turnoff (left) onto a three-mile loop along a scenic farm byway through the farm village of **Preston.** Here is little more than farmhouses and fields, a creamery, cemetery, and a big piece of peace.

In another eight miles you come to US 6; from there, Ely is 23 miles east.

TO CALIENTE

Delamar

Back at the junction of US 93 and NV 318, heading to Caliente, US 93 cuts across **Sixmile Flat,** then climbs into the **Pahroc Range.** Climbing up to **Pahroc Summit** (just under 5,000 feet), you enter sage country, and then, oddly enough, pass through a forest of Joshua trees. Farther along, even more oddly, is a little interface zone with the Joshuas growing right next to the junipers—something you don't see very often in Nevada. Beyond there you head up into the **Delamar Range.**

About 24 miles east of Alamo, you come to a dirt road on the south side of the highway proclaiming Delamar 15 miles. This straight-arrow dirt road heading southwest is well graded and an easy passage for passenger vehicles. The broad Delamar Valley, one of the most striking in the state, is west of the Delamar Mountains. John and Alvin Ferguson made the first strike of record here in 1891. Using a monkey wrench, they broke a small piece of quartzite from a ledge, which proved to be high-grade ore. They

named their claim the Monkey Wrench for the incident. On April 1, 1892, Frank Wilson and D. A. Reeves discoverd the April Fool Mine in the same area. The town of Reeves was laid out below the mine, but the name was later changed to De Lamar (Delamar) when Capt. John R. De Lamar, a Dutch immigrant, purchased the group of mines in 1893.

Delamar was a principal gold-mining center that supported a thriving business district of stores, saloons, theaters, and professional offices. As many as 120 mule-drawn freight wagons were ceaselessly employed in importing supplies from the nearest railroad at Milford, Utah. Through 1908, the Delamar Mine had an estimated production of $25 million, even though it suffered from one of the worst working conditions in Nevada mining history. Improper ventilation permitted silica dust to waft continuously through the mines and mills with fatal results for many of the workmen. Three months was enough to kill a miner in Delamar from silicosis, and the town became notorious as a widow-maker. This accounts for the large size of the cemetery here.

Today, nothing much remains at the site except old stone walls, a crumbling mill, and a large cemetery, from which many of the old tombstones have been stolen by souvenir seekers. The rock ruins, crowded as they are into the shallow canyon above the mine dumps, make a fascinating picnic site. Have no fears: none of the deadly silica dust remains.

From Delamar, you can continue southwest on the dirt road to Alamo, or return to US 93 to the north and drive on in to Caliente. Six miles from the Delamar turnoff you top **Oak Springs Summit** (6,237 feet). A campground a short distance off the south side of the highway has picnic tables, grills, and a green shady picnic area. It's a nice cool place at high elevation to enjoy a rest and a picnic, and to listen to Air Force jets streaking up and down Pahranagat Valley.

From here you start dropping down to Caliente. One last scenic treat awaits before town; **Newman Canyon** has high, sheer sandstone cliffs, some of them completely vertical and smooth. This is but a warm-up, however, to Rainbow Canyon on the other side of town.

CALIENTE AND VICINITY

Petroglyphs in Meadow Valley indicate that a native population used this lush region for hunting, traveling, and artwork. The first Anglo settlers were farmers and ranchers; the Culverwells bought a large tract in 1879. On this property Caliente was founded, and the Harriman-Clark Railroad War was waged.

This southeast corner of Nevada, too far to connect with the transcontinental main line in northern Nevada, was neglected by the railroads until late in the 19th century. In 1894, E.H. Harriman's Union Pacific surveyed a route between Salt Lake City and Los Angeles. At the turn of the century the Union Pacific's subsidiary, Oregon Shortline, resumed work on the route, laying track southward from Utah to Meadow Valley. There, however, it was stopped short by William Clark's upstart San Pedro, Los Angeles and Salt Lake Railroad, which claimed title to the narrow right-of-way south of the Culverwell ranch. Each company deployed thugs to interfere with its competitor's progress. The inevitable violence ensued in Clover Valley with shovels and axe handles—the only major confrontation between railroads in Nevada history. A federal judge sided with Harriman, who shortly thereafter reluctantly went into partnership with Clark. Beginning again in 1903, together they continued construction south toward the little ranch known as Las Vegas—along the dangerous Meadow Valley Wash. Caliente was created as a division point on the San Pedro, Los Angeles and Salt Lake Railroad, thanks to the abundant water gushing out of springs near the Wash, which quelled the unslakable thirst of the steam engines.

Company row houses were built north of the repair shops and offices, and the new town enjoyed a continuous prosperity up through the '40s. The only disruptions were railroad related. The disastrous floods of 1907, for example, required a million dollars' worth of repairs, only to be washed away again in the terrible flood of 1910, which wrecked 100 miles of track. (Two million was spent after that to raise the roadbed; little damage reccurred.) The branch line between Caliente and Pioche ran a full 60 years, 1907–67. The bell might have tolled for Caliente

in 1948 when dieselization replaced steamification and the maintenance yards were moved to Las Vegas. But US 93 had already been built through town, three state parks were created nearby, agriculture continued to contribute, and the railroad never abandoned Caliente completely. Freight trains rumble through town regularly.

Today, Caliente has a vitality all its own. The streets follow an orderly company-town grid, with two main business streets downtown, one on each side of the wide railroad right-of-way. The hot springs for which the town was founded and named are one of the surprise treats in the state. That, along with the depot mural, Rainbow Canyon, and the singularly unstressed residents, makes Caliente (pronounced like the Spanish—but with an American West inflection: "cally," which rhymes with Sally, and "anti," as in freeze) an undiscovered gem in this southeastern-Nevada corridor full of undiscovered gems.

Sights

Start out at the Union Pacific Railroad Station, built in 1923 for $83,000, once the nerve center of the railroad, now the nerve center of the town. City Hall, the library (open Mon.–Fri. 9 A.M.–4 P.M.), and the Chamber of Commerce (775/726-3129, open weekdays 9 A.M.–6 P.M.) all share the lovely building. The pièce de résistance in the depot and town is the historical mural in the lobby. The big painting covers the history between 1864 and 1914 of the entire southern section of Nevada, from Pioche in the northeast to Las Vegas in the south and all the way up to Tonopah in the west—with a lot of detail. Locals Mary Ellen Sadovich and Rett Hastings designed and painted it. The depot is also open on Saturday and Sunday; stop in to the lobby and pick up the brochures from the info rack. Also check out the EPA's radiation-monitoring apparatus outside the depot; it comes complete with a printout of the level of microentgens for southern Nevada (almost always within the range of normal background radiation for the U.S.).

Lots of local buildings have been standing since aught-five and six; consult the walking tour brochure. Wander around the two main streets, and be sure to peek into the post office to see the beautiful wooden interior, solid walls and counters, and a pretty wall of P.O. boxes. Near the corner of Market and Culverwell in back of town, the community church and elementary school are attractive historical structures. Also pass the Underhill rock apartments (take a right off Clover St. beyond town), built in 1907 and still in use. Union Pacific railroad row houses, standing grandly on Spring St. just north of town, were built in 1905; notice the two choices of floor plans.

Rainbow Canyon and Kershaw-Ryan State Park

Beginning at the intersection of US 93 and NV 317 at the south end of Caliente by the Mormon Church lies Rainbow Canyon (a.k.a. Meadow Valley), one of the most beautiful canyons in all of southern Nevada. Mark your mileage at this point because many of the most interesting sites can only be located by knowing the miles you've driven from this intersection. You come around the corner, pass under the first of many trestles, and then you're there, in this stunning and remarkable wash. The cliff rock is volcanic tuff, which settled over all of Nevada 34 million years ago; hot mineralized water flowing through cracks and faults accounts for the glorious colors: iron the reds and yellows, copper the blues and greens, manganese the black, and plain ash the white. Many elements combine to make this one of the most scenic (and least known) roads in the state: the dips in the road in the flood zones; the many railroad trestles and bridges; the idyllic ranches, farms, big trees, and creek; the petroglyphs and other historical sites; and of course the sheer and colorful canyon walls.

Two miles into Rainbow Canyon you come to **Kershaw-Ryan State Park,** a small park that was recently opened for the first time since it was destroyed by flash floods in the summer of 1984. The entrance to this gem is a well-marked graded dirt road leading east into a box canyon off NV 317. The park is closed from 10 P.M. to 7 A.M. No overnight camping is allowed, but this is a beautiful place to spend the day.

The park is 240 acres of cliff and canyon country, liberally shaded by groves of ash and cottonwood and laced with hiking trails. The rugged cliff walls enclosing the canyon are heavily overgrown with scrub oak and wild grapevines. The sound of running water is everywhere since the end wall of the canyon has a series of seeps that send water trickling down its face to be caught in a pond and little brook at its base. This protected canyon is early to feel spring returning and late to feel the cold touch of winter, making it a good place to visit during most of the year.

The park has modern restrooms amid a profusion of ivy and grass. The picnic area has tables and barbecue grills. Just above the picnic area is a small wading pool for children. Above that is a beautiful seep dripping water from the canyon wall in an undercut that creates a beautiful hanging garden of riparian plantlife including grapevines. Two short hikes (one a mile and the other a quarter mile) lead to other springs and lush canyons. The fees are $3 per day, group use $15, seniors free. The fine for failing to pay at the self pay station is $2.

Continuing down Rainbow Canyon, at mile 3.8 you come to the Old Conway Ranch, which was turned into a public golf course that went bankrupt, but there's talk of it reopening in the future. At mile 5.0, you arrive at Etna Cave. Park on the right shoulder, walk under the train trestle, and follow the sandy wash though the tunnel for about 400 feet, then look up to the left on the tan cliff face. This site has been an archaeological dig since the 1930s when a profusion of Indian artifacts were found that document 5,000 years of native habitat. The artifacts are currently collecting dust in the basement of a museum in San Francisco, but efforts are being made to reclaim them for a Lincoln County museum. The San Francisco folk did not manage to make off with the abundant petroglyphs and pictographs carved and painted into the cliff face.

At mile 6.0 you come to the Tennile Ranch. Tennile sold the ranch to a Las Vegas man who conducts stress-management classes at the beautiful ranch house. The place is now called the Longhorn Cattle Company. At mile 8.7 you come upon the the remains of Stein Power Station, a steam-generated power plant that supplied electrical power to the mines between 1902 and 1909. Farther up this road are the remains of the old Delamar pumping station and pipeline, which pumped water over the high cliffs to Delamar on the other side of the mountains to the west.

At mile 11.0 you come to a vantage point where you can view the few remaining pinion pines and juniper trees, which were much more abundant in the canyon prior to being cut down for fuel and building materials at the turn of the century. This stand has grown back after the intensive uses of the past.

At mile 14.7 watch for a turnoff to the left just after crossing under another railroad trestle. Park off the road and take a short drive (0.7 mile) up a good dirt road into Grapevine Canyon. Bear left at the fork. Park at the barbecue-pit area and enjoy a picnic under the shade of huge ash and hackberry trees. Walk back down the road about 100 feet, then follow the well-marked foot trail up the slope to some tuff overhang. You'll spot another abundance of petroglyphs and pictographs dating back thousands of years. More such artifacts can be found along the cliff face and on the south side of Grapevine Canyon.

At mile 17.5, just past the railroad bridge, look for a short dirt road on the right. Park and walk north along this access road about 400 feet. You'll see a small railroad tie structure and Tunnel No. 5, dated 1911–1925. Look west and uphill from the structure. You should see several dark-stained talus blocks strewn along the hillside with petroglyphs of bighorn sheep carved on the top and sides.

At mile 19.9, park along the right shoulder of NV 317 and look for a boulder covered with petroglyphs. Across the highway lush willows dominate a wetland zone and protect the stream bank from erosion by flooding. They also provide food for deer, beaver, and livestock.

At mile 20.2 you come to Bradshaw's "End of the Rainbow" Ranch, which was established in the 1880s, and is the only ranch in the canyon still owned by family of the original settler. The pavement ends here. If your visit occurs in the fall, you might be able to pick a bucket of Jonathan or Delicious apples in the ranch's orchard. Check for a sign on the ranch gate for the dates when End of the Rainbow is open to the public. In another few miles Rainbow Canyon starts to peter out and becomes an ordinary desert wash. The stream that you've followed all the way down the canyon either dries up or goes underground.

Elgin and Carp
The old railroad station of Elgin has been absorbed into the ranching community at the south end of Rainbow Canyon where the pavement turns to dirt. Little is left of the old station facilities.

Continuing down Rainbow Canyon along what is now a dirt road, you come to Carp, which was a station on the main line of the Union Pacific and a local community, first settled in 1907. Like Elgin, not much is left of Carp today: only the shells of two concrete buildings and the foundations of a few wood-frame houses. The place has become a garbage dump and milling place for free-range cattle.

This dirt road continues down the barren desert valley and comes into the back side of Moapa on I-15 about 35 miles later. All along this road are the remains of frequent Union Pacific way stations, but nothing else of much interest.

Kane Springs Valley Road
This road starts at the south end of Rainbow Canyon where the paved road turns into dirt and ends 38 miles (45–50 mph) southwest on US 93. It's a shortcut or a good circle tour for anyone traveling between Caliente and Las Vegas. It's also a great drive across high desert with clean clear air and lots of yucca. As you traverse the high-desert green valley running between the Meadow Valley Mountains on the south and the Delamar Mountains on the north, shut off your air conditioning, open your windows, and taste, smell, and feel the desert. Don't seal yourself off from it. Toward the end the Sheep Range keeps growing bigger and bigger dead ahead.

Beaver Dam State Park
One of Nevada's loveliest and most remote state parks is accessed from Caliente. The park is so irrepressibly cheerful a place that the long dusty drive to get there is a small price to pay for a visit. The 1,713-acre park is set high in mountain pine forests. Hiking trails wind under the trees and cliffs and through the canyons. Spring-fed Beaver Dam Reservoir is stocked with fish and anglers may try their luck along the cottonwood-lined stream leading to the reservoir or in the small reservoir itself; no boating services or facilities have been developed. Swimmers are welcome to try the reservoir. There are picnic sites and both developed and primitive campsites in the park, though both picnicking and camping are permitted anywhere you find a spot you like. There is no visitor center here,

and no concessions; bring everything you'll need.

The well-marked turnoff for the state park is 5.3 miles north of Caliente on US 93. For the next 25 miles the well-graded dirt road climbs gently into pinion pine country. However, you can't travel faster than 35–40 mph because the road twists and turns a great deal and you don't know what's coming up around the next turn or over the next hilltop. After 14 miles you come to a fork in the road. Stay on the left branch to Beaver Dam. The right branch, which rapidly becomes 4WD territory, goes to the dry remains of Matthews Canyon Reservoir, then winds its way though the mountains south into Utah backcountry.

After another 4.5 miles you cross the Union Pacific tracks. Four miles later you come to the beginning of a steep incline down the side of Pine Ridge into Beaver Dam State Park. While it may look like a nail-biting ride, any passenger vehicle can make it with no trouble. From this point it's three miles to the campground. Do what the stop sign says (yes, a stop sign out here) and register. The park is open April 15–Oct. 15. Fees are $8 a day to camp and $3 for day use. Group use reservations are $15 and senior NV residents (with permit) can camp for free.

There are a number of campgrounds available. The first (to the left) is the best of the lot, with 40 sites, tables, grills, running water, porta-potties, cut and cured firewood, and camping spots for RVs. All the other campgrounds are much more primitive.

The road through the campground drops down a steep grade; at the bottom is parking and the trailhead for a half-mile hike along narrow trail to the Beaver Dam Reservoir, better known as Schroeder Lake. Passenger vehicles would do better not to chance the hill; park at the top and hike down instead. It's only a few hundred feet (of loose gravel) and you may have some trouble with traction coming back up.

The reservoir has a lot of over and undergrowth as well as a couple of rather large beaver dams. You can hike all the way around to the dam and camp on the earthen dike, providing a beautiful view of both the lake and the stream and canyon below. There are numerous other hikes available in the area. The Hamblin Ranch is not far up canyon from the reservoir, or you can follow the wash from the dam down quite a ways and enjoy the lush flora and abundant fauna in the area.

Practicalities

Caliente has three motels with a grand total of 45 rooms. The **Rainbow Canyon,** 884 A St., 775/726-3291, charges $31–40; **Shady Motel,** 450 Front, 775/726-3106, charges $33–40. Or follow the signs across the railroad tracks north of town and stay at **Caliente Hot Springs Motel,** 775/726-3777 or 800/748-4785, where the hot spring baths are located. The room rate includes use of the baths; if you're not spending the night, you can use the baths from 8 A.M. to 10 P.M. for $5. These are spacious private cubicles with five- by five-foot Roman tubs, about three feet deep; fire-hydrant faucets fill them up in four minutes flat. This water, at 105 degrees or so, is so soft, so sulphur-free, and so seductive that you easily pass the pickling point. The baths are a bit frayed around the edges these days, but if you can look beyond some missing tiles, a little dirt in the tubs, and 20-year-old paint, you'll have a mighty good time.

Young's RV, US 93 behind the BLM office, 775/726-3418, is the only bona fide RV park between Las Vegas and Ely on US 93. Spaces are wide, with trees and grass at each. Facilities are limited, but it's right in town. There are 27 spaces for motor homes, all with full hookups; 16 are pull-throughs. Tents are allowed (separate grassy area). Restrooms have flush toilets and hot showers; sewage disposal is available. Reservations are accepted; the fee is $7 for tents and $12 per vehicle.

The **Knotty Pine** coffee shop is on Front St., open weekdays 6 A.M.–9 P.M., till 10 Friday and Saturday. A bar with pool table adjoins. Something typically local is bound to be going on inside. The **Branding Iron,** on Clover St. across the tracks, is similar, open 6 A.M.–9 P.M., till 2 on Sunday, closed Monday; bacon and eggs $4.50, burgers $2.75, fried chicken $8, steaks $11. Foodtown supermarket is next door. **Carl's Sandwich Shop** next to the old Scott Hotel is a great old-time soda fountain, with a big U-shaped counter and sundaes, floats, and freezes ($2); you can also get a variety of burgers (try the Ortega pepper burger) for little more than $2. There's also **Susie's Charbroiled Grill,** serving breakfast, subs, tacos, and burgers.

That Little Shop in Caliente is a gift-and-book store down the street from Foodtown, open at 9 A.M., selling souvenirs, cards, paperbacks, and travel guides.

PANACA

Drive north on US 93 through Meadow Valley between the **Cedar Range** on the east and the **Chief Range** on the west. After 14 miles the high desert turns amazingly green (in summer). Lush irrigated fields of grains and vegetables, barns, farm equipment, stacks of hay, feedlots, long fences, and farmers frame the landscape, much as they have for 130 years. One of the oldest villages in the state, Panaca (pan-ACK-uh) was founded in 1864 by Latter-day Saints missionaries and colonists. The town's name was an Anglicized version of *pan-nuk-ker,* a Southern Paiute word meaning metal or wealth. The Panaker Ledge was actually at Pioche, and the boomtown of Bullionville thrived slightly north of Panaca between 1870 and 1875 until it was supplanted by Pioche.

As usual, the two groups made uneasy neighbors, with the miners disrespectful of the Mormons' water rights, religious beliefs, and lifestyle, and the Mormons disapproving of the miners' lawlessness and faithlessness. Even so, a mutual dependence arose as the miners provided an excellent market for Mormon produce, and both groups defended a common interest against Indian threats. In fact, this yin-yang relationship between the valley farmers and the mountain miners was so complete that it's hard to write about one without the other; Pioche and Panaca today remain excellent reminders of that typical frontier tension. Of course, the boom at Bullionville—five mills and the narrow-gauge Pioche and Bullionville short line notwithstanding—lasted a mere half-dozen years. Pioche, as well, finally settled down to a semblance of law and order by the mid-1870s, and real quiet arrived with the inevitable decline of the mining boom.

Some serious dust, however, was stirred up after an 1866 survey revealed Panaca to be within Nevada's boundaries, not Utah's or Arizona's, to which the townspeople had already paid taxes. Panacans thought it unjust for Neva-da to try and collect back taxes from them, and many left in protest. But the town itself persisted as it always had and always would, through the vagaries of desert, miners, Indians, tax collectors, and persecution. To pause here is to enter a timelessness felt nowhere so strongly in the rest of the state.

Sights

At the corner of US 93 and NV 319 are **Skittles and Vittles** cafe and a Texaco station. Turn right from the highway and poke into town along Main St., which becomes four lanes downtown. You pass **Algiers Market** on the way in (groceries and gas). Peek into the **Mercantile**, established in 1868 on the corner of 4th, then go up a block and take a left on 5th. Notice the Italian Victorianate house on the east corner; this was the second house of N.J. Wadsworth, a member of one of the founding families. On the west corner is an interesting red-brick house, built in 1871. Take the first left onto E St., then mosey along past the gymnasium and ballfield, which dominate the town and where you'll find the whole populace during a basketball or baseball game, past the schools and church, all presided over by the incongruous but striking chalk formation known as Court Rock. This public square is a graphic example of how seriously this town takes its education, religion, and civic responsibilities. Go right at the stop sign across from the big two-story frame house. Take your first left on D St., go to the end, and take a left onto 2nd St. at Henry Matthews' home. Look back for a view of this pretty house, built in stages. Go two blocks to Main St.; a right returns you to the highway.

Now go back to the corner of Main St. and 5th and take a right. Bear around to the right of the school athletic field, and stay on 5th after the pavement ends. Drive through the back of town, past big backyard gardens, some with tall corn growing in late summer, past some sand dunes, and head toward the tallest cottonwood tree about a half mile in the distance. This is **Panaca Spring,** whose warm sweet water is part of Meadow Valley Wash, which makes this farm valley possible. It's deep and warm, with kids swimming all hours, and a beautiful view of the valley and mountains beyond.

Cathedral Gorge State Park

Only a mile north of Panaca on US 93 and 165 miles north of Las Vegas is this state park, yet another unexpected delight on the run up eastern Nevada (which even Las Vegas, considering itself the gateway to such far-away and out-of-state places as Death Valley and the Grand Canyon, has yet to discover!). Take a left into the park; at the fork a right goes to the gorgeous gorge, a left goes around to the campground. Like Valley of Fire, Cathedral Gorge (1,578 acres) is more a place to exercise the imagination than your legs and lungs. Simply put, it's a wash, a cut in the earth's skin, that over the eons has been weathered and eroded into a fantasy land. What separates it from countless other washes and gulches is that its walls are made of a chalky-soft suede-colored bentonite clay, which has created the pillars, gargoyles, wedding cakes, fortresses, hunchbacked men, dragons, palaces, melting elephants, and, of course, cathedrals. Baroque architectural elements— lacy, filigreed, fluted, and feathered—decorate its walls.

A million years ago, this valley was covered by a lake, into which streams washed silt, clay, ash, and other decomposed volcanic and igneous products from rock outcrops surrounding the valley. These sediments were eventually deposited on the lake bottom up to 1,500 feet deep, the coarser materials at the edges and the finer in the deep middle. Then faulting in the mountains at the southern end of the lake allowed the water to slowly seep away, carving the canyon deeper along the fault line. After the lake dried up and exposed the bed, the sun, wind, and rain did the rest.

More recently, some evidence shows the presence of Basket Maker Indians a few thousand years ago; the Paiute passed through. The wash was named, for obvious reasons, in 1894 by a local woman; in the 1920s, Shakespearean passion plays, local pageants, and fairs made use of the dramatic backdrop. The whole thing was designated a state park in 1935, along with the three other original Nevada state parks.

Park at the pull-out near the signboard at the main part of the gorge. Notice the horizontal line running along the formation; the darker rock on top is compacted clay hardened by lime from decomposing limestone, while the light greenish rock below is the siltstone from the middle of the lake. The hard clay protects the soft siltstone from accelerated erosion, which is believed to have already worn away roughly 1,000 feet of deposits from the lake bed.

From here, hikes disappear into Moon and Canyon caves, narrow passageways with walls so tight that they almost create natural bridges. Best time for pictures is in the evening, as the cliffs face west. A one-mile trail continues from the end of the paved road to under Miller Point Overlook (see below); a four-mile nature trail leads through the desert and around to the campground; signs along the way identify plants and animals in the lower gorge.

Cathedral Gorge

DEKE CASTLEMAN

Cathedral Gorge knows no real visiting season. It's open year round. There is no visitor center, no concessions, nothing but the campground, shaded picnic areas in strategic locations, drinking water, restrooms and the magic of your imagination.

The campground is a pleasant spot, with introduced Russian olive and locust trees. In spring, the Russian olives bear a little yellow flower in the spring, which gives the susceptible locals a bad case of hayfever; birds love to eat the pea-size olives, but can't quite digest them. Elevation is 5,000 feet. There are 22 sites for tents or self-contained motor homes up to 30 feet; the two pull-throughs can handle longer. Piped drinking water, flush toilets, heavenly showers, sewage disposal, public telephones, picnic tables, grills, and fire pits are provided. The maximum stay is 14 days. Day use fee is $3 and it's $7 to camp. Bundles of firewood are for sale for $2. Call the State Parks District Office in Panaca, 775/728-4467, for more information.

To Pioche

Another mile north from the main entrance is **Miller Point Overlook,** with a superlative view of the whole wash, plus four sheltered picnic tables, pit toilets, and explanatory signs.

The historical sign for **Bullionville** stands between the entrance and Miller Point. Beyond Miller Point, the road begins to climb into the juniper forest on the slopes of the Highland Range. In a few miles you pass the Castleton Cutoff, then in three miles take a left at the fork to go up into Pioche.

PIOCHE

They came in waves from Virginia City across the corrugated Great Basin of central Nevada—prospectors in search of rich lodes, miners in search of eternal veins, speculators in search of boomtown profits, and camp followers in search of new lives to lead. First Austin in the Toiyabe Mountains in 1862, then Eureka in the Diamond Mountains in 1864, then Hamilton in the White Pine Mountains in 1868, and finally Pioche in the Highland Range in 1869 all mushroomed atop promising ore bodies in the rush to

riches eastward across the new state.

Pioche (pronounced pee-OACH and named after a San Francisco financier who bankrolled the original strike) quickly gained notoriety as one of the most dangerous towns on the western frontier, described in terms usually reserved for Bodie or Tombstone. Here, the distinction between law enforcement and law breaking was determined by your particular side of the gun. And since Pioche attracted the most violent and anarchistic frontier element, inevitably groups of "regulators" were organized to protect the various claims, which further contributed to the mayhem. Pioche's enduring (and dubious) claim to fame is the 40–50 men who died of violence or accident before anyone lived long enough to expire of natural causes. Records show that two men were punished during this time. And then, during a particularly rowdy celebration in 1871, a fire got out of control and touched off an explosion of 300 powder kegs, killing a dozen, wounding a score, and destroying nearly the entire town.

By the mid-1870s, after the Lincoln County seat was transferred from Hiko to Pioche and the population had increased to 12,000, some order had been established on the streets and in the mines. One explanation credits (or blames) the influx of women to the town; they married the miners and settled them down. In fact, it got to the point where men were afraid of "walking down the street for fear of coming home married," and the Single Men's Protective Association was formed in 1876 to help "the bachelors withstand the wiles of the fair sex."

Behind the scenes, meanwhile, unchecked corruption reigned supreme. In the freewheeling days at the peak of the boom, county officials developed a fondness for expenses (to build the courthouse, for example) far beyond their capacity to raise revenues. They floated bonds, printed local scrip, and quickly doomed the county to 70 years of debt. Part of the problem was that the citizens weren't interested in paying taxes, especially in the decline period of the late 1870s. This situation prompted the sheriff to assume tax-collection responsibilities, which helped line his and his cronies' pockets. The courthouse, which cost $26,000 to build in 1871, was finally paid off in 1938—at an accrued cost of nearly a million smackeroos.

EASTERN NEVADA TOUR DEVELOPMENT

With the proper promotion and packaging, southeastern Nevada would make a perfect one-week bus tour. More historic, scenic, artistic, and recreational attractions are concentrated between Las Vegas and Ely than in any other comparable stretch in the state. Start with two nights in Las Vegas, one of the easiest places in the world to fly to, and an exciting destination itself. On the third morning, head straight over to Lake Mead, and take North Shore Road by the bays, marinas, and springs; have a rest stop at Echo Bay or Overton Beach. Serve a box picnic at Valley of Fire State Park, and visit the Lost City Museum in Overton after lunch. Then settle down to a two-hour bus ride up US 93 to Alamo and Ash Springs (rest, snack, and swimming stop). Arrive an hour later in Caliente to get settled into motel rooms and have dinner. Afterward, meet at the Spanish railroad depot to hear historian Mary Ellen Sadovich and artist Rett Hastings talk about their stunning mural depicting southern Nevada history. Then enjoy cocktails in Rainbow Canyon at sunset, and finish up with an evening at the Hot Springs Motel, with its large private mineral Roman tubs and swimming pool.

The fourth day, have breakfast in Caliente, take a short swing through Mormon Panaca, one of the oldest towns in the state, then spend the rest of the morning hiking around the unique, accessible, and thrilling Cathedral Gorge State Park. Picnic there, then run up to Pioche for massive mining remains, two museums, shops, rest stop, and snack. Next, sit back for an afternoon ride to Ely. Motel, dinner, city tour that evening.

On the fifth morning, take the tour through the Nevada Northern's freight yards, then ride the Ghost Train to Ruth or McGill. If there's time, the group could easily go to Cave Lake State Park up in the mountains, or the Ward Charcoal Ovens in the desert. Dinner, free night in Ely.

The sixth morning leave for Great Basin National Park and Lehman Caves: take the cave tour, drive up the mountain, have a picnic lunch, spend the afternoon hiking, head down to Baker for dinner at the Outlaw, then drive back to the motels in Ely. The seventh day, bus down to Las Vegas (250 miles) on NV 318 via Preston, Lund, and Hiko, which parallels US 93 mile for mile, only one valley east. There the group can disband, and the people can fly out at their convenience. Options out of Las Vegas for further travel are manifold.

Pioche's boom-and-bust cycles have continued ever since. Mines and short lines came and went; a small boom developed when cheap power reached Pioche from Hoover Dam just before WW II. The war effort also kept the mines open and producing manganese and tungsten. Since then Pioche has managed to stay alive in large part due to highway traffic, some mining, ranching, and farming. Historical signs and sites, the visitors center and library, two museums, the tramway structure, and a couple of motels and cafes will keep you happily occupied for an afternoon and complete your tour of the "Lincoln County Tri-Towns"—the orderly railroad company town, the virtuous Mormon farming community, and the rough-and-tumble mining boomtown—within an hour's drive of each other on US 93.

Sights

At the fork you have your choice of two routes: the higher, westerly road, newly paved and newly named Business 93 or NV 321, goes left into Pioche (6,060 feet up in the hills), and the lower, easterly one bypasses the town. The lower bypass runs under the tramway **buckets** suspended on the cable between the mine and the mill. The upper road takes you right to the **headframe** of the aerial tramway built by the Pioche Mine Company in 1923. The weight of the buckets carrying ore down to the mill helped propel the empty buckets back up to the mine. A five-horsepower engine (about the size of one that turns a large washing machine) got the whole thing going. According to the historical sign at the site, the cost of delivering ore to the mill by the tramway in the late 1920s was six cents a ton. Slide down to the 80-foot-high structure to see where the small motor turned the little pulley that turned the big pulley that hooked up to the small gear that turned the bigger and biggest gears that helped propel the cable and its dozens of buckets. The whole monstrous structure—headframe, gears, cable, and buckets—is in the very same place it's been since the tram was shut down for the last time, 60 years ago. Climb around on it at your own risk, but if the risk doesn't bother you, it's lungle-gym heaven.

Stop in at the **Commerce Cottage,** at the top of Main St., 775/962-5544, open weekdays 11 A.M.–3 P.M., weekends 10 A.M.–2 P.M., for a historical map and plenty of handouts on Pioche. Down Main St. from the visitors center is the **library,** open Mon.–Fri. noon–4 P.M. (1–5 P.M. on Tuesday), 775/962-5244.

Next door is the **Lincoln County Museum,** open 9 A.M.–4 P.M., closed Monday, 775/962-5207. This place has a fine collection of artifacts, which completely fills two large rooms. Most of the first room is occupied by mining material: pretty calcite and aragonite (like that from Lehman Caves), case after case of minerals from Lincoln County, a blacklight display, plus taxidermied birds, guns, medicines, 1910 embalmer's certificate, printing press, clocks, and invaluable bound books of the Lincoln County *Record* from 1920–60. The second room illustrates Pioche in its heyday, with black-and-white photos and a big map of town from the 1870s and '80s. Finally there are the obligatory pioneer kid's bedroom, a kitchen, plus antique pianos, organs, Wurlitzers. Admission is free, but this place is worth two bucks for sure.

Take Main St. through town. At the fork of Main and Pioche are the **Commercial Club** and **Amsden Building,** both of which by some miracle managed to survive fires, explosions, and gunfights, and are now two of the oldest buildings in Nevada. Two doors down from them is the old firehouse. The **Gem** movie theater actually shows first-run films Thursday, Friday, and Saturday nights at 8. It uses the original 1930s equipment and has 300 seats, with a balcony and even an old-fashioned "cry room," a glass-enclosed booth for weepy kids.

Next door is the **Thompson Opera House.** The interior still has the original footlights, seats, and scalloped picture frames, plus an adit to an old mining tunnel running out the back. Money to shore up the foundation has been raised and the work was underway as this book went to press. Since Main St. was paved and designated Business 93, federal money for historical preservation has for the first time also been made available to the Opera House.

Down the street are the **Wells Fargo Building**

and a **miner's cabin,** with the local historical signs in front. Take a right on Comstock St. to get to the cemetery, with its renowned Boot Row. Come back to Main and keep going down to the "new" courthouse; take a left in front, past Dinky, the little railroad engine that once could, to **Memorial Park,** which has kiddie toys, swimming pool (with brand new tiles on the bottom), tennis courts, and RV parking.

Also around town are the **General Store** and **mercantile, antique store** and **art gallery,** and **craft and gift shop.**

Million Dollar Courthouse

This is one of Nevada's ultimate symbols of a boom-bust economy and mentality. Originally designed to cost $16,000, overruns forced the price up to $26,000 when it was finally completed in 1876. Discounted bonds to finance the construction immediately put the county deep in the red, from which it took nearly 70 years to recover. By 1890, officials had yet to make a payment on the principal, and interest had accrued to the tune of $400,000—nearly 70% of the assessed value of the entire county! The state refused to allow the county to default, and the commissioners refinanced the debt, by then $650,000, in 1907. They finally finished paying off the bonds in 1938, four years after the building itself had been condemned, and the same year a new courthouse was constructed.

It's open Sun.–Thurs. 10 A.M.–5 P.M., Friday and Saturday 9 A.M.–5 P.M., April–October. Walk in, sign in, and the volunteer will take you around the building: through the historical photo room, sheriff's office, DA's office, and assessor's office. Upstairs are the fire department's room, the judge's office, and the courtroom. The judge's bench and nearby chairs are original. From there you head out the back door to the jailhouse—the middle cell has the original bunk and leg iron. The jailhouse is possibly the most graphic evidence remaining of the tough hombres that hung around this town 120 years ago. New to the courthouse in 1994 was a series of large watercolors painted in the late 1800s and early 1900s by one R.G. Schofield, a watchmaker and jeweler by trade.

Echo Canyon State Recreation Area

This state park, with a reservoir and campground, is four miles east on NV 322 (or the Mt. Wilson

National Backcountry Byway), then eight miles southeast on NV 86. This narrow two-lane road winds around and then drops fast into a beautiful and inappropriately named **Dry Valley,** part of the Meadow Valley Wash water system. You pass by well-irrigated and verdantly green alfalfa fields, and then approach the small earthen dam stretching across Echo Canyon on the far side of the valley. When you arrive at the park, take a right to get to the ranger station and group picnic area (in a prime spot at the bottom of the backside of the dam); drive straight ahead and past the earthen dam, which is about 40–50 feet high and holds back a fairly large body of water, to get to the campground. The campground has 34 big sites, lush with tall sagebrush, plus piped drinking water, flush toilets (turned off end of October), sewage disposal, public telephones, picnic tables under roofed shelters, barbecue and fire pits; the fees are $3 day use, $8 per night camping, firewood for sale $2. The maximum stay is 14 days. The elevation is 5,800 feet. No reservations. Contact Park Headquarters at 775/962-5103 or the State Parks District Office, 775/728-4467.

The reservoir is fed from the northeast by a stream that flows through a long narrow farming community dedicated to growing hay. The canyon in which the park is set has high walls of volcanic tuff, which has been eroded and carved by time, wind and rain. The reservoir is stocked with rainbows and crappies (the campground has a fish-cleaning shed). Boating costs $1 per day.

The road continues into Echo Canyon up the wash, under big white sandstone walls—100 feet high with eroded pinnacles. It emerges in **Rose Valley,** another beautiful little basin full of alfalfa fields hemmed in by hills and canyon walls. At Rose Valley Ranch is a T-intersection: to the left, the road climbs a mile back up to NV 322; instead, go right through another lesser canyon into **Eagle Valley** for more of the same farm-canyon scenery.

Continue on this good dirt road all the way to **Ursine,** a stunning little farm town with huge cottonwoods and fruit trees, idyllic farmhouses, horses and sheep along the creek that runs right through, kids and dogs in the road. This is as bucolic and pastoral a village as you could ever imagine. You pick up the NV 322 pavement again at the far end of Ursine; take a right. **Eagle Valley Resort,** 775/962-5293, has 40 spaces for motor homes, 36 with full hookups and no pull-throughs. Tents are allowed (separate grassy area). The fee is $7.50 for tents and $11.50–15 per RV. The grocery store and bar (slots, video poker) are across the highway. Beyond the resort, You wind around **Eagle Canyon** past the precarious gravel- and slate-covered slopes of the **White Rock Mountains** until you reach Spring Valley Recreation Area.

Spring Valley Recreation Area

Spring Valley has the same facilities as Echo Canyon: dam, reservoir, campground. A canyon cliff forms about 15% of the dam wall. This park is bigger and more crowded, and older, drier, less attractive. There's pretty good fishing (for rainbow and cutthroat trout and grebe) at the

65-acre reservoir—indicated by the large number of anglers around the lake. There's a five trout limit; the trout are 3–4 inches when released and grow three inches per year. Docking and launching facilities are available. The reservoir water is muddy, precluding swimming, but you can see the springs that feed it bubbling up under the surface of the lake.

Horsethief Gulch Campground has 37 campsites for tents or self-contained motor homes up to 28 feet. Piped drinking water, flush toilets, showers, sewage disposal, fish-cleaning shed, public telephones, picnic tables, grills, and fire pits are provided. There's a 14-day limit, which many people, presumably, use up. No reservations fees are $10 overnight, $3 day use, boating $2 per day, $2 firewood. Contact Park Headquarters at 775/962-5102 or the State Parks District Office, 775/728-4467.

The road continues along the reservoir, though the pavement ends at the dam. The rez gets marshy quite quickly, and then just like that it's gone. The road of course keeps going and going and going (you'll need the Nevada Map Atlas to explore back here) and when you finally get to the end, there's the pink Eveready bunny banging away on his big bass drum.

Practicalities

Pioche has 13 motel rooms and a few hotel rooms. **Motel Pioche** is on Lacour St. up from the old courthouse, 775/962-5245, charging $31–42. The **Hutchings Motel** is on US 93, 775/962-5404, charging $30 and up. The **Overland Hotel**, on Main St., 775/962-5895, charges $25 d; the bar here has an unusual antique interior.

The **Silver Cafe**, Main St., is open daily 7 A.M.–9 P.M., till 10 P.M. in the summer. The **Frontier House** across the street, open 6:30 A.M.–9 P.M., closed Tuesday, has $3.50 bacon and eggs and quarter-pounders, meat loaf for $5, sirloin for $8, and T-bone for $13.

Frontier Foods grocery store is open Mon.–Sat. 8 A.M.–6 P.M., Sunday 9 A.M.–6 P.M. A few video poker machines sit in front.

If anything exciting is going on in town, it'll probably be at the Alamo Club; also look into the Nevada Club, which has 10 slot machines.

The **Book Mine** is still going strong, just down the hill from the old Courthouse, 775/962-5408.

This used and antiquarian bookstore is run by Martha Lauritzen, a delightful woman who retired to Pioche from Los Angeles and has never been so busy. The store is in an old house that used to be the offices of the mining company, then the power company. The "concrete room" houses all the company records, along with a big safe. Martha's daughter Leah helps out these days, when she's not making wild junk metal sculptures. The Book Mine's hours are generally afternoons on the weekends, but do stop by to see if anybody's there at odd times: it basically opens when Martha gets the inclination and closes when she runs out of steam.

To Ely

Head north on US 93 out of Pioche along the **Bristol Range,** then up long **Lake Valley.** To the east lies the **Wilson Creek Range.** East of that is **Camp Valley,** and east of that are the **White Rock Mountains**—then you're in Utah. Around the cutoff to **Wildhorse,** you leave the Bristols behind and come into the **Fairview Hills,** on the west. Climb up a little into some single-leaf piñon pine. Go by **Mt. Wilson**—named not, according to popular belief, after Mr. Wilson of "Dennis the Menace" fame. At the Pony Springs rest area, you leave the Fairviews behind and come to **Grassy Mountain.** The **Schell Creeks** start down here, west of Grassy Mountain and its **Muleshoe Valley,** and run up to Ely and beyond. Bid Grassy Mountain adieu and say bonjour to **Dutch John Mountain,** at 8,860 feet. Say sayonara to Dutch John and say shalom to the mighty Schell Creeks, which still border Lake Valley. Here the road cuts east, up and over the minor **Fortification Range** at **Lake Valley Summit** (6,140 feet), then heads down into **Spring Valley,** with the giant **Snake Range** to the east, massive **Wheeler Peak** standing guard.

Just north US 93, US 50, and NV 6 join, 50 and 6 from the east, and 93 from the south. They all run together into Ely, then split up again. Here you start climbing way up into the Schell Creeks (Connors Pass, 7,722 feet), and between mid-June and mid-August you might not get snowed on. Beyond the summit, the Schell Creeks are now on the east (right), and the Egans are on the west, as you make the last run up Cave Valley into Ely, at 6,435 feet above sea level.

SOUTH OF LAS VEGAS

BLACK CANYON

Black Canyon, which starts at the base of Hoover Dam and extends downriver to Katherine, is the nearest river running to Las Vegas. If you want to take a commercial raft trip, call Black Canyon Raft Tours (see "River Tours" under "Hoover Dam" earlier in this chapter). If you're looking to run the river from the base of the dam on your own, you have to get a permit from the U.S. Department of Interior's Bureau of Reclamation for access via Portal Road on dam property. The Bureau of Reclamation only allows two groups of 15 people each to access the river per day: one at 8 A.M. and the second at 10:30 A.M. All popular dates, such as weekends and holidays, are booked up a year or more in advance. You can acquire a permit to put in at Portal Road during the week with a mere two or three weeks' notice, and you may also be able to snag a cancellation. For more information on accessing the Colorado River from Portal Road, call the Reclamation reservation department at 702/293-8204, Mon.–Fri. 8 A.M.–4 P.M. PST, or if there's no response at that number, contact Dan Jenson, Hoover Dam Visitor's Center Manager, at 702/294-3513. The 24-hour emergency phone number is 702/293-8932.

Other put-in and take-out points include Cottonwood Cove and Eldorado Canyon on the Nevada side, Willow Beach and Katherine Landing on the Arizona side. Once on the river, there are many exciting places to visit and things to do. Our river tour will begin at the base of the dam as if you had launched at Portal Road. If you launch from any other point you can come upriver to enjoy these locations.

Life jackets must be worn during the entire trip down Black Canyon to Chalk Cliffs at marker 43. The water below the dam is 53 degrees Fahrenheit all year, warming up as it goes farther downriver toward Eldorado Canyon, where it widens out and is warm enough for swimming in the summer. Navigational markers (day boards) are posted on the shores of the river: red triangles with even numbers on the Arizona side,

green squares with odd numbers on the Nevada side. These markers indicate the approximate distance, in miles, from Davis Dam at the extreme southern end of Lake Mojave. Also look for bighorn sheep on the cliffs along the river throughout Black Canyon. Sighting them provides the sharp-eyed observer a special opportunity to see these majestic animals in their natural environment.

Remember that the water level in the canyon can fluctuate considerably during the day, sometimes as much as 4–6 vertical feet, depending on releases from Hoover Dam. When stopping to camp, picnic, or explore, small craft should be pulled well up out of the water and larger craft should be well anchored on shore above any highwater marks to prevent being stranded.

Sights

There are hundreds of interesting places in Black Canyon. Below are ten of the best.

Sauna Cave: A few hundred yards below the Portal Road launch site on the Nevada side of the river is a long gravel spit with tamarisk bushes. At the end of a lagoon just past the spit are some rain caves on the west wall. Some drops of water are hot, while others are cold. During the construction of Hoover Dam, workers started to drill a tunnel at this site; however, they encountered hot water (122 degrees F) and had to abandon the site.

Goldstrike Canyon: At the entrance to the lagoon on the left is a small very hot spring (123 degrees F). The mouth of Goldstrike Canyon is 50 yards below the entrance to the lagoon on the Nevada side. A short walk up this canyon leads to hot pools and a hot waterfall that is about as hot as a person can stand. Various algae are responsible for the vivid green colors on the rocks. The rock formations are spectacular and there are many hot pools. The rocks and pebbles in the hot stream are sharp and tennis shoes are advised. (**Caution:** *Naegleria fowleri*, an amoeba common to thermal pools, can enter the human body through the nose, causing a rare infection and possible death. Do not allow water from the hot springs or associated streams to enter your nose. Do not dive into or submerse your head in any thermal water in this recreation area.)

After leaving Goldstrike Canyon, inexperienced boaters, especially canoeists, should line their craft past the rock reef, or paddle upstream far enough to get over to the Arizona side, where the water is less turbulent.

A hot waterfall is located within a few feet of the river about 100 yards below Goldstrike Canyon on the Arizona side. This waterfall is larger and not as hot as the one in Goldstrike Canyon. Just past the waterfall is a palm tree. The palm, which is not native to Black Canyon, was planted around 1970 by G. W. Paulin, who loved these canyons and spent much time exploring the river.

Boy Scout Canyon: About a third of a mile south of the Mile 62 marker is a sandy beach at the mouth of a large canyon on the Nevada side. Hot springs and hot pools are about a half mile up the canyon. The stream goes underground before it reaches the river.

Ringbolt Rapids: When approaching Ringbolt Rapids, watch for a large iron ring set into the rock on the Arizona side about 50 yards above the rapids (marker 60) and 15–20 feet above the high-water mark. This is one of many ringbolts that were placed in the canyon walls and used to winch steamboats up through the rapids from 1865 to 1890. The construction at Davis Dam, 60 miles downstream and the resulting Lake Mojave significantly tamed these rapids, which at one time were one of the most challenging on the Colorado River. These rapids are adjacent to White Rock Canyon and the Arizona Hot Springs on the Arizona side of the river (see entry for White Rock Canyon.)

Gauging Station: An old gauging station can be seen clinging to the Nevada canyon wall at mile 54.25. The gauging station was used prior to and during construction of Hoover Dam for monitoring the water levels, flow rate, and silt content of the Colorado. A cable car provided access to the gauging station from the Arizona side. Just across the river on the Arizona side is the trail and catwalk used by the resident engineers who were responsible for gathering the data at the gauging station to travel from their residence to the Station. The catwalk can be seen high up on the sheer walls above the river and is unsafe

for access. A second cable car across a side canyon enabled the engineers to go from the trail over to the catwalk. The foundations of the gauger's house and garage are located just down the river at about mile 53.

Willow Beach Fish Hatchery: The buildings on the Arizona bank just before mile 52 are a part of the Willow Beach National Fish Hatchery. The buoys floating on the Arizona shore mark an area that is closed to all water craft including canoes and kayaks (see entry for Willow Beach.) The Willow Beach area extends for about a half mile along the Arizona shore. If you're terminating your trip at Willow Beach, boat to the south end at the harbor past the marinas, and bring your vessel to shore at the south end of the parking lot. There is convenient vehicle access to this location and you will not come into conflict with other boaters as you remove your boat from the water. South of Willow Beach the river is still narrow and cold; it continues flowing through the deep canyon for about 3.5 miles. Life jackets must still be worn while underway.

Monkey Hole: The point where the river widens is known as Monkey Hole. With a bit of imagination, the rock formation high on the Arizona shore kinda sorta resembles a monkey. Just below Monkey Hole and Mile 48, the Mead-Liberty powerlines cross the river.

Windy Canyon: The stretch of river between Mile 45 and 44A is known as Windy Canyon. On occasion up-river winds become quite strong in this area, when this canyon more than earns its name. Canoes and other small boats are recommended to check the wind currents before venturing below Willow Beach, the last take-out point before Windy Canyon. Below Mile 44A, the river spreads out into Copper Basin; several canyons open out in this area, providing good places to camp.

Chalk Cliffs: Just below Squaw Peaks on the Nevada side are the Chalk Cliffs. A navigational light and Marker 43 high on the Nevada side mark the mouth of Black Canyon. Life jackets are not required to be worn below this point, but their continued use is strongly recommended as the river current is still strong at this point.

Eldorado Canyon: Eldorado Canyon is on the Nevada side at about Mile 39. The take-out point used is a quarter-mile-long uphill portage to the road. This was the site of a large flash flood in 1974 that wiped out the facilities at Eldorado Canyon; they were never replaced.

For those intrepid boaters who wish to continue south of Eldorado Canyon, be prepared for open water, possible very windy conditions, and extreme temperature ranges. Cottonwood Cove is 17 miles distant and Katherine Landing is 40 miles.

Nelson and Vicinity

Head out from Las Vegas on US 93/95, either via Boulder Hwy. or I-515. You go through Henderson and over Railroad Pass, then drop down to Eldorado Valley, where US 95 turns off (right) and aims due south on a flat, straight, and fast stretch of blacktop. The **McCullough Range** keeps you company on the west; after a while the **Eldorado Range** comes up on the east. Down the road a piece the small **Highland Range** cuts in front of the McCulloughs. Roughly 30 miles southeast of Las Vegas is the turnoff for NV 165; 12 miles south of there on a good paved road lies Nelson, a veritible living ghost town that dates back to the mid-1800s. The town is named for Charles Nelson, a prospector who was murdered at his mine in 1897 by an Indian named Ahvote.

The town of Nelson was established in 1905, seven miles to the west of the original settlement at the mouth of the infamous Eldorado Canyon, near the Techatticup mine. Today Nelson hosts a combination bar and cafe, trailer hookups, and a gas station that is more or less open or closed depending on the whims of the owner. The principal attraction is the spectacular descent into town through a narrow squeeze of tipped and tumbled rock after the long climb over the gentle slope from US 95. All reds and blacks toward sundown, the canyon suggests the entrance to hell—it's a fitting (and magnificent) tribute to a place many considered its equivalent.

One of the biggest mining booms in Nevada history originated with the discovery of gold and silver here in 1859. Soon rich mines were developed and the original community of Eldorado was laid out. During its early years, Eldorado was a rough-and-tumble camp; not even a killing would bring the sheriff to the camp, because he was over 200 miles away and would take his own life in his hands trying to get there. Besides, once he was there, his life remained in jeopardy as long as he tried to control the crowd that was used to making its own law and doling out its own justice at the end of a gun or rope.

The old town of Eldorado was a landing place for the sternwheelers that came up from Yuma. The most noted of these ships was the *Mojave,* which brought up supplies and returned with ore. The ore was reduced in a 15-stamp mill located at the dock, which created a roar that was heard up and down the canyon. During its reign, more than 45,000 ounces of fine gold were taken from this area. In later years the tailings of the mines were processed at a cyanide mill seen in the journey down the canyon across from the Texaco station. Wild burros are prolific in the canyon, attesting to the prospecting activity in the canyon. The original site of Eldorado was submerged when Davis Dam was built and Lake Mojave was created. However, three of the largest old mines—the Techatticup, the Wall Street, and the Savage, as well as many old structures, including the ruins of the cyanide plant—are left.

At one point Eldorado was renamed Nelson and reached a respectable population of 600. The current population is about 40, mostly retired folk who live the hot summer serenity and a few old half-baked sourdoughs who never give up. From the town of Nelson, you can continue down to the end of the canyon on a two-lane asphalt road that gets worse each year. Unless Clark County decides to resurface and reinforce it, one day it will disappear into the desert wash along which it runs. After seven miles you get to the end of road; it's blocked off about half a mile from the river's edge. This is flash flood country. In 1974 a flash flood completely destroyed the launch dock and marina that sat here. You can still put-in and take-out here, but you have to portage your craft the half mile to the water. It is not recommended to come down here during flash flood season!

When you come to the sign marked Dead End, the road to the right takes you down to the wash trailhead and parking. The road to the left takes you to an overlook that provides a spectacular view of the river and hills on both sides of the river. But be careful. On windy days, which happen frequently, you could easily lose your balance and be blown into one of the washes.

Knob Hill and Tule Springs

Twenty-three miles south of the junction of US 95 and NV 165 is another road leading to Nelson. This unpaved road, referred to by locals as a "dirt freeway" because it's so well graded and maintained, cuts across the front of the Ireteba Peaks, part of the Eldorado Mountains, then switches past many of the old mines making up the Eldorado Mining District, and comes into Nelson from the southwest. About halfway along this road, it crosses a powerline road, recognizable by the string of gigantic power transmission towers. Turn east on the powerline road, another well-maintained dirt road, and travel to the summit of Knob Hill (4,550 feet), at the north end of the Ireteba Peaks. Another road juts to the southeast a short distance to Tule Springs.

You'll recognize the area by the old windmill and concrete reservoir dating back to the turn of the century. The view of the Colorado River and surrounding canyons is magnificent. There are no restrictions on camping in this desert beauty, but it is primitive camping, which means you must bring your own water and other supplies. There are no picnic tables, no grills, no toilet facilites, nor is there any water. Neither the windmill nor the well work anymore. You must also pack out your trash. This is worth a visit if you're into off-road travel and camping, and it's eminently accessible by passenger vehicle.

This area can also be reached directly from Nelson by means of a 10-mile dirt and gravel road in good condition. The road winds up and out of the hilly terrain behind the tiny community. At the apex a panoramic view of Nelson and mine tailings is well worth seeing.

SEARCHLIGHT AND VICINITY

Thirty-six miles from the junction where US 95 cuts south is the town of **Searchlight,** right on the highway. Gold was discovered here in 1897. In 1902 a narrow-gauge railroad was built from the town down to the mill on the Colorado River near the site of Cottonwood Cove. The peak year for mining was in 1907, but production continued all the way up to 1940; in all $4.5 million in gold was recovered.

Today, the Searchlight **Nugget** is a good place to break up the trip from Las Vegas to Laughlin. Have a snack or a pop at the big coffee shop, which actually dwarfs the casino; the casino cage also serves as the cashier for the restaurant. The Searchlight Nugget is famous for its 10-cent cup of coffee (it's actually 11 cents when you add in the sales tax). The bar is pretty classy. Notice the turquoise cow heads with polished horns hanging on the hearth, and the posters of the Calgary Stampede in the poker room.

The Searchlight Historic Museum and Mining Park is at 200 Michael Wendoll Way, 702/297-1201, open Mon.–Fri. 9 A.M.–5 P.M., Saturday 9 A.M.–1 P.M., donation. When you walk into this museum, you trigger a recording, and though no one else is generally around, a voice starts talking to you—eerie but cool. Check out the displays and historical photographs on the history of Searchlight—how the town was named, local personalities and famous people, mostly Nevada politicians who have some connection to the area, minerals in the neighborhood, the railroad story, and more. Outside is a historic mining park.

Also in town are a Chevron station, Coulton's General Store, a dozen billboards for Laughlin, and two motels. The **El Rey Lodge** at the corner of Hobson, 702/297-1144, has 21 rooms and charges $32–54; the **Renteria Motel,** 702/297-1581, has 18 rooms and charges $25–35.

Also here is the turnoff onto NV 164 to Cottonwood Cove on Lake Mojave, 14 miles east. **Cottonwood Cove Resort and Marina,** 702/297-1464, is a full-scale motel-RV park-resort, with 24 motel rooms at $80–85, a large campground of 75 RV sites ($10) and 150 tent sites ($5), showers, picnic area, boating, fishing, swimming, and playground.

West of Searchlight

NV 164 runs west from Searchlight and winds its way across the California border and the small town of Nipton, and eventually terminates at I-15 at Mountain Pass. Seven miles west of Searchlight, turn left (south) on Walking Box Ranch Road. About three-quarters of a mile down the road you come to a sign on the right that says Castle Mountain Venture 18 miles. Operated by Viceroy Gold Operations, Castle Mountain is a commercial gold mine. Immediately to the left is Walking Box Ranch, a beautiful mission-style set of buildings. Walking Box Ranch was built in the 1930s by legendary silent film stars Rex Bell and Clara Bow, seeking a refuge from the bright lights of Hollywood and Paramount Pictures. Many film stars, including Clark Gable, Errol Flynn, Charles Coburn, and Lionel Barrymore, visited this unique ranch. Rex Bell went on to become Lt. Gov. of Nevada and Stewart Bell, his son, is currently Clark County District Attorney. The ranch grounds are private property and you're not welcome there; it's owned by the Viceroy Company in conjunction with the Nature Conservancy to preserve it for future generations.

East of Searchlight

From Searchlight, you take NV 164 (Cove Road) straight down a 14-mile grade to Lake Mojave. It would be a breeze of a bike ride from Searchlight to Cottonwood Cove; you can coast almost all the way down. But it would be a death ride back up. You pass through a teddy bear cholla forest on Cove Road. Teddy bear cholla is the spiniest, but most handsome, many believe, of all cactus. The spines are painful and difficult to remove. Packrats use the prickly joints for protection around their nests.

At the bottom of Cove Road is **Cottonwood Cove,** a small little settlement on Lake Mojave. Here you'll find a trailer village, RV park, Park Service campground, motel, cafe, convenience store, Chevron gas station, and marina. There's also a Park Service interpretive center, with water fountains, handouts, and some history and ecology. You'll learn about the narrow-gauge railroad that ran from the Quartet Mine in Searchlight down to the Colorado River, where steamboats picked up the gold; also check out the water-in-the-desert exhibit: kangaroo rats, for example, have such efficient kidneys that the animal never has to drink water, obtaining all the moisture it needs from the seeds it eats. There's a short desert discovery trail around the building; pick up a brochure for an explanation of the sites marked with modern-day pictoglyphs. You'll get a good look at silver cholla, prickly pear, hedgehog, ocotillo, cottontop cactus, and of course, screwbean mesquite.

The **Cove Cafe** is a cozy little full-service restaurant, open for breakfast, lunch, and dinner, with some fuzzy black-and-white photographs on the south wall; bacon and eggs $5, burgers $4–6.50, T-bone $14. The 24-room Cottonwood Cove Resort, 702/297-1464, charges $55–95 d; the front yard is the lake, the back yard is a grassy lawn. The Cottonwood Cove RV Park has 75 spaces for motor homes, all with full hookups; 15 are pull-throughs. Tents are not allowed. Restrooms have flush toilets and hot showers. The RV park is the epitome of "desert landscaping" (bring sunscreen), but the sites are wide enough to park a boat next to an RV. There are some activities (shuffleboard, horseshoes, volleyball, etc.), but the main action is on the water: houseboat, deck cruiser, and motorboat rentals, fishing, waterskiing, canoeing, and of course swimming. Reservations are accepted (for pull-throughs). The fee is $17–20 for two people.

The **Cottonwood Cove Campground** has 144 campsites for tents or self-contained motor homes up to 35 feet; there are two sections, upper and lower. The upper campground is strictly desert; the lower campground is on the other side of the parking lot from the sandy beach (and six picnic tables under shelters): big sites (dirt), big trees (cottonwoods, palms, willows), paved access road. Piped drinking water, flush toilets, sewage disposal, laundry, picnic tables, grills, and fire rings are provided. The maximum stay is 90 days. No reservations are taken. The fee is $8 per site.

Cal-Nev-Ari

Ten miles south of Searchlight lies Cal-Nev-Ari, a hamlet of trailers and shade trees that stretches along the highway for a bit. This is one of the more unusually founded towns in the state, built around an old WW II practice airstrip by Slim and Nancy Kidwell in 1965. The whole story is posted on the wall just inside the cafe. Also inside the main building in town are a bar, slot machines, and the post office (open afternoon weekdays). The cafe recently installed a sunroom fronted by a series of flags. Out in back are the runway and hangar.

Across the street is **Blue Sky Motel,** 702/297-9289, with 10 rooms at $31–41. In the vicinity of the motel are an RV park, market (with a couple of big saguaro in front), and laundromat.

One mile south of town is the Christmas Tree Pass cutoff (see "Grapevine and Christmas Tree" under "Around Laughlin" later in this chapter). Eight miles south of there is the turn (left) onto NV 163 to Laughlin, featuring four laudable lanes (newly paved in 1994) the 20 miles up and over the Newberry Mountains and down to the Colorado River and Laughlin. Davis Dam is on the left, the tall single smokestack from the power plant on the right, and the high-rise hotels right in between on the river.

LAUGHLIN

What it is about godforsaken patches of the Nevada desert that gives men visions of booming metropolises is hard to say. Abe Curry bought a tiny trading post in Eagle Valley to launch the capital city of a state that didn't even exist. Myron Lake bought a collapsing bridge and proceeded to found the world's biggest little city. And Don Laughlin bought a bankrupt bait shop and built, in a few short years, one of the largest gambling centers in the country. Maybe it's water. All three pioneers had rivers—the Carson, Truckee, and Colorado—in common. Maybe it's heat—the scorching, absorbing, blinding swelter that gives rise to sugar-plum fairies, pink elephants, and mirages of gold mines. Probably it's destiny—the Great Basin and Mojave are littered with the ghosts of hundreds of boomtowns whose founding fathers dreamed of the prosperity and posterity that only a select few have achieved. Whatever it is, Don Laughlin came, invested, and conquered, giving life to a namesake town site the likes of which Nevada hasn't seen for exactly 100 years.

Don Laughlin was born in 1933 and grew up in Owatonna, Michigan. By the time he was in the ninth grade, he already had a successful business supplying pinball machines, jukeboxes, and slots (legal at the time) to nearby bars and restaurants. He moved to Las Vegas at the age of 21 and worked as a bartender and dealer for a couple of years, then bought the 101 Club, a small bar in North Las Vegas that afforded him the opportunity to get a gaming license. In 1966 he sold the bar and began looking around for a place to start an empire—a predictable ambition for any 33-year-old entrepreneur with Las Vegas cash and a gaming license burning a hole in his pocket. Soon he'd spotted Sandy

Point, a small beach on the Colorado River where the southern tip of Nevada wedges between California and Arizona in the fierce Sonoran desert. At the time the only business was a baked and bankrupt bait shop, familiar only to a handful of anglers from broiling Bullhead City, Arizona, across the river. Laughlin bought six acres of land at the end of a sandy road for $250,000 ($35,000 down). Along with the land came the bait shop, an eight-room motel (Laughlin's family occupied half of it), and a six-seat bar. But it was his unrestricted gaming license that put Laughlin in the black, and an Irish postal official who put "Laughlin" on the map. According to legend, the inspector, O'Reilly, listened to Laughlin's suggestions of Riverside and Casino for the name of the town, but settled on Laughlin instead, for the Irish ring of it. Today Don jokes that Laughlin was named after his mother.

The Riverside

Both Laughlins struggled for the first decade or so; banks laughed at Don's loan applications. But Southern California Edison built a coal-fired power plant just up the hill from the river, expanding the population base. Slowly, people from Needles, Kingman, Lake Havasu, and even as far away as San Bernardino and Flagstaff began frequenting the homegrown little river resort-casino as an alternative to corporate Las Vegas. By 1976, the Riverside Hotel had expanded to 100 rooms and 300 slots. The growth of Bullhead City, Arizona, right across the Colorado River, kept pace; its population increased from 600 in 1966 to more than 6,000 in 1976, as employees, retirees, and snowbirds moved in, attracted by the weather, the water, and the wagering. In 1982, the Colorado River Commission began developing housing and recreational facilities nearby, then Clark County installed water and sewer systems, and growth rapidly snowballed, so to speak.

By 1984, the Riverside was a 14-story, 350-room hotel, accompanied by half a dozen other casinos lining the river—and little else. In that year Laughlin had a grand total of 95 residents—the temp. still higher than the pop. and one casino for every 16 townspeople! The rest of the 3,000 employees lived on the Arizona side (by then Bullhead City had surpassed the 15,000 mark), commuting across the river by way of the

Davis Dam bridge or the casino ferries, and gaining an hour in the process (Arizona is on Mountain Time, but unlike Jackpot and Wendover, Laughlin sticks to Pacific Time).

The Boom

But the mid-'80s was just the beginning of the boom. Don Laughlin proceeded to spend more than a million of his own dollars in road improvements, $3 million to build the new bridge from Bullhead City to his hotel (then had a little trouble getting Nevada to take it over), and $6 million to expand the airport across the river. Meanwhile, developers began throwing up condos, apartments, shopping centers, even a school and library. And the casinos kept coming: Sam's Town Gold River opened in 1985 (the name was changed, along with the management, in 1992 to Gold River Resort; and then again in 1998 to River Palms Resort); Circus Circus's Colorado Belle opened in July 1987, right next door to its sister the Edgewater. Harrah's gorgeous Del Rio Hotel opened in mid-1988, and a big Flamingo Hilton opened in August 1990. Steve Wynn paid $40 million for Del Webb's Nevada Club (now the Golden Nugget), vastly improved the interior, and built a 300-room tower. Parking garages have now been built at every joint.

The Flamingo is the largest hotel with 2,000 rooms; Harrah's is second largest, having expanded to nearly 1,700. Ramada Express recently completed a $75 million, 1,100-room expansion (for a total of 1,500), and Don Laughlin's own Riverside just put the finishing touches on a 28-story, 792-room addition, for a total of 1,450.

Gambling revenues began dropping slightly in Laughlin in 1994, due to intense competition from the new megajoints on the Las Vegas Strip, but it's too early to wonder if it will become an ongoing trend. More competition, however, has just arrived, however, and not from the north, but from the south. The Fort Mojave Tribe opened the Avi Hotel-Casino eight miles south of Laughlin right on the state line, with plans to expand immediately; eventually, the development will encompass a 4,000-acre master-planned community in California, Arizona, and Nevada. The new boomtown is called Aha Macav.

Laughlin is one of the hottest spots in the country, logging in with the second-highest record temperatures, right behind Laredo, Texas. On June 29, 1994, the official thermometer at Laughlin's Clark County Fire Department station registered a sizzling 125 degrees, breaking Nevada's highest recorded temperature (in 1954) by two degrees. But in another way, Laughlin is pretty cool. You'll immediately notice how airy and bright the casinos are, thanks to the big picture windows overlooking the river. Their more comfortable and less claustrophobic atmosphere makes you wonder what Las Vegas has against natural light. Also, inside the Riverside and Del Rio casinos, you can snap pictures to your heart's content. The hotel rooms can be 50% cheaper than comparable ones in Las Vegas. And food here, like the cheap hotel rooms, expansive casinos, cooperative weather, and playful river, is user-friendly.

CASINOS

Orientation

From the Nevada corner of the Laughlin bridge it's exactly a mile to the town's only traffic light at the Ramada Express, then another mile exactly to Harrah's Del Rio. Between March and November, unless you're a camel it's a long sweaty walk from one end to the other, even if you take the fine riverwalk behind the casinos between the Riverside and the Golden Nugget. You can take the public bus, CAT, which runs along the Strip every hour ($1). You can also catch a water taxi to five of the hotels. Or grab a cab to where you want to go. But easiest, as always, is to drive. You can park in the Riverside lot to see it, then park in the Flamingo structure to see the Hilton, Ramada Express, Edgewater, Colorado Belle, Pioneer, and Golden Nugget, then drive to River Palms Resort, and on to Harrah's.

Riverside

Start your tour, naturally enough, at Don Laughlin's front-runner Riverside Hotel. The Riverside, being Laughlin's first, has the Greyhound bus depot, a movie theater (newly expanded to six cinemas), a showroom and headliner room, and the old post office. It's an older establishment, comparatively speaking, so it's somewhat claustrophobic and always *very* crowded with regulars.

Colorado River casinos

JOHN ELK III

It has one of the state's only scenic pits—which runs along the back of the casino, over the sunken bar, looking out the big picture windows onto the Colorado.

The Riverside has a 24-hour coffee shop, buffet, snack bar, and prosaically but practically named Prime Rib Room and Gourmet Room. The showroom features headliners and traveling productions, such as "Legends in Concert." Something a little wild is almost always going in Loser's Lounge: rock 'n' roll, amateur striptease, drinking. Check out the stooge gallery, featuring the Hindenberg, the Titanic, and a big poster of the famous Las Vegas horror movie, *Attack of the 50-Foot Woman.* There's also a Western dance hall, where a DJ spins the country tunes, the local country station holds contests and country-and-western fans learn to line dance.

Flamingo Hilton

This 2,000-room hotel, with its trademark purple and pink neon, and nearly 8,000 pink-tinted windows, opened in August 1990. Its casino, in the Laughlin tradition, is wide open and airy, with high ceilings and good ambient light. Club Flamingo is a good-sized lounge with 400 seats; you can almost see, and clearly hear, the performers from the casino; lately, "American Superstars" has been playing here.

Regency

This sweet little casino provides the tattered edge to Laughlin, with a sort of downtown Las Vegas feel about it. Completely dwarfed by the Flamingo's five-story parking structure and the Edgewater's 1,000-room tower, the Regency is a smoky little grind joint, with four blackjack tables, a funky snack bar, and restaurant serving unexpected food, such as frog's legs, pepper steak, and crab, for less than $10. The Regency could be, proportionately speaking, the smallest casino between the two biggest casinos in Nevada.

Edgewater

This Circus Circus hotel grew to nearly 1,500 rooms when its 1,000-room tower, right on the river, opened in 1992. The casino is about 50 times larger inside than it looks from the outside: sprawling, airy, roomy. Downstairs are the buffet, 24-hour coffee shop, and a typical Hickory Pit steakhouse in the Circus Circus mold. The sports book has room for 400. The snack bar is a great place to get big sandwiches, shrimp cocktails, and strawberry shortcake.

Colorado Belle

Another Circus Circus establishment, this hotel-casino is an anomaly in Nevada: a riverboat casino actually right on a river. The smokestacks soar 21 stories, strobe lights turn the paddlewheel, and a bridge over a little moat fronts the main entrance. Inside it's red-flocked wallpaper, riveted stacks for beams, fancy cut-glass chandeliers, major period murals and paintings, and a sweeping staircase with wood and brass banisters. The big Riverboat Lounge at the south end gets the boat rocking at night.

Upstairs are the restaurants and snack shop, gift shop, candy shop, and arcade.

Pioneer

This is the other grind joint in Laughlin (along with the Regency), with low ceilings, closely packed slots, dark, crowded. The Pioneer has a buffet that, especially on the weekends, lines them up out the back door, along with **Granny's** restaurant upstairs from the main desk. The big neon River Ric, third in the unholy trinity of Vegas Vic and Wendover Will, waves with both arms, winks with one eye, and puffs on the perfect cigarette.

Ramada Express

Across the street sits this big hotel-casino, the only hotel (so far) on the east side of the Strip. Catch Old No. 7, "the Gambler," at the new depot in front of the hotel for a 10-minute three-quarter-mile ride around the parking lot. The trip takes you fairly high above the action and supplies convenient transportation from the covered parking lot down to the casino and street. It runs every 15 minutes on the quarter hour 10 A.M.–10 P.M. (till 11 on weekends); cost of your ticket is one smile. A fog machine simulates smoke from the stack and engine; sound effects, such as the roar of fire in the engine's boiler and whoosh of air brakes, add to the effect.

Cameras are welcome inside. The original casino wing is set up like a giant depot. The whole joint is full of railroad memorabilia; employees are called "the crew," the gift shop is train-oriented, the carpet looks like railroad track, and the bus boys greet you with "Welcome aboard." When the slot attendants announce their wares, it sounds like "Train! Train!" till you finally figure out they're saying "Change! Change!"

The air in the casino actually *circulates,* thanks to hundreds of ceiling fans, and track lighting (along with the eyes-in-the-sky) is suspended from black pipe from the high round ceiling. The acoustics are so muffled that you can have a conversation with the crap dealer, and there's even a water fountain right in the front vestibule! Ramada Express has taste and

good designers.

Golden Nugget

You walk in through a familiar tropical atrium that was inspired by (or left over from) the Las Vegas Mirage: verdant foliage, curvy palms, rocky waterfalls—humid. Duck down the alleyway to the right for the Gilded Cage, in which five animated birds do French showtunes every 15 minutes 10 A.M.–10 P.M. It's about as tasteful as such a thing can be (though you still feel pretty silly standing there watching it). Have a coconut cocktail at Tarzan's Lounge, which generally showcases the best lounge bands in Laughlin and doubles as a comedy club (all free).

River Palms Resort

You walk through the front doors onto the mezzanine level, overlooking the casino and looking out over a slew of neon signs of mines. Up here are slots, a bar, and an ice cream parlor. Down a level you'll find the main casino, the Lodge resturant, the buffet, Palace Theater, Gaming Society slot club, Cody's Lounge, front desk, bingo parlor, sports book, and bake shop that, altogether, are larger than Cal-Nev-Ari. On the lowest (river) level are Pasta Cucina, the video arcade, and the doors to the dock.

Harrah's Laughlin

Harrah's Mexican-theme hotel, Laughlin's southernmost hotel-casino so far, is in a league all its own—as classy as you would expect a Harrah's to be. Opened in the summer of 1988, Harrah's simple white walls, painted with green and purple flora, the strolling mariachi bands, and the overhead decorations create a festive south-of-the-border feel.

Club La Bamba gets some classy and brassy entertainers, with the river as a backdrop. Cisco's Party Zone is Harrah's trademark fun pit—loud, low limit. Harrah's also boasts the only official swimming beach along the Strip on the Nevada side, and it's open to the public.

Bay Shore Inn

Newest lodging in Laughlin, this 100-room hotel on Casino Dr. near the intersection with the Needles Hwy. offers mostly video poker and the Lazy River Lounge.

AROUND LAUGHLIN

Suburbs

Continue south along Casino Dr. from the Bay Shore, and take a right onto the Needles Hwy. (US 95). Here is Laughlin town, which consists of numerous new subdivisions with names such as Laughlin Estates, Laughlin Bay Village, South Pointe, Crown Point, South Bay, El Mirage, Rio Vista, Palm Terrace, and Las Palmas. Also along this stretch are a new post office, brand new round library, high school and elementary school, and the El Mirage shopping center. Edison Way runs past the Mojave Generating Station, which at night is lit up all the way around with one tall stack blowing white smoke, and the sanitation plant on its way back down to the Strip.

Davis Dam

Take a right onto NV 163 from Needles Hwy. and drop down to the river. Pass Sportsman's Park and drive onto Davis Dam and Power-house. This dam, the second of three in the Lower Colorado Dams Project (along with Hoover 67 miles north and Parker 80 miles south), was completed in 1953 at a cost of $67 million. Like Hoover Dam, its functions are to regulate the Colorado River water (often to the dismay of Laughlin tour-boat operators), pro-duce 1–2 billion kilowatt-hours of electricity, irri-gate nearby farmland, and provide recreational opportunities to residents and visitors on long, thin Lake Mojave behind it. It was named after Arthur Davis, the Bureau's director between 1914 and 1932. The dam is earth-filled, 200 feet high, 1,600 feet across, and has five turbines. NV 163 crosses the crest and joins AZ 68; the new bridge just north of the Riverside cuts a full 20 miles off the commute from Bullhead City to Laughlin. Self-guided tours are open to the pub-lic daily 7:30 A.M.–3:30 P.M. (Mountain Time)—recorded narration, maps, and views of the power plant. For more information, write Chief, Davis Dam, Bullhead City, AZ 86430.

Katherine Landing

A quarter mile east on the Arizona side of the dam, take a left. A 3.5-mile scenic drive winds through some hills down to **Lake Mojave Resort and Marina,** 702/754-3245, on long, thin Lake Mojave. The lake stretches 67 miles north, backing up all the way to Hoover Dam. It's hemmed in by Pyramid, Painted, Eldorado, and Black canyons. Its 44 square miles of surface area mark a beautiful deep-blue contrast to the dull beige desert. The resort is pleasingly green, with a big campground, motel, gas station, ranger station, fish-cleaning facilities and ice machine, marina, houseboat rentals, Tail of the Whale restaurant (open 7 A.M.–8 P.M.—bacon and eggs $4.50, burgers and sandwiches $3.50, dinners $10 average), and a small beach for swimming. Fish you might catch include channel catfish, carp, black crappie, green and bluegill sunfish, and big-ass bass. Not much for landlubbers to do down here, except camp in an idyllic setting and take a dip, but it's worth the drive just for the view or to stick your toes in.

Grapevine and Christmas Tree

Head north on Casino Dr. or Needles Hwy. and go left (west) on NV 163. In 3.5 miles turn right onto an unmarked sandy road; in 20 yards a sign gives you the distances to Grapevine Canyon (two miles), **West Boundary** of Lake Mead Recreation Area (7.3 miles), and US 95 (15 miles—but really 17). Go the two miles and turn left into the Grapevine Canyon parking lot; step out of the car and into some remote and forbidding desert. A trail heads up the canyon, which is full of petroglyphs and has a little stream that (supposedly) runs year-round. Nice hike. Then continue north on the dusty, 25-mph road through the Newberry Mountains, bearing left (west) at the intersection to Pipe Spring. An open-mouth rock greets you after a while—dying of thirst. Turn back to see the skull after the ag-onizing death. This is some spectacular desert and sandstone scenery. Somewhere (not sign-posted) you cross **Christmas Tree Pass** at 3,500 feet. The road gets pretty rough and nar-row and twisty, but there are plenty of side roads down to primitive camping spots. Don't despair: the road is much smoother and wider and faster as you make your run due west down to US 95.

PRACTICALITIES

Accommodations

At last count, there were a little more than

11,000 rooms in Laughlin itself, and another goodly amount in Bullhead City across the river. Though around 4,000 of them have opened in the past few years, the total rooms still don't go very far in accommodating nearly 500,000 visitors a month. And the season here is year-round, with older snowbirds in the winter and younger river rats in the summer (120° notwithstanding!). Also, the hotel rooms can be amazingly cheap, which ensures vacancy rates that you need a micrometer to measure. So, as always, make your reservations early. If you can't get one, call over to the Bullhead City Chamber of Commerce for a motel room (see below; also see Moon Publications' *Arizona Handbook* by Bill Weir).

Colorado Belle, 2100 Casino Dr., 702/298-4000 or 800/47-RIVER, $16–75; Edgewater, 2020 Casino Dr., 702/298-2453 or 800/67-RIVER, $18–69; Flamingo Hilton, 1900 Casino Dr., 702/298-5111 or 800/FLAMING, $25–89; River Palms Resort, 2700 Casino Dr., 702/298-2242 or 800/835-7904, $15–300; Golden Nugget, 2300 Casino Dr., 702/298-7111 or 800/237-1739, $21–99; Harrah's, 2900 Casino Dr., 702/298-4600 or 800/447-8700, $25–100; Pioneer, 2200 Casino Dr., 702/298-2442 or 800/634-3469, $17–55; Ramada Express, 2100 Casino Dr., 702/298-4200 or 800/2-RAMADA, $16–49; and Riverside, 1650 Casino Dr., 702/298-2535 or 800/227-3849, $17–109.

Camping and RVing

Nevada side, there is one RV park, Riverside RV Park, just up Laughlin Cutoff Rd. across from the little Regency, 702/298-2535. It charges $16 a night for one of 600 spaces with full hookups, has showers and a laundry on the property, and allows the use of all the Riverside Hotel's resort amenities.

In Arizona, Davis Camp Park is a mile or so south of Davis Dam—go right on AZ 68 and follow it around to the left; 602/754-4606. Enter and pay at the guard station: $13 for one of 95 spaces and full hookups, $7 for tent camping, $2 for day use (8 A.M.–8 P.M.). Take a right to get to the tent and beach area, a left for the RV park and day-use picnic facilities. This is a 355-acre Mojave County park, a relaxing place to meet people, eat, breathe, watch the river go by, get into the river, and dig the view of the strip. High-

ly recommended. Bullhead City also has a KOA and three private RV parks.

Food

Food in Laughlin is good, plentiful, cheap, and has some variety, with a major in meat and a minor in Italian and Mexican.

The nicest room in town for ambience is the Lodge at River Palms Resort, 702/835-7904, open 5-11 P.M. (midnight Friday and Saturday), with tasteful stone and log architecture, a comfortable bar with piano, and outside seating. Caesar salad is $4, clams casino $7; blackened redfish, red snapper, halibut, shrimp, chicken, game hen, and duck are $11–15, steaks, blackened filet, and cioppino are $16–20. Pasta Cucina, downstairs at River Palms Resort, serves $5–6 pasta, $6 pizza, $7–9 chicken and veal parmesan, and $10 N.Y. steak. River Palms Resort also has a 24-hour coffee shop, buffet, and Mexican snack bar.

Ramada Express is proud of its promenade, where you can duck into Ramada Expresso, Passaggio Italian Gardens, and the Steakhouse. Passaggio offers Italian sandwiches, pasta, pizza, chicken, veal, and eggplant in the $8–12 range. The Steakhouse features Caesar salad for $3.75 and a good lobster and shiitake mushroom appetizer for $6.75; salads are served from the gambling-train salad cart, with entrees of chicken, swordfish, veal, and steaks $13–20, and rack of lamb, lobster thermidor, and king crab $20–25. Ramada Express also has a 24-hour coffee shop, buffet, and snack bar.

For California Kitchen-style pizza, pasta, mesquite burgers, and salads in the $3–7 range, try Jane's Grill at the Golden Nugget. There's also a good deli with New York-style sandwiches for around $3.50. Or head downstairs for the buffet and 24-hour coffee shop.

Harrah's has William Fisk's, a steakhouse with whole artichoke heart for $5, mussels for $6, and smoked salmon for $7, along with beef, lamb, veal, fish, and quail entrees for around $17. Guadalaja Harrah's next door is the most cleverly named bar in town. Also here are a buffet, 24-hour coffee shop, Hacienda Mexican restaurant, and Gringo's Grill snack bar (burgers $1.50–3).

The Edgewater's Winner's Circle Deli has an awesome shrimp cocktail served on a paper plate for $1.50, plus a $2 hot dog, $1.50 bowl of chili, and big $3 sandwiches.

Upstairs at the Colorado Belle are **Mark Twain's,** serving barbecue chicken and ribs in the $7.50–10 range; **Mississippi Lounge** oyster bar, serving oysters and clams on the half shell for $5.50, seafood sampler $10, steamed clams $10 a dozen, crab melt sandwich $5; the **Orleans Room** steakhouse, serving steak and seafood in the $12–19 range; and buffet.

The **Alta Villa** and **Beef Baron** restaurants are similar to the restaurants of the same name at the Las Vegas Flamingo; the former is like an Italian town square, with pasta, chicken, beef, and fish $10–17; the latter serves ribs, prime rib, steaks, and barbecue chicken for $9–15. The Flamingo also has a 24-hour coffee shop, buffet, '50s-style diner, and Burger King.

Fishing

Striped bass are the big thing around here—30 pounds isn't uncommon. The world's record (inland) striper was landed at Bullhead City: 59.5 pounds! May is the best time to fish for them; they run north from Lake Havasu starting in March. There's a bass derby all summer on the river and a few rainbows might be lurking in the cold water right below the dam. Or head down to Katherine Landing and strike up a conversation about the crappies, carpies, and catfish.

Tours

Three tour boats cruise the Colorado, as long as there's enough water downriver—the Bureau of Reclamation controls the levels, often not to the liking of the tour-boat operators. The *Fiesta Queen* departs daily 11 A.M.–6:30 P.M. (winter hours may vary) from the dock outside the River Palms Resort on 75-minute cruises downstream and back, $10 adult, $6 children, under three free. The *Little Belle,* a 150-passenger side-

DOVER PUBLICATIONS, INC.

wheeler, departs daily March-Dec. from the Edgewater dock for a 75-minute cruise, 11:30 A.M.–6:30 P.M., adults $10, children $6, under three free. The **USS** *Riverside* is a luxury casino cruiser designed to be able to pass under the Laughlin Bridge for a look at Davis Dam. It departs from the Riverside dock for 75-minute cruises 10:30 A.M.–6:30 P.M. (and 8:30 P.M. on Saturday); $10/$6.

Information

Most of the real-life activities take place in or around the **El Mirage Shopping Center,** five miles from the strip inland. The library, post office, supermarket, video store, etc., are in the vicinity.

The Laughlin Chamber of Commerce/Convention and Visitors Authority **visitor center** is in a little trailer across from the Flamingo, 1725 Casino Dr., 702/298-2214; the Bullhead City **Chamber** is on US 95 just next door (south) to Bullhead Community Park for some good brochure hunting, 602/754-4121.

AHA MACAV

The Fort Mojave Tribe owns 33,300 acres of land in Nevada, Arizona, and California at the tri-state tip south of Laughlin, and holds water rights to 129,000 acre-feet annually. The tribe, which consists of around 900 Native Americans, is developing its 4,000 acres in Nevada into a master-planned community called Aha Macav, which means "People of the River." The tribe signed an 85-year lease with a development company to build Mojave Valley Resort on nearly 500 acres of its primest Nevada real estate, which has a mile of Colorado riverfront, and on 800 acres in Arizona, with a mile and a half on the river. The Nevada side of the resort, which will be accessible from US 95 six miles south of Laughlin, will consist of four hotel-casinos with 5,300 rooms, an 18-hole golf course, 650 residential units, and a 1,600-space RV park. The Arizona side will have another 18-hole golf course, another RV park and mobile home subdivision, a marina, and 3,400 residential units. Mojave Valley Resort, when completed, will combine the lush landscaping and golf courses reminiscent of Palm Springs, the hotel-casino atractions of Las Vegas and Laughlin, and the recreational benefits of the Colorado River.

The $3 million bridge over the Colorado connecting the two sides of the resort has been completed, as has the paving of the one-mile gravel access road off US 95 to Aha Macav is imminent.

So basically, what we have here is the newest town in Nevada. Aha Macav is not quite a boom-town, since it has a master plan, but it's a safe bet that it will make a fair amount of noise, especially if all goes according to plan and it winds up before long with the 30,000 or so residents that it's planned for. That's bigger than Laughlin. That's even bigger than Elko. Stay tuned.

FURTHER INFORMATION

LAS VEGAS MAJOR HOTELS

Please see "Hotels" in the "Accommodations" section of Las Vegas chapter for tips on how and when to book a hotel.

HOTEL	ADDRESS	(702)	(800)	RATES
Alladin	3667 Las Vegas Blvd. S	736-7114	877/333-WISH	$100-800
Alexis Park	37 E. Harmon Ave.	796-3300	800/453-8000	125-1000
Arizona Charlie's	740 S. Decatur	258-5200	800/342-2629	40-70
Bally's	3645 Las Vegas Blvd. S	739-4111	800/634-3434	100-1000
Barbary Coast	3539 Las Vegas Blvd. S	737-7111	800/634-6755	60-250
Bellagio	3600 Las Vegas Blvd. S	693-7111	888/987-3456	225-1600
Binion's Horseshoe	128 Fremont	382-1600	800/622-6468	45-70
Boomtown	3333 Blue Diamond Rd.	263-7777	800/588-7711	50-85
Boulder Station	4111 Boulder Hwy.	432-7777	800/683-7777	55-100
Bourbon Street	120 E. Flamingo	737-7200	800/634-6956	40-85
Caesars Palace	3570 Las Vegas Blvd. S	731-7110	800/634-6661	100-350
California	12 Ogden Ave.	385-1222	800/634-6255	50-70
Casino Royale	3411 Las Vegas Blvd. S	737-3500	800/854-7666	40-140
Circus Circus	2880 Las Vegas Blvd. S	734-0410	800/634-3450	40-200
Continental	4100 Paradise	737-5555	800/634-6641	40-140
Debbie Reynolds	305 Convention Center	734-0711	800/633-1777	60-300
El Cortez	600 Fremont	385-5200	800/634-6703	25-60
Excalibur	3850 Las Vegas Blvd. S	597-7777	800/937-7777	60-200
Fiesta	2400 N. Rancho	631-7000	800/731-7333	60-150
Fitzgeralds	301 Fremont	388-2400	800/274-5825	50-100
Flamingo Hilton	3555 Las Vegas Blvd. S	733-3111	800/732-2111	75-300
Four Queens	202 Fremont	385-4011	800/634-6045	60-200
Fremont	200 Fremont	385-3232	800/634-6460	35-85
Frontier	3120 Las Vegas Blvd. S	794-8200	800/634-6966	40-90
Gold Coast	4000 W. Flamingo	367-7111	800/331-5334	50-80
Gold Spike	400 E. Ogden	384-8444	800/634-6703	22-36
Golden Gate	1 Fremont	382-3510	800/426-1906	35-80

LAS VEGAS MAJOR HOTELS (Continued)

HOTEL	ADDRESS	(702)	(800)	RATES
Golden Nugget	129 Fremont	385-7111	800/634-3454	65-350
Hard Rock	4455 Paradise	693-5000	800/634-6765	100-250
Harrah's	3475 Las Vegas Blvd. S	369-5000	800/427-7247	60-375
Holiday Inn/Boardwalk	3750 Las Vegas Blvd. S	735-2400	800/635-4581	70-100
Imperial Palace	3535 Las Vegas Blvd. S	731-3311	800/634-6441	50-300
Lady Luck	206 N. Third	477-3000	800/523-9582	45-120
Las Vegas Club	18 Fremont	385-1664	800/634-6532	45-150
Las Vegas Hilton	3000 Paradise	732-5155	800/732-7117	100-300
Luxor	3900 Las Vegas Blvd. S	262-4000	800/288-1000	65-350
Main Street Station	300 N. Main	387-1896	800/634-6255	35-60
Mandalay Bay	3960 Las Vegas Blvd. S	632-5000	877/632-7800	200-600
Maxim	160 E. Flamingo	731-4300	800/634-6987	50-125
MGM Grand	3799 Las Vegas Blvd. S	891-1111	800/929-1111	75-300
Mirage	3400 Las Vegas Blvd. S	791-7171	800/627-6667	90-450
Monte Carlo	3770 Las Vegas Blvd. S	730-7777	800/311-8999	60-200
Nevada Palace	5255 Boulder Hwy.	458-8810	800/634-6283	35-100
New York–New York	3790 Las Vegas Blvd. S	740-6969	800/693-6763	100-250
Orleans	4500 W. Tropicana	365-7111	800/675-3267	75-100
Palace Station 2411	W. Sahara	367-2411	800/634-3101	45-350
Paris	3655 Las Vegas Blvd. S	946-7000	888/266-5687	150-1500
Plaza	1 Main	386-2110	800/634-6575	40-90
Polo Towers	3745 Las Vegas Blvd. S	261-1000	800/935-2233	90-400
Rio	3700 W. Flamingo	252-7600	800/752-9746	60-350
Rivera	2901 Las Vegas Blvd. S	734-5110	800/634-6753	65-200
Royal	99 Convention Center	735-6117	800/634-6118	50-140
Sahara	2535 Las Vegas Blvd. S	737-2111	800/634-6666	50-150
Sam's Town	5111 Boulder Hwy.	456-7777	800/634-6371	55-300
San Remo	115 E. Tropicana	739-7000	800/522-7366	50-200
Santa Fe	4949 N. Rancho	658-4900	800/872-6823	40-75
Showboat	2800 E. Fremont	385-9163	800/826-2800	40-150
Stardust	3000 Las Vegas Blvd. S	732-6111	800/634-6757	40-350
Stratosphere	2000 Las Vegas Blvd. S	380-7777	800/998-6937	40-250
Sun Coast	9090 Alta Dr.	636-7111	877/677-7111	60-90

LAS VEGAS MAJOR HOTELS (Continued)

HOTEL	ADDRESS	(702)	(800)	RATES
Texas Station	2101 Texas Star	631-1000	800/654-8888	40-90
Treasure Island	3300 Las Vegas Blvd. S	894-7111	800/949-7444	65-300
Tropicana	3801 Las Vegas Blvd. S	739-2222	800/634-4000	60-200
Vacation Village	6711 Las Vegas Blvd. S	897-1700	800/658-5000	30-70
Westward Ho	2900 Las Vegas Blvd. S	731-2900	800/634-6803	40-70
Venetian	3355 Las Vegas Blvd. S	414-1000	888/2-VENICE	100-1000

LAS VEGAS MOTELS

Please see "Motels" in the "Accommodations" section of Las Vegas chapter for descriptions of areas and for tips on how and when to book a motel. Call for current rates.

SOUTH OF DOWNTOWN

NAME	ADDRESS	PHONE (702)
Boulevard	525 Las Vegas Blvd. S	384-6090
Normandie	708 Las Vegas Blvd. S	382-1002
Desert Star	1210 Las Vegas Blvd. S	384-7172
High Hat	1300 Las Vegas Blvd. S	382-8080

UPPER STRIP—FROM VEGAS WORLD TO STARDUST

NAME	ADDRESS	PHONE (702)
Holiday House	2211 Las Vegas Blvd. S	732-2468
Fun City	2233 Las Vegas Blvd. S	731-3155
El Mirador	2310 Las Vegas Blvd. S	384-6570

LOWER STRIP—FROM FRONTIER TO BEYOND HACIENDA

NAME	ADDRESS	PHONE (702)
La Concha	2955 Las Vegas Blvd. S	735-1255
Tam O'Shanter	3317 Las Vegas Blvd. S	735-7331
Center Strip	3688 Las Vegas Blvd. S	739-6066
White Sands	3889 Las Vegas Blvd. S	736-2515
Glass Pool	4613 Las Vegas Blvd. S	739-6636
Casa Malaga	4615 Las Vegas Blvd. S	736-2226
Silver Sands	4617 Las Vegas Blvd. S	736-2545

NORTH OF DOWNTOWN

NAME	ADDRESS	PHONE (702)
Golden Inn	120 Las Vegas Blvd. N	384-8204
Travel Inn	217 Las Vegas Blvd. N	384-3040
Knotty Pine	1900 Las Vegas Blvd. N	624-8300
Crest	207 N. 6th	382-5642
Town Lodge	225 N. 7th	386-7988
Vista	209 N. 7th	382-4920
Downtowner	129 N. 8th	384-1441

EAST FREMONT—FROM DOWNTOWN TO SAM'S TOWN

NAME	ADDRESS	PHONE (702)
City Center	700 E. Fremont	382-4766
Fergusons	1028 E. Fremont	382-3500
Travelers	1100 E. Fremont	384-7121
Lucky	1111 E. Fremont	384-1311
Las Vegas	1200 E. Fremont	382-8131
Gables	1301 E. Fremont	384-1637
Lucky Lady	1308 E. Fremont	385-1093
Valley	1313 E. Fremont	384-6890
Blue Angel	2110 E. Fremont	386-9500
La Palm	2512 E. Fremont	384-5874
Lamplighter	2805 E. Fremont	382-8791
Capri	3245 E. Fremont	457-1429
Lucky Cuss	3305 E. Fremont	457-1929
Ponderosa	3325 E. Fremont	457-0422

LAS VEGAS WEEKLY MOTELS
(WITH KITCHEN)

*Please see "Weekly Motels" in the "Accommodation" section
of the Las Vegas chapter for more on weekly motels.*

NAME	ADDRESS	PHONE (702)
Budget Suites	Stardust Rd.	732-1500
Crest	207 N. Sixth	382-5642
Downtowner	129 N. 8th	384-1441
Fun City	2233 Las Vegas Blvd. S	731-3155
Glass Pool	4613 Las Vegas Blvd. S	739-6636
Holiday Royale	4505 Paradise	733-7676
Hops	3412 Paradise	732-2494
King Albert	Albert St.	732-1555
Somerset House	294 Convention Center	735-4411
Tod	1508 Las Vegas Blvd. S	477-0022

BOOKLIST

For an exhaustive bibliography of books about Nevada and gambling, see *Nevada—An Annotated Bibliography* by Stanley Paher, Nevada Publications, 1980; and *Gambling Bibliography* by Jack Gardner, Gale Research Company, 1980. Although both were published over 20 years ago, they are still the most comprehensive general bibliographies available.

For a large number of Nevada titles published in the 20 years since the two bibliographies, contact **University of Nevada Press**, Mailstop 166, Reno, NV 89557-0076, tel. 775/784-6573 or 877/NV-BOOKS, www.nvbooks.nevada.edu . Huntington Press, 3687 S. Procyon Ave., Las Vegas, NV 89103, tel. 800/244-2224, www.huntingtonpress.com and www.greatstuff4gamblers.com, Nevada's largest commercial publisher, is another fine resource.

For the best current books about gambling, write or call for catalogs from the Gambler's Bookstore, 1 E. 1st St. (corner 1st and Virginia Streets), Reno, NV 89501, tel. 775/825-7778 or 800/748-5797, www.gamblerhome.com, or the Gambler's Book Club, 630 S. 11th St., Las Vegas, NV 89101, tel. 800/634-6243, www.gamblersbook.com. Huntington Press, mentioned above, publishes and distributes a number of books about gambling.

A visit to any bookstore specializing in Nevada themes will turn up many books on interesting Nevada-related topics including the California Trail, the Pony Express, Native Americans, the Basques (check out the University of Nevada Press's Basque series), ghost towns, the natural history and geology of the Great Basin, ghost towns. Larger museums usually offer a good selection of Nevada-related books.

TRAVEL AND DESCRIPTION

Castleman, Deke. *Nevada*. Oakland: Compass American Guides, 2000. Travel guidebook with information for travelers on everything from Las Vegas lights to the most remote ghost towns and nature spots, with color photos.

Castleman, Deke, and Gayen Wharton and Tom Wharton. *Utah & Nevada Camping: The Complete Guide to More Than 36,000 Campsites*. San Francisco: Foghorn Press, 1996. Covers every campground in Nevada (180 total) and Utah (430), listing and describing all the public and private campgrounds and RV parks in both states.

Dickerson, Richard. *Nevada Angler's Guide— Fish Tails in the Sagebrush*. Portland: Frank Amato Publications, 1997. A handy, useful, and authoritative guide to 116 of the most accessible fishing spots in Nevada

Glass, Mary Ellen, and Al Glass. *Touring Nevada: A Historic and Scenic Guide*. Reno: University of Nevada Press, 1983. An excellent guide, well organized into specific "circle tours" for people who are interested in the historical significance of the sights of Nevada.

Graham, Jefferson. *Vegas—Live And In Person*. New York: Abbeville Press, 1969. This large format, profusely photographed book lives up to its name. Graham's brief history carries him right up to Las Vegas live—games, high rollers, movers and shakers, entertainers, waitresses, bellmen, maitre d's, wedding chapel owners, and signmakers.

Grubbs, Bruce. *Hiking Nevada*. Helena, Montana: Falcon Publishing, 1994. Good guidebook for hikes all around Nevada; includes maps.

Hall, Shawn. *Old Heart of Nevada: Ghost Towns and Mining Camps of Elko County*. Reno: University of Nevada Press, 1998. Identifies and locates the ghost towns and old mining camps of Elko County, and recounts their colorful histories. Divides Elko County into five easily accessible regions, lists the historic sites within each region, and provides directions to reach them.

Hall, Shawn. *Preserving the Glory Days: Ghost Towns and Mining Camps of Nye County, Nevada.* Reno: University of Nevada Press, 1999. Nevada's largest and least-populated county is also the site of many of the state's most colorful ghost towns and mining camps. A lively, informative record of Nevada's isolated interior, this book provides historical information on nearly 200 sites and a current assessment of each one, with clear directions for locating each site.

Hall, Shawn. *Romancing Nevada's Past: Ghost Towns and Historic Sites of Eureka, Lander, and White Pine Counties.* Reno: University of Nevada Press, 1994. History of 175 significant sites, with historic photos and an update on the present condition of each ghost town or landmark, and easy-to-follow directions to each one.

Hart, John. *Hiking The Great Basin.* San Francisco: Sierra Club Books, 1980. An indispensable guidebook for anyone wanting to explore the back country of Nevada. Wonderfully written, accurate and detailed, superb attitude.

Kelsey, Michael. *Hiking and Climbing in Great Basin National Park.* Provo, UT: Kelsey Publishing, 1988. The best book available on hiking Great Basin Park. Nearly 50 hikes with maps and photos for each.

Moreno, Richard. *Roadside History of Nevada.* Missoula, Montana: Mountain Press Publishing Company, 2000. Memorable tales of Nevada's places and people, written with a historian's nose for details and a traveler's sense of fun, with 140 photos and detailed maps showing how to get to every place mentioned. Written by the friendly, personable, and knowledgeable publisher of *Nevada* magazine.

Parr, Barry. *Hiking the Sierra Nevada.* Helena, Montana: Falcon Publishing, 1999. Gook hiking book for the Sierras.

Perry, John, and Jane Greverus. *Guide to the Natural Areas of New Mexico, Arizona, and Nevada.* San Francisco: Sierra Club Books, 1985. This handy book has information on 82 BLM, Forest Service, State Park, and state and federal Wildlife Department lands.

Schwartz, J.R. *Best Cat Houses in Nevada.* Los Altos, CA: Straight Arrow Publishing, 1987. A guide to 36 brothels in Nevada.

Tingley, Joseph V. and Kris Ann Pizarro. *Traveling America's Loneliest Road: A Geologic and Natural History Tour through Nevada along U.S. Highway 50.* Reno: University of Nevada Press, 2000. A guide to geologic features and other points of interest along U.S. Highway 50 between Lake Tahoe and Great Basin National Park.

Toll, David W. *The Complete Nevada Traveler.* Virginia City, NV: Gold Hill Publishing Company, 1999. Subtitled "The affectionate and intimately detailed guidebook to the most interesting state in America," this guidebook offers narrative about places to visit around the state, with historic and recent black-and-white photos. An interesting book for visitors, but does not try to comprehensively cover nuts-and-bolts travel info such as places to stay, places to eat, transportation, etc.

White, Michael C. *Nevada Wilderness Areas and Great Basin National Park—A Hiking and Backpacking Guide.* Berkeley: Wilderness Press, 1997. If you want to explore any of Nevada's 13 rugged, remote, and primitive wilderness areas, you must have this book.

GAMBLING

Anderson, Ian. *Turning The Tables On Las Vegas.* New York: Vintage Books, 1976. "Ian Anderson" was a pseudonym for R. Kent London, a highly successful and anonymous card counter. Goes into extraordinary detail about playing and betting strategies, camouflage, interaction with the pit personnel, and maintaining a winning attitude. Required reading for aspiring counters.

Bass, Thomas. *Eudaemonic Pie.* New York: Houghton Mifflin, 1985. A true hippie adventure story about a group of physicists at U.C. Santa Cruz who invented a computer that fit in a shoe to beat the casino at roulette.

Compton, Jeffrey. *Las Vegas Advisor Guide to Slot Clubs.* Las Vegas: Huntington Press, 1995. A must for anyone who plays any gaming machines, this is the only book that covers all the slot clubs of Las Vegas. Second edition due out in January 2001.

Ortiz, Darwin. *On Casino Gambling.* New York: Dodd, Mead & Company, 1986. One of the best-written and most useful how-to books for playing casino games.

Rubin, Max. *Comp City—a Guide to Free Las Vegas Vacations.* Las Vegas: Huntington Press, 1994. A former casino executive, Rubin quit his job to write this book, revealing the best-kept secrets in the casino industry about comps (free rooms, food, beverage, shows, etc.). Second edition due out in February 2001.

Scott, Jean. *The Frugal Gambler.* Las Vegas: Huntington Press, 1998. The world's pre-eminent low-rolling casino buster reveals her secrets for staying free at hotel-casinos, beating casino promotions, eating and drinking on the house, and getting bumped from airplanes and flying free.

Solkey, Lee. *Dummy Up and Deal.* Las Vegas: Gamblers Book Club, 1980. Written by a Las Vegan who earned a degree in urban ethnology and dealt blackjack for seven years as part of her "field study." Talks with great authority about the dealer culture, language, territorial domains, and the dealer relationship with the casino.

HISTORY

Cahlan, Florence Lee, and John F. Cahlan. *Water—A History of Las Vegas.* Las Vegas: Las Vegas Water District, 1975. Written by the longtime publisher of the Las Vegas *Review-Journal* and his reporter-wife, this is a sprawling, two-volume history of Las Vegas that "shows how its evolution as a city closely paralleled the development of its water."

Carlson, Helen S. *Nevada Place Names: A Geographical Dictionary.* Reno: University of Nevada Press, 1974. Recently re-issued, this classic book of place-name facts is spiced with plenty of history, folklore and legend.

Demaris, Ovid. *The Vegas Legacy.* New York: Dell Publishing, 1983. By one of the co-authors of *The Green Felt Jungle,* this is a story, *very* loosely based on actual Nevada history, about a presidential convention taking place in Las Vegas and how the Nevada powers that be attempt to install their totally corrupt favorite son as the candidate.

DeQuille, Dan. *The Big Bonanza.* New York: Random House, 1980. The story of the discovery and development of Nevada's fabulous Comstock Lode, written by Mark Twain's friend and fellow reporter on Virginia City's *Territorial Enterprise* newspaper. An American classic, first published in 1876.

Dodd, Charles H. and Jeff Gnass. *California Trail: Voyage of Discovery—The Story Behind the Scenery.* Las Vegas: KC Publications, 1996. Well illustrated with excellent color photos, this book tells the story and follows the path of the California Trail, which stretched from Missouri to California. More than 200,000 immigrants passed through Nevada headed westward on this trail from around 1828 to 1869.

Findlay, John. *People of Chance—Gambling in American Society from Jamestown to Las Vegas.* Lincoln, Nebraska: University of Nebraska Press, 1986. Written by a Pennsylvania State University history professor, this incredible book is not only *the* best book on the evolution of American gambling, but also one of the great books on American history itself.

Ford, Jean, Betty Glass, and Martha Gould. *Women in Nevada History: An Annotated Bibliography of Published Sources.* Reno: Nevada Women's History Project, 2000. An excellent resource for finding out everything you ever wanted to know about women in the Silver State's history.

Hulse, James W. *The Silver State.* Reno: University of Nevada Press, Second Edition, 1998. This cohesive and readable history provides students and general readers with an accessible account of Nevada's colorful history, exploring many dimensions of Nevada's experience and its peoples.

James, Ronald M. *The Roar and the Silence: A History of Virginia City and the Comstock Lode.* Reno: University of Nevada Press, 1998. This lively, thoughtful book chronicles the area's history from its earliest days through the early 20th century, when the lode finally gave out and the Comstock sank into silent decay, and up to the present, when Virginia City and its environs found new life, first as a community of bohemians and artists, and more recently as a tourist attraction.

Kasindorf, Jeanie. *The Nye County Brothel Wars.* New York: Linden Press, 1985. Spellbinding account of how an "outsider," who tried to open and run a brothel in Pahrump, Nevada (60 miles from Las Vegas, just on the other side of the Clark County Line), ran afoul of the Nye County Sheriff's Department, District Attorney, established whorehouse owners, and their henchmen, and how his battle against harassment, arrest, attempted murder, low- and high-level corruption, white slavery, and racketeering eventually was taken up by the FBI and U.S. Attorney and tried in federal court.

Kling, Dwayne. *The Rise of the Biggest Little City: An Encyclopedic History of Reno Gaming, 1931-1981.* Reno: University of Nevada Press, 1999. The first 50 years of Reno's gaming and gambling industry, written by a long-time gaming executive and illustrated with historic photos.

Knepp, Donn. *Las Vegas—the Entertainment Capital.* Menlo Park, CA: Lane Publishing, 1987. This Sunset Pictorial book concentrates on the glamour and glitter of the casino entertainment industry. Hundreds of black and whites and color plates illustrate Las Vegas's long and fascinating larger-than-life heritage—collected and captioned by this writer and photographer for the famous Las Vegas News Bureau.

Land, Barbara, and Myrick Land. *A Short History of Las Vegas.* Reno: University of Nevada Press, 1999. A lively history, illustrated with historic and recent photographs, telling the story of the Las Vegas area from the earliest visitors 11,000 years ago up to the present.

Land, Barbara, and Myrick Land. *A Short History of Reno.* Reno: University of Nevada Press, 1995. An entertaining and anecdotal history of Reno's colorful past and the larger-than-life characters who left their mark on the city, illustrated with dozens of black-and-white photos.

Laxalt, Robert. *Nevada—A History.* New York: W.W. Norton & Company, 1977. This is a very personal, lyrical, and selective account of the history and shape of the state by one of Nevada's best-known and best-loved writers.

Lewis, Oscar. *The Town That Died Laughing.* Reno: University of Nevada Press, 1986. The story of Austin, Nevada—rambunctious early-day mining camp—and its renowned newspaper, the *Reese River Reveille.*

McCracken, Robert D. *Las Vegas: The Great American Playground.* Reno: University of Nevada Press, 1997. Traces the city's history from its first Native American occupants more than 10,000 years ago to its present status as a premier tourist destination, illustrated with historical photos.

McDonald, Douglas. *Virginia City and the Silver Region of the Comstock Lode.* Las Vegas: Nevada Publications, 1982. Another in the long list of excellent historicals from Stanley Paher's press. Very well written and nicely illustrated.

Moehring, Eugene P. *Resort City in the Sunbelt: Las Vegas, 1930-2000 (Second Edition).* Reno: University of Nevada Press, 2000. In this new edition, renowned historian Moehring provides a comprehensive history, description and analysis of Las Vegas's development since the 1930s, and also provides insight into the city's future. Indispensable for Las Vegas researchers.

Nicklas, Michael L. *Great Basin: The Story Behind the Scenery.* Las Vegas: KC Publications, 1996. One in a series of interesting books with excellent color photos on various places around the West.

Nevada—A Guide to the Silver State. Portland: Binfords and Mort, 1940. One of 50 books in the famous WPA American Guide Series, and 60 years later still indispensable to modern-day domestic historians and researchers.

Paher, Stanley W. *Las Vegas: As It Began—As It Grew.* Las Vegas: Nevada Publications, 1971. This outstanding history, with hundreds of fascinating b & w's and half a dozen historical maps, covers in detail the popular history of Las Vegas from the Old Spanish Trail up through the building of Hoover Dam.

Paher, Stanley W. *Nevada: Ghost Towns & Mining Camps.* Las Vegas: Nevada Publications, 1970. The Bible of Nevada ghost towns, with good black-and-white photos and bibliography.

Ralston, Jon. *The Anointed One: An Inside Look at Nevada Politics.* Las Vegas: Huntington Press, 2000. Kenny Guinn was elected the governor of Nevada in a 1998 landslide, but the outcome was determined long before a single voter stepped into a polling booth. Written by Nevada's foremost political reporter, this book is a biting commentary on the inner workings of the Nevada political machine.

Reid, Ed, and Ovid Demaris. *The Green Felt Jungle.* New York: Pocket Books, 1964. The classic book in the Diatribe style of indicting Las Vegas as "a corrupt jungle of iniquity."

Roske, Ralph. *Las Vegas: A Desert Paradise.* Tulsa: Continental Heritage Press, 1986. A spectacular picture book, affectionately written by a history professor at UNLV.

Rowley, William D. *Reno—Hub of Washoe County.* CA: Windsor Publications, 1984. An excellently written and illustrated history of Reno, in the context of broader times. Highly recommended.

Shaner, Lora. *Madam: Chronicles of a Nevada Cathouse.* Las Vegas: Huntington Press, 1999. A first-hand look into Nevada's sex-for-money industry, written by a former madam. Piercing character studies of the "working girls" and the men who purchase their services, as well as poignant sketches of day-to-day life in a legal brothel.

Sifakis, Carl. *Mafia Encyclopedia.* New York: Facts on File Publications, 1987. Entries on scores of top underworld personalities and locales, including Las Vegas, Moe Dalitz, Bugsy Siegel, Gus Greenbaum, Virginia Hill, and Johnny Roselli.

Sloan, Jim. *Nevada—True Tales of the Neon Wilderness.* Salt Lake City: University of Utah Press, 1993. Eleven stories covering some of Nevada's biggest headline-grabbing events of the past few decades, written by a reporter and editor for the *Reno Gazette-Journal.*

Townley, John M. *Tough Little Town on the Truckee: Reno.* Reno: Great Basin Studies Center, 1983. Sprawling and brilliant book on Reno's environment and early history.

Vogliotti, Gabriel R. *The Girls of Nevada.* Secaucus, NJ: Citadel Press, 1975. One of the best books ever written on Nevada, including the complete rundown of prostitution issues, a great bio of Joe Conforte, and a stunningly unique history of Las Vegas.

Wolfe, Tom. *The Kandy-Kolored Tangerine-Flaked Streamlined Baby.* New York: Farrar, Strauss & Giroux, 1965. The Las Vegas chapter in this big book of essays is perhaps the classic look at the city as the ultimate expression of the new culture—glamour, entertainment, art—style!—that emerged from 1960s' America.

BIOGRAPHY

Canfield, Gae Whitney. *Sarah Winnemucca of the Northern Paiutes.* Norman, Oklahoma: University of Oklahoma Press, 1983. Biography of the daughter of Chief Winnemucca, whose book *Life Among the Piutes* became a classic.

Garrison, Omar. *Howard Hughes in Las Vegas.* Secaucus, NJ: Lyle Stuart, 1970. Everything about this troubled, mysterious billionaire is gripping. But this book, centered around the four years Hughes spent sequestered on the ninth floor of the Desert Inn, is especially eye-opening, shedding light on the public events and private life of the recluse, as he set about to buy and redesign the city that may well have been "his true spiritual home."

Hillyer, Katharine. *Mark Twain: Young Reporter in Virginia City.* Reno: Nevada Publications, Second Edition, 1997. Tells the story Twain's life as a young reporter in Virginia City, which was the beginning of his literary career.

Hopkins, Sarah Winnemucca. *Life Among the Piutes: Their Wrongs and Claims.* Reno: University of Nevada Press, 1994. Daughter of Chief Winnemucca, born around 1844, writes the story of her life and her people.

Seagraves, Anne. *High-Spirited Women of the West.* Hayden, Idaho: Wesanne Publications, 1992. Includes stories about the lives of several women important in Nevada's history, including Sarah Winnemucca, Jeanne Elizabeth Wier and Helen Jane Wiser Stewart.

Anne Seagraves has written several good books about women in the West, all published by Wesanne Publications, including *Women of the Sierra* (1990), *Women Who Charmed the West* (1991), *Soiled Doves: Prostitution in the Early West* (1994), and *Daughters of the West* (1996).

Twain, Mark. *Mark Twain's Virginia City, Nevada Territory, in the 1860's.* Golden, Colorado: Outbooks, 1982. Reprint of material first published in 1872, with original illustrations, in which Twain tells of his journey across the continent by stagecoach in 1861 with his brother Orion, and their later adventures in Nevada, particularly Twain's sojourn as a newspaper reporter in Virginia City.

Twain, Mark. *Roughing It.* Berkeley: University of California Press, 1996. Twain's account of his life in the West, including his sojourns in Nevada, first published in 1868.

Williams, George III. *Mark Twain: His Life in Virginia City, Nevada.* Dayton, NV: Tree by the River Publishing, 1992. Tells the story of Mark Twain's time in Virginia City, with many stories of the town and historic photos. George Williams III has written many fine books about Virginia City, Mark Twain, and Nevada history, all available from the same publisher.

NATURAL HISTORY

Anderson, Steve, et al. *Ruby Mountain Flora: A Guide to Common Plants of the Ruby Mountains and East Humboldt Range.* Elko: Humboldt National Forest Interpretive Association, 1998. Excellent book for identifying plants, with fine color photos.

Clark, Jeanne L. *Nevada Wildlife Viewing Guide.* Helena, Montana: Falcon Press, 1993. Guide to 55 sites around the state for viewing Nevada's varied birds, mammals, reptiles and endangered fish, with maps, directions, and descriptions of both the wildlife viewing areas and the animals, with excellent color photos.

Fiero, Bill. *Geology of the Great Basin.* Reno: University of Nevada Press, 1986. One in a comprehensive and in-depth series of half a dozen large and beautiful books on the Great Basin.

Haase, John. *Big Red.* New York: Pinnacle Books, 1980. Towering novel about the building of Boulder-Hoover Dam, from the point of view of Frank Crowe, the dam's chief engineer. As monumental and epic a book as the dam itself.

Lanner, Ronald M. *Trees of the Great Basin.* Reno: University of Nevada Press, 1984.

McPhee, John. *Basin and Range.* New York: Farrar, Strauss and Giroux, 1980. Another stunning job by this master author. Here he takes the entire history of geology and relates it to a drive along I-80 through northern Nevada, and manages to tell the tale in 215 pages. Breathtaking.

Ryser, Fred A. Jr. *Birds of the Great Basin.* Reno: University of Nevada Press, 1985.

Sigler, William, and John Sigler. *Fishes of the Great Basin.* Reno: University of Nevada Press, 1987.

Taylor, Ronald J. *Sagebrush Country: A Wildflower Sanctuary.* Missoula, Montana: Mountain Press Publishing, 1992. Excellent book for identifying plants, with fine color photos.

Tilford, Gregory L. *Edible and Medicinal Plants of the West.* Missoula, Montana: Mountain Press Publishing, 1997. Excellent book for identifying plants, with fine color photos.

Trimble, Stephen. *The Sagebrush Ocean: A Natural History of the Great Basin.* Reno: University of Nevada Press, 1999. This noted writer and photographer mixes eloquent accounts of personal experiences with clear explication of natural history., and his photos capture some of the most spectacular but least-known scenery in the western states. An excellent general introduction to the ecology and spirit of the Great Basin.

FICTION & LITERATURE

McLaughlin, Mark. *Sierra Stories: True Tales of Tahoe.* Carnelian Bay, CA: Mic Mac Publishing. Volume 1, 1997; Volume 2, 1998. Stories about Lake Tahoe and the Tahoe area.

McMurtry, Larry. *The Desert Rose.* New York: Simon and Schuster, 1983. An affectionate and poignant little character study of an aging showgirl and her ties—men, daughter, neighbors, friends, and co-workers—that McMurtry wrote over a three-week period during a lull in the writing of his epic *Lonesome Dove*.

Puzo, Mario. *Fool's Die.* New York: Putnam, 1978. A sprawling, semi-autobiographical novel about a writer who starts out as an orphan, gets married and raises a family in New York, makes a pilgrimage to Las Vegas, and publishes a blockbuster novel that is turned into a box-office smash. Contains some of the best writing in fiction about a Las Vegas hotel owner and his right-hand assistant, scams on both sides of the gaming table, and casino color.

Puzo, Mario. *Inside Las Vegas.* New York: Charter Books, 1977. A short, stream-of-consciousness look at gambling, girls, and glamour by this famous novelist, himself a heavy, but not degenerate, gambler.

Thompson, Hunter S. *Fear and Loathing in Las Vegas.* New York: Random House, 1998. Thompson's classic novel.

Tronnes, Mike (Editor). *Literary Las Vegas: The Best Writing About America's Most Fabulous City.* New York: Henry Holt & Company, 1995. A collection of previously published articles about Sin City by two dozen of America's top wordsmiths: Tom Wolfe, Hunter S. Thompson, John Gregory Dunne, Joan Didion, Noel Coward, Michael Herr, and many more.

MAGAZINES

Nevada. 401 N. Carson St., Suite 100, Carson City, NV 89701-4291, tel. 775/687-5416, www.nevadamagazine.com. Published continuously (though under several names) since 1936, this bimonthly contains an extraordinary amount of coverage on the 36th state, with proportionate attention paid to Las Vegas. Good writing and photography, great production, and the "Events" section alone is worth the subscription price.

Range. P.O. Box 639, Carson City, NV 89702, tel. 775/884-2200 or 800/726-4348, www.rangemagazine.com. This quarterly magazine focuses on creating a public awareness about the positive presence of ranchers on the nation's rangelands.

Las Vegas Advisor. Published by Huntington Press, 3687 S. Procyon Ave., Las Vegas, NV 89103, tel. 800/244-2224, www.huntingtonpress.com and www.greatstuff4gamblers.com. Monthly magazine covering where to go, where to stay, where to eat, entertainment, tournaments, special events and so on in Las Vegas. Subscribers get a coupon book offering valuable savings.

NEVADA CASINOS

NEVADA CASINOS BY REGION

INDEX

MUSEUMS

ABOUT THE AUTHOR

Deke Castleman adopted Nevada in 1988 when he began working on the first edition of *Nevada Handbook*.

Since then, he's produced five more editions of *Nevada*, six editions of Compass *Las Vegas*, ten editions of Fodor's *Las Vegas*, and one measly edition of Compass *Nevada*. He's the senior editor of Huntington Press, the largest commercial book publisher in Nevada, which also publishes the award-winning *Las Vegas Advisor* monthly newsletter. He lives in Reno with his beautiful wife and three perfect sons.

ABOUT THE UPDATERS

Nancy Keller has been making a living traveling and writing guidebooks for 16 years, mostly working for Lonely Planet, where her titles have included *California & Nevada, Mexico, Central America on a Shoestring, Guatemala, Belize & Yucatan - La Ruta Maya, New Zealand, Tonga, Rarotonga & the Cook Islands,* and *South Pacific.* This update of the *Moon Handbooks: Nevada* is her first book with Moon.

Kathleen Dodge braced herself against the grips of temptation and addictive impulses to update the Las Vegas and the Southern Corner chapter of this Nevada Handbook. Previously Kathleen has written and edited guidebooks to California and Las Vegas for Fodor's, as well as authored a number of their European travel guides. Kathleen lives in Berkeley.

AVALON TRAVEL

publishing

How far will our travel guides take you? As far as you want.

Discover a rhumba-fueled nightspot in Old Havana, explore prehistoric tombs in Ireland, hike beneath California's centuries-old redwoods, or embark on a classic road trip along Route 66. Our guidebooks deliver solidly researched, trip-tested information—minus any generic froth—to help globetrotters or weekend warriors create an adventure uniquely their own.

And we're not just about the printed page. Public television viewers are tuning in to Rick Steves' new travel series, Rick Steves' Europe. On the Web, readers can cruise the virtual black top with Road Trip USA author Jamie Jensen and learn travel industry secrets from Edward Hasbrouck of The Practical Nomad. With Foghorn AnyWare eBooks, users of handheld devices can place themselves "inside" the content of the guidebooks.

In print. On TV. On the Internet. In the palm of your hand.
We supply the information. The rest is up to you.

Avalon Travel Publishing
Something for everyone

www.travelmatters.com

Avalon Travel Publishing guides are available at your favorite book or travel store.

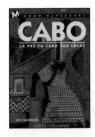

MOON HANDBOOKS provide comprehensive

coverage of a region's arts, history, land, people, and social issues in addition to detailed practical listings for accommodations, food, outdoor recreation, and entertainment. Moon Handbooks allow complete immersion in a region's culture—ideal for travelers who want to combine sightseeing with insight for an extraordinary travel experience in destinations throughout North America, Hawaii, Latin America, the Caribbean, Asia, and the Pacific.

WWW.MOON.COM

Rick Steves shows you where to travel and how to travel—all while getting the most value for your dollar. His Back Door travel philosophy is about making friends, having fun, and avoiding tourist rip-offs.

Rick's been traveling to Europe for more than 25 years and is the author of 22 guidebooks, which have sold more than a million copies. He also hosts the award-winning public television series *Rick Steves' Europe*.

WWW.RICKSTEVES.COM

ROAD TRIP USA

Getting there is half the fun, and Road Trip USA guides are your ticket to driving adventure. Taking you off the interstates and onto less-traveled, two-lane highways, each guide is filled with fascinating trivia, historical information, photographs, facts about regional writers, and details on where to sleep and eat—all contributing to your exploration of the American road.

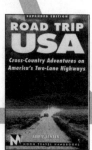

*"[Books] so full of the pleasures of the American road,
you can smell the upholstery."*
~BBC radio

WWW.ROADTRIPUSA.COM

FOGHORN OUTDOORS guides are for campers, hikers, boaters, anglers, bikers, and golfers of all levels of daring and skill. Each guide focuses on a specific U.S. region and contains site descriptions and ratings, driving directions, facilities and fees information, and easy-to-read maps that leave only the task of deciding where to go.

"Foghorn Outdoors has established an ecological conservation standard unmatched by any other publisher."
~Sierra Club

WWW.FOGHORN.COM

TRAVEL SMART guidebooks are accessible, route-based driving guides focusing on regions throughout the United States and Canada. Special interest tours provide the most practical routes for family fun, outdoor activities, or regional history for a trip of anywhere from two to 22 days. Travel Smarts take the guesswork out of planning a trip by recommending only the most interesting places to eat, stay, and visit.

"One of the few travel series that rates sightseeing attractions. That's a handy feature. It helps to have some guidance so that every minute counts."
~San Diego Union-Tribune

CiTY·SMaRT™ guides are written by local authors with hometown perspectives who have personally selected the best places to eat, shop, sightsee, and simply hang out. The honest, lively, and opinionated advice is perfect for business travelers looking to relax with the locals or for longtime residents looking for something new to do Saturday night.

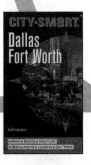

U.S.~METRIC CONVERSION

1 inch =	2.54 centimeters (cm)
1 foot =	.304 meters (m)
1 yard =	0.914 meters
1 mile =	1.6093 kilometers (km)
1 km =	.6214 miles
1 fathom =	1.8288 m
1 chain =	20.1168 m
1 furlong =	201.168 m
1 acre =	.4047 hectares
1 sq km =	100 hectares
1 sq mile =	2.59 square km
1 ounce =	28.35 grams
1 pound =	.4536 kilograms
1 short ton =	.90718 metric ton
1 short ton =	2000 pounds
1 long ton =	1.016 metric tons
1 long ton =	2240 pounds
1 metric ton =	1000 kilograms
1 quart =	.94635 liters
1 US gallon =	3.7854 liters
1 Imperial gallon =	4.5459 liters
1 nautical mile =	1.852 km

To compute celsius temperatures, subtract 32 from Fahrenheit and divide by 1.8. To go the other way, multiply celsius by 1.8 and add 32.

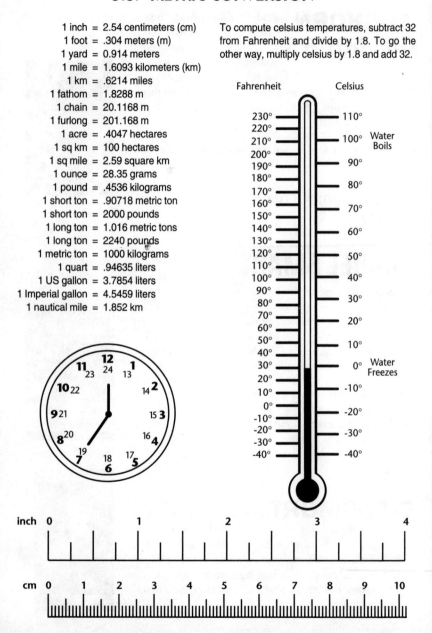

Will you have enough stories to tell your grandchildren?

Yahoo! Travel

Do You YAHOO!?